WISCONSIN
· BLUE BOOK ·

2019 · 2020

Published biennially by
the Wisconsin Legislative Reference Bureau

To view a pdf of the 2019–2020 *Wisconsin Blue Book*, go to
http://legis.wisconsin.gov/lrb/blue-book

Wisconsin Legislative Reference Bureau
One East Main Street, Suite 200, Madison, WI 53703
http://legis.wisconsin.gov/lrb
©2019 Joint Committee on Legislative Organization, Wisconsin Legislature
All rights reserved. Published 2019.
Printed in the United States of America

ISBN 978-1-7333817-0-3

Sold and distributed by:
Document Sales Unit
Department of Administration
2310 Darwin Road
Madison, WI 53704
608-243-2441, 800-362-7253
DOADocumentSalesInformation@wisconsin.gov

Front cover: On August 22, 2018, Wisconsin veterans honored the families of their fallen comrades during the dedication of a Gold Star Memorial on capitol grounds. Gold stars first came to represent fallen service members during World War I, when American families made and displayed "service flags," upon which blue stars signified family members serving, and gold stars signified those who died. Today, the Gold Star Memorial pays tribute to the Wisconsinites who sacrificed their lives—and the families who sacrificed their loved ones—in service of the nation. JOE KOSHOLLEK, LEGISLATIVE PHOTOGRAPHER

Back cover: This poster honored Company G of the First Wisconsin Infantry Regiment, mustered into service in July 1917 at Camp Douglas, Wisconsin, and redesignated as the 127th Infantry within the 32nd Division. During World War I, Company G fought in several battles in France, and were later commended for "fighting like demons" at the Battle of Chateau-Thierry under the command of General John Pershing. Surviving members of this company arrived home to Madison on May 17, 1919. Together, they and their fallen comrades were among the 118,000 Wisconsinites who served during World War I. WHS IMAGE ID 130839

Tony Evers
Office of the Governor

July 2019

Dear Readers:

As a kid who grew up in Plymouth, met my wife in kindergarten, took her to junior prom, and went from working in a cheese factory to teaching science to becoming state superintendent, I was incredibly humbled to be sworn in as the forty-sixth governor of the great state of Wisconsin this year.

The *Wisconsin Blue Book* allows us to reflect on our history, how far we have come, and the work we have yet to do. At a time of great division and increasing polarity, it has never been more important to create and maintain a more aware and engaged citizenry, foster accountability and transparency, and promote a greater understanding of all the things that we have in common. It is essential that we return to governing and leading with kindness and respect, empathy and compassion, and integrity and civility, and that we embrace discourse and dialogue that make us better people and better citizens. These are not Republican or Democratic values—these are our Wisconsin values that have made our state great.

The *Blue Book* is an important reminder that we are more than the sum of our differences and that what unites us is far, far greater than what divides us. So, whether you are a farmer, a small business owner, a teacher inspiring kids to be thoughtful and engaged citizens, someone who is considering a career in public service, or a constituent who wants to learn more about your elected officials, or you are interested in Wisconsin's rich history and traditions, the *Blue Book* serves as a helpful resource to learn about, respect, and appreciate, not just our state, but each other, so we can keep moving Wisconsin forward, together.

Thank you for picking up a copy. Happy reading and On, Wisconsin!

Sincerely,

Tony Evers

Tony Evers
Governor

INTRODUCTION

In the summer of 1919, the Wisconsin Legislature enacted laws to provide for temporary support for World War I veterans with disabilities, cash bonuses for service, and bonuses for veterans to pursue education. Wisconsin led the nation 100 years ago with these new programs, many of which were precursors for later federal legislation, such as the GI Bill. At the time, passage of these veterans programs was far from guaranteed: it was an uphill battle for advocates to convince legislators of the distinct challenges veterans faced and there were political divisions in the legislature, intense conflict between the legislature and the governor, and legal challenges in the courts. The realization of these programs required coalition building in the legislature, mobilization and involvement of the public, and development of novel constitutional arguments.

In the 2019–20 *Wisconsin Blue Book* feature article, "A Hero's Welcome," LRB analyst Jillian Slaight tells the story of "a watershed moment in Wisconsin history," when the 1919 Wisconsin Legislature overcame discord to enact innovative veterans legislation following World War I. "A Hero's Welcome" is a story about political statesmanship and an energetic legislature; it is also about the sacrifices of the Wisconsin veterans who served their country in combat only to return home to face political divisions over how their military service should be recognized and rewarded.

The 2019–20 *Blue Book* also contains the biographies of all legislators, descriptions of executive and judicial branch agencies, and vital statistics on Wisconsin. The *Blue Book* is an introduction to Wisconsin state and local government and the most comprehensive source for information about the State of Wisconsin. Composing the *Blue Book* requires agency-wide collaboration, involving all LRB staff to write essays, update tables, and assemble and organize material about the legislature and state and local government. The LRB's legal and research expertise is unmatched, and three people deserve special recognition: Kira Langoussis Mochal, Nancy Warnecke, and Lauren Jackson. Their leadership has been invaluable, and I am grateful for their contributions.

Richard A. Champagne, Chief
Wisconsin Legislative Reference Bureau

TABLE OF CONTENTS

3 About Wisconsin

4 Statistics and Reference

1

ELECTED OFFICIALS

INDEX OF BIOGRAPHIES

Tony Evers, Governor

Democrat

Biography: Born Plymouth, Wisconsin, November 5, 1951; married; 3 children, 9 grandchildren. ▪ Graduate Plymouth High School, 1969; B.S., University of Wisconsin-Madison, 1973; M.S., University of Wisconsin-Madison, 1976; Ph.D., University of Wisconsin-Madison, 1986. ▪ Former teacher; technology coordinator; principal, Tomah; superintendent of schools, Oakfield, Verona; CESA 6 administrator, Oshkosh; deputy state superintendent of public instruction. ▪ Former member: Wisconsin Association of CESA Administrators; Wisconsin Association of School District Administrators; University of Wisconsin Board of Regents; Wisconsin Technical College System Board; Council of Chief State School Officers. ▪ Elected state superintendent 2009–17.

Current office: Elected governor 2018.

Contact: eversinfo@wisconsin.gov; 608-266-1212; PO Box 7863, Madison, WI 53707-7863.

Mandela Barnes, Lieutenant Governor
Democrat

Biography: Born Milwaukee, Wisconsin, December 1, 1986. ▪ Graduate John Marshall High School (Milwaukee) 2003; attended Alabama A&M University 2003–08. ▪ Deputy Director of Strategic Engagement at the State Innovation Exchange; Lead Organizer of MICAH (Milwaukee Innercity Congregations Allied for Hope). ▪ Member: National Lieutenant Governors Association; Democratic Lieutenant Governor's Association; NewDEAL Leader (Climate Policy Group Co-Chair); NAACP Milwaukee Branch; Kappa Alpha Psi Fraternity, Inc. ▪ Elected to Assembly 2012–15.

Current office: Elected lieutenant governor 2018.

Contact: ltgov@wisconsin.gov; 608-266-3516; PO Box 2043 Madison, WI 53701.

Joshua L. Kaul, Attorney General
Democrat

Biography: Born Mount Lebanon, Pennsylvania, February 2, 1981; married; 2 children. ▪ Graduate Goodrich High School (Fond du Lac) 1999; B.A. in Economics and History, Yale University, 2003; J.D., Stanford Law School, 2006. ▪ Former attorney; Assistant United States Attorney. ▪ Former president of Stanford Law Review.

Current office: Elected attorney general 2018. Member ex officio: Board of Commissioner of Public Lands.

Contact: 608-266-1221; PO Box 7857, Madison, WI 53707-7857.

Carolyn Stanford Taylor, State Superintendent of Public Instruction, nonpartisan office

Biography: Born Marks, Mississippi, March 3, 1957; married; 5 children, 5 grandchildren. ▪ Graduate Quitman County High School; B.S., University of Wisconsin-Madison, 1978; M.S., University of Wisconsin-Madison, 1979. ▪ Former assistant state superintendent; principal and teacher in the Madison Metropolitan School District. ▪ Member: Madison Alumnae Chapter of Delta Sigma Theta Sorority. ▪ Former member: Wisconsin Education Association Council Board of Directors; Madison Teachers Inc. Board of Directors; Families And Schools Together (FAST) Board and FAST National Board; Forward Service Corporation Board of Directors; Children Come First Committee (chair); Governor's Justice Commission; University of Wisconsin Board of Visitors.

Current office: Appointed state superintendent 2019 to fill vacancy created by election of Tony Evers as governor. Member of Governor's Early Childhood Advisory Council and Governor's Commission on Offender Re-entry.

Contact: dpistatesuperintendent@dpi.wi.gov; 608-266-3390; 125 S. Webster Street, Madison, WI 53703.

Sarah Godlewski, State Treasurer

Democrat

Biography: Born Eau Claire, Wisconsin, November 9, 1981; married. ▪ Graduate Eau Claire Memorial High School, 2000; B.A. in Peace and Conflict Resolution, George Mason University, 2004; Master of Public Administration candidate, University of Pennsylvania; National Security Fellow, Air War College, 2013; Certificates in Public Treasury Management and Finance, Pepperdine Graziadio Business School and National Institute of Public Finance, 2017. ▪ Former national security project manager; director of strategy and performance; investor; entrepreneur. ▪ Former member: UNICEF Advocacy Leadership Committee (chair); Congressional Bipartisan Post Traumatic Stress Disorder Task Force; U.S. Fund for UNICEF (board member);

Arlington Academy of Hope (board secretary); George Mason University College of Visual and Performance Arts (board member).

Current office: Elected state treasurer 2018. Member ex officio: Board of Commissioners of Public Lands; Wisconsin Insurance Security Fund.

Contact: Treasurer@wisconsin.gov; 608-266-1714; B38 West State Capitol, Madison, WI 53701.

Douglas J. La Follette, Secretary of State
Democrat

Biography: Single. ▪ B.S. in Chemistry, Marietta College, 1963; M.S. in Chemistry, Stanford University, 1964; Ph.D. in Organic Chemistry, Columbia University, 1967. ▪ Former director of training and development with an energy marketing company; assistant professor, University of Wisconsin-Parkside; public affairs director, Union of Concerned Scientists; owner and operator of a small business; research associate, University of Wisconsin-Madison. ▪ Member: American Solar Energy Society; Audubon Society; Friends of the Earth; Phi Beta Kappa. ▪ Former member: Council of Economic Priorities; American Federation of Teachers; Federation of American Scientists; Lake Michigan Federation; Southeastern Wisconsin Coalition for Clean Air; Clean Wisconsin (formerly Wisconsin Environmental Decade, founder). ▪ Elected to Senate 1972.

Current office: Elected secretary of state 1974 and 1982. Reelected since 1986. Member ex officio: Board of Commissioners of Public Lands.

Contact: doug.lafollette@wisconsin.gov; 608-266-8888 (press 3); PO Box 7848, Madison, WI 53707-7848.

▪ ▪ ▪

Ann Walsh Bradley

Biography: Born Richland Center, Wisconsin, July 5, 1950; married; 4 children. ▪ Graduate Richland Center High School; B.A. Webster College (St. Louis, Missouri); J.D. University of Wisconsin-Madison (Knapp Scholar), 1976. ▪ Former high school teacher, practicing attorney, and Marathon County circuit court judge. ▪ Member: Board of Managerial Trustees, International Association of Women Judges; elected member of the American Law Institute; state coordinator for iCivics; Wisconsin Bench Bar Committee; University of Wisconsin Law School Board of Visitors; American Bar Association; State Bar of Wisconsin; Federal-State Judicial Council; lecturer for the American Bar Association's Asian Law Initiative, International Judicial Academy, and Institute of International Education. ▪ Former member: Board of Directors, National Association of Women Judges; Board of Directors and vice chair, International Judicial Academy; Board of Directors, International Association of Women Judges; American Judicature Society; National Conference on Uniform State Laws; Wisconsin Judicial College (associate dean and faculty); Wisconsin Rhodes Scholarship Committee (chair); Wisconsin Judicial Council; Wisconsin Equal Justice Task Force; Wisconsin Judicial Conference (executive committee, legislative committee, judicial education committee); Civil Law Committee (executive committee); Task Force on Children and Families; Board of Directors, Wisconsin State Public Defender; Committee on the Administration of Courts. ▪ Recipient: American Judicature Society's *Herbert Harley Award; Business and Professional Woman of the Year; Business Woman of the Year Athena Award; Women in the Law Award.*

Current office: Elected to Supreme Court 1995. Reelected 2005 and 2015.

Patience Drake Roggensack, Chief Justice

Biography: Born Joliet, Illinois, July 7; married; 3 children. ▪ Graduate Lockport Township High School; B.A. Drake University; J.D. University of Wisconsin-Madison Law School (cum laude). ▪ Former practicing attorney. ▪ Participation: Commissioner, Uniform Laws Commission; Fellow, American Bar Foundation; Wisconsin Judicial Council; Supreme Court Rules Procedure Committee;

Supreme Court Finance Committee; Committee for Public Trust and Confidence in the Courts; American Bar Association; State Bar Association of Wisconsin; Western District of Wisconsin Bar Association (past president); Dane County Bar Association, served on Personnel Review Board (supreme court delegate); 2005 Judicial Conference (cochair); 2005 Statewide Bench Bar Conference (cochair). ▪ Board service on: YMCA; YWCA; Wisconsin Center for Academically Talented Youth; Olbrich Botanical Society; International Women's Forum (past president); A Fund For Women; Friends of the Arboretum. ▪ Court of Appeals judge, District IV (1996–2003). Served on Judicial Conference (legislative liaison); Publication Committee for the Court of Appeals; State Court/Tribal Court Planning Committee (cochair); Personnel Review Board (appeals court delegate).

Current office: Elected to Supreme Court 2003. Reelected 2013. Elected chief justice May 1, 2015. Reelected 2017.

Annette K. Ziegler

Biography: Born Grand Rapids, Michigan, March 6, 1964; married with children. ▪ Graduate Forest Hills Central High School; B.A. in Business Administration and Psychology, Hope College (Holland, Michigan), 1986; J.D. Marquette University Law School, 1989. ▪ Former practicing attorney (civil litigation), 1989–95. Pro bono special assistant district attorney, Milwaukee County, 1992, 1996. Assistant U.S. attorney, Eastern District of Wisconsin, 1995–97. Washington County Circuit Court judge, 1997–2007. Court of Appeals District II (Judicial Exchange Program 1999). Deputy chief judge, Third Judicial District. Judicial faculty at various seminars. ▪ Court liaison, Board of Bar Examiners. Member, Supreme Court Finance Committee. Commissioner, Uniform State Laws Commission. ▪ Member: State Bar of Wisconsin; American Bar Association; American Law Institute (elected member); American Bar Foundation (fellow); International Women's Forum; Washington County Bar Association; Milwaukee County Bar Association; Eastern District of Wisconsin Bar Association; Boys & Girls Club of Washington County (trustee board president); Marquette University Law School Advisory Board; Rotary Club West Bend. ▪ Former member: Wisconsin Judicial Council; State Bar of Wisconsin Bench & Bar Committee; Governor's Juvenile Justice Commission; Criminal Benchbook Committee; Criminal Jury Instruction Committee; Legal Association for Women; James E. Doyle American Inn of Court.

Current office: Elected to Supreme Court 2007. Reelected 2017.

Rebecca Grassl Bradley

Biography: Born Milwaukee, Wisconsin, August 2, 1971. ▪ Graduate Divine Savior Holy Angels High School; Honors B.S. in Business Administration and Business Economics, Marquette University, 1993; J.D. University of Wisconsin-Madison, 1996. ▪ Former practicing attorney, 1996–2012; Milwaukee County Circuit Court judge, appointed 2012, elected 2013; District I Court of Appeals judge, appointed 2015. ▪ Member: Supreme Court Finance Committee; Supreme Court Legislative Committee; Board of Advisors, Federalist Society, Milwaukee Lawyers Chapter; Wisconsin State Advisory Committee, U.S. Commission on Civil Rights. ▪ Former member: Board of Governors, St. Thomas More Lawyers Society; Wisconsin Juvenile Jury Instructions Committee; Wisconsin Juvenile Benchbook Committee; Milwaukee Trial Judges Association; Wisconsin Trial Judges Association. ▪ In private practice: American Arbitration Association arbitrator; chair, Business Law Section, State Bar of Wisconsin.

Current office: Appointed to Supreme Court October 2015 to fill vacancy created by death of Justice N. Patrick Crooks. Elected to full term 2016.

Daniel Kelly

Biography: Born Santa Barbara, California, 1964; married; 5 children. ▪ Graduate B.S. Political Science and Spanish, Carroll College, 1986; J.D. Regent University Law School (Virginia Beach, Virginia), 1991, where he was editor-in-chief of the Law Review. ▪ Former shareholder in one of Wisconsin's oldest and largest law firms; law clerk for Wisconsin Court of Appeals Judge Ralph Adam

Fine (1991–92); law clerk and staff attorney, Office of Special Masters, U.S. Court of Federal Claims (1992–96). ▪ Member: Board of Advisors, Federalist Society, Milwaukee Lawyers Chapter; Wisconsin State Advisory Committee, U.S. Commission on Civil Rights; President's Advisory Council, Carroll University. ▪ Former member: Old World Wisconsin Foundation (board member); Milwaukee Forum.

Current office: Appointed to Supreme Court July 2016 to fill vacancy created by resignation of Justice David T. Prosser.

Rebecca Frank Dallet

Biography: Born Cleveland, Ohio, July 15, 1969; married, 3 children. ▪ Graduated B.A. in Economics *summa cum laude* with honors, The Ohio State University, 1991;

J.D. *summa cum laude*, Case Western Reserve University School of Law, 1994. ▪ Law Clerk for U.S. Magistrate Judge Aaron Goodstein, Eastern District of Wisconsin, 1994–96; Assistant District Attorney, Milwaukee County, 1996–99 and 2002–07; Special Assistant United States Attorney 1999–2002; Adjunct Law Professor, Marquette University Law School, 2005–08; Presiding Court Commissioner, Milwaukee County, 2007–08; Milwaukee

County Circuit Court Judge 2008–18. ▪ Member: Chair, Judicial Education Committee; Court Liaison, Access to Justice Commission; Faculty, National Institute on Domestic Violence; Trainer, VoteRunLead; National Board of Trial Advocacy, James E. Doyle Inn of Court (board member); Milwaukee Bar Association. ▪ Former member: Wisconsin Criminal Jury Instruction Committee; Associate Dean, Wisconsin Judicial College; Association of Women Lawyers (secretary); Milwaukee Trial Judges' Association (president); Eastern District of Wisconsin Bar Association (ex officio director); Legislative Council Special Committee on Sexually Violent Person Commitments 2004, 2012; Milwaukee Jewish Federation (board membe); Congregation Shalom (youth leader and educator). ▪ Recipient: Phi Beta Kappa; Merit Scholar, Case Western Reserve University School of Law; *Order of the Coif*; Whitehouse Leadership Project Women Rule! 2005; *Pasch Meritorious Service Award* 2005; Woman in the Law Honoree 2012; *Dallet Youth Award* 2014; *Woman of Influence Award* 2019.

Current office: Elected to Supreme Court 2018.

Brian Hagedorn

Biography: Born Brookfield, Wisconsin, January 21, 1978; married; 5 children. ▪ Graduate Wauwatosa West High School, 1996; B.A. in Philosophy, Trinity International University, 2000; J.D. Northwestern University School of Law, 2003. ▪ Former attorney in private practice (2006–09); Wisconsin Supreme Court law clerk for Justice Michael Gableman (2009–10); Assistant Attorney General at Wisconsin Department of Justice (2010–11); Chief Legal Counsel for the Office of Governor Scott Walker (2010–15); Wisconsin Court of Appeals judge, District II (2015–19). ▪ Memberships in State Bar of Wisconsin Bench Bar Committee; State Claims Board; Wisconsin Judicial Commission; Federalist Society. ▪ Recipient: *Alumnus of the Year* 2014, Trinity International University.

Current office: Elected to Supreme Court 2019.

U.S. CONGRESSIONAL DELEGATION

Tammy Baldwin, U.S. Senator
Democrat

Biography: Born Madison, Wisconsin, February 11, 1962. Voting address: Madison, Wisconsin. ▪ Graduate Madison West High School; A.B. in Mathematics and Government, Smith College (Massachusetts), 1984; J.D., University of Wisconsin-Madison, 1989. ▪ Former practicing attorney, 1989–92. ▪ Madison City Council, 1986; Dane County Board, 1986–94. ▪ State legislative service: Elected to Assembly, 78th District, 1992–96 (served until January 4, 1999).

Congress: Elected to U.S. House of Representatives 1998. Reelected 2000–10. Elected to U.S. Senate since 2012. Committee assignments, 116th Congress: Appropriations and its subcommittees on Agriculture, Rural Development, Food and Drug Administration, and Related Agencies; on Department of Defense; on Department of Homeland Security; on Departments of Labor, Health and Human Services, and Education, and Related Agencies; and on Military Construction and Veterans Affairs, and Related Agencies. Commerce, Science and Transportation and its subcommittees on Communications, Technology, Innovation, and the Internet; on Manufacturing, Trade, and Consumer Protection; on Science, Oceans, Fisheries, and Weather; and on Transportation and Safety. Health, Education, Labor, and Pensions and its subcommittees on Employment and Workplace Safety and on Primary Health and Retirement Security.

Contact: Washington—202-224-5653; 709 Hart Senate Office Building, Washington, D.C. 20510. Eau Claire—715-832-8424; 500 South Barstow Street, Suite LL2, Eau Claire, WI 54701. Green Bay—920-498-2668; 1039 West Mason Street, Suite 119, Green Bay, WI 54303. La Crosse—608-796-0045; 205 5th Avenue South, Room 216, La Crosse, WI 54601. Madison—608-264-5338; 30 West Mifflin Street, Suite 700, Madison, WI 53703. Milwaukee—414-297-4451; 633 West Wisconsin Avenue, Suite 1920, Milwaukee, WI 53203. Ashland—715-450-3754; PO Box 61, Ashland, WI 54806.

Website: www.baldwin.senate.gov

Ron Johnson, U.S. Senator
Republican

Biography: Born Mankato, Minnesota, April 8, 1955; 3 children. Voting address: Oshkosh, Wisconsin. ▪ Graduate Edina High School, 1973; B.S.B., University of Minnesota, 1977. ▪ Former CEO, plastics manufacturing company. ▪ Former member: Partners in Education Council, Oshkosh Chamber of Commerce (business cochair); Oshkosh Opera House Foundation (treasurer); Lourdes Foundation (board president); Diocese of Green Bay Finance Council; Oshkosh Chamber of Commerce Board of Directors (chair-elect); Oshkosh Area Community Foundation Investment Council.

Congress: Elected to U.S. Senate 2010. Reelected 2016. Committee assignments, 116th Congress: Homeland Security and Governmental Affairs (chair); its Permanent Subcommittee on Investigations; and its subcommittees on Federal Spending Oversight and Emergency Management; and on Regulatory Affairs and Federal Management. Budget. Commerce, Science, and Transportation and its subcommittees on Communications, Technology, Innovation, and the Internet; on Manufacturing, Trade, and Consumer Protection; on Science, Oceans, Fisheries, and Weather; and on Security. Foreign Relations and its subcommittees on Europe and Regional Security Cooperation (chair); on East Asia, the Pacific, and International Cybersecurity Policy; and on Africa and Global Health Policy.

Contact: Washington—202-224-5323; 328 Hart Senate Office Building, Washington, D.C. 20510. Milwaukee—414-276-7282; 517 East Wisconsin Avenue, Suite 408, Milwaukee, WI 53202. Oshkosh—920-230-7250; 219 Washington Avenue, Suite 100, Oshkosh, WI 54901. Madison—608-240-9629; 5315 Wall Street, Suite 110; Madison, WI 53718.

Website: www.ronjohnson.senate.gov

U.S. Congressional Districts

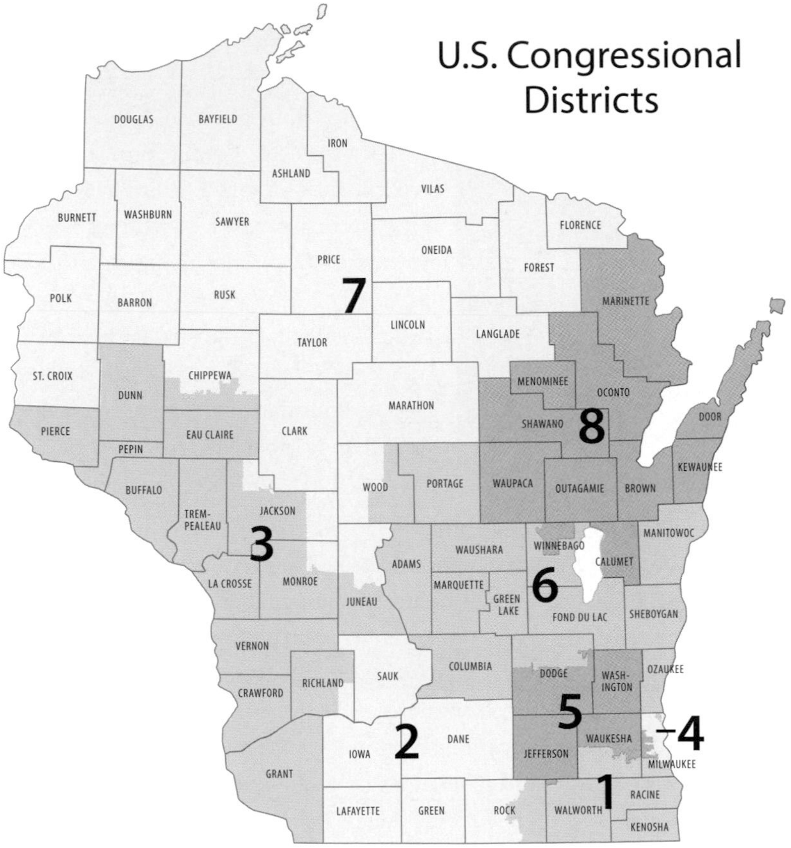

Bryan Steil, U.S. Representative
Republican, 1st Congressional District

Biography: Born Janesville, Wisconsin, March 3, 1981. Voting address: Janesville, Wisconsin. ▪ Graduate Janesville Craig High School; B.S. in Business Administration, Georgetown University, 2003; J.D., University of Wisconsin-Madison, 2007. ▪ Former attorney; businessman. ▪ Member: St. John Vianney Parish. ▪ Former member: University of Wisconsin Board of Regents.

Congress: Elected to U.S. House of Representatives 2018. Committee assignments, 116th Congress: Financial Services and its subcommittees on Housing, Community Development and Insurance; on Diversity and Inclusion; and on Oversight and Investigations.

Contact: Washington—202-225-3031; 1408 Longworth House Office Building, Washington, D.C. 20515. Janesville—608-752-4050; 20 South Main Street, Suite 10, Janesville, WI 53545. Kenosha—262-654-1901; Somers Village/Town Hall, 7511 12th Street, Somers, WI 53171. Racine—262-637-0510; Racine County Courthouse, Room 101; 730 Wisconsin Avenue; Racine, WI 53403.

Website: https://steil.house.gov

Mark Pocan, U.S. Representative

Democrat, 2nd Congressional District

Biography: Born Kenosha, Wisconsin, August 14, 1964; married. Voting address: Town of Vermont, Wisconsin. ▪ Graduate Mary D. Bradford High School (Kenosha); B.A., University of Wisconsin-Madison, 1986. ▪ Small businessperson. ▪ State legislative service: Elected to Assembly, 78th District, 1998–2010 (served until January 3, 2013).

Congress: Elected to U.S. House of Representatives 2012. Reelected since 2014. Committee assignments, 116th Congress: Appropriations and its subcommittees on Labor, Health and Human Services, Education, and Related Agencies; on Energy and Water Development, and Related agencies; and on Agriculture, Rural Development, Food and Drug Administration and Related Agencies. Select Committee on the Modernization of Congress.

Contact: Washington—202-225-2906; 1421 Longworth House Office Building, Washington, D.C. 20515. Beloit—608-365-8001; 100 State Street, 3rd floor, Beloit, WI 53511. Madison—608-258-9800; 10 East Doty Street, Suite 405, Madison, WI 53703.

Website: http://pocan.house.gov

Ron Kind, U.S. Representative

Democrat, 3rd Congressional District

Biography: Born La Crosse, Wisconsin, March 16, 1963; married; 2 children. Voting address: La Crosse, Wisconsin. ▪ Graduate Logan High School; B.A., Harvard University, 1985; M.A., London School of Economics (England); J.D., University of Minnesota Law School, 1990. ▪ Attorney. Former La Crosse County assistant district attorney and State of Wisconsin special prosecutor. ▪ Member: U.S. Supreme Court Bar; State Bar of Wisconsin and

La Crosse County Bar Association; Association of State Prosecutors; Democratic Party; Wisconsin Harvard Club (board of directors); Boys and Girls Club of Greater La Crosse (board of directors); Coulee Council on Alcohol and Other Drug Abuse (board of directors); Moose Club; Optimist Club.

Congress: Elected to U.S. House of Representatives 1996. Reelected since 1998. Committee assignments, 116th Congress: Ways and Means and its subcommittees on Health and on Trade.

Contact: Washington—202-225-5506; 1502 Longworth House Office Building, Washington, D.C. 20515-4906. Eau Claire—715-831-9214; 131 S. Barstow Street, Suite 301, Eau Claire, WI 54701. La Crosse—608-782-2558; 205 5th Avenue South, Suite 400, La Crosse, WI 54601.

Website: https://kind.house.gov

Gwendolynne S. Moore, U.S. Representative

Democrat, 4th Congressional District

Biography: Born Racine, Wisconsin, April 18, 1951; 3 children. Voting address: Milwaukee, Wisconsin. ▪ Graduate North Division High School (Milwaukee); B.A. in Political Science, Marquette University, 1978; certification in Credit Union Management, Milwaukee Area Technical College, 1983. ▪ Former housing officer with Wisconsin Housing and Economic Development Authority; development specialist with Milwaukee City Development; program and planning analyst with Wisconsin Departments of Employment Relations and Health and Social Services. ▪ Member: National Black Caucus of State Legislators; National Conference of State Legislatures—Host Committee, Milwaukee 1995; National Black Caucus of State Legislators—Host Committee (chair) 1997; Wisconsin Legislative Black and Hispanic Caucus (chair since 1997). ▪ State legislative service: Elected to Assembly 1988 and 1990; elected to Senate 1992, 1996, and 2000. Senate President Pro Tempore 1997, 1995 (effective 7/15/96).

Congress: Elected to U.S. House of Representatives 2004. Reelected since 2006. Committee assignments, 116th Congress: Ways and Means and its subcommittees on Oversight; on Select Revenue Measures; and on Worker and Family Support.

Contact: Washington—202-225-4572; 2252 Rayburn House Office Building, Washington, D.C. 20515. Milwaukee—414-297-1140; 250 East Wisconsin Avenue, Suite 950, Milwaukee, WI 53202.

Website: https://gwenmoore.house.gov

F. James Sensenbrenner, Jr., U.S. Representative

Republican, 5th Congressional District

Biography: Born Chicago, Illinois, June 14, 1943; married; 2 children, 1 grandchild. Voting address: Menomonee Falls, Wisconsin. ▪ Graduate Milwaukee Country Day School, 1961; A.B., Stanford University, 1965; J.D., University of Wisconsin-Madison Law School, 1968. ▪ Attorney. Former assistant to State Senate Majority Leader Jerris Leonard and to U.S. Congressman Arthur Younger. ▪ Member: State Bar of Wisconsin; Riveredge Nature Center; American Philatelic Society; Waukesha County Republican Party. ▪ Former member: Whitefish Bay Jaycees; Shorewood Men's Club. ▪ Recipient: Government of Japan *Order of the Rising Sun, Gold and Silver Star*; European Parliament *Schuman Medal*. ▪ State legislative service: Elected to Assembly 1968–74. Elected to Senate in April 1975 special election. Reelected in 1976. Assistant minority leader 1977.

Congress: Elected to U.S. House of Representatives 1978. Reelected since 1980. Committee assignments, 116th Congress: Judiciary and its subcommittees on Crime, Terrorism and Homeland Security; and on Antitrust, Commercial and Administrative Law. Foreign Affairs and its subcommittees on Europe, Eurasia, Energy, and the Environment; and on Africa, Global Health, Global Human Rights and International Organizations.

Contact: Washington—202-225-5101; 2449 Rayburn House Office Building, Washington, D.C. 20515-4905. Brookfield—262-784-1111; 800-242-1119 (toll free) 120 Bishops Way, Room 154, Brookfield, WI 53005-6294.

Website: http://sensenbrenner.house.gov

Glenn Grothman, U.S. Representative

Republican, 6th Congressional District

Biography: Born Milwaukee, Wisconsin, July 3, 1955. Voting address: Glenbeulah, Wisconsin. ▪ Graduate Homestead High School (Mequon); B.B.A.; J.D., University of Wisconsin-Madison. ▪ Former practicing attorney. ▪ Member: Kiwanis—West Bend, Early Risers; Loyal Order of the Moose—West Bend; Kettle Moraine Symphony (board member); ABATE of Wisconsin; Rotary Club of Fond du Lac. ▪ Recipient: The Association of Mature

American Citizens *Friend of AMAC*; International Food Distributors Association *Thomas Jefferson Award* 2016; American Conservative Union *Award for Conservative Achievement* 2015; FreedomWorks *Freedom Fighter Award* 2016; *Asian American Hotel Owners Association Award* 2015; U.S. Chamber of Commerce *Spirit of Enterprise Award* 2014; National Retail Federation *Hero on Main Street* 2016, 2015; WMC *Exemplar Awar*d for work on manufacturing tax credit 2012; Wisconsin Farm Bureau's *Friend of Farm Bureau Award* 2016; NFIB *Guardian of Small Business Award* 2016. ▪ State legislative service: Elected to Assembly in December 1993 special election. Reelected 1994–2002. Elected to Senate 2004. Reelected 2008–12. Assistant Majority Leader 2013, 2011; Assistant Minority Leader 2009; Minority Caucus Chair 2007; Majority Caucus Vice Chair 2003, 2001, 1999.

Congress: Elected to U.S. House of Representatives since 2014. Committee assignments, 116th Congress: Education and Labor and its subcommittees on Early Childhood, Elementary, and Secondary Education; and on Higher Education and Workforce Investment. Oversight and Reform, and its subcommittees on Government Operations and on Economic and Consumer Policy.

Contact: Washington—202-225-2476; 1427 Longworth House Office Building, Washington, D.C. 20515. Fond du Lac—920-907-0624; 24 West Pioneer Road, Fond du Lac, WI 54935.

Website: https://grothman.house.gov

Sean P. Duffy, U.S. Representative
Republican, 7th Congressional District

Biography: Born October 3, 1971; married; 7 children. Voting address: Weston, Wisconsin. ▪ Graduate Hayward High School; B.A. in Business Marketing, St. Mary's (Winona, Minnesota), 1994; J.D., William Mitchell College of Law, 1999. ▪ Attorney. Former special prosecutor and district attorney, Ashland County.

Congress: Elected to U.S. House of Representatives 2010. Reelected since 2012. Committee assignments, 116th Congress: Financial Services and its subcommittees on Housing, Community Development, and Insurance; and on Investor Protection, Entrepreneurship, and Capital Markets.

Contact: Washington—202-225-3365; 1714 Longworth House Office Building, Washington, D.C. 20515. Hayward—715-392-3984; 15569 Railroad Street, Suite 302, Hayward, WI 54843. Hudson—715-808-8160; 502 2nd Street, Suite 202, Hudson, WI 54016. Wausau—715-298-9344; 208 Grand Avenue, Wausau, WI 54403.

Website: https://duffy.house.gov

Mike Gallagher, U.S. Representative
Republican, 8th Congressional District

Biography: Born Green Bay, Wisconsin, March 3, 1984. Voting address: Green Bay, Wisconsin. ▪ A.B., Princeton University; Master's in Security Studies, Georgetown University; Ph.D. in International Relations, Georgetown University. Iraq War Veteran, intelligence officer, served in U.S. Marine Corps 2006–13. ▪ Former staffer, U.S. Senate Foreign Relations Committee; senior global market strategist at a fuel management services company.

Congress: Elected to U.S. House of Representatives since 2016. Committee assignments, 116th Congress: Armed Services and its subcommittees on Seapower and Projection Forces; and on Intelligence and Emerging Threats and Capabilities. Transportation and Infrastructure and its subcommittees on Aviation; on Coast Guard and Maritime Transportation; and on Highways and Transit.

Contact: Washington—202-225-5665; 1230 Longworth House Office Building, Washington, D.C. 20515. De Pere—920-301-4500; 1702 Scheuring Road, Suite B, De Pere, WI 54115.

Website: https://gallagher.house.gov

■ ■ ■

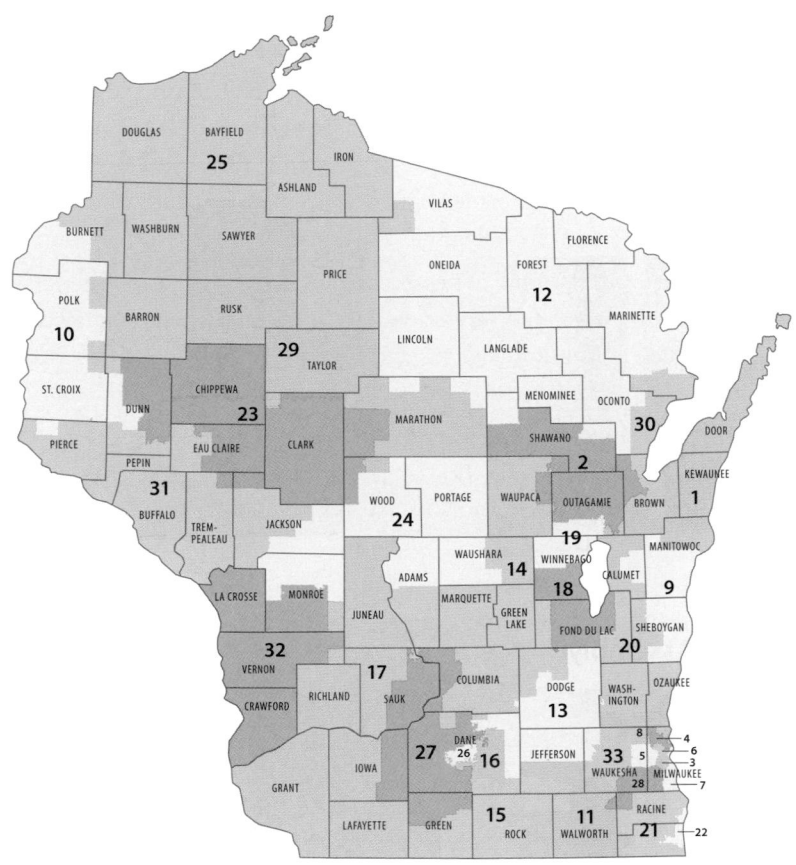

State Senate Districts

The Wisconsin Constitution requires the state legislature to redraw the state assembly and senate districts, based on population, following each U.S. Census. To fulfill this requirement, the state legislature passed 2011 Wisconsin Act 43 to establish the current senate districts. The Wisconsin Constitution additionally requires that senate districts be "convenient contiguous territory" and that "no assembly district [be] divided in the formation of a senate district." Under 2011 Wisconsin Act 43, each senate district comprises three consecutive assembly districts: for example, Senate District 1 is comprised of Assembly Districts 1, 2, and 3.

2019 State Senate Officers

President Roth

President Pro Tempore
Marklein

Majority Leader
Fitzgerald

Assistant Majority
Leader Feyen

Minority Leader
Shilling

Assistant Minority
Leader Bewley

Chief Clerk Renk

Sergeant at Arms Blazel

2019 State Assembly Officers

Speaker Vos

Speaker Pro Tempore
August

Majority Leader
Steineke

Assistant Majority
Leader Felzkowski

Minority Leader Hintz

Assistant Minority
Leader Hesselbein

Chief Clerk Fuller

Sergeant at Arms
Tonnon Byers

Senate District 1
Assembly Districts 1, 2, 3

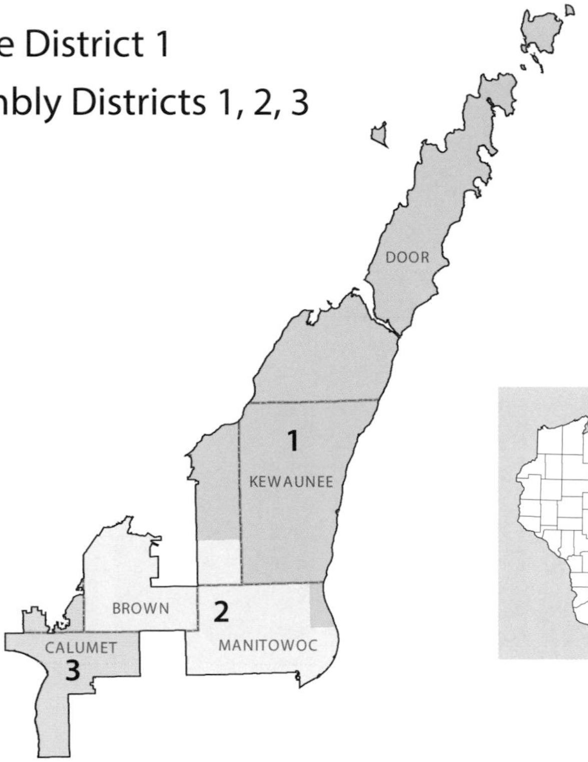

DOOR

1

KEWAUNEE

BROWN

2

CALUMET

MANITOWOC

3

1

André Jacque, Senate District 1
Republican

Biography: Born Beaver Dam, Wisconsin, October 13, 1980; married; 5 children. Voting address: De Pere, Wisconsin. ▪ Graduate Green Bay Southwest High School, 1999; B.S. University of Wisconsin-Madison, 2003; graduate certificate from UW-Madison La Follette School of Public Affairs. ▪ Former communications and planning director, and environmental consultant. ▪ Member: Wisconsin Council on Domestic Abuse; Wisconsin Small Business Environmental Council; Family & Childcare Resources of Northeast Wisconsin (board member); Green Bay Area Crime Stoppers (board member); Van Handel Foundation for Families of Children with Special Needs (board member); Golden House Domestic Abuse Shelter Community Leadership Council; Brown County Taxpayers Association; Knights of Columbus. ▪ Former member: Wisconsin Higher Educational Aids Board, 2001–03. ▪ Recipient: Wisconsin Coalition Against Domestic Violence *Legislative Champion Award*; Wisconsin

Counties Association *Outstanding Legislator Award*; Pro-Life Wisconsin *Legislator of the Year*; NFIB *Guardian of Small Business Award*; Wisconsin Family Council *William Wilberforce Freedom Award*; Brown County Crime Prevention Foundation *Crimefighter Award*; Manitowoc County Substance Abuse Prevention Coalition IMPACT Recognition; Wisconsin Coalition of Virtual School Families *Shining Star of Education Reform*; Phillips Foundation *Distinguished Young Conservative Leader of the Year*; Green Bay Area Chamber of Commerce *Legislator of the Year*; Mothers Against Drunk Driving (MADD) *Legislator of the Year*; Oral Health Partnership *Children's Health Champion*; Wisconsin Towns Association *Friend of Towns*; Wisconsin Professional Police Association *Legislator of the Year*; Wisconsin Chiefs of Police Association *Legislator of the Year*; U.S. Chamber of Commerce Institute for Legal Reform *State Legislative Achievement Award*.

Legislature: Elected to Assembly 2010–2016. Elected to Senate 2018. Committee assignments, 2019: Local Government, Small Business, Tourism and Workforce (chair); Judiciary and Public Safety (vice chair); Agriculture, Revenue and Financial Institutions; Health and Human Services; Joint Committee on Information Policy and Technology (co-chair); Joint Legislative Council; Legislative State Supported Programs Study and Advisory Committee. Additional appointments: Child Abuse and Neglect Prevention Board; Council on Tourism; Wisconsin Housing and Economic Development Authority.

Contact: Sen.Jacque@legis.wisconsin.gov; 608-266-3512; Room 7 South, State Capitol, PO Box 7882, Madison, WI 53707.

Joel C. Kitchens, Assembly District 1
Republican

Biography: Born Washington, D.C., September 20, 1957; married; 3 children, 1 grandchild. Voting address: Sturgeon Bay, Wisconsin. ▪ Graduate Ballard High School, Louisville, Kentucky, 1975; B.S. Ohio State University, 1979; D.V.M. Ohio State University, 1983. ▪ Large animal veterinarian. ▪ Member: Sturgeon Bay Moravian Church; Wisconsin Veterinary Medical Association; American Veterinary Medical Association; Sturgeon Bay Rotary Club. ▪ Former member: Sturgeon Bay Board of Education, 2000–14.

Legislature: Elected to Assembly since 2014. Committee assignments, 2019: Environment (chair); Education (vice chair); Agriculture; Financial Institutions; Tourism.

April 1987 special election. Reelected since 1988. Committee assignments, 2019: Natural Resources and Energy (chair); Transportation, Veterans and Military Affairs; Joint Legislative Audit Committee (co-chair); Speaker's Task Force on Water Quality.

Contact: Sen.Cowles@legis.wisconsin.gov; 608-266-0484; 800-334-1465 (toll free); 920-448-5092 (district); Room 118 South, State Capitol, PO Box 7882, Madison, WI 53707-7882.

David Steffen, Assembly District 4
Republican

Biography: Born October 12, 1971; married; 1 child. Voting address: Howard, Wisconsin. ▪ Graduate Ashwaubenon High School, 1990; B.A. in Political Science, University of Wisconsin-Madison, 1995. ▪ Small business owner. ▪ Membership: McPherson Eye Research Institute (advisory council member); U.S. Global Leadership Coalition (advisory council member); Howard Small Business Partnership (founder); Howard Go Green Save Green Initiative (founder, chair); Ashwaubenon Business Association (president); Prevent Blindness—Northeastern Wisconsin (president); Team Lambeau (executive director); Green Bay Area Chamber of Commerce State and Federal Issues Committee (chair). ▪ Village of Howard Board of Trustees, 2007–15; Brown County Board of Supervisors, 2012–15.

Legislature: Elected to Assembly since 2014. Committee assignments, 2019: Criminal Justice and Public Safety; Energy and Utilities (vice chair); Government Accountability and Oversight (chair); Insurance; Local Government.

Contact: Rep.Steffen@legis.wisconsin.gov; 608-266-5840; 888-534-0004 (toll free); Room 21 North, State Capitol, PO Box 8953, Madison, WI 53708.

Jim Steineke, Assembly District 5
Republican

Biography: Born Milwaukee, Wisconsin, November 23, 1970; married; 3 children. Voting address: Kaukauna, Wisconsin. ▪ Graduate Wauwatosa West High School, 1989; attended University of Wisconsin-Milwaukee and University of Wisconsin-Oshkosh. ▪ Realtor; salesman. ▪ Member: Realtors Association of Northeast Wisconsin; Wisconsin Realtors Association.

- Town of Vandenbroek supervisor, 2005–07; town chair, 2007–11. Outagamie County supervisor, 2006–11.

Legislature: Elected to Assembly since 2010. Leadership positions: Majority Leader 2019, 2017, 2015; Assistant Majority Leader 2013. Committee assignments, 2019: Assembly Organization (vice chair); Employment Relations (vice chair); Rules (chair); Joint Committee on Employment Relations; Joint Committee on Legislative Organization; Joint Legislative Council.

Contact: Rep.Steineke@legis.wisconsin.gov; 608-266-2418; 888-534-0005 (toll free); Room 115 West, State Capitol, PO Box 8953, Madison, WI 53708.

Gary Tauchen, Assembly District 6
Republican

Biography: Born Rice Lake, Wisconsin, November 23, 1953; single. Voting address: Bonduel, Wisconsin.
- Graduate Bonduel High School, 1971; attended University of Wisconsin-Madison, 1971–72; B.S. in Animal Science, University of Wisconsin-River Falls, 1976.
- Dairy farmer. ▪ Member: Wisconsin Farm Bureau; Badger AgVest, LLC (former director); Professional Dairy Producers of Wisconsin (former director); Dairy Business Association; Wisconsin Livestock Identification Consortium (former director, former chair); Brown, Shawano, Outagamie, Waupaca County Republican Party; Shawano Area Chamber of Commerce; Shawano County Dairy Promotions (former director); Cooperative Resources International (former vice chair); AgSource Cooperative Services (former chair); National Dairy Herd Improvement Association (former director); University of Wisconsin Center for Dairy Profitability (former chair); Shawano Rotary; Major, Wisconsin Wing, Civil Air Patrol Legislative Squadron (official Auxiliary of the U.S. Air Force).

Legislature: Elected to Assembly since 2006. Leadership positions: Minority Caucus Sergeant at Arms 2009. Committee assignments, 2019: Agriculture (chair); State Affairs (vice chair); Energy and Utilities; Family Law; International Affairs and Commerce; Tourism.

Contact: Rep.Tauchen@legis.wisconsin.gov; 608-266-3097; 888-529-0006 (toll free); Room 13 West, State Capitol, PO Box 8953, Madison, WI 53708.

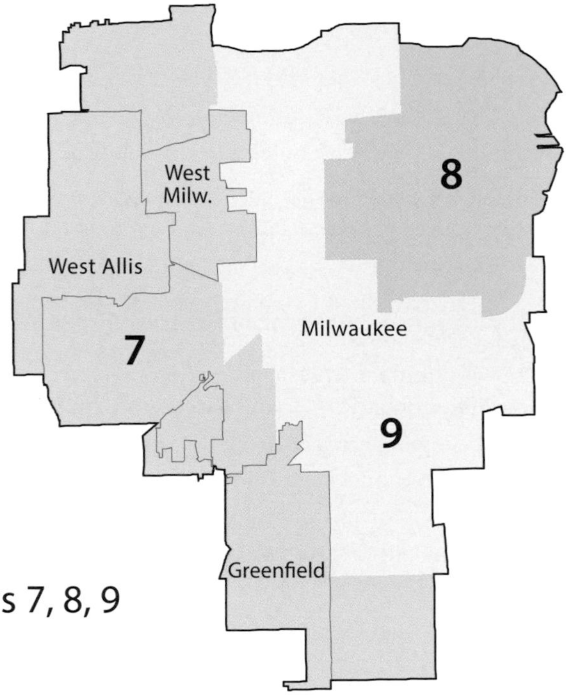

Senate District 3
Assembly Districts 7, 8, 9

Tim Carpenter, Senate District 3
Democrat

Biography: Born Milwaukee, Wisconsin. Voting address: Milwaukee, Wisconsin. ▪ Graduate Pulaski High School; B.A. in Political Science and History, University of Wisconsin-Milwaukee; M.A. in Public Policy and Public Administration, La Follette School of Public Affairs, University of Wisconsin-Madison; Milwaukee Police Department Citizen Academy, 2018. ▪ Full-time legislator. ▪ Member: Sierra Club; Jackson Park Neighborhood Association; Story Hill Neighborhood Association; Milwaukee VA Soldiers Home Advisory Council; Milwaukee LGBT Community Center; Wisconsin Humane Society; Polish Center of Wisconsin; Democratic Party. ▪ Recipient:

Mothers Against Drunk Driving *Legislator of the Year*; Wisconsin Professional Police Association *Law Enforcement Honor Roll*; Wisconsin League of Conservation Voters *Conservation Champion*; several Wisconsin Environmental Decade *Clean 16* awards; Shepherd Express *Best State Legislator*; Wisconsin Public Health Association's *Champion of Public Health*; Coalition of Wisconsin Aging Groups *Award for Service to Seniors*; Wisconsin Professional Fire Fighters *Legislator of the Year.*

Legislature: Elected to Assembly 1984–2000. Elected to Senate since 2002. Leadership positions: Senate President Pro Tempore, 2011–2013; Assembly Speaker Pro Tempore, 1993–1994. Committees, 2019: Economic Development, Commerce and Trade; Health and Human Services; Transportation, Veterans and Military Affairs; Joint Committee on Information Policy and Technology; Joint Legislative Audit Committee. Additional appointments: Wisconsin Economic Development Corporation Board; State Fair Park Board; Transportation Projects Commission; Governor's Council on Domestic Abuse.

Contact: Sen.Carpenter@legis.wisconsin.gov; 608-266-8535; Room 109 South, State Capitol, PO Box 7882, Madison, WI 53707.

Daniel G. Riemer, Assembly District 7
Democrat

Biography: Born Milwaukee, Wisconsin, December 10, 1986; married, 1 child. Voting address: Milwaukee, Wisconsin. ▪ Graduate Rufus King High School (Milwaukee), 2005; B.A. University of Chicago, 2009; J.D. University of Wisconsin Law School, 2013. ▪ Full-time legislator. ▪ Member: Wisconsin State Bar Association; World Economic Forum: Global Shapers, Milwaukee Hub; Eisenhower Fellows.

Legislature: Elected to Assembly since 2012. Committee assignments, 2019: Health; Insurance; Medicaid Reform and Oversight; Veterans and Military Affairs; Ways and Means; Joint Survey Committee on Tax Exemptions.

Contact: Rep.Riemer@legis.wisconsin.gov; 608-266-1733; 888-529-0007 (toll free); Room 122 North, State Capitol, PO Box 8953, Madison, WI 53708.

JoCasta Zamarripa, Assembly District 8

Democrat

Biography: Born Milwaukee, Wisconsin, March 8, 1976. Voting address: Milwaukee, Wisconsin. ▪ Graduate St. Joan Antida High School (Milwaukee), 1994; BFA University of Wisconsin-Milwaukee, 2005. ▪ Full-time legislator. Former nonprofit professional.

Legislature: Elected to Assembly since 2010. Leadership positions: Minority Caucus Vice Chair 2015, 2013. Committee assignments, 2019: Campaigns and Elections; Housing and Real Estate; International Affairs and Commerce; Jobs and the Economy; Small Business Development; State Affairs.

Contact: Rep.Zamarripa@legis.wisconsin.gov; legis.wisconsin.gov/assembly/zamarripa; Twitter: @repjocasta; Facebook: Rep.Zamarripa; 608-267-7669; 888-534-0008 (toll free); Room 112 North, State Capitol, PO Box 8953, Madison, WI 53708.

Marisabel Cabrera, Assembly District 9

Democrat

Biography: Born Milwaukee, Wisconsin, December 12, 1975; single. Voting address: Milwaukee, Wisconsin. ▪ Graduate Nathan Hale High School, 1993; B.A. in Spanish and Latin American Iberian Studies, University of Wisconsin-Madison, 1998; J.D. Michigan State University College of Law, 2002. ▪ Small business owner; immigration attorney. ▪ Member: City of Milwaukee Fire and Police Commission (chair); Voces de la Frontera; Democratic Party of Wisconsin; Democratic Party of Milwaukee County; State Bar of Wisconsin; State Bar of Florida. ▪ Former member: Centro Hispano of Milwaukee Board of Directors; Latino Caucus of the Democratic Party of Wisconsin (chair).

Legislature: Elected to Assembly 2018. Committee assignments, 2019: Constitution and Ethics; Consumer Protection; Criminal Justice and Public Safety; International Affairs and Commerce; Judiciary; Small Business Development; State Affairs.

Contact: Rep.Cabrera@legis.wisconsin.gov; 608- 266-1707; 888-534-0009 (toll free); Room 16 West, State Capitol, PO Box 8952, Madison, WI 53708.

Senate District 4
Assembly Districts 10, 11, 12

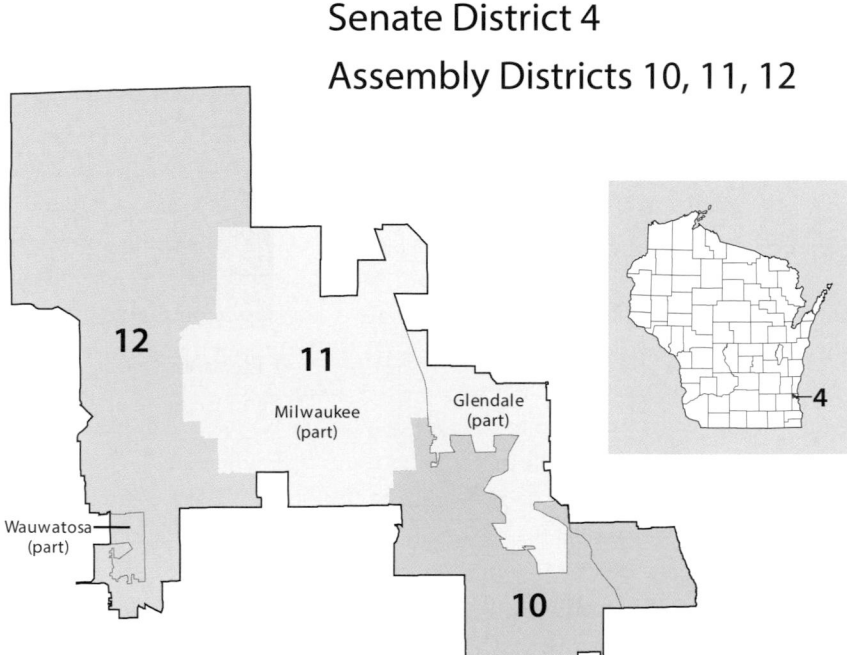

Lena C. Taylor, Senate District 4
Democrat

Biography: Born Milwaukee, Wisconsin, July 25, 1966; 1 child. Voting address: Milwaukee, Wisconsin. ▪ Graduate Rufus King High School (Milwaukee), 1984; B.A. in English, University of Wisconsin-Milwaukee, 1990; J.D., Southern Illinois University-Carbondale, 1993. ▪ Attorney.

Member: Alpha Kappa Alpha (Wisconsin State Connection Coordinator); National Organization of Black Elected Legislative Women; National Black Caucus of State Legislators; NAACP.

Legislature: Elected to Assembly in April 2003 special election. Elected to Senate since 2004. Committee assignments, 2019: Insurance, Financial Services, Government Oversight and Courts; Judiciary and Public Safety; Utilities and Housing; Joint Review Committee on Criminal Penalties.

Contact: Sen.Taylor@legis.wisconsin.gov; Facebook: Senator Lena Taylor; Twitter: @sentaylor; 608-266-5810; 414-342-7176 (district); Room 5 South, State Capitol, PO Box 7882, Madison, WI 53707-7882.

David Bowen, Assembly District 10
Democrat

Biography: Born Milwaukee, Wisconsin, January 28, 1987; married. Voting address: Milwaukee, Wisconsin. ▪ Graduate MPS Bradley Technology High School, 2005; Scholar of Education Policy and Community Studies at the University of Wisconsin-Milwaukee. ▪ Member: Milwaukee County Juvenile Detention Alternative Initiative Advisory Committee; Beyond the Bell Milwaukee (steering committee); Black Youth Project 100; African American Breastfeeding Network (advisory board); Democratic Party of Wisconsin (Vice Chair); State Innovation Exchange; Democratic National Committee State Leader (Super Delegate); People for the American Way Foundation (board); Association of State Democratic Chairs (Midwest Caucus Vice Chair); Young Elected Officials Network; National Black Caucus of State Legislators; National Caucus of State Legislators; Black Millennial Political Convention. ▪ Former member: American Legacy Foundation Activism Fellow. ▪ Recipient: Public Allies Alumni of the Year *Change Maker Award* 2013; Community Action Program *Executive Champion Against Poverty*; Young Elected Officials Network *Leader of the Year—Public Service Leadership Award*; Amani Neighborhood Award; Northwest Side CDC *Unsung Hero Award* 2014; Safe and Sound Borchert Field C.A.R.E.S. *Certificate for Outstanding Community Building Advocate*; Conservation Champion Award 2015–16, 2017–18. ▪ Milwaukee County Board of Supervisors, 2012–14.

Legislature: Elected to Assembly since 2014. Committee Assignments, 2019: Children and Families; Community Development; Corrections; Education.

Contact: Rep.Bowen@legis.wisconsin.gov; 608-266-7671; 888-534-0010 (toll free); Room 126 North, State Capitol, PO Box 8952, Madison, WI 53708.

Jason M. Fields, Assembly District 11
Democrat

Biography: Born Milwaukee, Wisconsin, January 29, 1974; married. Voting address: Milwaukee, Wisconsin. ▪ Graduate Milwaukee Lutheran High School, 1992; B.S. in Business Management, Cardinal Stritch University, 2014. ▪ CEO of investment firm; certified financial education instructor (CFEI). Former stockbroker; investment banker; business owner. ▪

Member: Prince Hall Masons; Alpha Phi Alpha Fraternity, Inc.; Independent Order of Odd Fellows; Elks Lodge of Milwaukee #46; International Society of Business Leaders.

Legislature: Elected to Assembly 2004–10. Reelected since 2016. Committee assignments, 2019: Community Development; Energy and Utilities; Financial Institutions; Jobs and the Economy; Workforce Development.

Contact: Rep.Fields@legis.wisconsin.gov; 608-266-3756; 888-534-0011 (toll free); Room 320 West, State Capitol, PO Box 8952, Madison, WI 53708.

LaKeshia N. Myers, Assembly District 12
Democrat

Biography: Born Milwaukee, Wisconsin, May 21, 1984; single. Voting address: Milwaukee, Wisconsin. ▪ Graduate Rufus King High School, 2002; B.A. in Political Science, Alcorn State University, 2006; M. Ed., Strayer University, 2009; Ed.D., Argosy University, 2016. ▪ Educator; small business owner. Former subcommittee clerk, U.S. House of Representatives; former legislative aide, Wisconsin State Senate. ▪ Member: Alcorn State University National Alumni Association (Milwaukee Chapter Vice President); Alpha Kappa Alpha Sorority, Inc.; Democratic Party of Wisconsin; Historically Black College/University Alumni United (President); Milwaukee Metropolitan Alliance of Black School Educators; National Education Association; National Association for the Advancement of Colored People; Wisconsin African American Chamber of Commerce. ▪ Former member: College Democrats of America (National Membership Director, 2005–06); Phi Delta Kappa International; National Council of Negro Women.

Legislature: Elected to Assembly 2018. Committee assignments, 2019: Agriculture; Education; Federalism and Interstate Relations; Labor and Integrated Employment; Regulatory Licensing Reform; Tourism; Speaker's Task Force on Adoption.

Contact: Rep.Myers@legis.wisconsin.gov; 608-266-5813; 888-534-0012 (toll free); 262-297-3291 (district); Room 3 North, State Capitol, PO Box 8953, Madison, WI 53708.

Senate District 5
Assembly Districts 13, 14, 15

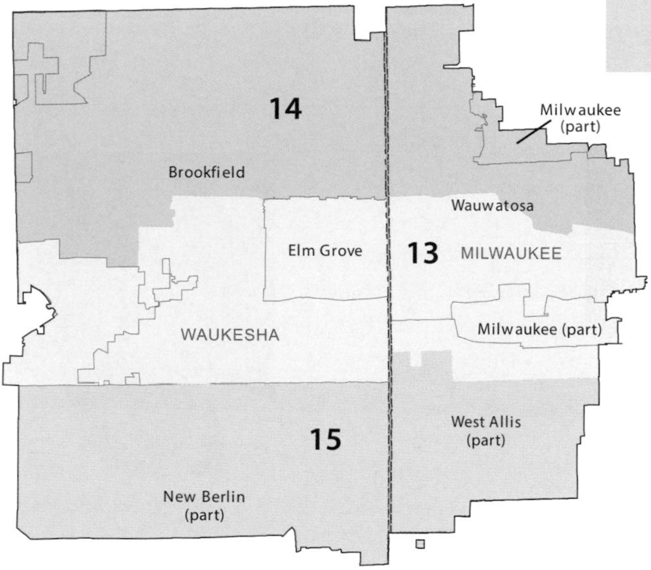

Dale Kooyenga, Senate District 5
Republican

Biography: Born Oak Lawn, Illinois, February 12, 1979; married; 4 children. Voting address: Brookfield, Wisconsin. ▪ Graduate Chicago Christian High School, 1997; A.A., Moraine Valley Community College, 2000; B.A., Lakeland College, 2000; M.B.A., Marquette University, 2007. ▪ Certified public accountant. Member U.S. Army Reserve, 2005–present. Iraq War veteran. ▪ Member: American Legion; American Institute of Certified Public Accountants; Wisconsin Institute of Certified Public Accountants.

Legislature: Elected to Assembly 2010–2016. Elected to Senate 2018. Committee assignments, 2019: Education; Elections, Ethics and Rural Issues; Committee on Health and Human Services (vice chair); Universities, Technical Colleges,

Children and Families (chair); Joint Committee on Information Policy and Technology; Joint Survey Committee on Tax Exemptions (co-chair).

Contact: Sen.Kooyenga@legis.wisconsin.gov; 608-266-2512; 866-817-6061 (toll free); Room 310 South, State Capitol, PO Box 7882, Madison, WI 53707.

Rob Hutton, Assembly District 13
Republican

Biography: Born Milwaukee, Wisconsin, April 7, 1967; married; 4 children. Voting address: Brookfield, Wisconsin. ▪ Graduate Brookfield East High School, 1985; B.A. in History, University of Wisconsin-Whitewater, 1990. ▪ 20 years executive business experience. ▪ Waukesha County supervisor, 2005–12.

Legislature: Elected to Assembly since 2012. Committee assignments, 2019: Corrections (vice chair); Federalism and Interstate Relations; Government Accountability and Oversight; International Affairs and Commerce (chair); Substance Abuse and Prevention; Joint Review Committee on Criminal Penalties (co-chair).

Contact: Rep.Hutton@legis.wisconsin.gov; 608-237-9113; 888 534-0013 (toll free); Room 220 North, State Capitol, PO Box 8952, Madison, WI 53708.

Robyn Dorianne Beckley Vining, Assembly District 14
Democrat

Biography: Born Wright Patterson Air Force Base, Ohio, November 11, 1976; married; 2 children. Voting address: Wauwatosa, Wisconsin. ▪ Attended Westlake High School, Austin, Texas; graduated James Madison High School, Vienna, Virginia, 1995; B.A. in Psychology and B.A. in Studio Art, James Madison University, 1999; M.A. in Religion, Trinity Evangelical Divinity School, 2002. ▪ Current small business owner and photographer. Former pastor; church planter; youth minister. ▪ Member: Exploit No More (co-founder, executive board member).

Legislature: Elected to Assembly 2018. Committee assignments, 2019: Children and Families; Financial Institutions; Health; Small Business Development; Speaker's Task Force on Adoption.

Contact: Rep.Vining@legis.wisconsin.gov; 608-266-9180; 888-534-0014; Room 321 West, State Capitol, PO Box 8953, Madison, WI 53708.

Joe Sanfelippo, Assembly District 15
Republican

Biography: Born Milwaukee, Wisconsin, February 26, 1964; married; 3 children. Voting address: New Berlin, Wisconsin. ▪ Graduate Thomas More High School, 1982; attended Marquette University, 1982–84. ▪ Small businessman; currently operates a small Christmas tree farm. Owned and operated a landscaping business for 20 years. ▪ Member: St. John the Evangelist Parish, Greenfield. ▪ Milwaukee County Board of Supervisors, 2008–12.

Legislature: Elected to Assembly since 2012. Committee assignments, 2019: Health (chair); Campaigns and Elections (vice chair); Financial Institutions; Mental Health; Transportation; Community Development. Additional appointments, 2019: Wisconsin Center District Board; Evidence-Based Health Policy Project Legislative Advisory Board.

Contact: Rep.Sanfelippo@legis.wisconsin.gov; 608-266-0620; 888-534-0015 (toll free); Room 314 North, State Capitol, PO Box 8953, Madison, WI 53708.

Senate District 6
Assembly Districts 16, 17, 18

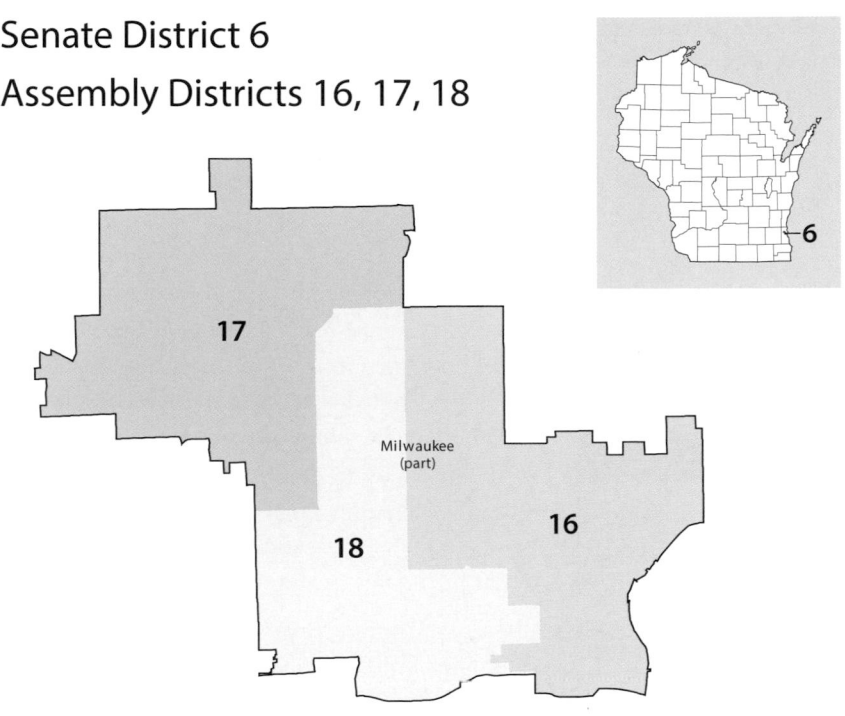

LaTonya Johnson, Senate District 6
Democrat

Biography: Born Somerville, Tennessee, June 22; 1 child. Voting address: Milwaukee, Wisconsin. ▪ Graduate Bay View High School, 1990; B.S. in Criminal Justice, Tennessee State University, 1997; attended University of Wisconsin–Milwaukee, 1990–92. ▪ Full-time legislator. Former family child care provider/owner, 2002–12; insurance agent, 2000–02; financial employment planner, 1997–2000. ▪ Member: AFSCME Wisconsin Child Care Providers Together Local 502 (former president); AFSCME District Council 48 (former vice president); African American Chamber of Commerce; Emerge Wisconsin, Class of 2012; CBTU—Coalition of Black Trade Unionists; Milwaukee Democratic Legislative Caucus (former chair); Wisconsin Women in Government (former board member); Wisconsin Legislative Black Caucus.

Legislature: Elected to Assembly 2012 and 2014. Elected to Senate 2016. Committee assignments, 2019: Education; Finance; Public Benefits, Licensing and State-Federal Relations; Joint Committee on Finance.

Contact: Sen.Johnson@legis.wisconsin.gov; 608-266-2500; 877-474-2000 (toll free); 414-313-1241 (district); Room 19 South, State Capitol, PO Box 7882, Madison, WI 53707-7882.

Kalan Haywood, Assembly District 16
Democrat

Biography: Born Milwaukee, Wisconsin, June 5, 1999; single. Voting address: Milwaukee, Wisconsin. ▪ Graduate Rufus King International Baccalaureate High School, 2017; B.A. in Business Administration, Cardinal Stritch University, 2017–present. ▪ Full-time legislator. Former nonprofit consultant. ▪ Member: City of Milwaukee Restorative Justice Advisory Committee (chair); BlackCEO Milwaukee Chapter (vice president); Determined Young Investors (president). Former member: City of Milwaukee Youth Council (president).

Legislature: Elected to Assembly 2018. Committee assignments, 2019: Housing and Real Estate; International Affairs and Commerce; Veterans and Military Affairs; Ways and Means; Workforce Development.

Contact: Rep.Haywood@legis.wisconsin.gov; 608-266-3786; 888-534-0016; 608-266-3487 (district); Room 16 West, State Capitol, PO Box 8952, Madison, WI 53708.

David Crowley, Assembly District 17
Democrat

Biography: Born Milwaukee, Wisconsin, May 14, 1986; married; 2 children. Voting address: Milwaukee, Wisconsin. ▪ Graduate Bay View High School; attended University of Wisconsin-Milwaukee. ▪ Former executive assistant/ policy director to Senator Nikiya Harris Dodd, Wisconsin Legislature; legislative assistant to Milwaukee County Supervisor Nikiya Harris; field organizer for the Democratic Party of Wisconsin; African American statewide organizer for Feingold Senate Committee. ▪ Member: ACLU-Milwaukee Chapter Board (chair 2014–16); YMCA of Greater Milwaukee; Americorps/Public Allies Alumni; Prince Hall F&A Mason, Asher Lodge #7; Urban League of Young Professionals; Community Brainstorming Conference; NAACP.

Legislature: Elected to Assembly 2016. Committee assignments, 2019: Criminal

Justice and Public Safety; Energy and Utilities; State Affairs; Transportation; Workforce Development.

Contact: Rep.Crowley@legis.wisconsin.gov; 608-266-5580; 888-534-0017 (toll free); Room 5 North, State Capitol, PO Box 8952, Madison, WI 53708.

Evan Goyke, Assembly District 18

Democrat

Biography: Born Neenah, Wisconsin, November 24, 1982; married. Voting address: Milwaukee, Wisconsin. ▪ Graduate Edgewood High School (Madison), 2001; B.A. in Political Science, St. John's University (Minnesota), 2005; J.D., Marquette University Law School, 2009. ▪ Attorney. Former state public defender. ▪ Member: Historic Concordia Neighborhood Association (board member); Progressive Community Health Center (former board member); State Bar of Wisconsin; Eagle Scout, Boy Scouts of America; Milwaukee Democratic Delegation (former chair); Milwaukee Young Lawyers Association (former board member). ▪ Former member: American Federation of Teachers Local 4822.

Legislature: Elected to Assembly since 2012. Committee assignments, 2019: Corrections; Finance; Joint Committee on Finance; Joint Review Committee on Criminal Penalties.

Contact: Rep.Goyke@legis.wisconsin.gov; 608-266-0645; 888-534-0018 (toll free); Room 111 North, State Capitol, PO Box 8952, Madison, WI 53708.

Senate District 7
Assembly Districts 19, 20, 21

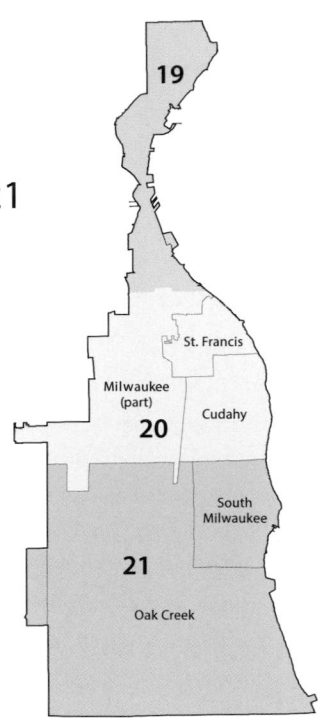

Chris Larson, Senate District 7
Democrat

Biography: Born Milwaukee County, Wisconsin, November 12, 1980; married; 2 children. Voting address: Milwaukee, Wisconsin. ▪ Graduate Thomas More High School, 1999; degree in Finance, University of Wisconsin-Milwaukee, 2007. ▪ Full-time legislator. Former business manager. ▪ Member: American Civil Liberties Union; University of Wisconsin-Milwaukee Alumni Association; League of Conservation Voters; Bay View Neighborhood Association; Planned Parenthood Advocates of Wisconsin; Sierra Club; Humboldt Park Friends; South Side Business Club of Milwaukee; Bay View Historical Society; Arbor Day Foundation; TriWisconsin; Badgerland Striders; Bay View Lions Club; Lake Park Friends; MPTV Friends. ▪ Former member: Airport Area Economic Development Group; Young Elected Officials; Coalition to Save the Hoan Bridge (cofounder); WISPIRG (campus intern). ▪ Milwaukee County Board of Supervisors, 2008–10.

Legislature: Elected to Senate since 2010. Leadership positions: Minority Leader

2013. Committee assignments, 2019: Administrative Rules; Agriculture, Revenue and Financial Institutions; Education; Universities, Technical Colleges, Children and Families; Joint Committee for Review of Administrative Rules; Joint Survey Committee on Tax Exemptions.

Contact: Sen.Larson@legis.wisconsin.gov; 608-266-7505; 800-361-5487 (toll free); Room 20 South, State Capitol, PO Box 7882, Madison, WI 53707-7882.

Jonathan Brostoff, Assembly District 19
Democrat

Biography: Born September 25, 1983; married; 1 child. Voting address: Milwaukee, Wisconsin. ▪ B.A. in Political Science, University of Wisconsin-Milwaukee, 2011. ▪ Full-time legislator. Former district director for Senator Larson; backup shift supervisor, Pathfinders; program director, SDC Family Support Center; public ally, AmeriCorps; volunteer, Street Beat, Big Brothers Big Sisters, Casa Maria. ▪ Member: Bay View Neighborhood Association; Historic Water Tower Neighborhood Association; Planned Parenthood; Urban Ecology Center. ▪ Former member: ACLU-Wisconsin (board member); Tikkun Ha-Ir (board member); Democratic Party of Milwaukee County (board member); America's Black Holocaust Museum (board member).

Legislature: Elected to Assembly since 2014. Committee assignments, 2019: Aging and Long-Term Care; Constitution and Ethics; Family Law; Mental Health; Regulatory Licensing Reform; Speaker's Task Force on Suicide Prevention.

Contact: Rep.Brostoff@legis.wisconsin.gov; 608-266-0650; 888-534-0019 (toll free); Room 17 West, State Capitol, PO Box 8952, Madison, WI 53708.

Christine Sinicki, Assembly District 20
Democrat

Biography: Born Milwaukee, Wisconsin, March 28, 1960; married; 2 children. Voting address: Milwaukee, Wisconsin. ▪ Graduate Bay View High School; Bowhay Institute Fellow, La Follette School, University of Wisconsin-Madison, 2001; Flemming Fellow, Center for Policy Alternatives, 2003. ▪ Former small business manager. ▪ Member: American Council of Young Political Leaders (Delegate to Israel and Palestine, 2001); Milwaukee Committee on Domestic Violence and Sexual Assault; Major, Wisconsin Wing, Civil Air Patrol Legislative Squadron (official Auxiliary of the U.S. Air Force); Milwaukee City Council Parents and Teachers Association; Bay View Historical Society; Bay View Neighborhood Association; State Assembly Milwaukee Caucus (chair 2005, 2003). ▪ Former member: Delegate—U.S. President Electoral College, 2000; State Minimum Wage Council (governor's appointee), 2005; Assembly Democratic Task Force on Working Families (chair), 2003. ▪ Recipient: Wisconsin Environmental Decade Clean 16 2000; Wisconsin Ob/Gyn Physicians' *Legislator of the Year* 2000; Wisconsin Coalition Against Domestic Violence DV Diva 2003; Wisconsin Department of Veterans Affairs *Certificates of Commendation* 2006, 2005; Wisconsin League of Conservation Voters *Conservation Champion* 2017, 2015, 2013, 2011, 2009, 2007; Wisconsin Women's Alliance Legislation Award 2009–10; Professional Firefighters of Wisconsin *Legislator of the Year* 2010; Wisconsin Grocers Association *Friend of Grocers* 2010; Cudahy Veterans' *Service Award* 2010; AMVETS State Legislative *Advocacy Award* 2011; Mothers Against Drunk Driving *Legislator of the Year* 2018. ▪ Milwaukee School Board, 1991–98.

Legislature: Elected to Assembly since 1998. Leadership positions: Minority Caucus Sergeant at Arms 2019, 2017; Minority Caucus Secretary 2001. Committee assignments, 2019: Labor and Integrated Employment; State Affairs; Consumer Protection; Forestry, Parks and Outdoor Recreation; Government Accountability and Oversight; Veterans and Military Affairs; Committee to Celebrate the Centennial Anniversary of Wisconsin's Ratification of the 19th Amendment.

Contact: Rep.Sinicki@legis.wisconsin.gov; 608-266-8588; 888-534-0020 (toll free); 414-481-7667 (district); Room 114 North, State Capitol, PO Box 8953, Madison, WI 53708.

Jessie Rodriguez, Assembly District 21
Republican

Biography: Born Puerto el Triunfo, El Salvador, July 5, 1977; married. Voting address: Oak Creek, Wisconsin. ▪ Graduate Alexander Hamilton High School (Milwaukee), 1996; B.A., Marquette University, 2002. ▪ Full-time legislator. Former analyst for a supermarket company; outreach coordinator for a nonprofit. ▪ Member: Major, Wisconsin Wing, Civil Air Patrol Legislative Squadron (official Auxiliary of the U.S. Air Force).

Legislature: Elected to Assembly in November 2013 special election. Reelected since 2014. Leadership positions: Majority Caucus Secretary 2019, 2017, 2015.

Committee assignments, 2019: Education; Energy and Utilities; Family Law (chair); Health; International Affairs and Commerce.

Contact: Rep.Rodriguez@legis.wisconsin.gov; 608-266-0610; 888-534-0021 (toll free); Room 204 North, State Capitol, PO Box 8953, Madison, WI 53708

Senate District 8
Assembly Districts 22, 23, 24

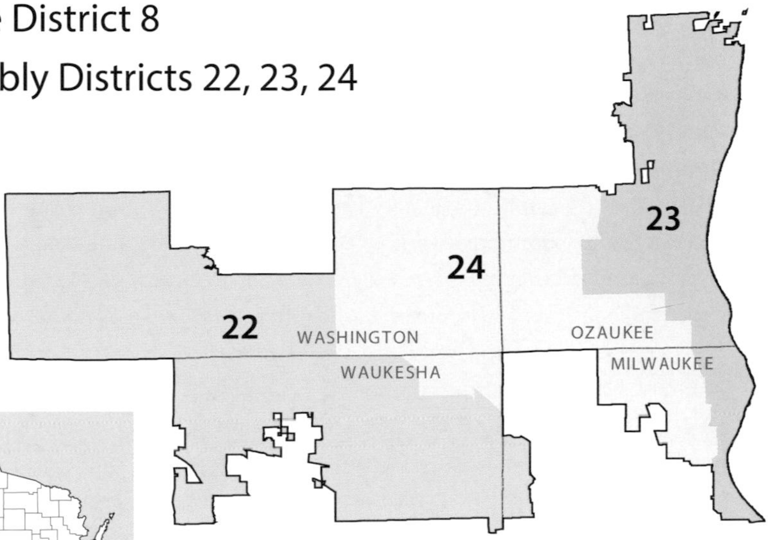

Alberta Darling, Senate District 8
Republican

Biography: Born Hammond, Indiana, April 28; widowed; 2 children, 3 grandchildren. Voting address: River Hills, Wisconsin. ▪ Graduate University of Wisconsin-Madison; postgraduate work University of Wisconsin-Milwaukee. ▪ Former teacher and marketing director. ▪ Member: North Shore Rotary; College Savings Program Board (EdVest); Junior League of Milwaukee (former president); Wisconsin Children's Caucus (cofounder); Milwaukee Child Welfare Partnership Council; NCSL Budgets and Revenue standing committee (vice chair); Fostering Futures Policy Advisory Council; NCSL Task Force on State and Local Taxation. ▪ Former member: Next Door Foundation; Public Policy Forum; Wisconsin Strategic Planning Council for Economic Development; Greater Milwaukee Committee; Goals for Greater Milwaukee 2000 Project (executive committee); United Way Board (chair, allocations committee); TEMPO Professional Women's Organization; Future Milwaukee (president); Milwaukee Forum; Children's Service Society of Wisconsin (board of directors); American Red Cross of Wisconsin (executive committee, board of directors); League of Women Voters; Today's Girl Tomorrow's Woman; Boys & Girls Club (founder); NCSL Education Committee (chair); YMCA (board member). ▪ Recipient: *Shining Star of Education Reform*; Hispanic Chamber of Commerce *Government Advocates Award*; Greater Milwaukee Committee *Leadership Award*; Leukemia and Lymphoma Society *Legislative Leadership Award*; Wisconsin Manufacturers and Commerce *Working for Wisconsin*; American Conservative Union Foundation *Defender of Liberty Award*; Wisconsin Grocer's Association *Friend of Grocers*; Coalition of Wisconsin Aging Groups *Tommy G. Thompson Award for Service*; RightWisconsin *Iron Lady Award, Margaret Thatcher Award*; *Wisconsin Charter Champion Award*; National MS Hall of Fame Inductee; American Cancer Society *Legislative Champion*; Fair Air Coalition *Friend of Education*; Metropolitan Milwaukee Association of Commerce *Champion of Commerce*; Wisconsin Head Start Directors Association *Award of Excellence*; National Association of Community Leadership *Leadership Award*; United Way *Gwen Jackson Leadership Award*; St. Francis Children's Center *Children Service Award*.

Legislature: Elected to Assembly in May 1990 special election. Reelected November 1990. Elected to Senate since 1992. Committee assignments, 2019: Education (vice chair); Finance (chair); Judiciary and Public Safety; Universities, Technical Colleges, Children and Families; Joint Committee on Employment Relations; Joint Committee on Finance (co-chair); Joint Legislative Audit Committee; Joint Legislative Council.

Contact: Sen.Darling@legis.wisconsin.gov; 608-266-5830; Room 317 East, State Capitol, PO Box 7882, Madison, WI 53707-7882.

Janel Brandtjen, Assembly District 22
Republican

Biography: Born Milwaukee, Wisconsin, March 27; married; 2 children. Voting address: Menomonee Falls, Wisconsin. ▪ Graduate Marshall High School; B.B.A. in Finance and Marketing, University of Wisconsin-Milwaukee, 1988. ▪ Business owner. ▪ Member: Republican Party of Waukesha, Washington, and Milwaukee

Counties; Republican Women of Waukesha, Washington, and Milwaukee Counties; National Rifle Association (lifetime member); Immanuel Lutheran Church. ▪ Recipient: *Wisconsin Pro-Life Legislator of the Year* 2016; Wisconsin Family Action *Friend of Family, Life and Liberty* 2016; Associated Builders & Contractors Building Wisconsin Award 2016, 2018; MMAC *Champion of Commerce* 2015–16, 2017–18; WDA *Dental Academy Award* 2015, 2017; WMC *Working for Wisconsin Award* 2015–16, 2017–18; ABATE of Wisconsin award for outstanding support of motorcyclists, 2018. ▪ Waukesha County supervisor, 2008–16.

Legislature: Elected to Assembly since 2014. Committee assignments, 2019: Small Business Development (chair); Community Development (vice chair); Government Accountability and Oversight (vice chair); Campaigns and Elections; Corrections; Public Benefit Reform; Science and Technology; Workforce Development; Joint Committee on Information Policy and Technology.

Contact: Rep.Brandtjen@legis.wisconsin.gov; 608-267-2367; 888-534-0022 (toll free); Room 12 West, State Capitol, PO Box 8952, Madison, WI 53708.

Jim Ott, Assembly District 23
Republican

Biography: Born Milwaukee, Wisconsin, June 5, 1947; married; 2 sons, 1 grandchild. Voting address: Mequon, Wisconsin. ▪ Graduate Milwaukee Washington High School, 1965; B.S., University of Wisconsin-Milwaukee, 1970; M.S., University of Wisconsin-Milwaukee, 1975; J.D., Marquette University, 2000. ▪ Full-time legislator. Former broadcast meteorologist and instructor

at University of Wisconsin-Parkside; Served in U.S. Army, 1970–73; Vietnam veteran. ▪ Member: State Bar of Wisconsin; American Meteorological Society; Mequon/Thiensville Noon Rotary; Mequon/Thiensville Chamber of Commerce; American Legion; Ozaukee County Republican Party; North Shore Branch Milwaukee County Republican Party; Lumen Christi Catholic Church (past parish council president). ▪ Recipient: National Weather Service *Public Service Award* 2006; Archbishops Vatican II *Service Award* 1999; Vietnam Campaign Medal and Meritorious Unit Citation; Emerging Political Leaders Program; BILLD Leadership Fellow; MADD *Legislator of the Year* 2016, 2015, 2013; Wisconsin Chiefs of

Police Association True Friend of the Law Enforcement Community 2016; Trout Unlimited recognition 2015; MMAC *Champion of Commerce* 2016, 2015.

Legislature: Elected to Assembly since 2006. Committee assignments, 2019: Administrative Rules; Criminal Justice and Public Safety; Judiciary (chair); Veterans and Military Affairs; Joint Committee for Review of Administrative Rules.

Contact: Rep.OttJ@legis.wisconsin.gov; 608-266-0486; 888-534-0023 (toll free); Room 317 North, State Capitol, PO Box 8953, Madison, WI 53708-8953.

Dan Knodl, Assembly District 24
Republican

Biography: Born Milwaukee, Wisconsin, December 14, 1958; 4 children, 3 grandchildren. Voting address: Germantown, Wisconsin. ▪ Graduate Menomonee Falls East High School, 1977; attended University of Wisconsin-Madison. ▪ Resort owner. ▪ Member: Ozaukee Washington Land Trust; Pike Lake Sportsmen's Club; Pike Lake Protection District (member 2000–present, secretary 2010–17, chair, 2017–present); Menomonee Falls Optimist Club; Knights of Columbus; St. Boniface Parish. ▪ Pike Lake Protection District 2000–present (secretary); Washington County Board, 2006–08.

Legislature: Elected to Assembly since 2008. Leadership positions: Majority Caucus Chair 2019, 2017. Assistant Majority Leader 2015, 2011. Committee assignments, 2019: Assembly Organization; Rules; State Affairs; Joint Committee on Information Policy and Technology (co-chair).

Contact: Rep.Knodl@legis.wisconsin.gov; 608-237-9124; 888-529-0024 (toll free); Room 218 North, State Capitol, PO Box 8952, Madison, WI 53708.

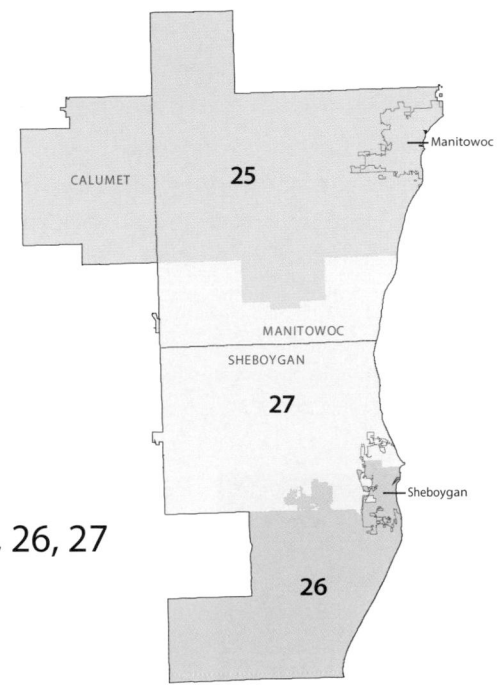

Senate District 9
Assembly Districts 25, 26, 27

Devin LeMahieu, Senate District 9
Republican

Biography: Born Sheboygan, Wisconsin, August 8, 1972; single. Voting address: Oostburg, Wisconsin. ▪ Graduate Sheboygan County Christian High School, 1991; B.A. in Business Administration and Political Science, Dordt College (Sioux Center, Iowa), 1995. ▪ Publisher/owner, Lakeshore Weekly. ▪ Member: Oostburg Chamber of Commerce; Sheboygan County Chamber of Commerce; Bethel OPC (deacon); NRA (life member). ▪ Recipient: Wisconsin Wildlife Association *State Conservation Legislator of the Year*, 2015; League of Wisconsin Municipalities *Strong Municipal Supporter*, 2016; Wisconsin Cemetery and Cremation Association *Legislator of the Year*, 2016; Wisconsin Counties Association *Outstanding Legislator Award*, 2016; Wisconsin Academy of Family Physicians *Friend of Family Medicine*, 2016; ABC of Wisconsin *Building Wisconsin Award*, 2018; Wisconsin Grocers Association Friend of Grocers, 2016; Wisconsin Builders Association *Friend of Housing*, 2016; WMC *Working for Wisconsin*, 2018; MMAC *Champion of Commerce*, 2017–18; Wisconsin Coalition for International Adoption *Friend of International Adoption*, 2016; *Friend of Nursing*

Award, 2018; *Reining in Government Award*, 2018. ▪ Sheboygan County Board supervisor, 2006–15, Human Resources Committee, 2006–15 (chair, 2010–14), Finance Committee, 2012–15, Executive Committee, 2010–12.

Legislature: Elected to Senate since 2014. Committee assignments, 2019: Utilities and Housing (chair); Sporting Heritage, Mining & Forestry (vice chair); Public Benefits, Licensing & State-Federal Relations; Joint Committee on Finance; Joint Survey Committee on Retirement Systems; Joint Committee on Law Revision. Additional appointments, 2019: Wisconsin Aerospace Authority Board.

Contact: Sen.LeMahieu@legis.wisconsin.gov; SenatorDevin.com; Facebook: Senator Devin LeMahieu; Twitter: @senatordevin; 608-266-2056; 888-295-8750 (toll free); Room 409 South, State Capitol, PO Box 7882, Madison, WI 53707-7882.

Paul Tittl, Assembly District 25
Republican

Biography: Born Delavan, Wisconsin, November 23, 1961; married; 2 children, 3 grandchildren. Voting address: Manitowoc, Wisconsin. ▪ Graduate Lincoln High (Manitowoc), 1980. ▪ Owner, vacuum and sewing center. ▪ Member: National Rifle Association. ▪ Former member: Eagles Manitowoc; Manitowoc County Home Builders Association; Economic Development Corporation; Wastewater Treatment Facility Board; Manitowoc Crime Prevention Committee; Community Development Authority; Safety Traffic and Parking Commission; Wisconsin Utility Tax Association, 2009–13; WCA Taxation and Finance Steering Committee, 2010–13; WCA Judicial and Public Safety Steering Committee, 2010–13. ▪ Manitowoc City Council, 2004–08 (president 2006–07); Manitowoc County Board of Supervisors, 2006–13 (chair 2010–12).

Legislature: Elected to Assembly since 2012. Committee assignments, 2019: Mental Health (chair); Consumer Protection (vice chair); Veterans and Military Affairs; Sporting Heritage; Jobs and the Economy; International Affairs and Commerce; Speaker's Task Force on Suicide Prevention.

Contact: Rep.Tittl@legis.wisconsin.gov; 608-266-0315; 888-529-0025 (toll free); Room 219 North, State Capitol, PO Box 8953, Madison, WI 53708.

Terry Katsma, Assembly District 26
Republican

Biography: Born Sheboygan, Wisconsin, April 23, 1958; married; 3 children, 6 grandchildren. Voting address: Oostburg, Wisconsin. ▪ Graduate Sheboygan

County Christian High School, 1976; B.A. in Business Administration, Dordt College (Sioux Center, Iowa), 1980; M.B.A., Marquette University, 1985. ▪ Full-time legislator. Former community bank president and CEO. ▪ Member: Oostburg State Bank Board of Directors (former president and CEO); Oostburg Chamber of Commerce (former president-elect); Oostburg Christian Reformed Church (elder); Random Lake Area Chamber of Commerce; Republican Party of Sheboygan County; NRA; Sheboygan County Chamber of Commerce; YMCA of Sheboygan County Board of Managers. ▪ Former member: Trinity Christian College Board of Trustees (Palos Heights, Illinois—treasurer); Dordt College Board of Trustees (vice chair); Sheboygan County Christian High School (board president); Oostburg Christian School Board (secretary); Oostburg Community Education Foundation; Oostburg Kiwanis Club (president); Workbound, Inc. (president).

Legislature: Elected to Assembly since 2014. Committee assignments, 2019: Finance; Financial Institutions; Joint Committee on Finance.

Contact: Rep.Katsma@legis.wisconsin.gov; 608-266-0656; 888-529-0026 (toll free); Room 306 East, State Capitol, PO Box 8952, Madison, WI 53708.

Tyler Vorpagel, Assembly District 27
Republican

Biography: Born Plymouth, Wisconsin, March 24, 1985; married; 1 child. Voting address: Plymouth, Wisconsin. ▪ Graduate Plymouth High School, 2003; B.A. in Political Science, B.S. in Public Administration, University of Wisconsin-Green Bay, 2007; Completed 2016 Emerging Leader Program at University of Virginia Darden School of Business. ▪ Full-time legislator. Former district director, Congressman Tom Petri. ▪ Member: Sheboygan County Youth Apprenticeship Grant Advisory Committee; Sheboygan Elks #299; National Association of Parliamentarians; NCSL State Chair; Republican Party of Sheboygan County (former member of executive committee); 6th District Republican Party (former vice chair); Republican Party of Wisconsin (former member of executive committee); Major, Wisconsin Wing, Civil Air Patrol Legislative Squadron (official Auxiliary of the U.S. Air Force). ▪ Former member: Plymouth Rotary; Exchange Club (president).

Legislature: Elected to Assembly since 2014. Committee assignments, 2019: Children and Families; Federalism and Interstate Relations (chair); International Affairs and Commerce; State Affairs; Transportation.

Contact: Rep.Vorpagel@legis.wisconsin.gov; 608-266-8530; 888-529-0027 (toll free); Room 127 West, State Capitol, PO Box 8953, Madison, WI 53708.

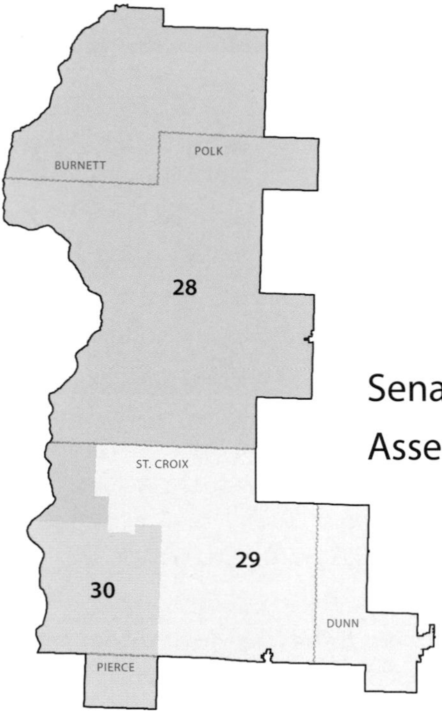

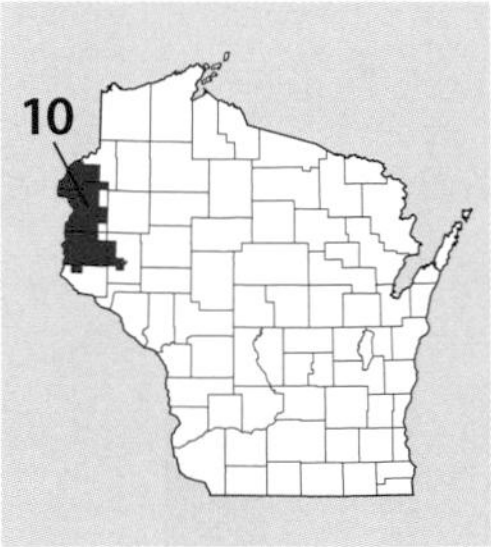

Senate District 10
Assembly Districts 28, 29, 30

Patty Schachtner, Senate District 10
Democrat

Biography: Born Somerset, Wisconsin, April 1, 1960; married; 6 children, 10 grandchildren. Voting address: Somerset, Wisconsin. ▪ Graduate Somerset High School, 1978; Wisconsin Indianhead Technical College (EMT Basic, EMT Intermediate, EMS Adult Educator). ▪ St. Croix County Chief Medical Examiner. Former Health Care Provider, Somerset High School; Medicolegal Death Investigator, St. Croix County; EMT, New Richmond Ambulance and Rescue; Town of Star Prairie Town Supervisor (2010–14). ▪ Board member: Turningpoint Wisconsin; Somerset Community Food Pantry. ▪ Former member: Somerset School District School Board (2015–18); Rotary Club of New Richmond; Wisconsin Coroners and Medical Examiners Association; Western Saddle Club Association; St. Anne's Parent Group; St. Croix Valley Restorative Justice; Championship Pulling Series (president); Greater Stillwater Chamber of Commerce (director); Suicide Prevention Task Force of St. Croix County (cofounder).

Legislature: Elected in January 2018 special election. Committee assignments, 2019: Education; Local Government, Small Business, Tourism and Workforce Development; Universities, Technical Colleges, Children and Families.

Contact: Sen.Schachtner@legis.wisconsin.gov; 608-266-7745; Room 3 South, State Capitol, PO Box 7882, Madison, WI 53707.

Gae Magnafici, Assembly District 28
Republican

Biography: Born Amery, Wisconsin, July 14, 1952; married; 2 children ; 3 grandchildren. Voting address: Dresser, Wisconsin. ▪ Graduate Amery High School, 1970; A.A. in Applied Science, Sauk Valley Community College (Dixon, Illinois), 1982. ▪ Small business owner. Former mental health technician; registered nurse.

Legislature: Elected to Assembly 2018. Committee assignments, 2019: Aging and Long-Term Care; Constitution and Ethics; Health; Jobs and the Economy; Mental Health; Substance Abuse and Prevention (vice chair); Tourism.

Contact: Rep.Magnafici@legis.wisconsin.gov; 608-267-2365; 888-534-0028; Room 7 West, State Capitol, PO Box 8953, Madison, WI 53708.

Rob Stafsholt, Assembly District 29
Republican

Biography: Born St. Croix County, Wisconsin; single; 1 child. Voting address: New Richmond, Wisconsin. ▪ Graduate New Richmond Public Schools; attended University of Wisconsin-Eau Claire, University of Wisconsin-River Falls. ▪ Small business owner of residential rental and real estate investment company; farmer; assistant coach for the New

Richmond-Somerset High School trap team. Former co-owner of a salad and food dressings manufacturing and sales company; mortgage loan originator. ▪ Member: Farm Bureau; National Rifle Association (life member); New Richmond Chamber of Commerce; Sportsmen's Alliance; SCI. ▪ Former Member: Erin Prairie Township Planning Commission; Wisconsin Bear Hunters' Association (board of directors); Wisconsin Association of Mortgage Brokers; NWTF.

Legislature: Elected to Assembly since 2016. Committee assignments, 2019: Colleges and Universities; Financial Institutions (vice chair); Insurance; Medicaid Reform and Oversight; Sporting Heritage (chair); Speaker's Task Force on Suicide Prevention; Speaker's Task Force on Adoption.

Contact: Rep.Stafsholt@legis.wisconsin.gov; 608-266-7683; 888-529-0029 (toll free); Room 17 North, State Capitol, PO Box 8953, Madison, WI 53708.

Shannon Zimmerman, Assembly District 30
Republican

Biography: Born Madison, Wisconsin, March 15, 1972; married; 2 children. Voting address: River Falls, Wisconsin. ▪ Attended Augusta High School; Chippewa Valley Technical College; University of Wisconsin-Milwaukee. ▪ Founder and CEO, language translation company; small business owner. Coached youth football for 7 years. ▪ Member: University of Wisconsin-River Falls Foundation Board; University of Wisconsin-River Falls Chancellor's Advisory Committee; Rotary. ▪ Former member: Wisconsin Department of Workforce Development Board.

Legislature: Elected to Assembly since 2016. Committee assignments, 2019: Finance; Joint Committee on Finance.

Contact: Rep.Zimmerman@legis.wisconsin.gov; 608-266-1526; 888-529-0030 (toll free); Room 320 East, State Capitol, PO Box 8953, Madison, WI 53708.

Senate District 11
Assembly Districts 31, 32, 33

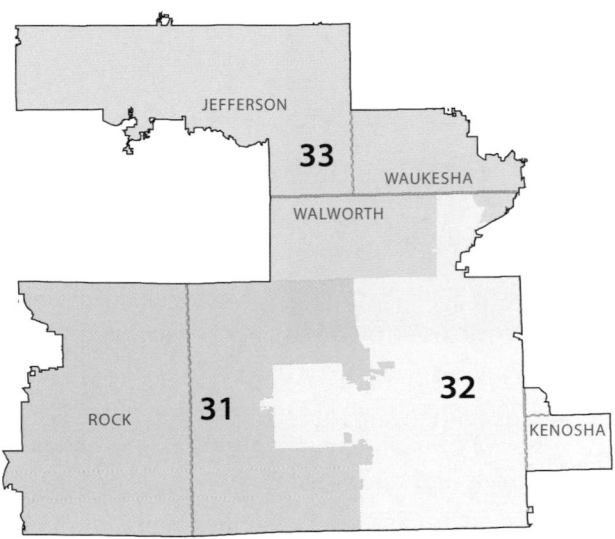

Stephen L. Nass, Senate District 11
Republican

Biography: Born Whitewater, Wisconsin, October 7, 1952. Voting address: Whitewater, Wisconsin.

- Graduate Whitewater High School; B.S. University of Wisconsin-Whitewater, 1978; M.S. Ed. in School Business Management, University of Wisconsin-Whitewater, 1990. - Owner, rental property business. Former payroll benefits analyst and information analyst/negotiator. Member of Wisconsin Air National Guard (retired, CMSgt, 33 years of service), served in Middle East in Operations Desert Shield and Desert Storm. - Member: American Legion; Veterans of Foreign Wars. - Former member: University of Wisconsin-Whitewater Board of Visitors, 1979–89. - Whitewater City Council, 1977–81.

Legislature: Elected to Assembly 1990–2012. Elected to Senate since 2014. Committee assignments, 2019: Administrative Rules (chair); Education; Labor and

Regulatory Reform (chair); Universities, Technical Colleges, Children and Families (vice chair); Joint Committee for Review of Administrative Rules (co-chair).

Contact: Sen.Nass@legis.wisconsin.gov; 608-266-2635; Room 10 South, State Capitol, PO Box 7882, Madison, WI 53707-7882.

Amy Loudenbeck, Assembly District 31
Republican

Biography: Born Midland, Michigan, September 29, 1969; married. Voting address: Clinton, Wisconsin. ▪ Graduate Hinsdale Central High School (Hinsdale, Illinois), 1987; B.A. in Political Science, International Relations, University of Wisconsin-Madison, 1991; studied abroad in Kingston, Jamaica. ▪ Former chamber of commerce executive, compliance manager, environmental/engineering services project manager. ▪ Member: Wisconsin Family Impact Seminar (advisory board member); Wisconsin DNR Green Tier Advisory Board. ▪ Former member: Town of Linn Fire Department. ▪ Town of Clinton supervisor, 2010–12.

Legislature: Elected to Assembly since 2010. Committee assignments, 2019: Finance (vice chair); Joint Committee on Finance (co-vice chair); Joint Committee on Information Policy and Technology. Additional appointments, 2019: State Capitol and Executive Residence Board (vice chair).

Contact: Rep.Loudenbeck@legis.wisconsin.gov; 608-266-9967; 888-529-0031 (toll free); Room 304 East, State Capitol, PO Box 8952, Madison, WI 53708.

Tyler August, Assembly District 32
Republican

Biography: Born Wisconsin, January 26, 1983; single. Voting address: Lake Geneva, Wisconsin. ▪ Graduate Big Foot High School, 2001; attended University of Wisconsin-Eau Claire and University of Wisconsin-Madison; completed 2012 Emerging Leader Program at University of Virginia Darden School of Business. ▪ Full-time legislator. Former chief of staff to Representative Thomas Lothian. ▪ Member: Republican Party of Wisconsin (former board member); First Congressional District Republican Party (former chair); Republican Party of Walworth County (former chair, vice chair); National

Rifle Association. ▪ Recipient: American Conservative Union *Defender of Liberty* 2012; GOPAC *Emerging Leader* 2012.

Legislature: Elected to Assembly since 2010. Leadership positions: Speaker Pro Tempore 2019, 2017, 2015, 2013. Committee assignments, 2019: Assembly Organization; Government Accountability and Oversight; Insurance; Rules; Joint Legislative Council; Joint Survey Committee on Tax Exemptions (co-chair).

Contact: Rep.August@legis.wisconsin.gov; 608-266-1190; Room 119 West, State Capitol, PO Box 8952, Madison, WI 53708.

Cody J. Horlacher, Assembly District 33
Republican

Biography: Born Burlington, Wisconsin, April 10, 1987; married, 1 child. Voting address: Mukwonago, Wisconsin. ▪ Graduate East Troy High School, 2006; B.A. in Marketing, University of Wisconsin-Whitewater, 2010; J.D., Marquette University Law School, 2014. ▪ Attorney; Partner of Horlacher Necci Law Firm. Former special prosecutor, Walworth County; former assistant district attorney, Walworth County. ▪ Member: Wisconsin Historical Society (Board of Curators); YMCA of Mukwonago; YMCA of Greater Waukesha County; Mukwonago Area Chamber of Commerce; Sportsmen's Caucus; Carroll University President's Advisory Council; Wisconsin State Bar; Old World Wisconsin Foundation (board of trustees); NCSL Occupational Licensing Consortium; Polish Heritage Alliance. ▪ Former member: Walworth County Republican Party (secretary, vice chair, chair); Federalist Society.

Legislature: Elected to Assembly since 2014. Committee assignments, 2019: Criminal Justice and Public Safety; Federalism and Interstate Relations; Judiciary (vice chair); Regulatory Licensing Reform (chair); Sporting Heritage.

Contact: Rep.Horlacher@legis.wisconsin.gov; 608-266-5715; 888-529-0033 (toll free); Room 214 North, State Capitol, PO Box 8952, Madison, WI 53708.

Senate District 12
Assembly Districts 34, 35, 36

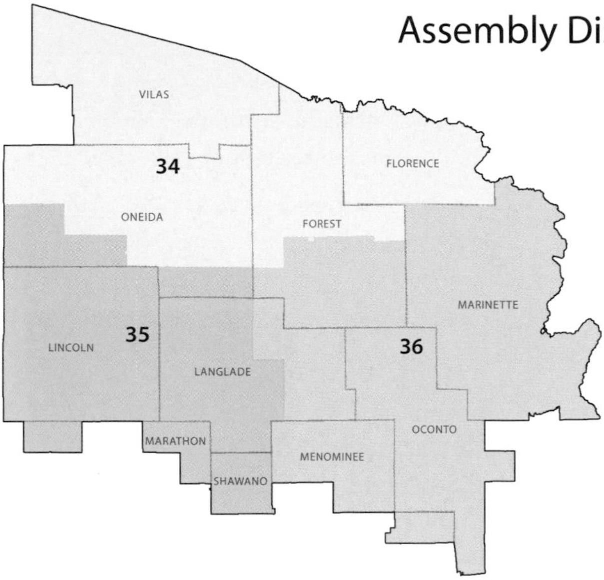

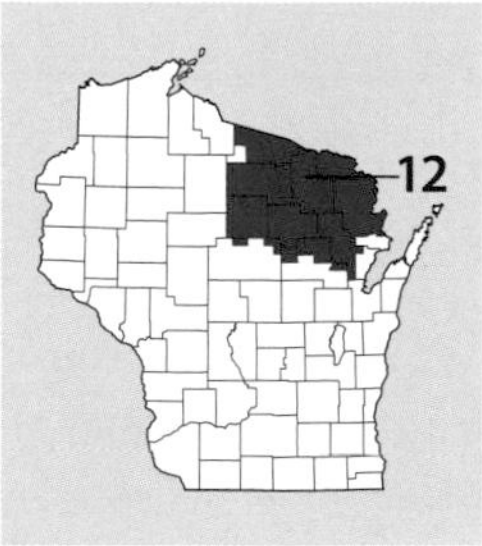

Tom Tiffany, Senate District 12
Republican

Biography: Born Wabasha, Minnesota, December 30, 1957; married; 3 children. Voting address: Town of Minocqua, Wisconsin. ▪ Graduate Elmwood High School, 1976; B.S. in Agricultural Economics, University of Wisconsin-River Falls, 1980. ▪ Dam tender, Wisconsin Valley Improvement Company. ▪ Member: National Rifle Association; Ruffed Grouse Society. ▪ Town of Little Rice supervisor, 2009–13.

Legislature: Elected to Assembly 2010. Elected to Senate since 2012. Committee assignments, 2019: Elections, Ethics and Rural Issues (vice chair); Finance; Local Government, Small Business, Tourism and Workforce Development; Committee on Sporting Heritage, Mining and Forestry (chair); Joint Committee on Finance; Joint Survey Committee on Tax Exemptions.

Contact: Sen.Tiffany@legis.wisconsin.gov; 608-266-2509; Room 316 South, State Capitol, PO Box 7882, Madison, WI 53707-7882.

Rob Swearingen, Assembly District 34
Republican

Biography: Born Oneida County, Wisconsin, July 23, 1963; married; 2 children. Voting address: Rhinelander, Wisconsin. ▪ Graduate Rhinelander High School, 1981. ▪ Restaurant owner/operator. ▪ Member: Tavern League of Wisconsin (former president, zone vice president, district director); American Beverage Licensees (former member, board of directors); Oneida County Tavern League (former president, vice president); Rhinelander Chamber of Commerce; Oneida County Republican Party.

Legislature: Elected to Assembly since 2012. Committee assignments, 2019: Forestry, Parks and Outdoor Recreation; Small Business Development; State Affairs (chair); Tourism (vice chair); Joint Survey Committee on Tax Exemptions. Additional appointments: Building Commission.

Contact: Rep.Swearingen@legis.wisconsin.gov; 608-266-7141; 888-534-0034 (toll free); Room 123 West, State Capitol, PO Box 8953, Madison, WI 53708.

Mary J. Felzkowski, Assembly District 35
Republican

Biography: Born Tomahawk, Wisconsin, September 25, 1963; married; 5 children. Voting address: Irma, Wisconsin. ▪ Graduate Tomahawk High School, 1981; B.S. in Finance and Economics, University of Wisconsin-River Falls, 1986. ▪ Insurance agency owner. ▪ Member: Tomahawk Main Street, Inc. (former president); Tomahawk Regional Chamber of Commerce; Tomahawk Child Care (former president); National Alliance for Insurance Education and Research (board member); NRA (lifetime member); Professional Insurance Agents of Wisconsin (former board member, secretary, treasurer, vice president, president, national director).

Legislature: Elected to Assembly since 2012. Leadership positions: Assistant Majority Leader 2019. Committee assignments, 2019: Joint Survey Committee on Retirement Systems; Health; Forestry, Parks and Outdoor Recreation; Sporting Heritage.

Contact: Rep.Felzkowski@legis.wisconsin.gov; 608-266-7694; 888-534-0035 (toll free); Room 309 North, State Capitol, PO Box 8952, Madison, WI 53708; PO Box 321, Tomahawk, WI 54487 (district).

Jeffrey L. Mursau, Assembly District 36

Republican

Biography: Born Oconto Falls, Wisconsin, June 12, 1954; married; 4 children, 11 grandchildren. Voting address: Crivitz, Wisconsin. ▪ Graduate Coleman High School, 1972; attended University of Wisconsin-Oshkosh. ▪ Small business owner; electrical contractor. ▪ Member: Crivitz Ski Cats waterski team (advisor, former president); Crivitz Lions Club; Crivitz, Wisconsin-Crivitz, Germany Sister City Organization (former director); Wings Over Wisconsin; St. Mary's Catholic Church; Fourth Degree Knights of Columbus; Friends of Governor Thompson State Park; Master Loggers Certifying Board. ▪ Recipient: Crivitz Business Association *Citizen of the Year* 1994. ▪ Crivitz Village President, 1991–2004.

Legislature: Elected to Assembly since 2004. Committee assignments, 2019: Forestry, Parks and Outdoor Recreation (chair); Agriculture; Education; Sporting Heritage; Tourism; Speaker's Task Force on Adoption; Special Committee on State-Tribal Relations (chair).

Contact: Rep.Mursau@legis.wisconsin.gov; 608-266-3780; 888-534-0036 (toll free); Room 113 West, State Capitol, PO Box 8953, Madison, WI 53708.

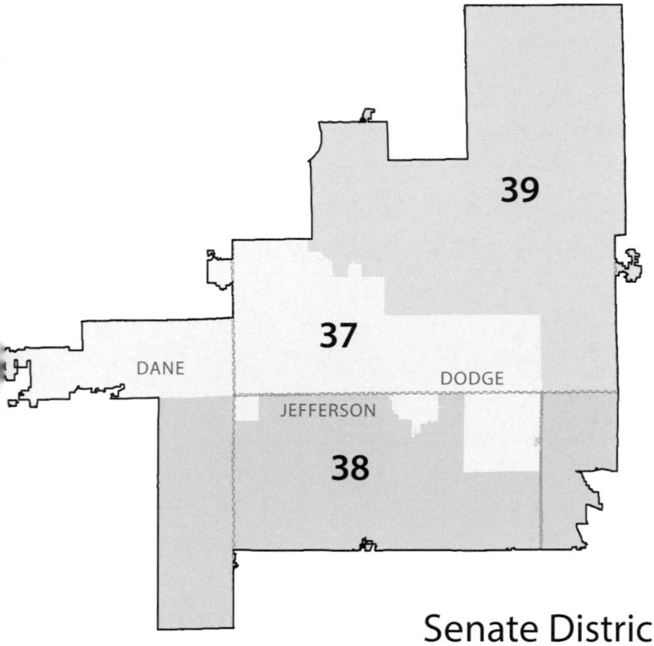

39

37

DANE

DODGE

JEFFERSON

38

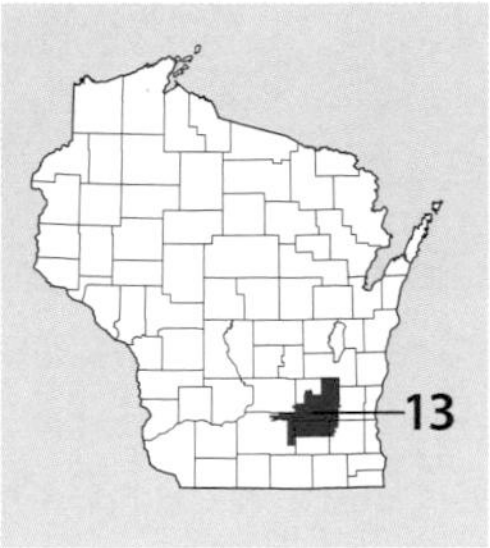

13

Senate District 13
Assembly Districts 37, 38, 39

Scott L. Fitzgerald, Senate District 13
Republican

Biography: Born Chicago, Illinois, November 16, 1963; married; 3 children. Voting address: Juneau, Wisconsin. ▪ Graduate Hustisford High School, 1981; B.S. in Journalism, University of Wisconsin-Oshkosh, 1985; U.S. Army Armor Officer Basic Course, 1985; U.S. Army Command and General Staff College. ▪ Former associate newspaper publisher; U.S. Army Reserve Lieutenant Colonel (retired). ▪ Member: Dodge County Republican Party (chair, 1992–94); Juneau Lions Club; Reserve Officers Association; Knights of Columbus.

Legislature: Elected to Senate since 1994. Leadership positions: Majority Leader 2019, 2017, 2015, 2013, 2011 (through 7/24/12); Minority Leader 2011 (effective 7/24/12), 2009, 2007; Majority Leader 9/17/04 to 11/10/04. Committee assignments, 2019: Senate Organization (chair); Joint Committee on Employment Relations; Joint Committee on Legislative Organization; Joint Legislative Council.

Contact: Sen.Fitzgerald@legis.wisconsin.gov; 608-266-5660; Room 211 South, State Capitol, PO Box 7882, Madison, WI 53707-7882.

John Jagler, Assembly District 37
Republican

Biography: Born Louisville, Kentucky, November 4, 1969; married; 3 children. Voting address: Watertown, Wisconsin. ▪ Graduate Oak Creek High School, 1987; Trans-American School of Broadcasting (Madison), 1989; attended University of Wisconsin-Parkside, 1987–88. ▪ Realtor; owner, family-run natural dog treat company; owner, communications consulting company. Former radio morning show host, news anchor; communications director, Assembly Speaker Jeff Fitzgerald. ▪ Member: Honorable Order of Kentucky Colonels; Watertown Elks Club. ▪ Former member: Radio TV News Directors Association; Milwaukee Press Club.

Legislature: Elected to Assembly since 2012. Committee assignments, 2019: Education; Housing and Real Estate (chair); Insurance; Mental Health (vice chair); Rules; State Affairs.

Contact: Rep.Jagler@legis.wisconsin.gov; 608-266-9650; 888-534-0037 (toll free); Room 316 North, State Capitol, PO Box 8952, Madison, WI 53708.

Barbara Dittrich, Assembly District 38
Republican

Biography: Born Milwaukee, Wisconsin, May 21, 1964; married; 3 children. Voting address: Oconomowoc, Wisconsin. ▪ Graduate Hamilton High School (Sussex) 1982; attended Waukesha County Technical College, 1983; attended University of Wisconsin-Milwaukee, 1986. ▪ Non-profit leader (16 years). Former financial advisor (13 years); small business owner.

▪Member: Oconomowoc Area Chamber of Commerce; Crosspoint Community Church. ▪ Former member: Great Lakes Hemophilia Foundation (board of directors); Christian Council on Persons with Disabilities (board of directors); Lutheran Homes of Oconomowoc (personnel committee member); St. Catherine of Alexandria (parish council treasurer); Oconomowoc Area Chamber of Commerce (ambassador); NORD Rare Disease Day (ambassador).

Legislature: Elected to Assembly 2018. Committee assignments, 2019: Financial Institutions; Jobs and the Economy; Labor and Integrated Employment; Medicaid Reform and Oversight; Small Business Development; Ways and Means; Workforce Development (vice chair).

Contact: Rep.Dittrich@legis.wisconsin.gov; 608-266-8551; 888-534-0038 (toll free); Room 19 North, State Capitol, PO Box 8952, Madison, WI 53708.

Mark L. Born, Assembly District 39
Republican

Biography: Born Beaver Dam, Wisconsin, April 14, 1976; married; 1 child. Voting address: Beaver Dam, Wisconsin. ▪ Graduate Beaver Dam High School, 1994; B.A. in Political Science and History, Gustavus Adolphus College (St. Peter, Minnesota), 1998. ▪ Full-time legislator. Former corrections supervisor, Dodge County Sheriff's Department. ▪ Member: Downtown Beaver Dam, Inc.; Friends of Horicon Marsh; Beaver Dam Area Arts Association; Dodge County Historical Society (vice president); Leadership Beaver Dam Steering Committee; Beaver Dam Lake Improvement Association (former vice president); Republican Party of Dodge County (former chair); Beaver Dam Elks Lodge 1540. ▪ Beaver Dam Fire and Police Commission, 2003–05; Beaver Dam City Council, 2005–09.

Legislature: Elected to Assembly since 2012. Committee assignments, 2019: Finance; Rules; Joint Committee on Finance. Additional appointments: State Building Commission.

Contact: Rep.Born@legis.wisconsin.gov; 608-266-2540; 888-534-0039 (toll free); Room 324 East, State Capitol, PO Box 8952, Madison, WI 53708.

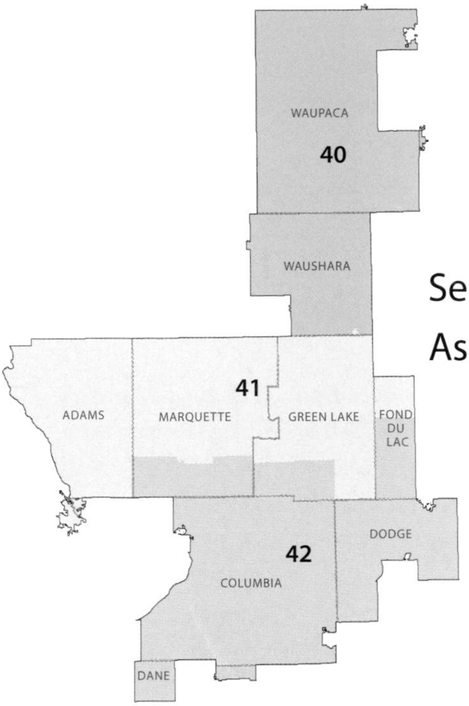

Senate District 14
Assembly Districts 40, 41, 42

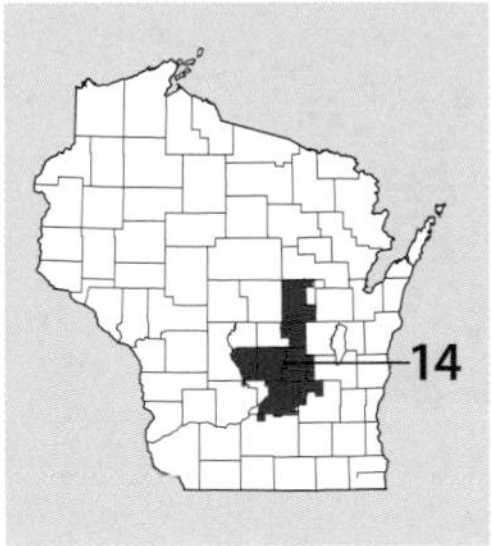

Luther S. Olsen, Senate District 14
Republican

Biography: Born Berlin, Wisconsin, February 26, 1951; married. Voting address: Ripon, Wisconsin. ▪ Graduate Berlin High School, 1969; B.S., University of Wisconsin-Madison, 1973; Wisconsin Rural Leadership Program Group IV, 1990–92. ▪ Partner in farm supply dealerships. ▪ Member: University of Wisconsin Hospital & Clinics Authority (UWHCA) Board of Directors, serving on Finance, Audit, and Executive Committees; Conservative Leaders for Education; Education Commission of the States (ECS) Executive Committee; National Conference of State Legislatures (NCSL) Education Committee, Agriculture Task Force, Education Policy Work Group, and International Education Study Group. ▪ Former member: Waushara County Fair Board (director); Family Health/La Clinica director, 1995–99. ▪ Berlin Area School Board, 1976–97 (president 1986–95).

Legislature: Elected to Assembly 1994–2002. Elected to Senate since 2004. Committee assignments, 2019: Education (chair); Finance (vice chair); Natural

Resources and Energy (vice chair); Universities, Technical Colleges, Children and Families; Joint Committee on Finance (vice chair); Joint Legislative Council. Additional appointments: Education Commission of the States; Educational Communications Board; State Capitol and Executive Residence Board; Claims Board.

Contact: Sen.Olsen@legis.wisconsin.gov; 608-266-0751; 800-991-5541 (toll free); Room 122 South, State Capitol, PO Box 7882, Madison, WI 53707-7882.

Kevin David Petersen, Assembly District 40
Republican

Biography: Born Waupaca, Wisconsin, December 14, 1964; married; 2 children. Voting address: Waupaca, Wisconsin. ▪ Graduate Waupaca High School, 1983; B.S.M.E., University of New Mexico, 1989. ▪ Co-owner of family-run electronics corporation. Served in U.S. Navy sub service, 1983–94; Persian Gulf War veteran; U.S. Naval Reserve member, 1994–2008. ▪ Member: Waupaca County Republican Party; Waushara County Republican Party; VFW Post 1037 (life member); AMVETS Post 1887 (life member); American Legion Post 161; Manawa Chamber of Commerce; Waupaca Area Chamber of Commerce; New London Area Chamber of Commerce; National Rifle Association. ▪ Former Town of Dayton supervisor, 2001–07.

Legislature: Elected to Assembly since 2006. Committee assignments, 2019: Energy and Utilities; Financial Institutions; Insurance (chair); Public Benefit Reform (vice chair); Science and Technology (vice chair); Ways and Means.

Contact: Rep.Petersen@legis.wisconsin.gov; 608-266-3794; 888-947-0040 (toll free); Room 105 West, State Capitol, PO Box 8953, Madison, WI 53708.

Joan Ballweg, Assembly District 41
Republican

Biography: Born Milwaukee, Wisconsin, March 16, 1952; married; 3 children, 3 grandchildren. Voting address: Markesan, Wisconsin. ▪ Graduate Nathan Hale High School (West Allis), 1970; attended University of Wisconsin-Waukesha; B.A. in Elementary Education, University of Wisconsin-Stevens Point, 1974. ▪ Co-owner of farm equipment business. Former first grade teacher. ▪ Member: Council of State Governments (chair-elect 2019, chair 2020); Midwest Legislative Conference (chair 2016); Markesan Chamber of Commerce (former treasurer); Waupun Chamber of Commerce; Green Lake County Farm Bureau; Waupun Memorial Hospital (board of directors, former chair); Agnesian HealthCare Enterprises LLC management committee (former secretary); volunteer, Markesan District Schools; Markesan PTA (former president); Markesan AFS Chapter (hosting coordinator, president, former host family, liaison). ▪ Former member: FEMA V Regional Advisory Council. ▪ Markesan City Council, 1987–91; mayor of Markesan, 1991–97.

Legislature: Elected to Assembly since 2004. Leadership positions: Majority Caucus Chair 2013, 2011. Committee assignments, 2019: Review of Administrative Rules (chair); Children and Families; Colleges and Universities; International Affairs and Commerce; Jobs and the Economy; Mental Health; Regulatory Licensing Reform (vice chair); Rules; Tourism; Joint Committee for Review of Administrative Rules (co-chair); Joint Legislative Council; Speaker's Task Force on Suicide Prevention (chair).

Contact: Rep.Ballweg@legis.wisconsin.gov; 608-266-8077; 888-534-0041 (toll free); Room 210 North, State Capitol, PO Box 8952, Madison, WI 53708.

Jon Plumer, Assembly District 42
Republican

Biography: Born Sterling, Illinois, March 1, 1955; married; 4 children, 7 grandchildren. Voting address: Lodi, Wisconsin. ▪ Graduate West High School, 1973. ▪ Small business owner, Plumer Karate America. Former route salesman for Kraft Foods for 30 years. ▪ Member: Lodi Area EMS Commission; Lodi Optimist Club; Project SEARCH (board member); Town of Lodi Board Supervisor; Columbia County Board Supervisor; Lodi Knights of Columbus. ▪ Former member: Lodi & Lake Wisconsin Chamber of Commerce (3-term president).

Legislature: Elected to Assembly in June 2018 special election. Reelected November 2018. Committee assignments, 2019: Aging and Long-Term Care; Agriculture; Family Law; Rural Development; Substance Abuse and Prevention (chair); Tourism; Transportation.

Contact: Rep.Plumer@legis.wisconsin.gov; 608-266-3404; 888-534-0042 (toll-free); Room 18 North, State Capitol, PO Box 8953, Madison, WI 53708.

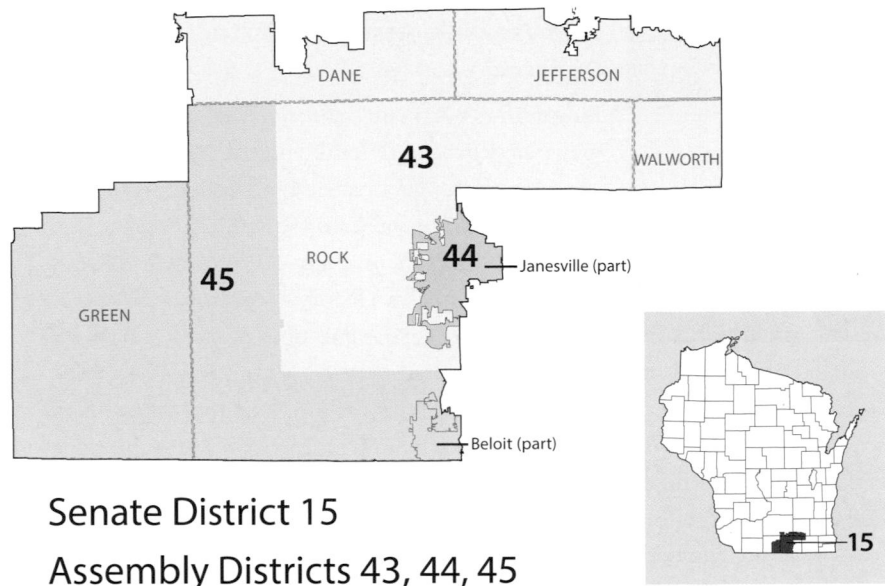

Senate District 15
Assembly Districts 43, 44, 45

Janis Ringhand, Senate District 15
Democrat

Biography: Born Madison, Wisconsin, February 13, 1950; married; 2 children, 5 grandchildren, 3 great-grandchildren. Voting address: Evansville, Wisconsin. ▪ Graduate Evansville High School, 1968; Associate Degree Madison Area Technical College, 1985. ▪ Full-time legislator. Former accountant for small businesses; executive director of nonprofit. ▪ Member: Evansville Chamber of Commerce; Evansville Energy Independence Team. ▪ Former member: Stoughton Hospital Board (chair); Creekside Place, Inc. (board of directors); Evansville Community Partnership (secretary). ▪ Evansville City Council, 1998–2002, 2008–10; Mayor of Evansville, 2002–06.

Legislature: Elected to Assembly 2010–12. Elected to Senate since 2014. Leadership positions: Minority Caucus Vice Chair 2019, 2017; Minority Caucus Secretary 2013. Committee assignments, 2019: Agriculture, Revenue and Financial Institutions; Economic Development, Commerce and Trade; Labor and Regulatory Reform. Additional appointments: Building Commission (Administrative Affairs Subcommittee chair).

Contact: Sen.Ringhand@legis.wisconsin.gov; 608-266-2253; Room 108 South, State Capitol, PO Box 7882, Madison, WI 53707-7882.

Don Vruwink, Assembly District 43
Democrat

Biography: Born Auburndale, Wisconsin, June 12, 1952; married; 1 child. Voting address: Milton, Wisconsin. ▪ Graduate Auburndale High School, 1970; B.A. in Broad Field Social Studies, Political Science and Coaching Minor, University of Wisconsin-Stevens Point, 1975; M.A. in History, University of Wisconsin-Whitewater, 1986. ▪ Full-time legislator; substitute teacher; softball and baseball umpire. Retired teacher, Milton School District; Former Parks and Recreation Director, City of Milton; Former Milton High School basketball, football and softball coach. ▪ Member: Farm Bureau; League of Conservation Voters. ▪ Recipient: Channel 3000 Top Notch Teacher, 2011; Milton Athletic Hall of Fame, 2011; Wisconsin Fastpitch Coaches Hall of Fame, 2014; Milton Chamber of Commerce *Lifetime Achievement Award*, 2014; Wisconsin Property Taxpayers *Property Taxpayer Champion Award*, 2018; Wisconsin Educational Technology Leaders *Education Technology Appreciation Award*, 2018. ▪ Milton City Council 2011–15 (president 2015); Milton School Board 2016–19 (acting president 2019).

Legislature: Elected to Assembly since 2016. Committee assignments, 2019: Agriculture; Education; Government Accountability and Oversight; International Affairs and Commerce; Rural Development; Tourism. Additional appointments, 2019: Dairy Task Force 2.0; Special Committee on the Investment and Use of School Trust Funds.

Contact: Rep.Vruwink@legis.wisconsin.gov; 608-266-3790; 888-534-0043 (toll free); Room 6 North, State Capitol, PO Box 8953, Madison, WI 53708.

Debra Kolste, Assembly District 44
Democrat

Biography: Born O'Neill, Nebraska, June 20, 1953; married; 3 children. Voting address: Janesville, Wisconsin. ▪ Graduate Kimball County High School (Kimball, Nebraska), 1971; B.S. in Medical Technology, University of Nebraska, 1975. ▪ Full-time legislator. Former medical technologist. ▪ Member: League of Women Voters; Friends of Rotary Botanical Gardens; Janesville Performing Arts Center (board member). ▪ Former member: Mercy Health Systems Volunteers (president); Rock Futbol Soccer League (founding board member); PTO Board; PTA Board; YMCA of Northern Rock County Board of Directors. ▪ Janesville School Board, 2000–09.

Legislature: Elected to Assembly since 2012. Committee assignments, 2019: Agriculture; Health; Medicaid Reform and Oversight; Mental Health; Rules; Substance Abuse and Prevention; Transportation; Speaker's Task Force on Suicide Prevention.

Contact: Rep.Kolste@legis.wisconsin.gov; 608-266-7503; 888-947-0044 (toll free); Room 107 North, State Capitol, PO Box 8952, Madison, WI 53708.

Mark Spreitzer, Assembly District 45
Democrat

Biography: Born Evanston, Illinois, December 16, 1986, married. Voting address: Beloit, Wisconsin. ▪ Graduate Northside College Preparatory High School (Chicago, Illinois), 2005; B.A. in Political Science, Beloit College, 2009; Bowhay Institute for Legislative Leadership Development, 2017; State Legislative Leaders Foundation Emerging Leaders Program, 2017. ▪ Full-time legislator. Former assistant director of alumni and parent relations and annual support, Beloit College. ▪ Member: United Church of Beloit (deacons board); Welty Environmental Center (board president); Young Democrats of Wisconsin; New Leaders Council (advisory board); Young Elected Officials Network; National Caucus of Environmental Legislators; Great Lakes Legislative Caucus; Major, Wisconsin Wing, Civil Air Patrol Legislative Squadron (official Auxiliary of the U.S. Air Force). ▪ Former member: Community Action, Inc. of Rock and Walworth Counties (board member); City of Beloit Appointment Review Committee (chair). ▪ Recipient: Wisconsin League of Conservation Voters *Conservation Champion* 2015–16 and 2017–18; Wisconsin Economic Development Association *Champion of Economic Development Award* 2017–18; Wisconsin Farmers Union *Friend of the Family Farmer* 2017; Rock River Coalition *Protector Award* 2017; Fair Wisconsin *Community Advocate of the Year* 2014. ▪ Beloit City Council, 2011–15 (president, 2014–15).

Legislature: Elected to Assembly since 2014. Leadership positions: Minority Caucus Chair 2019, 2017. Committee assignments, 2019: Agriculture; Assembly Organization; Campaigns and Elections; Criminal Justice and Public Safety; Forestry, Parks and Outdoor Recreation; Local Government; Rules; Sporting Heritage.

Contact: Rep.Spreitzer@legis.wisconsin.gov; 608-266-1192; 888-534-0045 (toll free); Room 113 North, State Capitol, PO Box 8953, Madison, WI 53708.

Senate District 16
Assembly Districts 46, 47, 48

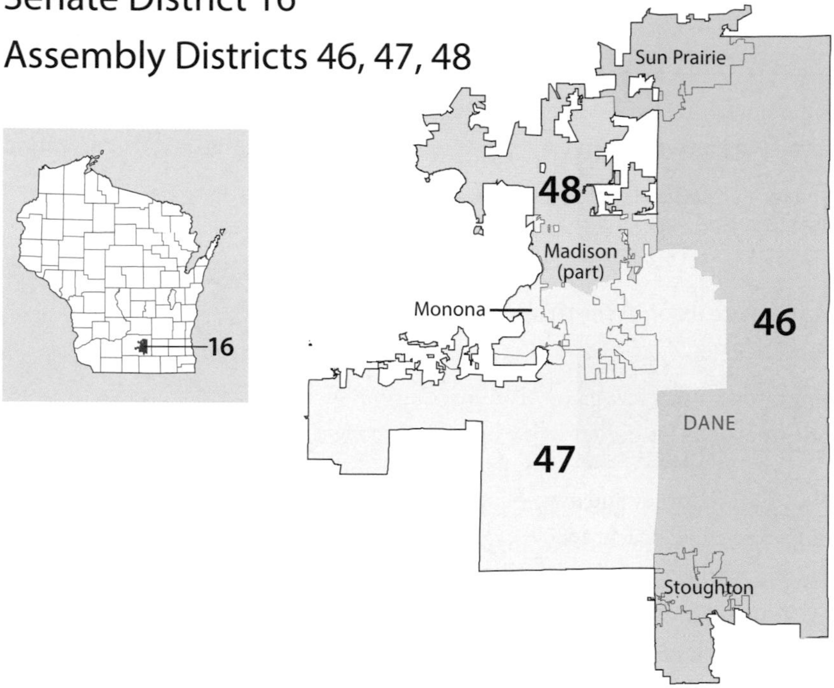

Mark Miller, Senate District 16
Democrat

Biography: Born Boston, Massachusetts, February 1, 1943. Voting address: Monona, Wisconsin. ▪ Graduate Middleton High School; B.S., University of Wisconsin-Madison; Bowhay Institute for Legislative Leadership Development (BILLD), 1999; Flemming Fellows Leadership Institute, 2002. ▪ Former military pilot; Wisconsin Air National Guard, 1966–95 (retired Lieutenant Colonel); former real estate property manager. ▪ Dane County Board of Health, 1998–2004; Board of Health for Madison and Dane County, 2004–07; Dane County Board of Supervisors, 1996–2000.

Legislature: Elected to Assembly 1998–2002. Elected to Senate since 2004. Leadership positions: Minority Caucus Chair 2019, 2017; Minority Leader 2011 (through 7/17/12); Majority Leader 2011 (effective 7/17/12); Majority Caucus Chair 2007. Committee assignments, 2019: Elections, Ethics and Rural Issues; Local Government, Small Business, Tourism and Workforce Development; Natural Resources and Energy; Joint Legislative Council; Speaker's Task Force on Water Quality.

Contact: Sen.Miller@legis.wisconsin.gov; 608-266-9170; 608-221-2701 (district); Room 106 South, State Capitol, PO Box 7882, Madison, WI 53707-7882.

Gary Alan Hebl, Assembly District 46

Democrat

Biography: Born Madison, Wisconsin, May 15, 1951; married; 3 children, 2 grandsons. Voting address: Sun Prairie, Wisconsin. ▪ Graduate Sun Prairie High School, 1969; B.A. in Political Science, University of Wisconsin-Madison, 1973; Gonzaga University Law School, 1976; Bowhay Institute, 2008; Council of State Government 2018 Henry Toll Fellowship Program, alumnus. ▪ Attorney and owner of a title insurance company. Sacred Hearts eighth grade basketball coach, 1980–99. ▪ Member: Wisconsin League of Conservation Voters; Dane County Bar Association; Wisconsin Bar Association; Sun Prairie Optimist Club (former president); Sun Prairie Chamber of Commerce (former president); UW Flying Club (former board chair); AOPA; EAA Young Eagles Program; Knights of Columbus (fourth degree member); Sun Prairie Cable Access Board; YMCA (former president); Sun Prairie Public Library Board (former president); Sacred Heart Parish Council (former trustee); Sun Prairie Quarterback Club (former president); Major, Wisconsin Wing, Civil Air Patrol Legislative Squadron (official Auxiliary of the U.S. Air Force). ▪ Recipient: State Bar of Wisconsin *Scales of Justice Award* 2009–10; Wisconsin Dietetic Association *Nutrition Champion Award* 2010; Pharmacy Society of Wisconsin Legislator of the Year 2010, 2009; Sun Prairie Star poll *Best Attorney in Sun Prairie* 2008–16; *James J. Reininger Award* for lifetime achievement 2008; Wisconsin Association of PEG Channels *Friend of Access Award* 2010, 2007; Wisconsin League of Conservation Voters *Conservation Champion* 2013–14, 2011–12, 2009–10, 2005–06; Sun Prairie Exchange Club *Book of Golden Deeds Award* 2003; Chamber of Commerce *Judith Krivsky Business Person of the Year Award* 2002; Sun Prairie Business and Education Partnership *Outstanding Small Business of the Year* 2001; Sun Prairie High School Wall of Success 2015.

Legislature: Elected to Assembly since 2004. Committee assignments, 2019: Constitution and Ethics; Education; Environment; Judiciary; Joint Committee for Review of Administrative Rules. Additional appointments: Commission on Uniform State Laws.

Contact: Rep.Hebl@legis.wisconsin.gov; 608-266-7678; Room 120 North, State Capitol, PO Box 8952, Madison, WI 53708.

Jimmy Anderson, Assembly District 47
Democrat

Biography: Born El Paso, Texas, August 26, 1986; raised in Patterson, California. Voting address: Fitchburg, Wisconsin. ▪ Graduate Patterson High School, 2004; B.A., summa cum laude, California State University, Monterey Bay, 2008; J.D., University of Wisconsin Law School, 2012. ▪ Nonprofit director. ▪ Member: Wisconsin State Bar Association.

Legislature: Elected to Assembly since 2016. Committee assignments, 2019: Colleges and Universities; Environment; Health; Judiciary; Medicaid Reform and Oversight; Science and Technology; Speaker's Task Force on Suicide Prevention.

Contact: Rep.Anderson@legis.wisconsin.gov; 608-266-8570; 888-302-0047 (toll free); Room 9 North, State Capitol, PO Box 8952, Madison, WI 53708.

Melissa Sargent, Assembly District 48
Democrat

Biography: Born Madison, Wisconsin, March 28, 1969; 4 sons. Voting address: Madison, Wisconsin. ▪ Graduate Madison East High School, 1987; B.A., University of Wisconsin-Madison, 1991. Graduate Bowhay Institute for Legislative Leadership Development; Emerging Leaders Program, University of Virginia, 2014; Toll Fellowship, 2015. ▪ Small business owner. ▪

Member: Women in Government; WiLL/WAND; Emerge Wisconsin (board of directors); Dane County Democratic Party; Democratic Party; Make Room for Youth; Friends of Cherokee Marsh; BSA Glacier's Edge Council (board of directors) ▪ Former member: Midwest Shiba Inu Dog Rescue (president); Gompers PTO (president). ▪ Recipient: National Federation of Women Legislators *Woman of Excellence*; WiLL *Pacesetter Award*; Arc Dane County *Elected Official of the Year* 2014; Citizen Action *Activist Achievement Award* 2014; *Eleanor Roosevelt Award* nominee 2013; Wisconsin League of Conservation Voters *Conservation Champion* 2016, 2014. ▪ Dane County Board of Supervisors, 2010–14.

Legislature: Elected to Assembly since 2012. Committee assignments, 2019: Audit; Mental Health; Science and Technology; Small Business Development; Substance Abuse and Prevention; Joint Committee on Information Policy and Technology; Joint Legislative Audit Committee; Speaker's Task Force on Suicide Prevention.

Additional appointments: State Capitol and Executive Residence Board; Committee to Celebrate the Centennial Anniversary of Wisconsin's Ratification of the 19th Amendment (executive committee member).

Contact: Rep.Sargent@legis.wisconsin.gov; 608-266-0960; Room 11 North, State Capitol, PO Box 8953, Madison, WI 53708.

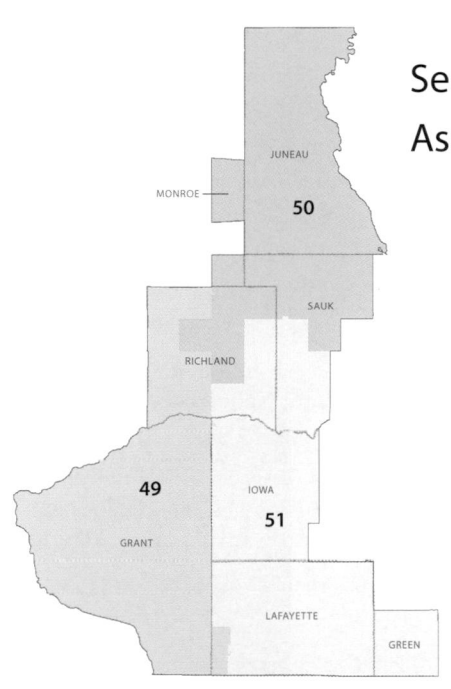

Senate District 17
Assembly Districts 49, 50, 51

Howard Marklein, Senate District 17
Republican

Biography: Born Madison, Wisconsin, October 3, 1954; married; 2 children, 3 stepchildren, 5 grandchildren. Voting address: Spring Green, Wisconsin. ▪ Graduate River Valley High School (Spring Green), 1972; B.B.A., University of Wisconsin-Whitewater, 1976. ▪ Certified public accountant (CPA); certified fraud examiner (CFE). ▪ Member: St. John's Catholic Church Spring Green (finance committee member); Taliesin Preservation Inc. Board of Trustees (treasurer); National Rifle Association. ▪ Former member: University of Wisconsin-Whitewater National Alumni Association (president);

University of Wisconsin-Whitewater Foundation (board of directors president); Fort HealthCare Board of Directors (chair, treasurer); Fort Atkinson Rotary Club (president); Fort Atkinson Chamber of Commerce (president); Whitewater Chamber of Commerce (president); Dodgeville Chamber of Commerce (vice president). ▪ Recipient: WMC *Working for Wisconsin Award* 2018, 2016, 2014, 2012; MMAC *Champion of Commerce Award* 2018, 2016, 2014, 2012; Wisconsin Pork Association *Distinguished Service Award* 2013; Wisconsin Newspaper Association *Badger Award* 2013; Wisconsin Aquaculture Association *Legislator of the Year* 2013; Dairy Business Association *Legislative Excellence Award* 2018, 2016, 2012; Wisconsin Auto Collision Technicians Association *Legislator of the Year* 2016; Wisconsin Towns Association *Friend of Towns* 2016; Associated General Contractors *Legislator of the Year* 2016; Wisconsin Counties Association *Outstanding Legislator* 2018, 2016; Wisconsin Builders Association *Friend of Housing* 2018, 2016, 2015; Wisconsin Association of Local Health Departments and Boards & Wisconsin Public Health Association *Friend of Public Health* 2018, 2016; Wisconsin Hospitals Association *Health Care Advocate Award* 2018; Associated Builders and Contractors *Building Wisconsin Award* 2018, 2014; League of Wisconsin Municipalities *Municipal Champion Award* 2018, 2016; National Federation of Independent Businesses *Guardian of Small Business Award* 2018; University of Wisconsin-Platteville *Friend of the University Award* 2018; Wisconsin Grocers Association *Friend of Grocers* 2018; Wisconsin Agri-Business Association *Friend of Wisconsin Agri-Business* 2018; Wisconsin ATV/UTV Association *President's Award* 2017; Wisconsin State Telecommunications Association *Excellence in Legislative Leadership Award* 2018.

Legislature: Elected to Assembly 2010–12. Elected to Senate since 2014. Committee assignments, 2019: Agriculture, Revenue and Financial Institutions (chair); Transportation, Veterans and Military Affairs (vice chair); Natural Resources and Energy; Joint Committee on Finance; Joint Legislative Council. Additional appointments, 2019: Mississippi River Parkway Commission; Transportation Projects Commission.

Contact: Sen.Marklein@legis.wisconsin.gov; 608-266-0703; Room 8 South, State Capitol, PO Box 7882, Madison, WI 53707-7882.

Travis Tranel, Assembly District 49
Republican

Biography: Born Dubuque, Iowa, September 12, 1985; married; 5 children. Voting address: Cuba City, Wisconsin. ▪ Graduate Wahlert Catholic High School

(Dubuque, Iowa), 2004; B.A. Loras College (Dubuque, Iowa), 2007. ▪ Dairy farmer, small business owner. ▪ Member: St. Joseph Sinsinawa Parish Council, 2010–12 (president, 2011–12); Wisconsin Farm Bureau; Knights of Columbus; National Rifle Association; Platteville Regional Chamber of Commerce; Grant County Republican Party. ▪ Recipient: DBA *Legislative Excellence Award* 2018, 2016, 2014, 2012; WMC *Working for Wisconsin Award* 2018, 2016, 2014, 2012; MMAC *Champion of Commerce Award* 2014, 2012; WAFP *Friends of Family Medicine* 2014; WATA *Ambassador Award* 2015; University of Wisconsin-Platteville *Friend of the University Award* 2018; WEDA *Champion of Economic Development Award* 2018.

Legislature: Elected to Assembly since 2010. Committee assignments, 2019: Tourism (chair); Colleges and Universities (vice chair); Agriculture; Energy and Utilities; Insurance; Small Business Development; Speaker's Task Force on Water Quality. Additional appointments, 2019: Governor's Council on Tourism.

Contact: Rep.Tranel@legis.wisconsin.gov; 608-266-1170; 888-872-0049 (toll free); Room 302 North, State Capitol, PO Box 8953, Madison, WI 53708.

Tony Kurtz, Assembly District 50
Republican

Biography: Born Columbus, Ohio, December 23, 1966. Voting address: Wonewoc, Wisconsin. ▪ B.S. in Professional Aeronautics, Embry-Riddle Aeronautical University, 1989; M.S. in International Relations, Troy State University (Troy, Alabama), 1997. ▪ Organic grain farmer. Former U.S. Army attack helicopter pilot 1985–2005, retired from active duty as a Chief Warrant Officer Four (CW4); Persian Gulf War veteran; Iraq War veteran. ▪ Member: Veterans of Foreign Wars (life member); Military Officers Association of America (life member); American Legion; Wisconsin Farm Bureau; Organic Farmers Association; Juneau County Republican Party.

Legislature: Elected to Assembly 2018. Committee assignments, 2019: Agriculture; Corrections; Environment; Health (vice chair); Rural Development; Veterans and Military Affairs; Speaker's Task Force on Suicide Prevention; Speaker's Task Force on Water Quality.

Contact: Rep.Kurtz@legis.wisconsin.gov; 608-266-8531; 888-534-0050; Room 418 North, State Capitol, PO Box 8952, Madison, WI 53708.

Todd Novak, Assembly District 51
Republican

Biography: Born Dodgeville, Wisconsin, April 23, 1965; 2 children. Voting address: Dodgeville, Wisconsin. ▪ Graduate Iowa-Grant High School, 1983; attended Southwest Technical College, 1983–85. ▪ Former government/associate newspaper editor, 1990–2014. ▪ Member: Wisconsin League of Municipalities; NRA; Wisconsin Farm Bureau. ▪ Former member: Iowa County Humane Society (founding member, treasurer); Wisconsin Newspaper Association; National Newspaper Association. ▪ Recipient: Gathering Waters *Policymaker of the Year*; WISCAP *William Steiger Human Services Award*; MMAC *Champion of Commerce*; WMC *Working for Wisconsin Award*; WNA *Legislative Service Award*; WCA *Outstanding Legislator Award*; WPHCA *Friend of Community Health Centers*; WAFP *Friend of Family Medicine Award*; LWM Municipal Champion Award; CEF (Clean Energy Service) *Clean Energy Champion*; University of Wisconsin-Platteville *Friend of the University Award* 2018. ▪ Southwest Regional Planning Commission, 2012–present; Mayor of Dodgeville, 2012–present.

Legislature: Elected to Assembly since 2014. Committee assignments, 2019: Local Government (chair); Speaker's Task Force on Water Quality (chair); Agriculture (vice chair); Criminal Justice and Public Safety; Environment; Mental Health; Rural Development.

Contact: Rep.Novak@legis.wisconsin.gov; 608-266-7502; 888-534-0051 (toll free); Room 310 North, State Capitol, PO Box 8953, Madison, WI 53708.

Senate District 18
Assembly Districts 52, 53, 54

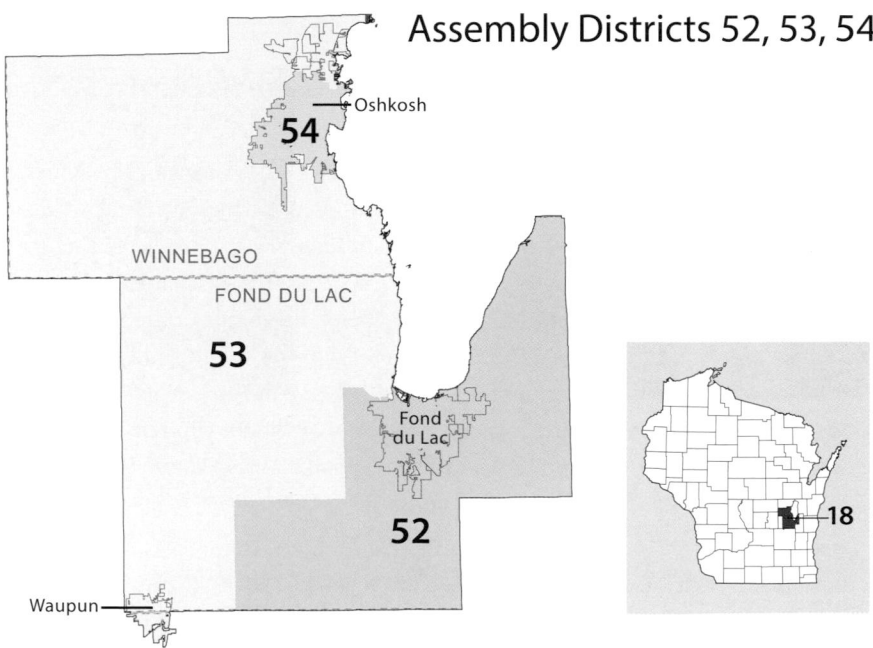

Dan Feyen, Senate District 18
Republican

Biography: Born New Holstein, Wisconsin; married; 2 children. Voting address: Fond du Lac, Wisconsin. ▪ Graduate New Holstein High School, 1986; Diploma in Printing, Fox Valley Technical College, 1988. ▪ Print and bindery coordinator. ▪ Member: Knights of Columbus; Elks Club; Major, Wisconsin Wing, Civil Air Patrol Legislative Squadron (official Auxiliary of the U.S. Air Force); Fond du Lac County Republican Party (former chair); Fond du Lac Noon Rotary Club; 6th District Republican Party (former chair). ▪ Former member: Jaycees Fond du Lac County (past president); Fond du Lac Advisory Parks Board.

Legislature: Elected to Senate 2016. Leadership positions: Assistant Majority Leader 2019. Committee assignments, 2019: Economic Development, Commerce and Trade (chair); Insurance, Financial Services, Government Oversight and Courts; Senate Organization; Utilities and Housing (vice chair); Joint Committee on Legislative Organization.

Contact: Sen.Feyen@legis.wisconsin.gov; 608-266-5300; Room 306 South, State Capitol, PO Box 7882, Madison, WI 53707-7882.

Jeremy Thiesfeldt, Assembly District 52
Republican

Biography: Born Fond du Lac, Wisconsin, November 22, 1966; married; 4 children. Voting address: Fond du Lac, Wisconsin. ▪ Graduate Kettle Moraine Lutheran High School (Jackson), 1985; B.S. in Elementary Education, Martin Luther College, 1989; attended University of Minnesota, 1992–93. ▪ Full-time legislator. Former teacher. ▪ Member: Fond du Lac Noon Rotary; Fond du Lac County Republican Party; Redeemer Lutheran Church, Thrivent Financial; National Rifle Association; Leadership Fond du Lac Alumni; Wisconsin Farm Bureau. ▪ Former member: Fond du Lac City Council, 2005–10.

Legislature: Elected to Assembly since 2010. Committee assignments, 2019: Constitution and Ethics; Committee on Education (chair); Judiciary; Transportation.

Contact: Rep.Thiesfeldt@legis.wisconsin.gov; 608-266-3156; 888-529-0052 (toll free); Room 223 North, State Capitol, PO Box 8953, Madison, WI 53708.

Michael Schraa, Assembly District 53
Republican

Biography: Born Fort Carson, Colorado, April 17, 1961; married; 3 children. Voting address: Oshkosh, Wisconsin. ▪ Graduate Oshkosh North High School, 1979; attended University of Wisconsin-Oshkosh, 1980–82. ▪ Restaurant owner. Former stock broker/investment advisor. ▪ Member: Winnebago County Republican Party (executive board); Fond du Lac County Republican Party; Calvary SonRise Church (Oshkosh); Wisconsin Independent Businesses; NRA; Winnebago County Farm Bureau; Fond du Lac County Farm Bureau. ▪ Former member: Southwest Rotary; NFIB; Oshkosh Jaycees; Big Brothers Big Sisters; Exchange Club.

Legislature: Elected to Assembly since 2012. Committee assignments, 2019: Corrections (chair); Federalism and Interstate Relations (vice chair); Criminal Justice and Public Safety; Labor and Integrated Employment; Public Benefit Reform;

Science and Technology; State Affairs Committee; Speaker's Task Force on Suicide Prevention. Additional appointments: Juvenile Corrections Grant Committee; Juvenile Corrections Study Committee.

Contact: Rep.Schraa@legis.wisconsin.gov; 608-267-7990; 888-534-0053 (toll free); Room 107 West, State Capitol, PO Box 8953, Madison, WI 53708.

Gordon Hintz, Assembly District 54
Democrat

Biography: Born Oshkosh, Wisconsin, November 29, 1973; married; 2 children. Voting address: Oshkosh, Wisconsin. ▪ Graduate Oshkosh North High School, 1992; B.A., Hamline University (St. Paul, Minnesota), 1996; M.P.A., University of Wisconsin-Madison, 2001. ▪ Municipal consultant. Former legislative staff assistant, U.S. Representative Jay Johnson, U.S. Senator Herb Kohl; former management and budget analyst, City of Long Beach, California; former instructor, Political Science Department, University of Wisconsin-Oshkosh. ▪ Member: Oshkosh Rotary Club; First Congregational Church; Oshkosh Public Museum; Winnebagoland Housing Coalition; Winnebago County Safe Streets Committee; Winnebago County Democratic Party; Oshkosh Food Co-op; Wisconsin Family Impacts Seminars.

Legislature: Elected to Assembly since 2006. Leadership positions: Minority leader 2019. Committee assignments, 2019: Assembly Organization; Employment Relations; Rules; Joint Committee on Employment Relations; Joint Committee on Legislative Organization; Joint Legislative Council; Joint Survey Committee on Retirement Systems.

Contact: Rep.Hintz@legis.wisconsin.gov; www.gordonhintz.com; Facebook: Gordon Hintz; Twitter: @GordonHintz; 608-266-2254; 888-534-0054 (toll free); 920-232-0805 (district); Room 201 West, State Capitol, PO Box 8952, Madison, WI 53708.

Senate District 19
Assembly Districts 55, 56, 57

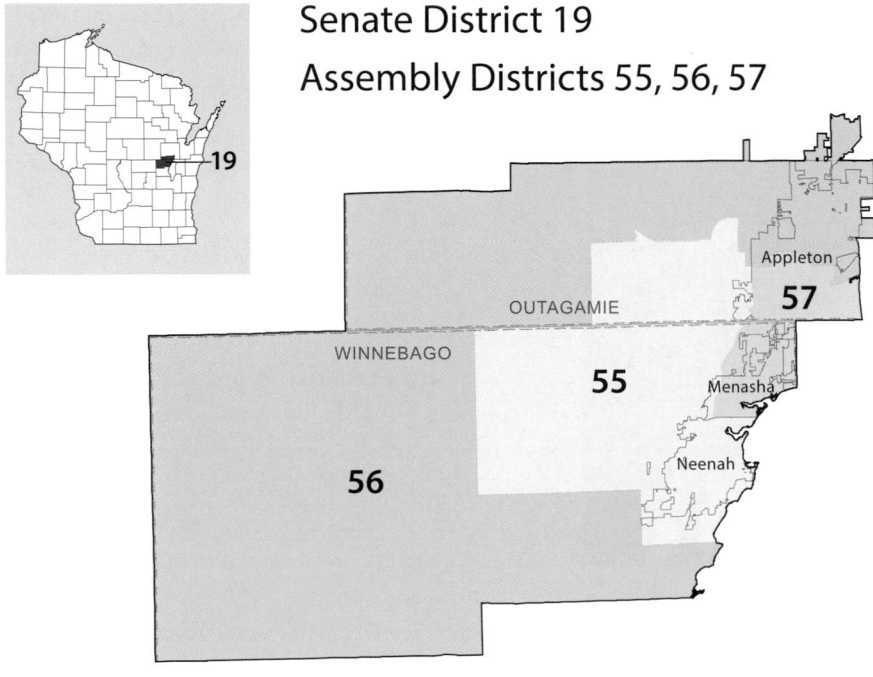

Roger Roth, Senate District 19
Republican

Biography: Born Appleton, Wisconsin, February 5, 1978; married; 4 children. Voting address: Appleton, Wisconsin. ▪ Graduate St. Mary Central High School (Menasha), 1996; B.S. in History, University of Wisconsin-Oshkosh, 2001. ▪ Self-employed home builder; First lieutenant in the Wisconsin Air National Guard. Iraq War veteran. ▪ Member: American Legion; AMVETS; Veterans of Foreign Wars.

Legislature: Elected to Assembly 2006–08. Elected to Senate since 2014. Leadership positions: President of the Senate 2019, 2017. Committee assignments, 2019: Senate Organization; Joint Committee on Employment Relations (co-chair); Joint Committee on Legislative Organization (co-chair); Joint Legislative Council (co-chair).

Contact: Sen.Roth@legis.wisconsin.gov; 608-266-0718; Room 220 South, State Capitol, PO Box 7882, Madison, WI 53707-7882.

Mike Rohrkaste, Assembly District 55
Republican

Biography: Born Dayton, Ohio, September 24, 1958; married; 2 children. Voting address: Neenah, Wisconsin. ▪ Graduate Chaminade-Julienne High School (Dayton, Ohio), 1976; B.S., Michigan State University, 1980; Masters in Labor and Industrial Relations, Michigan State University, 1982. ▪ Full-time legislator. Former chief human resources officer; vice president of human resources; over 30 years business/human resources experience. ▪ Member: YMCA of Fox Cities (board member); Samaritans Counseling Center Fox Valley (board member); Neenah Club; Fox Cities Morning Rotary; Calvary Bible Church. ▪ Former member: Fox Valley Christian Academy (board member).

Legislature: Elected to Assembly since 2014. Committee assignments, 2019: Finance; Joint Committee on Finance.

Contact: Rep.Rohrkaste@legis.wisconsin.gov; 608-266-5719; 888-534-0055 (toll free); Room 321 East, State Capitol, PO Box 8953, Madison, WI 53708.

Dave Murphy, Assembly District 56
Republican

Biography: Born Appleton, Wisconsin, November 26, 1954; married; 2 children. Voting address: Greenville, Wisconsin. ▪ Graduate Hortonville High School, 1972; University of Wisconsin-Fox Valley, 1972–74; Wisconsin School of Real Estate, 1975. ▪ Full-time legislator. Former owner, fitness center and agribusiness; real estate broker. ▪ Member: Greenville Lions Club; Immanuel Lutheran Church. ▪ Former member: Paper Valley Soccer Club (vice president).

Legislature: Elected to Assembly since 2012. Committee assignments, 2019: Campaigns and Elections; Colleges and Universities (chair); Financial Institutions; Health; Housing and Real Estate; Transportation; Workforce Development.

Contact: Rep.Murphy@legis.wisconsin.gov; 608-266-7500; 888-534-0056 (toll free); 318 North, State Capitol, PO Box 8953, Madison, WI 53708.

Amanda Stuck, Assembly District 57
Democrat

Biography: Born Appleton, Wisconsin, December 16, 1982; married; 2 children. Voting address: Appleton, Wisconsin. ▪ Graduate Appleton North High School, 2001; attended Fox Valley Technical College; B.A. in Political Science, University of Wisconsin-Oshkosh, 2007; Master of Public Administration degree, University of Wisconsin-Oshkosh, 2012. ▪ Full-time legislator; part-time substitute teacher and school bus driver. Former housing specialist, Appleton Housing Authority; legislative aide, Congressman Steve Kagan; rural mail carrier. ▪ Member: Wisconsin Future Caucus (cochair); CSG Midwest Legislative Conference Economic Development Committee; Outagamie County Local Emergency Planning Commission; Major, Wisconsin Wing, Civil Air Patrol Legislative Squadron (official Auxiliary of the U.S. Air Force); CESA 6 Women Leading Wisconsin (planning committee member); Kaleidoscope Academy (board member); Respite Care Association of Wisconsin (board member); Neighborhood Housing, Inc. (board member); Menasha Rotary; Neenah-Menasha Elks Lodge.

Legislature: Elected to Assembly since 2014. Committee assignments, 2019: Energy and Utilities; Housing and Real Estate; Insurance; Jobs and the Economy; Regulatory Licensing Reform; Sporting Heritage; Joint Committee on Information Policy and Technology.

Contact: Rep.Stuck@legis.wisconsin.gov; 608-266-3070; 888-534-0057 (toll free); Room 4 West, State Capitol, PO Box 8953, Madison, WI 53708.

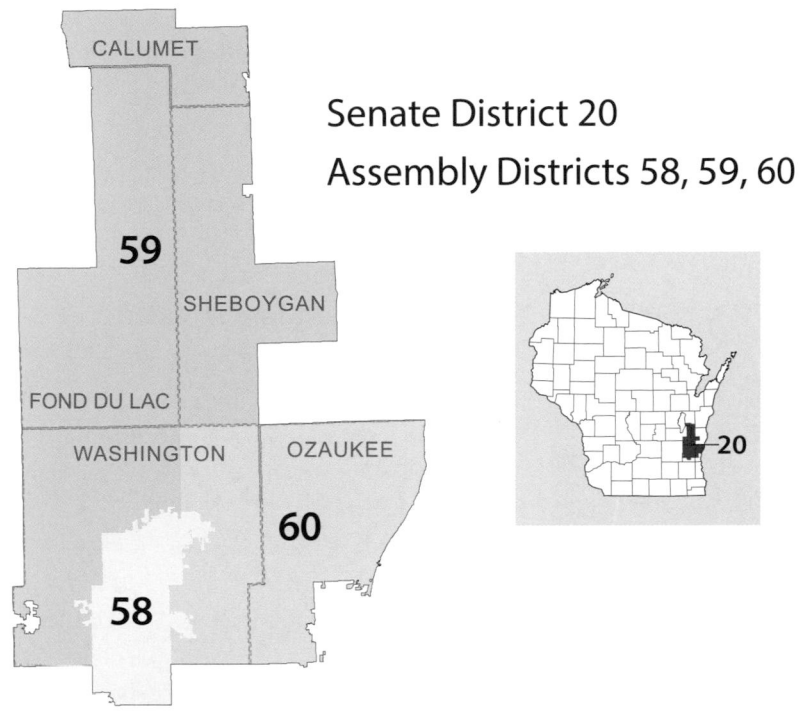

Senate District 20
Assembly Districts 58, 59, 60

Duey Stroebel, Senate District 20
Republican

Biography: Born Cedarburg, Wisconsin, September 1, 1959; married; 8 children. Voting address: Town of Cedarburg, Wisconsin. ▪ Graduate Cedarburg High School, 1978; B.B.A., University of Wisconsin-Madison, 1984; M.S., University of Wisconsin-Madison, 1987. ▪ Real estate. ▪ Member: Ozaukee Board of Realtors; Cedarburg Chamber of Commerce; Greater Cedarburg Foundation (former president); Concordia University President's Council; Farm Bureau; ABATE of Wisconsin; West Bend Chamber of Commerce; Saukville Chamber of Commerce. ▪ Former member: City of Cedarburg Downtown Ad Hoc Committee; Ozaukee Bank and Cornerstone Bank (board of directors). ▪ Town of Cedarburg Parks Commission, 2001–04; Town of Cedarburg Planning Commission, 2003–05; Cedarburg School Board, 2007–12.

Legislature: Elected to Assembly in May 2011 special election. Reelected 2012. Elected to Senate in April 2015 special election. Reelected 2016. Committee assignments, 2019: Administrative Rules (vice chair); Finance; Government Operations, Technology and Consumer Protection (chair); Insurance, Financial Services,

Government Oversight and Courts (vice chair); Sporting Heritage, Mining and Forestry; Joint Committee for Review of Administrative Rules (vice chair); Joint Committee on Finance.

Contact: Sen.Stroebel@legis.wisconsin.gov; SenatorStroebel.com; Twitter: @SenStroebel; Facebook: Senator Duey Stroebel; 608-266-7513; 800-662-1227 (toll free); Room 18 South, State Capitol, PO Box 7882, Madison, WI 53707-7882.

Rick Gundrum, Assembly District 58
Republican

Biography: Born Nenno, Wisconsin, September 4; married; 2 stepchildren, 4 grandchildren. Voting address: Slinger, Wisconsin. ▪ Graduate Hartford Union High School; A.D., University of Wisconsin-Washington County; B.S. in Radio-TV-Film, University of Wisconsin-Oshkosh. ▪ Business owner in broadcast media. ▪ Member: St. Peter Catholic Church; Washington County Republican Party; Slinger Advancement Association; Washington County Agricultural & Industrial Society; Slinger Housing Authority; Village of Slinger Board of Trustees (2009–present). ▪ Former Chair: East Wisconsin Counties Railroad Consortium; Washington County Aging & Disability Resource Board; Washington County Board of Health; Washington-Ozaukee County Joint Board of Health; Washington County Board (2016–18). ▪ Former Member: Waukesha-Ozaukee-Washington Workforce Development Board of Directors; Wisconsin Counties Association Board of Directors; Wisconsin Counties Utility Tax Association Board of Directors; Washington County Board of Supervisors, 2006–18.

Legislature: Elected to Assembly in January 2018 special election. Reelected November 2018. Committee assignments, 2019: Aging and Long-Term Care (chair); Children and Families; Insurance; Labor and Integrated Employment; Local Government (vice chair); Workforce Development.

Contact: Rep.Gundrum@legis.wisconsin.gov; 608-264-8486; 888-534-0058 (toll free); Room 304 North, State Capitol, PO Box 8952, Madison, WI 53708.

Timothy S. Ramthun, Assembly District 59
Republican

Biography: Born Kewaskum, Wisconsin, March 13, 1957; married; 2 children, 8 grandchildren. Voting address: Campbellsport, Wisconsin. ▪ Graduate Kewaskum school district, 1975; MBTI Business Training Institute, 1983; diplomas in Project

Management and Six Sigma (green), Project Management Institute, 1999; diplomas in Organizational Efficiency, Operational Quality, and Service Execution, American Management Association, 1994–96. ▪ Former executive business management consultant; vice president and directorship roles for multiple Fortune 100 and Fortune 500 companies that specialized in manufacturing, technology, finance, education, supply-chain service, and delivery and call center operations. ▪ Member: Kewaskum School District School Board (past president); the Heritage Foundation.

Legislature: Elected to Assembly 2018. Committee assignments, 2019: Children and Families (vice chair); Community Development; Constitution and Ethics; Education; Public Benefit Reform; Ways and Means; Speaker's Task Force on Water Quality.

Contact: Rep.Ramthun@legis.wisconsin.gov; 608-266-9175; 888-534-0059 (toll free); 262-305-0713 (district); Room 409 North, State Capitol, PO Box 8953, Madison, WI 53708.

Robert Brooks, Assembly District 60
Republican

Biography: Born Rockford, Illinois, July 13, 1965; married; 2 children. Voting address: Saukville, Wisconsin. ▪ Graduate Orfordville Parkview High School, 1983; attended University of Wisconsin-La Crosse, 1983–86. ▪ Real estate broker since 1990, restaurant/tavern owner. ▪ Former member: Stars and Stripes Honor Flight (board of directors); Wisconsin County Mutual (board of directors); Wisconsin Board of Realtors; Ozaukee County Tavern League (board of directors). ▪ Former commissioner, Southeastern Wisconsin Regional Planning Commission; Ozaukee County Board, 2000–14.

Legislature: Elected to Assembly since 2014. Leadership positions: Assistant Majority Leader 2017. Committee assignments, 2019: Joint Legislative Council (co-chair); Housing and Real Estate; Judiciary; Local Government; Medicaid Reform and Oversight (vice chair); Ways and Means; Speaker's Task Force on Water Quality.

Contact: Rep.Rob.Brooks@legis.wisconsin.gov; 608-267-2369; 888-534-0060 (toll free); Room 216 North, State Capitol, PO Box 8952, Madison, WI 53708.

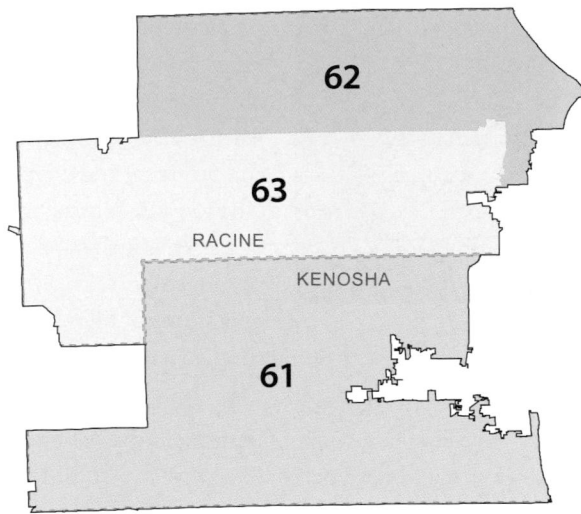

Senate District 21
Assembly Districts 61, 62, 63

Van H. Wanggaard, Senate District 21
Republican

Biography: Born Ft. Leavenworth, Kansas, April 1952; married; 2 children, 3 grandchildren. Voting address: Racine, Wisconsin. ▪ Graduate Racine Lutheran High School, 1970; Racine Police Academy; Wisconsin State Patrol Academy Accident Investigation; Northwestern University Traffic Institute—Reconstruction; U.S. Coast Guard National SAR School; attended John F. Kennedy University, California; University of Wisconsin-Extension; University of Wisconsin-Parkside; Green Bay Technical College; Milwaukee Area Technical College; Fox Valley Technical College. ▪ Full-time legislator. Retired traffic investigator, Racine Police Department; adjunct instructor, Gateway Technical College and Northwestern Traffic Institute; police liaison and security, Racine Unified School District. ▪ Member: National Rifle Association (life member); Racine County Line Rifle Club (board of directors); Racine Police Credit Union (former president, vice president); Major, Wisconsin Wing, Civil Air Patrol Legislative

Squadron (official Auxiliary of the U.S. Air Force). ▪ Former member: Racine Zoological Society (board of directors); Racine Jaycees; Racine Police Explorers (advisor); Traffic Accident Consultants, Inc. (board of directors); Association of SWAT Personnel; Racine Innovative Youth Service (board); Hostage Negotiation Team, RAPD; Racine Junior Deputy Sheriffs Association; Racine Alateen (advisor); National Association for Search and Rescue (PSAR chair). ▪ Racine Police and Fire Commission, 2003–13 (chair, vice chair, secretary); Racine County Board, 2002–11.

Legislature: Elected to Senate 2010. Reelected since 2014. Leadership positions: Majority Caucus Vice Chair 2017, 2015; Majority Caucus Chair 2019, 2017. Committee assignments, 2019: Judiciary and Public Safety (chair); Labor and Regulatory Reform (vice chair); Utilities and Housing; Joint Review Committee on Criminal Penalties (co-chair). Additional appointments: Juvenile Corrections Grant Committee; Judicial Council; Midwest Interstate Passenger Rail Commission; Prison Facilities Planning Committee; Historical Society Board of Curators.

Contact: Sen.Wanggaard@legis.wisconsin.gov; 608-266-1832; 866-615-7510 (toll free); Room 313 South, State Capitol, PO Box 7882, Madison, WI 53707-7882.

Samantha Kerkman, Assembly District 61
Republican

Biography: Born Burlington, Wisconsin, March 6, 1974; 2 children. Voting address: Village of Salem Lakes, Wisconsin. ▪ Graduate Wilmot High School; B.A., University of Wisconsin-Whitewater, 1996. ▪ Member: Kenosha Area Business Alliance; Twin Lakes Chamber and Area Business Association; Twin Lakes American Legion Auxiliary Post 544; St. Alphonsus Catholic Church. ▪ Former member: Burlington Area Chamber of Commerce; Powers Lake Sportsmens Club; VFW Auxiliary, Bloomfield Center Post 5830.

Legislature: Elected to Assembly since 2000. Leadership positions: Majority Caucus Sergeant at Arms 2019, 2017, 2015, 2013, 2011. Committee assignments, 2019: Audit (chair); Children and Families; Federalism and Interstate Relations; Judiciary; Ways and Means; Joint Legislative Audit Committee (co-chair).

Contact: Rep.Kerkman@legis.wisconsin.gov; 608-266-2530; 888-529-0061 (toll free); 262-279-1037 (district); Room 315 North, State Capitol, PO Box 8952, Madison, WI 53708; PO Box 156, Powers Lake, WI 53159 (district).

Robert O. Wittke, Jr., Assembly District 62

Republican

Biography: Born Racine, Wisconsin, September 23, 1957; married; 4 children. Voting address: Racine, Wisconsin. ▪ Graduate William Horlick High School (Racine, Wisconsin), 1975; B.A., University of Wisconsin-Eau Claire, 1980. ▪ Tax professional for 35 years, specializing in corporate taxation. ▪ Former member: Racine Unified School District Board, 2016–19 (past president).

Legislature: Elected to the Assembly 2018. Committee assignments, 2019: Colleges and Universities; Education; Jobs and the Economy; Science and Technology; Ways and Means (vice chair).

Contact: Rep.Wittke@legis.wisconsin.gov; 608-266-0731; 888-534-0062 (toll free); 262-417-0045 (district); Room 412 North, State Capitol, PO Box 8953, Madison, WI 53708.

Robin J. Vos, Assembly District 63

Republican

Biography: Born Burlington, Wisconsin, July 5, 1968. Voting address: Burlington, Wisconsin. ▪ Graduate Burlington High School, 1986; University of Wisconsin-Whitewater, 1991. ▪ Owner of several small businesses. Former congressional district director; former legislative assistant. ▪ Member: President-Elect of the National Conference of State Legislatures and the Vice Chair of the State Legislative Leaders Foundation. Rotary Club (past president); Racine/Kenosha Farm Bureau; Knights of Columbus; Racine County Republican Party; Racine Area Manufacturers and Commerce; Union Grove Chamber of Commerce; Burlington Chamber of Commerce. ▪ University of Wisconsin Board of Regents, 1989–91; Racine County Board, 1994–2004 (former chair of Finance and Personnel committees).

Legislature: Elected to Assembly since 2004. Leadership positions: Speaker of the Assembly 2019, 2017, 2015, 2013; co-chair of the Joint Committee on Finance 2011.

Contact: Rep.Vos@legis.wisconsin.gov; SpeakerVos.com; 608-266-9171; 888-534-0063 (toll free); 608-282-3663 (fax); Room 217 West, State Capitol, PO Box 8953, Madison, WI 53708.

Senate District 22
Assembly Districts 64, 65, 66

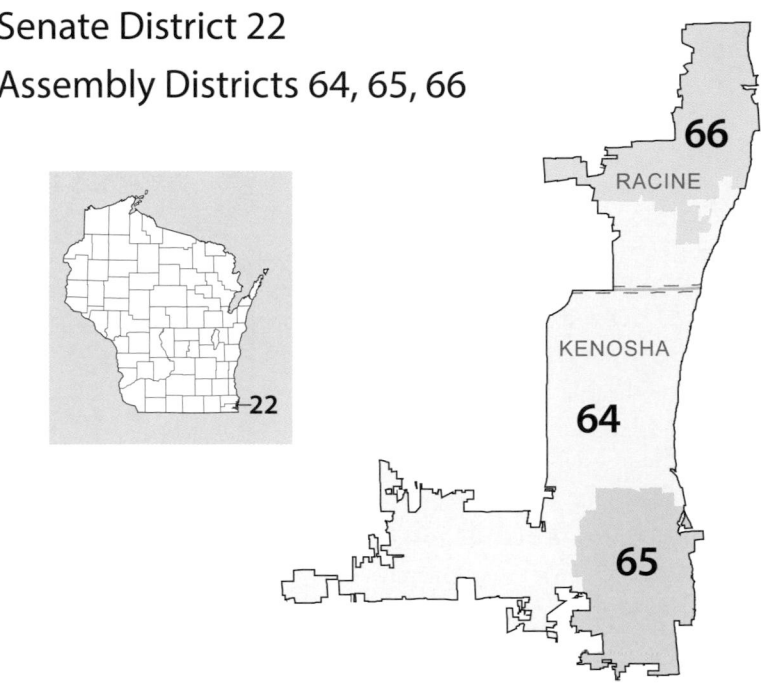

Robert W. Wirch, Senate District 22
Democrat

Biography: Born Kenosha, Wisconsin, November 16, 1943; married; 2 children. Voting address: Somers, Wisconsin. ▪ Graduate Mary D. Bradford High School; B.A., University of Wisconsin-Parkside, 1970. ▪ Full-time legislator. ▪ Former factory worker and liaison to JTPA programs; served in Army Reserve, 1965–71. ▪ Member: Danish Brotherhood; Kenosha Sport Fishing and Conservation Association; Democratic Party of Wisconsin. ▪ Former member: Kenosha Boys and Girls Club (board of directors). ▪ Kenosha County supervisor, 1986–94 (served on Health and Human Services Committee, Welfare Board, and Developmental Disabilities Board).

Legislature: Elected to Assembly 1992. Reelected 1994. Elected to Senate since 1996. Leadership positions: Minority Caucus Chair 2003. Committee assignments, 2019: Administrative Rules; Government Operations, Technology and Consumer Protection; Labor and Regulatory Reform; Sporting Heritage, Mining and Forestry; Joint Committee for Review of Administrative Rules.

Contact: Sen.Wirch@legis.wisconsin.gov; 608-267-8979; 262-694-7379 (district); 888-769-4724 (office hotline); Room 127 South, State Capitol, PO Box 7882, Madison, WI 53707-7882.

Tip McGuire, Assembly District 64
Democrat

Biography: Born Somers, Wisconsin. Voting address: Kenosha, Wisconsin. ▪ Graduate St. Catherine's High School (Racine), 2005; B.A., Marquette University, 2009; J.D., University of Wisconsin Law School, 2017. ▪ Attorney. Former legislative aide to Representative Peter Barca; Kenosha County special prosecutor; Milwaukee County assistant district attorney. ▪ Member: State Bar of Wisconsin. ▪ Former member: Kenosha Public Library Foundation Board (president of board of directors); National Alliance on Mental Illness (NAMI) of Kenosha County (board member).

Legislature: Elected to Assembly in April 2019 special election. Committee assignments, 2019: Community Development; Criminal Justice and Public Safety; Labor and Integrated Employment; State Affairs; Ways and Means.

Contact: Rep.McGuire@legis.wisconsin.gov; 608-266-5504; 888-534-0064 (toll free); Room 15 West, State Capitol, PO Box 8953, Madison, WI 53708.

Tod Ohnstad, Assembly District 65
Democrat

Biography: Born Eau Claire, Wisconsin, May 21, 1952; married. Voting address: Kenosha, Wisconsin. ▪ Graduate Altoona Public High School, 1970; attended University of Wisconsin-Parkside. ▪ Former member: UAW Local 72 (chair of trustees, shop committeeman, bargaining committee, executive board). ▪ City of Kenosha alderman, 2008–14.

Legislature: Elected to Assembly since 2012. Committee assignments, 2019: Jobs and the Economy; Labor and Integrated Employment; State Affairs; Ways and Means; Workforce Development.

Contact: Rep.Ohnstad@legis.wisconsin.gov; 608-266-0455; 888-534-0065 (toll free); Room 128 North, State Capitol, PO Box 8953, Madison, WI 53708.

Greta Neubauer, Assembly District 66
Democrat

Biography: Born Racine, Wisconsin, September 13, 1991. Voting Address: Racine, Wisconsin. ▪ Graduate the Prairie School, 2010; B.A. in History, Middlebury College, 2015. ▪ Former legislative aide to State Representative Cory Mason; Fossil Fuel Divestment Student Network (director and cofounder); Divest Middlebury (cofounder and organizer); 350.org (fellow). ▪ Member: Racine Hospitality Center (board chair); Racine Interfaith Coalition; Visioning Greater Racine; NAACP-Racine Branch; Great Lakes Legislative Caucus; National Caucus of Environmental Legislators; Planned Parenthood; Democratic Party of Racine County.

Legislature: Elected to Assembly in January 2018 special election. Reelected November 2018. Committee assignments, 2019: Environment; International Affairs and Commerce; Jobs and the Economy; Public Benefit Reform; Science and Technology; Transportation.

Contact: Rep.Neubauer@legis.wisconsin.gov; 608-266-0634; 888-534-0066 (toll free); Room 8 North, State Capitol, PO Box 8953, Madison, WI 53708.

Senate District 23
Assembly Districts 67, 68, 69

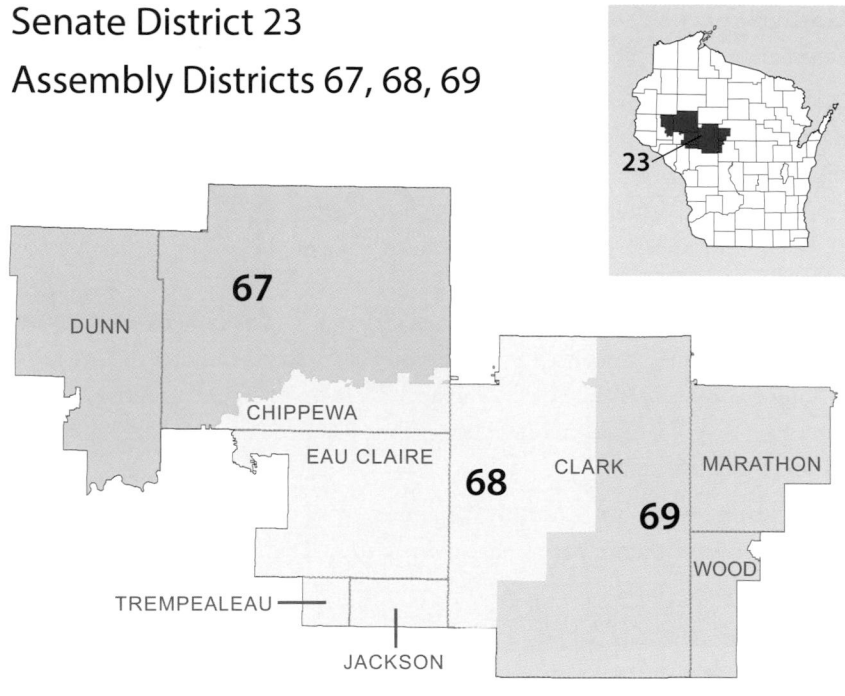

Kathy Bernier, Senate District 23
Republican

Biography: Born Eau Claire, Wisconsin, April 29, 1956; 3 children, 6 grandchildren. Voting address: Lake Hallie, Wisconsin. ▪ Graduate Chippewa Falls Senior High School, 1974; B.A., University of Wisconsin-Eau Claire, 1998; Certificate in Public Management Essentials, University of Wisconsin-Green Bay, 2005. ▪ Member: U.S. Elections Assistance Commission Board of Advisors; Chippewa Falls, Eau Claire, and Marshfield Chambers of Commerce; Lake Hallie Optimists Club; National Foundation for Women Legislators (State Director); American Legislative Exchange Council; Assembly of State Legislatures; National Conference of State Legislatures, Elections and Redistricting Committee; Wisconsin County Clerks Association (lifetime member). ▪ Former member: Wisconsin Women in Government; Wisconsin County Constitutional Officers; Chippewa County Humane Association; Kiwanis Noon Club. ▪ Chippewa County Clerk, 1999–2011; Village of Lake Hallie trustee, 2007–11 and 2015–16.

Legislature: Elected to Assembly 2010–2016. Elected to Senate 2018. Committee assignments, 2019: Agriculture, Revenue and Financial Institutions; Education; Elections, Ethics and Rural Issues (chair); Local Government, Small Business, Tourism and Workforce Development (vice chair); Joint Survey Committee on Retirement Systems (co-chair).

Contact: Sen.Bernier@legis.wisconsin.gov; 608-266-7511; Room 319 South, State Capitol, PO Box 7882, Madison, WI 53707.

Robert Summerfield, Assembly District 67
Republican

Biography: Born Eau Claire, Wisconsin, February 24, 1980; raised Bloomer, Wisconsin; married; 3 children. Voting address: Bloomer, Wisconsin. ▪ Graduate Bloomer High School, 1998; B.S. in Business Administration, University of Wisconsin-Stout, 2002. ▪ Small business owner; supper club manager. ▪ Member: Bloomer Chamber of Commerce; Bloomer Rod & Gun; Tavern League of Wisconsin; Chippewa County Tavern League; NRA; Good Shepherd Lutheran Church (Bloomer, Wisconsin).

Legislature: Elected to Assembly since 2016. Committee assignments, 2019: Colleges and Universities; International Affairs and Commerce (vice chair); Medicaid Reform and Oversight (chair); Small Business Development; State Affairs; Tourism; Veterans and Military Affairs; Speaker's Task Force on Water Quality.

Contact: Rep.Summerfield@legis.wisconsin.gov; 608-266-1194; 888-534-0067 (toll free); Room 308 North, State Capitol, PO Box 8953, Madison, WI 53708.

Jesse James, Assembly District 68
Republican

Biography: Born Eau Claire, Wisconsin, April 16, 1972; married; 4 children. Voting address: Altoona, Wisconsin. ▪ Graduate Eau Claire North High School, 1990; Chippewa Valley Technical College, Eau Claire (associate degree in Police Science, 2001; Emergency Medical Responder, 2015; Entry level, Fire I, Fire II Firefighter, 2016); University of Wisconsin-Madison Command College (Certified Public Manager, 2017). ▪ Small business owner. Served in the U.S. Army Air Defense, 1990–93; U.S. Army Reserves (Medic),

1993–96; Persian Gulf War veteran; Former warehouse specialist; police officer; SWAT team member; firefighter. ▪ Member: Jacob's Well Security Team Advisor/ Trainer. ▪ Former member: Boy Scouts of America (Cubmaster); YMCA (basketball coach); AYSO (soccer coach); Eau Claire United Soccer Club (soccer coach).

Legislature: Elected to the Assembly 2018. Committee assignments, 2019: Children and Families; Corrections; Environment; Family Law (vice chair); Small Business Development; Substance Abuse and Prevention; Veterans and Military Affairs; Speaker's Task Force on Suicide Prevention.

Contact: Rep.James@legis.wisconsin.gov; 608-266-9172; 888-534-0068 (toll free); Room 9 West; State Capitol; PO Box 8952; Madison, WI 53708.

Bob Kulp, Assembly District 69
Republican

Biography: Born Elkhart, Indiana, March 21, 1966; married; 7 children, 12 grandchildren. Voting address: Stratford, Wisconsin. ▪ Roofing and insulation contractor. ▪ Member: National Roofing Contractors Association (past vice chairman); Construction Specifications Institute—Wausau Chapter (past president); Small Business Administration Regulatory Fairness Board (former board member); Wausau Area Builders Association (former member, governmental committee); Noon Rotary Club of Marshfield.

Legislature: Elected to Assembly in November 2013 special election. Reelected since 2014. Committee assignments, 2019: Jobs and the Economy; Rural Development (vice chair); State Affairs; Transportation (chair); Ways and Means; Workforce Development; Speaker's Task Force on Adoption.

Contact: Rep.Kulp@legis.wisconsin.gov; 608-267-0280; 888-534-0069 (toll free); Room 15 West, State Capitol, PO Box 8952, Madison, WI 53708.

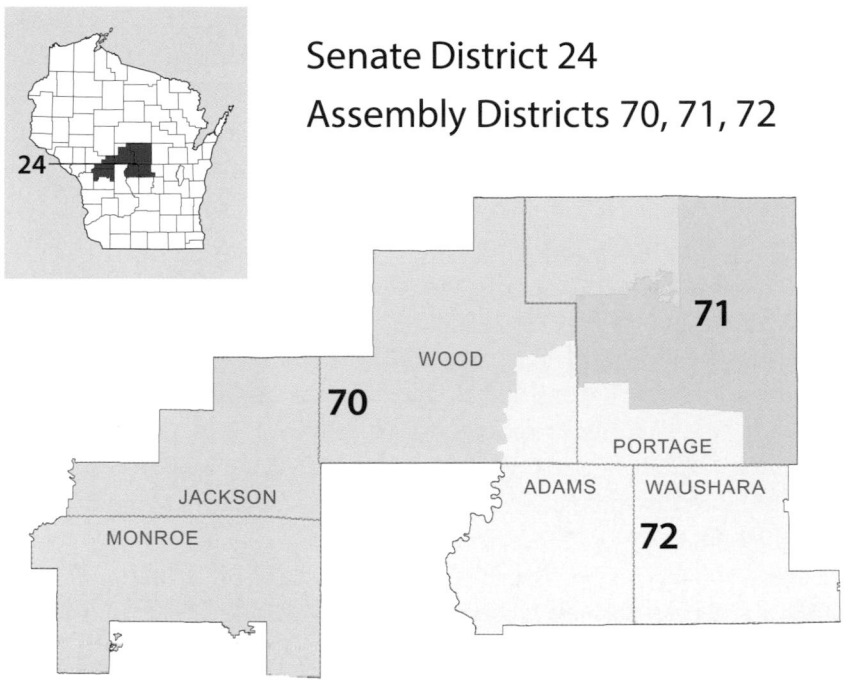

Senate District 24
Assembly Districts 70, 71, 72

Patrick Testin, Senate District 24
Republican

Biography: Born Madison, Wisconsin, June 9, 1988; married. Voting address: Stevens Point, Wisconsin. ▪ Graduate Marinette High School, 2006; B.S. in Political Science, University of Wisconsin-Stevens Point, 2011. ▪ Sales professional for Wisconsin-based wine distributor. ▪ Member: Stevens Point Elk Lodge 641; Ignite Leadership Network of Portage County.

Legislature: Elected to Senate 2016. Leadership positions: Majority Caucus Vice Chair 2019, 2017. Committee assignments, 2019: Health and Human Services (chair); Economic Development, Commerce and Trade (vice chair); Agriculture, Revenue and Financial Institutions; Joint Committee on Information Policy and Technology; Speaker's Task Force on Water Quality. Additional appointments: Building Commission, Council on Alcohol and Other Drug Abuse and Interstate Compact on Educational Opportunity for Military Children.

Contact: Sen.Testin@legis.wisconsin.gov; 608-266-3123; Room 131 South, State Capitol, PO Box 7882, Madison, WI 53707-7882.

Nancy Lynn VanderMeer, Assembly District 70
Republican

Biography: Born Evergreen Park, Illinois, December 15, 1958; married. Voting address: Tomah, Wisconsin. ▪ Graduate Evergreen Park Community High School, 1976; B.S. in Psychology, University of Wisconsin-La Crosse, 1988; Bowhay Institute for Legislative Leadership Development class of 2017. ▪ Former automobile dealer; small business owner; family dairy farmer. ▪ Member: Jackson County Local Emergency Planning Commission; Farm Bureau; Gloria Dei Lutheran Church (former council president); Tomah Chamber of Commerce (former board of directors member); NRA; American Legion Auxiliary; board of directors of the nonprofit Handishop Industries; Monroe County Mental Health Coalition; American Association of University Women—Tomah Chapter. ▪ Former member: Tomah Memorial Hospital board of directors (former officer); American Business Women's Association (former president). ▪ Recipient: Sparta Area School District *Certificate of Recognition* 2015; Wisconsin Child Support Enforcement Association *Legislative Award* 2016; Wisconsin Academy of Family Physicians *Friend of Family Medicine* 2016; Dairy Business Association *Legislative Excellence Award* 2018, 2017, 2016; Wisconsin Library Association *Wisconsin Library Champion* 2016; National Foundation for Women Legislators *Elected Women of Excellence Award* 2017; U.S. Army War College Commandant's National Security Program *Certificate of Leader Development* 2017; Tomah AAUW *Mary E. Wedin Women's History Month Award* 2018; NCSL Early Learning Fellow 2018.

Legislature: Elected to Assembly since 2014. Committee assignments, 2019: Agriculture; Consumer Protection; Health; Labor and Integrated Employment (vice chair); Mental Health; Rural Development (chair); Tourism; Veterans and Military Affairs (vice chair); Speaker's Task Force on Suicide Prevention.

Contact: Rep.VanderMeer@legis.wisconsin.gov; 608-266-8366; 888-534-0070 (toll free); Room 11 West, State Capitol, PO Box 8953, Madison, WI 53708.

Katrina Shankland, Assembly District 71
Democrat

Biography: Born Wausau, Wisconsin, August 4, 1987; single. Voting address: Stevens Point, Wisconsin. ▪Graduate Wittenberg-Birnamwood High School, 2005; attended University of Wisconsin-Marathon County, 2004–05, and Marquette University, 2005–06; B.A. in Political Science, University of Wisconsin-Madison,

2009; completed graduate work at UW-Stevens Point, 2017–19. ▪ Full-time legislator. Former nonprofit professional. ▪ Member: Born Learning Advocacy and Awareness Steering Committee; Wisconsin Legislative Children's Caucus; Wisconsin Legislative Sportsmen's Caucus; National Caucus of Environmental Legislators; Young Elected Officials Network; Council of State Governments Henry Toll Fellow, 2013; Major, Wisconsin Wing, Civil Air Patrol Legislative Squadron (official Auxiliary of the U.S. Air Force).

Legislature: Elected to Assembly since 2012. Leadership positions: Assistant Minority Leader 2015. Committee assignments, 2019: Audit; Colleges and Universities; Environment; Workforce Development; Joint Legislative Audit Committee; Speaker's Task Force on Water Quality (vice chair).

Contact: Rep.Shankland@legis.wisconsin.gov; 608-267-9649; 888-534-0071 (toll free); Room 304 West, State Capitol, PO Box 8953, Madison, WI 53708.

Scott S. Krug, Assembly District 72
Republican

Biography: Born Wisconsin Rapids, Wisconsin, September 16, 1975; married; 6 children. Voting address: Rome, Wisconsin. ▪ Graduate Lincoln High School, 1993; attended University of Wisconsin-Stevens Point; A.D., Mid-State Technical College, 1999; B.A.S. in Psychology, University of Wisconsin-Green Bay, 2008. ▪ Employment and training specialist. Former Wood County drug court coordinator, jail discharge planner; Juneau County sheriff's deputy. ▪ Member: Heart of Wisconsin Chamber of Commerce; Wisconsin Rapids Rotary. ▪ Recipient: Wisconsin Industrial Energy Group *Legislator of the Year Award* 2014; Dairy Business Association *Legislative Excellence Award* 2014, 2012; Wisconsin Paper Council *Legislator of the Year* 2014; Child Support Enforcement Association *Legislator of the Year* 2014; League of Conservation Voters *Honor Roll* 2014; Wisconsin Troopers Association *Legislator of the Year* 2014; Wisconsin Counties Association *Outstanding Legislator* 2014; WMC *Working for Wisconsin Award* 2016, 2014, 2012; Third Congressional District *State Legislator of the Year* 2012.

Legislature: Elected to Assembly since 2010. Committee assignments, 2019: Colleges and Universities; Criminal Justice and Public Safety; Environment; Forestry, Parks and Outdoor Recreation (vice chair); Government Accountability and

Oversight; International Affairs and Commerce; Public Benefit Reform (chair); Speaker's Task Force on Water Quality.

Contact: Rep.Krug@legis.wisconsin.gov; 608-266-0215; 888-529-0072 (toll free); Room 207 North, State Capitol, PO Box 8952, Madison, WI 53708.

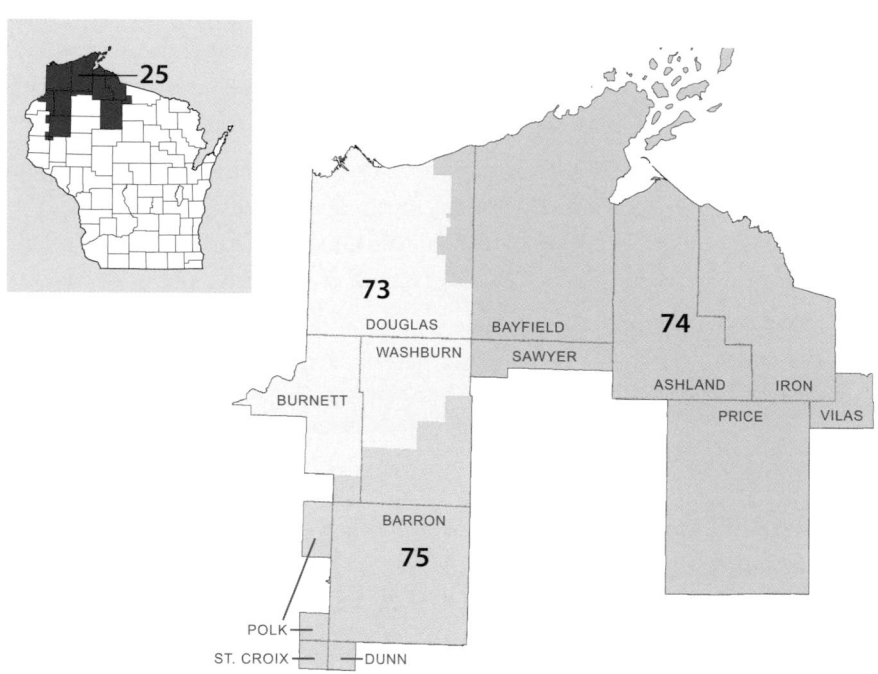

Senate District 25
Assembly Districts 73, 74, 75

Janet Bewley, Senate District 25
Democrat

Biography: Born Painesville, Ohio, November 10, 1951; married; 5 children, 5 grandchildren. Voting address: Mason, Wisconsin. ▪ Graduate James Ford Rhodes High School (Cleveland, Ohio), 1969; B.A., Case Western Reserve University, 1973; M. Ed., University of Maine, 1977. ▪ Full-time legislator. Former Community Relations Officer, Wisconsin Housing and Economic Development Authority; former Dean of Students, Northland College; former executive director, Mary H. Rice Foundation. ▪ Member: Original cast member at Lake Superior Big Top Chautauqua and current member of the Rittenhouse Chamber Singers; Wisconsin Family Impact Seminar (advisory board member); Wisconsin Paper Caucus (vice chair); Democratic National Committee. ▪ Former Member: Governor's Task Force on Opioid Abuse; Fostering Futures Policy Advisory Committee. ▪ Recipient: Wisconsin Association of Free & Charitable Clinics *Legislative Advocate of the Year* 2019; Professional Fire Fighters of Wisconsin *Legislator of the Year* 2018; Wisconsin Economic Development Association *Champion of Economic Development* 2018; Wisconsin Builders Association *Friend of Housing* 2018, 2016, 2014; Wisconsin Electric Cooperative Association *Enlightened Legislator of the Year* 2018; Wisconsin League of Conservation Voters *Conservation Champion* 2018, 2014, 2012; Wisconsin Brewers Guild *Friend of Wisconsin Craft Brewers* 2013. ▪ Ashland City Council, 2007–09.

Legislature: Elected to Assembly 2010–12. Elected to Senate since 2014. Leadership positions: Assistant Minority Leader 2017. Committee assignments, 2019: Education; Senate Organization; Universities, Technical Colleges, Children and Families; Utilities and Housing; Joint Committee on Legislative Organization; Joint Legislative Audit Committee. Additional appointments: State Council on Alcohol and Other Drug Abuse; Governor's Council on Tourism; Wisconsin Housing and Economic Development Authority Board; Wisconsin Council on Forestry; Special Committee on State-Tribal Relations.

Contact: Sen.Bewley@legis.wisconsin.gov; 608-266-3510; 800-469-6562 (toll free); Room 126 South, State Capitol, PO Box 7882, Madison, WI 53707-7882.

Nick Milroy, Assembly District 73
Democrat

Biography: Born Duluth, Minnesota, April 15, 1974; married; 3 children. Voting address: South Range, Wisconsin. ▪ Graduate Superior Senior High School, 1992; B.S., University of Wisconsin-Superior, 1998; attended University of Wisconsin-Eau Claire, 1999–2000. ▪ Full-time legislator. Former fisheries biologist; Served in U.S. Navy, 1992–94, U.S. Naval Reserve, 1994–2000; deployed to Persian Gulf during Operation Southern Watch. ▪ Member: Great Lakes Legislative Caucus of the Council of State Governments; Wisconsin Chapter of the Congressional Sportsmen's Foundation (co-chair); National

Conference of Environmental Legislators; Douglas County Democratic Party (former secretary). ▪ Former member: Lake Superior Binational Forum; St. Louis River Watershed TMDL Partnership (board of directors); American Fisheries Society; Duluth-Superior Metropolitan Interstate Council (policy board member); Head of the Lakes Fair (board of directors). ▪ Superior City Council, 2005–09.

Legislature: Elected to Assembly since 2008. Committee assignments, 2019: Forestry, Parks and Outdoor Recreation; Rural Development; Sporting Heritage; Veterans and Military Affairs.

Contact: Rep.Milroy@legis.wisconsin.gov; 608-266-0640; 888-534-0073 (toll free); Room 104 North, State Capitol, PO Box 8953, Madison, WI 53708.

Beth Meyers, Assembly District 74
Democrat

Biography: Born Ashland, Wisconsin, May 29, 1959; married; 2 children. Voting address: Bayfield, Wisconsin. ▪ Graduate Bayfield High School, 1977; B.S., Northland College (Ashland, Wisconsin), 1989. ▪ Full-time legislator. Former executive director, CORE Community Resources; Former board member Apostle Islands Area Community Fund. ▪ Bayfield County Board of Supervisors, 2010–15 (Executive Committee; Personnel Committee; Library Board chair; County Tribal Relations Committee vice chair; Northern Wisconsin Community Action Program Committee vice chair; Health Department Committee chair).

Legislature: Elected to Assembly since 2014. Leadership positions: Minority Caucus Secretary 2019, 2017, 2015. Committee assignments, 2019: Aging and Long-Term Care; Energy and Utilities; Financial Institutions; Transportation; Speaker's Task Force on Suicide Prevention. Additional appointments: Governor's Council on Forestry; Wisconsin Public Utility Board; Great Lakes-St. Lawrence Legislative Caucus Executive Committee.

Contact: Rep.Meyers@legis.wisconsin.gov; 608-266-7690; 888-534-0074 (toll free); Room 7 North, State Capitol, PO Box 8953, Madison, WI 53708.

Romaine Robert Quinn, Assembly District 75

Republican

Biography: Born Rice Lake, Wisconsin, July 30, 1990. Voting address: Cameron, Wisconsin. ▪ Graduate Rice Lake High School, 2009; interdisciplinary B.A. in Political Science with emphasis on Public Leadership, University of Wisconsin-Green Bay, 2014; attended University of Wisconsin-Barron County and University of Wisconsin-Eau Claire. ▪ Full-time legislator. Former Coca-Cola salesman. ▪ Rice Lake City Council, 2009–10; mayor of Rice Lake, 2010–12.

Legislature: Elected to Assembly since 2014. Leadership positions: Majority Caucus Vice Chair 2019, 2017. Committee assignments, 2019: Science and Technology (chair); Sporting Heritage (vice chair); Colleges and Universities; Education; Housing and Real Estate; Regulatory Licensing Reform; Rural Development.

Contact: Rep.Quinn@legis.wisconsin.gov; 608-237-9175; 888-534-0075 (toll free); Room 323 North, State Capitol, PO Box 8953, Madison, WI 53708.

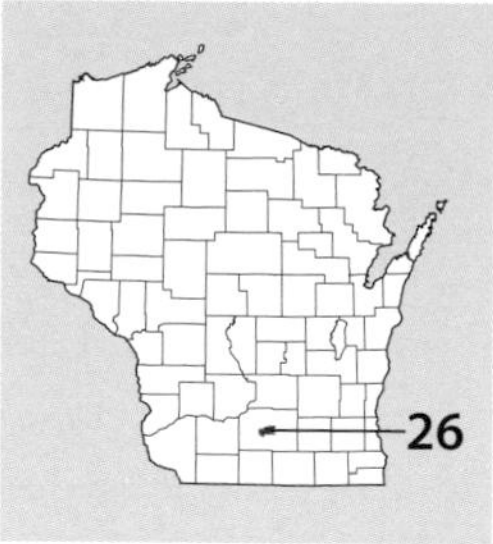

Senate District 26
Assembly Districts 76, 77, 78

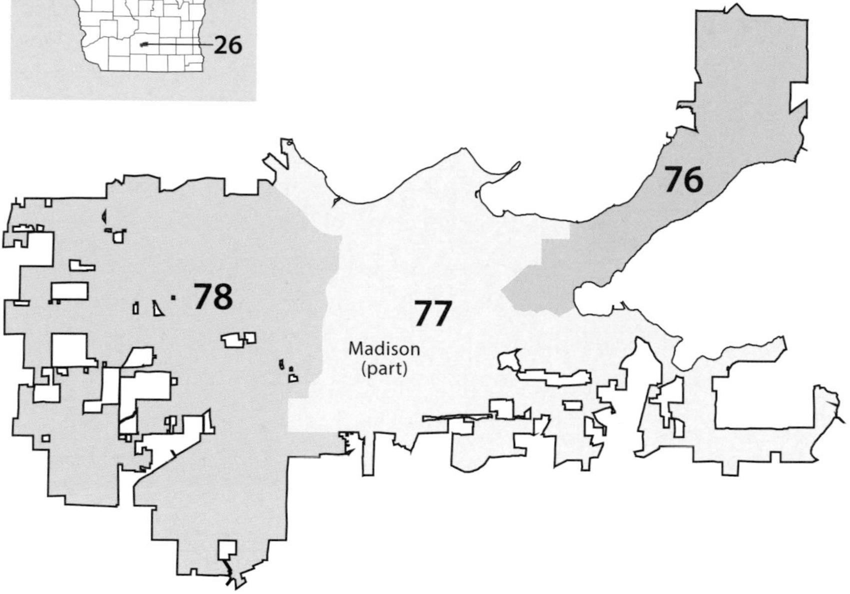

26

76

78

77

Madison
(part)

Fred Risser, Senate District 26
Democrat

Biography: Born Madison, Wisconsin, May 5, 1927; married; 3 children. Voting address: Madison, Wisconsin. ▪ Attended Carleton College (Minnesota), University of Wisconsin-Madison; B.A., University of Oregon, 1950; LL.B., University of Oregon, 1952. ▪ Attorney. World War II veteran; Navy. ▪ Member: State Bar of Wisconsin and Oregon and Dane County Bar Associations; NCSL (past member National Executive Committee); CSG (past member National Executive Committee, Midwestern Conference chair 1993, 1982). ▪ Presidential Elector 2012, 2008, 1964.

Legislature: Elected to Assembly 1956–60. Elected to Senate in 1962 special election. Reelected since 1964. Longest serving legislator in Wisconsin history and longest serving state legislator in U.S. history. Leadership positions: President of the Senate 2011 (effective 7/17/12), 2009, 2007, 2001, 1999, 1997 (effective 1/15/97 to 4/20/98), 1995 (effective 7/9/96), also 1979 to 4/20/93; Comajority Leader 2001 (effective 10/22/02); Assistant Minority Leader 1995 (effective 1/5/95 to 7/12/96), 1993 (effective 4/20/93), also 1965; Senate President Pro Tempore 1977, 1975; Minority Leader 1967–73. Committee assignments, 2019: Agriculture, Revenue and Financial Institutions; Insurance, Financial Services, Government Oversight and Courts; Judiciary and Public Safety; Joint Legislative Council.

Contact: Sen.Risser@legis.wisconsin.gov; 608-266-1627; Room 130 South, State Capitol, PO Box 7882, Madison, WI 53707-7882.

Chris Taylor, Assembly District 76
Democrat

Biography: Born January 13, 1968, Los Angeles, California; married; 2 children. Voting address: Madison, Wisconsin. ▪ Graduate Birmingham High School (Van Nuys, California), 1986; B.A., University of Pennsylvania, 1990; J.D., University of Wisconsin Law School, 1995. ▪ Full-time legislator. Former public policy director, Planned Parenthood of Wisconsin and practicing attorney. ▪ Member: State Bar of Wisconsin; Wisconsin League of Conservation Voters; Planned Parenthood Advocates of Wisconsin; Planned Parenthood Federation; Sierra Club; Democratic Party of Wisconsin. ▪ Former member: Public Interest Law Board (legislative subcommittee chair).

Legislature: Elected to Assembly in August 2011 special election. Reelected since 2012. Committee assignments, 2019: Federalism and Interstate Relations; Finance; Public Benefit Reform; Joint Committee on Finance; Joint Legislative Council.

Contact: Rep.Taylor@legis.wisconsin.gov; 608-266-5342; Room 306 West, State Capitol, PO Box 8953, Madison, WI 53708.

Shelia Stubbs, Assembly District 77
Democrat

Biography: Born February 22, 1971, Camden, Arkansas; married; 6 children. Voting address: Madison, Wisconsin. ▪ Graduate: Beloit Memorial High School; B.A. in Political Science, Tougaloo College; B.S. in Criminal Justice Administration, *magna cum laude*, Mount Senario College; Masters of Science & Management, Cardinal Stritch University. ▪ Full-time legislator; member of the Dane County Board of Supervisors, serving the 23rd district; first African American woman to chair a Dane County standing committee and to hold the leadership position of vice chair of the Board, currently serving on the following committees: Personnel & Finance Committee (chair); UW-Extension Committee (co-chair); Racial Disparities Sub-Committee; Greater Madison Convention & Visitors Board of Directors; Tamara D. Grigsby Office of Equity and Inclusion Advisory Board; Alliant Energy Center Redevelopment Committee; Dane County Youth in Government (mentor). Former special education teacher; adjunct professor; probation and parole agent; match support specialist. ▪ Member: National Association of Counties (NACo) (Justice and Public Safety Steering Committee, Vice chair of Law Enforcement Committee); first African American woman to serve on a NACo committee representing Wisconsin; Women of NACo (WON) Secretary; Bridge-Lake Point Neighborhood Association (president); Madison Alumnae Chapter of Delta Sigma Theta Sorority, Inc.; NAACP Dane County Branch; End Time Ministries International (co-founder and ordained pastor). ▪ Former member: Black Caucus Chair, Democratic Party of Wisconsin; Wisconsin Counties Association (Board of Directors, chair and vice chair of the Judicial and Public Safety Steering Committee, first African American woman to serve as steering committee chair); NAACP Madison Branch (first vice president); Wisconsin NAACP Conference of Branches (third vice president); Madison Youth Council of the NAACP (chartering member, youth advisor). ▪ Recipient: *Who's Who Among High School Students*; Wisconsin Women of Color Network, Inc. *Woman of Achievement Award* 2014; *National Dean's List*; Broadway-Simpson-Waunona Neighborhood Center Fifth Annual Pride Festival *Spirit Award* 1998; Dane County Human Services *Friends of Joining Forces for Families Award*; *"MISS NAACP"* 1992 at Tougaloo College; NAACP Madison Branch *W.E.B. DuBois Advocates Award* 2004; Now Faith Ministries *100 Women in White Award*; *Genesis Social Services Corporation & The Black Women's Expo Award* 2008; *100 Black Men of Madison Award* 2015; Democratic Party of Wisconsin *Eleanor Roosevelt Award* 2014; Madison 365 Black Power *The 44 Most Influential African Americans in Wisconsin* 2016; Community Building and Advocacy for Social Justice Building the Generation Gap *Community Leader Champion Award* 2018; Madison Metropolitan Chapter of the Links, Inc. *Community Award* 2017; Democratic Party of Dane County *Midge Miller Award for Outstanding Elected Official* 2019; YWCA *Woman of Distinction Award* 2019.

Legislature: Elected to Assembly 2018. Committee assignments, 2019: Colleges and Universities; Corrections; Criminal Justice and Public Safety; Insurance; State Affairs; Tourism.

Contact: Rep.stubbs@legis.wisconsin.gov; 608-266-3784; 888-534-0077; Room 18 West, State Capitol, PO Box 8953, Madison, WI 53708.

Lisa Subeck, Assembly District 78
Democrat

Biography: Born Chicago, Illinois, June 17, 1971; single. Voting address: Madison, Wisconsin. ▪ Graduate Rich Central High School, 1989; B.A., University of Wisconsin-Madison, 1993. ▪ Full-time legislator. Former early childhood education/Head Start program manager; technical college instructor; nonprofit executive director. ▪ Member: National Foundation of Women Legislators (Wisconsin state director); Women's Legislative Network of the National Conference of State Legislatures (executive board member). ▪ Former member: American Federation of Teachers. ▪ Recipient: National Foundation of Women Legislators *Woman of Excellence*; Wisconsin League of Conservation Voters *Conservation Champion*; Breastfeeding Coalition of South Central Wisconsin *Breastfeeding Advocate Award*. ▪ City of Madison Common Council, 2011–15.

Legislature: Elected to Assembly since 2014. Committee assignments, 2019: Campaigns and Elections; Children and Families; Community Development; Energy and Utilities; Health; Local Government; Public Benefit Reform; Speaker's Task Force on Adoption (vice chair).

Contact: Rep.Subeck@legis.wisconsin.gov; 608-266-7521; 888-534-0078 (toll free); Room 109 North, State Capitol, PO Box 8953, Madison, WI 53708.

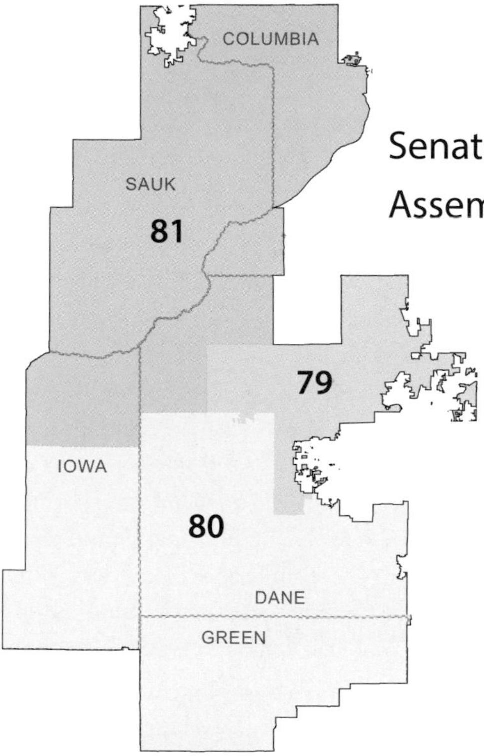

COLUMBIA

SAUK

81

Senate District 27
Assembly Districts 79, 80, 81

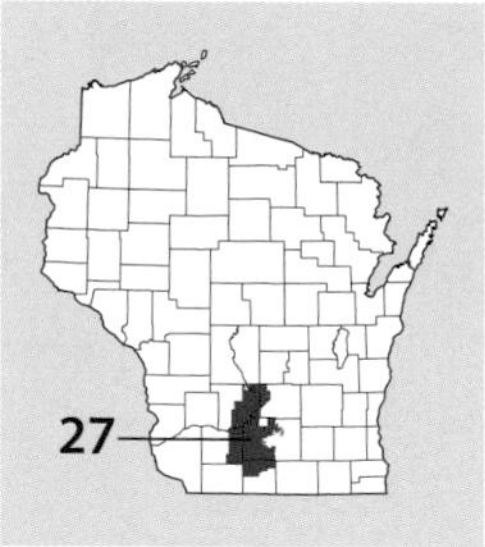

79

IOWA

80

27

DANE

GREEN

Jon B. Erpenbach, Senate District 27
Democrat

Biography: Born Middleton, Wisconsin, January 28, 1961; married; 2 children. Voting address: West Point, Wisconsin. ▪ Graduate: Middleton High School; attended University of Wisconsin-Oshkosh, 1979–81. ▪ Former communications director; legislative aide; radio personality; short order cook; meat packer; truck driver; and City of Middleton recreation instructor.

Legislature: Elected to Senate since 1998. Leadership positions: Minority Leader 2003. Committee assignments, 2019: Finance; Health and Human Services; Joint Committee on Finance; Joint Committee on Information Policy and Technology; Joint Legislative Council; Joint Survey Committee on Retirement Systems.

Contact: Sen.Erpenbach@legis.wisconsin.gov; 608-266-6670; 888-549-0027 (district, toll free); Room 415 South, State Capitol, PO Box 7882, Madison, WI 53707-7882.

Dianne Hesselbein, Assembly District 79
Democrat

Biography: Born Madison, Wisconsin, March 10, 1971; married; 3 children. Voting address: Middleton, Wisconsin. ▪ Graduate La Follette High School (Madison), 1989; B.S., University of Wisconsin-Oshkosh, 1993; M.A., Edgewood College, 1996. ▪ Full-time legislator. ▪ Member: Dane County Democratic Party; Friends of Pheasant Branch; Middleton Action Team; VFW Auxiliary Council; Girl Scouts troop leader. ▪ Former member: Parent Teacher Organization (president); Boy Scouts of America (cubmaster); Monona Terrace Convention and Community Center Board; Clean Wisconsin. ▪ Middleton-Cross Plains Area School District Board, 2005–08; Dane County Board, 2008–14.

Legislature: Elected to Assembly since 2012. Leadership positions: Assistant Minority Leader 2019, 2017. Committee assignments, 2019: Assembly Organization; Colleges and Universities; Financial Institutions; Insurance; Rules; Sporting Heritage; Veterans and Military Affairs; Joint Committee on Legislative Organization; Joint Legislative Council.

Contact: Rep.Hesselbein@legis.wisconsin.gov; 608-266-5340; Room 119 North, State Capitol, PO Box 8952, Madison, WI 53708.

Sondy Pope, Assembly District 80
Democrat

Biography: Born Madison, Wisconsin, April 27, 1950; married. Voting address: Mount Horeb, Wisconsin. ▪ Graduate River Valley High School; attended Madison Area Technical College and Edgewood College. ▪ Former Associate Director of the Foundation for Madison's Public Schools. ▪ Member: National Caucus of Environmental Legislators; Wisconsin Congress of

Parents and Teachers (Honorary Life Member); Midwestern Higher Education Compact Commission; Fellow, Bowhay Institute, La Follette School, University of Wisconsin-Madison; Fellow, Flemming Institute, Center for Policy Alternatives; Oakhill Correctional Institution Advisory Board; WiLL/WAND National Women's Leadership; State Innovation Exchange; Agrace Hospice Care Patient and Family Partnership Council; Agrace Hospice Care Ethics Committee.

Legislature: Elected to Assembly since 2002. Committee assignments, 2019: Consumer Protection; Education; Government Accountability and Oversight; Rules; Small Business Development; Speaker's Task Force on Water Quality.

Contact: Rep.Pope@legis.wisconsin.gov; 608-266-3520; 888-534-0080 (toll free); Room 118 North, State Capitol, PO Box 8953, Madison, WI 53708.

Dave Considine, Assembly District 81
Democrat

Biography: Born Janesville, Wisconsin, March 29, 1952; married; 5 children. Voting address: Baraboo, Wisconsin. ▪ Graduate Mukwonago Union High School, 1970; B.S. in Education, University of Wisconsin-Whitewater, 1974; certificate in EBD, University of Wisconsin-Madison, 1990; M.A. in Education, Viterbo University, 2005; certificates—instructor certificate, autism spectrum, and enhanced verbal skills, Crisis Prevention Institute (Milwaukee), 2008, 2010, 2013. ▪ Full-time legislator. Former dairy goat farmer; special education teacher. ▪ Member: Columbia County Democratic Party; Pheasants Forever; Ducks Unlimited. ▪ Former member: Baraboo Education Association (president); American Dairy Goat Association (judge); Wisconsin Dairy Goat Association (president); Crisis Prevention Institute (instructor).

Legislature: Elected to Assembly since 2014. Committee assignments, 2019: Agriculture; Education; Mental Health; Rural Development; Transportation.

Contact: Rep.Considine@legis.wisconsin.gov; 608-266-7746; 888-534-0081 (toll free); Room 303 West, State Capitol, PO Box 8952, Madison, WI 53708.

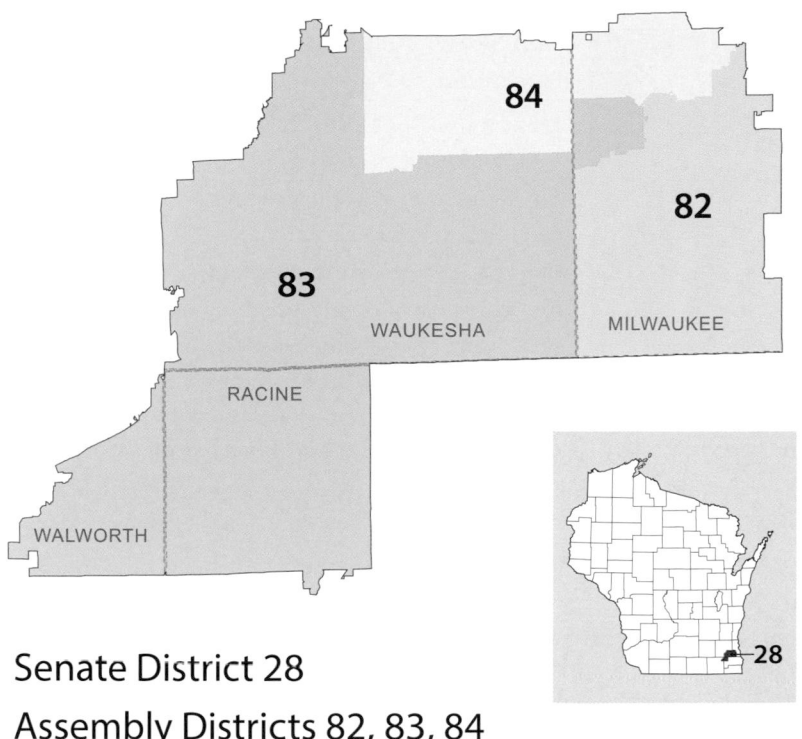

Senate District 28
Assembly Districts 82, 83, 84

David Craig, Senate District 28
Republican

Biography: Born Waukesha, 1979; married; 6 children. Voting address: Town of Vernon, Wisconsin. ▪ Graduate Wisconsin Lutheran High School, 1997; attended University of Wisconsin-Waukesha; B.A., University of Wisconsin-Milwaukee, 2002. ▪ Real Estate Agent. Former aide to Congressman Paul Ryan. ▪ Village of Big Bend trustee, 2008–10.

Legislature: Elected to Assembly in May 2011 special election. Reelected 2012, 2014. Elected to Senate 2016. Committee assignments, 2019: Administrative Rules; Government Operations, Technology and Consumer Protection; Insurance, Financial Services, Government Oversight and Courts (chair); Public Benefits, Licensing and State-Federal Relations (vice chair); Joint Committee for Review of Administrative Rules.

Contact: Sen.Craig@legis.wisconsin.gov; 608-266-5400; Room 104 South, State Capitol, PO Box 7882, Madison, WI 53707-7882.

Ken Skowronski, Assembly District 82

Republican

Biography: Born Milwaukee, Wisconsin, May 31, 1938; widowed; 2 children. Voting address: Franklin, Wisconsin. ▪ Graduate Boys Tech High School, 1958; journeyman carpenter, MATC (Milwaukee), 1961; NARI certified remodeler. ▪ General contractor; radio host, monthly talk show; 4-H construction skills instructor; seminar speaker, Wisconsin Burglar and Fire Alarm Association and WPR. Wisconsin Air National Guard, 1956–62. ▪ Member: Milwaukee/NARI Foundation (trustee, former president); Franklin Noon Lions Club (trustee, former president); Polish Heritage Alliance (board member); Knights of Columbus (former deputy grand knight); National Rifle Association (endowment life member); Ducks Unlimited (patron member); Rocky Mountain Elk Foundation (life member); South Suburban Chamber of Commerce (former board member); Milwaukee/NARI Chapter (former president); NARI National Foundation/NRF (former president). ▪ Former member: Franklin Lions Club (president); NKBA Wisconsin/Upper Michigan Chapter (treasurer); City of Franklin Plan Commission; City of Franklin Economic Development Commission (chair); City of Franklin Community Development Authority; City of Franklin 50th Anniversary Committee (chair). ▪ Recipient: City of Franklin *Distinguished Service Award* 1983; Lions Clubs International *Melvin Jones Fellowship Award* 1995; Remodeling Magazine *Big 50 Industry Impact Award* 1992; National Brand Names Foundation *First Place Remodelers Award* 1972; Milwaukee/NARI Chapter *Hank Fenderbosh Award* 1995; *Harold Hammerman Award* (nominee) 1994–95; *Lifetime Achievement Award* 2002, 1997; VFW Department of Wisconsin *Legislator of the Year Award* 2018–19. ▪ Alderman, City of Franklin 2005–14.

Legislature: Elected to Assembly in December 2013 special election. Reelected since 2014. Committee assignments, 2019: Consumer Protection; Health; International Affairs and Commerce; Local Government; Small Business Development; Sporting Heritage; Transportation; Veterans and Military Affairs (chair).

Contact: Rep.Skowronski@legis.wisconsin.gov; 608-266-8590; 888-534-0082 (toll free); Room 209 North, State Capitol, PO Box 8953, Madison, WI 53708.

Chuck Wichgers, Assembly District 83

Republican

Biography: Born Milwaukee, Wisconsin, July 4, 1965; married; 8 children; grandfather. Voting address: Muskego, Wisconsin. ▪ Graduate Muskego High School,

1983; Waukesha County Technical College, 1984–85. ▪ Practiced medical sales offering conservative options for pain management. Coach for softball, basketball, football. Volunteer, along with wife and children, assisting nursing home residents to get to weekly religious services. Education curriculum watchdog. Former occupations in sales and marketing, and in entrepreneurship and management. ▪ Member: Various pro-life groups across Wisconsin; church committees and organizations. ▪ Former Member: Muskego Hoops Booster Club (cofounder); Moose Club; Preserve Muskego (president); Janesville Road Reconstruction Advisory Committee. ▪ City of Muskego alderman, 1999–2002; Waukesha County supervisor, 1999–2002.

Legislature: Elected to Assembly since 2016. Committee assignments, 2019: Constitution and Ethics (chair); Education; Forestry, Parks and Outdoor Recreation; Government Accountability and Oversight; Health; Medicaid Reform and Oversight.

Contact: Rep.Wichgers@legis.wisconsin.gov; 608-266-3363; 888-534-0083 (toll free); Room 306 North, State Capitol, PO Box 8953, Madison, WI 53708.

Michael Kuglitsch, Assembly District 84
Republican

Biography: Born Milwaukee, Wisconsin, February 3, 1960; married; 4 children. Voting address: New Berlin, Wisconsin. ▪ Graduate New Berlin West High School, 1978; B.A. in Business, University of Wisconsin-Whitewater, 1983. ▪ Business consultant. ▪ Former member: Wisconsin Restaurant Association (president); Bowling Centers Association of Wisconsin (president); New Berlin Chamber of Commerce (president).

Legislature: Elected to Assembly since 2010. Committee assignments, 2019: Energy and Utilities (chair); Environment; Government Accountability and Oversight; State Affairs; Rules; Joint Survey Committee on Retirement Systems.

Contact: Rep.Kuglitsch@legis.wisconsin.gov; 608-267-5158; 888-534-0084 (toll free); Room 129 West, State Capitol, PO Box 8952, Madison, WI 53708.

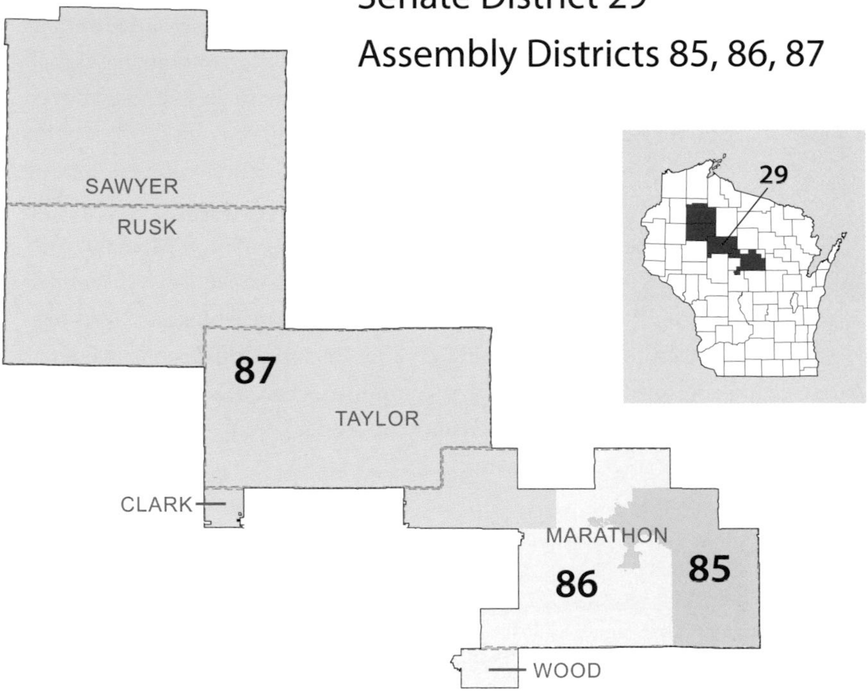

Senate District 29
Assembly Districts 85, 86, 87

Jerry Petrowski, Senate District 29
Republican

Biography: Born Wausau, Wisconsin, June 16, 1950; married; 4 children, 3 grandchildren. Voting address: Marathon, Wisconsin. ▪ Graduate Newman High School (Wausau); attended University of Wisconsin-Marathon County and Northcentral Technical College. ▪ Former ginseng, dairy, and beef farmer. Served in Army Reserve, 1968–74. ▪ Member: Seventh Congressional District, Marathon, Wood, Taylor, Rusk, Sawyer, Price, Lincoln, Portage, and Shawano County Republican Parties; Farm Bureau; National Rifle Association; Friends of Rib Mountain; Wausau Elks; Marathon Lions. ▪ Former member: Wisconsin Rifle and Pistol Association; International Brotherhood of Electrical Workers Local #1791; Childcare Connection Board; Department of Transportation Law Enforcement Advisory Council; Marathon County Hunger Coalition. ▪ Recipient: American Heart Association *Legislator of the Year* 2018, 2016, 2014; End Domestic Abuse Wisconsin *Legislative Leader Award* 2014; Wisconsin

VFW *Legislator of the Year* 2014; Wisconsin American Legion *Legislator of the Year* 2014; Wisconsin Vietnam Veterans *Legislator of the Year* 2002; Wisconsin Department of Veterans Affairs *Certificate of Commendation* 2005; Wisconsin Towns Association *Friend of Wisconsin Towns Award* 2016, 2014, 2011; Wisconsin Counties Association *Outstanding Legislator Award* 2014; Wisconsin Economic Development Association *Working for Wisconsin Award* 2018; Wisconsin Urban and Rural Transit Association *Legislative Statesman of the Year* 2014; Wisconsin Professional Police Association *Legislator of the Year* 2014; Wisconsin Troopers Association *Legislator of the Year* 2014, 2003; Center for Driver's License Recovery and Employability *Legislative Champion Award* 2014; State Bar of Wisconsin *Scales of Justice Award* 2014; Wisconsin Dental Association *Legislative Champion Award* 2013 & *Award of Honor* (Mission of Mercy) 2011; Wisconsin Academy of Family Physicians *Friend of Family Medicine Award* 2016, 2014; American Academy of Pediatrics *Childhood Legislative Advocate of the Year* 2005; Wisconsin Council on Physical Disabilities *Appreciation Award* 2014; Wisconsin Primary Health Care Association *Community Health Center Friend Award* 2018; Wisconsin Public Health Association *Friend of Public Health Award* 2016; Wisconsin Electric Cooperatives Association *Enlightened Legislator of the Year* 2013; Wisconsin Farm Bureau *Friend of Agriculture Award* 2006, 2004; Wisconsin Dairy Business Association *Legislative Excellence Award* 2018, 2014, 2012, 2010, 2008; Wisconsin Grocers Association *Friend of the Grocers Award* 2016, 2014, 2012, 2008, 2006; Wisconsin Pork Association *Distinguished Public Service Award* 2016; Wisconsin Builders Association *Friend of Housing Award* 2018, 2016, 2013, 2006; Associated Builders and Contractors of Wisconsin *Building Wisconsin Award* 2014; State Farm Insurance *Golden Car Seat Award* 2007; Chiropractic Society of Wisconsin *Legislator of the Year* 2014, *Champion for Chiropractic Award* 2018, 2017, 2016, 2015; 3M *Award of Appreciation* 2001; Wisconsin Paper Council *Champion of Paper Award* 2007; Wisconsin Technical College System *Legislator of the Year Award* 2016; Wisconsin Technical College District Boards Association *Legislator of the Year* 2016; UWSP Paper Science Foundation *Friends of the Foundation Award* 2005; WMC *Working for Wisconsin Award* 2018, 2016, 2014, 2012, 2002, 2000; MMAC *Champion of Commerce Award* 2016, 2014; The American Conservative Union *Defender of Liberty Award* 2013; Wisconsin Ginseng Board Assistance to the *Wisconsin Ginseng Industry Award* 2005; Wisconsin Bear Hunters Association Hero Award 2014, 2012.

Legislature: Elected to Assembly 1998–2010. Elected to Senate in June 2012 special election. Reelected since 2014. Leadership positions: Majority Caucus Sergeant at Arms 2003–07. Committee assignments, 2019: Transportation, Veterans and Military Affairs (chair); Agriculture, Revenue and Financial Institutions (vice chair); Economic Development, Commerce and Trade; Joint Legislative Council. Additional appointments, 2019: Building Commission; Transportation Projects Commission; Council on Highway Safety; Migrant Labor Council; Rustic Roads Board.

Contact: Sen.Petrowski@legis.wisconsin.gov; 608-266-2502; Room 123 South, State Capitol, PO Box 7882, Madison, WI 53707-7882.

Patrick Snyder, Assembly District 85
Republican

Biography: Born Boone, Iowa, October 10, 1956; married; 2 children, 3 grandchildren. Voting address: Schofield, Wisconsin. ▪ Graduate Oelwein Community High School (Iowa), 1974; Degree in Communications, University of Iowa, 1974–78. ▪ Former congressional staffer for Congressman Sean Duffy; radio host for WSAU. ▪ Member: Wausau Noon Rotary; ELKS Club; United Way's Hunger Coalition and Housing and Homelessness Committee; Marathon County Health Department's Alcohol and Other Drugs (AOD) Committee; Marathon County Department of Social Services' Administrative Review Panel. ▪ Former member: St. Therese Parish Council. ▪ Former alder for the City of Schofield.

Legislature: Elected to Assembly since 2016. Committee assignments, 2019: Aging and Long-Term Care; Children and Families (chair); Community Development; Corrections; Jobs and the Economy (vice chair); Mental Health; Workforce Development.

Contact: Rep.Snyder@legis.wisconsin.gov; 608-266-0654; 888-534-0085 (toll free); Room 307 North, State Capitol, PO Box 8953, Madison, WI 53708.

John Spiros, Assembly District 86
Republican

Biography: Born Akron, Ohio, July 28, 1961; married; 5 children (1 son-in-law), 4 grandchildren. Voting address: Marshfield, Wisconsin. ▪ Graduate Marietta High School (Marietta, Ohio), 1979; A.A.S. in Criminal Justice, MTCC (Omaha, Nebraska), 1985. ▪ Vice president, safety and claims management for a transportation company in Marshfield, Wisconsin. Served in U.S. Air Force, 1979–85, SAC "Elite" guard. ▪ Member: Trucking Industry Defense Association (board president 2015–17; executive committee

2013–18); Wisconsin Farm Bureau; Marshfield Elks Club. ▪ City of Marshfield alderman, 2005–13.

Legislature: Elected to Assembly since 2012. Committee assignments, 2019: Criminal Justice and Public Safety (chair); Transportation (vice chair); International Affairs and Commerce; Joint Legislative Council.

Contact: Rep.Spiros@legis.wisconsin.gov; 608-266-1182; 888-534-0086 (toll free); Room 212 North, State Capitol, PO Box 8953, Madison, WI 53708.

James W. Edming, Assembly District 87
Republican

Biography: Born Ladysmith, Wisconsin, November 22, 1945; married; 3 sons, 2 granddaughters, 1 great-granddaughter. Voting address: Glen Flora, Wisconsin. ▪ Graduate Flambeau High School (Tony), 1964; Teacher's Certificate Taylor County Teacher's College, 1967; attended University of Wisconsin-Superior, University of Wisconsin-Eau Claire, University of Wisconsin-Menomonie, University of Wisconsin-Barron County. ▪ Convenience store owner; metal stamping company owner; farmer. Former frozen pizza manufacturer. ▪ Member: 3rd degree Master Mason; 32nd degree Scottish Rite; Shriner; NRA (gun instructor); Model T Ford Club; Wisconsin Self Storage Association; St. Joseph's Hospital Advisory Council (Chippewa Falls) 2018–present; Rusk County Hospital Board, 1980–82, 2010–18. ▪ Rusk County Board of Supervisors, 1976–87.

Legislature: Elected to Assembly since 2014. Committee assignments, 2019: Labor and Integrated Employment (chair); Small Business Development (vice chair); Agriculture; Consumer Protection; Forestry, Parks & Outdoor Recreation; Health; Sporting Heritage; Veterans and Military Affairs.

Contact: Rep.Edming@legis.wisconsin.gov; 608-266-7506; 888-534-0087 (toll free); Room 109 West, State Capitol, PO Box 8952, Madison, WI 53708.

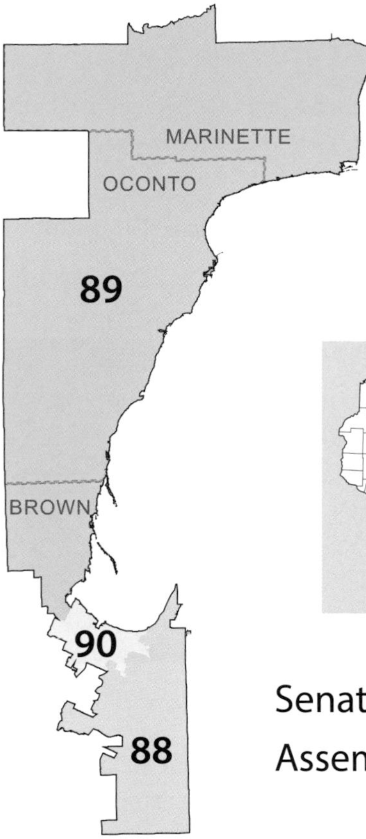

MARINETTE

OCONTO

89

30

BROWN

90

88

Senate District 30
Assembly Districts 88, 89, 90

Dave Hansen, Senate District 30
Democrat

Biography: Born Green Bay, Wisconsin, December 18, 1947; married; 3 children, 11 grandchildren. Voting address: Green Bay, Wisconsin. ▪ Graduate Green Bay West High School; B.S., University of Wisconsin-Green Bay, 1971. ▪ Full-time legislator. Former teacher; Former truck driver for Green Bay Department of Public Works; Former Teamsters Union steward. ▪ Former member: Brown County Human Services Board (chair); N.E.W. Zoo Advisory Board; Brown County Education and Recreation Committee (chair); Great Lakes Compact Commission. ▪ Brown County Board supervisor, 1996–2002.

Legislature: Elected to Senate since 2000. Leadership positions: Assistant Minority Leader 2015, 2013, 2011, 2005, 2003; Majority Leader 2009 (effective 12/15/10);

Assistant Majority Leader 2011 (effective 7/24/12), 2009, 2007. Committee assignments, 2019: Natural Resources and Energy; Public Benefits, Licensing and State-Federal Relations; Transportation, Veterans and Military Affairs.

Contact: Sen.Hansen@legis.wisconsin.gov; 608-266-5670; 866-221-9395 (toll free); 920-391-2000 (district); Room 323 South, State Capitol, PO Box 7882, Madison, WI 53707-7882.

John J. Macco, Assembly District 88
Republican

Biography: Born Green Bay, Wisconsin, September 23, 1958; married; 2 children, 6 grandchildren. Voting address: De Pere, Wisconsin. ▪ Graduate Green Bay Southwest High School, 1976; attended NWTC and University of Wisconsin-Green Bay. ▪ Founder of regional financial planning group; Founder of regional retail franchise; Business consultant. ▪ Member: National Rifle Association. ▪ Former member: American Cancer Society of Wood County; Old Main Street Marshfield; Old Main Street De Pere; Old Main Street Green Bay; U.S. Ski Patrol; Aircraft Owners and Pilots Association; Deacon and Church Elder at Central Church, Green Bay.

Legislature: Elected to Assembly since 2014. Committee assignments, 2019: Ways and Means (chair); Audit (vice chair); Campaigns and Elections; Jobs and the Economy; Regulatory Licensing Reform; Workforce Development; Joint Legislative Audit Committee.

Contact: Rep.Macco@legis.wisconsin.gov; 608-266-0485; 888-534-0088 (toll free); Room 208 North, State Capitol, PO Box 8953, Madison, WI 53708.

John Nygren, Assembly District 89
Republican

Biography: Born Marinette, Wisconsin, February 27, 1964; married; 3 children. Voting address: Marinette, Wisconsin. ▪ Graduate Marinette High School, 1982; attended University of Wisconsin-Marinette. ▪ Insurance and financial representative. Former restaurant owner and operator. ▪ Member: Jaycees (lifetime member, former chapter, state, U.S. president); Marinette Elks Club; Marinette Moose Lodge; Marinette Kiwanis (former president);

Marinette County Republican Party (former chair). ▪ City of Marinette Recreation and Planning Board, 2003–06.

Legislature: Elected to Assembly since 2006. Committee assignments, 2019: Audit; Employment Relations; Finance (chair); Substance Abuse and Prevention; Joint Committee on Employment Relations; Joint Committee on Finance (co-chair); Joint Legislative Audit Committee; Joint Legislative Council.

Contact: Rep.Nygren@legis.wisconsin.gov; 608-266-2343; 888-534-0089 (toll free); Room 308 East, State Capitol, PO Box 8953, Madison, WI 53708.

Staush Gruszynski, Assembly District 90
Democrat

Biography: Born Marinette, Wisconsin, February 13, 1985; married; 1 child. Voting address: Green Bay, Wisconsin. ▪ Graduate Marinette High School, 2003; B.S. in Political Science and Public Administration, University of Wisconsin-Oshkosh, 2008. ▪ Full-time legislator and county board supervisor. Former conservation nonprofit professional. ▪ Member: Brown County Board of Supervisors; Democratic Party of Brown County; Green Bay Trout Unlimited (board of directors, former president); Wisconsin Conservation Congress (delegate, former Brown County chair); University of Wisconsin-Oshkosh Political Science Alumni Association (former president).

Legislature: Elected to Assembly 2018. Committee assignments, 2019: Forestry, Parks and Outdoor Recreation; Local Government; Rural Development; Sporting Heritage; Tourism; Speaker's Task Force on Water Quality.

Contact: Rep.Gruszynski@legis.wisconsin.gov; 608-266-0616; 888-534-0090; Room 15 West, State Capitol, PO Box 8952, Madison, WI 53708.

Senate District 31
Assembly Districts 91, 92, 93

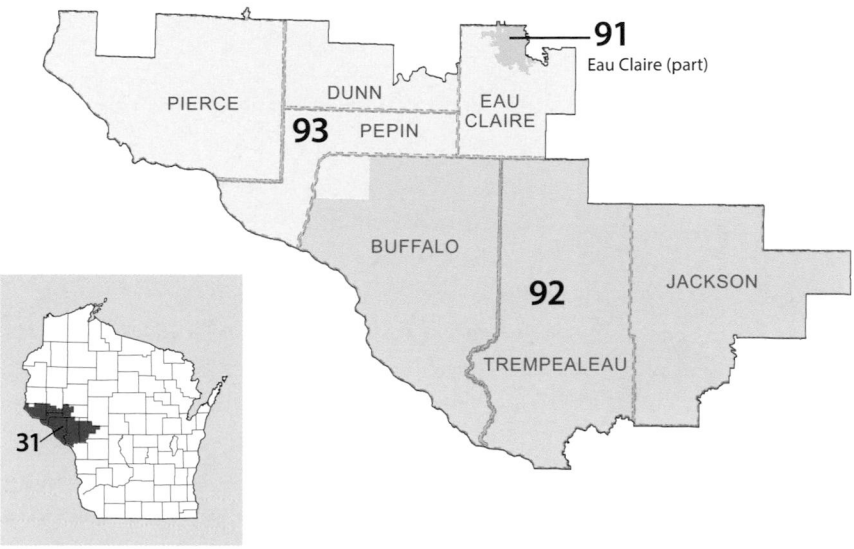

Jeff Smith, Senate District 31
Democrat

Biography: Born Eau Claire, Wisconsin, March 15, 1955; married; 2 children. Voting address: Eau Claire, Wisconsin. ▪ Graduate Eau Claire North High School, 1973. ▪ Former owner/operator of window cleaning business, 1973–2011; Chairman of Town of Brunswick, 2001–07; community organizer for Western Wisconsin Organizing Cooperative of Citizen Action, 2016–18. ▪ Former member: Eau Claire Area Chamber of Commerce; Valley Gospel Choir (president); Eau Claire Male Chorus; Eau Claire Kiwanis Club; Eau Claire Area School District Parent Advisory Committee (founder and chair); Eau Claire Family Resource Center board; Governor's Task Force for Educational Excellence; Wisconsin PTA state board; DPI Parent Leadership Corps; Wisconsin Alliance for Excellent Schools; Township Fire Department board (vice president); Tainter-Menomin Lake Improvement Association board; UW Extension Community Partner Advisory Group.

Legislature: Elected to Assembly 2006–08. Elected to Senate 2018. Committee assignments, 2019: Agriculture, Revenue and Financial Institutions; Elections,

Ethics and Rural Issues; Government Operations, Technology and Consumer Protection; Sporting Heritage, Mining and Forestry.

Contact: Sen.Smith@legis.wisconsin.gov; 608- 266-8546; 715-600-3307 (district); Room 22 South, State Capitol, PO Box 7882, Madison, WI 53707.

Jodi Emerson, Assembly District 91
Democrat

Biography: Born Eau Claire, Wisconsin, August 3, 1972; married; 2 children. Voting address: Eau Claire, Wisconsin. ▪ Graduate Eau Claire Memorial High School, 1990; studied biotechnology, University of Wisconsin-River Falls, 1990–92. ▪ Former anti-human trafficking advocate. ▪ Member: Eau Claire Area Chamber of Commerce; Wisconsin Anti-Human Trafficking Consortium. Former member: Wisconsin Human Trafficking Advisory Council; Wisconsin Anti-Human Trafficking Task Force; Wisconsin Parent Teacher Association; Girl Scouts; Eastside Hill Neighborhood Association Steering Committee.

Legislature: Elected to Assembly 2018. Committee assignments, 2019: Aging and Long-Term Care; Colleges and Universities; Criminal Justice and Public Safety; Family Law; International Affairs and Commerce.

Contact: Rep.Emerson@legis.wisconsin.gov; 608-266-7461; 888-534-0091; 715-456-9355 (district); Room 322 West, State Capitol, PO Box 8952, Madison, WI 53708.

Treig E. Pronschinske, Assembly District 92
Republican

Biography: Born Eau Claire, Wisconsin, July 7, 1978; married; 1 child. Voting address: Mondovi, Wisconsin. ▪ Graduate Memorial High School, 1996; degree in Construction Management, Chippewa Valley Technical College, 1997. ▪ Small business owner; general construction contractor. ▪ Member: Mondovi Fire Department (volunteer firefighter); Gilmanton Community Club. ▪ Former member: Mondovi Youth Baseball Association (president); Mondovi Ambulance Commission 2014–18; Big Brothers Big Sisters; Junior Achievement volunteer. ▪ Mayor of Mondovi, 2014–18.

Legislature: Elected to Assembly 2016. Committee assignments, 2019: Consumer Protection (chair); Aging and Long-Term Care; Agriculture; Children and Families; Family Law; Forestry, Parks and Outdoor Recreation; Housing and Real Estate; Rural Development.

Contact: Rep.Pronschinske@legis.wisconsin.gov; 608-266-7015; 888-534-0092 (toll free); Room 20 North, State Capitol, PO Box 8953, Madison, WI 53708.

Warren Petryk, Assembly District 93
Republican

Biography: Born Eau Claire, Wisconsin, January 24, 1955; married. Voting address: Eleva, Wisconsin. ▪ Eagle Scout, November 1969; Badger Boys State, 1972; Graduate and valedictorian, Boyceville High School, 1973; attended University of Wisconsin-Stout; earned B.A. with highest honors University of Wisconsin-Eau Claire, 1978. ▪ Worked 15 years in community relations for United Cerebral Palsy of West Central Wisconsin; cofounder of musical entertainment group "The Memories" (started 1972). ▪ Member: Eau Claire, Menomonie, Ellsworth, and Prescott Chambers of Commerce; National Rifle Association; Eau Galle-Rush River, Ellsworth, Durand, Rock Falls, and Arkansaw Sportsmen's Clubs; Wisconsin Farm Bureau; Cleghorn Lions Club; Chippewa Valley Council of Boy Scouts of America (board of directors). ▪ Recipient: Wisconsin Veterans of Foreign Wars *Legislator of the Year* 2013; Wisconsin AMVETS *Veteran's Advocate of the Year* 2014; Wisconsin Electrical Cooperative Association *Most Enlightened Legislator* 2016; Wisconsin School Nutrition Association *Legislator of the Year* 2016, 2018; Wisconsin Manufacturers and Commerce *Working for Wisconsin Award* (every term); Dairy Business Association *Legislative Excellence Award* (every term); Wisconsin Economic Development Association *Champion of Economic Development Award* 2018.

Legislature: Elected to Assembly since 2010. Committee assignments, 2019: Workforce Development (chair); Aging and Long-Term Care (vice chair); Colleges and Universities; Energy and Utilities; Financial Institutions; Insurance; Labor and Integrated Employment; Substance Abuse and Prevention; Veterans and Military Affairs.

Contact: Rep.Petryk@legis.wisconsin.gov; 608-266-0660; 888-534-0093 (toll free); Room 103 West, State Capitol, PO Box 8953, Madison, WI 53708.

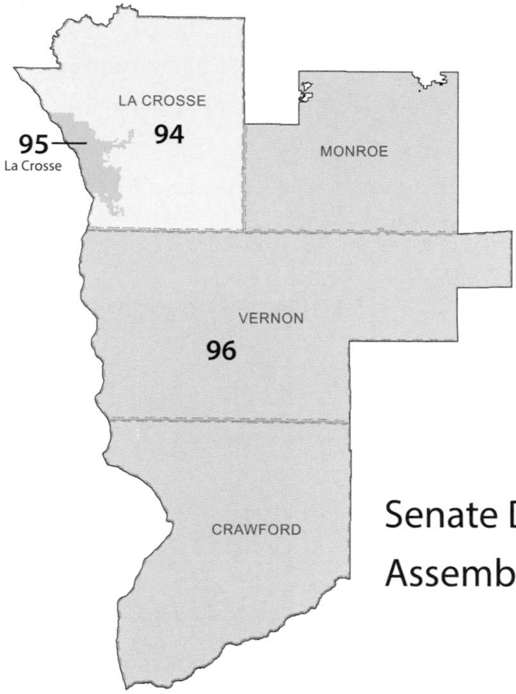

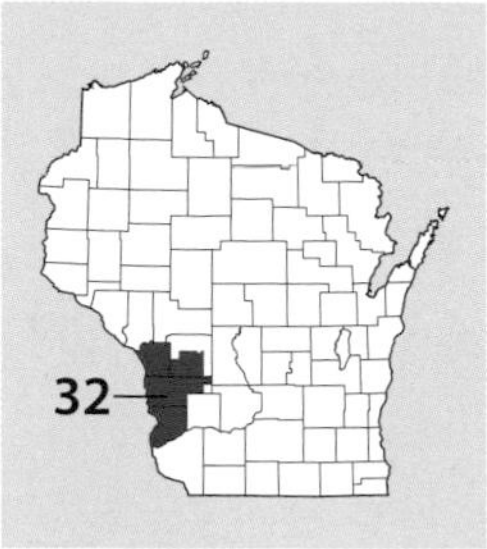

LA CROSSE

95 94

La Crosse

MONROE

VERNON

96

32

CRAWFORD

Senate District 32
Assembly Districts 94, 95, 96

Jennifer Shilling, Senate District 32
Democrat

Biography: Born Oshkosh, Wisconsin, July 4; married; 2 children. Voting address: La Crosse, Wisconsin. ▪ Graduate Buffalo Grove High School (Illinois); B.A. in Political Science and Public Administration, University of Wisconsin-La Crosse, 1992. ▪ Former congressional aide and legislative aide. ▪ Member: University of Wisconsin-La Crosse Alumni Association (former president); League of Women Voters of the La Crosse Area; La Crosse County Democratic Party (former chair); University of Wisconsin-La Crosse Chancellor's Community Council; La Crosse Area Chamber of Commerce; La Crosse County Local Emergency Planning Committee; Vernon Women's Alliance; Viroqua Chamber Main Street. ▪ La Crosse County Board, 1990–92.

Legislature: Elected to Assembly 2000–10. Elected to Senate in August 2011 special election. Reelected since 2012. Leadership positions: Minority Leader 2019, 2017, 2015; Minority Caucus Sergeant at Arms 2005. Committee assignments, 2019: Senate Organization; Joint Committee on Employment Relations; Joint

Committee on Legislative Organization; Joint Legislative Council.

Contact: Sen.Shilling@legis.wisconsin.gov; 608-266-5490; 800-385-3385 (toll free); Room 206 South, State Capitol, PO Box 7882, Madison, WI 53707-7882.

Steve Doyle, Assembly District 94

Democrat

Biography: Born La Crosse, Wisconsin, May 21, 1958; married; 2 children. Voting address: Onalaska, Wisconsin. ▪ Graduate Aquinas High School, 1976; B.A., University of Wisconsin-La Crosse, 1980; J.D., University of Wisconsin Law School, 1986. ▪ Attorney. Former instructor, University of Wisconsin-La Crosse. ▪ Former member: Family Resource Center (board member); Family and Children's Center (board member); Coulee Region Humane Society (board member, president). ▪ La Crosse County Board, 1986–present (chair, 2002–11).

Legislature: Elected to Assembly in May 2011 special election. Reelected since 2012. Leadership positions: Minority Caucus Vice Chair 2019, 2017. Committee assignments, 2019: Family Law; Financial Institutions; Insurance; Speaker's Task Force on Suicide Prevention (vice chair); Speaker's Task Force on Adoption.

Contact: Rep.Doyle@legis.wisconsin.gov; 608-266-0631; 888-534-0094 (toll free); Room 124 North, State Capitol, PO Box 8952, Madison, WI 53708.

Jill Billings, Assembly District 95

Democrat

Biography: Born Rochester, Minnesota, January 19, 1962; 2 children. Voting address: La Crosse, Wisconsin. ▪ Graduate Stewartville High School, 1980; B.A., Augsburg College (Minneapolis), 1989; Council of State Governments: BILLD Fellow 2012, Toll Fellow 2014, current member of Health and Human Services Committee. ▪ Full-time legislator. Former teacher of English and Citizenship to Hmong adults. ▪ Member: Wisconsin Legislative Children's Caucus (co-chair); Wisconsin Family Impact Seminar Advisors Committee; Viterbo University Board of Advisors; University of Wisconsin-La Crosse Chancellor's Community Council; League of Women Voters of the La Crosse

Area; Preservation Alliance of La Crosse; La Crosse Alliance to HEAL. ▪ La Crosse County Board, 2004–12.

Legislature: Elected to the Assembly in November 2011 special election. Reelected since 2012. Committee assignments, 2019: Children and Families; Colleges and Universities; Government Accountability and Oversight; Substance Abuse and Prevention; Tourism; Joint Legislative Council; Wisconsin 19th Amendment Celebration Committee. Additional appointments: Child Abuse and Neglect Prevention Board; Historical Society Board of Curators; Governor's Council on Tourism; State Council on Alcohol and Other Drug Addiction; Wisconsin Mississippi River Parkway Commission.

Contact: Rep.Billings@legis.wisconsin.gov; 608-266-5780; 888-534-0095 (toll free); Room 307 West, State Capitol, PO Box 8952, Madison, WI 53708.

Loren Oldenburg, Assembly District 96
Republican

Biography: Born Viroqua, Wisconsin, September 8, 1965; married. Voting address: Viroqua, Wisconsin. ▪ Graduate Viroqua High School, 1984; attended University of Wisconsin-La Crosse, 1984–87. ▪ Dairy farmer. ▪ Member: Chaseburg Cenex Co-op (19 years, current president of the board); Viroqua Church of Christ (trustee). ▪ Former Harmony Town Board Supervisor; Harmony Town Board Chairman; Westby Co-op Creamery board member and president.

Legislature: Elected to the Assembly 2018. Committee assignments, 2019: Consumer Protection; Energy and Utilities; Environment (vice chair); Rural Development; Workforce Development; Speaker's Task Force on Suicide Prevention.

Contact: Rep.Oldenburg@legis.wisconsin.gov; 608-266-3534; 888-534-0096 (toll free); Room 10 West, State Capitol, PO Box 8953, Madison, WI 53708.

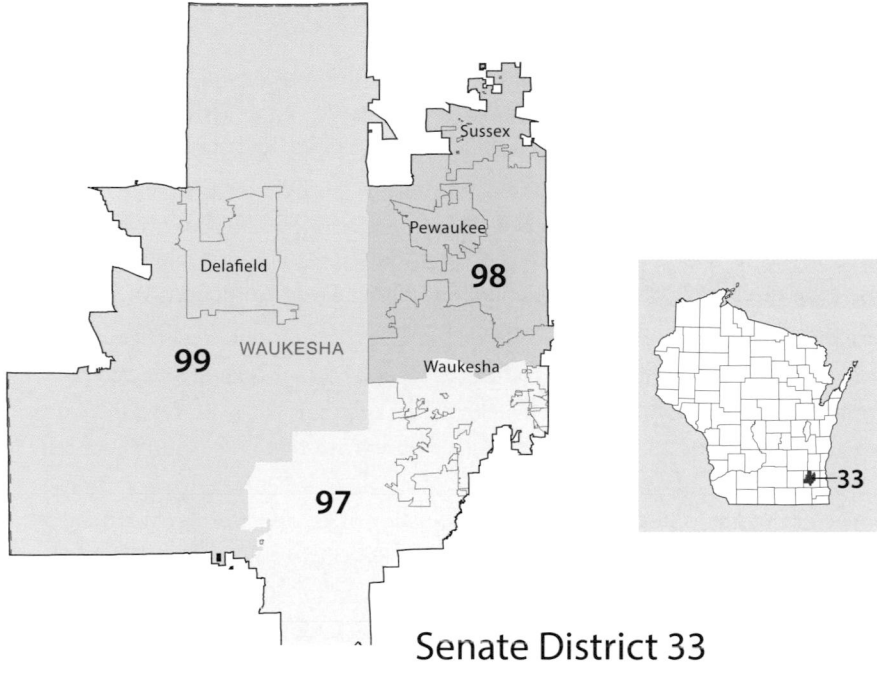

Senate District 33
Assembly Districts 97, 98, 99

Chris Kapenga, Senate District 33
Republican

Biography: Voting address: Delafield, Wisconsin. ▪ B.S. in Accountancy, Calvin College (Grand Rapids, Michigan), 1994. ▪ Business owner; Certified public accountant.

Legislature: Elected to Assembly 2010–14. Elected to Senate in July 2015 special election. Reelected 2018. Committee assignments, 2019: Government Operations, Technology and Consumer Protection (vice chair); Labor and Regulatory Reform; Public Benefits, Licensing and State-Federal Relations (chair); Joint Legislative Audit Committee.

Contact: Sen.Kapenga@legis.wisconsin.gov; 608-266-9174; 800-863-8883 (toll free); Room 15 South, State Capitol, PO Box 7882, Madison, WI 53707-7882.

Scott Allen, Assembly District 97

Republican

Biography: Born Racine, Wisconsin, December 18, 1965; married; 2 children. Voting address: Waukesha, Wisconsin. ▪ Graduate Kettle Moraine High School, 1984; attended University of Wisconsin-Oshkosh, University of Wisconsin-Waukesha; B.A., University of Wisconsin-Milwaukee, 1989; Master of Public Administration and Master of Planning, University of Southern California, 1992. ▪ Sales and leadership speaker, trainer, and coach. Co-owner of a printing and promotional products business. Former Realtor sales director, home builder, and risk management analyst; Served in U.S. Army Reserve, 1984–90. ▪ Member: Republican Party of Waukesha County; Spring Creek Church; Carroll University President's Advisory Committee; La Casa de Esperanza Advisory Board. ▪ Former member: Greater Milwaukee Association of Realtors (former board member); Wisconsin Realtors Association; National Association of Realtors; Waukesha Civic Theatre (president). ▪ Waukesha County Community Development Block Grant Board, 2010–14. Alderman, City of Waukesha, 1998–2001.

Legislature: Elected to Assembly since 2014. Committee assignments, 2019: Community Development (chair); Constitution and Ethics (vice chair); Housing and Real Estate (vice chair); Financial Institutions; Science and Technology; Small Business Development; Veterans and Military Affairs; Workforce Development; Regulatory and Licensing Reform; Transportation. Additional appointments: Wisconsin Housing and Economic Development Authority Board.

Contact: Rep.Allen@legis.wisconsin.gov; 608-266-8580; 888-534-0097 (toll free); Room 8 West, State Capitol, PO Box 8952, Madison, WI 53708.

Adam Neylon, Assembly District 98

Republican

Biography: Born Elgin, Illinois, December 30, 1984; married; 2 children. ▪ Graduate H.D. Jacobs High School, 2003; B.A. Carroll University, 2008; Council of State Governments, 2014 Bowhay Institute for Legislative Leadership Development (BILLD) Fellow. ▪ Small business owner. Former legislative staffer for U.S. Representative Jim Sensenbrenner and Republican leadership in the Wisconsin Assembly. ▪ Member: Wisconsin Future Caucus;

100th Anniversary Capitol Commemorative Commission; President's Advisory Council at Carroll University; Republican Party of Waukesha County (former youth chair); National Rifle Association. ▪ Recipient: Wisconsin Economic Development Association *Champion of Economic Development Award* 2018; Associated Builders and Contractors, Inc. *Building Wisconsin Award* 2018; American Conservative Union *Conservative Achievement Award* 2015–16, 2013–14; Metropolitan Milwaukee Association of Commerce *Champion of Commerce Award* 2015–16, 2013–14; Wisconsin Dairy Business Association *Legislative Excellence Award* 2015; Wisconsin Manufacturers and Commerce *Working for Wisconsin Award* 2015–16, 2013–14; Wisconsin Family Action *Friend of Family, Life & Liberty Award* 2015–16.

Legislature: Elected to Assembly in April 2013 special election. Reelected since 2014. Committee assignments, 2019: Review of Administrative Rules (vice chair); Constitution and Ethics; Energy and Utilities; Insurance (vice chair); Jobs and the Economy (chair); Medicaid Reform and Oversight; Joint Committee for Review of Administrative Rules.

Contact: Rep.Neylon@legis.wisconsin.gov; 608-266-5120; 888-534-0098 (toll free); Room 125 West, State Capitol, PO Box 8953, Madison, WI 53708.

Cindi S. Duchow, Assembly District 99
Republican

Biography: Born Waukesha, Wisconsin; married; 2 children. Voting address: Pewaukee, Wisconsin. ▪ Graduate Catholic Memorial High School, 1977; B.S., University of Wisconsin-Madison, 1981. ▪ Former manager and fashion specialist for national retailers. ▪ Member: St. Anthony's Church; Republican Party of Waukesha County, Leadership Circle; Volunteer Service Club of Pewaukee Lake (former president); Member: Kettle Moraine Curling Club; Pewaukee Yacht Club. ▪ Former member: Waukesha Youth Hockey Association board. ▪ Town of Delafield supervisor, 2013–16.

Legislature: Elected to Assembly in September 2015 special election. Reelected since 2016. Committee assignments, 2019: Financial Institutions (chair); College and Universities; Community Development; Criminal Justice and Public Safety; Family Law; Insurance; International Affairs and Commerce; Local Government; Small Business Development; Speaker's Task Force on Suicide Prevention.

Contact: Rep.Duchow@legis.wisconsin.gov; 608-266-3007; 888-534-0099 (toll free); Room 221 North, State Capitol, PO Box 8952, Madison, WI 53708.

Chief Clerks and Sergeants at Arms

Jeffrey Renk, Senate Chief Clerk

Biography: Born Wauwatosa, Wisconsin, January 31, 1960; married; 1 child. Voting address: Fitchburg, Wisconsin. ▪ Graduate Wauwatosa West High School, 1978; attended University of Wisconsin-Milwaukee, 1978–80; B.A. in Political Science, University of Wisconsin-Madison, 1984. ▪ Former Senate Assistant Chief Clerk, 2004–12; computer programmer, Legislative Technology Services Bureau, 1998–2004; Assembly chief clerk staff, 1988–98; Assembly messenger, 1983–88. Member: American Society of Legislative Clerks and Secretaries. Former member: National Association of Legislative Information Technology.

Current office: Elected Senate Chief Clerk 2013. Reelected since 2015.

Contact: 608-266-2517; Room B20 Southeast, State Capitol, PO Box 7882, Madison, WI 53707-7882.

Edward (Ted) A. Blazel, Senate Sergeant at Arms

Biography: Born Quincy, Illinois, June 14, 1972; married; 2 children. Voting address: Madison, Wisconsin. ▪ Graduate Quincy Senior High School, 1990; B.A. St. Norbert College (De Pere), 1994; M.A. Marquette University, 1998. ▪ Member: National Legislative Service and Security Association; Madison Area Youth Soccer Association (board member).

Current office: Elected Senate Sergeant at Arms 2003. Reelected since 2005.

Contact: 608-266-1801; Room B35 South, State Capitol, PO Box 7882, Madison, WI 53707-7882.

Patrick E. Fuller, Assembly Chief Clerk

Biography: Born Toledo, Ohio, February 24, 1954; married; 1 child. Voting address: Ridgeway, Wisconsin. ▪ Graduate St. Francis de Sales High School (Toledo), 1972; B.E. University of Toledo, 1980; M.B.A. Touro University International (Los Alamitos, CA), 2001. ▪ Former director, Wisconsin Troops to Teachers Program, Wisconsin Department of Veterans Affairs, 1998–2000. Vietnam Era and Operation Desert Storm veteran. Served in U.S. Marine Corps, 1972–86; U.S. Army, 1986–97. Member: NRA; Second Marine Division Association; Veterans of Foreign Wars; Disabled Veterans of America; American Legion; Force Recon Association; 75th Ranger Regiment Association.

Current office: Elected Assembly Chief Clerk 2003. Reelected since 2005.

Contact: Patrick.Fuller@legis.wisconsin.gov; 608-266-1501; Suite 401, Risser Justice Center, 17 West Main Street, Madison, WI 53703.

Anne Tonnon Byers, Assembly Sergeant at Arms

Biography: Born Green Bay, Wisconsin, December 14, 1968; married; 2 children. Voting address: McFarland, Wisconsin. ▪ Graduate Green Bay East High School, 1987; attended University of Wisconsin-Green Bay; B.S. University of Wisconsin-Madison, 1991; University of Wisconsin Certified Public Management Program, 2001. ▪ Former Assembly Assistant Sergeant at Arms, 1998–2010; office manager for Assembly Sergeant, 1993–98. Member: Boy Scout Troop 53.

Current office: Elected Assembly Sergeant at Arms 2011. Reelected since 2013.

Contact: Anne.TonnonByers@legis.wisconsin.gov; 608-266-1503; Room 411 West, State Capitol, PO Box 8952, Madison, WI 53708-8952.

▪ ▪ ▪

2

UNITS OF STATE GOVERNMENT

THE LEGISLATURE

Officers of the Senate
President: Roger Roth
President pro tempore: Howard L. Marklein

Majority leader: Scott L. Fitzgerald
Assistant majority leader: Dan Feyen
Majority caucus chair: Van H. Wanggaard
Majority caucus vice chair: Patrick Testin

Minority leader: Jennifer Shilling
Assistant minority leader: Janet Bewley
Minority caucus chair: Mark Miller
Minority caucus vice chair: Janis A. Ringhand

Chief clerk: Jeffrey Renk
Sergeant at arms: Edward A. Blazel

Officers of the Assembly
Speaker: Robin J. Vos
Speaker pro tempore: Tyler August

Majority leader: Jim Steineke
Assistant majority leader: Mary Felzkowski
Majority caucus chair: Dan Knodl
Majority caucus vice chair: Romaine Quinn
Majority caucus secretary: Jessie Rodriguez
Majority caucus sergeant at arms: Samantha Kerkman

Minority leader: Gordon Hintz
Assistant minority leader: Dianne Hesselbein
Minority caucus chair: Mark Spreitzer
Minority caucus vice chair: Steve Doyle
Minority caucus secretary: Beth Meyers
Minority caucus sergeant at arms: Christine Sinicki

Chief clerk: Patrick E. Fuller
Sergeant at arms: Anne Tonnon Byers

Legislative hotline: 608-266-9960; 800-362-9472
Website: www.legis.wisconsin.gov
Number of employees: 195 (senate, includes the 33 senators); 368 (assembly, includes the 99 representatives)
Total budget 2017–19: $153,001,200 (includes the legislative service agencies)

The 33 members of the state senate are elected for four-year terms, and each senator represents more than 170,000 Wisconsinites.

Overview

Wisconsin's legislature makes the laws of the state. The legislature also controls the state's purse strings: no money can be paid out of the treasury unless the legislature enacts a law that specifically appropriates it. At the same time, the legislature is required to raise revenues sufficient to pay for the state's expenditures, and it is required to audit the state's accounts. The legislature can remove any elective office holder in state government, including the governor, from office for wrongdoing. It can also remove a judge or supreme court justice from office for any reason that, in its judgment, warrants it. The legislature can override the governor's veto of legislation. Finally, the legislature has charge of the two avenues by which the Wisconsin Constitution can be amended: the legislature can propose amendments for the people to vote on, and it can set in motion the process for calling a constitutional convention.

The legislature has two houses: the senate and the assembly. The senate is composed of 33 senators, each elected for a four-year term from a different senate district. The assembly is composed of 99 representatives, each elected for a two-year term from a different assembly district. Each senate district comprises the combined territory of three assembly districts. Elections are held in November of each even-numbered year. The terms of 17 senate seats expire in alternate even-numbered years from the terms of the other 16. If a midterm vacancy occurs in the office of senator or representative, it is filled through a special election called by the governor.

All 99 members of the state assembly take their oath of office on Inauguration Day on January 7, 2019. Each legislator also signs the book pictured at the center on the table, carrying on a tradition that originated with statehood.

A new legislature is sworn in to office in January of each odd-numbered year, and it meets in continuous session for the full biennium until its successor is convened. The 2019 legislature is the 104th Wisconsin Legislature. It convened on January 7, 2019, and will continue until January 4, 2021.

Apparatus for conducting business

Rules. The Wisconsin Constitution prescribes a number of specific procedural requirements for the legislature (for example, that each house must keep and publish a journal of its proceedings and that a roll-call vote, rather than a voice vote, must be taken in certain circumstances). For the most part, however, the legislature determines for itself the manner in which it conducts its business. Each house of the legislature has adopted rules that codify its own practices, and the two houses have adopted joint rules that deal with relations between the houses and administrative proceedings common to both. Either house can change its own rules by passing a resolution, and the two houses can change the joint rules by passing a joint resolution.

A joint session of the legislature is held in February to hear the governor's budget address. The address is held in the Assembly Chamber, where representatives greet and host their colleagues from the senate. *(from left)* Representative Amanda Stuck, Senator Jennifer Shilling, Senate President Roger Roth, and Senate Majority Leader Scott Fitzgerald.

Officers. Each house elects from among its members a presiding officer and an officer to stand in for the presiding officer as needed. The presiding officer or stand-in chairs the house's meetings and authenticates the house's acts, orders, and proceedings. In the senate, these officers are the president and president pro tempore; in the assembly, they are the speaker and speaker pro tempore.

Each house also elects two individuals who are not legislators to serve as the house's chief clerk and sergeant at arms. The chief clerk is the clerk for the house's meetings. The chief clerk also manages the house's paperwork, records, and general operations. The sergeant at arms maintains order in and about the house's meeting chamber and supervises the house's messengers.

Within each house, the members from each political party organize as a caucus and elect officers to coordinate their activity. Caucus officers include the majority leader and assistant majority leader and the minority leader and assistant minority leader.

The senate majority leader and the assembly speaker play major, and roughly parallel, roles in guiding the activities of their houses as a result of special responsibilities that the rules in their houses assign to their offices. These responsibilities include appointing the members of committees, determining what business will be scheduled for the house's meetings, and making staffing and budget decisions for the house's operations.

Committees. The legislature does much of its work in committees. Legislative committees study proposed legislation to determine whether it should be given further consideration by the houses. They review the performance and expenditures of state agencies. And they conduct inquiries to inform the public and the legislature about important issues facing the state.

Each committee is assigned a general area of responsibility or a particular matter to look into and, within the scope of its assignment, can hold hearings to gather information and executive sessions (deliberative meetings) to decide what recommendations and reports it will make. Some committees can do more than make recommendations and reports. (For example, the Joint Committee on Finance can approve requests from state agencies for supplemental funding.) With rare exceptions, all committee proceedings are open to the public.

Each house has its own committees, and the two houses together have joint committees. Usually, every member of the legislature serves on at least one committee. Each house committee includes members from the two major political parties, but more of the members are from the majority party. On a joint committee, which includes members from both houses, more of the members from each house are from the majority party in that house. For some members on some committees, membership is automatic and based on another office that they hold (ex officio membership), but otherwise, committee members are appointed. The senate majority leader and the assembly speaker make the appointments in their respective houses but honor the nominations of the minority leader for the minority party appointments. They also designate the committee chairs and the joint committee cochairs, except when those positions are held ex officio.

The standing committees in each house operate through the legislature's entire biennial session. They are created under or pursuant to the rules of the house and consist exclusively of legislators from the house. Most of the standing committees have responsibility for one or more specific subject areas—for example, "transportation" or "health." However, the Committee on Senate Organization has organizational responsibilities: it schedules and determines the agendas for the senate's meetings, and it decides matters pertaining to the senate's personnel, expenditures, and general operations. In the assembly, these organizational responsibilities fall, respectively, to the Assembly Committee on Rules and the Committee on Assembly Organization.

In addition to the standing committees in the houses, there are 10 joint standing committees, which likewise operate through the entire biennial session. These committees are created in the statutes rather than under the legislature's rules. Three of these committees include nonlegislators in addition to the legislators from both houses. The responsibilities of each of the joint standing committees are described on pages 148–66.

(left) Assembly Minority Leader Gordon Hintz appears before the Committee on Ways and Means to state his party's position on a bill in early February. *(right)* Representatives Lisa Subeck and Melissa Sargent, both of Madison, compare notes at a meeting of the Wisconsin Legislative Children's Caucus, a bipartisan effort to create evidence-informed public policy to improve the lives of Wisconsin children.

Special committees can also be appointed in either house or by the two houses jointly. Committees of this type are created to study a problem or conduct an investigation and report their findings to the house or the legislature. Special committees cease to exist when they have completed their assignments.

Meetings. Early in the biennial session, the legislature adopts a joint resolution to establish its session schedule. The session schedule specifies the floorperiods for the session. A floorperiod is a day or span of days that is reserved for meetings of the full houses. Committees can meet on any day. When a house meets during a floorperiod, it meets in regular session.

The legislature can also call itself into extraordinary session for any day or span of days. The call requires a majority vote of the members of the committee on organization in each house, the adoption of a joint resolution in both houses, or a joint petition signed by a majority of the members of each house. In addition, the call must specify what business can be considered during the session. An extraordinary session can have the effect of extending a floorperiod so that it begins earlier or ends later than originally scheduled. An extraordinary session can also overlap a floorperiod, and a house can meet in extraordinary session and in regular session at different times during the same day.

The governor can call the legislature into special session at any time. When the legislature convenes in special session, it can act only upon the matters specified in the governor's call. Special sessions can occur during floorperiods and during extraordinary sessions, and a house can meet in special session and in regular or extraordinary session at different times during the same day.

Notices and records. Each house issues a calendar for each of its meetings. The calendar lists the business that will be taken up at the meeting.

The legislature publishes on the Internet a schedule of committee activities that indicates the time, place, and business scheduled for each committee meeting. Each house keeps a record of its actions known as the daily journal.

The legislature issues the *Bulletin of the Proceedings of the Wisconsin Legislature* periodically during the biennial session. Each issue contains a cumulative record of actions taken on bills, resolutions, and joint resolutions; information on administrative rule changes; and a listing of statutes affected by acts.

Employees. Each house employs staff for its members and staff to take care of general administrative matters. In addition, the legislature maintains five service agencies to provide it with legal advice; bill drafting services; budgetary, economic, and fiscal analysis; public policy analysis; research and information services; committee staffing; auditing services; and information technology advice and services.

How a bill becomes a law

A bill is a formal document that proposes to make a new law or change an existing law. For a bill to become a law, two things must happen: (1) the bill must be en-

Assistant Minority Leader Dianne Hesselbein (*left*) discusses an amendment to a bill with Majority Leader Jim Steineke on the assembly floor. The leaders of each party work together to ensure that action during the floorperiod follows legislative rules.

JOE KOSHOLLEK, LEGISLATIVE PHOTOGRAPHER

Senator LaTonya Johnson of Milwaukee (*foreground*) makes a point to her colleagues as Senate President Roger Roth (*top*) presides over the action in the chamber. Senator Dave Hansen of Green Bay (*far right*) and Senate Chief Clerk Jeff Renk (*far left*), as well as other staff members of the chief clerk's office, listen in.

acted—that is, it must be passed in identical form by both houses of the legislature and either agreed to by the governor or passed again with a two-thirds vote by both houses over the governor's veto, and (2) the enacted bill must be published.

First reading. A bill takes the first step toward becoming a law when a member or committee of the legislature introduces it in the member's house. This is done by filing the bill with the chief clerk. The chief clerk then assigns the bill its bill number (for example, Assembly Bill 15), and the presiding officer refers the bill to a standing committee or joint standing committee.

A bill must be given three readings on three different days before the house can pass it. Each reading is followed by a different stage in the house's deliberation process. Introduction and referral to committee are considered a bill's first reading and are followed by committee review.

Committee review. When a bill is referred to a committee, it remains in the committee until the committee reports it out to the house, the bill is rereferred, or the house acts to withdraw it. The committee chair (or cochairs in a joint committee) determines whether the committee will meet to consider a bill and, if so, whether it will hold a hearing or an executive session or both. In the senate, though not in the assembly, a bill that has not received a public hearing cannot be placed on the calendar for a meeting of the full house unless the Committee on Senate Organization waives the public hearing requirement. And in both houses, a committee cannot report a bill out to the house unless it holds an executive session.

A committee holds a hearing on a bill to gather information, either from the public at large or from specifically invited persons. A committee holds an executive session on a bill to decide what recommendation it will to make to the house. The committee can recommend passage of the bill as originally introduced, passage of the bill with amendments, passage of a substitute amendment, or rejection of the bill. Unless it recommends rejection, the committee reports the bill, together with its recommendation, out to the house. In limited circumstances (such as a tie vote), a committee can report a bill without a recommendation.

Senate Minority Caucus Chair Mark Miller asks a question at a meeting of the Speaker's Task Force on Water Quality. The task force was created in the wake of reports about the contamination of private wells in southwest Wisconsin. Such task forces study specific issues and make recommendations on policy to address those issues.

If a bill is reported out by a committee, or if it is withdrawn from a committee by the house, it is generally sent to the house's scheduling committee—the Committee on Senate Organization or the Assembly Committee on Rules—so that it can be scheduled for consideration at a meeting of the house. Sometimes, however, a bill is referred to another committee for that committee to review. In such cases, the bill remains in that other committee, just as it did in the previous committee, until it is reported out or withdrawn.

Scheduling. A bill that reaches a scheduling committee cannot advance further unless the scheduling committee schedules it for a meeting of the house or the house acts to withdraw it. The scheduling committee is not required to schedule the bill for a meeting of the house. If the house withdraws a bill from the scheduling committee, the bill is automatically scheduled for a future meeting of the house. (In the senate, it is placed on the calendar for the senate's next succeeding meeting; in the assembly, it is placed on the calendar for the assembly's second succeeding meeting.) If a bill is scheduled for a meeting of the house, it can be given its second reading at that meeting.

Second reading. A bill's second reading is a formal announcement that the chief clerk makes at the time when the bill is about to be considered. Following this announcement, the house debates and votes on amendments and substitute amendments to the bill (any that the standing committee recommended and any that are offered by members). This stage ends if the house votes affirmatively to engross the bill. Such a vote means that the house has decided on the final form that the bill will take and is ready to consider passage of the bill in that final form. However, the house cannot proceed to consider passage until the bill has been given its third reading—and this must be done on a different day. However, and this is often the case, the house can suspend this restriction by a unanimous voice vote or a two-thirds roll call vote. If the house does not suspend the restriction, the bill is automatically scheduled for a future meeting of the house. (In the senate, it is placed on the calendar for the senate's next succeeding meeting; in the assembly, it is placed on the calendar for the assembly's second succeeding meeting.)

Third reading. A bill's third reading, like its second, is a formal announcement that the chief clerk makes at the time when the bill is about to be considered. Following this announcement, the house debates whether the bill, in its final form previously determined by the house, should be passed. Members can only speak for and against passage; no further amendments can be offered. When debate on the bill ends, the members of the house vote. If the bill is passed, it is ready to be messaged to the other house. Messaging occurs automatically following a reconsideration period specified in the rules of the house, unless, within that period, the house chooses to reconsider its action in passing the bill. (In the senate, the reconsideration period extends through the senate's next meeting; in the assembly, it extends through the seventh order of business at the assembly's next meeting.) Generally, only a member who voted for passage can make a motion for reconsideration. Alternatively, the house can suspend its rules to message the bill immediately, by a unanimous voice vote or a two-thirds roll call vote.

Action in the second house. When the bill is received in the other house, it goes through substantially the same process as in the first house. If the second house ultimately passes the bill, which it can do with or without additional amendments, it messages the bill back to the house of origin.

Subsequent action in the houses. If the second house adopted additional amendments, the house of origin must determine whether it agrees to those amendments. If the house of origin rejects or amends the amendments, it can message the bill back to the second house. The houses can message the bill back and forth repeatedly until it has been passed in identical form by both houses. Alternatively, the houses can create a conference committee to develop a compromise version of the bill. If the conference committee proposes a compromise version, the houses can vote on it but cannot adopt additional amendments. The compromise version is considered in the second house first; if it passes in the second house, it is messaged to the house of origin.

Action by the governor. If a bill is passed in identical form by both houses, it is sent to the governor. The governor has six days (excluding Sundays) in which to take action on a bill after receiving it. If the governor takes no action, the bill is enacted on the seventh day. If the governor signs the bill, the bill is enacted on the day it is signed. If the governor vetoes the bill, it goes back to the house of origin. If the governor signs the bill but vetoes part of it—which is permitted in the case of appropriation bills—the signed part is enacted on the day it is signed, and the vetoed part goes back to the house of origin.

Publication and effective date. A bill or part of a bill that has been enacted is called an act. An act becomes a law when it is published in the manner prescribed by the legislature. The legislature has provided for each act to be published on the Internet no later than the day after its date of enactment. An act goes into effect on the second day after its date of enactment, unless the act specifies that it goes into effect on a different date.

Veto override. A bill or part of a bill that the governor has vetoed can become a law if the legislature passes it again over the governor's veto. The procedure is different than when the bill was passed the first time. The only question considered is passage, and this question can be taken up immediately; the three-readings process is not repeated, and amendments cannot be offered. In addition, passage requires a two-thirds vote in each house, rather than a simple majority vote. Any action on a veto begins in the house of origin. If a vote is taken in the house of origin and two-thirds of the members present and voting agree to pass the vetoed bill or vetoed part of a bill, the bill or part is messaged to the other house. If a vote is taken in the second house and two-thirds of the members present and voting agree to pass the bill or part, the bill or part is enacted on the day the vote is taken. The enacted bill or part is then published and becomes a law in the same way as other acts. If either house does not take a vote or fails to muster a two-thirds vote, the bill or part advances no further, and the governor's veto stands.

Senate standing committees

Administrative Rules Nass, *chair*; Stroebel, *vice chair*; Craig; Larson, *ranking minority member*; Wirch

Agriculture, Revenue and Financial Institutions Marklein, *chair*; Petrowski, *vice chair*; Testin, Jacque, Bernier; Smith, *ranking minority member*; Ringhand, Risser, Larson

Economic Development, Commerce and Trade Feyen, *chair*; Testin, *vice chair*; Petrowski; Ringhand, *ranking minority member*; Carpenter

Education Olsen, *chair*; Darling, *vice chair*; Nass, Kooyenga, Bernier; Larson, *ranking minority member*; Bewley, Johnson, Schachtner

Elections, Ethics, and Rural Issues Bernier, *chair*; Tiffany, *vice chair*; Kooyenga; Miller, *ranking minority member*; Smith

Finance Darling, *chair*; Olsen, *vice chair*; Tiffany, Marklein, Stroebel, LeMahieu; Erpenbach, *ranking minority member*; Johnson

Government Operations, Technology and Consumer Protection Stroebel, *chair*; Kapenga, *vice chair*; Craig; Wirch, *ranking minority member*; Smith

Health and Human Services Testin, *chair*; Kooyenga, *vice chair*; Jacque; Erpenbach, *ranking minority member*; Carpenter

Insurance, Financial Services, Government Oversight and Courts Craig, *chair*; Stroebel, *vice chair*; Feyen; Risser, *ranking minority member*; Taylor

Speaker Pro Tempore Tyler August (*center*) confers with Representative Chris Taylor (*right*) during a break in assembly floor action. The minority party works with leadership to make sure that all voices are heard on an issue. Representative John Nygren (*left*) is the chair of the Joint Finance Committee.

The standing committees of each house handle much of the work related to legislative proposals and holding public and informational hearings, as well as giving final recommendations on the passage of bills. Representative Jessie Rodriguez (*left*) chairs the Assembly Committee on Family Law, and Senator Kathleen Bernier (*right*) chairs the Senate Committee on Elections, Ethics and Rural Issues.

Judiciary and Public Safety Wanggaard, *chair*; Jacque, *vice chair*; Darling; Risser, *ranking minority member*; Taylor

Labor and Regulatory Reform Nass, *chair*; Wanggaard, *vice chair*; Kapenga; Wirch, *ranking minority member*; Ringhand

Local Government, Small Business, Tourism and Workforce Development Jacque, *chair*; Bernier, *vice chair*; Tiffany; Schachtner, *ranking minority member*; Miller

Natural Resources and Energy Cowles, *chair*; Olsen, *vice chair*; Marklein; Miller, *ranking minority member*; Hansen

Public Benefits, Licensing and State-Federal Relations Kapenga, *chair*; Craig, *vice chair*; LeMahieu; Johnson, *ranking minority member*; Hansen

Senate Organization Fitzgerald, *chair*; Roth, *vice chair*; Feyen; Shilling, *ranking minority member*; Bewley

Sporting Heritage, Mining and Forestry Tiffany, *chair*; LeMahieu, *vice chair*; Stroebel; Wirch, *ranking minority member*; Smith

Transportation, Veterans and Military Affairs Petrowski, *chair*; Marklein, *vice chair*; Cowles; Carpenter, *ranking minority member*; Hansen

Universities, Technical Colleges, Children and Families Kooyenga, *chair*; Nass, *vice chair*; Darling, Olsen; Bewley, *ranking minority member*; Larson, Schachtner

Utilities and Housing LeMahieu, *chair*; Feyen, *vice chair*; Wanggaard; Taylor, *ranking minority member*; Bewley

Assembly standing committees

Administrative Rules Ballweg, *chair*; Neylon, Ott; Hebl, *ranking minority member*; Taylor

Speaker's Task Force on Adoption Dittrich, *chair*, other appointments pending

Aging and Long-Term Care Gundrum, *chair*; Petryk, *vice chair*; Pronschinske, Snyder, Plumer, Magnafici; Meyers, *ranking minority member*; Brostoff, Emerson

Agriculture Tauchen, *chair*; Novak, *vice chair*; Kurtz, Tranel, Kitchens, VanderMeer, Mursau, Edming, Pronschinske, Plumer; Considine, *ranking minority member*; Vruwink, Kolste, Spreitzer, Myers

Assembly Organization Vos, *chair*; Steineke, *vice chair*; Felzkowski, August, Knodl; Hintz, *ranking minority member*; Hesselbein, Spreitzer

Audit Kerkman, *chair*; Macco, *vice chair*; Nygren; Sargent, *ranking minority member*; Shankland

Campaigns and Elections Tusler, *chair*; Sanfelippo, *vice chair*; Brandtjen, Macco, Sortwell, Murphy; Zamarripa, *ranking minority member*; Subeck, Spreitzer

Children and Families Snyder, *chair*; Ramthun, *vice chair*; Kerkman, Ballweg, Vorpagel, Pronschinske, Gundrum, James; Subeck, *ranking minority member*; Billings, Bowen, Vining

Colleges and Universities Murphy, *chair*; Tranel, *vice chair*; Duchow, Ballweg, Wittke, Summerfield, Stafsholt, Krug, Quinn, Petryk; Shankland, *ranking minority member*; Billings, Stubbs, Emerson, Hesselbein, Anderson

Community Development Allen, *chair*; Brandtjen, *vice chair*; Snyder, Duchow, Sanfelippo, Ramthun; Fields, *ranking minority member*; Bowen, McGuire

Constitution and Ethics Wichgers, *chair*; Allen, *vice chair*; Thiesfeldt, Magnafici, Neylon, Ramthun; Hebl, *ranking minority member*; Brostoff, Cabrera

Consumer Protection Pronschinske, *chair*; Tittl, *vice chair*; Skowronski, Edming, VanderMeer, Oldenburg; Pope, *ranking minority member*; Sinicki, Cabrera

Representative John Spiros chairs the Assembly Committee on Criminal Justice and Public Safety. He listens to testimony at a public hearing on a variety of related issues in March 2019.

Corrections Schraa, *chair*; Hutton, *vice chair*; Brandtjen, Snyder, James, Kurtz; Bowen, *ranking minority member*; Goyke, Stubbs

Criminal Justice and Public Safety Spiros, *chair*; Sortwell, *vice chair*; Ott, Steffen, Horlacher, Duchow, Novak, Schraa, Krug; Crowley, *ranking minority member*; Spreitzer, Emerson, Stubbs, McGuire

Education Thiesfeldt, *chair*; Kitchens, *vice chair*; Jagler, Wittke, Rodriguez, Tusler, Mursau, Quinn, Ramthun, Wichgers; Pope, *ranking minority member*; Bowen, Considine, Hebl, Vruwink, Myers

JOE KOSHOLLEK, LEGISLATIVE PHOTOGRAPHER

Employment Relations Vos, *chair*; Steineke, *vice chair*; Nygren; Hintz, *ranking minority member*

Energy and Utilities Kuglitsch, *chair*; Steffen, *vice chair*; Rodriguez, Sortwell, Petersen, Tauchen, Tranel, Oldenburg, Petryk, Neylon, Vorpagel; Meyers, *ranking minority member*; Crowley, Subeck, Stuck, Fields

Environment Kitchens, *chair*; Oldenburg, *vice chair*; Tusler, Novak, Kurtz, James, Kuglitsch, Krug; Hebl, *ranking minority member*; Anderson, Shankland, Neubauer

Family Law Rodriguez, *chair*; James, *vice chair*; Duchow, Tauchen, Plumer, Pronschinske; Doyle, *ranking minority member*; Brostoff, Emerson

Federalism and Interstate Relations Vorpagel, *chair*; Schraa, *vice chair*; Kerkman, Hutton, Horlacher; Taylor, *ranking minority member*; Myers

Finance Nygren, *chair*; Loudenbeck, *vice chair*; Born, Rohrkaste, Katsma, Zimmerman; Taylor, *ranking minority member*; Goyke

Financial Institutions Duchow, *chair*; Stafsholt, *vice chair*; Dittrich, Allen, Sanfelippo, Petryk, Katsma, Murphy, Petersen, Kitchens; Doyle, *ranking minority member*; Meyers, Hesselbein, Fields, Vining

Forestry, Parks and Outdoor Recreation Mursau, *chair*; Krug, *vice chair*; Pronschinske, Felzkowski, Swearingen, Edming, Wichgers, Tusler; Milroy, *ranking minority member*; Spreitzer, Sinicki, Gruszynski

Government Accountability and Oversight Steffen, *chair*; Brandtjen, *vice chair*; Krug, Wichgers, Kuglitsch, August, Hutton; Pope, *ranking minority member*; Sinicki, Vruwink, Billings

Health Sanfelippo, *chair*; Kurtz, *vice chair*; Rodriguez, Edming, Skowronski, Wichgers,

(from left) Representatives Terry Katsma of Oostburg, Don Vruwink of Milton, and Jeremy Thiesfeldt of Fond du Lac share a bipartisan conversation at the State of the State address in January.

GREG ANDERSON, LEGISLATIVE PHOTOGRAPHER

GREG ANDERSON, LEGISLATIVE PHOTOGRAPHER

Representative Sondy Pope of Mount Horeb *(left)* and Senate Assistant Minority Leader Janet Bewley of Mason greet each other on Inauguration Day 2019.

Murphy, VanderMeer, Felzkowski, Magnafici; Kolste, *ranking minority member*; Riemer, Subeck, Anderson, Vining

Housing and Real Estate Jagler, *chair*; Allen, *vice chair*; Quinn, Brooks, Murphy, Pronschinske; Stuck, *ranking minority member*; Zamarripa, Haywood

Insurance Petersen, *chair*; Neylon, *vice chair*; Duchow, Jagler, Petryk, Tusler, Tranel, Steffen, August, Stafsholt, Gundrum; Riemer, *ranking minority member*; Doyle, Hesselbein, Stuck, Stubbs

International Affairs and Commerce Hutton, *chair*; Summerfield, *vice chair*; Tusler, Skowronski, Vorpagel, Rodriguez, Tittl, Duchow, Ballweg, Tauchen, Krug, Spiros; Vruwink, *ranking minority member*; Neubauer, Zamarripa, Cabrera, Emerson, Haywood

Jobs and the Economy Neylon, *chair*; Snyder, *vice chair*; Dittrich, Kulp, Tittl, Macco, Wittke, Magnafici, Ballweg; Ohnstad, *ranking minority member*; Neubauer, Stuck, Fields, Zamarripa

Judiciary Ott, *chair*; Horlacher, *vice chair*; Thiesfeldt, Brooks, Tusler, Kerkman; Anderson, *ranking minority member*; Hebl, Cabrera

Labor and Integrated Employment Edming, *chair*; VanderMeer, *vice chair*; Petryk, Schraa, Dittrich, Gundrum; Sinicki, *ranking minority member*; Ohnstad, McGuire

Local Government Novak, *chair*; Gundrum, *vice chair*; Duchow, Steffen, Skowronski, Brooks; Spreitzer, *ranking minority member*; Subeck, Gruszynski

Medicaid Reform and Oversight Summerfield, *chair*; Brooks, *vice chair*; Neylon, Dittrich, Wichgers, Stafsholt; Riemer, *ranking minority member*; Kolste, Anderson

Representative Robyn Vining (*left*) of Wauwatosa and Representative Shelia Stubbs of Madison, both Democrats, are two of eighteen freshman representatives to the assembly in the 2019 legislature. Representative Stubbs is also the first African American state legislator to represent the Madison area.

Mental Health Tittl, *chair*; Jagler, *vice chair*; Ballweg, Novak, Sanfelippo, Snyder, VanderMeer, Magnafici; Considine, *ranking minority member*; Kolste, Sargent, Brostoff

Public Benefit Reform Krug, *chair*; Petersen, *vice chair*; Brandtjen, Schraa, Ramthun, Sortwell; Subeck, *ranking minority member*; Neubauer, Taylor

Regulatory Licensing Reform Horlacher, *chair*; Ballweg, *vice chair*; Allen, Sortwell, Macco, Quinn; Brostoff, *ranking minority member*; Stuck, Myers

Rules Steineke, *chair*; Vos, *vice chair*; August, Felzkowski, Knodl, Ballweg, Kuglitsch, Jagler, Born; Hintz, *ranking minority member*; Hesselbein, Spreitzer, Doyle, Pope, Kolste

Rural Development VanderMeer, *chair*; Kulp, *vice chair*; Novak, Kurtz, Quinn, Oldenburg, Pronschinske, Plumer; Vruwink, *ranking minority member*; Milroy, Considine, Gruszynski

Science and Technology Quinn, *chair*; Petersen, *vice chair*; Allen, Wittke, Schraa, Brandtjen; Neubauer, *ranking minority member*; Anderson, Sargent

Small Business Development Brandtjen, *chair*; Edming, *vice chair*; Tranel, James, Allen, Swearingen, Summerfield, Duchow, Dittrich, Skowronski; Sargent, *ranking minority member*; Zamarripa, Pope, Vining, Cabrera

Sporting Heritage Stafsholt, *chair*; Quinn, *vice chair*; Tittl, Edming, Felzkowski, Mursau, Skowronski, Tusler, Horlacher; Milroy, *ranking minority member*; Stuck, Spreitzer, Hesselbein, Gruszynski

State Affairs Swearingen, *chair*; Tauchen, *vice chair*; Jagler, Schraa, Knodl, Kuglitsch,

JOE KOSHOLLEK, LEGISLATIVE PHOTOGRAPHER

Republican Representative Tony Kurtz of Wonewoc makes his first speech on the floor of the legislature in January. A legislator's first speech is traditionally greeted with applause from his or her colleagues.

Summerfield, Kulp, Vorpagel; Sinicki, *ranking minority member*; McGuire, Ohnstad, Crowley, Stubbs, Cabrera

Substance Abuse and Prevention Plumer, *chair*; Magnafici, *vice chair*; Petryk, Hutton, James, Nygren; Kolste, *ranking minority member*; Sargent, Billings

Speaker's Task Force on Suicide Prevention Ballweg, *chair*; Doyle, *vice chair*; Shraa, Tittl, VanderMeer, Stafsholt, Duchow, James, Oldenburg, Kurtz; Sargent, *ranking minority member*; Kolste, Anderson, Brostoff, Meyers

Tourism Tranel, *chair*; Swearingen, *vice chair*; Ballweg, Tauchen, Summerfield, Kitchens, Magnafici, Mursau, VanderMeer, Plumer; Billings, *ranking minority member*; Vruwink, Myers, Gruszynski, Stubbs

Transportation Kulp, *chair*; Spiros, *vice chair*; Thiesfeldt, Allen, Sanfelippo, Vorpagel, Murphy, Skowronski, Plumer; Kolste, *ranking minority member*; Crowley, Meyers, Neubauer, Considine

Veterans and Military Affairs Skowronski, *chair*; VanderMeer, *vice chair*; Allen, Petryk, Edming, Kurtz, Summerfield, Ott, Tittl, James; Hesselbein, *ranking minority member*; Riemer, Milroy, Sinicki, Haywood

Speaker's Task Force on Water Quality Novak, *chair*; Shankland, *vice chair*; Tranel, Kitchens, Krug, Felzkowski, Summerfield, Ramthun, Kurtz, Brooks, Pope, Gruszynski, Senators Testin, Cowles, Jacque, Miller

JOE KOSHOLLEK, LEGISLATIVE PHOTOGRAPHER

Senator Alberta Darling (*center*) has cochaired the powerful Joint Committee on Finance for five continuous sessions. Representative John Nygren (*left*) has been cochair since 2013, and Joe Malkasian (*right*) is the committee clerk.

Ways and Means Macco, *chair*; Wittke, *vice chair*; Kerkman, Brooks, Kulp, Petersen, Dittrich, Ramthun; Riemer, *ranking minority member*; Ohnstad, Haywood, McGuire

Workforce Development Petryk, *chair*; Dittrich, *vice chair*; Murphy, Allen, Brandtjen, Kulp, Macco, Snyder, Gundrum, Oldenburg; Shankland, *ranking minority member*; Fields, Crowley, Ohnstad, Haywood

Joint legislative committees and commissions

Joint committees and commissions are created by statute and include members from both houses. Three joint committees include members who are not legislators. Commissions include gubernatorial appointees and, in two cases, the governor.

Joint Committee for Review of Administrative Rules

Senators: Nass, *cochair*; Stroebel, Craig; Larson, *ranking minority member*; Wirch
Representatives: Ballweg, *cochair*; Neylon, Ott; Hebl, *ranking minority member*; C. Taylor
Senator Nass: Sen.Nass@legis.wisconsin.gov; 608-266-2635; Room 10 South, State Capitol, PO Box 7882, Madison, WI 53707-7882
Representative Ballweg: Rep.Ballweg@legis.wisconsin.gov; 608-266-8077; Room 210 North, State Capitol, PO Box 8952, Madison, WI 53708-8952

The Joint Committee for Review of Administrative Rules must review proposed rules and may object to the promulgation of rules as part of the legislative oversight of the rule-making process. It also may suspend rules that have been promulgated; suspend or extend the effective period of emergency rules; and order an agency to put policies in rule form. Following standing committee review, a proposed rule must be referred to the joint committee. The joint committee must meet to review proposed rules that receive standing committee objections, and may meet to review any rule received without objection. The joint committee generally has 30 days to review the rule, but that period may be extended in certain cases. The joint committee may concur or nonconcur in the standing committee's action or may on its own accord object to a proposed rule or portion of a rule. If it objects or concurs in a standing committee's objection, it must introduce bills concurrently in both houses to prevent promulgation of the rule. If either bill is enacted, the agency may not adopt the rule unless specifically authorized to do so by a subsequent legislative enactment. The joint committee may also request that an agency modify a proposed rule. The joint committee may suspend a rule that was previously promulgated after holding a public hearing. Within 30 days following the suspension, the joint committee must introduce bills concurrently in both houses to repeal the suspended rule. If either bill is enacted, the rule is repealed and the

Assembly Speaker Robin Vos (*center*) and Senator Van Wanggaard (*right*) take part in the annual Research in the Rotunda event, which allows undergraduate students from the University of Wisconsin System to bring the results of their work directly to state leadership.

GREG ANDERSON, LEGISLATIVE PHOTOGRAPHER

Senate Minority Leader Jennifer Shilling directs her party's response to the policy agenda of the majority. On Girl Scout Advocacy Day in March 2019, Senator Shilling and Representative Joan Ballweg, (*left*) were made the leaders of Honorary Troop 1912.

agency may not promulgate it again unless authorized by a subsequent legislative action. If both bills fail to pass, the rule remains in effect. The joint committee receives notice of any action in a circuit court for declaratory judgments about the validity of a rule and may intervene in the action with the consent of the Joint Committee on Legislative Organization. The joint committee is composed of five senators and five representatives, and the membership from each house must include representatives of both the majority and minority parties.

State of Wisconsin Building Commission

Governor: Tony Evers, *chair*
Senators: Petrowski, Ringhand, Testin
Representatives: Swearingen, *vice chair;* Billings, Born

Other members: Summer Strand (citizen member appointed by governor)
Nonvoting advisory members from Department of Administration: Naomi De Mers (administrator, Division of Facilities Development), *commission secretary;* Kevin Trinastic, R. J. Binau, David Erdman, Jillian Vessely
Contact: 608-266-1855; 101 East Wilson Street, 7th Floor, Madison, WI 53703; PO Box 7866, Madison, WI 53707-7866

The State of Wisconsin Building Commission coordinates the state building program, which includes the construction of new buildings; the remodeling, renovation, and maintenance of existing facilities; and the acquisition of lands and capital equipment. The commission determines the projects to be incorporated into the building program and biennially makes recommendations concerning the building program to the legislature, including the amount to be appropriated in the biennial budget. The budget for the state building program for 2015–17 was $848,728,000. The commission oversees all state construction, except highway development. In addition, the commission may authorize expenditures from the State Building Trust Fund for construction, remodeling, maintenance, and planning of future development. The commission has supervision over all matters relating to the contracting of state debt. All transactions for the sale of instruments that result in a state debt liability must be approved by official resolution of the commission. The eight-member commission includes three senators and three representatives. Both the majority and minority parties in each house must be represented, and one legislator from each house must also be a member of the State Supported Programs Study and Advisory Committee. The governor serves as chair. One citizen member serves at the pleasure of the governor. The Department of Administration provides staffing for the commission, and several department employees serve as nonvoting, advisory members.

Joint Review Committee on Criminal Penalties

Senators: Wanggaard, *cochair*; L. Taylor, *ranking minority member*
Representatives: Hutton, *cochair*; Goyke, *ranking minority member*
Other members: Josh Kaul (attorney general); Kevin A. Carr (secretary of corrections); Kelli S. Thompson (state public defender); James T. Bayorgeon, David G. Deininger (reserve judges appointed by supreme court); Bradley Gehring, Maury Straub (public members appointed by governor)

Senator Wanggaard: Sen.Wanggaard@legis.wisconsin.gov; 608-266-1832; Room 313 South, State Capitol, PO Box 7882, Madison, WI 53707-7882
Representative Hutton: Rep.Hutton@legis.wisconsin.gov; 608-267-9836; Room 220 North, State Capitol, PO Box 8952, Madison, WI 53708-8952

Representative Ken Skowronski of Franklin celebrates the Midwestern tradition of Paczki Day in his Capitol office. Paczki are filled donuts that originate from a Polish tradition of using up fat, sugar and fruit just before the Lenten season.

JOE KOSHOLLEK, LEGISLATIVE PHOTOGRAPHER

The Joint Review Committee on Criminal Penalties reviews any bill that creates a new crime or revises a penalty for an existing crime when requested to do so by the chair of a standing committee in the house of origin to which the bill was referred. The presiding officer in the house of origin may also request a report from the joint committee if the bill is not referred to a standing committee. Reports of the joint committee on bills submitted for its review concern the costs or savings to public agencies; the consistency of proposed penalties with existing penalties; whether alternative language is needed to conform the proposed penalties to existing penalties; and whether any acts prohibited by the bill are already prohibited under existing law. Once a report is requested for a bill, a standing committee may not vote on the bill and the house of origin may not pass the bill before the joint committee submits its report or before the 30th day after the request is made, whichever is earlier. The joint committee includes one majority and one minority party member from each house of the legislature; the members from the majority party serve as cochairs. The attorney general, secretary of corrections, and state public defender serve ex officio. The supreme court appoints one reserve judge residing somewhere within judicial administrative districts 1 to 5 and another residing within districts 7 to 10. The governor appoints two public members—an individual with law enforcement experience and an elected county official.

Joint Committee on Employment Relations

Senators: Roth, *cochair*; Fitzgerald, Darling; Shilling, *ranking minority member*
Representatives: Vos, *cochair*; Steineke, Nygren; Hintz, *ranking minority member*
Contact: Legislative Council Staff, 608-266-1304; 1 East Main Street, Suite 401, Madison, WI 53703-3382

The Joint Committee on Employment Relations approves all changes to the collective bargaining agreements that cover state employees represented by unions, and the compensation plans for nonrepresented state employees. These plans and agreements include pay adjustments; fringe benefits; performance awards; pay equity adjustments; and other items related to wages, hours, and conditions of employment. The committee also approves the assignment of certain unclassified positions to the executive salary group ranges. The Division of Personnel Management in the Department of Administration submits the compensation plans for nonrepresented employees to the committee. One plan covers all nonrepresented classified employees and certain officials outside the classified service, including legislators, justices of the supreme court, court of appeals judges, circuit court judges, constitutional officers, district attorneys, heads of executive agencies, division administrators, and others designated by law. The faculty and academic staff of the University of Wisconsin System are covered by a separate compensation plan, which is based on recommendations made by the University of Wisconsin Board of Regents. After public hearings on the nonrepresented employee plans, the committee may modify the plans, but the committee's modifications may be disapproved by the governor. The committee may set aside the governor's disapproval by a vote of six committee members. In

GREG ANDERSON, LEGISLATIVE PHOTOGRAPHER

Senator Lena Taylor (*left*) and Senate President Roger Roth, on different sides of the aisle politically, share a laugh before serious debate begins in the senate.

the case of unionized employees, the Division of Personnel Management or, for University of Wisconsin bargaining units, the Board of Regents or the University of Wisconsin-Madison, submits tentative agreements negotiated between it and certified labor organizations to the committee. If the committee disapproves an agreement, it is returned to the bargaining parties for renegotiation. When the committee approves an agreement for unionized employees, it introduces those portions requiring legislative approval in bill form and recommends passage without change. If the legislature fails to pass the bill, the agreement is returned to the bargaining parties for renegotiation. The committee is composed of eight members: the presiding officers of each house; the majority and minority leaders of each house; and the cochairs of the Joint Committee on Finance. It is assisted in its work by the Legislative Council Staff and the Legislative Fiscal Bureau.

Joint Committee on Finance

Senators: Darling, *cochair*; Olsen, *vice chair*; Tiffany, Marklein, Stroebel, LeMahieu; Erpenbach, *ranking minority member*; Johnson

Representatives: Nygren, *cochair*; Loudenbeck, *vice chair*; Born, Rohrkaste, Katsma, Zimmerman; C. Taylor, *ranking minority member*; Goyke

Senator Darling: Sen.Darling@legis.wisconsin.gov; 608-266-5830; Room 317 East, State Capitol, PO Box 7882, Madison, WI 53707-7882

Representative Nygren: Rep.Nygren@legis.wisconsin.gov; 608-266-2343; Room 309 East, State Capitol, PO Box 8953, Madison, WI 53708-8953

The Joint Committee on Finance examines legislation that deals with state income and spending. The committee also gives final approval to a wide variety of state payments and assessments. Any bill introduced in the legislature that appropriates money, provides for revenue, or relates to taxation must be referred to the committee. The committee introduces the biennial budget as recommended by the governor. After holding a series of public hearings and executive sessions, it submits its own version of the budget as a substitute amendment to the governor's budget bill for consideration by the legislature. At regularly scheduled quarterly meetings, the committee considers agency requests to adjust their budgets. It may approve a request for emergency funds if it finds that the legislature has authorized the activities for which the appropriation is sought. It may also transfer funds between existing appropriations and change the number of positions authorized to an agency in the budget process. When required, the committee introduces

Freshman Representative Greta Neubauer (*left*) of Racine chats with Milwaukee Representative Evan Goyke, who began his legislative career three sessions ago.

GREG ANDERSON, LEGISLATIVE PHOTOGRAPHER

legislation to pay claims against the state, resolve shortages in funds, and restore capital reserve funds of the Wisconsin Housing and Economic Development Authority to the required level. As an emergency measure, it may reduce certain state agency appropriations when there is a decrease in state revenues. The committee is composed of the eight senators on the Senate Finance Committee and the eight representatives on the Assembly Finance Committee. It includes members of the majority and minority party in each house. The cochairs are appointed in the same manner as are the chairs of standing committees in their respective houses.

Joint Committee on Information Policy and Technology

Senators: Jacque, *cochair*; Testin, Kooyenga; Carpenter, *ranking minority member*; Erpenbach

Representatives: Knodl, *cochair*; Loudenbeck, Brandtjen; Sargent, *ranking minority member*; Stuck

Senator Jacque: Sen.Jacque@legis.wisconsin.gov; 608-266-3512; Room 7 South, State Capitol, PO Box 7882, Madison, WI 53707-7882

Representative Knodl: Rep.Knodl@legis.wisconsin.gov; 608-266-3796; Room 218 North, State Capitol, PO Box 8952, Madison, WI 53708-8952

The Joint Committee on Information Policy and Technology reviews information management practices and technology systems of state and local units of government to ensure economic and efficient service, maintain data security and integrity, and protect the privacy of individuals who are subjects of the databases. It studies the effects of proposals by the state to expand existing information technology or implement new technologies. With the concurrence of the Joint Committee on Finance, it may direct the Department of Administration to report on any information technology system project that could cost $1 million or more in the current or succeeding biennium. The committee may direct the Department of Administration to prepare reports or conduct studies and may make recommendations to the governor, the

Senate President Pro Tempore Howard Marklein (*left*) of Spring Green confers with Senator Dewey Stroebel of Saukville during the February 2019 floorperiod.

JOE KOSHOLLEK, LEGISLATIVE PHOTOGRAPHER

legislature, state agencies, or local governments based on this information. The University of Wisconsin Board of Regents is required to submit a report to the committee semiannually, detailing each information technology project in the University of Wisconsin System costing more than $1 million or deemed "high-risk" by the board. The committee may make recommendations on the identified projects to the governor and the legislature. The committee is composed of three majority and two minority party members from each house of the legislature.

Joint Legislative Audit Committee

Senators: Cowles, *cochair*; Darling (cochair, Joint Committee on Finance), Kapenga; Bewley, *ranking minority member*; Carpenter

Representatives: Kerkman, *cochair*; Macco, Nygren (cochair, Joint Committee on Finance); Sargent, *ranking minority member*; Shankland

Senator Cowles: Sen.Cowles@legis.wisconsin.gov; 608-266-0484; Room 118 South, State Capitol, PO Box 7882, Madison, WI 53707-7882

Representative Kerkman: Rep.Kerkman@legis.wisconsin.gov; 608-266-2530; Room 315 North, State Capitol, PO Box 8952, Madison, WI 53708-8952

The Joint Legislative Audit Committee advises the Legislative Audit Bureau, subject to general supervision of the Joint Committee on Legislative Organization. The committee is composed of the cochairs of the Joint Committee on Finance, plus two majority and two minority party members from each house of the legislature. The committee evaluates candidates for the office of state auditor and makes recommendations to the Joint Committee on Legislative Organization, which selects the auditor. The committee may direct the state auditor to undertake specific audits and review requests for special audits from individual legislators or standing committees, but no legislator or standing committee may interfere with the auditor in the conduct of an audit. The committee reviews each report of the Legislative Audit Bureau and then confers with the state auditor, other legislative committees, and the audited agencies on the report's findings. It may propose corrective action and direct that follow-up reports be submitted to it. The committee may hold hearings on audit reports, request the Joint Committee on Legislative Organization to investigate any matter within the scope of the audit, and request investigation of any matter relative to the fiscal and performance responsibilities of a state agency. If an audit report cites financial deficiencies, the head of the agency must report to the Joint Legislative Audit Committee on remedial actions taken. Should the agency head fail to report, the committee may refer the matter to the Joint Committee on Legislative Organization and the appropriate standing committees. When the committee determines that legislative action is needed, it may refer the necessary information to the legislature or a standing committee. It can also request information from a committee on action taken or seek advice

Representatives Katrina Shankland (*left*) and JoCasta Zamarripa have been colleagues in the Assembly for four sessions. Together they applaud a guest at the February budget address.

of a standing committee on program portions of an audit. The committee may introduce legislation to address issues covered in audit reports.

Joint Legislative Council

Senators: Roth (senate president) *cochair*; Fitzgerald (majority leader), Darling (cochair, Joint Committee on Finance), Marklein (president pro tempore), Petrowski, Olsen, Jacque; Shilling (minority leader), *ranking minority member*; Erpenbach (ranking minority member, Joint Committee on Finance), Risser, Miller

Representatives: Brooks, *cochair*; Vos (assembly speaker), Steineke (majority leader), August (speaker pro tempore), Nygren (cochair, Joint Committee on Finance), Ballweg, Spiros; Hintz (minority leader), *ranking minority member*; Hesselbein, Billings, C. Taylor

Legislative Council Staff: Anne Sappenfield, *director*; Jessica Karls-Ruplinger, *deputy director*; Scott Grosz, *rules clearinghouse director*; Margit Kelley, *rules clearinghouse assistant director*

Contact: leg.council@legis.wisconsin.gov; 608-266-1304; 1 East Main Street, Suite 401, Madison, WI 53703-3382

Website: http://lc.legis.wisconsin.gov

Publications: *General Report of the Joint Legislative Council to the Legislature*; *State Agency Staff with Responsibilities to the Legislature*; *Wisconsin Legislator Briefing Book*; *Directory of Joint Legislative Council Committees*; *Comparative Retirement Study*; *A Citizen's Guide to Participation in the Wisconsin State Legislature*; rules clearinghouse reports; staff briefs; information memoranda on substantive issues considered by council committees; staff memoranda; amendment and act memoranda.

Number of employees: 34.17

Total budget 2017–19: $7,955,500

The Joint Legislative Council creates special committees made up of legislators and members of the public to study various problems of state and local government. Study topics are selected from requests presented to the council by law, joint resolution, and individual legislators. After research, expert testimony, and public hearings, the study committees draft proposals and submit them to the council, which must approve those drafts it wants introduced in the legislature as council bills. The council is assisted in its work by the Legislative Council Staff. The staff provides legal and research assistance to all of the legislature's substantive standing committees and joint statutory committees (except the Joint Committee on Finance) and assists individual legislators on request. The staff operates the rules clearinghouse to review proposed administrative rules and assists standing committees in their oversight of rulemaking. The staff also assists the legislature in identifying and responding to issues relating to the Wisconsin Retirement System. By law, the Legislative Council Staff must be strictly nonpartisan and must observe the confidential nature of the research and drafting requests it receives. The law requires that state agencies and local governmental units cooperate fully with the council staff in its carrying out of its statutory duties. The Joint Committee on Legislative Organization appoints the director of the Legislative Council Staff from outside the classified service. The director appoints the other staff members from outside the classified service. The council consists of 22 legislators. The majority of them serve ex officio, and the remainder are appointed in the same manner as members of standing committees. The president of the senate and the speaker of the assembly serve as cochairs, but each may designate another member to serve as cochair and each may decline to serve on the council. The council operates two permanent statutory committees and various special committees appointed to study selected subjects.

PERMANENT COMMITTEES OF THE COUNCIL

Special Committee on State-Tribal Relations Representative Mursau, *chair*; Senator Vinehout, *vice chair*; Senators Bewley, Carpenter, Petrowski, L. Taylor; Representatives Considine, Edming; Dee Ann Allen (Lac du Flambeau Band of Lake Superior Chippewa Indians), Gary Besaw (Menominee Indian Tribe of Wisconsin), Wilfrid Cleveland (Ho-Chunk Nation), Ned Daniels, Jr. (Forest County Potawatomi Community), Michael Decorah (St. Croix Chippewa Indians of Wisconsin), Shannon Holsey (Stockbridge-Munsee Community), Chris McGeshick (Sokaogon Chippewa Community), Richard Peterson (Red Cliff Band of Lake Superior Chippewa Indians), Lisa Summers (Oneida Nation), Jason Weaver (Lac Courte Oreilles Tribal Governing Board)

State-Tribal Relations Technical Advisory Committee Tom Bellavia (Department of

Justice), Kelly Jackson (Department of Transportation), David O'Connor (Department of Public Instruction), Michele Allness (Department of Natural Resources), Andrew Evenson (Department of Workforce Development), Thomas Ourada (Department of Revenue), Gail Nahwahquaw (Department of Health Services), Stephanie Lozano (Department of Children and Families)

The Special Committee on State-Tribal Relations is appointed by the Joint Legislative Council each biennium to study issues related to American Indians and the Indian tribes and bands in this state and develop specific recommendations and legislative proposals relating to such issues. Legislative membership includes not fewer than six nor more than 12 members with at least one member of the majority and the minority party from each house. The council appoints no fewer than six and no more than 11 members from names submitted by federally recognized Wisconsin Indian tribes or bands or the Great Lakes Inter-Tribal Council. The council may not appoint more than one member recommended by any one tribe or band or the Great Lakes Inter-Tribal Council. The Technical Advisory Committee, consisting of representatives of eight major executive agencies, assists the Special Committee on State-Tribal Relations.

Law Revision Committee Senators Wanggaard, *cochair,* LeMahieu, Risser, L.Taylor; Representatives Ott, *cochair,* August, Riemer, Wachs

The Law Revision Committee is appointed each biennium by the Joint Legislative Council. The membership of the committee is not specified, but it must include majority and minority party representation from each house. The committee reviews minor, remedial changes to the statutes as proposed by state agencies and reviews opinions of the attorney general and court decisions declaring a Wisconsin statute unconstitutional, ambiguous, or otherwise in need of revision. It considers proposals by the Legislative Reference Bureau to correct statutory language and session laws that conflict or need revision, and it may submit recommendations for major law revision projects to the Joint Legislative Council. It also serves as the repository for interstate compacts and agreements and makes recommendations to the legislature regarding revision of such agreements.

SPECIAL COMMITTEES OF THE COUNCIL REPORTING IN 2018

Legislative Council Study Committee on Alcohol Beverage Enforcement

Representative Swearingen *chair*; Senator Feyen, *vice chair*; Senator Johnson; Representative Zamarripa, Joe Bartolotta, Sarah Botham, Angie Bowe, Andrew Bowman, William Glass, Evan Hughes, Roger Johnson, Paul Lucas, John Macy, Pete Madland, Mike Wittenwyler

The study committee is directed to review the structure and staffing of the Department of Revenue's efforts to enforce Wisconsin's alcohol beverage laws found in ch. 125, Stats., and compare the regulatory and enforcement structure of alcohol law enforcement efforts in other states. The committee shall further examine whether establishments and venues that serve alcohol are properly licensed to do so. The committee may recommend legislation that ensures the proper enforcement of alcohol beverage laws, including increased clarity and education.

Legislative Council Study Committee on Bail and Conditions of Pretrial Release Senator Wanggaard, *chair*; Senator Risser, *vice chair*; Representatives Duchow, Tusler; Jennifer Dorow, Adam Gerol, Scott Horne, Gary King, Jane Klekamp, Joseph McCleer, Paul Susienka, Kelli Thompson, Maxine White

The study committee is directed to review Wisconsin's pretrial release system, including considerations for courts in imposing monetary bail and for denying pretrial release. The committee shall review relevant Wisconsin constitutional and statutory provisions and best practices implemented by Wisconsin counties and other states, including use of risk assessment tools for informing pretrial detention decisions. The committee is directed to recommend legislation regarding bail and pretrial release that enhances public safety, respects constitutional rights of the accused, considers costs to local governments, and incorporates evidence-based strategies.

Legislative Council Study Committee on Child Placement and Support Representative R. Brooks, *chair*; Senator L. Taylor, *vice chair*; Senator Kapenga; Representatives Brandtjen, Stuck; Maureen Atwell, Tony Bickel, Mark Fremgen, Jenna Gormal, Tiffany Highstrom, Benjamin Kain, Jim Sullivan, Thomas Walsh

The study committee is directed to review the standards under current law for determining periods of physical placement and child support obligations. The committee may consider alternatives to current law concerning physical placement, including a rebuttable presumption that equal placement is in the child's best interest. The committee may also consider whether the current standard for determining child support adequately and equitably provides for the support of children and alternative models for determining child support obligations.

Legislative Council Study Committee on Direct Primary Care Senator Darling, *chair*; Representative Nygren, *vice chair*; Senators Johnson, Tiffany; Representatives Felzkowski, Kolste; Greg Banaszynski, Coreen Dicus-Johnson, Suzanne Gehl, Maureen McNally, Dr. Tim Murray, Mark Rakowski, Elizabeth Trowbridge, Bob Van Meeteren

The study committee is directed to review the emergence of "direct primary care" as a healthcare delivery option and assess its potential impact on the healthcare delivery system and health outcomes in the state. The committee shall recommend legislation regarding requirements for direct primary care arrangements in the private market. In addition, the committee is directed to review options for incorporation of direct primary care arrangements into the fee-for-service and managed-care parts of the Medical Assistance (MA) program and assess

GREG ANDERSON, LEGISLATIVE PHOTOGRAPHER

Wisconsin is home to the longest-serving state legislator in the country, as well as one of the youngest state legislators in the nation; Senator Fred Risser (*left*) has more than 60 years of experience, and Representative Kalan Haywood just began his legislative career.

its potential impact on the functionality, efficiency, and effectiveness of service delivery and health outcomes in both parts of the MA program. The committee shall recommend legislation regarding a direct primary care pilot in the MA program, including an evaluation of the impact of the pilot on service delivery and health outcomes for participating individuals and the MA program as a whole.

Legislative Council Study Committee on Minor Guardianships Representative Steineke, *chair*; Senator Johnson, *vice chair*; Representatives Kolste, Tittl; Susan Conwell, Megan DeVore, Henry Plum, Theresa Roetter, Michael Rosborough, Carrie Schneider, Gretchen Viney

The study committee is directed to examine ch. 54, Stats., concerning guardianship of minors and adults, and recommend legislation that creates procedures

JOE KOSHOLLEK, LEGISLATIVE PHOTOGRAPHER

Senator Janis Ringhand (*left*) and Representative Mark Spreitzer work together for the residents of South Central Wisconsin in both houses of the legislature. Senator Ringhand represents the larger population of over 172,000 people across five counties, while Representative Spreitzer's more than 57,000 constituents are concentrated in the areas around Beloit, Brodhead, and Evansville.

specific to guardianship of a minor. The committee may consider whether any new provisions should apply to guardianship of a minor's person, estate, or both.

Legislative Council Study Committee on Property Tax Assessment Practices

Senator Olsen, *chair*; Representative Allen, *vice chair*; Senators Cowles, Ringhand; Representatives Considine, Gundrum; Ed Catani, Jeff Hoffman, Don Millis, Jeff Nooyen, Amy Seibel, Rocco Vita

The study committee is directed to review current property tax assessment practices, including the review of statutory, administrative, and judicial directives on assessment practices and the consistency of assessment practices throughout the state. Following its review, the committee shall recommend legislation to revise and clarify property tax assessment practices, including recommendations regarding the role of comparable sales and market segments in assessments and the assessment of leased property.

Legislative Council Study Committee on the Identification and Management of Dyslexia

Representative Kulp, *chair*; Senator Schachtner, *vice chair*; Senator Tiffany; Representatives Rohrkaste, Stuck; Nancy Dressel, Steven Dykstra, Donna S. Hejtmanek, Ann Malone, Brenda Warren, Michael Weber

The study committee is directed to review current screening, identification, school intervention, and treatment protocols for dyslexia in K-12 schools; to examine the effects of current state statutes and regulations on literacy outcomes for students with dyslexia; and to evaluate the effects of dyslexia on literacy outcomes in the state. The committee shall study recent research on evidence-based instructional techniques for students with dyslexia; determine the components and costs of successful dyslexia education practices and laws in other states; and identify institutional obstacles to academic attainment for these students. The committee shall consider legislation to implement screening for characteristics of dyslexia in early grades; to ensure that reading instruction and intervention practices incorporate relevant research findings from the University of Wisconsin; to improve the partnership between parents, educators, counselors, and others on early identification and effective interventions for dyslexic learners; and to enhance statewide access to updated resources and training on dyslexic education.

Legislative Council Study Committee on the Investment and Use of the School Trust Funds Representative Katsma, *chair*; Senator L. Taylor, *vice chair*; Senator Stroebel; Representatives Vruwink; Kim Bannigan, Jerry Derr, Stephen Eager, Don Merkes, Steve O'Malley

The study committee is directed to review the statutes governing the investment of the trust funds administered by the Board of Commissioners of Public Lands (BCPL), including the loan programs administered by BCPL. The Study Committee shall assess whether current statutes adequately ensure the effective investment and appropriate use of the proceeds of the funds, and recommend legislation for necessary changes.

Legislative Council Study Committee on the Use of Police Body Cameras Senator Testin, *chair*; Representative C. Taylor, *vice chair*; Senator Larson; Representative Spiros; Kevin Croninger, Catherine Dorl, James Friedman, Ben Hart, Mike Kass, Jeff Klatt

The study committee is directed to review law enforcement policies regarding the use of body cameras and recommend legislation to establish uniform procedures regarding the retention and release of body camera video for state and local law enforcement agencies.

Joint Committee on Legislative Organization

Senators: Roth (senate president), *cochair*; Fitzgerald (majority leader), Feyen (assistant majority leader); Shilling (minority leader), Bewley (assistant minority leader)

Representatives: Vos (assembly speaker), *cochair*; Steineke (majority leader), Felzkowski (assistant majority leader); Hintz (minority leader), Hesselbein (assistant minority leader)

Contact: Legislative Council Staff, 608-266-1304; 1 East Main Street, Suite 401, Madison, WI 53703-3382

The Joint Committee on Legislative Organization is the policy-making body for the Legislative Audit Bureau, the Legislative Fiscal Bureau, the Legislative Reference Bureau, and the Legislative Technology Services Bureau. In this capacity, it assigns tasks to each bureau, approves bureau budgets, and sets the salary of bureau heads. The committee selects the four bureau heads, but it acts on the recommendation of the Joint Legislative Audit Committee when appointing the state auditor. The committee also selects the director of the Legislative Council Staff. The committee may inquire into misconduct by members and employees of the legislature. It oversees a variety of operations, including the work schedule for the legislative session, computer use, space allocation for legislative offices and legislative service agencies, parking on the State Capitol Park grounds, and sale and distribution of legislative documents. The committee recommends which newspaper should serve as the official state newspaper for publication of state legal notices. It advises the Elections Commission on its operations and, upon recommendation of the Joint Legislative Audit Committee, may investigate any problems the Legislative Audit Bureau finds during its audits. The committee may employ outside consultants to study ways to improve legislative staff services and organization. The ten-member committee consists of the presiding officers and party leadership of both houses. The committee has established a Subcommittee on Legislative Services to advise it on matters pertaining to the legislative institution, including the review of computer technology purchases. The Legislative Council Staff provides staff assistance to the committee.

Joint Survey Committee on Retirement Systems

Senators: Bernier, *cochair*; LeMahieu; Erpenbach
Representatives: Felzkowski, *cochair*; Kuglitsch; Hintz
Other members: Charlotte Gibson (assistant attorney general appointed by attorney general), Robert J. Conlin (secretary of employee trust funds), Mark V. Afable (insurance commissioner), Tim Pederson (public member appointed by governor)
Contact: Legislative Council Staff, 608-266-1304; 1 East Main Street, Suite 401, Madison, WI 53703-3382

The Joint Survey Committee on Retirement Systems makes recommendations on legislation that affects retirement and pension plans for public officers and employees, and its recommendations must be attached as an appendix to each retirement bill. Neither house of the legislature may consider such a bill until the committee submits a written report that describes the proposal's purpose, probable costs, actuarial effect, and desirability as a matter of public policy. The ten-member committee includes two majority party members and one minority party member from each house of the legislature. An experienced actuary from the Office of the Commissioner of Insurance may be designated to serve in the

The Joint Legislative Audit Committee can direct the state auditor to perform specific audits on state agencies, and it can hold hearings on audit reports. Senator Chris Kapenga (*right*) speaks during a public hearing in February. Senator Alberta Darling (*background*) as the co-chair of the Joint Committee on Finance, is an ex officio member.

commissioner's place on the committee. The public member cannot be a participant in any public retirement system in the state and is expected to "represent the interests of the taxpayers." Appointed members serve four-year terms unless they lose the status upon which the appointment was based. The committee is assisted by the Legislative Council Staff in the performance of its duties, but may contract for actuarial assistance outside the classified service.

Joint Survey Committee on Tax Exemptions

Senators: Kooyenga, *cochair*; Tiffany; Larson
Representatives: August, *cochair*; Swearingen; Riemer
Other members: Peter Barca (secretary of revenue), Paul Connell (Department of Justice representative appointed by attorney general), Kimberly Shaul (public member appointed by governor)
Contact: Legislative Council Staff, 608-266-1304; 1 East Main Street, Suite 401, Madison, WI 53703-3382

The Joint Survey Committee on Tax Exemptions considers all legislation related to the exemption of persons or property from state or local taxes. It is assisted by the Legislative Council Staff. Any legislative proposal that provides a tax exemption must be referred to the committee immediately upon introduction. Neither house of the legislature may consider the proposal until the committee has issued its report, attached as an appendix to the bill, describing the proposal's legality, desirability as public policy, and fiscal effect. In the course of its review, the committee is authorized to conduct investigations, hold hearings, and subpoena witnesses. For an executive budget bill that provides a tax exemption, the committee must prepare its report within 60 days. The committee includes two majority party members and one minority party member from each house of the legislature. The public member must be familiar with the tax problems of local government. Members' terms expire on January 15 of odd-numbered years.

Transportation Projects Commission

Governor: Tony Evers, *chair*
Senators: Cowles, Marklein, Petrowski; Carpenter, Hansen
Representatives: Krug, Spiros, 1 vacancy; Spreitzer, Riemer
Other members: Jean Jacobson, Barbara Fleisner LaMue (citizen members appointed by governor)
Nonvoting members: Craig Thompson (secretary of transportation)
Commission secretary: Craig Thompson
Contact: bshp.dtim@dot.wi.gov; 608-267-9617; Bureau of State Highway Programs, 4822 Madison Yards Way, 6th Floor South, Madison, WI 53705

The Transportation Projects Commission includes three majority party and two minority party members from each house of the legislature. The commission reviews Department of Transportation recommendations for major highway projects. The department must report its recommendations to the commission by September 15 of each even-numbered year, and the commission, in turn, reports its recommendations to the governor or governor-elect, the legislature, and the Joint Committee on Finance before December 15 of each even-numbered year. The department must also provide the commission with a status report on major transportation projects every six months. The commission also approves the preparation of environmental impact or assessment statements for potential major highway projects.

Commission on Uniform State Laws

Members: Joanne Huelsman (former state senator), *chair*; Aaron Gary (designated by Legislative Reference Bureau chief), *secretary*; Senator Risser; Representatives Hebl, Tusler; Margit Kelley (designated by Legislative Council Staff director); David Zvenyach, Justice Annette Kingsland Ziegler (public members appointed by governor); David Cullen (former state representative), Justice David T. Prosser, Jr. (ULC life members appointed by commission)
Contact: aaron.gary@legis.wisconsin.gov; 608-504-5850; 1 East Main Street, Suite 200, Madison, WI 53701-2037

The Commission on Uniform State Laws examines subjects on which interstate uniformity is desirable, cooperates with the national Uniform Law Commission, and advises the legislature on uniform laws and model laws. The commission consists of four current or former legislators, two public members, and two

Collegiality among the different parties and houses of the legislature is a key element of the functioning of government. Representative Chris Taylor (*left*) shares a moment with her former colleague in the assembly, Senator Dale Kooyenga (*right*).

members representing legislative service agencies. The commission may also appoint as members individuals who have attained the status of Life Members of the national Uniform Law Commission.

Legislative service agencies

Legislative Audit Bureau

State auditor: Joe Chrisman
Deputy state auditor for performance evaluation: Paul Stuiber
Audit directors: Kendra Eppler, Sherry Haakenson, Erin Scharlau, Carolyn Stittleburg, Dean Swenson
Contact: AskLAB@legis.wisconsin.gov; 608-266-2818; 877-FRAUD-17 (fraud, waste, and mismanagement hotline); 22 East Mifflin Street, Suite 500, Madison, WI 53703-2512
Website: http://legis.wisconsin.gov/lab
Publications: Audit reports of individual state agencies and programs; biennial reports.
Number of employees: 86.80
Total budget 2017–19: $17,223,300

The Legislative Audit Bureau is responsible for conducting financial and program audits to assist the legislature in its oversight function. The bureau performs financial audits to determine whether agencies have conducted and reported their financial transactions legally and properly. It undertakes program audits to analyze whether agencies have managed their programs efficiently and effectively and have carried out the policies prescribed by law. The bureau's authority extends to executive, legislative, and judicial agencies; authorities created by the legislature; special districts; and certain service providers that receive state funds. The bureau may audit any county, city, village, town, or school district at the request of the Joint Legislative Audit Committee. The bureau provides an annual audit opinion on the state's comprehensive financial statements by the Department of Administration and prepares audits and reports on the financial transactions and records of state agencies at the state auditor's discretion or at the direction of the Joint Legislative Audit Committee. The bureau maintains a toll-free number to receive reports of fraud, waste, and mismanagement in state government. Typically, the bureau's program audits are conducted at the request of the Joint Legislative Audit Committee, initiated by the state auditor, or required by legislation. The reports are reviewed by the Joint Legislative Audit Committee, which may hold hearings on them and may introduce legislation in response to audit recommendations. The director of the bureau is the state auditor, who is appointed by the Joint Committee on Legislative Organization upon the recommendation of the Joint Legislative Audit Committee. Both the state auditor and the bureau's staff are appointed from outside the classified service and are strictly nonpartisan.

STATUTORY ADVISORY COUNCIL

Municipal Best Practices Reviews Advisory Council Steve O'Malley, Adam Payne (representing the Wisconsin Counties Association); Mark Rohloff (representing the League

Senate Assistant Majority Leader Dan Feyen (*left*), elected in 2016, speaks with Democratic Senator Robert Wirch, who has been a member of that body since 1996.

GREG ANDERSON, LEGISLATIVE PHOTOGRAPHER

of Wisconsin Municipalities); Richard Nawrocki (representing the Wisconsin Towns Association). (All are appointed by the state auditor.)

The Municipal Best Practices Reviews Advisory Council advises the state auditor on the selection of county and municipal service delivery practices to be reviewed by the state auditor. The state auditor conducts periodic reviews of procedures and practices used by local governments in the delivery of governmental services; identifies variations in costs and effectiveness of such services between counties and municipalities; and recommends practices to save money or provide more effective service delivery. Council members are chosen from candidates submitted by the organizations represented.

Legislative Council Staff

Director: Anne Sappenfield
Deputy director: Jessica Karls-Ruplinger
Rules clearinghouse director: Scott Grosz
Rules clearinghouse assistant director: Margit Kelley
Contact: leg.council@legis.wisconsin.gov; 608-266-1304; 1 East Main Street, Suite 401, Madison, WI 53703-3382
Website: http://lc.legis.wisconsin.gov

See the entry for the Joint Legislative Council, beginning on page 157.

Legislative Fiscal Bureau

Director: Robert Wm. Lang
Assistant director: David Loppnow
Program supervisors: Jere Bauer, Paul Ferguson, Charles Morgan, Sean Moran, Al Runde
Supervising analysts: Jon Dyck, Rachel Janke
Administrative assistant: Becky Hannah
Supervising program assistant: Sandy Swain
Contact: fiscal.bureau@legis.wisconsin.gov; 608-266-3847; 1 East Main Street, Suite 301, Madison, WI 53703
Website: http://legis.wisconsin.gov/lfb
Publications: Biennial budget and budget adjustment summaries; summaries of state agency budget requests; cumulative and comparative summaries of the governor's proposals, Joint Committee on Finance provisions and legislative amendments, and separate summaries of legislative amendments when necessary; summary of governor's partial vetoes. Informational reports on various state programs, budget issue papers, and revenue estimates. (Reports and papers available on the Internet and upon request.)
Number of employees: 35.00
Total budget 2017–19: $7,984,800

The Legislative Fiscal Bureau develops fiscal information for the legislature, and its services must be impartial and nonpartisan. One of the bureau's principal duties is to staff the Joint Committee on Finance and assist its members. As part of this responsibility, the bureau studies the state budget and its long-range implications, reviews state revenues and expenditures, suggests alternatives to the committee and the legislature, and prepares a report detailing earmarks in the budget bill. In addition, the bureau provides information on all other bills before the committee and analyzes agency requests for new positions and appropriation supplements outside of the budget process. The bureau provides fiscal information to any legislative committee or legislator upon request. On its own initiative, or at legislative direction, the bureau may conduct studies of any financial issue affecting the state. To aid the bureau in performing its duties, the director or designated employees are granted access to all state departments and to any records maintained by the agencies relating to their expenditures, revenues, operations, and structure. The Joint Committee on Legislative Organization is the policy-making body for the Legislative Fiscal Bureau, and it selects the bureau's director. The director is assisted by program supervisors responsible for broadly defined subject areas of government budgeting and fiscal operations. The director and all bureau staff are chosen outside the classified service.

Legislative Reference Bureau

Chief: Richard A. Champagne
Deputy chief: Cathlene M. Hanaman
Legal services manager: Joe Kreye
Administrative services manager: Wendy L. Jackson
Contact: 608-266-3561 (legal); 608-266-0341 (research and analysis); 1 East Main Street, Suite 200, Madison; PO Box 2037, Madison, WI 53701-2037
Website: http://legis.wisconsin.gov/lrb
Publications: Wisconsin Statutes; Laws of Wisconsin; Wisconsin Administrative Code and Register; *Wisconsin Blue Book*; informational, legal, and research reports.
Number of employees: 60.00
Total budget 2017–19: $11,947,900

The Legislative Reference Bureau provides nonpartisan, confidential bill drafting and other legal services to the Wisconsin Legislature. The bureau employs a staff of attorneys and editors who serve the legislature and its members and who draft and prepare all legislation, including the executive budget bill, for introduction in the legislature. Bureau attorneys also draft legislation at the request of state agencies. The bureau publishes all laws enacted during each biennial legislative session and incorporates the laws into the Wisconsin Statutes. The bureau prints the Wisconsin Statutes every two years and updates continuously the Wisconsin Statutes on the Wisconsin Legislature's Internet site. The bureau publishes and updates the Wisconsin Administrative Code and the Wisconsin Administrative Register on the Internet site. The Legislative Reference Bureau employs research

Coordination between both houses of the legislature is crucial to keeping proposals on track. Senator Van Wanggaard (*center*) speaks to Representatives Evan Goyke (*left*) and Michael Schraa (*right*) during a particularly busy floorperiod in 2018.

analysts who provide research and analysis services to the legislature. Bureau analysts and librarians also provide information services to the legislature and the public. The bureau publishes the *Wisconsin Blue Book* and informational, legal, and research reports. The bureau responds to inquiries from legislators, legislative staff, and the public on current law and pending legislation and the operations of the legislature and state government. The bureau operates a legislative library that contains an extensive collection of materials pertaining to Wisconsin government and politics. The bureau compiles and publishes the Assembly Rules, Senate Rules, and Joint Rules. The bureau maintains for public inspection the drafting records of all legislation introduced in the Wisconsin Legislature, beginning with the 1927 session. The Joint Committee on Legislative Organization is the policy-making body for the Legislative Reference Bureau, and it selects the bureau chief. The chief employs all bureau staff. The chief and the bureau staff serve outside the classified service.

Legislative Technology Services Bureau

Director: Jeff Ylvisaker
Deputy director: Nate Rohan
Enterprise operations manager: Matt Harned
Geographic information systems manager: Tony Van Der Wielen
Software development manager: Doug DeMuth
Technical services team lead: Cade Gentry
Contact: 608-264-8582; 17 West Main Street, Suite 200, Madison, WI 53703
Website: http://legis.wisconsin.gov/ltsb

Number of employees: 43.00
Total budget 2017–19: $8,752,400

The Legislative Technology Services Bureau provides confidential, nonpartisan information technology services and support to the Wisconsin Legislature. The bureau creates, maintains, and enhances specialized software used for bill drafting, floor session activity, and committee activity, managing constituent interactions, producing the Wisconsin Statutes and the Wisconsin Administrative Code, and publishing the *Wisconsin Blue Book*. It supports the publication of legislative documents including bills and amendments, house journals, daily calendars, and the *Bulletin of the Proceedings*. The bureau also maintains network infrastructure, data center operations, electronic communications, desktops, laptops, printers, and other technology devices. It keeps an inventory of computer hardware and software assets and manages technology replacement schedules. It supports the redistricting project following each decennial U.S. Census and provides mapping services throughout the decade. The bureau also supports the legislature during floor sessions, delivers audio and video services, manages the technology for the Wisconsin Legislature's websites, and offers training services for legislators and staff in the use of information technology. The bureau's director is appointed by the Joint Committee on Legislative Organization and has overall management responsibilities for the bureau. The director appoints bureau staff; both the director and the staff serve outside the classified service.

Office of the Governor

Governor: Tony Evers
Chief of staff: Maggie Gau
Location: 115 East, State Capitol, Madison
Contact: EversInfo@wisconsin.gov; 608-266-1212; PO Box 7863, Madison, WI 53707-7863
Website: https://evers.wi.gov
Number of employees: 37.25
Total budget 2017–19: $7,421,400

The governor is the state's chief executive. Voters elect the governor and lieutenant governor on a joint ballot to a four-year term. Most of the individuals, commissions, and boards that head the major executive branch agencies are appointed by, and serve at the pleasure of, the governor, although many of these appointments require senate confirmation. The governor reviews all bills passed by the legislature and can veto an entire bill or veto parts of a bill containing an appropriation. A two-thirds vote of the members present in each house of the legislature is required to override the governor's veto. In addition, the governor can call the legislature into special session to deal with specific legislation.

On April 11, Governor Tony Evers signed Executive Order 19, creating the Committee to Celebrate the Centennial Anniversary of Wisconsin's Ratification of the 19th Amendment. The 19th Amendment affirmed the right of women to vote in state and federal elections. Evers is joined by the women of the legislature, the supreme court, and his cabinet, all of whom are appointed as members of the committee.

GREG ANDERSON, LEGISLATIVE PHOTOGRAPHER

If a vacancy occurs in the state senate or assembly, state law directs the governor to call a special election. Vacancies in elective county offices and judicial positions can be filled by gubernatorial appointment for the unexpired terms or until a successor is elected. The governor may dismiss sheriffs, district attorneys, coroners, and registers of deeds for cause.

Finally, the governor serves as commander in chief of the Wisconsin National Guard when it is called into state service during emergencies, such as natural disasters and civil disturbances.

Subordinate statutory boards, councils, and committees

STATE COUNCIL ON ALCOHOL AND OTHER DRUG ABUSE

The State Council on Alcohol and Other Drug Abuse coordinates and reviews the efforts of state agencies to control and prevent alcohol and drug abuse. It evaluates program effectiveness, recommends improved programming, educates people about the dangers of drug abuse, and allocates responsibility for various alcohol and drug abuse programs among state agencies. The council also reviews and provides an opinion to the legislature on proposed legislation that relates to alcohol and other drug abuse policies, programs, or services.

COUNCIL ON MILITARY AND STATE RELATIONS

The Council on Military and State Relations assists the governor by working with the state's military installations, commands and communities, state agencies, and economic development professionals to develop and implement strategies designed to enhance those installations. It advises and assists the governor on issues related to the location of military installations and assists and cooperates with state agencies to determine how those agencies can better serve military communities and families. It also assists the efforts of military families and their support groups regarding quality-of-life issues for service members and their families.

COUNCIL ON VETERANS EMPLOYMENT

The Council on Veterans Employment advises and assists the governor and state agencies with the recruitment and employment of veterans so as to increase veteran employment in state government.

Independent entities attached for administrative purposes

DISABILITY BOARD

Members: Tony Evers (governor), Patience Roggensack (chief justice of the supreme court), Senator Roth (senate president), Senator Shilling (senate minority leader),

Representative Vos (assembly speaker), Representative Hintz (assembly minority leader), Robert Golden (dean, UW Medical School)

The Disability Board is authorized to determine when a temporary vacancy exists in the office of the governor, lieutenant governor, secretary of state, treasurer, state superintendent of public instruction, or attorney general because the incumbent is incapacitated due to illness or injury.

Nongovernmental entities with gubernatorial appointments

WISCONSIN HUMANITIES COUNCIL

Executive director: Dena Wortzel
Contact: contact@wisconsinhumanities.org; 608-262-0706; 3801 Regent Street, Madison, WI 53705
Website: www.wisconsinhumanities.org

The Wisconsin Humanities Council is an independent affiliate of the National Endowment for the Humanities. It is supported by state, federal, and private funding. Its mission is to create and support programs that use history, culture, and discussion to strengthen community life in Wisconsin. The governor appoints six members to the council. Other members are elected by the council.

THE MEDICAL COLLEGE OF WISCONSIN, INC.

President and CEO: John R. Raymond, Sr.
Contact: 414-955-8225; 8701 Watertown Plank Road, Milwaukee, WI 53226
Website: www.mcw.edu
State appropriation 2017–19: $20,304,900

The Medical College of Wisconsin, Inc., is a private nonprofit institution located in Milwaukee that operates a school of medicine, school of pharmacy, and graduate school of biomedical sciences. The college receives state funds for education, training, and research; for its family medicine residency program; and for cancer research. The college is required to fulfill certain reporting requirements concerning its finances, student body, and programs. The governor appoints two members to the board of trustees with the advice and consent of the senate.

Governor's special committees

The committees listed below were created by executive order to conduct studies and provide advice. Members serve at the governor's pleasure. These committees submit final reports to the governor or governor-elect prior to the beginning of a new gubernatorial term and, unless continued by executive order, expire on the fourth Monday of January of the year in which a new gubernatorial term begins.

COUNCIL ON AUTISM

Aligned to: Department of Health Services; 1 West Wilson Street, Madison, WI 53703
Contact: Andrea Jacobson; AndreaL.Jacobson@dhs.wisconsin.gov; 608-261-5998
Website: https://autismcouncil.wisconsin.gov

Created by Governor Jim Doyle in 2005 and continued by Governor Evers, the Council on Autism advises the Department of Health Services on strategies for implementing statewide support and services for children with autism. A majority of its members are parents of children with autism or autism spectrum disorders.

BICYCLE COORDINATING COUNCIL

Aligned to: Department of Transportation; 4822 Madison Yards Way, 6th Floor South,
Madison, WI 53705
Contact: Jill Mrotek Glenzinski; jill.mrotekglenzinski@dot.wi.gov; 608-267-7757

Created by Governor Tommy G. Thompson in 1991 and continued most recently by Governor Evers, the Bicycle Coordinating Council's concerns include encouraging the use of the bicycle as an alternative means of transportation, promoting bicycle safety and education, promoting bicycling as a recreational and tourist activity, and disseminating information about state and federal funding for bicycle programs.

COMMITTEE TO CELEBRATE THE CENTENNIAL ANNIVERSARY OF WISCONSIN'S RATIFICATION OF THE 19TH AMENDMENT

This Committee was created by Governor Evers in April 2019 to educate the public and plan events related to Wisconsin becoming the first state to ratify the 19th Amendment, which granted women in the United States the right to vote.

GOVERNOR'S TASK FORCE ON CAREGIVING

Aligned to: Department of Health Services; 1 West Wilson Street, Madison, WI 53703
Contact: Carrie Molke; carrie.molke@dhs.wisconsin.gov; 608-267-5267

This Task Force was created by Governor Evers in 2019. It is charged with developing solutions and strategies for hiring and retaining a direct care workforce, increasing access to direct care services, developing a registry of home care providers, and supporting families providing such care.

WISCONSIN COASTAL MANAGEMENT COUNCIL

Aligned to: Department of Administration; 101 East Wilson Street, PO Box 8944, Madison,
WI 53708-8944
Contact: Michael Friis; michael.friis@wisconsin.gov; coastal@wisconsin.gov; 608-267-7982
Website: https://doa.wi.gov/Pages/LocalGovtsGrants/CoastalAdvisoryCouncil.aspx

The Wisconsin Coastal Management Council was created by acting Governor Martin J. Schreiber in 1977 to comply with provisions of the federal Coastal Zone

Management Act of 1972 and to implement Wisconsin's Coastal Management Program. It was continued most recently by Governor Evers. The council advises the governor with respect to Wisconsin's coastal management efforts.

CRIMINAL JUSTICE COORDINATING COUNCIL

Aligned to: Department of Justice; 608-266-1221; PO Box 7857, Madison, WI 53707-7857
Website: https://cjcc.doj.wi.gov

Created by Governor Walker in 2012, and continued by Governor Evers, the Criminal Justice Coordinating Council is tasked with assisting the governor in directing, collaborating with, and coordinating the services of state, local, and private actors in the criminal justice system to increase public safety and the system's efficiency and effectiveness. Members of the council represent various aspects of the state's criminal justice system.

GOVERNOR'S COMMITTEE FOR PEOPLE WITH DISABILITIES

Aligned to: Department of Health Services; 1 West Wilson Street, Room 551, Madison, WI 53703
Contact: Maia Stitt; maia.stitt@dhs.wisconsin.gov; 608-266-3118
Website: https://gcpd.wisconsin.gov/

The Governor's Committee for People with Disabilities, in its present form, was established in 1976 by Governor Patrick J. Lucey and has since been continued by each succeeding governor. The committee's functions include advising the governor on a broad range of issues affecting people with disabilities, including involvement in the workforce, reviewing legislation affecting people with disabilities, and promoting public awareness of the needs and abilities of people with disabilities.

EARLY CHILDHOOD ADVISORY COUNCIL

Aligned to: Department of Children and Families; 201 East Washington Avenue, 2nd Floor, PO Box 8916, Madison, WI 53708-8916
Contact: Amanda Reeve; Amanda.Reeve@wisconsin.gov; 608-422-6079
Website: https://dcf.wisconsin.gov/ecac

Governor Jim Doyle created the Early Childhood Advisory Council in 2008 in accordance with federal law, and Governor Evers has continued it. The council advises the governor on the development of a comprehensive statewide early childhood system by, among other things, conducting needs assessments, developing recommendations for increasing participation of children in early childhood services, assessing the capacity of higher education to support the development of early childhood professionals, and making recommendations for the improvement of early learning standards.

EARLY INTERVENTION INTERAGENCY COORDINATING COUNCIL

Aligned to: Department of Health Services; 1 West Wilson Street, Room 418, Madison, WI 53707

Contact: Deborah Rathermel; deborah.rathermel@dhs.wisconsin.gov; 608-266-9366

Website: https://b3icc.wisconsin.gov

First established by Governor Tommy G. Thompson in 1987, re-established by Governor Thompson in 1998, and continued most recently by Governor Evers, the Early Intervention Interagency Coordinating Council was created pursuant to federal law. The council assists the Department of Health Services in the development and administration of early intervention services, referred to as the "Birth to Three Program," for infants and toddlers with developmental delays and their families. The council's members include parents of children with disabilities.

JOINT ENFORCEMENT TASK FORCE ON PAYROLL FRAUD AND WORKER MISCLASSIFICATION

Aligned to: Department of Workforce Development; 201 E. Washington Avenue, Madison; PO Box 7972, Madison, WI 53707-7972

The Joint Enforcement Task Force was created by Governor Evers to coordinate the investigation and enforcement of worker misclassification issues, which can result in underpayment of wages, payroll taxes, unemployment insurance contributions and workers' compensation insurance. The Department of Workforce Development will work with the departments of Revenue, Justice, the Office of the Commissioner of Insurance, and other relevant agencies.

GOVERNOR'S COUNCIL ON FINANCIAL LITERACY

Aligned to: Department of Financial Institutions, Office of Financial Literacy; PO Box 8861, Madison, WI 53708-8861

Contact: David Mancl, *executive director*; david.mancl@dfi.wisconsin.gov; 608-261-9540

Website: www.wdfi.org/ymm/govcouncilfinlit

Created by Governor Jim Doyle in 2005 and continued by Governor Evers, the Governor's Council on Financial Literacy works with state agencies, private entities, and nonprofit associations to improve financial literacy among Wisconsin citizens. The council also promotes the financial literacy awareness and education campaign called Money Smart Week.

GOVERNOR'S HEALTH EQUITY COUNCIL

Aligned to: Department of Health Services; 1 West Wilson Street, Madison, WI 53703

Contact: Jeanne Ayers; jeanne.ayers@dhs.wisconsin.gov; 608-267-7828

This Council was created by Governor Evers in 2019. The council is tasked with developing a plan to reduce and eliminate health disparities in Wisconsin by the year 2030. The plan must address factors such as race, economic status, education, geography and history of incarceration in health disparities.

HISTORICAL RECORDS ADVISORY BOARD

Aligned to: State Historical Society of Wisconsin; 816 State Street, Madison, WI 53706
Contact: Matthew Blessing; matthew.blessing@wisconsinhistory.org; 608-264-6480
Website: https://wisconsinhistory.org/Records/Article/CS3558

Continued most recently by Governor Evers, the Historical Records Advisory Board enables the state to participate in a grant program of the National Historical Publications and Records Commission. The board also promotes the availability and use of historic records as a key to understanding American culture.

HOMELAND SECURITY COUNCIL

Contact: 608-242-3075; 2400 Wright Street, PO Box 14587, Madison, WI 53708-0587
Website: http://hsc.wi.gov

Created by Governor Jim Doyle in 2003 and continued by Governor Evers, the Homeland Security Council advises the governor and coordinates the efforts of state and local officials concerning the prevention of and response to potential threats to the homeland security of Wisconsin.

INDEPENDENT LIVING COUNCIL OF WISCONSIN

Executive director: Mike Bachhuber
Contact: director@ilcw.org; 608-256-9257; 866-656-4010 (toll free); 3810 Milwaukee Street, Madison, WI 53714
Website: www.wis-il.net/council

Governor Tommy G. Thompson created the Independent Living Council of Wisconsin in 1994; Governor Jim Doyle established the council as a nonprofit entity in 2004. Governor Evers has continued it. In coordination with the Division of Vocational Rehabilitation in the Department of Workforce Development, the council maintains the state's plan for independent living services for people with disabilities. The majority of the council's members are persons with disabilities. At least one member must be a director of a center for independent living, and at least one member must represent Native American vocational rehabilitation programs.

GOVERNOR'S INFORMATION TECHNOLOGY EXECUTIVE STEERING COMMITTEE

Aligned to: Department of Administration; 101 East Wilson Street, PO Box 7864, Madison, WI 53707
Contact: Vicky Short; vicky.short@wisconsin.gov

Governor Walker created the Governor's Information Technology Executive Steering Committee in 2013. It is responsible for the effective and efficient application of information technology assets across state agencies.

GOVERNOR'S JUDICIAL SELECTION ADVISORY COMMITTEE

Aligned to: Office of the Governor; Room 115 East, State Capitol, PO Box 7863, Madison, WI 53707-7863

Contact: Ryan Nilsestuen; ryan.nilsestuen1@wisconsin.gov; 608-266-9676

Governor Walker created the Governor's Judicial Selection Advisory Committee in 2011. The committee recommends candidates to the governor to fill judicial vacancies in the state courts.

GOVERNOR'S JUVENILE JUSTICE COMMISSION

Aligned to: Department of Justice; PO Box 7857, Madison, WI 53707-7857

Contact: Allison Budzinski; allison.budzinski@wisconsin.gov

Governor Tommy G. Thompson created the Juvenile Justice Advisory Group in 1989. In 1991, he recreated it as the Governor's Juvenile Justice Commission, which was continued most recently by Governor Evers. The commission distributes federal grant moneys for the improvement of the juvenile justice system in the state. It also advises the governor and the legislature concerning juvenile justice issues.

GOVERNOR'S COUNCIL ON PHYSICAL FITNESS AND HEALTH

Aligned to: Office of the Governor; Room 115 East, State Capitol, PO Box 7863, Madison, WI 53707-7863

Contact: Noah Roberts; noah.roberts@wisconsin.gov; 608-261-2163

Governor Anthony Earl established the Governor's Council on Physical Fitness and Health in 1983, and Governor Walker recreated it in 2012. It was continued by Governor Evers in 2019. The council develops policy recommendations to improve the status of and educate the public concerning children's health, physical fitness, and nutrition. The council also encourages obesity prevention for all state residents.

STATE REHABILITATION COUNCIL

Aligned to: Department of Workforce Development, Division of Vocational Rehabilitation; 800-442-3477; 201 East Washington Avenue, PO Box 7852, Madison, WI 53707-7852

Website: http://dwd.wisconsin.gov/dvr/wrc

Created by Governor Tommy G. Thompson in 1999 and continued most recently by Governor Evers, the State Rehabilitation Council advises the Department of Workforce Development on a statewide vocational rehabilitation plan for disabled individuals required by federal law.

WISCONSIN SHARED SERVICES EXECUTIVE COMMITTEE

Aligned to: Department of Administration; 101 East Wilson Street, Madison WI 53707

The Committee was created by Governor Walker in 2018. The committee is charged with establishing a shared services business model to deliver high-quality human resources and payroll and benefits services to all state agencies.

WISCONSIN TECHNOLOGY COMMITTEE
Aligned to: Wisconsin Technology Council; 455 Science Drive, Suite 240, Madison, WI 53711
Contact: Tom Still; 608-442-7557
Website: http://wisconsintechnologycouncil.com

Created by Governor Walker in 2011, the Wisconsin Technology Committee consists of the members of the Wisconsin Technology Council, a nonprofit corporation that was created by state legislation but later removed from the statutes. The committee provides a means by which the council can coordinate with state government. The council assists the state in promoting the creation, development, and retention of science-based and technology-based businesses.

TELECOMMUNICATIONS RELAY SERVICE COUNCIL
Aligned to: Public Service Commission; 4822 Madison Yards Way, Madison, WI 53705
Contact: Billy Mauldin; billy.mauldin@wisconsin.gov; 608-234-4781

Created by Governor Tommy G. Thompson in 1990 and continued most recently by Governor Evers, the Telecommunications Relay Service Council advises the state concerning telecommunications relay service, including with respect to rates and availability. The members include one speech-impaired person, one hearing-impaired person, one speech-impaired and hearing-impaired person, and one person not having a speech or hearing impairment.

GOVERNOR'S COUNCIL ON WORKFORCE INVESTMENT
Aligned to: Department of Workforce Development; 414-874-1680; 201 E. Washington Avenue, Madison, WI 53703; PO Box 7972, Madison, WI 53707-7972
Website: www.wi-cwi.org

Governor Tommy G. Thompson created the Governor's Council on Workforce Investment in 1999. Governor Scott Walker reconstituted the council in 2015 as a result of changes to federal law. The council is charged with carrying out certain duties and functions established under federal law governing state workforce development boards, including recommending strategies that align workforce development resources to support economic development, promoting programs to increase the number of skilled workers in the workforce and provide resources to job seekers, and recommending strategies that align workforce development resources to support economic development.

Office of the Lieutenant Governor

Lieutenant governor: Mandela Barnes
Chief of staff: Fred Ludwig
Location: 19 East, State Capitol, Madison
Contact: ltgov@wisconsin.gov; 608-266-3516; PO Box 2043, Madison, WI 53702-2043

OFFICE OF THE GOVERNOR

Lieutenant Governor Mandela Barnes (*left*) is the first African American to hold that office in Wisconsin. Barnes and Governor Evers (*right*) have held listening sessions around the state in order to hear the policy and budget priorities of Wisconsin citizens.

Website: www.ltgov.wisconsin.gov
Number of employees: 5.00
Total budget 2017–19: $764,200

The lieutenant governor is the state's second-ranking executive officer, a position analogous to that of the vice president of the United States. If the incumbent governor dies, resigns, or is removed from office, the lieutenant governor becomes governor for the balance of the unexpired term. The lieutenant governor serves as acting governor while the governor is unable to perform the duties of the office due to impeachment, incapacitation, or absence from the state. If there is a vacancy in the office of lieutenant governor, the governor must nominate a successor to serve, upon confirmation by both the senate and assembly, for the remainder of the unexpired term.

The governor may designate the lieutenant governor to represent the governor's office on any statutory board, commission, or committee on which the governor is entitled to membership, on any nonstatutory committee established by the governor, and on any intergovernmental body created to maintain relationships with federal, state, and local governments or regional agencies. The governor may ask the lieutenant governor to coordinate certain state services and programs the governor is directed by law to coordinate.

Voters elect the governor and lieutenant governor on a joint ballot to four-year terms. Candidates are nominated independently in the partisan August primary, but voters cast a combined ballot for the two offices in the November election.

Department of Administration

Department secretary: Joel Brennan
Deputy secretary: Chris Patton
Location: State Administration Building; 101 East Wilson Street, Madison
Contact: 608-266-1741; PO Box 7864, Madison, WI 53707-7864
Website: doa.wi.gov
Number of employees: 1,371.27
Total budget 2017–19: $1,902,337,900

The Department of Administration is administered by a secretary who is appointed by the governor with the advice and consent of the senate.

The department provides a wide range of services to other state agencies, including personnel management, payroll, accounting systems, and legal services. The department administers the state civil service system. The department administers the state's information system, procurement policies and contracts, fleet transportation, and risk management. It oversees the state's buildings and leased office space, as well as statewide facilities project planning and analysis. The department oversees the Capitol Police. It administers a federal and state funded low-income household energy assistance program and offers program assistance and funds to address homelessness and support affordable housing, public infrastructure, and economic development opportunities. It provides fiscal and policy analysis to the governor for development of executive budget proposals. It regulates racing, charitable gaming, and Indian gaming. The department advises the Building Commission and the governor on the issuance of state debt. It administers finances for the clean water revolving loan fund program. Finally, the department provides a variety of services to the public and state, local, and tribal governments.

Subordinate statutory boards, councils, and committees

COUNCIL ON AFFIRMATIVE ACTION

Chair: Adin Palau
Contact: angelal.nash@wisconsin.gov; 608-266-0713; 101 E. Wilson Street, 4th Floor, Madison, WI 53703
Website: https://dpm.wi.gov/Pages/HR_Admin/State-Council-on-Affirmative-Action-Diversity-Awards.aspx

The Council on Affirmative Action advises the administrator of the Division of Personnel Management in the department, evaluates affirmative action programs throughout the classified service, seeks compliance with state and federal regulations, and recommends improvements in the state's affirmative action efforts.

CERTIFICATION STANDARDS REVIEW COUNCIL

Chair: Sharon Mertens

The Certification Standards Review Council reviews the Department of Natural Resources laboratory certification and registration program and makes recommendations on programs for testing water, wastewater, waste material, soil, and hazardous substances.

COUNCIL ON SMALL BUSINESS, VETERAN-OWNED BUSINESS AND MINORITY BUSINESS OPPORTUNITIES

The Council on Small Business, Veteran-Owned Business and Minority Business Opportunities advises the department on how to increase the participation of small businesses, veteran-owned businesses, and minority businesses in state purchasing.

STATE EMPLOYEES SUGGESTION BOARD

Contact: WIEmployeeSuggestionProgram@wisconsin.gov; State Employee Suggestion Program, Division of Personnel Management, 101 E. Wilson St., 4th Floor, PO Box 7855, Madison, WI 53707-7855
Website: http://suggest.wi.gov

The State Employees Suggestion Board administers an awards program to encourage unusual and meritorious suggestions and accomplishments by state employees that promote economy and efficiency in government functions.

Independent entities attached for administrative purposes

BOARD ON AGING AND LONG-TERM CARE

Chair: Tanya L. Meyer
Executive director: Heather A. Bruemmer
Contact: boaltc@wisconsin.gov; 608-246-7013; Ombudsman Program, 800-815-0015; Medigap Helpline, 800-242-1060; Part D Helpline, 855-677-2783; 1402 Pankratz Street, Suite 111, Madison, WI 53704
Website: http://longtermcare.wi.gov
Number of employees: 42.50
Total budget 2017–19: $6,671,600

The Board on Aging and Long-Term Care reports to the governor and the legislature on matters relating to long-term care for the aged and disabled. The board monitors the development and implementation of federal, state, and local laws and regulations related to long-term care facilities and investigates complaints from persons receiving long-term care. The board operates the Medigap Helpline, which provides information on insurance designed to supplement Medicare.

OFFICE OF BUSINESS DEVELOPMENT

Director: Tia Torhorst

Contact: DOAOBD@wisconsin.gov; 608-267-7873; PO Box 7864, Madison, WI 53707
Website: https://doa.wi.gov/obd

The Office of Business Development provides administrative support to the Small Business Regulatory Review Board.

CLAIMS BOARD

Chair: Corey Finkelmeyer
Secretary: Amy Kasper
Contact: patricia.reardon@wisconsin.gov; 608-264-9595; PO Box 7864, Madison, WI 53707-7864
Website: http://claimsboard.wi.gov/
Number of employees: 0.00
Total budget 2017–19: $50,000

The Claims Board investigates and makes recommendations on all money claims against the state for $10 or more. The findings and recommendations are reported to the legislature, and no claim may be considered by the legislature until the board has made its recommendation.

ELECTRONIC RECORDING COUNCIL

Chair: Sharon Martin
Contact: sharon.martin@co.washington.wi.us; 262-335-4318; Electronic Recording Council, c/o Secretary's Office, Department of Administration, 101 E. Wilson Street, PO Box 7864, Madison, WI 53707-7864
Website: http://ercwis.wi.gov/

The Electronic Recording Council adopts standards regarding the electronic recording of real estate documents to be promulgated by rule by the department.

DIVISION OF HEARINGS AND APPEALS

Administrator: Brian Hayes
Location: 4822 Madison Yards Way, 5th Floor North, Madison
Contact: dhamail@wisconsin.gov; 608-266-7709; PO Box 7875, Madison, WI 53707-7875
Website: www.doa.wi.gov/divisions/Hearings-and-Appeals
Number of employees: 88.65
Total budget 2017–19: $21,697,700

The Division of Hearings and Appeals decides contested proceedings for the Department of Natural Resources, cases arising under the Department of Justice's Crime Victim Compensation Program, and appeals related to actions of the Departments of Health Services, Children and Families, Safety and Professional Services, and Agriculture, Trade and Consumer Protection. It hears appeals from the Department of Transportation, including those related to motor vehicle dealer licenses, highway signs, motor carrier regulation, and disputes arising between motor vehicle dealers and manufacturers. The division conducts hearings for the Department of Corrections on probation, parole, and extended supervision revocation and juvenile aftercare supervision. It handles contested cases for the Department of Public Instruction, the Department of Employee Trust Funds, and the Low-Income Home Energy Assistance Program of the Department of Administration. Other agencies may contract with the division for hearing services.

INTERAGENCY COUNCIL ON HOMELESSNESS

Acting Director: Michael Basford
Contact: james.langdon@wisconsin.gov; 608-264-6109
Website: https://doa.wi.gov/Pages/AboutDOA/ICH.aspx

The Interagency Council on Homelessness is tasked with establishing and periodically reviewing a statewide policy with the purpose of preventing and ending homelessness in Wisconsin.

INCORPORATION REVIEW BOARD

Chair: Dawn Vick
Location: 101 East Wilson Street, 9th Floor, Madison
Contact: wimunicipalboundaryreview@wi.gov; 608-264-6102; PO Box 1645, Madison, WI 53701
Website: https://doa.wi.gov/Pages/LocalGovtsGrants/IncorporationReviewBoard.aspx

The Incorporation Review Board reviews petitions for incorporating territory as a city or village to determine whether the petition meets certain statutory standards and is in the public interest.

LABOR AND INDUSTRY REVIEW COMMISSION

Chair: David Falstad
Location: Public Broadcasting Building, 3319 West Beltline Highway, Madison
Contact: lirc@wisconsin.gov; 608-266-9850; PO Box 8126, Madison, WI 53708-8126
Website: http://lirc.wisconsin.gov
Number of employees: 18.70
Total budget 2017–19: $6,179,100

The Labor and Industry Review Commission reviews the decisions of the Department of Workforce Development related to unemployment insurance, fair employment, and public accommodations and decisions of the Department of Workforce Development and the Division of Hearings and Appeals related to worker's compensation. The commission also hears appeals about discrimination in postsecondary education involving a person's physical condition or developmental disability.

NATIONAL AND COMMUNITY SERVICE BOARD

Chair: Paula Horning
Executive director: Jeanne M. Duffy

Contact: servewisconsin@wisconsin.gov; 608-261-6716; 1 West Wilson Street, Room B274, Madison, WI 53703
Website: www.servewisconsin.wi.gov
Number of employees: 5.00
Total budget 2017–19: $8,593,600

The National and Community Service Board prepares a plan for providing national service programs (which must ensure outreach to organizations serving underrepresented populations) and provides a system to recruit and place participants in national service programs. The board receives and distributes funds from governmental and private sources and acts as an intermediary between the Corporation for National and Community Service and local agencies.

BOARD FOR PEOPLE WITH DEVELOPMENTAL DISABILITIES

Executive Director: Beth Swedeen
Chair: Pam Malin
Contact: jennifer.neugart@wisconsin.gov; 608-266-7826; 888-332-1677 (toll free); 608-266-6660 (TTY); 101 East Wilson Street, Room 219, Madison, WI 53703
Website: http://wi-bpdd.org
Number of employees: 8.00
Total budget 2017–19: $3,087,000

The Board for People with Developmental Disabilities advises the department, other state agencies, the legislature, and the governor on matters related to developmental disabilities. The board also administers a program to foster the employment of individuals with disabilities and provide specific, targeted supports to businesses, school districts, and vocational agencies that demonstrate how coworkers can provide internal support to coworkers with disabilities.

PUBLIC RECORDS BOARD

Chair: Matthew Blessing
Contact: 101 East Wilson Street, Madison, WI 53703
Website: http://publicrecordsboard.wi.gov

The Public Records Board is responsible for the preservation of important state records, the cost-effective management of records by state agencies, and the orderly disposition of state records that have become obsolete. State agencies must have written approval from the board to dispose of records they generate or receive.

SMALL BUSINESS REGULATORY REVIEW BOARD

Contact: DOAOBD@wisconsin.gov
Website: https://doa.wi.gov/Pages/DoingBusiness/SBRRB.aspx

The Small Business Regulatory Review Board reviews state agency rules and guidelines, proposed rules, and emergency rules to determine whether they place an unnecessary burden on small businesses.

JOE KOSHOLLEK, LEGISLATIVE PHOTOGRAPHER

The State Capitol and Executive Residence Board is made of up citizens and state officers who help ensure the integrity of the buildings, furnishings, and grounds of both buildings. The board is pictured at the executive residence, or "Governor's Mansion," that sits on Lake Mendota and has been the home of the governor's family for over 50 years. It was purchased by the state in 1949 for $47,500.

STATE CAPITOL AND EXECUTIVE RESIDENCE BOARD

Members: Senator Risser, *chair*, Senator Olsen, Senator Roth, Representative Loudenbeck, Representative Born, Debra Alton, Laurel Brown, Jim Draeger, John Fernholz, Arlan Kay, Kathryn Neitzel, Marijo Reed, Ron Siggelkow, Cindy Torstveit, Paula Vellum, 1 vacancy

Website: https://doa.wi.gov/Pages/Capitol/State-Capitol-and-Executive-Residence-Board-(SCERB).aspx

The State Capitol and Executive Residence Board (SCERB) ensures the architectural and decorative integrity of the buildings, decorative furniture, furnishings, and grounds of the capitol and executive residence and directs the continuing and consistent maintenance of the properties. No renovations, repairs (except of an emergency nature), installation of fixtures, decorative items, or furnishings for the ground and buildings of the capitol or executive residence may be performed by or become the property of the state by purchase wholly or in part from state funds, or by gift, loan or otherwise, until approved by the board as to design, structure, composition, and appropriateness.

Increasing awareness of and concern for preserving and protecting the special nature of the people's buildings led to the creation of a mechanism for ensuring that the public interest and appropriate standards be carefully considered when altering or redecorating historic facilities. Building upon the State Capitol Restoration Guidelines prepared in 1980 by the Department of Administration's Division of State Facilities, the Legislature's Joint Committee on Legislative Organization in 1987 approved the Capitol Master Plan, which envisioned a full-scale renovation of the Capitol, balancing the integrity of the building with the need

GREG ANDERSON, LEGISLATIVE PHOTOGRAPHER

Capitol Tour Guide Jim Schaff, in his signature white shirt, green vest, and plaid tie, has been a familiar face in the building since 1999. Schaff is retiring in 2019 after 20 years of regaling students and tourists with stories about the State Capitol building and its history.

to maintain it as a modern, functioning seat of government. After approval of the plan by SCERB and the State of Wisconsin Building Commission, renovation of the Capitol, whose construction had been completed in 1917, commenced in 1990 and concluded in 2001. The project included extensive updating and improvements to the plumbing, electrical, and heating and cooling systems and largely restored office spaces to their original décor. The board is also responsible for overseeing the upkeep of the Classical Revival home on the shores of Lake Mendota in the Village of Maple Bluff that has served as the official residence of the governor's family for over 50 years.

STATE USE BOARD

Chair: Jean Zweifel
Contact: doadeosbopprograms@wisconsin.gov; 608-266-5462 or 608-266-5669;
  Bureau of Procurement, Division of Enterprise Operations, PO Box 7867, Madison, WI
  53707-7867
Website: http://stateuseprogram.wi.gov/
Number of employees: 1.50
Total budget 2017–19: $276,500

The State Use Board oversees state purchases of goods and services from charitable organizations or nonprofit institutions that employ individuals with severe disabilities for at least 75 percent of the direct labor used in providing the goods or services.

TAX APPEALS COMMISSION

Members: Elizabeth Kessler, Lorna Hemp Boll, David L. Coon
Contact: Nancy Batz, *legal assistant*, nancy.batz@wisconsin.gov, 608-266-9754; Bonnie
  Jorstad, *legal clerk*, bonnie.jorstad@wisconsin.gov, 608-266-1391 (main line); 5005
  University Avenue, Suite 110, Madison, WI 53705
Number of employees: 5.00
Total budget 2017–19: $1,141,200

The Tax Appeals Commission hears and decides appeals of assessments and determinations made by the Department of Revenue involving state-imposed taxes and state tax assessments of manufacturing property. The commission also adjudicates disputes between taxpayers and the Department of Transportation regarding certain motor vehicle taxes and fees. In addition, the commission has jurisdiction over cases involving the reasonableness of municipally imposed fees. The commission's decisions may be appealed to circuit court.

DIVISION OF TRUST LANDS AND INVESTMENTS

Executive secretary: Jonathan B. Barry
Deputy secretary: Tom German
Location: 101 East Wilson Street, 2nd Floor, Madison
Contact: bcplinfo@wisconsin.gov; 608-266-1370; PO Box 8943, Madison, WI 53708-8943
Website: http://bcpl.wisconsin.gov

The Division of Trust Lands and Investments assists the Board of Commissioners of Public Lands in its work and is under the direction and supervision of that board. The division is headed by an executive secretary who is appointed by the board. See the entry for the Board of Commissioners of Public Lands beginning on page 222.

SOLID WASTE FACILITY SITING BOARD

Chair: Dale Shaver
Executive director: Brian Hayes
Location: 4822 Madison Yards Way, 5th Floor North, Madison, WI 53705-9100
Contact: dhamail@wisconsin.gov; 608-266-7709; PO Box 7875, Madison, WI 53707-7875
Website: https://doa.wi.gov/Pages/LicensesHearings/DHAWasteFacilitySitingBoard.aspx
Number of employees: 0.00
Total budget 2017–19: $91,000

The Solid Waste Facility Siting Board supervises a mandated negotiation-arbitration procedure between applicants for new or expanded solid or hazardous waste facility licenses and local committees composed of representatives from the municipalities affected by proposed facilities. It is authorized to make final awards in arbitration hearings and can enforce legal deadlines and other obligations of applicants and local committees during the process.

WOMEN'S COUNCIL

Chair: Mary Jo Baas
Executive director: Christine Lidbury
Contact: womenscouncil@wisconsin.gov; 608-266-2219; 101 East Wilson Street, 9th Floor, Madison, WI 53702
Website: http://womenscouncil.wi.gov
Number of employees: 1.00
Total budget 2017–19: $290,600

The Women's Council identifies barriers that prevent women in Wisconsin from participating fully and equally in all aspects of life. The council advises state agencies about how current and emerging state policies, laws, and rules have an impact on women; recommends changes to the public and private sectors and initiates legislation to further women's economic and social equality and improve this state's tax base and economy; and disseminates information on the status of women.

Department of Agriculture, Trade and Consumer Protection

Board of Agriculture, Trade and Consumer Protection: Miranda Leis, *chair*
Department secretary: Brad Pfaff
Deputy secretary: Randy Romanski
Location: 2811 Agriculture Drive, Madison
Contact: 608-224-5012; PO Box 8911, Madison, WI 53708-8911
Website: https://datcp.wi.gov
Number of employees: 630.29
Total budget 2017–19: $193,595,700

The Department of Agriculture, Trade and Consumer Protection is directed and supervised by the Board of Agriculture, Trade and Consumer Protection and is administered by a secretary. The members of the board and the secretary are appointed by the governor with the advice and consent of the senate.

The department regulates agriculture, trade, and commercial activity in Wis-

Robbie Daily, a Weights and Measures Petroleum System Specialist, checks the gauge readings of the underground storage tank monitor at a retail gas station. The Department of Agriculture, Trade and Consumer Protection regulates commercial activity and enforces consumer protection laws in Wisconsin.

DEPARTMENT OF AGRICULTURE, TRADE AND CONSUMER PROTECTION

consin for the protection of the state's citizens. It enforces the state's primary consumer protection laws, including those relating to deceptive advertising, unfair business practices, and consumer product safety. The department oversees the enforcement of Wisconsin's animal health and disease control laws and conducts a variety of programs to conserve and protect the state's vital land, water, and plant resources. The department licenses and inspects food-related businesses to ensure the safety of food produced or sold in Wisconsin. The department administers financial security programs to protect agricultural producers, facilitates the marketing of Wisconsin agricultural products in interstate and international markets, and promotes agricultural development.

Subordinate statutory boards, councils, and committees

AGRICULTURAL PRODUCER SECURITY COUNCIL

Contact: Eric Hanson; eric.hanson@wisconsin.gov; 608-224-4968

The Agricultural Producer Security Council advises the department on the administration and enforcement of the agricultural producer security program, which reimburses grain, milk, and vegetable producers and grain warehouse keepers if a purchaser defaults on payment.

FARM TO SCHOOL COUNCIL

Contact: Charlotte Litjens; charlotte.litjens@wisconsin.gov; 608-224-5017

The Farm to School Council advises the department regarding the promotion and administration of farm to school programs and reports to the legislature on the needs of those programs.

FERTILIZER RESEARCH COUNCIL

Website: https://frc.soils.wisc.edu

The Fertilizer Research Council provides funding, with the department secretary's final approval, to the University of Wisconsin System for fertilizer-related research projects. The research projects are funded from a portion of the sales of fertilizer and soil or plant additives in Wisconsin.

VETERINARY EXAMINING BOARD

Chair: Philip C. Johnson

Contact: datcpveb@wi.gov; 608-224-4353; PO Box 8911, Madison, WI 53708-8911

The Veterinary Examining Board determines the education and experience required for obtaining veterinary licenses and veterinary technician certifications and develops and evaluates examinations for obtaining these licenses and certifications. The board also establishes and enforces standards of professional conduct for veterinarians and veterinary technicians.

Independent entities attached for administrative purposes

LAND AND WATER CONSERVATION BOARD

Chair: Mark E. Cupp
Contact: Lisa Trumble; lisa.trumble@wi.gov; 608-224-4617; Christopher Clayton; christopher.clayton@wi.gov; 608-224-4630

The Land and Water Conservation Board advises the secretary and department regarding soil and water conservation and animal waste management. It reviews and makes recommendations to the department on county land and water resource plans and funding allocations to county land conservation committees. The board also advises the University of Wisconsin System about needed research and education programs related to soil and water conservation and assists the Department of Natural Resources with issues related to runoff from agriculture and other rural sources of pollution.

LIVESTOCK FACILITY SITING REVIEW BOARD

Members: Lee Engelbrecht, Scott Godfrey, Raymond Diederich, Bob Selk, Bob Topel, Scott Sand, Jerome Gaska
Contact: SitingBoard@wisconsin.gov; 608-224-5026

The Livestock Facility Siting Review Board may review certain decisions made by political subdivisions relating to the siting or expansion of livestock facilities such as feedlots. An aggrieved person may challenge the decision of a city, village, town, or county government approving or disapproving the siting or expansion of a livestock facility by requesting that the board review the decision. If the board determines that a challenge is valid, it must reverse the decision of the governmental body. The decision of the board is binding on the governmental body, but either party may appeal the board's decision in circuit court.

Department of Children and Families

Department secretary: Emilie Amundson
Deputy secretary: Jeff Pertl
Assistant Secretary: Danielle Melfi
Location: 201 East Washington Avenue, 2nd Floor, Madison
Contact: dcfweb@wisconsin.gov; 608-422-7000; PO Box 8916, Madison, WI 53703-8916
Website: https://dcf.wisconsin.gov
Number of employees: 783.16
Total budget 2017–19: $2,573,778,500

The Department of Children and Families is administered by a secretary who is appointed by the governor with the advice and consent of the senate.

The department provides or oversees county provision of various services to assist children and families, including services for children in need of protection or services, adoption and foster care services, the licensing of facilities that provide out-of-home care for children, background investigations of child caregivers, child abuse and neglect investigations, and community-based juvenile justice services. The department administers the Wisconsin Works (W-2) public assistance program, including the Wisconsin Shares child care subsidy program, the YoungStar child care quality improvement program, the child support enforcement and paternity establishment program, and programs related to the federal Temporary Assistance to Needy Families (TANF) income support program. The department also works to ensure that families have access to high quality and affordable early childhood care and education and administers the licensing and regulation of child care centers.

Subordinate statutory boards, councils, and committees

READ TO LEAD DEVELOPMENT COUNCIL

Website: https://dcf.wisconsin.gov/readtolead

The Read to Lead Development Council makes recommendations to the secretary of children and families and the state superintendent of public instruction regarding recipients of literacy and early childhood development grants. It annually submits a report on its operation to the appropriate standing committees of the legislature.

GOVERNOR'S COUNCIL ON DOMESTIC ABUSE

Contact: Kaitlin Tolliver; 608-422-6962
Website: https://dcf.wisconsin.gov/domesticabuse

The Council on Domestic Abuse reviews applications for domestic abuse services grants, advises the department and the legislature on matters of domestic abuse policy, and, in conjunction with the Judicial Conference, develops forms for filing petitions for domestic abuse restraining orders and injunctions.

RATE REGULATION ADVISORY COMMITTEE

Contact: DCFCWLRateReg@wisconsin.gov
Website: https://dcf.wisconsin.gov/ratereg

The Rate Regulation Advisory Committee advises the department regarding rates for child welfare agencies, residential care centers, and group homes.

Independent entities attached for administrative purposes

CHILD ABUSE AND NEGLECT PREVENTION BOARD

Chair: Teri Zywicki

Executive director: Michelle M. Jensen
Contact: PreventionBoard@wisconsin.gov; 608-266-6871; 110 East Main Street, Suite 810, Madison, WI 53703-3316
Website: https://preventionboard.wi.gov
Number of employees: 6.00
Total budget 2017–19: $6,317,400

The Child Abuse and Neglect Prevention Board administers the Children's Trust Fund, which was created to develop and fund strategies that prevent child maltreatment in Wisconsin. In addition, the board recommends to the governor, the legislature, and state agencies changes needed in state programs, statutes, policies, budgets, and rules to reduce child abuse and neglect and improve coordination among state agencies.

MILWAUKEE CHILD WELFARE PARTNERSHIP COUNCIL

Chair: Michele Bria
Contact: dcfmilwaukeechildwelfare@wisconsin.gov; Bridget Chybowski, 414-343-5781; 635 North 26th Street, Milwaukee, WI 53233
Website: https://dcf.wisconsin.gov/mcps/partnership-council

The Milwaukee Child Welfare Partnership Council makes recommendations to the department and the legislature regarding policies and plans to improve the child welfare system in Milwaukee County.

Department of Corrections

Department secretary: Kevin A. Carr
Deputy secretary: Amy Pechacek
Location: 3099 East Washington Avenue, Madison
Contact: 608-240-5000; PO Box 7925, Madison, WI 53707-7925
Website: www.doc.wi.gov
Number of employees: 10,124.97
Total budget 2017–19: $2,479,354,300

The Department of Corrections is administered by a secretary who is appointed by the governor with the advice and consent of the senate. The department administers Wisconsin's state prisons, community corrections programs, and juvenile corrections programs. It supervises the custody and discipline of all inmates and operates programs to rehabilitate offenders and reintegrate them into society. It also supervises offenders on probation, parole, and extended supervision; monitors compliance with deferred prosecution programs; and may make recommendations for pardons or commutations of sentence when requested by the governor. The department maintains the sex offender registry and monitors sex offenders and sexually violent persons who are subject to GPS tracking.

Subordinate statutory boards, councils, and committees

CORRECTIONS SYSTEM FORMULARY BOARD

The Corrections System Formulary Board establishes written guidelines, to be applied uniformly throughout the state's correctional institutions, for making therapeutic alternate drug selections for prisoners.

Independent entities attached for administrative purposes

INTERSTATE ADULT OFFENDER SUPERVISION BOARD

Chair: Joselyn Lopéz, *commissioner/compact administrator*
Contact: docdccic@wisconsin.gov, 608-240-5388 (Interstate Compact Office);
joselyn.lopez@wisconsin.gov, 608-240-5333; 3099 East Washington Avenue, Madison, WI 53704
Website: https://doc.wi.gov/Pages/AboutDOC/CommunityCorrections/
InterstateCompact.aspx

The Interstate Adult Offender Supervision Board appoints the Wisconsin representative to the Interstate Commission for Adult Offender Supervision. The board advises and exercises oversight and advocacy concerning the state's participation in the Interstate Compact for Adult Offender Supervision and on the operation of the compact within this state.

COUNCIL ON OFFENDER REENTRY

Chair: Silvia Jackson
Contact: Michele Krueger; michele.krueger@wisconsin.gov; 608-240-5072
Website: https://doc.wi.gov/Pages/AboutDOC/ReentryUnit.aspx (Council annual reports)

The Council on Offender Reentry coordinates reentry initiatives across the state, including by promoting collaboration in the provision of transition services and training opportunities, identifying funding sources, and developing methods of information sharing.

PAROLE COMMISSION

Chair: John Tate II
Location: 3099 East Washington Avenue, Madison
Contact: ParoleCommission@wisconsin.gov; 608-240-7280; PO Box 7960, Madison, WI 53707-7960
Website: https://doc.wi.gov/Pages/AboutDOC/ParoleCommission.aspx

The Parole Commission conducts regularly scheduled interviews to consider the parole of eligible inmates and is responsible for notifying victims and law enforcement about parole decisions.

PRISON INDUSTRIES BOARD

Members: Bill G. Smith, *president*, James Jackson, Kevin A. Carr, James Langdon, Lenard Simpson, 4 vacancies

Location: 3099 East Washington Avenue, Madison
Contact: 608-240-5200; P.O. Box 8990, Madison, WI 53708
Website: http://www.shopbsi.com/

The Prison Industries Board develops a plan for the manufacture and marketing of prison industry products and the provision of prison industry services and research and development activities.

STATE BOARD FOR INTERSTATE JUVENILE SUPERVISION

Chair: Christopher Dee
Contact: Casey Gerber, *compact administrator/commissioner*, casey.gerber@wisconsin.gov; 608-240-5918
Websites: https://doc.wi.gov/Pages/AboutDOC/JuvenileCorrections/InterstateCompact.aspx; https://www.juvenilecompact.org/midwest/wisconsin

The State Board for Interstate Juvenile Supervision advises and exercises oversight and advocacy concerning the state's participation in the Interstate Compact for Juveniles and on the operation of the compact within this state.

Educational Communications Board

Chair: Rolf Wegenke
Executive director: Marta Bechtol
Contact: 608-264-9600; 3319 West Beltline Highway, Madison, WI 53713

A crew replaces the antenna on the WHLA-TV tower near La Crosse. The Educational Communications Board maintains the infrastructure of the state's public broadcasting system.

EDUCATIONAL COMMUNICATIONS BOARD

Website: https://www.ecb.org
Number of employees: 55.18
Total budget 2017–19: $38,199,600

The Educational Communications Board oversees the statewide public broadcasting system. It plans, constructs, operates, and maintains the infrastructure necessary for the state's public radio and television networks and oversees operation of the Emergency Alert System, the Amber Alert System, National Weather Service transmitters, a telecommunication operations center, and other transmitters and satellite facilities. The board operates the statewide Wisconsin Public Radio and Wisconsin Public Television services in partnership with the University of Wisconsin-Extension.

Elections Commission

Commissioners: Dean Knudson, *chair*; Beverly Gill, Julie M. Glancey, Ann S. Jacobs, Jodi Jensen, Mark L. Thomsen
Administrator: Meagan Wolfe
Location: 212 East Washington Avenue, 3rd Floor, Madison
Contact: elections@wi.gov; 608-266-8005; 866-VOTE-WIS (toll-free voter help line); PO Box 7984, Madison, WI 53707-7984
Website: https://elections.wi.gov
Number of employees: 25.75
Total budget 2017–19: $8,974,800

The Elections Commission consists of six members and can include additional members in certain circumstances. The majority leader of the senate, the speaker of the assembly, and the minority leaders of the senate and assembly each appoint one member. The governor appoints two members who were formerly county or municipal clerks, selecting one each from lists prepared by the legislative leadership of the two major political parties. If another political party qualified for a separate ballot and received at least 10 percent of the vote in the most recent gubernatorial election, the governor must appoint an additional member selected from a list prepared by that party. The governor's appointees must be confirmed by a majority of the members of the senate, but they can serve on the commission prior to confirmation. The commission appoints an administrator to direct and supervise the commission's staff. This appointment must be confirmed by the senate, but the commission can select a person to serve as interim administrator while the confirmation is pending. The administrator serves as the chief election officer of the state.

The commission is responsible for ensuring compliance with state election laws and with the federal Help America Vote Act of 2002, which established certain requirements regarding the conduct of federal elections in the state. In this capacity, the commission trains and certifies all municipal clerks and chief election inspectors in the state to promote uniform election procedures. In addition, the commission is responsible for the design and maintenance of the statewide voter registration system. Every municipality in the state must use this system to administer federal, state, and local elections.

Department of Employee Trust Funds

Employee Trust Funds Board: Wayne Koessl, *chair*
Department Secretary: Robert J. Conlin
Deputy Secretary: A. John Voelker
Location: North Tower, 8th Floor, Hill Farms State Office Building, 4822 Madison Yards Way, Madison
Contact: 608-266-3285; 877-533-5020 (toll free); PO Box 7931, Madison, WI 53707-7931
Website: etf.wi.gov
Number of employees: 272.20
Total budget 2017–19: $93,278,000

The Department of Employee Trust Funds is directed and supervised by the Employee Trust Funds Board. The board consists of 13 members, one of whom is the governor (or a designee). The department is administered by a secretary who is appointed by the board.

The department administers various benefit programs available to state and local public employees, including the Wisconsin Retirement System, health and life insurance programs for active and retired employees of the state and participating local governments, a deferred compensation program, and employee-funded reimbursement account plans. The department serves all state employees and teachers and most municipal employees, with the notable exceptions of employees of the City of Milwaukee and Milwaukee County.

The Employee Trust Funds Board sets policy for the department; appoints the department secretary; approves tables used for computing benefits, contribution rates, and actuarial assumptions; authorizes all annuities except for disability; approves or rejects the department's administrative rules; and generally oversees benefit programs administered by the department, except the group insurance and deferred compensation programs.

Subordinate statutory boards, councils, and committees

DEFERRED COMPENSATION BOARD

Website: http://etf.wi.gov/boards/board_dc.htm

The Deferred Compensation Board oversees the deferred compensation plans offered to state and local employees and contracts with deferred compensation plan providers.

GROUP INSURANCE BOARD

Website: http://etf.wi.gov/boards/board_gib.htm

The Group Insurance Board oversees the group health, life, income continuation, and other insurance programs offered to state employees, covered local employees, and retirees.

TEACHERS RETIREMENT BOARD

Website: http://etf.wi.gov/boards/board_tr.htm

The Teachers Retirement Board advises the Employee Trust Funds Board about retirement matters related to teachers, approves administrative rules related to teachers, authorizes the payment of disability annuities for teachers, and hears appeals of staff determinations regarding disability annuities for teacher participants.

WISCONSIN RETIREMENT BOARD

Website: http://etf.wi.gov/boards/board_wr.htm

The Wisconsin Retirement Board advises the Employee Trust Funds Board about retirement matters related to state and local general and protective employees and performs the same functions for these employees as the Teachers Retirement Board does for teachers.

Ethics Commission

Commissioners: Katie McCallum, *chair*, Tamara Packard, *vice chair*, Mac Davis, David R. Halbrooks, Pat Strachota, Timothy Van Akkeren

Administrator: Daniel Carlton

Location: 101 E. Wilson Street, Suite 127, Madison

Contact: Ethics@wi.gov (general agency and code of ethics questions); CampaignFinance @wi.gov (campaign finance); ETHLobbying@wi.gov (lobbying); 608-266-8123; PO Box 7125, Madison, WI 53707-7125

Website: https://ethics.wi.gov; https://cfis.wi.gov (Campaign Finance Information System); https://lobbying.wi.gov (Eye On Lobbying)

Number of employees: 8.00

Total budget 2017–19: $2,653,700

The Ethics Commission consists of six members and may include additional members in certain circumstances. The majority leader of the senate, the speaker of the assembly, and the minority leaders of the senate and assembly each appoint one member. The governor appoints two members who were formerly elected judges, selecting one each from lists prepared by the legislative leadership of the two major political parties. If another political party qualified for a separate ballot and received at least 10 percent of the vote in the most recent gubernatorial election, the governor must appoint an additional member selected from a list prepared by that party. The governor's appointees must be confirmed by a majority of the members of the senate, but they can serve on the commission prior to confirmation. The commission appoints an administrator to direct and supervise the commission's staff. The senate must confirm this appointment, but the commission may select a person to serve as interim administrator while the confirmation is pending.

The commission administers Wisconsin's campaign finance laws, lobbying laws, and ethics laws. The commission is the campaign finance filing officer for political organizations that are required to file campaign finance reports with the state, and provides forms, training materials, and assistance to local campaign filing officers (municipal, county, and school district clerks). Lobbyists must obtain a license from the commission; and organizations that employ a lobbyist must register and file reports with the commission detailing the time and money they spend on lobbying. State officials, candidates, and nominees must annually file with the commission statements detailing their economic interests.

Cheryl Rapp, a college affordability specialist at the Department of Financial Institutions, discusses Edvest accounts with school counselor Dana Guetschow at a conference in Shell Lake. Edvest is the state's college savings plan.

Department of Financial Institutions

Department secretary: Kathy Blumenfeld
Deputy secretary: Cheryll Olson-Collins
Contact: 608-261-9555; 4822 Madison Yards Way, North Tower, Madison, WI 53705
Website: www.wdfi.org
Number of employees: 141.54
Total budget 2017–19: $37,035,300

The Department of Financial Institutions is administered by a secretary who is appointed by the governor with the advice and consent of the senate. The department regulates state-chartered banks, savings banks, and savings and loan associations. The department also registers securities and securities industry members and regulates securities offerings, securities industry operations, corporate takeovers, and franchise offerings. It examines and files organizational documents and annual reports for corporations, limited liability companies, and other business entities. It also licenses and regulates the mortgage banking industry and other financial service providers, including payday lenders, high-interest consumer lenders, collection agencies, check cashing services, check sellers, credit counseling and debt settlement services, and automobile sales finance companies. The department administers the Uniform Commercial Code filing system and the Wisconsin Consumer Act. It also issues notary public commissions and registers trademarks, trade names, and brands. It registers and regulates charitable organizations, persons involved with solicitations on behalf of charitable organizations, and professional employer organizations. It also issues video service franchises to cable television operators.

Subordinate statutory boards, councils, and committees

BANKING REVIEW BOARD

The Banking Review Board advises the Division of Banking in the department on matters related to banks and banking and reviews the division's administrative actions.

SAVINGS INSTITUTIONS REVIEW BOARD

The Savings Institutions Review Board advises the Division of Banking in the department on matters related to savings banks and savings and loan associations and reviews the division's administrative actions.

Independent entities attached for administrative purposes

OFFICE OF CREDIT UNIONS

Director: Kim Santos
Credit Union Review Board: Colleen Woggon, Lisa M. Greco, Danny Wollin, Christopher P. Butler, Sherri O. Stumpf
Location: 4822 Madison Yards Way, Madison
Contact: 608-261-9543; PO Box 14137, Madison, WI 53708
Website: www.wdfi.org/fi/cu

The Office of Credit Unions regulates state-chartered credit unions. The Credit Union Review Board advises the Office of Credit Unions on matters relating to credit unions and reviews the office's administrative actions.

COLLEGE SAVINGS PROGRAM BOARD

Administrator: James DiUlio
Contact: 608-264-7899; PO Box 8861, Madison, WI 53708
Website: http://529.wi.gov

The College Savings Program Board administers the Edvest and Tomorrow's Scholar programs, which provide for tax-advantaged investment accounts used to pay higher education expenses. The Board also has continuing responsibility for a legacy college tuition units program.

Department of Health Services

Department secretary: Andrea Palm
Deputy secretary: Julie Willems Van Dijk
Location: Wilson Street State Human Services Building, 1 West Wilson Street, Madison
Contact: 608-266-1865; 1 West Wilson Street, Madison, WI 53707
Website: www.dhs.wisconsin.gov
Number of employees: 6,176.89
Total budget 2017–19: $23,946,286,400

The Department of Health Services is administered by a secretary who is appointed by the governor with the advice and consent of the senate.

The Department of Health Services administers a wide range of services to clients in the community and at state institutions; regulates certain care providers, including emergency medical services practitioners; oversees vital records, including birth, death, marriage, and divorce certificates; and supervises and consults with local public and voluntary agencies. The department promotes and protects public health in Wisconsin through various services and regulations addressing environmental and occupational health, family and community health, chronic and communicable disease prevention and control, and programs relating to maternal and child health. The department provides access to health care for low-income persons, the elderly, and people with disabilities and administers the Medical Assistance (Medicaid), BadgerCare Plus, SeniorCare, chronic disease aids, general relief, and FoodShare programs. Additionally, the department administers programs that provide long-term support for the elderly and people with disabilities, including Family Care, IRIS, Aging and Disability Resource Centers, and Pathways to Independence. The department licenses and regulates programs and facilities that provide health, long-term care, and mental health and substance abuse services, including assisted living facilities, nursing homes, home health agencies, and facilities serving people with developmental disabilities, including three state-operated centers for persons with developmental disabilities. The department administers programs to meet mental health and substance abuse prevention, diagnosis, early intervention, and treatment needs in community and institutional settings, including two state-owned, inpatient mental health institutes, Mendota Mental Health Institute and Winnebago Mental Health Institute. Mendota Mental Health Institute houses a secure treatment unit to meet the mental health needs of male adolescents from the Department of Corrections' juvenile institutions. The department also operates the Wisconsin Resource Center as a medium security facility for mentally ill prison inmates whose treatment needs cannot be met by the Department of Corrections and provides treatment at the Sand Ridge Secure Treatment Center for individuals civilly committed under the sexually violent persons law.

Subordinate statutory boards, councils, and committees

COUNCIL ON BIRTH DEFECT PREVENTION AND SURVEILLANCE

Contact: Peggy Helm-Quest; peggy.helmquest@dhs.wisconsin.gov; 608-267-2945
Website: https://cbdps.wisconsin.gov

The Council on Birth Defect Prevention and Surveillance makes recommendations to the department regarding the administration of the Wisconsin Birth Defects Registry, which documents diagnoses and counts the number of birth defects for children up to age two. The council advises what birth defects are to be reported; the content, format, and procedures for reporting; and the contents of the aggregated reports.

COUNCIL ON BLINDNESS

Contact: Ann Sievert, *director*; dhsobvi@dhs.wisconsin.gov; 608-266-2536
Website: https://scob.wisconsin.gov

The Council on Blindness makes recommendations to the department and other state agencies on services, activities, programs, investigations, and research that affect persons who are blind or visually impaired.

COUNCIL FOR THE DEAF AND HARD OF HEARING

Contact: Hollie Barnes Spink, *director*; hollie.barnesspink@dhs.wisconsin.gov;
    608-247-5343
Website: https://dhhcouncil.wisconsin.gov

The Council for the Deaf and Hard of Hearing advises the department on the provision of effective services to persons who are deaf, hard-of-hearing, or deaf-blind.

COUNCIL ON MENTAL HEALTH

Contact: WCMH@wisconsin.gov
Website: https://mhc.wisconsin.gov

The Council on Mental Health advises the department, governor, and legislature on mental health programs; provides recommendations on the expenditure of federal mental health block grants; reviews the department's plans for mental health services; and serves as an advocate for the mentally ill.

PUBLIC HEALTH COUNCIL

Contact: DHSPublicHealthCouncil@wisconsin.gov
Website: https://publichealthcouncil.wisconsin.gov

The Public Health Council advises the department, the governor, the legislature, and the public on progress made in the implementation of the department's ten-year public health plan and coordination of responses to public health emergencies.

TRAUMA ADVISORY COUNCIL

Contact: Caitlin Washburn; caitlin.washburn@dhs.wisconsin.gov; 608-266-0601
Website: https://stac.wisconsin.gov

The Trauma Advisory Council advises the department on developing and implementing a statewide trauma care system.

Other statutorily required advisory entities

MEDICAID PHARMACY PRIOR AUTHORIZATION ADVISORY COMMITTEE

The Medicaid Pharmacy Prior Authorization Advisory Committee advises the department on issues related to prior authorization decisions concerning prescription drugs on behalf of Medical Assistance recipients.

NEWBORN SCREENING ADVISORY GROUP: UMBRELLA COMMITTEE

Contact: Tami Horzewski; tami.horzewski@dhs.wisconsin.gov; 608-266-8904
Website: http://www.slh.wisc.edu/clinical/newborn/program-information/
wisconsin-newborn-screening-advisory-group/

The Newborn Screening Advisory Umbrella Committee advises the department regarding a statutorily required program that generally requires that newborn infants receive blood or other diagnostic tests for congenital and metabolic disorders.

QUALITY ASSURANCE AND IMPROVEMENT COMMITTEE

The Quality Assurance and Improvement Committee makes recommendations for the disbursement of civil money penalties funds allocated for improving the quality of care in Wisconsin nursing homes.

Independent entities attached for administrative purposes

EMERGENCY MEDICAL SERVICES BOARD

Chair: Jerry Biggart
Contact: dhsemssmail@dhs.wisconsin.gov; 608-266-1568
Website: https://www.dhs.wisconsin.gov/ems/boards/meetings.htm

The Emergency Medical Services Board appoints an advisory committee of physicians to advise the department on the selection of the state medical director for emergency medical services and to review that person's performance. The board also advises the director on medical issues; reviews emergency medical service statutes and rules concerning the transportation of patients; and recommends changes to the department and the Department of Transportation.

COUNCIL ON PHYSICAL DISABILITIES

Chair: Benjamin Barrett
Contact: Lisa Sobczyk; lisa.sobczyk@dhs.wisconsin.gov; 608-266-9354; TTY/TDD/Relay: WI Relay 711
Website: https://cpd.wisconsin.gov

The Council on Physical Disabilities develops and modifies the state plan for services to persons with physical disabilities. The council advises the secretary of health services, recommends legislation, encourages public understanding of the needs of persons with physical disabilities, and promotes programs to prevent physical disability.

Higher Educational Aids Board

Members: Stephen Willett, *chair*; Robert T. Welch, *vice chair*; Jeff Cichon, *secretary*; Jose Delgado, Kelsey C. Fenske, Nathaniel Helm-Quest, Alex M. Hipler, Jennifer Kammerud, Logan M. Kossel, Timothy Opgenorth, 1 vacancy
Nonvoting members: Paul Trebian, Russell Swagger
Executive secretary: Connie Hutchison
Location: 4822 Madison Yards Way, Seventh floor, Madison
Contact: HEABmail@wi.gov; 608-267-2206; PO Box 7885, Madison, WI 53707-7885
Website: http://heab.state.wi.us
Number of employees: 10.00
Total budget 2017–19: $289,543,100

The Higher Educational Aids Board consists of the superintendent of public instruction and ten members appointed by the governor without senate confirmation. The board has added one nonvoting member to represent tribal colleges. The governor appoints the board's executive secretary. The board is responsible for administering the state's higher education student financial aid system and also enters into certain interstate agreements relating to higher education.

Independent entities attached for administrative purposes

DISTANCE LEARNING AUTHORIZATION BOARD

Members: Rolf Wegenke, *chair*, Ray Cross, *vice chair*, Dawn Crim, Morna Foy, 1 vacancy (tribal college representative)
Contact: Connie Hutchison; connie.hutchison@wi.gov; 608-267-2206
Website: Http://heab.wi.gov/dlab

The Distance Learning Authorization Board administers this state's participation in the State Authorization Reciprocity Agreement (SARA), an interstate agreement related to state authorization and oversight of postsecondary institutions that offer educational programs to students located in other states. As provided in SARA, the board reviews, authorizes, and monitors eligible postsecondary institutions with respect to their distance learning programs such as online classes offered to out-of-state students.

State Historical Society of Wisconsin

Board of Curators: Gregory Huber, *president*; Angela Bartell, *president-elect*; Brian Rude, *past president*; Walter Rugland, *treasurer*; Dave Anderson, Representative Billings, Mary Buestrin, Ramona Gonzalez, Mary Jane Herber, Representative Horlacher, Joanne Huelsman, Carol McChesney Johnson, Alli Karrels, James Klauser, Thomas Maxwell, Susan McLeod, Catherine Orton, Lowell Peterson, Senator Risser, , Phillip Schauer, Donald Schott, Thomas Shriner, Jr., Robert Smith, Leonard Sobczak, Greg Summers, John Thompson, Chia Youyee Vang, Senator Wanggaard, Terri Yoho, Aharon Zorea
Director: Christian Overland
Location: 816 State Street, Madison (archives and library); 30 North Carroll Street, Madison (museum)
Contact: 608-264-6400 (general); 608-264-6535 (library); 608-264-6460 (archives); 608-264-6555 (museum); 608-264-6493 (historic preservation); 608-264-6515 (programs and outreach); 816 State Street, Madison, WI 53706
Website: www.wisconsinhistory.org
Number of employees: 135.04
Total budget 2017–19: $55,962,900

The State Historical Society of Wisconsin, also known as the Wisconsin Historical Society, is both a state agency and a membership organization. The society's Board of Curators includes eight statutory appointments and up to 30 members who are selected according to the society's constitution and bylaws. Three board members are appointed by the governor with the advice and consent of the senate. The board selects the society's director, who serves as administrative head and as secretary to the board.

The mission of the society is to help connect people to the past. The society has a statutory duty to collect and preserve historical and cultural resources related to Wisconsin and to make them available to the public. To meet these objectives, the society maintains a major history research collection in Madison and in 13 area research centers, including the Northern Great Lakes Visitor Center. The society also operates the Wisconsin Historical Museum in Madison, the Circus World Museum, and nine other museums and historic sites throughout the state, as well as a field services office in Eau Claire. The society provides statewide school services programs and public history programming such as National History

STATE HISTORICAL SOCIETY OF WISCONSIN

Visitors enjoy a ride in an omnibus at the Wade House historic site, a stagecoach inn from the 1850s that sits at the halfway point between Sheboygan and Fond Du Lac.

Day, and collaborates with other agencies such as Wisconsin Public Television to deliver history programming to the public. The society provides technical services and advice to approximately 400 affiliated local historical societies throughout the state. The society conducts, publishes, and disseminates research on Wisconsin and U.S. history and serves as the state's historic preservation office, which facilitates the preservation of historic structures and archaeological sites and administers the state and national registers of historic places. The society is also responsible for implementation of the state's Burial Sites Preservation Law.

Independent entities attached for administrative purposes

BURIAL SITES PRESERVATION BOARD

Members: Melinda Young, *chair*; Cynthia Stiles, *vice chair*; David J. Grignon, Jennifer Haas, Christian Overland, Katherine Stevenson, Corina Williams
Nonvoting member: John H. Broihahn
Contact: Amy Rosebrough; amy.rosebrough@wisconsinhistory.org; 608-264-6494; 816 State Street, Madison, WI 53706
Website: https://www.wisconsinhistory.org/Records/Article/CS3252

The Burial Sites Preservation Board assists in the administration of the state's burial sites laws. The board's duties include determining which Indian tribes in Wisconsin have an interest in burial sites, approving applicants for a registry of persons interested in burial sites, reviewing decisions of the Wisconsin Historical

Society director to record burial sites in the catalog or to remove land from the burial sites catalog, reviewing decisions on permit applications to disturb burial sites, and reviewing decisions regarding the disposition of human remains and burial objects removed from burial sites.

HISTORIC PRESERVATION REVIEW BOARD

Members: Neil Prendergast, *chair*; Melinda Young, *vice chair*; Bruce T. Block, Carlen Hatala, Carol McChesney Johnson, Dan J. Joyce, Kubet Luchterhand, David V. Mollenhoff, Sissel Schroeder, Valentine J. Schute, Jr., Daniel J. Stephans, Paul Wolter, Donna Zimmerman, 2 vacancies

Contact: Peggy Veregin; peggy.veregin@wisconsinhistory.org; 608-264-6501; 816 State Street, Madison, WI 53706

Website: https://www.wisconsinhistory.org/Records/Article/CS3564

The Historic Preservation Review Board approves nominations to the Wisconsin State Register of Historic Places and the National Register of Historic Places upon recommendation of the state historic preservation officer. The board approves the distribution of federal grants-in-aid for preservation and approves the state preservation plan, advises the State Historical Society, and requests comments from planning departments of affected cities, villages, towns, counties, local landmark commissions, and local historical societies regarding properties being considered for nomination to the state and national registers.

Office of the Commissioner of Insurance

Commissioner: Mark V. Afable
Deputy commissioner: Nathan Houdek
Location: 125 South Webster Street, Madison
Contact: 608-266-3585; 800-236-8517 (toll free); PO Box 7873, Madison, WI 53707-7873
Website: https://oci.wi.gov
Email contacts by subject: https://oci.wi.gov/Pages/AboutOCI/EmailAdd.aspx
Number of employees: 141.00
Total budget 2017–19: $222,205,500

The Office of the Commissioner of Insurance is administered by the commissioner of insurance, who is appointed by the governor with the advice and consent of the senate. The office supervises the insurance industry in Wisconsin. The office is responsible for examining insurance industry financial practices and market conduct, licensing insurance agents, reviewing policy forms for compliance with state insurance statutes and regulations, investigating consumer complaints, and providing consumer information.

The office administers two segregated insurance funds: the State Life Insurance Fund and the Injured Patients and Families Compensation Fund. The State

the State Historical Society of Wisconsin Endowment Trust Fund, the Injured Patients and Families Compensation Fund, the Tuition Trust Fund, and the UW System Trust Funds.

Department of Justice

Attorney general: Josh Kaul
Deputy attorney general: Eric Wilson
Location: 114 East, State Capitol (attorney general's office); 17 West Main Street, Madison (Department of Justice)
Contact: 608-266-1221; PO Box 7857, Madison, WI 53707-7857
Website: www.doj.state.wi.us
Number of employees: 695.14
Total budget 2017–19: $376,536,300

The Department of Justice is headed by the attorney general, a constitutional officer who is elected on a partisan ballot to a four-year term. The department provides legal advice and representation, investigates criminal activity, and provides various law enforcement services for the state. The department appears for the state and prosecutes or defends civil and criminal actions and proceedings in the court of appeals or the supreme court in which the state is interested or a party. The department prosecutes or defends all civil cases sent or remanded to any circuit court in which the state is a party. The department also represents the state in criminal cases on appeal in federal court.

Subordinate statutory boards, councils, and committees

CRIME VICTIMS COUNCIL

Members: Michelle Arrowood, Ave M. Bie, Tania M. Bonnett, Thomas Eagon, Jane E. Graham Jennings, Chief Kurt D. Heuer, Scott L. Horne, Connie Klick, Dione Knop, Charles S. McGee, Jennifer L. Noyes, Mallory E. O'Brien, Michael S. Rogowski, Kari Sasso, Stephen T'Kach
Contact: ocvs@doj.state.wi.us
Website: https://www.doj.state.wi.us/ocvs/not-crime-victim/crime-victims-council

The Crime Victims Council provides advice and recommendations to the attorney general on the rights of crime victims, how to improve the criminal justice response to victims, and other issues affecting crime victims.

Independent entities attached for administrative purposes

CRIME VICTIMS RIGHTS BOARD

Chair: Timothy Gruenke
Contact: cvrb@doj.state.wi.us

Website: https://www.doj.state.wi.us/ocvs/victim-rights/crime-victims-rights-board

The Crime Victims Rights Board has the authority to review complaints filed by a crime victim that allege that a public official, public employee, or public agency violated the victim's rights. The board may issue a private or public reprimand for a violation, seek appropriate equitable relief on behalf of a victim, or bring a civil action to assess a forfeiture for an intentional violation. The board may issue a report or recommendation concerning the rights of crime victims and the provision of services to crime victims.

LAW ENFORCEMENT STANDARDS BOARD

Chair: Christopher Domagalski
Contact: Stacy Lenz, Training and Standards Bureau deputy director; lenzse@doj.state.
  wi.us; 608-267-3870; 17 West Main St., PO Box 7070, Madison, WI 53707-7070
Website: https://wilenet.org
Curriculum Advisory Committee: Ron Cramer, Nate Dreckman, Joe Fath, Sara Gossfeld-
  Benzing, Mike Hartert, Greg Leck, Mike Lukas, Paul Matl, Richard Oliva, Mark Podoll,
  Jerry Staniszewski, Todd Thomas, Ron Tischer, Sam Wollin,

The Law Enforcement Standards Board sets minimum education and training standards for law enforcement and tribal law enforcement officers. The board certifies persons who meet professional standards as qualified to be law enforcement, tribal law enforcement, jail, or juvenile detention officers. The board consults with other government agencies regarding the development of training schools and courses, conducts research to improve law enforcement and performance, and evaluates governmental units for compliance with board standards.

The Curriculum Advisory Committee advises the Law Enforcement Standards Board on the establishment of curriculum requirements for training of law enforcement, tribal law enforcement, and jail and secure detention officers.

Department of Military Affairs

Commander in chief: Tony Evers (governor)
Adjutant general: Major General Donald P. Dunbar
Deputy adjutant general for army: Brigadier General Joane K. Mathews
Deputy adjutant general for air: Brigadier General Gary L. Ebben
Administrator, Division of Emergency Management: Brian M. Satula
Location: 2400 Wright Street, Madison
Contact: 608-242-3000 (general); 800-335-5147 (toll free); 800-943-0003 (24-hour hotline
  for emergencies and hazardous materials spills); PO Box 8111, Madison, WI 53708-8111
Websites: http://dma.wi.gov (Department of Military Affairs and Wisconsin National
  Guard); https://dma.wi.gov/DMA/wem (Division of Emergency Management)
Number of state employees: 490.30

DEPARTMENT OF MILITARY AFFAIRS

A Wisconsin Army National Guard soldier delivers sandbags to Madison residents during the historic flooding of late summer 2018.

Total state budget 2017–19:
$232,821,200 (An additional $230 million (approximately) annually in federal funding pays for National Guard salaries, benefits, and training.)

The governor is the commander in chief of the state's military forces, which are organized as the Wisconsin National Guard within the Department of Military Affairs. The department is directed by an adjutant general who is appointed by the governor without senate advice and consent. The department also includes the Division of Emergency Management, which is headed by an administrator who is appointed by the governor with the advice and consent of the senate.

The Wisconsin National Guard is maintained by both the federal and the state governments. (When it is called up in an active federal duty status, the president of the United States, rather than the governor, becomes its commander in chief.) The federal mission of the National Guard is to provide trained units to the U.S. Army and U.S. Air Force in time of war or national emergency. Its state mission is to assist civil authorities, protect life and property, and preserve peace, order, and public safety in times of natural or human-caused emergencies. The federal government provides arms and ammunition, equipment and uniforms, major outdoor training facilities, pay for military and support personnel, and training and supervision. The state provides personnel; conducts training as required under the National Defense Act; and shares the cost of constructing, maintaining, and operating armories and other military facilities.

The Division of Emergency Management coordinates the development and implementation of the state emergency operations plan; provides assistance to local jurisdictions in the development of their programs and plans; administers private and federal disaster and emergency relief funds; administers the Wisconsin Disaster Fund; and maintains the state's 24-hour duty officer reporting and response system. The division also conducts training programs in emergency planning for businesses and state and local officials, as well as educational programs for the general public. It also prepares for off-site radiological emergencies at nuclear power plants and provides assistance for various emergencies such as prison disturbances and natural disasters.

Independent entities attached for administrative purposes

INTEROPERABILITY COUNCIL

Chair: Matthew Joski
Website: https://dma.wi.gov/DMA/oec/programs/interop

The Interoperability Council develops strategies and makes recommendations on how to achieve and operate a statewide public safety interoperable communication system.

Department of Natural Resources

Natural Resources Board: Frederick Prehn, *chair*
Department secretary: Preston D. Cole
Deputy secretary: Elizabeth Kluesner
Location: State Natural Resources Building (GEF 2), 101 South Webster Street, Madison
Contact: 888-936-7463 (TTY access via relay 711); PO Box 7921, Madison, WI 53707-7921
Website: http://dnr.wi.gov
Number of employees: 2,500.60
Total budget 2017–19: $1,086,916,300

The Department of Natural Resources is directed and supervised by the Natural Resources Board and is administered by a secretary. The members of the board and the secretary are appointed by the governor with the advice and consent of the senate.

The department is responsible for implementing state and federal laws that protect and enhance Wisconsin's natural resources, including its air, land, water, forests, wildlife, fish, and plants. It coordinates the many state-administered programs that protect the environment and provides a full range of outdoor recreational opportunities for Wisconsin residents and visitors.

Subordinate statutory boards, councils, and committees

DRY CLEANER ENVIRONMENTAL RESPONSE COUNCIL

The Dry Cleaner Environmental Response Council advises the department on matters relating to the Dry Cleaner Environmental Response Program, which is administered by the department and which provides awards to dry cleaning

DEPARTMENT OF NATURAL RESOURCES

Visitors to the overlook at Wyalusing State Park in Grant County can view the meeting point of the Wisconsin and Mississippi Rivers.

establishments for assistance in the investigation and cleanup of environmental contamination.

COUNCIL ON FORESTRY

The Council on Forestry advises the governor, legislature, department, and other state agencies on topics relating to forestry in Wisconsin, including protection from fire, insects, and disease; sustainable forestry; reforestation and forestry genetics; management and protection of urban forests; increasing the public's knowledge and awareness of forestry issues; forestry research; economic development and marketing of forestry products; legislation affecting forestry; and staff and funding needs for forestry programs.

METALLIC MINING COUNCIL

The Metallic Mining Council advises the department on matters relating to the reclamation of mined land and the disposal of metallic mine-related waste. The council is currently inactive.

NATURAL AREAS PRESERVATION COUNCIL

The Natural Areas Preservation Council advises the department on matters pertaining to the protection of natural areas that contain native biotic communities and habitats for rare species. It also makes recommendations about gifts or purchases for the state natural areas system.

NONMOTORIZED RECREATION AND TRANSPORTATION TRAILS COUNCIL

The Nonmotorized Recreation and Transportation Trails Council carries out studies and advises the governor, the legislature, the department, and the Department of Transportation on matters relating to nonmotorized recreation and transportation trails.

OFF-HIGHWAY MOTORCYCLE COUNCIL

The Off-Highway Motorcycle Council makes recommendations to the department on matters relating to off-highway motorcycle corridors and routes and the operation of off-highway motorcycles.

OFF-ROAD VEHICLE COUNCIL

The Off-Road Vehicle Council advises the department, the Department of Transportation, the governor, and the legislature on all matters relating to all-terrain vehicle trails and routes.

SMALL BUSINESS ENVIRONMENTAL COUNCIL

The Small Business Environmental Council advises the department on the effectiveness of assistance programs to small businesses that enable the businesses to comply with the federal Clean Air Act. It also advises on the fairness and effectiveness of air pollution rules promulgated by the department and the U.S. Environmental Protection Agency regarding their impact on small businesses.

SNOWMOBILE RECREATIONAL COUNCIL

The Snowmobile Recreational Council carries out studies and makes recommendations to the governor, the legislature, the department, and the Department of Transportation regarding all matters affecting snowmobiling.

SPORTING HERITAGE COUNCIL

The Sporting Heritage Council advises the governor, the legislature, and the Natural Resources Board about issues relating to hunting, trapping, fishing, and other types of outdoor recreation activities.

STATE TRAILS COUNCIL

The State Trails Council advises the department about the planning, acquisition, development, and management of state trails.

WETLAND STUDY COUNCIL

The Wetland Study Council conducts research and develops recommendations on a range of topics involving wetland policy, procedures, regulations, and financing, including the implementation and effectiveness of statewide wetland mitigation programs; statewide incentive programs for creating, restoring, and enhancing wetlands; providing statewide wetland trainings; and methods of financing wetland mitigation requirements for local units of government.

Other statutorily required advisory entities

FIRE DEPARTMENT ADVISORY COUNCIL

The Fire Department Advisory Council was chartered in 1994 as an official advisory council to the state forester. The purpose of the council is to strengthen partnerships between the department and the rural fire service in Wisconsin. The council advises and assists the state forester on operational issues relating to the department's forest fire management program to provide for an effective rural community fire protection program. In addition, the council provides fundamental guidance on the administration of the Forest Fire Protection Grant.

URBAN FORESTRY COUNCIL

The Urban Forestry Council advises the state forester and the department on the best ways to preserve, protect, expand, and improve Wisconsin's urban and community forest resources. The council gives awards to outstanding individuals, organizations, and communities that further urban forestry in Wisconsin.

Independent entities attached for administrative purposes

GROUNDWATER COORDINATING COUNCIL

Chair: James Zellmer

The Groundwater Coordinating Council advises state agencies on the coordination of nonregulatory programs relating to groundwater management. Member agencies exchange information regarding groundwater monitoring, budgets for groundwater programs, data management, public information efforts, laboratory analyses, research, and state appropriations for research.

INVASIVE SPECIES COUNCIL

Chair: Thomas Buechel

The Invasive Species Council conducts studies relating to controlling invasive species and makes recommendations to the department regarding a system for classifying invasive species under the department's statewide invasive species control program and regarding procedures for awarding grants to public and private agencies engaged in projects to control invasive species.

LAKE MICHIGAN COMMERCIAL FISHING BOARD

Members: Charles W. Henriksen, Richard R. Johnson, Michael LeClair, Mark Maricque, Dan Pawlitzke, Brent Schwarz, Todd Stuth

The Lake Michigan Commercial Fishing Board reviews applications for transfers of commercial fishing licenses between individuals, establishes criteria for allotting catch quotas to individual licensees, assigns catch quotas when the department establishes special harvest limits, and assists the department in establishing criteria for identifying inactive license holders.

LAKE SUPERIOR COMMERCIAL FISHING BOARD

Members: Bill Bodin, Maurine Halvorson, Craig Hoopman, Bob Nelson, 1 vacancy

The Lake Superior Commercial Fishing Board reviews applications for transfers of commercial fishing licenses between individuals, establishes criteria for allotting catch quotas to individual licensees, assigns catch quotas when the department establishes special harvest limits, and assists the department in establishing criteria for identifying inactive license holders.

LOWER WISCONSIN STATE RIVERWAY BOARD

The Lower Wisconsin State Riverway Board is responsible for protecting and preserving the scenic beauty and natural character of the riverway. The board reviews permit applications for buildings, walkways and stairways, timber harvests, nonmetallic mining, utility facilities, public access sites, bridges, and other structures in the riverway and issues permits for activities that meet established standards.

COUNCIL ON RECYCLING

Chair: David Keeling

The Council on Recycling promotes implementation of the state's solid waste reduction, recovery, and recycling programs; helps public agencies coordinate programs and exchange information; advises state agencies about creating administrative rules and establishing priorities for market development; and advises the department and the University of Wisconsin System about education and research relating to solid waste recycling. The council also works with the packaging industry on standards for recyclable packaging and works with counties, municipalities, and the auto service industry to promote the recycling of oil filters. The council advises the department about statewide public information activities and advises the governor and the legislature.

WISCONSIN WATERWAYS COMMISSION

Chair: Roger Walsh

The Wisconsin Waterways Commission conducts studies to determine the need for recreational boating facilities; approves financial aid to local governments for development of recreational boating projects, including the acquisition of weed harvesters; and recommends administrative rules for the recreational facilities boating program.

Affiliated entity

CONSERVATION CONGRESS

The Conservation Congress is a publicly elected citizen advisory group, and its district leadership council advises the Natural Resources Board on all matters under the board's jurisdiction.

Office of the State Public Defender

Public Defender Board: Daniel M. Berkos, *chair*
State public defender: Kelli S. Thompson
Deputy state public defender: vacancy
Location: 17 South Fairchild Street, 5th Floor, Madison
Contact: 608-266-0087; PO Box 7923, Madison, WI 53707-7923
Website: www.wispd.org
Number of employees: 615.85
Total budget 2017–19: $ 176,751,100

The Office of the State Public Defender provides legal representation to indigent persons and to persons otherwise entitled to such representation. The state public defender, who must be a member of the state bar, serves at the pleasure of the Public Defender Board. Board members are appointed by the governor with the advice and consent of the senate.

Attorneys are assigned by the state public defender to persons charged with a crime that may be sentenced by imprisonment and to other cases, such as cases involving paternity determinations, termination of parental rights, emergency detentions, involuntary commitments, modification of bifurcated sentences, and certain appeals.

Department of Public Instruction

State superintendent of public instruction: Carolyn Stanford Taylor
Deputy state superintendent: Mike Thompson
Location: State Education Building (GEF 3), 125 South Webster Street, Madison
Contact: 608-266-3390; 800-441-4563 (toll free); PO Box 7841, Madison, WI 53707-7841
Website: www.dpi.wi.gov
Number of employees: 642.00
Total budget 2017–19: $14,228,084,600

The Department of Public Instruction is headed by the state superintendent of public instruction, a constitutional officer who is elected on the nonpartisan spring ballot for a term of four years. The department provides guidance and technical assistance to support public elementary and secondary education in Wisconsin. The department also administers the Milwaukee, Racine, and Statewide Parental Choice Programs; the Special Needs Scholarship Program; the open enrollment program; and a number of educational and other services for children and their families.

The department offers a broad range of programs and professional services to local school administrators and staff. It also reviews and approves educator preparation programs and licenses teachers, pupil services personnel, administrators, and library professionals. The department distributes state and federal aids to supplement local tax revenue, improve curriculum and school operations, ensure education for children with disabilities, offer professional guidance and counseling, and develop school and public library resources. The department also administers the Wisconsin Educational Services Program for the Deaf and Hard of Hearing and the Wisconsin Center for the Blind and Visually Impaired.

Finally, the department provides assistance for the development and improvement of public and school libraries. The department fosters interlibrary cooperation and resource sharing and promotes information and instructional technology in schools and libraries. The department also acts as a state-level clearinghouse for interlibrary loan requests; administers BadgerLink (https://badgerlink.dpi.wi.gov), the statewide full-text database project that allows access to thousands of magazines, newsletters, newspapers, pamphlets, and historical documents; and, in collaboration with other Wisconsin library organizations, manages BadgerLearn, the statewide portal that provides continuing education resources for library professionals.

Subordinate statutory boards, councils, and committees

STATE SUPERINTENDENT'S ADVISORY COUNCIL ON ALCOHOL AND OTHER DRUG ABUSE PROBLEMS

Contact: Brenda Jennings; brenda.jennings@dpi.wi.gov

The council advises the governor, the legislature, and state agencies about programs to prevent or reduce alcohol, tobacco, and other drug abuse.

BLIND AND VISUAL IMPAIRMENT EDUCATION COUNCIL

Contact: 608-758-6100

Website: http://www.wcbvi.k12.wi.us/outreach/state-superintendents-advisory-council

The Blind and Visual Impairment Education Council provides advice on educational and library services to blind and visually impaired people and provides advice on the services of the Wisconsin Center for the Blind and Visually Impaired.

DEAF AND HARD-OF-HEARING EDUCATION COUNCIL

Contact: Marla Walsh; marla.walsh@wsd.12k.wi.us
Website: https://dpi.wi.gov/sped/program/deaf-hard-of-hearing/advisory

The Deaf and Hard-of-Hearing Education Council advises the state superintendent on issues related to pupils who are hearing impaired and informs the state superintendent about services, programs, and research that could benefit those pupils.

COUNCIL ON LIBRARY AND NETWORK DEVELOPMENT

Contact: Alison Hiam; 608-266-6439
Website: https://dpi.wi.gov/coland

The Council on Library and Network Development advises the state superintendent and the administrator of the Division for Libraries and Technology to ensure that all state citizens have access to library and information services.

PROFESSIONAL STANDARDS COUNCIL FOR TEACHERS

Website: https://dpi.wi.gov/tepdl/programs/psc

The Professional Standards Council for Teachers advises the state superintendent regarding licensing and evaluating teachers; the evaluation and approval of teacher education programs; the status of teaching in Wisconsin; school board practices to develop effective teaching; peer mentoring; evaluation systems; alternative dismissal procedures; and alternative procedures for the preparation and licensure of teachers.

SCHOOL DISTRICT BOUNDARY APPEAL BOARD

Contact: Janice Zmrazek; janice.zmrazek@dpi.wi.gov; 608-266-2803
Website: https://dpi.wi.gov/sms/school-district-boundary-appeal-board

Panels consisting of three or seven members of the School District Boundary Appeal Board hear appeals related to school district creation and dissolution, annexation, and boundary disputes.

COUNCIL ON SPECIAL EDUCATION

Contact: Jennifer Mims Howell; mimshjn@milwaukee.k12.wi.us; 414-438-3648
Website: https://dpi.wi.gov/sped/council

The Council on Special Education advises the state superintendent on matters related to meeting the needs and improving the education of children with disabilities.

Board of Commissioners of Public Lands

Members: Douglas J. La Follette (secretary of state), Sarah Godlewski (state treasurer), Joshua L. Kaul (attorney general)

Division of Trust Lands and Investments: Jonathan B. Barry, *executive secretary*; Tom German, *deputy secretary*; Richard Sneider, *chief investment officer*
Location: 101 East Wilson Street, 2nd Floor, Madison
Contact: 608-266-1370; PO Box 8943, Madison, WI 53708-8943
Website: https://bcpl.wisconsin.gov
Number of employees: 9.50
Total budget 2017–19: $3,358,200

The Board of Commissioners of Public Lands is a body established in the Wisconsin Constitution. The board is composed of the secretary of state, state treasurer, and attorney general. The board manages the state's remaining trust lands, manages trust funds primarily for the benefit of public education, and maintains the state's original 19th-century land survey and land sales records. The board is assisted in its work by the Division of Trust Lands and Investments, an entity attached to the Department of Administration for administrative purposes.

The board holds title to nearly 76,000 acres of school trust lands. These lands are managed for timber production, natural area preservation, and public use. The board manages four trust funds, totaling over $1 billion in assets. The largest of these is the Common School Fund. The principal of this fund continues to grow through the collection of fees, fines, and forfeitures that accrue to the state. The board invests the moneys of this fund in state and municipal bonds. It also loans moneys from this fund directly to Wisconsin municipalities and school districts through the State Trust Fund Loan Program. These loans are used for economic development, school repairs and improvements, local infrastructure and utilities, and capital equipment and vehicles. The net earnings of the Common School Fund are distributed annually by the Department of Public Instruction to all of Wisconsin's public school districts and provide the sole source of state aid for public school library media and resources. The other trust funds are used to support the University of Wisconsin and the state's general fund.

Public Service Commission

Members: Rebecca Cameron Valcq, *chair*; Mike Huebsch, Ellen Nowak
Executive assistant to the chair: Kathy Endres
Location: 4822 Madison Yards Way, North Tower—6th Floor, Madison
Contact: pscrecordsmail@wisconsin.gov (general); PSCPublicRecordsRequest@Wisconsin.gov (public records requests); 608-266-5481; 888-816-3831 (toll free); 608-266-2001 (consumer complaints); 800-225-7729 (consumer complaints, toll free); PO Box 7854, Madison, WI 53707-7854
Website: http://psc.wi.gov
Number of employees: 153.25
Total budget 2017–19: $71,351,500

The Public Service Commission consists of three commissioners appointed by the governor with the advice and consent of the senate for six-year terms. The governor appoints one of the commissioners as chair for a two-year term. A commissioner may not have a financial interest in a railroad, public utility, or water carrier; may not be a candidate for public office; and is subject to certain restrictions regarding political activity.

The commission is responsible for regulating Wisconsin's public utilities and ensuring that utility services are provided to customers safely, reliably, and at prices reasonable to both ratepayers and utility owners. The commission also regulates the rates and services of electric, natural gas distribution, water, and municipal combined water and sewer utilities. The commission's responsibilities include determining levels for adequate and safe service; overseeing compliance with renewable energy and energy conservation and efficiency requirements; approving public utility bond sales and stock offerings; and approving mergers, consolidations, and ownership changes regarding public utilities. The commission also considers applications for major construction projects, such as power plants, transmission lines, and wind farms. In addition to ensuring public utility compliance with statutes, administrative codes, and record-keeping requirements, commission staff investigates and mediates consumer complaints.

The commission has limited jurisdiction over landline telecommunications providers and services. The commission certifies various types of telecommunications providers; manages the Universal Service Fund; handles some wholesale disputes between telecommunications providers; and administers telephone numbering resources. In general, the commission has no jurisdiction over electric cooperatives, liquefied petroleum gas, fuel oil, wireless telephone, or cable television. Although the commission has no jurisdiction over Internet service, it does provide oversight for statewide broadband mapping and planning and makes grants for constructing broadband infrastructure in underserved areas. Also, the commission has enforcement authority for Digger's Hotline violations involving natural gas or other hazardous materials.

Subordinate statutory boards, councils, and committees

UNIVERSAL SERVICE FUND COUNCIL

Contact: Holly O'Higgins, Universal Service Fund director; hollyohiggins@wisconsin.gov; 608-267-9486; PO Box 7854, Madison, WI 53707-7854

The Universal Service Fund Council advises the commission on the administration of the Universal Service Fund. The purposes of the fund include assisting low-income customers, customers in areas where telecommunications service costs are relatively high, and customers with disabilities in obtaining affordable access to basic telecommunications services. The Universal Service Fund director acts as the liaison between the Public Service Commission and the council.

WIND SITING COUNCIL

The Wind Siting Council advises the commission on the promulgation of rules relating to restrictions that a political subdivision may impose on the installation or use of a wind energy system, including setback requirements that provide reasonable protection from any health effects. The council also surveys the peer-reviewed scientific research regarding the health impacts of wind energy systems and studies state and national regulatory developments regarding the siting of wind energy systems.

Independent entities attached for administrative purposes

OFFICE OF THE COMMISSIONER OF RAILROADS

Commissioner of railroads: Yash Wadhwa
Location: 4822 Madison Yards Way, Suite S633, Madison
Contact: 608-261-8221; PO Box 7854, Madison, WI 53707-7854
Website: http://ocr.wi.gov
Number of employees: 6.00
Total budget 2017–19: $ 1,117,700

The governor appoints the commissioner of railroads with the advice and consent of the senate for a six-year term. The commissioner may not have a financial interest in railroads or water carriers and may not serve on or under any committee of a political party. The Office of the Commissioner of Railroads enforces regulations related to railway safety and determines the safety of highway crossings, including the adequacy of railroad warning devices. The office also has authority over the rates and services of intrastate water carriers.

Department of Revenue

Department secretary: Peter Barca
Deputy secretary: David Casey
Location: 2135 Rimrock Road, Madison
Contact: 608-266-2772 (office phone); 608-266-2486 (individuals); 608-266-2776 (businesses); PO Box 8906, Madison, WI 53708-8906
Website: www.revenue.wi.gov
Number of employees: 1,182.03
Total budget 2017-19: $421,581,300

The Department of Revenue is administered by a secretary who is appointed by

DEPARTMENT OF REVENUE

The Department of Revenue provides services to taxpayers by administering the state's tax laws.

the governor with the advice and consent of the senate. The department administers all major state tax laws except the insurance premiums tax and enforces the state's alcohol beverage and tobacco laws. It estimates state revenues, forecasts state economic activity, helps formulate tax policy, and administers the Wisconsin Lottery. The department also determines the equalized value of taxable property and assesses manufacturing and telecommunications company property for property tax purposes. It administers local financial assistance programs and assists local governments in their property assessments and financial management. The department also oversees Wisconsin's Unclaimed Property program to match taxpayers with unclaimed financial assets.

Subordinate statutory boards, councils, and committees

STATE BOARD OF ASSESSORS

The State Board of Assessors investigates objections to the amount, valuation, or taxability of real or personal manufacturing property, as well as objections to the penalties issued for late filing or nonfiling of required manufacturing property report forms.

FARMLAND ADVISORY COUNCIL

The Farmland Advisory Council advises the department on implementing use-value assessment of agricultural land and reducing the expansion of urban sprawl. It reports annually to the legislature on the usefulness of use-value assessment as a way to preserve farmland and reduce the conversion of farmland to other uses. The council also recommends changes to the shared revenue formula to compensate local governments adversely affected by use-value assessment.

Independent entities attached for administrative purposes

INVESTMENT AND LOCAL IMPACT FUND BOARD

Chair: Peter Barca

The Investment and Local Impact Fund Board administers the Investment and Local Impact Fund, created to help municipalities alleviate costs associated with social, educational, environmental, and economic impacts of metalliferous mineral mining. The board certifies to the Department of Administration the amount of the payments to be distributed to municipalities from the fund. It also provides funding to local governments throughout the development of a mining project.

Department of Safety and Professional Services

Department secretary: Dawn B. Crim
Deputy secretary: Nia Trammell
Contact: 608-266-2112; 4822 Madison Yards Way, Madison, WI 53705
Website: http://dsps.wi.gov
Number of employees: 236.14
Total budget 2017–19: $111,889,200

The Department of Safety and Professional Services is administered by a secretary who is appointed by the governor with the advice and consent of the senate.

The department administers and enforces laws to ensure safe and sanitary conditions in public and private buildings, including by reviewing plans and performing inspections of commercial buildings and certain of their components and systems.

The department is also responsible for ensuring the safe and competent practice of various licensed occupations and businesses in Wisconsin. The department provides direct regulation or licensing of certain occupations and businesses. In addition, numerous boards are attached to the department that are responsible for regulating other occupations and businesses. In general, these boards determine the education and experience required for credentialing, develop and evaluate examinations, and establish standards for professional conduct. The department or the relevant board may reprimand a credential holder in a field that it regulates; limit, suspend, or revoke the credential of a practitioner who violates laws or rules; and, in some cases, impose forfeitures. The department provides administrative services to the boards and policy assistance in such areas as evaluating and establishing new professional licensing programs, creating routine procedures for legal proceedings, and adjusting policies in response to public needs. The department also investigates and prosecutes complaints against credential holders and assists with drafting administrative rules.

Under DSPS's Educational Approval Program, DSPS is also responsible for approving and overseeing most private, for-profit postsecondary schools offering educational programs or occupational training in this state; in-state private, nonprofit colleges and universities incorporated after 1991; and out-of-state postsecondary institutions offering distance education to Wisconsin residents if the institution is not located in a state participating in the State Authorization Reciprocity Agreement (see Distance Learning Authorization Board for more information on SARA).

Subordinate statutory boards, councils, and committees

AUTOMATIC FIRE SPRINKLER SYSTEM CONTRACTORS AND JOURNEYMEN COUNCIL

Contact: Yolanda Y. McGowan; yolanda.mcgowan@wisconsin.gov; 608-266-8419

The Automatic Fire Sprinkler System Contractors and Journeymen Council advises the department on rules for credentials required for installing and maintaining automatic fire sprinkler systems.

COMMERCIAL BUILDING CODE COUNCIL

Contact: Yolanda Y. McGowan; yolanda.mcgowan@wisconsin.gov; 608-266-8419

The Commercial Building Code Council advises the department on rules relating to public buildings and buildings that are places of employment. The council also reviews and makes recommendations pertaining to the department's rules for constructing, altering, adding to, repairing, and maintaining those types of buildings.

CONTROLLED SUBSTANCES BOARD

Contact: Debra Sybell; debra.sybell@wisconsin.gov; 608-267-7223

The Controlled Substances Board classifies controlled substances into schedules that regulate the prescription, use, and possession of controlled substances. The board also approves special use permits for controlled substances.

CONVEYANCE SAFETY CODE COUNCIL

Contact: Yolanda Y. McGowan; yolanda.mcgowan@wisconsin.gov; 608-266-8419

The Conveyance Safety Code Council makes recommendations to the department pertaining to safety standards for elevators, escalators, and similar conveyances.

MANUFACTURED HOUSING CODE COUNCIL

Contact: Yolanda Y. McGowan; yolanda.mcgowan@wisconsin.gov; 608-266-8419

The Manufactured Housing Code Council makes recommendations to the department pertaining to standards for the construction, installation, and sale of manufactured homes.

PLUMBERS COUNCIL

Contact: Yolanda Y. McGowan; yolanda.mcgowan@wisconsin.gov; 608-266-8419

The Plumbers Council advises the department on rules for credentials required for plumbing.

SIGN LANGUAGE INTERPRETER COUNCIL

Contact: Debra Sybell; debra.sybell@wisconsin.gov; 608-267-7223

The Sign Language Interpreter Council advises the department on rules for the practice of sign language interpreters and grants temporary and permanent exemptions from a department-issued license for sign language interpreters.

UNIFORM DWELLING CODE COUNCIL

Contact: Yolanda Y. McGowan; yolanda.mcgowan@wisconsin.gov; 608-266-8419

The Uniform Dwelling Code Council reviews and makes recommendations for department rules regarding the construction and inspection of one-family and two-family dwellings and regarding continuing education, examinations, and financial responsibility for building contractors. The council also reviews complaints about building inspectors and recommends disciplinary action to the department. In addition, the council reviews and makes recommendations for department rules regarding modular homes.

Independent entities attached for administrative purposes

These are the occupation and business regulating boards described in the write-up of the department given above. (In each case, the occupations or businesses regulated are indicated by the entity's name.)

ACCOUNTING EXAMINING BOARD

Chair: John S. Scheid
Contact: Christian Albouras; christian.albouras@wisconsin.gov; 608-261-5406

EXAMINING BOARD OF ARCHITECTS, LANDSCAPE ARCHITECTS, PROFESSIONAL ENGINEERS, DESIGNERS AND PROFESSIONAL LAND SURVEYORS

Chair: Rosheen Styczinski
Architect section chair: Steven L. Wagner
Designer section chair: vacancy
Engineer section chair: Mark E. Mayer
Landscape architect section chair: Rosheen M. Styczinski
Land surveyor section chair: Bruce D. Bowden
Contact: Christian Albouras; christian.albouras@wisconsin.gov; 608-261-5406

ATHLETIC TRAINERS AFFILIATED CREDENTIALING BOARD (affiliated to Medical Examining Board)

Members: Jay J. Davide, Kurt A. Fielding, John J. Johnsen, Gregory S. Vergamini, 2 vacancies

Contact: Yolanda Y. McGowan; yolanda.mcgowan@wisconsin.gov; 608-266-8419

AUCTIONEER BOARD

Chair: Jerry L. Thiel

Contact: Debra Sybell; debra.sybell@wisconsin.gov; 608-267-7223

CEMETERY BOARD

Members: Kathleen M. Cantu, Patricia A. Grathen, Francis J. Groh, John M. Reinemann, Bernard G. Schroedl, 1 vacancy

Contact: Debra Sybell; debra.sybell@wisconsin.gov; 608-267-7223

CHIROPRACTIC EXAMINING BOARD

Chair: Patricia A. Schumacher

Contact: Yolanda Y. McGowan; yolanda.mcgowan@wisconsin.gov; 608-266-8419

COSMETOLOGY EXAMINING BOARD

Chair: Vicky L. McNally

Contact: Christian Albouras; christian.albouras@wisconsin.gov; 608-261-5406

DENTISTRY EXAMINING BOARD

Chair: Matthew R. Bistan

Contact: Christian Albouras; christian.albouras@wisconsin.gov; 608-261-5406

DIETITIANS AFFILIATED CREDENTIALING BOARD (affiliated to Medical Examining Board)

Chair: Tara L. LaRowe

Contact: Yolanda Y. McGowan; yolanda.mcgowan@wisconsin.gov; 608-266-8419

FUNERAL DIRECTORS EXAMINING BOARD

Chair: Marc A. Eernisse

Contact: Debra Sybell; debra.sybell@wisconsin.gov; 608-267-7223

EXAMINING BOARD OF PROFESSIONAL GEOLOGISTS, HYDROLOGISTS AND SOIL SCIENTISTS

Chair: William N. Mode

Geologist section chair: William N. Mode

Hydrologist section chair: Randall J. Hunt

Soil scientist section: (all seats currently vacant)

Contact: Debra Sybell; debra.sybell@wisconsin.gov; 608-267-7223

HEARING AND SPEECH EXAMINING BOARD

Chair: Thomas K. Krier

Contact: Yolanda Y. McGowan; yolanda.mcgowan@wisconsin.gov; 608-266-8419

MARRIAGE AND FAMILY THERAPY, PROFESSIONAL COUNSELING AND SOCIAL WORK EXAMINING BOARD

Chair: Bridget C. Ellingboe
Marriage and family therapist section chair: vacancy
Professional counselor section chair: Tammy H. Scheidegger
Social worker section chair: vacancy
Contact: Debra Sybell; debra.sybell@wisconsin.gov; 608-267-7223

MASSAGE THERAPY AND BODYWORK THERAPY AFFILIATED CREDENTIALING BOARD (affiliated to Medical Examining Board)

Members: Elizabeth C. Krizenesky, 6 vacancies
Contact: Yolanda Y. McGowan; yolanda.mcgowan@wisconsin.gov; 608-266-8419

MEDICAL EXAMINING BOARD

Chair: Kenneth B. Simons
Contact: Yolanda Y. McGowan; yolanda.mcgowan@wisconsin.gov; 608-266-8419
Advisory councils assisting the board: Council on Anesthesiologists Assistants, Michael L. Bottcher, *chair*; Perfusionists Examining Council, Shawn E. Mergen, *chair*; Council on Physician Assistants, Jennifer L. Jarrett, *chair*; Respiratory Care Practitioners Examining Council, William D. Rosandick, *chair*

BOARD OF NURSING

Chair: Peter J. Kallio
Contact: Debra Sybell; debra.sybell@wisconsin.gov; 608-267-7223

NURSING HOME ADMINISTRATOR EXAMINING BOARD

Members: Kathleen E. Bertram, Brittany M. Cobb, Charles D. Hawkins, Susan Kinast-Porter, Jessica Radtke
Contact: Yolanda Y. McGowan; yolanda.mcgowan@wisconsin.gov; 608-266-8419

OCCUPATIONAL THERAPISTS AFFILIATED CREDENTIALING BOARD (affiliated to Medical Examining Board)

Chair: Brian B. Holmquist
Contact: Yolanda Y. McGowan; yolanda.mcgowan@wisconsin.gov; 608-266-8419

OPTOMETRY EXAMINING BOARD

Chair: Ann Meier Carli
Contact: Yolanda Y. McGowan; yolanda.mcgowan@wisconsin.gov; 608-266-8419

PHARMACY EXAMINING BOARD

Chair: Philip J. Trapskin
Contact: Debra Sybel; debra.sybell@wisconsin.gov; 608-267-7223

PHYSICAL THERAPY EXAMINING BOARD

Chair: Shari L. Berry
Contact: Yolanda Y. McGowan; yolanda.mcgowan@wisconsin.gov; 608-266-8419

PODIATRY AFFILIATED CREDENTIALING BOARD (affiliated to Medical Examining Board)

Members: Jeffrey L. Giesking, Thomas R. Komp, 2 vacancies

Contact: Yolanda Y. McGowan; yolanda.mcgowan@wisconsin.gov; 608-266-8419

PSYCHOLOGY EXAMINING BOARD

Members: Rebecca C. Anderson, Marcus P. Desmonde, Daniel A. Schroeder, Peter I. Sorce, David W. Thompson, 1 vacancy

Contact: Debra Sybell; debra.sybell@wisconsin.gov; 608-267-7223

RADIOGRAPHY EXAMINING BOARD

Chair: Donald A. Borst

Contact: Yolanda Y. McGowan; yolanda.mcgowan@wisconsin.gov; 608-266-8419

REAL ESTATE APPRAISERS BOARD

Chair: Carl N. Clementi

Contact: Yolanda Y. McGowan; yolanda.mcgowan@wisconsin.gov; 608-266-8419

REAL ESTATE EXAMINING BOARD

Chair: Robert L. Webster

Contact: Christian Albouras; christian.albouras@wisconsin.gov; 608-261-5406

Advisory councils assisting the board: Council on Real Estate Curriculum and Examinations, Casey C. Clickner, *chair*

Office of the Secretary of State

Secretary of state: Douglas La Follette
Location: B41 West, State Capitol, Madison
Contact: statesec@wisconsin.gov; 608-266-8888; PO Box 7848, Madison, WI 53707-7848
Website: www.sos.state.wi.us
Number of employees: 2.00
Total budget 2017–19: $531,400

The secretary of state is a constitutional officer elected for a four-year term by partisan ballot in the November general election. The secretary of state maintains the official acts of the legislature and governor and keeps the Great Seal of the State of Wisconsin, affixing it to all official acts of the governor. Along with the attorney general and the state treasurer, the secretary of state serves on the Board of Commissioners of Public Lands. The secretary of state may also be called upon to act as governor under certain circumstances, for example, if the sitting governor dies or resigns and there is a vacancy in the office of lieutenant governor.

Office of the State Treasurer

State treasurer: Sarah Godlewski
Location: Room B38 West, State Capitol, Madison
Mailing address: PO Box 7871 Madison, WI 53707
Contact: Treasurer@wisconsin.gov; 608-266-1714
Website: https://statetreasurer.wisconsin.gov
Number of employees: 1.00
Total budget 2017–19: $227,000

The state treasurer is a constitutional officer elected for a four-year term by partisan ballot in the November general election. The state treasurer signs certain checks and financial instruments and helps to promote the state's unclaimed property program. Along with the attorney general and secretary of state, the state treasurer serves on the Board of Commissioners of Public Lands.

Technical College System

Technical College System Board: S. Mark Tyler, *president*
System president: Morna K. Foy
Location: 4622 University Avenue, Madison
Contact: communications@wtcsystem.edu; 608-266-1207; PO Box 7874, Madison, WI
    53707-7874
Website: https://wtcsystem.edu
Number of employees: 56.00
Total budget 2017–19: $1,114,151,700

The Technical College System Board is the coordinating and oversight agency for the Technical College System. The governor, with the advice and consent of the senate, appoints 10 of the board's 13 members, 9 to serve six-year terms and a technical college student to serve a two-year term. The remaining members are the state superintendent of public instruction, the secretary of workforce development, and the president of the Board of Regents of the University of Wisconsin System (but each of these officers may designate another individual to serve in his or her place).

    The board establishes statewide policies for the educational programs and services provided by the state's 16 technical college districts. (The districts, in turn, are responsible for the direct operation of the technical colleges, including setting academic and grading standards and hiring instructional staff for their programs.) The board defines, approves, evaluates, and reviews educational programs; provides guidance to the technical college districts in developing financial policies and standards; distributes state and federal aid; sets student fees;

The Wisconsin Technical College System is responsible for training students for a variety of careers. (*left*) The Fire Service Training program trains professional and volunteer firefighters. (*right*) The short-term truck driving program prepares individuals for careers on the road.

sets standards for and approves building projects; oversees district budgets and enrollments; coordinates state and federal grant programs and student financial aid; and supports services for students.

The board also coordinates with the University of Wisconsin System on programming and college transfer courses and with other state agencies on vocational and technical education programs and apprentice training.

Department of Tourism

Department secretary: Sara Meaney
Deputy secretary: Anne Sayers
Location: 201 West Washington Avenue, 2nd Floor, Madison
Contact: tourinfo@travelwisconsin.com; 608-266-2161; 800-432-8747; 608-266-7621 (information for the tourism industry); PO Box 8690, Madison, WI 53708-8690
Websites: www.travelwisconsin.com (information for tourists); http://industry.travelwisconsin.com (information for the tourism industry)
Number of employees: 30.00
Total budget 2017–19: $31,005,800

The Department of Tourism is administered by a secretary who is appointed by the governor with the advice and consent of the senate. The department formulates and implements a statewide marketing strategy to promote travel to Wisconsin's scenic, historic, natural, agricultural, educational, and recreational attractions. The department coordinates its efforts with public and private organizations and provides assistance to travel-related and recreational industries and their consumers. The department also does the following: (1) makes grants to local governments, American Indian organizations, and nonprofits for tourist information centers and marketing projects; (2) provides marketing services to state agencies; and (3) coordinates its economic development activities with the Wisconsin Economic Development Corporation and makes annual reports to the legislature assessing those activities.

Subordinate statutory boards, councils, and committees

ARTS BOARD

Chair: Kevin Miller
Executive director: George Tzougros
Location: 201 West Washington Avenue, second floor, Madison
Contact: artsboard@wisconsin.gov; 608-266-0190; PO Box 8690, Madison, WI 53708-8690
Website: https://artsboard.wisconsin.gov
Number of employees: 4.00
Total budget 2017–19: $3,247,200

The Arts Board studies and assists artistic and cultural activities in the state, assists communities in developing their own arts programs, and plans and implements financial support programs for individuals and organizations engaged in the arts, including creation and presentation grants, folk art apprenticeships, creative communities grants, and challenge grants to organizations that exceed fundraising goals. The board also provides matching grants to local arts agencies and municipalities through the Wisconsin Regranting Program.

Kayakers view the rock formations at the Apostle Islands north of Bayfield. Hundreds of thousands of visitors to the area contribute millions of tourist dollars to the local economy.

DEPARTMENT OF TOURISM

COUNCIL ON TOURISM

Chair: Paul Upchurch
Website: http://industry.travelwisconsin.com/about-the-department/
governors-council-on-tourism

The Council on Tourism advises the secretary on tourism, including assisting in the formulation of the statewide marketing strategy. The council also develops and adopts a plan for encouraging Wisconsin-based companies to promote the state in their advertisements.

Independent entities attached for administrative purposes

KICKAPOO RESERVE MANAGEMENT BOARD

Chair: Ronald M. Johnson
Executive director: Marcy West
Contact: kickapoo.reserve@krm.state.wi.us; 608-625-2960; S3661 State Highway 131,
La Farge, WI 54639
Website: http://kvr.state.wi.us
Number of employees: 4.00
Total budget 2017–19: $1,936,800

The Kickapoo Reserve Management Board manages the approximately 8,600-acre Kickapoo Valley Reserve through a joint management agreement with the Ho-Chunk Nation. The Kickapoo Valley Reserve exists to preserve and enhance the area's environmental, scenic, and cultural features and provides facilities for the use and enjoyment of visitors. Subject to the approval of the governor, the board may purchase land for inclusion in the reserve and may trade land in the reserve under certain conditions. The board also may lease land for purposes consistent with the management of the reserve or for agricultural purposes.

STATE FAIR PARK BOARD

Chair: John Yingling
Chief executive officer: Kathleen O'Leary
Contact: wsfp@wistatefair.com; 414-266-7000; 414-266-7100 (ticket office); 640 South 84th
Street, West Allis, WI 53214
Website: https://wistatefair.com/wsfp/
Number of employees: 47.00
Total budget 2017–19: $46,864,100

The State Fair Park Board manages the Wisconsin State Fair Park, including the development of new facilities. The park provides a permanent location for the annual Wisconsin State Fair and for major sports events, agricultural and industrial expositions, and other programs of civic interest.

Department of Transportation

Secretary: Craig Thompson
Deputy secretary: Paul Hammer
Location: Hill Farms State Office Building, 4822 Madison Yards Way, Madison
Contact: information.dmv@dot.wi.gov; Office of Public Affairs, 608-266-3581; Driver
   Services and Vehicle Services, 608-264-7447; PO Box 7910, Madison, WI 53707-7910
Website: https://wisconsindot.gov
Number of employees: 3,441.11
Total budget 2017–19: $6,099,061,000

The Department of Transportation is administered by a secretary who is appointed by the governor with the advice and consent of the senate.

The department is responsible for the planning, promotion, and protection of all transportation systems in the state. Its major responsibilities involve highways, motor vehicles, motor carriers, traffic law enforcement, railroads, waterways, mass transit, and aeronautics. The department issues vehicle titles and registrations and individual identification cards and examines and licenses drivers. The department works with several federal agencies in the administration of federal transportation aids. It also cooperates with departments at the state level in travel promotion, consumer protection, environmental analysis, and transportation services for elderly and handicapped persons.

Subordinate statutory boards, councils, and committees

The Wisconsin Division of Motor Vehicles administers driving tests to citizens in every county. It issued more than 300,000 driver's licenses in 2018.

DEPARTMENT OF TRANSPORTATION

COUNCIL ON HIGHWAY SAFETY

Acting Chair: John Mesich
Location: 4822 Madison Yards Way, 9th Floor South, Madison, WI 53705
Contact: Diana Guinn; diana.guinn@dot.wi.gov; 608-709-0093

The Council on Highway Safety advises the department secretary about on highway safety matters.

RUSTIC ROADS BOARD

Chair: Marion Flood
Contact: Liat Bonneville, Rustic Roads coordinator; WIRusticRoads@dot.wi.gov; 608-267-3614; 4822 Madison Yards Way, 6th Floor South, PO Box 7913, Madison, WI 53705

Website: https://wisconsindot.gov/Pages/travel/road/rustic-roads/create.aspx

The Rustic Roads Board oversees the application and selection process of locally nominated county highways and local roads for inclusion in the Rustic Roads network system. The Rustic Roads program is a partnership between local officials and state government to showcase some of Wisconsin's most picturesque and lightly traveled roadways for the leisurely enjoyment of hikers, bikers, and motorists.

COUNCIL ON UNIFORMITY OF TRAFFIC CITATIONS AND COMPLAINTS

Chair: Mark Conroy
Location: 4822 Madison Yards Way, 2nd Floor South, Madison
Contact: Mark Conroy; markk.conroy@dot.wi.gov; 608-264-7345

The Council on Uniformity of Traffic Citations and Complaints recommends forms used for traffic violations citations.

University of Wisconsin System

Board of Regents: Robert Atwell, John Robert Behling, Scott Beightol, José Delgado, Michael M. Grebe, Eve Hall, Mike Jones, Tracey L. Klein, Regina Millner, Janice Mueller, Drew Petersen, Cris Peterson, Jason R. Plante, Ryan L. Ring, Carolyn Stanford Taylor, S. Mark Tyler, Gerald Whitburn
Executive director and corporate secretary: Jess Lathrop
System Administration: Raymond W. Cross, *president*
Contact: 608-262-2321; 1700 Van Hise Hall, 1220 Linden Drive, Madison, WI 53706
Website: www.wisconsin.edu
Number of employees: 35,338.49
Total budget 2017–19: $12,162,114,900

The University of Wisconsin System is governed by an 18-member Board of Regents, which consists of 14 citizen members, two student members, the president of the Technical College System Board or his or her designee, and the state superintendent of public instruction. The citizen and student members are appointed by the governor subject to senate confirmation. The Board of Regents appoints the president of the UW System, who has executive responsibility for system operation and management. The Board of Regents also appoints the chancellors for each four-year university and one chancellor who administers both UW Colleges and the UW-Extension.

The prime responsibilities of the UW System are teaching, public service, and research. The system provides postsecondary academic education for more than 170,000 students, including more than 150,000 undergraduates. The system consists of 13 four-year universities, 13 two-year colleges, and a statewide extension program known as the UW-Extension. All of the four-year universities offer bachelor's degrees. Two of the four-year universities (UW-Madison and UW-Milwaukee) offer comprehensive master's and doctoral degree programs, including professional doctorate degrees. The remaining four-year universities (UW-Eau Claire, UW-Green Bay, UW-La Crosse, UW-Oshkosh, UW-Parkside, UW-Platteville, UW-River Falls, UW-Stevens Point, UW-Stout, UW-Superior, and UW-Whitewater) offer more limited master's degree programs and some also offer associate degrees and clinical/professional doctorate degrees in select areas. The two-year colleges, known collectively as the UW Colleges, function administratively as one institution and offer Associate of Arts and Sciences (AAS) degrees at each campus as well as transfer programs for students wishing to satisfy general education requirements and then transfer to a four-year UW institution. Many two-year colleges also offer bachelor's degrees in certain fields of study through collaboration with various four-year UW institutions. In addition, UW Colleges offers an entirely online AAS degree program through UW Colleges Online. The UW-Extension, administratively joined with UW Colleges, provides statewide access to system resources and research in partnership with all system campuses, counties, tribal governments, and other public and private organizations.

In November 2017, the Board of Regents passed a resolution authorizing the UW System president to restructure the UW Colleges and UW-Extension. Under the proposed reorganization, all 26 campuses of the UW System would remain

Jake Hendley, a UW-Stout computer science–game design major from Flossmoor, Illinois, speaks with a recruiter at a 2017 career conference. UW-Stout reported that after six months, 98.2 percent of 2016–17 graduates were either employed or continuing their education.

open, but the 13 two-year colleges would be joined with the four-year universities and UW-Extension functions would be assigned to either UW-Madison or the UW System administration.

UW-MADISON

Chancellor: Rebecca M. Blank
Contact: 608-262-9946; 500 Lincoln Drive, Madison, WI 53706
Website: www.wisc.edu

UW-MILWAUKEE

Chancellor: Mark Mone
Contact: 414-229-4331; PO Box 413, Milwaukee, WI 53201
Website: www.uwm.edu

UW-EAU CLAIRE

Chancellor: James Schmidt
Contact: 715-836-2327; 105 Garfield Avenue, Eau Claire, WI 54702
Website: www.uwec.edu

UW-GREEN BAY

Chancellor: Gary L. Miller
Contact: 920-465-2207; 2420 Nicolet Drive, Green Bay, WI 54311
Website: www.uwgb.edu

UW-LA CROSSE

Chancellor: Joe Gow
Contact: 608-785-8004; 1725 State Street, La Crosse, WI 54601
Website: www.uwlax.edu

UW-OSHKOSH

Chancellor: Andrew J. Leavitt
Contact: 920-424-0200; 800 Algoma Boulevard, Oshkosh, WI 54901
Website: www.uwosh.edu

UW-PARKSIDE

Chancellor: Deborah Ford
Contact: 262-595-2211; PO Box 2000, Kenosha, WI 53141
Website: www.uwp.edu

UW-PLATTEVILLE

Chancellor: Dennis J. Shields
Contact: 608-342-1234; 1 University Plaza, Platteville, WI 53818
Website: www.uwplatt.edu

UW-RIVER FALLS

Chancellor: Dean Van Galen

Contact: 715-425-3201; 410 South Third Street, River Falls, WI 54022
Website: www.uwrf.edu

UW-STEVENS POINT

Chancellor: Bernie L. Patterson
Contact: 715-346-2123; 2100 Main Street, Stevens Point, WI 54481
Website: www.uwsp.edu

UW-STOUT

Chancellor: Bob Meyer
Contact: 715-232-2441; 712 South Broadway, Menomonie, WI 54751
Website: www.uwstout.edu

UW-SUPERIOR

Chancellor: Renée Wachter
Contact: 715-394-8223; Belknap and Catlin Avenue, Superior, WI 54880
Website: www.uwsuper.edu

UW-WHITEWATER

Chancellor: Cheryl Green (interim)
Contact: 262-472-1918; 800 West Main Street, Whitewater, WI 53190
Website: www.uww.edu

Programs required by statute

OFFICE OF THE STATE CARTOGRAPHER

State cartographer: Howard Veregin
Contact: sco@wisc.edu; 608-262-3065; 384 Science Hall, 550 North Park Street, Madison, WI 53706
Website: www.sco.wisc.edu

GEOLOGICAL AND NATURAL HISTORY SURVEY

Director and state geologist: Ken Bradbury
Contact: 608-262-1705; 3817 Mineral Point Road, Madison, WI 53705
Website: http://wgnhs.uwex.edu

UW CENTER FOR AGRICULTURAL SAFETY AND HEALTH

Director: Cheryl Skjolaas
Contact: 608-265-0568
Website: http://fyi.uwex.edu/agsafety

WISCONSIN CENTER FOR ENVIRONMENTAL EDUCATION

Director: vacancy
Contact: wcee@uwsp.edu; 715-346-4973; WCEE—110 TNR, 800 Reserve Street, Stevens Point, WI 54481
Website: www.uwsp.edu/cnr-ap/wcee

AREA HEALTH EDUCATION CENTERS

Director: vacancy
Contact: ahec@ahec.wisc.edu; 608-263-1712; 4251 Health Sciences Learning Center, 750 Highland Avenue, Madison, WI 53705
Website: www.ahec.wisc.edu

WISCONSIN STATE HERBARIUM

Director: Kenneth Cameron
Contact: kmcameron@wisc.edu; 608-262-2792; Birge Hall, 430 Lincoln Drive, Madison, WI 53706
Website: http://herbarium.wisc.edu

PSYCHIATRIC HEALTH EMOTIONS RESEARCH INSTITUTE

Director: Ned Kalin
Contact: 608-232-3171; 6001 Research Park Boulevard, Madison, WI 53719
Website: https://www.psychiatry.wisc.edu/research/heri/

ROBERT M. LA FOLLETTE SCHOOL OF PUBLIC AFFAIRS

Director: Susan Yackee
Contact: info@lafollette.wisc.edu; 608-262-3581; 1225 Observatory Drive, Madison, WI 53706
Website: www.lafollette.wisc.edu

STATE SOILS AND PLANT ANALYSIS LABORATORY

Director: Andrew Stammer
Contact: soil-lab@mailplus.wisc.edu; 715-387-2523; 2611 Yellowstone Drive, Marshfield, WI 54449
Website: https://uwlab.soils.wisc.edu

INSTITUTE FOR URBAN EDUCATION

Chair: Linda Post (interim)
Contact: lpost@uwm.edu; 414-229-2629; 321 Enderis Hall, UW-Milwaukee, 2400 East Hartford Avenue, Room 568, Milwaukee, WI 53211
Website: https://uwm.edu/education/engagement/institute-urban-edu/

JAMES A. GRAASKAMP CENTER FOR REAL ESTATE

Executive director: Mark Eppli
Contact: mark.eppli@wisc.edu; 608-263-1000; Grainger Hall, 975 University Avenue, Madison, WI 53706
Website: https://bus.wisc.edu/centers/james-a-graaskamp-center-for-real-estate

SCHOOL OF VETERINARY MEDICINE

Dean: Mark D. Markel
Contact: 608-263-6716; 2015 Linden Drive West, Madison, WI 53706
Website: www.vetmed.wisc.edu

Subordinate statutory boards, councils, and committees

LABORATORY OF HYGIENE BOARD

Members: Robert Corliss, Steve Geis, Barry Irmen, Gil Kelley, Jeff Kindrai, James Morrison, Richard Moss, Chuck Warzecha, 3 vacancies
Nonvoting member and laboratory director: James Schauer
Contact: 608-890-0288 (Administrative Office); 608-262-6386 and 800-862-1013 (Clinical Laboratories); 800-442-4618 (Environmental Health Laboratory); 800-446-0403 (Occupational Health Laboratory); 800-462-5261 (Proficiency Testing); 2601 Agriculture Drive, Madison, WI 53718-6780
Website: www.slh.wisc.edu
Number of employees: 309.75
Total budget 2017–19: $67,089,200

The Laboratory of Hygiene Board oversees the Laboratory of Hygiene, which provides laboratory services in the areas of water quality, air quality, public health, and contagious diseases for state agencies, local health departments, physicians, veterinarians, and others to prevent and control diseases and environmental hazards. Attached to UW-Madison, the laboratory provides facilities for teaching and research in the fields of public health and environmental protection.

RURAL HEALTH DEVELOPMENT COUNCIL

Contact: 608-261-1883; 800-385-0005, Ext. 1; Wisconsin Office of Rural Health, 310 North Midvale Boulevard, Suite 301, Madison, WI 53705
Website: http://www.worh.org/rhdc

The Rural Health Development Council consists of 17 members appointed by the governor, with the advice and consent of the senate, for five-year terms and the secretary of health services or his or her designee. The council advises the Board of Regents on matters related to loan assistance programs for physicians, dentists, and other health care providers.

Independent entities attached for administrative purposes

PUBLIC LEADERSHIP BOARD

Members: Robert Cook, Scott Jensen, Gerard Randall, Dean Stensberg, Jason Thompson, Robin Vos
Director: Ryan J. Owens
Contact: thompsoncenter@wisc.edu; 608-265-4087; 214 North Hall, 1050 Bascom Mall, Madison, WI 53706
Website: https://thompsoncenter.wisc.edu/

The Public Leadership Board appoints, upon joint recommendation of the chancellor of UW-Madison and the dean of the College of Letters and Science at UW-Madison, the director of the Tommy G. Thompson Center on Public Leadership at UW-Madison. The mission of the center is to facilitate research, teaching, outreach, and policy reform regarding effective public leadership throughout all universities of the UW System. The board approves the center's budget and must allocate at least $500,000 annually for speaking engagements at campuses other than UW-Madison.

VETERINARY DIAGNOSTIC LABORATORY BOARD

Members: Charles Czuprynski, Casey Davis, Alissa Grenawalt, Darlene Konkle, Paul Kunde, Sandra Madland, Mark Markel, Jim Meronek, Ray Pawlisch
Nonvoting member and laboratory director: Keith Poulsen
Contact: 608-262-5432; 800-608-8387; 445 Easterday Lane, Madison, WI 53706
Website: www.wvdl.wisc.edu
Number of employees: 94.50
Total budget 2017–19: $19,226,400

The Veterinary Diagnostic Laboratory Board oversees the Veterinary Diagnostic Laboratory, which provides animal health testing and diagnostic services on a statewide basis for all types of animals. The laboratory may also participate in research, education, and field services related to animal health.

Department of Veterans Affairs

Department secretary: Mary M. Kolar
Deputy secretary: James Bond
Board of Veterans Affairs: Larry Kutschma, *chair*
Location: 2135 Rimrock Road, Madison
Contact: 608-266-0517; 1-800-WIS-VETS (toll free); PO Box 7843, Madison, WI 53707-7843
Website: https://dva.wi.gov
Number of employees: 1,269.20
Total budget 2017–19: $280,944,700

The Department of Veterans Affairs is administered by a secretary who must be a veteran and is appointed by the governor with the advice and consent of the senate. The department includes the Board of Veterans Affairs, consisting of nine members who must be veterans and are appointed by the governor with the advice and consent of the senate. The board advises the secretary on the promulgation of administrative rules necessary to carry out the powers and duties of the department.

The department administers an array of grants, benefits, programs, and services for eligible veterans, their families, and organizations that serve veterans. It operates the Wisconsin veterans homes at Chippewa Falls, King, and Union Grove, which provide short-term rehabilitation and long-term skilled nursing care to eligible veterans (and, to the extent of their resources, to the spouses

DEPARTMENT OF VETERAN AFFAIRS

A resident of the Wisconsin Veterans Home at King enjoys her time at a family carnival. The Department of Veterans Affairs operates three homes for veterans and their families in Wisconsin.

and parents of veterans). The department also operates the Southern Wisconsin Veterans Memorial Cemetery at Union Grove, the Northern Wisconsin Veterans Memorial Cemetery near Spooner, and the Central Wisconsin Veterans Memorial Cemetery at King. Finally, the department operates the Wisconsin Veterans Museum in Madison.

Subordinate statutory boards, councils, and committees

COUNCIL ON VETERANS PROGRAMS

Chair: Larry Hill
Website: https://dva.wi.gov/Pages/aboutWdva/CouncilonVeteransPrograms.aspx
The Council on Veterans Programs studies and presents policy alternatives and recommendations to the Board of Veterans Affairs.

Department of Workforce Development

Department secretary: Caleb Frostman
Deputy secretary: JoAnna Richard
Location: 201 East Washington Avenue, Madison
Contact: 608-266-3131; PO Box 7946, Madison, WI 53707-7946
Website: https://dwd.wisconsin.gov

Number of employees: 1,608.05
Total budget 2017–19: $702,301,400

The Department of Workforce Development is administered by a secretary who is appointed by the governor with the advice and consent of the senate.

The department administers the unemployment insurance program and oversees the worker's compensation program. The department also operates the state's job center network (https://jobcenterofwisconsin.com); manages the Fast Forward worker training grant program; operates adult and youth apprenticeship programs; collects, analyzes, and distributes labor market information; monitors migrant workers services; provides vocational rehabilitation services to help people with disabilities achieve their employment goals; and offers comprehensive employment and training programs and services to youth and adults, including veterans with service-connected disabilities. Finally, the department enforces wage and hour laws; leave and benefits laws; child labor laws; civil rights laws; plant closing laws; and laws regulating migrant labor contractors and camps.

Subordinate statutory boards, councils, and committees

WISCONSIN APPRENTICESHIP ADVISORY COUNCIL

Cochairs: Terry Hayden, Henry Hurt
Contact: 608-266-3332; PO Box 7972, Madison, WI 53707-7972
Website: https://dwd.wisconsin.gov/apprenticeship/advisory_council.htm

The Wisconsin Apprenticeship Advisory Council advises the department on matters pertaining to Wisconsin's apprenticeship system.

COUNCIL ON MIGRANT LABOR

Contact: 608-266-0002; PO Box 7972, Madison, WI 53707-7972

The Governor's Council on Migrant Labor advises the department and other state officials about matters affecting migrant workers.

SELF-INSURERS COUNCIL

Contact: 608-266-8327; PO Box 7901, Madison, WI 53707-7901
Website: https://dwd.wisconsin.gov/wc/councils/self-insured/

The Self-Insurers Council assists the department in administering the self-insurance program, under which an employer can be permitted to cover its worker's compensation costs directly rather than by purchasing insurance. The council ensures that those employers applying for self-insurance are financially viable and monitors the financial status of employers in the self-insurance pool.

UNEMPLOYMENT INSURANCE ADVISORY COUNCIL

Chair: Janell Knutson

Lieutenant Governor Mandela Barnes (*left*) joins Department of Workforce Development Secretary Caleb Frostman (*second from left*) at the WE Energies operations yard in West Allis. Their tour of the facilities kicked off Career and Technical Education Month in February 2019.

Contact: 608-267-1405; PO Box 8942, Madison, WI 53708-8942
Website: https://dwd.wisconsin.gov/uibola/uiac/

The Unemployment Insurance Advisory Council provides advice and counsel to the department and the legislature about unemployment insurance matters, including by providing advice and recommendations with respect to proposed changes to the unemployment insurance law.

WORKER'S COMPENSATION ADVISORY COUNCIL

Chair: Steve Peters
Contact: 608-266-6841; PO Box 7901, Madison, WI 53707-7901
Website: https://dwd.wisconsin.gov/wc/councils/wcac/

The Council on Worker's Compensation provides advice and counsel to the department and the legislature about worker's compensation matters, including by providing advice and recommendations with respect to proposed changes to the worker's compensation law.

HEALTH CARE PROVIDER ADVISORY COMMITTEE

Chair: Steve Peters
Contact: 608-266-6841; PO Box 7901, Madison, WI 53707-7901
Website: https://dwd.wisconsin.gov/wc/councils/wcac/Health_Care_Providers/Health_comm.htm

The Health Care Provider Advisory Committee advises the department and the

Council on Worker's Compensation on the standards that the department uses when it determines whether treatment provided to an injured employee was necessary treatment that is compensable by worker's compensation insurance.

Independent entities attached for administrative purposes

EMPLOYMENT RELATIONS COMMISSION
Chair: James J. Daley
Chief legal counsel: Peter G. Davis
Location: 2418 Crossroads Drive, Suite 1000, Madison
Contact: werc@werc.state.wi.us; 608-243-2424
Website: http://werc.wi.gov
Number of employees: 6.00
Total budget 2017–19: $ 2,274,700

The Employment Relations Commission promotes collective bargaining and peaceful labor relations in the private and public sectors. The commission determines various types of labor relations cases and issues decisions arising from state employee civil service appeals. The commission also provides mediation and grievance arbitration services as well as training and assistance to parties interested in labor-management cooperation and a consensus approach to resolving labor relations issues.

Authorities

Wisconsin Aerospace Authority (inactive)

The Wisconsin Aerospace Authority is directed to promote and develop the state's space-related industry and coordinate these activities with governmental entities, the aerospace industry, businesses, educational organizations, and the Wisconsin Space Grant Consortium.

Wisconsin Economic Development Corporation

Board of directors chair: Lisa Mauer
Chief executive officer: Mark Hogan
Chief operating officer: Tricia Braun
Location: 201 West Washington Avenue, Madison
Contact: 608-210-6700; PO Box 1687, Madison, WI 53701
Website: https://wedc.org/
Total state appropriation 2017–19: $83,601,400

The Wisconsin Economic Development Corporation is a public corporation that develops, implements, and administers programs to provide business support and

DEPARTMENT OF WORKFORCE DEVELOPMENT

The Wisconsin Economic Development Corporation assisted the Diversified Manufacturing Corporation in identifying a location in Prescott to accommodate the company's growth. The WEDC also authorized up to $520,000 in state tax credits to help the company move to Wisconsin.

expertise and financial assistance to companies that are investing and creating jobs in Wisconsin and to promote new business start-ups and business expansion and growth in the state. The authority was established in 2011 and assumed many of the functions previously performed by the former Department of Commerce. WEDC is governed by an 18-member board that consists of six appointees of the governor, ten appointees of legislative leaders—four appointees each of the speaker of the assembly and senate majority leader and one appointee each of the minority leaders of both houses, and the secretaries of administration and revenue as nonvoting members. WEDC may issue bonds and incur other debt to achieve its public purposes. WEDC's bonds and other debt do not create a debt of the state.

Fox River Navigational System Authority

Board of directors chair: S. Timothy Rose
Chief executive officer: Jeremy Cords
Contact: 920-759-9833; 1008 Augustine Street, Kaukauna, WI 54130-1608
Website: www.foxlocks.org

The Fox River Navigational System Authority is a public corporation that is responsible for the rehabilitation, repair, and management of the navigation system on or near the Fox River, and it may enter into contracts with third parties to operate the system. The authority may charge fees for services provided to watercraft owners and users of navigational facilities, enter into contracts with nonprofit organizations to raise funds, and contract debt, but it may not issue bonds. Annually, the authority must submit an audited financial statement to the Department of Administration. The authority is governed by a nine-member board of directors that includes six appointees of the governor, two each from Brown, Outagamie, and Winnebago Counties.

Wisconsin Health and Educational Facilities Authority

Board of directors chair: James Dietsche
Executive director: Dennis P. Reilly
Contact: info@whefa.com; 262-792-0466; 18000 West Sarah Lane, Suite 300, Brookfield, WI 53045-5841
Website: www.whefa.com

The Wisconsin Health and Educational Facilities Authority is a public corporation governed by a seven-member board whose members are appointed by the governor and confirmed by the senate. No more than four of the members may be of the same political party. The governor appoints the chair.

WHEFA issues bonds on behalf of private nonprofit facilities to help them finance their capital costs. The authority has no taxing power. WHEFA's bonds are not a debt, liability, or obligation of the State of Wisconsin or any of its subdivisions. The authority may issue bonds to finance any qualifying capital project, including new construction, remodeling, and renovation; expansion of current facilities; and purchase of new equipment or furnishings. WHEFA may also issue bonds to refinance outstanding debt.

Wisconsin Housing and Economic Development Authority

Board of directors chair: Ivan Gamboa
Executive director: Joaquin J. Altoro
Contact: info@wheda.com; 608-266-7884 or 800-334-6873 (Madison); 414-227-4039 or 800-628-4833 (Milwaukee); PO Box 1728, Madison, WI 53701-1728; 201 West Washington Avenue, Suite 700, Madison, WI 53703; 611 West National Avenue, Suite 110, Milwaukee, WI 53204 (Milwaukee office)
Website: www.wheda.com

The Wisconsin Housing and Economic Development Authority is a public corporation governed by a 12-member board that includes six appointees of the governor and four legislators representing both parties and both houses. WHEDA administers numerous loan programs and other programs and projects that provide housing and related assistance to Wisconsin residents, including single and multifamily housing for individuals and families of low and moderate income, and that promote and support home ownership. WHEDA also finances loan guarantees and administers other programs to support business and agricultural development in the state. WHEDA issues bonds to support its operations, which, however, do not create a debt of the state.

Lower Fox River Remediation Authority (inactive)

The Lower Fox River Remediation Authority is a public corporation that is authorized to issue assessment bonds for eligible waterway improvement costs, which generally include environmental investigation and remediation of the Fox River extending from Lake Winnebago to the mouth of the river in Lake Michigan, and including any portion of Green Bay in Lake Michigan that contains sediments discharged from the river.

University of Wisconsin Hospitals and Clinics Authority

Board of directors chair: Gary Wolter
Chief executive officer: Alan Kaplan
Contact: 608-263-6400 or 800-323-8942; 600 Highland Avenue, Madison, WI 53792
Website: www.uwhealth.org

The University of Wisconsin Hospitals and Clinics Authority is a public corporation governed by a 16-member board of directors that includes the cochairs of the Joint Committee on Finance and six appointees of the governor. The authority operates the UW Hospital and Clinics, including the American Family Children's Hospital, and related clinics and health care facilities. Through the UW Hospital and Clinics and its other programs, the authority delivers health care, including care for the indigent; provides an environment for instruction of physicians, nurses, and other health-related disciplines; sponsors and supports health care research; and assists health care programs and personnel throughout the state.

The authority is self-financing. It derives much of its income from charges for clinical and hospital services. The authority also may issue bonds to support its operations, which, however, do not create a debt of the state, and may seek financing from the Wisconsin Health and Educational Facilities Authority.

Nonprofit corporations

Bradley Center Sports and Entertainment Corporation (inactive)

The Bradley Center Sports and Entertainment Corporation is a public nonprofit corporation that was created as an instrumentality of the state to receive and operate the Bradley Center, a sports and entertainment facility located in Milwaukee County and donated by the Bradley Center Corporation. The Bradley Center was the home of the Milwaukee Bucks basketball team from 1988 to 2018 and hosted other sporting events as well as numerous entertainment shows and concerts. The Bradley Center has been replaced by a new facility, the Fiserv Forum, which is owned and operated by the Wisconsin Center District, a local governmental entity (see page 256).

Wisconsin Artistic Endowment Foundation (inactive)

The Wisconsin Artistic Endowment Foundation is a public nonprofit corporation that was created by the legislature for the purpose of supporting the arts, distributing funds, and facilitating the conversion of donated property into cash to support the arts. The foundation may not be dissolved except by an enactment of the legislature.

Regional planning commissions

Regional planning commissions advise cities, villages, towns, and counties on the planning and delivery of public services to the residents of a defined region, and they prepare and adopt master plans for the physical development of the region they serve.

The commissions may conduct research studies; make and adopt plans for the physical, social, and economic development of the region; provide advisory services to local governmental units and other public and private agencies; and coordinate local programs that relate to their objectives. The functions of commissions are solely advisory to the political subdivisions comprising the region.

Currently, there are nine regional planning commissions serving all but five of the state's 72 counties. Their boundaries are based on factors including common topographical and geographical features; the extent of urban development; the existence of special or acute agricultural, forestry, or other rural problems; and the existence of physical, social, and economic problems of a regional character.

Regional planning commissions have developed and assisted with projects in areas including rail and air transportation, waste disposal and recycling, highways, air and water quality, farmland preservation and zoning, land conservation and reclamation, outdoor recreation, parking and lakefront studies, and land records modernization.

Membership of regional planning commissions varies according to conditions defined by statute. The commissions are funded through state and federal planning grants, contracts with local governments for special planning services, and a statutorily authorized levy of up to 0.003 percent of equalized real estate value charged to each local governmental unit.

Wisconsin's regional planning commissions have established the Association of Wisconsin Regional Planning Commissions. The association's purposes include assisting the study of common problems and serving as an information clearinghouse.

Regional planning commission areas

Bay-Lake Regional Planning Commission

Counties in region: Brown, Door, Florence, Kewaunee, Manitowoc, Marinette, Oconto, Sheboygan
Chair: Mike Hotz
Executive director: Cindy J. Wojtczak
Contact: 920-448-2820; 425 South Adams Street, Suite 201, Green Bay, WI 54301
Website: www.baylakerpc.org

Capital Area Regional Planning Commission

Counties in region: Dane
Chair: Larry Palm
Deputy director: Steve Steinhoff
Contact: info@capitalarearpc.org; 608-266-4137; City-County Building, 210 Martin Luther King Jr. Boulevard, Room 362, Madison, WI 53703
Website: www.capitalarearpc.org

East Central Wisconsin Regional Planning Commission

Counties in region: Calumet, Fond du Lac, Green Lake (not participating), Marquette (not participating), Menominee, Outagamie, Shawano, Waupaca, Waushara, Winnebago
Chair: Jerry Erdmann
Executive director: Eric W. Fowle
Contact: 920-751-4770; 400 Ahnaip Street, Suite 100, Menasha, WI 54952-3100
Website: www.ecwrpc.org

Mississippi River Regional Planning Commission

Counties in region: Buffalo, Crawford, Jackson, La Crosse, Monroe, Pepin, Pierce, Trempealeau, Vernon
Chair: James Kuhn
Executive director: Gregory D. Flogstad
Contact: plan@mrrpc.com; 608-785-9396; 1707 Main Street, Suite 435, La Crosse, WI 54601
Website: www.mrrpc.com

North Central Wisconsin Regional Planning Commission

Counties in region: Adams, Forest, Juneau, Langlade, Lincoln, Marathon, Oneida, Portage (not participating), Vilas, Wood
Chair: Paul Millan
Executive director: Dennis L. Lawrence
Contact: info@ncwrpc.org; 715-849-5510; 210 McClellan Street, Suite 210, Wausau, WI 54403
Website: www.ncwrpc.org

Northwest Regional Planning Commission

Counties in region: Ashland, Bayfield, Burnett, Douglas, Iron, Price, Rusk, Sawyer, Taylor, Washburn
Participating tribal nations: Bad River, Lac Courte Oreilles, Lac du Flambeau, Red Cliff, St. Croix
Chair: Douglas Finn
Executive director: Sheldon Johnson
Contact: info@nwrpc.com; 715-635-2197; 1400 South River Street, Spooner, WI 54801
Website: www.nwrpc.com

Southeastern Wisconsin Regional Planning Commission

Counties in region: Kenosha, Milwaukee, Ozaukee, Racine, Walworth, Washington, Waukesha
Chair: Charles L. Colman
Executive director: Kevin Muhs
Contact: sewrpc@sewrpc.org; 262-547-6721; W239 N1812 Rockwood Drive, PO Box 1607, Waukesha, WI 53187-1607
Website: www.sewrpc.org

Southwestern Wisconsin Regional Planning Commission

Counties in region: Grant, Green, Iowa, Lafayette, Richland
Chair: Jeanetta Kirkpatrick
Executive director: Troy Maggied
Contact: info@swwrpc.org; 608-342-1636; 20 South Court Street, Platteville, WI 53818
Website: www.swwrpc.org

West Central Wisconsin Regional Planning Commission

Counties in region: Barron, Chippewa, Clark, Dunn, Eau Claire, Polk, St. Croix
Chair: John L. Frank
Executive director: Lynn Nelson
Contact: wcwrpc@wcwrpc.org; 715-836-2918; 800 Wisconsin Street, Building D2, Room 401, Mail Box 9, Eau Claire, WI 54703
Website: www.wcwrpc.org

Other regional entities

Professional Football Stadium District

Board of directors chair: Chuck Lamine
Executive director: Pat Webb
Contact: 920-965-6997; 1229 Lombardi Avenue, At Lambeau Field, Green Bay, WI 54304

The Professional Football Stadium District is an owner and landlord of Lambeau Field, the designated home of the Green Bay Packers football team. It is a local governmental unit that may acquire, construct, equip, maintain, improve, operate, and manage football stadium facilities or hire others to do the same. Maintenance and operation of the stadium is governed by provisions of the Lambeau Field Lease Agreement by and among the district; Green Bay Packers, Inc.; and the City of Green Bay. The district board consists of seven members who are appointed by local elected officials.

Southeast Wisconsin Professional Baseball Park District

Governing board chair: Don Smiley
Executive director: Michael R. Duckett
Contact: contact@millerparkdistrict.com; 414-902-4040
Website: www.millerparkdistrict.com

The Southeast Wisconsin Professional Baseball Park District is the majority owner of Miller Park, the home of the Milwaukee Brewers Baseball Club. It is a local governmental unit that may acquire, construct, maintain, improve, operate, and manage baseball park facilities, which include parking lots, garages, restaurants, parks, concession facilities, entertainment facilities, and other related structures.

The district is also authorized to issue bonds for certain purposes related to baseball park facilities. To pay off the bonds, the district may impose a sales tax and a use tax. A city or county within the district's jurisdiction may make loans or grants to the district, expend funds to subsidize the district, borrow money for baseball park facilities, or grant property to the state dedicated for use by a professional baseball park.

The district includes Milwaukee, Ozaukee, Racine, Washington, and Waukesha counties. The district's governing board consists of 13 members appointed by the governor and elected officials from within its jurisdiction. The governor appoints the chair of the governing board.

Wisconsin Center District

Board of directors chair: James Kanter
President and CEO: Marty Brooks
Contact: 414-908-6000; 400 West Wisconsin Avenue, Milwaukee, WI 53203
Website: www.wcd.org

The Wisconsin Center District is a local governmental unit that may acquire, construct, and operate an exposition center and related facilities; enter into contracts and grant concessions; mortgage district property and issue bonds; and invest funds as the district board considers appropriate. The Wisconsin Center District operates the University of Wisconsin-Milwaukee Panther Arena, the Milwaukee Theatre, and the Wisconsin Center. It also assists in the development and construction of sports and entertainment facilities, including a new arena for the Milwaukee Bucks, which opened in August 2018. Once the new sports and entertainment facilities are completed, the Wisconsin Center District will oversee the demolition of the Bradley Center, the previous large-event arena for the Milwaukee area.

The district is funded by operating revenue and special sales taxes on hotel rooms, restaurant food and beverages, and car rentals within its taxing jurisdiction. The district board has 17 members, including legislative leaders, local government finance officials, and members who are appointed by the governor, Milwaukee County executive, city of Milwaukee mayor, and city of Milwaukee common council president.

Interstate compacts

Wisconsin has entered with other states into various interstate compacts, under which the compacting states agree to coordinate their activities related to a particular matter according to uniform guidelines or procedures. Some of these compacts include provisions creating an interstate entity made up of representatives from the compacting states, while others do not.

Interstate entities created by interstate compacts

EDUCATION COMMISSION OF THE STATES

Wisconsin delegation: Tony Evers (governor), *chair*
Contact: 303-299-3600; 700 Broadway Street, Suite 810, Denver, CO 80203
Website: www.ecs.org

The Education Commission of the States was established to foster national cooperation among executive, legislative, educational, and lay leaders of the various states concerning education policy and the improvement of state and local education systems. The seven-member Wisconsin delegation includes the governor and the state superintendent of public instruction.

GREAT LAKES COMMISSION

Wisconsin delegation: Stephen Galarneau, *chair*
Executive director: Darren Nichols
Contact: 734-971-9135; 1300 Victors Way, Suite 1350, Ann Arbor, MI 48108
Website: www.glc.org

The Great Lakes Commission was established under the Great Lakes Basin Compact to promote the orderly, integrated, and comprehensive development, use, and conservation of the water and related natural resources of the Great Lakes basin and St. Lawrence River. Its members include the eight Great Lakes states of Illinois, Indiana, Michigan, Minnesota, New York, Ohio, Pennsylvania, and Wisconsin, with associate member status for the Canadian provinces of Ontario and Québec. A three-member delegation, appointed by the governor, represents Wisconsin on the commission. The commission develops and recommends the adoption of policy positions by its members and offers advice on issues such as clean energy, climate change, habitat and coastal management, control of aquatic invasive species, water quality, and water resources.

GREAT LAKES PROTECTION FUND

Wisconsin representatives to the board of directors: Kevin Shafer
Executive director: J. David Rankin
Contact: 847-425-8150; 1560 Sherman Avenue, Suite 1370, Evanston, IL 60201
Website: www.glpf.org

The Great Lakes Protection Fund is a private nonprofit corporation, the members of which are the governors of Illinois, Michigan, Minnesota, New York, Ohio, Pennsylvania, and Wisconsin. The purpose of the corporation is to finance projects for the protection and cleanup of the Great Lakes. The corporation is managed by a board of directors composed of two representatives from each member state. The governor appoints the two Wisconsin representatives.

GREAT LAKES-ST. LAWRENCE RIVER BASIN WATER RESOURCES COUNCIL

Wisconsin members: Tony Evers (governor)
Executive director: David Naftzger
Contact: cglg@cglg.org; 312-407-0177; 20 North Wacker Drive, Suite 2700, Chicago, IL 60606
Website: www.glslcompactcouncil.org

The Great Lakes-St. Lawrence River Basin Water Resources Council is charged with aiding, promoting, and coordinating the activities and programs of the Great Lakes states concerning water resources management in the Great Lakes-St. Lawrence River basin. The council may promulgate and enforce rules and regulations as may be necessary for the implementation and enforcement of the Great Lakes-St. Lawrence River Basin Water Resources Compact. The legally binding compact governs withdrawals, consumptive uses, conservation and efficient use, and diversions of basin water resources, and the council may initiate legal actions to compel compliance with the compact. In addition, the council must review and approve proposals from certain parties for the withdrawal, diversion, or consumptive use of water from the basin that is subject to the compact.

Under the compact, the governors from the states of Illinois, Indiana, Michigan, Minnesota, New York, Ohio, Pennsylvania, and Wisconsin jointly pursue intergovernmental cooperation and consultation to protect, conserve, restore, improve, and effectively manage the waters and water dependent natural resources of the basin. The governor serves as Wisconsin's representative on the council.

GREAT LAKES-ST. LAWRENCE RIVER WATER RESOURCES REGIONAL BODY

Wisconsin members: Tony Evers (governor)
Executive director: David Naftzger
Contact: cglg@cglg.org; 312-407-0177; 20 North Wacker Drive, Suite 2700, Chicago, IL 60606
Website: www.glslregionalbody.org

The Great Lakes-St. Lawrence River Water Resources Regional Body is an entity charged with aiding and promoting the coordination of the activities and programs of the Great Lakes states and provinces concerned with water resources management in the Great Lakes and St. Lawrence River basin. The regional body may develop procedures for the implementation of the Great Lakes-St. Lawrence River Basin Sustainable Water Resources Agreement, which is a good-faith agreement between Great Lakes states and provinces that governs the withdrawal, consumptive use, conservation and efficient use, and diversion of basin water resources. The regional body must review and approve proposals from certain parties for the withdrawal, diversion, or consumptive use of water from the basin that is subject to the agreement.

The members of the regional body are the governors from the states of Illinois, Indiana, Michigan, Minnesota, New York, Ohio, Pennsylvania, and Wisconsin, and the premiers of Ontario and Québec. The members of the body jointly pursue intergovernmental cooperation and consultation to protect, conserve, restore, improve, and manage the waters and water dependent natural resources of the basin.

INTERSTATE COMMISSION FOR JUVENILES

Wisconsin members: Casey Gerber (compact administrator, Department of Corrections); Joy Swantz (deputy compact administrator, Department of Corrections)
Executive director: Marylee Underwood
Contact: icjadmin@juvenilecompact.org; 859-721-1061; 836 Euclid Avenue, Suite 322, Lexington, KY 40502
Website: www.juvenilecompact.org

The Interstate Commission for Juveniles was established under the Interstate Compact for Juveniles. The compact is designed to coordinate the supervision of juveniles on probation and parole who move across state lines and assists states in returning youth who run away, escape, or abscond across state lines. The commission has the authority to promulgate rules that have the force of law and enforce compliance with the compact.

INTERSTATE COMMISSION OF NURSE LICENSURE COMPACT ADMINISTRATORS

Wisconsin member: Thomas Ryan (executive director, Wisconsin Medical Examining Board)
Contact: info@ncsbn.org; 312-525-3600; 111 East Wacker Drive, Suite 2900, Chicago, IL 60601
Website: https://www.ncsbn.org/

The Interstate Commission of Nurse Licensure Compact Administrators was established under the Enhanced Nurse Licensure Compact. The compact authorizes a nurse licensed in a member state to practice nursing in any other member state without obtaining a license in that state. The commission administers the compact and has the authority to promulgate rules that have the force of law.

INTERSTATE INSURANCE PRODUCT REGULATION COMMISSION

Wisconsin member: Mark Afable (commissioner of insurance)
Contact: 202-471-3962; 444 North Capitol Street, NW, Hall of the States, Suite 700, Washington, DC 20001-1509
Website: www.insurancecompact.org

The Interstate Insurance Product Regulation Commission was established under the Interstate Insurance Product Regulation Compact. The compact's purposes are to promote and protect the interest of consumers of, and establish uniform standards for, annuity, life, disability income, and long-term care insurance products; establish a central clearinghouse for the review of those insurance products and related matters such as advertising; and improve the coordination of regulatory resources and expertise among the various insurance agencies of the member states.

INTERSTATE MEDICAL LICENSURE COMPACT COMMISSION

Wisconsin member: Kenneth Simons, *chair*
Contact: imlccexecutivedirector@imlcc.net; 303-898-1144; 5306 South Bannock Street #205, Littleton, CO 80120
Website: https://imlcc.org

The Interstate Medical Licensure Compact Commission was established under the Interstate Medical Licensure Compact. The compact provides an expedited process for physicians to become licensed to practice medicine in member states. The commission administers the compact and has the authority to promulgate rules that have the force of law.

INTERSTATE WILDLIFE VIOLATOR COMPACT BOARD OF ADMINISTRATORS

Wisconsin member: Jennifer McDonough (compact administrator, Department of Natural Resources)
Contact: Wisconsin Department of Natural Resources; 608-267-0859; PO Box 7921, Madison, WI 53707-7921
Website: https://www.naclec.org/wvc#

The Interstate Wildlife Violator Compact is intended to promote compliance with laws and rules relating to the management of wildlife resources in the member states. The compact establishes a process for handling a wildlife resources law violation by a nonresident in a member state as if the violator were a resident of that state. The compact also requires each member state to recognize the revocation or suspension of an individual's wildlife resources privileges in another member state. The compact board of administrators resolves all matters relating to the operation of the compact.

LOWER ST. CROIX MANAGEMENT COMMISSION

Wisconsin member: Dan Baumann (designated by secretary of natural resources)
Contact: Department of Natural Resources, West Central Region; 715-839-3722; 1300 West Clairemont Avenue, Eau Claire, WI 54701

The Lower St. Croix Management Commission was created to provide a forum for discussion of problems and programs associated with the Lower St. Croix National Scenic Riverway. It coordinates planning, development, protection, and management of the riverway between Wisconsin, Minnesota, and the U.S. government.

MIDWEST INTERSTATE LOW-LEVEL RADIOACTIVE WASTE COMMISSION

Wisconsin member: Paul Schmidt (chief, Radiation Protection Section, Department of Health Services)

Contact: paul.schmidt@dhs.wisconsin.gov; 608-267-4792; PO Box 2659, Madison, WI 53701-2659
Website: www.midwestcompact.org

The Midwest Interstate Low-Level Radioactive Waste Commission administers the Midwest Interstate Low-Level Radioactive Waste Compact. The compact is an agreement between the states of Indiana, Iowa, Minnesota, Missouri, Ohio, and Wisconsin that provides for the cooperative and safe disposal of commercial low-level radioactive waste.

MIDWEST INTERSTATE PASSENGER RAIL COMMISSION

Wisconsin members: Tony Evers (governor); Senator Miller; 2 vacancies
Contact: miprc@miprc.org; 630-925-1922; 701 East 22nd Street, Suite 110, Lombard, IL 60148
Website: www.miprc.org

The Midwest Interstate Passenger Rail Commission brings together state leaders from the members of the Midwest Interstate Passenger Rail Compact to advocate for passenger rail improvements. The commission also works to educate government officials and the public with respect to the advantages of passenger rail. The current members of the compact are Illinois, Indiana, Kansas, Michigan, Minnesota, Missouri, Nebraska, North Dakota, and Wisconsin.

MIDWESTERN HIGHER EDUCATION COMMISSION

Wisconsin members: Representative Ballweg; Senator Nass; Rolf Wegenke; Morna K. Foy (alternate); Sean P. Nelson (alternate); 2 vacancies
Contact: 612-677-2777; 105 Fifth Avenue South, Suite 450, Minneapolis, Minnesota 55401
Website: www.mhec.org

The Midwestern Higher Education Commission was organized to further higher educational opportunities for residents of states participating in the Midwestern Higher Education Compact. The commission may enter into agreements with states, universities, and colleges to provide student programs and services. The commission also studies the compact's effects on higher education.

MILITARY INTERSTATE CHILDREN'S COMPACT COMMISSION

Wisconsin commissioner: Shelley Joan Weiss
Contact: mic3info@csg.org; 859-244-8000; 1776 Avenue of The States, Lexington, KY 40511
Website: www.mic3.net

The Military Interstate Children's Compact Commission oversees implementation of the Interstate Compact on Educational Opportunity for Military Children. The compact is intended to facilitate the education of children of military families and remove barriers to educational success due to frequent moves and parent deployment.

The commission is composed of one commissioner from each of the compacting states. In each compacting state, a council or other body in state government administers the compact within that state. In Wisconsin, the compact is administered by the State Council on the Interstate Compact on Educational Opportunity for Military Children.

MISSISSIPPI RIVER PARKWAY COMMISSION

Wisconsin commission: Sherry Quamme, *chair*
Contact: mrpc@pilchbarnet.com; 866-763-8310; 701 East Washington Avenue, #202, Madison, WI 53703
Website: https://mrpcmembers.com

The Mississippi River Parkway Commission coordinates the development and preservation of Wisconsin's portion of the Great River Road corridor along the Mississippi River. It advises state and local agencies on maintaining and enhancing the scenic, historic, economic, and recreational assets within the corridor and works with similar commissions in other Mississippi River states and the province of Ontario. The 16-member Wisconsin commission includes 12 voting members. Four of these are legislative members who represent the two major political parties in each house, and eight others are appointed by the governor. The four nonvoting members are ex officio, consisting of the secretaries of tourism, natural resources, and transportation and the director of the historical society. The commission selects its own chair to act as Wisconsin's sole voting representative at national meetings of the Mississippi River Parkway Commission.

UPPER MISSISSIPPI RIVER BASIN ASSOCIATION

Wisconsin representative: Steve Galarneau
Executive director: Kirsten Wallace
Contact: 651-224-2880; 415 Hamm Building, 408 St. Peter Street, St. Paul, MN 55102
Website: www.umrba.org

The Upper Mississippi River Basin Association is a nonprofit regional organization created by Illinois, Iowa, Minnesota, Missouri, and Wisconsin to facilitate cooperative action regarding the basin's water and related land resources. The association consists of one voting member from each state and sponsors studies of river-related issues, cooperative planning for use of the region's resources, and an information exchange. The organization also enables the member states to develop regional positions on resource issues and to advocate for the basin states' collective interests before the U.S. Congress and federal agencies. The association is involved with programs related to commercial navigation, ecosystem restoration, water quality, aquatic nuisance species, hazardous spills, flood risk management, water supply, and other water resource issues. Six federal agencies with major water resources responsibilities serve as advisory members: the Environmental

Protection Agency, the U.S. Army Corps of Engineers, and the U.S. departments of Agriculture, Homeland Security, the Interior, and Transportation.

Interstate compacts without interstate entities

INTERSTATE COMPACT ON ADOPTION AND MEDICAL ASSISTANCE

Requires each member state to cooperate with other states to ensure that children with special needs who were adopted in or from another member state receive medical and other benefits. The Department of Children and Families administers the compact in Wisconsin.

INTERSTATE COMPACT FOR ADULT OFFENDER SUPERVISION

Creates cooperative procedures for individuals placed on parole, probation, or extended supervision in one state to be supervised in another state if certain conditions are met. The Department of Corrections administers the compact in Wisconsin.

INTERSTATE CORRECTIONS COMPACT

Authorizes Wisconsin to contract with member states for the confinement of Wisconsin inmates in those states and to receive inmates from member states. The Department of Corrections administers the compact in Wisconsin.

INTERSTATE AGREEMENT ON DETAINERS

Allows a member state to obtain temporary custody of an individual incarcerated in another member state to conduct a trial on outstanding charges.

EMERGENCY MANAGEMENT ASSISTANCE COMPACT

Authorizes member states to provide mutual assistance to other states in an emergency or disaster declared by the governor of the affected state. Under the compact, member states cooperate in emergency-related training and formulate plans for interstate cooperation in responding to a disaster. The Division of Emergency Management in the Department of Military Affairs administers the compact in Wisconsin.

INTERSTATE COMPACT ON MENTAL HEALTH

Facilitates treatment of patients with mental illness and mental disabilities by the cooperative action of the member states, to the benefit of the patients, their families, and society.

INTERSTATE COMPACT ON THE PLACEMENT OF CHILDREN

Provides a uniform legal and administrative framework governing the interstate placement of abused, neglected, or dependent children, the interstate placement of children through independent or private adoption, and the interstate placement of any child into residential treatment facilities. The Department of Children and Families administers the compact in Wisconsin.

INTERSTATE AGREEMENT ON QUALIFICATION OF EDUCATIONAL PERSONNEL

Authorizes a state education official designated by each member state to contract with other member states to recognize the credentials of educators from those member states and facilitate the employment of qualified educational personnel.

Wisconsin Supreme Court

Justices: Patience Drake Roggensack, *chief justice;* Ann Walsh Bradley, Annette Kingsland
  Ziegler, Rebecca Grassl Bradley, Daniel Kelly, Rebecca Frank Dallet, Brian Hagedorn
Clerk of the supreme court: Sheila Reiff
Supreme court commissioners: Nancy Kopp, Julie Rich, David Runke, Mark Neuser,
  Laureen Bussan, Kendra Wochos, Sonja Umberger
Location: Room 16 East, State Capitol, Madison (supreme court); 110 East Main Street,
  Suite 215, Madison (clerk)
Contact: 608-266-1880 (clerk); 608-266-7442 (commissioners); PO Box 1688, Madison, WI
  53701-1688
Website: https://wicourts.gov/courts/supreme/index.htm
Number of employees: 38.50
Total budget 2017–19: $ 11,059,400

The Wisconsin Supreme Court is the highest court in Wisconsin's court system. It is the final authority on matters pertaining to the Wisconsin Constitution and the highest tribunal for all actions begun in the state court system, except those involving federal constitutional issues appealable to the U.S. Supreme Court. In addition, it has regulatory and administrative authority over all courts and the practice of law in the state. In this capacity, it establishes procedural rules and codes of conduct for the courts and for the practice of law, and it regulates and disciplines attorneys, judges, and justices.

The supreme court consists of seven justices elected for ten-year terms. They are chosen in statewide elections on the nonpartisan April ballot and take office on the following August 1. The Wisconsin Constitution provides that only one justice can be elected in any single year. In the event of a vacancy, the governor may appoint a person to serve until an election can be held to fill the seat.

The justices elect one of themselves to be the chief justice for a term of two years. The chief justice serves as administrative head of the court system. Any four justices constitute a quorum for conducting court business.

The court decides which cases it will hear. The supreme court exercises its appellate jurisdiction to review a decision of a lower court if three or more justices approve a petition for review, if the court decides on its own motion to review a matter that has been appealed to the court of appeals, or if the court accepts a petition for bypass or a certification from the court of appeals. The majority of cases advance from the circuit court to the court of appeals before reaching the supreme court, but the supreme court can bypass the court of appeals, either on its own motion or at the request of the parties; in addition, the court of appeals may certify a case to the supreme court, asking the high court to take the case directly from the circuit court. The court accepts cases on bypass or on certification if four of more justices approve. Further, although rarely granted, a person may file a petition requesting the supreme court to exercise its superintending authority over actions and proceedings both in the circuit courts and court of appeals. The supreme court may also exercise original jurisdiction as the first court to hear a case if four or more justices approve a petition requesting it to do so.

The supreme court does not take testimony. Instead, it decides cases on the basis of written briefs and oral argument. The court is required by statute to deliver its decisions in writing, and it may publish them as it deems appropriate.

Wisconsin Court of Appeals

Chief judge: Lisa S. Neubauer
Clerk of the court of appeals: Sheila Reiff
Location: 110 East Main Street, Suite 215, Madison (clerk)
Contact: 608-266-1880; PO Box 1688, Madison, WI 53701-1688
Website: https://wicourts.gov/courts/appeals/index.htm
Number of employees: 75.50
Total budget 2017–19: $ 22,321,600

DISTRICT I

Kitty K. Brennan, *presiding judge*; Joan F. Kessler, William W. Brash III, Timothy G. Dugan
Contact: 414-227-4680; 330 East Kilbourn Avenue, Suite 1020, Milwaukee, WI 53202-3161

DISTRICT II

Paul F. Reilly, *presiding judge*; Lisa S. Neubauer, Mark D. Gundrum, vacant
Contact: 262-521-5230; 2727 North Grandview Boulevard, Suite 300, Waukesha, WI
53188-1671

DISTRICT III

Lisa K. Stark, *presiding judge*; Thomas M. Hruz, Mark A. Seidl
Contact: 715-848-1421; 2100 Stewart Avenue, Suite 310, Wausau, WI 54401

DISTRICT IV

Brian W. Blanchard, JoAnne F. Kloppenburg, Michael R. Fitzpatrick, Jennifer Nashold,
vacancy
Contact: 608-266-9250; 10 East Doty Street, Suite 700, Madison, WI 53703-3397

The Wisconsin Court of Appeals consists of 16 judges serving in four districts. The Wisconsin Supreme Court appoints one of these judges to be the chief judge and to serve as administrative head of the court of appeals for a three-year term. The clerk of the supreme court serves as the clerk for the court of appeals.

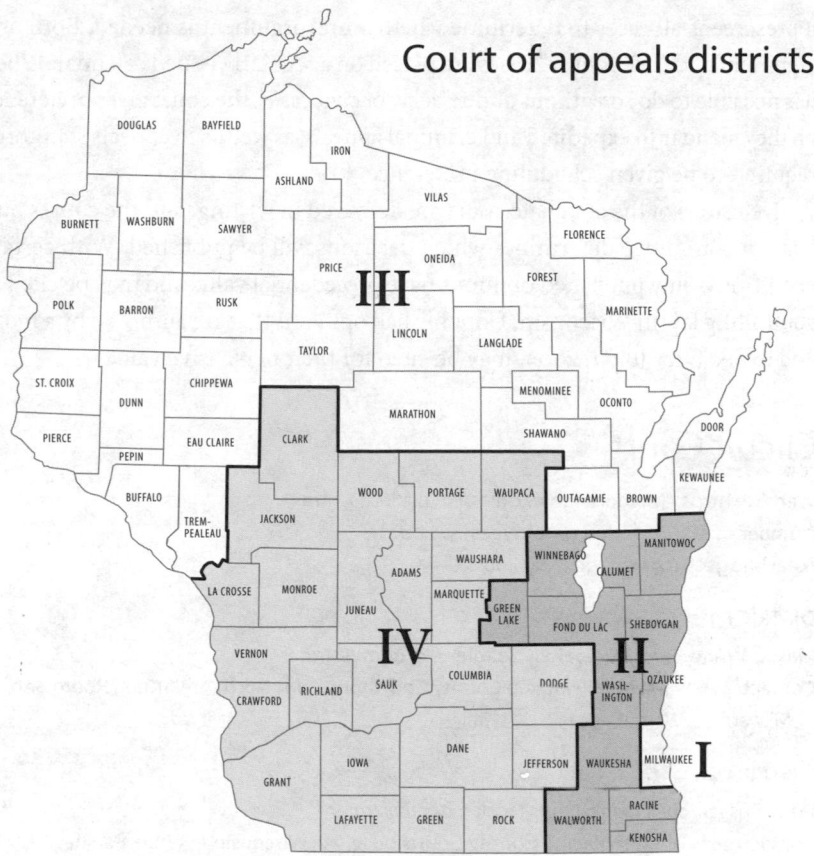

Court of appeals districts

Court of appeals judges are elected for six-year terms in the nonpartisan April election and begin their terms of office on the following August 1. They must reside in the district from which they are elected. Only one court of appeals judge may be elected in a district in any one year. In the event of a vacancy, the governor may appoint a person to serve until an election can be held to fill the seat.

The court of appeals has appellate jurisdiction, as well as original jurisdiction to issue prerogative writs. The court also has supervisory authority over all actions and proceedings except those of the supreme court. The final judgments and orders of a circuit court may be appealed to the court of appeals as a matter of right. Other judgments or orders may be appealed upon leave of the appellate court.

The court usually sits as a three-judge panel to dispose of cases on their merits. However, a single judge may decide certain categories of cases, including juvenile cases; small claims; municipal ordinance and traffic violations; and mental health and misdemeanor cases. No testimony is taken in the appellate court. The court relies on the trial court record and written briefs in deciding a case, and it prescreens all cases to determine whether oral argument is needed. Both oral argument and "briefs only" cases are placed on a regularly issued calendar. When it is possible to do so without undue delay of civil cases, the court gives preference on the calendar to expedited and criminal appeals, as well as to appeals statutorily required to be given scheduling preference.

Decisions of the appellate court are delivered in writing, and the court's publication committee determines which decisions will be published. With certain exceptions, only published opinions have precedential value and may be cited as controlling law in Wisconsin. Unpublished opinions that are authored by a judge and issued after July 1, 2009, may be cited for their persuasive value.

Circuit Court

Website: https://wicourts.gov/courts/circuit/index.htm
Number of state-funded employees: 527.00
Total budget 2017–19: $203,586,400

DISTRICT 1

Maxine White, *chief judge*; Holly Szablewski, *administrator*
Contact: 414-278-5115; Milwaukee County Courthouse, 901 North 9th Street, Room 609, Milwaukee, WI 53233-1425

DISTRICT 2

Jason Rossell, *chief judge*; Louis Moore, *administrator*
Contact: 262-636-3133; Racine County Courthouse, 730 Wisconsin Avenue, Racine, WI 53403-1274

DISTRICT 3

Jennifer Dorow, *chief judge*; Michael Neimon, *administrator*
Contact: 262-548-7209; Waukesha County Courthouse, 515 West Moreland Boulevard, Room C-359, Waukesha, WI 53188-2428

DISTRICT 4

Barbara Hart Key, *chief judge*; Jon Bellows, *administrator*
Contact: 920-424-0027; District Court Administrator's Office, 415 Jackson Street, Room 510, Oshkosh, WI 54903-2808

DISTRICT 5

William E. Hanrahan, *chief judge*; Theresa Owens, *administrator*
Contact: 608-267-8820; Dane County Courthouse, 215 South Hamilton Street, Room 6111, Madison, WI 53703-3290

DISTRICT 6

District 6 was eliminated by supreme court order effective July 31, 2018.

DISTRICT 7

Robert Van De Hey, *chief judge*; Patrick Brummond, *administrator*
Contact: 608-785-9546; La Crosse County Law Enforcement Center, 333 Vine Street, Room 3504, La Crosse, WI 54601-3296

DISTRICT 8

James Morrison, *chief judge*; Thomas Schappa, *administrator*
Contact: 920-448-4281; District Court Administrator's Office, 414 East Walnut Street, Suite 100, Green Bay, WI 54301-5020

DISTRICT 9

Greg Huber, *chief judge*; Susan Byrnes, *administrator*
Contact: 715-842-3872; District Court Administrator's Office, 2100 Stewart Avenue, Suite 310, Wausau, WI 54401

DISTRICT 10

Maureen Boyle, *chief judge*; Donald Harper, *administrator*
Contact: 715-245-4104; District Court Administrator's Office, 1101 Carmichael Road, Suite 1260; Hudson, WI 54016

The circuit court is the trial court of general jurisdiction in Wisconsin. It has original jurisdiction in both civil and criminal matters unless exclusive jurisdiction is given to another court. It also reviews state agency decisions and hears appeals from municipal courts. Jury trials are conducted only in circuit courts.

The circuit court consists of numerous judges serving in 69 circuits. Each circuit consists of the territory of a single county, except for three two-county

Wisconsin Supreme Court Chief Justice Patience Drake Roggensack, standing, makes opening remarks during the Court's Justice on Wheels visit at the Monroe County Justice Center in Sparta on Friday, October 12, 2018. Other justices, left to right: Justice Daniel Kelly, Justice Annette Kingsland Ziegler, Justice Shirley S. Abrahamson, Justice Ann Walsh Bradley, Justice Rebecca Grassl Bradley, and Justice Rebecca Frank Dallet.

TOM SHEEHAN, WISCONSIN SUPREME COURT

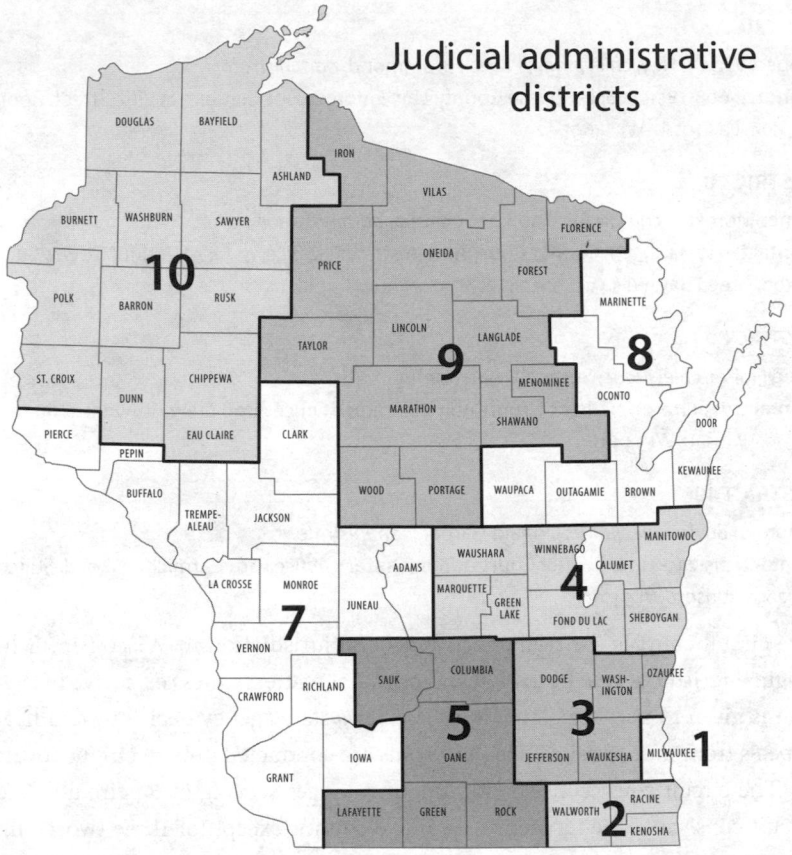

Judicial administrative districts

circuits (Buffalo-Pepin, Florence-Forest, and Menominee-Shawano). Because of the varying size of their caseloads, some circuits have a single judge, while others have multiple judges. Each judge in a circuit holds court separately—circuit judges do not sit as a panel to hear cases—and each judgeship is called a branch of the circuit. As of August 1, 2018, there were a total of 249 circuit court branches in the state.

Circuit judges are elected for six-year terms on a nonpartisan basis in the April election and take office the following August 1. The governor may fill circuit court vacancies by appointment, and the appointees serve until a successor is elected. The state pays the salaries of circuit judges and court reporters. It also covers some of the expenses for interpreters, guardians ad litem, judicial assistants, court-appointed witnesses, and jury per diems. Counties bear the remaining expenses for operating the circuit courts.

Effective July 31, 2018, the circuit court is divided into nine administrative districts, each supervised by a chief judge appointed by the supreme court from the district's circuit judges. A judge usually cannot serve more than three successive two-year terms as chief judge. The chief judge has authority to assign judges, manage caseflow, supervise personnel, and conduct financial planning. The chief judge in each district appoints a district court administrator from a list of candidates supplied by the director of state courts. The administrator manages the nonjudicial business of the district at the direction of the chief judge.

Circuit court commissioners are appointed by the circuit court to assist the court, and they must be attorneys licensed to practice law in Wisconsin. They may be authorized by the court to conduct various civil, criminal, family, small claims, juvenile, and probate court proceedings. Their duties include issuing summonses, arrest warrants, or search warrants; conducting initial appearances; setting bail; conducting preliminary examinations and arraignments; imposing monetary penalties in certain traffic cases; conducting certain family, juvenile, and small claims court proceedings; hearing petitions for mental commitments; and conducting uncontested probate proceedings. On their own authority, court commissioners may perform marriages, administer oaths, take depositions, and issue subpoenas and certain writs.

The statutes require the circuit court for Milwaukee County to have full-time family, small claims, and probate court commissioners. In all other counties, the circuit court is required to have a family court commissioner.

Municipal Court

Website: https://wicourts.gov/courts/municipal/index.htm

The legislature has authorized cities, villages, and towns to establish municipal courts to exercise jurisdiction over municipal ordinance violations that have monetary penalties. Municipal courts also have the authority to handle first offense Operating While Under the Influence cases. In addition, municipal courts may rule on the constitutionality of municipal ordinances.

Municipal courts can have multiple branches (judges who hold court separately), and two or more municipalities can form a joint court. As of October 2017, there were 240 municipal courts with 242 municipal judges, as well as 7 reserve judges. There were 70 joint courts, serving from two to 17 municipalities. The cities of Milwaukee and Madison have the state's only full-time municipal courts.

Upon convicting a defendant, the municipal court may order payment of a forfeiture plus costs, fees, and surcharges, or it may order community service in lieu of a forfeiture. In general, municipal courts may also order restitution up to $10,000. In certain cases, a municipal court may suspend or revoke a driver's license.

If a defendant fails to pay a forfeiture or make restitution, the municipal court may suspend the driver's license or order the defendant to jail. Municipal court decisions may be appealed to the circuit court for the county where the offense occurred.

Municipal judges are elected at the nonpartisan April election and take office on May 1. The term of office is four years, unless the municipality has adopted a charter ordinance designating a different term of at least two years, but less than four years. The governing body determines the judge's salary. There is no state requirement that the office be filled by an attorney, but a municipality may enact such a qualification by ordinance. If a municipal judge is ill, disabled, or temporarily absent, the municipal judge may temporarily designate another municipal judge to handle the matter, subject to an order of the chief judge of the circuit court administrative district containing the municipality. In other circumstances, such as when a judge is disqualified, the chief judge of the circuit court administrative district may designate another municipal judge to handle a matter. Finally, if a municipal judge is incompetent, unable or fails to act, the chief justice of the supreme court may assign cases to another municipal judge, a former municipal judge, or a former circuit court judge.

Auxiliary entities

Office of the Director of State Courts

Director of state courts: Randy Koschnick
Deputy director for court operations: Diane Fremgen
Deputy director for management services: Dean Stensberg
Location: Room 16 East, State Capitol, Madison (director); 110 East Main Street, Madison (staff)
Contact: 608-266-6828 (director); PO Box 1688, Madison, WI 53701-1688 (director); 110 East Main Street, Madison, WI 53703-3356 (staff)
Website: https://wicourts.gov/courts/offices/director.htm
Number of employees: 147.75
Total budget 2017–19: $44,205,300

The director of state courts is appointed by the supreme court and is the chief nonjudicial officer of the Wisconsin court system. The director is responsible for the management of the court system and advises the supreme court, particularly on matters relating to improvements to the court system. The director supervises most state-level court personnel; develops the court system's budget; and directs the courts' work on legislation, public information, and information systems. This office also controls expenditures; allocates space and equipment; supervises judicial education, interdistrict judicial assignments at the circuit court level, and planning and research; and administers the medical malpractice mediation system.

Judge Christopher R. Foley, Milwaukee County Circuit Court, testifies before the Assembly Committee on Family Law about legislation affecting conditions for the restoration of parental rights. The legislation was introduced by the Speaker's Task Force on Foster Care and eventually signed into law as 2017 Act 256.

State Bar of Wisconsin

Board of Governors, officer members: Christopher Earl Rogers, *president*; Jill M. Kastner, *president-elect*; Paul G. Swanson, *past president*; Starlyn Rose Tourtillott, *secretary*; John E. Danner, *treasurer*; Odalo J. Ohiku, *chair of the board*

Board of Governors, district elected members: Steven Conrad Harvey, Kori L. Ashley, Andrew P. Beilfuss, Brittany C. Grayson, Rochelle Johnson-Bent, Elizabeth Kerstin Miles, Amy Elizabeth Wochos, Karen Marie Bauer, Daniel J. Blinka, Gregg M. Herman, Lisa M. Lawless, Krista G. LaFave Rosolino, Nicholas C. Zales, Kathleen A. Brost, Mary Lynne Donohue, Craig R. Steger, Jesse Blocher, John P. Macy, Timothy T. Kay, Bradley Yanke, Joel D. Skinner, Jr., Truscenialyn Brooks, Jeff Goldman, Laura Skilton Verhoff, Katie R. York, Kathleen Chung, Patricia Epstein Putney, Sam Wayne, Charles Stertz, Howard J. Bichler, Jane Ellen Bucher, Robert G. Barrington, Sherry Coley, Gretchen G. Rosenke, Amanda J. Ley

Executive director: Larry J. Martin

Location: 5302 Eastpark Boulevard, Madison

Contact: service@wisbar.org; 608-257-3838 (general); 800-362-9082 (lawyer referral and information service); PO Box 7158, Madison, WI 53707-7158

Website: www.wisbar.org

The State Bar of Wisconsin is a mandatory professional association of all attorneys who hold a Wisconsin law license. In order to practice law in the state, attorneys must be admitted to practice by the full Wisconsin Supreme Court or by a single justice and must also join the State Bar. The governance and structure of the

State Bar are established by the supreme court. The State Bar works to maintain and promote professional standards, improve the administration of justice and the delivery of legal services, and provide continuing legal education to lawyers. The State Bar conducts legal research in substantive law, practice, and procedure and develops related reports and recommendations. It also maintains the roll of attorneys, collects mandatory assessments imposed by the supreme court for supreme court boards and to fund civil legal services for the poor, and performs other administrative services for the judicial system.

State Law Library

State law librarian: Julie Tessmer Robinson
Deputy law librarian: Amy Crowder
Location: 120 Martin Luther King, Jr. Blvd., 2nd Floor, Madison
Contact: wsll.ref@wicourts.gov (reference); 800-322-9755 (toll free); 608-266-1600 (circulation); 608-267-9696 (reference); PO Box 7881, Madison, WI 53707
Website: http://wilawlibrary.gov

The State Law Library is a public library open to all citizens of Wisconsin. The library supports the information needs of the justices, judges, and staff of the Wisconsin court system. The library is administered by the supreme court, which appoints the state law librarian and determines the rules governing library access. The library acts as a consultant and resource for circuit court libraries throughout the state. Milwaukee County and Dane County contract with the State Law Library for management and operation of their courthouse libraries (the Milwaukee County Law Library and the Dane County Law Library).

The library's collection features session laws, statutory codes, case reporters, administrative rules, and legal indexes of the U.S. government, all 50 states, and U.S. territories. It also includes legal and bar periodicals and legal treatises and encyclopedias relevant to all major areas of law. As a federal depository library, it selects federal documents to complement the legal collection. The collection circulates to judges and court staff, attorneys, legislators, and government personnel. The library offers reference, legal research guidance, and document delivery services, as well as training in the use of legal research tools, databases, and websites.

Lawyer Regulation System

Office of Lawyer Regulation: Keith L. Sellen, *director*
Preliminary Review Committee: Nora Platt, *chair*
Special Preliminary Review Panel: Bruce F. Ehlke, *chair*
Board of Administrative Oversight: Gary J. Vandomelen, *chair*
Location: 110 East Main Street, Suite 315, Madison
Contact: 608-267-7274; 877-315-6941 (toll free); PO Box 1648, Madison, WI 53701-1648

Number of employees: 27.50
Total budget 2017–19: $6,543,400
Website: https://www.wicourts.gov/courts/offices/olr.htm

The Lawyer Regulation System assists the supreme court in supervising the practice of law and protecting the public from professional misconduct by persons practicing law in Wisconsin. The system includes several entities.

The Office of Lawyer Regulation receives and evaluates all complaints, inquiries, and grievances related to attorney misconduct or medical incapacity. The office is headed by a director who is appointed by the supreme court. The office must investigate any grievance that appears to support an allegation of possible attorney misconduct or incapacity, and the attorney in question must cooperate with the investigation. After investigation, the director decides whether the matter should be forwarded to the Preliminary Review Committee, be dismissed, or be diverted for alternative action. The director may also obtain the attorney's consent to a private or public reprimand.

If the director does forward a matter to the Preliminary Review Committee and a panel of that committee determines there is cause to proceed, the director may seek disciplinary action, ranging from agreement to a private reprimand to filing a formal complaint with the supreme court that requests private or public reprimand, license suspension or revocation, monetary payment, or imposing conditions on the continued practice of law. An attorney may be offered alternatives to formal disciplinary action, including mediation, fee arbitration, law office management assistance, evaluation and treatment for alcohol and other substance abuse, psychological evaluation and treatment, monitoring of the attorney's practice or trust account procedures, continuing legal education, ethics school, or the multistate professional responsibility examination.

Formal disciplinary actions for attorney misconduct are filed by the director with the supreme court, which appoints an attorney or reserve judge to be the referee for each such action. Referees conduct hearings on complaints of attorney misconduct, petitions alleging attorney medical incapacity, and petitions for reinstatement. They make findings, conclusions, and recommendations and submit them to the supreme court for review and appropriate action. Only the supreme court has the authority to suspend or revoke a lawyer's license to practice law in Wisconsin.

If the director receives an allegation of misconduct or incapacity pertaining to an attorney who works in or is retained to assist the Lawyer Regulation System, the director must refer the matter to a special investigator. Special investigators are attorneys who are appointed by the supreme court and who are not currently working in or retained by the Lawyer Regulation System. The special investigator commences an investigation if he or she determines there is enough information to support a possible finding of cause to proceed on the allegation, but otherwise may close the matter. After an investigation, the special investigator can dismiss the matter or submit an investigative report to the Special Preliminary Review Panel. If this panel determines, after receiving an investigative report from a special investigator, that there is cause to proceed, the special investigator can proceed to file a complaint with the supreme court and prosecute the matter personally or may assign that responsibility to counsel retained by the director for such purposes.

The Board of Administrative Oversight monitors and assesses the performance of the Lawyer Regulation System and reports its findings to the supreme court. The board reviews with the supreme court the operation of the Lawyer Regulation System, proposes for consideration by the supreme court substantive and procedural rules related to the regulation of lawyers, and proposes to the supreme court the annual budget for the Office of Lawyer Regulation, after consulting with the director of that office.

Board of Bar Examiners

Vice Chair: Judith G. McMullen
Director: Jacquelynn B. Rothstein
Location: 110 East Main Street, Suite 715, Madison
Contact: bbe@wicourts.gov; 608-266-9760; PO Box 2748, Madison, WI 53701-2748
Website: https://wicourts.gov/courts/offices/bbe.htm
Number of employees: 8.00
Total budget 2017–19: $ 1,679,400

The Board of Bar Examiners administers all bar admissions; it writes and grades the bar examination, reviews motions for admission on proof of practice, and conducts character and fitness investigations of all candidates for admission to the bar, including diploma privilege graduates. The board also administers the Wisconsin mandatory continuing legal education requirement for attorneys.

Judicial Commission

Members: Mark Barrette, Eileen Burnett, William E. Cullinan, Frank J. Daily, Brian K. Hagedorn, Kendall M. Kelley, Steve C. Miller, Joseph L. Olson, Robert H. Papke
Executive director: Jeremiah C. Van Hecke
Contact: judcmm@wicourts.gov; 608-266-7637; 110 East Main Street, Suite 700, Madison, WI 53703-3328
Website: https://wicourts.gov/judcom
Number of employees: 2.00
Total budget 2017–19: $607,600

Wisconsin Supreme Court Chief Justice Patience Drake Roggensack discusses the structure and role of the court system with freshmen legislators as part of the Legislature's New Member Institute held Dec. 5, 2018. The new legislators also visited the Supreme Court Conference Room, where the chief justice discussed the process used to take and decide cases.

The Judicial Commission conducts investigations regarding allegations that a justice, judge, or court commissioner has committed misconduct or has a permanent disability that substantially impairs his or her judicial performance.

The commission's investigations are confidential. If the commission finds probable cause that a justice, judge, or court commissioner has engaged in misconduct or has a disability that substantially impairs his or her judicial performance, the commission must file a formal complaint of misconduct or a petition regarding disability with the supreme court.

The commission then prosecutes a proceeding against the judge before a three-judge panel or, if the commission so requested when it filed the complaint or petition, before a jury. The panel of judges, or a single judge to preside over a jury proceeding, is selected by the chief judge of the court of appeals. If the proceeding was held before a panel, the supreme court reviews the panel's findings of fact, conclusions of law, and recommended disposition and determines the appropriate discipline in cases of misconduct or appropriate action in cases of permanent disability. If the proceeding was held before a jury, the presiding judge files the jury verdict and his or her recommendations regarding appropriate discipline for misconduct or appropriate action for permanent disability with the supreme court for the court's review.

Judicial Conduct Advisory Committee

Members: D. Todd Ehlers, *chair*; Dan Conley, William J. Domina, Anton Jamieson, Joan F. Kessler, Daniel P. Koval, Victor Manion, Randy Morrissette II, Maxine A. White
Contact: 608-266-6828; PO Box 1688, Madison, WI 53701-1688
Website: https://wicourts.gov/courts/committees/judicialconduct.htm

The Judicial Conduct Advisory Committee gives formal advisory opinions and informal advice regarding whether actions judges are contemplating comply with the Code of Judicial Conduct. It also makes recommendations to the supreme court about amending of the Code of Judicial Conduct or the rules governing the committee.

Judicial Conference

Website: https://wicourts.gov/courts/committees/judicialconf.htm

The Judicial Conference is composed of all supreme court justices, court of appeals judges, circuit court judges, and reserve judges; three municipal court judges designated by the Wisconsin Municipal Judges Association; three judicial representatives of tribal courts designated by the Wisconsin Tribal Judges Association; one circuit court commissioner designated by the Family Court Commissioner Association; and one circuit court commissioner designated by the Judicial Court Commissioner Association.

The Judicial Conference meets at least once a year to recommend improvements in administration of the justice system; conduct educational programs for its members; adopt revised deposit and bail schedules for misdemeanors and traffic offenses, violations of Department of Natural Resources and University of Wisconsin rules, trespass to land, certain alcohol and tobacco violations, harassment, drug paraphernalia offenses, and safety violations; and adopt forms necessary for the administration of certain court proceedings.

The Judicial Conference has several standing committees, including committees to prepare model civil, criminal, and juvenile jury instructions. The Judicial Conference may also create study committees to examine particular topics. These study committees must report their findings and recommendations to the next annual meeting of the Judicial Conference. Study committees usually work for one year, unless extended by the Judicial Conference.

Judicial Council

Members: Annette Kingsland Ziegler (justice designated by supreme court); Randy Koschnick (director of state courts); Michael R. Fitzpatrick (justice designated by court of appeals), Eugene A. Gasiorkiewicz, Robert P. Van De Hey, Jeffrey A. Wagner, Scott R. Needham (circuit court judges designated by Judicial Conference); Senator Van H. Wanggaard (chairperson, senate judicial committee); Representative Jim Ott (chairperson, assembly judicial committee); R. Duane Harlow (designated by attorney general); Sarah Walkenhorst Barber (designated by Legislative Reference Bureau chief); Steven Wright (faculty member designated by UW Law School dean); Thomas L. Shriner, Jr. (faculty member designated by Marquette University Law School dean); Devon M. Lee (designated by state public defender); William Gleisner, Sherry D. Coley, Margo Kirchner, John R. Orton (State Bar members selected by State Bar); Christian Gossett (district attorney appointed by governor); Benjamin J. Pliskie (public member appointed by governor)

Contact: 414-651-3182; PO Box 1001, Brookfield, WI 53008-1001
Website: http://wilawlibrary.gov/judicialcouncil/index.htm
Number of employees: 0.00
Total budget 2017–19: $0

The Judicial Council advises the supreme court, the governor, and the legislature on any matter affecting the administration of justice in Wisconsin, and it may recommend changes in the jurisdiction, organization, operation, or business methods of the courts that would result in a more effective and cost-efficient court system. The council studies the rules of pleading, practice, and procedure and advises the supreme court about changes that will simplify procedure and promote efficiency.

Judicial Education Committee

Members: Chief Justice Patience Drake Roggensack, *chair*; Justice Rebecca Dallet; Thomas R. Hruz (designated by court of appeals chief judge); Randy Koschnick (director of state courts); Jennifer R. Dorow, Eugene A. Gasiorkiewicz, Jill J. Karofsky, Maria S. Lazar, Jason A. Rossell, Robert R. Russell, Mary E. Triggiano, Thomas J. Walsh (circuit court judges appointed by supreme court); John C. Moore, Sara Scullen (circuit court commissioners appointed by supreme court); Jini M. Jasti (designated by UW Law School dean); Thomas Hammer (designated by Marquette University Law School dean), Lisa K. Stark (dean, Wisconsin Judicial College)

Director of Office of Judicial Education: Karla Baumgartner
Contact: JED@wicourts.gov; 608-266-7807; Office of Judicial Education, 110 East Main Street, Suite 200, Madison, WI 53703-3328
Website: https://wicourts.gov/courts/committees/judicialed.htm

The Judicial Education Committee approves educational programs for the purpose of continuing education requirements mandated for the judiciary by the supreme court. All supreme court justices and commissioners, appeals court judges and staff attorneys, and circuit court judges and commissioners must earn 60 credit hours of continuing education every six years in approved educational programs. Different credit-hour requirements apply to reserve judges and municipal court judges. The committee monitors compliance with the continuing education requirements and refers instances of noncompliance to the supreme court. The committee is assisted in its work by the Office of Judicial Education in the Office of the Director of State Courts, which also plans and conducts educational seminars for judges and tracks credits earned by judges.

Planning and Policy Advisory Committee

Chair: Patience Drake Roggensack (chief justice of the supreme court)
Contact: 608-266-3121; 110 East Main Street, Suite 410, Madison, WI 53703
Website: https://wicourts.gov/courts/committees/ppac.htm

The Planning and Policy Advisory Committee advises the Wisconsin Supreme Court and the director of state courts on planning and policy and assists in a continuing evaluation of the administrative structure of the court system. It participates in the budget process of the Wisconsin judiciary and appoints a subcommittee to confer with the supreme court and the director of state courts in the court's review of the budget. The committee meets at least quarterly, and the supreme court meets with the committee annually. The director of state courts participates in committee deliberations, with full floor and advocacy privileges, but is not a member of the committee and does not have a vote.

3

ABOUT WISCONSIN

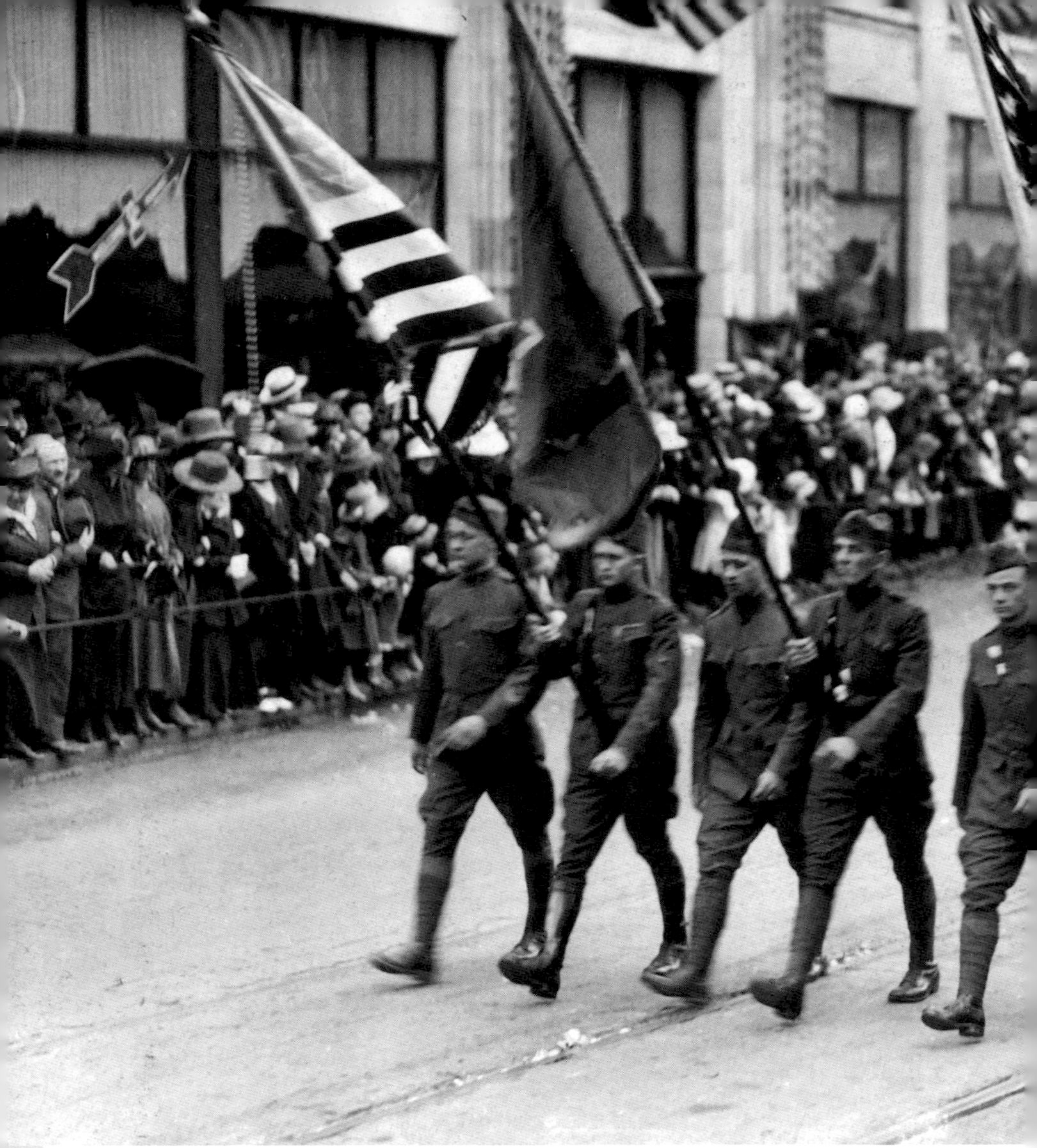

WHS IMAGE ID 103418 *(TOP)* WHS IMAGE ID 26240

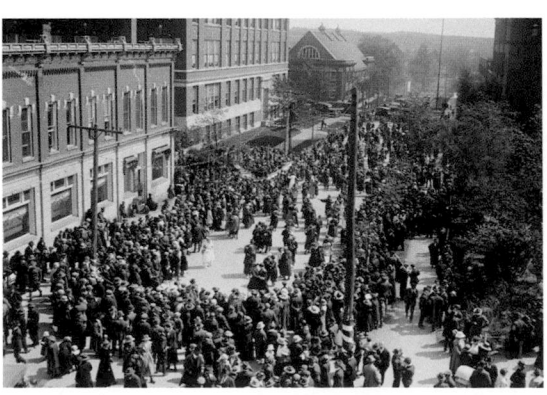

As Wisconsin soldiers demobilized, policymakers reevaluated the meaning of wartime service—and fiercely debated how the state should recognize veterans' sacrifices. (*above*) Crowds assembled in Milwaukee to welcome the 32nd Division after its return from France in 1919. (*left*) Menomonie residents celebrated local members of the Wisconsin National Guard who served during the Great War.

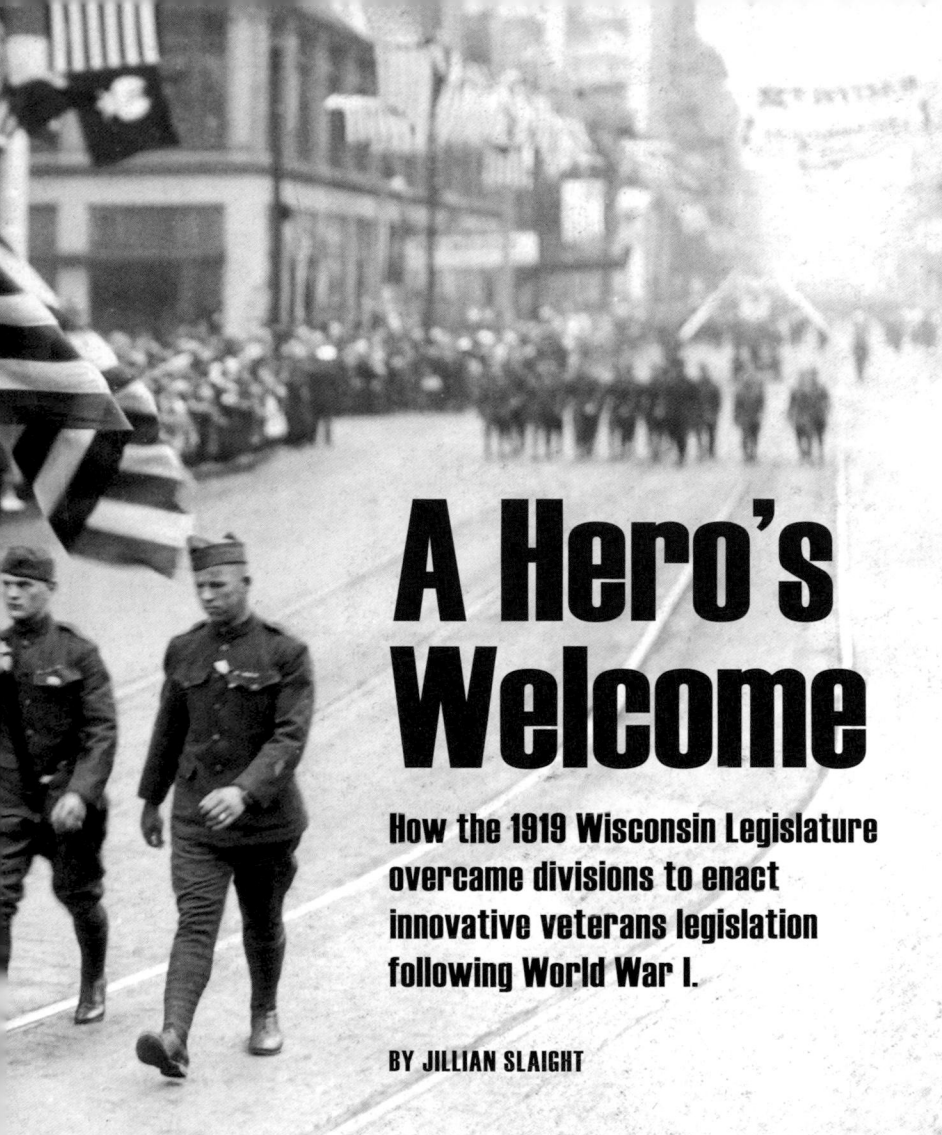

A Hero's Welcome

How the 1919 Wisconsin Legislature overcame divisions to enact innovative veterans legislation following World War I.

BY JILLIAN SLAIGHT

The Great War seemed strangely distant to Ira Lee Peterson, even as his unit camped mere miles from the front lines in France. Between drills and marches, the twenty-two-year-old Wisconsinite swam in streams, wrote letters home, and slept underneath the stars in apple orchards. Even in the trenches, the morning of Sunday, June 16, 1918, was "so quiet . . . that all one could hear was the rats running around bumping into cans and wire." Peterson sat reading a book until a "whizzing sound" cut through the silence, announcing a bombardment that sent him and his comrades scurrying "quick as gophers" into their dugout.[1] After this "baptism with shell fire," Peterson suffered a succession of horrors: mustard gas inhalation, shrapnel wounds, and a German

Before 1914, faith in scientific progress led people to believe that twentieth-century war would be less brutal. In reality, new technologies resulted in unprecedented death and disability. (*left*) American soldiers suffered the effects of chemical warfare despite training in the use of gas masks. (*right*) Life in the trenches also meant frequent exposure to enemy shellfire—as these men from Antigo soon discovered.

sniper's bullet. "I feel like a stranger on earth," he later reflected, adding, "we are veterans now and ready for anything."[2]

To their surprise, many veterans found themselves less ready for the challenges that awaited them *off* the battlefield. "I have found it more difficult to get used to civilian life than it was to become used to the army," Peterson confided in May, 1919.[3] He and hundreds like him returned home with minimal discharge pay and poor job prospects. Physical and psychological traumas further compounded these problems. When state legislators convened in Madison for the 1919 legislative session, they assumed the demanding task of crafting policy that not only acknowledged the sacrifices these men made for their country, but also eased their transition back into civilian life.

On the centennial of the 1919 session, this article tells the story of how Wisconsin legislators enacted groundbreaking veterans policy that would serve as a model nationwide. Together, the bills they passed—which encompassed disability compensation, cash payments, and educational investments—exemplified a stronger commitment to veterans than ever before. The accomplishments of the 1919 Legislature placed Wisconsin at the forefront of innovative change, even anticipating the future GI Bill.

Part I of this story begins during World War I, when critics condemned Wisconsin as a bastion of pacifists and pro-German sympathizers. The state's embattled reputation motivated legislators to prove their patriotism with legislation in support of the war effort—and later, in support of veterans. With the end of the war, legislators soon realized the challenges veterans policy would entail;

members of a welcome committee in New York relayed dispiriting news about the obstacles soldiers encountered upon arriving stateside.

Part II turns to the Legislature itself, tracing key policies from inception to implementation. Early on, legislators made only halting progress, reluctant to pass wide-sweeping bills with staggering price tags. They underestimated the extent to which Wisconsinites would support generous veterans policies, even at the cost of higher taxes. Ultimately, returning soldiers secured the enactment of these policies by reframing debates about the meaning and value of wartime service.

Finally, Part III explores the legacy of the most noteworthy veterans bills enacted in 1919. It describes veterans' personal experiences with newly founded programs, outlines how these programs outshone their predecessors, and identifies ways in which Wisconsin surpassed other state and federal policies.

The veterans policies passed in 1919 represented a watershed moment in Wisconsin history. But this outcome was hardly guaranteed. It was the product of a hard-fought legislative process, one in which the public participated at every turn. Heated debates jeopardized the enactment of this legislation but simultaneously invited scrutiny and revision that made enacted policies more generous, accessible, and popular over the long term. Accordingly, this article not only depicts a specific moment in state history, but also tells a broader story about how the people of Wisconsin and their representatives reached wide-sweeping consensus on a divisive issue.

I

IN 1916, AMERICANS remained sheltered from the horrors of war that they heard and read about daily. That year, the Battle of Verdun alone had claimed 350,000 French and 330,000 Germans.[4] Thousands of miles away, Wisconsin men and women—especially those of German descent, under pressure to renounce their native country—hoped the conflict would end before ensnaring the United States. After the United States entered the war in April 1917, critics increasingly regarded Wisconsin—and its firebrand anti-war politicians—as insufficiently patriotic, even labelling it the "Traitor State." Wisconsin's embattled reputation motivated state legislators to enact laws that proved their patriotism—not only during the war, but also during the session that followed in 1919.

From late 1914 through 1916, Wisconsin politicians lobbied for peace in ways that eventually cast suspicion on the state. Governor Emanuel Philipp, a stalwart Republican, opposed American entry into the war, but advocated for "preparedness," arguing that the nation should ready itself for war, even while standing on the sidelines.[5] By contrast, U.S. Senator Robert La Follette attacked the war hounds. The progressive Republican—and Philipp's rival for control of the party—condemned the "predatory special interests" pressuring the country to declare war, namely businesses that stood to profit from industrial mobilization. Still, he offered a less trenchant critique than Victor Berger, a prominent Socialist and Milwaukee newspaper editor, who characterized war as an aggressive instrument of capitalism.[6] Such staunch commitment to neutrality barely raised eyebrows in the early part of 1916. Indeed, President Woodrow Wilson won reelection later that year on a campaign that boasted, "He Kept Us Out of War."

Soon, however, many Americans experienced a change of heart. At the

BRINGING IT HOME.

President Wilson championed neutrality during his 1916 reelection campaign, but changed course after a series of German submarine attacks in early 1917.

start of 1917, Germany intensified its submarine attacks against unarmed cargo ships. A chorus of voices now called for war. Despite this change in public opinion, Wisconsin's politicians in Washington still insisted on neutrality. In a speech on the Senate floor on April 4, Senator La Follette protested that the American people had made clear their "deep-seated conviction that the United States should not enter the European war."[7] Their representatives in government, he argued, must obey the popular will. But the senator failed to sway his colleagues, who voted 82 to 6 to approve President Wilson's declaration of war. On April 6, the House of Representatives concurred, with most Wisconsin members voting in the minority.[8]

These votes came to haunt Wisconsin. It hardly mattered that support for American entry into war remained scant in many states outside the northeast.[9] By advertising their neutrality, Wisconsin politicians summoned a barrage of criticism that their state was unpatriotic at best and traitorous at worst. This reaction opened new rifts within the state's political landscape. Even before his fiery April speech, La Follette embarrassed some of his constituents; "Whenever he speaks in the Senate," an editorial in the *Eau Claire Leader* lamented, "Wisconsin groans and hides her face."[10] Both La Follette and Philipp exacerbated the problem when they expressed opposition to conscription—the former on principle, the latter out of concern that it would turn popular opinion against the war effort.[11] Every slight note of dissension seemed to chip away at the state's good name.

Even if its politicians had enthusiastically embraced the war effort, Wisconsin's demographics placed its loyalty in question. The 1910 census classified the vast majority of Wisconsin residents as foreign-born or having at least one foreign-born parent. Of these, half were German by birth or blood, easily surpassing lineage groups from other parts of Europe.[12] These proportions raised alarms among Americans for whom pro-war patriotism and anti-German sentiment had become seamlessly intertwined.

German Americans found their actions subject to intense scrutiny even before the official declaration of war. In February 1917, the German-American Alliance of Milwaukee issued a statement affirming its neutrality, but pledging to support the United States if it waged war against Germany. Like many of his peers, member Otto Schilffarth felt compelled to profess his undivided loyalty even while expressing apprehension about the dilemma such a choice entailed: "We are Americans first of all, although we hate to see our country fight against the land of our birth."[13] As entry into the conflict appeared more and more inevitable, some German Americans shifted strategy, organizing patriotic rallies in Milwaukee.[14]

This cartoon depicts the Kaiser honoring Senator La Follette for his anti-war stance. Some Americans viewed pacifists as German sympathizers at best, traitors at worst.

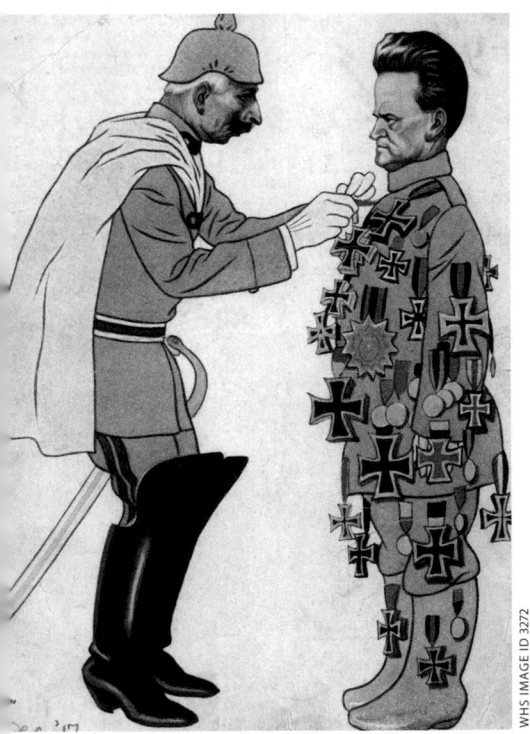

WHS IMAGE ID 3272

This strategy may have softened opinions of German Americans, but did nothing to protect Germans who were not yet naturalized. Under banner headlines announcing "War Is Declared," late edition newspapers on April 6 published Wilson's proclamation restricting "alien enemies," i.e., nonnaturalized German males 14 years of age and older.[15] Immigrants likely received this news with equal parts fear and uncertainty. How broadly would these restrictions be applied? Could the slightest mistake brand someone a traitor? Responding to these concerns, the United States Attorney General, Thomas Watt Gregory, offered

Where Disloyalty in Wisconsin Chiefly Centres

"SEDITION MAP"
PREPARED BY
THE WISCONSIN LOYALTY LEAGUE
The shaded areas show the districts most infected with Pro-Germanism.

For the first time, probably, in the history of the country it has been necessary to map the sedition of a State of the American Union. The Loyalist Legion of Wisconsin, after an investigation lasting about six months, located in certain counties of the State certain centres of pro-Germanism and active or silent disloyalty. It purposes to be only a rough and general indication of the way in which Wisconsin is rotten spotted. There are counties not indicated by the shading where strong sympathy for Germany, and very active backing for La Follette is manifest, but on the whole the counties marked represent the most violent hostility to the President's policy and to the war aims of the nation. These are the counties in which Thompson, La Follette's candidate for the Senatorship, received his heaviest vote and where Victor Berger rolled up a large vote.

Hyperpatriot groups claimed to expose "pro-Germanism" within Wisconsin by identifying "infected" areas of the state. Unsurprisingly, most of these areas were counties with sizeable German immigrant populations.

sobering advice: "Obey the law; keep your mouth shut."[16] Wisconsin papers published comparatively reassuring headlines in subsequent days and weeks; the *La Crosse Tribune-Press* announced "Aliens Are Safe Here" and "Department of Justice Official Says Peaceful Non-Citizens Have Nothing to Fear." But the content of these articles often undercut the headlines, reporting on a "round-up of German citizens and sympathizers" and noting that "every pro-German utterance is anti-American."[17]

This mood of mistrust transformed into outright hostility over the course of the spring. To the dismay of Wisconsin Germans, President Wilson made little effort to sooth suspicion of immigrant residents. Instead, his Flag Day speech that year sowed paranoia that Germany had "filled our unsuspecting communities with vicious spies and conspirators."[18] Wilson also warned against "generous naturalization laws" that allowed foreigners to "[pour] the poison of disloyalty into the very arteries of our national life."[19] Statements like these placed impossible demands on naturalized immigrants, pressuring them to assimilate while simultaneously categorizing them as "other," no matter

WHS IMAGE ID 132826

German immigrants and their American-born children found themselves subject to intense scrutiny and suspicion as potential agents of "Kaiserism." This series ran in the Milwaukee Journal despite that city's German heritage.

WHS IMAGE ID 131044

Though there were efforts to suppress it, an accepted use of the German language during the war was to promote the purchase of war bonds, as in this poster from Sheboygan County.

After the official declaration of war, anti-German suspicion manifested itself in efforts to suppress use of the German language. President Wilson himself referred to German conspirators' efforts "to corrupt the opinion of our people" in his Flag Day speech. The notion that foreign-born residents sought to sway public opinion on the Kaiser's behalf ultimately justified strict censorship of the press. Federal laws like the Trading Act of 1917 compelled German newspaper editors to publish all editions of their papers in both German and English, a requirement that strained the foreign language press in Wisconsin.

Source: John D. Stevens, "When Sedition Laws Were Enforced: Wisconsin in World War I," Wisconsin Academy of Sciences, Arts and Letters 58 (1970), 39–60.

The war placed immigrants in a difficult position—stigmatized as "other" while simultaneously expected to sacrifice for the war effort. This poster called on immigrants to support their adoptive country by conserving food.

FOOD WILL WIN THE WAR

You came here seeking Freedom
You must now help to preserve it

WHEAT is needed for the allies
Waste nothing

UNITED STATES FOOD ADMINISTRATION

WHS IMAGE ID 125090

(*left*) Posters for Liberty Loan bonds suggested that purchasing them would "prove" one's patriotism. (*top*) Local events—like this parade in Hartford—reinforced the same message.

ARE YOU 100% AMERICAN? PROVE IT BUY U.S. GOVERNMENT BONDS THIRD LIBERTY LOAN

WHS IMAGE ID 130958

how hard they strove to become American.

In all, thousands of Wisconsin citizens attracted scrutiny by virtue of their ethnicity.[20] Soon, the state itself—by virtue of its foreign-born populations—found its loyalty questioned. The *Milwaukee Journal* reported that businessmen in eastern cities considered Milwaukee a "hotbed of sedition," devoting a three-part series to these allegations in February.[21] Rather than reject these charges outright, prominent Milwaukee figures largely accepted them but blamed "pro-German fanatics and extremists."[22] Months later, an Indiana newspaper levied similar accusations against the entire state, inventing the term the "Traitor State" and decrying Wisconsin's alleged "pro-Germanism."[23] In hindsight, such scathing attacks proved exceptional. At the time, however, they reverberated loudly.[24]

Recruits from Antigo trained at Camp Douglas, Wisconsin, before shipping out to France as part of the 107th Trench Mortar Battery Company. Despite the state's draft registration rate of 98 percent, critics continued to question Wisconsin's patriotism throughout the war.

These allegations exasperated Governor Philipp. "To undertake to fight all the falsehoods that have been circulated concerning the state," he complained, "is not unlike fighting the wind."[25] In this atmosphere, the governor himself stood on shaky ground. The son of Swiss immigrants near Sauk City, he rose from humble origins to accumulate a fortune from refrigerated train cars and came to embody the state's business interests. His company helped carry Wisconsin-made beer across the country, and Philipp forged close ties with the Schlitz family, among other German American brewers.[26] Those associations carried him into office in 1914, but imperiled his popularity in 1917. For all these reasons, Philipp sought to prove not only the state's patriotism, but his own.

As early as mid-April, Governor Philipp signed into law a bill establishing the nation's first State Council of Defense (Chapter 82, Laws of 1917). This body would support the federal war effort by addressing potential labor, food, and fuel shortages and promoting the purchase of Liberty Bonds.[27] By June, Philipp had also shepherded legislation through both houses of the Legislature to provide monthly financial support for dependents of enlisted men for the duration of the war (Chapter 487, Laws of 1917). That same month, an impressive 98 percent of Wisconsin's draft-age men had registered, by comparison to about 92 percent nationwide.[28] Meanwhile, Wisconsinites raised over $360 million for the war effort, vastly exceeding bond quotas set by the federal government.[29]

But no proof of patriotism silenced the state's critics. Worse, the most potent

WHS IMAGE ID 132128

Even children contributed to the war effort; for example, these boys from Milwaukee's Riverside High School collected periodicals to send to the troops in France.

accusations of disloyalty came from within the state. Self-styled patriots filled the ranks of the fiercely pro-war Wisconsin Defense League, which hurled accusations at public figures and private citizens alike. In one incendiary speech during an August 1917 gathering, a member argued that seditious men "should be shot down or hanged."[30] Occasionally, words like these escalated into outright violence, as in several incidents in which masked men tarred and feathered individuals who they believed were German.[31]

More commonly, concerned citizens reported neighbors and acquaintances whom they suspected of disloyalty to the authorities. These accusations carried serious consequences: federal laws promised prison sentences to those found guilty of disparaging the war effort. In one instance, a Wisconsin farmer and father to seven children faced a year in prison for dissuading young men from registering for the draft. "We have no business in this war," he reportedly said, adding, "We went into it to protect the money that was loaned to the Allies." Under the Espionage Act of June 1917, thirty-two Wisconsinites would be indicted for characterizing the conflict as a "Rich man's war," and another thirty-six for speaking positively of Germany. Although small, these numbers dwarfed comparative figures for other states.[32] Wisconsinites clearly placed inordinate pressure on themselves to root out disloyalty in their midst.

Suspicion also pervaded the political domain, where candidates questioned their rivals' patriotism as a matter of course. The Loyalty Legion formed in 1917

Within the Legislature, concerns about loyalty culminated in a Senate vote to expel Socialist Frank Raguse of Milwaukee for uttering purportedly disloyal remarks in April 1917. The German American legislator had invoked the sinking of the USS Maine in 1898—a catalyst of the Spanish-American war—to imply that war hawks manipulated "the destruction of property or the destruction of lives" to drum up support for war. Raguse also questioned the uneven toll that war took: his brother lost a leg during the Spanish-American conflict and had to "[cut] down a tree to make himself a wooden leg," whereas President William McKinley remained "[surrounded] by silks and satins." Legislators clearly hoped to advertise their own patriotism by punishing a colleague who dared doubt the war effort. In retrospect, they silenced one of the few who foretold the problems legislators would collectively face when a generation of men returned from war broken in body and spirit.

Source: Kathleen R. Kepner, Seating, Unseating and Censuring Members of the Wisconsin Legislature, 1842–1955, Informational Bulletin 154 (Madison, WI: Wisconsin Legislative Reference Library, June 1956).

for the purpose of defeating purportedly unpatriotic politicians, or "slackers" as the Legion termed them. The group cast a wide net, disparaging any public figure who failed to conform to its "inflexible . . . standard of loyalty."[33] It targeted progressive Republicans like Senator La Follette, as well as Socialist Victor Berger, who ran for the U.S. Senate late in 1917.[34] Although some Legion-endorsed candidates flopped, Republican Irvine Lenroot defeated Berger by echoing Legion principles, touting Wisconsin's war record while castigating "socialist, pacifist, and other theoretical objectors to the sentiment of war."[35]

Even Governor Philipp faced allegations of insufficient patriotism. State Senator Roy Wilcox of Eau Claire mocked his reputation as a "War Governor" when he challenged Philipp in the 1918 Republican gubernatorial primary. Philipp fought back, deriding Wilcox as the "Tar and Feather Candidate" and repudiating vigilante justice of any kind. Ultimately, Philipp eked out a primary win over Wilcox, but not without a draining fight.[36]

Privately, some public figures expressed discomfort with hyperpatriotic political bluster. In personal correspondence, one state assemblyman wrote of Wilcox, "He may be patriotic enough, but in my estimation it is what a man does and not what he says that counts for patriotism." To illustrate this point, he contrasted Wilcox with his only son, who had joined the service and would personally help "win

(*above*) A sign in Monroe identified alleged "slackers"—people thought to be insufficiently patriotic— alongside an effigy of the Kaiser. (*below*) Elsewhere, self-professed patriots derided anti-war political candidates like Victor Berger—seen here in campaign materials defaced to represent Berger as a Russian Bolshevik and German sympathizer.

this war."[37] Publicly, most hesitated to take any stand that might attract negative attention. One Stoughton lawyer reflected in August 1918, "it behooves anyone with a German strain of blood in his veins to be exceedingly careful not to give politician demagogues an opportunity to charge him with being pro-German and disloyal."[38] However baseless they may have been, accusations of pro-Germanness remained rampant. Granted, they were not always effective, as Socialist Victor Berger eventually won a seat in Congress in November 1918.[39]

When the conflict came to a halt on November 11, 1918, people across the state shared a collective sense of relief; the bloody battles overseas had ended, and the war of words on the home front might soon cease as well. Fights over loyalty had derailed productive policy making and sapped the energy of politicians and constituents alike. But the memories of these tense times remained fresh long after the Armistice, and the sting of "Traitor State" accusations lingered. Before the 1919 legislative session even began, Wisconsin politicians eyed it as their final chance to combat the state's "maligned" reputation and prove its patriotism once and for all.[40]

Shortly after German representatives signed an agreement to cease fighting at precisely 11:11 am on November 11, 1918, telegrams announcing the Armistice

Wisconsinites celebrated the end of war with impromptu parades on November 11, 1918. This New Lisbon parade included a soldier who had returned stateside after suffering the effects of chemical warfare.

WHS IMAGE ID 37430

zipped across the Atlantic, reaching the Midwest in the middle of the night. But its late night arrival did not stop the news from causing a stir. In Madison, hundreds emerged from their homes for a spontaneous "nightly procession" that lasted until daybreak. A report in the *Capital Times* depicted it as a parade of sorts, with "Tin pans, tea kettles, old dish pans tied on the back of automobiles, girls hanging on every available perch of every car on the streets, flags galore, noise more than galore," and some still sporting their pajamas.[41] In nearby Janesville, unlikely revelers participated in "wild scenes" at 2:00 am: "Elderly women who have not left their homes for months were seen dancing the latest steps with young youths on the streets."[42] Impromptu gatherings elsewhere featured drums, bugles, and even "the Kaiser in effigy."[43] The following day, a writer for the *Eau Claire Leader* humorously remarked that "mother looks in vain for tubs to do the belated washing," as every pot, pan, or tub had been "commandeered" as a makeshift drum the prior evening.[44] Across the state, Wisconsinites expressed collective euphoria, bursting through the silence of night with joyous, unrestrained noise.

One group was notably absent among these riotous crowds: soldiers. Most would not return until spring 1919. Until then, men like Columbia County native Elton Morrison wrote long letters home from Germany and France. Although they would not stoop to complain, the troops "would like to be home tomorrow and are anxiously waiting for that order," Morrison told his parents on Christmas Eve.[45] Frustratingly, the United States lacked the ships to bring back its boys; they

Across the state, people gathered in the streets to express collective euphoria at the news of an armistice. Here, Menomonie residents marched downtown, led by women triumphantly carrying an American flag.

WHS IMAGE ID 88625

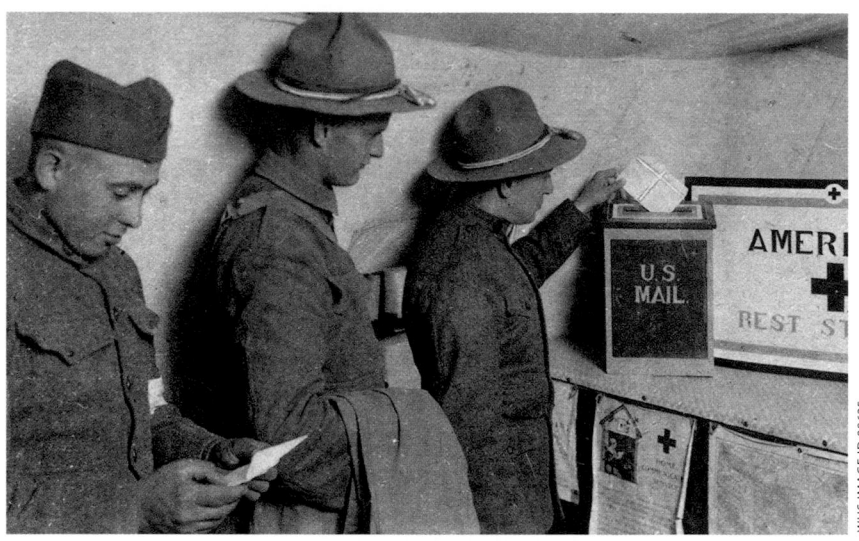

(*above*) Throughout the war, soldiers posted their letters home at Red Cross canteens. (*below*) In the months following the Armistice, those letters increasingly expressed impatience to return home. Most servicemen did not leave France until late April or early May 1919—like these soldiers from Antigo.

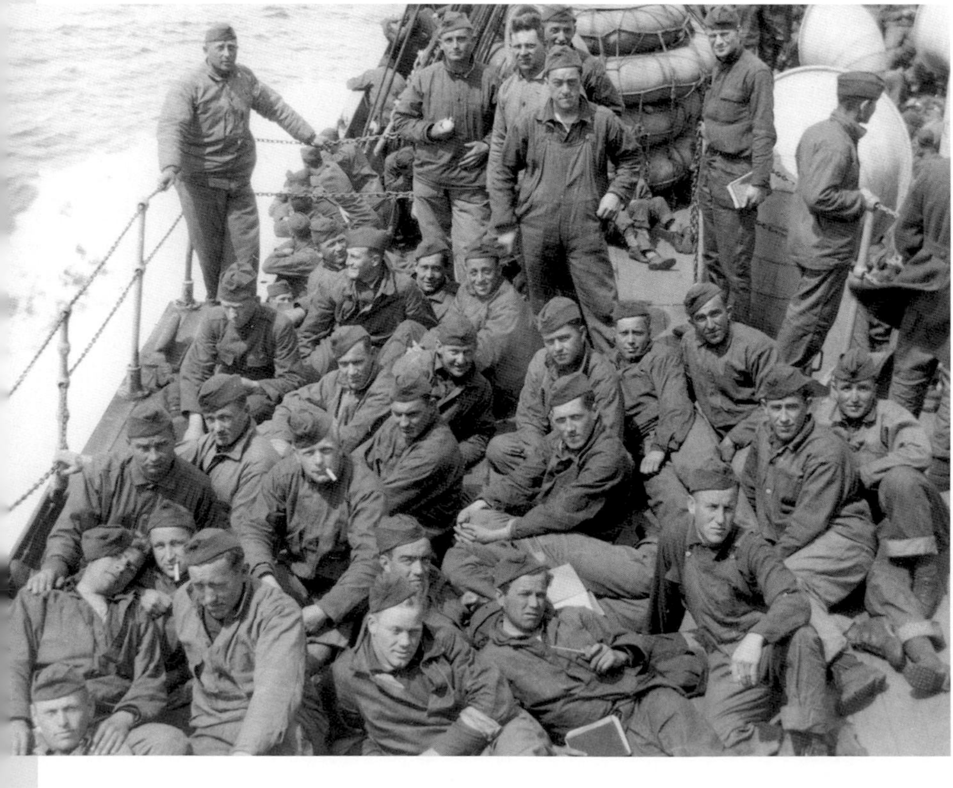

WILLIAM WESSA, LANGLADE COUNTY HISTORICAL SOCIETY

had crossed the Atlantic on English vessels, now busy delivering Australians home. Ultimately, converted American cargo ships—and former German ships—carried Americans to the East Coast, with most leaving Europe between April and August 1919.[46] In the interim, the troops *and* their families became increasingly impatient. Loved ones pressured public officials to bring the boys home.[47] As the planting season approached, farmers also demanded their return. "A great many of our soldiers over there are farmers," an Evansville man told Governor Philipp, "which are very much needed from the first of April on."[48]

This delay—although exasperating to many—may have been a boon to legislators. It provided time to study and debate policies that would help soften servicemen's landing in Wisconsin. Help in this endeavor came from an unexpected source: a group of Wisconsin-born women who spearheaded an effort to welcome Wisconsin soldiers as they arrived in New York.[49] This group became the governor's and Legislature's first source of information about the unanticipated problems veterans faced, financial hardship chief among them. Ultimately, these women helped position veterans policy not only as a means to reestablish the state's reputation, but also as a necessary acknowledgment of the servicemen who had sacrificed their own safety for that of the country.

It all began with a Wisconsin transplant to New York who expressed concern that her home state was not measuring up to its Midwestern peers. In late February 1919, Mary Sabin penned a letter to Governor Philipp, informing him that various states had designated meeting places in Manhattan where servicemen could congregate while awaiting their discharges. At a "Hall of States" located in a spacious private residence at 27 West 25th Street, women volunteers from these states welcomed the boys who had already returned with doughnuts and warm coffee. But Wisconsin had made no such effort, and Sabin politely but insistently asked Philipp to request an appropriation from the Legislature, lest the state's inaction expose it to unfavorable comparisons.[50] Her appeal succeeded. Within a fortnight, Philipp signed a bill granting $5,000 toward welcoming Wisconsin servicemen in New York.[51]

By mid-March, a speedily formed welcome committee had been "officially recognized" in the Hall of States.[52] Katherine Frederickson, President of the Wisconsin Women's Society, took the helm as committee secretary,[53] and recruited remaining committee members by March 21.[54] From the start, she won high praise from Wisconsin Adjutant General Orlando Holway, who complimented Frederickson and treasurer Mary Foote as being "very practical and business like."[55] These remarks confirmed a tendency for officials in Madison to bestow full trust in the volunteers on the ground to direct the funds in whatever way they saw fit.[56]

Volunteers keenly understood that those funds should be directed toward

WHS IMAGE ID 132118

Members of the state's welcome committee in New York assisted soldiers in myriad ways—supplying stamps and stationery for letters home, providing local Wisconsin newspapers, and helping secure discharges.

soldiers' basic needs. George Russell, an insurance magnate and colonel in the Wisconsin State Guard,[57] explained to Philipp that soldiers had little cash on hand and invariably wound up broke after arriving stateside:

> Any man who has been in New York recently and has had his heart's strings torn seeing thousands upon thousands of these brave boys aimlessly wandering around the streets, thousands upon thousands of them crippled, feels that we have let down too much. We sent these boys off with bands and promises, and not enough real necessary assistance and interest is being taken in them upon their return.[58]

With these words, Russell suggested a larger dilemma: policymakers had not foreseen the dismal condition of soldiers upon their return or planned for their reintegration into civilian life.

Russell did not propose solutions, but reminded Philipp that "people do not want any Wisconsin boys returning from France penniless alone." Accordingly, the committee would keep Wisconsin men afloat—financially and emotionally—until they returned home. It would not only provide material assistance to soldiers, but "a little companionship among their own people."[59]

To this end, the committee would need to advertise the welcome headquarters as widely as possible. Members posted notices at train and ferry stations, sent radiograms to ships offshore, and wrote letters to Wisconsin soldiers laid up in nearby hospitals.[60] Once at the Hall of States, servicemen could take warm baths, launder their clothes, write letters on free stationery, and eat hot breakfasts. The Hall was conveniently located near accommodations where beds cost a mere twenty-five cents per night—fees the welcome committee would pay for those who could not afford them.[61] The return of the 32nd Division—which boasted the largest number of Wisconsin men—remained several weeks away, but some sixty soldiers from Wisconsin had already enjoyed these amenities by late March.[62]

During this same period, the committee publicized Wisconsin's patriotism by participating in parades to welcome newly arriving troops. For example, Mary Foote directed $100 toward a wreath on display at festivities celebrating the 27th Division.[63] She and her colleagues continued to stress the importance of welcome festivities ahead of the arrival of the 32nd Division in early May. "We would like to do the State proud on that occasion," Frederickson wrote just a week before its slated entry into New York. Ultimately, she helped persuade Philipp to personally greet the troops of the 32nd Division in New York with "as royal a welcome as possible."[64] In this instance, committee members shaped the governor's understanding of demobilization, convincing him that formal ceremonies showed servicemen that their state government supported them wholeheartedly.

By this measure, the welcome ceremony proved a triumph. Although some ships carrying the 32nd Division were diverted to Boston, others landed in New York, where festivities proceeded as planned.[65] Newspapers back home reported that on May 5, the governor's guestrooms at the Pennsylvania Hotel teemed with officers from the 127th Infantry, including Major George O'Connell of Madison, whose battalion members fought "like demons" at the Battle of Château Thierry.[66] The following day, the governor proceeded to Camp Merritt, New Jersey, to meet Major General Haan and survey the 32nd Division. Haan told Philipp, "They are a pretty good crowd of fighters"—a comment that likely pleased the once-embattled "Traitor State" governor. Following his inspection, the governor welcomed the troops:

> Boys, Wisconsin has always given good soldiers to the nation. You men lived up to all the fine traditions of the past, and the brilliant record you made—and God knows it was a great sacrifice—will live forever.[67]

After other formal appearances and an official parade, the welcome committee hosted more lighthearted fare, including a comedy show at the Hippodrome.[68]

These festivities succeeded so well in advertising the welcome center that the trickle of men into the Hall of States quickly became a torrent. From a mere sixty men in late March, Frederickson reported a total of 1,110 visitors by June.[69] By July

The Wisconsin welcome committee hosted frequent outings to places like Luna Park, a Brooklyn amusement park, to stave off homesickness among soldiers awaiting discharge in New York.

1, that figure rose to 1,475.[70] Most of these men were happy to return stateside, but anxious to be home. "We have lived and slept in mud up to our knees and gone without food and drink for hours," Leo Levenick exclaimed, "just to get one more glimpse of the old state capitol."[71]

Against this backdrop, volunteers at Wisconsin's headquarters in the Hall of States sought to keep men like Levenick busy and entertained. The committee covered subway and bus fare for anyone who wished to explore the city. It also paid for theater tickets at venues like the Winter Garden, where $1.75 treated a soldier to the top entertainers of his day, or Luna Park, a theme park on Coney Island.[72] In addition to these excursions, servicemen could chat with "volunteer hostesses" who staffed the Hall of States between 9 am and 10 pm. There, homesick men could also read about goings-on in their native towns and cities from around ninety local newspapers.[73] As Katherine Frederickson put it, "[we] do all we can to make the stricken heroes from our home state comfortable."[74]

In many respects, Frederickson and her allies served as stand-ins for the boys' mothers. They doted on servicemen to relieve women back home who agonized about the well-being of their distant sons. "No Wisconsin mother need worry," Frederickson told the *Wisconsin State Journal*, "about the attention her son receives while in an army hospital here." She added reassuringly, "We have the names of every boy and call upon him twice daily."[75] The same women exhibited motherly persistence toward men who initially declined their assistance. Mary Sabin remarked that some men would "go without a meal rather than say they are hungry," adding that she used "adroit questioning to get facts from them." Even reluctant recipients of help, Sabin continued, would be "made to feel at home."[76] Observers noticed and appreciated this quasi-maternal dynamic. Early on, Adjutant General Holway commented that a "society of ladies" was uniquely capable of forging close relationships on a short-term basis.[77]

On the basis of such relationships, volunteers provided material and emotional support to men who were acutely vulnerable. For example, Bernard Dostal discovered his wallet was stolen just moments after learning his father had died. "They were holding up funeral arrangements until they heard from him," Frederickson explained in a letter to Governor Philipp that described Dostal as "very depressed." Springing to action, the committee not only supplied the serviceman's train fare home to Milwaukee, but also purchased him a new pair of shoes.[78] Frederickson and her colleagues not only helped servicemen return home, but also found accommodations for Wisconsin men and women who travelled to New York City to personally welcome their boys.[79] Clearly, committee members understood the importance of family reunion among men long isolated from their loved ones.

In the various roles they played, volunteers served as important conduits between servicemen and the state. They kept Governor Philipp abreast of the challenges facing newly returned troops, and alerted him to problems he might solve through his personal intervention. In one instance, Katherine Frederickson alerted Governor Philipp to the case of Otto Brown, an Eau Claire man who desperately sought his discharge so he could return home to support his wife and three children. Brown's father had looked after his son's

Letters attest to the welcome committee volunteers' success in establishing meaningful relationships with soldiers. Here, Benjamin Kemmerer, struggling to use a typewriter, accidentally addressed Katherine Frederickson as "My dear Mr Frederickson."

family during the war, but his sudden death in November 1918 jeopardized their well-being.[80] A reply from the governor's office promised prompt contact with Brown's commanding officer to secure his discharge.[81]

In another instance, Frederickson recruited Philipp's help in defense of Private Samuel Simon of Milwaukee, who faced charges of desertion after failing to return from leave due to health problems.[82] Frederickson felt Simon lacked the mental capacity to grasp the gravity of his actions. She also knew the soldier had no other advocates, and thus took up his case wholeheartedly: "He clings to me as his only friend and I assure you, I will leave no stone unturned to see that justice is done him."[83] Meanwhile, Frederickson fielded letters written by Simon's younger sister on behalf of their parents. "My father and mother want to

THE AMERICAN RED CROSS

U. S. Debarkation Hospital No. 3
Sixth Avenue and 18th Street
New York City

Many soldiers like Sam Simon came to regard welcome committee volunteers as surrogate mothers—women who fiercely advocated on their behalf.

WISCONSIN HISTORICAL SOCIETY ARCHIVES

know if you will please help Sam," the girl wrote in large, scrawling letters: "my mother feels so sorry for Sam she crys every day for him. . . . We have so much work and we need Sam so bad."[84] In the meantime, the committee supplied Simon with stamps and a fountain pen to ensure he kept his parents apprised of his situation.[85] Ultimately, Frederickson prompted Philipp to help secure Simon a lighter sentence in lieu of prison time at Fort Leavenworth.[86]

Responses from men like Simon illustrate the committee's success in making men feel at home before their return to Wisconsin. Simon poured out profuse thanks in long letters from his hospital bed. "Well a fellow always meets a good friend," he told Frederickson, "but you are the best one of them all." To another member of the welcome committee, he professed, "you shure are good to me your just like a mother."[87] Like Simon, other men—some clearly unaccustomed to writing letters—expressed their thanks upon returning home. John Kronberger praised "the great work you's are doing there for those coming home," adding, "you can't imagin how much we injoyed that time which you ladies had for US."[88] W. C. Smith echoed the same sentiments, thanking the committee for keeping him afloat until his "happy reunion" with his wife: "When I arrived in New York I was still far from home, and I certainly appreciated the kindness shown me by you."[89] Servicemen and volunteers were not the only ones pleased with the welcome effort; legislators recognized the committee's success with an additional appropriation of $5,000 and a joint resolution honoring their work.[90] Joint Resolution 62 cited the "enthusiastic praise" of Wisconsin's servicemen for the women who "made them feel at home as soon as they landed upon our shores."

Although temporary by nature, the welcome committee created an impression among servicemen that the state would look after them over the long term.[91] It also provided valuable insight into the challenges these men faced, including financial insecurity and emotional trauma. This insight, in turn, could inform effective veterans policy. But what policies precisely would adequately address these challenges? And who would pay for them? Reaching consensus on these questions proved more complicated than handing out coffee, doughnuts, and newspapers. As the committee members worked long hours in New York, legislators in Madison struggled to match their efforts in the spring and summer of 1919.

II

BACK HOME, THE spirit of spontaneous Armistice celebrations had carried over into 1919, and Wisconsinites sloughed off months of tension about who was adequately loyal, patriotic, and American. But new debates embroiled the state, and the end of war hardly softened the tenor of public dialogue. As Wisconsinites waged an ongoing battle against the deadly Influenza virus, they also dealt with divisive issues like temperance, women's suffrage, labor disruptions, and the perceived threat of Bolshevism following the Russian Revolution of 1917.[92] Disagreements on these issues carried over into debates about veterans legislation, which stalled as members of the Legislature argued over the best means to recognize veterans and simultaneously serve the state—for example, by preventing unemployment or addressing farm labor shortages. Key proposals gathered momentum only as soldiers returned home to Wisconsin and voiced their opinions, often to challenge legislators' assumptions about them.

Those confrontations remained on the distant horizon when legislators first convened in Madison in January 1919. Governor Emanuel Philipp greeted returning and newly elected legislators on January 9 with an address that laid out his agenda for the 1919 session.[93] Philipp began by touting the state's war record and

WHS IMAGE ID 43009

Governor Philipp (seated at center of desk, with secretary L. C. Whittet seated to his right) praised Wisconsin soldiers but declined to make veterans policy a key part of his agenda as the 1919 legislative session began.

the impressive number of Wisconsin men who had served. These men, he declared, deserved government loans to clear and cultivate land for their own benefit. However, he implied that responsibility for such a program fell to the federal government.[94] Then, without sketching further plans with respect to veterans, Philipp transitioned to other matters: settlement of wage disputes, privatization of railroads, and foreign language education in grade school.[95]

Veterans featured only marginally on the governor's list of priorities, and their concerns soon became lost in a sea of legislative proposals. Early reports forecast that an unprecedented number of bills would be introduced in the 1919 session on a vast array of issues.[96] The *Capital Times* confirmed these predictions, announcing in mid-February that an "avalanche" of legislation was in play—about two hundred bills, many pertaining to labor relations and railroads.[97] By then, the Legislature had received the formal report of the Special Legislative Committee on Reconstruction, responsible for devising "a comprehensive social and economic welfare program of Reconstruction after the war."[98] This report touched on a wide range of issues, including collective bargaining, farming cooperatives, rural schools, the eight-hour workday, and women in the workplace. But soldiers seemed to be an afterthought, meriting only a brief mention in one paragraph.[99]

Why was veterans policy so far down the list of policymakers' concerns? An editorial published months later in the *Wisconsin State Journal* pointed blame in one direction: "Political jealousies have been batted about like ping pong balls," the author complained, "and legislators have maneuvered for political advantage or to register political spite." Political ambitions had quashed "big, broad, constructive and patriotic measures" simply because they failed to serve a personal career or party faction. The author even alleged that some members had "[chosen] to kill good legislation rather than give their opponents credit for doing good things." Granted, the Legislature had considered an astounding amount of legislation by then—but its main failing, the author concluded, was its inability to move on matters pertaining to ex-soldiers.[100]

Meanwhile, legislators contended with the clock. The 32nd Division remained in Europe, but some discharged men had already arrived stateside by January 1919, and their circumstances troubled legislators. As Senator Lawrence Cunningham of Beloit informed his colleagues, France's heroes were arriving home to cities like Madison without "money . . . to buy a square meal."[101] The same men also faced the distinct possibility of unemployment.[102] They had risked their lives overseas, only to miss out on the wartime economic boom back home. Charles McCarthy, head of Wisconsin's Legislative Reference Library, put it this way: "they have sort of lost step in the procession while they have been away."[103] Successful legislation, he reasoned, would reward both their patriotic deeds and help them keep pace in the "procession."

Granted, many returned servicemen were eligible for newly created federal programs. However, these programs focused primarily on rehabilitating the

---

Governor Philipp faced another unexpected dilemma during the spring of 1919. After arriving in New York, some Wisconsin servicemen simply stayed there. "The boys in many cases will not go home," Mary Sabin informed Philipp. This revelation confounded the governor, who replied, "It is not clear to us just why Wisconsin men would ask for employment in New York City." Katherine Frederickson explained that the "attractions of a city like New York" compelled some to stay. (In hindsight, scholars have pointed to well-paying urban industrial jobs as another deciding factor.) Whatever the cause, the governor and his allies devised strategies to lure reluctant servicemen home, including coordinating with local chambers of commerce to secure jobs for them. Above all, Philipp relied on the welcome committee in New York to make the boys "genuinely homesick for their own people."

Source: Wisconsin Historical Society Archives, Mss JC, Emanuel Philipp Papers, Box 6, folders 1 and 2.

quarter of a million men who returned home wounded and disabled.[104] Many of these men could not resume their prior professions, a reality that jeopardized their position as breadwinners. Against this backdrop, the federal government sought to support families while remaking disabled men into self-sufficient workers.[105] Two policies attempted to fulfill these goals. First, the War Risk Insurance Act of 1917 compensated American service personnel for "loss of life or personal injury by the risks of war." Soldiers who purchased policies paid for them as deductions from their paychecks. Those who lost their lives ensured that their dependents would receive monthly support payments, continuing until children reached adulthood or wives remarried. Those who returned home sick or injured would receive monthly payments for the duration of their disability, capped at twenty years.[106] Second, the Soldiers Rehabilitation Act of 1918 entitled disabled servicemen to training and education toward future employment.[107] The Federal Board for Vocational Education promised not only to aid injured men, but to make them superior to their pre-war selves. "If he is willing to learn," one informational brief boasted, "he can usually get a better position than he had before entering the service."[108]

Although more comprehensive than their predecessors, federal programs did not address the hardships of all former servicemen as they transitioned back into civilian life. Some state legislators recognized this oversight as an opportunity. Senator Cunningham encouraged his colleagues to assist Wisconsin soldiers and thereby set a standard for other states. He told the *Wisconsin State Journal*,

Here, soldiers convalesced in a French church used as a hospital during the war. Few men escaped combat physically or psychologically unscathed, and in all, about a quarter of a million American men returned home wounded.

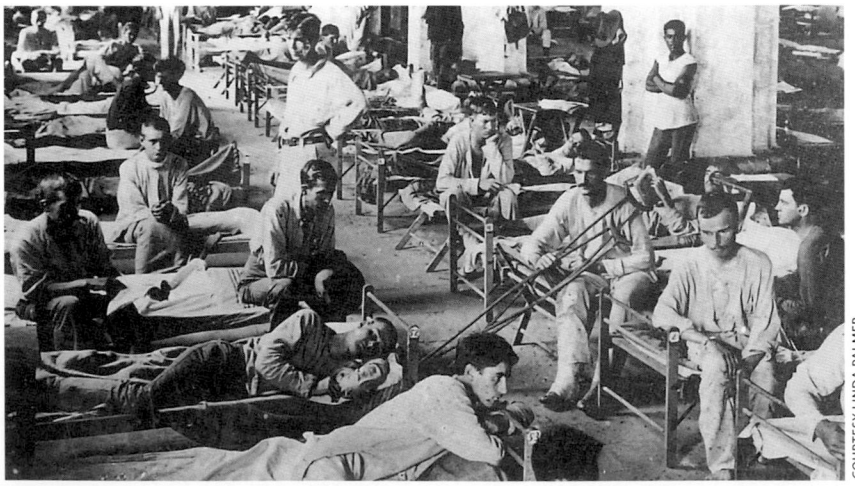

COURTESY LINDA PALMER

JOBS for FIGHTERS

BUREAU
for
RETURNING
SOLDIERS
and
SAILORS
--
WALK IN

U.S.
Employment
Service
and
Co-operating
Agencies

If You Need a Job
If You Need a Man
Inform the Official Central Agency
The Service is Free
The United States Employment Service
Bureau for Returning Soldiers and Sailors
THIS CHURCH IS HELPING

WHS IMAGE ID 130790

The federal government urged employers to hire former servicemen who had missed out on the wartime economic boom and returned home with minimal discharge pay.

"I am strongly in favor of Wisconsin taking the lead in showing the nation how the returning heroes should be treated."[109] To this end, Cunningham recruited Charles McCarthy to draft legislation that would grant those who served a one-time cash benefit equivalent to three months' pay. The governor would make individual appropriations of $25,000 to pay for the program incrementally.[110] By early March, the *Wisconsin State Journal* proclaimed that people "all over the state and nation" had requested copies of Cunningham's bill, implying the legislation would serve widely as a model.[111] But the bonus proposal barely made waves within the state Legislature, fighting for attention against a deluge of bills that flooded both houses.[112]

Other legislators, for example, supported alternative forms of cash relief. Representative Albert Pullen of Fond du Lac—who had served in the Medical Reserve Corps during the war—protested that Cunningham's bill paid greater sums to higher ranking men, for whom three months' pay was considerably higher.[113] He proposed a bill that based payments on duration of service, allotting $10 to each serviceman per month served.[114] At the same time, other members of both houses approved of cash relief, but believed the federal government should provide it.[115]

Meanwhile, additional legislation addressed another arena in which servicemen had "lost step in the procession," as McCarthy put it: education. Senator Ray Nye of Superior noted that the conflict had cut short the college careers of many young servicemen. In early February, he introduced a bill that would help those men resume their studies by waiving tuition at state institutions.[116] The policy proposal was novel, albeit limited—after all, it offered assistance only to those already able to access higher education. But it also promised to delay the reentry of certain men into the workforce—and stave off potential spikes in the unemployment rate—by diverting them to college.

WHS IMAGE ID 33439

During the war, women built army trucks at the Four Wheel Drive Auto Company in Clintonville. Most employers expected women to leave these positions once the soldiers returned.

The federal War Risk Insurance program reflected Progressive Era ideals and echoed state legislation in workers' compensation and workplace safety. If dangerous work made a man unable to support himself or his family, his employer—in this case, the government—would step in to help him fulfill his duties as a husband or father. The program also reflected deep-seated social values, especially faith in a model of family within which men earned wages and women oversaw household tasks like cooking, cleaning, and childcare. The war endangered this model by raising the possibility that women whose husbands had died or become disabled might seek employment outside the home as a matter of necessity. But monthly War Risk Insurance payments averted the problem, ensuring that women would remain in the domestic sphere and not infringe unnecessarily upon the predominantly male working world.

Source: K. Walter Hickel, "War, Region, and Social Welfare: Federal Aid to Servicemen's Dependents in the South, 1917–1921," *Journal of American History* 87 (2001), 1362–1391.

Similarly, farming-oriented programs sought to assist soldiers while addressing larger labor issues. Elsewhere across the West, lawmakers devised policies designed to stall mass migration to urban industrial centers and simultaneously fill rural labor shortages. In North Dakota, for example, a newly created "Returned Soldiers' Fund" promised financial assistance to aspiring farmers.[117] Veterans like Ben Mooney, equipped with a "mechanical arm" following injuries suffered at the Battle of Cantigy, became homesteaders with the state's sponsorship.[118] With men like Mooney in mind, the Wisconsin Assembly created a committee in February to investigate the possibility of acquiring agricultural lands for former soldiers for whom "exorbitant prices" otherwise posed barriers.[119] That same month, Representative Pullen drafted a bill to help servicemen purchase land or find employment in rural areas of the state.[120] Ultimately, Representative Orrin Fletcher of La Crosse authored the bill that gained the most traction.[121] It provided for an agricultural loan program operated by a state board that would exercise the power of eminent domain and procure land on the state's behalf. The sole responsibilities of approved participants would be to farm the land, keep the property in "good order," insure the land and buildings against fire, and make regular loan payments. On the whole, the bill sought to eliminate "the evil of unemployment" through land ownership.[122]

But the proposal faced objections that such a program would stifle soldiers' work ethic. Unconvinced by the example of Ben Mooney, Fletcher's colleagues worried that generous loans would attract loafers. F. W. Ploetz of Coloma professed his admiration for the returning soldier, but asserted that the bill "would tempt him into a life of idleness."[123] This claim likely perplexed Fletcher, a farmer keenly aware of the backbreaking effort the profession entailed. Still, many legislators subscribed to the logic that any form of direct support would suppress soldiers' drive to work.

That notion was not isolated to legislators, but shared widely throughout the state. Although only a trickle of men had returned to the state by April, their would-be employers issued recurring complaints to the governor about ex-soldiers' supposed laziness. Their correspondence conveyed a collective accusation that this younger generation of men felt themselves entitled to cushy jobs and unreasonably high wages. Farmer H. T. Christenson reported in March that "it is impossible this spring to get help on the farm" because young men refused hard, physical labor; "they want Uncle Sam to feed them or give them a soft job, short hours and big pay." At the rates they demanded—$65 per month, plus room and board—he groused, "We might as well give them the farm."[124]

Factory owners also bemoaned the work ethic of ex-servicemen. Industrialist Theodore Vilter fielded frequent letters from members of his Milwaukee community requesting employment for former soldiers.[125] But these men often quit upon learning their wages. Some, he grumbled, desired $40 a week.[126] Worse, "soldier boys" often shunned work in favor of "soliciting," that is, "going around the houses pleading with the house wife to buy this and that and the other thing."[127] To Vilter, high expectations posed more significant problems than unemployment. As he put it, "It will require some talking and some education to get these boys away from their ideas."[128] State support would only embolden the boys and their "ideas."

Soldiers themselves told a different story. Their testimonies suggested that an abrupt return to the working world following months of hardship could provoke distress. Ira Peterson confirmed the challenges of readjustment in a letter to Katherine Frederickson back in New York. Peterson explained that he had initially accepted a "strenuous position" but came close to a "nervous breakdown." As a result, he opted for temporary work as a desk clerk at the YMCA in Madison. His advice for fellow soldiers? "It is better that they do some light work at first than to be idle."[129] Although advising against it, Peterson framed idleness differently than employers like Vilter. It was not evidence of laziness, but the natural inclination of men whose lives in the service were both regimented and traumatic. Other servicemen echoed the same sentiment. "I stay out until 12 each night," John Kronberger confided in a letter, "just to see how it all feels again."[130] Released from the constraints of military life, men like Kronberger sought to enjoy their newly regained autonomy. Employment was not foremost in their minds.

Perspectives like these remained absent from debates at the state capitol before the arrival of the 32nd Division in early May. Still, pressure had steadily mounted for the Joint Committee on Finance to "do something more substantial than play bands and cheer."[131] Well-attended hearings indicated that the servicemen who had already come home largely supported the cash bonus.[132] Correspondence from the Wisconsin welcome committee confirmed enthusiasm for this policy among soldiers and sailors waylaid in New York.[133] In early May, the Joint Committee on Finance hosted another round of hearings on the cash bonus, merging myriad competing proposals into a single bill.[134] Under this new legislation, the amount of the bonus would reflect an individual's length of service during the conflict.

By late May, servicemen had finally arrived in Wisconsin *en masse*. There, they confronted the claims legislators made about them, and powerfully asserted the sacrifices they had made for their country. As an example, one ex-soldier drew a stark contrast between conditions in the trenches and those in munitions factories. He reminded readers of the *Milwaukee Journal*, "We sacrificed our lives, parents, wives, sweethearts, friends, our all, to make the world safe." Nevertheless, he continued, "We (the returned heroes) worked for $30 a month while the men at home were paid enormous wages."[135] Members of the Legislature seemed to ignore these sacrifices when they complained of "idleness" and "soft jobs." Together, testimonies like these posed a powerful counterweight to arguments about soldiers' supposedly lacking work ethic.

Those arguments—voiced by their state legislators—may have shocked servicemen after their warm welcome in New York. Still, disparaging comments did not dissuade them from participating in debates about the proper way to recognize their service. After months of legislative delay, soldiers and sailors began to apply pressure that would shape the fate of veterans policy to come.

By June, legislators had begun to better understand veterans' needs, but they still wrangled with cost. Was the public willing to reward its war heroes with a cash

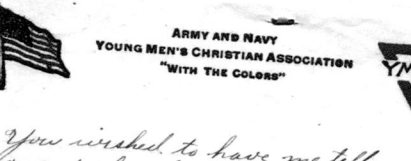

In this letter, Ira Peterson described his difficult transition to civilian life in 1919. Taking a job shortly after returning home to Madison had provoked a "nervous breakdown." Still, some employers characterized ex-soldiers' reluctance to work as evidence of laziness, rather than trauma.

bonus even if it meant paying higher taxes? This question immobilized legislators, fearful of the potential unpopularity of an expensive mandate. Meanwhile, they made progress on significant, but less sweeping legislation, precisely because cost posed fewer obstacles. Ultimately, Governor Philipp proposed a solution to the cash bonus stalemate; if passed by both houses, the bonus would be submitted to the people of Wisconsin for their approval. This referendum plan worked in wildly unpredictable ways. First, it dredged up wartime doubts about Philipp's patriotism and prompted questions about his commitment to the men who had helped win the war. Second, it revealed the extent to which legislators had underestimated their constituents' support for veterans.

Policymakers had assumed that most Wisconsinites would balk at the bonus's imposing price tag, despite soldiers' resounding enthusiasm for the policy. Governor Philipp's office predicted that the sums necessary to finance such a measure

WILLIAM WESSA, LANGLADE COUNTY HISTORICAL SOCIETY

The 107th Trench Mortar Battery Company marched down Fifth Avenue in Antigo upon their return home. Wisconsinites welcomed their "boys" with great fanfare, but legislators were unsure whether the same people would willingly shoulder a heavier tax burden to fund costly veterans policies.

were "so great" that raising them through a tax levy would be "inadvisable."[136] The Joint Committee on Finance confirmed these concerns in May, estimating that the bonus would cost $10 million at minimum.[137] Its members initially proposed to foot the bill by popular subscription, much like war bonds. Each county would be responsible for raising a portion of the total goal of $12 million.[138] Authors of this plan explained that it avoided tax levies that potentially ran afoul of the state constitution.[139] Still, legislative progress lagged. Although ultimately recommended for passage, the bill suffered delays in the Senate.[140] Some members seemed to hope that the federal government would resolve the issue first; a resolution adopted on June 26 urged the U.S. Congress "to enact legislation providing adequate compensation for soldiers, sailors and marines."[141]

While they fumbled for a solution on the cash bonus, legislators moved forward with less costly policies. The most significant of these was a program to aid disabled servicemen awaiting delayed War Risk Insurance payments from the federal government. In theory, policyholders were supposed to have received their first monthly checks, but in practice, few had. State legislators grasped the urgency of providing short-term support for these men and their families, and the Joint Committee on Finance recommended an appropriation of $500,000 to pay up to $30 per month to "sick, wounded or disabled soldiers, sailors or marines during their period of convalescence."[142] Shortly after the bill's passage in early July, the newly founded Service Recognition Board began processing applications for temporary relief.[143]

This bill joined a host of smaller, piecemeal measures passed earlier in the session. Those included temporary aid for indigent soldiers, as well as preference to Great War veterans in civil service hiring.[144] Legislators acknowledged soldiers whose high school educations were interrupted by the war, granting diplomas to those who missed their final semester of instruction.[145] For the dead, legislators took steps to ensure "proper and decent care" of gravesites. Other legislation enabled counties and local municipalities to construct memorials honoring their fallen hometown heroes.[146]

Despite progress on these other policies, the cash bonus remained at an impasse. Recognizing this inertia, Governor Philipp floated a new strategy in late June; he proposed to fund the bonus through a tax levy *after* asking the people of the state to approve the levy at a referendum. This method provided a compelling solution to legislators, who would shift responsibility for a potentially unpopular tax off of themselves and onto voters. If enacted, the multimillion-dollar appropriation would be "the largest that ever was made in a state of two and one-half million people," the governor said in a message to the Assembly. "While we all feel grateful to our soldier boys for their patriotic services," he continued, "I feel that we should not appropriate these tremendous sums of money without consulting the people." Immediately following the governor's speech, Representative Thomas Nolan of Rock County introduced a bill "embodying the idea of the executive" that slated the referendum for late August.[147]

This moment represented a turning point after which members of both the press and the Legislature politicized the bonus in ways that brought more veterans into the debate. Few journalists were more vocal than Fred Holmes—a former state representative, progressive Republican, and correspondent for the *Capital Times*.[148] Holmes portrayed the proposed referendum as a poison pill—a way for Philipp to quash the cash bonus without vetoing it himself. Legislators like Senator John Conant of Marquette County agreed, characterizing the referendum as "simply a way of getting out of paying these boys."[149] According to the *Wisconsin State Journal*, Conant hardly stood alone, as other legislators heaped "bitter criticism" on Philipp during debate on the bill.[150]

Why would Philipp seek the bonus' failure, as these critics alleged? The editorial pages of the *Capital Times* pointed the finger at big business interests.[151] Taxes to fund the cash bonus would fall disproportionately on industry, and critics assumed that Philipp—a magnate himself—secretly sided with his prosperous peers. One characteristic editorial railed against "the hungry horde of profiteers who grind the faces of the poor." Another pilloried politicians "loud in their acclaim of the heroism of the Wisconsin soldier" until asked to make sacrifices on the soldier's behalf.[152] The referendum plan had threatened to pit soldiers against taxpayers, but a handful of vocal critics portrayed the proposal as one that pit soldiers against big business—and challenged policymakers to choose sides.

Still more voices in the Legislature and the press opposed the referendum on the grounds that it demeaned soldiers. Senator Oscar Olson of Blanchardville, among others, believed that the vote reduced proud military men to beggars. "The soldiers are not the kind of men who will go to the polls and ask for a gratuity," Olson explained in a floor speech: "The very suggestion of such a procedure is repugnant to their manhood and an insult to their sense of fairness and justice." Olson concluded by reminding his colleagues that during the war, soldiers had earned minimal pay while people back home

THE DISABLED MAN CAN WIN

YOUR LOCAL AMERICAN RED CROSS HOME SERVICE SECTION KNOWS HOW

HOLDEN

WHS IMAGE ID 132634

While Wisconsin legislators bickered over a cash bonus for veterans, they managed to pass legislation to support disabled servicemen who were unable to work.

prospered. By publishing his speech in its entirety, the *Wisconsin State Journal* indicated its support for his position.[153] Overall, proponents of Philipp's plan found few allies in the press.

Meanwhile, a new round of debate around the referendum proved damaging for legislators who opposed the bonus. Speaking against the measure, Representative John Markham of Independence predicted that men who received the bonus would decline work. "As long as the soldiers have any money," he reportedly said, "they will refuse to take off their coats and put their shoulders to the wheel." Instead, they would "warm the benches."[154] These comments inadvertently galvanized veterans around the issue. In short order, the *Wisconsin State Journal* published soldiers' indignant replies. One letter included the following remarks:

If these men who think we are a lot of loafers want to experience a little of what we went through let them pick out some cold rainy night in November, then go out in the woods or field and dig a little hole deep enough to lay in and shelter their body and head and then have three or four men try and sneak up on him from in front with high powered rifles with the intention of killing him or being killed themselves. Let them lay there night after night with nothing but the dismal pattering of the rain and the whine of shells and the terrible concussion as one bursts near him, killing one or two of his buddies."

Another soldier reminded Markham "We were not 'bench warmers' going over the top."[155] Whether or not the referendum plan constituted an intentional attempt to kill the bonus, debate on the subject resulted in increasingly vocal support for the bonus from soldiers and civilians alike.

Ultimately, a compromise bill passed both houses on July 14. The bill provided a cash bonus for soldiers, sailors, marines, and nurses who had served during the war "as a token of appreciation of the character and spirit of their patriotic service." This "token" amounted to $10 per month of service, and payments to deceased service personnel would be directed to their surviving spouses, dependents, or parents.[156] Critics conceded the issue of the referendum, which remained a key provision of the legislation. Perhaps they gambled that public support had turned toward the soldiers. Moreover, by successfully lobbying to push the vote back from August 19 to September 2, bonus boosters won more time to consolidate this support.[157]

The governor had successfully overseen the bill's passage, but in the process, his political rivals had reframed the issue and cornered him into supporting the bonus at all costs. Philipp found himself hard pressed to prove that he supported soldiers over big business—and lest he confirm suspicions to the contrary, he actively campaigned for the bonus throughout July and August. Newspapers favorable to Philipp reported that he participated in an "organized campaign" to sway voters, and dismissed accusations that he opposed the measure "but lacked the courage to kill it."[158]

That summer, legislators of all political persuasions bent over backward to publicly promote the bonus.[159] Newspapers also encouraged Wisconsin voters to cast their ballots for the bonus. "Now is the time," read one *Capital Times* piece, "for every man to talk with his neighbor on the justice of the soldier bonus plan."[160] Elsewhere, journalists emphasized that soldiers had sacrificed prosperity and suffered extreme hardships. As one *Wisconsin State Journal* writer put it, servicemen endured "death and rats and lice" only to earn "one-quarter to one-half what they would have earned had they remained safely at home—as WE DID." The bonus promised not only to compensate for their "pitiably inadequate fighting wage," but also to help secure them "a new start."[161]

At this point, legislators had made assumptions about what sacrifices the public would make for the sake of returning soldiers without any means of gauging public opinion, lacking the tools of modern polling. This uncertainty heightened the suspense leading up to September 2. Would the people enthusiastically endorse the "token of appreciation" for those who so valiantly served the war effort? Or would a resounding "no" further blemish Wisconsin's tarnished wartime reputation?

The supporters prevailed. When Wisconsinites opened their newspapers to read the vote results on September 3, they discovered that the measure had passed by a decisive margin, 165,762 votes to 57,324.[162] Some newspapers published vote counts by the county, as if to praise (or shame) certain localities. The *Milwaukee Journal*, for example, publicized that in working-class "down town wards," the bonus passed 6 to 1 and 9 to 1, compared to a 3 to 1 vote in "well-to-do" wards.[163] This outcome may have surprised legislators. After all, many of their reservations about the policy had stemmed from the assumption that the public would not wish to foot the bill for such far-reaching policy. In short, they had underestimated public support for veterans.

As quickly as legislators realized their miscalculation, they moved to enact another wide-sweeping policy on the heels of the cash bonus's success: the educational bonus. Earlier that summer, both houses had passed a bill to make grants of $30 per month to any soldier, sailor, or marine who wished to pursue his college degree. This monthly value exceeded that of the cash bonus ($10 per month) as an incentive to pursue education.[164] But Governor Philipp had vetoed the measure on the grounds that it treated veterans unequally, excluding those who had not completed high school. This latter group stood to receive only $240 each from the cash bonus, whereas educational bonus recipients could receive as much as $1,080. Philipp pressed legislators to craft an educational bonus for all, "regardless of their educational qualifications." He suggested funding "special schools" where former servicemen might complete their elementary education among other adults, rather than children. In the meantime, he recommended that the state conduct research on soldiers' educational aspirations in order to better serve them.[165]

Within days of Philipp's veto, state officials hastened to devise and send questionnaires to former servicemen. The resultant document, mailed on July 25, briefly described the concept of the educational bonus before asking simply, "do you intend to take advantage of this offer?" The form then instructed respondents who answered in the affirmative to name the institutions they might attend.[166] The State Board of Education processed responses almost immediately, but the compiled data was limited at best. Questionnaires reached only a small subset of the 118,000 men who served, and fewer than five thousand men returned completed forms.[167] Those problems aside, completed forms attested to the measure's popularity. A majority of respondents (72 percent) expressed interest in the educational bonus, and of those, many sought nonuniversity education, preferring the "special schools" Philipp had proposed.[168]

With this data in hand, Philipp met with the State Board of Education on August 21 and tasked the agency with providing policy recommendations ahead of the September 4 special session he had called for the Legislature to reconsider the issue. Ultimately, the agency's recommendations mirrored Philipp's stated priorities, i.e., that the legislation should "provide the widest kind of educational opportunity under the most elastic conditions." It should accommodate the most people possible by facilitating education full-time, part-time, in-person, long-distance, nights, summers, and at grade school, high school, undergraduate, and graduate levels. Moreover, the agency recommended expanding proposed legislation to cover nurses.[169]

Ultimately, the governor's veto had made the proposal even more radical and far-reaching. Program costs would be higher than those for the cash bonus, including not only direct payments to recipients, but state investments in special schools, correspondence courses, and increased administration and instruction. All told, the State Board of Education projected a price tag of about $3.6 million the first year and $2.7 million the second year, sums that required taxes over and above those funding the cash bonus.[170]

Legislators confronted these imposing costs when they reconvened for the special session. Just two days earlier, however, Wisconsin voters had pledged to support veterans, even if doing so entailed a heavier tax burden. The results of the cash bonus referendum seemed to tip the scales in favor of its educational counterpart. Moreover, the proposal positioned education as a right veterans had earned in sacrificing their safety for the nation—a novel idea at the time. Its passage presented yet another opportunity to prove the state's commitment to—and investment in—its returning heroes.

With these considerations in mind, legislators overwhelmingly approved the measure. One senator and twenty-two representatives voted against the bill, arguing that the costs were too burdensome. Still, the *Milwaukee Sentinel* confidently reported that, "There was never any doubt about the passage of the bill at the special session."[171] Governor Philipp promptly signed Chapter 5, Laws of 1919 Special Session, into law, entitling service personnel who enlisted before November 1, 1918, to $30 for each month enrolled at an educational institution, a benefit capped at nine months per year over four consecutive years.

Together, Philipp's veto and the cash bonus referendum secured the fate of the educational bonus. The veto paved the way for the program's expansion and

WHS IMAGE ID 86880

Socialist legislators—seen here outside the state capitol in 1919—opposed the country's entry into war in 1917 and attracted their colleagues' criticism as a result. War politics continued to divide members of the 1919 Legislature, which meant that each enacted bill was the product of hard-won consensus.

delayed legislators' vote on the issue until September. By then, the cash bonus referendum had affirmed voters' commitment to veterans and made passage of the educational bonus much more likely.

Even after enactment, the bonuses faced another hurdle: legal challenge. Over the summer, public officials had disagreed over whether the bonuses violated the state constitution, particularly various sections under article VIII, which delineated the state's power to raise and spend funds.[172] Senator Timothy Burke, for example, reminded his colleagues that taxes could be collected for public purposes only, and questioned "whether the courts would hold [the cash bonus] to be a public purpose." By contrast, Attorney General John J. Blaine confidently affirmed the measure's constitutionality.[173] Only the state supreme court could lay to rest the question of whether the bonuses passed constitutional muster. But the court might invalidate these laws, crushing the hard-won consensus legislators had finally reached on veterans policy and destroying the achievements they relied on to restore Wisconsin's reputation.

Earlier in the session, concerns about constitutionality had torpedoed other popular proposals. Representative Fletcher's agricultural land grant program, for example, underwent several rounds of revision for this reason. Early drafts risked contravening public purpose spending requirements because they restricted loans to soldiers, sailors, and nurses. Later drafts addressed this issue by expanding eligibility to include any unemployed persons as "public necessity" demanded.[174] Attorney General Blaine reassured members of the Legislature that the bill aimed "to prevent or minimize unemployment," and those goals constituted "public purposes."[175] But critics remained unconvinced.[176] Siding with them, Governor Philipp vetoed the version that passed both houses, citing the constitutional prohibition against "internal improvements."[177]

On similar grounds, bonus legislation faced legal challenge—orchestrated by the governor himself—immediately following the September referendum and special session. Philipp depicted the suit as a "friendly" action designed to avoid "the results that might follow if at some later date a taxpayer . . . should come to the court and the court should set aside either or both statutes."[178] To this end, he asked David Atwood to serve as plaintiff. Atwood was managing editor of the *Janesville Gazette* and Philipp's appointee to the State Printing Board; his grandfather and namesake had founded the *Wisconsin State Journal*.[179] Madison attorney Harry Butler would argue on Atwood's behalf, as Blaine refused to represent him.[180] Atwood himself appeared to be a reluctant challenger at best. A front-page article in the *Wisconsin State Journal* stated, "Atwood has no bone to pick with the soldiers," and implied that he had been pressured to act as plaintiff.[181] Even Philipp characterized the challenge as a mere formality, reassuring soldiers that they should not "feel in the least alarmed."[182] Despite these claims, the suit revived accusations that Governor Philipp and his allies secretly wished to defeat the bonuses—if not by popular vote, then by judicial intervention. Such rhetoric indicated that to many Wisconsinites the bonuses signified something more than legislation. Instead, they stood for the state's collective endorsement of expansive veterans policy. In this context, the suit not only challenged the laws, but the will of the people.

Mobilizing behind the bonuses once again, progressive politicians and members of the press publicized the matter as a battle between humble soldiers and big business interests. Attorney General Blaine characterized the plaintiff as a pawn of private parties, pushed into filing a "friendly" suit on behalf of less-than-friendly interests.[183] The *Capital Times* depicted the suit as a veiled attempt to block the law from going into effect, describing Butler as "one of the ablest corporation lawyers in the state" and "a friend of the profiteers."[184]

Accusations like these seemed to strike a nerve. In a letter to the editor dated October 15, Governor Philipp insisted that he "was not importuned either by big business or little business to have these laws tested by the court." If indeed he had truly opposed the bonuses, Philipp told readers, he would have vetoed both measures. The letter concluded with a jab at armchair policymakers: "It is all well for a man who has no responsibility to talk loud about what ought to be done or what he would do." The governor, unlike his detractors, had sworn an oath to obey the constitution and would not shirk this responsibility.[185]

The court challenge had once again placed Philipp on the defensive. As with the referendum, anything but a positive outcome for the bonuses threatened to confirm his critics' allegations. As the *Wisconsin State Journal* worded it, a decision striking down either piece of legislation would amount to "political suicide" on Philipp's part.[186] Criticism of the governor's position on the bonus now broadened to encompass his entire record in office. The *Capital Times*, for example, dismissed Philipp as a man who "has great wealth and lacks vision," and "can not see over and beyond the mere dollar measure of greatness."[187] Privately, some Wisconsinites dredged up wartime allegations of his "pro-hun" stance and inadequate patriotism.[188]

More problematically, the lawsuit also threatened the reputation of the state constitution itself. A decision overturning the bonuses, read one piece in the *Capital Times*, would prove that "the constitution is a protection for the rich and a stern instrument to keep the common people in their place."[189] Other papers spoke in less hyperbolic terms, simply expressing confidence that the legislation would be upheld and entertaining no other possible outcome.[190] Whatever the justices decided, the people had already decided in the bonuses' favor. This sentiment represented a sea change in thinking about veterans benefits—a radical shift from prior decades when people across the country complained loudly about the costs of veterans pensions.[191] Practically speaking, it also placed enormous pressure on the justices of the state supreme court to affirm the law.

On the morning of November 8, 1919, the justices filed into a courtroom "crowded by ex-soldiers" to hear oral arguments that lasted nearly seven hours.[192] Attorney Harry Butler opened, speaking for the plaintiff, David

Long after the war ended, Governor Emmanuel Philipp faced accusations of insufficient patriotism for his allegedly lukewarm attitude toward veterans policies.

WHS IMAGE ID 32600

Atwood. Butler disputed the notion that the bonuses fulfilled a public purpose because they encouraged voluntary military service; such service was made to the United States, not Wisconsin, and benefitted the federal government rather than the state.[193] This argument echoed an idea that members of the Legislature had articulated earlier in the session, i.e., that the nation, not the state, owed soldiers for their service.

Defending the cash bonus, Deputy Attorney General M. B. Olbrich disputed Butler's conception of public purposes, arguing that the national war effort fell under this category. To this end, the cash bonus enhanced patriotism among the general population and would aid further war efforts by encouraging service in the armed forces.[194] In short, Olbrich argued for an expansive, rather than restrictive, notion of public purposes—one that encompassed general incentives to military service.

Olbrich then yielded the floor to Charles H. Crownhart, an attorney speaking on behalf of 305 ex-soldiers seeking the educational bonus.[195] Crownhart emphasized that soldiers themselves had neither asked nor campaigned for these laws: "These defendants seek no charity and they wish no gifts as such from the state treasury." He then proceeded to establish legal and historical precedents to prove that the bonus fulfilled a public purpose, even invoking ancient Rome to argue that reward for soldiers' sacrifices was a "public duty," and that governments failing to perform this duty "[had] already begun to decay."[196] With this remark, Crownhart touched on the anxieties of those who believed the bonuses' failure would stain the state's reputation.

By this point in the afternoon, the patience of all present had worn thin. When Senator Roy Wilcox requested to speak as a "friend of the court," one justice jokingly replied, "you are no friend of the court if you want to talk now!" provoking bursts of laughter in the courtroom. Wilcox spoke for a mere five minutes, and the session concluded around 5 o'clock.[197]

The first decision came swiftly on November 17—just over a week after oral arguments. Justice James Kerwin wrote the opinion, confirming that the cash bonus *did* constitute a public benefit. "When a war is waged by the nation," Kerwin explained, "those supporting it are performing service as well for their respective states as for the nation." Moreover, Kerwin noted the Legislature's "very broad discretion" to tax and concluded that the additional taxes to fund the bonuses were not "arbitrary or whimsical."[198]

The court simultaneously ruled in favor of the educational bonus, although that opinion came months later, in February 1920.[199] In it, Justice Aad John Vinje asserted the public purpose the legislation performed by inspiring future volunteers: "The main purpose was to stimulate patriotism, to

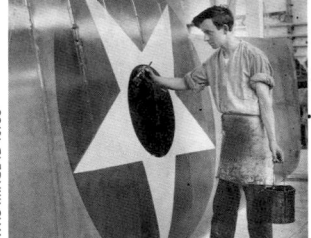

WHS IMAGE ID 10758

April 6, 1917

Congress votes overwhelmingly to declare war against Germany. Later in the year, it will vote to declare war against Austria-Hungary as well.

WHS IMAGE ID 132646

November 11, 1918

The war stops with the declaration of an armistice. It will end formally when the Treaty of Versailles is signed in June 1919.

WHS IMAGE ID 54244

May 1919

Most soldiers of the 32nd Division return stateside, arriving in Boston and New York, and Governor Philipp welcomes them at Camp Merritt, New Jersey. Many will struggle to resume their civilian lives.

WHS IMAGE ID 25348

July 14, 1919

Members of the Wisconsin Legislature vote to pass a bill that would provide a cash bonus to all Wisconsin veterans (Chapter 667, Laws of 1919). On September 2, Wisconsinites will approve the required referendum on the bonus..

WHS IMAGE ID 45142

November 17, 1919

Nine days after hearing oral arguments in the legal challenges to the cash and educational bonus laws, the Wisconsin Supreme Court rules that both laws are constitutional.

April 4, 1917

Two days after President Wilson asks Congress to declare war against Germany, U.S. Senator Robert La Follette urges his colleagues in the Senate against going to war. Many Wisconsinites blame La Follette for exacerbating perceptions of Wisconsin as an unpatriotic state.

February 1918

The 32nd Division—made up of soldiers from Wisconsin and Michigan—arrives in France. Since the declaration of war by Congress, 98 percent of eligible Wisconsin men have registered for the draft, compared to 92 percent nationwide.

March 4, 1919

Both houses of the Wisconsin Legislature pass an appropriation of $5,000 to fund "a committee to welcome Wisconsin soldiers" in New York (Chapter 22, Laws of 1919).

June 1919

Wisconsin legislators enact a bill to provide temporary support to veterans with disabilities (Chapter 452, Laws of 1919).

September 4, 1919

The Wisconsin Legislature convenes in special session to consider—and ultimately pass—an educational bonus program for returning veterans (Chapter 5, Laws of 1919 Special Session).

quicken the perception in our citizens that there is a sacred duty to defend the government in term of need." Vinje also dismissed the argument that the draft made such "stimulation" unnecessary. To this end, he evoked French heroism during an early allied victory: "[T]hink you the French soldiers at the battle of the Marne exclaimed 'They shall not pass,' because they were drafted, or because they loved France?" To this rhetorical question, he answered, "their heroic and successful defense sprang from desire, not from compulsion."[200]

As with the referendum, the court decisions reassured the widening circle of Wisconsinites who shared a stake in the bonuses. One lawyer wrote confidently to attorney Charles Crownhart that this outcome would surely redeem the state's "unenviable reputation" during the war. Despite that reputation, he noted with some relief, "its Supreme Court has at all times been pro-American."[201] Similar sentiments echoed in official state publications. The official mouthpiece of the State Board of Education heaped praise on the justices and declared that the bonus laws "brought glory to the name of Wisconsin."[202]

Over just a few months, Wisconsinites had reached consensus on the importance of veterans policies. Until November, however, few veterans had reaped any benefits. Now, having overcome court challenges, the bonuses could finally take effect. Wisconsin veterans would learn how these policies measured up to their lofty goals in subsequent days, months, and years.

III

THREE POLICIES ENACTED during the 1919 legislative session proved exemplary, each in its own way: temporary disability payments marked a turning point from an earlier, Civil War-era program; the cash bonus outshone the federal government's commitment to veterans in the aftermath of the war; and the educational bonus not only surpassed similar programs adopted by other states, but also inspired future federal legislation. No program was perfect—and administrators sometimes underestimated the challenges veterans faced. Together, however, they signaled the state's unprecedented commitment to its veterans.

Chapter 452, Laws of 1919, supported disabled soldiers awaiting War Risk Insurance payments, and in so doing, continued a tradition for the state government to serve as a resource for veterans struggling to access federal benefits. Following the Civil War, the state adjutant general served as an intermediary between Wisconsin and Washington as disabled Union Army veterans sought federal pensions.[203] Through the adjutant general, soldiers and their surviving family members requested the proof of service required to file an application. But many among them proved ill-equipped to cut through the "voluminous amount of red tape" the process entailed.[204] Meanwhile, no formalized system existed to process these requests in an efficient and timely manner.

By contrast, a glimpse into records related to Chapter 452 reveals a vastly more effective system. The Service Recognition Board developed standard forms prompting applicants to provide required information in an orderly, straightforward way. Acknowledging mistakes of the past, administrators ensured that the application process itself posed no barriers to benefits. To more easily answer inquiries about individual applications, they retained all files and correspondence within folders labelled with applicants' names. Moreover, they kept in frequent contact with aid beneficiaries to inform them of any changes in their status or benefits.[205]

Facing fewer bureaucratic hoops than their Union Army forebears, Great War veterans promptly accessed benefits that bridged the gap before federal funds kicked in. As an example, Gustave Hildebrandt of Beloit suffered from what his doctor described as a "deformed, painful right ankle and foot" resulting from bullet wounds. Hildebrandt planned to begin training in electrical work as soon as he felt "physically able to enter," but in the meantime, he received $30 per month from the state. After five months, that support ceased when his $80 per month War Risk Insurance payments began.[206] In another case, August Buchholz of Ripon accepted lower paying clerical work after a gunshot wound to the abdomen prevented him from resuming his former occupation as a paper hanger. The state supplemented his salary until January 1, 1920, when he began receiving federal funds.[207]

Administrators often addressed recipients with harsh words, but their tone belied a level of support previously unavailable to veterans. For example, a letter from the Service Recognition Board reminded Oscar Dettmeyer that his $30 monthly allowance was "temporary only and should in no manner be considered as a pension." The same letter reprimanded the veteran for failing to pursue his War Risk Insurance benefits, and counseled him against becoming dependent on state support. At the same time, the administrator spelled out what Dettmeyer should do next, instructing him to contact his local Red Cross to settle the claim and expedite federal funds.[208] This approach likely borrowed from rehabilitation theories that advocated for stirring injured men into self-sufficiency rather than treating them as objects of charity.

Of course, this program recognized only the physical wounds of war as obstacles to rehabilitation. The Service Recognition Board followed the lead of the Bureau of War Risk Insurance in defining disability with reference to "capacity for productive labor."[209] Application questions centered around work and training, asking "Are you well and strong enough to work?" Nowhere did they address psychological barriers to rehabilitation. A Milwaukee veteran named Leo Kwasniewski attempted to explain as much in his response to a letter scolding him for failing to work:

> I am wholly dependent upon [state aid] for help as I am not able to work at my former occupation, that of a motorman, because of my general nervousness. I am improving, but still have spells of nervousness and weakness come over me lasting for a period of four or five days.[210]

It is possible that "nervousness" referred to the condition eventually known as "shell shock" and later called Post-Traumatic Stress Disorder (PTSD). Whatever the case, Kwasniewski's remarks hint at the ways post–World War I veterans programs—at both state and federal levels—ignored thorny problems like mental injury and trauma.

These issues aside, Chapter 452 provided a much-needed safety net for disabled Wisconsin servicemen. The law enabled its beneficiaries to support themselves and their families during the summer and fall of 1919, long before other policies materialized, and its efficient administration helped veterans access aid without undue delay or confusion. In this instance, state policy succeeded because it complemented an existing federal program, recognizing that program's shortcomings—namely, a slow, bureaucratic process—and intervening to fill the gap.

The cash bonus bill—Chapter 667, Laws of 1919—pledged support for veterans in ways that notably surpassed the federal government. Earlier in 1919, Wisconsin legislators had looked to Congress to provide some form of lump sum payment to demobilized servicemen. When no policy materialized, they moved ahead with their own legislation. Over the long term, this comparatively prompt action worked to Wisconsin's favor. The cash bonus of 1919 affirmed the state's appreciation of veterans' sacrifices during the war and preempted protest against the state based on claims to the contrary. Meanwhile, failure to pass a satisfactory federal bonus led to resentment and outright revolt against their representatives in Washington, D.C., who seemed to have forgotten the heroes of the Great War.

In Washington, as in Madison, advocates for the bonus insisted that it would place returning soldiers on an even footing with civilians who had benefited from the wartime boom in industry. But opponents argued that it would discourage work by offering an easy handout.[211] Veterans groups lobbied for bonuses through the 1920s and '30s, but each interwar president opposed the policy and vetoed

WHS IMAGE ID 49240

Federal rehabilitation programs promoted the idea that wives, mothers, sisters, and "sweethearts" could help wounded men overcome their disabilities with tough love. Brochures asked women, "Are you going to spoil him and pamper him with your pity? Do you want him to be dependent upon you, and possibly later an object of charity, dissatisfied with life, broken in spirit?" The intended reply was "no." A woman should restore her broken hero by prodding him to become "self-supporting" and "self-respected." This message was premised on the notion that anyone could overcome disability with the right mental attitude, a theory popularized by Elizabeth Upham of Milwaukee-Downer College. Upham argued that the "chief obstacle" to recovery was not physical disability, but "the mental condition which the physical handicap is apt to bring about." This theory created potentially unrealistic expectations among disabled servicemen and their loved ones.

Sources: Federal Board for Vocational Education, To the Sweethearts, Sisters, Wives, and Mothers of Discharged Soldiers and Sailors (Washington: Government Printing Office, December 1918); Elizabeth G. Upham, Desirability of vocational education and direction for disabled soldiers (Madison, WI: University of Wisconsin Extension Service, September 1917).

successful legislation. Congress occasionally overrode vetoes to pass compromise measures, but these paltry concessions embittered veterans groups and culminated in mass protests. During the summer of 1932, thousands of veterans assembled in a "Bonus Army" that encamped in Washington, D.C. Problems had worsened with the onset of the Depression, when veterans disproportionally faced unemployment.[212] "This generation," writes historian Jennifer Keene, "faced the prospect of starting over, not just once, but twice in their lives."[213] Realistically, a federal bonus could not have preempted these problems. But federal inaction only embittered veterans unable to attain lasting economic stability after returning home in 1919.

State-level action on the bonus helped avert the tense confrontations that had occurred at the federal level. With Chapter 667, Wisconsin joined several other state legislatures that recognized the policy's value as a goodwill measure, worth its high price.[214] Over time, the state granted monthly payments to 116,000 veterans and their families. These payments amounted to an astounding total of $20,748,462, which far exceeded initial estimates.[215]

Despite resounding support for the bonus in 1919, its popularity declined within Wisconsin and few lobbied to reintroduce the policy in the wake of World War II. This change of heart did not reflect disapproval of the policy itself, but anger over perceived mishandling of bonus funds. Almost immediately, the Legislature diverted surplus tax revenues toward programs unrelated to veterans.[216] For example, Chapter 30, Laws of 1920 Special Session, allocated over $1 million to build the Wisconsin General Hospital.[217] Later legislation tapped the bonus fund to support the University Medical School. Although certain bill provisions directly assisted veterans in some way, critics objected that any diversion of bonus funds amounted to a broken promise.[218] By the early 1930s, a group of legislators pushed to renew the state's commitment to its veterans and cease unrelated diversions of bonus funds.[219] But the reputation of the cash bonus would not recover before the state sent soldiers off to fight in another global conflict.

Still, the policy had very likely played an important role in individual veterans' lives, easing the transition into civilian life and relieving pressure to find immediate employment. That said, its legacy remains difficult to discern, largely because the state did not compile data about use of the cash bonus the same way it had for other programs. Names of cash bonus recipients were quietly entered into administrative rolls, unseen beyond state agency offices.

The educational bonus—Chapter 5, Laws of 1919 Special Session—benefitted enormously from the fact that people across the state witnessed it in action. The mere presence of soldiers, sailors, marines, and nurses in classrooms, libraries, and laboratories reminded Wisconsinites of the pledge their lawmakers had made to these men and women. Participation lent itself easily to publicity—an unforeseen feature of the policy that enhanced its reputation and ultimately positioned it as a model for future federal legislation.

From the start, the educational bonus prompted enthusiastic reports. Fred Holmes penned one particularly glowing tribute, highlighting the case of Frank Kupris, one of the program's earliest enrollees. After surviving the Battle of the Somme, his next challenge was graduating from high school. The thirty-one-year-old had emigrated with his parents from Russia at a young age and was quick to contrast the educational opportunities of his homeland with those of his adopted country: "In Russia, there are no chances for any kind of education for a self-supporting man. But I found that it is not so in this country."[220] In clear terms, Kupris revealed the capacity of education, like military service, to Americanize immigrants and instill them with fierce patriotism. His comments demonstrated the bonus' great potential; by solidifying newcomers' allegiance to the nation, it would dispel the kinds of doubts about patriotism that Wisconsin had endured during the war.

As of January 1920, some three hundred of Kupris's peers filled high school classrooms, with hundreds more opting to pursue college educations. Of that group, 1,829 enrolled at the University of Wisconsin, 465 at Marquette University, and 393 at the Milwaukee School of Engineering. Other beneficiaries dotted the country at schools like Harvard or the University of Chicago. Those who worked or remained homebound took night classes (300) or correspondence courses (1,223).[221] In the program's first nine months, the state disbursed $811,580 to applicants.[222]

Women received these funds as well, though state statistics are silent on precisely how many participated. In the program's infancy, state officials often spoke of beneficiaries using male pronouns exclusively, as if forgetting that the legislation included female nurses. But as the policy went into practice, agency publications increasingly mentioned women. For example, a State Board of Education publication detailing course subjects did so under the heading, "Special Classes and Short Courses for Ex-Service Men and Women."[223] Despite this effort, the press primarily portrayed the educational bonus as an opportunity for soldiers, sailors, and marines.

How well did these men and women adjust to academic life? School administrators across the state weighed in, and the State Board of Education publicly reproduced their comments. On balance, testimonies conveyed confidence in these students, even if they did not dramatically outpace their civilian peers as GI Bill beneficiaries would following World War II. For example, the Engineering College at the University of Wisconsin compiled grade statistics to report that bonus recipients performed slightly better than the general population in most subjects. A less precise assessment from Ripon College judged bonus students to be "a little better" than the average, and another from Beloit College as "rather better." One administrator from Campion College in Prairie du Chien offered only lukewarm praise: "While none are brilliant, and one or two have shown a lassitude and wandering of mind, the majority have gone at their work with determination."[224]

Schools held former service personnel to high standards; they closely monitored attendance and performance, notifying the Board of Education of circumstances that warranted cessation of funds. University of Wisconsin students who attended classes "irregularly" prompted formal faculty decisions that they be "dropped." Those students received terse notifications from the faculty secretary, informing them, "you will not receive any educational bonus." At the same time, faculty also mobilized to bend the rules for exceptional students. Although Herman Deutsch had enrolled in fewer credits than required, the UW History Department advocated on his behalf; as the chair explained, Deutsch performed "investigation of such quality" that the department had authorized him to conduct independent scholarly research on a full-time basis.[225]

To faculty and administrators, exceptional students like Deutsch embodied the legislation's promise and potential. For him and others, military service became a pathway to an education he could not otherwise afford. Success stories like these prompted positive assessments of the program as a whole. As one Stevens Point State Normal School official put it, "I honestly believe that the law is a fine one and that the students are measuring up to the spirit of the law."[226]

The spirit of the law itself seemed to surpass that of any other state legislation. Before the bonus became law, the Wisconsin Legislative Reference Library identified similar policies in neighboring states, but most either limited eligibility or restricted benefits to higher education only. For example, Iowa provided a public college education only to those men whose service began before they reached the age of twenty-one; Minnesota law covered tuition at state colleges and universities to men and women who served in the armed forces or Red Cross.[227] Nationwide, only Oregon came close, passing a bill to provide broad, flexible educational benefits. Even so, its funding fell short of Wisconsin's educational bonus.[228] Wisconsin stood poised to offer universally accessible educational benefits in a way no other state had to date. Unsurprisingly, the State Board of Education fielded inquiries about the bonus from other states following its enactment in September 1919.[229]

In subsequent years, nationwide reporting championed the policy's ingenuity and generosity. The *New York Times*, for example, provided a state-by-state comparison of veterans benefits and singled out Wisconsin as having created "the most comprehensive educational program worked out by any State."[230] A piece in Henry Ford's journalistic mouthpiece, the *Dearborn Independent*, dubbed it "the most comprehensive piece of bonus legislation offering educational opportunity adopted by any of the states."[231] More recently, historians have singled out the policy as evidence that Wisconsin "went beyond the federal government" in terms of the benefits it provided to veterans.[232]

Why was the educational bonus so remarkable? Other policies focused on practical issues, like preventing unemployment or other forms of distress. This policy was idealistic by comparison, framing education as both a pathway to employment and a valid investment in itself. Board of Education publications consistently emphasized that work need not preclude the pursuit of knowledge.

Some college administrators hinted that soldiers' readjustment to student life proved more difficult than they would publicly acknowledge. An official from Lawrence College described educational bonus recipients as producing "good average work" after an initial period of "considerable restlessness." Another observed that "it was difficult for them to settle down to work" at the start of the semester, when most performed "quite poorly." Nevertheless, he added, "most of these men have retrieved themselves since then." These comments echoed the same sentiments soldiers like Ira Peterson had expressed in their letters back to the welcome committee in New York. As Peterson put it, it was "more difficult to get used to civilian life than it was to become used to the army."

Sources: University of Wisconsin–Madison Archives, Series 5/2/7 S41M9: World War I Bonus Records, 1919–1939; Wisconsin Historical Society Archives, Mss JC, Emanuel Philipp Papers, Box 6, folder 2.

After all, distance learning courses were available in subjects ranging from plant histology and bookkeeping to Shakespeare and railway engineering. These publications normalized the pursuit of education at all ages, reasoning, "the education of man . . . is never finished." Indeed, the man who neglected his education did so at his peril: "He must either progress and go forward, or he begins to retrograde and rust and consequently falls behind his fellows."[233] Never before had the state so resoundingly endorsed the importance of adult education.

Moreover, the educational bonus repaid the sacrifices soldiers had made to their country, wagering that such an investment would serve the state over the long term. Specifically, those who implemented the policy framed it as a means to produce more active participants in democracy. As Edward A. Fitzpatrick of the State Board of Education explained to recipients, the policy prolonged their "public duty" by demanding "a further investment of your time and your money to fit yourself to become even a better citizen, and to render in peace time the quality of service you rendered in war." An early report on implementation reinforced this message with a potent epigram that referred to knowledge as "the precursor and protector of republican institutions."[234] The educational bonus ensured that ex-servicemen continued to share a stake in their country's future, both on and off the battlefield.

Over succeeding decades, the popularity of this policy and its underlying principles helped reshape ideas around the value of education and the meaning

Although the educational bonus law expired on July 1, 1924, legislators in subsequent sessions revived its spirit. Chapter 305, Laws of 1931, extended benefits to orphaned children of otherwise eligible applicants who had fallen in action or died from war-related causes. Beneficiaries of this law included sisters Dorothy and Betty Jean King of Green Bay, who pursued coursework in pharmacy and physical education at the University of Wisconsin in 1932. Their father, George, had died nearly ten years earlier as the result of injuries incurred overseas.

Source: Wisconsin Historical Society Archives, Series 1566 MAD 3/39/H7: Orphans' educational bonus applications, 1919–1945, Box 1.

of military service. Historian Jennifer Keene explains that, across the nation, veterans' battles for recognition paved the way for a reimagining of soldiers' relationship to the state. Policymakers and members of the public increasingly understood that they owed a great debt to those who had sacrificed individual safety for that of the country. With this bar set, when servicemen returned from Europe in the wake of World War II, they reaped the benefits of this new way of thinking: unprecedented access to education. The GI Bill, one of the most important legislative accomplishments of the twentieth century, enabled this generation to pursue higher education in greater numbers than ever before. As Keene concludes, "For the first and perhaps only time, wartime military service became a stepping-stone to a better life."[235] From this vantage point, Wisconsin's educational bonus served as an important precursor to the GI Bill.

Epilogue

With memories of the welcome committee fresh in his mind, Ira Lee Peterson wrote a letter of thanks to Katherine Frederickson in New York after he returned home to Wisconsin in the spring of 1919. "I was entertained so nicely at the Hall of States," he told her, identifying himself as the "unusually tall solder" with a diamond ring.[236] In fact, Frederickson made such a positive impression on Peterson, that he would eventually follow her lead. By early 1924, the Red Cross had formally recognized his work organizing "many entertainments for disabled war veterans" at the psychiatric hospital in Mendota.[237] The former soldier who had relied on the YMCA to send letters home from France now served as its membership secretary in Madison, helping fellow veterans in that role and as an active member of the American Legion.[238] Remarkably, when the United States entered World War II, Peterson answered the call of duty a second time, this time serving with the Air Force.[239]

Peterson and others like him embodied the spirit of veterans legislation enacted by the 1919 Wisconsin Legislature. These innovative policies looked forward rather than backwards; they did not reward past deeds, but sought to "stimulate patriotism" in the uncertain future.[240] On this score, the personal biographies of many World War I veterans, Peterson included, bear testimony to the success of these laws. Moreover, Wisconsin legislators—unlike their predecessors or peers in other states—came to understand that successful rehabilitation to civilian life required more than short-term material assistance. Instead, they implemented more comprehensive programs that affirmed the value of veterans' service to the state and the nation. To achieve this goal, legislators invested in veterans' physical health, financial stability, and education. Although far from complete, legislation enacted in 1919 formed a solid foundation upon which veterans policy continued to evolve over the next century. ▨

NOTES

1. Ira Peterson, "Journal of a World War Veteran," *Wisconsin Magazine of History* 8 (1924), 199–220: 214.

2. Ira Peterson, "Journal of a World War Veteran," *Wisconsin Magazine of History* 8 (1924), 328–348: 334.

3. Letter from Ira L. Peterson to Katherine Frederickson, May 14, 1919. Wisconsin Historical Society (WHS) Archives, Mss JC, Emanuel Philipp Papers, Box 6, folder 2.

4. For a brief but helpful overview, see Chapter 26 of Jackson J. Spielvogel, *Western Civilization: A Brief History Volume II: Since 1300* (New York: West/Wadsworth, 1999). See also David Kennedy, *Over Here: The First World War and American Society* (Oxford: Oxford University Press, 1982).

5. Richard L. Pifer with Marjorie Hannon Pifer, *The Great War Comes to Wisconsin: Sacrifice, Patriotism, and Free Speech in a Time of Crisis* (Madison, WI: Wisconsin Historical Society Press, 2017), 49–50. See also Robert S. Maxwell, Emanuel L. Philipp: Wisconsin Stalwart (Madison: State Historical Society of Wisconsin, 1959), 113.

6. Paul Glad, *The History of Wisconsin, Volume 5: War, A New Era, and Depression, 1914–1940* (Madison, WI: Wisconsin Historical Society Press, 1990), 21/9/11.

7. "La Follette's speech in the U.S. Senate against the entry of the United States into the World War, April 4, 1917," *Congressional Record—Senate* (Washington: U.S. Government Printing Office, 1917), 223–236.

8. Pifer, The Great War Comes to Wisconsin, 65.

9. Kennedy, Over Here, 21–22.

10. Eau Claire Leader, March 16, 1917. Cited from the original in Lorin Lee Cary, "The Wisconsin Loyalty Legion, 1917–1918," *Wisconsin Magazine of History* 53 (1969), 33–50: 34.

11. Glad, *History of Wisconsin, Volume 5*, 24.

12. Department of Commerce and Labor, *Thirteenth Census of the United States Taken in the Year 1910: Statistics for Wisconsin* (Washington: U.S. Government Printing Office, 1913), 593–4.

13. "Pledge Loyalty of Allegiance," *Milwaukee Journal*, February 8, 1917.

14. Mary Antonette Henke, "World War I: Dissent and Discord in Milwaukee" (master's thesis, Loyola University Chicago, 1966), 88.

15. "War Is Declared," *Wisconsin State Journal*, April 6, 1917.

16. "Obey Law; Keep Mouth Shut," *Grand Rapids Daily Leader*, April 10, 1917; "Good Advice," *Racine Journal News*, April 11, 1917.

17. "Uncle Sam Generous Says Attorney Wolfe Aliens Are Safe Here," *La Crosse Tribune and Leader Press*, April 15, 1917.

18. Woodrow Wilson, The President's Flag Day Address: *With Evidence of Germany's Plans* (Washington: U. S. Government Printing Office, 1917), 4.

19. Quoted in Kennedy, *Over Here*, 24.

20. For a brief synopsis, see David Zonderman, "Over Here: The Wisconsin Homefront during World War I," *Wisconsin Magazine of History* 77 (1994), 296–300.

21. Alvin P. Kletzsch, a prominent Milwaukee businessman and chairman of the German-American Bazaar Association, relayed this news, "Says City Has a Black Eye," *Milwaukee Journal*, February 21, 1917, WHS Library, Microfilm P70-2227.

22. "'Black Eye' Due to Fanatics?" *Milwaukee Journal*, February 23, 1917.

23. "The Traitor State," *Princeton Democrat* (Indiana), July 17, 1917. Another article seems to indicate that the editorial had also been published in the Louisville, Kentucky *Courier-Journal*, and possibly elsewhere, "Governor Philipp Defends State's War Record," *Eau Claire Sunday Leader*, July 29, 1917.

24. Many thanks to Leslie Bellais of the Wisconsin Historical Society for sharing her valuable insight concerning the use and perceptions of the term "Traitor State" in 1917.

25. Pifer, *The Great War Comes to Wisconsin*, 210.

26. Maxwell, *Emanuel Philipp*, xiii/125/32.

27. Glad, *History of Wisconsin, Volume 5*, 29; Karen Falk, "Public Opinion in Wisconsin during World War I," *The Wisconsin Magazine of History* 25 (1942), 389–407: 399.

28. Falk, "Public Opinion in Wisconsin during World War I," 390. Of those nearly 220,000 men, 118,000 would serve. Pifer, *The Great War Comes to Wisconsin*, 203.

29. Glad, *History of Wisconsin, Volume 5*, 45.

30. Ibid., 28.

31. See, for example, "Another Tar and Feather Party Is Staged," *Ashland Daily Press*, April 11, 1918.

32. Federal laws included the Threats Against the President Act, Selective Service Act, Espionage Act, Trading-with-the-Enemy Act, and the Sabotage Act. See John D. Stevens, "When Sedition Laws Were Enforced: Wisconsin in World War I," *Wisconsin Academy of Sciences, Arts and Letters* 58 (1970), 39–60.

33. Cary, "The Wisconsin Loyalty Legion, 1917–1918," 33.

34. Glad, *History of Wisconsin, Volume 5*, 42.

35. Irvine L. Lenroot, "The War Loyalty of Wisconsin," *The Forum*, June 1918, 695–702.

36. Pifer, *The Great War Comes to Wisconsin*, 212–4; Maxwell, *Emanuel Philipp*, 175; Glad, *History of Wisconsin, Volume 5*, 50–2.

37. Letter from John T. Williams to Charles D. Rosa, August 20, 1918, WHS Archives, Mss VV, Charles D. Rosa Papers, Box 1.

38. Letter from H. A. Huber to Charles D. Rosa, August 15, 1918, WHS Archives, Mss VV, Charles D. Rosa Papers, Box 1.

39. Cary, "The Wisconsin Loyalty Legion, 1917–1918," 43.

40. Charles McCarthy, head of the Wisconsin Legislative Reference Library, described the state as "maligned" despite its notable contributions to the war effort. Letter from Charles McCarthy to James S. Benn, February 18, 1919, WHS Archives, Mss KU Series A, Charles McCarthy Papers, Box 18, folder 1.

41. "Joy Reigns in Madison," *Capital Times*, November 11, 1918.

42. "Citizens Go Wild as News of Truce is Received Here," *Janesville Daily Gazette*, November 11, 1918.

43. "Peace Celebration Greatest Event Ever Witnessed," *Sheboygan Press*, November 12, 1918.

44. "Overjoyed Crowds Here Celebrate Victory Day: Parades Then Carnival," *Eau Claire Leader*, November 12, 1918.

45. Letter from Elton Morrison, December 24, 1918, WHS Archives, Mss 97.153, Elton Morrison Papers, folder 14.

46. Burl Noggle, *Into the Twenties: The United States from Armistice to Normalcy* (Urbana, IL: University of Illinois Press, 1974), 14.

47. As an example, see Walter Kohler's letter to Governor Philipp, February 1919, WHS Archives, Mss JC, Emanuel Philipp Papers, Box 6, folder 1.

48. A. H. Roepke to Emanuel Philipp, January 21, 1919, WHS Archives, Mss JC, Emanuel Philipp Papers, Box 6, folder 1. The agricultural sector had already lost 2.5 million workers to military and industry following the nation's entry into war. See Harry Schwartz, "Farm Labor Adjustments after World War I," *Journal of Farm Economics* 25 (February 1943), 269–277: 269.

49. Mrs. Victor Frederickson, "History of the Wisconsin Women's Society in New York, 1916 to 1936" (n.d.), 7, WHS Pamphlet Collection 54-6189. Of twenty-two members listed, five were men.

50. Letter from Mary Sabin to Governor Philipp, February 22, 1919, WHS Archives, Mss JC, Emanuel Philipp Papers, Box 6, folder 1.

51.Letter from L. C. Whittet to A. H. Wilkinson dated February 28, 1919; Letter from L. C. Whittet to Mary Sabin, March 5, 1919, WHS Archives, Mss JC, Emanuel Philipp Papers, Box 6, folder 1. Chapter 22, Laws of 1919 was published on March 14, 1919.

52. Telegram from Mary Sabin to L. C. Whittet, March 16, 1919, WHS Archives, Mss JC, Emanuel Philipp Papers, Box 6, folder 1.

53. Telegram from Katherine Frederickson to Emanuel Philipp, March 15, 1919, WHS Archives, Mss JC, Emanuel Philipp Papers, Box 6, folder 1.

54. Letter from Mary Sabin to L. C. Whittet, March 21, 1919, WHS Archives, Mss JC, Emanuel Philipp Papers, Box 6, folder 1.

55. Letter from Orlando Holway to Emanuel Philipp, March 31, 1919, WHS Archives, Mss JC, Emanuel Philipp Papers, Box 6, folder 1.

56. Letter from L. C. Whittet to Mary Sabin, March 5, 1919, WHS Archives, Mss JC, Emanuel Philipp Papers, Box 6, folder 1.

57. John William Leonard, ed., *Who's Who in America, Volume 11* (1920), 2459.

58. Letter from L. Grieb, Secretary to George Russell, to Emanuel Philipp, March 5, 1919; Letter from George Russell to Emanuel Philipp, March 11, 1919, WHS Archives, Mss JC, Emanuel Philipp Papers, Box 6, folder 1.

59. The appropriation would be a "revolving fund rather than one that is gradually exhausted," since most men repaid small loans after returning to Wisconsin. Letter from L. Grieb, Secretary to George Russell, to Emanuel Philip, March 5, 1919; Letter from George Russell to Emanuel Philipp, March 11, 1919, WHS Archives, Mss JC, Emanuel Philipp Papers, Box 6, folder 1.

60. Letter from Orlando Holway to L. C. Whittet, March 7, 1919; Letter from Mary Sabin to L. C. Whittet, March 21, 1919, WHS Archives; Letter from Katherine Frederickson to L. C. Whittet, March 27, 1919; Letter from Katherine Frederickson to L. C. Whittet, March 27, 1919; Letter from Mary Sabin to L. C. Whittet, March 21, 1919, WHS Archives, Mss JC, Emanuel Philipp Papers, Box 6, folder 1.

61. Letter from L. Grieb, Secretary to George Russell, to Emanuel Philipp, March 5, 1919; Letter from George Russell to Emanuel Philipp, March 11, 1919, WHS Archives, Mss JC, Emanuel Philipp Papers, Box 6, folder 1.

62. Letter from Katherine Frederickson to L. C. Whittet, March 27, 1919, WHS Archives, Mss JC, Emanuel Philipp Papers, Box 6, folder 1.

63. Telegram from E. L. Philipp to Mary Sabin, March 14, 1919; Letter from Mary Sabin to Emanuel Philipp, March 26, 1919, WHS Archives, Mss JC, Emanuel Philipp Papers, Box 6, folder 1.

64. Letter from Katherine Frederickson to L. C. Whittet, April 28, 1919; L. C. Whittet to Katherine Frederickson, April 30, 1919, WHS Archives, Mss JC, Emanuel Philipp Papers, Box 6, folder 2.

65. Both the Executive II Wilhelmina and the Battleship Georgia were diverted to Boston, at which point the men were sent to Camp Devens, west of Boston. Still, other men arrived in New York on May 5, 6, and 10. Memoranda, undated [May 1, 1919]; Telegram from Adjutant General Harris to Adjutant General Holway, May 2, 1919, WHS Archives, Mss JC, Emanuel Philipp Papers, Box 6, folder 2.

66. G. Earl Wallis, "Major O'Connell Lauds Madison Heroes," *Wisconsin State Journal*, May 6, 1919.

67. "Governor in Visit to Camp Welcomes Men," *Capital Times*, May 7, 1919.

68. "Madison Boys Leave Merrit Thursday," *Wisconsin State Journal*, May 7, 1919, Letter from Katherine Frederickson to L. C. Whittet, April 28, 1919; Letter from C. C. Smith to Lt. Col. James McCully, May 14, 1919, WHS Archives, Mss JC, Emanuel Philipp Papers, Box 6, folder 2.

69. Additionally, volunteers had paid nearly one hundred in-person visits to men in hospitals. "Report of Work Done at Headquarters up to June 1st, 1919," Wisconsin Headquarters, Hall of States, WHS Archives, Mss JC, Emanuel Philipp Papers, Box 6, folder 2.

70. "Report of Work Done at Headquarters up to July 1st, 1919," Wisconsin Headquarters, Hall of States, WHS Archives, Mss JC, Emanuel Philipp Papers, Box 6, folder 2.

71. "Madison Boys Leave Merrit Thursday," *Wisconsin State Journal*, May 7, 1919.

72. "Wisconsin Committee to Welcome Returning Soldiers," WHS Archives, Series 304, MAD 4/44/I1; "Report of Work Done at Headquarters up to July 1st, 1919," Wisconsin Headquarters, Hall of States, WHS Archives, Mss JC, Emanuel Philipp Papers, Box 6, folder 2. For more on the Winter Garden, see William D. Miller, *Pretty Bubbles in the Air: America in 1919* (Urbana, IL: University of Illinois Press, 1991), 109/113.

73. "Report of Work Done at Headquarters up to July 1st, 1919," Wisconsin Headquarters, Hall of States, WHS Archives, Mss JC, Emanuel Philipp Papers, Box 6, folder 2.

74. G. Earl Wallis, "Major O'Connell Lauds Madison Heroes," *Wisconsin State Journal*, May 6, 1919.

75. Ibid.

76. Letter from Mary Sabin to Emanuel Philipp, April 8, 1919, WHS Archives, Mss JC, Emanuel Philipp Papers, Box 6, folder 2.

77. Letter from Orlando Holway to Emanuel Philipp, March 31, 1919, WHS Archives, Mss JC, Emanuel Philipp Papers, Box 6, folder 1.

78. A grateful Dostal later wrote a letter of thanks, promising to pay the money back. Letter from Katherine Frederickson to Emanuel Philipp, June 2, 1919; Letter from Katherine Frederickson to Emanuel Philipp, June 17, 1919, WHS Archives, Mss JC, Emanuel Philipp Papers, Box 6, folder 2.

79. "Report of Work Done at Headquarters up to June 1st, 1919," Wisconsin Headquarters, Hall of States, WHS Archives, Mss JC, Emanuel Philipp Papers, Box 6, folder 2.

80. Letter from Katherine Frederickson to L. C. Whittet, April 23, 1919, WHS Archives, Mss JC, Emanuel Philipp Papers, Box 6, folder 2.

81. Unsigned letter to Katherine Frederickson, April 25, 1919, WHS Archives, Mss JC, Emanuel Philipp Papers, Box 6, folder 2.

82. Telegram from Katherine Frederickson to Emanuel Philip, May 27, 1919, WHS Archives, Mss JC, Emanuel Philipp Papers, Box 6, folder 2.

83. Letter from Katherine Frederickson to Emanuel Philipp, June 2, 1919, WHS Archives, Mss JC, Emanuel Philipp Papers, Box 6, folder 2.

84. Letter from Anna Simon to Katherine Frederickson, June 9, 1919, WHS Archives, Mss JC, Emanuel Philipp Papers, Box 6, folder 2.

85. Sam Simon to unnamed recipient, June 10, 1919, WHS Archives, Mss JC, Emanuel Philipp Papers, Box 6, folder 2.

86. "Report of Work Done at Headquarters up to July 1st, 1919," Wisconsin Headquarters, Hall of States, WHS Archives, Mss JC, Emanuel Philipp Papers, Box 6, folder 2.

87. Sam Simon to unnamed recipient, June 9, 1919; Sam Simon to unnamed recipient, June 10, 1919, WHS Archives, Mss JC, Emanuel Philipp Papers, Box 6, folder 2.

88. Letter from John Kronberger to Mrs. B. R. Clawson, June 14, 1919, WHS Archives, Mss JC, Emanuel Philipp Papers, Box 6, folder 2.

89. Letter from W. C. Smith to Katherine Frederickson, May 22, 1919, WHS Archives, Mss JC, Emanuel Philipp Papers, Box 6, folder 2.

90. L. C. Whittet to Katherine Frederickson, May 15, 1919, WHS Archives, Mss JC, Emanuel Philipp Papers, Box 6, folder 2. Additional appropriations were enacted under Chapter 387, Laws of 1919.

91. The welcome effort formally ceased on September 15.

92. See, for example, "Chapter 2: An Uneasy Peace Comes to Wisconsin" in Glad, *History of Wisconsin, Volume 5*, 55–82.

93. News of the governor's inauguration would be overshadowed by the death of former president Theodore Roosevelt. "Gov. Philipp Begins his Third Term," *Capital Times*, January 6, 1919.

94. "Philipp Proposes State Fair Wages Board for Future," *La Crosse Tribune and Leader Press*, January 9, 1919.

95. The front page of the *Journal* provided a useful summary of his points. "What Governor Advocates in Message," *Wisconsin State Journal*, January 9, 1919.

96. "Under the Big Dome," *Wisconsin State Journal*, January 9, 1919.

97. "Avalanche of Bills on Final Assembly Day," *Capital Times*, February 12, 1919.

98. Policymakers in Washington, D.C., frequently deployed the term "reconstruction" following the war to encompass a broad range of policies—especially nationalizing industry, reforming labor practice, and investing government resources in infrastructure—that would remake the country anew. But little would come of the so-called Reconstruction Congress of 1919, which reasserted the pre-war status quo. See Noggle, *Intro the Twenties*, 44–53; Chapter 5 of Kennedy, *Over Here*.

99. This committee had formed as the result of a resolution adopted during the February 1918 special session. Roy P. Wilcox, Chairman, "Report of Special Legislative Committee on Reconstruction," filed in Wisconsin State Legislature, February 5, 1919, WHS, Government Documents, Z3 Rec.1 1919.

100. Granted, newspapers—as we will discuss later—were highly politicized, and often subsidized in part or full by elected officials who used them as mouthpieces to advocate for certain policies. "In Mid-June" (Editorial), *Wisconsin State Journal*, June 11, 1919.

101. "Asks State to Give Soldiers Bonus," *Wisconsin State Journal*, February 13, 1919.

102. Unemployment rates among servicemen exceeded 40 percent according to a 1919 estimate by the War Department. Nancy Gentile Ford, "'Put Fighting Blood in Your Business': The U.S. War Department and the Reemployment of World War I Soldiers," in *Veterans' Policies, Veterans' Politics: New Perspectives on Veterans in the Modern United States*, ed. Stephen R. Ortiz (University Press of Florida, 2014), 121. Still, the federal government would soon cease job placement services provided through the U.S. Employment Service, despite warnings from Wisconsin employers that doing so would wreak "extreme hardship on returning soldiers." WHS Archives, Series 1702 MAD 3/43/B6, "Emergency employment situation in Wisconsin, 1918–1919." On U.S. Employment Service functions, see Henry P. Guzda, "The U.S. Employment Service at 50: It too had to wait its turn," Monthly Labor Review (June 1983), 12–19.

103. Letter from Charles McCarthy to Fred Keppel, Third Assistant Secretary of War, February 17, 1919, WHS Archives, Mss KU Series A, Charles McCarthy Papers, Box 18, folder 1.

104. John M. Kinder, *Paying With Their Bodies: American War and the Problem of the Disabled Veteran* (Chicago: University of Chicago Press, 2015), 5; John Maurice Clark, *The Costs of the World War to the American People* (New Haven: Yale University Press, 1931), 188.

105. For a broad discussion of rehabilitation's goals, see Beth Linker, *War's Waste: Rehabilitation in World War I America* (Chicago: University of Chicago Press, 2011).

106. The act was initially passed in June but became known as the War Risk Insurance Act following October 1917 revisions. Quoted from the original in Samuel McCune Lindsay, "Purpose and Scope of War Risk Insurance," *The Annals of the American Academy of Political and Social Science* 79 (1918), 52–68: 53. See also Jessica Adler, *Burdens of War: Creating the United States Veterans Health System* (Baltimore: The Johns Hopkins University Press, 2017), 13; Kinder, *Paying with Their Bodies*, 63–4; Thomas B. Love, "The Social Significance of War Risk Insurance," *The Annals of the American Academy of Political and Social Science* 79 (1918), 46–51. Within five years of the armistice, the Bureau of War Risk Insurance would field more than 930,000 applications from policyholders. K. Walter Hickel, "Medicine, Bureaucracy, and Social Welfare: The Politics of Disability Compensation for American Veterans of World War I," in *The New Disability History: American Perspectives*, ed. Paul K. Longmore and Lauri Umansky (New York: New York University Press, 2001), 236–267: 238.

107. Kathlyn L. Reed, "History of Federal Legislation for Persons With Disabilities," *American Journal of Occupational Therapy* 46 (1992), 397–408, 398; Vocational Rehabilitation Act, Pub. L. No. 65-178 (1918), https://www.loc.gov; "Vocational Education," Monthly Labor Review 10 (1920), 138–153: 139.

108. "Every Disabled Soldier and Sailor Should Know," *Journal of Education* 89 (May 22, 1919), 578.

109. "Asks State to Give Soldiers Bonus," *Wisconsin State Journal*, February 13, 1919.

110. "Rough notes on Senator Cunningham's bill providing three month's pay for soldiers," February 13, 1919, WHS Archives, Mss KU Series A, Charles McCarthy Papers, Box 25.

111. "Under the Big Dome," *Wisconsin State Journal*, March 6, 1919.

112. *Capital Times* buried the bill's introduction in a short notice on the 7th page of the paper. "3 Months' Pay for Soldiers," *Capital Times*, February 12, 1919. See also Fred Holmes, "Has Plan to Aid Returning Yanks," *Stevens Point Daily Journal*, February 17, 1919.

113. Paul F. Hunter, ed., *The Wisconsin Blue Book, 1919* (Madison: Democrat Printing Co. State Printer, 1919), 467.

114. "Senate Reconsiders 'Secrecy' Vote," *Wisconsin State Journal*, March 5, 1919.

115. Both houses passed resolutions like 1919 Joint Resolution 13, "Urging the Congress of the United States to enact necessary legislation to allow soldiers, sailors and marines, who served in the war against Germany and her allies, six months' pay after discharge."

116. Fred Holmes, "Has Plan to Aid Returning Yanks," *Stevens Point Daily Journal*, February 17, 1919.

117. Chapter 55, Laws of 1919. *Laws Passed by the Special Session of the Sixteenth Legislative Assembly of the State of North Dakota* (Bismarck, ND: Bismarck Tribune Company, 1920), 94–5.

118. "League State Has Real Soldier Plan," *Nonpartisan Leader*, March 10, 1919, LRB, Theobald Legislative Library Clippings Collection, 359.82 Z.

119. "Land Clearing Aid Asked in House," *Wisconsin State Journal*, February 11, 1919.

120. The bill would appropriate $500,000 to create a Wisconsin Soldier Settlement fund. "Asks State to Give Soldiers Bonus," *Wisconsin State Journal*, February 13, 1919.

121. "The Soldier and His Bonus Are Live Subjects," *Oshkosh Daily Northwestern*, June 4, 1919; "Senate to Pass on the Soldiers' Bonus Law," *Racine Journal News*, June 13, 1919.

122. "Rough notes of a bill," n.d. [1919]; "A Bill," n.d. [1919], WHS Archives, Mss KU, Charles McCarthy Papers, Box 25. Early drafts included nurses but later drafts excluded them from eligibility.

123. "Soldier Air Bill Is Returned," *Wisconsin State Journal*, May 13, 1919.

124. Letter from H. T. Christenson to Emanuel Philipp, March 21, 1919, WHS Archives, Mss JC, Emanuel Philipp Papers, Box 6, folder 1. Ultimately, American farmers would raise wages 40 percent to compete with industrial pay. Harry Schwartz, "Farm Labor Adjustments after World War I," *Journal of Farm Economics* 25 (February 1943), 269–277: 269.

125. See Euring Brian Roberts, "Theodore Vilter," unpublished manuscript accessed on May 11, 2018, http://www.hevac-heritage.org.

126. Letters from Neele B. Neelen to Theodore Vilter, March 20 and 21, 1919, WHS Archives, Mss JC, Emanuel Philipp Papers, Box 6, folder 1.

127. Letter from Theodore Vilter to Emanuel Philipp, April 4, 1919; letter from Theodore Vilter to George Bruce, April 4, 1919, WHS Archives, Mss JC, Emanuel Philipp Papers, Box 6, folder 2.

128. Letter from Theodore Vilter to Emanuel Philipp, March 22, 1919, WHS Archives, Mss JC, Emanuel Philipp Papers, Box 6, folder 1.

129. Letter from Ira L. Peterson to Katherine Frederickson, May 14, 1919, WHS Archives, Mss JC, Emanuel Philipp Papers, Box 6, folder 2.

130. Letter from John Kronberger to Mrs. B. R. Clawson, June 14, 1919, WHS Archives, Mss JC, Emanuel Philipp Papers, Box 6, folder 2.

131. "Bonus Assured Badger Fighters," *Racine Journal News*, April 11, 1919.

132. "A large delegation of soldiers" had already attended earlier March hearings of the same bills. "Soldiers to Attend Senate Hearing," *Wisconsin State Journal*, March 10, 1919.

133. Katherine Frederickson reported that she had been "asked repeatedly" about the bonus. Letter from Katherine Frederickson to L. C. Whittet, April 23, 1919, WHS Archives, Mss JC, Emanuel Philipp Papers, Box 6, folder 2.

134. "Soldier Bonus Problem," *Grand Rapids Tribune*, May 1, 1919.

135. "Soldier Defends State Bonus for Returning Yanks," *Milwaukee Journal*, June 1, 1919.

136. Unsigned letter to Katherine Frederickson, April 25, 1919, WHS Archives, Mss JC, Emanuel Philipp Papers, Box 6, folder 2.

137. "Soldier Bonus Problem," *Grand Rapids Tribune*, May 1, 1919.

138. B. A. Hoffman, "State Drive to Pay War Bonuses," *Wisconsin State Journal*, May 20, 1919. See also, "Show Appreciation," *Door County Advocate*, May 23, 1919.

139. "Report of the Sub-committee of the Finance Committee of the Wisconsin Legislature Relating to Bonuses for Soldiers and Sailors," (Madison, WI: Assembly Chief Clerk, May 27, 1919).

140. "Two Vital Bills Up Before Senate," *Wisconsin State Journal*, June 8, 1919; "Senate to Pass on the Soldiers' Bonus Law," *Racine Journal News*, June 13, 1919.

141. 1919 Joint Resolution 85, WHS Archives, Mss 403, Charles Crownhart Papers, Box 7, folder 1.

142. "Will Print Copies of Soldier Aid Plan," *Capital Times*, May 23, 1919; "To Ask $500,000 of Senate to Aid Crippled Soldiers," *Eau Claire Leader*, May 27, 1919.

143. Chapter 452, Laws of 1919.

144. Chapter 42, published March 28, 1919, "relating to temporary aid for honorably discharged indigent soldiers, sailors and marines"; Chapter 18, published March 14, 1919, "relating to preference to veterans in the civil service."

145. Chapter 427, Laws of 1919.

146. Chapter 336, published June 20, 1919; Chapter 598, published July 24, 1919.

147. Fred Holmes, "Philipp Requests Referendum Vote on Soldier Bonus," *La Crosse Tribune and Leader Press*, June 30, 1919.

148. Holmes served as a correspondent for 19 or 31 papers covering the capitol. Paul F. Hunter, ed., *The Wisconsin Blue Book, 1919* (Madison: Democrat Printing Co. State Printer, 1919), 450; Biographical note, WHS Archives, Mss OC, Fred Holmes Papers, Box 1. Like most reporters of this period, he was closely associated with a political faction and openly advocated for policies and politicians. Burt, "'Conflicts of Interests,'" 97–8.

149. "Double Cross is Charged in Soldier Bill," *Capital Times*, July 9, 1919, TBL, Clippings Collection, 359.82 Z.

150. "Referendum Bonus Plan Hits Snag," *Wisconsin State Journal*, July 9, 1919, LRB, Theobald Legislative Library Clippings Collection, 359.82 Z.

151. Former state representative William Evjue founded his paper in 1917 as a statement of protest against the *Wisconsin State Journal* after that paper withdrew its support from Robert La Follette due to his anti-war position. The paper frequently broadcast progressive criticisms of stalwart Republicans like Governor Philipp. Elizabeth Burt, "'Conflicts of Interests': Covering Reform in the Wisconsin Press, 1910–1920," *Journalism History* 26 (Fall 2000), 95–107: 101. See also Falk, "Public Opinion in Wisconsin during World War I," 396; William Theodore Evjue, *A Fighting Editor* (Wells Print Company, 1968), 301.

152. "Finis," *Capital Times*, July 14, 1919; "Starting to Gig," *Capital Times*, July 18, 1919, LRB, Theobald Legislative Library Clippings Collection, 359.82 Z.

153. "Substitute Dies After Fights," *Wisconsin State Journal*, July 15, 1919, LRB, Theobald Legislative Library Clippings Collection, 359.82 Z.

154. Later, Markham would dispute the stenographer's account of his remarks in an effort to reverse the damage these remarks caused. "Substitute Dies After Fights," *Wisconsin State Journal*, July 15, 1919, LRB, Theobald Legislative Library Clippings Collection, 359.82 Z.

155. "Mr. Markham Forgets, Say Returned Badger Heroes," *Wisconsin State Journal*, July 16, 1919, LRB, Theobald Legislative Library Clippings Collection, 359.82 Z.

156. Chapter 667, Laws of 1919. *The Wisconsin Blue Book, 1962* (Madison: State of Wisconsin, 1962), 232–233.

157. "Bill Passes Both Houses Minus Fight," *Capital Times*, July 16, 1919, LRB, Theobald Legislative Library Clippings Collection, 359.82 Z.

158. "Legislators Plan Bonus Campaign," *Milwaukee Sentinel*, July 22, 1919, LRB, Theobald Legislative Library Clippings Collection, 359.82 Z.

159. "Bonus for Wisconsin Soldiers Has Indorsement [*sic*] of Legislative Members," *Milwaukee Sentinel*, August 26, 1919, LRB, Theobald Legislative Library Clippings Collection, 359.82 Z.

160. "Starting to Gig," *Capital Times*, July 18, 1919, LRB, Theobald Legislative Library Clippings Collection, 359.82 Z.

161. "The Soldier Speaks to You," *Wisconsin State Journal*, August 26, 1919, LRB, Theobald Legislative Library Clippings Collection, 359.82 Z.

162. *The Wisconsin Blue Book, 1962* (Madison: State of Wisconsin, 1962), 234.

163. "Soldiers Bonus Vote Carries," *Milwaukee Journal*, September 3, 1919. See also "State Vote Is 5 to 1 For Bonus," *Wisconsin State Journal*, September 3, 1919, LRB, Theobald Legislative Library Clippings Collection, 359.82 Z.

164. Fred Holmes, "Has Plan to Aid Returning Yanks," *Stevens Point Daily Journal*, February 17, 1919.

165. Emanuel L. Philipp, "The Governor's Veto Message," July 19, 1919, TBL, Clippings Collection, 359.6 Z. This request was formally affirmed by law: Chapter 699, published August 8, 1919, "relating to the adjutant general and the securing of information concerning Wisconsin residents who fought in the war against Germany and her allies."

166. Circular letter from O. Holway, Wisconsin Adjutant General, to all Wisconsin veterans, dated July 25, 1919, LRB, Theobald Legislative Library Clippings Collection, 359.6 Z.

167. "Educational Opportunities for Soldiers and Sailors," *Wisconsin's Educational Horizon* 2 (September 1919), 9–10.

168. "Soldiers Favor Education Bill," *Wisconsin News*, August 19, 1919, LRB, Theobald Legislative Library, Clippings Collection, 359.6 Z.

169. "Educational Opportunities for Soldiers and Sailors," *Wisconsin's Educational Horizon* 2 (September 1919), 23–24.

170. "Educational Opportunities for Soldiers and Sailors," *Wisconsin's Educational Horizon* 2 (September 1919).

171. "Soldiers' Aid Bill Passes Legislature," *Milwaukee Sentinel*, September 6, 1919, LRB, Theobald Legislative Library, Clippings Collection, 359.6 Z.

172. *The Wisconsin Blue Book, 1917* (Madison: Democrat Printing Company State Printer, 1917), 25–6.

173. "Bill Passes Both Houses Minus Fight," *Capital Times*, July 16, 1919, "State Bonus to Soldiers Held Valid," *Wisconsin State Journal*, August 25, 1919, LRB, Theobald Legislative Library Clippings Collection, 359.82 Z.

174. Copy of letter from John J. Blaine to Orin [*sic*] Fletcher, April 2, 1919, WHS Archives, Mss KU, Charles McCarthy Papers, Box 25.

175. Fred Holmes, "Senate Has Measure to Provide Lands for Returned Troops," *Janesville Daily Gazette*, April 9, 1919. See also "Fletcher Offers Bill of Sweeping Character to Give Soldiers Land," *La Crosse Tribune and Leader*

Press, April 11, 1919; copy of letter from John J. Blaine to Orin [*sic*] Fletcher, April 2, 1919, WHS Archives, Mss KU, Charles McCarthy Papers, Box 25.

176. "Fletcher of *La Crosse Fathers Bill to Give Land to Veterans of the State*," La Crosse Tribune and Leader Press, June 19, 1919; William Kirsch "Fletcher Bill Is Unconstitutional? Faces Veto, Rumor," *Wisconsin State Journal*, July 29, 1919.

177. "Wisconsin Legislature Completes Its Work and Adjourns Sine Die," *Racine Journal News*, July 31, 1919.

178. Fred L. Holmes, "Start Action in Supreme Court Today," *Capital Times*, October 15, 1919, LRB, Theobald Legislative Library Clippings Collection, 359.82 Z.

179. "Bonus Test Leader Has 200-LB Smile," *Wisconsin State Journal*, October 16, 1919.

180. Fred L. Holmes, "Start Action in Supreme Court Today," *Capital Times*, October 15, 1919; "Titles of Bonus Test Cases Now in Supreme Court," unidentified newspaper, n.d., LRB, Theobald Legislative Library Clippings Collection, 359.82 Z.

181. "Bonus Test Leader Has 200-LB Smile," *Wisconsin State Journal*, October 16, 1919.

182. Fred L. Holmes, "Start Action in Supreme Court Today," *Capital Times*, October 15, 1919, LRB, Theobald Legislative Library Clippings Collection, 359.82 Z.

183. John J. Blaine, "Rewarding Soldiers By Bonus," *La Follette Magazine* 11 (December 1919), LRB, Theobald Legislative Library Clippings Collection, 359.82 Z.

184. "Who Is to Blame," *Capital Times*, October 16, 1919; "The Governor Is Peeved," *Capital Times*, October 17, 1919, LRB, TLL Clippings Collection, 359.82 Z.

185. Letter from E. L. Philipp to William T. Evjue, dated October 15, 1919, as published in *Capital Times*, October 16, 1919, LRB, TLL Clippings Collection, 359.82 Z. The governor later tried to emphasize these points by promising to call a special session if the laws were declared unconstitutional after all. "Assurance Is Given on Soldier Aid," *Wisconsin State Journal*, October 16, 1919, LRB, TLL Clippings Collection, 359.82 Z.

186. "Pay the Soldiers Now," *Wisconsin State Journal*, October 23, 1919, LRB, TLL Clippings Collection, 359.82 Z.

187. "A Tragedy and a Disgrace," *Capital Times*, October 25, 1919, LRB, TLL Clippings Collection, 359.82 Z.

188. Letter from H. H. Dean to Charles Crownhart, November 19, 1919, WHS Archives, Mss 403, Charles Crownhart Papers, Box 7, folder 1.

189. "Sovereign: The People or the Profiteers," *Capital Times*, October 20, 1919, LRB, TLL Clippings Collection, 359.82 Z.

190. "Pay the Soldiers Now," *Wisconsin State Journal*, October 23, 1919, LRB, TLL Clippings Collection, 359.82 Z.

191. See, for example, Carl R. Fish, "Back to Peace in 1865," *American Historical Review* 24 (1919), 435–443.

192. "Ex-Soldiers Pack Chambers at Bonus Case," *The Madison Democrat*, November 9, 1919, LRB, TLL Clippings Collection, 359.82 Z.

193. "Here Is Gist of Arguments of Lawyers in Bonus Cases," *The Madison Democrat*, November 9, 1919, LRB, TLL Clippings Collection, 359.82 Z.

194. "Here Is Gist of Arguments of Lawyers in Bonus Cases," *The Madison Democrat*, November 9, 1919, LRB, TLL Clippings Collection, 359.82 Z.

195. "Ex-Soldiers Pack Chambers at Bonus Case," *The Madison Democrat*, November 9, 1919, LRB, TLL Clippings Collection, 359.82 Z. Some of these men had already enrolled at the University of Wisconsin, but received no monthly reimbursement while the legislation remained in legal limbo. "Nye Act Students May Be Forced Out," *Milwaukee Sentinel*, October 21, 1919, LRB, TLL Clippings Collection, 359.6 Z.

196. "State of Wisconsin in Supreme Court, August Term 1919" No. 160-161 (Madison, WI: Blied Printing Company, 1919), 2–6, WHS Archives, Mss 403, Charles Crownhart Papers, Box 7, folder 1. Crownhart had read Legislative Reference Library materials on court challenges to similar legislation in Connecticut (where a bonus was struck down) and Massachusetts (where a bonus was maintained). Irma Hochstein, "Citations and Quotations From Various Cases in the States of the U.S. Upholding or Disputing the Constitutionality of Acts Appropriating Money Rewards to Soldiers in Recognition for Services" (Madison, WI: Wisconsin Legislative Reference Library, October 1919), WHS Archives, Mss 403, Charles Crownhart Papers, Box 7, folder 1.

197. "Ex-Soldiers Pack Chambers at Bonus Case," *The Madison Democrat*, November 9, 1919, LRB, TLL Clippings Collection, 359.82 Z.

198. State Ex. Rel. Atwood v. Johnson, State Treasurer, et al. Supreme Court of Wisconsin, 170 Wis. 218, 175 N.W. 589 (1919).

199. "Legality of School Aid Explained," *Wisconsin State Journal*, February 10, 1920, LRB, TLL Clippings Collection, 359.6 Z.

200. State Ex Rel. Atwood v. Johnson, State Treasurer, et al. Supreme Court of Wisconsin, 170 Wis. 251, 176 N.W. 224 (1920).

201. Letter from H. H. Dean to Charles Crownhart, November 19, 1919, WHS Archives, Mss 403, Charles Crownhart Papers, Box 7, folder 1.

202. "Education as Wars Reward: A Wisconsin Contribution," *Wisconsin's Educational Horizon* 2 (January 1920), 1.

203. As of 1862, federal laws provided pensions for men with disabilities "incurred as a direct consequence of . . . military duty. Within decades, the federal pension extended to include nearly all veterans with the Dependent Pension Act of 1890. Theda Skocpol, *Protecting Soldiers and Mothers: The Political Origins of Social Policy in the United States* (Cambridge: Harvard University Press, 1996), 126, 108–110. See also Mary Dearing, *Veterans in Politics: The Story of the G.A.R.* (Baton Rouge, LA: Louisiana State University Press, 1952); William H. Glasson, *Federal Military Pensions in the United States* (New York: Oxford University Press, 1918).

204. Various factors—illiteracy, poverty, and unfamiliarity with pension laws—raised barriers to successful pension applications. See WHS Archives, Series 1927, Box 29 (January 1879).

205. In the post–Civil War era, the adjutant general organized pension-related correspondence by date, which meant that letters pertaining to a single soldier were often scattered across multiple places, rather than an individual file.

206. WHS Archives, Series 1567: Disabled soldiers correspondence, 1919–1923, Box 1, case #24 (Gustave Hildebrandt).

207. WHS Archives, Series 1567: Disabled soldiers correspondence, 1919–1923, Box 1, case #4 (August Buchholz).

208. WHS Archives, Series 1567: Disabled soldiers correspondence, 1919–1923, Box 1, case #17 (Oscar Dettmeyer).

209. Hickel, "Medicine, Bureaucracy, and Social Welfare," 236.

210. WHS Archives, Series 1567: Disabled soldiers correspondence, 1919–1923, Box 1, case #35 (Leo Kwasniewski).

211. Jennifer D. Keene, *Doughboys, the Great War, and the Remaking of America* (Baltimore: The Johns Hopkins University Press, 2001), 162–3. For a concise summary of bonus legislation's proponents and opponents, see Chapter 5 of John F. Cogan, *The High Cost of Good Intentions: A History of U.S. Federal Entitlement Programs* (Stanford: Stanford University Press, 2017). See also Chapter 1 of Glenn Altschuler and Stuart Blumin, *The GI Bill: The New Deal for Veterans* (Oxford: Oxford University Press, 2009).

212. The 1924 World War Adjusted Compensation Act provided for deferred compensation to veterans, but provoked protest in 1932 when veterans sought to cash out benefits that would otherwise only be available upon death or in the year 1945. In 1936, Congress successfully overrode President Roosevelt's veto to enable veterans to access their benefits early. Altschuler, *The GI Bill*, 35–6. For more on veterans' groups efforts to lobby for these measures, see Stephen R. Ortiz, "The 'New Deal' for Veterans: The Economy Act, the Veterans of Foreign wars, and the Origins of New Deal Dissent," The Journal of Military History 70 (2006), 415–438.

213. Keene, *Doughboys*, 182.

214. Henry D. Morgan, "Financing of State Veterans' Bonuses," *National Tax Journal* 1 (1938), 233–240: 1.

215. H. Rupert Theobald, editor, *The Wisconsin Blue Book, 1962* (Madison: State of Wisconsin, 1962), 231–238.

216. These funds were deposited in the Service Recognition Fund. "A thumbnail history of Wisconsin veterans' legislation" (Madison: Legislative Reference Bureau, 1998), 4.

217. This law made no mention of veterans, except to credit them for financing the facility. Later legislation allied the hospital more closely to veterans' causes, including Chapter 63, Laws of 1929, "giving war veterans a preference in admission to the Wisconsin general hospital," and Chapter 146, Laws of 1929, providing veterans care "at the clinic cost rate" at the general hospital. Later laws revised rates related to these provisions (Chapter 330, Laws of 1939; Chapter 507, Laws of 1957), and 1985 Act 29 repealed these provisions.

218. Some of the surplus tax revenues would be used to construct Camp Minnewawa, Chapter 356, Laws of 1925, "a restoration camp for sick and disabled veterans of the world war."

219. Their efforts resulted in Chapter 442, Laws of 1933, asserting the state's "obligation to provide hospitalization for all indigent, disabled and honorably discharged soldiers, sailors, marines or nurses." H. Rupert Theobald, editor. *The Wisconsin Blue Book, 1962* (Madison: State of Wisconsin, 1962), 231–238.

220. "Education as Wars Reward: A Wisconsin Contribution," *Wisconsin's Educational Horizon* 2 (January 1920), 16–17.

221. Later reports noted that the Board of Education had not originally intended to place participants at out-of-state institutions, but did so from October 1919 onward in cases where students could not access the specific kind of education or training they sought within the state. In some instance, high-volume of out-of-state placement alerted the University of Wisconsin to program areas it might expand, like architecture and veterinary science. "Education as Wars Reward: A Wisconsin Contribution," *Wisconsin's Educational Horizon* 2 (January 1920), 17–19;

"The First Year of Wisconsin's Educational Bonus Law, 1919–1920," *Wisconsin's Educational Horizon* 3 (November 1920), 10/19–23.

222. "The First Year of Wisconsin's Educational Bonus Law, 1919–1920," *Wisconsin's Educational Horizon* 3 (November 1920), 45.

223. "Special Classes and Short Courses for Ex-Service Men and Women," *Wisconsin's Educational Horizon* 3 (September 1920), 2–4.

224. "The First Year of Wisconsin's Educational Bonus Law, 1919–1920," 25–6.

225. UW-Madison Archives, Series 5/2/7 S41M9: World War I Bonus Records, 1919–1939.

226. "The First Year of Wisconsin's Educational Bonus Law, 1919–1920," 26–7.

227. Iowa law (Chapter 160, Laws of 1919); Minnesota law (Chapter 338, Laws of 1919); Hazel Rasmussen, "Digest of Legislation of Various States Relating to State Aid to Soldiers and Sailors to Enable Such Persons to Secure or Complete an Education, With Complete Text of Laws of Minnesota, North Dakota and Oregon Appended" (Madison, WI: Legislative Reference Library, August 22, 1919), WHS Archives, Mss 403, Charles Crownhart Papers, Box 7, folder 1.

228. Oregon's policy provided up to $25/month and no more than $200/year for up to four years ($800 total versus $1080 in Wisconsin). "Educational Opportunities for Soldiers and Sailors," *Wisconsin's Educational Horizon* 2 (September 1919), 30. See also "Soldiers' Bonus in Foreign Countries: Extracts from Magazine Articles," Legislative Reference Library (Madison, WI: 1921).

229. "Education as Wars Reward: A Wisconsin Contribution," *Wisconsin's Educational Horizon* 2 (January 1920), 17.

230. William E. Hannan, "What States Have Done for Soldiers: While Federal Program Is Still in Doubt Bonuses and Educational Opportunities Have Been Provided in Sixteen States," *New York Times*, 5 September 1920 (New York, NY), XX2. See also "College Education Bonus: Wisconsin Offers It to Ex-Service Men Who Are Eligible," *New York Times*, 5 September 1920 (New York, NY), W22.

231. Bruce R. McCoy, "Making the Soldier Bonus a State Investment: Wisconsin Paying Its Debt of Gratitude by Educational Plan," *Dearborn Independent*, February 11, 1922.

232. Altschuler, *The GI Bill*, 36.

233. "Free Correspondence Study Courses for Ex-Service Men and Women," *Wisconsin's Educational Horizon* 3 (September 1920), 4–6.

234. "Educational Opportunities for Soldiers and Sailors," *Wisconsin's Educational Horizon* 2 (September 1919), 1–3.

235. Keene, *Doughboys*, 205.

236. Letter from Ira L. Peterson to Katherine Frederickson, May 14, 1919, WHS Archives, Mss JC, Emanuel Philipp Papers, Box 6, folder 2.

237. The hospital is now known as the Mendota Mental Health Institute but was formerly called the Wisconsin Hospital for the Insane. "Peterson Thanked for Entertaining War Vets," *Capital Times*, January 2, 1924.

238. Peterson had worked at the YMCA in Madison before the war began. *Wisconsin State World: Young Men's Christian Associations* 29 (1915), 17. He frequently organized Memorial Day events in Brainerd, MN, and returned to Whitewater as a guest speaker at the Whitewater Legion in 1962. "First Duty of American Legion," *Brainerd Daily Dispatch*, May 29, 1929; "Graves Decorated Beautifully for Rites Tomorrow," *Brainerd Daily Dispatch*, May 29, 1930; "Teacher Is New Head of Whitewater Legion," *Janesville Daily Gazette*, June 8, 1962.

239. "Obituaries: Lt. Col. I. L. Peterson," *Janesville Daily Gazette*, August 31, 1965. See also Ancestry.com. *U.S., Find A Grave Index, 1600s–Current* [database online] (Provo, UT: Ancestry.com Operations, Inc., 2012).

240. "Legality of School Aid Explained," *Wisconsin State Journal*, February 10, 1920, TBL, Clippings Collection, 359.6 Z.

Legislation to combat the opioid crisis in Wisconsin

BY LAUREN JACKSON

Overview

For several years, the epidemic of opioid abuse has been prominent in news headlines and legislative agendas across the country. Many health, law enforcement, and political institutions have labeled the significant impact of opioid abuse on human lives and state resources a crisis. The Wisconsin Legislature responded in a bipartisan manner over the past three sessions by passing large packages of legislation aimed at opioid abuse treatment, prevention, and awareness. This report discusses the opioid epidemic at the national and state levels and the Wisconsin Legislature's response in the 2013, 2015, and 2017 legislative sessions.

Background on the opioid crisis

From the late 1990s to the present, the sale of opioid analgesics, overdose deaths, and substance abuse–related treatment involving opioid analgesics have risen rapidly.[1] Opioids include illegal substances like heroin as well as prescription drugs such as fentanyl, oxycodone, hydrocodone, codeine, and morphine. Popular painkillers like OxyContin and Vicodin combine an opioid with another analgesic such as aspirin, acetaminophen, or ibuprofen. During the mid-1990s, opioid analgesics, specifically OxyContin, were marketed to doctors as being less likely to be abused;[2] as a result, prescriptions for such drugs soared during this period. The federal government began to take notice of this rise, as well as the potential for abuse, in the early 2000s.[3] By the time the epidemic was widely reported by the media, the abuse of opioid painkillers had taken a widespread toll across communities large and small, affecting drug overdose rates, crime rates, and medical costs.

Reports from the Centers for Disease Control on the increase of both opioid prescriptions and opioid drug abuse prompted several states to act. In Wisconsin, the State Council on Alcohol and Other Drug Abuse (SCAODA) organized workgroups on both prescription drug abuse (in 2010) and related heroin abuse (2013). Reports issued in January 2012[4] and July 2014[5] identified issues concerning opioid abuse and called for strategies and community efforts to combat the epidemic. While many of the suggested strategies involved implementation on a local scale, others required statewide action and indicated the need for state legislation. Representative John Nygren (R-89), from Marinette, took the lead in the legislature; northern Wisconsin was hit particularly hard by the opioid abuse epidemic, and the representative's own family was affected by the crisis.[6] The assembly used these personal experiences and the information gathered in the SCAODA reports to create a package of proposals to present to the full legislature aimed at stemming the tide of opioid-related drug abuse.

2013-14 legislation

The first wave of legislation representing the Wisconsin Legislature's strategy to combat opioid abuse was introduced in a group of bills presented as the HOPE (Heroin and Opioid Prevention and Education) Agenda. Representative Nygren was the lead author of the seven bills in the package: four were introduced in October 2013, three were introduced in January 2014, and all carried bipartisan support. These bills proposed laws that mirrored the strategies and recommendations proposed in the SCAODA reports on prescription drug abuse and heroin abuse. The first four bills focused on responding to incidents of opioid overdose, addressing issues related to obtaining and disposing of opioid prescriptions, and expanding or creating treatment programs on the local level.

Arguably the most high-profile bill of the first HOPE Agenda package was 2013 Assembly Bill 446 (2013 Wisconsin Act 200), which focused on the administration of Naloxone, commercially known as Narcan, by safety officers and Good Samaritans. Naloxone is an opioid antagonist used in emergency situations to counter the effects of an opioid overdose. The bill, as amended in committee, provided the opportunity for training first responders, emergency medical technicians, and police and fire officers in the administration of the drug as a way to lower the mortality rate of heroin and prescription opioid overdoses; in addition, it required EMTs to carry a supply of Naloxone and keep records of how it is administered. The bill also allowed physicians to prescribe Naloxone to trained individuals who were attempting to assist a person at risk of an overdose. Finally, it created immunity from civil and criminal liability for prescribers and administrators of Naloxone, with certain exceptions.

Like Assembly Bill 446, 2013 Assembly Bill 447 (2013 Wisconsin Act 194) took on an immediate problem of the opioid epidemic: addressing the fear of criminal prosecution that is sometimes a hindrance to those who would otherwise summon help for another person in the event of an overdose.[7] In its amended form, the bill provided a person immunity from criminal prosecution for possession of a controlled substance and possession of drug paraphernalia if that person acted as an "aider" to someone suffering from a drug overdose. This meant that a companion of someone experiencing an overdose would be immune from possession charges if he or she took the overdosing person to the emergency room or called emergency services in order to aid them. Known popularly as the "911 Good Samaritan law," the proposal was developed from the recommendations of SCAODA and the Department of Justice.[8]

The remaining two bills introduced in October, 2013 Assembly Bills 445 (2013 Wisconsin Act 199) and 448 (2013 Wisconsin Act 198), focused on preventing prescription opioid abuse. In AB 445, lawmakers grappled with prescription fraud by requiring a person to show identification when picking up a prescription for a schedule II or schedule III drug.[9] In addition, the bill required that the pharmacist record the name of the person and send that information to the Prescription Drug Monitoring Program (PDMP)[10], which maintains information on all monitored prescription drugs dispensed to patients in the state.[11] Misuse of prescriptions was also addressed in AB 448, which authorized and regulated drug disposal programs through the Department of Justice and local governments. Drug disposal programs are aimed at getting unused prescription painkillers out of the hands of children or household members that would misuse them, since many people do not consider prescription drugs to be as dangerous as illegal narcotics and might use leftover doses of the drugs in a non-prescribed manner.

The final three bills of the first HOPE Agenda package focused on the ways that people who abuse opioids are sanctioned or receive treatment. Assembly Bills 668 and 701 expanded existing treatment programs by increasing funding and created pilot treatment programs in underserved areas. Assembly Bill 702 aimed to create a system of short-term but impactful sanctions for habitual drug offenders who violate probation or parole by possessing drugs.

In 2013 Assembly Bill 668 (2013 Wisconsin Act 197), the legislature used programs that the state already had in place to help solve the opioid crisis. Treatment Alternatives and Diversion (TAD) programs overseen by the Department of Justice (DOJ) have been an effective tool against drug and alcohol abuse. In TAD programs, district attorneys and judges may offer someone the opportunity to receive substance abuse treatment instead of jail or prison time. The TAD programs' potential was expanded under AB 668, which allotted an additional $1.5 million for the DOJ to provide grants to counties for TAD programs. The bill also required reports from both counties and the DOJ to continue to determine the effectiveness of the TAD programs.

The opioid epidemic affected all areas of the state, but hit rural areas of Wisconsin especially hard because many of those areas did not have treatment networks already established or as easily accessible as urban areas. 2013 Assembly Bill 701 (2013 Wisconsin Act 195) identified the rural areas most in need of help and created pilot programs to treat individuals from those communities who had opi-oid abuse issues. The proposal required the Department of Health Services (DHS) to establish two or three regional treatment programs in "rural and underserved, high-need areas." The department used specific benchmarks to determine which areas of the state to define as "rural," "underserved," and "high-need."[12] Once it determined which areas fit those guidelines, the DHS then reviewed proposals to create treatment programs. The treatment programs had to include specific components, including (1) an assessment of individuals in need to determine the type of treatment that was required and, if necessary, the transitioning of those individuals to a licensed residential program; (2) a residential program that provided counseling, medication-assisted treatment, and abstinence-based treatment; and (3) the transition of individuals, once they completed treatment, to county-based or private care. The programs were not allowed to offer methadone treatment. Contracts with three treatment organizations, located in northeastern, north central, and northwestern Wisconsin, were executed in June 2015.[13]

While treatment and diversion options for people with substance abuse issues were the focus of 2013 Assembly Bills 668 and 701, Assembly Bill 702 (2013 Wis-consin Act 196) created "swift and certain" punishments for those on extended supervision, parole, or probation, or subject to a deferred prosecution agreement, who possessed or attempted to possess a narcotic drug under schedule I or II. The bill, fashioned after a Hawaiian initiative, required the Department of Corrections (DOC) to create a system of short-term sanctions for violations of release and to take into account several factors when using such sanctions, including the objective in imposing the sanction, correction of the offender's behavior, the safety of the community, flexibility, and the impact on the offender's family members and his or her employment. This "rapid response model" is based on research that finds that an offender who knows a violation has immediate consequences is less likely to reoffend.[14]

All seven bills of the 2013–14 HOPE Agenda passed unanimously or on a voice vote in both houses of the legislature, and all seven were signed by the governor on April 7, 2014. The legislation passed in the 2013 session created or expanded laws, programs, and grants, establishing a baseline from which the state could confront the opioid crisis on many levels, from prevention to treatment. But that work was only just beginning, as an epidemic decades in the making would require the implementation of many different strategies and a combination of government and community resources.

2015–16 legislation

A second package of HOPE Agenda bills was introduced in the 2015 session, with

Representative Nygren again the lead author. The package built on the legislation of the previous session, expanding access to Naloxone, broadening the reporting requirements for the PDMP, allocating more money to TAD programs, and creating a number of other laws to allow the state to rein in opioid abuse in Wisconsin.

Access to the opioid antagonist Naloxone was further expanded under 2015 Assembly Bill 427 (2015 Wisconsin Act 115). The bill authorized a physician to issue a standing order to one or more persons and allowed a pharmacist to dispense Naloxone under that standing order. The law essentially allows a pharmacy to sell Naloxone to patients without a specific written prescription and further clarifies the intentions of the 2013 law.[15] The bill was signed into law on December 8, 2015. In the fall of 2017, the chief medical officer at the DHS signed a statewide standing order for Wisconsin pharmacies, effective September 2017.[16]

2015 legislation increased the use of Wisconsin's PDMP to monitor prescription opioid use in Wisconsin. Three bills were introduced to specify what information must be submitted to the PDMP, and by whom, and how the Controlled Substances Board (CSB) was to use the information that was collected. Under 2015 Assembly Bill 364 (2015 Wisconsin Act 266), the amount of time that physicians have to report that a prescription was filled was shortened from seven days to twenty-four hours. This measure was to help prevent "doctor-shopping" by patients attempting to fill their prescription at more than one pharmacy before anything was noticed in the PDMP system.[17] The bill also required practitioners to review the records of a patient in the PDMP before issuing an opioid prescription. That provision will sunset in April 2020. Other parts of the bill specified how and when information gathered by the PDMP could be disclosed to law enforcement, medical professionals, and certain other individuals. This bill and several others in the 2015–16 HOPE Agenda package were signed into law on March 17, 2016.

Similarly, 2015 Assembly Bill 365 (2015 Wisconsin Act 268) required law enforcement officers to report to the PDMP the inappropriate or illegal use of monitored prescription drugs, opioid-related drug overdoses, and reports of stolen prescription drugs. The report must include names and birthdates of the individuals involved. The PDMP must then disclose that information to the relevant practitioners, pharmacists, and others.

2015 Assembly Bill 766 (2015 Wisconsin Act 267) tasked the CSB with reporting the PDMP-collected data. A quarterly review of the PDMP with actual and projected outcomes, as well as quarterly and annual reports on the results of the quarterly reviews, must be submitted to the Department of Safety and Professional Services (DSPS) until the end of 2020. Contracting with an analytics firm, the CSB will use the PDMP data to "detect problematic behaviors" of doctors, pharmacists, and patients related to opioid prescriptions. In order to deal with the "problematic" behaviors detected by the PDMP data, 2015 Assembly Bill 660 (2015 Wisconsin Act 269) allowed several of the licensing boards under the umbrella of DSPS, including the Medical Examining Board, to create best practices for prescribing controlled substances. The goal was to reduce the "overprescribing" of opioids by medical professionals.[18] The Medical Examining Board published its opioid prescribing guidelines in August 2017.[19] The guidelines recommended that if physicians prescribe opioids for treating acute pain, they do so only in low doses, and in most cases for fewer than three days. It also discouraged the use of oxycodone due to studies indicating its addictive qualities.

In an effort to prevent the proliferation of "pill mills" in the state,[20] 2015 Assembly Bill 366 (2015 Wisconsin Act 265) gave the DHS oversight of pain management clinics. The bill generally defined a "pain clinic" as a privately owned facility that devotes the majority of its practice to pain management and prescribes opioids for that purpose, with certain exceptions. Further, the bill gave the DHS the authority to set certification and operation requirements for pain clinics. The DHS can also penalize pain clinics that no longer comply with the certification rules by revoking their certification and imposing a $1,000 forfeiture per day for continued violations. The law also specifies that pain clinics may accept only a traceable method of payment from patients.

The legislature also gathered more information from methadone clinics in the state. Methadone is a prescribed drug used to treat substance abuse patients by tapering them off of opioid narcotics. Because of the nature of their work, methadone clinics have the ability to provide a wealth of information related to opioid substance abusers' behavior and their treatment outcomes. 2015 Assembly Bill 367 (2015 Wisconsin Act 262) requires methadone clinics to annually send information to the DHS[21] related to staffing ratios at each clinic; relapse rates; how far patients are traveling to get to the clinic; the number of patients receiving behavioral health services in addition to methadone treatment; and other relevant statistical information. The clinics must ensure that individual patients cannot be identified in these reports.

The 2015 HOPE Agenda package also expanded treatment options for those dealing with opioid substance abuse by providing further funding for TAD programs and aligning Wisconsin statutes on opioid treatment services with federal standards. 2015 Assembly Bill 657 (2015 Wisconsin Act 388) transferred $2 million from the DHS to the DOJ in the 2015–16 fiscal year to use as grant money for TAD programs. The law also specified that a TAD program cannot prohibit a person from participating in the program if that person is using an FDA-approved medication for the treatment of substance abuse. 2015 Assembly Bill 659 (2015 Wisconsin Act 263) updated Wisconsin's oversight of opioid treatment programs, as state statutes were previously more stringent than federal regulations. Under prior DHS rules, opioid treatment services were certified for two years, compared to three years under federal rules; DHS rules also required such services to directly employ all counselors, while federal rules allowed for substance abuse counseling services to be contracted out. The law also removed DHS restrictions on where and how long a patient receives treatment.

Assembly Bill 658 (2015 Wisconsin Act 264) was also introduced in the 2015 legislative session and prohibited the use of a masking agent in order to pass a lawfully administered drug test. The penalty for using, possessing, or advertising a masking agent is a fine up to $500, 30 days' imprisonment, or both. People who deliver or manufacture a masking agent can receive up to a $1,000 fine, 90 days in jail, or both.

Though the HOPE Agenda bills were the primary tool used to address the opioid epidemic, the legislature also used its budgetary approval power. Sections of the 2015–17 budget act (2015 Wisconsin Act 55) provided funds to support substance abuse programs. For example, the budget allocated $5,386,300 in the 2016–17 fiscal year to extend Wisconsin Medicaid coverage to residential substance abuse services.[22] This extension of services was based on the idea that the living environment of someone in recovery contributes significantly to his or her chances of successfully changing habits.[23] In addition, the DOC was charged with implementing a pilot program for offenders with an opiate addiction. The program would provide these offenders with a monthly Vivitrol injection alongside other rehabilitation programming and treatments. The budget appropriated $1,670,400 ($876,700 per fiscal year) for this purpose for 2015–17 and placed it in the Joint Committee on Finance's (JCF) supplemental appropriation. Upon submitting a detailed plan for the pilot program, the DOC could request the release of funds from the JCF.[24] The DOC submitted its plan in a report on December 9, 2015.

Tomah VA scandal

While bipartisan work in the legislature was addressing the opioid crisis, a scandal broke concerning the Tomah Veterans Administration Hospital in west-central Wisconsin. In January 2015, the Center for Investigative Reporting published a story on the surge of prescriptions for opioids under the then-chief of staff, as well as the death of a patient who was reported to be on more than a dozen drugs.[25] The report described a culture of fear among employees that kept them from questioning the use of prescription narcotics and complaints of overmedicated patients who were drowsy or fell asleep during therapy sessions. Two families believed their sons had died because of the amount of drugs given to them by doctors at the Tomah VA. According to the report, prescriptions for opiates such as hydrocodone, oxycodone, methadone, and morphine rose from 50,000 in 2004 to 712,000 in 2012. This news story was a reflection of larger issues faced by the Veterans Administration in recent years, as well as the nationwide scourge of opioid painkiller addiction, and it also shone a light on how invasive and damaging the epidemic had become at the local level. It was affecting chronic pain patients and their families in communities around the state of Wisconsin.

The scandal evoked responses at the state and federal levels. Congressional hearings were called for and eventually held in late March 2015, with both of Wisconsin's U.S. senators allowed to participate in the questioning.[26] It was also reported by the La Crosse Tribune on March 14 that several congressional offices had been contacted by whistleblowers regarding the prescription opioid issues at Tomah well before 2015, but staffers either failed to notify the congressperson or senator or mishandled the information. The Office of Inspector General at the Veterans Administration was also faulted for how it handled its investigation into the whistleblower allegations. Many other hearings and investigations were opened as a result of the revelations about the Tomah VA, and the publicity surrounding the scandal gave new urgency to the efforts of state government to face the issue of opioid abuse.

Governor's task force on opioid abuse and special session

With the final piece of legislation of the 2015–16 HOPE Agenda signed in April 2016, several state efforts to combat the opioid epidemic were well on their way to making a difference in communities around the state. With more state funds and better data resources, the DHS and the DOJ could begin to measure treatment efforts. But, as the Tomah VA scandal demonstrated, the work on the opioid crisis was still ongoing. In early 2016, the National Governor's Association (NGA) began a coordinated effort to reduce the use of opioid painkillers by developing prescribing protocols. In July 2016, the Association announced that 46 governors, including Wisconsin Governor Scott Walker, had signed "A Compact to Fight Opioid Addiction," committing the signing states to developing prescription guidelines, raising awareness of the issue through various channels of communication, and reducing barriers to treatment services.[27]

In September 2016, the governor issued an executive order creating the Governor's Task Force on Opioid Abuse. The governor appointed Representative Nygren and Lieutenant Governor Rebecca Kleefisch as co-chairs of the task force; they were to lead a group that included the attorney general; the secretaries of the Departments of Corrections, Health Services, and Safety and Professional Services; the Commissioner of Insurance; members of the legislature from each party (Senator Leah Vukmir, Senator Janet Bewley, and Representative Jill Billings); members of law enforcement and public health and state medical societies and organizations; and residents of Wisconsin personally affected by the opioid crisis.[28] The task force was charged with advising and assisting the governor and coordinating the fight against the opioid epidemic. To gather information, the task force held meetings in Green Bay, Westin, La Crosse, and Madison in 2016 and in Milwaukee, Minocqua, Wausau, and again Madison in 2017.

In addition to the task force, Executive Order #214 called on the state health officer to issue a public health advisory on opioid abuse. The advisory was issued "to inform the public of the alarming statistics" related to the opioid crisis.[29] In the executive order, the DHS was also directed to use its powers under the statutes[30] "to do what is reasonable and necessary for the prevention and suppression of opioid abuse." The DHS was also ordered to provide staff support to the task force. A total of eight state agencies were required to develop "agency steering committees" to develop a strategic plan to address opioid abuse and coordinate with the task force.

The task force submitted a report to the governor in January 2017 with a list of recommendations for tackling the opioid crisis. The recommendations offered ideas for legislation but also for programs, funding, and grants at the state and local levels, actions that could be initiated at the executive agency level, and community and medical industry best practices. The recommendations built on both the achievements of the HOPE Agenda and the information received by the task force in 2016. As a direct result of the task force report, Governor Walker issued Executive Order #230, calling for a special session of the legislature focused on opioid abuse. The eleven points enumerated in the executive order mirrored the report's recommendation and were all introduced as separate pieces of legislation. The special session convened in January 2017 and concluded in June 2017. All eleven bills passed, and they were signed on July 17, 2017.

Special Session Assembly Bill 1 (2017 Wisconsin Act 29) provided civil immunity for school employees to administer Naloxone to students experiencing an overdose. The bill was based on statutes that allow school personnel to administer epinephrine in the case of anaphylactic shock.[31] It also built on the HOPE Agenda's 2013 911 Good Samaritan law. The original bill was amended to include residence hall directors employed by the UW System, the Technical College System, and private colleges. Special Session Assembly Bill 3 (2017 Wisconsin Act 33) expanded the 2013 911 Good Samaritan law by extending immunity to the "aided" (the person experiencing an overdose) from revocation of parole, probation, or extended supervision if that person completed a treatment program or, if a program was not available or was financially prohibitive, agreed to spend 15

drug trafficking. The law also appropriated $500,000 in federal grant money in the 2018–19 fiscal year for programs to provide evidence-based substance abuse prevention to at-risk children and their families. Additionally, the law authorized two additional attorney positions in the DOJ to assist district attorneys in prosecuting drug-related offenses. Finally, the law created a provision that allows the courts to order a person convicted under the Uniform Controlled Substances Act to attend a victim impact panel that demonstrates the adverse effects of substance abuse. The second law, 2017 Assembly Bill 907 (2017 Wisconsin Act 262), focused on health care providers and education on substance abuse. The law specified who is allowed to treat alcohol and substance abuse as a specialty. It also created the Behavioral Health Review Committee appointed by the DSPS to semiannually review the requirements to obtain a license in substance abuse counseling, social work, marriage and family therapy, or certain other professions in the behavioral health field. It also provided the Department of Children and Families with $50,000 to develop an online resource for social workers who deal with substance abuse. Further, the law provided $250,000 in the 2018–19 fiscal year to increase the number of students in graduate psychiatric nursing education at the University of Wisconsin–Madison, creating more opportunities for people to become mental health professionals. It also required school boards to incorporate prescription drug abuse awareness into health instruction programs. Both bills were signed into law in April 2018, bringing the total number of opioid-related laws enacted under the HOPE Agenda to 30.[40]

Through innovative diversion programs, legislation, and administrative directives, the legislative, executive, and judicial branches are continually working together to respond to the opioid crisis. The legislature's role will continue to be vital, as funding programs through the budget and through grant moneys will be a significant factor in determining who gets treatment and how that treatment is administered. This collaborative effort has led the federal government to look to Wisconsin for strategies to implement in the wake of the opioid crisis.[41] The bipartisan efforts within the Wisconsin Legislature have contributed to a wave of innovative actions to reduce the devastation caused by opioid abuse in America and have confronted an expansive, complex issue that continues to deeply affect people around the state. ☒

NOTES

1. Centers for Disease Control, "Vital Signs: Overdoses of Prescription Opioid Pain Relievers—United States, 1999–2008," November 4, 2011, https://www.cdc.gov/mmwr/preview/mmwrhtml/mm6043a4.htm?s_cid=mm6043a4_w.

2. Esch, Caitlin, "How one sentence helped set off the opioid crisis," Marketplace, December 13, 2017, https://www.marketplace.org/2017/12/13/health-care/uncertain-hour/opioid.

3. U.S. Government Accountability Office, *Prescription Drugs: OxyContin Abuse and Diversion and Efforts to Address the Problem*, GAO-04-110, December 2003, https://www.gao.gov/new.items/d04110.pdf.

4. Wisconsin State Council on Alcohol and Other Drug Abuse, Prevention Committee, Controlled Substances Workgroup, *Reducing Wisconsin's Prescription Drug Abuse: A Call to Action*, January 2012, https://scaoda.wisconsin.gov/scfiles/prevspf/FINAL01032012CSWReport.pdf.

5. Wisconsin State Council on Alcohol and Other Drug Abuse, Prevention Committee, Heroin Ad-hoc Committee, *Wisconsin's Heroin Epidemic: Strategies and Solutions*, July 2014, https://scaoda.wisconsin.gov/scfiles/docs/SCAODAHeroinReportFinal063014.pdf.

6. Opoien, Jessie, "Led by state Rep. John Nygren, Wisconsin families caught in heroin's grasp fight back," *The Capital Times*, December 2, 2015.

7. Harsdorf, Sheila, testimony on 2013 Assembly Bill 447, hearing materials submitted to Legislative Council, January 9, 2014, 6.

8. Nygren, John, testimony on 2013 Assembly Bill 447, hearing materials submitted to Legislative Council, January 9, 2014, 3.

9. "Schedule" refers to the lists in Chapter 961, Wisconsin Statutes, *Uniform Controlled Substances Act*. Several types of synthetic opiates and substances related to opium can be found in schedules II and III.

10. The PDMP was authorized in 2009 Wisconsin Act 362, and was established by federal funds; it began collecting information and issuing reports in 2013.

11. The requirement to supply the recorded name was implemented in April 2017. Wisconsin Department of Safety and Professional Services, "Wisconsin ePDMP," March 20, 2017, https://content.govdelivery.com/accounts/WIDSPS/bulletins/18d9900.

12. Wisconsin Department of Health Services, *Opioid Treatment Programs: 2016 Report to the Legislature*, April 2016, 3.

13. Ibid., 5.

14. Harsdorf, Sheila, testimony on 2013 Assembly Bill 702, hearing materials submitted to Legislative Council, February 6, 2014, 10.

15. Julal, Nicole, testimony on 2015 Assembly Bill 427, hearing materials submitted to Legislative Council, October 22, 2015, 4–5.

16. Wisconsin Department of Health Services, "Opioids: Standing Order for Naloxone," September 2017, https://www.dhs.wisconsin.gov/opioids/standing-order.htm.

17. Schimel, Brad, testimony on 2015 Assembly Bill 364, hearing materials submitted to Legislative Council, October 14, 2015, 5.

18. Governor's Task Force on Opioid Abuse, *Combating Opioid Abuse: A Report to the Governor, 2016*, January 2017, 6.

19. Wisconsin Medical Examining Board, Wisconsin Medical Examining Board Opioid Prescribing Guideline, August 16, 2017.

20. Governor's Task Force on Opioid Abuse, *Combating Opioid Abuse: A Report to the Governor, 2016*, January 2017, 5.

21. DHS certifies methadone treatment centers under s. DHS 75.15, Wisconsin Administrative Code.

22. Sections 1808 and 1809 of 2015 Wisconsin Act 55, http://docs.legis.wisconsin.gov/2015/related/acts/55.

23. Dyck, John, Paper #352, 2015–17 Biennial Budget Papers, Wisconsin Legislative Fiscal Bureau, May 21, 2016.

24. Section 9108 (1d) of 2015 Wisconsin Act 55, http://docs.legis.wisconsin.gov/2015/related/acts/55.

25. Glantz, Aaron, "Opiates handed out like candy to 'doped-up' veterans at Wisconsin VA," *Reveal from the Center for Investigative Reporting*, January 8, 2015, https://www.revealnews.org/article-legacy/opiates-handed-out-like-candy-to-doped-up-veterans-at-wisconsin-va.

26. Gilbert, Craig, "VA official vows accountability at Tomah site," *Milwaukee Journal Sentinel*, March 27, 2015.

27. National Governor's Association, *A Compact to Fight Opioid Addiction*, July 2016, https://www.nga.org/cms/news/2016/opioid-compact.

28. Executive Order #214, issued September 22, 2016.

29. Wisconsin Department of Health Services, Division of Public Health, *Public Health Advisory*, September 26, 2016, https://www.dhs.wisconsin.gov/opioids/opioid-public-health-advisory.pdf.

30. Section 250.04, Wisconsin Statutes.

31. Kulow, Chris, testimony on January 2017 Special Session Assembly Bill 1, hearing materials submitted to Legislative Council, March 2, 2017, 9.

32. The bill also required the aided to be offered a deferred prosecution agreement that included a treatment program.

33. Nygren, John, testimony on January 2017 Special Session Assembly Bill 3, hearing materials submitted to Legislative Council, March 8, 2017, 1.

34. The law was later modified through the budget bill, 2017 Wisconsin Act 59, sections 378k, 2265t, and 9220 (1m).

35. Nygren, John, testimony on January 2017 Special Session Assembly Bill 9, hearing materials submitted to Legislative Council, March 8, 2017, 2.

36. Schimel, Brad, testimony on January 2017 Special Session Assembly Bill 10, hearing materials submitted to Legislative Council, March 2, 2017, 6–7.

37. Nygren, John, testimony on January 2017 Special Session Assembly Bill 5, hearing materials submitted to Legislative Council, March 8, 2017, 1–2.

38. Section 961.22 (2), Wisconsin Statutes.

39. Governor's Task Force on Opioid Abuse, *Combating Opioid Abuse: A Report to the Governor, 2017*, January 2018, 8–9.

40. Office of Representative John Nygren, "HOPE Agenda Bills Signed by Governor Walker" [Press Release], April 9, 2018.

41. WISN 12 News, "Federal government looks to Wisconsin for help in battling opioid epidemic," updated March 21, 2018, http://www.wisn.com/article/federal-government-looks-to-wisconsin-for-help-in-battling-opioid-epidemic/19554241.

Elections in Wisconsin

Purposes and days

Wisconsin holds elections for a variety of purposes and, depending on the purpose, on a variety of days.

FILLING THE STATE'S ELECTIVE OFFICES

To fill its elective offices, Wisconsin holds elections on four regular election days.

The general election. On the Tuesday after the first Monday in November of every even-numbered year, Wisconsin elects individuals to fill its partisan elective offices. The elections held on this day are referred to collectively as the "general election."

The partisan offices in Wisconsin are U.S. senator, U.S. representative, state senator, state representative, governor, lieutenant governor, attorney general, secretary of state, state treasurer, and the county-level offices of district attorney, county clerk, sheriff, clerk of circuit court, register of deeds, treasurer, coroner (in counties that have one), and surveyor (in counties in which the office is elective).

The voters of the entire state elect Wisconsin's U.S. senators, governor, lieutenant governor, attorney general, secretary of state, and state treasurer. The voters of each congressional, senate, and assembly district elect that district's U.S. representative, state senator, or state representative. The voters of each county elect that county's clerk, sheriff, clerk of circuit court, register of deeds, treasurer, coroner, and surveyor and the district attorney for the prosecutorial unit serving the county. (For the prosecutorial unit that serves Menominee and Shawano counties, the voters of both counties elect the district attorney.)

The terms of office for the partisan offices are not all the same length and do not all expire on the same day or in the same year. Accordingly, only some of the partisan offices will be up for election at any particular general election—those, namely, for which the currently running term of office will expire before the next general election is held.

The ballot at each general election lists the offices that are up for election and, under each office, the candidates for the office who have qualified to be listed. Next to each candidate's name, the ballot lists the name of the political party or the principle that the candidate represents.

An individual who wishes to be listed as a candidate on the ballot must file, no later than the June 1 preceding the general election, 1) a declaration of candidacy indicating the office that the individual seeks and the political party or the principle that he or she proposes to represent and 2) nomination papers signed by a prescribed number of voters residing in the governmental jurisdiction or election district that the office serves. In addition, the individual must win a partisan primary election if he or she proposes to represent one of the "recognized" political parties (see below). By contrast, an individual who does not propose to represent a recognized political party will be listed on the general election ballot without participating in a partisan primary election. Such an individual is called an "independent candidate."

The candidate who receives the most votes cast for a particular office at the general election fills that office when the currently running term of office expires.

The partisan primary. Prior to the general election, on the second Tuesday in August of every even-numbered year, Wisconsin holds primary elections to select the individuals who will be listed on the general election ballot as the candidates of the "recognized" political parties. The elections held on this day are referred to collectively as the "partisan primary."

A political party qualifies as a recognized political party in one of three situations:

- A candidate of the political party won at least 1 percent of the votes cast in Wisconsin, either for a statewide office at the last general election at which the office of governor was up for election or for U.S. president at the most recent general election, and the political party was a recognized political party for that election.

- An individual representing the political party as an independent candidate won at least 1 percent of the votes cast in Wisconsin, either for a statewide office at the last general election at which the office of governor was up for election or for U.S. president at the most recent general election, and the political party requests recognized status no later than the April 1 preceding the partisan primary.

- The political party submits, no later than the April 1 preceding the partisan primary, a petition requesting recognized status signed by at least 10,000 Wisconsin voters, including at least 1,000 from each of at least three congressional districts.

A separate primary ballot is prepared for each recognized political party. Each party's ballot lists all of the offices that will be filled at the general election and, under each office, the individuals, if any, who have filed to be candidates for the office and have proposed, in their declarations of candidacy, to represent the party.

A voter at the partisan primary is given a ballot for each of the recognized political parties but can vote on just one of them. The voter can pick any party's ballot for this purpose—voters in Wisconsin are not asked to declare a party affiliation when registering or voting and are not obliged in any other way to pick a particular party's ballot. However, if a voter votes on the ballots of more than one party, none of the voter's votes will be counted.

The individual who receives the most votes cast for a particular office on the ballots of a particular party is selected thereby as that party's candidate for that office at the general election, and his or her name, together with the party's name, will be listed under the office on the general election ballot.

The partisan primary is the exclusive means by which a recognized political party can select a candidate to be listed on the general election ballot. The party must accept as its candidate the individual selected by the voters who vote its ballots. Moreover, if no individual is listed under a particular office on a party's partisan primary ballot (because no one who filed to be a candidate for the office proposed to represent that party), the party will not have a candidate for that office listed on the general election ballot.

The spring election. On the first Tuesday in April of every year, Wisconsin elects individuals to fill its nonpartisan elective offices. The elections held on this day are referred to collectively as the "spring election."

The nonpartisan offices in Wisconsin are state superintendent of public instruction; supreme court justice; court of appeals judge; circuit court judge; county executive (in counties that have one); county supervisor; county comptroller (in Milwaukee); every elective town, village, and city office; and school board member.

The voters of the entire state elect Wisconsin's state superintendent of public instruction and supreme court justices. The voters of each court of appeals district elect that district's judges. The voters of each county elect the county's county executive (if any) and county comptroller (in Milwaukee) and the circuit court judges for the circuit that serves the county. (For circuits that serve two counties, the voters of both counties elect the circuit court judges.) The voters of each county supervisory district elect that district's county supervisor. The voters of each town elect that town's officers. Village trustees and city alders can be elected at large by the voters of the entire village or city or from election districts by the voters residing in each election district. All other village and city officers are elected at large by the voters of the entire village or city. School board members can be elected at large by the voters of the entire school district, from election districts by the voters residing in each election district, or from election districts by the voters of the entire school district.

Just as with the partisan offices, the terms of office for the nonpartisan offices

individuals, one from each of Wisconsin's eight congressional districts and two more from anywhere in the state.

A slate can be determined in two ways. For the candidates of the recognized political parties, the slates are determined at a special convention held at the state capitol on the first Tuesday in the October preceding the general election. The convention consists of certain officials holding partisan elective offices in state government—the governor, lieutenant governor, attorney general, secretary of state, state treasurer, and those state senators whose seats are not up for election— together with the individuals who will be listed on the general election ballot as the candidates of the recognized political parties for the offices of state senator and state representative. The convention participants meet separately according to the parties they belong to, and each party designates a slate of presidential electors for its pair of candidates for president and vice president. The state chair of each party then certifies that party's slate to the Elections Commission.

By contrast, each pair of independent candidates for U.S. president and vice president designates its own slate of presidential electors in its nomination papers.

The slate of presidential electors of the candidate pair that wins the most votes at Wisconsin's general election becomes Wisconsin's delegation to the Electoral College. On the Monday after the second Wednesday in the December following the general election, this delegation assembles in the state capitol and casts its votes as members of that body.

At the spring election. On the day of the spring election, in presidential election years, Wisconsin conducts its presidential preference primary.

This primary is advisory, rather than binding. Wisconsin's voters indicate which individual they would like a political party to select as its candidate for U.S. president, but Wisconsin law does not require the party's Wisconsin members to vote for that individual at the party's national convention. Rather, the party conducts its convention according to rules that it determines for itself, and it can select its presidential candidate using any mechanism it chooses.

A political party qualifies to participate in Wisconsin's presidential preference primary only if 1) it was a recognized political party (see above, page 360) at Wisconsin's last general election, 2) it had a candidate for governor at that election, and that candidate won at least 10 percent of the votes cast for that office, and 3) its state chair certifies to the Elections Commission, no later than the second Tuesday in the December preceding the presidential preference primary, that the party will participate.

A separate presidential preference primary ballot is prepared for each participating political party. Each party's ballot lists the individuals who wish to be selected as the party's candidate for president and have qualified to be listed.

An individual can qualify to be listed on a party's presidential preference primary ballot in two ways. The individual can be certified by a special committee that meets in the state capitol on the first Tuesday in the January preceding the presidential preference primary. This committee consists of the state chair, one national committeeman, and one national committeewoman of each participating political party; the speaker and the minority leader of the state assembly; the president and the minority leader of the state senate; and an additional member selected by the rest of the committee to be its chair. The committee identifies, for each of the participating political parties, the individuals who are generally recognized in the national media as the party's candidates for U.S. president and any additional individuals that the committee believes should be listed as candidates on the party's ballot. The committee must certify these candidates to the Elections Commission no later than the Friday following its meeting.

Alternatively, an individual can submit to the Elections Commission, no later than the last Tuesday in January, a petition requesting to be listed as a candidate on a party's ballot. The petition must be signed by a prescribed number of voters from each of Wisconsin's congressional districts.

A voter at the spring election is given a presidential preference primary ballot for each of the participating political parties but can vote on just one of them. As at the partisan primary, the voter can pick any party's ballot to vote on and is not obliged, based on party affiliation or any other criteria, to pick the ballot of a particular party.

FILLING A MIDTERM VACANCY

A "special election" can be held to fill a midterm vacancy in certain elective offices. This kind of election can be held on one of the four regular election days or on a different day.

A vacancy in the office of U.S. senator, U.S. representative, state senator, or state representative can be filled only by a special election called by the governor. A vacancy in the office of attorney general, state superintendent of public instruction, secretary of state, or state treasurer can be filled either by a special election called by the governor, if the vacancy occurs more than six months before the term of office expires, or by appointment by the governor, regardless of when the vacancy occurs. (A vacancy in the office of supreme court justice, court of appeals judge, circuit court judge, district attorney, sheriff, coroner, or register of deeds can be filled only by appointment by the governor.)

In some county and municipal offices, a vacancy can be filled either by a special election or by appointment, at the discretion of the local governing body.

An individual who wishes to be listed as a candidate on a special election ballot must file a declaration of candidacy and nomination papers and must also win a special primary election if one is required. For a partisan office, a special primary must be held for each of the recognized political parties if it is the case for any one of them that two or more individuals have proposed in their declarations of candidacy to represent it. For a nonpartisan office, a special primary must be held if three or more individuals file to be candidates.

RECALLING AN ELECTED OFFICIAL FROM OFFICE

A "recall election" can be held to decide whether an elected official will be recalled from office before his or her term of office expires and, if so, who will serve in his or her place for the remainder of the term. This kind of election can be held on one of the four regular election days or on a different day. However, a recall election cannot be held before an official has served one year of his or her term. In addition, no more than one recall election can be held for the same official during a single term of office.

A recall election is held only if voters of the governmental jurisdiction or election district that elected an official file a petition to recall the official. The petition must be signed by a number of voters equal to at least 25 percent of the vote cast for governor in the jurisdiction or district at the last election for governor. In addition, if the petition seeks the recall of a city, village, town, or school district official, it must assert a reason that is related to the duties of the office.

Other than the official named in the recall petition, an individual who wishes to be listed as a candidate on a recall election ballot must file a declaration of candidacy and nomination papers and might also have to win a recall primary election if one is required. The official named in the recall petition might similarly have to win a recall primary but otherwise will be listed on the recall election ballot automatically (unless he or she resigns).

For a partisan office, a recall primary must be held for each recognized political party for which it is the case that two or more individuals, who might include the official named in the recall petition, seek to be listed as its candidate on the recall election ballot. If only one individual seeks to be listed as a party's candidate, the individual will be listed as such without a primary being held for that party.

For a nonpartisan office, a recall primary must be held if three or more individuals, who might include the official named in the recall petition, seek to be listed as candidates on the recall election ballot. In contrast to other nonpartisan primaries, if one individual receives over 50 percent of the votes cast at the recall primary, no further election is held, and that individual fills the office for the remaining term.

APPROVING OR REJECTING A PROPOSAL

A "referendum" can be held in Wisconsin to approve or reject a proposal (rather than to choose an individual to fill an office). This kind of election can be held on one of the four regular election days or on a different day.

A referendum can be binding or nonbinding. In the one case, a proposal is implemented automatically if approved by a majority of the voters voting at the referendum; in the other, the voters' approval or rejection of a proposal is merely advisory.

At the state level, binding referenda can be held on proposals 1) to amend the state constitution, 2) to extend the right to vote, 3) to allow the state to contract public debt in excess of the limit imposed by the state constitution, and 4) to permit an act of the legislature to take effect when the legislature has provided that the act's taking effect is contingent upon voter approval.

A referendum ballot presents the referendum proposal in the form of a yes-or-no question, and the voter votes the ballot by marking "yes" or "no." The question on the ballot summarizes the effect of the proposal. The full text of the proposal along with an explanation of its effect must be posted at the polling place.

Administration

The responsibility for administering elections is distributed across several levels of government.

Elections Commission. The state Elections Commission oversees and facilitates the performance of elections-related functions by officials at lower levels of government. The commission:

- Determines the format that must be used for ballots.
- Certifies all equipment and materials used to record votes at elections.
- Trains and certifies officials at lower levels of government.
- Maintains the electronic statewide voter registration list.

The Elections Commission also performs certain functions related to state and national elections. The commission:

- Determines which candidates for elective offices in state and national government qualify to be listed on the ballot. Such candidates must file with the commission their declarations of candidacy, nomination papers, and other documents that demonstrate that they are qualified.
- Tabulates the votes cast in the state at each election held to fill an office in state or national government or to vote on a state referendum.

County clerk. The county clerk performs certain functions related to county, state, and national elections. In Wisconsin's most populous county, Milwaukee, a special commission performs these functions instead. The county clerk:

- Determines which candidates for elective offices in county government qualify to be listed on the ballot. Such candidates must file with the county clerk their declarations of candidacy, nomination papers, and other documents that demonstrate that they are qualified.
- Prepares the ballots for elections held to fill offices in county, state, and national government and to vote on county and state referenda and distributes these ballots to the municipalities (cities, villages, and towns) located within the county.
- Processes voter registrations for county residents who ask to register at the county clerk's office and forwards the information obtained to the municipal clerk of the municipality in which the registrant resides so that the municipal clerk can update the electronic statewide registration list. (In some cases, a county clerk, by agreement with a municipal clerk, acts in place of the municipal clerk as that clerk's agent for the performance of all registration functions, including updating the statewide registration list.)
- Tabulates the votes cast in the county at each election held to fill an office in county, state, or national government or to vote on a county or state referendum.
- Reports to the Elections Commission the votes cast in the county related to a state or national election.

Municipal clerk. The municipal clerk—i.e., the city, village, or town clerk—performs certain functions related to municipal, county, state, and national elections. In Wisconsin's most populous city, Milwaukee, a special commission performs these functions instead. The municipal clerk:

- Determines which candidates for elective offices in municipal government qualify to be listed on the ballot. Such candidates must file with the municipal clerk their declarations of candidacy, nomination papers, and other documents that demonstrate that they are qualified.
- Prepares the ballots for elections held to fill offices in municipal government and to vote on municipal referenda.
- Processes voter registrations for residents of the municipality and updates the electronic statewide registration list to reflect the information obtained.
- Provides the ballots for each election to the voters who desire to vote and receives the ballots back from those voters when they cast them. Only the municipal clerk provides ballots to voters and receives cast ballots back; county clerks and the Elections Commission do not.
- Operates polling places in the municipality on the day of an election. Only the municipal clerk operates polling places; county clerks and the Elections Commission do not.

- Tabulates the votes cast in the municipality at each election held to fill an office in municipal, county, state, or national government or to vote on a municipal, county, or state referendum.
- Reports to the county clerk of each county in which the municipality is located the votes cast in the municipality related to a county, state, or national election.

The municipal clerk also handles most matters related to elections held by school districts that are located in whole or part within the municipality. However, the school district clerk determines which candidates for school district elective offices qualify to be listed on the ballot, and such candidates must file with the school district clerk their declarations of candidacy, nomination papers, and other documents that demonstrate that they are qualified.

Voting

Eligibility. To vote at an election in Wisconsin, an individual must be a U.S. citizen, must be 18 years of age or older, and must reside in the governmental jurisdiction or election district for which the election is held. For example, an individual must reside in a particular county to vote at an election held to elect that county's sheriff and must reside in a particular supervisory district within the county to vote at an election held to elect that district's member of the county board of supervisors.

To establish residence for voting purposes, an individual must reside at the same address for at least ten consecutive days[2] prior to the election at which he or she wishes to vote.

An individual who moves to a new address in Wisconsin during the ten days preceding an election is considered, for that election, to reside at his or her former address if the individual had established residence at the former address before the move. The individual can vote at the election only if the former address is located within the governmental jurisdiction or election district for which the election is held.

An individual who has resided in Wisconsin for less than ten days but who is otherwise eligible to vote can vote for U.S. president and vice president only, under a special procedure.

Certain individuals are not eligible to vote at any election:

- An individual who has been convicted of treason, felony, or bribery, unless the individual has been pardoned or has completed his or her sentence—including any parole, probation, or extended supervision—for the crime.
- An individual who has been adjudicated incompetent by a court, unless the court has determined that the individual is competent to exercise the right to vote.

In addition, an individual is not eligible to vote at a particular election if the individual has bet upon the result of the election.

Registration. Registration is the means by which an individual demonstrates that he or she is eligible to vote. With limited exceptions, an individual must register to vote before he or she will be allowed to vote.

To register, an individual must fill out, sign, and submit a registration form and present acceptable proof of residence.

On the registration form, the individual must:

- Provide his or her name and date of birth; current address; previous address; and the number and expiration date of his or her Wisconsin driver's license or identification card, if any, or the last four digits of his or her social security number, if any.
- Indicate whether he or she has been convicted of a felony for which he or she has not been pardoned and, if so, whether he or she is incarcerated or on parole, probation, or extended supervision.
- Indicate whether he or she is currently registered to vote at an address other than the current one.
- Certify that he or she is a U.S. citizen, will be 18 years of age or over on the day of the next election, and will have resided at his or her current address for at least ten consecutive days prior to that day.

Registrants are not asked to indicate a political party affiliation.

Documents that qualify as proof of residence include:

- A current and valid Wisconsin driver's license or identification card.
- A student identification card accompanied by a fee receipt dated within the preceding nine months.
- A property tax bill or receipt for the current or previous year.
- A bank statement.
- A utility bill for a period beginning no earlier than 90 days before the date of registration.

Through the third Wednesday preceding an election, an eligible voter can register in person at the office of the municipal clerk or county clerk, by mail with the municipal clerk, or via an electronic registration system maintained by the Elections Commission and accessible at myvote.wi.gov.[3] After that Wednesday and through the Friday preceding the election, an eligible voter can register only in person at the office of the municipal clerk (or of the county clerk, if the county clerk is acting as the municipal clerk's agent for registration purposes). After that Friday, an eligible voter who still has not registered and who wishes to vote at the election must register on the day of the election at his or her polling place.

The Elections Commission maintains an electronic list of all eligible voters who are registered to vote in Wisconsin. Every municipal clerk (or county clerk acting as the agent of a municipal clerk) who processes a registration for an eligible voter must update the list via an interface provided by the Elections Commission to reflect the information obtained. The list updates automatically to reflect registrations submitted via the electronic registration system.

An individual who has registered once does not need to register again, unless the individual changes his or her name or address. However, an individual's registration can be suspended if the individual has not voted for four years and fails to respond to a mailed postcard that asks whether he or she wishes to continue his or her registration. The Elections Commission sends out the postcards to such voters every two years.

Military voters who are residents of Wisconsin, as well as their spouses and dependents who reside with or accompany them, are not required to register as a prerequisite to voting. In addition, an individual who has resided in Wisconsin for less than ten days, but who is otherwise eligible to vote, can vote for U.S. president and vice president without being registered. Similarly, a former Wisconsin resident who has moved to another state and is not eligible to vote in the new state can, if he or she is otherwise eligible to vote, vote a Wisconsin absentee ballot for U.S. president and vice president without being registered, during the 24 months after the move.

Voter registration information is generally open to public inspection. However, voters who are victims of certain crimes, such as domestic abuse, sexual assault, and stalking, can request confidential voter status. If a voter qualifies for this status, the municipal clerk updates the electronic statewide registration list to indicate that the voter's registration must be kept confidential and issues a confidential voter identification card to the voter.

Photo identification. With few exceptions,[4] a registered voter (or an eligible voter exempt from registration) who wishes to vote at an election in Wisconsin must present acceptable proof of identification in order to obtain a ballot. In most cases, photo identification is required. Acceptable forms of photo identification include:

- A Wisconsin driver's license or identification card issued by the Wisconsin Department of Transportation.
- A U.S. passport.
- A Veterans Affairs identification card.
- A photo identification card issued by a Wisconsin university, college, or technical college, if certain conditions are satisfied.

Individuals who have a religious objection to being photographed can obtain and present a Wisconsin driver's license or identification card issued without a photo. In addition, an individual who has had to surrender his or her driver's license to a law enforcement officer within 60 days of the election can present in place of the driver's license the citation or notice that he or she received. A confidential voter can present his or her confidential voter identification card instead of photo identification.

Voting at a polling place. Polling places are operated by the municipal clerk and are open for voting only on the day of an election. Each address in a municipality is served by a designated polling place, and a voter can vote only at the polling place that serves his or her address. (If a registered voter has moved within Wisconsin during the ten days preceding an election, he or she is considered to reside at his or her former address for that election and can vote only at the polling place that serves the former address.) Each polling place is staffed by poll workers who have been trained by the municipal clerk. Each polling place is supplied with duplicate "poll lists," which are generated from the electronic statewide registration list, of all eligible voters served by the polling place who registered before the day of the election. Each polling place is also supplied with ballots that are specific to the elections at which voters served by the polling place are eligible to vote.

When an individual comes to a polling place to vote, a poll worker asks him or her to state his or her name and address and to present proof of identification. (A confidential voter can present his or her confidential voter identification card without stating anything or can state just his or her name and the serial number of the card without presenting anything.) A poll worker confirms that the individual's name and address are listed in the poll list, that the name on the proof of identification is consistent with the name on the poll list, and that any photograph on the proof of identification reasonably resembles the individual.[5] The individual is then required to sign the poll list, unless he or she cannot sign due to a physical disability.

Following these preliminaries, the poll workers assign the individual a voter number, record the number on both copies of the poll list, and give the individual a paper ballot or a card that will permit the voter to access an electronic ballot on a voting machine.

The voter takes the ballot or card to a voting booth and marks the paper ballot, or marks an electronic ballot via an interface on a voting machine, to indicate his or her votes. After marking a paper ballot, the voter casts it by depositing it through a slot into a locked ballot box or by feeding it into an optical scanning machine. (An optical scanning machine reads and tabulates electronically the votes marked on a paper ballot and stores the ballot in a locked compartment.) After marking an electronic ballot, the voter verifies a record of his or her votes that the voting machine prints on a paper tape, then casts the ballot by giving a direction via the machine's interface. (A voting machine records a voter's votes in its electronic memory, tabulates them electronically, and advances the paper tape so that the paper record of the voter's votes is stored within a locked compartment.)

Voting by absentee ballot. A registered voter (or an eligible voter exempt from registration) who is unwilling or unable to vote at his or her polling place on the day of an election can vote by absentee ballot instead.

To obtain an absentee ballot, the voter must submit a written request to the municipal clerk. This can be done in person at the clerk's office or at an alternate site designated by the clerk. It can also be done by mail, email, or fax. In-person requests must be made prior to the Monday preceding the election; other requests, in most cases, must be made no later than the Thursday preceding the election.

An in-person requester must present acceptable proof of identification to the municipal clerk or an individual designated by the clerk before he or she will be issued a ballot. Most other requesters must submit a copy of their proof of identification with their request for a ballot.[6]

To cast an absentee ballot, the voter must mark his or her votes on the ballot and seal the marked ballot in a special envelope that is provided with the ballot. The voter must take these actions in the presence of a witness. The voter must also show the unmarked ballot to the witness prior to marking it and must make sure that no one, including the witness, sees the votes that he or she marks. After the ballot is sealed in the special envelope, the voter and the witness must sign a certification that is printed on the special envelope—the voter to attest that he or she is eligible to vote the ballot, will not cast any other ballot at the election, and followed the required procedures in voting the ballot; and the witness to attest that the voter followed the required procedures in voting the ballot. If the ballot was requested in person, the voter must return it before leaving the municipal clerk's office or alternate site. In these cases, the municipal clerk or an individual designated by the clerk serves as the witness. If the ballot was requested in another way, the voter must seal the special envelope containing the ballot in a second envelope[7] and either mail it or deliver it in person to the municipal clerk so that it is received by the municipal clerk no later than the day of the election.

Campaign finance regulation

Wisconsin regulates campaign finance—the spending of money on campaigning and the giving of money to others to spend on campaigning—in several ways:

- Only a particular kind of entity, called a "committee," is allowed to use money that it has accepted from others to engage in campaign spending and campaign giving. If the amount of money exceeds a specified threshold, a committee must register and file reports of its financial activity.[8]

- Limits are placed on who can give money to a committee and how much money can be given.
- Limits are also placed on some campaign spending, and some campaign spending is subject to special disclosure requirements.

Three kinds of campaigning are covered by the regulations: express advocacy related to a candidate for elective office in state or local government,[9] campaigning related to a state or local referendum question, and campaigning related to the recall of an elected official in state or local government.[10]

COMMITTEES

A "committee" is a group of two or more individuals that comes together, or an organization that is established, specifically for the purpose of accepting money from others[11] and using the money for campaign spending and campaign giving. An entity that is not formed specifically for that purpose—for example, a business or a social club—cannot accept money from others to use for campaign spending or campaign giving, and neither can an individual acting alone. However, such an entity or individual could set up a committee as a separate entity that would be able to do those things.

Registration. A committee must register with a state or local filing officer before it accepts or disburses money above a specified threshold. Wisconsin's regulations distinguish seven types of committee (described in a moment) and specify a different threshold for each type. When a committee registers, it must identify the type of committee it is. It must also identify a single depository account that it will use to accept and disburse money and an individual who will be in charge of the account.

A "candidate committee" is a committee formed by a candidate to campaign for his or her election. A candidate cannot accept or disburse any money except through his or her candidate committee. In addition, a candidate can have only one candidate committee for any one office that he or she seeks. However, the candidate can be the individual in charge of the candidate committee depository account. (For that matter, the candidate can be the sole member of the candidate committee—an exception to the rule that a committee consists of two or more individuals.) A candidate's candidate committee must register with the appropriate filing officer[12] as soon as the candidate qualifies[13] to be considered a candidate.

A "political party" is a committee that qualifies for a separate partisan primary ballot—in other words, it is a "recognized" political party. (See page 360, above.) Local affiliates of a recognized political party that are authorized to operate under the same name are also considered political parties. A political party must register with the Ethics Commission before it accepts or disburses any money in a calendar year. (An entity that calls itself a political party, but that does not meet the criteria just described, would have to register as a different type of committee.)

A "legislative campaign committee" is a committee that is formed by state senators or state representatives of a particular political party to support candidates for legislative office by engaging in express advocacy on their behalf and by giving money to their candidate committees. A legislative campaign committee must register with the Ethics Commission before it accepts or disburses any money in a calendar year.

A "political action committee," or "PAC," is a committee, other than a candidate committee, political party, or legislative campaign committee, that 1) is formed to engage in express advocacy; 2) might do this independently or in coordination with a candidate, candidate committee, political party, or legislative campaign committee;[14] 3) might also campaign for and against referenda; and 4) might also give money to other committees. A PAC must register with the Ethics Commission if it accepts or disburses more than $2,500 in a calendar year.

An "independent expenditure committee," or "IEC," is a committee, other than a candidate committee, political party, or legislative campaign committee, that 1) is formed to engage in express advocacy; 2) will do this independently only and not in coordination with a candidate, candidate committee, political party, or legislative campaign committee; 3) might also campaign for and against referenda; and 4) might also give money to other committees, but will not give money to a candidate committee or to a committee that is able to give the money subsequently to a candidate committee. An IEC must register with the Ethics Commission if it accepts or disburses more than $2,500 in a calendar year.

A "referendum committee" is a committee that 1) is formed specifically to campaign for or against a referendum and 2) will not attempt to influence how voters vote with respect to a candidate. A referendum committee must register with the appropriate filing officer[15] if it accepts or disburses more than $10,000 in a calendar year.

A "recall committee" is a committee that is formed specifically to campaign for or against the recall of an elected official. A recall committee must register with the appropriate filing officer[16] if it accepts or disburses more than $2,000 in a calendar year. However, if a recall committee intends to gather signatures on a recall petition, it must register beforehand, regardless of whether it has accepted or disbursed any money.

Reporting financial activity. Each registered committee must file with its filing officer regular reports of its financial activity. Reports are due every January

15 and July 15. A report is also due on the fourth Tuesday in September of an even-numbered year if a committee accepts or disburses money for campaigning related to a partisan office or a referendum that will be held on the day of the partisan primary or general election. Other reports are required in advance of each primary and election with respect to which a committee accepts or disburses money. All of a committee's reports are made public within two days of their filing.

Each report must include, among other things:

- A listing of each gift of money received from an individual, specifying the amount and date of the gift and the name and address of the individual.
- A listing of each gift of money received from a committee, specifying the amount and date of the gift and the name and address of the committee.
- A listing of any other income received from any source, specifying the amount, date, and type of the income and the name and address of the source.
- A listing of each gift of money given to another committee, specifying the amount and date of the gift and the name and address of the committee.
- A listing of each other disbursement of money made to any individual or entity, specifying the amount, date, and purpose of the disbursement and the name and address of the individual or entity.

CAMPAIGN GIVING LIMITS

Campaign giving consists of giving money to a committee (necessarily, since an entity that is not a committee cannot use money given by others for campaigning). Wisconsin's regulations place limits on who can give money to a committee and how much money can be given. The limits apply simultaneously to the giver and the recipient; both are guilty if the latter accepts a gift that violates a limit.

Generally, only individuals and committees are allowed to give money to a committee. However, corporations, labor unions, cooperative associations, and federally recognized American Indian tribes can also give money in certain cases—but not to a candidate committee and not to a committee that is able to give the money subsequently to a candidate committee.

Giving to a candidate committee. An individual can give up to $20,000 to the candidate committee of a candidate for a statewide office (governor, lieutenant governor, attorney general, superintendent of public instruction, secretary of state, state treasurer, or supreme court justice). Other limits apply to other offices, including $2,000 for state senator and $1,000 for state representative.

A candidate committee can give to another candidate committee up to the same amount as an individual can give. However, the candidate committees of candidates who are running together for governor and lieutenant governor can give unlimited amounts to each other.

A candidate can give unlimited amounts to his or her own candidate committee.

A political party or legislative campaign committee can give unlimited amounts to a candidate committee.

A PAC can give up to $86,000 to the candidate committee of a candidate for governor. Other limits apply to other offices, including $26,000 for lieutenant governor; $44,000 for attorney general; $18,000 for superintendent of public instruction, secretary of state, state treasurer, or supreme court justice; $2,000 for state senator; and $1,000 for state representative.

No one else can give money to a candidate committee.

Giving to a political party or legislative campaign committee. An individual, candidate committee, political party, or legislative campaign committee can give unlimited amounts to a political party or a legislative campaign committee.

A PAC can give up to $12,000 in a calendar year to a political party or legislative campaign committee.

No one else can give money to a political party or legislative campaign committee, unless the political party or legislative campaign committee has established a segregated fund of money that will not be spent on express advocacy or given to a candidate committee. An individual, candidate committee, political party, or legislative campaign committee can give unlimited amounts to such a fund. A PAC can give up to $12,000 in a calendar year to such a fund (in addition to the other money it can give to a political party or legislative campaign committee). A corporation, labor union, cooperative association, or American Indian tribe can also give up to $12,000 in a calendar year to such a fund (even though it cannot otherwise give money to a political party or legislative campaign committee).

Giving to a PAC. An individual, candidate committee, political party, legislative campaign committee, or PAC can give unlimited amounts to a PAC. No one else can give money to a PAC.

Giving to an IEC. An individual, candidate committee, political party, legislative campaign committee, PAC, or IEC can give unlimited amounts to an IEC. A corporation, labor union, cooperative association, or American Indian tribe can also give unlimited amounts to an IEC. No one else can give money to an IEC.

Giving to a referendum committee. Individuals and committees can give unlimited amounts to a referendum committee. A corporation, labor union, cooperative association, or American Indian tribe can also give unlimited amounts to a referendum committee. No one else can give money to a referendum committee.

Giving to a recall committee. Individuals and committees other than IECs or referendum committees can give unlimited amounts to a recall committee. No one else can give money to a recall committee.

CAMPAIGN SPENDING LIMITS

Individuals, committees, and entities that are not committees can generally spend unlimited amounts on campaigning that they do themselves. The exception is spending on express advocacy that is coordinated with a candidate, candidate committee, political party, or legislative campaign committee.[17] (See note 14 for the criteria that define coordination.) Spending of this kind is treated as a gift given to the candidate committee of the candidate who is benefitted by the express advocacy. As such, it is subject to the limits that apply to giving to a candidate committee.

CAMPAIGN SPENDING SPECIAL DISCLOSURE REQUIREMENTS

Special disclosures are required for some kinds of campaign spending. These are the only disclosures that individuals and entities that are not committees must make about their campaign spending.[18] Committees, by contrast, must also report their campaign spending in the regular reports they file covering all of their financial activity.

Specific reporting of certain communications. If an individual, PAC, IEC, or entity that is not a committee spends $2,500 or more to make express advocacy communications during the 60 days preceding a primary or election, the individual, PAC, IEC, or entity must report that spending to the Ethics Commission within 72 hours after the first $2,500 has been spent and within 72 hours after any additional expenditure. Reports must specify the date, amount, recipient, and purpose of each expenditure, as well as the name of and office sought by any candidate who is the subject of the express advocacy (but these details are not required for the expenditures made prior to reaching the $2,500 threshold). The reports are made public within two days of their filing.

Candidate committees, political parties, and legislative campaign committees are not required to report these expenditures other than in their regular financial activity reports.

Information required in certain communications. If an individual, committee, or other entity spends money to make an express advocacy communication or to make a communication to influence the outcome of a recall effort, the individual, committee, or entity must include in the communication the phrase, "Paid for by," followed by the name of the individual, committee, or other entity.[19] For individuals and entities that are not committees, this requirement applies only to a communication whose cost exceeds $2,500. BB

NOTES

1. An alternative mechanism exists by which an individual can qualify to be listed on the spring election ballot. A town or village (but no other type of governmental jurisdiction) can hold a special meeting called a caucus to select the individuals who will be the candidates at the spring election for the town's or village's offices. The caucus must be held on or between the January 2 and the January 21 preceding the spring election. The caucus is open to the public, but only the eligible voters of the town or village can participate. The caucus participants propose one or more individuals to be the candidates for each office and vote, if the total number of proposed candidates for a particular office is more than two (or is more than twice the number of seats to be filled), to determine which ones will be the candidates. An individual who is selected at a caucus to be a candidate for a town or village office must subsequently file a declaration of candidacy in order to be listed on the spring election ballot.

2. Wisconsin changed the required number of days of consecutive residence from ten to 28 in 2011, but a U.S. district court found this change to be unconstitutional in 2016. Wisconsin appealed the court's finding, but as of August 2018 the appeal remained pending.

3. To register via the electronic registration system, an individual must possess a current and valid Wisconsin driver's license or identification card. The system requires the individual to enter his or her name, address, and date of birth together with the number of the driver's license or identification card. If the system confirms that the individual's information matches the records of the state Department of Transportation pertaining to the driver's license or identification card, the system permits the individual to register by 1) filling out and submitting an electronic version of the registration form, 2) "signing" the form by authorizing the use of a copy of the signature that he or she provided when applying for the driver's license or identification card, and 3) using as proof of residence the number of his or her driver's license or identification card.

4. Military voters (members of a uniformed service who are residents of Wisconsin and their spouses and dependents who reside with or accompany them) and overseas voters (former Wisconsin residents who no longer reside in the U.S. but remain U.S. citizens) can obtain and vote a Wisconsin absentee ballot without providing proof of identification. Overseas voters are entitled to vote for offices in national government only (U.S. president, vice president, senator, and representative).

5. If an individual's name and address are not listed in the poll list, the poll worker will determine whether the voter is at the wrong polling place or is at the correct polling place but not registered. In the one case, the poll worker will direct the voter to the correct polling place; in the other, the poll worker will tell the voter where to go so that he or she can register.

If an individual's name and address are listed in the poll list but a poll worker believes that the name on the proof of identification is not consistent with the name on the poll list, or that a photograph on the proof of identification does not reasonably resemble the individual, the poll worker must challenge the individual. The individual must reply to the challenge under oath in order to obtain a ballot. If the poll worker does not withdraw the challenge, the individual must also take an oath that he or she is eligible to vote the ballot, and a poll worker must make a note in the poll list and on the ballot before issuing it. The individual's votes will be considered valid unless the election officials responsible for counting the votes determine beyond a reasonable doubt, based on evidence presented, that the individual was not eligible to vote or was not properly registered.

If an individual's name and address are listed in the poll list but the individual is unable or unwilling to present proof of identification, he or she is given an opportunity to cast a provisional ballot, rather than a regular ballot. The voter must sign a certification attesting that he or she is eligible to vote the ballot. The provisional ballot will not be counted unless the voter subsequently presents the proof of identification. The voter can return to the polling place to do this, until 8:00 p.m. when the polls close, or the voter can bring the proof of identification to the municipal clerk's office, until 4:00 p.m. on the Friday following the election.

6. Military and overseas voters are exempt from this requirement. (See note 4.)

7. If the ballot was requested by email or fax, the voter must also include in the second envelope a signed, printed copy of the request.

8. Another kind of entity, called a "conduit," is subject to similar requirements. Conduits do not spend money on campaigning themselves, nor do they give money to others to spend on campaigning. Rather, they hold money on behalf of givers and pass it on to a committee at the direction of those givers.

9. Express advocacy is communication that 1) uses words such as "vote for," "elect," "support," "vote against," "defeat," or "oppose" with reference to a clearly identified candidate and 2) unambiguously relates to the election or defeat of that candidate. Communication that refers to a candidate but that does not qualify as express advocacy would not, by itself, subject the communicator to Wisconsin's regulations, even if the communication was intended to influence voters' opinion of the candidate.

10. Not covered by the regulations is campaigning related to a candidate for elective office in national government. That kind of campaigning is regulated under federal law. There is no national-level referendum or recall process.

11. The money that a committee accepts from others can consist exclusively of money provided by the committee's own members; the committee is an entity distinct from its individual members. A committee is formed, therefore, whenever individuals pool their money to engage in campaign spending or campaign giving, regardless of how informal a decision-making process they follow or how little campaign spending or giving they actually do.

12. The Ethics Commission, if the candidate is seeking office in state government, or a county, municipal, or school district clerk, if the candidate is seeking office in local government.

13. Based on one of the following criteria: 1) filing nomination papers, 2) being certified as the nominee of a political party or a village or town caucus, 3) accepting or disbursing any money in an effort to win a primary or election, or 4) being an incumbent elective office holder.

14. Under Wisconsin law, coordination exists in only two situations: 1) a candidate, candidate committee, political party, or legislative campaign committee communicates directly with an individual or with an entity other than a political party or legislative campaign committee to specifically request that the individual or entity make an expenditure for express advocacy, and the individual or entity explicitly assents before making the expenditure; or 2) a candidate, candidate committee, political party, or legislative campaign committee exercises control over an expenditure made for express advocacy by an individual or by an entity other than a political party or legislative campaign committee or exercises control over the content, timing, location, form, intended audience, number, or frequency of the express advocacy.

15. The Ethics Commission, for a statewide referendum, or a county, municipal, or school district clerk, for a local one.

16. The Ethics Commission, if the petition pertains to an official in state government, or a county, municipal, or school district clerk, if it pertains to an official in local government.

17. Also, some entities that enjoy tax-exempt status under federal law, based on the fact that they have limited themselves to specific activities, would lose that status if they were to spend money on campaigning. In addition, a registered committee cannot spend money on a kind of campaigning that is inconsistent with the type of committee that it has registered as.

18. Campaign giving is a different story. For every gift of money that an individual or entity makes to a committee, the individual or entity must disclose to the committee the information (such as name and address) that the committee needs to complete its financial activity reports, and those reports, in turn, are made public soon after they are filed.

19. An additional phrase—"Not authorized by any candidate or candidate's agent or committee"—must be included in an express advocacy communication that is made independently, rather than in coordination with a candidate, candidate committee, political party, or legislative campaign committee.

Local government in Wisconsin

Government in Wisconsin includes not only the state government, but also numerous local governments that exist and operate under the authority of the state government. Some local governments are "general purpose districts," which have broad authority to administer a particular locale, while others are "special purpose districts," whose authority is limited to the performance of a specific function.

General purpose districts

Counties and municipalities—towns, villages, and cities—are Wisconsin's general purpose districts. The territory of the state is divided into counties, and it is also divided into towns, villages, and cities. Towns lie entirely within the boundaries of counties, but villages and cities can lie across county boundaries.

Historically, counties were created to be administrative subdivisions of the state. Towns were created within counties to enable sparsely populated areas to provide basic services for themselves, whereas villages and cities were created to enable population centers, wherever they had formed, to govern their local affairs.

Today, counties continue to act as the local arm of state government, and towns continue to be providers of basic services, but all general purpose districts have some authority to make decisions about their local affairs.

General purpose districts determine their own budgets and raise money to pay for their operations by establishing fees, imposing property taxes on real property within their boundaries, and incurring debt.

Counties. Wisconsin has 72 counties. County boundaries are drawn by the legislature and specified in state law. County boundary lines generally run north to south and east to west or follow major physical features (such as rivers).

The governing body of a county is the county board. The county board is composed of supervisors who are elected from election districts within the county for two-year terms at the nonpartisan spring election. Each county decides for itself how many supervisors it will have (subject to a statutory maximum that is based on a county's population), and whether their terms will be concurrent or staggered.

In addition to the county board, counties are required to have a central administrative officer. For this purpose, a county can create the office of county executive or county administrator, or it can designate an individual holding an existing elective or appointive office (other than county supervisor) to serve also as the county's administrative coordinator.

population density have been met, the petition is forwarded to the state's Incorporation Review Board. If that board determines that the incorporation is in the public interest, a referendum on the incorporation is held in the territory that is proposed to be incorporated. If the referendum is approved, the city or village is established.

The governing body of a city is the common council, which is composed of alders and, in cities that have one, a mayor. The alders are elected at the nonpartisan spring election. Each city decides for itself how many alders it will have, whether they will be elected at large or from election districts, what the term of office will be, and whether terms will be staggered or concurrent. The mayor is elected at large at the nonpartisan spring election for a term decided by the city. The mayor presides over meetings of the common council but has no vote, except to break a tie.

Cities use two forms of executive organization. In most cities, the mayor is the chief executive officer. The mayor can veto the council's actions and has a general responsibility to ensure that the laws are obeyed and that city officials and employees carry out their duties. Specific responsibilities, however, vary from city to city. In some cities, for example, the mayor proposes an annual budget for the city, but in others the council develops the budget itself. Similarly, the mayor might have authority to appoint many or few of a city's appointive positions.

In place of a mayor, ten cities have created the position of city manager. A city manager is appointed (and can be removed) by the common council. A city manager can attend, but does not preside or vote at, meetings of the council and cannot veto its actions. The responsibilities of a city manager include proposing an annual budget and appointing department heads, unless the common council defines the position differently.

City officers other than alders and the mayor or city manager can be elected or appointed, as decided by the city. If elected, they are elected at the nonpartisan spring election.

The governing body of a village is the village board, which is composed of trustees and a village president. Trustees are elected at the nonpartisan spring election for staggered terms. Each village decides for itself how many trustees it will have, whether they will be elected at large or from election districts, and what the term of office will be. The village president is elected at large at the nonpartisan spring election, for a term decided by the village. The village president presides over meetings of the village board and votes as a trustee. The president also acts on behalf of the board in certain matters.

Villages do not have a separate elected executive officer, but ten villages have created the position of village manager to perform much the same role as a city manager performs in a city. A village manager is appointed (and can be removed) by the village board.

Village officers other than the trustees, president, and village manager (if any) can be elected or appointed, as decided by the village. If elected, they are elected at the nonpartisan spring election.

Cities and villages, like towns, provide basic services. These include fire protection, road maintenance, and police service. To a greater extent than towns or counties, however, cities and villages have broad authority to make local policy. Some powers are granted expressly in state statutes. Among the most characteristic of these are powers related to land use regulation, including authority to make rules that limit land uses in particular areas and that limit the kinds of structures that can be built or maintained in the city or village and authority to grant exceptions to the rules.

Beyond the authority granted in the statutes, however, cities and villages possess "home rule" powers conferred by the state constitution. The home rule provision states that cities and villages have the authority to "determine their local affairs and government, subject only to this constitution and to such enactments of the legislature of statewide concern as with uniformity shall affect every city or every village." While it is not clear exactly what powers the provision grants to cities and villages or to what extent it prohibits the state from restricting local powers, the provision is typically understood to allow cities and villages to take action on local matters without specific authorization from the state. That is, conversely to the situation with towns or counties, cities and villages can take such action unless specifically prohibited from doing so.

An additional power exercised only by cities and villages is the power of annexation: the power to detach territory from a town and attach it to the city or village. There are several different procedures by which an annexation can take place. Usually, all of the owners of property in the territory to be annexed sign on to a petition for annexation that is filed with the annexing city or village. If the petition meets certain statutory requirements and the governing body of the city or village enacts an ordinance approving the annexation, the territory becomes part of the city or village. In most cases, a town has no power to prohibit an annexation of part of its territory (but it can challenge the legality of an annexation in court).

Although cities and villages ordinarily have the same powers and duties, the legislature has imposed special requirements on "1st class" cities, including specific standards for budgeting, public employment, and police and fire department administration. Milwaukee is Wisconsin's only 1st class city currently.

Special purpose districts

Wisconsin has over 1,100 special purpose districts. The legislature has created some special purpose districts directly, and it has also authorized general purpose districts to create certain types of special purpose districts. Although a special purpose district exists only to perform a special function, the scope of its authority and its impact on the people who reside within its jurisdiction can be great. For example, some school districts have jurisdiction over the education of tens of thousands of children and some metropolitan sewerage districts manage sewage for hundreds of thousands of people. Other special purpose districts, however, such as certain public inland lake protection and rehabilitation districts, have authority over a very small geographic area and directly affect only a very small number of people.

School districts. Wisconsin has 443 school districts, which collectively cover the entire territory of the state. District boundaries can be modified, including by subdividing or consolidating existing districts, so long as no territory of the state is left outside of a district. Boundary modifications are typically initiated by the affected districts and might require ratification by referendum. The governing body of a school district is the school board. School board members are elected at the nonpartisan spring election, usually to staggered three-year terms. The number of members on a school board varies between three and eleven, and school board members can be elected at large or from election districts. School districts operate primary and secondary schools and otherwise provide educational services to the children who reside in the district. School districts are authorized to levy property taxes and to incur debt.

Technical college districts. Wisconsin has 16 technical college districts, which collectively cover the entire territory of the state. The number of districts and their boundaries were originally determined by a predecessor of the state Technical College System Board, and that board has the power to reorganize the districts. Technical college districts are governed by boards of nine members who are appointed for staggered three-year terms. Depending on the district, the appointments are made by a committee composed of the county board chairs of the counties that lie within the district or by a committee composed of the school board presidents of the school districts that lie within the district. For the Milwaukee Area Technical College District, the appointing committee is composed of the Milwaukee county executive and the Milwaukee, Ozaukee, and Washington county board chairs. Technical college districts operate technical colleges that provide postsecondary education and occupational training to persons who enroll in their programs. Districts are authorized to charge tuition and other fees, levy property taxes, and incur debt.

Metropolitan sewerage districts. Wisconsin has seven metropolitan sewerage districts. The legislature created the Milwaukee Metropolitan Sewerage District (MMSD) in the Milwaukee area. State law authorizes general purpose districts in the rest of the state to create their own metropolitan sewerage districts.

Sewerage districts plan, design, construct, maintain, and operate sewerage systems for the collection, transmission, disposal, and treatment of both sewage and storm water. An 11-member commission governs the MMSD, and five-member commissions govern other sewerage districts. Commissioners of the MMSD are appointed to staggered three-year terms by officials of the municipalities located in Milwaukee County. Commissioners of other sewerage districts are generally appointed to staggered five-year terms by the county board of the county in which the district is located. Funds for a district's projects and operations are generated from property taxes assessed against property located in the district, from the issuance of bonds, and from user fees that are paid by the individuals and businesses that use the district's services. A large district, like the MMSD, provides services both to people who live within its jurisdiction and to people whose municipalities have contracted with it for its services.

Professional sports team stadium districts. Wisconsin has three professional sports team stadium districts. The Southeast Wisconsin Professional Baseball Park District was created by the legislature in 1995 and was authorized to issue bonds to acquire, construct, own, and operate a baseball park and related facilities. The district built, and is the majority owner of, Miller Park, the home stadium of the Milwaukee Brewers baseball team. To pay off the bonds, and to pay for stadium maintenance, the district is authorized to impose a sales tax within the district's jurisdiction, which consists of the counties of Milwaukee, Ozaukee, Racine, Waukesha, and Washington. The district is governed by a board of 13 members: six appointed by the governor, three for two-year terms and three for four-year terms; two appointed by and serving at the pleasure of the Milwaukee county executive for indefinite terms; and one each appointed by and serving at the pleasure of the Racine county executive, Waukesha county executive, Ozaukee county board chair, Washington county board chair, and Milwaukee mayor.

The Professional Football Stadium District was created by the legislature in 1999 and was authorized to issue bonds to finance the renovation of Lambeau Field, the home stadium of the Green Bay Packers football team. To pay off the bonds, the district was authorized to impose a sales tax within the district's jurisdiction, which consists of Brown County. The sales tax was imposed until September 2015, at which time sufficient money had been collected to repay the bonds and to set aside a required reserve fund. Although its purpose has been carried out, the district continues to exist. The district is governed by a board of seven members who are appointed for concurrent two-year terms by elected local officials, including the mayor of Green Bay and the Brown county executive.

The Wisconsin Center District was created in 1994 by the City of Milwaukee under a state law that permits general purpose districts in the state to create a kind of special purpose district called a local exposition district. The district was authorized to issue bonds to build, own, and operate certain entertainment facilities in Milwaukee. (These facilities are known today as the Milwaukee Theatre, Wisconsin Center, and UW-Milwaukee Panther Arena.) To pay off the bonds, the district is authorized to impose special sales taxes in Milwaukee County on hotel rooms, on food and beverages sold in restaurants and taverns, and on car rentals. Operating revenues of the facilities pay for the district's operations. In 2015, the legislature expanded the district's purpose, altered its governance structure, and authorized it to issue bonds to finance the development and construction of a professional basketball arena for the Milwaukee Bucks basketball team. The state, the City of Milwaukee, and Milwaukee County are required to provide the district the money that the district will need to pay off the bonds. The district is governed by a board of 17 members, including the state assembly speaker and minority leader, the state senate majority leader and minority leader, and appointees of the governor, the Milwaukee mayor, the Milwaukee common council president, and the Milwaukee county executive.

Other special purpose districts. State law also authorizes the creation of other types of special purpose districts. These include agricultural drainage districts, sanitary districts, public inland lake protection and rehabilitation districts, sewer utility districts, solid waste management systems, long-term care districts, water utility districts, and mosquito control districts. ▣

Public education in Wisconsin

2018–19 school year

The Wisconsin Constitution requires the legislature to make available to all children in the state a free uniform basic education. (Article X, section 3.) At the same time, the constitution does not prohibit the legislature from creating additional forms of publicly funded education; nor does it require the additional forms, if any, to be available to all children, to be entirely free, or to provide the same basic education as the legislature must make available to all children. (*Davis v. Grover*, 166 Wis. 2d 501, 539, 480 N.W.2d 460, 474 (1992) and *Jackson v. Benson*, 218 Wis. 2d 835, 895, 578 N.W.2d 602, 628 (1998).) This article describes first the general educational system that the legislature has established to meet its obligation under the constitution and then each of the currently existing additional forms of publicly funded education that the legislature has also created.

The general system

In Wisconsin, every child resides within a school district and is entitled to a free education at a public school operated by that school district. The education provided at the public school must conform to requirements specified in state law.

Wisconsin is organized into 421 school districts. Each school district is governed by a school board whose members are elected by the residents of the district. For the purpose of operating public schools, school districts can, among other things, own and lease property; employ teachers and other personnel; and contract for the provision of services. Funding for school district operations comes primarily from state aid and property taxes levied by each district, but also from federal aid and miscellaneous fees, sales, and interest earnings. The amount of general state aid that a school district receives is based on several factors, including the number of pupils enrolled in the district's schools. State law limits the total amount of revenue that a school district can raise each year from general state aid, the state aid it receives for computers, and the property taxes it levies. However, a school district can exceed its revenue limit if it obtains voter approval at a referendum. School districts also receive aid for specified purposes, known as categorical aids, that are not counted toward revenue limits.

State law sets out general educational goals for children attending public schools and requires school districts to provide educational programs that will enable students to attain those goals. State law requires school districts to specify to the student in the particular course. Parents are responsible for transporting their student to and from the school in the other school district, unless a course is being taken to implement the IEP of a student with a disability. Parents can apply to DPI for financial aid to offset the cost of transportation based on need.

EARLY COLLEGE CREDIT PROGRAM

The Early College Credit Program (ECCP) allows a student who is attending public or private high school to take college courses at a University of Wisconsin System institution, a tribally controlled college, or a private, nonprofit institution of higher education in Wisconsin. A student can indicate on their application whether they want to take the class for high school credit, college credit, or both. The ECCP does not include courses taken at a public or private high school for college credit, commonly known as dual enrollment.

If the course a student takes is for high school credit, and if the course is not comparable to a course offered by the school district or private school, then the student pays nothing. The Department of Workforce Development and the school district or private school split the cost. The student pays for each course that the student takes for college credit only, although this cost is reduced. The student also pays for each course that the school board or private school governing board finds to be comparable to an existing course at the student's school, or that the student does not successfully complete. Parents are responsible for providing transportation to and from courses under the ECCP, but can apply to DPI for financial assistance based on need.

TECHNICAL COLLEGE DUAL CREDIT

Wisconsin allows students who are attending a public school in grade 11 or 12 to take courses at a technical college. If the course is taken for high school credit and if the course is not comparable to a course at the student's high school but is eligible for credit, then the district will pay for the student's tuition, fees, and books. Parents are responsible for providing transportation to and from courses at the technical college, unless a course is being taken to implement a student's IEP. If a student with a disability applies to the program, they may be denied if the cost of their participation would impose an undue burden on the school district.

CHARTER SCHOOLS

A charter school is a type of public school that is operated by an organization who contracts with an entity empowered to authorize charter schools. Currently, all school districts and several other entities have this power. The contract describes the school's educational program and governance structure and specifies the facilities and funds that will be available to it. The authorizing entity can revoke a charter school contract if the charter school operator fails to comply with the terms of the contract. The authorizing entity can also revoke the contract if the children attending the charter school fail to make sufficient progress towards attaining the general educational goals set out in state law for children attending public schools. Outside of the contract's terms, charter schools are largely exempt from state education laws that apply to other public schools. Charter schools must be free to students, like other public schools.

Charter schools are not exempt from state education laws that pertain to public health and safety. In addition, all professional employees of a charter school who have direct contact with students or involvement with the instructional program must hold a license or permit to teach issued by DPI, with two exceptions: teachers at virtual charter schools and high school grade teachers who are faculty at an institution of higher learning may not need licenses, under certain conditions.

Charter school operators must report the same kinds of information to DPI as school districts and administer the same standardized tests to their students as school districts must administer to students in other public schools. In addition, DPI must include performance evaluations of charter schools in the annual school and school district accountability report.

As public schools, charter schools are subject to federal laws pertaining to education, the education of children with disabilities, and civil rights.

School district charter schools. A charter school established by a school district is a public school of that school district, even though the school district does not directly operate the charter school. As a result, a school district charter school is subject to school district policies, except as otherwise negotiated in the charter contract. A student who attends a school district charter school is enrolled in the school district just the same as if the student attended a school that the school district operated directly. The school district receives the same amount of state aid or the same full-time open enrollment transfer payment for the child, and the school district has the same duties if the student is a child with a disability. However, a school district cannot require a student to attend a charter school and must provide other public school attendance arrangements for a student who does not wish to attend a charter school. A school district that establishes a charter school pays the charter school operator an amount negotiated in the charter contract to operate the charter school.

A school district can also establish a "virtual" charter school, which is a kind of charter school at which all or a portion of the instruction is provided on the Internet. A virtual charter school is considered to be located in the school district that establishes it, even if it has no physical presence there. In contrast to the situation with a bricks-and-mortar school, it is feasible under the Full-Time Open Enrollment Program for children who reside anywhere in the state to attend a virtual charter school. A teacher for a virtual charter school is not required to have a license from DPI, if the teacher is licensed to teach the grade and subject they are teaching in the state from which the online course is provided.

Independent charter schools. Several entities other than school districts can authorize independent charter schools. This includes the chancellors of any institution in the University of Wisconsin System, the City of Milwaukee, any technical college district board, the county executive of Waukesha County, the College of Menominee Nation, the Lac Courte Oreilles Ojibwa Community College, and the Office of Educational Opportunity in the University of Wisconsin System.

An independent charter school established by one of these entities is not part of any school district. Accordingly, an independent charter school is not subject to any school district's policies. If a child with a disability attends an independent charter school, the charter school operator is subject to the same federal laws pertaining to the education of such children as a school district would be and must evaluate the child, develop an IEP, offer the child an educational setting in which it will provide the special education and services specified in the IEP, and regularly reevaluate the child and revise the IEP. None of the chartering entities may establish or contract with a virtual charter school.

The state pays an independent charter school operator a set amount for each student attending the independent charter school. However, for an independent charter school authorized by the College of Menominee Nation or the Lac Courte Oreilles Ojibwa Community College, the per student amount in each school year is tied to a type of federal aid provided to tribal schools.

PARENTAL CHOICE PROGRAMS

Under a parental choice program (sometimes called a "voucher" program), the state makes a payment to a private school, on behalf of a student's parent, for the student to attend the private school. There are three parental choice programs in Wisconsin: the Milwaukee Parental Choice Program, which has been in existence since 1989; the Racine Parental Choice Program, which was created in the 2011–13 biennial budget act; and the Statewide Parental Choice Program, which was created in the 2013–15 biennial budget act.

Each of these programs is available to children whose family income, at the time that the child first participates, is below a specified level (three times the federal poverty level for the Milwaukee and Racine programs and 2.2 times that level for the statewide program). A child must reside in the city of Milwaukee to participate in the Milwaukee program, in the Racine Unified School District to participate in the Racine program, and anywhere else in the state to participate in the statewide program. Except in certain circumstances, a child cannot participate in the Racine or statewide program if the child was attending a private school in the previous school year other than as a participant in one of those programs. In addition, a temporary limit has been imposed on the number of children from each school district who can participate in the statewide program. This limit was 3 percent of a school district's student membership in the 2018–19 school year. The limit increases by one percentage point each school year until the 2025–26 school year and ceases to apply after that.

A private school that wishes to participate in a parental choice program must report to DPI, by the January 10 preceding each school year of participation, the number of spaces it has for choice students and pay an annual fee. Additional requirements apply to a private school that has been in continuous operation in this state for less than 12 consecutive months or provides education to fewer than 40 students divided into two or fewer grades.

A student who wishes to participate in a parental choice program must apply to a participating private school during specific enrollment periods. The private school may reject an applicant only if the spaces it has for choice students are full. If a private school rejects an application, the applicant can transfer his or her application to another participating private school. A private school must generally accept applicants on a random basis, but may give preference to applicants who participated in a parental choice program in the previous school year, siblings of such applicants, and siblings of applicants whom the private school has accepted for the current school year on a random basis.

A participating private school must satisfy all state health and safety laws and codes that are applicable to public schools and federal laws prohibiting discrimination on the basis of race, color, or national origin. It must satisfy at least one of four achievement standards to continue participating in the program, and it may not require a choice student to participate in any religious activity. The private school must also provide a prescribed minimum number of hours of direct student instruction in each grade. Additionally, all of the private school's teachers and administrators must have a bachelor's or higher degree, or a license issued by DPI, unless they are only teaching or administrating rabbinical courses.

Participating private schools must report the same kinds of information to DPI as school districts must report, but only with respect to the choice students attending them. They must also administer the same standardized tests to their choice students as school districts must administer to public school students. In addition, DPI must include an evaluation of each participating private school's performance with respect to its choice students in the annual school and school district accountability report.

A private school cannot charge tuition to a choice student unless the student's family income exceeds a set percentage of the federal poverty line. A private school can charge a choice student fees related to certain expenses (such as social and extracurricular activities, musical instruments, meals, and transportation) but cannot take adverse action against a choice student or the student's family if the fees are not paid.

SPECIAL NEEDS SCHOLARSHIP PROGRAM

Under the Special Needs Scholarship Program, the state makes a payment (the scholarship) to a private school, on behalf of the parent of a child with a disability, for the child to attend the private school. In the 2018-19 school year, the scholarship amount was $12,431. Beginning in the 2019-20 school year, if a student has participated in the program for a year, the scholarship amount can be the actual costs incurred by the private school, if that is greater than the standard scholarship amount. There is no limit on the amount of additional tuition or fees a private school may charge a child who receives a scholarship under the program.

A child with a disability is eligible for a scholarship under the program if three conditions are met. First, the child must have an IEP or services plan in effect. (A services plan outlines the services that a school district has agreed to provide to a child with a disability whose parent has enrolled the child in a private school rather than in the school district.) Second, the child's parent or guardian must consent to make the child available for reevaluation upon request of the child's school district of residence. And third, the private school that the child wishes to attend with the scholarship must be accredited or approved as a private school by DPI and must have notified DPI of its intent to participate in the program.

A private school that wishes to participate in the program must notify DPI of the number of spaces it has available for children who receive a scholarship under the program. A participating private school must accept applications under the program on a first-come first-served basis, but may give preference to siblings of students who are already attending the private school if it receives more applications than the number of spaces it has available.

A participating private school must implement, for each child that receives a scholarship, either 1) the IEP or services plan that the child's school district of residence developed in its most recent reevaluation of the child or 2) a modified version of that IEP or services plan agreed to between the private school and the child's parent. The private school must also provide the child with any related services agreed to between the private school and the child's parent that are not included in the child's IEP or services plan. A child with a disability who attends a private school under the program is not entitled to all the special education and related services to which he or she would be entitled under state and federal law if he or she attended a public school.

A participating private school must comply with all health and safety laws that apply to public schools; must provide each child who applies for a scholarship with a profile of the private school's special education program; and must submit to DPI an annual school financial information report.

Unless it is also participating in a parental choice program, a private school participating in the Special Needs Scholarship Program is not required to report to DPI the kinds of information that school districts must report or to administer to any of its students the standardized tests that school districts must administer to public school students, and no performance evaluation of the private school is included in the annual school and school district accountability report.

Once awarded, a scholarship continues until the child graduates from high school or until the end of the school term in which the child attains the age of 21, whichever comes first, unless upon reevaluation by the child's school district of residence, it is determined that the child is no longer a child with a disability. In that case, the child can continue to receive a scholarship under the program, but the amount of the scholarship is reduced to the per student amount paid under the parental choice programs. ⯀

The legislature and the state budget

The legislature has the power of the purse. In Wisconsin, the state government may not spend a single dollar without the legislature specifically authorizing the expenditure by law. The manner in which the legislature controls the expenditure of state funds is through its appropriation power, which is a power granted to the legislature under the Wisconsin Constitution. In the 1936 case Finnegan v. Dammann, the Wisconsin Supreme Court defined an appropriation as "the setting aside from the public revenue of a certain sum of money for a specified object, in such a manner that the executive officers of the government are authorized to use that money, and no more, for that object, and no other."[1] It is the legislature that directs the governor and the executive branch in determining what state moneys are to be spent and the purposes for which they may be spent.

The most consequential exercise of the legislature's appropriation power is the enactment of the state budget. The biennial budget bill is easily the most significant piece of legislation that is enacted during the entire legislative session. This is the case for two reasons. First, the biennial budget bill appropriates almost all dollars that will be expended by state government during the two fiscal years covered by the bill. These dollars consist mostly of state taxes and revenues, program and license fees, and federal moneys allocated to Wisconsin. In 2019 Wisconsin Act 9, the state budget act for the 2019–21 fiscal biennium, the legislature authorized the expenditure of over $81 billion in total state government spending from all revenue sources. The second reason for the significance of the biennial budget bill is that it contains most of the governor's public policy agenda for the entire legislative session. The biennial budget bill is generally considered the one bill that "must pass" in order to sufficiently fund state government operations and programs during the fiscal years covered in the bill. As such, there is a strong incentive for the governor, as well as for legislators, to include in the biennial budget bill the major public policy items supported by the governor and the legislators. The state budget process is therefore unequaled in its significance for the operations of state government and for its effects on the people of Wisconsin.

The state budget process: core principles

There are several core principles to the state budget process in Wisconsin. First, the state budget is a biennial budget, covering two fiscal years of state government operations and programs, with each fiscal year beginning on July 1 and ending on June 30. Many states have a "drop-dead" date by which a new state budget must be enacted in order for state government to continue to operate. Wisconsin does not have such a deadline. In Wisconsin, if a new state budget is not enacted by June 30 of the odd-numbered year, state government continues to operate and its programs are funded, but only at the prior year's appropriation amounts. The governor and the legislature strive to enact the state budget bill before July 1 of the odd-numbered year, but there is little short-term fiscal impact if that deadline is not met.

Second, Wisconsin uses what is known as program budgeting, in which executive branch state agencies are assigned to different functional areas and generally lump-sum appropriations are made to the agencies to fund the programs. The biennial budget bill therefore lists the overall amounts appropriated for agency operations and programs, but does not contain the level of expenditure detail that one might find in a state that uses a so-called "line-item" budget, in which each agency expenditure is specifically budgeted by line in the bill. This level of detail is not found in the biennial budget bill in Wisconsin; instead, it appears in accompanying budget documents, which are not law but which do capture the intentions of the governor and the legislature in budget deliberations. Consequently, that portion of the biennial bill that sets the expenditure levels of state operations and programs is roughly 200 pages in length, which is typically about 15 to 20 percent of the total number of pages of recent biennial budget bills.

Third, the Wisconsin Constitution requires that the legislature "provide for an annual tax sufficient to defray the estimated expenses of the state for each year."[2] What this means in practice is that Wisconsin has a balanced-budget requirement, in which state expenditures must equal revenues received by the state. Generally speaking, at each stage of the budget process, in which different versions of the budget are formulated and considered, each version of the budget must be balanced by having proposed state expenditures in any fiscal year be less than or equal to anticipated state revenues. This is a real constraint on state budgeting, one that is not found at the federal level.

Finally, the Wisconsin Constitution grants the governor partial veto power over appropriation bills. This partial veto power allows the governor to reduce amounts appropriated to state agencies for their operations and programs by writing in a lower amount, and allows the governor, with limitations, to delete specific words and digits within newly created statutory text in appropriation bills. The governor can thus police the legislature's budget actions. While this power has been curtailed in recent years by amendments to the constitution, the governor still can reduce all state expenditures, or the expenditures of any specific state agency, with the stroke of a pen, subject only to an override of his or her actions by a two-thirds vote of each house of the legislature—an event that last occurred in 1985.

The state budget process: an overview of executive action

The provision for a biennial executive budget bill was created by Chapter 97, Laws of 1929[3], and it has applied to all legislative sessions since 1931. Prior to that time, the governor was not responsible for submitting an executive budget bill to the legislature; individual bills were introduced for each department. The legislature delegated the biennial budget task to the governor for understandable reasons. As head of the executive branch, the governor can assess and coordinate the expenditure needs of each executive branch agency. In addition, the growth in state government in the twentieth century resulted in a level of public policy and budgetary expertise in the executive branch that is generally not available in the legislative branch, which has a much smaller professional staff. Requiring the governor to produce the budget bill allows the legislature to work from a document that may require modification, because of different legislative public policy or budgetary priorities, but which already contains numerous budgetary matters and details that the legislature need not address. The governor's budget is a solid foundation on which the legislature can build its version of the budget, a process which serves both the governor and the legislature well.

To begin the biennial budget process, in the summer of each even-numbered year, the State Budget Office in the Department of Administration submits budget instructions to executive-branch agencies, establishing the manner of submitting budget requests and informing them of any broad fiscal or policy goals that the governor intends the state agencies to achieve. By September 15, state agencies must submit their budget requests to the State Budget Office for review by that office, the state budget director, and the governor. By November 20, the Department of Administration publishes a compilation and summation of the agency budget requests, as well as estimated revenues to the state for the current and forthcoming fiscal biennia. The State Budget Office oversees the preparation of legislation to achieve the governor's budget and policy recommendations. In this endeavor, the State Budget Office works closely with legal counsel at the Legislative Reference Bureau—the legislature's bill-drafting agency—to draft the statutory language that will ultimately be incorporated into the governor's budget bill. Throughout the process, the governor is briefed on individual items in the budget bill, and the bill is complete only when the governor has signed off on the items in the bill. The governor is then required to deliver the budget bill to the legislature no later than the last Tuesday in January of each odd-numbered year, but the legislature regularly moves this deadline back into

February to allow the governor to make changes in the bill once more accurate revenue estimates for the current and forthcoming fiscal biennia are available in late January. When the budget bill is delivered to the legislature, the governor addresses the legislature on the proposals contained in the bill, which more often than not are the key public policy goals of the governor's administration for the entire legislative session.

The first thing to note about the production of the executive budget bill is the role of the State Budget Office. The State Budget Office is headed by the state budget director and consists of about 25 budget analysts who serve in classified civil service positions. These analysts serve both Republican and Democratic gubernatorial administrations in a strictly nonpartisan and highly professional manner and are able to provide independent review of state agency funding requirements, as well as fashion fiscal and nonfiscal policies to achieve the governor's political and public policy aims. The State Budget Office translates the governor's public policy goals into workable and funded programs.

The second thing to note about the production of the executive budget bill is that the State Budget Office works directly with nonpartisan legal counsel in the Legislative Reference Bureau to prepare statutory text that achieves the governor's policy goals. The Legislative Reference Bureau has about 20 licensed attorneys with subject matter and legal expertise in virtually all policy areas. This is significant. The governor's budget bill is drafted in a professional, nonpartisan manner, so that the legislators need only focus on the public policies in the bill and not worry about the bill's legal quality or effectiveness. In addition, when the legislature takes up the governor's budget bill, the Legislative Reference Bureau attorneys who originally drafted the governor's provisions in the bill will be the ones who draft the legislature's alternatives. In this way, often the very same attorneys are working on the same language in the bill throughout the process. The legislature can thus count on experienced and competent legal counsel to prepare its budget bill in an accurate, high-quality, and nonpartisan manner.

Finally, it is important to note the political uses of the executive budget bill. The budget bill is by far the longest and most complex bill before the legislature during the entire biennial session. In recent years the bill has grown substantially in length. From 1961 to 1986, the executive budget bills averaged 367 pages in length. From 1987 to 2017, in contrast, the executive budget bills averaged 1,524 pages in length. This is more than a fourfold increase in the size of the executive budget bill. The 2017 executive budget bill was just under 1,000 pages in length.

The executive budget bill is now a blueprint for the legislature for taking up the governor's goals for public policy change. When the governor steps up to the assembly podium, usually in early or mid-February, to present the budget address

the governor for signing. As mentioned earlier, the governor has partial veto power over appropriation bills and will use that power to modify what the legislature has wrought in the bill. The governor can reduce appropriations, as well as modify some statutory text. The extent to which the governor will partially veto the bill also depends on a number of factors, such as the partisan makeup of the legislature, the degree to which the governor agrees with what the legislature has done, and whether the governor has made agreements in negotiations with the legislature over what can and cannot be vetoed. Once the governor has signed the bill into law, the budget-making process is concluded, as the only other possible step is for the legislature to override one or more of the governor's partial vetoes—an action, as mentioned earlier, that has not happened since 1985.

Concluding considerations

The state budget-making process is truly a year-long event, beginning in the summer of each even-numbered year when the State Budget Office sends budget instructions to the state agencies, and concluding the following summer with the enactment of the biennial budget act. The process is characterized both by careful deliberation and by frenzied, all-night sessions and meetings. The budget bill is the work product of the governor, every elected member of the Senate and the Assembly, and numerous professional staff in both the executive and legislative branches. There is never an "easy" budget, as each fiscal biennium presents its own unique budgetary and political challenges. But there is never complete gridlock, as the legislature does complete its work. Sometimes the budget will be late, especially when the two houses are controlled by different political parties, but in the end Wisconsin will have a state budget. ▩

NOTES

1. Finnegan v. Dammann, 220 Wis. 143, 148, 264 N.W. 622 (1936).

2. Wisconsin Constitution, article VIII, section 5.

3. This would have been called Act 97 if it took effect today; before 1983, a bill that was enacted into law was called a "chapter" rather than an "act."

4. Woodrow Wilson, Congressional Government, A Study in American Politics (1885).

Significant enactments of the 2017 Legislature

Administrative law

Act 57 (SB-15) makes changes regarding the promulgation of administrative rules by state agencies, including:

1. Requiring agencies to submit all statements of scope for proposed rules to the Department of Administration for review before they are submitted to the governor for approval.

2. Creating a process that allows the Joint Committee for Review of Administrative Rules (JCRAR) or a cochairperson of JCRAR to contract for the preparation of an independent economic impact analysis by a third party for an agency's proposed rule.

3. Prohibiting an agency from promulgating any rule with estimated costs of $10 million or more over any two-year period unless the agency reduces the estimated cost of the rule or a law is passed authorizing the rule to be promulgated.

Act 108 (AB-317) makes changes concerning administrative rules promulgated by state agencies, including allowing JCRAR to direct an agency to prepare a retrospective economic impact analysis on its existing rules.

Act 158 (AB-330) prohibits an agency that has not taken any action to exercise rule-making authority in ten years or more from promulgating administrative rules unless such promulgation is subsequently authorized in legislation.

Act 369 (SB-884) provides limitations on agency rule-making authority and allows JCRAR to suspend rules multiple times. The act also includes provisions regarding the adoption by agencies of guidance documents and requires agency publications to include citations to applicable provisions. Finally, the act prohibits agencies from seeking deference to agency interpretations of law and prohibits such deference from being accorded in reviews of agencies' administrative proceedings.

Agriculture

Act 100 (SB-119) allows people to grow, process, transport, sell, and take possession of industrial hemp to the greatest extent allowed under federal law. The act requires the Department of Agriculture, Trade and Consumer Protection to create a pilot program to study the growth, cultivation, and marketing of industrial hemp and to create a licensing and registration system for industrial hemp-related activities. The act also exempts certain industrial hemp-related activities from prosecution under the state's controlled substances laws.

Buildings and safety

Act 243 (AB-770) prohibits a city, village, town, or county from making or enforcing an ordinance that does not conform to the Uniform Dwelling Code and allows the owner of a dwelling to waive any provision in a contract with a city, village, town, or county that requires the owner to comply with such an ordinance. If the owner waives the provision, it is void and unenforceable.

Business and consumer law

Act 77 (SB-298) creates a category of business corporation identified as a benefit corporation. A benefit corporation must have a purpose of creating public benefit and must have a benefit director on its board.

Act 177 (SB-404) creates, for college students who form a business start-up, an exemption to the Department of Financial Institutions filing fee to form a limited liability company.

Act 318 (AB-811) directs the Wisconsin Economic Development Corporation to collaborate with state agencies for the purpose of attracting talent to this state.

Act 369 (SB-884) makes changes to laws relating to economic development, including the following:

1. Increases the number of members and alters the composition of the WEDC board. Under the act, the legislative appointees to the board need not be legislators and serve four-year terms. Additionally, the legislative appointees constitute a majority of the board until September 1, 2019, after which the speaker of the assembly and senate majority leader each lose one appointee.

2. Eliminates the cap on the number of enterprise zones WEDC may designate for purposes of the enterprise zone tax credit program, but requires that WEDC get approval from the Joint Committee on Finance before designating a new zone.

Children

Act 47 (SB-35) adds juvenile correctional officers to the list of professionals who must report suspected abuse and neglect of children.

Act 59 (AB-64) does the following:

1. Allows counties to contract with other counties to perform certain child welfare intake services.

2. Grants juvenile courts exclusive jurisdiction over any child who is, or is at a substantial risk of becoming, a victim of child sex trafficking.

3. Increases from 16 to 18 the age below which persons sentenced to a state prison must, under certain circumstances, be placed at a juvenile correctional facility or secured residential care center for children and youth.

Act 143 (AB-843) requires all persons who under current law are mandatory reporters of suspected child abuse or neglect to also report to a law enforcement agency if the person believes in good faith, based on a threat made by an individual seen in the course of professional duties regarding violence in or targeted at a school, that there is a serious and imminent threat to the health or safety of a student or school employee or the public.

Act 185 (AB-953) does all of the following:

1. Requires the state to close the Type 1 juvenile correctional facilities at the Lincoln Hills School and the Copper Lake School by January 1, 2021.

2. Requires the Department of Corrections, subject to the approval of the Joint Committee on Finance, to establish new Type 1 juvenile correctional facilities to hold certain juveniles adjudicated delinquent and placed under the supervision of DOC.

3. Creates a $40 million grant program to establish new county-run, secured residential care centers for children and youth to hold certain juveniles adjudicated delinquent and placed under the supervision of the county.

4. Transfers all youth that were housed at the Lincoln Hills School and the Copper Lake School to the appropriate new facility created under the act.

Act 308 (SB-52) removes the three-year limit on the amount of time DOC may place certain juveniles participating in the Serious Juvenile Offender Program in a Type 1 juvenile correctional facility or a secured residential care center for children and youth.

Corrections

Act 33 (Jr7 SS AB-3) provides that a person who is on parole, probation, or extended supervision may not have his or her parole, probation, or extended supervision revoked for possession of a controlled substance or paraphernalia if he or she assists a person who is suffering from a drug overdose by summoning an emergency service provider or by bringing that person to an emergency service provider.

Courts and civil actions

Act 58 (Au7 SS AB-1) establishes an expedited appeal procedure under which a party may, as a matter of right, appeal a judgment or order of the trial court relating to a decision by a state or local official, board, commission, condemnor, authority, or department concerning an Electronics and Information Technology

Manufacturing Zone. The act also provides that any circuit court judgment or order related to an EITM zone is automatically stayed pending appeal, though a party may request to have the stay modified or vacated.

Act 235 (AB-773) shortens the statute of limitations for an action for injury to character from six years to three years; for an action for injury resulting from improvements to real property from ten years to seven years; and for an action upon a liability created by statute when a different limitation is not prescribed by law and for an action for relief on the ground of fraud from six years to three years.

Crime

Act 4 (SB-10) provides that a person may possess cannabidiol in a form without a psychoactive effect (CBD oil) if the person has a certification issued by a physician within the previous year stating that the person possesses the CBD oil to treat a medical condition.

Act 25 (Jr7 SS AB-4) prohibits certain narcotics designated as schedule V controlled substances from being dispensed without a prescription.

Act 54 (SB-133) makes it a Class I felony to possess, and a Class H felony to use, a credit card scanner with the intent to commit identity theft. The act also provides an exemption from civil liability for an owner of an ATM or gas pump who has had a credit card scanner installed on his or her machine without permission.

Act 60 (AB-335) adds fentanyl analogs that are not already schedule I controlled substances to the list of synthetic opioids under that schedule and reorganizes some substances from the general synthetic opioids category to the specific fentanyl analog category under that schedule.

Act 145 (SB-408) makes it a Class G felony to purchase a firearm with the intent to transfer it to a person who is prohibited from possessing a firearm (straw purchasing) or to illegally furnish or possess a firearm for a person who is prohibited from possessing a firearm. The act also increases the penalty for providing false information on a firearm background check form from a misdemeanor to a Class H felony if the false information is regarding whether the person is purchasing the firearm with the intent of transferring it to a person who is prohibited from possessing a firearm. The act also subjects a person to a mandatory minimum period of confinement in prison of four years if the person is convicted of illegally possessing a firearm or convicted of another crime involving a firearm and, within five years prior to that conviction, he or she had been convicted of either three misdemeanors or one felony.

Act 211 (SB-61) changes the procedure for forfeiture of property after it has been seized in relation to a crime. With certain exceptions, the act provides that property may be forfeited only after a person has been convicted of the crime related to the forfeiture action and only if a court finds that the property seized is proportional to the crime committed. If the person is acquitted, the charges against the person are dismissed, or no criminal charges are filed within six months of the initiation of the forfeiture proceeding, the court must order the return of the property within 30 days. The act requires seized property to be returned to innocent owners of the property unless the owners were involved with or knowledgeable about the crime related to his or her property. In addition, the act allows the court, upon petition by a person whose property was seized but not yet forfeited, to return the property to the person under certain circumstances. Further, the act requires a law enforcement agency to sell forfeited property and divide the proceeds as specified in the act.

Act 272 (AB-825) makes it a Class H felony to intentionally threaten or cause bodily harm to an attorney or the family member of an attorney because of his or her role in child welfare or family law cases.

Domestic relations

Act 59 (AB-64) requires that individuals seeking to form new domestic partnerships apply on or after August 1, 2009, but no later than April 1, 2018. The act prohibits county clerks from issuing declarations of domestic partnership to individuals who apply after April 1, 2018.

Economic development

Act 58 (Au7 SS AB-1) authorizes the Wisconsin Economic Development Corporation to designate an Electronics and Information Technology Manufacturing Zone. Under the act, WEDC may certify one or more businesses that begin operations in the EITM zone to claim up to a total of $2,850,000,000 in refundable tax credits in connection with job creation and capital investment in the EITM zone and the state. The EITM zone designation may last for up to 15 years.

Act 59 (AB-64) eliminates a prohibition against WEDC issuing new loans. Instead, the act prohibits WEDC from issuing certain forgivable loans and requires that WEDC's new lending programs adhere to commonly accepted commercial lending practices.

Education

HIGHER EDUCATION

Act 29 (Jr7 SS AB-1) grants immunity to a residence hall director who administers

year in which the pupil is applying for the SNSP and that the open enrollment application was denied.

b. Eliminates the requirement that a pupil must have been enrolled in a public school in Wisconsin for the entire school year immediately preceding the school year for which the pupil is applying for the SNSP.

6. Makes the following changes related to independent charter schools:

a. Requires DPI to make summer school payments, in the same manner DPI makes summer school payments to private schools participating in a PCP, to independent charter schools for children who attend summer school.

b. Expands independent charter school authorizers to include any UW chancellor and any technical college district board.

c. Eliminates geographic restrictions for a charter school authorized by the Office of Educational Opportunity in the UW System.

d. Eliminates the restrictions on charter schools authorized by the Gateway Technical College District Board.

7. Beginning in the 2018–19 school year, modifies the Youth Options Program, other than that portion of the program governing a pupil's attendance at a technical college, to create the Early College Credit Program (ECCP). The ECCP allows a public or private high school pupil to enroll in an institution of higher education for the purpose of taking nonsectarian courses.

8. Allows a faculty member of an institution of higher education to teach in a public high school, including a charter school operating only high school grades, without a license or permit from DPI if the faculty member satisfies certain criteria.

9. Limits the dates on which a school board may schedule a referendum seeking approval to raise the school district's revenue limit or issue bonds to the spring primary or election or the partisan primary or election unless the school district has experienced a natural disaster, in which case the school board may schedule a special referendum within six months of the natural disaster.

Act 141 (AB-835), beginning in the 2018–19 school year, increases sparsity aid payments for eligible school districts to $400 per pupil. Subject to restrictions related to failed operating referenda, the act also increases the revenue ceiling to $9,400 in the 2018–19 school year and then by $100 in each school year thereafter until the revenue ceiling is $9,800 in the 2022–23 school year.

Elections

Act 120 (AB-153) allows a candidate to petition for a recount if the candidate trails the leading candidate by no more than 1 percent of the total votes cast for the office sought by the candidates. The act also increases the per diem compensation for a member of the Elections Commission or Ethics Commission from $27 to

$115 for each day on which the member attends or participates in a meeting of the member's commission.

Act 369 (SB-884) does all of the following:

1. Modifies current law regarding the absentee ballot voting procedures for military and overseas electors so that the law is in substantial compliance with the federal Uniformed and Overseas Citizens Absentee Voting Act. The act also provides that an individual signing the witness certification for an absentee ballot cast by a military or overseas elector need not be a U.S. citizen.

2. Codifies an administrative rule adopted by the Government Accountability Board, now the Elections Commission, which allows an individual to use an identification card issued by a technical college in this state as a valid form of voter identification.

3. Codifies administrative rules adopted by the Department of Transportation regarding the petition process for acquiring a valid voter identification card.

Eminent domain

Act 59 (AB-64) changes eminent domain law by prohibiting the acquisition of property by condemnation for certain purposes, including establishing or extending recreational trails or bicycle lanes.

Act 243 (AB-770) makes changes to the eminent domain law with respect to calculating the amount of just compensation for property that is condemned and with respect to payments made in addition to just compensation. The act creates new categories of costs for which a condemnee must be compensated if that condemnee incurs expenses to make the condemnee's new property comparable to the condemned property and restricts the amount of additional payments made if the condemnor is a village, town, or city.

Employment

Act 58 (Au7 SS AB-1) requires the Department of Workforce Development to allocate $20,000,000 in the 2019–21 fiscal biennium to provide funding, through grants or other means, to facilitate worker training and employment in this state, subject to approval by JCF.

Act 59 (AB-64) repeals the prevailing wage law, which required that certain laborers, workers, mechanics, and truck drivers employed on the site of certain state projects of public works be paid at the prevailing wage rate.

Environment

Act 10 (SB-76) provides that a person with a high capacity well permit does not need to obtain additional approval from the Department of Natural Resources to repair, replace, reconstruct, or transfer ownership of the high capacity well unless taking these actions would be inconsistent with the person's high capacity well permit. The act also requires DNR to evaluate and model the hydrology of three specific lakes, and allows DNR to evaluate and model the hydrology of any navigable lakes or navigable streams at risk of significant water loss within three specific small watersheds. After completing its evaluation and modeling, DNR may recommend that the legislature adopt special measures relating to groundwater withdrawal within the areas that DNR studied.

Act 58 (Au7 SS AB-1) provides that a determination regarding the issuance of any permit or approval for a new manufacturing facility within an Electronics and Information Technology Manufacturing Zone does not require an environmental impact statement.

Act 70 (SB-173) relates to the regulation of brownfields, which are abandoned commercial or industrial properties that are contaminated with pollution. The act exempts a person who owns property where a hazardous vapor is emitted from the soil or groundwater from the requirement to remediate the environment, under certain limited circumstances.

Act 134 (AB-499) makes the following changes to the state's nonferrous metallic mining regulations:

1. Repeals what is commonly called the "mining moratorium," which prohibited DNR from issuing any sulfide ore mining permits in this state until DNR could determine that at least one sulfide ore mine had operated anywhere in the United States or Canada for at least ten years and had been closed for at least ten years without resulting in groundwater or surface water pollution.

2. Prohibits DNR from enforcing groundwater enforcement standards at any point below the point in the bedrock at which the groundwater is not reasonably capable of being used for human consumption.

3. Allows DNR to approve a high capacity well that DNR determines would ordinarily result in the unreasonable detriment of public or private water supplies or the unreasonable detriment of public rights in the waters of the state if DNR includes conditions in the high capacity well approval or mining permit to ensure that those detriments will not occur, including a requirement that the applicant provide a replacement water supply or temporarily augment the quantity of water in the affected water body.

Act 159 (SB-466) prohibits DNR from including the air monitoring site located at Kohler-Andrae State Park in the state's initial monitoring network plan for 2018 and requires DNR to request a waiver of the relevant provisions of the federal Clean Air Act that may be implicated by discontinuing the use of the monitor.

Financial institutions

Act 72 (AB-283) allows financial institutions to conduct or participate in savings promotions in which depositors are offered a chance to win prizes. The act specifies that these savings promotions are not a prohibited form of gambling.

Health and human services

FOODSHARE

Act 59 (AB-64) makes changes regarding the law relating to the FoodShare program, including:

1. If certain criteria are met, prohibiting certain individuals and parents who refuse to cooperate in obtaining child support or determining the paternity of a child or who are delinquent in child support payments and do not satisfy an exception from being eligible for FoodShare benefits.

2. Imposing an eligibility limit for FoodShare of $25,000 in liquid assets for certain individuals, if the federal government does not disallow such a limit, and requiring the Department of Health Services to operate a financial record matching program to verify assets of FoodShare recipients.

3. Applying current-law requirements for drug screening, testing, and treatment to all able-bodied adults participating in the FoodShare employment and training program, known as FSET, regardless of whether they have dependents.

4. Allowing DHS to require able-bodied adults to participate in FSET.

5. Expunging certain unused FoodShare benefits.

Act 264 (Jr8 SS AB-2) requires DHS to require all able-bodied adults who are not already employed to participate in FSET to the extent allowed by the federal government.

Act 266 (Jr8 SS AB-6) requires DHS to create and implement a payment system based on performance for entities that administer FSET. The act also requires DHS to establish and implement a pilot program to provide discounts on fresh produce and other healthy foods from retailers.

Act 269 (Jr8 SS AB-3) creates an asset limit such that to be eligible for FoodShare an individual may have a single residence worth no more than 200 percent of the statewide median home value, excluding agricultural land, and a combined equity value of vehicles, excluding business vehicles, of no more than $20,000.

HEALTH

Act 133 (AB-96) allows certain individuals to obtain a prescription for and provide or administer epinephrine auto-injectors to individuals experiencing anaphylaxis.

MEDICAL ASSISTANCE

Act 59 (AB-64) makes changes to the laws related to the Medical Assistance program, including:

1. Making changes to the income eligibility and premium methodology for the Medical Assistance Purchase Plan program, known as MAPP, and changing to 100 percent of the federal poverty line the income limit for Medical Assistance program eligibility for certain elderly, blind, or disabled individuals who are medically needy.

2. Eliminating the ambulatory surgical center assessment and requiring DHS to develop a plan to increase Medical Assistance program reimbursement rates to ambulatory surgical centers.

3. Requiring DHS to submit a waiver amendment request to the federal government to provide employment and training services for childless adults who are eligible for Medical Assistance.

Act 268 (Jr8 SS AB-8) requires an able-bodied adult to cooperate with paternity and child support determinations, obtain child support, or pay any required child support to be eligible for Medical Assistance.

Act 370 (SB-886) prohibits DHS from submitting a request to the federal government for a waiver or modification of a waiver or for authorization to implement a pilot program or demonstration project unless legislation directing the submission has been enacted. The act establishes a procedure giving the Joint Committee on Finance review authority over steps in the process of submitting such a request to the federal government and over submission of amendments to the Medical Assistance state plan and changes in the Medical Assistance reimbursement rate for or the making of supplemental payments to providers of Medical Assistance services.

MENTAL HEALTH AND DEVELOPMENTAL DISABILITIES

Act 26 (Jr7 SS AB-7) expands two grant programs to provide grants for expanding and creating fellowship programs in addiction medicine or addiction psychiatry.

Act 27 (Jr7 SS AB-8) requires DHS to create two or three regional programs to treat opioid and opiate and methamphetamine addiction in underserved, high-need areas.

Act 28 (Jr7 SS AB-9) requires DHS to create and administer an addiction medicine consultation program to assist participating clinicians in caring for patients with substance use addiction. Consultation services through the program may be provided by teleconference, video conference, e-mail, or other mode of communication.

Act 34 (Jr7 SS AB-5) extends to persons who are drug dependent certain programs established by DHS that apply to alcoholics. The act extends emergency detention and involuntary commitment procedures that apply currently to alcoholics and intoxicated persons to persons incapacitated by drug use and persons who habitually lack self-control as to drug use.

Act 143 (AB-843) exempts from the state's requirements for confidentiality of patient health information the disclosure of any threat made by a patient regarding violence in or targeted at a school if the disclosure is a good faith effort to prevent or lessen a serious and imminent threat to the health and safety of a student or school employee or the public.

Act 184 (AB-539) changes the process for determining the residency of a person who is being placed on supervised release after having been involuntarily committed to DHS as a sexually violent person. The act eliminates the ability of the court to choose a county other than the person's county of residence to prepare a report for the placement of the person. The act also requires that the report identify one appropriate residence for the person rather than identify prospective residential options for the person.

WISCONSIN WORKS AND WISCONSIN SHARES

Act 59 (AB-64) does the following:

1. Expands existing controlled substance screening, testing, and treatment requirements to certain Wisconsin Works (W-2) work experience programs, applies the requirements to all adult members of an individual's W-2 group, and, if an individual fails to satisfy the requirements, requires DCF to pay monthly benefits to a protective payee for the benefit of the individual's dependent children.

2. Authorizes individuals who receive case management services after moving from W-2 employment to unsubsidized employment to receive a subsidy for up to 12 months.

3. Provides continued eligibility for families receiving child care subsidies under Wisconsin Shares so that if a family's gross income exceeds 200 percent of the federal poverty line, the family's copayment increases, but the family is not disqualified from receiving a benefit.

Act 269 (Jr8 SS AB-3) creates an asset limit such that to be eligible for FoodShare an individual may have a single residence worth no more than 200 percent of the statewide median home value, excluding agricultural land, and a combined equity value of vehicles, excluding business vehicles, of no more than $20,000. The act allows DHS to create a hardship exemption to the asset limitation. The act also requires DHS and the Department of Children and Families to review death record databases to identify deceased participants in public benefits programs.

Housing

Act 74 (AB-234) creates the Interagency Council on Homelessness, whose purpose is to establish, periodically review, and coordinate statewide policy to prevent and end homelessness.

Act 265 (Jr8 SS AB-4) requires, to the extent allowed under federal law, employment and substance abuse-related screening of residents of public housing and the establishment of employability plans for certain unemployed or underemployed residents of public housing.

Insurance

Act 138 (SB-770) establishes the Wisconsin Healthcare Stability Plan, which provides reinsurance to health carriers whose costs for an enrolled individual exceed a specified amount.

Justice

Act 32 (Jr7 SS AB-2) increases the amount of grant moneys awarded to counties that provide alternatives to prosecution and incarceration for criminal offenders who abuse alcohol and other drugs, expands the grant program to more counties, and creates a pilot program to divert nonviolent offenders to a treatment option instead of prosecution and incarceration.

Act 35 (Jr7 SS AB-10) authorizes four new criminal investigation agent positions at the Department of Justice to focus on drug interdiction and drug trafficking.

Act 143 (AB-843) creates the Office of School Safety in DOJ to award grants to schools to improve school safety, create model practices for school safety, compile blueprints and GIS maps for all schools, and offer training to school staff on school safety.

Act 175 (SB-473) creates an alert for missing veterans at risk that parallels the alerts for missing children at risk (commonly known as the Amber Alert) and missing adults at risk (commonly known as the Silver Alert).

Act 369 (SB-884) limits the authority of the attorney general to compromise or discontinue civil actions prosecuted by DOJ and to compromise or settle certain civil actions for injunctive relief or involving a consent decree defended by DOJ, by requiring that the attorney general obtain approval of a legislative intervenor in the action, if any, or if none, approval from JCF. In actions involving certain statutory challenges, the attorney general, the assembly speaker, the senate president, and the senate majority leader must be served with a copy of the proceeding and the attorney general, the assembly, the senate, and the legislature are each entitled to be heard. When certain statutory challenges are raised in state or federal court, the act allows the state assembly, senate, and legislature to intervene as a matter of right at any time. The act also requires the attorney general to deposit all settlement funds into the general fund and eliminates the DOJ Office of the Solicitor General.

Local government

Act 3 (SB-3) prohibits local units of government from engaging in certain practices in letting bids for public works contracts, including requiring that a bidder enter into an agreement with a labor organization or an agreement that requires the bidder or bidder's employees to become members of, or pay any dues or fees to, a labor organization.

Act 58 (Au7 SS AB-1) excludes from the calculation of a municipality's budget, for purposes of receiving an expenditure restraint payment, expenditures of grant payments to the municipality for the costs associated with developing an Electronics and Information Technology Manufacturing Zone in the municipality. The act also creates special provisions that apply to a tax incremental district created by a city or village in an EITM zone, expands the use of design-build construction, creates new incorporation procedures for certain towns, and creates new provisions related to bonding and the use of sales and use tax revenues that apply to a county in which there is an EITM zone.

Act 59 (AB-64) requires a lodging marketplace, as defined in the act, to register with the Department of Revenue for the collection of sales and use tax and local room tax revenues, expands the applicability of a local room tax to the owners of short-term rentals, and restricts a local government's ability to prohibit or restrict a person from renting out the person's residential dwelling.

Act 67 (AB-479) makes changes to local government zoning authority, including limiting the authority of a political subdivision to prohibit a property owner from conveying an ownership interest in a substandard lot or from using a substandard lot as a building site under certain circumstances. A substandard lot is one that met applicable lot size requirements when it was created but does not meet current requirements.

Act 137 (SB-48) allows cities, villages, towns, and counties to make loans or enter into third-party financing agreements for property owners to replace customer-side water service lines containing lead. The act also creates an exception to a prohibition against political subdivision involvement in private construction contracts. The exception applies to ancillary work performed in replacing utility-side water service lines containing lead.

Act 207 (AB-836) changes the standard for what constitutes "populous counties" in certain statutory provisions from counties having a population of 500,000 or more to counties having a population of 750,000 or more.

Act 327 (AB-748) prohibits local governments from doing any of the following:
1. Requiring any person to accept certain collective bargaining provisions or waive the person's rights under the National Labor Relations Act or state labor law.
2. Imposing additional occupational licensing requirements on a person who works in any profession that is regulated by the state.
3. Enacting or enforcing ordinances related to wage claims and collections, employee hours and overtime, employment benefits, or an employer's right to solicit salary information of prospective employees.

Natural resources

CONSERVATION

Act 71 (SB-421) allows previously authorized but unobligated bonding authority under the stewardship program to be obligated for critical health and safety-related water infrastructure projects in state parks.

FISH AND GAME

Act 14 (SB-46) requires DNR to issue wild turkey hunting licenses and tags to resident disabled veterans and to recipients of the Purple Heart medal without using the cumulative preference system required under current law.

Act 41 (SB-68) provides that, after any confirmed positive test for chronic wasting disease or bovine tuberculosis, the DNR rule prohibiting feeding deer may be in effect for no longer than three years in the county where the tested animal was located or no longer than two years in neighboring counties.

Act 44 (SB-257) allows a person of any age to apply for a preference point under the cumulative preference system for issuing Class A bear hunting licenses. Under prior law, a person had to be at least ten years old to apply for a preference point.

Act 62 (AB-455) eliminates the requirement that a person be at least ten years old to hunt under the hunting mentorship program and eliminates the limit on the number of hunting devices that a mentor and the person hunting with the mentor may have in their possession while hunting.

NAVIGABLE WATERS AND WETLANDS

Act 21 (AB-160) exempts certain fish farming activities from needing a permit to discharge into artificial wetlands created for fish farming purposes. If a wetland permit is needed for fish farming activities, the act limits DNR's review of practicable alternatives. The act also exempts certain activities in a registered fish farm from needing a permit to construct, dredge, or enlarge an artificial water body that is near a navigable waterway. Also under the act, a certain commercial fish farm in Langlade County does not need to allow a minimum amount of water to flow through a dam on a navigable stream if the water is later returned to the navigable stream.

Act 58 (Au7 SS AB-1) prohibits DNR from requiring a permit for any of the following activities that relate to the construction, access, or operation of a new manufacturing facility located in an EITM zone:

1. The deposit of any material or placement of any structure on the bed of any navigable water.

2. The construction, placement, or maintenance of a bridge or culvert in, on, or over navigable waters.

3. The construction, dredging, or enlargement of any artificial water body that connects with or will be located within 500 feet of the ordinary high-water mark of an existing navigable waterway.

4. The grading or removal of topsoil from the bank of any navigable waterway where the area exposed will exceed 10,000 square feet.

5. The changing of the course of or straightening of a navigable stream.

6. The discharge of dredged material or fill material into a nonfederal wetland that is located in an EITM zone if any adverse impacts are compensated at a ratio of two acres per each acre impacted.

Act 118 (AB-497) prohibits DNR from requiring mitigation as a condition of a wetland individual permit issued to a public utility unless the discharge authorized by the permit will result in a permanent fill of more than 10,000 square feet of wetland.

PARKS, FORESTRY, AND RECREATION

Act 59 (AB-64) does all of the following:

1. Eliminates the forestation state property tax (mill tax).

2. Increases most state park and forest daily parks admission fees by up to $5 and increases the range of nightly camping fees in state parks and forests by up to $10, both at the secretary of natural resources's discretion.

Occupational regulation

Act 81 (SB-108) does the following regarding barbers, cosmetologists, and related professionals:

1. Eliminates continuing education requirements, except as part of the disciplinary process, and instead requires as a condition of license renewal that a licensee review a digest e-mailed by Department of Safety and Professional Services that describes changes to laws affecting the practice of those professions.

2. Eliminates the requirement that an applicant for a reciprocal license have 4,000 hours of experience in the licensed practice, and instead requires those applicants to complete a course about laws that apply to the applicant's practice.

Act 88 (AB-188) makes changes regarding the educational requirements that must be satisfied in order to receive a certified public accounting certificate or to take the CPA examination. The act also allows the Accounting Examining Board to participate in certain national data-sharing programs regarding licensees. Finally, the act allows the board to establish continuing education requirements that must be satisfied in order to renew a CPA license.

Act 165 (SB-84) provides immunity to certain persons, including drug manufacturers and physicians, when an investigational drug, device, or biological product that has not yet been approved for use by the federal Food and Drug Administration is provided to an eligible patient, subject to various requirements and limitations.

Act 319 (AB-733) reduces the fee for obtaining an initial occupational credential by 90 percent for a person whose family income does not exceed 180 percent of the federal poverty line.

Public utilities

Act 59 (AB-64) increases funding for broadband expansion grants and requires the Public Service Commission to (1) prioritize grants for areas without access to Internet service at specified upload and download speeds; (2) prioritize grants for projects that do not delay broadband service to neighboring areas; and (3) consider impacts on home access to health care and educational opportunities and impacts on duplication of existing broadband infrastructure.

Real estate

Act 67 (AB-479) prohibits a housing cooperative or homeowners' association from preventing a member of the organization from displaying the flag of the United States on the member's residential property.

Act 222 (AB-118) makes changes to the laws governing the cataloging of properties that are known or believed to contain human remains (burial sites) by the Wisconsin Historical Society. Properties that have been cataloged as burial sites are generally prohibited from being disturbed.

State government

STATE BUILDING PROGRAM

Act 59 (AB-64) authorizes an additional $655,013,200 in general obligation bonding authority during the 2017–19 fiscal biennium for new or revised state building projects.

Act 185 (AB-953) authorizes $25,000,000 in general fund supported borrowing for the construction of Type 1 juvenile correctional facilities statewide; $15,000,000 in general fund supported borrowing for an expansion to the Mendota Juvenile Treatment Center; and $40,000,000 in general fund supported borrowing for grants to counties for the establishment of county-run, secured residential care centers for children and youth.

STATE CONTRACTING

Act 3 (SB-3) prohibits the state, when soliciting bids for goods, services, or construction contracts, from requiring a bidder to enter into an agreement with a labor organization, consider whether a bidder has entered into such an agreement, or require a bidder to enter into an agreement that requires the bidder or bidder's employees to become members of, or pay any dues or fees to, a labor organization.

Act 132 (AB-205) requires the Department of Administration, when entering into or renewing a state lease for real property, to conduct a cost-benefit analysis comparing the proposed lease to the purchase of the space or another suitable space and to evaluate comparable lease options within at least a ten-mile radius to ensure that the proposed lease rates do not exceed lease rates on comparable properties or the market rate by more than 5 percent.

Act 248 (AB-553) prohibits the state and local governments from becoming involved in a boycott of Israel and prohibits the state from contracting with persons that participate in such a boycott.

STATE EMPLOYMENT AND FRINGE BENEFITS

Act 191 (AB-128) prohibits the Group Insurance Board from providing coverage for abortions in a group insurance plan or as part of a benefit offered on a self-insured basis.

STATE FINANCE

Act 59 (AB-64) increases from $5,285,000,000 to $6,785,000,000 the amount of public debt that may be issued to refund any outstanding tax-supported or self-amortizing public debt for facilities.

GENERAL STATE GOVERNMENT

Act 83 (AB-165) provides for the appointment of delegates to a convention called by Congress under Article V of the U.S. Constitution to amend the constitution if the legislatures of at least two-thirds of the states adopt resolutions applying for such a call.

Act 226 (SB-488) allows an individual to use a tribal identification card to sell scrap metal to scrap dealers, used home furnishings to an antique dealer, or secondhand items to a pawnbroker or dealer; to purchase alcohol, cigarettes, or tobacco products; as proof of residence for voter registration; and to purchase certain prescribed controlled substances from a pharmacist.

Act 369 (SB-884) provides that if the Senate rejects a nominee for an office or position that requires senate confirmation, the person may not be renominated for the same office or position during the same legislative biennium.

Taxation

Act 58 (Au7 SS AB-1) does all of the following related to taxation:

1. Authorizes the Wisconsin Economic Development Corporation to certify one or more businesses that begin operations in an Electronics and Information Technology Manufacturing Zone to claim refundable tax credits in connection with job creation and capital investment in the zone and in the state.

2. Provides a sales and use tax exemption for the purchase of building materials, supplies, and services acquired solely for or used solely in the construction of facilities located in the EITM zone if the capital expenditures for such construction may be claimed as an income or franchise tax credit, as certified by WEDC.

Act 59 (AB-64) changes laws related to taxation as follows:

1. Exempts from the personal property tax machinery, tools, and patterns, not including such items used in manufacturing. The act also provides an annual

state aid payment to each taxing jurisdiction equal to the amount of the personal property tax imposed on such items by the taxing jurisdiction for the January 1, 2018, assessment.

2. Eliminates the state forestation property tax for the purpose of acquiring, preserving, and developing the forests of the state and provides for the annual transfer of an amount from the general fund to the conservation fund equal to the revenue that the tax would have generated if still in effect.

3. Repeals the sales and use tax on Internet access services, effective on July 1, 2020.

4. Eliminates the alternative minimum tax for taxable years beginning after December 31, 2018.

5. Allows the current $5,000 individual income tax deduction for adoption expenses to be claimed for adoptions finalized in other states and countries.

Act 68 (AB-480) provides that a property owner's refusal to allow an assessor to enter the person's residence does not preclude the person from appearing before the local board of review to object to the property's valuation. The act also prohibits the assessor from increasing the property's valuation based solely on the property owner's refusal to allow entry.

Act 190 (AB-402) provides a sales and use tax exemption for sales to a state veterans organization.

Act 367 (SB-798) provides a onetime sales and use tax rebate based on a person's eligible dependent children and a sales tax holiday in August for the sale of clothing, school supplies, and personal computers.

Act 368 (SB-883) modifies current law as follows:

1. Allows the state to require certain out-of-state sellers to collect the sales tax from in-state consumers, consistent with the recent U.S. Supreme Court case, *South Dakota v. Wayfair, Inc.* 585 U.S. ___ (2018). An out-of-state seller must collect the tax if its annual gross sales into this state exceed $100,000 or if its annual number of separate sales transactions into this state is 200 or more. The act also requires that the projected increase in sales tax collections from out-of-state sellers be used to reduce the individual income tax rates for 2019, based on a determination by the Department of Revenue, as approved by the Joint Committee on Finance.

2. Allows a partnership, limited liability company, or tax-option corporation to elect to be taxed, for state income tax purposes, at the entity level rather than have the partners, members, or shareholders taxed at the individual level. This election would result in having the entities taxed at a higher corporate rate, but would allow the entities to claim offsetting tax benefits for federal tax purposes.

Protection to create a 'veteran farmer assistance and outreach program to help veterans, and family members of veterans who died in service or are missing in action, integrate into the field of agriculture. The act also requires DATCP and the Department of Veterans Affairs to create a logotype that can be used on agricultural products produced by veterans or family members of veterans who died in service or are MIA.

Act 122 (SB-47) authorizes certification of a disabled veteran-owned business for state procurement and other purposes regardless of the degree of severity of the veteran's service-connected disability.

Act 195 (AB-422) creates the Hire Heroes program, which provides subsidized work opportunities for veterans.

Constitutional amendments

PROPOSED STATE CONSTITUTIONAL AMENDMENTS

Enrolled Joint Resolution 7 (SJR-3), proposed by the 2017 legislature on second consideration, would have eliminated the Office of the State Treasurer from the constitution and replaced the state treasurer with the lieutenant governor on the Board of Commissioners of Public Lands. The amendment was rejected by the voters on April 3, 2018.

Enrolled Joint Resolution 13 (SJR-53), proposed by the 2017 legislature on first consideration, expands in various ways the rights of crime victims under the Wisconsin Constitution. To become a part of the constitution, the 2019 legislature must concur in the amendment and the amendment must then be ratified by the voters.

PROPOSED FEDERAL CONSTITUTIONAL AMENDMENTS

Assembly Joint Resolution 20, adopted by the 2017 legislature, declares that the state of Wisconsin recognizes the rules and procedures adopted by the Assembly of State Legislatures as the official rules and procedures for a convention under Article V of the U.S. Constitution.

Assembly Joint Resolution 21, adopted by the 2017 legislature, constitutes an application to Congress for a convention under Article V of the U.S. Constitution for the purpose of amending the Constitution to require the federal government to operate on a balanced budget. An Article V convention requires the application of at least two-thirds of the states. ▣

Significant decisions of the Wisconsin Supreme Court and Court of Appeals

January 2017 to December 2018

Substantial fault standard under unemployment insurance

In *Operton v. Labor and Industry Review Commission*, 2017 WI 46, 375 Wis. 2d 1, 894 N.W.2d 426, the supreme court held that Lela Operton's conduct did not satisfy the "substantial fault" standard enacted by the legislature and therefore did not disqualify her from receiving unemployment insurance (UI) benefits after her termination from employment.

In 2013, the Wisconsin Legislature enacted various changes to the UI law as part of the 2013-15 state budget act. Among the changes was a provision that disqualified an individual from receiving UI benefits if he or she was terminated for "substantial fault." The act defined substantial fault as "those acts or omissions of an employee over which the employee exercised reasonable control and which violate reasonable requirements of the employee's employer." The act, however, also included three enumerated exceptions to the standard, which, if satisfied, were not to be considered substantial fault. One such exception provided that substantial fault did not include "[o]ne or more inadvertent errors made by the employee." Also included in the act were changes to the even more severe misconduct standard, which had long been governed by the landmark case *Boynton Cab Co. v. Neubeck*, 237 Wis. 249, 296 N.W. 636 (1941). The act codified the *Boynton Cab* standard into the statutes and also delineated a number of additional specific grounds for which a person could be found to have committed misconduct.

The case concerned the application of the substantial fault standard to Operton, who worked as a clerk at a Walgreen's store from 2012 to 2014. During her employment, Operton made a number of errors that resulted in monetary losses to Walgreen's, the last of which was her acceptance of a stolen credit card for payment for a loss of nearly $400. Operton was terminated and applied for UI benefits, which Walgreen's contested. The Department of Workforce Development (DWD) found in an initial determination that Operton's errors had constituted misconduct. On appeal, however, a DWD administrative law judge found that Operton's conduct constituted substantial fault, not misconduct, a finding upheld by the Labor and Industry Review Commission (LIRC) on appeal. Operton appealed further, with the circuit court upholding LIRC's findings and determination. The court of appeals, however, reversed the circuit court, finding that LIRC was owed no deference in its interpretation of the relatively new statute and that LIRC had erred in its construction of the statute.

LIRC appealed to the supreme court, which affirmed the holding of the court of appeals in an opinion written by Chief Justice Roggensack. In discussing the level of deference to be accorded to LIRC, the supreme court held that, because LIRC had not given an articulated interpretation of the statute, the court would not assign a level of deference and would proceed to interpret the statute under established principles of statutory construction. The court then proceeded to analyze the text of the substantial fault exception for inadvertent errors, noting the lack of limitations on the exception, and found that Operton's conduct represented a series of inadvertent errors, each of a similar, but distinct, nature. Because of this, the court found that Operton's conduct fell within the one or more inadvertent errors exception and was therefore not considered substantial fault under the statute.

Three justices each wrote separate concurring opinions, each of which addressed the issue of agency deference. Justice Abrahamson concurred in an opinion joined by Justice A.W. Bradley; Justice Ziegler concurred in a separate opinion; and Justice R.G. Bradley concurred in an opinion joined by Justice Gableman and Justice Kelly. In her concurring opinion, Justice Abrahamson also criticized language in the majority opinion suggesting that inadvertent errors that were repeated or for which warning had been given could constitute substantial fault.

Mining permit

In *AllEnergy Corporation v. Trempealeau County Environment & Land Use Committee*, 2017 WI 52, 375 Wis. 2d 329, 895 N.W.2d 368, the supreme court held that the Trempealeau County Environment & Land Use Committee properly denied AllEnergy Corporation's request to open a frac sand mine. Frac sand is a special type of sand used in fracking, also known as hydraulic fracturing. In fracking, explosives are used to create cracks deep underground. Water, chemicals, and frac sand are then injected into the cracks to hold them open to allow oil or natural gas to seep out into wells.

AllEnergy wanted to open a frac sand mine in Trempealeau County. However, the desired site was located in an agriculture zoning district. Trempealeau County's zoning ordinance allowed frac sand mining in an agriculture zoning district as a conditional use, which meant that AllEnergy needed to obtain a conditional use permit from the county before opening the mine.

Under the county's zoning ordinance, the Trempealeau County Environment

& Land Use Committee could approve a conditional use permit only if the committee determined that "the proposed use at the proposed location will not be contrary to the public interest and will not be detrimental or injurious to the public health, public safety, or character of the surrounding area." The ordinance also included factors to consider when determining whether to grant or deny a conditional use permit, specifically: whether the mine would be a "wise use of the natural resources of the county"; the "aesthetic implications of the siting of such a mine at [that] location"; and "the impacts of such a mining operation on the general health, safety and welfare of the public."

The committee held a public hearing on AllEnergy's application for a conditional use permit. The committee identified conditions that could be placed on the proposed permit to address environmental and health concerns raised during the public hearing. However, the committee ultimately denied AllEnergy's application for the conditional use permit.

AllEnergy sought review in the circuit court, which upheld the committee's decision to deny the permit. The court of appeals also upheld the denial, and AllEnergy appealed to the Wisconsin Supreme Court.

The supreme court issued a split decision. In a lead opinion written by Justice Abrahamson and joined by Justice A.W. Bradley, and in a concurrence written by Justice Ziegler and joined by Chief Justice Roggensack, the four justices rejected AllEnergy's argument that the committee had exceeded its jurisdiction when the committee denied the conditional use permit. The court held that the committee had properly considered and applied the factors required to be considered under the county's zoning ordinance, including use of the county's natural resources, aesthetic implications, and impacts on the general health, safety, and welfare of the public, as well as adverse effects on the environment, including water quality, groundwater, and wetlands.

The court also rejected AllEnergy's argument that the committee's decision was arbitrary and capricious because it was not based on sufficient evidence. The court found that there was sufficient evidence in the record supporting the committee's decision.

Justice Abrahamson and Justice A.W. Bradley went further, examining and rejecting AllEnergy's argument that the zoning ordinance's requirement to consider the impacts of the mine on "the general health, safety and welfare of the public" was unconstitutionally vague and its argument that an applicant for a conditional use permit has a right to that permit if the applicant meets the conditions of the ordinance and if any adverse impacts can be addressed by imposing conditions on the permit.

Justice Kelley, joined by Justice Gableman and Justice R.G. Bradley, dissented.

In their view, the fact that Trempealeau County's zoning ordinance allowed frac sand mining as a conditional use within an agriculture zoning district meant that the county had already determined that frac sand mining was an appropriate use of the property in question. The dissenting justices believed that the only question, then, was whether there were conditions that could be imposed on the proposed mine that would alleviate the environmental and health concerns that had been raised. The dissenting justices would have reversed the decision of the lower court and remanded the matter back to the committee for further proceedings.

Failure to correct inaccurate criminal history report

In *Teague v. Schimel*, 2017 WI 56, 375 Wis. 2d 458, 896 N.W.2d 286, the supreme court held that the Department of Justice's failure to prospectively correct an inaccurate criminal history report constituted a violation of procedural due process.

The Department of Justice (DOJ) is required by statute to maintain a centralized criminal history database of individuals who have come into contact with Wisconsin's criminal justice system and to provide a criminal history report to anyone who requests one. Although the database contains fingerprints and can be searched by fingerprint, a name-based search of the database is faster, cheaper, and easier to perform than a fingerprint-based search.

Dennis Teague's name was listed as an alias of another individual in the DOJ's criminal history database after the other individual allegedly stole Teague's identity. Therefore, any time a name-based search was requested for Teague, the DOJ's report indicated that he had a criminal record when, in fact, he did not. DOJ was aware that its criminal history reports were unreliable and was aware of Teague's situation. DOJ's procedure for an individual who is the subject of a false report is for the individual to request an "innocence letter" from DOJ. The innocence letter verifies that a fingerprint-based search of DOJ's criminal history database shows that, as of the date of the letter, the individual has no criminal history. However, because the innocence letter does not remove the associative information from the database, the innocence letter does not cover any future criminal activity in Teague's case that is committed by the individual with Teague's name listed as an alias.

Teague, along with two other similarly aggrieved individuals, challenged the actions of DOJ on the grounds that DOJ is required by statute to correct its record production when it inaccurately ascribes a criminal history to an innocent person and that failure to correct the false report violates both procedural and substantive due process.

Section 19.70, Wisconsin Statutes, provides that an individual may challenge the accuracy of a record that contains personally identifiable information pertaining to the individual that is maintained by an authority—in this case, DOJ—and, if the authority agrees that the information is incorrect, the authority must correct the information. In an opinion written by Justice Kelly, the supreme court considered this statutory requirement but determined that, although it applied to his case, it was not an adequate remedy for Teague because the statute only provides retroactive correction and does not offer prospective relief.

The court next found that DOJ's practices deprived Teague of his right to due process of law. The court stated that, because the stigma caused by DOJ's criminal history search report imposes a tangible burden on Teague's ability to obtain or exercise a variety of rights and opportunities recognized by state law, he has been deprived of a liberty interest, and the procedural safeguards found in section 19.70, Wisconsin Statutes, and DOJ's innocence letter were insufficient to protect that liberty interest.

Because the court found that procedural due process was violated, the court did not engage in an analysis of whether substantive due process was violated in the case. The court remanded the case to the circuit court to determine an appropriate remedy.

Justice Abrahamson concurred in an opinion joined by Justice A.W. Bradley. Justice Gableman concurred in a separate opinion joined by Chief Justice Roggensack. Justice Ziegler dissented.

Property tax assessment

In *Milewski v. Town of Dover*, 2017 WI 79, 377 Wis. 2d 38, 899 N.W.2d 303, the supreme court held that property owners were entitled to a hearing to contest their property tax assessment even though they did not allow a tax assessor to view the interior of their home.

Vincent Milewski and Morganne MacDonald (the Milewskis) owned property in the Town of Dover. As part of a town-wide revaluation program, the assessor requested permission to view the Milewskis' property, but the Milewskis refused to allow the assessor to view the inside of their home. The assessor later increased the assessed value of the Milewskis' property by 12 percent, and the Milewskis filed an objection with the board of review based on excessive assessment. The board of review refused to hear the objection, relying on state law that prohibits a property owner from challenging a property tax assessment if the owner refused to allow an assessor to view the property. The Milewskis sued claiming that the law was unconstitutional as applied to them.

The supreme court issued a split decision. In the lead opinion written by Justice Kelly and joined by Justice R.G. Bradley, the two justices concluded that the town, by requiring the Milewskis to allow the assessor to view the interior of their property as a precondition to challenging their property tax assessment, violated the Milewskis' due process rights. In reaching that conclusion, the lead opinion found that an assessor "viewing" the interior of a building conducts a search within the meaning of the Fourth Amendment to the U.S. Constitution and that the search would be unconstitutional without a warrant or consent.

Chief Justice Roggensack concurred in the mandate that the Milewskis were entitled to a hearing to contest their tax assessment; however, the concurrence did not address the constitutional issues raised in the lead opinion. Rather, the concurring opinion concluded that the Milewskis complied with the property-viewing requirement by allowing the assessor to view the exterior of their property.

Justice Ziegler also concurred in the mandate in a separate opinion joined by Justice Gableman. The concurring opinion objected to the lead opinion relying on a doctrine that the parties did not address in their briefing and concluded that the case should be decided on narrow grounds.

Justice Abrahamson dissented in an opinion joined by Justice A.W. Bradley. The dissent agreed that an assessor entering a building to view its interior is a search under the Fourth Amendment. The dissent concluded, however, that the Milewskis were afforded due process. According to the dissent, the challenged statutes offered the Milewskis an inducement to consent to the assessor's search by imposing a reasonable and constitutional limit on the ability of the property owners to contest the amount of the assessment if the property owners prevent the assessor from having an actual view of the property.

Building permit rule

In *Golden Sands Dairy LLC v. Town of Saratoga*, 2018 WI 61, 381 Wis. 2d 704, 913 N.W.2d 118, the supreme court expanded the building permit rule to cover all land identified in a building permit application as part of the project.

Golden Sands Dairy LLC obtained a building permit from the town of Saratoga to build seven farm structures on 100 acres of land that comprised part of more than 6,300 acres of land that Golden Sands owned or was under contract to purchase for a planned farming operation. After Golden Sands filed the application, the town enacted a zoning ordinance that prohibited agricultural uses such as those proposed by Golden Sands. Golden Sands asked the court for a declaration that, even though the zoning for the land had changed, Golden Sands had a vested right to use all of the land identified in the application for agricultural purposes.

In a majority opinion written by Justice Gableman, the supreme court held that the building permit rule applied and extended to all land identified in Golden Sands' application, including the land upon which no actual building construction was planned. The majority noted that Wisconsin has long followed a doctrine known as the "building permit rule," which provides a vested right to an applicant to build a structure upon the filing of a building permit application that strictly conforms to all applicable zoning regulations. Because the rule creates a definite moment in time at which rights vest, it is commonly referred to as a "bright-light" rule. Under the building permit rule, an applicant's rights are vested even if the zoning regulations change before the application is granted or before the building is constructed. The court noted that the purpose of the bright-line rule is to create predictability for land owners, purchasers, developers, municipalities, and the courts by balancing a municipality's need to regulate land use with a land owner's interest in developing property under an existing zoning classification.

The majority concluded that the policy underlying the building permit rule supported extending the rule to all land specifically identified in a building permit application. In other words, the court held that the building permit rule gives an applicant a vested right to use all land specifically identified in a building permit application consistent with zoning regulations in effect at the time a building permit application is filed if the application strictly conforms to all applicable zoning regulations.

The majority limited the scope of its ruling by specifying that any vested rights in the land would expire when the building permit expires. Thus, any land not in use at the time a building permit expires would not benefit from the building permit rule, and future use of that land must comply with any zoning ordinances then in effect.

Justice Abrahamson dissented in an opinion joined by Justice A.W. Bradley.

Challenges to the use of tax incremental financing by a municipality

In *Voters with Facts v. City of Eau Claire*, 2018 WI 63, 382 Wis. 2d 1, 913 N.W.2d 131, the supreme court dismissed challenges regarding the use of tax incremental financing (TIF) to support redevelopment projects in the city of Eau Claire but allowed challenges to be brought under the more limited method of certiorari review.

The case arose out of the use of TIF to finance a redevelopment project in downtown Eau Claire known as the Confluence Project. Under current Wisconsin law, a municipality can use TIF to create a tax incremental district (TID), and the increased taxes that are paid by property owners within the TID because of development in the TID and the resulting rise in property values are then allocated to pay back certain costs incurred by the creating municipality. The expansion or creation of a TID may occur only if the municipality adopts findings that the property satisfies one of four criteria, one of which is that at least 50 percent of the property is blighted. In addition, a TID must be approved by a joint review board (JRB), which must find that development would not occur without the use of a TID.

In the fall of 2014, the city of Eau Claire's Common Council voted to expand an existing TID and create a new TID to support the Confluence Project, finding that not less than 50 percent of the areas in question were blighted areas as defined in the statute. In addition, the JRB made the requisite findings that the development would not occur without the TIDs.

The plaintiffs brought suit, alleging that the city's and JRB's findings were not supported by any evidence and that they were lacking a public purpose under the constitution's public purpose doctrine and therefore void. The plaintiffs also made other allegations relating to the disbursement of cash grants pursuant to the project plan, including a claim that funds may be unlawfully used to destroy historic properties and a claim that cash grants functioned as a tax rebate in violation of the Wisconsin Constitution's uniformity clause. The plaintiffs sought both declaratory relief and certiorari review.

Following dismissal in the circuit court, the court of appeals ruled on the plaintiffs' claims, dismissing most of the claims on the grounds that the plaintiffs lacked standing but remanding for certiorari review of the city's and JRB's findings. The supreme court granted review and affirmed the court of appeal's decision, but on alternate grounds.

The supreme court first held that the findings of blight are legislative determinations that did not require any specified rationale or an itemization of supporting evidence and did not raise justiciable issues of fact or law. Therefore, the court wrote, because a court cannot issue a declaration regarding the wisdom of a legislative determination, the blight findings were not susceptible to an action for declaratory judgment. The court applied similar reasoning to findings of the JRB. In both cases, the court held, plaintiffs failed to state a case on which relief could be granted, even assuming that they had standing to bring those claims.

Regarding the uniformity clause claim, the court found that the plaintiffs had not made allegations sufficient to establish such a violation. The court also dismissed a claim regarding the potential use of TID funds for the destruction of historic buildings as having not stated sufficient factual grounds to bring a claim. The court therefore dismissed the complaint with respect to the claims for declaratory relief.

The court held, however, that what were deemed legislative determinations could be challenged through the method of common law certiorari review, which entails a more limited review and applies a presumption of correctness and validity as to the municipality's decision. The court therefore remanded the case to the circuit court for certiorari review of the determinations.

In a lengthy dissent, Justice R.G. Bradley, joined by Justice Kelly, wrote that the claims for declaratory relief should not have been dismissed. In her view, the findings made by the city were not legislative determinations but rather were matters involving factual determinations that could be reviewed by a court. The dissent would also not have dismissed the claim regarding the use of funds to destroy historic properties given the fact that money is fungible. They agreed, however, that the claim with respect to the uniformity clause was correctly dismissed, albeit on other grounds.

Agency deference

In *Tetra Tech EC, Inc. v. Wisconsin Department of Revenue*, 2018 WI 75, 382 Wis. 2d 496, 914 N.W.2d 21, the supreme court ended the longstanding judicial practice of deferring to administrative agencies' conclusions of law.

The Department of Revenue assessed a sales tax on petitioners for work that was performed by a subcontractor conducting environmental remediation of the Fox River. After a field audit, DOR determined that the work performed constituted "processing" of tangible personal property, a service subject to sales tax under Wisconsin law. The petitioners disagreed that the work performed— dewatering and desanding of dredged, contaminated sediment—should fall under the definition of "processing" under the statute. The circuit court and court of appeals sided with DOR, and Tetra Tech EC, Inc., and its subcontractor Lower Fox River Remediation, LLC, petitioned the supreme court for review.

Generally, when a court reviews a question of law, the court applies a de novo standard of review, meaning that the court will consider the question without deference to a lower court or other lower decision maker. However, prior to the supreme court's decision in Tetra Tech, courts granted interpretations of law by an administrative agency varying levels of deference, depending on whether the agency in question was charged by the legislature with administering the law, whether the agency employed expertise in forming its interpretation, and whether the agency's interpretation provided uniformity and consistency in the law's application. Under this test, a court reviewing an administrative agency's interpretation of law gave the agency's interpretation *great weight deference*, meaning that the court would adopt an agency's interpretation if it was reasonable, even if a more reasonable interpretation existed; *due weight deference*, meaning that the court may adopt an interpretation that the court found to be more reasonable than the agency's; or *no deference* at all.

In this case, the supreme court unanimously upheld DOR's interpretation of the statute. However, the court did so without granting, or even considering whether to grant, DOR any agency deference. Instead, the court, on its own initiative, determined to end altogether the practice of granting deference to administrative agencies on questions of law. In a lead opinion authored by Justice Kelly, the court offered a history of the agency deference doctrine, traced its roots and evolution from 1871 to the present day, reviewed the standards of great weight and due weight deference, and included a discussion of concerns raised by U.S. Supreme Court justices regarding the agency deference doctrine under federal law.

Justice Kelly's opinion offered several lines of reasoning for abandoning agency deference in Wisconsin, including that the practice violates both the separation of powers and due process; however, no part of this reasoning was agreed to by a majority of the justices. Thus, while the decision clearly ends administrative deference, the decision does so without clear reasoning by a majority. Separate concurrences authored by Justice A.W. Bradley, Justice Zeigler, and Justice Gableman each raised concerns with the lead opinion's reasoning and approach, including concerns regarding overturning well-established precedent and unnecessarily basing a decision on constitutional principles.

Cap on noneconomic damages in medical malpractice claims is constitutional

In *Mayo v. Wisconsin Injured Patients & Families Compensation Fund*, 2018 WI 78, 383 Wis. 2d 1, 914 N.W.2d 678, the supreme court held that the statutory $750,000 cap on noneconomic damages for victims of medical malpractice is constitutional.

In the 1970s, the Wisconsin Legislature established a system for paying claims alleging medical malpractice against health care providers. Under that system, health care providers must maintain a certain amount of liability insurance coverage and pay an annual assessment, which is deposited in the Wisconsin Injured Patients and Families Compensation Fund (the fund). The fund pays medical malpractice claims that exceed the health care provider's liability coverage, guaranteeing payment of 100 percent of all settlements and judgments for economic damages and up to $750,000 for noneconomic damages for each claim. The legislature has changed the cap at various times, most recently in response to a supreme court case, *Ferdon ex rel. Petrucelli v. Wisconsin Patients Compensation Fund*, 2005 WI 125, 184 Wis. 2d 573, 701 N.W.2d 440, which held that a previous $350,000 cap was facially unconstitutional.

This case arose when Ascaris Mayo visited an emergency room at a Milwaukee hospital complaining of abdominal pain and a high fever. A physician and physician's assistant advised her to follow up with her gynecologist and sent her home. Upon visiting a different emergency room the next day, Mayo was correctly diagnosed with sepsis caused by an untreated infection. Ultimately, all four of her limbs were amputated after many of her organs failed and her limbs developed dry gangrene.

Mayo and her husband sued, alleging medical malpractice and failure to provide proper information. A jury found that, though not negligent, neither the physician nor the physician's assistant gave Mayo adequate information regarding alternative diagnoses and treatment options and awarded economic damages of $8,842,096 and noneconomic damages of $15,000,000 to Mayo and $1,500,000 to her husband. The fund moved to reduce the noneconomic damages award to $750,000 as required under the statutory cap. The circuit court, relying on *Ferdon*, held that, while the cap was not facially unconstitutional, it was unconstitutional as applied to the Mayos on equal protection and due process grounds. The court of appeals, also relying on *Ferdon*, held the cap to be facially unconstitutional.

In an opinion by Chief Justice Roggensack, the supreme court reversed the court of appeals decision, overruled *Ferdon*, and held that the cap on noneconomic damages is constitutional, both facially and as applied to the Mayos. The supreme court held that *Ferdon*'s holding invaded the policy-making function of the legislature by creating a new but unclear standard of scrutiny. The court instead applied the rational basis standard of review and held that the legislature had a legitimate government interest in imposing the cap, supported by the legislature's stated policy objectives: controlling health care costs, encouraging physicians to practice in the state, limiting defensive medicine, making noneconomic damage payments predictable, and protecting the fund's integrity. The court also held that the cap is constitutional as applied to the Mayos because there was no evidence that they were treated differently than others similarly situated and dismissed the argument that the significant balance in the fund compared to the size of the award is relevant to the constitutional claim.

Justice A.W. Bradley dissented, joined by Justice Abrahamson, asserting that the cap on noneconomic damages violates the guarantee of equal protection because the cap treats the most severely injured differently than other injured people who are similarly situated. The dissent also argued that evidence in the record shows that the cap does not achieve the legislature's stated policy objectives and therefore lacks a rational basis.

Ability of State Superintendent of Public Instruction to choose own counsel

In *Koschkee v. Evers*, 2018 WI 82, 382 Wis. 2d 666, 913 N.W.2d 878, the supreme court held that the state superintendent of public instruction was entitled to his own representation in a case where a declaratory judgment was sought regarding the state superintendent's and the Department of Public Instruction's duty to comply with rule-making provisions contained in 2017 Wisconsin Act 57, also referred to as the "REINS Act."

In May 2011, Governor Scott Walker signed into law 2011 Wisconsin Act 21, which included provisions mandating that each agency, when proposing an administrative rule, obtain the governor's and, in one case, the Department of Administration's approval, in order for the agency to promulgate the rule. In *Coyne v. Walker*, 2016 WI 38, 368 Wis. 2d 444, 879 N.W.2d 520, the supreme court addressed whether these provisions were unconstitutional as applied to rules promulgated by the state superintendent, a constitutional office established by article X, section 1, of the Wisconsin Constitution, and the Department of Public Instruction, which is headed by the state superintendent (collectively, SPI). The case garnered five separate opinions, with a majority agreeing that the provisions were unconstitutional because they effectively gave the governor a veto power over the SPI's rules, but with a divergence on the reasoning and the broader issues implicated.

In August 2017, Governor Walker signed into law 2017 Wisconsin Act 57, which included a number of additional provisions affecting the rulemaking process, specifically including some changes to the process by which the governor receives and then approves initial "statements of scope" for rules pursuant to 2011 Act 21. In the following November, a number of petitioners filed an original action with the supreme court seeking a declaration that the SPI was required to comply with the provisions in Act 57. Upon the filing of the petition, a dispute arose between the SPI and the Department of Justice (DOJ) regarding who would represent the SPI in the action, with DOJ indicating that it supported the position taken by the petitioners and the SPI viewing the action as frivolous in light of the recent Coyne decision. After the SPI and DOJ made competing filings on the issue of representation, the supreme court granted the petition to commence the original action and subsequently heard oral argument on the issue of representation. The court ruled on the representation issue in an unsigned order issued approximately one month after the oral argument.

The court began its order by citing its superintending and administrative authority over the courts under article VII, section 3, of the Wisconsin Constitution and the court's power, which flows from that authority, to regulate the practice of law. Deciding a question of representation of a client before the court was, the court said, within the scope of that power and authority. Moving then to the merits of the representation issue, the court ruled that the SPI was entitled to its choice of counsel. The court cited a number of grounds for reaching its decision. First, the court said, there were ethical implications for DOJ attorneys if they were to take a position in the case with which the SPI did not agree, with the court citing a supreme court rule requiring a lawyer to withdraw from representation when discharged by a client. Second, the court observed, DOJ's position would effectively prohibit a constitutional officer, including potentially even a supreme court justice, from taking a position in court contrary to that of the attorney general, a view the court declined to adopt. Consequently, the court granted the SPI's motion to deny substitution of counsel and allowed the SPI to be represented by its own attorneys. The court also ruled that, despite his role in the contested provisions, the governor was not a necessary party to the action. In its order, the court did not address the underlying merits of the petition, leaving them for further argument.

Justice R.G. Bradley, in an opinion concurring in part and dissenting in part from the court's order and that was joined by two other justices, wrote that the majority's decision contradicted both the statutes and the constitution. Finding the constitution and the statutes to be silent on the issue of representation of the SPI in court, she viewed the issue as a matter of legislative prerogative, citing a number of authorities for the proposition that DOJ lawyers are generally the only attorneys authorized to appear in state courts on state matters. She also criticized the majority's invocation of its "ever-evolving" superintending authority in a case that was an original action before the supreme court itself, and not a lower court, cautioning that it allowed the court to use that power to disregard laws passed by the legislature. Finally, Justice R.G. Bradley dismissed the notion that there were ethical implications given that the state, and not the "nominal figurehead," was the real party in interest and that DOJ was statutorily designated to represent it.

Expunged OWI counts as prior OWI conviction

In *State v. Braunschweig*, 2018 WI 113, 384 Wis. 2d 742, 921 N.W.2d 199, a unanimous supreme court held that a prior expunged operating while intoxicated (OWI) conviction must be counted in determining the penalty for a later OWI conviction.

In 2011, Justin Braunschweig was convicted of injuring another person by operation of a vehicle while intoxicated. At the time of sentencing, the circuit court ordered the conviction expunged upon successful completion of the sentence, and the conviction was, in fact, expunged. Nearly five years after that conviction, Braunschweig was convicted of one count of OWI and one count of operating with a prohibited alcohol concentration (PAC), both as second offenses, relying on the 2011 conviction as the prior offense. Braunschweig appealed, claiming that an expunged conviction did not qualify as a prior offense for purposes of charging a later OWI or PAC as a second offense.

In an opinion written by Justice Ziegler, the supreme court affirmed the conviction. The court explained that, in Wisconsin, a first OWI-related offense is civil, but repeat offenses are criminal, and the penalties imposed increase for each subsequent offense. The question in the case was whether a conviction that had been expunged could be counted as a prior offense for purposes of imposing increased penalties.

The court's answer turned on the statutory definition of "conviction," which excludes a conviction that is vacated. The court explained that "vacating" a conviction and "expunging" a conviction are not equivalent. Under Wisconsin law, a conviction may be expunged only under limited circumstances. Expungement is available only if, among other things: 1) the defendant is under 25 years of age at the time the crime is committed; 2) the crime has a maximum period of imprisonment of six years; and 3) the sentencing court determines that the offender will benefit from, and that society will not be harmed by, expungement. If a conviction is expunged, the court seals the case and destroys all court records related to the conviction. Expungement, the supreme court explained, is designed to provide a second chance or a fresh start to an offender.

Vacating a conviction, on the other hand, invalidates a judgment or sentence as a result of jurisdictional, constitutional, or other defects. If a conviction is vacated, it is cancelled and null and void, and it is as if there had been no judgment in the first place. In short, vacating a conviction "invalidates the conviction itself, whereas expunction of a conviction merely deletes the evidence of the underlying conviction from court records."

Thus, the court reasoned, a conviction, even if it is expunged, is still a conviction that must be counted for purposes of determining the appropriate penalty for an OWI-related offense.

Finally, the court determined that, although the court record of the 2011 conviction had been destroyed and could not be considered in the current case, other records existed that could be used to prove the existence of the 2011 conviction. The court concluded that the state had proved the 2011 conviction by a preponderance of the evidence by introducing certified copies of driving records maintained by the Department of Transportation.

Municipal authority to regulate firearms

In *Wisconsin Carry, Inc. v. City of Madison*, 2017 WI 19, 373 Wis. 2d 543, 892 N.W.2d 233, the supreme court held that Wisconsin statute prohibits a city and any of its subunits from regulating firearms in a way that is more stringent than an analogous state statute.

In this case, the city of Madison, through its Transit and Parking Commission, adopted a rule that prohibited city bus passengers from bringing any item of a dangerous nature, including any pistol, rifle, knife, or sword, onto a city bus. Following adoption of this rule, the Wisconsin Legislature passed 2011 Wisconsin Act 35, which authorizes Wisconsin residents to carry a concealed weapon once he or she has obtained the required license. Additionally, section 66.0409, Wisconsin Statutes, also provides that no political subdivision may enact or enforce an ordinance or adopt a resolution that regulates firearms in a manner that is more stringent than a similar state statute. The question presented in this case was whether the city's Transit and Parking Commission, by enacting a rule, had enacted an ordinance or adopted a resolution and, if so, whether the rule regulating the carrying of weapons on board city buses was more stringent than state law and thus prohibited.

In a majority opinion written by Justice Kelly, the court held that the legislature's prohibition on a municipality from enacting an ordinance or resolution regarding firearms that is more stringent than state law necessarily includes a prohibition on any other type of legislation or action by a municipality that may result from the municipality's delegation of its legislative authority. The court concluded that the Transit and Parking Commission is a subunit of the city of Madison and that the commission is permitted to make rules only because the city has delegated its authority to the commission. Thus, the commission may only exercise authority that the city itself may also exercise. The court noted that any other conclusion would result in an absurd result allowing subunits of a city to regulate in a piecemeal fashion when the city itself, in a formal exercise of its power, may not. Therefore, the court concluded that the city through its Transit and Parking Commission had enacted an ordinance or resolution regarding firearms, and thus the court must examine whether the commission's rule was more stringent than state statutes on the topic of firearms.

The court addressed two statutes dealing with firearms to which the Transit and Parking Commission's rule could be compared. First, the court compared the rule to section 167.31 (2) (b) 1., Wisconsin Statutes, which prohibits the placing, possession, or transportation of a firearm in a vehicle unless the firearm is unloaded or a handgun. Because the Transit and Parking Commission's rule prohibited all carrying of firearms on buses, the court held that the rule was more stringent than the relevant statute and thus was prohibited under state law. The second statute to which the court compared the Transit and Parking Commission's rule was section 175.60, Wisconsin Statutes, which allows for a person to carry a concealed weapon anywhere in the state as long as the person complies with the state's licensing requirements. Though the statute does contain a few narrow exceptions, city buses are not mentioned in the statute. The court concluded that the Transit and Parking Commission's rule prohibiting the carrying of a weapon on a city bus was substantially more stringent than the state law on the same topic and was thus prohibited under state law.

Justice A.W. Bradley and Justice Abrahamson dissented, arguing that the court's settled rules of statutory interpretation require looking first to the plain language of the statute and that, when the plain language is clear, the inquiry must stop. The dissent argued that the plain language of the statute in question only applies to ordinances and resolutions and that the city Transit and Parking Commission's rule was neither an ordinance nor a resolution. The dissent argued that the majority opinion impermissibly looked beyond the plain language of the statute in an attempt to create meaning in the statute that the legislature had not contemplated.

Executive agency authority over judges

In *Gabler v. Crime Victims Rights Board*, 2017 WI 67, 376 Wis. 2d 147, 897 N.W.2d 384, the supreme court considered the constitutionality of an executive branch entity exercising authority to evaluate the actions of and impose discipline upon a judge exercising his or her judicial powers. The court held that "Wis. Stat. §§ 950.09 (2) (a), (2) (c)-(d), and (3) and 950.11 cannot constitutionally apply to judges because they invade two exclusive aspects of judicial authority: the judicial power vested in the unified court system and the disciplinary function vested in this court."

The case arose from a decision made by Circuit Court Judge William M. Gabler in January 2012 in a criminal action pending before him. Leigh M. Beebe was accused of sexual assault of two minors. Judge Gabler granted a motion for separate trials, and Beebe was convicted in the first trial in January 2012. The trial involving the second victim was scheduled for August 2012. The state requested that Judge Gabler sentence Beebe immediately for the first conviction. After expressly considering both the rights of the first victim, including the right to a "speedy disposition" of cases under section 950.04 (1v) (k), Wisconsin Statutes, and the rights of the defendant, Judge Gabler exercised his discretion to postpone sentencing in the first matter until completion of the second trial.

The first victim submitted a formal complaint to the Crime Victims Rights Board alleging that Judge Gabler's "decision to postpone sentencing abridged her speedy disposition under Wis. Stat. § 950.04 (1v) (k) and her rights to timely disposition and protection from the accused under Article I, Section 9m of the Wisconsin Constitution."

The board issued a probable cause determination concluding that Judge Gabler violated the victim's statutory and constitutional rights to a timely disposition by postponing the sentencing on the January 2012 conviction. The board then issued a Final Decision and Order, finding that Judge Gabler met the definition of "public employee" and "public official" for purposes of section 950.09 (2) (a), Wisconsin Statutes, and "was therefore subject to the Board's statutory authority to determine whether he violated the rights of a crime victim under Wis. Stat. ch. 950, Wis. Stat. ch. 938, or [A]rticle I, [S]ection 9m of the Wisconsin Constitution, and to impose a remedy for any rights violation found." The board concluded that Judge Gabler violated the first victim's constitutional right to timely disposition of the case in which she was a victim and, as a remedy, issued a Report and Recommendation directed to Judge Gabler consistent with its Final Decision and Order.

Judge Gabler sought circuit court review of the board's decision under chapter 227, Wisconsin Statutes. The circuit court reversed the board's decision and remanded the matter to the board with instructions to dismiss the complaint against Judge Gabler with prejudice. The board appealed. The supreme court subsequently granted Judge Gabler's petition to bypass the court of appeals.

In an opinion written by Justice R.G. Bradley, the supreme court first found that the challenged statutory provisions violate the separation of powers doctrine and are unconstitutional as applied to judges. The court framed the issue in the case as a fundamental constitutional question relating to separation of powers, stating: "May an executive agency, acting pursuant to authority delegated by the legislature, review a Wisconsin court's exercise of discretion, declare its application of the law to be in error, and then sanction the judge for making a decision the agency disfavors? Applying separation of powers principles, we conclude that the answer to this question is unequivocally no." The court found that it is the "province and duty of the judicial department to say what the law is" and that permitting an executive agency to review judges' decisions "for compliance with the victims' rights law would upend the constitutional structure of separated powers, which allocates independent judicial power to the courts." The court also found that allowing the board to impose penalties against a judge, including potential financial forfeitures, could interfere with judicial decision-making and would "contravene" the constitution's "careful allocation of governmental powers."

The court also found that the board's assertion of authority over judges was unconstitutional because it would infringe on the supreme court's exclusive authority to discipline judges, established under article VII, section 11, of the Wisconsin Constitution, which states that "[e]ach justice or judge shall be subject to reprimand, censure, suspension, removal for cause or for disability, by the supreme court pursuant to procedures established by the legislature." The court also noted that section 757.83 (1) (a), Wisconsin Statutes, establishes the judicial commission, which investigates and prosecutes allegations of judicial misconduct. The court stated that, if the commission's prosecution of a judge results in a recommendation for discipline, it is the supreme court that reviews the commission's findings and determines appropriate discipline. The court found that "[a]llowing the Board to take disciplinary action against judges under Wis. Stat. § 950.09 (2) (a), (c) and (d) would clearly contradict the constitution."

While acknowledging that the court does not decide constitutional questions if a case can be resolved on other grounds, the court found that this case was "incapable of resolution without deciding the constitutional conflict presented by the Board's exercise of its statutory powers."

Accordingly, the court affirmed the decision of the circuit court, holding that "Wis. Stat. §§ 950.09 (2) (a) and (2) (c)-(d) and (3) and 950.11 (2015-16) are unconstitutional with respect to judges" and that the board's actions against Judge Gabler were void. The court emphasized, however, that its holding "does not constrain individuals or groups from criticizing judges" and also reaffirmed the court's "commitment to upholding the crime victims' rights enshrined in our statutes and constitution."

Justice Abrahamson wrote separately, concurring in part and dissenting in part, finding that the majority could have, and should have, interpreted the relevant statutes in a manner to uphold the constitutionality of the statutes, stating that "[a]s properly interpreted, the challenged provisions of Chapter 950 are constitutional with respect to judges." Justice Abrahamson nonetheless concurred with the result of the case, finding that judges were *not* "public officials" within the meaning of the challenged statutes and that therefore the challenged statutory provisions were not applicable to judges.

Justice A.W. Bradley did not participate.

Lifetime GPS tracking for sex offenders

In two cases decided in 2018, Wisconsin courts considered and upheld the constitutionality of Wisconsin's lifetime global positioning system (GPS) tracking requirements for persons convicted of certain sex crimes.

In *State v. Muldrow*, 2018 WI 52, 381 Wis. 2d 492, 912 N.W.2d 74, the supreme court unanimously upheld a guilty plea where the defendant was not informed prior to the plea that he would be subjected to a lifetime GPS tracking requirement if he pled guilty.

DeAnthony Muldrow pled guilty to second-degree sexual assault, an offense that subjected him to the lifetime GPS tracking requirement under Wisconsin law. A guilty plea must be entered voluntarily, with full knowledge of the nature of the charge and the potential punishment if convicted. Under Wisconsin law, a court is statutorily required to notify a defendant of the nature of the charge and the punishment that may be imposed if he or she pleads guilty. Muldrow was not informed of the GPS requirement before he pled guilty, and so Muldrow moved to have his guilty plea withdrawn on the basis of a due process violation. The circuit court and court of appeals both held that the GPS tracking requirement did not constitute a "punishment," and therefore the court was not required to inform Muldrow before the plea was entered that he may be subjected to lifetime GPS monitoring.

The supreme court agreed that the lifetime GPS tracking requirement is not a "punishment." Under Wisconsin law, certain serious sex offenders are subject to the GPS tracking requirement. While it is referred to as a "lifetime" requirement, a court can terminate the requirement under the following circumstances: upon a petition to terminate tracking if the offender is permanently physically incapacitated, if the offender moves out of state, or after tracking has been in place for at least 20 years. In determining whether GPS tracking constitutes a punishment, the court analyzed whether the intent or effect of lifetime GPS tracking is punitive. The court found that GPS tracking did not meet the intent-effects test and therefore was not punitive in nature.

In its analysis, the court compared Wisconsin's GPS tracking requirement to a similar requirement under Michigan law. The court noted that, unlike the Michigan law, which fell under that state's penal statutes, Wisconsin's law fell under the statutes primarily concerning safeguards to protect the public from persons convicted of criminal content, with the stated intent to provide "a just, humane[,] and efficient program of rehabilitation of offenders." The court noted that the provisions allowing termination of tracking are "tailored to ensure that an offender is tracked only when he poses a threat to Wisconsin residents."

Having found that the intent of the GPS tracking was not punitive, the court turned to an analysis of whether the effect of the GPS tracking requirement was punitive. The court found that it was not because it did not involve a significant affirmative disability or restraint, has not historically been regarded as punishment, is not aimed at deterrence or retribution, and is not imposed based on new, uncharged criminal conduct, and that the tracking requirement has a rational relationship to a nonpunitive purpose.

In *Kaufman v. Walker*, 2018 WI App 37, 382 Wis. 2d 774, 915 N.W.2d 193, the court of appeals again upheld the lifetime GPS tracking requirement against a challenge that it 1) violates the ex post facto clause of the U.S. Constitution and its counterpart in the Wisconsin Constitution; 2) violates the Fourth Amendment of the U.S. Constitution; and 3) violates due process.

The *ex post facto* clause prohibits the passage of any law that would impose a punishment for a crime retroactively. Because James Kaufman was convicted for sex crimes in 1998 and the lifetime GPS tracking requirement was passed in

2005, Kaufman argued that the imposition of this requirement violated the *ex post facto* clause. However, the court of appeals noted that a law can be an *ex post facto* law only if it imposes punishment, and, as established by the supreme court under *Muldrow*, the GPS tracking requirement is not punitive. Therefore, the court of appeals reasoned, imposition of the law against Kaufman did not violate the ex post facto clause.

Second, Kaufman argued that the lifetime GPS tracking constituted an unreasonable search and violated his Fourth Amendment rights. The court of appeals disagreed, finding that the search was reasonable, that repeat sex offenders have diminished privacy expectations, and that Wisconsin has a particularly strong interest in reducing recidivism through the use of GPS tracking. The court of appeals further held that the GPS program services "the recognized 'special needs' of deterring future crimes and gathering information needed to solve them." Adopting the concurrence from a case out of the Seventh Circuit Court of Appeals that analyzed whether the Wisconsin GPS requirement violated the Fourth Amendment, the court in Kaufman's case stated that "in light of the State's special need to protect children from sex offenders, the GPS's relatively limited scope, and Kaufman's diminished expectation of privacy, the GPS monitoring program constitutes a special needs search."

Finally, the court responded to Kaufman's argument that the GPS tracking requirement violated due process because the statute does not require an individualized determination as to the reasonableness of the requirement in each case. The court did not agree with this argument, noting that the GPS requirement is imposed based on prior convictions rather than current dangerousness and therefore no further procedural protections are necessary.

Breach of contract; tenured professor

In *McAdams v. Marquette University*, 2018 WI 88, 383 Wis. 2d 358, 914 N.W.2d 708, the supreme court held that Marquette University breached its contract with a professor when it suspended him.

A student at Marquette University wanted the issue of gay rights to be open for discussion in a class. The graduate student teaching the class told the student, in an after-class conversation, that certain opinions were not appropriate and that homophobic comments would not be tolerated in the class. The student secretly recorded the conversation and provided a copy of the recording to John McAdams, a political science professor at Marquette. McAdams wrote a blog post criticizing the graduate student for foreclosing debate and included the graduate student's name and contact information. McAdams promoted the blog post and sent the recording of the graduate student to local and national news outlets and other bloggers. McAdams had previously used the idea of a mention on his blog as a threat to others at the university. The graduate student received a number of violent and threatening messages and ultimately transferred to another university.

A university hearing committee made up of seven tenured faculty members unanimously found that Marquette had cause to discipline McAdams and recommended that he be suspended for up to two semesters. The president of the university agreed and suspended McAdams for two semesters but also made McAdams's return contingent on writing a private letter of apology to the graduate student. McAdams refused to write the letter and sued the university for breach of contract.

The circuit court dismissed McAdams's complaint. The court held that McAdams had agreed in his contract to abide by the university's disciplinary procedure; that he was afforded due process during the faculty committee hearing; and that the committee's and university president's findings deserved deference.

The supreme court, in an opinion by Justice Kelly, reversed the circuit court. The supreme court decided not to defer to the committee's and president's findings because the university and McAdams never agreed that the university's discipline procedure would replace or limit their ability to litigate in court. The court also refused to defer because, while the faculty statutes included a detailed procedure for the faculty hearing committee to follow, the final decision on discipline was up to the university's president, and there were no procedures in the faculty statutes for how the president was to make that decision. The court also found that the faculty hearing committee's impartiality was tainted because one member had previously made her opinion about McAdams's actions public. Finally, the court noted that the faculty hearing committee was an advisory body only and that the court would not defer to advice.

Having decided not to defer to the faculty hearing committee or university president, the court went on to look at the merits of the case. The university's faculty handbook ensured the concept of academic freedom for university professors, including for statements made as a citizen outside the scope of a professor's university activities. The parties and the court relied on policy documents from the American Association of University Professors, which state that "a faculty member's expression of opinion as a citizen cannot constitute grounds for dismissal unless it clearly demonstrates the faculty member's unfitness for his or her position" and that "a final decision should take into account the faculty member's entire record as a teacher and scholar." The court interpreted this as a two-part test and looked exclusively at whether McAdams's blog post, taken by itself, clearly demonstrated that he was unfit for his position. The court noted that there is no law or university rule that prohibited McAdams from naming a student in a blog post, publishing a student's contact information, or distributing the secretly made recording of the student. The court held that the blog post did not clearly demonstrate that McAdams was unfit for his position and that the blog post was therefore protected under the doctrine of academic freedom. As such, the university breached its contract with McAdams when it suspended him. The court ordered the university to reinstate McAdams with back pay.

Justice A.W. Bradley, joined by Justice Abrahamson, dissented. In their view, the majority disregarded the "mutually agreed-upon and time-honored" shared governance process under which a university president relied on the findings of a committee made up of faculty peers and noted that the committee, not the court, observed the demeanor of witnesses and was in a position to assess credibility. The dissenting justices determined that "[t]he revealing of a student's contact information for the purpose of holding that student up for public ridicule and harassment is not a protected act of academic freedom." ▣

4

STATISTICS AND REFERENCE

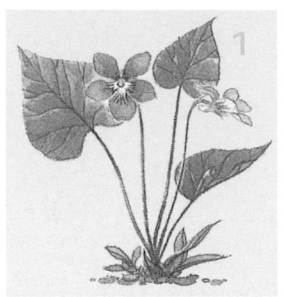

1. **State flower.** Wood violet (*Viola papilionacea*)

2. **State tree.** Sugar maple (*Acer saccharum*)

3. **State animal.** Badger (*Taxidea taxus*)

4. **State bird.** Robin (*Turdus migratorius*)

5. **State fish.** Muskellunge (*Esox masquinongy masquinongy Mitchell*)

6. **State dog.** American water spaniel

7. **State insect.** Honey bee (*Apis mellifera*)

8. **State domestic animal.** Dairy cow (*Bos taurus*)

9. **State wildlife animal.** White-tailed deer (*Odocoileus virginianus*)

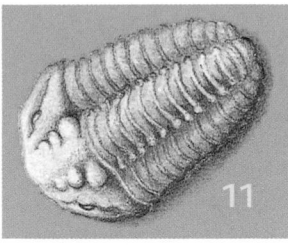

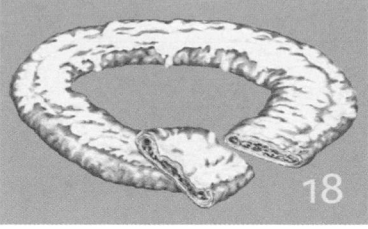

10. State symbol of peace. Mourning dove (*Zenaidura macroura carolinensis Linnaeus*)

11. State fossil. Trilobite (*Calymene celebra*)

12. State mineral. Galena (*lead sulfide*)

13. State rock. Red granite

14. State soil. Antigo silt loam (*Typic glossoboralf*)

15. State beverage. Milk

16. State fruit. Cranberry (*Vaccinium macrocarpon*)

17. State grain. Corn (*Zea mays*)

18. State pastry. Kringle

19. State dance. Polka

20. State dairy product. Cheese

Ginseng: Wisconsin's new state herb

Farmers have raised domesticated ginseng in Wisconsin for over a century. In 1904, the Fromm brothers pioneered ginseng farming in Wisconsin. After they successfully harvested and sold their first crop for $24 in 1909, other farmers began to replicate their process. Demand for American ginseng grew, and by 1919, Wisconsin had become the leading producer of ginseng in the nation.

Today, Wisconsin remains the leading producer of ginseng in both acreage and volume, and the state is known for producing some of the highest quality ginseng in the world. It is estimated that Wisconsin farmers produced over one million pounds of ginseng in 2017, which accounted for 98 percent of U.S. ginseng production and 10 percent of the world's supply. The vast majority of Wisconsin's ginseng production takes place in north-central Wisconsin, particularly in Marathon County, where the area's cool climate, rolling hills, and quality topsoil are ideal for raising ginseng.

Coat of arms. The large shield at the center of the coat of arms is divided into quarters on which appear symbols for agriculture (plow), mining (pick and shovel), manufacturing (arm and hammer), and navigation (anchor). At the center of the large shield, a small shield and the band that encircles it represent the United States coat of arms and symbolize Wisconsin's membership in and loyalty to the United States. Supporting the large shield from the sides are a sailor holding a coil of rope and a yeoman resting on a pick. These figures represent labor on water and land. At the base of the large shield, a horn of plenty represents prosperity and abundance, and a pyramid of 13 lead ingots represents mineral wealth and the 13 original states of the United States. Above the large shield appears a badger, the state animal, and above the badger appears the state motto, "Forward."

Great seal. The great seal consists of the state coat of arms; the words "Great Seal of the State of Wisconsin" in a curve above; and a line of 13 stars, representing the 13 original states of the United States, in a curve below, all enclosed within an ornamental border. The great seal is used to authenticate the official acts of the governor other than the governor's approval of laws.

Flag. The state flag consists of the state coat of arms; the word "Wisconsin" in white letters above; and the statehood date "1848" in white numbers below, all centered on a royal blue field.

State song. "On, Wisconsin," music by W. T. Purdy

On, Wisconsin! On, Wisconsin! Grand old badger state! We, thy loyal sons and daughters, Hail thee, good and great. ▪ On, Wisconsin! On, Wisconsin! Champion of the right, "Forward", our motto—God will give thee might!

State ballad. "Oh Wisconsin, Land of My Dreams," words by Erma Barrett, music by Shari A. Sarazin

Oh Wisconsin, land of beauty, with your hillsides and your plains, with your jackpine and your birch tree, and your oak of mighty frame. ▪ Land of rivers, lakes and valleys, land of warmth and winter snows, land of birds and beasts and humanity, oh Wisconsin, I love you so. ▪ Oh Wisconsin, land of my dreams. Oh Wisconsin, you're all I'll ever need. A little heaven here on earth could you be? Oh Wisconsin, land of my dreams. ▪ In the summer, golden grain fields; in the winter, drift of white snow; in the springtime, robins singing; in the autumn, flaming colors show. ▪ Oh I wonder who could wander, or who could want to drift for long, away from all your beauty, all your sunshine, all your sweet song? ▪ Oh Wisconsin, land of my dreams. Oh Wisconsin, you're all I'll ever need. A little heaven here on earth could you be? Oh Wisconsin, land of my dreams. ▪ And when it's time, let my spirit run free in Wisconsin, land of my dreams.

State waltz. "The Wisconsin Waltz," words and music by Eddie Hansen

Music from heaven throughout the years; the beautiful Wisconsin Waltz. Favorite song of the pioneers; the beautiful Wisconsin Waltz. ▪ Song of my heart on that last final day, when it is time to lay me away. One thing I ask is to let them play the beautiful Wisconsin Waltz. ▪ My sweetheart, my complete heart, it's for you when we dance together; the beautiful Wisconsin Waltz. I remember that September, before love turned into an ember, we danced to the Wisconsin Waltz. ▪ Summer ended, we intended that our l ives then would both be blended, but somehow our planning got lost. ▪ Memory now sings a dream song, a faded love theme song; the beautiful Wisconsin Waltz.

State tartan. The thread count of the state tartan is 44 threads muted blue; 6 threads scarlet; 4 threads muted blue; 6 threads gray; 28 threads black; 40 threads dark green; 4 threads dark yellow; 40 threads dark green; 28 threads black; 22 threads muted blue; and 12 threads dark brown (half sett with full count at the pivots).

Significant events in Wisconsin history

First nations

Wisconsin's original residents were Native American hunters who arrived here about 14,000 years ago. The area's first farmers appear to have been the Hopewell people, who raised corn, squash, and pumpkins around 2,000 years ago. They were also hunters and fishers, and their trade routes stretched to the Atlantic Coast and the Gulf of Mexico. Later arrivals included the Chippewa, Ho-Chunk (Winnebago), Mohican/Munsee, Menominee, Oneida, Potawatomi, and Sioux.

Under the flag of France

The written history of the state began with the accounts of French explorers. The French explored areas of Wisconsin, named places, and established trading posts; however, they were interested in the fur trade, rather than agricultural settlement, and were never present in large numbers.

1634 Jean Nicolet became the first known European to reach Wisconsin.

1654–59 Pierre-Esprit Radisson and Médart Chouart des Groseilliers became the first known fur traders in Wisconsin.

1661 Father René Ménard became the first missionary to set foot in Wisconsin.

1665 Father Claude Allouez founded a mission at La Pointe.

1668 Nicolas Perrot opened fur trade with Wisconsin Indians near Green Bay.

1672 Father Allouez and Father Louis André built the St. François Xavier mission at De Pere.

1673 Louis Jolliet and Father Jacques Marquette traveled the length of the Mississippi River.

1679 Daniel Greysolon Sieur du Lhut (Duluth) explored the western end of Lake Superior.

1689 Perrot asserts the sovereignty of France over various Wisconsin Indian tribes.

1690 Lead mines are discovered in Wisconsin and Iowa.

1701–38 The Fox Indian Wars occurred.

1755 Wisconsin Indians, under Charles Langlade, helped defeat British General Braddock during the French and Indian War.

1763 The Treaty of Paris is signed, making Wisconsin part of British colonial territory.

Under the flag of Great Britain

Wisconsin experienced few changes under British control. It remained the western edge of European penetration into the American continent, important only as a source of valuable furs for export. French traders plied their trade, and British and colonial traders began to appear, but Europeans continued to be visitors rather than settlers.

1763 Wisconsin Indians staged a revolt against the new and comparatively more hostile British regime.

1764 Charles Langlade—later known as the "Father of Wisconsin"—settled at Green Bay.

1766 Jonathan Carver explored various sites along the Mississippi River, including a Fox Indian settlement at Prairie du Chien.

1774 The Quebec Act made Wisconsin a part of the Province of Quebec.

1783 The second Treaty of Paris is signed, making Wisconsin a U.S. territory.

Achieving territorial status

In spite of the second Treaty of Paris, Wisconsin remained British in all but title until after the War of 1812. In 1815, the American army established control. Gradually, the British extinguished Indian title to the southeastern half of the state. Lead mining brought the first heavy influx of settlers and ended the dominance of the fur trade in the economy of the area. The lead mining period ran from about 1824 to 1861. Almost half of the 11,683 people who lived in the territory in 1836 were residents of the lead mining district in the southwestern corner of the state.

1787 Under the Northwest Ordinance of 1787, Wisconsin was made part of the Northwest Territory. The governing units for the Wisconsin area prior to statehood were:

1787–1800	Northwest Territory.
1800–1809	Indiana Territory.
1809–1818	Illinois Territory.
1818–1836	Michigan Territory.
1836–1848	Wisconsin Territory.

1795 Jacques Vieau established a trading post at Milwaukee, and outposts at Kewaunee, Manitowoc, and Sheboygan.

1804 William Henry Harrison's treaty with Indians at St. Louis extinguished Indian title to land in the lead region, which eventually became a contributing cause of the Black Hawk War.

1815 The War of 1812 concluded, leading to the abandonment of Fort McKay (formerly Fort Shelby) by the British.

1816 Astor's American Fur Company began operations in Wisconsin.

1819 Solomon Juneau bought Jacques Vieau's Milwaukee trading post.

1820 Rev. Jedediah Morse traveled to the Green Bay area to report on Indian tribes to the U.S. secretary of war. Lewis Cass, James Duane Doty, and Henry Schoolcraft made an exploratory trip through Wisconsin.

1821 Oneida, Stockbridge, Munsee, and Brothertown tribes began migrating to Wisconsin from the New York area.

1822 The first mining leases in southwest Wisconsin were issued.

1825 A treaty concluded at Prairie du Chien established tribal boundaries.

1827 The Winnebago War began and quickly ended with the surrender of Chief Red Bird to the United States.

1832 The Black Hawk War occurred.

1833 The second Treaty of Chicago between the United States and the Potawatomi granted the U.S. government the land between Lake Michigan and Lake Winnebago. The first Wisconsin newspaper, the *Green Bay Intelligencer*, was established.

1834 Land offices were established in Green Bay and Mineral Point. The first public road was laid.

1835 The first steamboat arrived in Milwaukee. The first bank in Wisconsin obtained its charter and later opened in Green Bay.

1836 President Andrew Jackson signed the act creating the Territory of Wisconsin on April 20. (Provisions of Ordinance of 1787 made part of the act.)

Wisconsin territory

Wisconsin's population had reached 305,000 by 1850. Newcomers were primarily migrants from New York and New England, or immigrants from England, Scotland, Ireland, Germany, and Scandinavia. New York's Erie Canal gave Wisconsin a water outlet to the Atlantic Ocean and a route for new settlers. Wheat was the primary cash crop for most of the newcomers.

State politics revolved around factions headed by James Doty and Henry Dodge. As political parties developed, the Democrats proved dominant throughout the period.

1836 Henry Dodge was appointed governor by President Andrew Jackson. The first session of the legislature was held, and Madison was chosen as permanent capital. (The capital had initially been located in Belmont.) Madison was surveyed and platted.

1837 Construction on the first capitol building began. The Panic of 1837 drove territorial banks to failure and initiated a five-year economic depression. The Winnebago Indians ceded all claims to land in Wisconsin. Imprisonment for debt was abolished.

1838 The territorial legislature met in Madison. The Milwaukee & Rock River Canal Company was chartered to create a canal connecting Lake Michigan to the Rock River and, accordingly, a waterway to the Mississippi River.

1841 James D. Doty was appointed governor by President John Tyler.

1842 Legislator James Vineyard shot and killed fellow legislator Charles Arndt in the capitol.

1844 Nathaniel P. Tallmadge was appointed governor by President Tyler. The Wisconsin Phalanx, a utopian commune, was established in Ceresco (later annexed by Ripon).

1845 Dodge was reappointed governor by President James Polk. Mormons settled in Voree (near Burlington). Swiss immigrants founded New Glarus.

1846 Congress passed the enabling act for the admission of Wisconsin as state.

The first constitutional convention met in Madison.

1847 The first proposed state constitution was rejected by the people. A second constitutional convention was held.

1848 The second proposed state constitution was adopted. President Polk signed a bill on May 29 making Wisconsin a state.

Early statehood

Heavy immigration continued, and the state remained largely agricultural. Slavery, banking laws, and temperance were the major political issues of the period. Despite the number of foreign immigrants, most political leaders continued to have ties to the northeastern United States, and New York state laws and institutions provided models for much of the activity of the early legislative sessions. Control shifted from the Democrats to the Republicans during this period.

1848 The legislature met on June 5, and Governor Nelson Dewey was inaugurated June 7. The University of Wisconsin was founded. Large-scale German immigration began.

1849 A school code was adopted, and the first free, tax-supported, graded school with a high school was established in Kenosha. The first telegram reached Milwaukee.

1850 The state opened the Wisconsin Institute for Education of the Blind at Janesville.

1851 The first railroad train ran from Milwaukee to Waukesha. The first state fair was held in Janesville.

1852 The Wisconsin School for the Deaf opened in Delavan. Prison construction begun at Waupun.

1853 Capital punishment was abolished following the controversial execution of John McCaffary in 1851.

1854 The Republican Party formed in Ripon. The first class graduated from the University of Wisconsin. Joshua Glover, a fugitive slave, was arrested in Racine, and the Wisconsin Supreme Court, in a related matter, declared the Fugitive Slave Law of 1850 unconstitutional. The Milwaukee and Mississippi Railroad reached Madison.

1856 Two candidates claimed themselves winners of a contested gubernatorial race. Coles Bashford took office only after acting Governor William Barstow was found to have committed election fraud.

1857 The first passenger train reached Prairie du Chien, connecting Milwaukee with the Mississippi River.

1858 Legislators uncovered bribery by former Governor Bashford and other members of the 1856 Legislature.

1859 Abraham Lincoln spoke at the state fair in Milwaukee.

1861 The U.S. Civil War began. A bank riot occurred in Milwaukee. The office of county superintendent of schools was created.

1862 Governor Louis P. Harvey drowned. Draft riots occurred.

1864 Chester Hazen founded the state's first cheese factory in Ladoga.

1865 The U.S. Civil War ends. Approximately 96,000 Wisconsin soldiers served in the war, and 12,216 died.

The maturing commonwealth

After the Civil War, Wisconsin matured into a modern political and economic entity. Heavy immigration continued, with composition remaining similar to the antebellum period until the end of the century, when Poles arrived in larger numbers.

The Republican Party remained in control of state government throughout the period, but was challenged by Grangers, Populists, Socialists, and Temperance candidates in addition to the Democratic Party and dissidents within the Republican Party. Temperance, the use of foreign languages in schools, railroad regulation, and currency reform were major political issues in the state.

In the 1880s and 1890s, dairying surpassed wheat culture to become the state's primary agricultural activity, with the University of Wisconsin's agricultural school becoming a national leader in the field of dairy science. From the 1870s to the 1890s, lumbering prospered in the north, accounting for one-fourth of all wages paid in the state at its peak. During the same period, Milwaukee developed a thriving heavy machinery industry, and the paper industry emerged in the Fox River Valley. The tanning and the brewing industries were also prominent.

1866 The Platteville Normal School (University of Wisconsin-Platteville) opened as the first teacher preparation institution in the state. The legislature formally named the University of Wisconsin a land-grant institution and incorporated an agricultural department.

1871 The Peshtigo fire resulted in over 1,000 deaths—the most fatalities by fire in U.S. history.

1872 The Wisconsin Dairymen's Association organized in Watertown.

1873 Milwaukee newspaper publisher and Wisconsin legislator Christopher Latham Sholes invented the typewriter. The Patrons of Husbandry, an agricultural organization nicknamed the Grangers, helped elect William R. Taylor as governor.

1874 The Potter Law, which limited railroad rates, was enacted—only to be repealed two years later.

1875 A free high school law was enacted. The State Industrial School for Girls was established in Milwaukee. Republican Harrison Ludington defeated Governor Taylor. Oshkosh, a leader in the lumber trade, was almost destroyed by fire.

1876 The community of Hazel Green was destroyed by a tornado.

1877 John Appleby patented a device to bind bundles of grain with twine, a significant contribution to automating agricultural production.

1882 The Wisconsin Constitution was amended to make legislative sessions biennial. The world's first hydroelectric plant was built in Appleton.

1883 Fire at the Newhall House in Milwaukee killed 71—the country's most lethal hotel fire. The south wing of the capitol extension collapsed; seven were killed. The legislature established the Agricultural Experiment Station at the University of Wisconsin. Wisconsin first observed Arbor Day.

1885 Gogebic iron range discoveries made Ashland a major shipping port.

1886 Strikes related to the eight-hour work day movement in Milwaukee culminated in confrontation with the militia at Bay View; five were killed. The University of Wisconsin established an agricultural short course.

1887 Marshfield was almost destroyed by fire.

1889 The Bennett Law, requiring classroom instruction in English, passed. In the "Edgerton Bible case," the Wisconsin Supreme Court prohibited reading and prayers from the King James Bible in public schools. Former Governor Jeremiah Rusk became the first U.S. secretary of agriculture.

1890 Stephen M. Babcock invented an easy and accurate test for milk butterfat content.

1891 The Bennett Law was repealed after bitter opposition from German Protestants and Catholics.

1893 The Wisconsin Supreme Court ordered the state treasurer to refund to the state interest on state deposits, which had customarily been retained by treasurers.

1897 Corrupt-practices legislation was enacted to regulate caucuses and prohibit bribery of voters. The Wisconsin Tax Commission was created.

1898 Wisconsin sent 5,469 men to fight in the Spanish-American War, suffering 134 losses.

1899 A new law prohibited railroads from giving public officials free rides. The New Richmond Tornado, the deadliest ever recorded in Wisconsin, killed 117 people.

The progressive era

The state's prominent role in the reform movements that swept the country at the beginning of the century gave Wisconsin national fame and its first presidential candidate. Republicans controlled the state legislature, but the Progressive and Stalwart factions fought continually for control of the party. Milwaukee consistently sent a strong Socialist contingent to the legislature.

Large-scale European immigration ended during this period, but ethnic groups retained strong individual identities and remained a significant force in the politics and culture of the state. Of those groups, Germans faced disproportionate suspicion and hostility during the two world wars.

Heavy machinery manufacturing, paper products, and dairying continued to drive the state economy. Meanwhile, lumbering faded in importance and brewing ground to a halt with the onset of Prohibition.

1900 Wisconsin's first state park, Interstate near St. Croix Falls, was established.

1901 First Wisconsin-born governor, Robert M. La Follette, was inaugurated. Agricultural education was introduced into rural schools. The Legislative Reference Library, which served as a model for other states and for the Library of Congress, was established and later renamed the Legislative Reference Bureau.

1904 A referendum vote approved popular election of primary candidates for state-level offices (in place of selection by party leaders). The state capitol burned down, destroying many records and state artifacts.

1905 The state civil service was established. An auto license law that required residents to register their automobiles and display license plates was enacted. A law was enacted that authorized the establishment of a state-owned sanitarium for tuberculosis patients. The Forestry Board and Railroad Commission were created.

1907 Construction on the current capitol building began.

1908 A referendum amended the Wisconsin Constitution to permit taxing the income of individuals and corporations.

1910 Milwaukee elected Emil Seidel as the first Socialist mayor of a major city in the United States. Eau Claire became the first Wisconsin city to adopt a commission form of government.

1911 The legislature enacted a bill to establish the state income tax. The Workmen's Compensation Act required employer compensation for on-the-job injuries. The legislature created a pension plan for public school teachers statewide. It also required every town, city, or village with a population of over 5,000 to establish an industrial school. The State Highway Commission was created to regulate the construction and inspection of highways and bridges, and to ensure highways would form continuous routes. The State Industrial Commission was formed to investigate and create administrative rules relating to industrial safety.

1913 Wisconsin ratified the Seventeenth Amendment, which provided that the people, rather than the state legislature, would directly elect U.S. senators.

1915 The Conservation Commission, the State Board of Agriculture, and the State Board of Education were created.

1917 The new capitol building was

completed at a final cost of over $7 million. Wisconsin sent approximately 120,000 soldiers to serve during World War I, of which nearly 4,000 died. Wisconsin was the first state to meet national draft requirements.

1919 Wisconsin ratified the Eighteenth Amendment, which established Prohibition, and was the first state to deliver the ratification of the Nineteenth Amendment, which granted American women the right to vote.

1921 Laws establishing Prohibition and equal rights for women were enacted.

1923 Military training at the University of Wisconsin was made optional, rather than compulsory.

1924 Robert M. La Follette, Sr., ran for president as the Progressive Party candidate and won the state of Wisconsin.

1925 Professor Harry Steenbock developed a way to increase vitamin D in certain foods and prompted the formation of the Wisconsin Alumni Research Foundation to ensure that his patent would benefit the University of Wisconsin.

1929 The legislature repealed all Wisconsin laws enforcing Prohibition.

1933 Dairy farmers orchestrated strikes to protest low milk prices. Wisconsin voted for the repeal of the Eighteenth Amendment (Prohibition).

1935 A researcher from the Forest Products Laboratory in Madison helped convict the kidnapper and murderer of Charles Lindbergh's son in 1932.

1942 Governor-elect Orland Loomis died; the Wisconsin Supreme Court decided that Lieutenant Governor Walter Goodland would serve as acting governor.

1941–45 Wisconsin sent over 330,000 to serve in World War II (including approximately 9,000 enlisted women), of whom about 8,000 died.

1946 The Wisconsin Progressive Party dissolved and rejoined the Republican Party.

The middle years of the twentieth century

After the demise of the Progressives, the Democratic Party began a gradual resurgence and, by the late 1950s, became strongly competitive for the first time in over a century. As the black population grew in urban areas of the state, discrimination in housing and employment became matters of increasing concern. Other issues included the growth in the size of state government, radicalism on the university campuses, welfare programs, and environmental questions. Tourism emerged as a major industry during this period.

1948 Wisconsin's Centennial Year.

1949 The legislature enacted a new formula for the distribution of state educational aids and classified school districts for this purpose.

1950 Approximately 132,000 Wisconsinites served during the Korean Conflict, and 747 died.

1951 Legislative districts were reapportioned to reflect the rapid growth of urban populations.

1957 A new law prohibited lobbyists from giving anything of value to a state employee.

1958 Professor Joshua Lederberg, a geneticist at the University of Wisconsin, won the Nobel Prize in Physiology or Medicine.

1959 Gaylord Nelson, the first Democratic governor since 1933, was inaugurated. The Circus World Museum was established in Baraboo. Famous Wisconsin architect Frank Lloyd Wright died.

1960 Dena Smith was elected state treasurer, becoming the first woman elected to statewide office in Wisconsin.

1961 The legislature initiated a long-range program of acquisition and improvement of state recreation facilities (the ORAP program). Menominee became Wisconsin's 72nd county when federal supervision of the Indian tribe terminated.

1962 Selective sales tax and income tax withholding were enacted. The Kohler Company recognized its workers' union after a record-long strike that began in 1954.

1963 John Gronouski, the state tax commissioner, was appointed U.S. postmaster general. State expenditures from all funds for the 1963–64 fiscal year topped $1 billion for the first time.

1964 The Wisconsin Supreme Court redistricted the legislative districts after the legislature and the governor failed to agree on a plan. Two National Farmers Organization members were killed in a demonstration at a Bonduel stockyard. The legislature enacted property tax relief for the elderly. The office of county superintendent of schools was abolished, but Cooperative Educational Service Agencies (CESAs) were created to provide regional services.

1965 The school compulsory attendance age was raised to 18. All parts of the state were placed into vocational school districts. County boards were reapportioned on the basis of population. A new state law prohibited discrimination in housing. The capitol building, in use since 1917, was officially dedicated after extensive remodeling and cleaning.

1966 The 1965 Legislature held the first full even-year regular session since 1882. Governor Warren P. Knowles called the National Guard to keep order during civil rights demonstrations in Wauwatosa. The Wisconsin Supreme Court upheld the Milwaukee Braves baseball team's move to Atlanta. A grand jury investigation of illegal lobbying activities in the legislature resulted in 13 indictments.

1967 The executive branch was reorganized. Legislators repealed a ban on colored oleomargarine. Civil disturbances broke out in Milwaukee in late July. Activists advocated for a Milwaukee open housing ordinance. Anti-war protests at the University of Wisconsin-Madison culminated in violence.

1968 A constitutional amendment permitted the legislature to meet as provided by law rather than once per biennium. The State University of Wisconsin at Oshkosh expelled 94 black students who confronted administrators about civil rights issues. Doctors performed Wisconsin's first heart transplant at St. Luke's Hospital in Milwaukee. The first successful bone marrow transplant that was not between identical twins was performed by a team of scientists and surgeons at UW-Madison.

1969 Wisconsin implemented a general sales tax in place of elective sales taxes. Father James Groppi led protests at the capitol on the opening day of a special legislative session on welfare and urban aids. The National Guard was called, and Groppi was cited for contempt and jailed. Student strikes at UW-Madison demanded a black studies department, and the National Guard was again activated. Wisconsin Congressional Representative Melvin R. Laird was appointed U.S. secretary of defense. Wisconsin's portion of the Interstate Highway System was completed.

1970 Anti-war protestors bombed the Army Mathematics Research Building at UW-Madison, resulting in one

death. "Old Main" at Wisconsin State University-Whitewater burned down in an apparent arson. State constitutional officers were elected to four-year terms for the first time in Wisconsin history following a constitutional amendment ratified in 1967. University of Wisconsin scientists, headed by Dr. Har Gobind Khorana, succeeded in the first total synthesis of a gene.

1971 The legislature enacted major shared tax redistribution, the merger of the University of Wisconsin and State University systems, and a revision of municipal employee relations laws.

1972 The legislature enacted comprehensive consumer protection, lowered the age of majority from 21 to 18, required an environmental impact statement for all legislation affecting the environment, repealed the railroad full crew law, and ratified the unsuccessful "equal rights" amendment to the U.S. Constitution. The state reached a record highway death toll of 1,168.

1973 A state constitutional amendment permitting bingo was adopted. Barbara Thompson became the first woman to hold the elective office of state superintendent of public instruction. The 1954 Menominee Termination Act was repealed by the U.S. Congress. The legislature enacted a state ethics code, repealed an oleomargarine tax, funded programs for the education of all children with disabilities, and established procedures for the informal probate of simple estates.

1974 The legislature enacted a comprehensive campaign finance act and strengthened the open meetings law. Democrats swept all constitutional offices and gained control of both houses of the 1975 Legislature for first time since 1893. Kathryn Morrison became the first woman elected to the state senate. The Hortonville School District fired striking teachers.

1964–75 165,400 Wisconsinites served in Vietnam; at least 1,161 were killed.

The late twentieth century

Democrats lost control of the senate in 1993 for the first time since 1974, and in 1995 they lost control of the assembly for the first time since 1970. Women began to be widely represented in the legislature for the first time in the 1990s.

Health care reform, welfare, the state's business climate, taxation, education, and prisons were the chief concerns of policymakers in the 1990s.

California challenged Wisconsin's dominance of the dairy industry. After an economic downturn in the 1980s, the 1990s saw a robust economy throughout most of the state, with Madison leading the entire country in employment for several months. The farm sector and brewing industry continued to experience difficulties.

Litigation and demonstrations over off-reservation resource rights of the Chippewa Indians continued throughout the 1980s, to be replaced by controversy over Indian gaming in the 1990s and into the new century.

1975 Menominee Indians occupied the Alexian Brothers Novitiate. The legislature made voter registration easier, established property tax levy limits on local governments, and eliminated statutory distinctions based on sex. UW-Madison scientist Dr. Howard Temin won the 1975 Nobel Prize in Physiology or Medicine. Exxon discovered sulfide zinc and copper deposits near Crandon.

1976 A U.S. district court judge ordered the integration of Milwaukee public schools. Ice storms caused $50.4 million in damages. The legislature established a system for compensating crime victims. Shirley S. Abrahamson was appointed the first woman on the Wisconsin Supreme Court.

1977 Governor Patrick Lucey was appointed as the ambassador to Mexico, and Lieutenant Governor Martin Schreiber became the acting governor. The first state employees' union strike lasted 15 days, leaving the National Guard to run Wisconsin prisons. Constitutional amendments authorized raffle games and revised the structure of the court system by creating a court of appeals. Legislation enacted included public support of elections campaigns, no-fault divorce, and an implied consent law for drunk driving.

1978 The Wisconsin Supreme Court allowed cameras in state courtrooms. Vel Phillips, elected as secretary of state, became Wisconsin's first black constitutional officer. The legislature enacted a hazardous waste management program.

1979 A constitutional amendment removed the lieutenant governor from serving as the president of the senate. A moratorium on tax collections gave state taxpayers a three-month "vacation" from taxes. Shirley Abrahamson became the first woman elected to the Wisconsin Supreme Court after having served by appointment for three years. The legislature established a school of veterinary medicine at UW-Madison.

1980 Eric Heiden of Madison broke several Olympic records when he won five gold medals for ice speed skating. Fort McCoy housed 14,250 Cuban refugees following the Mariel boatlift. Former Governor Patrick Lucey ran as an independent candidate for U.S. vice president. A state revenue shortfall led to a 4.4 percent cut in state spending.

1981 The U.S. Supreme Court ruled against Wisconsin's historic open primary. The legislature enacted stronger penalties for drunk driving and changes in mining taxes.

1982 State unemployment hit the highest levels since the Great Depression. Voters endorsed the first statewide referendum in the nation calling for a freeze on nuclear weapons. Stroh Brewery Company of Detroit acquired the Schlitz Brewing Company and closed all Milwaukee operations.

1983 The continued recession resulted in a budget including a 10 percent tax surcharge and a pay freeze for state employees. A law raising the minimum drinking age to 19 passed (to become effective in 1985). Inmates at Waupun State Prison took 15 hostages but released them uninjured the same day. Laws enacted included a "lemon law" on motor vehicle warranties and changes in child support collection procedures. The UW-Madison School of Veterinary Medicine enrolled its first class.

1984 The most powerful U.S. tornado of 1984 destroyed Barneveld, killing nine residents. The Democratic Party chose presidential convention delegates in caucuses rather than by a presidential preference primary because of new Democratic National Committee rules. Economic conditions began to improve from the low point of the previous two years.

1985 A Milwaukee plane crash killed 31. A major consolidation of state banks by large holding companies occurred. A state tax amnesty program was implemented for the first time.

1986 Farm land values fell across the state. Exxon dropped plans to develop a copper mine near Crandon. Legislation raised the drinking age to 21 and limited damages payable in malpractice actions. Protests against Ojibwa spearfishing intensified, and some lawmakers proposed suspending or eliminating Indian hunting and fishing rights.

1987 Voters approved a constitutional amendment allowing pari-mutuel betting and a state lottery. Laws enacted included a mandatory seatbelt law, antitakeover legislation, a gradual end to the inheritance and gift taxes, and a "learnfare" program designed to keep children of families on welfare in school.

1988 The first state lottery games began. Chrysler Corporation's automobile assembly plant in Kenosha, the nation's oldest car plant, closed. Mandatory family leave for employees was enacted.

1989 The legislature created the Department of Corrections, the Lower Wisconsin State Riverway, and a statewide land stewardship program.

1990 More than 1,400 Wisconsin National Guard and Reserve soldiers were called to active duty in the Persian Gulf crisis, and 10 died. Milwaukee's homicide rate broke records, raising concerns about drugs and crime. Laws enacted included a major recycling law and a Milwaukee Parental Choice voucher program for public and non-sectarian private schools.

1991 The price of milk hit its lowest point since 1978. The first state-tribal gambling compacts were signed. Governor Tommy G. Thompson vetoed a record 457 items in the state budget.

1992 A train derailed, spilling toxic chemicals and forcing the evacuation of over 22,000 people in Superior. Protests at six abortion clinics in Milwaukee led to hundreds of arrests. Laws enacted included parental consent requirements for abortion, health care reform, and the creation of a three-member Gaming Commission.

1993 President Bill Clinton appointed Wisconsin Congressman Les Aspin as secretary of defense and UW-Madison Chancellor Donna Shalala as secretary of health and human services. Thousands in Milwaukee became ill as a result of cryptosporidium in the water supply. California passed Wisconsin in milk production. Republicans won control of the state senate for the first time since 1974. Laws enacted included a 1999 sunset for traditional welfare programs, a cap on school spending, and permission to organize limited liability companies.

1994 Laws enacted include the removal of about $1 billion in public school operating taxes from property taxes, to take effect by 1997; a new framework for the Public Service Commission's regulation of telecommunication utilities; and granting towns most of the same powers exercised by cities and villages.

1995 Republicans won control of the state assembly for the first time since 1970. Elk were reintroduced in northern Wisconsin. A July heat wave contributed to 152 deaths.

1996 Governor Thompson's welfare reform plan, known as Wisconsin Works (W-2), received national attention. A train derailment forced the evacuation of Weyauwega. Pabst Brewing closed its

152-year-old brewery in Milwaukee. Following his tie-breaking vote in favor of the new Brewers stadium, State Senator George Petak was removed from office in the first successful legislative recall election in state history.

1997 Workers broke ground on Miller Park, the future home of the Milwaukee Brewers.

1998 Tammy Baldwin became the first Wisconsin woman and first openly gay woman elected to U.S. Congress. The U.S. Supreme Court upheld the constitutionality of the extension of Milwaukee Parental Choice school vouchers to religious schools. Laws enacted included a mining moratorium, new penalties for failure to pay child support, truth-in-sentencing, and penalties for substance abuse by expectant mothers.

1999 Laws enacted included requirements for local comprehensive plans, graduated drivers licensing, and a sales tax rebate. Supermax, the state's high security prison, opened at Boscobel. State unemployment reached a record low. Chronic wasting disease was detected in the state's deer herd.

2000 The legislature approved a local sales tax and revenue bonds for the renovation of Lambeau Field, home of the Green Bay Packers.

Recent years

2001 Governor Thompson ended a record 14 years in office and became U.S. secretary of health and human services. Lieutenant Governor Scott McCallum became governor and appointed State Senator Margaret Farrow as the first woman to serve as lieutenant governor. Extensive Mississippi River flooding occurred. Miller Park opened. Laws enacted included establishing a telemarketing "no call" list, wetland protection, and the "Senior-Care" prescription drug assistance plan.

2002 Barbara Lawton became the first woman elected lieutenant governor, and Peggy Lautenschlager became the first woman elected attorney general. The deadliest single traffic accident in state history killed 10 and injured almost 40 near Sheboygan. Several state legislators faced criminal charges following an investigation into legislative caucus staffs. Milwaukee County board members resigned or were recalled over a pension scandal.

2003 Jim Doyle became the first Democratic governor in 16 years. Controversy over the Crandon mine ended when local Indian tribes purchased land and mining rights. The renovated Lambeau Field opened. State Senator Gary George became the second legislator in Wisconsin history to be recalled. Wisconsin National Guard and Reserve units were activated for service in the Iraq War. Wisconsin held its first mourning dove hunt.

2004 Louis Butler, Jr., became the first black justice of the Wisconsin Supreme Court. The state government reduced its automobile fleet after allegations of misuse. Significant legislation included a livestock facility siting law and a revision to clean air and water laws intended to spur job creation. Voter turnout in the fall election was 73 percent, the highest in many years.

2005 The state minimum wage was increased. Wisconsin experienced a record 62 tornadoes during the year, including a record 27 on August 18, when tornadoes hit Viola, Stoughton, and other communities, resulting in one death and 27 injuries. Several current and former members of the legislature were convicted of illegal campaign activities.

2006 Immigration reform and the Iraq War were potent, divisive issues. The legislature limited the use of condemnation power for the benefit of private individuals. Voters approved a constitutional amendment limiting marriage to persons of the opposite sex. An advisory referendum in favor of the death penalty was also approved by the voters.

2007 The legislature modified ethics laws and elections regulations. Milwaukee-based Miller Brewing Company merged with Denver's Coors Brewing Company. The state budget passed in late October as one of the latest budgets in state history.

2008 A sharp economic downturn led to rising unemployment and the closing of the General Motors plant in Janesville. Louis Butler, Jr., became the first sitting Supreme Court justice to be defeated at the polls in 40 years, losing to Michael Gableman. Severe flooding hit southern Wisconsin. Flooding caused Lake Delton to drain, destroying nearby homes. The Great Lakes Compact received state and federal approval, regulating the use of Great Lakes water outside its watershed.

2009 Democrats opened the 99th Legislature with control of the governor's office and both houses of the legislature for the first time since the 1985 session. The ongoing economic crisis resulted in a projected budget deficit of $6 billion for the next biennium. More than 3,000 members of the Wisconsin National Guard prepared for mobilization to Iraq. A severe influenza outbreak resulted in 47 deaths.

2010 Several powerful tornadoes hit southern Wisconsin, severely damaging the Old World Wisconsin historic site. Republicans swept the November elections, capturing the governor's office and both houses of the legislature—the first time in over 70 years that partisan control of all three switched in the same election. Governor-elect Scott Walker declined $810 million in federal funds to build a high speed rail line between Madison and Milwaukee.

2011 Governor Walker's proposal to curtail collective bargaining rights for public workers led 14 Democrats to leave the state in order to deny the senate a quorum. Thousands of protesters surrounded the capitol to oppose the legislation, which was delayed for weeks before being enacted. Wisconsin remained in a state of political agitation into the summer as nine senators were the subject of recall elections; two senators were recalled. The legislature enacted a legislative redistricting plan for the first time in three decades, revamped the state's economic development efforts, and expanded the parental school choice program.

2012 Governor Walker, Lieutenant Governor Rebecca Kleefisch, and four senators were the subject of recall elections in the wake of the 2011 collective bargaining law. Walker, Kleefisch, and two senators were retained; one senator resigned; and one senator was defeated, giving the Democrats control of the senate. A period of severe heat and drought occurred in June and July. Republican Paul Ryan was nominated for U.S. vice president. In November elections, Republicans regained control of the state senate, and Tammy Baldwin became the first Wisconsin woman and first openly gay woman elected to the U.S. Senate.

2013 The legislature revised regulations for the mining of metallic ferrous minerals, easing the way for the construction of an iron mine in northern Wisconsin's Gogebic Range. Wisconsin's role as a major source of sand used in the "fracking" method of natural gas extraction presented questions for state and local quarry regulators. The winter of 2013–14 was the most severe in many years.

2014 Voters passed a constitutional amendment requiring that transportation fund resources be used only for transportation. Court rulings legalized same-sex marriage in Wisconsin. The deer harvest was the lowest in 30 years. Governor Walker denied the Menominee Nation permission to operate a casino in Kenosha.

2015 Senator Mary Lazich was elected president of the senate, becoming the first woman to be elected presiding officer of either house of the legislature. Efforts to open an iron mine in the Gogebic Range were abandoned. The legislature enacted "Right to Work" legislation, raised the speed limit to 70 miles per hour on certain highways, and approved funding for a new Milwaukee Bucks arena. Voters approved a constitutional amendment requiring the Wisconsin Supreme Court to elect its chief justice by majority vote. Governor Walker announced his candidacy for U.S. president in July but dropped out of the race in late September. Congressman Paul Ryan was elected Speaker of the House.

2016 The Wisconsin Elections Commission and the Wisconsin Ethics Commission replaced the Wisconsin Government Accountability Board. An outbreak of Elizabethkingia meningoseptica killed 18 people. In the presidential election, Republican Donald Trump became the first Republican presidential candidate to win Wisconsin since President Reagan in 1984.

Vote for governor in general elections since 1848

1848
Nelson Dewey[1]—D 19,875
John H. Tweedy[1]—W 14,621
Charles Durkee[1]—I 1,134
Total. 35,309

1849
Nelson Dewey—D 16,649
Alexander L. Collins—W . . 11,317
Warren Chase—I 3,761
Total. 31,759

1851
Leonard J. Farwell—W . . . 22,319
Don A. J. Upham—D 21,812
Total. 44,190

1853
William A. Barstow—D . . . 30,405
Edward D. Holton—R 21,886
Henry S. Baird—W 3,304
Total. 55,683

1855
William A. Barstow[2]—D . . 36,355
Coles Bashford—R 36,198
Total. 72,598

1857
Alexander W. Randall—R . 44,693
James B. Cross—D 44,239
Total. 90,058

1859
Alexander W. Randall—R . 59,999
Harrison C. Hobart—D . . . 52,539
Total. 112,755

1861
Louis P. Harvey—R 53,777
Benjamin Ferguson—D . . 45,456
Total. 99,258

1863
James T. Lewis—R. 72,717
Henry L. Palmer—D. 49,053
Total. 122,029

1865
Lucius Fairchild—R 58,332
Harrison C. Hobart—D . . . 48,330
Total. 106,674

1867
Lucius Fairchild—R 73,637
John J. Tallmadge—D . . . 68,873
Total. 142,522

1869
Lucius Fairchild—R 69,502
Charles D. Robinson—D . . 61,239
Total. 130,781

1871
Cadwallader C. Washburn—R
. . . . 78,301
James R. Doolittle—D . . . 68,910
Total. 147,274

1873
William R. Taylor—D 81,599
Cadwallader C. Washburn—R
. . . . 66,224
Total. 147,856

1875
Harrison Ludington—R . . 85,155
William R. Taylor—D 84,314
Total. 170,070

1877
William E. Smith—R. 78,759
James A. Mallory—D 70,486
Edward P. Allis—G. 26,216
Collin M. Campbell—S 2,176
Total. 178,122

1879
William E. Smith—R. . . . 100,535
James G. Jenkins—D 75,030
Reuben May—G. 12,996
Total. 189,005

1881
Jeremiah M. Rusk—R. . . . 81,754
N.D. Fratt—D. 69,797
T.D. Kanouse—Pro 13,225
Edward P. Allis—G 7,002
Total. 171,856

1884
Jeremiah M. Rusk—R . . . 163,214
N.D. Fratt—D. 143,945
Samuel D. Hastings—Pro . . 8,545
William L. Utley—G 4,274
Total. 319,997

1886
Jeremiah M. Rusk—R . . . 133,247
Gilbert M. Woodward—D 114,529
John Cochrane—PPop . . . 21,467
John Myers Olin—Pro . . . 17,089
Total. 286,368

1888
William D. Hoard—R . . . 175,696
James Morgan—D 155,423
E.G. Durant—Pro 14,373
D. Frank Powell—L 9,196
Total. 354,714

1890
George W. Peck—D 160,388
William D. Hoard—R . . . 132,068
Charles Alexander—Pro . . 11,246
Reuben May—UL 5,447
Total. 309,254

1892
George W. Peck—D 178,095
John C. Spooner—R . . . 170,497
Thomas C. Richmond—Pro 13,185
C.M. Butt—PPop. 9,638
Total. 371,559

1894
William H. Upham—R . . 196,150
George W. Peck—D 142,250
D. Frank Powell—PPop. . . 25,604
John F. Cleghorn—Pro . . . 11,240
Total. 375,449

1896
Edward Scofield—R. . . . 264,981
Willis C. Silverthorn—D . 169,257
Joshua H. Berkey—Pro. . . . 8,140
Christ Tuttrop—SL 1,306
Robert Henderson—Nat. . . . 407
Total. 444,110

1898
Edward Scofield—R. . . . 173,137
Hiram W. Sawyer—D . . . 135,353
Albinus A. Worsley—PPop. . 8,518
Eugene W. Chafin—Pro . . 8,078
Howard Tuttle—SDA 2,544
Henry Riese—SL. 1,473
Total. 329,430

1900
Robert M. La Follette—R. 264,419
Louis G. Bomrich—D . . . 160,674
J. Burritt Smith—Pro 9,707
Howard Tuttle—SD 6,590
Frank R. Wilke—SL 509
Total. 441,900

1902
Robert M. La Follette—R. 193,417
David S. Rose—D 145,818
Emil Seidel—SD 15,970
Edwin W. Drake—Pro. . . . 9,647
Henry E.D. Puck—SL 791
Total. 365,676

Vote for governor in general elections since 1848, continued

1904
Robert M. La Follette—R. 227,253
George W. Peck—D. . . . 176,301
William A. Arnold—SD . . . 24,857
Edward Scofield—NR. . . . 12,136
William H. Clark—Pro. 8,764
Charles M. Minkley—SL 249
Total. 449,570

1906
James O. Davidson—R . . 183,558
John A. Aylward—D . . . 103,311
Winfield R. Gaylord—SD . . 24,437
Ephraim L. Eaton—Pro. . . . 8,211
Ole T. Rosaas—SL 455
Total. 320,003

1908
James O. Davidson—R . . 242,935
John A. Aylward—D . . . 165,977
H.D. Brown—SD 28,583
Winfred D. Cox—Pro 11,760
Herman Bottema—SL 393
Total. 449,656

1910
Francis E. McGovern—R . 161,619
Adolph H. Schmitz—D . . 110,442
William A. Jacobs—SD . . . 39,547
Byron F. Van Keuren—Pro . .7,450
Fred G. Kremer—SL. 430
Total. 319,522

1912
Francis E. McGovern—R . 179,360
John C. Karel—D 167,316
Carl D. Thompson—SD. . . 34,468
Charles L. Hill—Pro 9,433
William H. Curtis—SL. 3,253
Total. 393,849

1914
Emanuel L. Philipp—R . . 140,787
John C. Karel—D 119,509
John J. Blaine—I. 32,560
Oscar Ameringer—SD . . . 25,917
David W. Emerson—Pro . . .6,279
John Vierthaler—I. 352
Total. 325,430

1916
Emanuel L. Philipp—R . . 229,889
Burt Williams—D 164,555
Rae Weaver—Soc 30,649
George McKerrow—Pro . . .9,193
Total. 434,340

1918
Emanuel L. Philipp—R . . 155,799
Henry A. Moehlenpah—D 112,576
Emil Seidel—SD 57,523
William C. Dean—Pro. 5,296
Total. 331,582

1920
John J. Blaine—R 366,247
Robert McCoy—D. 247,746
William Coleman—S 71,126
Henry H. Tubbs—Pro 6,047
Total. 691,294

1922
John J. Blaine—R 367,929
Arthur A. Bentley—ID . . . 51,061
Louis A. Arnold—S 39,570
M.L. Welles—Pro. 21,438
Arthur A. Dietrich—ISL. . . .1,444
Total. 481,828

1924
John J. Blaine—R 412,255
Martin L. Lueck—D 317,550
William F. Quick—S 45,268
Adolph R. Bucknam—Pro . 11,516
Severi Alanne—IW 4,107
Farrand K. Shuttleworth—IPR 4,079
Jose Snover—SL. 1,452
Total. 796,432

1926
Fred R. Zimmerman—R . 350,927
Charles Perry—I 76,507
Virgil H. Cady—D 72,627
Herman O. Kent—S. 40,293
David W. Emerson—Pro . . .7,333
Alex Gorden—SL 4,593
Total. 552,912

1928
Walter J. Kohler, Sr—R . . 547,738
Albert G. Schmedeman—D 394,368
Otto R. Hauser—S. 36,924
Adolph R. Bucknam—Pro . .6,477
Joseph Ehrhardt—IL 1,938
Alvar J. Hayes—IW 1,420
Total. 989,143

1930
Philip F. La Follette—R . . 392,958
Charles E. Hammersley—D 170,020
Frank B. Metcalfe—S 25,607
Alfred B. Taynton—Pro. . . 14,818
Fred B. Blair—IC 2,998
Total. 606,825

1932
Albert G. Schmedeman—D
. . . . 590,114
Walter J. Kohler, Sr—R . . 470,805
Frank B. Metcalfe—S 56,965
William C. Dean—Pro. 3,148
Fred B. Blair—Com 2,926
Joe Ehrhardt—SL 398
Total. 1,124,502

1934
Philip F. La Follette—P . . 373,093
Albert G. Schmedeman—D
. 359,467
Howard Greene—R 172,980
George A. Nelson—S . . . 44,589
Morris Childs—IC 2,454
Thomas W. North—IPro . . . 857
Joe Ehrhardt—ISL. 332
Total. 953,797

1936
Philip F. La Follette—P . . 573,724
Alexander Wiley—R. . . . 363,973
Arthur W. Lueck—D. . . . 268,530
Joseph F. Walsh—U 27,934
Joseph Ehrhardt—SL. 1,738
August F. Fehlandt—Pro. . .1,008
Total. 1,237,095

1938
Julius P. Heil—R 543,675
Philip F. La Follette—P . . 353,381
Harry W. Bolens—D. 78,446
Frank W. Smith—U 4,564
John Schleier, Jr—ISL. 1,459
Total. 981,560

1940
Julius P. Heil—R 558,678
Orland S. Loomis—P . . . 546,436
Francis E. McGovern—D . 264,985
Fred B. Blair—Com 2,340
Louis Fisher—SL. 1,158
Total. 1,373,754

1942
Orland S. Loomis—P . . . 397,664
Julius P. Heil—R 291,945
William C. Sullivan—D . . . 98,153
Frank P. Zeidler—S 11,295
Fred Bassett Blair—IC 1,092
Georgia Cozzini—ISL. 490
Total. 800,985

Vote for governor in general elections since 1848, continued

1944
Walter S. Goodland—R. . 697,740
Daniel W. Hoan—D 536,357
Alexander O. Benz—P . . . 76,028
George A. Nelson—S 9,183
Georgia Cozzini—I (ISL) . . . 1,122
Total. 1,320,483

1946
Walter S. Goodland—R. . 621,970
Daniel W. Hoan—D 406,499
Walter H. Uphoff—S 8,996
Sigmund G. Eisenscher—IC 1,857
Jerry R. Kenyon—ISL 959
Total. 1,040,444

1948
Oscar Rennebohm—R . . 684,839
Carl W. Thompson—D . . 558,497
Henry J. Berquist—PP . . . 12,928
Walter H. Uphoff—S 9,149
James E. Boulton—ISW 356
Georgia Cozzini—ISL 328
Total. 1,266,139

1950
Walter J. Kohler, Jr—R . . 605,649
Carl W. Thompson—D . . 525,319
M. Michael Essin—PP. 3,735
William O. Hart—S 3,384
Total. 1,138,148

1952
Walter J. Kohler, Jr—R . 1,009,171
William Proxmire—D . . . 601,844
M. Michael Essin—I 3,706
Total. 1,615,214

1954
Walter J. Kohler, Jr—R . . 596,158
William Proxmire—D . . . 560,747
Arthur Wepfer—I 1,722
Total. 1,158,666

1956
Vernon W. Thomson—R . 808,273
William Proxmire—D . . . 749,421
Total. 1,557,788

1958
Gaylord A. Nelson—D . . 644,296
Vernon W. Thomson—R . 556,391
Wayne Leverenz—I 1,485
Total. 1,202,219

1960
Gaylord A. Nelson—D . . 890,868
Philip G. Kuehn—R . . . 837,123
Total. 1,728,009

1962
John W. Reynolds—D. . . 637,491
Philip G. Kuehn—R 625,536
Adolf Wiggert—I 2,477
Total. 1,265,900

1964
Warren P. Knowles—R . . 856,779
John W. Reynolds—D. . . 837,901
Total. 1,694,887

1966
Warren P. Knowles—R . . 626,041
Patrick J. Lucey—D 539,258
Adolf Wiggert—I 4,745
Total. 1,170,173

1968
Warren P. Knowles—R . . 893,463
Bronson C. La Follette—D 791,100
Adolf Wiggert—I 3,225
Robert Wilkinson—I 1,813
Total. 1,689,738

1970
Patrick J. Lucey—D 728,403
Jack B. Olson—R. 602,617
Leo J. McDonald—A 9,035
Georgia Cozzini—I (SL). . . . 1,287
Samuel K. Hunt—I (SW) . . . 888
Myrtle Kastner—I (PLS) 628
Total. 1,343,160

1974
Patrick J. Lucey—D 628,639
William D. Dyke—R 497,189
William H. Upham—A . . . 33,528
Crazy Jim[3]—I. 12,107
William Hart—I (DS) 5,113
Fred Blair—I (C) 3,617
Georgia Cozzini—I (SL). . . . 1,492
Total. 1,181,685

1978
Lee S. Dreyfus—R 816,056
Martin J. Schreiber—D. . . 673,813
Eugene R. Zimmerman—C . 6,355
John C. Doherty—I 2,183
Adrienne Kaplan—I (SW) . . 1,548
Henry A. Ochsner—I (SL) . . . 849
Total. 1,500,996

1982
Anthony S. Earlv—D . . . 896,872
Terry J. Kohler—R 662,738
Larry Smiley—Lib 9,734
James P. Wickstrom—Con . 7,721
Peter Seidman—I (SW). . . . 3,025
Total. 1,580,344

1986
Tommy G. Thompson—R
. . . . 805,090
Anthony S. Earl—D 705,578
Kathryn A. Christensen—LF 10,323
Darold E. Wall—I. 3,913
Sanford Knapp—I 1,668
Total. 1,526,573

1990
Tommy G. Thompson—R
. . . . 802,321
Thomas A. Loftus—D. . . 576,280
Total. 1,379,727

1994
Tommy G. Thompson—R 1,051,326
Charles J.Chvala—D . . . 482,850
David S. Harmon—Lib . . . 11,639
Edward J. Frami—Tax. 9,188
Michael J. Mangan—I 8,150
Total. 1,563,835

1998
Tommy G. Thompson—R
. . . . 1,047,716
Ed Garvey—D 679,553
Jim Mueller—Lib 11,071
Edward J. Frami—Tax. . . . 10,269
Mike Mangan—I. 4,985
A-Ja-mu Muhammad—I . . 1,604
Jeffrey L. Smith—WG. 14
Total. 1,756,014

2002
Jim Doyle—D 800,515
Scott McCallum—R. . . . 734,779
Ed Thompson—Lib 185,455
Jim Young—WG. 44,111
Alan D. Eisenberg—I 2,847
Ty A. Bollerud—I. 2,637
Mike Mangan—I. 1,710
Aneb Jah Rasta Sensas-Utcha
Nefer-I—I 929
Total. 1,775,349

2006
Jim Doyle—D 1,139,115
Mark Green—R 979,427
Nelson Eisman—WG 40,709
Total. 2,161,700

2010
Scott Walker—R 1,128,941
Tom Barrett—D 1,004,303
Jim Langer—I 10,608
James James—I 8,273
Total[4]. 2,160,832

Vote for governor in general elections since 1848, continued

June 5, 2012 recall election		2014		2018	
Scott Walker—R	1,335,585	Scott Walker—R	1,259,706	Tony Evers—D	1,324,307
Tom Barrett—D	1,164,480	Mary Burke—D	1,122,913	Scott Walker—R	1,295,080
Hari Trivedi—I	14,463	Robert Burke—I (Lib)	18,720	Phillip Anderson—Lib	20,225
Total.	2,516,065	Dennis Fehr—I (Peo)	7,530	Maggie Turnbull—I	18,884
		Total.	2,410,314	Michael J. White—WG	11,087
				Arnie Enz—I (Wis)	2,745
				Total.	2,673,308

Note: A candidate whose party did not receive 1% of the vote for a statewide office in the previous election or who failed to meet the alternative requirement of section 5.62, Wis. Stats., is listed on the Wisconsin ballot as "independent." When a candidate's party affiliation is listed as "I," followed by a party designation in parentheses, "independent" was the official ballot listing, but a party designation was found by the Wisconsin Legislative Reference Bureau in newspaper reports.

Totals include scattered votes for other candidates.

A—American	ISL—Independent Socialist Labor	R—Republican
C—Conservative	ISW—Independent Socialist Worker	S—Socialist
Com—Communist	IW—Independent Worker	SD—Social Democrat
Con—Constitution	L—Labor	SDA—Social Democrat of America
D—Democrat	LF—Labor-Farm/Laborista-Agrario	SL—Socialist Labor
DS—Democratic Socialist	Lib—Libertarian	SW—Socialist Worker
G—Greenback	Nat—National	Tax—U.S. Taxpayers
I—Independent	NR—National Republic	U—Union
IC—Independent Communist	P—Progressive	UL—Union Labor
ID—Independent Democrat	Peo—People's	W—Whig
IL—Independent Labor	PLS—Progressive Labor Socialist	WG—Wisconsin Green
IPR—Independent Prohibition	PP—People's Progressive	Wis—Wisconsin Party
Republic	PPop—People's (Populist)	
IPro—Independent Prohibition	Pro—Prohibition	

1. Votes for Dewey and Tweedy are from 1874 *Blue Book*; Durkee vote is based on county returns, as filed in the Office of the Secretary of State, but returns from Manitowoc and Winnebago Counties were missing. Without these 2 counties, Dewey had 19,605 votes and Tweedy had 14,514 votes. 2. Barstow's plurality was set aside in *Atty. Gen. ex rel. Bashford v. Barstow*, 4 Wis. 567 (1855) because of irregularities in the election returns. 3. Legal name. 4. Total includes 6,780 votes for the Libertarian ticket, which had a candidate for lieutenant governor, but no candidate for governor.

Source: Canvass reports and Wisconsin Elections Commission records.

Wisconsin lieutenant governors since 1848

	Party	Service	Residence[1]
John E. Holmes	Democrat	1848–1850	Jefferson
Samuel W. Beall	Democrat	1850–1852	Taycheedah
Timothy Burns	Democrat	1852–1854	La Crosse
James T. Lewis	Republican	1854–1856	Columbus
Arthur McArthur[2]	Democrat	1856–1858	Milwaukee
Erasmus D. Campbell	Democrat	1858–1860	La Crosse
Butler G. Noble	Republican	1860–1862	Whitewater
Edward Salomon[3]	Republican	1862–1864	Milwaukee
Wyman Spooner	Republican	1864–1870	Elkhorn
Thaddeus C. Pound	Republican	1870–1872	Chippewa Falls
Milton H. Pettit[4]	Republican	1872–3/23/73	Kenosha
Charles D. Parker	Democrat	1874–1878	Pleasant Valley
James M. Bingham	Republican	1878–1882	Chippewa Falls
Sam S. Fifield	Republican	1882–1887	Ashland
George W. Ryland	Republican	1887–1891	Lancaster
Charles Jonas	Democrat	1891–1895	Racine
Emil Baensch	Republican	1895–1899	Manitowoc
Jesse Stone	Republican	1899–1903	Watertown
James O. Davidson[5]	Republican	1903–1907	Soldiers Grove
William D. Connor	Republican	1907–1909	Marshfield
John Strange	Republican	1909–1911	Oshkosh

Wisconsin lieutenant governors since 1848, continued

	Party	Service	Residence[1]
Thomas Morris	Republican	1911–1915	La Crosse
Edward F. Dithmar	Republican	1915–1921	Baraboo
George F. Comings.	Republican	1921–1925	Eau Claire
Henry A. Huber	Republican	1925–1933	Stoughton
Thomas J. O'Malley.	Democrat	1933–1937	Milwaukee
Henry A. Gunderson[6]	Progressive	1937–10/16/37	Portage
Herman L. Ekern[7].	Progressive	5/16/38–1939	Madison
Walter S. Goodland[8].	Republican	1939–1945	Racine
Oscar Rennebohm[9]	Republican	1945–1949	Madison
George M. Smith	Republican	1949–1955	Milwaukee
Warren P. Knowles	Republican	1955–1959	New Richmond
Philleo Nash	Democrat	1959–1961	Wisconsin Rapids
Warren P. Knowles	Republican	1961–1963	New Richmond
Jack Olson	Republican	1963–1965	Wisconsin Dells
Patrick J. Lucey	Democrat	1965–1967	Madison
Jack Olson	Republican	1967–1971	Wisconsin Dells
Martin J. Schreiber[10].	Democrat	1971–1979	Milwaukee
Russell A. Olson.	Republican	1979–1983	Randall
James T. Flynn.	Democrat	1983–1987	West Allis
Scott McCallum[11]	Republican	1987–2/1/01	Fond du Lac
Margaret A. Farrow[12]	Republican	5/9/01–2003	Pewaukee
Barbara Lawton.	Democrat	2003–2011	Green Bay
Rebecca Kleefisch	Republican	2011–2019	Oconomowoc
Mandela Barnes.	Democrat	2019–	Milwaukee

Note: Prior to 1971, the term of office was two years rather than four. Prior to 1885, the term of office began in January of an even-numbered rather than an odd-numbered year. Prior to 1979, lieutenant governors did not cease to hold the office of lieutenant governor while acting in place of a governor who had died or resigned.

1. Residence at the time of election.   2. Served as acting governor 3/21/1856 to 3/25/1856 during dispute over outcome of gubernatorial election.   3. Became acting governor on the death of Governor Harvey, 4/19/1862.   4. Died in office.   5. Became acting governor when Governor La Follette resigned, 1/1/1906.   6. Resigned.   7. Appointed to serve the rest of Gunderson's term.   8. Became acting governor on the death of Governor-elect Orland Loomis, 1/1/1943.   9. Became acting governor on the death of Governor Goodland, 3/12/1947.   10. Became acting governor when Governor Lucey resigned, 7/6/1977.   11. Became governor when Governor Thompson resigned, 2/1/2001.   12. Appointed to serve the rest of McCallum's term.

Source: Wisconsin Legislative Reference Bureau, *Wisconsin Blue Book*, various editions, and bureau records.

Wisconsin attorneys general since 1848

	Party	Service	Residence[1]
James S. Brown	Democrat	1848–1850	Milwaukee
S. Park Coon	Democrat	1850–1852	Milwaukee
Experience Estabrook	Democrat	1852–1854	Geneva
George B. Smith.	Democrat	1854–1856	Madison
William R. Smith	Democrat	1856–1858	Mineral Point
Gabriel Bouck.	Democrat	1858–1860	Oshkosh
James H. Howe[2]	Republican	1860–1862	Green Bay
Winfield Smith[3].	Republican	1862–1866	Milwaukee
Charles R. Gill	Republican	1866–1870	Watertown
Stephen Steele Barlow	Republican	1870–1874	Dellona
Andrew Scott Sloan	Republican	1874–1878	Beaver Dam
Alexander Wilson.	Republican	1878–1882	Mineral Point
Leander F. Frisby	Republican	1882–1887	West Bend
Charles E. Estabrook	Republican	1887–1891	Manitowoc
James L. O'Connor	Democrat	1891–1895	Madison
William H. Mylrea.	Republican	1895–1899	Wausau
Emmett R. Hicks	Republican	1899–1903	Oshkosh

Wisconsin attorneys general since 1848, continued

	Party	Service	Residence[1]
Lafayette M. Sturdevant.	Republican	1903–1907	Neillsville
Frank L. Gilbert	Republican	1907–1911	Madison
Levi H. Bancroft.	Republican	1911–1913	Richland Center
Walter C. Owen[4]	Republican	1913–1918	Maiden Rock
Spencer Haven[5]	Republican	1918–1919	Hudson
John J. Blaine.	Republican	1919–1921	Boscobel
William J. Morgan	Republican	1921–1923	Milwaukee
Herman L. Ekern	Republican	1923–1927	Madison
John W. Reynolds.	Republican	1927–1933	Green Bay
James E. Finnegan	Democrat	1933–1937	Milwaukee
Orlando S. Loomis	Progressive	1937–1939	Mauston
John E. Martin[2].	Republican	1939–6/1/48	Madison
Grover L. Broadfoot[6]	Republican	6/5/48–11/12/48	Mondovi
Thomas E. Fairchild[7].	Democrat	11/12/48–1951	Verona
Vernon W. Thomson	Republican	1951–1957	Richland Center
Stewart G. Honeck.	Republican	1957–1959	Madison
John W. Reynolds.	Democrat	1959–1963	Green Bay
George Thompson	Republican	1963–1965	Madison
Bronson C. La Follette	Democrat	1965–1969	Madison
Robert W. Warren[2].	Republican	1969–10/8/74	Green Bay
Victor A. Miller[8].	Democrat	10/8/74–11/25/74	St. Nazianz
Bronson C. La Follette[9]	Democrat	11/25/74–1987	Madison
Donald J. Hanaway.	Republican	1987–1991	Green Bay
James E. Doyle	Democrat	1991–2003	Madison
Peggy A. Lautenschlager	Democrat	2003–2007	Fond du Lac
J.B. Van Hollen.	Republican	2007–2015	Waunakee
Brad D. Schimel.	Republican	2015–2019	Waukesha
Josh Kaul.	Democrat	2019–	Madison

Note: Prior to 1971, the term of office was two years rather than four. Prior to 1885, the term of office began in January of an even-numbered rather than an odd-numbered year.

1. Residence at the time of election. 2. Resigned. 3. Appointed 10/7/1862 to serve the rest of Howe's term. 4. Resigned 1/7/1918. 5. Appointed to serve the rest of Owen's term. 6. Appointed to serve the rest of Martin's term. Resigned. 7. Attorney General-elect Fairchild appointed to serve the rest of Martin's term. 8. Appointed to serve the rest of Warren's term. Resigned. 9. Attorney General-elect La Follette appointed to serve the rest of Warren's term.

Source: Wisconsin Legislative Reference Bureau, *Wisconsin Blue Book*, various editions, and bureau records.

Wisconsin superintendents of public instruction since 1849

	Service	Residence[1]
Eleazer Root.	1849–1852	Waukesha
Azel P. Ladd	1852–1854	Shullsburg
Hiram A. Wright.	1854–1855	Prairie du Chien
A. Constantine Barry.	1855–1858	Racine
Lyman C. Draper	1858–1860	Madison
Josiah L. Pickard	1860–1864	Platteville
John G. McMynn	1864–1868	Racine
Alexander J. Craig	1868–1870	Madison
Samuel Fallows.	1870–1874	Milwaukee
Edward Searing.	1874–1878	Milton
William Clarke Whitford.	1878–1882	Milton
Robert Graham	1882–1887	Oshkosh
Jesse B. Thayer	1887–1891	River Falls
Oliver Elwin Wells.	1891–1895	Appleton
John Q. Emery.	1895–1899	Albion

Justices of the Wisconsin Supreme Court since 1836

	Service	Residence[1]
Judges during the territorial period		
Charles Dunn (Chief Justice)[2]	1836–1848	
William C. Frazier	1836–1838	
David Irvin	1836–1838	
Andrew G. Miller	1836–1848	
Circuit judges who served as justices 1848–1853[3]		
Alexander W. Stow	1848–1851 (C.J.)	Fond du Lac
Levi Hubbell	1848–1853 (C.J. 1851)	Milwaukee
Edward V. Whiton	1848–1853 (C.J. 1852–53)	Janesville
Charles H. Larrabee	1848–1853	Horicon
Mortimer M. Jackson	1848–1853	Mineral Point
Wiram Knowlton	1850–1853	Prairie du Chien
Timothy O. Howe	1851–1853	Green Bay
Justices since 1853		
Edward V. Whiton	1853–1859 (C.J.)	Janesville
Samuel Crawford	1853–1855	New Diggings
Abram D. Smith	1853–1859	Milwaukee
Orsamus Cole	1855–1892 (C.J. 1880–92)	Potosi
Luther S. Dixon[4]	1859–1874 (C.J.)	Portage
Byron Paine[4]	1859–1864, 1867–71	Milwaukee
Jason Downer[4]	1864–1867	Milwaukee
William P. Lyon[4]	1871–1894 (C.J. 1892–94)	Racine
Edward G. Ryan[4]	1874–1880 (C.J.)	Racine
David Taylor	1878–1891	Sheboygan
Harlow S. Orton	1878–1895 (C.J. 1894–95)	Madison
John B. Cassoday[4]	1880–1907 (C.J. 1895–07)	Janesville
John B. Winslow[4]	1891–1920 (C.J. 1907–20)	Racine
Silas U. Pinney	1892–1898	Madison
Alfred W. Newman	1894–1898	Trempealeau
Roujet D. Marshall[4]	1895–1918	Chippewa Falls
Charles V. Bardeen[4]	1898–1903	Wausau
Joshua Eric Dodge[4]	1898–1910	Milwaukee
Robert G. Siebecker[5]	1903–1922 (C.J. 1920–22)	Madison
James C. Kerwin	1905–1921	Neenah
William H. Timlin	1907–1916	Milwaukee
Robert M. Bashford[4]	Jan.–June 1908	Madison
John Barnes	1908–1916	Rhinelander
Aad J. Vinje[4]	1910–1929 (C.J. 1922–29)	Superior
Marvin B. Rosenberry[4]	1916–1950 (C.J. 1929–50)	Wausau
Franz C. Eschweiler[4]	1916–1929	Milwaukee
Walter C. Owen	1918–1934	Maiden Rock
Burr W. Jones[4]	1920–1926	Madison
Christian Doerfler[4]	1921–1929	Milwaukee
Charles H. Crownhart[4]	1922–1930	Madison
E. Ray Stevens	1926–1930	Madison
Chester A. Fowler[4]	1929–1948	Fond du Lac
Oscar M. Fritz[4]	1929–1954 (C.J. 1950–54)	Milwaukee
Edward T. Fairchild[4]	1929–1957 (C.J. 1954–57)	Milwaukee
John D. Wickhem[4]	1930–1949	Madison
George B. Nelson[4]	1930–1942	Stevens Point
Theodore G. Lewis[4]	Nov. 15–Dec. 5, 1934	Madison
Joseph Martin[4]	1934–1946	Green Bay
Elmer E. Barlow[4]	1942–1948	Arcadia
James Ward Rector[4]	1946–1947	Madison
Henry P. Hughes	1948–1951	Oshkosh
John E. Martin[4]	1948–1962 (C.J. 1957–62)	Green Bay

Justices of the Wisconsin Supreme Court since 1836, continued

	Service	Residence[1]
Grover L. Broadfoot[4].	1948–1962 (C.J. Jan.–May 1962)	Mondovi
Timothy Brown[4]	1949–1964 (C.J. 1962–64)	Madison
Edward J. Gehl	1950–1956	Hartford
George R. Currie[4].	1951–1968 (C.J. 1964–68)	Sheboygan
Roland J. Steinle[4].	1954–1958	Milwaukee
Emmert L. Wingert[4]	1956–1959	Madison
Thomas E. Fairchild.	1957–1966	Verona
E. Harold Hallows[4]	1958–1974 (C.J. 1968–74)	Milwaukee
William H. Dieterich	1959–1964	Milwaukee
Myron L. Gordon	1962–1967	Milwaukee
Horace W. Wilkie[4].	1962–1976 (C.J. 1974–76)	Madison
Bruce F. Beilfuss.	1964–1983 (C.J. 1976–83)	Neillsville
Nathan S. Heffernan[4]	1964–1995 (C.J. 1983–95)	Sheboygan
Leo B. Hanley[4].	1966–1978	Milwaukee
Connor T. Hansen[4]	1967–1980	Eau Claire
Robert W. Hansen	1968–1978	Milwaukee
Roland B. Day[4]	1974–1996 (C.J. 1995–96)	Madison
Shirley S. Abrahamson[4].	1976–2019 (C.J. 1996–2015)	Madison
William G. Callow.	1978–1992	Waukesha
John L. Coffey.	1978–1982	Milwaukee
Donald W. Steinmetz	1980–1999	Milwaukee
Louis J. Ceci[4].	1982–1993	Milwaukee
William A. Bablitch	1983–2003	Stevens Point
Jon P. Wilcox[4]	1992–2007	Wautoma
Janine P. Geske[4].	1993–1998	Milwaukee
Ann Walsh Bradley	1995–	Wausau
N. Patrick Crooks	1996–2015	Green Bay
David T. Prosser, Jr.[4]	1998–2016	Appleton
Diane S. Sykes[4]	1999–2004	Milwaukee
Patience D. Roggensack.	2003– (C.J. 2015–)	Madison
Louis B. Butler, Jr.[4]	2004–2008	Milwaukee
Annette K. Ziegler	2007–	West Bend
Michael J. Gableman.	2008–2018	Webster
Rebecca Grassl Bradley[4]	2015–	Milwaukee
Daniel Kelly[4].	2016–	North Prairie
Rebecca Frank Dallet	2018–	Whitefish Bay
Brian Hagedorn.	2019–	Oconomowoc

Note: The structure of the Wisconsin Supreme Court has varied. There were three justices during the territorial period. From 1848 to 1853, circuit judges acted as supreme court judges—five from 1848 to 1850 and six from 1850 to 1853. From 1853 to 1877, there were three elected justices. The number was increased to five in 1877, and to seven in 1903.

C.J.—chief justice.

1. Residence at the time of election or appointment.   2. Before 1889, the chief justice was elected or appointed to the position. From 1889 to 2015, the most senior justice seved as chief justice. From 2015 onward, the justices have elected one of themselves to be chief justice for a two-year term. 3. Circuit judges acted as Supreme Court justices from 1848 to 1853. 4. Initially appointed to the court. 5. Siebecker was elected April 7, 1903, but prior to inauguration for his elected term was appointed April 9, 1903, to fill the vacancy caused by the death of Justice Bardeen.

Sources: Wisconsin Legislative Reference Bureau, *Wisconsin Blue Book*, 1935, 1944, 1977; Wisconsin Elections Commission; Wisconsin Supreme Court, *Wisconsin Reports*, various volumes.

Senate presidents, or presidents pro tempore, and assembly speakers since 1848

Session	Senate presidents or presidents pro tempore[1]	Residence[2]	Assembly speakers	Residence[2]
1848.	—	—	Ninian E. Whiteside—D	Lafayette County
1849.	—	—	Harrison C. Hobart—D	Sheboygan
1850.	—	—	Moses M. Strong—D	Mineral Point
1851.	—	—	Frederick W. Horn—D	Cedarburg
1852. . . .	E.B. Dean, Jr.—D	Madison	James M. Shafter—W	Sheboygan
1853.	Duncan C. Reed—D	Milwaukee	Henry L. Palmer—D	Milwaukee
1854.	Benjamin Allen—D	Hudson	Frederick W. Horn—D	Cedarburg
1855.	Eleazor Wakeley—D	Whitewater	Charles C. Sholes—R	Kenosha
1856.	Louis Powell Harvey—R	Shopiere	William Hull—D	Grant County
1857.	—	—	Wyman Spooner—R	Elkhorn
1858.	Hiram H. Giles—R	Stoughton	Frederick S. Lovell—R	Kenosha County
1859.	Dennison Worthington—R	Summit	William P. Lyon—R	Racine
1860.	Moses M. Davis—R	Portage	William P. Lyon—R	Racine
1861.	Alden I. Bennett—R	Beloit	Amasa Cobb—R	Mineral Point
1862.	Frederick O. Thorp—D	West Bend	James W. Beardsley—UD	Prescott
1863.	Wyman Spooner—R	Elkhorn	J. Allen Barber—R	Lancaster
1864.	Smith S. Wilkinson—R	Prairie du Sac	William W. Field—U	Fennimore
1865.	Willard H. Chandler—U	Windsor	William W. Field—U	Fennimore
1866.	Willard H. Chandler—U	Windsor	Henry D. Barron—U	St. Croix Falls
1867.	George F. Wheeler—U	Nanuapa	Angus Cameron—U	La Crosse
1868.	Newton M. Littlejohn—R	Whitewater	Alexander M. Thomson—R	Janesville
1869.	George C. Hazelton—R	Boscobel	Alexander M. Thomson—R	Janesville
1870.	David Taylor—R	Sheboygan	James M. Bingham—R	Palmyra
1871.	Charles G. Williams—R	Janesville	William E. Smith—R	Fox Lake
1872.	Charles G. Williams—R	Janesville	Daniel Hall—R	Watertown
1873.	Henry L. Eaton—R	Lone Rock	Henry D. Barron—R	St. Croix Falls
1874.	John C. Holloway—R	Lancaster	Gabriel Bouck—D	Oshkosh
1875.	Henry D. Barron—R	St. Croix Falls	Frederick W. Horn—R	Cedarburg
1876.	Robert L.D. Potter—R	Wautoma	Sam S. Fifield—R	Ashland
1877.	William H. Hiner—R	Fond du Lac	John B. Cassoday—R	Janesville
1878.	Levi W. Barden—R	Portage	Augustus R. Barrows—GB	Chippewa Falls
1879.	William T. Price—R	Black River Falls	David M. Kelly—R	Green Bay
1880.	Thomas B. Scott—R	Grand Rapids	Alexander A. Arnold—R	Galesville
1881.	Thomas B. Scott—R	Grand Rapids	Ira B. Bradford—R	Augusta
1882.	George B. Burrows—R	Madison	Franklin L. Gilson—R	Ellsworth
1883.	George W. Ryland—R	Lancaster	Earl P. Finch—D	Oshkosh
1885.	Edward S. Minor—R	Sturgeon Bay	Hiram O. Fairchild—R	Marinette
1887.	Charles K. Erwin—R	Tomah	Thomas B. Mills—R)	Millston
1889.	Thomas A. Dyson—R	La Crosse	Thomas B. Mills—R	Millston
1891.	Frederick W. Horn—D	Cedarburg	James J. Hogan—D	La Crosse
1893.	Robert J. MacBride—D	Neillsville	Edward Keogh—D	Milwaukee
1895.	Thompson D. Weeks—R	Whitewater	George B. Burrows—R	Madison
1897.	Lyman W. Thayer—R	Ripon	George A. Buckstaff—R	Oshkosh
1899.	Lyman W. Thayer—R	Ripon	George H. Ray—R	La Crosse
1901.	James J. McGillivray—R	Black River Falls	George H. Ray—R	La Crosse
1903–05 . .	James J. McGillivray—R	Black River Falls	Irvine L. Lenroot—R	West Superior
1907.	James H. Stout—R	Menomonie	Herman L. Ekern—R	Whitehall
1909.	James H. Stout—R	Menomonie	Levi H. Bancroft—R	Richland Center
1911.	Harry C. Martin—R	Darlington	C.A. Ingram—R	Durand
1913.	Harry C. Martin—R	Darlington	Merlin Hull—R	Black River Falls
1915.	Edward T. Fairchild—R	Milwaukee	Lawrence C. Whittet—R	Edgerton
1917.	Timothy Burke—R	Green Bay	Lawrence C. Whittet—R	Edgerton
1919.	Willard T. Stevens—R	Rhinelander	Riley S. Young—R	Darien
1921.	Timothy Burke—R	Green Bay	Riley S. Young—R	Darien
1923.	Henry A. Huber—R	Stoughton	John L. Dahl—R	Rice Lake
1925.	Howard Teasdale—R	Sparta	Herman Sachtjen[3]—R	Madison
			George A. Nelson[3]—R	Milltown

Senate presidents, or presidents pro tempore, and assembly speakers since 1848, continued

Session	Senate presidents or presidents pro tempore[1]	Residence[2]	Assembly speakers	Residence[2]
1927.....	William L. Smith—R	Neillsville	John W. Eber—R	Milwaukee
1929.....	Oscar H. Morris—R	Milwaukee	Charles B. Perry—R	Wauwatosa
1931.....	Herman J. Severson—P	Iola	Charles B. Perry—R	Wauwatosa
1933.....	Orland S. Loomis—R	Mauston	Cornelius T. Young—D	Milwaukee
1935.....	Harry W. Bolens—D	Port Washington	Jorge W. Carow—P	Ladysmith
1937.....	Walter J. Rush—P	Neillsville	Paul R. Alfonsi—P	Pence
1939.....	Edward J. Roethe—R	Fennimore	Vernon W. Thomson—R	Richland Center
1941–43 ..	Conrad Shearer—R	Kenosha	Vernon W. Thomson—R	Richland Center
1945.....	Conrad Shearer—R	Kenosha	Donald C. McDowell—R	Soldiers Grove
1947.....	Frank E. Panzer—R	Brownsville	Donald C. McDowell—R	Soldiers Grove
1949.....	Frank E. Panzer—R	Brownsville	Alex L. Nicol—R	Sparta
1951–53 ..	Frank E. Panzer—R	Brownsville	Ora R. Rice—R	Delavan
1955.....	Frank E. Panzer—R	Brownsville	Mark Catlin, Jr.—R	Appleton
1957.....	Frank E. Panzer—R	Brownsville	Robert G. Marotz—R	Shawano
1959.....	Frank E. Panzer—R	Brownsville	George Molinaro—D	Kenosha
1961.....	Frank E. Panzer—R	Brownsville	David J. Blanchard—R	Edgerton
1963.....	Frank E. Panzer—R	Brownsville	Robert D. Haase—R	Marinette
1965.....	Frank E. Panzer—R	Brownsville	Robert T. Huber—D	West Allis
1967–69 ..	Robert P. Knowles—R	New Richmond	Harold V. Froehlich—R	Appleton
1971.....	Robert P. Knowles—R	New Richmond	Robert T. Huber[4]—D	West Allis
			Norman C. Anderson[4]—D	Madison
1973.....	Robert P. Knowles—R	New Richmond	Norman C. Anderson—D	Madison
1975.....	Fred A. Risser—D	Madison	Norman C. Anderson—D	Madison
1977–81 ..	Fred A. Risser—D	Madison	Edward G. Jackamonis—D	Waukesha
1983–89 ..	Fred A. Risser—D	Madison	Thomas A. Loftus—D	Sun Prairie
1991.....	Fred A. Risser—D	Madison	Walter J. Kunicki—D	Milwaukee
1993.....	Fred A. Risser[5]—D	Madison	Walter J. Kunicki—D	Milwaukee
	Brian D. Rude[5]—R	Coon Valley		
1995.....	Brian D. Rude[6]—R	Coon Valley	David T. Prosser, Jr.—R	Appleton
	Fred A. Risser[6]—D	Madison		
1997.....	Fred A. Risser[7]—D	Madison	Ben Brancel[8]—R	Endeavor
	Brian D. Rude[7]—R	Coon Valley	Scott R. Jensen[8]—R	Waukesha
1999.....	Fred A. Risser—D	Madison	Scott R. Jensen—R	Waukesha
2001.....	Fred A. Risser—D	Madison	Scott R. Jensen—R	Waukesha
2003–05 ..	Alan J. Lasee—R	De Pere	John Gard—R	Peshtigo
2007.....	Fred A. Risser—D	Madison	Michael D. Huebsch—R	West Salem
2009.....	Fred A. Risser—D	Madison	Michael J. Sheridan—D	Janesville
2011.....	Michael G. Ellis[9]—R	Neenah	Jeff Fitzgerald—R	Horicon
	Fred A. Risser[9]—D	Madison		
2013.....	Michael G. Ellis—R	Neenah	Robin J. Vos—R	Burlington
2015.....	Mary A. Lazich—R	New Berlin	Robin J. Vos—R	Burlington
2017–19 ..	Roger Roth—R	Appleton	Robin J. Vos—R	Burlington

Note: Political party indicated is for session elected and is obtained from newspaper accounts for some early legislators.

D–Democrat; GB–Greenback; P–Progressive; R–Republican; U–Union; UD–Union Democrat; W–Whig.

1. Prior to May 1, 1979, the president pro tempore is listed because the lieutenant governor, rather than a legislator, was the president of the senate under the constitution until that time. 2. Residence at the time of election. 3. Nelson was elected to serve at special session, 4/15/26 to 4/16/26, as Sachtjen had resigned. 4. Anderson was elected speaker 1/18/72 after Huber resigned 5. A new president was elected on 4/20/93 after a change in party control following two special elections. 6. A new president was elected on 7/9/96 after a change in party control following a recall election. 7. A new president was elected on 4/21/98 after a change in party control following a special election. 8. Jensen was elected speaker 11/4/97 after Brancel resigned. 9. A new president was elected on 7/17/12 after a change in party control following a recall election.

Sources: Senate and Assembly Journals; Wisconsin Legislative Reference Bureau records.

Majority and minority leaders of the Wisconsin Legislature since 1937

Session	Senate majority	Senate minority	Assembly majority	Assembly minority
1937...	Maurice Coakley—R	NA	NA	NA
1939...	Maurice Coakley—R	Philip Nelson—P	NA	Paul Alfonsi—P
1941...	Maurice Coakley—R	Cornelius Young—D	Mark Catlin, Jr.—R	Andrew Biemiller—P Robert Tehan—D
1943...	Warren Knowles[1]—R John Byrnes[1]—R	NA	Mark Catlin, Jr.—R	Elmer Genzmer—D Lyall Beggs—P
1945...	Warren Knowles—R	Anthony Gawronski—D	Vernon Thomson—R	Lyall Beggs—P Leland McParland—D
1947...	Warren Knowles—R	Robert Tehan—D	Vernon Thomson—R	Leland McParland—D
1949...	Warren Knowles—R	NA	Vernon Thomson—R	Leland McParland—D
1951...	Warren Knowles—R	Gaylord Nelson—D	Arthur Mockrud—R	George Molinaro—D
1953...	Warren Knowles—R	Henry Maier—D	Mark Catlin, Jr.—R	George Molinaro—D
1955...	Paul Rogan[2]—R	Henry Maier—D	Robert Marotz—R	Robert Huber—D
1957...	Robert Travis—R	Henry Maier—D	Warren Grady—R	Robert Huber—D
1959...	Robert Travis—R	Henry Maier—D	Keith Hardie—D	David Blanchard—R
1961...	Robert Travis—R	William Moser[3]—D	Robert Haase—R	Robert Huber—D
1963...	Robert Knowles—R	Richard Zaborski—D	Paul Alfonsi—R	Robert Huber—D
1965...	Robert Knowles—R	Richard Zaborski—D	Frank Nikolay—D	Robert Haase[4]—R Paul Alfonsi[4]—R
1967...	Jerris Leonard—R	Fred Risser—D	J. Curtis McKay—R	Robert Huber—D
1969...	Ernest Keppler—R	Fred Risser—D	Paul Alfonsi—R	Robert Huber—D
1971...	Ernest Keppler—R	Fred Risser—D	Norman Anderson[5]—D Anthony Earl[5]—D	Harold Froehlich—R
1973...	Raymond Johnson—R	Fred Risser—D	Anthony Earl—D	John Shabaz—R
1975...	Wayne Whittow[6]—D William Bablitch[6]—D	Clifford Krueger—R	Terry Willkom—D	John Shabaz—R
1977...	William Bablitch—D	Clifford Krueger—R	James Wahner—D	John Shabaz—R
1979...	William Bablitch—D	Clifford Krueger—R	James Wahner[7]—D Gary Johnson[7]—D	John Shabaz—R
1981...	William Bablitch[9]—D Timothy Cullen[9]—D	Walter Chilsen—R	Thomas Loftus—D	John Shabaz[8]—R Tommy Thompson[8]—R
1983...	Timothy Cullen—D	James Harsdorf—R	Gary Johnson—D	Tommy Thompson—R
1985...	Timothy Cullen—D	Susan Engeleiter—R	Dismas Becker—D	Tommy Thompson—R
1987...	Joseph Strohl—D	Susan Engeleiter—R	Thomas Hauke—D	Betty Jo Nelsen—R
1989...	Joseph Strohl—D	Michael Ellis—R	Thomas Hauke—D	David Prosser—R
1991...	David Helbach—D	Michael Ellis—R	David Travis—D	David Prosser—R
1993...	David Helbach[10]—D Michael Ellis[10]—R	Michael Ellis[10]—R David Helbach[10,11]—D Robert Jauch[11]—D	David Travis—D	David Prosser—R
1995...	Michael Ellis[13]—R Charles Chvala[13]—D	Robert Jauch[12]—D Charles Chvala[12,13]—D Michael Ellis[13]—R	Scott Jensen—R	Walter Kunicki—D
1997...	Charles Chvala[14]—D Michael Ellis[14]—R	Michael Ellis[14]—R Charles Chvala[14]—D	Steven Foti—R	Walter Kunicki[15]—D Shirley Krug[15]—D
1999...	Charles Chvala—D	Michael Ellis[16]—R Mary Panzer[16]—R	Steven Foti—R	Shirley Krug—D
2001...	Charles Chvala—D Russell Decker[17]—D Fred Risser[17]—D Jon Erpenbach[17]—D	Mary Panzer—R	Steven Foti—R	Shirley Krug—D Spencer Black[18]—D
2003...	Mary Panzer[19]—R Scott Fitzgerald[19]—R Dale Schultz[20]—R	Jon Erpenbach—D Judith Robson[20]—D	Steven Foti—R	James Kreuser—D
2005...	Dale Schultz—R	Judith Robson—D	Michael Huebsch—R	James Kreuser—D
2007...	Judith Robson—D Russell Decker[21]—D	Scott Fitzgerald—R	Jeff Fitzgerald—R	James Kreuser—D
2009...	Russell Decker[22]—D Dave Hansen[22]—D	Scott Fitzgerald—R	Thomas Nelson—D	Jeff Fitzgerald—R

Majority and minority leaders of the Wisconsin Legislature since 1937, continued

Session	Senate majority	Senate minority	Assembly majority	Assembly minority
2011...	Scott Fitzgerald—R	Mark Miller—D	Scott Suder—R	Peter Barca—D
	Mark Miller[23]—D	Scott Fitzgerald[23]—R		
2013...	Scott Fitzgerald—R	Chris Larson—D	Scott Suder[24]—R	Peter Barca—D
			Bill Kramer[25]—R	
			Pat Strachota—R	
2015...	Scott Fitzgerald—R	Jennifer Shilling—D	Jim Steineke—R	Peter Barca—D
2017...	Scott Fitzgerald—R	Jennifer Shilling—D	Jim Steineke—R	Peter Barca[26]—D
				Gordon Hintz[26]—D
2019	Scott Fitzgerald—R	Jennifer Shilling—D	Jim Steineke—R	Gordon Hintz—D

Note: Majority and minority leaders, who are chosen by the party caucuses in each house, were first recognized officially in the senate and assembly rules in 1963. Prior to the 1977 session, these positions were also referred to as "floor leader."

D–Democrat; P–Progressive; R–Republican. NA–Not available.

1. Knowles granted leave of absence to return to active duty in U.S. Navy; Byrnes chosen to succeed him on 4/30/1943. 2. Resigned after sine die adjournment. 3. Resigned 1/30/1962. 4. Haase resigned 9/15/1965; Alfonsi elected 10/4/1965. 5. Earl elected 1/18/1972 to succeed Anderson who became assembly speaker. 6. Whittow resigned 4/30/1976; Bablitch elected 5/17/1976. 7. Wahner resigned 1/28/1980; Johnson elected 1/28/1980. 8. Shabaz resigned 12/18/1981; Thompson elected 12/21/1981. 9. Bablitch resigned 5/26/1982; Cullen elected 5/26/1982. 10. Democrats controlled senate from 1/4/1993 to 4/20/1993 when Republicans assumed control after a special election. 11. Helbach resigned 5/12/1993; Jauch elected 5/12/1993. 12. Jauch resigned 10/17/1995; Chvala elected 10/24/1995. 13. Republicans controlled senate from 1/5/1995 to 6/13/1996 when Democrats assumed control after a recall election. 14. Democrats controlled the senate from 1/6/1997 to 4/21/1998 when Republicans assumed control after a special election. 15. Kunicki resigned 6/3/1998; Krug elected 6/3/1998. 16. Ellis resigned 1/25/2000; Panzer elected 1/25/2000. 17. Decker and Risser elected co-leaders 10/22/2002. Erpenbach elected leader 12/4/2002. 18. Black elected 5/1/2001. 19. Panzer resigned 9/17/2004; Fitzgerald elected 9/17/2004. 20. Schultz elected 11/9/2004; Robson elected 11/9/2004. 21. Decker elected 10/24/2007. 22. Hansen replaced Decker as leader, 12/15/2010. 23. After a resignation on 3/16/12 resulted in a 16–16 split, Fitzgerald and Miller served as co-leaders. A recall election gave Democrats control of the senate as of 7/17/12. 24. Suder resigned 9/3/13; Kramer elected 9/4/13. 25. Kramer removed 3/4/14; Strachota elected 3/4/14. 26. Barca resigned 9/19/17; Hintz elected 9/19/17.

Sources: Wisconsin Blue Book, various editions; Senate and Assembly Journals; newspaper accounts.

Chief clerks and sergeants at arms of the legislature since 1848

	Senate		Assembly	
Session	Chief clerk	Sergeant at arms	Chief clerk	Sergeant at arms
1848......	Henry G. Abbey	Lyman H. Seaver	Daniel N. Johnson	John Mullanphy
1849......	William R. Smith	F. W. Shollner	Robert L. Ream	Felix McLinden
1850......	William R. Smith	James Hanrahan	Alex T. Gray	E. R. Hugunin
1851......	William Hull	E. D. Masters	Alex T. Gray	C. M. Kingsbury
1852......	John K. Williams	Patrick Cosgrove	Alex T. Gray	Elisha Starr
1853......	John K. Williams	Thomas Hood	Thomas McHugh	Richard F. Wilson
1854......	Samuel G. Bugh	J. M. Sherwood	Thomas McHugh	William H. Gleason
1855......	Samuel G. Bugh	William H. Gleason	David Atwood	William Blake
1856......	Byron Paine	Joseph Baker	James Armstrong	Egbert Mosely
1857......	William H. Brisbane	Alanson Filer	William C. Webb	William C. Rogers
1858......	John L. V. Thomas	Nathaniel L. Stout	L. H. D. Crane	Francis Massing
1859......	Hiram Bowen	Asa Kinney	L. H. D. Crane	Emmanual Munk
1860......	J. H. Warren	Asa Kinney	L. H. D. Crane	Joseph Gates
1861......	J. H. Warren	J. A. Hadley	L. H. D. Crane	Craig B. Peebe
1862......	J. H. Warren	B. U. Caswell	John S. Dean	A. A. Huntington
1863......	Frank M. Stewart	Luther Bashford	John S. Dean	A. M. Thompson
1864......	Frank M. Stewart	Nelson Williams	John S. Dean	A. M. Thompson
1865......	Frank M. Stewart	Nelson Williams	John S. Dean	Alonzo Wilcox
1866......	Frank M. Stewart	Nelson Williams	E. W. Young	L. M. Hammond
1867......	Leander B. Hills	Asa Kinney	E. W. Young	Daniel Webster

Political composition of the Wisconsin Legislature since 1885, continued

Session[1]	Senate[2]					Assembly[3]				
	D	R	P	S	SD	D	R	P	S	SD
1921.	2	27	—	4	—	2	92	—	6	—
1923.	—	30	—	3	—	1	89	—	10	—
1925.	—	30	—	3	—	1	92	—	7	—
1927.	—	31	—	2	—	3	89	—	8	—
1929.	—	31	—	2	—	6	90	—	3	—
1931.	1	30	—	2	—	2	89	—	9	—
1933.	9	23	—	1	—	59	13	24	3	—
1935.	13	6	14	—	—	35	17	45	3	—
1937.	9	8	16	—	—	31	21	46	2	—
1939.	6	16	11	—	—	15	53	32	—	—
1941.	3	24	6	—	—	15	60	25	—	—
1943.	4	23	6	—	—	14	73	13	—	—
1945.	6	22	5	—	—	19	75	6	—	—
1947.	5	27	1	—	—	11	88	—	—	—
1949.	3	27	—	—	—	26	74	—	—	—
1951.	7	26	—	—	—	24	75	—	—	—
1953.	7	26	—	—	—	25	75	—	—	—
1955.	8	24	—	—	—	36	64	—	—	—
1957.	10	23	—	—	—	33	67	—	—	—
1959.	12	20	—	—	—	55	45	—	—	—
1961.	13	20	—	—	—	45	55	—	—	—
1963.	11	22	—	—	—	46	53	—	—	—
1965.	12	20	—	—	—	52	48	—	—	—
1967.	12	21	—	—	—	47	53	—	—	—
1969.	10	23	—	—	—	48	52	—	—	—
1971.	12	20	—	—	—	67	33	—	—	—
1973.	15	18	—	—	—	62	37	—	—	—
1975.	18	13	—	—	—	63	36	—	—	—
1977.	23	10	—	—	—	66	33	—	—	—
1979.	21	10	—	—	—	60	39	—	—	—
1981.	19	14	—	—	—	59	39	—	—	—
1983.	17	14	—	—	—	59	40	—	—	—
1985.	19	14	—	—	—	52	47	—	—	—
1987.	19	11	—	—	—	54	45	—	—	—
1989.	20	13	—	—	—	56	43	—	—	—
1991.	19	14	—	—	—	58	41	—	—	—
1993[4]	15	15	—	—	—	52	47	—	—	—
1995[4]	16	17	—	—	—	48	51	—	—	—
1997[4]	17	16	—	—	—	47	52	—	—	—
1999.	17	16	—	—	—	44	55	—	—	—
2001.	18	15	—	—	—	43	56	—	—	—
2003.	15	18	—	—	—	41	58	—	—	—
2005.	14	19	—	—	—	39	60	—	—	—
2007.	18	15	—	—	—	47	52	—	—	—
2009.	18	15	—	—	—	52	46	—	—	—
2011[4]	14	19	—	—	—	38	60	—	—	—
2013.	15	18	—	—	—	39	59	—	—	—
2015.	14	18	—	—	—	36	63	—	—	—
2017.	13	20	—	—	—	35	64	—	—	—
2019.	14	19	—	—	—	36	63	—	—	—

Note: The number of assembly districts was reduced from 100 to 99 beginning in 1973. There have been 33 senate districts since 1862. Any deviation of a session's total from these numbers indicates vacant seats.

— Represents zero; D–Democrat; P–Progressive; R–Republican; S–Socialist; SD–Social Democrat.

1. Political composition at inauguration.   2. Miscellaneous affiliations for senate seats not shown in the table are: one Independent and one People's (1887); one Independent and 2 Union Labor (1889).   3. Miscellaneous affiliations for assembly seats not shown: 3 Independent, 4 Independent Democrat, and 6 People's (1887); one Union Labor (1891); one Fusion (1897);

one Independent (1929, 2009, 2011); one Independent Republican (1933).   4. In the 1993, 1995, and 1997 Legislatures, majority control of the senate shifted during the session. On 4/20/93, vacancies were filled resulting in a total of 16 Democrats and 17 Republicans; on 6/16/96, there were 17 Democrats and 16 Republicans; on 4/19/98, there were 16 Democrats and 17 Republicans.   5. A series of recall elections during the session resulted in a switch in majority control of the senate, with 17 Democrats and 16 Republicans as of 7/16/12.

Sources: Pre-1943 data compiled from the Secretary of State, *Officers of Wisconsin: U.S., State, Judicial, Congressional, Legislative and County Officers*, 1943 and earlier editions, and the *Wisconsin Blue Book*, various editions. Later data compiled from Wisconsin Legislative Reference Bureau sources.

Wisconsin legislative sessions since 1848

	Opening/final adjournment	Days	Measures introduced			Bills vetoed[1] (overridden)	Laws enacted
			Bills	Joint res.	Res.		
1848.	6/5–8/21	78	217	—	—	—	155
1849.	1/10–4/2	83	428	—	—	2(1)	220
1850.	1/9–2/11	34	438	—	—	1	284
1851.	1/8–3/17	69	707	—	—	9	407
1852.	1/14–4/19	97	813	—	—	3(1)	504
1853.	1/12–7/13	183	1,145	—	—	6	521
1854.	1/11–4/3	83	880	—	—	2	437
1855.	1/10–4/2	83	955	—	—	6	500
1856.	1/9–10/14	288	1,242	—	—	1	688
1857.	1/14–3/9	55	895	—	—	—	517
1858.	1/13–5/17	125	1,364	157	342	28	436
1859.	1/12–3/21	69	986	113	143	9	680
1860.	1/11–4/2	83	1,024	69	246	2	489
1861.	1/9–4/17	99	857	100	235	2	387
1861 SS.	5/15–5/27	13	28	24	34	—	15
1862.	1/8–6/17	161	1,008	125	207	36[2](8)	514
1862 SS.	9/10–9/26	17	43	25	37	—	17
1863.	1/14–4/2	79	895	101	157	10(1)	383
1864.	1/13–4/4	83	835	66	141	—	509
1865.	1/11–4/10	90	1,132	82	190	2	565
1866.	1/10–4/12	93	1,107	64	208	5	733
1867.	1/9–4/11	93	1,161	97	161	2	790
1868.	1/8–3/6	59	987	73	119	2(2)	692
1869.	1/13–3/11	58	887	52	81	14(1)	657
1870.	1/12–3/17	65	1,043	54	89	2	666
1871.	1/11–3/25	74	1,066	55	82	4	671
1872.	1/10–3/26	77	709	79	124	2	322
1873.	1/8–3/20	72	611	62	122	4	308
1874.	1/14–3/12	58	688	91	111	2	349
1875.	1/13–3/6	53	637	39	93	2	344
1876.	1/12–3/14	63	715	57	115	2	415
1877.	1/10–3/8	58	720	59	95	4	384
1878.	1/9–3/21	72	735	79	134	2	342
1878 SS.	6/4–6/7	4	6	14	10	—	5
1879.	1/8–3/5	57	610	49	105	—	256
1880.	1/14–3/17	64	669	58	93	3	323
1881.	1/12–4/4	83	780	104	100	6	334
1882.	1/11–3/31	80	728	57	90	6	330
1883.	1/10–4/4	85	705	75	100	2	360
1885.	1/14–4/13	90	963	97	108	8	471
1887.	1/12–4/15	94	1,293	114	60	10	553
1889.	1/9–4/19	101	1,355	136	82	6(1)	529
1891.	1/14–4/25	102	1,216	137	91	10(1)	483
1892 SS.	6/28–7/1	4	4	7	16	—	1
1892 SS.	10/17–10/27	11	8	6	14	—	2
1893.	1/11–4/21	101	1,124	135	86	6	312

Wisconsin legislative sessions since 1848, continued

	Opening/final adjournment	Days	Measures introduced Bills	Joint res.	Res.	Bills vetoed[1] (overridden)	Laws enacted
1895.	1/9–4/20	102	1,154	139	88	—	387
1896 SS.	2/18–2/28	11	3	11	15	—	1
1897.	1/13–8/20	220	1,077	155	39	19(1)	381
1899.	1/11–5/4	114	910	113	40	3	357
1901.	1/9–5/15	127	1,091	81	39	24	470
1903.	1/14–5/23	130	1,115	65	81	23	451
1905.	1/11–6/21	162	1,357	134	101	22	523
1905 SS.	12/4–12/19	16	24	15	26	—	17
1907.	1/9–7/16	189	1,685	205	84	28(1)	677
1909.	1/13–6/18	157	1,567	213	49	22	550
1911.	1/11–7/15	186	1,710	267	37	15	665
1912 SS.	4/30–5/6	7	41	7	6	—	22
1913.	1/8–8/9	214	1,847	175	79	24	778
1915.	1/13–8/24	224	1,560	220	79	15	637
1916 SS.	10/10–10/11	2	2	8	4	—	2
1917.	1/10–7/16	188	1,439	229	115	18	679
1918 SS.	2/19–3/9	19	27	22	28	2	16
1918 SS.	9/24–9/25	2	2	6	9	—	2
1919.	1/8–7/30	204	1,350	268	100	39	703
1919 SS.	9/4–9/8	5	7	4	6	—	7
1920 SS.	5/25–6/4	11	46	10	22	2	32
1921.	1/12–7/14	184	1,199	207	93	41(1)	591
1922 SS.	3/22–3/28	7	10	7	12	1	4
1923.	1/10–7/14	186	1,247	215	93	52	449
1925.	1/14–6/29	167	1,144	200	115	73	454
1926 SS.	4/15–4/16	2	1	8	12	—	1
1927.	1/12–8/13	214	1,341	235	167	90(2)	542
1928 SS.	1/24–2/4	12	20	35	23	—	5
1928 SS.	3/6–3/13	8	13	9	17	—	2
1929.	1/9–9/20	255	1,366	278	185	44	530
1931.	1/14–6/27	165	1,429	291	160	56	487
1931 SS.	11/24/31–2/5/32	74	99	93	83	2	31
1933.	1/11–7/25	196	1,411	324	157	15	496
1933 SS.	12/11/33–2/3/34	55	45	160	53	—	20
1935.	1/9–9/27	262	1,662	346	190	27	556
1937.	1/13–7/2	171	1,404	228	127	10	432
1937 SS.	9/15–10/16	32	28	18	23	—	15
1939.	1/11–10/6	269	1,559	268	133	22	535
1941.	1/8–6/6	150	1,368	160	109	17	333
1943.	1/13/43–1/22/44	375	1,153	202	136	39(20)	577
1945.	1/10–9/6	240	1,156	208	109	30(5)	590
1946 SS.	7/29–7/30	2	2	6	14	—	2
1947.	1/8–9/11	247	1,220	195	97	10(1)	615
1948 SS.	7/19–7/20	2	—	5	11	—	—
1949.	1/12–9/13	245	1,432	188	86	17(2)	643
1951.	1/10–6/14	156	1,559	157	73	18	735
1953.	1/14–11/6	297	1,593	175	70	31(3)	687
1955.	1/12–10/21	283	1,503	256	74	38	696
1957.	1/9–9/27	262	1,512	246	71	35(1)	706
1958 SS.	6/11–6/13	3	3	7	13	—	3
1959.	1/14/59–5/27/60	500	1,769	272	84	36(4)	696
1961.	1/11/61–1/9/63	729	1,592	295	68	70(2)	689
1963.	1/9/63–1/13/65	736	1,619	241	110	72(4)	580
1963 SS.	12/10–12/12	3	8	10	10	—	3
1965 [3]	1/13/65–1/2/67	720	1,818	293	86	24(1)	666
1967.	1/11/67–1/6/69	727	1,700	215	61	18	355
1969.	1/6/69–1/4/71	729	2,014	232	101	34(1)	501

Wisconsin legislative sessions since 1848, continued

	Opening/final adjournment	Days	Measures introduced			Bills vetoed[1] (overridden)	Laws enacted
			Bills	Joint res.	Res.		
1969 SS[4]...........	9/29/69–1/17/70	111	5	5	8	—	1
1970 SS............	12/22	1	—	1	5	—	—
1971.............	1/4/71–1/1/73	729	2,568	291	121	32(3)	336
1972 SS...........	4/19–4/28	10	9	4	4	—	6
1973.............	1/1/73–1/6/75	736	2,501	277	126	13	332
1973 SS...........	12/17–12/21	5	3	2	6	—	2
1974 SS...........	4/29–6/13	46	12	1	4	—	6
1974 SS[5].........	11/19–11/20	2	2	—	—	—	1
1975.............	1/6/75–1/3/77	729	2,325	169	88	36(6)	414
1975 SS...........	12/9–12/11	3	13	1	2	1	6
1976 SS...........	5/18	1	2	2	3	—	1
1976 SS[5]..........	6/15–6/17	3	13	4	3	—	9
1976 SS...........	9/8	1	4	1	4	—	2
1977.............	1/3/77–1/3/79	730	2,053	182	48	21(4)	442
1977 SS...........	6/30	1	—	1	2	—	—
1977 SS...........	11/7–11/11	5	6	4	2	—	5
1978 SS[5]..........	6/13–6/15	3	2	5	2	—	2
1978 SS...........	12/20	1	2	4	2	—	2
1979.............	1/3/79–1/5/81	734	1,920	203	40	19(3)	350
1979 SS...........	9/5	1	10	3	2	—	5
1980 SS[6].........	1/22–1/25	4	8	3	2	—	—
1980 SS...........	6/3– 7/3	31	20	14	2	—	7
1981.............	1/5/81–1/3/83	729	1,987	176	70	10(2)	381
1981 SS[7]..........	11/4–11/17	14	6	3	2	—	3
1982 SS[7]..........	4/6–5/20	45	4	2	2	1	1
1982 SS[7]..........	5/26–5/28	3	13	7	2	—	9
1983.............	1/3/83–1/7/85	736	1,902	173	50	3	521
1983 SS...........	1/4–1/6	3	2	2	1	—	2
1983 SS...........	4/12–4/14	3	1	1	—	—	1
1983 SS...........	7/11–7/14	4	5	3	1	—	4
1983 SS...........	10/18–10/28	11	12	1	—	—	11
1984 SS...........	2/2–4/4	63	2	1	—	—	—
1984 SS...........	5/22–5/24	3	12	5	1	—	11
1985.............	1/7/85–1/5/87	729	1,624	171	41	7	293
1985 SS...........	3/19–3/21	3	6	1	—	—	3
1985 SS...........	9/24–10/19	26	22	1	—	—	17
1985 SS...........	10/31	1	1	3	—	—	1
1985 SS...........	11/20	1	24	2	—	—	12
1986 SS...........	1/27–5/30	124	1	4	—	—	1
1986 SS...........	3/24–3/26	3	1	1	—	—	1
1986 SS...........	5/20–5/29	10	44	3	—	—	12
1986 SS...........	7/15	1	3	1	—	—	2
1987[8]............	1/5/87–1/3/89	730	1,631	196	21	35	413
1987 SS...........	9/15–9/16	2	2	1	—	—	2
1987 SS...........	11/18/87–6/7/88	203	19	3	—	3	5
1988 SS...........	6/30	1	4	1	3	—	2
1989.............	1/3/89–1/7/91	735	1,557	244	45	35	361
1989 SS...........	10/10/89–3/22/90	164	52	6	—	—	7
1990 SS...........	5/15/90	1	7	1	—	—	—
1991.............	1/7/91–1/4/93	729	1,676	244	32	33	318
1991 SS...........	1/29/–7/4	157	16	1	—	—	2
1991 SS...........	10/15/91–5/21/92	220	9	2	—	—	1
1992 SS[6]..........	4/14–6/4	52	7	1	2	—	2
1992 SS...........	6/1	1	—	2	—	—	—
1992 SS...........	8/25–9/15	22	1	1	2	—	1
1993.............	1/4/93–1/3/95	730	2,147	207	47	8	491
1994 SS...........	5/18–5/19	2	6	1	—	—	3

Wisconsin legislative sessions since 1848, continued

	Opening/final adjournment	Days	Measures introduced			Bills vetoed[1] (overridden)	Laws enacted
			Bills	Joint res.	Res.		
1994 SS[9]	6/7–6/23	17	3	4	—	—	3
1995	1/3/95–1/6/97	735	1,780	163	38	4	467
1995 SS	1/4	1	1	1	—	—	1
1995 SS	9/5–10/12	36	1	1	—	—	1
1997	1/6/97–1/4/99	729	1,508	183	30	3	333
1998 SS[10]	4/21–5/21	31	13	2	2	—	5
1999[11]	1/4/99–1/3/01	731	1,498	168	52	5	196
1999 SS[5]	10/27–11/11	16	3	1	—	—	1
2000 SS	5/4–5/9	8	2	2	1	—	1
2001	1/3/01–1/6/03	734	1,436	174	75	—	106
2001 SS[5]	5/1–5/3	3	1	—	—	—	1
2002 SS[5]	1/22–7/8	168	1	2	7	—	1
2002 SS[5]	5/13–5/15	3	2	—	—	—	1
2003[12]	1/6/03–1/3/05	729	1,567	164	78	54	326
2003 SS	1/30–2/20	22	1	—	—	—	1
2005[13]	1/3/05–1/3/07	731	1,967	196	76	47	489
2005 SS	1/12–1/20	9	2	—	—	—	1
2006 SS	2/14–3/7	22	2	—	—	—	1
2007	1/3/07–1/5/09	733	1,574	230	50	1	239
2007 SS	1/11–2/1	22	2	1	—	—	1
2007 SS	10/15–10/23	9	2	—	—	—	—
2007 SS	12/11/07–5/14/08	156	1	1	—	—	—
2008 SS	3/12–5/14	65	1	4	2	—	1
2008 SS	4/17–5/15	29	1	4	2	—	1
2009[14]	1/5/09–1/3/11	729	1,720	221	44	6	406
2009 SS	6/24–6/27	4	1	—	—	—	—
2009 SS	12/16–3/4/10	79	2	—	—	—	—
2011[15]	1/3/11–1/7/13	735	1,325	211	48	—	267
2011 SS	1/4–9/27	267	27	1	3	—	12
2011 SS	9/29–12/8	71	48	—	—	—	7
2013	1/7/13–1/5/15	730	1,627	214	37	1	373
2013 SS	10/10–11/12	34	8	—	—	—	4
2013 SS	12/2–12/19	18	2	—	—	—	1
2014 SS	1/23–3/20	57	4	—	—	—	2
2015[16]	1/5/15–1/3/17	730	1,830	236	45	2	392
2017[17]	1/3/17–1/7/19	735	1960	237	39	—	349
2017 SS	1/5–6/14	161	22	—	—	—	11
2017 SS	8/1–9/15	46	2	—	1	—	1
2018 SS	1/18–2/27	41	20	—	—	—	9
2018 SS	3/15–3/29	15	6	—	—	—	—

— Represents zero; Res.–Resolution; SS–Special session.

1. Partial vetoes not included. See executive vetoes table. 2. Does not include 18 bills that the lieutenant governor asserted had been vetoed by pocket veto when the governor, to whom they had been sent, died without signing them. 3. Although 1965 Legislature adjourned to 1/11/67, terms automatically expired on 1/2/67. 4. Senate adjourned the special session 11/15/69; assembly, 1/17/70. 5. Special session met concurrently with regular session. 6. Legislature met concurrently in extraordinary and special session. 7. Legislature met concurrently in special session and extended floorperiod. 8. Extraordinary sessions held in February, September, and November 1987 and April, May, and June 1988. May 1988 extraordinary session ran concurrently with May 1988 veto review period and with June 1988 extraordinary session. 9. Extraordinary session held in June 1994. 10. Extraordinary session held in April 1998. 11. Extraordinary session held in April and May 2000. 12. Extraordinary sessions held in February, July, and August 2003; December 2003–February 2004; March 2004; May 2004; and July 2004. 13. Extraordinary sessions held in July 2005 and April 2006. 14. Extraordinary sessions held in February, May, June, and December 2009 and December 2010. 15. Extraordinary sessions held in June and July 2011. 16. Extraordinary sessions held in February, July, and November 2015. 17. Extraordinary sessions held in March, April, November, and December 2018.

Sources: *Bulletin of the Proceedings of the Wisconsin Legislature*, various editions; and Senate and Assembly Journals.

Executive vetoes since 1931

Session	Bills vetoed (overridden)	Partial vetoes (overridden)	Budget bill partial vetoes[1] (overridden)
1931.	58	2	12
1933.	15	1	12
1935.	27	4	—
1937.	10	1	—
1939[2]	22	4	1
1941.	17	1	1
1943.	39 (20)	1 (1)	—
1945.	30 (5)	2 (1)	1
1947.	10 (1)	1	1
1949.	17 (2)	2 (1)	—
1951.	18	—	—
1953[3]	31 (3)	4	2
1955.	38	—	—
1957.	35 (1)	3	2
1959.	36 (4)	1	—
1961.	70 (2)	3	2
1963.	72 (4)	1	—
1965.	24 (1)	4	1
1967.	18	5	—
1969.	34 (1)	11	27
1971.	32 (3)	8	12
1973.	13	18 (3)	38 (2)
1975.	37 (6)	22 (4)	42 (5)
1977.	21 (4)	16 (3)	67 (21)
1979.	19 (3)	9 (2)	45 (1)
1981[4]	11 (2)	11 (1)	121
1983.	3	11 (1)	70 (6)
1985.	7	7 (1)	78 (2)
1987.	38	20	290
1989.	35	28	208
1991.	33	13	457
1993.	8	24	78
1995.	4	21	112
1997.	3	8	152
1999.	5	10	255
2001.	—	3	315
2003.	54	10	131
2005.	47	2	139
2007.	1	4	33
2009.	6	5	81
2011.	—	3	50
2013.	1	4	57
2015.	2	5	104
2017.	—	4	98

— Represents zero.

1. The number of individual veto statements in the governor's veto message.   2. Attorney general ruled veto of 1939 SB-43 was void and it became law (see Vol. 28, *Opinions of the Attorney General*, p. 423).   3. 1953 AB-141, partially vetoed in two separate sections by separate veto messages, is counted as one.   4. Attorney general ruled several vetoes "ineffective" because the governor failed to express his objections (see Vol. 70, *Opinions of the Attorney General*, p. 189).

Source: Compiled by Wisconsin Legislative Reference Bureau from the *Bulletin of the Proceedings of the Wisconsin Legislature* and the Assembly and Senate Journals.

History of proposed constitutional amendments since 1854

Article	Section	Subject	Election result	Vote totals	Date	Proposed amendment
IV	4	Assemblymen, 2-year terms	rejected	6,549–11,580	Nov. 1854	1854 Ch. 89
IV	5	Senators, 4-year terms	rejected	6,348–11,885	Nov. 1854	1854 Ch. 89
IV	11	Biennial legislative sessions	rejected	6,752–11,589	Nov. 1854	1854 Ch. 89
V	5	Governor's salary, changed from $1,250 to $2,500 a year	rejected	14,519–32,612	Nov. 1862	1862 JR 6
IV	21	Change legislators' pay to $350 a year	ratified	58,363–24,418	Nov. 1867	1866 JR 3
V	5	Change governor's salary from $1,250 to $5,000 a year	ratified	47,353–41,764	Nov. 1869	1869 JR 2
V	9	Change lieutenant governor's salary to $1,000 a year	ratified	47,353–41,764	Nov. 1869	1869 JR 2
I	8	Grand jury system modified	ratified	48,894–18,606	Nov. 1870	1870 JR 3
IV	31, 32	Private and local laws, prohibited on 9 subjects	ratified	54,087–3,675	Nov. 1871	1871 JR 1
VII	4	Supreme court, 1 chief and 4 associate justices	rejected	16,272–29,755	Nov. 1872	1872 JR 8
XI	3	Indebtedness of municipalities limited to 5%	ratified	66,061–1,509	Nov. 1874	1873 JR 4
VII	4	Supreme court, 1 chief and 4 associate justices	ratified	79,140–16,763	Nov. 1877	1877 JR 1
VIII	2	Claims against state, 6-year limit	ratified	33,046–3,371	Nov. 1877	1877 JR 4
IV	4, 5, 11	Biennial sessions; assemblymen 2-year, senators 4-year terms	ratified	53,532–13,936	Nov. 1881	1881 AJR 7[1]
IV	21	Change legislators' pay to $500 a year	ratified	53,532–13,936	Nov. 1881	1881 AJR 7[1]
III	1	Voting residence 30 days; in municipalities voter registration	ratified	36,223–5,347	Nov. 1882	1882 JR 5
VI	4	County officers except judicial, vacancies filled by appointment	ratified	60,091–8,089	Nov. 1882	1882 JR 3
VII	12	Clerk of court, full term election	ratified	60,091–8,089	Nov. 1882	1882 JR 3
XIII	1	Political year; biennial elections	ratified	60,091–8,089	Nov. 1882	1882 JR 3
X	1	State superintendent, qualifications and pay fixed by legislature	rejected	12,967–18,342	Nov. 1888	1887 JR 4
VII	4	Supreme court, composed of 5 justices of supreme court	ratified	125,759–14,712	Apr. 1889	1889 JR 3
IV	31	Cities incorporated by general law	ratified	15,718–9,015	Nov. 1892	1891 JR 4
X	1	State superintendent, pay fixed by law	rejected	38,752–56,506	Nov. 1896	1895 JR 2
VII	7	Circuit judges, additional in populous counties	ratified	45,823–41,513	Apr. 1897	1897 JR 9
X	1	State superintendent, nonpartisan 4-year term, pay fixed by law	ratified	71,550–57,411	Nov. 1902	1901 JR 3
XI	4	General banking law authorized	ratified	64,836–44,620	Nov. 1902	1901 JR 2
XI	5	Banking law referenda requirement repealed	ratified	64,836–44,620	Nov. 1902	1901 JR 2
XIII	11	Free passes prohibited	ratified	67,781–40,697	Nov. 1902	1901 JR 9
VII	4	Supreme court, 7 justices, 10-year terms	ratified	51,377–39,857	Apr. 1903	1903 JR 7
III	1	Suffrage for full citizens only	ratified	85,838–36,733	Nov. 1908	1907 JR 25
V	10	Governor's approval of bills in 6 days	ratified	85,958–27,270	Nov. 1908	1907 JR 13
VIII	1	Income tax	ratified	85,696–37,729	Nov. 1908	1907 JR 29
VIII	10	Highways, appropriations for	ratified	116,421–46,739	Nov. 1908	1907 JR 18

Art.	Sec.	Amendment	Result	Vote	Date	Reference
IV	3	Apportionment after each federal census.	ratified	54,932–52,634	Nov. 1910	1909 JR 55
IV	21	Change legislators' pay to $1,000 a year.	rejected	44,153–76,278	Nov. 1910	1909 JR 7
VIII	10	Water power and forests, appropriations for [2]	rejected	62,468–45,924 [2]	Nov. 1910	1909 Ch. 514
VII	10	Judges' salaries, time of payment.	ratified	44,855–34,865	Nov. 1912	1911 JR 24
XI	3	City or county debt for lands, discharge within 50 years.	ratified	46,369–34,975	Nov. 1912	1911 JR 42
XI	3a	Public parks, playgrounds, etc.	ratified	48,424–33,931	Nov. 1912	1911 JR 48
IV	1	Initiative and referendum	rejected	84,934–148,536	Nov. 1914	1913 JR 22
IV	21	Change legislators' pay to $600 a year, 2 cents a mile for additional round trips	rejected	68,907–157,202	Nov. 1914	1913 JR 24
VII	6,7	Judicial circuits, decreased number, additional judges.	rejected	63,311–154,827	Nov. 1914	1913 JR 26
VIII	—	State annuity insurance.	rejected	59,909–170,338	Nov. 1914	1913 JR 35
VIII	—	State insurance	rejected	58,490–165,966	Nov. 1914	1913 JR 12
XI	—	Home rule of cities and villages	rejected	86,020–141,472	Nov. 1914	1913 JR 21
XI	1	Municipal power of condemnation.	rejected	61,122–154,945	Nov. 1914	1913 JR 25
XII	—	Constitutional amendments, submission after 3/5 approval by one legislature	rejected	71,734–160,761	Nov. 1914	1913 JR 17
XII	—	Constitution amended upon petition	rejected	68,435–150,215	Nov. 1914	1913 JR 22
XIII	—	Recall of civil officers.	rejected	81,628–144,386	Nov. 1914	1913 JR 15
IV	21	Legislators' pay fixed by law	rejected	126,243–132,258	Apr. 1920	1919 JR 37
VII	6,7	Judicial circuits, decreased number, additional judges.	rejected	113,786–116,436	Apr. 1920	1919 JR 92
I	5	Jury verdict, 5/6 in civil cases	ratified	171,433–156,820	Nov. 1922	1921 JR 17
VI	4	Sheriffs, no limit on successive terms	rejected	161,832–207,594	Nov. 1922	1921 JR 36
XI	—	Municipal indebtedness for public utilities.	rejected	105,234–219,639	Nov. 1922	1921 JR 37
IV	21	Change legislators' pay to $750 a year.	rejected	189,635–250,236	Apr. 1924	1923 JR 18
VII	7	Circuit judges, additional in populous counties	ratified	240,207–226,562	Nov. 1924	1923 JR 64
VIII	10	Forestry, appropriations for	ratified	336,360–173,563	Nov. 1924	1923 JR 57
XI	3	Home rule for cities and villages	ratified	299,792–190,165	Nov. 1924	1923 JR 34
V	5	Governor's salary fixed by law	ratified	202,156–188,302	Nov. 1926	1925 JR 52
XIII	12	Recall of elective officials.	ratified	205,868–201,125	Nov. 1926	1925 JR 16
IV	21	Change legislators' pay to $1,000 for session.	rejected	151,786–199,260	Apr. 1927	1927 JR 12
VIII	1	Severance tax: forests, minerals.	ratified	179,217–141,888	Apr. 1927	1927 JR 13
IV	21	Legislators' salary repealed; to be fixed by law.	ratified	237,250–212,846	Apr. 1929	1929 JR 6
VI	4	Sheriffs succeeding themselves for 2 terms	ratified	259,881–210,964	Apr. 1929	1929 JR 13
V	10	Item veto on appropriation bills	ratified	252,655–153,703	Nov. 1930	1929 JR 43
V	5	Governor's salary provision repealed; fixed by law	ratified	452,605–275,175	Nov. 1932	1931 JR 52
V	9	Lieutenant governor's salary repealed; fixed by law	ratified	427,768–267,120	Nov. 1932	1931 JR 53
VII	1	Wording of section corrected	ratified	436,113–221,563	Nov. 1932	1931 JR 58
XI	3	Municipal indebtedness for public utilities.	ratified	401,194–279,631	Nov. 1932	1931 JR 71
III	1	Women's suffrage	ratified	411,088–166,745	Nov. 1934	1933 JR 76
XIII	11	Free passes, permitted as specified.	ratified	365,971–361,799	Nov. 1936	1935 JR 98
VIII	1	Installment payment of real estate taxes	ratified	330,971–134,808	Apr. 1941	1941 JR 18

History of proposed constitutional amendments since 1854, continued

Article	Section	Subject	Election result	Vote totals	Date	Proposed amendment
VIII	15	Justice of peace, abolish office in first class cities	ratified	160,965–113,408	Apr. 1945	1945 JR 2
VIII	10	Aeronautical program	ratified	187,111–101,169	Apr. 1945	1945 JR 3
VI	4	Sheriffs, no limit on successive terms	rejected	121,144–170,131	Apr. 1946	1945 JR 47
IV	33	Auditing of state accounts	ratified	480,938–308,072	Nov. 1946	1945 JR 73
VI	2	Auditing (part of same proposal)	ratified	480,938–308,072	Nov. 1946	1945 JR 73
X	3	Public transportation of school children to any school	rejected	437,817–545,475	Nov. 1946	1945 JR 78
XI	2	Repeal; relating to exercise of eminent domain by municipalities	rejected	210,086–807,318	Nov. 1948	1947 JR 48
II	2	Prohibition on taxing federal lands repealed	rejected	245,412–297,237	Apr. 1949	1949 JR 2
VIII	10	Allow internal improvement debt for veterans' housing	ratified	311,576–290,736	Apr. 1949	1949 JR 1
II	2	Prohibition on taxing federal lands repealed	ratified	305,612–186,284	Apr. 1951	1951 JR 7
XI	3	City debt limit 8% for combined city and school purposes	ratified	313,739–191,897	Apr. 1951	1951 JR 6
IV	3, 4, 5	Apportionment based on area and population[3]	rejected	433,043–406,133 [3]	Apr. 1953	1953 JR 9
VII	9	Judicial elections to full terms	ratified	386,972–345,094	Apr. 1953	1953 JR 12
VII	24	Judges: qualifications, retirement	ratified	380,214–177,929	Apr. 1955	1955 JR 14
XI	3	School debt limit, equalized value	ratified	320,376–228,641	Apr. 1955	1955 JR 12
IV	26	Teachers' retirement benefits	ratified	365,560–255,284	Apr. 1956	1955 JR 17
VI	4	Sheriffs, no limit on successive terms	rejected	269,722–328,603	Apr. 1956	1955 JR 53
XI	3a	Municipal acquisition of land for public purposes	ratified	376,692–193,544	Apr. 1956	1955 JR 36
XIII	11	Free passes, not for public use	rejected	188,715–380,207	Apr. 1956	1955 JR 54
VIII	10	Port development	ratified	472,177–451,045	Apr. 1960	1959 JR 15
XI	3	Debt limit in populous counties, 5% of equalized valuation	ratified	686,104–529,467	Nov. 1960	1959 JR 32
IV	26	Salary increases during term for various public officers	rejected	297,066–307,575	Apr. 1961	1961 JR 11
IV	34	Continuity of civil government	ratified	498,869–132,728	Apr. 1961	1961 JR 10
VI	4	Sheriffs, no limit on successive terms	rejected	283,495–388,238	Apr. 1961	1961 JR 9
VIII	1	Personal property classified for tax purposes	ratified	381,881–220,434	Apr. 1961	1961 JR 13
XI	2	Municipal eminent domain, abolished jury verdict of necessity	ratified	348,406–259,566	Apr. 1961	1961 JR 12
XI	3	Debt limit 10% of equalized valuation for integrated aid school district	ratified	409,963–224,783	Apr. 1961	1961 JR 8
IV	3	"Indians not taxed" exclusion removed from apportionment formula	ratified	631,296–259,577	Nov. 1962	1961 JR 32
IV	23	County executive: 4-year term	ratified	527,075–331,393	Nov. 1962	1961 JR 64
VI	4	County executive: 2-year terms	ratified	527,075–331,393	Nov. 1962	1961 JR 64
IV	23a	County executive veto power	ratified	524,240–319,378	Nov. 1962	1961 JR 64
IV	3	Time for apportionment of seats in the state legislature	rejected	232,851–277,014	Apr. 1963	1963 JR 9
IV	26	Salary increases during term for justices and judges	rejected	216,205–335,774	Apr. 1963	1963 JR 7

Article	Section	Amendment	Action	Vote	Date	Resolution
XI	3	Equalized value debt limit	ratified	285,296–231,702	Apr. 1963	1963 JR 8
VIII	10	Maximum state appropriation for forestry increased	rejected	440,978–536,724	Apr. 1964	1963 JR 32
XI	3	Property valuation for debt limit adjusted	rejected	336,994–572,276	Apr. 1964	1963 JR 33
XII	1	Constitutional amendments, submission of related items in a single proposition	rejected	317,676–582,045	Apr. 1964	SS 1963 JR 1[4]
VI	4	Coroner and surveyor abolished in counties of 500,000	ratified	380,059–215,169	Apr. 1965	1965 JR 5
IV	24	Lotteries, definition revised	ratified	454,390–194,327	Apr. 1965	1965 JR 2
IV	13	Legislators on active duty in armed forces	ratified	362,935–189,641	Apr. 1966	1965 JR 14
VII	2	Establishment of inferior courts	ratified	321,434–216,341	Apr. 1966	1965 JR 50
VII	15	Justices of the peace abolished	ratified	321,434–216,341	Apr. 1966	1965 JR 50
XI	3	Special district public utility debt limit	ratified	307,502–199,919	Apr. 1966	1965 JR 51
I	23	Transportation of children to private schools	ratified	494,236–377,107	Apr. 1967	1965 JR 58
IV	26	Judicial salary increased during term	ratified	489,989–328,292	Apr. 1967	1967 JR 13
V	1m, 1n	4-year term for governor and lieutenant governor	ratified	534,368–310,478	Apr. 1967	1967 JR 17
V	3	Joint election of governor and lieutenant governor	ratified	507,339–312,267	Apr. 1967	1967 JR 10
VI	1m	4-year term for secretary of state	ratified	520,326–311,974	Apr. 1967	1967 JR 11
VI	1n	4-year term for state treasurer	ratified	514,280–314,873	Apr. 1967	1967 JR 14
VI	1p	4-year term for attorney general	ratified	515,962–311,603	Apr. 1967	1967 JR 10
VI	4	Sheriffs, no limit on successive terms	ratified	508,242–324,544	Apr. 1967	1967 JR 10
IV	11	Legislative sessions, more than one permitted in biennium	ratified	670,757–267,997	Apr. 1968	1967 JR 12
VII	24	Uniform retirement date for justices and circuit judges	ratified	734,046–215,455	Apr. 1968	1967 JR 48
VII	24	Temporary appointment of justices and circuit judges	ratified	678,249–245,807	Apr. 1968	1967 JR 56
VIII	10	Forestry appropriation from sources other than property tax	ratified	652,705–286,512	Apr. 1968	1967 JR 56
IV	23	Uniform county government modified	ratified	326,445–321,851	Apr. 1969	1967 JR 25
IV	23a	County executive to have veto power	ratified	326,445–321,851	Apr. 1969	1969 JR 2
VIII	7	State public debt for specified purposes allowed	ratified	411,062–258,366	Apr. 1969	1969 JR 2
I	24	Private use of school buildings	ratified	871,707–298,016	Apr. 1972	1969 JR 3
VI	23	County government systems authorized	ratified	571,285–515,255	Apr. 1972	1971 JR 27
VI	4	Coroner/medical examiner option	ratified	795,497–323,930	Apr. 1972	1971 JR 13
X	3	Released time for religious instruction	ratified	595,075–585,511	Apr. 1972	1971 JR 21
I	25	Equality of the sexes	rejected	447,240–520,936	Apr. 1973	1971 JR 28
VI	24	Charitable bingo authorized	ratified	645,544–391,499	Apr. 1973	1973 JR 5
IV	26	Increased benefits for retired public employees	ratified	396,051–315,545	Apr. 1974	1973 JR 3
VII	13	Removal of judges by 2/3 vote of legislature for cause	ratified	493,496–193,867	Apr. 1974	1973 JR 15
VIII	1	Taxation of agricultural lands	ratified	353,377–340,518	Apr. 1974	1973 JR 25
VIII	3,7	Public debt for veterans' housing	ratified	385,915–300,232	Apr. 1975	1975 JR 3
VIII	7,10	Internal improvements for transportation facilities[5]	rejected	342,396–341,291[5]	Apr. 1975	1975 JR 2
XI	3	Exclusion of certain debt from municipal debt limit	rejected	310,434–337,925	Apr. 1975	1973 JR 133

History of proposed constitutional amendments since 1854, continued

Article	Section	Subject	Election result	Vote totals	Date	Proposed amendment
XIII	2	Dueling: repeal of disenfranchisement	ratified	395,616–282,726	Apr. 1975	1975 JR 4
XI	3	Municipal indebtedness increased up to 10% of equalized valuation	rejected	328,097–715,420	Apr. 1976	1975 JR 6
VIII	7(2)(a), 10	Internal improvements for transportation facilities [5]	rejected	722,658–935,152	Nov. 1976 [5]	1975 JR 2
IV	24	Charitable raffle games authorized	ratified	483,518–300,473	Apr. 1977	1977 JR 6
VII	2	Unified court system [also affected I 21; IV 17, 26; VII 3–11, 14, 16–23; XIV 16(1)–(4)]	ratified	490,437–215,939	Apr. 1977	1977 JR 7
VII	5	Court of appeals created [also affected I 21(1); VII 2, 3(3); XIV 16(5)]	ratified	455,350–229,316	Apr. 1977	1977 JR 7
VII	11, 13	Court system disciplinary proceedings	ratified	565,087–151,418	Apr. 1977	1977 JR 7
VII	24	Retirement age for justices and judges set by law	ratified	506,207–244,170	Apr. 1977	1977 JR 7
IV	23	Town government uniformity	rejected	179,011–383,395	Apr. 1977	1977 JR 18
V	7, 8	Gubernatorial succession	ratified	538,959–187,440	Apr. 1978	1979 JR 3
XIII	10	Lieutenant governor vacancy	ratified	540,186–181,497	Apr. 1979	1979 JR 3
IV	9	Senate presiding officer	ratified	372,734–327,008	Apr. 1979	1979 JR 3
V	1	4-year constitutional officer terms (improved wording) [also affected V 1m, 1n; VI 1, 1m, 1n, 1p]	ratified	533,620–164,768	Apr. 1979	1979 JR 3
I	8	Right to bail [6]	ratified	505,092–185,405 [6]	Apr. 1981	1981 JR 8
XI	1, 4	Obsolete corporation and banking provisions	ratified	418,997–186,898	Apr. 1981	1981 JR 9
XI	3	Indebtedness period for sewage collection or treatment systems	ratified	386,792–250,866	Apr. 1981	1981 JR 7
XIII	12	Primaries in recall elections	ratified	366,635–259,820	Apr. 1981	1981 JR 6
VI	4	Counties responsible for acts of sheriff	ratified	316,156–219,752	Apr. 1982	1981 JR 15
I	1, 18	Gender-neutral wording [also affected X 1, 2]	ratified	771,267–479,053	Nov. 1982	1981 JR 29
IV	3	Military personnel treatment in redistricting	ratified	834,188–321,331	Nov. 1982	1981 JR 29
IV	4, 5	Obsolete 1881 amendment reference	ratified	919,349–238,884	Nov. 1982	1981 JR 29
IV	30	Elections by legislature	ratified	977,438–193,679	Nov. 1982	1981 JR 29
X	1	Obsolete reference to election and term of superintendent of public instruction	ratified	934,236–215,961	Nov. 1982	1981 JR 29
X	2	Obsolete reference to military draft exemption purchase; school fund	ratified	887,488–295,693	Nov. 1982	1981 JR 29
XIV	3	Obsolete transition from territory to statehood [also affected XIV 4–12; XIV 14, 15]	ratified	926,875–223,213	Nov. 1982	1981 JR 29
XIV	16(1)	Obsolete transitional provisions of 1977 court reorganization [also affected XIV 16(2), (3), (5)]	ratified	882,091–237,698	Nov. 1982	1981 JR 29
XIV	16(4)	Terms on supreme court effective date provision	ratified	960,540–190,366	Nov. 1982	1981 JR 29
I	1	Rewording to parallel Declaration of Independence	ratified	419,699–65,418	Apr. 1986	1985 JR 21
III	1–6	Revision of suffrage defined by general law	ratified	401,911–83,183	Apr. 1986	1985 JR 14
XIII	1	Modernizing constitutional text	ratified	404,273–82,512	Apr. 1986	1985 JR 14
XIII	5	Obsolete suffrage right on Indian land	ratified	381,339–102,090	Apr. 1986	1985 JR 14
IV	24(5)	Permitting pari-mutuel on-track betting	ratified	580,089–529,729	Apr. 1987	1987 JR 3
IV	24(6)	Authorizing the creation of a state lottery	ratified	739,181–391,942	Apr. 1987	1987 JR 4

Art.	Sec.	Description	Status	Vote	Date	JR
VIII	1	Authorizing income tax credits or refunds for property or sales taxes	rejected	405,765–406,863	Apr. 1989	1989 JR 2
V	10	Redefining the partial veto power of the governor	ratified	387,068–252,481	Apr. 1990	1989 JR 39
VIII	10	Providing housing for persons of low or moderate income	rejected	295,823–402,921	Apr. 1991	1991 JR 2
VIII	7(2)(a)1	Railways and other railroad facilities [also created VIII 10]	ratified	650,592–457,690	Apr. 1992	1991 JR 9
IV	26	Legislative and judiciary compensation, effective date	ratified	736,832–348,645	Apr. 1992	1991 JR 13
VIII	1	Residential property tax reduction	rejected	675,876–1,536,975	Nov. 1992	1991 JR 14
I	9m	Crime victims	ratified	861,405–163,087	Apr. 1993	1993 JR 2
IV	24	Gambling, limiting "lottery"; divorce under general law [also affected IV 31, 32]	ratified	623,987–435,180	Apr. 1993	1993 JR 3
I	3	Removal of unnecessary references to masculine gender [also affected I 3, 7, 9, 19, 21(2); IV 6, 12, 13, 23a; V 4, 6; VI 2; VII 1, 12; XI 3a; XIII 4, 11, 12(6)]	rejected	412,032–498,801	Apr. 1995	1995 JR 3
IV	24(6)(a)	Authorizing sports lottery dedicated to athletic facilities	rejected	348,818–618,377	Apr. 1995	1995 JR 2
VII	10(1)	Removal of restriction on judges holding nonjudicial public office after resignation during the judicial term	rejected	390,744–503,239	Apr. 1995	1995 JR 4
XIII	3	Eligibility to seek or hold public office if convicted of a felony or a misdemeanor involving violation of a public trust	ratified	1,292,934–543,516	Nov. 1996	1995 JR 28
I	25	Guaranteeing the right to keep and bear arms	ratified	1,205,873–425,052	Nov. 1998	1997 JR 21
VI	4(1), (3), (5), (6)	4-year term for sheriff; sheriffs permitted to hold nonpartisan office; allowed legislature to provide for election to fill vacancy during term	ratified	1,161,942–412,508	Nov. 1998	1997 JR 18
IV	24(3), (5), (6)	Distributing state lottery, bingo and pari-mutuel proceeds for property tax	ratified	648,903–105,976	Apr. 1999	1999 JR 2
VI	26	Right to fish, hunt, trap, and take game	ratified	668,459–146,182	Apr. 2003	2003 JR 8
VI	4(1), (3), (4)	4-year term for county clerks, treasurers, clerks of circuit court, district attorneys, coroners, elected surveyors, and registers of deeds [also affected VII 12]	ratified	534,742–177,037	Apr. 2005	2005 JR 2
XIII	13	Marriage between one man and one woman	ratified	1,264,310–862,924	Nov. 2006	2005 JR 30
V	10(1)(c)	Gubernatorial partial veto power	ratified	575,582–239,613	Apr. 2008	2007 JR 26
IV	9(2)	Department of transportation and transportation fund [also created VIII 11]	ratified	1,733,101–434,806	Nov. 2014	2013 JR 1
VIII	1	Election of chief justice of the supreme court	ratified	433,533–384,503	Apr. 2015	2015 JR 2
VI	1,3	Elimination of state treasurer [also affected X 7, 8 and XIV 17]	rejected	363,562–586,134	Apr. 2018	2017 JR7

Note: To amend the Wisconsin Constitution, it is necessary for two consecutive legislatures to adopt an identical amendment (known as "first consideration" and "second consideration") and for a majority of the electorate to ratify the amendment at a subsequent election. See Art. XII, Sec. 1. JR 41 of 1925, which became Joint Rule 16 of the Wisconsin Legislature, established a new procedure to incorporate the "submission to the people" clause into the proposal at second approval.

Since the adoption of the Wisconsin Constitution in 1848, the electorate has voted 145 out of 196 times to amend a total of 128 sections of the constitution (excluding the same vote for more than one item but including a vote that was later resubmitted by the legislature and two votes that were declared invalid by the courts). The Wisconsin Legislature adopted 158 acts or joint resolutions to submit these changes to the electorate.

Ch.–Chapter; JR–Joint resolution; SS–Special session.

1. No other number was assigned to this joint resolution. 2. Ratified but declared invalid by Supreme Court in *State ex rel. Owen v. Donald*, 160 Wis. 21 (1915). 3. Ratified but declared invalid by Supreme Court in *State ex rel. Thomson v. Zimmerman*, 264 Wis. 644 (1953). 4. Special session December 1964. 5. Recount resulted in rejection (342,132 to 342,309). However, the Dane County Circuit Court ruled the recount invalid due to election irregularities and required that the referendum be resubmitted to the electorate. Resubmitted to the electorate November 1976 by the 1975 Wisconsin Legislature through Ch. 224, s.145r, Laws of 1975. 6. As a result of a Dane County Circuit Court injunction, vote totals were certified April 7, 1982, by the Board of State Canvassers.

Sources: Official records of the Wisconsin Elections Commission; *Laws of Wisconsin*, 2017 and previous volumes.

Statewide referenda other than constitutional amendments since 1849

Subject	Election result	Vote totals	Date	Submitting law
Extend suffrage to colored persons [1]	Approved	5,265–4,075	Nov. 1849	1849 Ch. 137
State banks; advisory	Approved	31,289–9,126	Nov. 1851	1851 Ch. 143
General banking law.	Approved	32,826–8,711	Nov. 1852	1852 Ch. 479
Liquor prohibition; advisory	Approved	27,519–24,109	Nov. 1853	1853 Ch. 101
Extend suffrage to colored persons	Rejected	28,235–41,345	Nov. 1857	1857 Ch. 44
Amend general banking law; redemption of bank notes	Approved	27,267–2,837	Nov. 1858	1858 Ch. 98
Amend general banking law; circulation of bank notes	Approved	57,646–2,515	Nov. 1861	1861 Ch. 242
Amend general banking law; interest rate 7% per year	Approved	46,269–7,794	Nov. 1862	1862 Ch. 203
Extend suffrage to colored persons [1]	Rejected	46,588–55,591	Nov. 1865	1865 Ch. 414
Amend general banking law; taxing shareholders	Approved	49,714–19,151	Nov. 1866	1866 Ch. 102
Amend general banking law; winding up circulation.	Approved	45,796–11,842	Nov. 1867	1866 Ch. 143; 1867 JR 12
Abolish office of bank comptroller.	Approved	15,499–1,948	Nov. 1868	1868 Ch. 28
Incorporation of savings banks and savings societies	Approved	4,029–3,069	Nov. 1876	1876 Ch. 384
Women's suffrage upon school matters	Approved	43,581–38,998	Nov. 1886	1885 Ch. 211
Revise 1897 banking law; banking department under commission.	Rejected	86,872–92,607	Nov. 1898	1897 Ch. 303
Primary election law.	Approved	130,366–80,102	Nov. 1904	1903 Ch. 451
Pocket ballots and coupon voting systems.	Rejected	45,958–111,139	Apr. 1906	1905 Ch. 522
Women's suffrage	Rejected	135,545–227,024	Nov. 1912	1911 Ch. 227
Soldiers' bonus financed by 3-mill property tax and income tax.	Approved	165,762–57,324	Sept. 1919	1919 Ch. 667
Wisconsin prohibition enforcement act.	Approved	419,309–199,876	Nov. 1920	1919 Ch. 556
U.S. prohibition act (Volstead Act); memorializing Congress to amend	Approved	349,443–177,603	Nov. 1926	1925 JR 47
Repeal of Wisconsin prohibition enforcement act; advisory	Approved	350,337–196,402	Nov. 1926	1925 JR 47
Modification of Wisconsin prohibition enforcement act; advisory.	Approved	321,688–200,545	Apr. 1929	1929 JR 16
County distribution of auto licenses; advisory.	Rejected	183,716–368,674	Apr. 1931	1931 JR 11
Sunday blue law repeal; advisory.	Approved	396,436–271,786	Apr. 1932	1931 JR 114
Old-age pensions; advisory	Approved	531,915–154,729	Apr. 1934	SS 1933 JR 64
Teacher tenure law repeal; advisory	Approved	403,782–372,524	Apr. 1940	1939 JR 100
Property tax levy for high school aid; 2 mills of assessed valuation	Rejected	131,004–410,315	Apr. 1944	1943 Ch. 525
Daylight saving time; advisory.	Rejected	313,091–379,740	Apr. 1947	1947 JR 4
3% retail sales tax for veterans bonus; advisory	Rejected	258,497–825,990	Nov. 1948	1947 JR 62
4-year term for constitutional officers; advisory	Rejected	210,821–328,613	Apr. 1951	1951 JR 13
Apportionment of legislature by area and population; advisory.	Rejected	689,615–753,092	Nov. 1952	1951 Ch. 728

Subject	Election result	Vote totals	Date	Submitting law
New residents entitled to vote for president and vice president.	Approved	550,056–414,680	Nov. 1954	1953 Ch. 76
Statewide educational television tax-supported; advisory.	Rejected	308,385–697,262	Nov. 1954	1953 JR 66
Daylight saving time.	Approved	578,661–480,656	Apr. 1957	1957 Ch. 6
Ex-residents entitled to vote for president and vice president.	Approved	627,279–229,375	Nov. 1962	1961 Ch. 512
Gasoline tax increase for highway construction; advisory.	Rejected	150,769–889,364	Apr. 1964	SS 1963 JR 3
New residents entitled to vote after 6 months.	Approved	582,389–256,246	Nov. 1966	1965 Chs. 88,89
State control and funding of vocational education; advisory.	Rejected	292,560–409,789	Apr. 1969	1969 JR 4
Recreational lands bonding; advisory.	Approved	361,630–322,882	Apr. 1969	1969 JR 5
Water pollution abatement bonding; advisory.	Approved	446,763–246,968	Apr. 1969	1969 JR 5
New residents entitled to vote after 10 days.	Approved	1,017,887–660,875	Nov. 1976	1975 Ch. 85
Presidential voting revised.	Approved	782,181–424,386	Nov. 1978	1977 Ch. 394
Overseas voting revised.	Approved	658,289–524,029	Nov. 1978	1977 Ch. 394
Public inland lake protection and rehabilitation districts	Approved	1,210,452–355,024	Nov. 1980	1979 Ch. 299
Nuclear weapons moratorium and reduction; advisory.	Approved	641,514–205,018	Sept. 1982	1981 JR 38
Nuclear waste site locating; advisory.	Rejected	78,327–628,414	Apr. 1983	1983 JR 5
Gambling casinos on excursion vessels; advisory.	Rejected	465,432–604,289	Apr. 1993	1991 WisAct 321
Gambling casino restrictions; advisory.	Approved	646,827–416,722	Apr. 1993	1991 WisAct 321
Video poker and other forms of video gambling allowed; advisory.	Rejected	358,045–702,864	Apr. 1993	1991 WisAct 321
Pari-mutuel on-track betting continuation; advisory.	Approved	548,580–507,403	Apr. 1993	1991 WisAct 321
State-operated lottery continuation; advisory.	Approved	773,306–287,585	Apr. 1993	1991 WisAct 321
Extended suffrage in federal elections to adult children of U.S. citizens living abroad	Approved	1,293,458–792,975	Nov. 2000	1999 WisAct 182
Death penalty; advisory.	Approved	1,166,571–934,508	Nov. 2006	2005 JR 58

Note: Statewide referendum questions are submitted to the electorate by the Wisconsin Legislature: 1) to ratify a law extending the right of suffrage (as required by the state constitution); 2) to ratify a law that has been passed contingent on voter approval; or 3) to seek voter opinion through an advisory referendum. Since 1848, the Wisconsin Legislature has presented 53 referendum questions to the Wisconsin electorate through the passage of acts or joint resolutions; 39 were ratified. Prior to statehood, the territorial legislature sent four cuestions to the electorate, as follows: Formation of a state government, submitted by Territorial Laws 1846, page 5 (Jan.31), approved April 1846, 12,334 votes for, 2,487 against; Ratification of first constitution, submitted by Art. XIX, Sec. 9 of 1846 Constitution, rejected April 1847, 14,119 votes for, 20,231 against; Extend suffrage to colored persons, submitted by supplemental resolution to 1846 Constitution, rejected April 1847, 7,664 votes for, 14,615 against; Ratification of second constitution, submitted by Art. XIV, Sec. 9 of 1848 Constitution, approved March 1848, 16,799 votes for, 6,384 against.

Ch.–Chapter; JR–Joint resolution; SS–Special session.

1. In *Gillespie v. Palmer*, 20 Wis. 544 (1866), the Wisconsin Supreme Court ruled that Chapter 137, Laws of 1849, extending suffrage to colored persons, was ratified November 6, 1849.

Sources: Official records of the Wisconsin Elections Commission; *Laws of Wisconsin*, 2015 and previous volumes.

Wisconsin vote in presidential elections since 1848, continued

2004—10 electoral votes
John F. Kerry—D. 1,489,504
George W. Bush—R . . . 1,478,120
Ralph Nader—I (TBL). . . . 16,390
Michael Badnarik—Lib. . . . 6,464
David Cobb—WG 2,661
Walter F. Brown—I (SPW) . . . 471
James Harris—I (SW) 411
Total. 2,997,007

2008—10 electoral votes
Barack Obama—D . . . 1,677,211
John McCain—R. 1,262,393
Ralph Nader—I 17,605
Bob Barr—Lib 8,858
Chuck Baldwin—I (Con) . . . 5,072

Cynthia McKinney—WG. . . . 4,216
Jeffrey J. Wamboldt—I (WtP) . 764
Brian Moore—I (SocUSA) . . . 540
Gloria La Riva—I (S&L) 237
Total. 2,983,417

2012—10 electoral votes
Barack Obama—D . . . 1,620,985
Mitt Romney—R. 1,407,966
Gary Johnson—I (Lib) . . . 20,439
Jill Stein—I (Grn) 7,665
Virgil Goode—Con 4,930
Jerry White—I (SE) 553
Gloria La Riva—I (S&L) 526
Total. 3,068,434

2016—10 electoral votes
Donald J. Trump—R . . 1,405,284
Hillary Clinton—D. . . . 1,382,536
Gary Johnson—Lib 106,674
Jill Stein—WG 31,072
Darrell L. Castle—Con . . . 12,162
Monica Moorehead—I (WW)
. . . . 1,770
Rocky Roque De La Fuente—I (AD)
. . . . 1,502
Total. 2,976,150

Note: The party designation listed for a candidate is taken from the Congressional Quarterly *Guide to U.S. Elections*. A candidate whose party did not receive 1% of the vote for a statewide office in the previous election or who failed to meet the alternative requirement of section 5.62, Wis. Stats., must be listed on the Wisconsin ballot as "independent." In this listing, candidates whose party affiliations appear as "I," followed by a party designation in parentheses, were identified on the ballot simply as "independent" although they also provided a party designation or statement of principle.

Under the Electoral College system, each state is entitled to electoral votes equal in number to its total congressional delegation of U.S. Senators and U.S. Representatives.

Some totals include scattered votes for other candidates.

A—American (Know Nothing)
AD—American Delta
AFC—America First Coalition
Cit—Citizens
Com—Communist
Con—Constitution
CU—Constitutional Union
D—Democrat
ER—Independents for Economic
   Recovery
FS—Free Soil
G—Greenback
Gr—Grassroots
Grn—Green
I—Independent
IP—Independent Progressive
IS—Independent Socialist
ISL—Independent Socialist Labor
ISW—Independent Socialist
   Worker

LF—Labor-Farm/Laborista-
   Agrario
Lib—Libertarian
LR—Liberal Republican
NA—New Alliance
Nat—National
ND—National Democrat
NER—National Economic
   Recovery
NL—Natural Law
P—Progressive
Pop—Populist
PP—People's Progressive
PPop—People's (Populist)
Pro—Prohibition
R—Republican
Rfm—Reform
S—Socialist
SD—Social Democrat
SE—Socialist Equality

SL—Socialist Labor
S&L—Party for Socialism and
   Liberation
SocUSA—Socialist Party USA
SoD—Southern Democrat
SPW—Socialist Party of Wis.
SW—Socialist Worker
Tax—U.S. Taxpayers
TBL—The Better Life
3rd—Third Party
U—Union
UL—Union Labor
USL—U.S. Labor
W—Whig
WG—Wisconsin Greens
WIA—Wis. Independent Alliance
Wrk—Workers
WtP—We, the People
WW—Worker's World

Sources: Official records of the Wisconsin Elections Commission and Congressional Quarterly, *Guide to U.S. Elections*, 1994.

Wisconsin members of the U.S. Senate since 1848

Class 1	Term
Henry Dodge—D	1848–1857
James R. Doolittle—R	1857–1869
Matthew H. Carpenter—R.	1869–1875
Angus Cameron[1]—R	1875–1881
Philetus Sawyer—R	1881–1893
John Lendrum Mitchell—D	1893–1899
Joseph Very Quarles—R	1899–1905
Robert M. La Follette, Sr.[2]—R	1906–1925
Robert M. La Follette, Jr. [3]—R.	1925–1935
Robert M. La Follette, Jr.—P.	1935–1947
Joseph R. McCarthy—R	1947–1957
William Proxmire[4]—D	1957–1989
Herbert H. Kohl—D	1989–2013
Tammy Baldwin—D.	2013–

Class 3	Term
Isaac P. Walker—D.	1848–1855
Charles Durkee—UR	1855–1861
Timothy O. Howe—UR	1861–1879
Matthew H. Carpenter—R.	1879–1881
Angus Cameron[1]—R	1881–1885
John C. Spooner—R	1885–1891
William F. Vilas—D	1891–1897
John C. Spooner—R	1897–1907
Isaac Stephenson[5]—R	1907–1915
Paul O. Husting—D	1915–1917
Irvine L. Lenroot[6]—R.	1918–1927
John J. Blaine—R	1927–1933
F. Ryan Duffy—D	1933–1939
Alexander Wiley—R.	1939–1963
Gaylord A. Nelson—D	1963–1981
Robert W. Kasten, Jr.—R	1981–1993
Russell D. Feingold—D.	1993–2011
Ron Johnson—R.	2011–

Note: Each state has two U.S. Senators, and each serves a six-year term. They were elected by their respective state legislatures until passage of the 17th Amendment to the U.S. Constitution on April 8, 1913, which provided for popular election. Article I, Section 3, Clause 2, of the U.S. Constitution divides senators into three classes so that one-third of the senate is elected every two years. Wisconsin's seats were assigned to Class 1 and Class 3 at statehood.

D–Democrat; P–Progressive; R–Republican; UR–Union Republican.

1. Not a candidate for reelection to Class 1 seat, but elected 3/10/1881 to fill vacancy caused by death of Class 3 Senator Carpenter on 2/24/1881. 2. Elected 1/25/1905 but continued to serve as governor until 1/1/1906. 3. Elected 9/29/1925 to fill vacancy caused by death of Robert La Follette, Sr., on 6/18/1925. 4. Elected 8/27/1957 to fill vacancy caused by death of McCarthy on 5/2/1957. 5. Elected 5/17/1907 to fill vacancy caused by resignation of Spooner on 4/30/1907. 6. Elected 5/2/1918 to fill vacancy caused by death of Husting on 10/21/1917.

Source: Wisconsin Legislative Reference Bureau records.

Wisconsin members of the U.S. House of Representatives since 1848

	Party	District	Term	Residence
Adams, Henry C.	Rep.	2	1903–1906	Madison
Amlie, Thomas R	Rep., Prog.	1	1931–1933; 1935–1939	Elkhorn
Aspin, Les	Dem.	1	1971–1993	East Troy
Atwood, David	Rep.	2	1870–1871	Madison
Babbitt, Clinton	Dem.	1	1891–1893	Beloit
Babcock, Joseph W.	Rep.	3	1893–1907	Necedah
Baldus, Alvin.	Dem.	3	1975–1981	Menomonie
Baldwin, Tammy	Dem.	2	1999–2013	Madison
Barber, J. Allen	Rep.	3	1871–1875	Lancaster
Barca, Peter W	Dem.	1	1993–1995	Kenosha
Barnes, Lyman E	Dem.	8	1893–1895	Appleton
Barney, Samuel S	Rep.	5	1895–1903	West Bend
Barrett, Thomas M	Dem.	5	1993–2003	Milwaukee
Barwig, Charles	Dem.	2	1889–1895	Mayville
Beck, Joseph D	Rep.	7	1921–1929	Viroqua
Berger, Victor L	Soc.	5	1911–1913; 1919; 1923–1929	Milwaukee
Biemiller, Andrew J.	Dem.	5	1945–1947; 1949–1951	Milwaukee
Billinghurst, Charles	Rep.	3	1855–1859	Juneau
Blanchard, George W	Rep.	1	1933–1935	Edgerton

Wisconsin members of the U.S. House of Representatives since 1848, continued

	Party	District	Term	Residence
Boileau, Gerald J	Rep., Prog.	8, 7	1931–1939	Wausau
Bolles, Stephen	Rep.	1	1939–1941	Janesville
Bouck, Gabriel	Dem.	6	1877–1881	Oshkosh
Bragg, Edward S	Dem.	5, 2	1877–1883; 1885–1887	Fond du Lac
Brickner, George H	Dem.	5	1889–1895	Sheboygan Falls
Brophy, John C	Rep.	4	1947–1949	Milwaukee
Brown, James S	Dem.	1	1863–1865	Milwaukee
Brown, Webster E.	Rep.	9, 10	1901–1907	Rhinelander
Browne, Edward E	Rep.	8	1913–1931	Waupaca
Burchard, Samuel D	Dem.	5	1875–1877	Beaver Dam
Burke, Michael E	Dem.	6, 2	1911–1917	Beaver Dam
Bushnell, Allen R	Dem.	3	1891–1893	Madison
Byrnes, John W	Rep.	8	1945–1973	Green Bay
Cannon, Raymond J	Dem.	4	1933–1939	Milwaukee
Cary, William J.	Rep.	4	1907–1919	Milwaukee
Caswell, Lucien B	Rep.	2, 1	1875–1883; 1885–1891	Fort Atkinson
Cate, George W	Reform	8	1875–1877	Stevens Point
Clark, Charles B	Rep.	6	1887–1891	Neenah
Classon, David G	Rep.	9	1917–1923	Oconto
Cobb, Amasa	Rep.	3	1863–1871	Mineral Point
Coburn, Frank P.	Dem.	7	1891–1893	West Salem
Cole, Orasmus.	Whig	2	1849–1851	Potosi
Cook, Samuel A	Rep.	6	1895–1897	Neenah
Cooper, Henry Allen	Rep.	1	1893–1919; 1921–1931	Racine
Cornell, Robert J	Dem.	8	1975–1979	De Pere
Dahle, Herman B	Rep.	2	1899–1903	Mount Horeb
Darling, Mason C	Dem.	2	1848–1849	Fond du Lac
Davidson, James H.	Rep.	6, 8	1897–1913; 1917–1918	Oshkosh
Davis, Glenn R.	Rep.	2, 9	1947–1957; 1965–1975	Waukesha
Deuster, Peter V.	Dem.	4	1879–1885	Milwaukee
Dilweg, La Vern R	Dem.	8	1943–1945	Green Bay
Doty, James D	Dem.	3	1849–1853	Neenah
Duffy, Sean P.	Rep.	7	2011–	Wausau
Durkee, Charles	Free Soil	1	1849–1853	Kenosha
Eastman, Ben C	Dem.	2	1851–1855	Platteville
Eldredge, Charles A	Dem.	4, 5	1863–1875	Fond du Lac
Esch, John Jacob	Rep.	7	1899–1921	La Crosse
Flynn, Gerald T	Dem.	1	1959–1961	Racine
Frear, James A.	Rep.	10, 9	1913–1935	Hudson
Froehlich, Harold V.	Rep.	8	1973–1975	Appleton
Gallagher, Mike	Rep.	8	2017–	Green Bay
Gehrmann, Bernard J	Prog.	10	1935–1943	Mellen
Green, Mark A.	Rep.	8	1999–2007	Green Bay
Griffin, Michael	Rep.	7	1894–1899	Eau Claire
Griswold, Harry W	Rep.	3	1939–1941	West Salem
Grothman, Glenn.	Rep.	6	2015–	Glenbeulah
Guenther, Richard W.	Rep.	6, 2	1881–1889	Oshkosh
Gunderson, Steven.	Rep.	3	1981–1997	Osseo
Hanchett, Luther	Rep.	2	1861–1862	Plover
Haugen, Nils P.	Rep.	8, 10	1887–1895	Black River Falls
Hawkes, Charles, Jr.	Rep.	2	1939–1941	Horicon
Hazelton, George C	Rep.	3	1877–1883	Boscobel
Hazelton, Gerry W	Rep.	2	1871–1875	Columbus
Henney, Charles W	Dem.	2	1933–1935	Portage
Henry, Robert K.	Rep.	2	1945–1947	Jefferson
Hopkins, Benjamin F.	Rep.	2	1867–1870	Madison
Hudd, Thomas R	Dem.	5	1886–1889	Green Bay
Hughes, James	Dem.	8	1933–1935	De Pere

Wisconsin members of the U.S. House of Representatives
since 1848, continued

	Party	District	Term	Residence
Hull, Merlin	Prog.	7, 9	1929–1931; 1935–1953	Black River Falls
Humphrey, Herman L	Rep.	7	1877–1883	Hudson
Jenkins, John J	Rep.	10, 11	1895–1909	Chippewa Falls
Johns, Joshua L	Rep.	8	1939–1943	Appleton
Johnson, Jay	Dem.	8	1997–1999	New Franken
Johnson, Lester R.	Dem.	9	1953–1965	Black River Falls
Jones, Burr W	Dem.	3	1883–1885	Madison
Kading, Charles A.	Rep.	2	1927–1933	Watertown
Kagen, Steve.	Dem.	8	2007–2011	Appleton
Kasten, Robert W., Jr	Rep.	9	1975–1979	Waukesha
Kastenmeier, Robert W	Dem.	2	1959–1991	Sun Prairie
Keefe, Frank B	Rep.	6	1939–1951	Oshkosh
Kersten, Charles J.	Rep.	5	1947–1949; 1951–1955	Whitefish Bay
Kimball, Alanson M.	Rep.	6	1875–1877	Waushara
Kind, Ron.	Dem.	3	1997–	La Crosse
Kleczka, Gerald D.	Dem.	4	1984–2005	Milwaukee
Kleczka, John C	Rep.	4	1919–1923	Milwaukee
Klug, Scott L	Rep.	2	1991–1999	Madison
Konop, Thomas F	Dem.	9	1911–1917	Kewaunee
Kopp, Arthur W	Rep.	3	1909–1913	Platteville
Kustermann, Gustav	Rep.	9	1907–1911	Green Bay
La Follette, Robert M., Sr	Rep.	3	1885–1891	Madison
Laird, Melvin R	Rep.	7	1953–1969	Marshfield
Lampert, Florian	Rep.	6	1918–1930	Oshkosh
Larrabee, Charles H	Dem.	3	1859–1861	Horicon
Lenroot, Irvine L	Rep.	11	1909–1918	Superior
Lynch, Thomas	Dem.	9	1891–1895	Antigo
Lynde, William Pitt	Dem.	1, 4	1848–1849; 1875–1879	Milwaukee
Macy, John B.	Dem.	3	1853–1855	Fond du Lac
Magoon, Henry S	Rep.	3	1875–1877	Darlington
McCord, Myron H.	Rep.	9	1889–1891	Merrill
McDill, Alexander S	Rep.	8	1873–1875	Plover
McIndoe, Walter D	Rep.	6	1863–1867	Wausau
McMurray, Howard J	Dem.	5	1943–1945	Milwaukee
Miller, Lucas M	Dem.	6	1891–1893	Oshkosh
Minor, Edward S	Rep.	8, 9	1895–1907	Sturgeon Bay
Mitchell, Alexander	Dem.	1, 4	1871–1875	Milwaukee
Mitchell, John L.	Dem.	4	1891–1893	Milwaukee
Monahan, James G.	Rep.	3	1919–1921	Darlington
Moody, James P.	Dem.	5	1983–1993	Milwaukee
Moore, Gwen	Dem.	4	2005–	Milwaukee
Morse, Elmer A	Rep.	10	1907–1913	Antigo
Murphy, James W.	Dem.	3	1907–1909	Platteville
Murray, Reid F.	Rep.	7	1939–1953	Ogdensburg
Nelson, Adolphus P	Rep.	11	1918–1923	Grantsburg
Nelson, John Mandt	Rep.	2, 3	1906–1919; 1921–1933	Madison
Neumann, Mark W	Rep.	1	1995–1999	Janesville
Obey, David R	Dem.	7	1969–2011	Wausau
O'Konski, Alvin E	Rep.	10	1943–1973	Mercer
O'Malley, Thomas D. P.	Dem.	5	1933–1939	Milwaukee
Otjen, Theobald.	Rep.	4	1895–1907	Milwaukee
Paine, Halbert E.	Rep.	1	1865–1871	Milwaukee
Peavey, Hubert H.	Rep.	11, 10	1923–1935	Washburn
Petri, Thomas E	Rep.	6	1979–2015	Fond du Lac
Pocan, Mark	Dem.	2	2013–	Black Earth
Potter, John F	Rep.	1	1857–1863	East Troy
Pound, Thaddeus C.	Rep.	8	1877–1883	Chippewa Falls
Price, Hugh H	Rep.	8	1887	Black River Falls

Wisconsin members of the U.S. House of Representatives since 1848, continued

	Party	District	Term	Residence
Price, William T	Rep.	8	1883–1886	Black River Falls
Race, John A.	Dem.	6	1965–1967	Fond du Lac
Randall, Clifford E.	Rep.	1	1919–1921	Kenosha
Rankin, Joseph	Dem.	5	1883–1886	Manitowoc
Reilly, Michael K.	Dem.	6	1913–1917; 1930–1939	Fond du Lac
Reuss, Henry S.	Dem.	5	1955–1983	Milwaukee
Ribble, Reid J.	Rep.	8	2011–2017	Appleton
Roth, Toby	Rep.	8	1979–1997	Appleton
Rusk, Jeremiah M.	Rep.	6, 7	1871–1877	Viroqua
Ryan, Paul	Rep.	1	1999–2019	Janesville
Sauerhering, Edward	Rep.	2	1895–1899	Mayville
Sauthoff, Harry	Prog.	2	1935–1939; 1941–1945	Madison
Sawyer, Philetus	Rep.	5, 6	1865–1875	Oshkosh
Schadeberg, Henry C	Rep.	1	1961–1965; 1967–1971	Burlington
Schafer, John C	Rep.	4	1923–1933; 1939–1941	Milwaukee
Schneider, George J	Rep., Prog.	9, 8	1923–1933; 1935–1939	Appleton
Sensenbrenner, F. James, Jr.	Rep.	9, 5	1979–	Menomonee Falls
Shaw, George B	Rep.	7	1893–1894	Eau Claire
Sloan, A. Scott	Rep.	3	1861–1863	Beaver Dam
Sloan, Ithamar C	Rep.	2	1863–1867	Janesville
Smith, Henry.	Union Labor	4	1887–1889	Milwaukee
Smith, Lawrence H	Rep.	1	1941–1959	Racine
Somers, Peter J	Dem.	4	1893–1895	Milwaukee
Stafford, William H	Rep.	5	1903–1911; 1913–1919; 1921–1923; 1929–1933	Milwaukee
Stalbaum, Lynn E	Dem.	1	1965–1967	Racine
Steiger, William A	Rep.	6	1967–1978	Oshkosh
Steil, Bryan	Rep.	1	2019–	Janesville
Stephenson, Isaac	Rep.	9	1883–1889	Marinette
Stevenson, William H	Rep.	3	1941–1949	La Crosse
Stewart, Alexander	Rep.	9	1895–1901	Wausau
Sumner, Daniel H	Dem.	2	1883–1885	Waukesha
Tewes, Donald E	Rep.	2	1957–1959	Waukesha
Thill, Lewis D.	Rep.	5	1939–1943	Milwaukee
Thomas, Ormsby B	Rep.	7	1885–1891	Prairie du Chien
Thomson, Vernon W	Rep.	3	1961–1975	Richland Center
Van Pelt, William K	Rep.	6	1951–1963	Fond du Lac
Van Schaick, Isaac W	Rep.	4	1885–1887; 1889–1891	Milwaukee
Voigt, Edward	Rep.	2	1917–1927	Sheboygan
Washburn, Cadwallader C	Rep.	2 6	1855–1861; 1867–1871	Mineral Point, La Crosse
Wasielewski, Thaddeus F	Dem.	4	1941–1947	Milwaukee
Weisse, Charles H.	Dem.	6	1903–1911	Sheboygan Falls
Wells, Daniel, Jr	Dem.	1	1853–1857	Milwaukee
Wells, Owen A	Dem.	6	1893–1895	Fond du Lac
Wheeler, Ezra	Dem.	5	1863–1865	Berlin
Williams, Charles G	Rep.	1	1873–1883	Janesville
Winans, John	Dem.	1	1883–1885	Janesville
Withrow, Gardner R	Rep., Prog.	7, 3	1931–1939; 1949–1961	La Crosse
Woodward, Gilbert M	Dem.	7	1883–1885	La Crosse
Zablocki, Clement J	Dem.	4	1949–1983	Milwaukee

Dem.–Democrat; Prog.–Progressive; Rep.–Republican; Soc.–Socialist.

Sources: Wisconsin Legislative Reference Bureau, *Wisconsin Blue Book*, various editions; Congressional Quarterly, *Guide to U.S. Elections*, 1985; and official election records.

Wisconsin members of the U.S. House of Representatives since 1943, by district

District	Name	Party	Term	Residence
1	Lawrence H. Smith	Rep.	1941–1959	Racine
	Gerald T. Flynn	Dem.	1959–1961	Racine
	Henry C. Schadeberg	Rep.	1961–1965; 1967–1971	Burlington
	Lynn E. Stalbaum	Dem.	1965–1967	Racine
	Les Aspin[1]	Dem.	1971–1993	East Troy
	Peter W. Barca[1]	Dem.	1993–1995	Kenosha
	Mark W. Neumann	Rep.	1995–1999	Janesville
	Paul Ryan	Rep.	1999–2019	Janesville
	Bryan Steil	Rep.	2019–	Janesville
2	Harry Sauthoff	Prog.	1941–1945	Madison
	Robert K. Henry	Rep.	1945–1947	Jefferson
	Glenn R. Davis	Rep.	1947–1957	Waukesha
	Donald E. Tewes	Rep.	1957–1959	Waukesha
	Robert W. Kastenmeier	Dem.	1959–1991	Sun Prairie
	Scott L. Klug	Rep.	1991–1999	Madison
	Tammy Baldwin	Dem.	1999–2013	Madison
	Mark Pocan	Dem.	2013–	Black Earth
3	William H. Stevenson	Rep.	1941–1949	La Crosse
	Gardner R. Withrow	Rep.	1949–1961	La Crosse
	Vernon W. Thomson	Rep.	1961–1975	Richland Center
	Alvin Baldus	Dem.	1975–1981	Menomonie
	Steven Gunderson	Rep.	1981–1997	Osseo
	Ron Kind	Dem.	1997–	La Crosse
4[3]	Thaddeus F. Wasielewski	Dem.	1941–1947	Milwaukee
	John C. Brophy	Rep.	1947–1949	Milwaukee
	Clement J. Zablocki[2]	Dem.	1949–1983	Milwaukee
	Gerald D. Kleczka[2]	Dem.	1984–2005	Milwaukee
	Gwen Moore	Dem.	2005–	Milwaukee
5[3]	Howard J. McMurray	Dem.	1943–1945	Milwaukee
	Andrew J. Biemiller	Dem.	1945–1947; 1949–1951	Milwaukee
	Charles J. Kersten	Rep.	1947–1949; 1951–1955	Whitefish Bay
	Henry S. Reuss	Dem.	1955–1983	Milwaukee
	James P. Moody	Dem.	1983–1993	Milwaukee
	Thomas M. Barrett	Dem.	1993–2003	Milwaukee
	F. James Sensenbrenner, Jr.	Rep.	2003–	Menomonee Falls
6	Frank B. Keefe	Rep.	1939–1951	Oshkosh
	William K. Van Pelt	Rep.	1951–1965	Fond du Lac
	John A. Race	Dem.	1965–1967	Fond du Lac
	William A. Steiger[4]	Rep.	1967–1978	Oshkosh
	Thomas E. Petri[4]	Rep.	1979–2015	Fond du Lac
	Glenn Grothman	Rep.	2015–	Glenbeulah
7	Reid F. Murray	Rep.	1939–1953	Ogdensburg
	Melvin R. Laird[5]	Rep.	1953–1969	Marshfield
	David R. Obey[5]	Dem.	1969–2011	Wausau
	Sean P. Duffy	Rep.	2011–	Wausau
8	La Vern R. Dilweg	Dem.	1943–1945	Green Bay
	John R. Byrnes	Rep.	1945–1973	Green Bay
	Harold V. Froehlich	Rep.	1973–1975	Appleton
	Robert J. Cornell	Dem.	1975–1979	De Pere
	Toby Roth	Rep.	1979–1997	Appleton
	Jay Johnson	Dem.	1997–1999	New Franken
	Mark A. Green	Rep.	1999–2007	Green Bay
	Steve Kagen	Dem.	2007–2011	Appleton
	Reid J. Ribble	Rep.	2011–2017	Appleton

Wisconsin population by race, 2017

	Total	Percent
One race	5,652,246	97.5
White	4,942,176	85.3
Black or African American	370,335	6.4
American Indian and Alaska Native	49,261	0.8
Asian	159,530	2.8
Asian Indian	37,042	0.6
Chinese	25,412	0.4
Filipino	8,138	0.1
Japanese	1,922	0.0
Korean	7,927	0.1
Vietnamese	6,637	0.1
Other Asian[1]	72,452	1.3
Native Hawaiian and Other Pacific Islander	4,177	0.1
Native Hawaiian	863	0.0
Guamanian or Chamorro	789	0.0
Samoan	88	0.0
Other Pacific Islander[2]	2,437	0.0
Some other race	126,767	2.2
Two or more races	143,237	2.5

1. Other Asian alone, or two or more Asian categories.   2. Other Pacific Islander alone, or two or more Native Hawaiian and Other Pacific Islander categories.

Source: U.S. Census Bureau, *2017 American Community Survey 1-Year Estimates, ACS Demographic and Housing Estimates*, September 2018.

Wisconsin population by Hispanic and non-Hispanic origin, 2017

	Total	Percent
Not Hispanic or Latino[1]	5,397,636	93.1
One race	5,284,858	91.3
White	4,706,315	81.2
Black or African American	362,314	6.3
American Indian and Alaska Native	44,664	0.8
Asian	158,583	2.7
Native Hawaiian and Other Pacific Islander	3,622	0.1
Some other race	9,360	0.2
Two or more races	112,778	1.9
Hispanic or Latino[1] (of any race)	397,847	6.9
Mexican	286,985	5.0
Puerto Rican	60,781	1.0
Cuban	4,578	0.1
Other Hispanic or Latino	45,503	0.8

1. "Hispanic or Latino" refers to a person of Cuban, Mexican, Puerto Rican, South or Central American, or other Spanish culture or origin regardless of race.

Source: U.S. Census Bureau, *2017 American Community Survey 1-Year Estimates, ACS Demographic and Housing Estimates*, September 2018.

Wisconsin 2010 census by sex, race, and Hispanic origin

	Total population	Male	Female	White	Black or African American	American Indian/ Alaska Native	Asian or Pacific Islander	Some other race	Two or more races	Hispanic origin (any race)
Adams . . .	20,875	11,221	9,654	19,409	633	205	86	266	276	783
Ashland. . .	16,157	8,082	8,075	13,662	48	1,791	63	56	537	302
Barron. . . .	45,870	22,814	23,056	44,076	407	406	226	236	519	862
Bayfield. . .	15,014	7,716	7,298	13,024	46	1,435	49	29	431	158
Brown. . . .	248,007	122,658	125,349	214,415	5,491	6,715	6,828	9,155	5,403	17,985
Buffalo . . .	13,587	6,859	6,728	13,253	37	38	28	122	109	237
Burnett . . .	15,457	7,806	7,651	14,163	81	718	55	67	373	194
Calumet . .	48,971	24,543	24,428	46,187	246	203	1,047	705	583	1,690
Chippewa .	62,415	32,404	30,011	59,504	982	310	788	182	649	800
Clark.	34,690	17,577	17,113	33,338	80	174	135	773	190	1,292
Columbia. .	56,833	28,935	27,898	54,468	717	277	330	441	600	1,444
Crawford . .	16,644	8,575	8,069	16,080	296	39	66	36	127	150
Dane	488,073	241,411	246,662	413,631	25,347	1,730	23,201	12,064	12,100	28,925
Dodge . . .	88,759	46,679	42,080	83,294	2,381	385	513	1,309	877	3,522
Door.	27,785	13,679	14,106	26,839	144	162	116	249	275	671
Douglas. . .	44,159	22,087	22,072	41,166	486	868	384	82	1,173	494
Dunn	43,857	22,133	21,724	41,545	220	168	1,158	228	538	626
Eau Claire. .	98,736	48,351	50,385	91,946	874	471	3,328	519	1,598	1,804
Florence . .	4,423	2,262	2,161	4,306	10	31	14	14	48	37
Fond du Lac	101,633	49,926	51,707	95,674	1,305	471	1,169	1,700	1,314	4,368
Forest	9,304	4,724	4,580	7,690	76	1,256	24	32	226	138
Grant	51,208	26,636	24,572	49,655	588	103	317	221	324	649
Green	36,842	18,241	18,601	35,593	140	65	209	490	345	1,033
Green Lake	19,051	9,509	9,542	18,428	88	52	91	268	124	743
Iowa.	23,687	11,878	11,809	23,127	87	36	134	102	201	336
Iron	5,916	2,959	2,957	5,790	3	36	18	13	56	35
Jackson . . .	20,449	10,874	9,575	18,258	400	1,271	73	144	303	519
Jefferson . .	83,686	41,638	42,048	78,632	681	257	578	2,479	1,059	5,555
Juneau . . .	26,664	14,029	12,635	25,077	557	398	122	188	322	687
Kenosha . .	166,426	82,444	83,982	139,416	11,052	814	2,482	7,880	4,782	19,592
Kewaunee .	20,574	10,460	10,114	19,955	69	77	65	219	189	463
La Crosse. .	114,638	55,961	58,677	105,540	1,610	493	4,770	371	1,854	1,741
Lafayette . .	16,836	8,582	8,254	16,292	39	48	58	303	96	522
Langlade . .	19,977	10,032	9,945	19,267	72	191	63	100	284	324
Lincoln . . .	28,743	14,412	14,331	27,929	157	100	134	131	292	340
Manitowoc	81,442	40,489	40,953	76,402	442	450	2,060	1,069	1,019	2,565
Marathon. .	134,063	67,308	66,755	122,446	841	634	7,178	1,223	1,741	2,992
Marinette. .	41,749	20,758	20,991	40,559	108	238	227	176	441	522
Marquette .	15,404	7,808	7,596	14,920	77	86	68	126	127	391
Menominee	4,232	2,098	2,134	451	19	3,701	1	6	54	178
Milwaukee .	947,735	457,717	490,018	574,656	253,764	6,808	32,785	51,429	28,293	126,039
Monroe . . .	44,673	22,648	22,025	41,940	512	510	329	764	618	1,661
Oconto . . .	37,660	19,194	18,466	36,418	73	467	116	198	388	519
Oneida . . .	35,998	17,993	18,005	34,787	152	323	193	82	461	385
Outagamie	176,695	88,130	88,565	161,238	1,736	2,982	5,294	2,728	2,717	6,359
Ozaukee . .	86,395	42,340	44,055	82,010	1,177	208	1,529	483	988	1,956
Pepin	7,469	3,780	3,689	7,337	21	19	14	35	43	72
Pierce	41,019	20,420	20,599	39,614	232	151	308	201	513	623
Polk	44,205	22,177	22,028	42,807	96	454	166	226	456	656
Portage . . .	70,019	34,984	35,035	65,981	383	265	1,983	546	861	1,853
Price	14,159	7,180	6,979	13,750	39	54	126	42	148	153
Racine. . . .	195,408	96,771	98,637	155,731	21,767	781	2,174	10,046	4,909	22,546
Richland . .	18,021	9,042	8,979	17,540	82	46	99	119	135	360
Rock.	160,331	78,815	81,516	140,513	7,978	516	1,669	5,948	3,707	12,124
Rusk.	14,755	7,371	7,384	14,398	61	74	42	37	143	173
St. Croix. . .	84,345	42,218	42,127	80,914	552	313	923	483	1,160	1,692

Wisconsin 2010 census by sex, race, and Hispanic origin, continued

	Total popu- lation	Male	Female	White	Black or African Amer- ican	Amer- ican Indian/ Alaska Native	Asian or Pacific Islander	Some other race	Two or more races	Hispanic origin (any race)
Sauk	61,976	30,848	31,128	58,588	357	769	350	1,156	756	2,675
Sawyer . . .	16,557	8,393	8,164	13,123	77	2,757	49	42	509	268
Shawano . .	41,949	20,921	21,028	37,254	143	3,172	193	366	821	905
Sheboygan	115,507	58,010	57,497	103,861	1,684	444	5,345	2,297	1,876	6,329
Taylor	20,689	10,559	10,130	20,248	58	43	64	128	148	316
Trempealeau	28,816	14,638	14,178	27,230	62	63	127	1,086	248	1,667
Vernon . . .	29,773	14,854	14,919	29,085	109	61	99	145	274	394
Vilas	21,430	10,861	10,569	18,658	35	2,370	62	45	260	268
Walworth . .	102,228	51,237	50,991	93,935	980	308	888	4,604	1,513	10,578
Washburn .	15,911	7,924	7,987	15,343	36	186	65	49	232	208
Washington	131,887	65,393	66,494	126,317	1,155	401	1,445	1,052	1,517	3,385
Waukesha .	389,891	191,355	198,536	363,963	4,914	1,066	10,852	4,041	5,055	16,123
Waupaca . .	52,410	26,447	25,963	50,916	154	258	200	425	457	1,307
Waushara . .	24,496	12,893	11,603	23,012	454	131	108	509	282	1,329
Winnebago	166,994	83,952	83,042	154,445	2,975	1,036	3,880	2,188	2,470	5,784
Wood	74,749	36,777	37,972	71,048	393	587	1,328	593	800	1,680
Total.	**5,686,986**	**2,822,400**	**2,864,586**	**4,902,067**	**359,148**	**54,526**	**131,061**	**135,867**	**104,317**	**336,056**

Sources: U.S. Department of Commerce, U.S. Census Bureau, P.L. 94-171 Redistricting File, processed by Wisconsin Demographic Services Center and the Applied Population Laboratory of UW-Madison, May 2011.

Wisconsin American Indian population

Year	Total	Male	Female
1900.	8,372	4,321	4,051
1910.	10,142	5,231	4,911
1920.	9,611	4,950	4,661
1930.	11,548	5,951	5,597
1940.	12,265	6,354	5,911
1950.	12,196	6,274	5,922
1960.	14,297	7,195	7,102
1970.	18,924	9,251	9,673
1980.	29,320	14,489	14,831
1990.	38,986	19,240	19,746
2000[1]	47,228	23,462	23,766
2010.	54,526	27,212	27,314
2017.	50,094	25,293	24,801

1. Beginning with the 2000 Census, individuals were allowed to select more than one race.

Source: U.S. Census Bureau, 2013–2017 American Community Survey, 2010 Census Summary File 1, July 2011, and previous issues.

Wisconsin voting age population

	2018 estimate	2010 census	2010 not Hispanic or Latino,[1] by race							2010 Hispanic or Latino
			White	Black/African American	American Indian/Alaska Native	Asian	Pacific Islander	Some other	Two or more	
Adams . . .	17,580	17,454	15,935	598	203	90	6	8	26	588
Ashland. . .	12,459	12,413	10,718	39	1,416	44	4	7	18	167
Barron. . . .	36,507	35,720	34,325	291	392	177	7	10	24	494
Bayfield. . .	12,553	12,161	10,812	22	1,170	43	4	9	10	91
Brown. . . .	197,735	186,184	162,483	3,705	5,076	4,470	92	96	196	10,066
Buffalo . . .	10,779	10,566	10,306	18	60	26	1	17	2	136
Burnett . . .	12,568	12,375	11,496	46	660	41	6	8	11	107
Calumet . .	38,290	35,733	33,709	167	248	665	12	15	16	901
Chippewa .	49,922	47,706	45,395	864	361	535	11	11	26	503
Clark.	24,916	24,599	23,527	52	141	87	10	3	9	770
Columbia. .	44,307	43,566	41,505	621	270	247	27	15	16	865
Crawford . .	13,150	12,920	12,441	247	68	47	6	5	10	96
Dane	419,870	381,989	324,503	17,235	1,901	18,629	189	450	845	18,237
Dodge . . .	70,934	69,180	63,961	2,241	441	369	38	30	46	2,054
Door.	23,554	22,709	21,902	92	196	89	4	7	18	401
Douglas. . .	35,326	34,694	32,579	376	1,047	336	14	20	38	284
Dunn	35,798	34,798	33,112	200	225	786	16	13	38	408
Eau Claire. .	82,029	77,864	73,172	653	572	2,232	35	40	82	1,078
Florence . .	3,717	3,649	3,560	7	41	20	2	—	—	19
Fond du Lac	81,449	78,589	73,638	937	549	754	23	34	57	2,597
Forest	7,287	7,261	6,222	58	863	13	15	3	8	79
Grant	42,013	40,322	38,922	513	140	265	6	13	21	442
Green	28,313	27,889	26,912	101	83	140	8	15	14	616
Green Lake	14,931	14,663	14,027	57	65	63	5	3	13	430
Iowa.	18,150	17,798	17,377	58	63	100	8	12	8	172
Iron	5,000	4,935	4,845	5	48	15	—	—	4	18
Jackson . . .	16,282	15,818	14,148	379	878	46	19	8	15	325
Jefferson . .	65,025	63,829	59,160	502	318	470	16	32	40	3,291
Juneau . . .	21,613	20,991	19,592	513	343	94	4	8	9	428
Kenosha . .	126,827	123,597	101,744	7,217	769	2,031	80	144	255	11,357
Kewaunee .	16,065	15,725	15,256	49	102	40	5	14	14	245
La Crosse. .	94,715	90,176	83,999	1,149	576	3,172	33	58	100	1,089
Lafayette . .	12,757	12,487	12,053	18	53	37	—	—	4	322
Langlade . .	16,076	15,762	15,264	58	213	51	2	4	4	166
Lincoln . . .	22,811	22,441	21,916	63	136	104	15	16	9	182
Manitowoc	64,025	63,232	59,800	272	439	1,247	25	33	50	1,366
Marathon. .	103,805	101,194	94,081	527	625	4,105	43	41	97	1,675
Marinette. .	33,256	33,182	32,221	85	293	203	18	15	17	330
Marquette .	12,472	12,319	11,900	57	93	51	—	4	3	211
Menominee	2,905	2,853	423	10	2,338	1	—	—	1	80
Milwaukee .	721,878	711,358	433,061	168,280	5,644	23,660	331	790	2,476	77,116
Monroe. . .	34,660	33,003	31,038	366	420	229	34	13	22	881
Oconto . . .	30,191	29,228	28,308	50	450	95	5	12	11	297
Oneida . . .	30,031	29,359	28,454	134	373	150	16	7	10	215
Outagamie .	139,804	132,271	121,384	1,180	2,390	3,410	60	65	119	3,663
Ozaukee . .	68,571	66,023	62,520	878	239	1,123	26	32	65	1,140
Pepin	5,771	5,765	5,658	13	24	15	2	4	2	47
Pierce	33,056	31,860	30,766	187	185	280	6	17	17	402
Polk	34,241	33,705	32,677	77	394	119	5	23	26	384
Portage . . .	56,913	55,472	52,322	325	309	1,325	20	31	49	1,091
Price	11,506	11,460	11,164	13	103	52	36	7	1	84
Racine. . . .	149,308	146,898	115,625	15,037	867	1,693	54	113	220	13,289
Richland . .	13,903	13,821	13,417	52	65	67	2	8	5	205
Rock.	121,591	120,148	105,720	5,460	646	1,331	54	80	135	6,722

Wisconsin voting age population, continued

	2018 estimate	2010 census	White	Black/ African American	American Indian/ Alaska Native	Asian	Pacific Islander	Some other	Two or more	2010 Hispanic or Latino
					2010 not Hispanic or Latino,[1] by race					
Rusk	11,579	11,440	11,158	28	97	40	2	1	6	108
St. Croix . . .	65,323	61,462	59,021	394	358	638	19	36	44	952
Sauk	48,426	47,209	44,473	254	557	292	13	30	30	1,560
Sawyer . . .	13,483	13,103	10,799	64	2,046	38	2	5	5	144
Shawano . .	32,545	32,387	29,227	84	2,371	155	18	4	25	503
Sheboygan	89,310	87,925	79,347	1,305	499	3,064	32	48	78	3,552
Taylor	15,830	15,600	15,269	27	65	48	7	3	6	175
Trempealeau	22,832	21,831	20,622	40	71	95	3	5	7	988
Vernon . . .	22,506	21,895	21,414	76	89	75	7	8	12	214
Vilas	18,121	17,621	15,816	33	1,533	66	3	9	4	157
Walworth . .	80,274	78,228	70,164	769	352	682	34	35	56	6,136
Washburn .	12,852	12,679	12,231	22	246	46	2	2	7	123
Washington	103,784	99,510	95,331	765	414	1,022	22	51	66	1,839
Waukesha .	308,494	296,081	273,899	3,256	1,160	7,769	112	143	256	9,486
Waupaca . .	40,869	40,540	39,216	111	303	152	7	9	10	732
Waushara . .	19,853	19,662	18,231	440	158	82	9	6	1	735
Winnebago	134,811	130,862	121,239	2,336	1,105	2,655	58	62	132	3,275
Wood	58,489	57,745	55,161	240	503	857	16	17	30	921
Total	**4,498,576**	**4,347,494**	**3,753,673**	**242,398**	**47,511**	**93,260**	**1,826**	**2,897**	**6,107**	**199,822**

Note: The voting age population is 18 and older.

—Represents zero.

1. "Hispanic or Latino" represents ethnicity and includes people of Cuban, Mexican, Puerto Rican, South or Central American, or other Spanish culture or origin, regardless of race.

Sources: U.S. Census Bureau, P.L. 94–171 Redistricting File, as processed by the Wisconsin Legislative Technology Services Bureau, May 2011; Wisconsin Department of Administration, Demographic Services Center, *Official Final Estimates, 1/1/2018, Wisconsin Counties, with Comparison to Census 2010*, October 2018.

Wisconsin population by age group

Age (years)	Male 2010 census	Male 2017 estimate	Female 2010 census	Female 2017 estimate	Total 2010 census	Total 2017 estimate
Under 5	183,391	171,722	175,052	164,166	358,443	335,888
5–9	188,286	180,862	180,331	172,527	368,617	353,389
10–14	192,232	188,711	183,695	179,858	375,927	368,569
15–19	204,803	193,976	194,406	186,254	399,209	380,230
20–24	196,897	204,039	189,655	197,742	386,552	401,781
25–29	189,349	188,944	182,998	176,576	372,347	365,520
30–34	178,120	185,502	171,227	180,338	349,347	365,840
35–39	174,619	185,235	170,709	180,468	345,328	365,703
40–44	191,738	165,992	188,600	162,441	380,338	328,433
45–49	218,539	181,918	219,088	179,081	437,627	360,999
50–54	218,303	198,942	217,823	200,294	436,126	399,236
55–59	192,952	212,179	193,034	216,194	385,986	428,373
60–64	155,756	191,153	158,069	195,812	313,825	386,965
65–69	109,168	157,231	117,861	163,786	227,029	321,017
70–74	81,067	110,559	92,400	120,833	173,467	231,392
75–79	62,181	72,751	79,071	87,040	141,252	159,791

Wisconsin population by age group, continued

Age (years)	Male 2010 census	Male 2017 estimate	Female 2010 census	Female 2017 estimate	Total 2010 census	Total 2017 estimate
80–84	47,549	48,471	69,512	65,038	117,061	113,509
85 and over	37,450	44,551	81,055	84,297	118,505	128,848
All ages	2,822,400	2,882,738	2,864,586	2,912,745	5,686,986	5,795,483

Note: The median age was 38.5 in 2010 and 39.4 in 2017. The median age for males was 37.3 in 2010 and 38.4 in 2017. The median age for females was 37.9 in 2010 and 40.5 in 2017.

Source: U.S. Census Bureau, Population Division, *Annual Estimates of the Resident Population for Selected Age Groups by Sex for the United States, States, Counties and Puerto Rico Commonwealth and Municipios: April 1, 2010 to July 1, 2017*, June 2018.

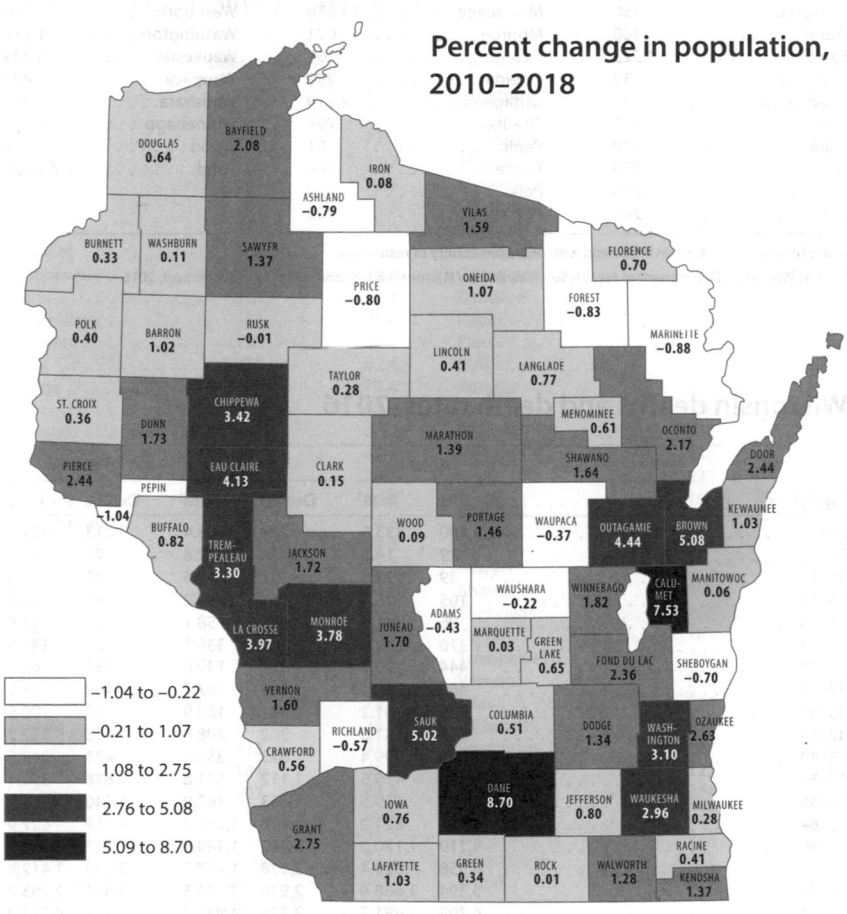

Percent change in population, 2010–2018

- −1.04 to −0.22
- −0.21 to 1.07
- 1.08 to 2.75
- 2.76 to 5.08
- 5.09 to 8.70

Basic data on Wisconsin counties

County (year created)[1]	County seat	Full value 2017 assessment ($1,000)[2]	Population 2018 estimate	% change[3]	2018 rank	Land area in sq. miles[4]	2018 population/ sq. mile
Adams (1848)	Friendship	2,513,048	20,786	-0.43	51[5]	645.7	32.2
Ashland (1860)	Ashland	1,214,386	16,030	-0.79	60	1,045.0	15.3
Barron (1859)	Barron	4,104,694	46,336	1.02	31	862.7	53.7
Bayfield (1845)	Washburn	2,556,036	15,327	2.08	64	1,477.9	10.4
Brown (1818)	Green Bay	20,863,711	260,616	5.08	4	529.7	492.0
Buffalo (1853)	Alma	1,157,109	13,699	0.82	67	671.6	20.4
Burnett (1856)	Meenon	2,619,978	15,508	0.33	62	821.9	18.9
Calumet (1836)	Chilton	4,002,112	52,658	7.53	27	318.2	165.5
Chippewa (1845)	Chippewa Falls	5,328,055	64,551	3.42	24	1,008.4	64.0
Clark (1853)	Neillsville	2,077,748	34,743	0.15	41	1,209.8	28.7
Columbia (1846)	Portage	5,350,207	57,125	0.51	26	765.5	74.6
Crawford (1818)	Prairie du Chien	1,196,983	16,737	0.56	59	570.7	29.3
Dane (1836)	Madison	60,784,158	530,519	8.70	2	1,197.2	443.1
Dodge (1836)	Juneau	6,375,763	89,949	1.34	17	875.6	102.7
Door (1851)	Sturgeon Bay	7,113,625	28,463	2.44	45	482.0	59.1
Douglas (1854)	Superior	3,430,449	44,443	0.64	33	1,304.1	34.1
Dunn (1854)	Menomonie	3,034,074	44,617	1.73	32	850.1	52.5
Eau Claire (1856)	Eau Claire	8,295,565	102,816	4.13	16	638.0	161.2
Florence (1881)	Florence	627,606	4,454	0.70	71	488.2	9.1
Fond du Lac (1836)	Fond du Lac	7,404,221	104,035	2.36	14	719.6	144.6
Forest (1885)	Crandon	1,113,815	9,227	-0.83	68	1,014.1	9.1
Grant (1836)	Lancaster	3,180,243	52,615	2.75	28	1,146.9	45.9
Green (1836)	Monroe	2,924,950	36,967	0.34	39	584.0	63.3
Green Lake (1858)	Green Lake	2,277,060	19,174	0.65	55	349.4	54.9
Iowa (1829)	Dodgeville	2,013,421	23,867	0.76	48	762.6	31.3
Iron (1893)	Hurley	944,743	5,921	0.08	70	758.2	7.8
Jackson (1853)	Black River Falls	1,649,337	20,800	1.72	50	987.7	21.1
Jefferson (1836)	Jefferson	6,948,834	84,352	0.80	20	556.5	151.6
Juneau (1856)	Mauston	2,080,178	27,117	1.70	46	766.9	35.4
Kenosha (1850)	Kenosha	14,655,093	168,700	1.37	8	272.0	620.2
Kewaunee (1852)	Kewaunee	1,661,921	20,786	1.03	51[5]	342.5	60.7
La Crosse (1851)	La Crosse	9,635,010	119,193	3.97	12	451.7	263.9
Lafayette (1846)	Darlington	1,149,154	17,010	1.03	57	633.6	26.8
Langlade (1879)	Antigo	1,688,212	20,131	0.77	54	870.6	23.1
Lincoln (1874)	Merrill	2,381,988	28,862	0.41	44	879.0	32.8
Manitowoc (1836)	Manitowoc	5,287,002	81,494	0.06	21	589.1	138.3
Marathon (1850)	Wausau	10,590,162	135,922	1.39	11	1,545.0	88.0
Marinette (1879)	Marinette	3,843,289	41,382	-0.88	37	1,399.4	29.6
Marquette (1836)	Montello	1,588,664	15,408	0.03	63	455.6	33.8
Menominee (1961)	Keshena	304,251	4,258	0.61	72	357.6	11.9
Milwaukee (1834)	Milwaukee	61,413,297	950,381	0.28	1	241.4	3,937.0
Monroe (1854)	Sparta	3,301,747	46,363	3.78	30	900.8	51.5
Oconto (1851)	Oconto	3,792,196	38,476	2.17	38	998.0	38.6
Oneida (1885)	Rhinelander	6,867,927	36,383	1.07	40	1,113.0	32.7
Outagamie (1851)	Appleton	14,882,910	184,541	4.44	6	637.5	289.5
Ozaukee (1853)	Port Washington	11,735,981	88,667	2.63	18	233.1	380.4
Pepin (1858)	Durand	616,445	7,391	-1.04	69	232.0	31.9
Pierce (1853)	Ellsworth	3,271,381	42,021	2.44	35	573.8	73.2
Polk (1853)	Balsam Lake	4,530,662	44,380	0.40	34	914.0	48.6
Portage (1836)	Stevens Point	5,718,796	71,038	1.46	23	800.7	88.7
Price (1879)	Phillips	1,376,984	14,046	-0.80	66	1,254.4	11.2
Racine (1836)	Racine	14,695,480	196,200	0.41	5	332.5	590.1
Richland (1842)	Richland Center	1,136,481	17,919	-0.57	56	586.2	30.6
Rock (1836)	Janesville	10,907,783	160,349	0.01	9	718.1	223.3
Rusk (1901)	Ladysmith	1,217,894	14,754	-0.01	65	913.6	16.1
St. Croix (1840)	Hudson	9,195,174	88,583	5.02	19	722.3	122.6
Sauk (1840)	Baraboo	7,120,479	62,822	1.37	25	830.9	75.6

Basic data on Wisconsin counties, continued

County (year created)[1]	County seat	Full value 2017 assessment ($1,000)[2]	Population 2018 estimate	% change[3]	2018 rank	Land area in sq. miles[4]	2018 population/ sq. mile
Sawyer (1883)	Hayward	3,496,215	16,828	1.64	58	1,257.3	13.4
Shawano (1853). . . .	Shawano	3,096,944	41,655	-0.70	36	893.1	46.6
Sheboygan (1836) . .	Sheboygan. . . .	9,228,846	115,924	0.36	13	511.3	226.7
Taylor (1875).	Medford	1,445,463	20,746	0.28	53	974.9	21.3
Trempealeau (1854) .	Whitehall	2,209,707	29,767	3.30	43	733.0	40.6
Vernon (1851)	Viroqua	1,956,310	30,248	1.60	42	791.6	38.2
Vilas (1893).	Eagle River	6,835,216	21,771	1.59	49	856.6	25.4
Walworth (1836) . . .	Elkhorn	14,156,955	103,535	1.28	15	555.1	186.5
Washburn (1883) . . .	Shell Lake	2,488,145	15,929	0.11	61	797.1	20.0
Washington (1836). .	West Bend	14,614,348	135,970	3.10	10	430.7	315.7
Waukesha (1846) . . .	Waukesha	54,158,132	401,446	2.96	3	549.6	730.4
Waupaca (1851). . . .	Waupaca	4,133,163	52,217	-0.37	29	747.7	69.8
Waushara (1851) . . .	Wautoma	2,513,511	24,441	-0.22	47	626.2	39.0
Winnebago (1840) . .	Oshkosh	12,909,955	170,025	1.82	7	434.5	391.3
Wood (1856).	Wisconsin Rapids	4,993,169	74,817	0.09	22	793.1	94.3
Total.		**525,984,546**	**5,816,231**	**2.27**		**54,157.8**	**107.4**

1. Counties are created by legislative act. Depending on the date, Wisconsin counties were created by the Michigan Territorial Legislature (1818–1836), the Wisconsin Territorial Legislature (1836–1848), or the Wisconsin State Legislature (after 1848). 2. Reflects actual market value of all taxable general property, including personal property and real estate, as determined by the Wisconsin Department of Revenue. 3. Change from 2010 U.S. census. 4. Determined by 2010 census. 5. Adams and Kewaunee counties tied for rank 51.

Sources: Wisconsin Department of Revenue, Division of State and Local Finance, *Town, Village, and City Taxes 2017: Taxes Levied 2017—Collected 2018*; Wisconsin Department of Administration, Demographic Services Center, *County Final Population Estimates*, October 2018; U.S. Census Bureau, *Census 2010 Summary File 1*, March 2015.

Population of legislative districts as created by 2011 Wisconsin Act 43[1]

District	2010 Population	Deviation from ideal[2] Total	Percent	District	2010 Population	Deviation from ideal[2] Total	Percent
SD-1	172,313	-20	-0.01	AD-16 . .	57,458	14	0.02
AD-1 . . .	57,220	-224	-0.39	AD-17 . .	57,354	-90	-0.16
AD-2 . . .	57,649	205	0.36	AD-18 . .	57,480	36	0.06
AD-3 . . .	57,444	0	0.00	SD-7	172,423	90	0.05
SD-2	172,461	128	0.07	AD-19 . .	57,546	102	0.18
AD-4 . . .	57,486	42	0.07	AD-20 . .	57,428	-16	-0.03
AD-5 . . .	57,470	26	0.04	AD-21 . .	57,449	5	0.01
AD-6 . . .	57,505	61	0.11	SD-8	172,356	23	0.01
SD-3	171,977	-356	-0.21	AD-22 . .	57,495	51	0.09
AD-7 . . .	57,498	54	0.09	AD-23 . .	57,579	135	0.23
AD-8[1] . .	57,196	-248	-0.43	AD-24 . .	57,282	-162	-0.28
AD-9[1] . .	57,283	-161	-0.28	SD-9	172,439	106	0.06
SD-4	172,425	92	0.05	AD-25 . .	57,322	-122	-0.21
AD-10 . .	57,428	-16	-0.03	AD-26 . .	57,581	137	0.24
AD-11 . .	57,503	59	0.10	AD-27 . .	57,536	92	0.16
AD-12 . .	57,494	50	0.09	SD-10	172,245	-88	-0.05
SD-5	172,421	88	0.05	AD-28 . .	57,467	23	0.04
AD-13 . .	57,452	8	0.01	AD-29 . .	57,537	93	0.16
AD-14 . .	57,597	153	0.27	AD-30 . .	57,241	-203	-0.35
AD-15 . .	57,372	-72	-0.13	SD-11	172,329	-4	0.00
SD-6	172,292	-41	-0.02	AD-31 . .	57,240	-204	-0.36

Population of legislative districts as created by 2011 Wisconsin Act 43[1], continued

District	2010 Population	Deviation from ideal[2] Total	Percent	District	2010 Population	Deviation from ideal[2] Total	Percent
AD-32 . .	57,524	80	0.14	AD-66 . .	57,545	101	0.18
AD-33 . .	57,565	121	0.21	SD-23	172,149	−184	−0.11
SD-12	172,381	48	0.03	AD-67 . .	57,239	−205	−0.36
AD-34 . .	57,387	−57	−0.10	AD-68 . .	57,261	−183	−0.32
AD-35 . .	57,562	118	0.20	AD-69 . .	57,649	205	0.36
AD-36 . .	57,432	−12	−0.02	SD-24	172,520	187	0.11
SD-13	172,387	54	0.03	AD-70 . .	57,552	108	0.19
AD-37 . .	57,507	63	0.11	AD-71 . .	57,519	75	0.13
AD-38 . .	57,493	49	0.08	AD-72 . .	57,449	5	0.01
AD-39 . .	57,387	−57	−0.10	SD-25	172,409	76	0.04
SD-14	171,988	−345	−0.20	AD-73 . .	57,453	9	0.02
AD-40 . .	57,366	−78	−0.14	AD-74 . .	57,494	50	0.09
AD-41 . .	57,337	−107	−0.19	AD-75 . .	57,462	18	0.03
AD-42 . .	57,285	−159	−0.28	SD-26	172,596	263	0.15
SD-15	172,496	163	0.09	AD-76 . .	57,617	173	0.30
AD-43 . .	57,443	−1	0.00	AD-77 . .	57,433	−11	−0.02
AD-44 . .	57,395	−49	−0.09	AD-78 . .	57,546	102	0.18
AD-45 . .	57,658	214	0.37	SD-27	172,449	116	0.07
SD-16	172,429	96	0.06	AD-79 . .	57,461	17	0.03
AD-46 . .	57,458	14	0.02	AD-80 . .	57,585	141	0.24
AD-47 . .	57,465	21	0.04	AD-81 . .	57,403	−41	−0.07
AD-48 . .	57,506	62	0.11	SD-28	172,218	−115	−0.07
SD-17	172,550	217	0.13	AD-82 . .	57,430	−14	−0.02
AD-49 . .	57,346	−98	−0.17	AD-83 . .	57,423	−21	−0.04
AD-50 . .	57,624	180	0.31	AD-84 . .	57,365	−79	−0.14
AD-51 . .	57,580	136	0.24	SD-29	172,292	−41	−0.02
SD-18	171,722	−611	−0.35	AD-85 . .	57,480	36	0.06
AD-52 . .	57,232	−212	−0.37	AD-86 . .	57,454	10	0.02
AD-53 . .	57,240	−204	−0.36	AD-87 . .	57,358	−86	−0.15
AD-54 . .	57,250	−194	−0.34	SD-30	172,798	465	0.27
SD-19	172,576	243	0.14	AD-88 . .	57,556	112	0.19
AD-55 . .	57,493	49	0.08	AD-89 . .	57,634	190	0.33
AD-56 . .	57,582	138	0.24	AD-90 . .	57,608	164	0.28
AD-57 . .	57,501	57	0.10	SD-31	172,338	5	0.00
SD-20	172,003	−330	−0.19	AD-91 . .	57,359	−85	−0.15
AD-58 . .	57,227	−217	−0.38	AD-92 . .	57,431	−13	−0.02
AD-59 . .	57,391	−53	−0.09	AD-93 . .	57,548	104	0.18
AD-60 . .	57,385	−59	−0.10	SD-32	172,122	−211	−0.12
SD-21	172,324	−9	−0.01	AD-94 . .	57,266	−178	−0.31
AD-61 . .	57,614	170	0.30	AD-95 . .	57,372	−72	−0.13
AD-62 . .	57,345	−99	−0.17	AD-96 . .	57,484	40	0.07
AD-63 . .	57,365	−79	−0.14	SD-33	172,288	−45	−0.03
SD-22	172,270	−63	−0.04	AD-97 . .	57,279	−165	−0.29
AD-64 . .	57,270	−174	−0.30	AD-98 . .	57,513	69	0.12
AD-65 . .	57,455	11	0.02	AD-99 . .	57,496	52	0.09

1. This table reflects modifications made to Assembly Districts 8 and 9 by the U.S. District Court for the Eastern District of Wisconsin in its decision in *Baldus vs. Members of the Wisconsin Government Accountability Board*, Case No. 11-CV-562, April 11, 2012.   2. Ideal senate district: 172,333. Ideal assembly district: 57,444.

Sources: U.S. Census Bureau, 2010 Census Redistricting Data (Public Law 94-171) Summary File, March 2011; Appendix to: 2011 Wisconsin Act 43. Assembly districts 8 and 9 population and deviations calculated by the Wisconsin Legislative Reference Bureau.

Wisconsin population by county and municipality

	2010 census	2018 esti- mate	% change		2010 census	2018 esti- mate	% change
Adams	20,875	20,786	-0.43	Doyle, town	453	471	3.97
Adams, city	1,967	1,918	-2.49	Haugen, village	287	284	-1.05
Adams, town	1,345	1,364	1.41	Lakeland, town	975	1,002	2.77
Big Flats, town.	1,018	1,037	1.87	Maple Grove, town. . . .	979	972	-0.72
Colburn, town.	223	231	3.59	Maple Plain, town	803	821	2.24
Dell Prairie, town	1,590	1,621	1.95	New Auburn, village (part)	20	33	65.00
Easton, town.	1,130	1,102	-2.48	Oak Grove, town	948	969	2.22
Friendship, village	725	742	2.34	Prairie Farm, town	573	596	4.01
Jackson, town	1,003	988	-1.50	Prairie Farm, village . . .	473	459	-2.96
Leola, town	308	305	-0.97	Prairie Lake, town.	1,532	1,528	-0.26
Lincoln, town	296	294	-0.68	Rice Lake, city	8,419	8,639	2.61
Monroe, town	398	408	2.51	Rice Lake, town	3,060	3,110	1.63
New Chester, town. . . .	2,254	2,057	-8.74	Sioux Creek, town	655	670	2.29
New Haven, town.	655	672	2.60	Stanfold, town	719	721	0.28
Preston, town	1,393	1,399	0.43	Stanley, town	2,546	2,570	0.94
Quincy, town	1,163	1,179	1.38	Sumner, town	798	815	2.13
Richfield, town	158	158	0.00	Turtle Lake, town	624	637	2.08
Rome, town	2,720	2,790	2.57	Turtle Lake, village (part)	957	947	-1.04
Springville, town	1,318	1,295	-1.75	Vance Creek, town	669	665	-0.60
Strongs Prairie, town. . .	1,150	1,166	1.39				
Wisconsin Dells, city (part)	61	60	-1.64	**Bayfield**	**15,014**	**15,327**	**2.08**
				Ashland, city (part). . . .	0	0	0.00
Ashland	**16,157**	**16,030**	**-0.79**	Barksdale, town.	723	731	1.11
Agenda, town	422	424	0.47	Barnes, town.	769	774	0.65
Ashland, city (part). . . .	8,216	8,082	-1.63	Bayfield, city	487	481	-1.23
Ashland, town.	594	589	-0.84	Bayfield, town.	680	705	3.68
Butternut, village.	375	369	-1.60	Bayview, town.	487	489	0.41
Chippewa, town	374	376	0.53	Bell, town.	263	278	5.70
Gingles, town	778	788	1.29	Cable, town	825	830	0.61
Gordon, town	283	288	1.77	Clover, town	223	220	-1.35
Jacobs, town.	722	720	-0.28	Delta, town	273	276	1.10
La Pointe, town	261	268	2.68	Drummond, town	463	434	-6.26
Marengo, town	390	392	0.51	Eileen, town	681	695	2.06
Mellen, city	731	710	-2.87	Grand View, town.	468	474	1.28
Morse, town	493	501	1.62	Hughes, town	383	391	2.09
Peeksville, town.	141	141	0.00	Iron River, town	1,123	1,173	4.45
Sanborn, town	1,331	1,317	-1.05	Kelly, town	463	473	2.16
Shanagolden, town . . .	125	125	0.00	Keystone, town	378	371	-1.85
White River, town.	921	940	2.06	Lincoln, town	287	291	1.39
				Mason, town.	315	324	2.86
Barron	**45,870**	**46,336**	**1.02**	Mason, village.	93	92	-1.08
Almena, town	858	853	-0.58	Namakagon, town	246	249	1.22
Almena, village	677	647	-4.43	Orienta, town	122	121	-0.82
Arland, town.	789	825	4.56	Oulu, town.	527	529	0.38
Barron, city.	3,423	3,341	-2.40	Pilsen, town	210	215	2.38
Barron, town.	873	870	-0.34	Port Wing, town.	368	378	2.72
Bear Lake, town.	659	661	0.30	Russell, town	1,279	1,443	12.82
Cameron, village	1,783	1,849	3.70	Tripp, town.	231	242	4.76
Cedar Lake, town	948	980	3.38	Washburn, city	2,117	2,104	-0.61
Chetek, city	2,221	2,181	-1.80	Washburn, town	530	544	2.64
Chetek, town	1,644	1,675	1.89				
Clinton, town	879	902	2.62	**Brown**.	**248,007**	**260,616**	**5.08**
Crystal Lake, town	757	767	1.32	Allouez, village	13,975	13,757	-1.56
Cumberland, city	2,170	2,167	-0.14	Ashwaubenon, village. .	16,963	16,795	-0.99
Cumberland, town	876	875	-0.11	Bellevue, village	14,570	15,423	5.85
Dallas, town	565	578	2.30	De Pere, city	23,800	24,699	3.78
Dallas, village	409	376	-8.07	Denmark, village	2,123	2,216	4.38
Dovre, town	849	880	3.65	Eaton, town	1,508	1,642	8.89

Wisconsin population by county and municipality, continued

	2010 census	2018 esti- mate	% change		2010 census	2018 esti- mate	% change
Glenmore, town	1,135	1,128	−0.62	Sand Lake, town	531	535	0.75
Green Bay, city	104,057	105,477	1.36	Scott, town	494	504	2.02
Green Bay, town	2,035	2,100	3.19	Siren, town	936	946	1.07
Hobart, village	6,182	9,261	49.81	Siren, village	806	789	−2.11
Holland, town	1,519	1,583	4.21	Swiss, town	790	789	−0.13
Howard, village (part)	17,399	19,508	12.12	Trade Lake, town	823	832	1.09
Humboldt, town	1,311	1,346	2.67	Union, town	340	343	0.88
Lawrence, town	4,284	5,286	23.39	Webb Lake, town	311	315	1.29
Ledgeview, town	6,555	7,948	21.25	Webster, village	653	649	−0.61
Morrison, town	1,599	1,611	0.75	West Marshland, town	367	369	0.54
New Denmark, town	1,541	1,564	1.49	Wood River, town	953	954	0.10
Pittsfield, town	2,608	2,752	5.52				
Pulaski, village (part)	3,321	3,336	0.45	**Calumet**	**48,971**	**52,658**	**7.53**
Rockland, town	1,734	1,834	5.77	Appleton, city (part)	11,088	11,680	5.34
Scott, town	3,545	3,655	3.10	Brillion, city	3,148	3,246	3.11
Suamico, village	11,346	12,676	11.72	Brillion, town	1,486	1,533	3.16
Wrightstown, town	2,221	2,293	3.24	Brothertown, town	1,329	1,331	0.15
Wrightstown, village (part)	2,676	2,726	1.87	Charlestown, town	775	778	0.39
				Chilton, city	3,933	3,894	−0.99
Buffalo	**13,587**	**13,699**	**0.82**	Chilton, town	1,143	1,158	1.31
Alma, city	781	774	−0.90	Harrison, town	10,839	0	−100.00
Alma, town	297	306	3.03	Harrison, village (part)[1]	NA	12,786	NA
Belvidere, town	396	393	−0.76	Hilbert, village	1,132	1,171	3.45
Buffalo, town	705	703	−0.28	Kaukauna, city (part)	0	0	0.00
Buffalo City, city	1,023	1,015	−0.78	Kiel, city (part)	309	317	2.59
Canton, town	305	315	3.28	Menasha, city (part)	2,209	2,771	25.44
Cochrane, village	450	442	−1.78	New Holstein, city	3,236	3,152	−2.60
Cross, town	377	387	2.65	New Holstein, town	1,508	1,514	0.40
Dover, town	486	500	2.88	Potter, village	253	250	−1.19
Fountain City, city	859	848	−1.28	Rantoul, town	798	817	2.38
Gilmanton, town	426	430	0.94	Sherwood, village	2,713	3,114	14.78
Glencoe, town	485	490	1.03	Stockbridge, town	1,456	1,508	3.57
Lincoln, town	162	179	10.49	Stockbridge, village	636	651	2.36
Maxville, town	309	313	1.29	Woodville, town	980	987	0.71
Milton, town	534	552	3.37				
Modena, town	354	359	1.41	**Chippewa**	**62,415**	**64,551**	**3.42**
Mondovi, city	2,777	2,757	−0.72	Anson, town	2,076	2,210	6.45
Mondovi, town	469	474	1.07	Arthur, town	759	773	1.84
Montana, town	284	286	0.70	Auburn, town	697	726	4.16
Naples, town	691	702	1.59	Birch Creek, town	517	528	2.13
Nelson, town	571	625	9.46	Bloomer, city	3,539	3,563	0.68
Nelson, village	374	376	0.53	Bloomer, town	1,050	1,094	4.19
Waumandee, town	472	473	0.21	Boyd, village	552	546	−1.09
				Cadott, village	1,437	1,456	1.32
Burnett	**15,457**	**15,508**	**0.33**	Chippewa Falls, city	13,661	14,049	2.84
Anderson, town	398	399	0.25	Cleveland, town	864	874	1.16
Blaine, town	197	195	−1.02	Colburn, town	856	894	4.44
Daniels, town	649	653	0.62	Cooks Valley, town	805	833	3.48
Dewey, town	516	513	−0.58	Cornell, city	1,467	1,445	−1.50
Grantsburg, town	1,136	1,144	0.70	Delmar, town	936	977	4.38
Grantsburg, village	1,341	1,317	−1.79	Eagle Point, town	3,053	3,193	4.59
Jackson, town	773	793	2.59	Eau Claire, city (part)	1,981	2,050	3.48
La Follette, town	536	530	−1.12	Edson, town	1,089	1,078	−1.01
Lincoln, town	309	313	1.29	Estella, town	433	436	0.69
Meenon, town	1,163	1,155	−0.69	Goetz, town	762	797	4.59
Oakland, town	827	849	2.66	Hallie, town	161	178	10.56
Roosevelt, town	199	202	1.51	Howard, town	798	798	0.00
Rusk, town	409	420	2.69				

Wisconsin population by county and municipality, continued

	2010 census	2018 esti- mate	% change		2010 census	2018 esti- mate	% change
Lafayette, town	5,765	6,069	5.27	Worden, town	666	684	2.70
Lake Hallie, village	6,448	7,029	9.01	York, town	886	876	−1.13
Lake Holcombe, town . .	1,031	1,042	1.07				
New Auburn, village (part)	528	517	−2.08	**Columbia**	**56,833**	**57,125**	**0.51**
Ruby, town.	494	497	0.61	Arlington, town.	806	810	0.50
Sampson, town	892	941	5.49	Arlington, village	819	829	1.22
Sigel, town.	1,044	1,046	0.19	Caledonia, town	1,378	1,413	2.54
Stanley, city (part)	3,602	3,643	1.14	Cambria, village.	767	760	−0.91
Tilden, town	1,485	1,519	2.29	Columbus, city (part) . .	4,991	5,127	2.72
Wheaton, town	2,701	2,788	3.22	Columbus, town	646	656	1.55
Woodmohr, town.	932	962	3.22	Courtland, town	525	529	0.76
				Dekorra, town.	2,311	2,335	1.04
Clark	**34,690**	**34,743**	**0.15**	Doylestown, village . . .	297	292	−1.68
Abbotsford, city (part). .	1,616	1,596	−1.24	Fall River, village	1,712	1,754	2.45
Beaver, town.	885	889	0.45	Fort Winnebago, town. .	825	825	0.00
Butler, town	96	95	−1.04	Fountain Prairie, town. .	887	893	0.68
Colby, city (part)	1,354	1,308	−3.40	Friesland, village	356	350	−1.69
Colby, town	874	896	2.52	Hampden, town	574	581	1.22
Curtiss, village.	216	210	−2.78	Leeds, town	774	774	0.00
Dewhurst, town.	323	336	4.02	Lewiston, town	1,225	1,228	0.24
Dorchester, village (part)	871	858	−1.49	Lodi, city	3,050	3,092	1.38
Eaton, town	712	714	0.28	Lodi, town	3,273	3,323	1.53
Foster, town.	95	97	2.11	Lowville, town.	1,008	1,015	0.69
Fremont, town	1,265	1,272	0.55	Marcellon, town	1,102	1,114	1.09
Grant, town	916	937	2.29	Newport, town	586	587	0.17
Granton, village.	355	353	−0.56	Otsego, town	693	692	−0.14
Green Grove, town	756	754	−0.26	Pacific, town	2,707	2,723	0.59
Greenwood, city	1,026	1,021	−0.49	Pardeeville, village	2,115	2,096	−0.90
Hendren, town	499	499	0.00	Portage, city	10,324	10,211	−1.09
Hewett, town	293	300	2.39	Poynette, village	2,528	2,528	0.00
Hixon, town	808	821	1.61	Randolph, town.	769	760	−1.17
Hoard, town	841	829	−1.43	Randolph, village (part) .	472	467	−1.06
Levis, town.	492	497	1.02	Rio, village	1,059	1,059	0.00
Longwood, town	858	860	0.23	Scott, town.	905	923	1.99
Loyal, city.	1,261	1,243	−1.43	Springvale, town	520	530	1.92
Loyal, town.	826	834	0.97	West Point, town	1,955	2,010	2.81
Lynn, town.	861	887	3.02	Wisconsin Dells, city (part)	2,440	2,420	−0.82
Mayville, town.	961	943	−1.87	Wyocena, town	1,666	1,681	0.90
Mead, town	321	337	4.98	Wyocena, village	768	738	−3.91
Mentor, town	584	583	−0.17				
Neillsville, city	2,463	2,399	−2.60	**Crawford**	**16,644**	**16,737**	**0.56**
Owen, city	940	923	−1.81	Bell Center, village	117	116	−0.85
Pine Valley, town	1,157	1,172	1.30	Bridgeport, town	990	1,027	3.74
Reseburg, town.	776	787	1.42	Clayton, town	958	933	−2.61
Seif, town.	172	171	−0.58	De Soto, village (part) . .	108	102	−5.56
Sherman, town	882	916	3.85	Eastman, town	739	757	2.44
Sherwood, town	220	225	2.27	Eastman, village	428	424	−0.93
Stanley, city (part)	6	6	0.00	Ferryville, village	176	190	7.95
Thorp, city	1,621	1,612	−0.56	Freeman, town	686	715	4.23
Thorp, town	808	828	2.48	Gays Mills, village.	491	504	2.65
Unity, town	878	900	2.51	Haney, town	309	318	2.91
Unity, village (part). . . .	139	137	−1.44	Lynxville, village	132	133	0.76
Warner, town	669	676	1.05	Marietta, town	470	491	4.47
Washburn, town	290	286	−1.38	Mount Sterling, village .	211	209	−0.95
Weston, town	699	699	0.00	Prairie du Chien, city. . .	5,911	5,869	−0.71
Withee, town	966	985	1.97	Prairie du Chien, town. .	1,073	1,069	−0.37
Withee, village	487	492	1.03	Scott, town.	462	482	4.33

Wisconsin population by county and municipality, continued

	2010 census	2018 estimate	% change		2010 census	2018 estimate	% change
Eden, village	875	903	3.20	Ellenboro, town	525	547	4.19
Eldorado, town	1,462	1,477	1.03	Fennimore, city	2,497	2,497	0.00
Empire, town	2,797	2,814	0.61	Fennimore, town	612	606	-0.98
Fairwater, village	371	364	-1.89	Glen Haven, town	417	415	-0.48
Fond du Lac, city	43,021	43,921	2.09	Harrison, town	495	504	1.82
Fond du Lac, town	3,015	3,859	27.99	Hazel Green, town	1,132	1,139	0.62
Forest, town	1,080	1,069	-1.02	Hazel Green, village (part)	1,243	1,248	0.40
Friendship, town	2,675	2,692	0.64	Hickory Grove, town	455	507	11.43
Kewaskum, village (part)	0	0	0.00	Jamestown, town	2,076	2,210	6.45
Lamartine, town	1,737	1,789	2.99	Lancaster, city	3,868	3,781	-2.25
Marshfield, town	1,138	1,154	1.41	Liberty, town	553	555	0.36
Metomen, town	741	730	-1.48	Lima, town	805	802	-0.37
Mount Calvary, village	762	568	-25.46	Little Grant, town	283	288	1.77
North Fond du Lac, village	5,014	5,203	3.77	Livingston, village (part)	657	648	-1.37
Oakfield, town	703	716	1.85	Marion, town	572	600	4.90
Oakfield, village	1,075	1,094	1.77	Millville, town	166	169	1.81
Osceola, town	1,865	1,860	-0.27	Montfort, village (part)	622	627	0.80
Ripon, city	7,733	7,802	0.89	Mount Hope, town	300	297	-1.00
Ripon, town	1,400	1,412	0.86	Mount Hope, village	225	226	0.44
Rosendale, town	695	705	1.44	Mount Ida, town	561	562	0.18
Rosendale, village	1,063	1,035	-2.63	Muscoda, town	769	772	0.39
Springvale, town	707	715	1.13	Muscoda, village (part)	1,249	1,218	-2.48
St. Cloud, village	477	471	-1.26	North Lancaster, town	509	531	4.32
Taycheedah, town	4,205	4,534	7.82	Paris, town	702	728	3.70
Waupun, city (part)	3,476	3,493	0.49	Patch Grove, town	339	343	1.18
Waupun, town	1,375	1,405	2.18	Patch Grove, village	198	201	1.52
				Platteville, city	11,224	12,268	9.30
Forest	**9,304**	**9,227**	**-0.83**	Platteville, town	1,509	1,563	3.58
Alvin, town	157	154	-1.91	Potosi, town	849	858	1.06
Argonne, town	512	520	1.56	Potosi, village	688	677	-1.60
Armstrong Creek, town	409	403	-1.47	Smelser, town	794	803	1.13
Blackwell, town	332	325	-2.11	South Lancaster, town	843	852	1.07
Caswell, town	91	89	-2.20	Tennyson, village	355	364	2.54
Crandon, city	1,920	1,837	-4.32	Waterloo, town	550	580	5.45
Crandon, town	650	661	1.69	Watterstown, town	330	343	3.94
Freedom, town	345	348	0.87	Wingville, town	357	368	3.08
Hiles, town	311	317	1.93	Woodman, town	185	195	5.41
Laona, town	1,212	1,197	-1.24	Woodman, village	132	129	-2.27
Lincoln, town	955	963	0.84	Wyalusing, town	346	353	2.02
Nashville, town	1,064	1,074	0.94				
Popple River, town	44	43	-2.27	**Green**	**36,842**	**36,967**	**0.34**
Ross, town	136	133	-2.21	Adams, town	530	539	1.70
Wabeno, town	1,166	1,163	-0.26	Albany, town	1,106	1,124	1.63
				Albany, village	1,018	1,008	-0.98
Grant	**51,208**	**52,615**	**2.75**	Belleville, village (part)	537	530	-1.30
Bagley, village	379	375	-1.06	Brodhead, city (part)	3,203	3,182	-0.66
Beetown, town	777	790	1.67	Brooklyn, town	1,083	1,135	4.80
Bloomington, town	350	361	3.14	Brooklyn, village (part)	465	459	-1.29
Bloomington, village	735	734	-0.14	Browntown, village	280	279	-0.36
Blue River, village	434	429	-1.15	Cadiz, town	815	802	-1.60
Boscobel, city	3,231	3,231	0.00	Clarno, town	1,166	1,159	-0.60
Boscobel, town	376	372	-1.06	Decatur, town	1,767	1,776	0.51
Cassville, town	416	409	-1.68	Exeter, town	2,023	2,087	3.16
Cassville, village	947	937	-1.06	Jefferson, town	1,217	1,222	0.41
Castle Rock, town	248	258	4.03	Jordan, town	641	630	-1.72
Clifton, town	385	396	2.86	Monroe, city	10,827	10,684	-1.32
Cuba City, city (part)	1,877	1,890	0.69	Monroe, town	1,245	1,269	1.93
Dickeyville, village	1,061	1,059	-0.19				

Wisconsin population by county and municipality, continued

	2010 census	2018 esti- mate	% change		2010 census	2018 esti- mate	% change
Monticello, village	1,217	1,218	0.08	Iron	5,916	5,921	0.08
Mount Pleasant, town . .	598	607	1.51	Anderson, town.	58	58	0.00
New Glarus, town.	1,335	1,379	3.30	Carey, town	163	161	-1.23
New Glarus, village. . . .	2,172	2,173	0.05	Gurney, town	159	165	3.77
Spring Grove, town . . .	874	904	3.43	Hurley, city.	1,547	1,512	-2.26
Sylvester, town	1,004	1,023	1.89	Kimball, town	498	500	0.40
Washington, town	809	820	1.36	Knight, town.	211	209	-0.95
York, town	910	958	5.27	Mercer, town	1,407	1,438	2.20
				Montreal, city	807	801	-0.74
Green Lake	**19,051**	**19,174**	**0.65**	Oma, town	289	303	4.84
Berlin, city (part)	5,435	5,494	1.09	Pence, town	163	163	0.00
Berlin, town	1,140	1,139	-0.09	Saxon, town	324	318	-1.85
Brooklyn, town	1,826	1,860	1.86	Sherman, town	290	293	1.03
Green Lake, city.	960	996	3.75				
Green Lake, town.	1,154	1,157	0.26	**Jackson**.	**20,449**	**20,800**	**1.72**
Kingston, town	1,064	1,085	1.97	Adams, town	1,342	1,382	2.98
Kingston, village	326	326	0.00	Albion, town.	1,210	1,241	2.56
Mackford, town.	560	559	-0.18	Alma, town.	1,044	1,103	5.65
Manchester, town	1,022	1,044	2.15	Alma Center, village . . .	503	501	-0.40
Markesan, city.	1,476	1,431	-3.05	Bear Bluff, town.	138	135	-2.17
Marquette, town	531	544	2.45	Black River Falls, city . . .	3,622	3,606	-0.44
Marquette, village	150	151	0.67	Brockway, town.	2,828	2,890	2.19
Princeton, city.	1,214	1,177	-3.05	City Point, town.	182	180	-1.10
Princeton, town.	1,434	1,443	0.63	Cleveland, town.	481	501	4.16
St. Marie, town	351	358	1.99	Curran, town.	343	314	-8.45
Seneca, town	408	410	0.49	Franklin, town.	448	458	2.23
				Garden Valley, town . . .	422	434	2.84
Iowa.	**23,687**	**23,867**	**0.76**	Garfield, town.	638	690	8.15
Arena, town	1,456	1,503	3.23	Hixton, town.	652	670	2.76
Arena, village	834	830	-0.48	Hixton, village.	433	427	-1.39
Avoca, village	637	620	-2.67	Irving, town	751	775	3.20
Barneveld, village.	1,231	1,258	2.19	Knapp, town.	299	313	4.68
Blanchardville, village				Komensky, town	509	529	3.93
(part)	177	177	0.00	Manchester, town	704	714	1.42
Brigham, town	1,034	1,076	4.06	Melrose, town	470	499	6.17
Clyde, town	306	312	1.96	Melrose, village	503	490	-2.58
Cobb, village.	458	467	1.97	Merrillan, village	542	520	-4.06
Dodgeville, city	4,693	4,700	0.15	Millston, town.	159	166	4.40
Dodgeville, town	1,708	1,709	0.06	North Bend, town	488	511	4.71
Eden, town.	355	366	3.10	Northfield, town	639	657	2.82
Highland, town	750	776	3.47	Springfield, town	623	609	-2.25
Highland, village	842	837	-0.59	Taylor, village	476	485	1.89
Hollandale, village	288	283	-1.74				
Linden, town	847	846	-0.12	**Jefferson**.	**83,686**	**84,352**	**0.80**
Linden, village.	549	538	-2.00	Aztalan, town	1,457	1,464	0.48
Livingston, village (part)	7	7	0.00	Cambridge, village (part)	109	108	-0.92
Mifflin, town.	585	590	0.85	Cold Spring, town	727	788	8.39
Mineral Point, city	2,487	2,488	0.04	Concord, town	2,072	2,072	0.00
Mineral Point, town . . .	1,033	1,055	2.13	Farmington, town	1,380	1,381	0.07
Montfort, village (part) .	96	97	1.04	Fort Atkinson, city	12,368	12,390	0.18
Moscow, town.	576	602	4.51	Hebron, town	1,094	1,111	1.55
Muscoda, village (part) .	50	37	-26.00	Ixonia, town	4,385	4,887	11.45
Pulaski, town	400	403	0.75	Jefferson, city	7,973	7,967	-0.08
Rewey, village.	292	287	-1.71	Jefferson, town	2,178	2,183	0.23
Ridgeway, town.	568	575	1.23	Johnson Creek, village. .	2,738	2,997	9.46
Ridgeway, village.	653	644	-1.38	Koshkonong, town	3,692	3,665	-0.73
Waldwick, town.	473	480	1.48	Lac La Belle, village (part)	1	1	0.00
Wyoming, town.	302	304	0.66	Lake Mills, city	5,708	5,953	4.29

Wisconsin population by county and municipality, continued

	2010 census	2018 estimate	% change		2010 census	2018 estimate	% change
Lake Mills, town	2,070	2,091	1.01	Twin Lakes, village	5,989	6,068	1.32
Milford, town	1,099	1,121	2.00	Wheatland, town	3,373	3,369	−0.12
Oakland, town	3,100	3,111	0.35	**Kewaunee . . . .**	**20,574**	**20,786**	**1.03**
Palmyra, town	1,186	1,174	−1.01	Ahnapee, town	940	937	−0.32
Palmyra, village	1,781	1,757	−1.35	Algoma, city	3,167	3,109	−1.83
Sullivan, town	2,208	2,213	0.23	Carlton, town	1,014	1,036	2.17
Sullivan, village	669	660	−1.35	Casco, town	1,165	1,208	3.69
Sumner, town	832	805	−3.25	Casco, village	583	598	2.57
Waterloo, city	3,333	3,362	0.87	Franklin, town	993	1,003	1.01
Waterloo, town	909	905	−0.44	Kewaunee, city	2,952	2,906	−1.56
Watertown, city (part) . .	15,402	15,366	−0.23	Lincoln, town	948	936	−1.27
Watertown, town	1,975	1,982	0.35	Luxemburg, town	1,469	1,519	3.40
Whitewater, city (part) . .	3,240	2,838	−12.41	Luxemburg, village. . . .	2,515	2,596	3.22
				Montpelier, town	1,306	1,333	2.07
Juneau	**26,664**	**27,117**	**1.70**	Pierce, town	833	833	0.00
Armenia, town	699	748	7.01	Red River, town	1,393	1,419	1.87
Camp Douglas, village. .	601	621	3.33	West Kewaunee, town. .	1,296	1,353	4.40
Clearfield, town	728	751	3.16	**La Crosse. . . . .**	**114,638**	**119,193**	**3.97**
Cutler, town	326	331	1.53	Bangor, town	615	625	1.63
Elroy, city	1,442	1,349	−6.45	Bangor, village	1,459	1,538	5.41
Finley, town	97	94	−3.09	Barre, town.	1,234	1,317	6.73
Fountain, town	555	589	6.13	Burns, town	947	957	1.06
Germantown, town . . .	1,471	1,675	13.87	Campbell, town.	4,314	4,324	0.23
Hustler, village	194	191	−1.55	Farmington, town	2,061	2,086	1.21
Kildare, town	681	711	4.41	Greenfield, town	2,060	2,153	4.51
Kingston, town	91	90	−1.10	Hamilton, town	2,436	2,490	2.22
Lemonweir, town	1,743	1,756	0.75	Holland, town	3,701	4,190	13.21
Lindina, town	718	719	0.14	Holmen, village	9,005	10,147	12.68
Lisbon, town.	912	919	0.77	La Crosse, city	51,320	52,282	1.87
Lyndon, town	1,384	1,404	1.45	Medary, town	1,461	1,524	4.31
Lyndon Station, village .	500	487	−2.60	Onalaska, city	17,736	18,788	5.93
Marion, town	426	430	0.94	Onalaska, town	5,623	5,803	3.20
Mauston, city	4,423	4,467	0.99	Rockland, village (part) .	594	679	14.31
Necedah, town	2,327	2,410	3.57	Shelby, town.	4,715	4,710	−0.11
Necedah, village	916	912	−0.44	Washington, town	558	538	−3.58
New Lisbon, city	2,554	2,583	1.14	West Salem, village. . . .	4,799	5,042	5.06
Orange, town	570	570	0.00	**Lafayette. . . . .**	**16,836**	**17,010**	**1.03**
Plymouth, town.	597	598	0.17	Argyle, town	436	452	3.67
Seven Mile Creek, town .	358	357	−0.28	Argyle, village	857	842	−1.75
Summit, town	646	666	3.10	Belmont, town	767	811	5.74
Union Center, village . .	200	197	−1.50	Belmont, village	986	1,000	1.42
Wisconsin Dells, city (part)	2	0	−100.00	Benton, town	504	522	3.57
Wonewoc, town.	687	693	0.87	Benton, village	973	957	−1.64
Wonewoc, village.	816	799	−2.08	Blanchard, town	264	276	4.55
Kenosha	**166,426**	**168,700**	**1.37**	Blanchardville, village (part)	648	639	−1.39
Brighton, town	1,456	1,461	0.34	Cuba City, city (part) . . .	209	220	5.26
Bristol, village	4,914	5,071	3.19	Darlington, city	2,451	2,391	−2.45
Genoa City, village (part).	6	6	0.00	Darlington, town	875	905	3.43
Kenosha, city	99,218	99,263	0.05	Elk Grove, town	551	578	4.90
Paddock Lake, village . .	2,992	2,972	−0.67	Fayette, town	376	418	11.17
Paris, town	1,504	1,510	0.40	Gratiot, town	550	562	2.18
Pleasant Prairie, village .	19,719	21,166	7.34	Gratiot, village	236	227	−3.81
Randall, town	3,180	3,201	0.66	Hazel Green, village (part)	13	13	0.00
Salem Lakes, village[4]. . .	14,478	14,531	0.37	Kendall, town	454	480	5.73
Somers, town	9,597	1,255	−86.92				
Somers, village[5].	NA	8,827	NA				

Wisconsin population by county and municipality, continued

	2010 census	2018 esti-mate	% change		2010 census	2018 esti-mate	% change
Lamont, town	314	315	0.32	Eaton, town	833	832	−0.12
Monticello, town	133	135	1.50	Francis Creek, village . .	669	664	−0.75
New Diggings, town . . .	502	519	3.39	Franklin, town	1,264	1,268	0.32
Seymour, town	446	451	1.12	Gibson, town	1,344	1,355	0.82
Shullsburg, city	1,226	1,209	−1.39	Kellnersville, village . . .	332	333	0.30
Shullsburg, town	354	351	−0.85	Kiel, city (part).	3,429	3,568	4.05
South Wayne, village. . .	489	485	−0.82	Kossuth, town	2,090	2,100	0.48
Wayne, town.	490	495	1.02	Liberty, town	1,281	1,289	0.62
White Oak Springs, town	118	123	4.24	Manitowoc, city.	33,736	33,692	−0.13
Willow Springs, town . .	758	771	1.72	Manitowoc, town.	1,083	1,111	2.59
Wiota, town	856	863	0.82	Manitowoc Rapids, town	2,150	2,149	−0.05
				Maple Grove, town	835	833	−0.24
Langlade.	**19,977**	**20,131**	**0.77**	Maribel, village	351	350	−0.28
Ackley, town.	524	526	0.38	Meeme, town	1,446	1,470	1.66
Ainsworth, town	469	462	−1.49	Mishicot, town	1,289	1,298	0.70
Antigo, city.	8,234	8,312	0.95	Mishicot, village	1,442	1,438	−0.28
Antigo, town.	1,412	1,411	−0.07	Newton, town	2,264	2,303	1.72
Elcho, town	1,233	1,241	0.65	Reedsville, village	1,206	1,185	−1.74
Evergreen, town	495	506	2.22	Rockland, town	1,001	1,017	1.60
Langlade, town	473	480	1.48	St. Nazianz, village	783	766	−2.17
Neva, town.	902	899	−0.33	Schleswig, town	1,963	2,019	2.85
Norwood, town	913	906	−0.77	Two Creeks, town.	437	432	−1.14
Parrish, town	91	91	0.00	Two Rivers, city	11,712	11,457	−2.18
Peck, town	349	367	5.16	Two Rivers, town	1,795	1,825	1.67
Polar, town.	984	998	1.42	Valders, village	962	953	−0.94
Price, town.	228	227	−0.44	Whitelaw, village	757	755	−0.26
Rolling, town	1,504	1,517	0.86				
Summit, town	163	161	−1.23	**Marathon . . . .**	**134,063**	**135,922**	**1.39**
Upham, town	676	678	0.30	Abbotsford, city (part). .	694	687	−1.01
Vilas, town	233	230	−1.29	Athens, village	1,105	1,101	−0.36
White Lake, village	363	361	−0.55	Bergen, town	641	635	−0.94
Wolf River, town	731	758	3.69	Berlin, town	945	938	−0.74
				Bern, town	591	604	2.20
Lincoln	**28,743**	**28,862**	**0.41**	Bevent, town	1,118	1,130	1.07
Birch, town.	594	592	−0.34	Birnamwood, village (part)	16	20	25.00
Bradley, town	2,408	2,459	2.12	Brighton, town	612	606	−0.98
Corning, town	883	886	0.34	Brokaw, village[6].	251	233	−7.17
Harding, town.	372	376	1.08	Cassel, town	911	924	1.43
Harrison, town	833	843	1.20	Cleveland, town.	1,488	1,511	1.55
King, town	855	882	3.16	Colby, city (part)	498	492	−1.20
Merrill, city.	9,661	9,646	−0.16	Day, town	1,085	1,092	0.65
Merrill, town.	2,980	3,032	1.74	Dorchester, village (part)	5	4	−20.00
Pine River, town.	1,869	1,874	0.27	Easton, town.	1,111	1,135	2.16
Rock Falls, town.	618	641	3.72	Eau Pleine, town	773	756	−2.20
Russell, town	677	684	1.03	Edgar, village	1,479	1,465	−0.95
Schley, town.	934	937	0.32	Elderon, town	606	618	1.98
Scott, town.	1,432	1,443	0.77	Elderon, village	179	174	−2.79
Skanawan, town	391	397	1.53	Emmet, town	931	944	1.40
Somo, town	114	116	1.75	Fenwood, village	152	145	−4.61
Tomahawk, city	3,397	3,314	−2.44	Frankfort, town	670	660	−1.49
Tomahawk, town	416	428	2.88	Franzen, town	578	590	2.08
Wilson, town.	309	312	0.97	Green Valley, town	541	548	1.29
				Guenther, town	341	345	1.17
Manitowoc	**81,442**	**81,494**	**0.06**	Halsey, town.	651	661	1.54
Cato, town	1,566	1,581	0.96	Hamburg, town	918	922	0.44
Centerville, town	645	647	0.31	Harrison, town	374	368	−1.60
Cleveland, village.	1,485	1,504	1.28	Hatley, village	574	612	6.62
Cooperstown, town . . .	1,292	1,300	0.62				

Wisconsin population by county and municipality, continued

	2010 census	2018 estimate	% change		2010 census	2018 estimate	% change
Hewitt, town	606	628	3.63	Wagner, town	681	701	2.94
Holton, town	873	879	0.69	Wausaukee, town.	1,066	1,115	4.60
Hull, town	750	739	-1.47	Wausaukee, village. . . .	575	563	-2.09
Johnson, town	985	987	0.20				
Knowlton, town.	1,910	1,942	1.68	**Marquette . . . .**	**15,404**	**15,408**	**0.03**
Kronenwetter, village . .	7,210	7,733	7.25	Buffalo, town	1,221	1,246	2.05
Maine, village[6]	2,337	2,338	0.04	Crystal Lake, town	484	493	1.86
Marathon, town.	1,048	1,040	-0.76	Douglas, town.	725	733	1.10
Marathon City, village . .	1,524	1,566	2.76	Endeavor, village	468	458	-2.14
Marshfield, city (part) . .	900	958	6.44	Harris, town	790	799	1.14
McMillan, town	1,968	2,018	2.54	Mecan, town.	686	691	0.73
Mosinee, city	3,988	4,008	0.50	Montello, city	1,495	1,454	-2.74
Mosinee, town	2,174	2,213	1.79	Montello, town	1,033	1,044	1.06
Norrie, town	976	991	1.54	Moundville, town.	552	562	1.81
Plover, town	689	689	0.00	Neshkoro, town	561	544	-3.03
Reid, town	1,215	1,243	2.30	Neshkoro, village	434	416	-4.15
Rib Falls, town.	993	998	0.50	Newton, town	547	554	1.28
Rib Mountain, town . . .	6,825	6,906	1.19	Oxford, town	885	891	0.68
Rietbrock, town	981	984	0.31	Oxford, village.	607	594	-2.14
Ringle, town	1,711	1,732	1.23	Packwaukee, town	1,416	1,406	-0.71
Rothschild, village	5,269	5,314	0.85	Shields, town	550	557	1.27
Schofield, city	2,169	2,206	1.71	Springfield, town	830	839	1.08
Spencer, town	1,581	1,631	3.16	Westfield, town	866	885	2.19
Spencer, village	1,925	1,932	0.36	Westfield, village	1,254	1,242	-0.96
Stettin, town.	2,554	2,579	0.98				
Stratford, village	1,578	1,607	1.84	**Menominee . . . .**	**4,232**	**4,258**	**0.61**
Texas, town	1,615	1,607	-0.50	Menominee, town	4,232	4,258	0.61
Unity, village (part). . . .	204	200	-1.96				
Wausau, city	39,106	39,024	-0.21	**Milwaukee. . . . .**	**947,735**	**950,381**	**0.28**
Wausau, town	2,229	2,332	4.62	Bayside, village (part) . .	4,300	4,254	-1.07
Weston, town	639	676	5.79	Brown Deer, village . . .	11,999	12,346	2.89
Weston, village	14,868	15,445	3.88	Cudahy, city	18,267	18,208	-0.32
Wien, town.	825	857	3.88	Fox Point, village	6,701	6,652	-0.73
				Franklin, city.	35,451	35,779	0.93
				Glendale, city	12,872	12,587	-2.21
Marinette	**41,749**	**41,382**	**-0.88**	Greendale, village	14,046	14,345	2.13
Amberg, town.	726	735	1.24	Greenfield, city	36,720	36,366	-0.96
Athelstane, town	504	512	1.59	Hales Corners, village . .	7,692	7,622	-0.91
Beaver, town.	1,146	1,167	1.83	Milwaukee, city (part) . .	594,833	595,555	0.12
Beecher, town.	724	737	1.80	Oak Creek, city	34,451	35,739	3.74
Coleman, village	724	723	-0.14	River Hills, village.	1,597	1,568	-1.82
Crivitz, village	984	953	-3.15	St. Francis, city	9,365	9,434	0.74
Dunbar, town	1,094	628	-42.60	Shorewood, village. . . .	13,162	13,315	1.16
Goodman, town	619	624	0.81	South Milwaukee, city. .	21,156	20,882	-1.30
Grover, town.	1,768	1,817	2.77	Wauwatosa, city	46,396	47,781	2.99
Lake, town	1,135	1,167	2.82	West Allis, city	60,411	59,590	-1.36
Marinette, city.	10,968	10,831	-1.25	West Milwaukee, village.	4,206	4,159	-1.12
Middle Inlet, town	840	842	0.24	Whitefish Bay, village . .	14,110	14,199	0.63
Niagara, city	1,624	1,586	-2.34				
Niagara, town	853	875	2.58	**Monroe. . . . .**	**44,673**	**46,363**	**3.78**
Pembine, town	889	893	0.45	Adrian, town.	762	795	4.33
Peshtigo, city	3,502	3,400	-2.91	Angelo, town	1,296	1,475	13.81
Peshtigo, town	4,057	4,127	1.73	Byron, town	1,342	1,362	1.49
Porterfield, town	1,971	2,007	1.83	Cashton, village.	1,102	1,107	0.45
Pound, town.	1,425	1,419	-0.42	Clifton, town.	690	702	1.74
Pound, village.	377	373	-1.06	Glendale, town	667	688	3.15
Silver Cliff, town.	491	507	3.26	Grant, town	495	503	1.62
Stephenson, town	3,006	3,080	2.46	Greenfield, town	707	719	1.70

Wisconsin population by county and municipality, continued

	2010 census	2018 estimate	% change		2010 census	2018 estimate	% change
Jefferson, town	819	880	7.45	Townsend, town	979	961	−1.84
Kendall, village	472	464	−1.69	Underhill, town	882	916	3.85
La Grange, town	2,007	2,006	−0.05	**Oneida**	**35,998**	**36,383**	**1.07**
Lafayette, town	396	415	4.80	Cassian, town	985	997	1.22
Leon, town.	1,086	1,141	5.06	Crescent, town	2,033	2,055	1.08
Lincoln, town	835	851	1.92	Enterprise, town	315	315	0.00
Little Falls, town	1,523	1,594	4.66	Hazelhurst, town	1,273	1,278	0.39
Melvina, village	104	103	−0.96	Lake Tomahawk, town. .	1,043	1,050	0.67
New Lyme, town	168	184	9.52	Little Rice, town.	306	318	3.92
Norwalk, village.	638	640	0.31	Lynne, town	141	136	−3.55
Oakdale, town.	772	794	2.85	Minocqua, town	4,453	4,511	1.30
Oakdale, village	297	289	−2.69	Monico, town	309	300	−2.91
Ontario, village (part)	0	0	0.00	Newbold, town	2,719	2,755	1.32
Portland, town	808	844	4.46	Nokomis, town	1,371	1,450	5.76
Ridgeville, town.	501	535	6.79	Pelican, town	2,764	2,816	1.88
Rockland, village (part) .	0	0	0.00	Piehl, town.	86	86	0.00
Scott, town.	135	132	−2.22	Pine Lake, town	2,740	2,763	0.84
Sheldon, town.	727	759	4.40	Rhinelander, city	7,798	7,825	0.35
Sparta, city.	9,522	10,058	5.63	Schoepke, town.	387	387	0.00
Sparta, town.	3,128	3,209	2.59	Stella, town	650	635	−2.31
Tomah, city	9,093	9,424	3.64	Sugar Camp, town	1,694	1,706	0.71
Tomah, town	1,400	1,434	2.43	Three Lakes, town	2,131	2,161	1.41
Warrens, village.	363	354	−2.48	Woodboro, town	813	838	3.08
Wellington, town	621	653	5.15	Woodruff, town	1,987	2,001	0.70
Wells, town.	519	540	4.05	**Outagamie**	**176,695**	**184,541**	**4.44**
Wilton, town.	1,027	1,076	4.77	Appleton, city (part) . . .	60,045	61,567	2.53
Wilton, village.	504	496	−1.59	Bear Creek, village	448	443	−1.12
Wyeville, village.	147	137	−6.80	Black Creek, town	1,259	1,246	−1.03
Oconto	**37,660**	**38,476**	**2.17**	Black Creek, village. . . .	1,316	1,309	−0.53
Abrams, town	1,856	1,920	3.45	Bovina, town	1,145	1,159	1.22
Bagley, town.	291	294	1.03	Buchanan, town	6,755	6,969	3.17
Brazeau, town.	1,284	1,308	1.87	Center, town.	3,402	3,564	4.76
Breed, town	712	732	2.81	Cicero, town	1,103	1,112	0.82
Chase, town	3,005	3,206	6.69	Combined Locks, village	3,328	3,525	5.92
Doty, town	260	267	2.69	Dale, town	2,731	2,852	4.43
Gillett, city	1,386	1,347	−2.81	Deer Creek, town	637	647	1.57
Gillett, town	1,043	1,018	−2.40	Ellington, town	2,758	2,999	8.74
How, town	516	536	3.88	Freedom, town	5,842	6,057	3.68
Lakewood, town	816	837	2.57	Grand Chute, town. . . .	20,919	22,701	8.52
Lena, town	727	717	−1.38	Greenville, town	10,309	11,785	14.32
Lena, village	564	552	−2.13	Harrison, village (part)[7] .	NA	0	NA
Little River, town	1,094	1,125	2.83	Hortonia, town	1,097	1,093	−0.36
Little Suamico, town. . .	4,799	5,182	7.98	Hortonville, village. . . .	2,711	2,744	1.22
Maple Valley, town	662	668	0.91	Howard, village (part) . .	0	0	0.00
Morgan, town	984	1,001	1.73	Kaukauna, city (part). . .	15,462	16,049	3.80
Mountain, town.	822	825	0.36	Kaukauna, town	1,238	1,296	4.68
Oconto, city	4,513	4,587	1.64	Kimberly, village	6,468	6,686	3.37
Oconto, town	1,335	1,357	1.65	Liberty, town	867	877	1.15
Oconto Falls, city	2,891	2,823	−2.35	Little Chute, village . . .	10,449	11,120	6.42
Oconto Falls, town	1,265	1,278	1.03	Maine, town	866	883	1.96
Pensaukee, town	1,381	1,395	1.01	Maple Creek, town	619	604	−2.42
Pulaski, village (part). . .	0	0	0.00	New London, city (part). .	1,610	1,713	6.40
Riverview, town.	725	733	1.10	Nichols, village	273	271	−0.73
Spruce, town	835	847	1.44	Oneida, town	4,678	4,729	1.09
Stiles, town	1,489	1,523	2.28	Osborn, town	1,170	1,209	3.33
Suring, village.	544	521	−4.23	Seymour, city	3,451	3,443	−0.23

Wisconsin population by county and municipality, continued

	2010 census	2018 estimate	% change		2010 census	2018 estimate	% change
Seymour, town	1,193	1,188	−0.42	Spring Valley, village (part)	1,346	1,341	−0.37
Shiocton, village	921	928	0.76	Trenton, town	1,829	1,847	0.98
Vandenbroek, town . . .	1,474	1,574	6.78	Trimbelle, town	1,679	1,684	0.30
Wrightstown, village (part)	151	199	31.79	Union, town	609	611	0.33
Ozaukee	**86,395**	**88,667**	**2.63**	**Polk . . . .**	**44,205**	**44,380**	**0.40**
Bayside, village (part) . .	89	85	−4.49	Alden, town	2,786	2,803	0.61
Belgium, town.	1,415	1,436	1.48	Amery, city.	2,902	2,878	−0.83
Belgium, village.	2,245	2,374	5.75	Apple River, town.	1,146	1,164	1.57
Cedarburg, city	11,412	11,628	1.89	Balsam Lake, town	1,411	1,389	−1.56
Cedarburg, town	5,760	5,927	2.90	Balsam Lake, village . . .	1,009	1,019	0.99
Fredonia, town	2,172	2,179	0.32	Beaver, town.	835	849	1.68
Fredonia, village	2,160	2,201	1.90	Black Brook, town	1,325	1,347	1.66
Grafton, town	4,053	4,159	2.62	Bone Lake, town	717	725	1.12
Grafton, village	11,459	11,803	3.00	Centuria, village	948	946	−0.21
Mequon, city	23,132	23,950	3.54	Clam Falls, town	596	611	2.52
Newburg, village (part) .	97	96	−1.03	Clayton, town	975	985	1.03
Port Washington, city . .	11,250	11,713	4.12	Clayton, village	571	564	−1.23
Port Washington, town .	1,643	1,659	0.97	Clear Lake, town	899	895	−0.44
Saukville, town	1,822	1,836	0.77	Clear Lake, village	1,070	1,093	2.15
Saukville, village	4,451	4,429	−0.49	Dresser, village	895	906	1.23
Thiensville, village	3,235	3,192	−1.33	Eureka, town.	1,649	1,675	1.58
				Farmington, town	1,836	1,855	1.03
Pepin	**7,469**	**7,391**	**−1.04**	Frederic, village	1,137	1,123	−1.23
Albany, town	676	677	0.15	Garfield, town	1,692	1,701	0.53
Durand, city	1,931	1,868	−3.26	Georgetown, town	977	996	1.94
Durand, town	742	747	0.67	Johnstown, town	534	526	−1.50
Frankfort, town	343	350	2.04	Laketown, town.	961	978	1.77
Lima, town	702	682	−2.85	Lincoln, town	2,208	2,207	−0.05
Pepin, town	721	737	2.22	Lorain, town	284	279	−1.76
Pepin, village	837	816	−2.51	Luck, town	930	927	−0.32
Stockholm, town	197	204	3.55	Luck, village	1,119	1,084	−3.13
Stockholm, village	66	62	−6.06	McKinley, town	347	355	2.31
Waterville, town	831	818	−1.56	Milltown, town	1,226	1,232	0.49
Waubeek, town	423	430	1.65	Milltown, village	917	911	−0.65
				Osceola, town	2,855	2,906	1.79
Pierce	**41,019**	**42,021**	**2.44**	Osceola, village	2,568	2,629	2.38
Bay City, village	500	489	−2.20	St. Croix Falls, city. . . .	2,133	2,090	−2.02
Clifton, town.	2,012	2,085	3.63	St. Croix Falls, town. . . .	1,165	1,170	0.43
Diamond Bluff, town. . .	469	454	−3.20	Sterling, town	790	775	−1.90
El Paso, town	681	704	3.38	Turtle Lake, village (part)	93	90	−3.23
Ellsworth, town	1,146	1,167	1.83	West Sweden, town . . .	699	697	−0.29
Ellsworth, village	3,284	3,323	1.19				
Elmwood, village	817	798	−2.33	**Portage. . . . .**	**70,019**	**71,038**	**1.46**
Gilman, town	959	992	3.44	Alban, town	885	882	−0.34
Hartland, town	827	857	3.63	Almond, town	680	666	−2.06
Isabelle, town	281	287	2.14	Almond, village	448	432	−3.57
Maiden Rock, town. . . .	589	604	2.55	Amherst, town	1,325	1,346	1.58
Maiden Rock, village. . .	119	117	−1.68	Amherst, village	1,035	1,059	2.32
Martell, town	1,185	1,201	1.35	Amherst Junction, village	377	379	0.53
Oak Grove, town	2,150	2,246	4.47	Belmont, town	616	626	1.62
Plum City, village	599	591	−1.34	Buena Vista, town	1,198	1,194	−0.33
Prescott, city.	4,258	4,227	−0.73	Carson, town	1,305	1,312	0.54
River Falls, city (part). . .	11,851	12,505	5.52	Dewey, town.	932	953	2.25
River Falls, town.	2,271	2,309	1.67	Eau Pleine, town	908	972	7.05
Rock Elm, town	485	488	0.62	Grant, town	1,906	1,927	1.10
Salem, town	510	517	1.37	Hull, town	5,346	5,401	1.03
Spring Lake, town	563	577	2.49	Junction City, village. . .	439	437	−0.46

Wisconsin population by county and municipality, continued

	2010 census	2018 estimate	% change		2010 census	2018 estimate	% change
Lanark, town.	1,527	1,549	1.44	**Richland**	**18,021**	**17,919**	**-0.57**
Linwood, town	1,121	1,130	0.80	Akan, town.	403	391	-2.98
Milladore, village (part) .	0	0	0.00	Bloom, town.	512	515	0.59
Nelsonville, village	155	155	0.00	Boaz, village	156	152	-2.56
New Hope, town	718	711	-0.97	Buena Vista, town	1,869	1,907	2.03
Park Ridge, village	491	497	1.22	Cazenovia, village (part)	314	305	-2.87
Pine Grove, town	937	927	-1.07	Dayton, town	693	681	-1.73
Plover, town	1,701	1,721	1.18	Eagle, town	531	520	-2.07
Plover, village	12,123	12,814	5.70	Forest, town	352	352	0.00
Rosholt, village	506	484	-4.35	Henrietta, town	493	492	-0.20
Sharon, town	1,982	2,032	2.52	Ithaca, town	619	637	2.91
Stevens Point, city	26,717	26,749	0.12	Lone Rock, village	888	873	-1.69
Stockton, town	2,917	3,000	2.85	Marshall, town	567	568	0.18
Whiting, village	1,724	1,683	-2.38	Orion, town	579	579	0.00
				Richland, town	1,379	1,350	-2.10
Price.	**14,159**	**14,046**	**-0.80**	Richland Center, city . . .	5,184	5,144	-0.77
Catawba, town	269	266	-1.12	Richwood, town	533	524	-1.69
Catawba, village	110	98	-10.91	Rockbridge, town	734	712	-3.00
Eisenstein, town	630	619	-1.75	Sylvan, town.	555	568	2.34
Elk, town	988	1,010	2.23	Viola, village (part)	477	472	-1.05
Emery, town	297	286	-3.70	Westford, town	530	528	-0.38
Fifield, town	901	894	-0.78	Willow, town.	579	586	1.21
Flambeau, town.	489	474	-3.07	Yuba, village.	74	63	-14.86
Georgetown, town	171	171	0.00				
Hackett, town	169	168	-0.59	**Rock**.	**160,331**	**160,349**	**0.01**
Harmony, town	222	220	-0.90	Avon, town.	608	590	-2.96
Hill, town	333	330	-0.90	Beloit, city	36,966	36,683	-0.77
Kennan, town	356	349	-1.97	Beloit, town	7,662	7,613	-0.64
Kennan, village	135	123	-8.89	Bradford, town	1,121	1,074	-4.19
Knox, town.	341	347	1.76	Brodhead, city (part). . .	90	92	2.22
Lake, town	1,128	1,111	-1.51	Center, town.	1,066	1,048	-1.69
Ogema, town	713	718	0.70	Clinton, town	930	941	1.18
Park Falls, city	2,462	2,471	0.37	Clinton, village	2,154	2,120	-1.58
Phillips, city	1,478	1,427	-3.45	Edgerton, city (part) . . .	5,364	5,477	2.11
Prentice, town.	475	470	-1.05	Evansville, city.	5,012	5,317	6.09
Prentice, village.	660	650	-1.52	Footville, village	808	816	0.99
Spirit, town	277	275	-0.72	Fulton, town.	3,252	3,337	2.61
Worcester, town.	1,555	1,569	0.90	Harmony, town	2,569	2,582	0.51
				Janesville, city.	63,575	63,570	-0.01
Racine	**195,408**	**196,200**	**0.41**	Janesville, town.	3,434	3,489	1.60
Burlington, city (part) . .	10,464	10,858	3.77	Johnstown, town	778	760	-2.31
Burlington, town	6,502	6,494	-0.12	La Prairie, town	834	816	-2.16
Caledonia, village.	24,705	25,021	1.28	Lima, town	1,280	1,281	0.08
Dover, town	4,051	4,193	3.51	Magnolia, town	767	748	-2.48
Elmwood Park, village . .	497	491	-1.21	Milton, city.	5,546	5,546	0.00
Mount Pleasant, village .	26,197	26,912	2.73	Milton, town.	2,923	2,979	1.92
North Bay, village.	241	234	-2.90	Newark, town	1,541	1,521	-1.30
Norway, town	7,948	8,013	0.82	Orfordville, village	1,442	1,440	-0.14
Racine, city.	78,860	77,807	-1.34	Plymouth, town.	1,235	1,163	-5.83
Raymond, village[8]	3,870	3,988	3.05	Porter, town	945	959	1.48
Rochester, village.	3,682	3,800	3.20	Rock, town.	3,196	3,182	-0.44
Sturtevant, village	6,970	6,615	-5.09	Spring Valley, town. . . .	746	741	-0.67
Union Grove, village . . .	4,915	4,978	1.28	Turtle, town	2,388	2,350	-1.59
Waterford, town	6,344	6,465	1.91	Union, town	2,099	2,114	0.71
Waterford, village.	5,368	5,503	2.51				
Wind Point, village	1,723	1,689	-1.97	**Rusk**.	**14,755**	**14,754**	**-0.01**
Yorkville, town[9]	3,071	3,139	2.21	Atlanta, town	592	570	-3.72

Wisconsin population by county and municipality, continued

	2010 census	2018 estimate	% change		2010 census	2018 estimate	% change
Big Bend, town	358	377	5.31	Somerset, town	4,036	4,238	5.00
Big Falls, town.	140	139	-0.71	Somerset, village	2,635	2,761	4.78
Bruce, village	779	767	-1.54	Spring Valley, village (part)	6	12	100.00
Cedar Rapids, town . . .	41	39	-4.88	Springfield, town	932	979	5.04
Conrath, village	95	87	-8.42	Stanton, town	900	888	-1.33
Dewey, town.	545	562	3.12	Star Prairie, town	3,504	3,583	2.25
Flambeau, town.	1,059	1,062	0.28	Star Prairie, village	561	553	-1.43
Glen Flora, village	92	84	-8.70	Troy, town	4,705	5,308	12.82
Grant, town	813	815	0.25	Warren, town	1,591	1,701	6.91
Grow, town	427	418	-2.11	Wilson, village.	184	187	1.63
Hawkins, town	153	161	5.23	Woodville, village.	1,344	1,319	-1.86
Hawkins, village.	305	300	-1.64				
Hubbard, town	204	202	-0.98	**Sauk. . . . .**	**61,976**	**62,822**	**1.37**
Ingram, village	78	80	2.56	Baraboo, city.	12,048	12,017	-0.26
Ladysmith, city	3,414	3,357	-1.67	Baraboo, town.	1,672	1,699	1.61
Lawrence, town.	311	305	-1.93	Bear Creek, town	595	611	2.69
Marshall, town	688	695	1.02	Cazenovia, village (part)	4	13	225.00
Murry, town	277	278	0.36	Dellona, town	1,552	1,578	1.68
Richland, town	232	231	-0.43	Delton, town	2,391	2,434	1.80
Rusk, town	525	546	4.00	Excelsior, town	1,575	1,570	-0.32
Sheldon, village.	237	231	-2.53	Fairfield, town.	1,077	1,083	0.56
South Fork, town	120	115	-4.17	Franklin, town.	652	661	1.38
Strickland, town	280	290	3.57	Freedom, town	447	457	2.24
Stubbs, town	579	583	0.69	Greenfield, town	932	936	0.43
Thornapple, town	774	793	2.45	Honey Creek, town	733	731	-0.27
Tony, village	113	109	-3.54	Ironton, town	660	660	0.00
True, town	296	295	-0.34	Ironton, village	253	255	0.79
Washington, town	339	358	5.60	La Valle, town	1,302	1,342	3.07
Weyerhaeuser, village . .	238	231	-2.94	La Valle, village	367	348	-5.18
Wilkinson, town.	40	41	2.50	Lake Delton, village	2,914	2,919	0.17
Willard, town	505	514	1.78	Lime Ridge, village	162	153	-5.56
Wilson, town.	106	119	12.26	Loganville, village	300	287	-4.33
				Merrimac, town	942	997	5.84
St. Croix	**84,345**	**88,583**	**5.02**	Merrimac, village	420	423	0.71
Baldwin, town.	928	955	2.91	North Freedom, village .	701	671	-4.28
Baldwin, village.	3,957	3,988	0.78	Plain, village	773	754	-2.46
Cady, town.	821	850	3.53	Prairie du Sac, town . . .	1,144	1,134	-0.87
Cylon, town	683	695	1.76	Prairie du Sac, village . .	3,972	4,152	4.53
Deer Park, village.	216	213	-1.39	Reedsburg, city	9,200	9,475	2.99
Eau Galle, town	1,139	1,225	7.55	Reedsburg, town	1,293	1,274	-1.47
Emerald, town.	853	852	-0.12	Rock Springs, village. . .	362	303	-16.30
Erin Prairie, town	688	685	-0.44	Sauk City, village	3,410	3,436	0.76
Forest, town	629	628	-0.16	Spring Green, town . . .	1,697	1,713	0.94
Glenwood, town	785	785	0.00	Spring Green, village . . .	1,628	1,630	0.12
Glenwood City, city . . .	1,242	1,208	-2.74	Sumpter, town	1,191	1,184	-0.59
Hammond, town	2,102	2,234	6.28	Troy, town	794	809	1.89
Hammond, village	1,922	1,874	-2.50	Washington, town	1,007	1,011	0.40
Hudson, city	12,719	13,877	9.10	West Baraboo, village . .	1,414	1,581	11.81
Hudson, town.	8,461	8,692	2.73	Westfield, town	571	547	-4.20
Kinnickinnic, town	1,722	1,779	3.31	Winfield, town.	856	865	1.05
New Richmond, city . . .	8,375	9,070	8.30	Wisconsin Dells, city (part)	175	303	73.14
North Hudson, village . .	3,768	3,758	-0.27	Woodland, town	790	806	2.03
Pleasant Valley, town . .	515	542	5.24				
Richmond, town	3,272	3,614	10.45	**Sawyer . . . .**	**16,557**	**16,828**	**1.64**
River Falls, city (part). . .	3,149	3,291	4.51	Bass Lake, town	2,377	2,421	1.85
Roberts, village	1,651	1,719	4.12	Couderay, town	401	395	-1.50
Rush River, town	508	500	-1.57	Couderay, village	88	83	-5.68
St. Joseph, town	3,842	4,020	4.63	Draper, town.	204	209	2.45

Wisconsin population by county and municipality, continued

	2010 census	2018 esti- mate	% change		2010 census	2018 esti- mate	% change
Edgewater, town	519	534	2.89	Sheboygan	115,507	115,924	0.36
Exeland, village	196	194	-1.02	Adell, village.	516	507	-1.74
Hayward, city	2,318	2,380	2.67	Cascade, village.	709	689	-2.82
Hayward, town	3,567	3,575	0.22	Cedar Grove, village . . .	2,113	2,104	-0.43
Hunter, town	678	691	1.92	Elkhart Lake, village . . .	967	1,002	3.62
Lenroot, town	1,279	1,341	4.85	Glenbeulah, village . . .	463	454	-1.94
Meadowbrook, town . .	131	139	6.11	Greenbush, town.	2,565	2,551	-0.55
Meteor, town	158	149	-5.70	Herman, town.	2,151	2,038	-5.25
Ojibwa, town	249	255	2.41	Holland, town	2,239	2,245	0.27
Radisson, town	405	406	0.25	Howards Grove, village .	3,188	3,245	1.79
Radisson, village	241	239	-0.83	Kohler, village.	2,120	2,105	-0.71
Round Lake, town	977	1,006	2.97	Lima, town.	2,982	2,975	-0.23
Sand Lake, town	813	832	2.34	Lyndon, town	1,542	1,553	0.71
Spider Lake, town	351	361	2.85	Mitchell, town.	1,304	1,303	-0.08
Weirgor, town	332	323	-2.71	Mosel, town	790	778	-1.52
Winter, town.	960	981	2.19	Oostburg, village	2,887	2,976	3.08
Winter, village	313	314	0.32	Plymouth, city.	8,445	8,686	2.85
				Plymouth, town.	3,195	3,228	1.03
Shawano.	**41,949**	**41,655**	**-0.70**	Random Lake, village . .	1,594	1,567	-1.69
Almon, town.	584	572	-2.05	Rhine, town	2,134	2,150	0.75
Angelica, town	1,793	1,818	1.39	Russell, town	377	362	-3.98
Aniwa, town	541	528	-2.40	Scott, town.	1,836	1,795	-2.23
Aniwa, village	260	244	-6.15	Sheboygan, city.	49,288	48,846	-0.90
Bartelme, town	819	798	-2.56	Sheboygan, town.	7,271	7,706	5.98
Belle Plaine, town	1,855	1,843	-0.65	Sheboygan Falls, city . .	7,775	7,951	2.26
Birnamwood, town. . . .	763	784	2.75	Sheboygan Falls, town .	1,718	1,743	1.46
Birnamwood, village (part)	802	781	-2.62	Sherman, town	1,505	1,511	0.40
Bonduel, village.	1,478	1,477	-0.07	Waldo, village	503	494	-1.79
Bowler, village.	302	287	-4.97	Wilson, town.	3,330	3,360	0.90
Cecil, village	570	562	-1.40				
Eland, village	202	195	-3.47	**Taylor.**	**20,689**	**20,746**	**0.28**
Fairbanks, town.	616	595	-3.41	Aurora, town.	422	429	1.66
Germania, town.	332	329	-0.90	Browning, town.	905	924	2.10
Grant, town	991	977	-1.41	Chelsea, town.	806	816	1.24
Green Valley, town	1,089	1,094	0.46	Cleveland, town.	268	259	-3.36
Gresham, village	586	584	-0.34	Deer Creek, town.	768	769	0.13
Hartland, town	904	900	-0.44	Ford, town	268	266	-0.75
Herman, town.	776	761	-1.93	Gilman, village	410	368	-10.24
Hutchins, town	600	585	-2.50	Goodrich, town	510	515	0.98
Lessor, town	1,263	1,282	1.50	Greenwood, town	638	639	0.16
Maple Grove, town	972	952	-2.06	Grover, town.	256	248	-3.13
Marion, city (part)	25	26	4.00	Hammel, town	713	730	2.38
Mattoon, village	438	424	-3.20	Holway, town	973	958	-1.54
Morris, town	453	447	-1.32	Jump River, town.	375	370	-1.33
Navarino, town	446	445	-0.22	Little Black, town	1,140	1,139	-0.09
Pella, town	865	875	1.16	Lublin, village	118	113	-4.24
Pulaski, village (part). . .	218	216	-0.92	Maplehurst, town.	335	328	-2.09
Red Springs, town	925	948	2.49	McKinley, town	458	463	1.09
Richmond, town	1,864	1,879	0.80	Medford, city	4,326	4,388	1.43
Seneca, town	558	552	-1.08	Medford, town	2,606	2,668	2.38
Shawano, city	9,305	9,175	-1.40	Molitor, town	324	331	2.16
Tigerton, village	741	725	-2.16	Pershing, town	180	176	-2.22
Washington, town	1,895	1,927	1.69	Rib Lake, town	852	869	2.00
Waukechon, town	1,021	1,047	2.55	Rib Lake, village.	910	885	-2.75
Wescott, town.	3,183	3,203	0.63	Roosevelt, town.	473	463	-2.11
Wittenberg, town.	833	823	-1.20	Stetsonville, village . . .	541	523	-3.33
Wittenberg, village. . . .	1,081	995	-7.96	Taft, town	430	422	-1.86
				Westboro, town.	684	687	0.44

Wisconsin population by county and municipality, continued

	2010 census	2018 estimate	% change		2010 census	2018 estimate	% change
Trempealeau	**28,816**	**29,767**	**3.30**	Webster, town.	778	812	4.37
Albion, town.	653	661	1.23	Westby, city	2,200	2,221	0.95
Arcadia, city	2,925	3,061	4.65	Wheatland, town	561	585	4.28
Arcadia, town	1,779	1,822	2.42	Whitestown, town	502	513	2.19
Blair, city	1,366	1,378	0.88				
Burnside, town	511	513	0.39	**Vilas**.	**21,430**	**21,771**	**1.59**
Caledonia, town	920	938	1.96	Arbor Vitae, town.	3,316	3,333	0.51
Chimney Rock, town. . .	241	232	-3.73	Boulder Junction, town .	933	949	1.71
Dodge, town.	389	384	-1.29	Cloverland, town	1,029	1,046	1.65
Eleva, village.	670	681	1.64	Conover, town.	1,235	1,247	0.97
Ettrick, town.	1,237	1,257	1.62	Eagle River, city	1,398	1,447	3.51
Ettrick, village	524	526	0.38	Lac du Flambeau, town .	3,441	3,477	1.05
Gale, town	1,695	1,756	3.60	Land O'Lakes, town . . .	861	879	2.09
Galesville, city	1,481	1,517	2.43	Lincoln, town	2,423	2,471	1.98
Hale, town	1,037	1,063	2.51	Manitowish Waters, town	566	587	3.71
Independence, city. . . .	1,336	1,383	3.52	Phelps, town.	1,200	1,266	5.50
Lincoln, town	823	844	2.55	Plum Lake, town	491	502	2.24
Osseo, city	1,701	1,707	0.35	Presque Isle, town	618	635	2.75
Pigeon, town	891	905	1.57	St. Germain, town	2,085	2,065	-0.96
Pigeon Falls, village . . .	411	403	-1.95	Washington, town	1,451	1,475	1.65
Preston, town	953	986	3.46	Winchester, town.	383	392	2.35
Strum, village	1,114	1,089	-2.24				
Sumner, town	810	845	4.32	**Walworth**	**102,228**	**103,535**	**1.28**
Trempealeau, town. . . .	1,756	1,894	7.86	Bloomfield, town	6,278	1,610	-74.35
Trempealeau, village. . .	1,529	1,842	20.47	Bloomfield, village[5] . . .	NA	4,703	NA
Unity, town	506	510	0.79	Burlington, city (part) . .	0	1	NA
Whitehall, city	1,558	1,570	0.77	Darien, town.	1,693	1,707	0.83
				Darien, village.	1,580	1,569	-0.70
Vernon	**29,773**	**30,248**	**1.60**	Delavan, city.	8,463	8,368	-1.12
Bergen, town	1,364	1,371	0.51	Delavan, town.	5,285	5,245	-0.76
Chaseburg, village	284	286	0.70	East Troy, town	4,021	4,048	0.67
Christiana, town	931	948	1.83	East Troy, village	4,281	4,414	3.11
Clinton, town	1,358	1,401	3.17	Elkhorn, city	10,084	9,973	-1.10
Coon, town	728	752	3.30	Fontana-on-Geneva Lake,			
Coon Valley, village. . . .	765	755	-1.31	village.	1,672	1,695	1.38
De Soto, village (part) . .	179	182	1.68	Geneva, town	4,993	5,068	1.50
Forest, town	634	648	2.21	Genoa City, village (part)	3,036	3,032	-0.13
Franklin, town.	1,140	1,177	3.25	Lafayette, town	1,979	1,990	0.56
Genoa, town.	789	802	1.65	La Grange, town	2,454	2,477	0.94
Genoa, village.	253	241	-4.74	Lake Geneva, city.	7,651	7,893	3.16
Greenwood, town	847	842	-0.59	Linn, town	2,383	2,447	2.69
Hamburg, town	973	989	1.64	Lyons, town	3,698	3,696	-0.05
Harmony, town	755	798	5.70	Mukwonago, village (part)	101	183	81.19
Hillsboro, city	1,417	1,401	-1.13	Richmond, town	1,884	1,889	0.27
Hillsboro, town	807	823	1.98	Sharon, town	907	894	-1.43
Jefferson, town	1,143	1,186	3.76	Sharon, village	1,605	1,576	-1.81
Kickapoo, town	626	667	6.55	Spring Prairie, town . . .	2,181	2,192	0.50
La Farge, village.	746	702	-5.90	Sugar Creek, town	3,943	3,930	-0.33
Liberty, town	252	269	6.75	Troy, town	2,353	2,369	0.68
Ontario, village (part) . .	554	544	-1.81	Walworth, town.	1,702	1,679	-1.35
Readstown, village. . . .	415	419	0.96	Walworth, village.	2,816	2,832	0.57
Stark, town.	363	385	6.06	Whitewater, city (part). .	11,150	11,966	7.32
Sterling, town	633	618	-2.37	Whitewater, town.	1,471	1,486	1.02
Stoddard, village	774	807	4.26	Williams Bay, village . . .	2,564	2,603	1.52
Union, town	700	722	3.14				
Viola, village (part)	222	222	0.00	**Washburn**	**15,911**	**15,929**	**0.11**
Viroqua, city	4,362	4,401	0.89	Barronett, town	442	449	1.58
Viroqua, town	1,718	1,759	2.39	Bashaw, town	946	958	1.27
				Bass Lake, town	505	527	4.36

Wisconsin population by county and municipality, continued

	2010 census	2018 esti-mate	% change		2010 census	2018 esti-mate	% change
Beaver Brook, town	713	725	1.68	Hartland, village	9,110	9,293	2.01
Birchwood, town	478	493	3.14	Lac La Belle, village (part)	289	295	2.08
Birchwood, village	442	431	-2.49	Lannon, village	1,107	1,204	8.76
Brooklyn, town	254	248	-2.36	Lisbon, town.	10,157	10,369	2.09
Casey, town	353	363	2.83	Menomonee Falls, village	35,626	37,574	5.47
Chicog, town	234	226	-3.42	Merton, town	8,338	8,449	1.33
Crystal, town	267	260	-2.62	Merton, village	3,346	3,629	8.46
Evergreen, town	1,135	1,134	-0.09	Milwaukee, city (part) . .	0	0	0.00
Frog Creek, town	130	126	-3.08	Mukwonago, town	7,959	8,024	0.82
Gull Lake, town	186	188	1.08	Mukwonago, village (part)	7,254	7,874	8.55
Long Lake, town	624	637	2.08	Muskego, city	24,135	24,812	2.81
Madge, town	508	518	1.97	Nashotah, village.	1,395	1,357	-2.72
Minong, town	917	936	2.07	New Berlin, city	39,584	40,349	1.93
Minong, village	527	523	-0.76	North Prairie, village . . .	2,141	2,214	3.41
Sarona, town	384	377	-1.82	Oconomowoc, city	15,759	16,889	7.17
Shell Lake, city	1,347	1,354	0.52	Oconomowoc, town . . .	8,408	8,679	3.22
Spooner, city	2,682	2,603	-2.95	Oconomowoc Lake, village	595	596	0.17
Spooner, town	706	726	2.83	Ottawa, town	3,859	3,917	1.50
Springbrook, town	445	439	-1.35	Pewaukee, city	13,195	14,436	9.41
Stinnett, town	246	235	-4.47	Pewaukee, village	8,166	7,983	-2.24
Stone Lake, town	508	502	-1.18	Summit, village[2]	4,674	4,754	1.71
Trego, town	932	951	2.04	Sussex, village.	10,518	11,114	5.67
				Vernon, town	7,601	7,651	0.66
Washington	**131,887**	**135,970**	**3.10**	Wales, village	2,549	2,566	0.67
Addison, town.	3,495	3,454	-1.17	Waukesha, city	70,718	71,731	1.43
Barton, town.	2,637	2,666	1.10	Waukesha, town	9,133	9,249	1.27
Erin, town	3,747	3,776	0.77				
Farmington, town	4,014	4,055	1.02	**Waupaca**	**52,410**	**52,217**	**-0.37**
Germantown, town . . .	254	246	-3.15	Bear Creek, town	823	807	-1.94
Germantown, village . .	19,749	20,183	2.20	Big Falls, village.	61	57	-6.56
Hartford, city (part). . . .	14,223	15,377	8.11	Caledonia, town	1,627	1,667	2.46
Hartford, town	3,609	3,570	-1.08	Clintonville, city.	4,559	4,477	-1.80
Jackson, town	4,134	4,437	7.33	Dayton, town	2,748	2,759	0.40
Jackson, village	6,753	7,035	4.18	Dupont, town	738	742	0.54
Kewaskum, town	1,053	1,069	1.52	Embarrass, village	404	371	-8.17
Kewaskum, village (part)	4,004	4,071	1.67	Farmington, town	3,974	3,886	-2.21
Milwaukee, city (part) . .	0	0	0.00	Fremont, town	597	595	-0.34
Newburg, village (part) .	1,157	1,157	0.00	Fremont, village	679	680	0.15
Polk, town	3,937	4,024	2.21	Harrison, town	468	473	1.07
Richfield, village	11,300	11,703	3.57	Helvetia, town.	636	633	-0.47
Slinger, village.	5,068	5,559	9.69	Iola, town.	971	989	1.85
Trenton, town	4,732	4,767	0.74	Iola, village.	1,301	1,276	-1.92
Wayne, town.	2,169	2,213	2.03	Larrabee, town	1,381	1,371	-0.72
West Bend, city	31,078	31,881	2.58	Lebanon, town	1,665	1,670	0.30
West Bend, town	4,774	4,727	-0.98	Lind, town	1,579	1,589	0.63
				Little Wolf, town	1,424	1,428	0.28
Waukesha	**389,891**	**401,446**	**2.96**	Manawa, city	1,371	1,327	-3.21
Big Bend, village	1,290	1,423	10.31	Marion, city (part)	1,235	1,210	-2.02
Brookfield, city	37,920	39,323	3.70	Matteson, town.	936	926	-1.07
Brookfield, town	6,116	6,497	6.23	Mukwa, town	2,930	2,969	1.33
Butler, village	1,841	1,824	-0.92	New London, city (part). .	5,685	5,753	1.20
Chenequa, village	590	593	0.51	Ogdensburg, village . . .	185	175	-5.41
Delafield, city	7,085	7,176	1.28	Royalton, town	1,434	1,444	0.70
Delafield, town	8,400	8,391	-0.11	St. Lawrence, town	710	702	-1.13
Dousman, village.	2,302	2,336	1.48	Scandinavia, town	1,066	1,077	1.03
Eagle, town	3,507	3,561	1.54	Scandinavia, village . . .	363	359	-1.10
Eagle, village	1,950	2,014	3.28	Union, town	806	802	-0.50
Elm Grove, village	5,934	5,921	-0.22	Waupaca, city	6,069	6,065	-0.07
Genesee, town	7,340	7,379	0.53				

Wisconsin population by county and municipality, continued

	2010 census	2018 estimate	% change		2010 census	2018 estimate	% change
Waupaca, town	1,173	1,196	1.96	Oshkosh, city	66,083	66,945	1.30
Weyauwega, city	1,900	1,882	−0.95	Oshkosh, town	2,475	2,482	0.28
Weyauwega, town	583	557	−4.46	Poygan, town	1,301	1,322	1.61
Wyoming, town.	329	303	−7.90	Rushford, town	1,561	1,582	1.35
				Utica, town.	1,299	1,325	2.00
Waushara	**24,496**	**24,441**	**−0.22**	Vinland, town	1,765	1,748	−0.96
Aurora, town.	985	999	1.42	Winchester, town	1,763	1,792	1.64
Berlin, city (part)	89	84	−5.62	Winneconne, town	2,350	2,422	3.06
Bloomfield, town	1,052	1,077	2.38	Winneconne, village . . .	2,383	2,447	2.69
Coloma, town	753	746	−0.93	Wolf River, town	1,189	1,202	1.09
Coloma, village	450	453	0.67				
Dakota, town	1,227	1,228	0.08	**Wood**	**74,749**	**74,817**	**0.09**
Deerfield, town	737	755	2.44	Arpin, town	929	962	3.55
Hancock, town	528	535	1.33	Arpin, village	333	321	−3.60
Hancock, village	417	401	−3.84	Auburndale, town	860	850	−1.16
Leon, town.	1,439	1,428	−0.76	Auburndale, village . . .	703	708	0.71
Lohrville, village	402	390	−2.99	Biron, village.	839	820	−2.26
Marion, town	2,038	2,039	0.05	Cameron, town	511	466	−8.81
Mount Morris, town . . .	1,097	1,115	1.64	Cary, town	424	418	−1.42
Oasis, town	389	399	2.57	Cranmoor, town	168	160	−4.76
Plainfield, town	550	544	−1.09	Dexter, town.	359	353	−1.67
Plainfield, village	862	847	−1.74	Grand Rapids, town . . .	7,646	7,748	1.33
Poy Sippi, town	931	909	−2.36	Hansen, town	690	687	−0.43
Redgranite, village	2,149	2,120	−1.35	Hewitt, village.	828	827	−0.12
Richford, town	612	644	5.23	Hiles, town.	167	168	0.60
Rose, town.	640	654	2.19	Lincoln, town	1,564	1,577	0.83
Saxeville, town	986	991	0.51	Marshfield, city (part) . .	18,218	18,139	−0.43
Springwater, town	1,274	1,280	0.47	Marshfield, town	764	784	2.62
Warren, town	668	662	−0.90	Milladore, town	690	679	−1.59
Wautoma, city.	2,218	2,151	−3.02	Milladore, village (part) .	276	272	−1.45
Wautoma, town.	1,278	1,277	−0.08	Nekoosa, city	2,580	2,547	−1.28
Wild Rose, village.	725	713	−1.66	Pittsville, city	874	869	−0.57
				Port Edwards, town . . .	1,427	1,412	−1.05
Winnebago	**166,994**	**170,025**	**1.82**	Port Edwards, village . .	1,818	1,773	−2.48
Algoma, town	6,822	6,956	1.96	Remington, town.	268	253	−5.60
Appleton, city (part) . . .	1,490	1,487	−0.20	Richfield, town	1,628	1,614	−0.86
Black Wolf, town	2,410	2,444	1.41	Rock, town.	855	861	0.70
Clayton, town	3,951	4,183	5.87	Rudolph, town	1,028	1,025	−0.29
Fox Crossing, village[10]. .	18,498	19,029	2.87	Rudolph, village	439	427	−2.73
Menasha, city (part) . . .	15,144	14,942	−1.33	Saratoga, town	5,142	5,179	0.72
Neenah, city	25,501	26,137	2.49	Seneca, town	1,120	1,103	−1.52
Neenah, town	3,237	3,572	10.35	Sherry, town.	803	805	0.25
Nekimi, town	1,429	1,424	−0.35	Sigel, town.	1,051	1,052	0.10
Nepeuskun, town.	710	738	3.94	Vesper, village.	584	579	−0.86
Omro, city	3,517	3,559	1.19	Wisconsin Rapids, city . .	18,367	18,587	1.20
Omro, town	2,116	2,287	8.08	Wood, town	796	792	−0.50

NA–Not available.

1. This part of this village was created from part of the town of the same name after April 1, 2010.   2. This village was created from the entire town of the same name after April 1, 2010; the 2010 figure reflects the data for the previously existing town. 3. Attached to the village of Kekoskee on October 5, 2018.   4. The town of Salem and the village of Silver Lake merged to become the village of Salem Lakes on February 14, 2017; the 2010 figure reflects the sum of the data for the previously existing town and village.   5. This village was created from part of the town of the same name after April 1, 2010.   6. Attached to the village of Maine on September 10, 2018.   7. This part of this village was created from part of the town of Buchanan after April 1, 2010. 8. This village was created from the entire town of the same name after April 2, 2019.   9. Became the village of Yorkville on April 18, 2018.   10. The village of Fox Crossing was created on April 20, 2016, from part of the town of Menasha. Subsequently, the village annexed the remainder of the town, except for three parcels that were annexed by the city of Menasha. The 2010 figure reflects the data for the previously existing town.

Sources: Wisconsin Department of Administration, Demographic Services Center, *January 1, 2018 Final Population Estimates*, October 2018; Wisconsin Department of Administration, Municipal Data System.

Wisconsin cities, January 1, 2018

City	Year incorporated	County	2010 census	2018 estimate	% change
One first class city (150,000 or more)[1]					
Milwaukee	1846	Milwaukee, Washington, Waukesha	594,833	595,555	0.12
15 second class cities (39,000–149,999)[1]					
Appleton	1857	Calumet, Outagamie, Winnebago	72,623	74,734	2.91
Eau Claire[2]	1872	Chippewa, Eau Claire	65,931	68,043	3.20
Fond du Lac[2] . . .	1852	Fond du Lac	43,021	43,921	2.09
Green Bay	1854	Brown.	104,057	105,477	1.36
Janesville[2]	1853	Rock.	63,575	63,570	–0.01
Kenosha	1850	Kenosha	99,218	99,263	0.05
La Crosse	1856	La Crosse	51,320	52,282	1.87
Madison	1856	Dane	233,209	252,546	8.29
Oshkosh[2]	1853	Winnebago	66,083	66,945	1.30
Racine.	1848	Racine.	78,860	77,807	–1.34
Sheboygan.	1853	Sheboygan.	49,288	48,846	–0.90
Waukesha	1895	Waukesha	70,718	71,731	1.43
Wausau	1872	Marathon	39,106	39,024	–0.21
Wauwatosa	1897	Milwaukee	46,396	47,781	2.99
West Allis	1906	Milwaukee	60,411	59,590	–1.36
33 third class cities (10,000–38,999)[1]					
Baraboo	1882	Sauk.	12,048	12,017	–0.26
Beaver Dam	1856	Dodge	16,214	16,861	3.99
Beloit[2]	1857	Rock.	36,966	36,683	–0.77
Brookfield	1954	Waukesha	37,920	39,323	3.70
Burlington	1900	Racine, Walworth.	10,464	10,859	3.77
Chippewa Falls . .	1869	Chippewa	13,661	14,049	2.84
Cudahy	1906	Milwaukee	18,267	18,208	–0.32
De Pere	1883	Brown.	23,800	24,699	3.78
Fort Atkinson[2] . . .	1878	Jefferson	12,368	12,390	0.18
Franklin.	1956	Milwaukee	35,451	35,779	0.93
Glendale	1950	Milwaukee	12,872	12,587	–2.21
Greenfield	1957	Milwaukee	36,720	36,366	–0.96
Hartford	1883	Dodge, Washington	14,223	15,384	8.16
Kaukauna	1885	Calumet, Outagamie.	15,462	16,049	3.80
Manitowoc.	1870	Manitowoc.	33,736	33,692	–0.13
Marinette.	1887	Marinette.	10,968	10,831	–1.25
Marshfield	1883	Marathon, Wood	19,118	19,097	–0.11
Menasha	1874	Calumet, Winnebago	17,353	17,713	2.07
Middleton	1963	Dane	17,442	20,472	17.37
Muskego	1964	Waukesha	24,135	24,812	2.81
Neenah	1873	Winnebago	25,501	26,137	2.49
New Berlin	1959	Waukesha	39,584	40,349	1.93
Oak Creek	1955	Milwaukee	34,451	35,739	3.74
Oconomowoc. . .	1875	Waukesha	15,759	16,889	7.17
Pewaukee	1999	Waukesha	13,195	14,436	9.41
River Falls.	1875	Pierce, St. Croix	15,000	15,796	5.31
Stevens Point . . .	1858	Portage.	26,717	26,749	0.12
Sun Prairie	1958	Dane	29,364	33,966	15.67
Superior	1858	Douglas.	27,244	27,257	0.05
Two Rivers[2]	1878	Manitowoc.	11,712	11,457	–2.18
Watertown.	1853	Dodge, Jefferson	23,861	23,945	0.35
West Bend	1885	Washington	31,078	31,881	2.58
Wisconsin Rapids	1869	Wood	18,367	18,587	1.20
141 fourth class cities (Under 10,000)[1]					
Abbotsford.	1965	Clark, Marathon.	2,310	2,283	–1.17
Adams	1926	Adams	1,967	1,918	–2.49
Algoma	1879	Kewaunee	3,167	3,109	–1.83

Wisconsin cities, January 1, 2018, continued

City	Year incor-porated	County	2010 census	2018 estimate	% change
Alma.	1885	Buffalo	781	774	−0.90
Altoona.	1887	Eau Claire.	6,706	7,682	14.55
Amery.	1919	Polk	2,902	2,878	−0.83
Antigo	1885	Langlade	8,234	8,312	0.95
Arcadia	1925	Trempealeau	2,925	3,061	4.65
Ashland.	1887	Ashland, Bayfield	8,216	8,082	−1.63
Augusta.	1885	Eau Claire.	1,550	1,521	−1.87
Barron.	1887	Barron.	3,423	3,341	−2.40
Bayfield	1913	Bayfield.	487	481	−1.23
Berlin	1857	Green Lake, Waushara	5,524	5,578	0.98
Black River Falls . .	1883	Jackson	3,622	3,606	−0.44
Blair	1949	Trempealeau	1,366	1,378	0.88
Bloomer	1920	Chippewa	3,539	3,563	0.68
Boscobel	1873	Grant	3,231	3,231	0.00
Brillion	1944	Calumet	3,148	3,246	3.11
Brodhead.	1891	Green, Rock	3,293	3,274	−0.58
Buffalo City	1859	Buffalo	1,023	1,015	−0.78
Cedarburg	1885	Ozaukee	11,412	11,628	1.89
Chetek	1891	Barron.	2,221	2,181	−1.80
Chilton	1877	Calumet	3,933	3,894	−0.99
Clintonville.	1887	Waupaca	4,559	4,477	−1.80
Colby	1891	Clark, Marathon.	1,852	1,800	−2.81
Columbus	1874	Columbia, Dodge.	4,991	5,127	2.72
Cornell	1956	Chippewa	1,467	1,445	−1.50
Crandon	1898	Forest	1,920	1,837	−4.32
Cuba City.	1925	Grant, Lafayette.	2,086	2,110	1.15
Cumberland	1885	Barron.	2,170	2,167	−0.14
Darlington	1877	Lafayette	2,451	2,391	−2.45
Delafield	1959	Waukesha	7,085	7,176	1.28
Delavan.	1897	Walworth.	8,463	8,368	−1.12
Dodgeville	1889	Iowa	4,693	4,700	0.15
Durand	1887	Pepin	1,931	1,868	−3.26
Eagle River	1937	Vilas	1,398	1,447	3.51
Edgerton	1883	Dane, Rock	5,461	5,613	2.78
Elkhorn	1897	Walworth.	10,084	9,973	−1.10
Elroy.	1885	Juneau	1,442	1,349	−6.45
Evansville.	1896	Rock	5,012	5,317	6.09
Fennimore	1919	Grant	2,497	2,497	0.00
Fitchburg.	1983	Dane	25,260	28,316	12.10
Fountain City . . .	1889	Buffalo	859	848	−1.28
Fox Lake	1938	Dodge	1,519	1,503	−1.05
Galesville.	1942	Trempealeau	1,481	1,517	2.43
Gillett	1944	Oconto	1,386	1,347	−2.81
Glenwood City . .	1895	St. Croix.	1,242	1,208	−2.74
Green Lake.	1962	Green Lake.	960	996	3.75
Greenwood	1891	Clark.	1,026	1,021	−0.49
Hayward	1915	Sawyer	2,318	2,380	2.67
Hillsboro	1885	Vernon	1,417	1,401	−1.13
Horicon.	1897	Dodge	3,655	3,721	1.81
Hudson	1857	St. Croix.	12,719	13,877	9.10
Hurley.	1918	Iron	1,547	1,512	−2.26
Independence. . .	1942	Trempealeau	1,336	1,383	3.52
Jefferson	1878	Jefferson	7,973	7,967	−0.08
Juneau	1887	Dodge	2,814	2,724	−3.20

Wisconsin cities, January 1, 2018, continued

City	Year incorporated	County	2010 census	2018 estimate	% change
Kewaunee	1883	Kewaunee	2,952	2,906	−1.56
Kiel	1920	Calumet, Manitowoc.	3,738	3,885	3.93
Ladysmith	1905	Rusk.	3,414	3,357	−1.67
Lake Geneva. . . .	1883	Walworth.	7,651	7,893	3.16
Lake Mills[2]	1905	Jefferson	5,708	5,953	4.29
Lancaster.	1878	Grant	3,868	3,781	−2.25
Lodi	1941	Columbia.	3,050	3,092	1.38
Loyal	1948	Clark.	1,261	1,243	−1.43
Manawa	1954	Waupaca	1,371	1,327	−3.21
Marion	1898	Shawano, Waupaca	1,260	1,236	−1.90
Markesan.	1959	Green Lake.	1,476	1,431	−3.05
Mauston	1883	Juneau	4,423	4,467	0.99
Mayville.	1885	Dodge	5,154	5,063	−1.77
Medford	1889	Taylor	4,326	4,388	1.43
Mellen	1907	Ashland.	731	710	−2.87
Menomonie	1882	Dunn	16,264	16,363	0.61
Mequon	1957	Ozaukee	23,132	23,950	3.54
Merrill.	1883	Lincoln	9,661	9,646	−0.16
Milton.	1969	Rock.	5,546	5,546	0.00
Mineral Point . . .	1857	Iowa.	2,487	2,488	0.04
Mondovi	1889	Buffalo	2,777	2,757	−0.72
Monona	1969	Dane	7,533	7,801	3.56
Monroe.	1882	Green	10,827	10,684	−1.32
Montello	1938	Marquette	1,495	1,454	−2.74
Montreal	1924	Iron	807	801	−0.74
Mosinee	1931	Marathon.	3,988	4,008	0.50
Neillsville.	1882	Clark.	2,463	2,399	−2.60
Nekoosa	1926	Wood	2,580	2,547	−1.28
New Holstein . . .	1926	Calumet	3,236	3,152	−2.60
New Lisbon	1889	Juneau	2,554	2,583	1.14
New London. . . .	1877	Outagamie, Waupaca	7,295	7,466	2.34
New Richmond . .	1885	St. Croix.	8,375	9,070	8.30
Niagara	1992	Marinette.	1,624	1,586	−2.34
Oconto	1869	Oconto	4,513	4,587	1.64
Oconto Falls	1919	Oconto	2,891	2,823	−2.35
Omro	1944	Winnebago	3,517	3,559	1.19
Onalaska	1887	La Crosse	17,736	18,788	5.93
Osseo	1941	Trempealeau	1,701	1,707	0.35
Owen	1925	Clark.	940	923	−1.81
Park Falls	1912	Price.	2,462	2,471	0.37
Peshtigo	1903	Marinette.	3,502	3,400	−2.91
Phillips	1891	Price.	1,478	1,427	−3.45
Pittsville	1887	Wood	874	869	−0.57
Platteville[2]	1876	Grant . . . . :	11,224	12,268	9.30
Plymouth.	1877	Sheboygan.	8,445	8,686	2.85
Port Washington .	1882	Ozaukee	11,250	11,713	4.12
Portage.	1854	Columbia.	10,324	10,211	−1.09
Prairie du Chien. .	1872	Crawford	5,911	5,869	−0.71
Prescott.	1857	Pierce	4,258	4,227	−0.73
Princeton.	1920	Green Lake.	1,214	1,177	−3.05
Reedsburg	1887	Sauk.	9,200	9,475	2.99
Rhinelander	1894	Oneida	7,798	7,825	0.35
Rice Lake	1887	Barron.	8,419	8,639	2.61
Richland Center. .	1887	Richland	5,184	5,144	−0.77
Ripon	1858	Fond du Lac	7,733	7,802	0.89

Wisconsin cities, January 1, 2018, continued

City	Year incorporated	County	2010 census	2018 estimate	% change
St. Croix Falls . . .	1958	Polk	2,133	2,090	−2.02
St. Francis	1951	Milwaukee	9,365	9,434	0.74
Schofield	1951	Marathon.	2,169	2,206	1.71
Seymour	1879	Outagamie.	3,451	3,443	−0.23
Shawano	1874	Shawano	9,305	9,175	−1.40
Sheboygan Falls .	1913	Sheboygan.	7,775	7,951	2.26
Shell Lake	1961	Washburn	1,347	1,354	0.52
Shullsburg	1889	Lafayette.	1,226	1,209	−1.39
South Milwaukee	1897	Milwaukee	21,156	20,882	−1.30
Sparta.	1883	Monroe	9,522	10,058	5.63
Spooner	1909	Washburn	2,682	2,603	−2.95
Stanley	1898	Chippewa, Clark	3,608	3,649	1.14
Stoughton	1882	Dane	12,611	12,854	1.93
Sturgeon Bay . . .	1883	Door.	9,144	9,363	2.40
Thorp	1948	Clark.	1,621	1,612	−0.56
Tomah	1883	Monroe	9,093	9,424	3.64
Tomahawk	1891	Lincoln	3,397	3,314	−2.44
Verona	1977	Dane	10,619	12,384	16.62
Viroqua	1885	Vernon	4,362	4,401	0.89
Washburn	1904	Bayfield.	2,117	2,104	−0.61
Waterloo	1962	Jefferson	3,333	3,362	0.87
Waupaca	1875	Waupaca	6,069	6,065	−0.07
Waupun	1878	Dodge, Fond du Lac	11,340	11,591	2.21
Wautoma.	1901	Waushara.	2,218	2,151	−3.02
Westby	1920	Vernon	2,200	2,221	0.95
Weyauwega	1939	Waupaca	1,900	1,882	−0.95
Whitehall.	1941	Trempealeau	1,558	1,570	0.77
Whitewater[2]	1885	Jefferson, Walworth	14,390	14,804	2.88
Wisconsin Dells . .	1925	Adams, Columbia, Juneau, Sauk.	2,678	2,783	3.92

1. A city is initially classified according to its population when it incorporates. If its population changes, a city can take action to change its classification, but if it does not take such action, its classification remains unchanged.   2. One of ten cities with a city manager.

Sources: Wisconsin Department of Administration, Demographic Services Center, *Official Final Estimates, 1/1/2018, Wisconsin Municipalities, with Comparison to Census 2010*, October 2018; League of Wisconsin Municipalities, *2018–2019 Directory of Wisconsin City and Village Officials*, July 2018; and data compiled by Wisconsin Legislative Reference Bureau.

Wisconsin villages, January 1, 2018

Village	Year incorporated	County	2010 census	2018 estimate	% change
Adell.	1918	Sheboygan.	516	507	−1.74
Albany	1918	Green	1,018	1,008	−0.98
Allouez	1986	Brown	13,975	13,757	−1.56
Alma Center	1902	Jackson.	503	501	−0.40
Almena	1945	Barron.	677	647	−4.43
Almond.	1905	Portage	448	432	−3.57
Amherst	1899	Portage	1,035	1,059	2.32
Amherst Junction	1912	Portage	377	379	0.53
Aniwa	1899	Shawano	260	244	−6.15
Arena	1923	Iowa.	834	830	−0.48
Argyle.	1903	Lafayette	857	842	−1.75
Arlington	1945	Columbia.	819	829	1.22

Wisconsin villages, January 1, 2018, continued

Village	Year incorporated	County	2010 census	2018 estimate	% change
Arpin	1978	Wood	333	321	-3.60
Ashwaubenon[1]	1977	Brown	16,963	16,795	-0.99
Athens	1901	Marathon	1,105	1,101	-0.36
Auburndale	1881	Wood	703	708	0.71
Avoca	1870	Iowa	637	620	-2.67
Bagley	1919	Grant	379	375	-1.06
Baldwin	1875	St. Croix	3,957	3,988	0.78
Balsam Lake	1905	Polk	1,009	1,019	0.99
Bangor	1899	La Crosse	1,459	1,538	5.41
Barneveld	1906	Iowa	1,231	1,258	2.19
Bay City	1909	Pierce	500	489	-2.20
Bayside[1]	1953	Milwaukee, Ozaukee	4,389	4,339	-1.14
Bear Creek	1902	Outagamie	448	443	-1.12
Belgium	1922	Ozaukee	2,245	2,374	5.75
Bell Center	1901	Crawford	117	116	-0.85
Belleville	1892	Dane, Green	2,385	2,401	0.67
Bellevue	2003	Brown	14,570	15,423	5.85
Belmont	1894	Lafayette	986	1,000	1.42
Benton	1892	Lafayette	973	957	-1.64
Big Bend	1928	Waukesha	1,290	1,423	10.31
Big Falls	1925	Waupaca	61	57	-6.56
Birchwood	1921	Washburn	442	431	-2.49
Birnamwood	1895	Marathon, Shawano	818	801	-2.08
Biron	1910	Wood	839	820	-2.26
Black Creek	1904	Outagamie	1,316	1,309	-0.53
Black Earth	1901	Dane	1,338	1,397	4.41
Blanchardville	1890	Iowa, Lafayette	825	816	-1.09
Bloomfield[2]	2011	Walworth	NA	4,703	NA
Bloomington	1880	Grant	735	734	-0.14
Blue Mounds	1912	Dane	855	961	12.40
Blue River	1916	Grant	434	429	-1.15
Boaz	1939	Richland	156	152	-2.56
Bonduel	1916	Shawano	1,478	1,477	-0.07
Bowler	1923	Shawano	302	287	-4.97
Boyceville	1922	Dunn	1,086	1,084	-0.18
Boyd	1891	Chippewa	552	546	-1.09
Brandon	1881	Fond du Lac	879	871	-0.91
Bristol	2009	Kenosha	4,914	5,071	3.19
Brokaw[3]	1903	Marathon	251	233	-7.17
Brooklyn	1905	Dane, Green	1,401	1,427	1.86
Brown Deer[1]	1955	Milwaukee	11,999	12,346	2.89
Brownsville	1952	Dodge	581	594	2.24
Browntown	1890	Green	280	279	-0.36
Bruce	1901	Rusk	779	767	-1.54
Butler	1913	Waukesha	1,841	1,824	-0.92
Butternut	1903	Ashland	375	369	-1.60
Cadott	1895	Chippewa	1,437	1,456	1.32
Caledonia	2005	Racine	24,705	25,021	1.28
Cambria	1866	Columbia	767	760	-0.91
Cambridge	1891	Dane, Jefferson	1,457	1,519	4.26
Cameron	1894	Barron	1,783	1,849	3.70
Campbellsport	1902	Fond du Lac	2,016	1,986	-1.49
Camp Douglas	1893	Juneau	601	621	3.33
Cascade	1914	Sheboygan	709	689	-2.82
Casco	1920	Kewaunee	583	598	2.57
Cashton	1901	Monroe	1,102	1,107	0.45
Cassville	1882	Grant	947	937	-1.06

Wisconsin villages, January 1, 2018, continued

Village	Year incorporated	County	2010 census	2018 estimate	% change
Iron Ridge	1913	Dodge	929	928	−0.11
Ironton	1914	Sauk	253	255	0.79
Jackson	1912	Washington	6,753	7,035	4.18
Johnson Creek	1903	Jefferson	2,738	2,997	9.46
Junction City	1911	Portage	439	437	−0.46
Kekoskee	1958	Dodge	161	158	−1.86
Kellnersville	1971	Manitowoc	332	333	0.30
Kendall	1894	Monroe	472	464	−1.69
Kennan	1903	Price	135	123	−8.89
Kewaskum	1895	Fond du Lac, Washington	4,004	4,071	1.67
Kimberly	1910	Outagamie	6,468	6,686	3.37
Kingston	1923	Green Lake	326	326	0.00
Knapp	1905	Dunn	463	459	−0.86
Kohler	1912	Sheboygan	2,120	2,105	−0.71
Kronenwetter	2002	Marathon	7,210	7,733	7.25
La Farge	1899	Vernon	746	702	−5.90
La Valle	1883	Sauk	367	348	−5.18
Lac La Belle	1931	Jefferson, Waukesha	290	296	2.07
Lake Delton	1954	Sauk	2,914	2,919	0.17
Lake Hallie	2003	Chippewa	6,448	7,029	9.01
Lake Nebagamon	1907	Douglas	1,069	1,084	1.40
Lannon	1930	Waukesha	1,107	1,204	8.76
Lena	1921	Oconto	564	552	−2.13
Lime Ridge	1910	Sauk	162	153	−5.56
Linden	1900	Iowa	549	538	−2.00
Little Chute	1899	Outagamie	10,449	11,120	6.42
Livingston	1914	Grant, Iowa	664	655	−1.36
Loganville	1917	Sauk	300	287	−4.33
Lohrville	1910	Waushara	402	390	−2.99
Lomira	1899	Dodge	2,430	2,491	2.51
Lone Rock	1886	Richland	888	873	−1.69
Lowell	1894	Dodge	340	329	−3.24
Lublin	1915	Taylor	118	113	−4.24
Luck	1905	Polk	1,119	1,084	−3.13
Luxemburg	1908	Kewaunee	2,515	2,596	3.22
Lyndon Station	1903	Juneau	500	487	−2.60
Lynxville	1899	Crawford	132	133	0.76
Maiden Rock	1887	Pierce	119	117	−1.68
Maine[6]	2015	Marathon	2,337	2,338	0.04
Maple Bluff	1930	Dane	1,313	1,299	−1.07
Marathon City	1884	Marathon	1,524	1,566	2.76
Maribel	1963	Manitowoc	351	350	−0.28
Marquette	1958	Green Lake	150	151	0.67
Marshall	1905	Dane	3,862	3,856	−0.16
Mason	1925	Bayfield	93	92	−1.08
Mattoon	1901	Shawano	438	424	−3.20
Mazomanie	1885	Dane	1,652	1,664	0.73
McFarland	1920	Dane	7,808	8,527	9.21
Melrose	1914	Jackson	503	490	−2.58
Melvina	1922	Monroe	104	103	−0.96
Menomonee Falls[1]	1892	Waukesha	35,626	37,574	5.47
Merrillan	1881	Jackson	542	520	−4.06
Merrimac	1899	Sauk	420	423	0.71
Merton	1922	Waukesha	3,346	3,629	8.46
Milladore	1933	Portage, Wood	276	272	−1.45
Milltown	1910	Polk	917	911	−0.65

Wisconsin villages, January 1, 2018, continued

Village	Year incorporated	County	2010 census	2018 estimate	% change
Minong	1915	Washburn	527	523	-0.76
Mishicot	1950	Manitowoc	1,442	1,438	-0.28
Montfort	1893	Grant, Iowa	718	724	0.84
Monticello	1891	Green	1,217	1,218	0.08
Mount Calvary	1962	Fond du Lac	762	568	-25.46
Mount Hope	1919	Grant	225	226	0.44
Mount Horeb	1899	Dane	7,009	7,240	3.30
Mount Pleasant	2003	Racine	26,197	26,912	2.73
Mount Sterling	1936	Crawford	211	209	-0.95
Mukwonago	1905	Walworth, Waukesha	7,355	8,057	9.54
Muscoda	1894	Grant, Iowa	1,299	1,255	-3.39
Nashotah	1957	Waukesha	1,395	1,357	-2.72
Necedah	1870	Juneau	916	912	-0.44
Nelson	1978	Buffalo	374	376	0.53
Nelsonville	1913	Portage	155	155	0.00
Neosho	1902	Dodge	574	569	-0.87
Neshkoro	1906	Marquette	434	416	-4.15
New Auburn	1902	Barron, Chippewa	548	550	0.36
Newburg	1973	Ozaukee, Washington	1,254	1,253	-0.08
New Glarus	1901	Green	2,172	2,173	0.05
Nichols	1967	Outagamie	273	271	-0.73
North Bay	1951	Racine	241	234	-2.90
North Fond du Lac	1903	Fond du Lac	5,014	5,203	3.77
North Freedom	1893	Sauk	701	671	-4.28
North Hudson	1912	St. Croix	3,768	3,758	-0.27
North Prairie	1919	Waukesha	2,141	2,214	3.41
Norwalk	1894	Monroe	638	640	0.31
Oakdale	1988	Monroe	297	289	-2.69
Oakfield	1903	Fond du Lac	1,075	1,094	1.77
Oconomowoc Lake	1959	Waukesha	595	596	0.17
Ogdensburg	1912	Waupaca	185	175	-5.41
Oliver	1917	Douglas	399	437	9.52
Ontario	1890	Vernon, Monroe	554	544	-1.81
Oostburg	1909	Sheboygan	2,887	2,976	3.08
Oregon	1883	Dane	9,231	10,078	9.18
Orfordville	1900	Rock	1,442	1,440	-0.14
Osceola	1886	Polk	2,568	2,629	2.38
Oxford	1912	Marquette	607	594	-2.14
Paddock Lake	1960	Kenosha	2,992	2,972	-0.67
Palmyra	1866	Jefferson	1,781	1,757	-1.35
Pardeeville	1894	Columbia	2,115	2,096	-0.90
Park Ridge	1938	Portage	491	497	1.22
Patch Grove	1921	Grant	198	201	1.52
Pepin	1860	Pepin	837	816	-2.51
Pewaukee	1876	Waukesha	8,166	7,983	-2.24
Pigeon Falls	1956	Trempealeau	411	403	-1.95
Plain	1912	Sauk	773	754	-2.46
Plainfield	1882	Waushara	862	847	-1.74
Pleasant Prairie	1989	Kenosha	19,719	21,166	7.34
Plover	1971	Portage	12,123	12,814	5.70
Plum City	1909	Pierce	599	591	-1.34
Poplar	1917	Douglas	603	611	1.33
Port Edwards	1902	Wood	1,818	1,773	-2.48
Potosi	1887	Grant	688	677	-1.60
Potter	1980	Calumet	253	250	-1.19
Pound	1914	Marinette	377	373	-1.06
Poynette	1892	Columbia	2,528	2,528	0.00

Wisconsin villages, January 1, 2018, continued

Village	Year incorporated	County	2010 census	2018 estimate	% change
Prairie du Sac	1885	Sauk.	3,972	4,152	4.53
Prairie Farm	1901	Barron.	473	459	−2.96
Prentice.	1899	Price.	660	650	−1.52
Pulaski	1910	Brown, Oconto, Shawano.	3,539	3,552	0.37
Radisson	1953	Sawyer	241	239	−0.83
Randolph.	1870	Columbia, Dodge.	1,811	1,792	−1.05
Random Lake	1907	Sheboygan.	1,594	1,567	−1.69
Raymond[7]	2019	Racine.	3,870	3,988	3.05
Readstown	1898	Vernon	415	419	0.96
Redgranite.	1904	Waushara.	2,149	2,120	−1.35
Reedsville	1892	Manitowoc.	1,206	1,185	−1.74
Reeseville	1899	Dodge	708	718	1.41
Rewey.	1902	Iowa.	292	287	−1.71
Rib Lake	1902	Taylor	910	885	−2.75
Richfield	2008	Washington	11,300	11,703	3.57
Ridgeland	1921	Dunn	273	270	−1.10
Ridgeway.	1902	Iowa.	653	644	−1.38
Rio.	1887	Columbia.	1,059	1,059	0.00
River Hills[1]	1930	Milwaukee	1,597	1,568	−1.82
Roberts	1945	St. Croix.	1,651	1,719	4.12
Rochester	1912	Racine.	3,682	3,800	3.20
Rockdale	1914	Dane	214	214	0.00
Rockland	1919	La Crosse, Monroe	594	679	14.31
Rock Springs.	1894	Sauk.	362	303	−16.30
Rosendale	1915	Fond du Lac	1,063	1,035	−2.63
Rosholt	1907	Portage.	506	484	−4.35
Rothschild	1917	Marathon.	5,269	5,314	0.85
Rudolph	1960	Wood	439	427	−2.73
St. Cloud	1909	Fond du Lac	477	471	−1.26
St. Nazianz	1956	Manitowoc.	783	766	−2.17
Salem Lakes[8]	2017	Kenosha	14,478	14,531	0.37
Sauk City	1854	Sauk.	3,410	3,436	0.76
Saukville	1915	Ozaukee	4,451	4,429	−0.49
Scandinavia	1894	Waupaca	363	359	−1.10
Sharon	1892	Walworth.	1,605	1,576	−1.81
Sheldon.	1917	Rusk.	237	231	−2.53
Sherwood	1968	Calumet	2,713	3,114	14.78
Shiocton	1903	Outagamie.	921	928	0.76
Shorewood[1]	1900	Milwaukee	13,162	13,315	1.16
Shorewood Hills	1927	Dane	1,565	2,238	43.00
Siren.	1948	Burnett	806	789	−2.11
Sister Bay.	1912	Door.	876	938	7.08
Slinger	1869	Washington	5,068	5,559	9.69
Soldiers Grove.	1888	Crawford	592	562	−5.07
Solon Springs	1920	Douglas.	600	597	−0.50
Somers[2]	2015	Kenosha	NA	8,827	NA
Somerset.	1915	St. Croix.	2,635	2,761	4.78
South Wayne	1911	Lafayette	489	485	−0.82
Spencer.	1902	Marathon.	1,925	1,932	0.36
Spring Green	1869	Sauk.	1,628	1,630	0.12
Spring Valley.	1895	Pierce, St. Croix	1,352	1,353	0.07
Star Prairie	1900	St. Croix.	561	553	−1.43
Stetsonville	1949	Taylor	541	523	−3.33
Steuben	1900	Crawford	131	122	−6.87
Stockbridge	1908	Calumet	636	651	2.36
Stockholm	1903	Pepin	66	62	−6.06
Stoddard	1911	Vernon	774	807	4.26
Stratford	1910	Marathon.	1,578	1,607	1.84

Wisconsin villages, January 1, 2018, continued

Village	Year incorporated	County	2010 census	2018 estimate	% change
Strum	1948	Trempealeau	1,114	1,089	-2.24
Sturtevant	1907	Racine.	6,970	6,615	-5.09
Suamico	2003	Brown.	11,346	12,676	11.72
Sullivan.	1915	Jefferson	669	660	-1.35
Summit.	2010	Waukesha	4,674	4,754	1.71
Superior	1949	Douglas.	664	654	-1.51
Suring.	1914	Oconto	544	521	-4.23
Sussex.	1924	Waukesha	10,518	11,114	5.67
Taylor	1919	Jackson.	476	485	1.89
Tennyson.	1940	Grant	355	364	2.54
Theresa	1898	Dodge	1,262	1,252	-0.79
Thiensville	1910	Ozaukee	3,235	3,192	-1.33
Tigerton	1896	Shawano	741	725	-2.16
Tony.	1911	Rusk.	113	109	-3.54
Trempealeau	1867	Trempealeau	1,529	1,842	20.47
Turtle Lake	1898	Barron, Polk	1,050	1,037	-1.24
Twin Lakes	1937	Kenosha	5,989	6,068	1.32
Union Center	1913	Juneau	200	197	-1.50
Union Grove	1893	Racine.	4,915	4,978	1.28
Unity	1903	Clark, Marathon.	343	337	-1.75
Valders	1919	Manitowoc.	962	953	-0.94
Vesper.	1948	Wood	584	579	-0.86
Viola.	1899	Richland, Vernon	699	694	-0.72
Waldo.	1922	Sheboygan.	503	494	-1.79
Wales	1922	Waukesha	2,549	2,566	0.67
Walworth.	1901	Walworth.	2,816	2,832	0.57
Warrens.	1973	Monroe	363	354	-2.48
Waterford	1906	Racine.	5,368	5,503	2.51
Waunakee	1893	Dane	12,097	13,675	13.04
Wausaukee.	1924	Marinette.	575	563	-2.09
Wauzeka	1890	Crawford	711	691	-2.81
Webster.	1916	Burnett	653	649	-0.61
West Baraboo	1956	Sauk.	1,414	1,581	11.81
Westfield	1902	Marquette	1,254	1,242	-0.96
West Milwaukee	1906	Milwaukee	4,206	4,159	-1.12
Weston	1996	Marathon.	14,868	15,445	3.88
West Salem	1893	La Crosse	4,799	5,042	5.06
Weyerhaeuser.	1906	Rusk.	238	231	-2.94
Wheeler.	1922	Dunn	348	343	-1.44
Whitefish Bay[1]	1892	Milwaukee	14,110	14,199	0.63
White Lake.	1926	Langlade	363	361	-0.55
Whitelaw	1958	Manitowoc.	757	755	-0.26
Whiting.	1947	Portage.	1,724	1,683	-2.38
Wild Rose.	1904	Waushara.	725	713	-1.66
Williams Bay	1919	Walworth.	2,564	2,603	1.52
Wilson.	1911	St. Croix.	184	187	1.63
Wilton.	1890	Monroe	504	496	-1.59
Wind Point	1954	Racine.	1,723	1,689	-1.97
Windsor[6]	2015	Dane	6,345	7,795	22.85
Winneconne.	1887	Winnebago	2,383	2,447	2.69
Winter.	1973	Sawyer	313	314	0.32
Withee	1901	Clark.	487	492	1.03
Wittenberg.	1893	Shawano	1,081	995	-7.96
Wonewoc	1878	Juneau	816	799	-2.08
Woodman	1917	Grant	132	129	-2.27
Woodville	1911	St. Croix.	1,344	1,319	-1.86
Wrightstown.	1901	Brown, Outagamie	2,827	2,925	3.47

Wisconsin villages, January 1, 2018, continued

Village	Year incor- porated	County	2010 census	2018 estimate	% change
Wyeville	1923	Monroe.	147	137	−6.80
Wyocena	1909	Columbia.	768	738	−3.91
Yorkville[9]	2018	Racine.	3,071	3,139	2.21
Yuba.	1935	Richland	74	63	−14.86

Note: There are 412 villages in Wisconsin as of April 2, 2019.

NA–Not available.

1. One of ten villages with an appointed village manager.   2. This village was created from part of a town after the date reflected by the 2010 data.   3. The village of Brokaw attached to the village of Maine on September 1, 2018.   4. The village of Fox Crossing was created on April 20, 2016, from part of the town of Menasha; the 2010 figure reflects data for the town of Menasha.   5. This village was created from parts of two towns after the date reflected by the 2010 data.   6. One of two villages that were created from a whole town after the date reflected by the 2010 data. The 2010 figure reflects the data for the previously existing town.   7. The village of Raymond was created from the entire town of the same name after April 2, 2019.   8. This village was created on February 14, 2017, by the merger of a whole village and a whole town. The 2010 figure reflects the combined data for the previously existing village and town.   9. The village of Yorkville was created on April 18, 2018, from the town of Yorkville. The 2010 and 2018 figures reflect data for the previously existing town.

Sources: Wisconsin Department of Administration, Demographic Services Center, *Official Final Estimates, 1/1/2018, Wisconsin Municipalities, with Comparison to Census 2010*, October 2018; Wisconsin Department of Administration, Municipal Data System, *Certificate of Incorporation: Village of Fox Crossing*, April 20, 2016; League of Wisconsin Municipalities, *2018–2019 Directory of Wisconsin City and Village Officials*, November 2018; and data compiled by Wisconsin Legislative Reference Bureau.

Wisconsin cities and villages over 10,000 population, January 1, 2018

City or village (county)	2018 estimate[1]	2010 census	% change	2018 rank	2010 non- white,[2] non- Hispanic	2010 Hispanic or Latino origin[3]
Cities						
Milwaukee (Milwaukee, Washington, Waukesha)	595,555	594,833	0.12	1	271,607	103,007
Madison (Dane).	252,546	233,209	8.29	2	40,798	15,948
Green Bay (Brown)	105,477	104,057	1.36	3	13,912	13,896
Kenosha (Kenosha).	99,263	99,218	0.05	4	14,121	16,130
Racine (Racine)	77,807	78,860	−1.34	5	20,362	16,309
Appleton (Calumet, Outagamie, Winnebago) . .	74,734	72,623	2.91	6	7,124	3,643
Waukesha (Waukesha)	71,731	70,718	1.43	7	5,321	8,529
Eau Claire (Chippewa, Eau Claire)	68,043	65,931	3.20	8	5,116	1,268
Oshkosh (Winnebago).	66,945	66,083	1.30	9	5,539	1,770
Janesville (Rock)	63,570	63,575	−0.01	10	3,689	3,421
West Allis (Milwaukee).	59,590	60,411	−1.36	11	5,094	5,770
La Crosse (La Crosse).	52,282	51,320	1.87	12	4,885	1,012
Sheboygan (Sheboygan)	48,846	49,288	−0.90	13	6,314	4,866
Wauwatosa (Milwaukee)	47,781	46,396	2.99	14	4,361	1,450
Fond du Lac (Fond du Lac)	43,921	43,021	2.09	15	2,695	2,742
New Berlin (Waukesha)	40,349	39,584	1.93	16	2,256	1,036
Brookfield (Waukesha)	39,323	37,920	3.70	17	3,545	853
Wausau (Marathon)	39,024	39,106	−0.21	18	5,891	1,149
Beloit (Rock)	36,683	36,966	−0.77	20	7,149	6,332
Greenfield (Milwaukee)	36,366	36,720	−0.96	21	3,043	3,087
Franklin (Milwaukee)	35,779	35,451	0.93	22	4,168	1,592
Oak Creek (Milwaukee)	35,739	34,451	3.74	23	3,282	2,582
Sun Prairie (Dane)	33,966	29,364	15.67	24	3,749	1,253
Manitowoc (Manitowoc)	33,692	33,736	−0.13	25	2,486	1,695
West Bend (Washington)	31,881	31,078	2.58	26	1,049	1,213
Fitchburg (Dane)	28,316	25,260	12.10	27	4,464	4,341

Wisconsin cities and villages over 10,000 population, January 1, 2018, continued

City or village (county)	2018 estimate[1]	2010 census	% change	2018 rank	2010 non-white,[2] non-Hispanic	2010 Hispanic or Latino origin[3]
Superior (Douglas).	27,257	27,244	0.05	28	2,166	382
Stevens Point (Portage).	26,749	26,717	0.12	30	1,946	696
Neenah (Winnebago)	26,137	25,501	2.49	31	1,163	967
Muskego (Waukesha)	24,812	24,135	2.81	33	529	545
De Pere (Brown).	24,699	23,800	3.78	34	1,207	511
Mequon (Ozaukee).	23,950	23,132	3.54	35	1,760	467
Watertown (Dodge, Jefferson).	23,945	23,861	0.35	36	706	1,731
South Milwaukee (Milwaukee).	20,882	21,156	-1.30	38	1,100	1,699
Middleton (Dane).	20,472	17,442	17.37	39	1,764	984
Marshfield (Marathon, Wood)	19,097	19,118	-0.11	42	796	452
Onalaska (La Crosse).	18,788	17,736	5.93	44	1,539	276
Wisconsin Rapids (Wood).	18,587	18,367	1.20	45	1,186	535
Cudahy (Milwaukee).	18,208	18,267	-0.32	46	1,142	1,769
Menasha (Calumet, Winnebago)	17,713	17,353	2.07	47	954	1,204
Oconomowoc (Waukesha)	16,889	15,759	7.17	48	422	559
Beaver Dam (Dodge).	16,861	16,214	3.99	49	502	1,210
Menomonie (Dunn)	16,363	16,264	0.61	51	1,176	276
Kaukauna (Calumet, Outagamie)	16,049	15,462	3.80	52	654	407
River Falls (Pierce, St. Croix).	15,796	15,000	5.31	53	673	270
Hartford (Dodge, Washington).	15,384	14,223	8.16	56	425	686
Whitewater (Jefferson, Walworth)	14,804	14,390	2.88	57	1,009	1,372
Pewaukee (Waukesha)	14,436	13,195	9.41	59	667	281
Chippewa Falls (Chippewa).	14,049	13,661	2.84	62	605	221
Hudson (St. Croix)	13,877	12,719	9.10	63	539	347
Stoughton (Dane)	12,854	12,611	1.93	67	554	230
Glendale (Milwaukee).	12,587	12,872	-2.21	71	2,499	465
Fort Atkinson (Jefferson)	12,390	12,368	0.18	72	315	1,128
Verona (Dane).	12,384	10,619	16.62	73	617	258
Platteville (Grant).	12,268	11,224	9.30	75	535	179
Baraboo (Sauk)	12,017	12,048	-0.26	76	487	446
Port Washington (Ozaukee)	11,713	11,250	4.12	78	457	347
Cedarburg (Ozaukee)	11,628	11,412	1.89	80	367	197
Waupun (Dodge, Fond du Lac)	11,591	11,340	2.21	81	1,651	217
Two Rivers (Manitowoc).	11,457	11,712	-2.18	82	536	224
Burlington (Racine, Walworth).	10,859	10,464	3.77	85	327	898
Marinette (Marinette)	10,831	10,968	-1.25	86	271	149
Monroe (Green)	10,684	10,827	-1.32	87	252	526
Portage (Columbia)	10,211	10,324	-1.09	89	811	414
Sparta (Monroe)	10,058	9,522	5.63	92	345	643
Villages						
Menomonee Falls (Waukesha).	37,574	35,626	5.47	19	2,789	697
Mount Pleasant (Racine)	26,912	26,197	2.73	29	2,714	2,181
Caledonia (Racine)	25,021	24,705	1.28	32	1,563	1,303
Pleasant Prairie (Kenosha)	21,166	19,719	7.34	37	1,141	1,332
Germantown (Washington)	20,183	19,749	2.20	40	1,334	400
Howard (Brown, Outagamie).	19,508	17,399	12.12	41	919	410
Fox Crossing (Winnebago)[4]	19,029	18,498	2.87	43	1,030	1,131
Ashwaubenon (Brown)	16,795	16,963	-0.99	50	1,375	471
Weston (Marathon)	15,445	14,868	3.88	54	1,670	301
Bellevue (Brown)	15,423	14,570	5.85	55	970	1,359
Salem Lakes (Kenosha)[5].	14,531	14,478	0.37	58	330	644
Greendale (Milwaukee).	14,345	14,046	2.13	60	805	667
Whitefish Bay (Milwaukee)	14,199	14,110	0.63	61	1,060	399
Allouez (Brown).	13,757	13,975	-1.56	64	1,252	383
Waunakee (Dane).	13,675	12,097	13.04	65	416	269

Wisconsin cities and villages over 10,000 population, January 1, 2018, continued

City or village (county)	2018 estimate[1]	2010 census	% change	2018 rank	2010 non-white,[2] non-Hispanic	2010 Hispanic or Latino origin[3]
Shorewood (Milwaukee)	13,315	13,162	1.16	66	1,416	447
Plover (Portage).	12,814	12,123	5.70	68	684	393
Harrison (Calumet, Outagamie)[6]	12,786	NA	NA	69	NA	NA
Suamico (Brown)	12,676	11,346	11.72	70	242	112
Brown Deer (Milwaukee)	12,346	11,999	2.89	74	4,358	471
Grafton (Ozaukee)	11,803	11,459	3.00	77	421	266
Richfield (Washington)	11,703	11,300	3.57	79	304	162
Little Chute (Outagamie)	11,120	10,449	6.42	83	337	327
Sussex (Waukesha).	11,114	10,518	5.67	84	431	249
DeForest (Dane)	10,221	8,936	14.38	88	467	325
Holmen (La Crosse)	10,147	9,005	12.68	90	827	96
Oregon (Dane)	10,078	9,231	9.18	91	344	204

NA–Not available.

1. Population estimates are based on the corrected 2010 Census totals. Race and ethnicity data have not been adjusted since the 2010 Census.   2. In the 2010 Census, respondents were allowed to choose more than one race. The column "nonwhite" includes all who chose at least one race other than white.   3. "Hispanic or Latino Origin" represents ethnicity and includes people of Cuban, Mexican, Puerto Rican, South or Central American, or other Spanish culture or origin, regardless of race. 4. The village of Fox Crossing was created on April 20, 2016, from part of the town of Menasha. The village subsequently annexed the remainder of the town, except for three parcels that were annexed by the city of Menasha. The 2010 figures reflect the data for the previously existing town.   5. The village of Salem Lakes was created on February 14, 2017, by the merger of the village of Silver Lake and the town of Salem.   The 2010 figures reflect the combined data for the previously existing village and town.   6. This village was created from parts of two towns after the date reflected by the 2010 data.

Sources: Wisconsin Department of Administration, Demographic Services Center, *Official Final Estimates, 1/1/2018, Wisconsin Municipalities, with Comparison to Census 2010,* October 2018, and *Population and Hispanic & Non-Hispanic Data, Wisconsin Municipalities, Census 2000 and 2010 Comparisons; Based on Census 2010 Geography,* March 2011.

Wisconsin towns over 2,500 population, January 1, 2018

Town (county)	2018 estimate	2010 census	% change	Town (county)	2018 estimate	2010 census	% change
Addison (Washington) . .	3,454	3,495	-1.17	Dayton (Waupaca)	2,759	2,748	0.40
Alden (Polk)	2,803	2,786	0.61	Delafield (Waukesha) . . .	8,391	8,400	-0.11
Algoma (Winnebago) . . .	6,956	6,822	1.96	Delavan (Walworth)	5,245	5,285	-0.76
Arbor Vitae (Vilas)	3,333	3,316	0.51	Dover (Racine)	4,193	4,051	3.51
Ashippun (Dodge)	2,617	2,559	2.27	Dunn (Dane).	4,927	4,931	-0.08
Barton (Washington) . . .	2,666	2,637	1.10	Eagle (Waukesha)	3,561	3,507	1.54
Beaver Dam (Dodge). . . .	4,029	3,962	1.69	Eagle Point (Chippewa) . .	3,193	3,053	4.59
Beloit (Rock)	7,613	7,662	-0.64	East Troy (Walworth). . . .	4,048	4,021	0.67
Bristol (Dane)	4,221	3,765	12.11	Ellington (Outagamie). . .	2,999	2,758	8.74
Brockway (Jackson)	2,890	2,828	2.19	Empire (Fond du Lac) . . .	2,814	2,797	0.61
Brookfield (Waukesha) . .	6,497	6,116	6.23	Erin (Washington)	3,776	3,747	0.77
Buchanan (Outagamie) . .	6,969	6,755	3.17	Farmington (Washington)	4,055	4,014	1.02
Burke (Dane).	3,327	3,284	1.31	Farmington (Waupaca) . .	3,886	3,974	-2.21
Burlington (Racine)	6,494	6,502	-0.12	Fond du Lac (Fond du Lac)	3,859	3,015	27.99
Campbell (La Crosse) . . .	4,324	4,314	0.23	Freedom (Outagamie). . .	6,057	5,842	3.68
Cedarburg (Ozaukee) . . .	5,927	5,760	2.90	Friendship (Fond du Lac) .	2,692	2,675	0.64
Center (Outagamie)	3,564	3,402	4.76	Fulton (Rock)	3,337	3,252	2.61
Chase (Oconto)	3,206	3,005	6.69	Genesee (Waukesha) . . .	7,379	7,340	0.53
Clayton (Winnebago) . . .	4,183	3,951	5.87	Geneva (Walworth)	5,068	4,993	1.50
Cottage Grove (Dane) . . .	3,895	3,875	0.52	Grafton (Ozaukee)	4,159	4,053	2.62
Dale (Outagamie).	2,852	2,731	4.43	Grand Chute (Outagamie)	22,701	20,919	8.52

Wisconsin towns over 2,500 population, January 1, 2018,
continued

Town (county)	2018 estimate	2010 census	% change	Town (county)	2018 estimate	2010 census	% change
Grand Rapids (Wood) . . .	7,748	7,646	1.33	Peshtigo (Marinette)	4,127	4,057	1.73
Greenbush (Sheboygan) .	2,551	2,565	-0.55	Pine Lake (Oneida)	2,763	2,740	0.84
Greenville (Outagamie) . .	11,785	10,309	14.32	Pittsfield (Brown)	2,752	2,608	5.52
Harmony (Rock).	2,582	2,569	0.51	Pleasant Springs (Dane). .	3,222	3,154	2.16
Hartford (Washington) . .	3,570	3,609	-1.08	Pleasant Valley (Eau Claire)	3,286	3,044	7.95
Hayward (Sawyer)	3,575	3,567	0.22	Plymouth (Sheboygan) . .	3,228	3,195	1.03
Holland (La Crosse).	4,190	3,701	13.21	Polk (Washington)	4,024	3,937	2.21
Hudson (St. Croix)	8,692	8,461	2.73	Randall (Kenosha)	3,201	3,180	0.66
Hull (Portage)	5,401	5,346	1.03	Rib Mountain (Marathon)	6,906	6,825	1.19
Ixonia (Jefferson)	4,887	4,385	11.45	Rice Lake (Barron)	3,110	3,060	1.63
Jackson (Washington) . . .	4,437	4,134	7.33	Richmond (St. Croix)	3,614	3,272	10.45
Janesville (Rock)	3,489	3,434	1.60	Rock (Rock)	3,182	3,196	-0.44
Koshkonong (Jefferson). .	3,665	3,692	-0.73	Rome (Adams)	2,790	2,720	2.57
Lac du Flambeau (Vilas). .	3,477	3,441	1.05	St. Joseph (St. Croix)	4,020	3,842	4.63
Lafayette (Chippewa) . . .	6,069	5,765	5.27	Saratoga (Wood)	5,179	5,142	0.72
Lawrence (Brown)	5,286	4,284	23.39	Scott (Brown)	3,655	3,545	3.10
Ledgeview (Brown)	7,948	6,555	21.25	Sevastopol (Door)	2,723	2,628	3.61
Lima (Sheboygan)	2,975	2,982	-0.23	Seymour (Eau Claire). . . .	3,340	3,209	4.08
Lisbon (Waukesha).	10,369	10,157	2.09	Sheboygan (Sheboygan) .	7,706	7,271	5.98
Little Suamico (Oconto). .	5,182	4,799	7.98	Shelby (La Crosse)	4,710	4,715	-0.11
Lodi (Columbia).	3,323	3,273	1.53	Somerset (St. Croix)	4,238	4,036	5.00
Lyons (Walworth).	3,696	3,698	-0.05	Sparta (Monroe)	3,209	3,128	2.59
Madison (Dane).	6,295	6,279	0.25	Springfield (Dane)	2,909	2,734	6.40
Medford (Taylor)	2,668	2,606	2.38	Stanley (Barron).	2,570	2,546	0.94
Menominee (Menominee)	4,258	4,232	0.61	Star Prairie (St. Croix) . . .	3,583	3,504	2.25
Menomonie (Dunn)	3,487	3,366	3.59	Stephenson (Marinette). .	3,080	3,006	2.46
Merrill (Lincoln).	3,032	2,980	1.74	Stettin (Marathon)	2,579	2,554	0.98
Merton (Waukesha)	8,449	8,338	1.33	Stockton (Portage)	3,000	2,917	2.85
Middleton (Dane).	6,440	5,877	9.58	Sugar Creek (Walworth). .	3,930	3,943	-0.33
Milton (Rock)	2,979	2,923	1.92	Taycheedah (Fond du Lac)	4,534	4,205	7.82
Minocqua (Oneida)	4,511	4,453	1.30	Trenton (Washington). . .	4,767	4,732	0.74
Mukwa (Waupaca)	2,969	2,930	1.33	Troy (St. Croix).	5,308	4,705	12.82
Mukwonago (Waukesha) .	8,024	7,959	0.82	Union (Eau Claire)	2,802	2,663	5.22
Neenah (Winnebago) . . .	3,572	3,237	10.35	Vernon (Waukesha)	7,651	7,601	0.66
Newbold (Oneida)	2,755	2,719	1.32	Washington (Eau Claire). .	7,355	7,134	3.10
Norway (Racine)	8,013	7,948	0.82	Waterford (Racine)	6,465	6,344	1.91
Oakland (Jefferson)	3,111	3,100	0.35	Waukesha (Waukesha) . .	9,249	9,133	1.27
Oconomowoc (Waukesha)	8,679	8,408	3.22	Wescott (Shawano).	3,203	3,183	0.63
Onalaska (La Crosse). . . .	5,803	5,623	3.20	West Bend (Washington) .	4,727	4,774	-0.98
Oneida (Outagamie)	4,729	4,678	1.09	Westport (Dane)	4,018	3,950	1.72
Oregon (Dane)	3,235	3,184	1.60	Wheatland (Kenosha) . . .	3,369	3,373	-0.12
Osceola (Polk)	2,906	2,855	1.79	Wheaton (Chippewa) . . .	2,788	2,701	3.22
Ottawa (Waukesha)	3,917	3,859	1.50	Wilson (Sheboygan)	3,360	3,330	0.90
Pacific (Columbia)	2,723	2,707	0.59	Yorkville (Racine)[1]	3,139	3,071	2.21
Pelican (Oneida)	2,816	2,764	1.88				

1. On April 18, 2018 the town of Yorkville became a village.

Source: Wisconsin Department of Administration, Demographic Services Center, *Official Final Estimates, 10/10/2018, Wisconsin Municipalities, with Comparison to Census 2010*, October 2018.

ELECTION RESULTS AND WISCONSIN PARTIES

Political parties qualifying for ballot status as of April 2019
in the order they will be listed on the ballot

Democratic Party of Wisconsin

15 N Pinckney Street, Suite 200, Madison, WI 53703; 608-255-5172; www.wisdems.org

Executive political director . . . . .Devin Remiker
Executive party operations director . . . . Breianna Hasenzahl-Reeder
Communications director . . . . Courtney Beyer
Party affairs director. . . . . .Will Hoffman
Digital communications director . . . . Chuck Engel
Data director . . . . Ali Nikseresht
Finance director . . . . Tom McCann
Membership manager. . . . . Gabriela Luna
Candidate services director . . . . Hannah Mullen
Compliance and operations managers . . . . .Dee Hanson, Joshua Rubin

State Administrative Committee
Party officers . . . . .Martha Laning, Sheboygan, *chair*; David Bowen, Milwaukee, *first vice chair*;
Mandela Barnes, Milwaukee, *second vice chair*; Meg Andrietsch, Racine, *secretary*;
Randy Udell, Madison, *treasurer*
National committee members. . . . . Martha Love, Milwaukee; Andrew Werthmann, Eau Claire;
Khary Penebaker, Hartland; Janet Bewley, Mason; Jason Rae,
College Democrats representative . . . . Shea Senger, Milwaukee
Young Democrats representative. . . . . .Sarah Smith, Milwaukee
Milwaukee County chair . . . . .Rob Hansen, Greenfield
At-large members . . . . Dian Palmer, Brookfield; Gretchen Lowe, Madison;
Michael Childers, La Pointe; Paul DeMain, Hayward;
David Duran, Lodi; Yee L. Xiong, Weston;
Mary Lang Sollinger, Madison; Penny Bernard Schaber, Appleton;
Melissa Lemke, Racine; Luke Fuszard, Middleton;
Sarah Lloyd, Wisconsin Dells; Ryan Greendeer, Black River Falls;
Gail Hohenstein, Green Bay
County Chairs Association chair. . . . . Peter Hellios, Granton
Assembly representative . . . . JoCasta Zamarripa, Milwaukee
Senate representative. . . . . Janis Ringhand, Evansville
CD 1 representative . . . . .Mary Jonker, Kenosha, *chair*; Matt Lowe, Muskego
CD 2 representative . . . . Christine Welcher, Stoughton, *chair*; Mike Martez Johnson, Madison
CD 3 representative . . . . .Lisa Herrmann, Eau Claire, *chair*; George Wilbur, La Farge
CD 4 representative . . . . Terrell Martin, Milwaukee, *chair*; Michelle Bryant, Milwaukee
CD 5 representative . . . . Justin Koestler, Waukesha, *chair*; Karen Kirsch, Greenfield
CD 6 representative . . . . Ben Stepanek, Oshkosh, *chair*; Debra Dassow, Cedarburg
CD 7 representative . . . . Melissa Schroeder, Merrill, *chair*; Paul Knuth, Rhinelander
CD 8 representative . . . . Mary Ginnebaugh, Green Bay, *chair*; Mark Waltman, Appleton

Republican Party of Wisconsin

PO Box 628250, Middleton, WI 53562; 608-257-4765; www.wisgop.org

Executive director . . . . Mark Jefferson
Political director . . . . .Phil Curry
Research and communications director. . . . . Charles Nichols
Finance director . . . . Richelle Wileman
Data and digital director . . . . David Bredemus
Grassroots director. . . . . Carlton Huffman
African American outreach director . . . . .Khenzer Senat
Hispanic outreach director. . . . . Mario Herrera

Political parties qualifying for ballot status as of April 2019, continued

Republican Party of Wisconsin, continued

Operation director . . . . .Jordan Wileman
Telemarketing manager. . . . . .Rich Dickie

Executive Committee

Party officers . . . . Andrew Hitt, Madison, *chair and first vice chair;*
Katie McCallum, Middleton, *second vice chair;* Laurie Forcier, Eau Claire, *third vice chair;*
Andrew Davis, Mikwaukee, *fourth vice chair;* Tyler August, Lake Geneva, *party secretary;*
Brian Westrate, Fall Creek, *party treasurer;* Tom Schreibel, Madison, *national committeeman;*
Mary Buestrin, River Hills, *national committeewoman*
Immediate past chair . . . . Brad Courtney, Whitefish Bay
At-large member . . . . Maripat Krueger, Menomonie
Wisconsin African American Council chair . . . . .Gerard Randall, Milwaukee
Wisconsin Republican Labor Council chair . . . . Van Wanggaard, Racine
Wisconsin Hispanic Heritage Council chair . . . . Ivan Gamboa, Greendale
CD 1 representative . . . . Kim Travis, Williams Bay, *chair;* Carol Brunner, Franklin, *vice chair*
CD 2 representative . . . . Kim Babler, Madison, *chair;* Tim McCumber, Merrimac, *vice chair*
CD 3 representative . . . . Bill Feehan, La Crosse, *chair;* Brian Westrate, Fall Creek, *vice chair*
CD 4 representative . . . . Bob Spindell, Milwaukee, *chair;* Doug Haag, Milwaukee, *vice chair*
CD 5 representative . . . . Kathy Kiernan, Richfield, *chair;* Keith Best, Waukesha, *vice chair*
CD 6 representative . . . . Darryl Carlson, Sheboygan, *chair;* Al Ott, Forest Junction, vice chair
CD 7 representative . . . . Jim Miller, Hayward, *chair;* Jesse Garza, Hudson, *vice chair*
CD 8 representative . . . . .Kelly Ruh, Green Bay, *chair;* Bill Berglund, Sturgeon Bay, *vice chair*

Libertarian Party of Wisconsin

PO Box 20815, Greenfield, WI 53220; 800-236-9236; www.lpwi.org

Executive Committee

Party officers . . . . Phillip Anderson, Madison, *chair;* Tyler Danke, Fremont, *vice chair;*
Rick Braun, Milwaukee, *secretary;* Adam Markert, Menasha, *treasurer*
At-large members . . . . .Chris Nass, Madison; Nathan Gall, Hayward
CD 1 representative . . . . .Jim Sewell, Oak Creek; Rachael Doan, *alternate*
CD 2 representative . . . . .Adam Grassnickle, Madison; Sasha Anderson, Madison, *alternate*
CD 3 representative . . . . Scott Noble, Stevens Point; Kevin Litten, Cadott, *alternate*
CD 4 representative . . . . .Matt Bughman, Milwaukee; Michael Chianese, Milwaukee, *alternate*
CD 5 representative . . . . Jeff Kortsch, Oconomowoc; Terry Virgil, Cambridge, *alternate*
CD 6 representative . . . . .Brian Defferding, Neenah; Daniel Bartelme, Neenah, *alternate*
CD 7 representative . . . . Robert Burke, Hudson; Trevor Massey, Dresser, *alternate*
CD 8 representative . . . . William Jacobson, Peshtigo

Wisconsin Green Party

PO Box 108, Madison, WI 53701; info@wisconsingreenparty.org; www.wisconsingreenparty.org

Coordinating Council

Party officers . . . . . Dave Schwab, *cochair;* Barbara Dahlgren, *cochair;* Keith Brumley, *recording secretary;*
Dace Zeps, *corresponding secretary;* Nathan Pelkey, *operations treasurer*
CD 1 representative . . . . .Joe Witkowiak, Greendale; Kevin Rydzik, Racine
CD 2 representative . . . . .vacant
CD 3 representative . . . . Michael White, La Crosse; Olga Anderson, La Crosse
CD 4 representative . . . . .Tom Rodman, Milwaukee
CD 5 representative . . . . Bruce Hinkforth, Oconomowoc
CD 6 representative . . . . Jeff Reese, Fond du Lac
CD 7 representative . . . . vacant
CD 8 representative . . . . .vacant

County vote for U.S. senator, August 14, 2018 partisan primary, continued

	Tammy Baldwin* (Dem.)	Charles Barman (Rep.)	Griffin Jones (Rep.)	George C. Lucia (Rep.)	Kevin Nicholson (Rep.)	Leah Vukmir (Rep.)	Total
Marinette.	1,984	149	163	373	2,455	1,904	7,029
Marquette	1,153	50	36	140	687	422	2,497
Menominee	303	3	1	7	33	35	382
Milwaukee	103,967	379	415	923	13,431	27,389	147,234
Monroe	2,384	120	101	212	2,398	1,052	6,278
Oconto	1,765	175	212	428	3,012	2,196	7,789
Oneida	2,971	137	131	281	2,195	1,856	7,593
Outagamie.	12,288	352	334	707	8,063	6,705	28,450
Ozaukee	7,972	102	89	240	4,278	8,118	20,839
Pepin	604	12	12	34	239	174	1,075
Pierce	2,683	61	67	214	785	816	4,631
Polk	2,573	156	250	552	1,485	997	6,013
Portage.	6,306	51	55	113	2,121	1,607	10,279
Price.	1,109	12	17	52	587	496	2,273
Racine.	16,029	134	157	383	6,927	9,001	32,719
Richland	1,401	24	26	57	423	273	2,204
Rock.	16,468	213	282	485	3,507	3,261	24,356
Rusk.	977	73	59	181	1,052	544	2,889
St. Croix.	4,903	143	200	526	2,354	1,800	9,950
Sauk.	5,952	152	100	292	1,870	1,241	9,607
Sawyer	1,286	54	62	216	826	463	2,911
Shawano	1,864	156	195	427	2,717	2,209	7,569
Sheboygan.	7,772	102	102	230	5,298	5,569	19,107
Taylor	837	76	76	185	1,074	780	3,029
Trempealeau	2,661	38	47	113	823	604	4,302
Vernon	3,317	43	53	103	949	614	5,093
Vilas	1,873	37	35	110	1,309	1,018	4,388
Walworth.	6,876	154	127	320	3,932	4,951	16,400
Washburn	1,157	161	187	431	1,128	550	3,622
Washington	6,757	250	235	474	7,124	12,963	27,806
Waukesha	26,647	392	390	823	18,057	40,062	86,519
Waupaca	2,993	85	79	213	2,607	1,829	7,816
Waushara.	1,205	106	118	211	1,812	1,396	4,849
Winnebago	11,537	152	184	272	5,884	4,590	22,664
Wood	5,319	191	178	308	3,968	2,531	12,496
Total.	**510,812**	**7,959**	**8,699**	**18,786**	**191,276**	**217,230**	**957,189**

Note: County totals include scattered votes in the following partisan primaries: Constitution, Democratic, Libertarian, Republican, and Wisconsin Green.

*Incumbent. Dem.–Democrat; Rep.–Republican.

Source: Official records of the Wisconsin Elections Commission.

County vote for U.S. senator, November 6, 2018 general election

	Tammy Baldwin* (Dem.)	Leah Vukmir (Rep.)	Total
Adams	4,537	4,854	9,399
Ashland.	4,533	2,351	6,892
Barron.	8,571	9,911	18,493
Bayfield.	5,541	3,233	8,775

County vote for U.S. senator, November 6, 2018 general election, continued

	Tammy Baldwin* (Dem.)	Leah Vukmir (Rep.)	Total
Brown	59,132	55,750	115,066
Buffalo	2,945	2,968	5,917
Burnett	3,239	4,289	7,528
Calumet	10,741	12,822	23,563
Chippewa	13,798	13,830	27,629
Clark	5,084	6,558	11,644
Columbia	15,230	11,674	26,940
Crawford	3,852	2,703	6,555
Dane	228,050	65,515	293,979
Dodge	16,007	21,482	37,490
Door	9,442	7,494	16,947
Douglas	11,689	6,925	18,622
Dunn	9,743	8,623	18,367
Eau Claire	29,614	18,957	48,642
Florence	729	1,438	2,167
Fond du Lac	19,065	25,496	44,602
Forest	1,879	2,062	3,944
Grant	10,554	8,860	19,420
Green	10,294	6,732	17,037
Green Lake	3,222	4,893	8,117
Iowa	7,270	3,835	11,114
Iron	1,459	1,605	3,064
Jackson	4,370	3,611	7,981
Jefferson	18,055	19,809	37,911
Juneau	4,658	5,429	10,096
Kenosha	38,296	29,181	67,589
Kewaunee	4,287	5,158	9,454
La Crosse	35,731	21,160	56,891
Lafayette	3,592	2,900	6,493
Langlade	3,889	5,239	9,128
Lincoln	6,463	6,901	13,379
Manitowoc	16,541	18,795	35,373
Marathon	29,084	32,661	61,813
Marinette	7,520	9,731	17,252
Marquette	3,337	3,791	7,134
Menominee	896	220	1,116
Milwaukee	280,426	111,684	392,858
Monroe	8,151	8,559	16,731
Oconto	7,042	10,392	17,449
Oneida	9,338	10,112	19,473
Outagamie	41,618	41,354	82,974
Ozaukee	21,464	29,480	51,010
Pepin	1,529	1,578	3,107
Pierce	9,216	8,247	17,466
Polk	8,299	10,245	18,544
Portage	20,170	14,510	34,725
Price	3,136	3,515	6,651
Racine	45,397	41,213	86,750
Richland	4,000	2,980	6,986
Rock	42,616	25,322	68,011
Rusk	2,654	3,381	6,046
St. Croix	18,765	21,069	39,864
Sauk	16,960	11,866	28,826
Sawyer	3,938	4,159	8,100
Shawano	7,414	10,438	17,852
Sheboygan	24,183	28,667	52,925

County vote for U.S. senator, November 6, 2018 general election, continued

	Tammy Baldwin* (Dem.)	Leah Vukmir (Rep.)	Total
Taylor	3,028	5,005	8,035
Trempealeau	6,526	5,633	12,168
Vernon	7,495	5,459	12,959
Vilas	5,308	7,166	12,491
Walworth	20,299	24,844	45,216
Washburn	3,664	4,190	7,858
Washington	23,072	47,102	70,175
Waukesha	84,147	136,190	220,630
Waupaca	9,509	12,792	22,316
Waushara	4,434	6,106	10,540
Winnebago	40,185	35,282	75,585
Wood	15,992	16,899	32,919
Total	**1,472,914**	**1,184,885**	**2,660,763**
% of total vote	**55.36**	**44.53**	

Note: County totals include scattered and write-in votes. Write-in candidate Mary Jo Walters received a total of 28 votes. Write-in candidate John Schiess received a total of 14 votes.

*Incumbent. Dem.–Democrat; Rep.–Republican.

Source: Official records of the Wisconsin Elections Commission.

District vote for U.S. representatives, August 14, 2018 partisan primary

First congressional district

County	Randy Bryce (Dem.)	Cathy Myers (Dem.)	Brad Boivin (Rep.)	Paul Nehlen (Rep.)	Nick Polce (Rep.)	Jeremy Ryan (Rep.)	Kevin Adam Steen (Rep.)	Bryan Steil (Rep.)
Kenosha	7,672	6,202	167	955	1,489	977	2,528	3,747
Milwaukee (part)	5,249	3,313	152	882	660	1,094	508	4,998
Racine	11,325	5,713	197	1,281	2,883	1,343	1,754	8,524
Rock (part)	5,192	4,546	78	660	630	369	232	2,509
Walworth (part)	3,641	2,678	116	1,304	2,019	854	585	3,940
Waukesha (part)	3,327	2,247	214	1,556	1,267	1,589	655	7,167
Total	**36,406**	**24,699**	**924**	**6,638**	**8,948**	**6,226**	**6,262**	**30,885**

Second congressional district

County	Mark Pocan* (Dem.)	Joey Wayne Reed (Rep.)
Dane	95,321	5
Green	3,315	0
Iowa	2,559	0
Lafayette	1,067	0
Richland (part)	232	0
Rock (part)	7,024	0
Sauk	5,728	9
Total	**115,246**	**14**

District vote for U.S. representatives, August 14, 2018 partisan primary, continued

Third congressional district

County	Ron Kind* (Dem.)	Steve Toft (Rep.)
Adams	1,581	1,430
Buffalo	1,126	777
Chippewa (part)	2,711	1,666
Crawford	1,466	679
Dunn	3,704	2,989
Eau Claire	10,628	4,465
Grant	3,003	1,733
Jackson (part)	1,847	816
Juneau (part)	1,202	1,050
La Crosse	10,853	4,793
Monroe (part)	2,167	3,018
Pepin	598	427
Pierce	2,645	1,836
Portage	6,243	2,843
Richland (part)	1,146	562
Trempealeau	2,683	1,510
Vernon	3,156	1,540
Wood (part)	2,884	3,634
Total	59,643	35,768

Fourth congressional district

County	George R. Gary (Dem.)	Gwen S. Moore* (Dem.)	Tim Rogers (Rep.)	Cindy Werner (Rep.)
Milwaukee (part)	9,468	76,991	8,912	7,122
Waukesha (part)	0	0	0	0
Total	9,468	76,991	8,912	7,122

Fifth congressional district

County	Ramon Garcia (Dem.)	Tom Palzewicz (Dem.)	F. James Sensenbrenner, Jr.* (Rep.)	Jennifer Hoppe Vipond (Rep.)
Dodge (part)	1	1,557	4,252	1,242
Jefferson	0	5,284	5,583	1,332
Milwaukee (part)	4	13,070	9,901	1,858
Walworth (part)	0	649	309	72
Washington	0	5,696	17,213	3,564
Waukesha (part)	0	16,936	36,139	8,943
Total	5	43,192	73,397	17,011

Sixth congressional district

County	Dan Kohl (Dem.)	Glenn Grothman* (Rep.)
Columbia	4,536	3,344
Dodge (part)	2,163	4,805
Fond du Lac	4,394	9,550

District vote for U.S. representatives, August 14, 2018 partisan primary, continued

Sixth congressional district, continued

County	Dan Kohl (Dem.)	Glenn Grothman* (Rep.)
Green Lake.	847	1,617
Manitowoc.	4,037	5,815
Marquette.	1,083	1,286
Milwaukee (part).	243	171
Ozaukee.	7,113	11,654
Sheboygan.	6,994	10,208
Waushara.	1,126	3,351
Winnebago (part).	9,326	8,684
Total.	**41,862**	**60,485**

Seventh congressional district

County	Margaret Engebretson (Dem.)	Brian Ewert (Dem.)	Bob Look (Dem.)	Sean P. Duffy* (Rep.)
Ashland.	1,420	647	0	834
Barron.	1,283	1,333	0	2,554
Bayfield.	1,583	923	0	1,014
Burnett.	660	313	0	2,047
Chippewa (part).	779	592	0	1,755
Clark.	518	733	0	2,948
Douglas.	2,722	1,069	0	1,766
Florence.	122	49	0	1,023
Forest.	263	152	0	1,718
Iron.	381	136	0	497
Jackson (part).	99	47	0	162
Juneau (part).	219	113	0	499
Langlade.	574	430	0	1,621
Lincoln.	907	817	0	4,158
Marathon.	4,363	4,351	10	10,360
Monroe (part).	116	61	0	453
Oneida.	1,407	1,439	1	4,319
Polk.	1,926	641	0	3,545
Price.	569	524	0	1,105
Rusk.	479	472	0	1,904
Sawyer.	760	513	0	1,685
St. Croix.	3,529	1,353	0	5,002
Taylor.	344	475	0	2,129
Vilas.	1,024	751	0	2,356
Washburn.	709	431	0	2,592
Wood (part).	438	1,920	0	2,662
Total.	**27,194**	**20,285**	**11**	**60,708**

Eighth congressional district

County	Beau Liegeois (Dem.)	Mike Gallagher* (Rep.)
Brown.	13,506	16,062
Calumet.	2,306	5,130

District vote for U.S. representatives, August 14, 2018 partisan primary, continued

Eighth congressional district, continued

County	Beau Liegeois (Dem.)	Mike Gallagher* (Rep.)
Door.	2,934	2,700
Kewaunee	1,124	1,583
Marinette.	1,767	4,859
Menominee	220	71
Oconto	1,573	5,820
Outagamie.	10,224	15,287
Shawano	1,625	5,433
Waupaca	2,632	4,575
Winnebago (part).	539	1,004
Total.	38,450	62,524

Note: County totals include scattered votes.

*Incumbent. Dem.–Democrat; Lib.–Libertarian; Rep.–Republican.

Source: Official records of the Wisconsin Elections Commission.

District vote for U.S. representatives, November 6, 2018 general election

First congressional district

County	Bryan Steil (Rep.)	Randy Bryce (Dem.)	Ken Yorgan (Ind.)
Kenosha	31,784	33,130	2,340
Milwaukee (part)	26,207	18,463	1,422
Racine.	44,412	39,337	2,859
Rock (part)	14,525	19,256	956
Walworth (part).	25,106	14,368	1,265
Waukesha (part)	35,458	12,954	1,164
Total.	177,492	137,508	10,006
% of total vote[1]	54.56	42.27	3.08

Second congressional district

County	Mark Pocan* (Dem.)	Joey Wayne Reed (write-in)
Dane	239,624	11
Green	12,121	2
Iowa.	8,454	10
Lafayette	4,564	1
Richland (part)	1,020	0
Rock (part).	23,574	1
Sauk.	19,759	4
Total.	309,116	29
% of total vote[1]	97.42	0.01

District vote for U.S. representatives, November 6, 2018 general election, continued

Eighth congressional district

County	Mike Gallagher* (Rep.)	Beau Liegeois (Dem.)
Brown.	69,402	45,320
Calumet	15,806	7,647
Door.	9,863	7,025
Kewaunee	6,490	2,951
Marinette.	12,017	5,273
Menominee	307	784
Oconto	12,734	4,722
Outagamie.	50,393	31,819
Shawano	12,739	5,070
Waupaca	15,360	6,888
Winnebago (part).	4,299	1,766
Total.	209,410	119,265
% of total vote[1]	63.69	36.28

Note: Write in candidates received the following totals: Joseph Kexel, 7 votes; Bradley Jason Burt, 1 vote; Rick Cruz, 8 votes; Ramon Garcia, 1 vote; Bob Look, 3 votes.

*Incumbent. Dem.–Democrat; Rep.–Republican; Lib.–Libertarian; Ind.--Independent.

1. Percentages do not add up to 100, as scattered and write-in votes have been omitted.

Source: Official records of the Wisconsin Elections Commission.

County vote for governor, August 14, 2018 partisan primary

	Democrat										Republican		Phillip Anderson (Lib.)	Michael J. White (WGR)	Total
	Tony Evers	Mahlon Mitchell	Kelda Helen Roys	Kathleen Vinehout	Mike McCabe	Matt Flynn	Paul R. Soglin	Andy Gronik	Dana Wachs	Josh Pade	Scott Walker*	Robert Meyer			
Adams	900	123	163	116	109	99	199	28	23	12	1,636	186	6	5	3,607
Ashland	1,015	154	150	165	285	199	44	37	24	9	845	118	5	2	3,055
Barron	1,564	152	126	314	172	211	42	71	44	12	2,521	174	14	4	5,422
Bayfield	1,219	191	159	263	481	125	48	42	28	8	1,004	94	8	3	3,673
Brown	8,735	1,599	1,932	859	1,155	1,389	737	235	135	56	16,492	1,316	73	35	34,772
Buffalo	410	28	27	542	57	40	23	12	14	6	827	62	3	8	2,061
Burnett	359	79	94	149	92	107	25	57	28	9	1,921	387	3	9	3,319
Calumet	1,480	194	395	120	292	187	128	42	15	13	5,051	639	15	4	8,579
Chippewa	2,412	241	215	747	242	272	53	51	89	14	3,778	305	17	6	8,444
Clark	815	51	73	160	106	87	38	12	26	5	2,852	582	6	5	4,819
Columbia	2,440	651	696	412	334	259	844	32	21	24	3,409	334	14	4	9,478
Crawford	706	83	38	318	205	78	99	18	11	8	736	89	5	3	2,397
Dane	40,135	12,098	19,983	11,155	10,003	2,354	8,531	304	236	155	17,590	1,818	219	120	124,786
Dodge	1,952	723	467	282	252	281	488	69	36	13	9,833	1,788	26	11	16,221
Door	1,999	211	394	413	166	229	151	38	14	6	2,694	242	8	3	6,571
Douglas	1,458	680	269	339	247	434	59	188	85	10	1,679	223	14	8	5,702
Dunn	1,604	194	196	777	388	232	65	70	81	18	3,060	514	21	6	7,227
Eau Claire	5,170	654	748	2,122	1,489	505	130	69	353	30	4,964	371	32	12	16,665
Florence	88	10	13	18	16	18	6	6	2	2	982	229	1	1	1,392
Fond du Lac	2,702	437	588	234	398	410	244	74	28	17	9,750	1,124	23	9	16,045
Forest	255	21	33	30	26	48	9	17	7	6	1,617	401	8	5	2,488
Grant	1,478	313	281	311	225	140	390	33	22	8	1,763	260	18	5	5,249
Green	1,519	371	457	393	257	198	535	27	11	4	1,678	191	8	4	5,656
Green Lake	462	76	91	61	61	75	87	15	7	5	1,618	146	7	3	2,716
Iowa	1,154	271	288	314	264	107	349	15	9	5	1,035	104	9	3	3,931
Iron	328	29	23	51	32	41	22	18	10	3	481	53	9	0	1,094
Jackson	697	82	44	908	130	79	38	28	20	6	1,037	90	11	4	3,174
Jefferson	2,663	925	715	448	516	331	754	68	22	16	6,902	432	19	11	13,829
Juneau	732	196	119	157	92	94	261	24	8	3	1,581	169	8	4	3,453
Kenosha	5,852	2,441	1,311	831	702	1,140	350	358	207	117	9,369	851	46	11	23,614

County vote for governor, August 14, 2018 partisan primary, continued

	Democrat										Republican				Total
	Tony Evers	Mahlon Mitchell	Kelda Helen Roys	Kathleen Vinehout	Mike McCabe	Matt Flynn	Paul R. Soglin	Andy Gronik	Dana Wachs	Josh Pade	Scott Walker*	Robert Meyer	Phillip Anderson (Lib.)	Michael J. White (WGR)	
Kewaunee	665	104	105	96	65	112	53	17	5	8	1,556	112	3	1	2,902
La Crosse	5,511	987	823	1,408	2,027	384	304	105	74	30	5,319	454	44	27	17,499
Lafayette	524	92	114	86	62	61	227	12	6	3	735	80	6	1	2,012
Langlade	636	83	86	57	77	70	22	30	10	3	1,592	135	14	0	2,817
Lincoln	1,037	137	161	115	99	111	37	45	27	6	3,733	1,103	4	1	6,629
Manitowoc	2,475	415	465	280	209	408	241	65	30	13	6,055	484	21	10	11,180
Marathon	5,471	510	1,383	481	505	478	201	118	87	25	10,242	789	47	19	20,374
Marinette	1,068	119	150	95	116	325	89	42	19	10	4,491	821	10	12	7,367
Marquette	444	163	101	84	64	78	250	20	9	4	1,241	137	3	2	2,605
Menominee	110	8	16	16	17	60	8	16	4	2	70	16	1	0	344
Milwaukee	35,708	39,914	15,292	4,246	4,839	7,799	2,926	1,325	832	498	40,663	2,174	207	135	156,705
Monroe	1,314	128	95	458	203	105	67	45	25	8	3,306	686	15	8	6,465
Oconto	1,008	116	129	83	128	196	77	34	17	4	5,184	1,088	10	7	8,084
Oneida	1,637	155	242	209	296	149	110	53	24	11	4,074	713	4	3	7,689
Outagamie	6,273	899	2,286	549	1,333	779	466	145	79	48	15,008	1,795	47	28	29,738
Ozaukee	3,597	1,108	1,331	405	540	704	319	93	58	42	12,350	443	29	6	21,037
Pepin	217	15	17	319	31	8	5	9	10	0	463	31	4	4	1,133
Pierce	822	201	213	824	324	173	48	72	24	9	1,854	178	10	6	4,759
Polk	1,106	162	161	465	240	250	46	108	57	14	3,298	508	33	11	6,460
Portage	3,684	654	805	492	563	332	180	77	53	31	3,698	322	22	12	10,933
Price	672	67	82	99	123	63	23	26	13	5	1,157	86	5	3	2,424
Racine	5,917	4,493	1,865	716	839	1,326	503	257	156	71	15,818	841	48	27	32,906
Richland	607	141	126	217	91	73	237	13	4	11	767	88	5	4	2,384
Rock	7,117	2,562	1,392	1,101	1,554	900	2,780	277	148	59	7,398	725	54	25	26,119
Rusk	567	38	32	127	78	73	14	22	17	5	1,819	273	6	5	3,076
St. Croix	1,906	352	513	906	536	404	99	153	95	17	5,018	409	35	11	10,468
Sauk	2,568	538	696	878	392	266	910	38	23	19	3,422	380	16	4	10,150
Sawyer	596	50	73	151	183	154	42	43	18	9	1,621	183	2	6	3,134
Shawano	975	111	207	130	141	176	73	44	14	6	4,933	884	18	14	7,728
Sheboygan	4,080	1,211	933	315	420	604	297	134	57	28	10,878	507	25	2	19,497

County vote for governor, August 14, 2018 partisan primary, continued

	Democrat										Republican				
	Tony Evers	Mahlon Mitchell	Kelda Helen Roys	Kathleen Vinehout	Mike McCabe	Matt Flynn	Paul R. Soglin	Andy Gronik	Dana Wachs	Josh Pade	Scott Walker*	Robert Meyer	Phillip Anderson (Lib.)	Michael J. White (WGR)	Total
Taylor	491	30	71	65	65	74	23	18	15	4	1,989	350	5	2	3,205
Trempealeau	1,178	95	80	1,011	198	131	46	32	28	9	1,568	139	9	9	4,539
Vernon	1,493	221	217	726	420	129	147	44	37	26	1,656	141	12	7	5,287
Vilas	1,043	86	156	140	235	91	69	36	15	5	2,406	111	4	1	4,399
Walworth	3,071	1,259	777	437	352	495	313	143	80	32	9,019	535	30	14	16,572
Washburn	565	62	73	154	119	101	25	57	20	6	2,326	656	9	1	4,179
Washington	2,945	1,191	923	365	410	621	238	119	60	24	20,128	1,041	27	8	28,102
Waukesha	12,644	4,428	4,381	1,513	1,225	1,978	1,062	324	197	116	57,389	2,509	90	35	87,954
Waupaca	1,485	223	296	204	374	239	145	60	12	13	4,417	465	20	6	7,962
Waushara	573	106	109	86	109	133	93	20	8	6	3,202	595	10	11	5,061
Winnebago	5,973	967	1,562	651	1,170	851	462	160	84	39	10,098	922	52	17	23,023
Wood	3,006	447	459	399	319	347	132	118	49	29	6,610	1,068	7	4	12,994
Total	225,082	87,926	69,086	44,168	39,885	31,580	28,158	6,627	4,216	1,908	417,276	38,269	1,673	817	997,334

Note: County totals include scattered votes. Democratic write-in candidate Paul Boucher received a total of ten votes. Republican write-in candidates Ryan Cason and Adam Nicholas Paul received, respectively, a total of 11 votes and a total of seven votes. Constitution write-in candidate Mark S. Grimek received a total of 11 votes.

*Incumbent. Lib.–Libertarian; WGR–Wisconsin Green.

Source: Official records of the Wisconsin Elections Commission.

County vote for lieutenant governor, August 14, 2018 partisan primary

	Democrat		Rebecca Kleefisch* (Rep.)	Patrick Baird (Lib.)	Tiffany Anderson (WGR)	Total
	Mandela Barnes	Kurt J. Kober				
Adams	871	651	1,619	6	4	3,153
Ashland.	1,150	634	755	5	1	2,548
Barron.	1,499	951	2,448	13	3	4,922
Bayfield.	1,581	624	936	7	3	3,154
Brown.	8,819	5,764	15,853	73	37	30,630
Buffalo	555	436	801	4	8	1,808
Burnett	550	354	1,910	2	9	2,826
Calumet	1,473	1,038	5,000	15	2	7,531
Chippewa	2,234	1,567	3,613	16	4	7,434
Clark.	683	503	2,757	6	5	3,957
Columbia	3,347	1,753	3,448	16	3	8,587
Crawford	815	586	716	4	3	2,125
Dane	71,083	22,386	17,173	214	123	111,375
Dodge	2,475	1,595	10,158	24	9	14,261
Door.	2,107	1,183	2,610	7	4	5,921
Douglas.	2,070	1,328	1,631	14	7	5,057
Dunn	2,120	1,309	3,143	20	8	6,600
Eau Claire.	6,610	3,206	4,823	33	10	14,732
Florence	103	63	980	1	1	1,149
Fond du Lac	2,541	2,032	9,570	27	9	14,199
Forest	205	177	1,550	7	4	1,948
Grant	1,835	1,102	1,850	18	6	4,822
Green	2,214	1,196	1,673	8	4	5,104
Green Lake.	503	346	1,619	6	3	2,480
Iowa.	1,711	812	1,046	9	2	3,589
Iron	302	190	474	3	0	969
Jackson	923	839	1,024	10	4	2,800
Jefferson	3,801	1,921	6,824	17	8	12,601
Juneau	881	615	1,616	8	6	3,142
Kenosha	7,382	4,584	9,112	43	11	21,202
Kewaunee	640	531	1,514	3	1	2,689
La Crosse.	6,479	3,532	5,163	44	25	15,245
Lafayette	640	411	738	6	2	1,800
Langlade	546	396	1,529	14	1	2,489
Lincoln	935	728	3,892	2	1	5,584
Manitowoc.	2,197	2,031	5,894	21	11	10,174
Marathon.	5,263	3,052	9,939	48	19	18,375
Marinette.	991	803	4,654	11	11	6,470
Marquette	655	411	1,288	3	2	2,361
Menominee	132	74	74	1	0	281
Milwaukee.	78,483	22,000	37,855	202	128	139,100
Monroe.	1,274	930	3,605	14	9	5,847
Oconto	852	742	5,517	8	7	7,130
Oneida	1,692	1,009	4,084	4	2	6,819
Outagamie.	7,130	4,127	14,995	51	27	26,330
Ozaukee	4,535	2,888	11,861	29	6	19,359
Pepin	352	189	456	1	3	1,001
Pierce	1,652	850	1,875	10	6	4,396
Polk	1,546	905	3,407	31	12	5,902
Portage.	3,870	2,127	3,320	21	11	9,360
Price.	593	390	1,067	5	3	2,058
Racine.	9,930	5,373	15,285	46	25	30,728
Richland	878	465	777	5	4	2,129
Rock.	10,343	5,885	7,378	53	19	23,736
Rusk.	521	344	1,797	5	5	2,676
St. Croix.	3,038	1,406	4,831	35	11	9,338

County vote for lieutenant governor, August 14, 2018 partisan primary, continued

	Democrat		Rebecca Kleefisch* (Rep.)	Patrick Baird (Lib.)	Tiffany Anderson (WGR)	Total
	Mandela Barnes	Kurt J. Kober				
Sauk.	3,740	1,994	3,452	15	4	9,206
Sawyer	749	428	1,585	1	6	2,773
Shawano	1,000	730	5,146	16	15	6,907
Sheboygan.	3,008	4,593	10,372	27	5	18,036
Taylor	430	330	1,997	5	2	2,768
Trempealeau	1,270	1,175	1,542	9	8	4,013
Vernon	1,919	1,115	1,641	11	7	4,700
Vilas.	1,038	654	2,301	3	1	4,002
Walworth.	4,007	2,462	8,777	28	13	15,317
Washburn	662	421	2,424	8	2	3,520
Washington	3,820	2,511	19,332	27	7	25,698
Waukesha	16,090	8,617	55,162	94	35	80,253
Waupaca.	1,616	1,166	4,477	20	7	7,298
Waushara.	664	445	3,389	8	8	4,514
Winnebago	6,679	3,998	9,771	49	17	20,565
Wood	2,553	2,011	6,525	6	4	11,099
Total.	326,855	153,994	407,420	1,636	793	892,672

Note: County totals include scattered votes. Democratic write-in candidates Corban Gehler and William Henry Davis III received, respectively, a total of 12 votes and a total of eight votes.

*Incumbent. Lib.–Libertarian; Rep.–Republican; WGR–Wisconsin Green.

Source: Official records of the Wisconsin Elections Commission.

County vote for governor and lieutenant governor, November 6, 2018 general election

	Tony Evers/ Mandela Barnes (Dem.)	Scott Walker*/ Rebecca Kleefisch* (Rep.)	Phillip Anderson/ Patrick Baird (Lib.)	Maggie Turnbull/ Wil Losch (Ind.)	Michael J. White/Tiffany Anderson (WGR)	Arnie Enz/ no candi-date (Ind.)	Total
Adams	3,892	5,209	68	67	42	11	9,291
Ashland.	4,168	2,584	49	58	48	9	6,920
Barron.	7,623	10,655	99	111	63	16	18,568
Bayfield.	5,152	3,458	51	85	43	7	8,797
Brown.	51,724	61,424	1,040	810	509	115	115,669
Buffalo	2,385	3,463	40	50	27	10	5,976
Burnett	2,742	4,664	31	108	33	10	7,588
Calumet	8,992	14,313	148	145	70	35	23,703
Chippewa	11,739	15,499	201	189	116	30	27,775
Clark.	4,015	7,469	74	77	69	10	11,714
Columbia.	14,124	12,363	212	197	111	17	27,034
Crawford	3,354	3,117	61	35	32	5	6,604
Dane	220,052	69,206	2,281	1,756	983	202	294,623
Dodge	13,552	23,516	276	245	143	78	37,810
Door.	8,151	8,536	112	102	63	11	16,979
Douglas.	11,034	7,251	151	191	109	13	18,759
Dunn	8,667	9,255	209	180	119	27	18,457
Eau Claire.	26,768	20,855	475	410	257	42	48,833
Florence	643	1,503	15	8	10	2	2,181
Fond du Lac	16,439	27,941	311	278	171	36	45,186
Forest	1,486	2,421	21	27	23	4	3,982
Grant	9,665	9,502	155	160	92	18	19,597
Green	9,378	7,333	130	127	100	16	17,090

Gubernatorial vote by county and municipality, November 6, 2018 general election, continued

	Scott Walker/ Rebecca Kleefisch (Rep.)	Tony Evers/ Mandela Barnes (Dem.)		Scott Walker/ Rebecca Kleefisch (Rep.)	Tony Evers/ Mandela Barnes (Dem.)
Bellevue, village	3,883	3,120	La Follette, town	139	108
De Pere, city	6,011	5,619	Lincoln, town	111	41
Denmark, village	564	353	Meenon, town.	305	184
Eaton, town	523	292	Oakland, town	287	211
Glenmore, town.	372	154	Roosevelt, town.	64	29
Green Bay, city	17,234	20,598	Rusk, town	130	69
Green Bay, town	794	349	Sand Lake, town	136	118
Hobart, village	2,533	1,603	Scott, town.	223	161
Holland, town	543	262	Siren, town.	312	152
Howard, village (part) . .	5,489	3,808	Siren, village.	191	117
Humboldt, town	454	238	Swiss, town	173	171
Lawrence, town.	1,973	1,017	Trade Lake, town	290	152
Ledgeview, town	2,468	1,538	Union, town	112	70
Morrison, town	600	166	Webb Lake, town	143	101
New Denmark, town. . .	516	303	Webster, village.	144	99
Pittsfield, town	1,024	471	West Marshland, town. .	118	48
Pulaski, village (part). . .	787	488	Wood River, town.	321	126
Rockland, town	667	309			
Scott, town.	1,178	835	**Calumet**	**14,313**	**8,992**
Suamico, village	4,313	2,273	Appleton, city (part) . . .	2,422	2,462
Wrightstown, town. . . .	749	348	Brillion, city	862	449
Wrightstown, village (part)	766	393	Brillion, town	511	181
			Brothertown, town. . . .	480	147
Buffalo	**3,463**	**2,385**	Charlestown, town	288	102
Alma, city.	184	171	Chilton, city	919	521
Alma, town.	68	80	Chilton, town	399	138
Belvidere, town	128	84	Harrison, town	0	0
Buffalo, town	217	134	Harrison, village (part). .	3,363	2,207
Buffalo City, city.	283	210	Hilbert, village	342	111
Canton, town	80	54	Kaukauna, city (part). . .	0	0
Cochrane, village	93	70	Kiel, city (part).	75	46
Cross, town	114	56	Menasha, city (part) . . .	764	659
Dover, town	95	73	New Holstein, city	867	528
Fountain City, city	204	159	New Holstein, town . . .	522	201
Gilmanton, town	100	67	Potter, village	96	25
Glencoe, town.	154	54	Rantoul, town	274	82
Lincoln, town	68	41	Sherwood, village	1,042	662
Maxville, town.	108	36	Stockbridge, town	554	231
Milton, town.	160	106	Stockbridge, village . . .	207	118
Modena, town.	85	64	Woodville, town	326	122
Mondovi, city	517	453			
Mondovi, town	110	81	**Chippewa**	**15,499**	**11,739**
Montana, town	93	30	Anson, town.	713	475
Naples, town	202	114	Arthur, town.	202	92
Nelson, town	168	103	Auburn, town	196	116
Nelson, village	63	65	Birch Creek, town.	183	97
Waumandee, town. . . .	169	80	Bloomer, city	947	536
			Bloomer, town	330	146
Burnett	**4,664**	**2,742**	Boyd, village.	121	102
Anderson, town.	124	51	Cadott, village.	276	267
Blaine, town	59	33	Chippewa Falls, city . . .	2,608	2,861
Daniels, town	210	101	Cleveland, town.	258	141
Dewey, town.	147	73	Colburn, town.	260	101
Grantsburg, town.	338	146	Cooks Valley, town	220	109
Grantsburg, village. . . .	313	168	Cornell, city	307	208
Jackson, town	274	213	Delmar, town	242	144

Gubernatorial vote by county and municipality, November 6, 2018 general election, continued

	Scott Walker/ Rebecca Kleefisch (Rep.)	Tony Evers/ Mandela Barnes (Dem.)		Scott Walker/ Rebecca Kleefisch (Rep.)	Tony Evers/ Mandela Barnes (Dem.)
Eagle Point, town	933	629	Thorp, city	363	242
Eau Claire, city (part) . . .	392	479	Thorp, town	164	85
Edson, town	221	144	Unity, town	174	79
Estella, town	134	56	Unity, village (part)	28	12
Goetz, town	205	166	Warner, town	144	63
Hallie, town	50	52	Washburn, town	98	35
Howard, town	216	156	Weston, town	179	86
Lafayette, town	1,736	1,351	Withee, town	183	82
Lake Hallie, village	1,608	1,350	Withee, village	121	85
Lake Holcombe, town . .	318	171	Worden, town	150	67
New Auburn, village (part)	113	62	York, town	189	90
Ruby, town	122	57	**Columbia**	**12,363**	**14,124**
Sampson, town	315	146	Arlington, town	212	219
Sigel, town	250	197	Arlington, village	215	229
Stanley, city (part)	422	290	Caledonia, town	358	475
Tilden, town	486	291	Cambria, village	136	145
Wheaton, town	768	579	Columbus, city (part) . .	985	1,392
Woodmohr, town	347	168	Columbus, town	203	125
			Courtland, town	149	84
Clark	**7,469**	**4,015**	Dekorra, town	650	684
Abbotsford, city (part) . .	331	197	Doylestown, village . . .	47	75
Beaver, town	167	66	Fall River, village	325	370
Butler, town	33	17	Fort Winnebago, town . .	268	214
Colby, city (part)	285	143	Fountain Prairie, town . .	214	202
Colby, town	162	72	Friesland, village	101	33
Curtiss, village.	38	2	Hampden, town	169	142
Dewhurst, town.	117	67	Leeds, town	214	220
Dorchester, village (part)	160	75	Lewiston, town	299	317
Eaton, town	169	63	Lodi, city	556	1,018
Foster, town	52	23	Lodi, town	894	966
Fremont, town	323	103	Lowville, town.	300	279
Grant, town	210	106	Marcellon, town	269	217
Granton, village.	91	57	Newport, town	203	152
Green Grove, town	119	53	Otsego, town	194	168
Greenwood, city	230	182	Pacific, town	740	725
Hendren, town	113	61	Pardeeville, village	416	449
Hewett, town	91	66	Portage, city	1,336	2,059
Hixon, town	118	66	Poynette, village	439	672
Hoard, town	134	45	Randolph, town.	313	82
Levis, town.	145	71	Randolph, village (part) .	126	73
Longwood, town	114	66	Rio, village	158	279
Loyal, city.	308	171	Scott, town.	173	127
Loyal, town.	171	51	Springvale, town	132	139
Lynn, town.	162	71	West Point, town	547	653
Mayville, town.	213	72	Wisconsin Dells, city (part)	482	550
Mead, town	79	37	Wyocena, town	413	439
Mentor, town	104	79	Wyocena, village	127	151
Neillsville, city	503	406			
Owen, city	189	181	**Crawford**	**3,117**	**3,354**
Pine Valley, town	347	176	Bell Center, village	18	26
Reseburg, town	78	68	Bridgeport, town	249	205
Seif, town.	46	43	Clayton, town	163	241
Sherman, town	210	66	De Soto, village (part) . .	20	18
Sherwood, town	64	65	Eastman, town	206	124
Stanley, city (part)	0	2	Eastman, village	80	47

Gubernatorial vote by county and municipality, November 6, 2018 general election, continued

	Scott Walker/ Rebecca Kleefisch (Rep.)	Tony Evers/ Mandela Barnes (Dem.)		Scott Walker/ Rebecca Kleefisch (Rep.)	Tony Evers/ Mandela Barnes (Dem.)
Ferryville, village	58	63	Montrose, town	226	423
Freeman, town	192	196	Mount Horeb, village	1,260	2,668
Gays Mills, village	88	118	Oregon, town	711	1,255
Haney, town	61	83	Oregon, village	1,791	3,961
Lynxville, village	39	34	Perry, town	151	313
Marietta, town	119	118	Pleasant Springs, town	769	1,167
Mount Sterling, village	32	46	Primrose, town	135	299
Prairie du Chien, city	822	1,027	Rockdale, village	34	80
Prairie du Chien, town	225	173	Roxbury, town	404	567
Scott, town	104	108	Rutland, town	407	754
Seneca, town	211	192	Shorewood Hills, village	143	1,285
Soldiers Grove, village	90	124	Springdale, town	455	755
Steuben, village	17	23	Springfield, town	706	855
Utica, town	127	167	Stoughton, city	1,877	4,721
Wauzeka, town	99	90	Sun Prairie, city	4,583	10,331
Wauzeka, village	97	131	Sun Prairie, town	520	750
			Vermont, town	174	388
Dane	**69,206**	**220,052**	Verona, city	2,018	5,193
Albion, town	427	609	Verona, town	449	751
Belleville, village (part)	277	687	Vienna, town	397	420
Berry, town	276	404	Waunakee, village	2,878	4,513
Black Earth, town	135	167	Westport, town	1,013	1,605
Black Earth, village	246	500	Windsor, village	1,644	2,487
Blooming Grove, town	242	670	York, town	169	206
Blue Mounds, town	226	321			
Blue Mounds, village	134	339	**Dodge**	**23,516**	**13,552**
Bristol, town	1,082	1,198	Ashippun, town	1,116	332
Brooklyn, village (part)	135	330	Beaver Dam, city	2,794	3,360
Burke, town	709	1,081	Beaver Dam, town	1,039	832
Cambridge, village (part)	280	552	Brownsville, village	217	86
Christiana, town	290	370	Burnett, town	298	133
Cottage Grove, town	884	1,358	Calamus, town	262	191
Cottage Grove, village	1,220	2,283	Chester, town	203	105
Cross Plains, town	392	535	Clyman, town	294	86
Cross Plains, village	697	1,422	Clyman, village	98	57
Dane, town	259	228	Columbus, city (part)	0	0
Dane, village	246	268	Elba, town	321	231
Deerfield, town	381	482	Emmet, town	511	161
Deerfield, village	419	779	Fox Lake, city	303	261
DeForest, village	1,639	3,176	Fox Lake, town	434	196
Dunkirk, town	441	711	Hartford, city (part)	4	1
Dunn, town	1,087	1,929	Herman, town	534	84
Edgerton, city (part)	26	29	Horicon, city	844	616
Fitchburg, city	2,994	10,312	Hubbard, town	626	288
Madison, city	22,437	119,530	Hustisford, town	563	168
Madison, town	229	2,034	Hustisford, village	355	136
Maple Bluff, village	342	639	Iron Ridge, village	294	124
Marshall, village	613	950	Juneau, city	482	370
Mazomanie, town	243	340	Kekoskee, village	370	119
Mazomanie, village	286	583	Lebanon, town	619	214
McFarland, village	1,487	3,356	Leroy, town	378	101
Medina, town	311	389	Lomira, town	447	108
Middleton, city	2,558	9,180	Lomira, village	695	291
Middleton, town	1,589	2,393	Lowell, town	337	161
Monona, city	1,053	4,171	Lowell, village	88	48

Gubernatorial vote by county and municipality, November 6, 2018 general election, continued

	Scott Walker/ Rebecca Kleefisch (Rep.)	Tony Evers/ Mandela Barnes (Dem.)		Scott Walker/ Rebecca Kleefisch (Rep.)	Tony Evers/ Mandela Barnes (Dem.)
Mayville, city.	1,346	786	Superior, town	485	595
Neosho, village	203	61	Superior, village.	121	197
Oak Grove, town	332	161	Wascott, town	238	219
Portland, town	325	204			
Randolph, village (part).	301	181	**Dunn**	**9,255**	**8,667**
Reeseville, village.	158	106	Boyceville, village.	215	147
Rubicon, town.	967	191	Colfax, town	306	220
Shields, town	210	84	Colfax, village	197	229
Theresa, town	422	123	Downing, village	51	30
Theresa, village	429	180	Dunn, town	348	296
Trenton, town	441	196	Eau Galle, town	222	128
Watertown, city (part). .	2,409	1,358	Elk Mound, town	468	310
Waupun, city (part). . . .	1,057	788	Elk Mound, village	148	156
Westford, town	390	273	Grant, town	136	84
			Hay River, town	157	108
Door.	**8,536**	**8,151**	Knapp, village	115	62
Baileys Harbor, town. . .	354	463	Lucas, town	195	134
Brussels, town	332	197	Menomonie, city	2,068	3,429
Clay Banks, town	123	105	Menomonie, town	804	704
Egg Harbor, town.	462	424	New Haven, town.	155	110
Egg Harbor, village. . . .	105	114	Otter Creek, town	130	93
Ephraim, village.	115	125	Peru, town	64	39
Forestville, town	308	221	Red Cedar, town	632	464
Forestville, village	135	96	Ridgeland, village	47	34
Gardner, town.	394	287	Rock Creek, town	296	180
Gibraltar, town	359	423	Sand Creek, town.	152	98
Jacksonport, town	285	231	Sheridan, town	138	78
Liberty Grove, town . . .	628	722	Sherman, town	277	165
Nasewaupee, town. . . .	672	449	Spring Brook, town. . . .	492	297
Sevastopol, town	1,013	796	Stanton, town	246	134
Sister Bay, village	293	366	Tainter, town.	692	585
Sturgeon Bay, city	2,018	2,440	Tiffany, town.	195	90
Sturgeon Bay, town . . .	261	219	Weston, town	145	110
Union, town	386	214	Wheeler, village.	46	46
Washington, town	293	259	Wilson, town.	118	107
Douglas	**7,251**	**11,034**	**Eau Claire**	**20,855**	**26,768**
Amnicon, town	234	321	Altoona, city	1,638	1,863
Bennett, town.	175	157	Augusta, city.	304	218
Brule, town.	122	222	Bridge Creek, town. . . .	309	205
Cloverland, town	55	43	Brunswick, town	523	444
Dairyland, town.	58	24	Clear Creek, town.	215	143
Gordon, town	215	194	Drammen, town	230	164
Hawthorne, town.	256	223	Eau Claire, city (part). . .	11,341	18,647
Highland, town	77	105	Fairchild, town	81	35
Lake Nebagamon, village	303	299	Fairchild, village.	105	62
Lakeside, town	161	168	Fall Creek, village.	323	322
Maple, town	107	193	Lincoln, town	319	218
Oakland, town	233	338	Ludington, town	290	218
Oliver, village	74	126	Otter Creek, town	140	80
Parkland, town	188	330	Pleasant Valley, town . .	1,196	807
Poplar, village	175	118	Seymour, town	972	802
Solon Springs, town . . .	249	254	Union, town	619	616
Solon Springs, village . .	130	155	Washington, town	2,144	1,877
Summit, town	175	326	Wilson, town.	106	47
Superior, city	3,420	6,427			

Gubernatorial vote by county and municipality, November 6, 2018 general election, continued

	Scott Walker/ Rebecca Kleefisch (Rep.)	Tony Evers/ Mandela Barnes (Dem.)		Scott Walker/ Rebecca Kleefisch (Rep.)	Tony Evers/ Mandela Barnes (Dem.)
Florence	1,503	643	Laona, town	294	182
Aurora, town.	291	137	Lincoln, town	273	183
Commonwealth, town. .	130	58	Nashville, town	296	230
Fence, town	82	22	Popple River, town	13	7
Fern, town	84	26	Ross, town	46	11
Florence, town	619	322	Wabeno, town.	219	159
Homestead, town	150	47			
Long Lake, town	70	22	**Grant**	**9,502**	**9,665**
Tipler, town	77	9	Bagley, village.	66	79
			Beetown, town	174	79
Fond du Lac.	**27,941**	**16,439**	Bloomington, town . . .	89	52
Alto, town	433	110	Bloomington, village . .	150	121
Ashford, town.	680	192	Blue River, village.	78	85
Auburn, town.	1,044	238	Boscobel, city	398	600
Brandon, village	239	117	Boscobel, town	74	75
Byron, town	613	250	Cassville, town	92	52
Calumet, town	538	208	Cassville, village	160	173
Campbellsport, village .	594	204	Castle Rock, town.	80	50
Eden, town.	429	111	Clifton, town.	59	55
Eden, village.	231	90	Cuba City, city (part) . . .	313	389
Eldorado, town	523	201	Dickeyville, village	231	189
Empire, town	1,074	531	Ellenboro, town.	152	99
Fairwater, village	89	41	Fennimore, city	400	487
Fond du Lac, city	8,933	7,320	Fennimore, town	109	85
Fond du Lac, town	1,184	661	Glen Haven, town	87	46
Forest, town	437	139	Harrison, town	139	80
Friendship, town	765	405	Hazel Green, town	255	285
Kewaskum, village (part)	0	0	Hazel Green, village (part)	210	248
Lamartine, town	640	266	Hickory Grove, town . . .	89	67
Marshfield, town	447	151	Jamestown, town.	517	350
Metomen, town.	268	90	Lancaster, city	697	671
Mount Calvary, village. .	179	87	Liberty, town	139	65
North Fond du Lac, village	1,022	879	Lima, town	163	137
Oakfield, town.	237	93	Little Grant, town.	72	40
Oakfield, village.	320	188	Livingston, village (part)	118	135
Osceola, town	732	215	Marion, town	98	87
Ripon, city	1,572	1,409	Millville, town	35	43
Ripon, town	469	246	Montfort, village (part) .	95	131
Rosendale, town	248	107	Mount Hope, town	47	28
Rosendale, village	340	148	Mount Hope, village . . .	28	28
St. Cloud, village	191	69	Mount Ida, town	131	75
Springvale, town	237	111	Muscoda, town	135	109
Taycheedah, town	1,797	777	Muscoda, village (part) .	185	227
Waupun, city (part). . . .	953	559	North Lancaster, town. .	154	73
Waupun, town	483	226	Paris, town	178	114
			Patch Grove, town	49	65
Forest.	**2,421**	**1,486**	Patch Grove, village . . .	26	33
Alvin, town.	65	21	Platteville, city.	1,682	2,545
Argonne, town	137	78	Platteville, town.	340	345
Armstrong Creek, town .	143	78	Potosi, town	189	161
Blackwell, town	42	27	Potosi, village	145	134
Caswell, town	34	11	Smelser, town	227	148
Crandon, city	412	229	South Lancaster, town. .	162	112
Crandon, town	162	118	Tennyson, village	67	67
Freedom, town	144	73	Waterloo, town	131	80
Hiles, town.	141	79	Watterstown, town. . . .	78	79

Gubernatorial vote by county and municipality, November 6, 2018 general election, continued

	Scott Walker/ Rebecca Kleefisch (Rep.)	Tony Evers/ Mandela Barnes (Dem.)		Scott Walker/ Rebecca Kleefisch (Rep.)	Tony Evers/ Mandela Barnes (Dem.)
Wingville, town	75	68	Brigham, town	199	371
Woodman, town	34	30	Clyde, town	66	115
Woodman, village	22	9	Cobb, village.	80	133
Wyalusing, town	78	80	Dodgeville, city	742	1,324
			Dodgeville, town	368	533
Green	**7,333**	**9,378**	Eden, town.	98	89
Adams, town	129	143	Highland, town	169	172
Albany, town	284	307	Highland, village	141	184
Albany, village.	120	263	Hollandale, village	30	100
Belleville, village (part) .	67	174	Linden, town	187	143
Brodhead, city (part). . .	507	592	Linden, village.	70	117
Brooklyn, town	291	356	Livingston, village (part)	2	0
Brooklyn, village (part) .	64	144	Mifflin, town.	120	107
Browntown, village . . .	55	39	Mineral Point, city	387	887
Cadiz, town	220	165	Mineral Point, town . . .	263	212
Clarno, town.	325	235	Montfort, village (part) .	19	25
Decatur, town	415	439	Moscow, town.	123	187
Exeter, town	391	675	Muscoda, village (part) .	8	5
Jefferson, town	319	230	Pulaski, town	78	59
Jordan, town	141	131	Rewey, village.	34	51
Monroe, city	1,785	2,513	Ridgeway, town.	120	204
Monroe, town	317	278	Ridgeway, village.	99	156
Monticello, village	189	353	Waldwick, town.	99	140
Mount Pleasant, town . .	131	177	Wyoming, town.	65	150
New Glarus, town.	318	441			
New Glarus, village. . . .	325	816	**Iron**	**1,785**	**1,264**
Spring Grove, town . . .	272	163	Anderson, town.	17	18
Sylvester, town	309	204	Carey, town	57	23
Washington, town	172	219	Gurney, town	43	34
York, town	187	321	Hurley, city.	303	278
			Kimball, town	136	124
Green Lake	**5,411**	**2,633**	Knight, town.	40	42
Berlin, city (part)	1,050	742	Mercer, town	605	316
Berlin, town	448	144	Montreal, city	179	171
Brooklyn, town	726	342	Oma, town	132	80
Green Lake, city.	287	184	Pence, town	42	44
Green Lake, town.	494	146	Saxon, town	105	63
Kingston, town	185	65	Sherman, town	126	71
Kingston, village	97	51			
Mackford, town	196	42	**Jackson**.	**4,129**	**3,713**
Manchester, town	237	71	Adams, town	380	317
Markesan, city.	371	173	Albion, town.	301	265
Marquette, town	161	66	Alma, town.	240	153
Marquette, village	56	24	Alma Center, village . . .	78	103
Princeton, city.	323	180	Bear Bluff, town	63	7
Princeton, town.	522	279	Black River Falls, city . . .	589	761
St. Marie, town	139	62	Brockway, town.	257	413
Seneca, town	119	62	City Point, town.	44	32
			Cleveland, town.	130	89
Iowa.	**4,289**	**6,674**	Curran, town.	65	66
Arena, town	287	449	Franklin, town.	71	75
Arena, village	125	231	Garden Valley, town . . .	135	64
Avoca, village	76	111	Garfield, town.	184	104
Barneveld, village.	207	366	Hixton, town.	155	98
Blanchardville, village			Hixton, village.	87	80
(part).	27	53	Irving, town	156	153

Gubernatorial vote by county and municipality, November 6, 2018 general election, continued

	Scott Walker/ Rebecca Kleefisch (Rep.)	Tony Evers/ Mandela Barnes (Dem.)		Scott Walker/ Rebecca Kleefisch (Rep.)	Tony Evers/ Mandela Barnes (Dem.)
Knapp, town	121	41	Lyndon, town	274	313
Komensky, town	24	105	Lyndon Station, village .	71	89
Manchester, town	200	132	Marion, town	133	61
Melrose, town	119	61	Mauston, city	619	677
Melrose, village	120	97	Necedah, town	668	333
Merrillan, village	90	95	Necedah, village	165	152
Millston, town.	51	36	New Lisbon, city	296	202
North Bend, town	124	100	Orange, town	142	88
Northfield, town	167	114	Plymouth, town.	167	119
Springfield, town	104	91	Seven Mile Creek, town .	81	68
Taylor, village	74	61	Summit, town.	177	115
			Union Center, village . .	47	37
Jefferson	**21,475**	**16,018**	Wisconsin Dells, city (part)	0	0
Aztalan, town	402	313	Wonewoc, town.	169	112
Cambridge, village (part)	11	27	Wonewoc, village.	156	119
Cold Spring, town	258	151			
Concord, town	773	322	**Kenosha**	**31,512**	**34,481**
Farmington, town	564	227	Brighton, town	549	253
Fort Atkinson, city	2,230	2,806	Bristol, village	1,708	854
Hebron, town	365	182	Genoa City, village (part)	0	0
Ixonia, town	1,865	625	Kenosha, city	13,497	21,910
Jefferson, city	1,545	1,451	Paddock Lake, village . .	709	454
Jefferson, town	649	382	Paris, town	559	274
Johnson Creek, village. .	792	559	Pleasant Prairie, village .	5,327	4,527
Koshkonong, town. . . .	1,078	729	Randall, town	982	501
Lac La Belle, village (part)	0	0	Salem Lakes, village . . .	3,620	2,121
Lake Mills, city.	1,332	1,690	Somers, town	234	223
Lake Mills, town.	598	589	Somers, village	1,950	1,963
Milford, town	347	228	Twin Lakes, village	1,344	874
Oakland, town	837	950	Wheatland, town	1,033	527
Palmyra, town.	496	202			
Palmyra, village	507	248	**Kewaunee**	**5,792**	**3,572**
Sullivan, town	847	350	Ahnapee, town	244	176
Sullivan, village	223	107	Algoma, city	627	661
Sumner, town	270	206	Carlton, town	354	163
Waterloo, city	680	692	Casco, town	381	176
Waterloo, town	296	187	Casco, village	159	72
Watertown, city (part) . .	3,451	1,997	Franklin, town.	297	198
Watertown, town.	728	273	Kewaunee, city	639	538
Whitewater, city (part). .	331	525	Lincoln, town	260	180
			Luxemburg, town.	562	203
Juneau	**5,689**	**4,247**	Luxemburg, village. . . .	656	383
Armenia, town	200	121	Montpelier, town	492	218
Camp Douglas, village. .	116	98	Pierce, town	231	182
Clearfield, town.	207	138	Red River, town	466	223
Cutler, town	109	52	West Kewaunee, town. .	424	199
Elroy, city	203	231			
Finley, town	37	21	**La Crosse.**	**23,537**	**32,103**
Fountain, town	160	116	Bangor, town	177	107
Germantown, town . . .	490	236	Bangor, village	303	325
Hustler, village	33	50	Barre, town.	418	226
Kildare, town	165	104	Burns, town	251	190
Kingston, town	14	1	Campbell, town.	959	1,195
Lemonweir, town.	380	262	Farmington, town	520	412
Lindina, town	184	172	Greenfield, town	561	525
Lisbon, town.	226	160	Hamilton, town	686	518

Gubernatorial vote by county and municipality, November 6, 2018 general election, continued

	Scott Walker/ Rebecca Kleefisch (Rep.)	Tony Evers/ Mandela Barnes (Dem.)		Scott Walker/ Rebecca Kleefisch (Rep.)	Tony Evers/ Mandela Barnes (Dem.)
Holland, town	1,184	1,014	Rolling, town	474	182
Holmen, village	1,944	2,197	Summit, town	54	23
La Crosse, city	7,611	15,982	Upham, town	283	144
Medary, town	436	487	Vilas, town	77	21
Onalaska, city	4,267	4,570	White Lake, village	66	61
Onalaska, town	1,540	1,406	Wolf River, town	281	125
Rockland, village (part) .	141	125	**Lincoln . . . .**	**7,865**	**5,335**
Shelby, town.	1,231	1,509	Birch, town.	130	83
Washington, town	135	139	Bradley, town	732	517
West Salem, village. . . .	1,173	1,176	Corning, town.	287	118
Lafayette.	**3,324**	**3,135**	Harding, town.	160	71
Argyle, town.	99	106	Harrison, town	314	190
Argyle, village.	123	180	King, town	311	251
Belmont, town	155	117	Merrill, city.	1,988	1,688
Belmont, village	201	193	Merrill, town.	911	536
Benton, town	122	77	Pine River, town.	635	353
Benton, village	146	210	Rock Falls, town.	228	132
Blanchard, town	61	91	Russell, town	173	105
Blanchardville, village			Schley, town.	301	116
(part)	93	203	Scott, town.	491	235
Cuba City, city (part) . . .	46	54	Skanawan, town	145	95
Darlington, city	318	482	Somo, town	38	29
Darlington, town	250	160	Tomahawk, city	744	665
Elk Grove, town	118	61	Tomahawk, town	152	99
Fayette, town	105	54	Wilson, town.	125	52
Gratiot, town	152	81	**Manitowoc . . . .**	**21,360**	**13,513**
Gratiot, village	42	42	Cato, town	561	244
Hazel Green, village (part)	3	4	Centerville, town	223	115
Kendall, town	99	63	Cleveland, village.	394	275
Lamont, town	70	65	Cooperstown, town . . .	448	202
Monticello, town	44	8	Eaton, town	304	121
New Diggings, town . . .	107	88	Francis Creek, village . .	184	116
Seymour, town	88	51	Franklin, town.	459	161
Shullsburg, city	174	264	Gibson, town	443	213
Shullsburg, town	79	60	Kellnersville, village . . .	81	53
South Wayne, village. . .	80	46	Kiel, city (part).	1,099	600
Wayne, town.	129	52	Kossuth, town.	649	366
White Oak Springs, town	34	18	Liberty, town	497	173
Willow Springs, town . .	184	127	Manitowoc, city.	7,044	5,767
Wiota, town	202	178	Manitowoc, town.	350	191
Langlade.	**5,712**	**2,825**	Manitowoc Rapids, town	867	421
Ackley, town.	172	69	Maple Grove, town. . . .	322	81
Ainsworth, town	172	77	Maribel, village	93	43
Antigo, city.	1,635	1,094	Meeme, town	536	229
Antigo, town.	475	196	Mishicot, town	406	185
Elcho, town	470	221	Mishicot, village	389	232
Evergreen, town	192	56	Newton, town.	847	334
Langlade, town	154	76	Reedsville, village	332	138
Neva, town.	272	126	Rockland, town	329	119
Norwood, town	316	113	St. Nazianz, village	208	76
Parrish, town	38	13	Schleswig, town	746	346
Peck, town	121	45	Two Creeks, town.	143	68
Polar, town	381	142	Two Rivers, city	2,368	2,079
Price, town	79	41	Two Rivers, town	550	323

Gubernatorial vote by county and municipality, November 6, 2018 general election, continued

	Scott Walker/ Rebecca Kleefisch (Rep.)	Tony Evers/ Mandela Barnes (Dem.)		Scott Walker/ Rebecca Kleefisch (Rep.)	Tony Evers/ Mandela Barnes (Dem.)
Valders, village	271	133	Spencer, village	421	293
Whitelaw, village	217	109	Stettin, town.	959	439
			Stratford, village	487	196
Marathon	**36,886**	**24,057**	Texas, town	562	299
Abbotsford, city (part). .	78	33	Unity, village (part). . . .	55	18
Athens, village	300	155	Wausau, city	7,577	7,891
Bergen, town	251	159	Wausau, town	771	433
Berlin, town	381	126	Weston, town	227	90
Bern, town	135	56	Weston, village	3,848	2,622
Bevent, town	312	226	Wien, town.	250	114
Birnamwood, village (part)	4	7			
Brighton, town	167	36	**Marinette**	**10,916**	**6,193**
Cassel, town	325	138	Amberg, town.	274	108
Cleveland, town.	472	199	Athelstane, town	202	90
Colby, city (part)	115	76	Beaver, town.	389	143
Day, town	372	142	Beecher, town.	244	112
Dorchester, village (part)	0	1	Coleman, village	201	109
Easton, town.	460	167	Crivitz, village	251	117
Eau Pleine, town	246	98	Dunbar, town	192	73
Edgar, village	400	228	Goodman, town	187	120
Elderon, town	208	97	Grover, town.	577	220
Elderon, village	43	22	Lake, town	349	182
Emmet, town	301	161	Marinette, city.	1,846	1,568
Fenwood, village	49	18	Middle Inlet, town	249	147
Frankfort, town	166	75	Niagara, city	314	219
Franzen, town	176	74	Niagara, town	285	130
Green Valley, town	214	96	Pembine, town	252	126
Guenther, town	137	58	Peshtigo, city	721	436
Halsey, town.	172	54	Peshtigo, town	1,244	752
Hamburg, town	278	113	Porterfield, town	596	298
Harrison, town	110	36	Pound, town.	445	168
Hatley, village	179	89	Pound, village	86	30
Hewitt, town.	216	92	Silver Cliff, town.	197	116
Holton, town	245	82	Stephenson, town	1,074	561
Hull, town	206	59	Wagner, town	244	117
Johnson, town	218	86	Wausaukee, town.	395	180
Knowlton, town.	701	360	Wausaukee, village. . . .	102	71
Kronenwetter, village . .	2,243	1,429			
Maine, village	926	490	**Marquette**	**4,143**	**2,911**
Marathon, town.	391	143	Buffalo, town	267	238
Marathon City, village . .	504	248	Crystal Lake, town	171	106
Marshfield, city (part) . .	196	148	Douglas, town.	251	186
McMillan, town	661	414	Endeavor, village	83	81
Mosinee, city	1,228	727	Harris, town	240	171
Mosinee, town	743	374	Mecan, town.	233	142
Norrie, town	326	171	Montello, city	290	304
Plover, town	216	89	Montello, town	341	207
Reid, town	394	210	Moundville, town.	136	106
Rib Falls, town.	412	107	Neshkoro, town	201	93
Rib Mountain, town . . .	2,510	1,452	Neshkoro, village	109	71
Rietbrock, town	287	120	Newton, town	142	76
Ringle, town	614	320	Oxford, town	257	163
Rothschild, village	1,463	1,151	Oxford, village	120	96
Schofield, city	514	423	Packwaukee, town	382	273
Spencer, town	464	227	Shields, town	195	107

Gubernatorial vote by county and municipality, November 6, 2018 general election, continued

	Scott Walker/ Rebecca Kleefisch (Rep.)	Tony Evers/ Mandela Barnes (Dem.)		Scott Walker/ Rebecca Kleefisch (Rep.)	Tony Evers/ Mandela Barnes (Dem.)
Springfield, town	234	153	Sparta, town	805	564
Westfield, town	250	157	Tomah, city	1,585	1,485
Westfield, village	241	181	Tomah, town	396	231
			Warrens, village	117	62
Menominee	**233**	**866**	Wellington, town	117	105
Menominee, town	233	866	Wells, town	168	90
			Wilton, town	123	78
Milwaukee	**124,055**	**262,124**	Wilton, village	87	103
Bayside, village (part) . .	982	1,711	Wyeville, village	33	21
Brown Deer, village . . .	2,026	4,302			
Cudahy, city	3,522	4,243	**Oconto**	**11,490**	**5,858**
Fox Point, village	1,691	2,570	Abrams, town	591	312
Franklin, city	10,930	7,208	Bagley, town	119	35
Glendale, city	2,523	5,060	Brazeau, town	492	207
Greendale, village	4,417	3,618	Breed, town	272	80
Greenfield, city	9,018	8,292	Chase, town	936	478
Hales Corners, village . .	2,254	1,655	Doty, town	133	62
Milwaukee, city (part) . .	42,264	167,350	Gillett, city	317	189
Oak Creek, city	8,845	7,185	Gillett, town	412	109
River Hills, village	591	488	How, town	201	63
St. Francis, city	1,967	2,701	Lakewood, town	340	164
Shorewood, village	1,752	6,399	Lena, town	224	86
South Milwaukee, city . .	4,405	4,608	Lena, village	119	77
Wauwatosa, city	11,276	15,711	Little River, town	320	143
West Allis, city	11,731	12,941	Little Suamico, town . . .	1,623	751
West Milwaukee, village.	444	914	Maple Valley, town	222	86
Whitefish Bay, village . .	3,417	5,168	Morgan, town	349	143
			Mountain, town	286	163
Monroe	**9,464**	**6,969**	Oconto, city	885	743
Adrian, town	238	115	Oconto, town	423	222
Angelo, town	322	186	Oconto Falls, city	643	357
Byron, town	263	168	Oconto Falls, town	392	189
Cashton, village	223	172	Pensaukee, town	439	234
Clifton, town	109	76	Pulaski, village (part) . . .	0	0
Glendale, town	188	98	Riverview, town	262	191
Grant, town	140	56	Spruce, town	268	125
Greenfield, town	217	109	Stiles, town	456	234
Jefferson, town	152	97	Suring, village	128	50
Kendall, village	80	67	Townsend, town	389	235
La Grange, town	542	366	Underhill, town	249	130
Lafayette, town	98	55			
Leon, town	347	170	**Oneida**	**11,248**	**7,850**
Lincoln, town	249	105	Cassian, town	340	264
Little Falls, town	374	237	Crescent, town	627	503
Melvina, village	18	10	Enterprise, town	143	65
New Lyme, town	59	29	Hazelhurst, town	444	338
Norwalk, village.	84	87	Lake Tomahawk, town. .	384	215
Oakdale, town.	187	107	Little Rice, town.	136	67
Oakdale, village	61	37	Lynne, town	57	25
Ontario, village (part) . .	0	0	Minocqua, town	1,883	1,012
Portland, town	223	138	Monico, town	86	32
Ridgeville, town.	135	97	Newbold, town	914	664
Rockland, village (part) .	0	0	Nokomis, town	446	329
Scott, town.	34	9	Pelican, town	755	583
Sheldon, town.	133	49	Piehl, town	24	17
Sparta, city	1,557	1,590			

Gubernatorial vote by county and municipality, November 6, 2018 general election, continued

	Scott Walker/ Rebecca Kleefisch (Rep.)	Tony Evers/ Mandela Barnes (Dem.)		Scott Walker/ Rebecca Kleefisch (Rep.)	Tony Evers/ Mandela Barnes (Dem.)
Forest, town	74	94	Glen Flora, village	19	13
Henrietta, town	93	115	Grant, town	177	118
Ithaca, town	131	125	Grow, town	142	35
Lone Rock, village	148	203	Hawkins, town	29	28
Marshall, town	153	115	Hawkins, village.	80	50
Orion, town	98	127	Hubbard, town	55	26
Richland, town	313	248	Ingram, village	15	15
Richland Center, city . . .	775	1,028	Ladysmith, city	666	495
Richwood, town	99	122	Lawrence, town.	78	30
Rockbridge, town	158	180	Marshall, town	117	45
Sylvan, town.	100	68	Murry, town	69	39
Viola, village (part)	75	91	Richland, town	64	35
Westford, town	115	123	Rusk, town	188	93
Willow, town.	106	104	Sheldon, village.	52	31
Yuba, village	8	16	South Fork, town	31	24
			Strickland, town	90	61
Rock.	**26,904**	**39,680**	Stubbs, town	161	107
Avon, town.	188	121	Thornapple, town	254	90
Beloit, city	3,842	7,240	Tony, village	28	14
Beloit, town.	1,823	1,864	True, town	83	54
Bradford, town	302	181	Washington, town	122	73
Brodhead, city (part) . . .	9	30	Weyerhaeuser, village . .	55	36
Center, town.	240	317	Wilkinson, town.	14	6
Clinton, town	287	126	Willard, town	134	71
Clinton, village	466	345	Wilson, town.	44	17
Edgerton, city (part) . . .	816	1,733			
Evansville, city.	756	1,802	**St. Croix**	**22,108**	**16,690**
Footville, village	165	193	Baldwin, town.	307	155
Fulton, town.	853	986	Baldwin, village	800	599
Harmony, town	634	773	Cady, town.	268	134
Janesville, city	9,832	16,497	Cylon, town	223	89
Janesville, town.	961	1,062	Deer Park, village	64	26
Johnstown, town	238	185	Eau Galle, town	371	211
La Prairie, town	230	179	Emerald, town.	198	117
Lima, town.	276	276	Erin Prairie, town	205	122
Magnolia, town	158	195	Forest, town	179	73
Milton, city.	1,019	1,477	Glenwood, town	201	78
Milton, town.	778	791	Glenwood City, city . . .	258	142
Newark, town	464	316	Hammond, town	710	314
Orfordville, village	242	354	Hammond, village	360	337
Plymouth, town.	292	294	Hudson, city	3,158	3,252
Porter, town	199	362	Hudson, town	2,480	1,664
Rock, town	511	657	Kinnickinnic, town	518	411
Spring Valley, town. . . .	201	164	New Richmond, city . . .	1,562	1,496
Turtle, town	723	519	North Hudson, village . .	983	937
Union, town	399	641	Pleasant Valley, town . .	136	100
			Richmond, town	928	591
Rusk.	**3,797**	**2,184**	River Falls, city (part) . . .	692	887
Atlanta, town	182	95	Roberts, village	354	332
Big Bend, town	140	87	Rush River, town	143	91
Big Falls, town.	42	28	St. Joseph, town	1,226	857
Bruce, village	161	113	Somerset, town	1,271	736
Cedar Rapids, town . . .	19	6	Somerset, village	492	346
Conrath, village	13	12	Spring Valley, village (part)	3	2
Dewey, town.	177	93	Springfield, town	256	160
Flambeau, town.	296	144			

Gubernatorial vote by county and municipality, November 6, 2018 general election, continued

	Scott Walker/ Rebecca Kleefisch (Rep.)	Tony Evers/ Mandela Barnes (Dem.)		Scott Walker/ Rebecca Kleefisch (Rep.)	Tony Evers/ Mandela Barnes (Dem.)
Stanton, town.	238	157	Hayward, city	491	384
Star Prairie, town	916	543	Hayward, town	870	701
Star Prairie, village	125	98	Hunter, town	190	154
Troy, town	1,681	1,162	Lenroot, town	411	315
Warren, town	503	268	Meadowbrook, town . .	57	12
Wilson, village.	47	34	Meteor, town	52	23
Woodville, village.	252	169	Ojibwa, town	84	61
			Radisson, town	138	59
Sauk.	**12,615**	**15,630**	Radisson, village	42	27
Baraboo, city.	1,858	3,090	Round Lake, town	380	234
Baraboo, town.	465	514	Sand Lake, town	251	197
Bear Creek, town	134	166	Spider Lake, town	162	107
Cazenovia, village (part)	0	2	Weirgor, town	125	59
Dellona, town	456	401	Winter, town.	303	204
Delton, town	507	559	Winter, village.	68	46
Excelsior, town	442	407			
Fairfield, town.	285	337	**Shawano.**	**11,478**	**6,121**
Franklin, town.	177	171	Almon, town.	182	71
Freedom, town	124	101	Angelica, town	613	234
Greenfield, town	262	296	Aniwa, town	167	52
Honey Creek, town. . . .	181	202	Aniwa, village	51	34
Ironton, town	146	107	Bartelme, town	62	220
Ironton, village	56	23	Belle Plaine, town	631	290
La Valle, town	423	302	Birnamwood, town. . . .	220	113
La Valle, village	91	63	Birnamwood, village (part)	168	96
Lake Delton, village . . .	462	539	Bonduel, village	423	198
Lime Ridge, village. . . .	34	46	Bowler, village.	62	35
Loganville, village	59	62	Cecil, village	198	101
Merrimac, town.	301	336	Eland, village	46	58
Merrimac, village	111	132	Fairbanks, town.	224	51
North Freedom, village .	102	113	Germania, town.	100	49
Plain, village.	191	195	Grant, town	317	85
Prairie du Sac, town . . .	301	297	Green Valley, town	329	139
Prairie du Sac, village . .	735	1,453	Gresham, village	127	115
Reedsburg, city	1,604	1,847	Hartland, town	274	73
Reedsburg, town	343	236	Herman, town.	243	109
Rock Springs, village. . .	69	55	Hutchins, town	171	58
Sauk City, village	552	1,114	Lessor, town	452	154
Spring Green, town . . .	433	536	Maple Grove, town. . . .	295	149
Spring Green, village . .	251	623	Marion, city (part)	5	1
Sumpter, town	155	185	Mattoon, village	80	29
Troy, town	222	183	Morris, town	122	77
Washington, town	185	124	Navarino, town	133	66
West Baraboo, village . .	262	350	Pella, town	314	116
Westfield, town	164	81	Pulaski, village (part). . .	39	25
Winfield, town.	253	191	Red Springs, town	171	235
Wisconsin Dells, city (part)	43	47	Richmond, town	665	284
Woodland, town	176	144	Seneca, town	163	71
			Shawano, city	1,809	1,433
Sawyer	**4,542**	**3,484**	Tigerton, village	190	92
Bass Lake, town	516	630	Washington, town	594	277
Couderay, town	73	52	Waukechon, town	356	129
Couderay, village	19	30	Wescott, town.	1,026	527
Draper, town.	74	56	Wittenberg, town.	265	137
Edgewater, town	204	94	Wittenberg, village. . . .	191	138
Exeland, village	32	39			

Gubernatorial vote by county and municipality, November 6, 2018 general election, continued

	Scott Walker/ Rebecca Kleefisch (Rep.)	Tony Evers/ Mandela Barnes (Dem.)		Scott Walker/ Rebecca Kleefisch (Rep.)	Tony Evers/ Mandela Barnes (Dem.)
Sheboygan	31,520	20,801	Stetsonville, village . . .	140	71
Adell, village.	177	42	Taft, town	80	45
Cascade, village.	236	96	Westboro, town.	255	76
Cedar Grove, village . . .	821	196			
Elkhart Lake, village . .	371	279	**Trempealeau**	**6,623**	**5,393**
Glenbeulah, village . . .	129	107	Albion, town.	167	136
Greenbush, town.	547	271	Arcadia, city	367	256
Herman, town.	632	252	Arcadia, town.	513	287
Holland, town.	1,080	299	Blair, city	207	220
Howards Grove, village .	1,160	570	Burnside, town	117	84
Kohler, village.	791	460	Caledonia, town	273	160
Lima, town.	1,219	371	Chimney Rock, town. . .	64	56
Lyndon, town	599	252	Dodge, town.	122	86
Mitchell, town.	471	198	Eleva, village.	132	144
Mosel, town.	272	141	Ettrick, town.	354	308
Oostburg, village	1,428	259	Ettrick, village.	140	115
Plymouth, city.	2,290	1,684	Gale, town	506	352
Plymouth, town.	1,187	560	Galesville, city.	345	311
Random Lake, village . .	554	219	Hale, town	295	207
Rhine, town	844	440	Independence, city. . . .	236	170
Russell, town	141	39	Lincoln, town	148	126
Scott, town.	741	181	Osseo, city	358	351
Sheboygan, city.	8,340	9,362	Pigeon, town	175	146
Sheboygan, town.	2,531	1,616	Pigeon Falls, village . . .	85	81
Sheboygan Falls, city . .	2,314	1,611	Preston, town	204	173
Sheboygan Falls, town .	648	257	Strum, village	184	237
Sherman, town	617	157	Sumner, town	244	174
Waldo, village	171	77	Trempealeau, town. . . .	535	399
Wilson, town.	1,209	805	Trempealeau, village. . .	431	414
			Unity, town	130	108
Taylor	**5,690**	**2,269**	Whitehall, city.	291	292
Aurora, town.	97	47			
Browning, town.	281	81	**Vernon**	**6,276**	**6,550**
Chelsea, town.	243	87	Bergen, town	359	343
Cleveland, town.	81	21	Chaseburg, village	74	58
Deer Creek, town.	239	46	Christiana, town	238	197
Ford, town	88	28	Clinton, town	126	85
Gilman, village	101	64	Coon, town	171	222
Goodrich, town.	158	55	Coon Valley, village. . . .	178	186
Greenwood, town	221	61	De Soto, village (part) . .	54	54
Grover, town.	84	21	Forest, town	132	78
Hammel, town	266	77	Franklin, town.	320	203
Holway, town	173	42	Genoa, town.	164	214
Jump River, town.	77	40	Genoa, village.	47	69
Little Black, town.	341	109	Greenwood, town	105	84
Lublin, village	30	15	Hamburg, town.	257	226
Maplehurst, town.	105	35	Harmony, town	162	154
McKinley, town	127	24	Hillsboro, city	262	262
Medford, city	997	632	Hillsboro, town.	199	87
Medford, town.	827	278	Jefferson, town.	330	270
Molitor, town	107	41	Kickapoo, town	119	122
Pershing, town	33	22	La Farge, village.	137	144
Rib Lake, town	240	94	Liberty, town	62	108
Rib Lake, village.	209	102	Ontario, village (part) . .	84	66
Roosevelt, town.	90	55	Readstown, village. . . .	82	54
			Stark, town.	95	101

Gubernatorial vote by county and municipality, November 6, 2018 general election, continued

	Scott Walker/ Rebecca Kleefisch (Rep.)	Tony Evers/ Mandela Barnes (Dem.)		Scott Walker/ Rebecca Kleefisch (Rep.)	Tony Evers/ Mandela Barnes (Dem.)
Sterling, town	186	82	Walworth, town	600	205
Stoddard, village	157	217	Walworth, village	667	430
Union, town	99	88	Whitewater, city (part) . .	1,595	2,577
Viola, village (part)	36	30	Whitewater, town	466	344
Viroqua, city	818	1,326	Williams Bay, village . . .	767	540
Viroqua, town	470	442			
Webster, town	117	197	**Washburn**	**4,461**	**3,292**
Westby, city	387	542	Barronett, town	106	81
Wheatland, town	146	134	Bashaw, town	313	194
Whitestown, town	103	105	Bass Lake, town	150	83
			Beaver Brook, town . . .	195	161
Vilas	**7,814**	**4,510**	Birchwood, town	234	89
Arbor Vitae, town	1,123	680	Birchwood, village	107	71
Boulder Junction, town .	420	247	Brooklyn, town	96	71
Cloverland, town	439	217	Casey, town	137	97
Conover, town.	505	251	Chicog, town	82	75
Eagle River, city	400	258	Crystal, town	89	46
Lac du Flambeau, town .	584	749	Evergreen, town	318	239
Land O'Lakes, town . . .	347	200	Frog Creek, town	40	26
Lincoln, town	976	420	Gull Lake, town	59	43
Manitowish Waters, town	330	144	Long Lake, town	215	172
Phelps, town.	492	208	Madge, town	169	139
Plum Lake, town	240	137	Minong, town	266	228
Presque Isle, town	323	188	Minong, village	114	70
St. Germain, town	785	396	Sarona, town	135	67
Washington, town	636	328	Shell Lake, city	314	321
Winchester, town	214	87	Spooner, city	454	443
			Spooner, town	240	158
Walworth	**27,088**	**17,394**	Springbrook, town	138	86
Bloomfield, town	350	240	Stinnett, town.	61	31
Bloomfield, village	1,083	545	Stone Lake, town	166	85
Burlington, city (part) . .	1	0	Trego, town	263	216
Darien, town.	513	230			
Darien, village.	344	228	**Washington**	**50,958**	**18,703**
Delavan, city.	1,513	1,410	Addison, town.	1,456	369
Delavan, town.	1,600	885	Barton, town.	1,174	390
East Troy, town	1,624	581	Erin, town	1,855	523
East Troy, village	1,394	699	Farmington, town	1,579	418
Elkhorn, city	2,244	1,598	Germantown, town . . .	106	47
Fontana-on-Geneva Lake, village.	623	358	Germantown, village . .	7,778	3,384
			Hartford, city (part). . . .	4,433	2,048
Geneva, town	1,574	936	Hartford, town	1,557	420
Genoa City, village (part)	628	338	Jackson, town	2,143	517
Lafayette, town	727	359	Jackson, village	2,572	886
La Grange, town	840	400	Kewaskum, town	496	149
Lake Geneva, city.	1,699	1,438	Kewaskum, village (part)	1,414	496
Linn, town	800	393	Milwaukee, city (part) . .	0	0
Lyons, town	1,108	538	Newburg, village (part) .	416	99
Mukwonago, village (part)	49	31	Polk, town	1,853	517
Richmond, town	548	356	Richfield, village	5,640	1,627
Sharon, town	301	139	Slinger, village.	1,965	683
Sharon, village	329	220	Trenton, town	2,060	572
Spring Prairie, town . . .	873	333	Wayne, town.	955	202
Sugar Creek, town	1,270	657	West Bend, city	9,369	4,677
Troy, town	958	386	West Bend, town	2,137	679

Gubernatorial vote by county and municipality, November 6, 2018 general election, continued

	Scott Walker/ Rebecca Kleefisch (Rep.)	Tony Evers/ Mandela Barnes (Dem.)		Scott Walker/ Rebecca Kleefisch (Rep.)	Tony Evers/ Mandela Barnes (Dem.)
Waukesha	**146,699**	**72,131**	Larrabee, town	397	197
Big Bend, village	548	182	Lebanon, town	507	267
Brookfield, city	14,907	8,366	Lind, town	490	208
Brookfield, town	2,423	1,331	Little Wolf, town	482	165
Butler, village	529	315	Manawa, city	288	128
Chenequa, village	277	58	Marion, city (part)	295	128
Delafield, city	2,814	1,336	Matteson, town	324	122
Delafield, town	3,765	1,347	Mukwa, town	922	540
Dousman, village	824	371	New London, city (part) .	1,080	876
Eagle, town	1,465	556	Ogdensburg, village . . .	50	22
Eagle, village	779	257	Royalton, town	474	176
Elm Grove, village	2,528	1,480	St. Lawrence, town	222	103
Genesee, town	3,272	1,199	Scandinavia, town	331	255
Hartland, village	3,270	1,505	Scandinavia, village . . .	83	69
Lac La Belle, village (part)	131	59	Union, town	231	82
Lannon, village	455	215	Waupaca, city	1,169	1,108
Lisbon, town.	4,489	1,521	Waupaca, town	367	202
Menomonee Falls, village	13,283	7,447	Weyauwega, city	363	220
Merton, town	3,856	1,089	Weyauwega, town	189	67
Merton, village	1,451	384	Wyoming, town.	109	46
Milwaukee, city (part) . .	0	0			
Mukwonago, town	3,361	1,102	**Waushara**	**6,719**	**3,742**
Mukwonago, village (part)	2,628	1,143	Aurora, town.	324	135
Muskego, city	9,956	4,026	Berlin, city (part)	23	16
Nashotah, village.	602	223	Bloomfield, town	348	138
New Berlin, city	14,904	8,032	Coloma, town	211	148
North Prairie, village . . .	958	279	Coloma, village	119	61
Oconomowoc, city	6,014	3,001	Dakota, town	324	136
Oconomowoc, town . . .	3,943	1,361	Deerfield, town	225	136
Oconomowoc Lake, village	283	67	Hancock, town	193	78
Ottawa, town	1,646	686	Hancock, village	85	65
Pewaukee, city	6,330	2,586	Leon, town.	498	252
Pewaukee, village	2,698	1,412	Lohrville, village	90	54
Summit, village	1,954	823	Marion, town	696	387
Sussex, village.	3,878	1,802	Mount Morris, town . . .	355	235
Vernon, town	3,535	1,151	Oasis, town	149	59
Wales, village	1,108	533	Plainfield, town	163	57
Waukesha, city	18,146	13,370	Plainfield, village	167	125
Waukesha, town	3,689	1,516	Poy Sippi, town	320	115
			Redgranite, village	183	122
			Richford, town	154	45
Waupaca	**13,909**	**8,143**	Rose, town	202	158
Bear Creek, town	249	81	Saxeville, town	359	187
Big Falls, village.	19	13	Springwater, town	458	277
Caledonia, town	599	279	Warren, town	175	108
Clintonville, city.	878	619	Wautoma, city.	343	281
Dayton, town	890	527	Wautoma, town.	402	229
Dupont, town	201	64	Wild Rose, village.	153	138
Embarrass, village	102	42			
Farmington, town	1,078	752	**Winnebago**	**38,368**	**35,610**
Fremont, town	242	95	Algoma, town	2,232	1,526
Fremont, village	273	102	Appleton, city (part) . . .	142	207
Harrison, town	140	67	Black Wolf, town	913	542
Helvetia, town.	239	102	Clayton, town	1,480	698
Iola, town.	322	177	Fox Crossing, village . . .	4,526	3,719
Iola, village.	304	242	Menasha, city (part) . . .	2,610	3,063

Gubernatorial vote by county and municipality, November 6, 2018 general election, continued

	Scott Walker/ Rebecca Kleefisch (Rep.)	Tony Evers/ Mandela Barnes (Dem.)		Scott Walker/ Rebecca Kleefisch (Rep.)	Tony Evers/ Mandela Barnes (Dem.)
Neenah, city	5,804	5,859	Grand Rapids, town . . .	2,361	1,696
Neenah, town	1,131	835	Hansen, town	270	103
Nekimi, town	502	239	Hewitt, village	269	149
Nepeuskun, town	268	120	Hiles, town	64	22
Omro, city	796	620	Lincoln, town	540	296
Omro, town	768	465	Marshfield, city (part) . .	4,058	3,479
Oshkosh, city	11,389	14,566	Marshfield, town	277	119
Oshkosh, town	888	554	Milladore, town	198	124
Poygan, town	462	229	Milladore, village (part) .	75	41
Rushford, town	500	266	Nekoosa, city	531	390
Utica, town	460	262	Pittsville, city	227	123
Vinland, town	683	402	Port Edwards, town . . .	365	254
Winchester, town	637	335	Port Edwards, village . .	485	385
Winneconne, town	915	499	Remington, town	85	33
Winneconne, village . . .	774	426	Richfield, town	499	225
Wolf River, town	488	178	Rock, town	292	136
			Rudolph, town	322	209
Wood	**18,871**	**13,638**	Rudolph, village	112	102
Arpin, town	257	134	Saratoga, town	1,423	997
Arpin, village	85	30	Seneca, town	314	223
Auburndale, town	286	94	Sherry, town	268	105
Auburndale, village . . .	179	97	Sigel, town	307	208
Biron, village	212	181	Vesper, village	160	79
Cameron, town	169	75	Wisconsin Rapids, city . .	3,600	3,231
Cary, town	142	68	Wood, town	269	140
Cranmoor, town	61	28	**State totals**	1,295,080	1,324,307
Dexter, town	109	62			

Note: Other governor/lieutenant governor tickets received the following votes: Phillip Anderson/Patrick Baird (Libertarian)—20,225; Maggie Turnbull/Wil Losch (Independent)—18,884; Michael J. White/Tiffany Anderson (Wisconsin Green)—11,087; Arnie Enz (Independent)—2,745; Ryan Cason (write-in)—4; William Henry Davis III (write-in)—3; Mark S. Grimek (write-in)—2; Richard Michael Turtenwald (write-in)—2; Paul Boucher (write-in)—1; Corban Gehler (write-in)—1; Robbie Hoffman (write-in)—1.

Source: Official records of the Wisconsin Elections Commission.

County vote for secretary of state, August 14, 2018 partisan primary

	Democrat		Republican		
	Doug La Follette*	Arvina Martin	Jay Schroeder	Spencer Zimmerman	Total
Adams	1,209	439	1,071	425	3,145
Ashland	1,262	635	522	204	2,628
Barron	1,829	752	1,614	654	4,855
Bayfield	1,557	889	625	269	3,341
Brown	10,224	4,985	10,091	3,974	29,334
Buffalo	780	303	531	230	1,846
Burnett	606	356	1,221	612	2,796
Calumet	1,760	854	3,331	1,249	7,195
Chippewa	2,902	1,131	2,372	952	7,360
Clark	947	326	1,834	835	3,943

County vote for secretary of state, August 14, 2018 partisan primary, continued

	Democrat		Republican		
	Doug La Follette*	Arvina Martin	Jay Schroeder	Spencer Zimmerman	Total
Columbia.	3,826	1,442	2,063	1,084	8,423
Crawford	1,053	412	463	221	2,149
Dane	58,400	37,403	9,667	5,059	110,806
Dodge	2,944	1,218	6,263	2,803	13,230
Door.	2,288	1,191	1,731	615	5,832
Douglas.	2,385	1,244	1,071	492	5,202
Dunn	2,399	1,205	2,061	900	6,565
Eau Claire.	7,058	3,479	2,912	1,401	14,890
Florence	112	61	645	257	1,075
Fond du Lac	3,343	1,462	5,960	2,368	13,141
Forest.	297	126	977	408	1,809
Grant	2,093	943	1,171	551	4,765
Green.	2,526	971	1,010	510	5,025
Green Lake.	618	264	1,140	355	2,379
Iowa.	1,862	751	663	281	3,568
Iron	391	144	307	131	973
Jackson.	1,333	624	646	289	2,892
Jefferson.	3,940	1,942	4,092	1,678	11,674
Juneau	1,155	406	1,073	436	3,081
Kenosha	8,689	4,261	5,538	2,398	20,935
Kewaunee	832	379	1,029	394	2,634
La Crosse.	7,324	3,489	3,254	1,430	15,499
Lafayette.	826	283	457	203	1,771
Langlade.	765	244	1,077	328	2,414
Lincoln	1,237	499	2,873	937	5,561
Manitowoc.	3,175	1,268	3,578	1,694	9,732
Marathon.	6,186	2,492	6,407	2,551	17,667
Marinette.	1,406	509	3,226	1,164	6,307
Marquette	795	354	883	338	2,371
Menominee	147	138	51	16	352
Milwaukee.	62,907	37,419	21,690	8,718	131,201
Monroe.	1,654	688	2,440	987	5,774
Oconto	1,217	467	3,922	1,331	6,939
Oneida	2,025	828	2,795	942	6,608
Outagamie.	7,624	4,014	9,908	3,641	25,188
Ozaukee.	5,194	2,393	7,428	2,287	17,330
Pepin	350	226	314	115	1,005
Pierce.	1,599	979	1,195	588	4,363
Polk.	1,660	862	2,240	1,030	5,792
Portage.	4,446	1,890	2,025	847	9,225
Price.	828	262	689	281	2,060
Racine.	10,090	5,487	9,294	3,776	28,721
Richland	1,021	383	515	211	2,130
Rock.	11,859	4,678	4,324	2,389	23,295
Rusk.	696	252	1,204	472	2,626
St. Croix.	2,689	2,073	2,842	1,755	9,377
Sauk.	4,203	1,712	2,188	1,015	9,118
Sawyer.	773	459	1,099	371	2,705
Shawano.	1,216	602	3,790	1,143	6,752
Sheboygan.	5,283	2,348	6,311	2,529	16,501
Taylor.	564	249	1,247	603	2,665
Trempealeau	1,990	644	1,022	426	4,085
Vernon.	2,185	1,045	1,068	447	4,753
Vilas.	1,256	530	1,605	518	3,912
Walworth.	4,356	2,256	5,744	2,030	14,414
Washburn	762	362	1,570	732	3,430

County vote for secretary of state, August 14, 2018 partisan primary, continued

	Democrat		Republican		
	Doug La Follette*	Arvina Martin	Jay Schroeder	Spencer Zimmerman	Total
Washington	4,537	1,938	12,191	4,214	22,883
Waukesha	17,467	7,967	32,193	11,366	69,174
Waupaca.......................	2,066	853	3,228	996	7,151
Waushara......................	847	304	2,249	918	4,318
Winnebago	7,352	3,723	6,548	2,448	20,097
Wood..........................	3,823	1,363	4,046	1,996	11,229
Total..........................	327,020	169,130	254,424	101,818	853,986

Note: County totals include scattered votes. Wisconsin Green write-in candidate Brad Karas received a total of 11 votes.

*Incumbent

Source: Official records of the Wisconsin Elections Commission.

County vote for secretary of state, November 6, 2018 general election

	Doug La Follette* (Dem.)	Jay Schroeder (Rep.)	Total
Adams	4,104	5,094	9,198
Ashland.......................................	4,294	2,493	6,792
Barron..	7,995	10,300	18,301
Bayfield.......................................	5,315	3,368	8,684
Brown..	55,195	57,858	113,139
Buffalo	2,628	3,191	5,822
Burnett	2,959	4,515	7,474
Calumet	9,758	13,457	23,216
Chippewa	12,529	14,607	27,136
Clark...	4,599	6,786	11,388
Columbia.....................................	14,368	12,211	26,598
Crawford	3,567	2,925	6,493
Dane	219,538	69,184	289,150
Dodge	14,527	22,440	36,969
Door..	8,480	8,141	16,634
Douglas.......................................	11,243	7,269	18,521
Dunn	9,019	9,118	18,138
Eau Claire.....................................	27,636	20,088	47,772
Florence	676	1,475	2,151
Fond du Lac	17,631	26,649	44,310
Forest	1,635	2,197	3,835
Grant	9,772	9,378	19,156
Green...	9,595	7,144	16,749
Green Lake....................................	2,836	5,211	8,050
Iowa..	6,819	4,124	10,948
Iron	1,366	1,669	3,035
Jackson.......................................	4,041	3,824	7,865
Jefferson	16,781	20,437	37,245
Juneau	4,249	5,710	9,964
Kenosha	35,781	30,829	66,673
Kewaunee	3,926	5,420	9,355
La Crosse.....................................	33,060	22,663	55,723
Lafayette.....................................	3,347	3,071	6,419
Langlade......................................	3,395	5,630	9,036

County vote for secretary of state, November 6, 2018 general election, continued

	Doug La Follette* (Dem.)	Jay Schroeder (Rep.)	Total
Lincoln	5,662	7,439	13,113
Manitowoc	15,354	19,388	34,761
Marathon	26,567	34,239	60,850
Marinette	6,662	10,356	17,020
Marquette	3,044	4,006	7,056
Menominee	847	237	1,084
Milwaukee	269,143	113,770	383,488
Monroe	7,347	9,182	16,545
Oconto	6,276	10,936	17,223
Oneida	8,540	10,553	19,112
Outagamie	38,391	43,109	81,504
Ozaukee	19,801	30,480	50,332
Pepin	1,374	1,683	3,057
Pierce	8,421	8,899	17,323
Polk	7,635	10,803	18,439
Portage	19,075	14,916	34,018
Price	2,916	3,662	6,578
Racine	42,821	42,705	85,614
Richland	3,648	3,253	6,906
Rock	40,630	26,068	66,765
Rusk	2,418	3,565	5,988
St. Croix	17,267	22,365	39,659
Sauk	15,870	12,468	28,338
Sawyer	3,662	4,372	8,035
Shawano	6,416	11,164	17,580
Sheboygan	22,949	29,289	52,293
Taylor	2,650	5,209	7,864
Trempealeau	5,864	6,088	11,959
Vernon	6,898	5,891	12,792
Vilas	4,901	7,464	12,371
Walworth	18,499	26,200	44,731
Washburn	3,374	4,401	7,778
Washington	20,697	48,749	69,446
Waukesha	77,918	139,149	217,239
Waupaca	8,540	13,441	21,990
Waushara	3,939	6,461	10,400
Winnebago	37,353	36,980	74,405
Wood	14,719	17,618	32,353
Total	**1,380,752**	**1,235,034**	**2,617,948**

Note: County totals include scattered votes. Wisconsin Green write-in candidate Brad Karas received a total of 60 votes.

*Incumbent. Dem.–Democrat; Rep.–Republican.

Source: Official records of the Wisconsin Elections Commission.

County vote for attorney general, August 14, 2018 partisan primary

	Josh Kaul (Dem.)	Brad Schimel* (Rep.)	Terry Larson (Con.)	Total
Adams	1,428	1,550	2	2,982
Ashland	1,575	719	3	2,302
Barron	1,996	2,413	3	4,419

County vote for attorney general, August 14, 2018 partisan primary, continued

	Josh Kaul (Dem.)	Brad Schimel* (Rep.)	Terry Larson (Con.)	Total
Bayfield	2,158	917	1	3,081
Brown	13,207	15,388	3	28,685
Buffalo	980	772	1	1,756
Burnett	901	1,893	7	2,801
Calumet	2,307	4,903	1	7,212
Chippewa	3,573	3,502	4	7,082
Clark	1,089	2,666	—	3,757
Columbia	4,573	3,389	1	7,985
Crawford	1,328	719	5	2,052
Dane	83,965	16,812	32	101,341
Dodge	3,610	9,911	2	13,525
Door	2,998	2,532	2	5,543
Douglas	3,388	1,564	—	4,963
Dunn	3,323	3,080	1	6,404
Eau Claire	9,616	4,661	4	14,334
Florence	151	957	—	1,109
Fond du Lac	4,218	9,249	2	13,482
Forest	363	1,519	1	1,885
Grant	2,709	1,824	3	4,547
Green	2,990	1,638	2	4,640
Green Lake	805	1,599	2	2,409
Iowa	2,363	1,026	3	3,407
Iron	459	466	1	927
Jackson	1,768	1,004	3	2,775
Jefferson	5,125	6,606	3	11,766
Juneau	1,382	1,597	2	2,992
Kenosha	11,237	8,811	8	20,138
Kewaunee	1,103	1,473	1	2,577
La Crosse	9,315	4,987	11	14,313
Lafayette	972	709	2	1,687
Langlade	886	1,498	4	2,388
Lincoln	1,529	3,811	—	5,361
Manitowoc	3,970	5,671	5	9,670
Marathon	7,669	9,660	6	17,378
Marinette	1,687	4,596	11	6,296
Marquette	1,047	1,275	3	2,327
Menominee	236	67	—	303
Milwaukee	85,546	35,463	39	121,904
Monroe	2,078	3,537	2	5,633
Oconto	1,506	5,486	5	7,000
Oneida	2,510	3,954	5	6,500
Outagamie	10,307	14,769	10	25,087
Ozaukee	6,693	11,497	2	18,229
Pepin	516	440	1	957
Pierce	2,462	1,853	3	4,321
Polk	2,389	3,381	4	5,774
Portage	5,440	3,186	1	8,643
Price	934	1,035	—	1,969˙
Racine	13,183	14,739	14	28,037
Richland	1,233	744	10	1,987
Rock	14,651	7,165	10	21,916
Rusk	832	1,757	1	2,591
St. Croix	4,430	4,697	22	9,175
Sauk	5,096	3,373	10	8,479
Sawyer	1,086	1,551	3	2,644
Shawano	1,587	5,100	6	6,694
Sheboygan	6,715	9,914	5	16,681

County vote for attorney general, August 14, 2018 partisan primary, continued

	Josh Kaul (Dem.)	Brad Schimel* (Rep.)	Terry Larson (Con.)	Total
Taylor	728	1,930	2	2,664
Trempealeau	2,433	1,493	2	3,937
Vernon	2,793	1,601	10	4,415
Vilas	1,524	2,246	1	3,777
Walworth	5,798	8,489	6	14,329
Washburn	1,011	2,375	8	3,396
Washington	5,678	18,705	2	24,387
Waukesha	21,812	53,377	11	75,446
Waupaca	2,643	4,423	2	7,071
Waushara	1,068	3,356	3	4,428
Winnebago	9,670	9,429	3	19,163
Wood	4,603	6,300	6	10,910
Total	**432,954**	**394,799**	**354**	**830,745**

Note: County totals include scattered votes.
*Incumbent. —Represents zero; Con.–Constitution; Dem.–Democrat; Rep.–Republican.
Source: Official records of the Wisconsin Elections Commission.

County vote for attorney general, November 6, 2018 general election

	Josh Kaul (Dem.)	Brad Schimel* (Rep.)	Terry Larson (Con.)	Total
Adams	3,818	5,243	208	9,269
Ashland	4,089	2,527	117	6,736
Barron	7,511	10,447	382	18,341
Bayfield	5,113	3,403	120	8,636
Brown	51,557	60,756	2,112	114,479
Buffalo	2,362	3,322	158	5,843
Burnett	2,835	4,466	208	7,509
Calumet	9,025	14,059	399	23,483
Chippewa	11,347	15,341	735	27,423
Clark	4,077	7,147	322	11,546
Columbia	13,391	12,696	518	26,614
Crawford	3,292	3,092	164	6,548
Dane	214,831	73,022	3,535	291,571
Dodge	13,379	23,504	628	37,511
Door	8,232	8,311	288	16,836
Douglas	11,034	7,191	360	18,590
Dunn	8,537	9,139	506	18,182
Eau Claire	26,483	20,547	1,198	48,252
Florence	632	1,479	27	2,138
Fond du Lac	16,778	27,366	669	44,825
Forest	1,489	2,296	78	3,866
Grant	9,080	9,787	379	19,248
Green	8,858	7,662	347	16,875
Green Lake	2,686	5,294	112	8,093

County vote for attorney general, November 6, 2018 general election, continued

	Josh Kaul (Dem.)	Brad Schimel* (Rep.)	Terry Larson (Con.)	Total
Iowa.	6,374	4,473	206	11,058
Iron	1,298	1,702	39	3,039
Jackson.	3,742	3,947	233	7,922
Jefferson.	15,735	21,352	616	37,714
Juneau	3,985	5,808	220	10,014
Kenosha	33,940	31,774	1,368	67,132
Kewaunee	3,548	5,694	158	9,404
La Crosse.	31,717	23,357	1,213	56,287
Lafayette.	2,919	3,370	131	6,421
Langlade.	3,023	5,870	196	9,089
Lincoln	5,185	7,733	262	13,185
Manitowoc.	13,937	20,343	732	35,025
Marathon.	24,242	36,317	1,055	61,635
Marinette.	6,174	10,683	335	17,192
Marquette.	2,777	4,151	156	7,088
Menominee	827	255	25	1,107
Milwaukee.	257,775	123,389	6,994	388,539
Monroe.	6,729	9,402	478	16,610
Oconto	5,721	11,284	340	17,351
Oneida	8,094	10,886	338	19,331
Outagamie.	36,062	45,074	1,497	82,633
Ozaukee	18,749	31,496	571	50,848
Pepin	1,287	1,700	81	3,068
Pierce	8,231	8,723	465	17,422
Polk	7,429	10,607	418	18,454
Portage.	17,940	15,876	616	34,444
Price.	2,623	3,847	131	6,601
Racine.	39,721	44,945	1,581	86,302
Richland	3,401	3,425	154	6,982
Rock.	38,415	27,241	1,502	67,201
Rusk.	2,167	3,675	164	6,013
St. Croix.	16,947	21,991	860	39,805
Sauk.	14,943	13,182	572	28,697
Sawyer	3,437	4,471	147	8,055
Shawano	6,011	11,366	355	17,732
Sheboygan.	20,687	30,886	1,064	52,657
Taylor	2,294	5,493	153	7,941
Trempealeau	5,338	6,375	300	12,015
Vernon	6,440	6,100	286	12,827
Vilas	4,647	7,660	151	12,462
Walworth.	17,414	26,761	809	45,002
Washburn	3,244	4,419	157	7,822
Washington	18,734	50,428	927	70,089
Waukesha	70,711	146,321	2,688	219,837
Waupaca.	7,900	13,852	458	22,217
Waushara.	3,748	6,561	185	10,494
Winnebago	35,815	37,933	1,427	75,207
Wood	13,389	18,417	654	32,467
Total.	**1,305,902**	**1,288,712**	**47,038**	**2,642,851**

Note: County totals include scattered votes.

*Incumbent. Con.–Constitution; Dem.–Democrat; Rep.–Republican.

Source: Official records of the Wisconsin Elections Commission.

County vote for state treasurer, August 14, 2018 partisan primary

	Democrat			Republican			
	Sarah Godlewski	Dawn Marie Sass	Cynthia Kaump	Travis Hartwig	Jill Millies	Andrew Zuelke (Con.)	Total
Adams	630	534	389	1,035	441	3	3,036
Ashland.	718	616	481	503	210	5	2,538
Barron.	987	823	653	1,683	592	3	4,745
Bayfield.	975	680	567	618	276	1	3,117
Brown.	5,962	4,614	3,494	9,692	4,325	4	28,156
Buffalo	332	463	236	544	210	1	1,788
Burnett	343	344	242	1,268	565	6	2,768
Calumet	996	879	566	3,373	1,278	1	7,094
Chippewa	1,631	1,176	976	2,508	822	4	7,123
Clark.	491	431	245	1,837	803	—	3,809
Columbia.	2,541	1,283	1,098	2,291	870	2	8,095
Crawford	556	530	285	503	180	5	2,060
Dane	42,580	24,844	19,238	10,336	4,514	33	101,920
Dodge	1,738	1,252	967	6,535	2,623	1	13,118
Door.	1,275	1,012	790	1,560	770	2	5,417
Douglas.	1,415	1,085	969	1,068	487	—	5,029
Dunn	1,462	1,025	893	2,134	815	2	6,331
Eau Claire.	5,550	2,286	2,160	3,131	1,170	4	14,349
Florence	48	58	56	610	289	—	1,061
Fond du Lac	1,820	1,615	1,031	6,057	2,419	5	12,958
Forest	144	141	101	935	400	1	1,728
Grant	1,196	974	677	1,309	441	3	4,606
Green	1,530	910	784	1,125	421	2	4,782
Green Lake.	362	292	183	1,128	370	2	2,338
Iowa.	1,215	691	559	720	244	2	3,442
Iron	192	198	114	308	119	1	932
Jackson	622	691	506	693	239	5	2,756
Jefferson	2,482	1,758	1,288	4,447	1,428	2	11,432
Juneau	641	488	364	1,077	439	2	3,023
Kenosha	4,990	3,816	3,249	5,495	2,473	10	20,095
Kewaunee	488	363	305	1,025	388	1	2,570
La Crosse	4,275	3,060	2,465	3,165	1,518	11	14,496
Lafayette	473	319	246	514	156	2	1,713
Langlade	367	373	212	1,050	336	3	2,342
Lincoln	829	452	375	2,534	1,284	—	5,486
Manitowoc.	1,704	1,361	1,093	4,045	1,360	5	9,580
Marathon.	3,898	2,269	1,972	6,287	2,704	6	17,173
Marinette.	686	627	490	3,205	1,148	9	6,167
Marquette	508	313	293	936	291	3	2,345
Menominee	64	103	84	44	22	—	317
Milwaukee	38,432	33,368	23,296	22,961	8,708	40	127,427
Monroe	775	834	581	2,385	1,052	2	5,635
Oconto	582	541	462	3,723	1,545	7	6,863
Oneida	1,174	831	617	2,843	1,052	7	6,548
Outagamie.	4,599	3,836	2,565	9,488	4,202	9	24,699
Ozaukee	3,120	2,312	1,542	7,747	2,317	5	17,070
Pepin	257	169	122	308	110	1	967
Pierce	1,004	786	668	1,255	516	2	4,233
Polk	834	879	738	2,345	935	4	5,735
Portage	2,840	1,660	1,288	2,120	775	—	8,701
Price	438	340	235	720	252	1	1,986
Racine.	5,813	4,548	4,111	9,951	3,466	12	27,981
Richland	589	471	255	534	181	3	2,033
Rock.	6,936	4,872	3,618	4,542	2,184	10	22,216
Rusk.	369	292	221	1,250	416	1	2,549

County vote for state treasurer, August 14, 2018 partisan primary, continued

	Democrat			Republican			
	Sarah Godlewski	Dawn Marie Sass	Cynthia Kaump	Travis Hartwig	Jill Millies	Andrew Zuelke (Con.)	Total
St. Croix.	1,840	1,456	1,251	3,195	1,370	22	9,156
Sauk.	2,620	1,590	1,203	2,305	911	7	8,637
Sawyer	505	346	314	1,074	409	2	2,653
Shawano.	604	618	492	3,771	1,167	5	6,657
Sheboygan.	2,910	2,535	1,754	6,615	2,403	7	16,262
Taylor.	318	272	176	1,312	541	2	2,622
Trempealeau	895	1,042	577	1,071	368	1	3,961
Vernon	1,339	894	728	1,107	391	7	4,478
Vilas.	662	562	416	1,626	527	1	3,799
Walworth.	2,317	2,206	1,672	5,810	2,056	5	14,102
Washburn	457	330	264	1,570	719	6	3,347
Washington	2,401	2,067	1,559	12,694	4,134	3	22,860
Waukesha	9,797	7,658	6,062	33,721	11,466	10	68,949
Waupaca	1,083	993	679	3,210	1,016	4	6,992
Waushara.	398	403	290	2,271	877	2	4,241
Winnebago	4,576	3,400	2,369	6,193	2,726	4	19,301
Wood.	1,831	1,502	1,434	4,094	1,921	6	10,789
Total.	201,031	148,362	112,255	261,139	100,153	350	825,284

Note: County totals include scattered votes.
—Represents zero; Con.–Constitution; Dem.–Democrat; Rep. Republican.
Source: Official records of the Wisconsin Elections Commission.

County vote for state treasurer, November 6, 2018 general election

	Sarah Godlewski (Dem.)	Travis Hartwig (Rep.)	Andrew Zuelke (Con.)	Total
Adams	3,896	4,997	275	9,168
Ashland.	4,194	2,418	109	6,722
Barron.	7,636	10,226	420	18,284
Bayfield.	5,197	3,286	142	8,626
Brown.	52,570	56,746	3,280	112,671
Buffalo	2,512	3,144	140	5,797
Burnett.	2,889	4,436	147	7,472
Calumet	9,150	13,321	613	23,084
Chippewa	11,874	14,623	621	27,118
Clark.	4,137	6,791	368	11,296
Columbia.	13,334	12,003	704	26,053
Crawford	3,368	2,935	152	6,455
Dane	213,387	68,403	5,114	287,156
Dodge	13,456	22,385	902	36,743
Door.	8,188	7,917	391	16,500
Douglas.	11,063	7,004	356	18,427
Dunn	8,684	8,942	481	18,107
Eau Claire.	27,108	19,369	1,266	47,768
Florence	648	1,453	37	2,138
Fond du Lac	16,495	26,274	1,120	43,902
Forest	1,523	2,191	82	3,798
Grant	8,956	9,665	444	19,069
Green	8,790	7,310	486	16,592

District vote for state senators, general and special elections

Senate district	Assembly districts	Party	Candidates	Vote	% of total[1]
January 16, 2018 special election					
10	1, 2, 3	Democrat	Patty Schachtner	12,249	54.60
		Republican	Adam Jarchow	9,909	44.17
		Libertarian	Brian J. Corriea	273	1.22
June 12, 2018 special election					
1	1, 2, 3	Democrat	Caleb Frostman	14,606	51.38
		Republican	André Jacque	13,801	48.55
November 6, 2018 general election					
1	1, 2, 3	Republican	André Jacque	47,289	54.50
		Democrat	Caleb Frostman*	39,414	45.42
3	7, 8, 9	Democrat	Tim Carpenter*	36,875	97.40
5	13, 14, 15	Republican	Dale Kooyenga	47,836	51.15
		Democrat	Julie Henszey	45,591	48.75
7	19, 20, 21	Democrat	Chris Larson*	56,198	66.25
		Republican	Jason Red Arnold	28,459	33.55
9	25, 26, 27	Republican	Devin LeMahieu*	44,680	58.47
		Democrat	Kyle Whelton	31,684	41.47
11	31, 32, 33	Republican	Steve Nass*	59,512	95.89
		Independent	Steven Michael Johnson (write-in)	53	0.09
13	37, 38, 39	Republican	Scott Fitzgerald*	49,668	59.07
		Democrat	Michelle Zahn	34,385	40.90
15	43, 44, 45	Democrat	Janis Ringhand*	53,458	96.59
		Republican	Gregory Alan Neumann (write-in)	4	0.01
17	49, 50, 51	Republican	Howard Marklein*	37,465	54.10
		Democrat	Kriss Marion	31,757	45.86
19	55, 56, 57	Republican	Roger Roth*	43,493	53.23
		Democrat	Lee Snodgrass	38,179	46.73
21	61, 62, 63	Republican	Van H. Wanggaard*	48,603	58.01
		Democrat	Lori Hawkins	35,111	41.91
23	67, 68, 69	Republican	Kathy Bernier	42,958	59.17
		Democrat	Chris Kapsner	29,637	40.82
25	73, 74, 75	Democrat	Janet Bewley*	39,624	51.06
		Republican	James Bolen	37,960	48.92
27	79, 80, 81	Democrat	Jon B. Erpenbach*	64,605	66.16
		Republican	Casey Helbach	32,992	33.79
29	85, 86, 87	Republican	Jerry Petrowski*	49,657	64.22
		Democrat	Richard Pulcher	27,627	35.73
31	91, 92, 93	Democrat	Jeff Smith	40,073	51.67
		Republican	Mel Pittman	35,684	46.01
		Independent	Aaron Elaine Camacho	1,776	2.29
33	97, 98, 99	Republican	Chris Kapenga*	68,759	96.85

*Incumbent.

1. Percentages do not add up to 100, as scattered votes have been omitted.

Source: Official records of the Wisconsin Elections Commission.

District vote for representatives to the assembly, partisan and special primaries

Assem. district	Party	Candidates	Vote
December 19, 2017 special primary			
58 . . .	Dem.	Dennis D. Degenhardt	444
	Rep.	Rick Gundrum	1,252
	Rep.	Tiffany Koehler	984
	Rep.	Steve Stanek	942
	Rep.	Spencer Zimmerman	37
66 . . .	Dem.	Greta Neubauer	1,518
	Dem.	John Tate, II	1,301
May 15, 2018 special primary			
42 . . .	Dem.	Ann Groves Lloyd	754
	Rep.	Colleen J. Locke-Murphy	142
	Rep.	Jon Plumer	1,418
	Rep.	Darren W. Schroeder	333
	Rep.	Spencer Zimmerman	116
August 14, 2018 partisan primary			
1 . . .	Rep.	Joel C. Kitchens*	5,008
2 . . .	Dem.	Mark Grams	2,970
	Rep.	Dean Raasch	2,221
	Rep.	Shae Sortwell	2,708
	Lib.	Kevin A. Bauer	18
3 . . .	Dem.	Scott Gavin	3,117
	Rep.	Ron Tusler*	4,490
4 . . .	Dem.	Terry Lee	3,629
	Rep.	David Steffen*	4,015
5 . . .	Dem.	Matt Lederer	2,669
	Rep.	Jim Steineke*	4,936
6 . . .	Dem.	Richard Sarnwick	1,453
	Dem.	William J. Switalla	929
	Rep.	Gary Tauchen*	6,564
	Lib.	Mike Hammond	29
7 . . .	Dem.	Daniel G. Riemer*	4,403
	Lib.	Matthew J. Bughman	12
8 . . .	Dem.	JoCasta Zamarripa*	1,292
	Rep.	Angel C. Sanchez	198
9 . . .	Dem.	Marisabel Cabrera	1,982
	Dem.	Josh Zepnick*	1,110
10 . . .	Dem.	David Bowen*	7,546
11 . . .	Dem.	Jason M. Fields*	5,063
12 . . .	Dem.	Frederick P. Kessler*	2,545
	Dem.	LaKeshia N. Myers	3,709
13 . . .	Dem.	Dennis Raymond McBride	5,158
	Rep.	Rob Hutton*	5,929
14 . . .	Dem.	Robyn Vining	6,210
	Rep.	Matt Adamczyk	3,580
	Rep.	Linda Boucher	614
	Rep.	Robin Moore	2,619
	Rep.	Joshua Parr	508
	Lib.	Rick Braun	23

Assem. district	Party	Candidates	Vote
15 . . .	Dem.	Lillian Cheesman	3,784
	Rep.	Joe Sanfelippo*	4,757
16 . . .	Rep.	Rick Banks	977
	Dem.	Brandy Bond	367
	Dem.	Kalan Haywood	2,324
	Dem.	Danielle McClendon-Williams	454
	Dem.	Supreme Moore Omokunde	2,079
17 . . .	Dem.	David C. Crowley*	6,528
18 . . .	Dem.	Evan Goyke*	4,797
	Dem.	Travis Spell	1,601
19 . . .	Dem.	Jonathan Brostoff*	9,446
20 . . .	Dem.	Christine M. Sinicki*	6,328
21 . . .	Dem.	Gabriel A Gomez	4,081
	Rep.	Jessie Rodriguez	3,597
22 . . .	Dem.	Aaron Matteson	3,322
	Rep.	Janel Brandtjen*	6,899
	Rep.	Michele Divelbiss	33
23 . . .	Dem.	William A. Demet	594
	Dem.	Andy Lamb	2,478
	Dem.	Liz Sumner	5,360
	Rep.	Jim Ott*	6,551
24 . . .	Dem.	Emily Siegrist	5,431
	Rep.	Dan Knodl*	6,069
25 . . .	Dem.	Jennifer Estrada	2,554
	Rep.	Paul Tittl*	4,111
26 . . .	Dem.	Rebecca Clarke	3,369
	Rep.	Terry Katsma*	4,912
27 . . .	Dem.	Nanette Bulebosh	3,744
	Rep.	Tyler Vorpagel*	4,733
28 . . .	Dem.	Kim Butler	3,061
	Rep.	Gae Magnafici	4,665
29 . . .	Dem.	John Rocco Calabrese	3,222
	Rep.	Robert Stafsholt*	3,155
	Lib.	Brian Corriea	21
30 . . .	Dem.	Barry Hammarback	3,615
	Rep.	Shannon Zimmerman*	3,000
31 . . .	Dem.	Brittany Keyes	4,299
	Rep.	Amy Loudenbeck*	4,376
32 . . .	Dem.	Katherine R. Gaulke	3,179
	Rep.	Tyler August*	4,709
33 . . .	Dem.	Brandon White	3,206
	Rep.	Cody J. Horlacher*	4,841
34 . . .	Dem.	Chris Meier	4,002
	Rep.	Rob Swearingen*	7,425
35 . . .	Dem.	Mark A. Martello	2,851
	Rep.	Mary Czaja-Felzkowski*	6,223
36 . . .	Dem.	Tim Comer	2,571
	Rep.	Jeffrey L. Mursau*	8,072
	W.Gr.	Wendy Gribben	1

District vote for representatives to the assembly, partisan and special primaries, continued

Assem. district	Party	Candidates	Vote
37	Dem.	Matt Taylor	404
	Rep.	John Jagler*	4,843
38	Dem.	Melissa Winker	4,332
	Rep.	Barbara Dittrich	5,272
39	Dem.	Elisha Barudin	2,436
	Rep.	Mark L. Born*	6,557
40	Dem.	Erin Tracy	2,987
	Rep.	Kevin Petersen*	5,463
41	Dem.	Frank T. Buress	3,171
	Rep.	Joan Ballweg*	3,997
42	Dem.	Ann Groves Lloyd	4,158
	Rep.	Jon Plumer	4,439
43	Dem.	Don Vruwink*	5,753
	Rep.	Gabriel Szerlong	2,297
44	Dem.	Deb Kolste*	6,367
45	Dem.	Mark Spreitzer*	4,005
	Lib.	Reese Wood	18
46	Dem.	Gary Hebl*	7,440
47	Dem.	Jimmy Anderson*	9,233
48	Dem.	Melissa Agard Sargent*	11,494
49	Dem.	Mike Mooney	3,218
	Rep.	Travis Tranel*	2,122
50	Dem.	Arthur L. Shrader	3,655
	Rep.	Tony Kurtz	3,260
51	Dem.	Jeffrey Wright	4,686
	Rep.	Todd Novak*	2,468
52	Dem.	Kevin Booth	2,507
	Rep.	Jeremy Thiesfeldt*	5,144
53	Dem.	Joe Lavrenz	2,405
	Rep.	Michael Schraa*	4,180
54	Dem.	Gordon Hintz*	3,913
55	Dem.	Dan Schierl	3,579
	Rep.	Mike Rohrkaste*	4,026
56	Dem.	John Cuff	1,687
	Dem.	Diana Lawrence	2,424
	Rep.	Dave Murphy*	5,852
57	Dem.	Amanda Stuck*	4,346
58	Dem.	Dennis D. Degenhardt	2,634
	Rep.	Rick Gundrum*	7,261
59	Rep.	Ty Bodden	2,556
	Rep.	Ken Depperman	709
	Rep.	Rachel Mixon	2,164
	Rep.	Timothy S. Ramthun	2,851
60	Dem.	Chris Rahlf	3,519
	Rep.	Robert Brooks*	7,355
61	Dem.	Gina Walkington	3,651
	Rep.	Samantha Kerkman*	4,481
62	Dem.	John Lehman	4,903

Assem. district	Party	Candidates	Vote
	Rep.	John S. Leiber	1,885
	Rep.	Robert Wittke	3,931
63	Dem.	Joel Jacobsen	3,813
	Rep.	Robin Vos*	5,395
64	Dem.	Peter W. Barca*	4,978
	Con.	Thomas Harland	6
65	Dem.	Tod Ohnstad*	4,333
66	Dem.	Greta Neubauer*	4,134
67	Dem.	Wren Keturi	3,775
	Rep.	Rob Summerfield*	3,887
68	Dem.	Wendy Sue Johnson	3,607
	Rep.	Jesse James	3,228
69	Rep.	Bob Kulp*	4,198
70	Dem.	Cari Fay	3,060
	Rep.	Nancy Lynn VanderMeer*	4,814
71	Dem.	Katrina Shankland*	5,436
72	Dem.	David Gorski	3,702
	Rep.	Scott S. Krug*	5,839
73	Dem.	Nick Milroy*	4,524
	Rep.	Jeffery L. Monaghan	7
74	Dem.	Beth Meyers*	6,573
	Rep.	Jeffrey Fahl	3,384
75	Dem.	Ali Holzman	3,213
	Rep.	Romaine Robert Quinn*	4,122
76	Dem.	Chris Taylor*	12,882
77	Dem.	Mark Garthwaite	968
	Dem.	John Imes	1,222
	Dem.	Shabnam Lotfi	5,612
	Dem.	Shelia Stubbs	7,760
78	Dem.	Lisa Subeck*	12,069
79	Dem.	Dianne Hesselbein*	9,723
80	Dem.	Sondy Pope*	9,213
81	Dem.	Dave Considine*	5,790
82	Rep.	Ken Skowronski*	4,479
	Lib.	Jason J. Sellnow	14
83	Dem.	Jim Brownlow	3,123
	Rep.	Chuck Wichgers*	6,486
84	Dem.	Erica Flynn	3,936
	Rep.	Mike Kuglitsch*	5,007
85	Dem.	Alyson Leahy	3,769
	Rep.	Patrick Snyder*	3,457
86	Dem.	Nancy Stencil	3,458
	Rep.	Brent Jacobson	2,103
	Rep.	John Spiros*	3,855
87	Dem.	Elizabeth Riley	2,129
	Dem.	Tom Wymore	858
	Rep.	James W. Edming*	5,782

District vote for representatives to the assembly, partisan and special primaries, continued

Assem. district	Party	Candidates	Vote
88	Dem.	Tom Sieber.	3,381
	Rep.	John Macco*.	3,469
89	Dem.	Ken Holdorf	2,429
	Rep.	John Nygren*	5,747
90	Dem.	Staush Gruszynski	2,530
91	Dem.	Jodi Emerson	2,648
	Dem.	Eric Larsen	1,778
	Dem.	Rich Postlewaite	814
	Dem.	Thomas Vue	1,890
	Rep.	Echo Reardon	1,928
92	Dem.	Desiree Gearing-Lancaster . .	1,580
	Dem.	Rob Grover.	2,645
	Dem.	Max Hart	1,224
	Rep.	Treig E. Pronschinske*	2,989
93	Dem.	Charlene Charlie Warner . . .	4,181
	Rep.	Warren Petryk*	3,599

Assem. district	Party	Candidates	Vote
94	Dem.	Steve Doyle*.	4,818
	Rep.	Albert Rohland	2,891
95	Dem.	Jill Billings*.	6,065
96	Dem.	Paul Buhr.	3,102
	Dem.	Alicia Leinberger	2,693
	Rep.	Loren Oldenburg	3,393
97	Rep.	Scott Allen*	4,626
98	Rep.	Mary Larson	0
	Rep.	Adam Neylon*	6,130
99	Rep.	Cindi Duchow*	7,424

April 2, 2019 special primary

64	Dem.	Tip McGuire	2,433
	Dem.	Gina Walkington	1,740
	Dem.	Spencer Zimmerman	243
	Rep.	Mark Stalker	2,822

*Incumbent. Assem.–Assembly; Con.–Constitution; Dem.–Democrat; Lib.–Libertarian; Rep.–Republican; W.Gr.–Wisconsin Green.
Source: Official records of the Wisconsin Elections Commission.

District vote for representatives to the assembly, general and special elections

Assembly district	Party	Candidates	Vote	% of total[1]
January 16, 2018 special election				
58	Republican	Rick Gundrum.	2,453	56.64
	Democrat	Dennis D. Degenhardt.	1,878	43.36
66	Democrat	Greta Neubauer.	831	100
June 12, 2018 special election				
42	Republican	Jon Plumer.	5,712	53.16
	Democrat	Ann Groves Lloyd.	4,834	44.99
	Independent	Gene Rubinstein	199	1.85
November 6, 2018 general election				
1	Republican	Joel C. Kitchens*	20,651	68.38
	Independent	Roberta Thelen	9,519	31.52
2	Republican	Shae Sortwell	15,014	54.82
	Democrat	Mark Grams	10,118	36.94
	Independent	Jeff Dahlke.	1,494	5.45
	Libertarian	Kevin A. Bauer.	745	2.72
3	Democrat	Scott Gavin	11,775	42.63
	Republican	Ron Tusler*.	15,847	57.36
4	Republican	David Steffen*.	15,291	54.81
	Democrat	Terry Lee	12,585	45.11
5	Republican	Jim Steineke*	17,175	61.06
	Democrat	Matt Lederer.	10,952	38.94
6	Republican	Gary Tauchen*	15,028	61.59

District vote for representatives to the assembly, general and special elections, continued

Assembly district	Party	Candidates	Vote	% of total[1]
	Democrat	Richard Sarnwick.	7,693	31.53
	Libertarian	Mike Hammond.	1,675	6.87
7	Democrat	Daniel G. Riemer*.	15,187	78.28
	Libertarian	Matthew J. Bughman	3,953	20.38
8	Democrat	JoCasta Zamarripa*	7,384	81.70
	Republican	Angel C. Sanchez.	1,639	18.13
9	Democrat	Marisabel Cabrera	11,453	97.96
10	Democrat	David Bowen*.	20,961	99.11
11	Democrat	Jason M. Fields*.	17,162	98.75
12	Democrat	LaKeshia N. Myers	17,428	98.45
13	Republican	Rob Hutton*.	16,617	51.41
	Democrat	Dennis Raymond McBride	15,662	48.45
14	Democrat	Robyn Vining	16,597	48.58
	Republican	Matt Adamczyk.	16,459	48.18
	Libertarian	Rick Braun	691	2.02
	Independent	Steven Shevey.	402	1.18
15	Republican	Joe Sanfelippo*.	15,089	56.11
	Democrat	Lillian Cheesman.	11,768	43.76
16	Democrat	Kalan Haywood.	16,861	98.80
17	Democrat	David C. Crowley*	20,820	99.04
18	Democrat	Evan Goyke*.	17,426	98.99
19	Democrat	Jonathan Brostoff*.	27,543	97.50
20	Democrat	Christine Sinicki*.	20,245	96.09
21	Republican	Jessie Rodriguez*.	14,280	54.66
	Democrat	Gabriel A. Gomez.	11,806	45.20
22	Republican	Janel Brandtjen*	21,153	64.25
	Democrat	Aaron Matteson.	11,738	35.65
	Republican	Michele Divelbiss (write-in)	2	0.01
23	Republican	Jim Ott*.	18,321	51.93
	Democrat	Liz Sumner.	16,939	48.01
24	Republican	Dan Knodl*	17,650	53.63
	Democrat	Emily Siegrist	15,244	46.33
25	Republican	Paul Tittl*.	14,785	62.02
	Democrat	Jennifer Estrada.	9,042	37.93
26	Republican	Terry Katsma*.	14,485	58.02
	Democrat	Rebecca Clarke.	10,466	41.92
27	Republican	Tyler Vorpagel*	16,533	59.61
	Democrat	Nanette Bulebosh	11,186	40.33
28	Republican	Gae Magnafici.	14,441	59.01
	Democrat	Kim Butler	10,028	40.98
29	Republican	Rob Stafsholt*.	12,523	54.70
	Democrat	John Rocco Calabrese.	9,750	42.58
	Libertarian	Brian Corriea.	620	2.71
30	Republican	Shannon Zimmerman*	15,240	53.91
	Democrat	Barry Hammarback.	13,015	46.03
31	Republican	Amy Loudenbeck*.	15,299	57.47
	Democrat	Brittany Keyes.	11,305	42.46
32	Republican	Tyler August*	14,813	59.22

District vote for representatives to the assembly, general and special elections, continued

Assembly district	Party	Candidates	Vote	% of total[1]
	Democrat	Katherine R. Gaulke	10,182	40.70
	Republican	Jeremiah Sutton (write-in)	2	0.01
33	Republican	Cody J. Horlacher*	17,236	62.73
	Democrat	Brandon White	10,219	37.19
34	Republican	Rob Swearingen*	19,699	61.91
	Democrat	Chris Meier	12,096	38.02
35	Republican	Mary Czaja-Felzkowski*	16,380	62.74
	Democrat	Mark A. Martello	9,714	37.21
36	Republican	Jeffrey L. Mursau*	16,938	66.99
	Democrat	Tim Comer	8,338	32.98
37	Republican	John Jagler*	19,616	96.00
38	Republican	Barbara Dittrich	18,056	57.58
	Democrat	Melissa Winker	13,286	42.36
39	Republican	Mark L. Born*	15,940	63.38
	Democrat	Elisha Barudin	9,210	36.62
40	Republican	Kevin Petersen*	15,794	64.32
	Democrat	Erin Tracy	8,759	35.67
41	Republican	Joan Ballweg*	15,257	62.92
	Democrat	Frank T. Buress	8,984	37.05
42	Republican	Jon Plumer*	15,299	57.67
	Democrat	Ann Groves Lloyd	11,209	42.25
43	Democrat	Don Vruwink*	16,241	61.14
	Republican	Gabriel Szerlong	10,288	38.73
44	Democrat	Deb Kolste*	18,005	97.47
45	Democrat	Mark Spreitzer*	14,198	79.10
	Libertarian	Reese Wood	3,496	19.47
46	Democrat	Gary Hebl*	24,011	97.22
47	Democrat	Jimmy Anderson*	25,706	98.02
48	Democrat	Melissa Agard Sargent*	27,794	98.22
49	Republican	Travis Tranel*	12,858	58.87
	Democrat	Mike Mooney	8,968	41.05
50	Republican	Tony Kurtz	12,379	54.53
	Democrat	Arthur L. Shrader	9,658	42.55
	Independent	James Krus	659	2.90
51	Republican	Todd Novak*	12,445	50.65
	Democrat	Jeff Wright	12,113	49.29
52	Republican	Jeremy Thiesfeldt*	15,164	61.64
	Democrat	Kevin Booth	9,427	38.31
53	Republican	Michael Schraa*	15,160	63.20
	Democrat	Joe Lavrenz	8,812	36.74
54	Democrat	Gordon Hintz*	18,019	94.04
55	Republican	Mike Rohrkaste*	15,122	55.15
	Democrat	Dan Schierl	12,283	44.80
56	Republican	Dave Murphy*	18,033	59.82
	Democrat	Diana Lawrence	12,110	40.17
57	Democrat	Amanda Stuck*	16,946	98.20
58	Republican	Rick Gundrum*	20,471	70.98
	Democrat	Dennis D. Degenhardt	8,368	29.02

District vote for representatives to the assembly, general and special elections, continued

Assembly district	Party	Candidates	Vote	% of total[1]
59	Republican	Timothy S. Ramthun	23,339	99.30
60	Republican	Robert Brooks*	20,702	64.86
	Democrat	Chris Rahlf	11,182	35.03
61	Republican	Samantha Kerkman*	16,606	61.87
	Democrat	Gina Walkington	10,207	38.03
62	Republican	Robert Wittke	16,035	54.87
	Democrat	John Lehman	13,161	45.04
63	Republican	Robin Vos*	16,775	61.00
	Democrat	Joel Jacobsen	10,705	38.93
64	Democrat	Peter W. Barca*	16,773	78.32
	Constitution	Thomas Harland	4,441	20.74
65	Democrat	Tod Ohnstad*	14,456	96.82
66	Democrat	Greta Neubauer*	14,450	97.01
67	Republican	Rob Summerfield*	15,970	61.78
	Democrat	Wren Keturi	9,878	38.22
68	Republican	Jesse James	14,129	57.59
	Democrat	Wendy Sue Johnson	10,394	42.37
69	Republican	Bob Kulp*	17,257	91.28
	Democrat	Kathleen M. Rulka (write-in)	1,576	8.34
70	Republican	Nancy Lynn VanderMeer*	15,027	61.91
	Democrat	Cari Fay	9,223	38.00
71	Democrat	Katrina Shankland*	20,548	97.75
72	Republican	Scott S. Krug*	14,773	57.32
	Democrat	David Gorski.	10,992	42.65
73	Democrat	Nick Milroy*	18,510	96.95
	Republican	Jeffery L. Monaghan (write-in).	16	0.08
74	Democrat	Beth Meyers*	15,738	56.16
	Republican	Jeffrey Fahl.	12,276	43.81
75	Republican	Romaine Robert Quinn*	14,925	62.18
	Democrat	Ali Holzman	9,078	37.82
76	Democrat	Chris Taylor*	36,891	98.43
	Libertarian	Thomas Leager (write-in)	0	0.00
77	Democrat	Shelia Stubbs	29,347	98.68
78	Democrat	Lisa Subeck*	30,044	98.06
79	Democrat	Dianne Hesselbein*	28,079	97.58
80	Democrat	Sondy Pope*	26,189	97.69
81	Democrat	Dave Considine*	19,766	98.64
82	Republican	Ken Skowronski*	18,039	67.97
	Libertarian	Jason J. Sellnow.	8,300	31.28
83	Republican	Chuck Wichgers*	22,351	69.85
	Democrat	Jim Brownlow	9,624	30.08
84	Republican	Mike Kuglitsch*	16,684	57.44
	Democrat	Erica Flynn	12,341	42.48
85	Republican	Patrick Snyder*	13,791	55.25
	Democrat	Alyson Leahy	11,150	44.67
86	Republican	John Spiros*	17,174	59.80
	Democrat	Nancy Stencil	10,575	36.83
	Independent	Michael A. Tauschek	945	3.29

District vote for representatives to the assembly, general and special elections, continued

Assembly district	Party	Candidates	Vote	% of total[1]
87	Democrat	Elizabeth Riley.	8,027	33.84
	Republican	James W. Edming*	15,682	66.12
88	Republican	John Macco*	14,628	53.31
	Democrat	Tom Sieber.	12,793	46.62
89	Republican	John Nygren*	17,091	66.85
	Democrat	Ken Holdorf	8,461	33.10
90	Democrat	Staush Gruszynski	12,994	96.34
91	Democrat	Jodi Emerson	17,512	66.47
	Republican	Echo Reardon	8,798	33.39
92	Republican	Treig E. Pronschinske*	12,955	55.13
	Democrat	Rob Grover.	10,537	44.84
93	Republican	Warren Petryk*	15,935	58.20
	Democrat	Charlene Charlie Warner	11,435	41.76
94	Democrat	Steve Doyle*.	17,498	60.20
	Republican	Albert Rohland	11,567	39.80
95	Democrat	Jill Billings*.	21,989	100.00
96	Republican	Loren Oldenburg	12,327	51.65
	Democrat	Paul Buhr.	11,536	48.34
97	Republican	Scott Allen*	18,945	96.03
98	Republican	Adam Neylon*	23,005	97.11
	Republican	Mary Larson (write-in).	0	0.00
99	Republican	Cindi Duchow*	26,251	97.94

April 30, 2019 special election

64	Democrat	Tip McGuire	4,096	62.35
	Republican	Mark Stalker.	2,467	37.56

*Incumbent.

1. Percentages do not add up to 100, as scattered votes have been omitted.

Source: Official records of the Wisconsin Elections Commission.

County vote for supreme court justice, February 20, 2018 spring primary

	Rebecca Dallet	Michael Screnock	Tim Burns	Total
Adams	405	845	221	1,473
Ashland.	371	361	388	1,120
Barron.	679	1,471	520	2,676
Bayfield.	599	610	771	1,980
Brown.	6,365	9,293	3,167	18,851
Buffalo	260	400	173	833
Burnett.	258	612	182	1,052
Calumet	959	1,882	378	3,220
Chippewa	1,075	1,909	790	3,783
Clark.	504	1,152	255	1,911
Columbia.	1,975	2,430	1,365	5,781
Crawford	399	498	282	1,181
Dane	40,163	13,322	23,616	77,186

County vote for supreme court justice, February 20, 2018 spring primary, continued

	Rebecca Dallet	Michael Screnock	Tim Burns	Total
Dodge	1,857	4,650	944	7,451
Door.	1,382	1,285	589	3,260
Douglas.	728	798	592	2,120
Dunn	1,022	1,335	760	3,117
Eau Claire.	2,930	2,682	2,430	8,057
Florence	64	184	44	292
Fond du Lac	1,989	4,935	949	7,873
Forest	110	361	100	572
Grant	1,084	1,270	671	3,029
Green	1,188	1,165	877	3,231
Green Lake.	350	923	161	1,434
Iowa.	945	779	640	2,365
Iron	206	294	122	622
Jackson.	406	580	233	1,219
Jefferson	2,507	4,565	1,234	8,310
Juneau	541	1,082	432	2,057
Kenosha	4,534	5,245	1,741	11,542
Kewaunee	596	1,043	262	1,901
La Crosse.	3,924	2,673	2,042	8,639
Lafayette.	554	539	421	1,515
Langlade.	427	817	152	1,396
Lincoln	641	1,167	336	2,163
Manitowoc.	2,178	3,997	1,052	7,262
Marathon.	3,050	5,014	1,399	9,471
Marinette.	664	1,447	310	2,421
Marquette	373	847	225	1,445
Menominee	20	30	15	65
Milwaukee.	37,516	30,485	13,886	82,050
Monroe.	864	1,293	457	2,619
Oconto	652	1,571	316	2,542
Oneida	956	1,649	714	3,322
Outagamie.	5,175	6,624	2,391	14,190
Ozaukee	4,001	9,064	1,081	14,159
Pepin	109	227	176	512
Pierce.	694	995	530	2,219
Polk	781	1,381	526	2,688
Portage.	3,030	2,561	1,645	7,245
Price.	361	682	207	1,250
Racine.	5,446	10,386	2,310	18,162
Richland	636	732	513	1,882
Rock.	4,660	4,263	2,996	11,939
Rusk.	318	730	167	1,216
St. Croix.	1,456	2,226	980	4,677
Sauk.	2,171	2,794	1,443	6,408
Sawyer	247	632	379	1,258
Shawano.	864	1,937	402	3,203
Sheboygan.	3,353	7,204	1,201	11,764
Taylor.	259	885	127	1,271
Trempealeau	527	673	275	1,475
Vernon	986	1,147	780	2,913
Vilas.	596	1,279	436	2,316
Walworth.	2,550	5,330	1,183	9,084
Washburn	313	656	390	1,362
Washington	3,169	13,309	1,293	17,771
Waukesha	14,124	40,933	4,435	59,556
Waupaca.	1,149	2,188	496	3,833
Waushara.	450	1,117	168	1,735
Winnebago	3,853	5,206	1,802	10,870

County vote for supreme court justice, February 20, 2018 spring primary, continued

	Rebecca Dallet	Michael Screnock	Tim Burns	Total
Wood	1,720	2,931	962	5,613
Total.	191,268	247,582	95,508	534,980

Note: County totals include scattered votes.
Source: Official records of the Wisconsin Elections Commission.

County vote for supreme court justice, April 3, 2018 spring election

	Rebecca Dallet	Michael Screnock	Total
Adams	1,892	1,912	3,806
Ashland.	1,903	940	2,856
Barron.	2,762	3,123	5,889
Bayfield.	2,862	1,550	4,412
Brown.	21,445	17,458	38,962
Buffalo	1,463	1,645	3,111
Burnett	1,020	1,406	2,426
Calumet	3,545	3,701	7,249
Chippewa	5,158	4,949	10,107
Clark.	2,248	2,911	5,163
Columbia.	6,271	4,889	11,174
Crawford	1,603	1,143	2,750
Dane	107,788	25,276	133,189
Dodge	6,613	8,780	15,393
Door.	4,374	2,663	7,044
Douglas.	4,044	2,422	6,478
Dunn	2,943	2,429	5,372
Eau Claire.	11,266	6,371	17,652
Florence	223	378	601
Fond du Lac	6,625	8,693	15,318
Forest	811	976	1,791
Grant	3,807	3,170	6,986
Green	4,693	2,847	7,553
Green Lake.	1,335	1,913	3,249
Iowa.	3,233	1,643	4,883
Iron	798	829	1,629
Jackson.	1,335	1,055	2,390
Jefferson	7,023	7,668	14,704
Juneau	2,157	2,600	4,763
Kenosha	11,865	9,104	20,995
Kewaunee	2,625	2,701	5,326
La Crosse.	11,721	5,785	17,506
Lafayette	2,005	1,668	3,678
Langlade	1,111	1,413	2,524
Lincoln	2,897	2,777	5,681
Manitowoc.	8,418	8,292	16,725
Marathon.	11,039	10,845	21,905
Marinette.	2,939	3,402	6,341
Marquette	1,346	1,748	3,095
Menominee	93	55	148
Milwaukee.	85,948	44,747	130,850
Monroe.	3,085	3,171	6,263
Oconto	2,388	2,943	5,337

County vote for supreme court justice, April 3, 2018 spring election, continued

	Rebecca Dallet	Michael Screnock	Total
Oneida	3,736	3,373	7,120
Outagamie	14,049	11,164	25,213
Ozaukee	9,597	13,643	23,251
Pepin	743	718	1,461
Pierce	3,460	2,996	6,456
Polk	2,992	3,411	6,403
Portage	7,456	4,436	11,902
Price	1,879	1,988	3,867
Racine	14,872	15,840	30,753
Richland	1,831	1,536	3,367
Rock	15,075	9,463	24,562
Rusk	1,214	1,524	2,740
St. Croix	6,114	6,067	12,199
Sauk	6,971	5,376	12,347
Sawyer	1,194	1,323	2,518
Shawano	2,352	3,041	5,393
Sheboygan	9,792	11,919	21,733
Taylor	1,090	1,709	2,800
Trempealeau	2,545	1,974	4,525
Vernon	3,307	2,489	5,798
Vilas	2,107	2,426	4,537
Walworth	7,855	9,257	17,135
Washburn	1,382	1,582	2,966
Washington	8,822	19,925	28,747
Waukesha	31,598	57,346	89,001
Waupaca	3,496	3,842	7,341
Waushara	1,618	2,197	3,816
Winnebago	13,510	10,319	23,856
Wood	6,471	5,933	12,404
Total	**555,848**	**440,808**	**997,485**

Note: County totals include scattered votes.
Source: Official records of the Wisconsin Elections Commission.

County vote for supreme court justice, April 2, 2019 spring election

	Brian Hagedorn	Lisa Neubauer	Total
Adams	2,401	1,911	4,313
Ashland	1,262	1,943	3,209
Barron	4,657	3,075	7,737
Bayfield	1,841	3,009	4,852
Brown	27,027	24,031	51,092
Buffalo	1,442	1,154	2,599
Burnett	1,953	1,118	3,071
Calumet	6,136	3,857	9,993
Chippewa	6,159	4,654	10,813
Clark	3,596	2,007	5,603
Columbia	5,801	6,794	12,609
Crawford	1,343	1,642	2,985
Dane	31,741	120,151	152,044
Dodge	11,782	6,123	17,905

County vote for supreme court justice, April 2, 2019 spring election, continued

	Brian Hagedorn	Lisa Neubauer	Total
Door	4,508	5,266	9,778
Douglas	3,102	4,067	7,179
Dunn	3,744	3,543	7,287
Eau Claire	8,396	11,764	20,175
Florence	595	288	883
Fond du Lac	14,268	8,051	22,319
Forest	1,265	748	2,015
Grant	3,999	4,125	8,131
Green	3,420	4,942	8,369
Green Lake	2,795	1,296	4,091
Iowa	2,255	3,973	6,231
Iron	1,139	988	2,130
Jackson	1,711	1,650	3,361
Jefferson	11,219	8,198	19,423
Juneau	2,537	1,799	4,340
Kenosha	12,086	11,352	23,454
Kewaunee	2,862	1,687	4,549
La Crosse	8,885	13,848	22,733
Lafayette	1,593	1,738	3,331
Langlade	2,493	1,333	3,826
Lincoln	3,200	2,256	5,457
Manitowoc	10,192	6,059	16,260
Marathon	16,483	11,271	27,771
Marinette	5,162	2,962	8,124
Marquette	2,101	1,476	3,579
Menominee	113	209	322
Milwaukee	56,541	93,569	150,246
Monroe	4,532	3,872	8,413
Oconto	5,634	2,906	8,540
Oneida	4,642	3,692	8,347
Outagamie	19,663	15,766	35,429
Ozaukee	16,962	10,092	27,074
Pepin	708	597	1,305
Pierce	3,129	3,095	6,226
Polk	5,037	3,479	8,516
Portage	6,782	8,003	14,795
Price	2,214	1,656	3,870
Racine	21,025	15,927	36,985
Richland	1,721	1,949	3,670
Rock	11,376	16,864	28,261
Rusk	2,018	1,246	3,270
St. Croix	7,329	5,938	13,279
Sauk	5,922	7,723	13,645
Sawyer	1,983	1,444	3,428
Shawano	5,531	2,662	8,193
Sheboygan	15,665	9,338	25,011
Taylor	2,609	1,129	3,739
Trempealeau	2,850	2,882	5,737
Vernon	2,878	3,382	6,261
Vilas	3,659	2,559	6,221
Walworth	12,322	7,685	20,024
Washburn	1,876	1,439	3,315
Washington	28,088	9,446	37,534
Waukesha	79,071	36,303	115,428
Waupaca	6,916	3,983	10,906
Waushara	3,328	1,753	5,081
Winnebago	17,690	16,526	34,249

County vote for supreme court justice, April 2, 2019 spring election, continued

	Brian Hagedorn	Lisa Neubauer	Total
Wood	9,449	7,170	16,628
Total.	**606,414**	**600,433**	**1,207,569**

Note: County totals include scattered votes.

Source: Official records of the Wisconsin Elections Commission.

District vote for court of appeals judges, April 3, 2018 spring election

District I

County	Timothy G. Dugan*	Total
Milwaukee	70,346	71,487
Total.	**70,346**	**71,487**

District IV

County	JoAnne F. Kloppenburg*	Total
Adams	2,619	2,635
Clark	3,863	3,883
Columbia.	8,091	8,324
Crawford	2,185	2,199
Dane	99,060	100,761
Dodge	10,586	10,586
Grant	5,473	5,517
Green	5,606	5,708
Iowa	3,925	3,973
Jackson	1,862	1,862
Jefferson	9,582	9,963
Juneau	3,835	3,858
La Crosse	12,638	12,638
Lafayette	2,882	2,893
Marquette	2,331	2,374
Monroe	5,084	5,136
Portage	8,096	8,172
Richland	2,656	2,665
Rock	17,650	17,953
Sauk.	8,820	8,820
Vernon	4,631	4,658
Waupaca	5,733	5,785
Waushara.	2,895	2,925
Wood	8,916	8,916
Total.	**239,019**	**242,204**

Note: County totals include scattered votes.

*Incumbent.

Source: Official records of the Wisconsin Elections Commission.

District vote for court of appeals judges, April 2, 2019 spring election

District II

County	Mark Gundrum*	Total
Calumet	7,192	7,192
Fond du Lac	15,570	15,574
Green Lake	3,296	3,304
Kenosha	14,691	14,992
Manitowoc	12,187	12,291
Ozaukee	18,178	18,389
Racine	24,172	24,434
Sheboygan	17,706	17,813
Walworth	14,451	14,624
Washington	28,548	28,548
Waukesha	79,064	79,850
Winnebago	23,686	23,973
Total	**258,741**	**260,984**

District III

County	Lisa K. Stark*	Total
Ashland	2,181	2,201
Barron	6,176	6,194
Bayfield	3,425	3,441
Brown	36,048	36,302
Buffalo	2,136	2,145
Burnett	2,383	2,383
Chippewa	8,197	8,197
Door	6,893	6,932
Douglas	5,233	5,288
Dunn	5,785	5,785
Eau Claire	15,323	15,480
Florence	652	652
Forest	1,412	1,417
Iron	1,588	1,595
Kewaunee	3,595	3,595
Langlade	2,883	2,883
Lincoln	3,957	3,977
Marathon	19,621	19,776
Marinette	6,448	6,448
Menominee	197	198
Oconto	7,097	7,097
Oneida	5,912	5,945
Outagamie	25,722	25,722
Pepin	1,052	1,052
Pierce	4,980	5,003
Polk	6,938	6,938
Price	2,766	2,766
Rusk	2,516	2,537
St. Croix	9,892	9,982
Sawyer	2,704	2,720
Shawano	6,599	6,599
Taylor	2,719	2,721
Trempealeau	4,752	4,779
Vilas	4,368	4,401
Washburn	2,523	2,540
Total	**224,673**	**225,691**

Vote for circuit judges, April 3, 2018 spring election, continued

Counties in circuit	Branch	Candidates	Vote
Wood	2	Nicholas J. Brazeau, Jr.*	9,361

— Means the circuit has only one branch. *Incumbent.
Source: Official records of the Wisconsin Elections Commission.

Vote for circuit judges, February 19, 2019 spring primary

Counties in circuit	Branch	Candidates	Vote
Ozaukee	2	Steve Cain	2,728
		Angela C. Foy	2,771
		Mark E. Larson.	1,754
		James Wawrzyn.	853

Source: Official records of the Wisconsin Elections Commission.

Vote for circuit judges, April 2, 2019 spring election

Counties in circuit	Branch	Candidates	Vote
Brown.	3	Tammy Jo Hock*	36,134
	7	Timothy A. Hinkfuss*	36,900
Dane	16	Rhonda L. Lanford*.	103,480
Dodge	3	Joseph G. Sciascia*.	13,303
Jefferson	1	William V. Gruber*	13,004
	2	William F. Hue*	13,239
La Crosse	1	Ramona A. Gonzalez*	15,852
	2	Elliott M. Levine*	16,258
	3	Todd W. Bjerke*.	16,579
	4	Scott L. Horne*	16,978
Lincoln	2	Robert R. Russell*.	4,297
Manitowoc.	1	Mark R. Rohrer*.	12,629
Marinette.	2	James A. Morrison*	6,867
Marquette	—	Chad A. Hendee.	2,885
Milwaukee	11	David C. Swanson*.	87,138
	26	William S. Pocan*.	87,258
	36	Laura A. Crivello*.	87,994
	40	Andrew A. Jones*.	53,407
		Danielle Shelton	71,649
	41	Audrey K. Skwierawski*.	85,654
Monroe	1	Todd L. Ziegler*.	7,354
Ozaukee	2	Steve Cain	14,800
		Angela C. Foy	10,650
Racine.	3	Maureen M. Martinez*.	24,151
	7	Jamie M. McClendon	12,512
		Jon E. Fredrickson*.	18,606
Rock.	1	Karl R. Hanson*	19,396
	2	Derrick A. Grubb*.	19,185
	4	Daniel T. Dillon*.	18,977
St. Croix.	2	Edward F. Vlack*	10,174
Waukesha	1	Michael O. Bohren*	75,867
	6	Brad D. Schimel*	81,363

— Means the circuit has only one branch. *Incumbent.
Source: Official records of the Wisconsin Elections Commission.

WISCONSIN OFFICIALS AND EMPLOYEES

State officers appointed by the governor, May 15, 2019

911 Subcommittee
Scott Behn. . . . . .expires 7/1/19
Andrew Faust 7/1/19
Kirk A. Gunderson 7/1/19
Joseph B. Nash 7/1/19
Kristina Page 7/1/19
Robert C. Whitaker 7/1/19
Richard A. Buntrock 7/1/20
John Dejung. 7/1/20
Melvin Frank 7/1/20
Danielle Miller 7/1/20
Douglas J. Wenzlaff 7/1/20
Kathleen Whitbeck 7/1/20
Dena Clark. 7/1/21
John Cummings 7/1/21
Rodney D. Olson 7/1/21
Jean M. Pauk 7/1/21
Cullen Peltier 7/1/21
Mark Podoll 7/1/21
Marcie R. Rainbolt 7/1/21

Accounting Examining Board[1] ($25/day[2])
Gerald Denor . . . . expires 7/1/17
John Scheid 7/1/19
Susan Strautmann[3] 7/1/20
Robert Misey[3] 7/1/21
John Reinemann[5] 7/1/21
David K. Schlichting[5] 7/1/22
Joan Phillips[3] 7/1/23

Adjutant General (group 6 salary[2])
Major Gen. Donald P. Dunbar . . . . . .expires 9/1/12

Administration, Department of, secretary[1] (group 8 salary[2])
Joel T. Brennan[3]. . . . . expires at governor's pleasure

Adult Offender Supervision Board, Interstate
Nick Korger . . . . .expires 5/1/19
Jay C. Laufenberg 5/1/19
Michael Bohren 5/1/21
vacancy

Adult Offender Supervision, Interstate Compact Administrator
Joselyn Lopez. . . . . .expires 5/1/21

Aerospace Authority, Wisconsin[1] inactive

Affirmative Action, Council on
David Dunham . . . . .expires 7/1/11
Eileen Hocker. 7/1/11
Sandra Ryan. 7/1/11
Ronald Shaheed 7/1/11
Nancy Vue. 7/1/11
Thresessa Childs 7/1/12
Janice Hughes 7/1/12
John Magerus. 7/1/12
James Parker 7/1/12

Yolanda Santos Adams 7/1/12
Lakshmi Bharadwaj 7/1/13

Aging and Long-Term Care, Board on[1]
Dale B. Taylor[5] . . . . expires 5/1/20
Valerie A. Palarski 5/1/21
Barbara Bechtel 5/1/22
Tanya L. Meyer 5/1/22
Michael Brooks[3] 5/1/23
James Surprise[5] 5/1/23
vacancy

Agriculture, Trade and Consumer Protection, Board of[1] (not to exceed $35/day nor $1,000/year[2])
Dennis Badtke . . . . .expires 5/1/19
Nicole Hansen 5/1/19
Dean Strauss 5/1/21
Kurt Hallstrand 5/1/21
Paul Palmby. 5/1/21
Gregory Zwald 5/1/21
Paul M. Bauer. 5/1/23
Andrew S. Diercks 5/1/23
Miranda Leis 5/1/23

Agriculture, Trade and Consumer Protection, Department of, secretary[1] (group 6 salary[2])
Brad M. Pfaff[3] . . . . . expires at governor's pleasure

Alcohol and Other Drug Abuse, State Council on
Norman Briggs . . . . .expires 7/1/19
Sandy Hardie 7/1/19
Michael R. Knetzger. 7/1/21
Caroline M. Miller 7/1/21
Thai Vue .7/1/21
Mary Ann Gerrard 7/1/23
Katie Domina . . . . . expires at governor's pleasure
Christine A. Ullstrup. . . . . governor's pleasure

Architects, Landscape Architects, Professional Engineers, Designers and Professional Land Surveyors, Examining Board of[1] ($25/day[2])
Michael J. Kinney . . . . .expires 7/1/12
Daniel Fedderly 7/1/13
Rosheen Styczinski 7/1/13
Bruce Bowden 7/1/14
Steven Hook 7/1/14
Andrew Gersich 7/1/15
Kenneth D. Arneson. 7/1/18
Mark Mayer 7/1/18
Matthew D. Wolfert 7/1/18
Michael J. Heberling 7/1/19
Christina C. Martin. 7/1/19
Tim Garland 7/1/20
Kristine Cotharn 7/1/21
Joseph D. Frasch 7/1/21
Karl Linck[3] 7/1/21
Dennis Myers[5] 7/1/21
Steven Wagner 7/1/21
9 vacancies

State officers appointed by the governor, May 15, 2019, continued

Artistic Endowment Foundation[1] inactive

Arts Board
Ann Brunner . . . . expires 5/1/20
Mary Gielow 5/1/20
Brian Kelsey 5/1/20
Frederick Schwertfeger 5/1/20
John H. Potter. 5/1/21
Gerard Randall 5/1/21
Robert Wagner 5/1/21
La'Ketta D. Caldwell 5/1/22
Karen A. Hoffman 5/1/22
Susan Lipp. .5/1/22
Kevin M. Miller 5/1/22
Mary K. Reinders 5/1/22
Lynn Richie .5/1/22
Jennifer Schwarzkopf 5/1/22
Matthew J. Wallock 5/1/22

Athletic Trainers Affiliated Credentialing Board[1]
($25/day[2])
Jay J. Davide. . . . . .expires 7/1/18
Kurt Fielding[3] 7/1/19
Gregory Vergamini[5] 7/1/20
Jack J. Johnsen[5] 7/1/21
2 vacancies

Auctioneer Board[1] ($25/day[2])
Ronald Polacek . . . . .expires 5/1/13
Heather Berlinski 5/1/16
Jerry Thiel 5/1/18
Bryce L. Hansen[5] 5/1/20
Randy J. Stockwell 5/1/20
Stanley D. Jones[5]. 5/1/22
vacancy

Banking Review Board[1] ($25/day, not exceed
$1,500/year[2])
Debra R. Lins . . . . .expires 5/1/19
Thomas J. Pamperin 5/1/20
Daniel M. Riebe. 5/1/22
Thomas E. Spitz. 5/1/22
Robert C. Gorsuch[6] 5/1/23

**Bradley Center Sports and Entertainment
Corporation, Board of Directors of the[1]** inactive

Building Commission
Summer Strand. . . . . expires at governor's pleasure

Burial Sites Preservation Board ($25/day[2])
Corina Williams . . . . .expires 7/1/10
David Grignon 7/1/14
Melinda Young 7/1/15
Katherine P. Stevenson 7/1/19
Cynthia Stiles 7/1/20
Jennifer R. Haas. 7/1/21

Cemetery Board[1] ($25/day[2])
Kathleen Cantu. . . . . .expires 7/1/12
Francis J. Groh[3] 7/1/20
John Reinemann[5] 7/1/20
Patricia Grathen[5] 7/1/22

Bernard Schroedl[5] 7/1/22
vacancy

Child Abuse and Neglect Prevention Board
Kari A. Christenson . . . . .expires 5/1/19
Paula J. Breese 5/1/20
Bernice C. Day 5/1/20
Mary E. Triggiano 5/1/20
Vicki M. Tylka 5/1/20
Molly J. Jasmer 5/1/22
Jennifer Kleven 5/1/22
Michael McHorney 5/1/22
Jennifer L. Noyes 5/1/22
Teri B. Zywicki. 5/1/22
Katie Domina . . . . . expires at governor's pleasure

Children and Families, Department of, Secretary[1]
(group 6 salary[2])
Emilie Amundson[3] . expires at governor's pleasure

Chiropractic Examining Board[1] ($25/day[2])
James Fortier[3]. . . . . .expires 7/1/20
Scott D. Bautch 7/1/21
Bryan R. Gerondale 7/1/21
Juli McNeely. 7/1/21
James M. Damrow[3] 7/1/23
Jeffrey A. King[3] 7/1/23

Circus World Museum Foundation[1]
David Hoffman . . . . expires at governor's pleasure

Claims Board
Katie Ignatowski . . . expires at governor's pleasure

College Savings Program Board[1]
John Wheeler . . . . .expires 5/1/15
Robert Kieckhefer 5/1/19
William L. Oemichen 5/1/19
Alberta Darling 5/1/21
Rob Kreibich 5/1/21
Kimberly Shaul 5/1/21

Commercial Building Code Council
Hunter Bohne . . . . .expires 7/1/15
Samuel Lawrence 7/1/16
Corey Rockweiler 7/1/16
Peter Scheuerman 7/1/16
Kevin Bierce 7/1/17
David Enigl .7/1/17
Steve Klessig 7/1/17
Irina Ragozin 7/1/17
Steven Howard 7/1/18
Brian J. Rinke 7/1/18

Controlled Substances Board
Subhadeep Barman. . . . . .expires 5/1/19
Alan Bloom .5/1/20

Conveyance Safety Code Council
Ronald P. Mueller. . . . . expires 7/1/17
Jennie L. Macaluso. 7/1/18
Keith S. Misustin 7/1/18
Brian Rausch 7/1/19

State officers appointed by the governor, May 15, 2019, continued

Paul S. Rosenberg 7/1/19
Kenneth R. Smith 7/1/19
Harold A. Thurmer. 7/1/19
Steven L. Ketelboeter. 7/1/20

Corrections, Department of, Secretary[1] (group 8 salary[2])
Kevin A. Carr[3] . . . . . expires at governor's pleasure

Cosmetology Examining Board[1] ($25/day[2])
Kristin Allison . . . . .expires 7/1/16
Suresh Misra 7/1/18
Gail Sengbusch. 7/1/18
Vicky McNally[5] 7/1/20
Georgianna Halverson[3]. 7/1/23
4 vacancies

Credit Union Review Board[1] ($25/day, not exc. $1,500 per yr.[2])
Danny Wollin . . . . .expires 5/1/19
Christopher P. Butler 5/1/20
Sherri O. Stumpf 5/1/21
Colleen Woggon 5/1/22
Lisa M. Greco[5] 5/1/23

Credit Unions, Office of, Director (group 3 salary[2])
Kim Santos . . . . . . expires at governor's pleasure

Crime Victims Rights Board
Rebecca St. John. . . . . .expires 5/1/19

Criminal Penalties, Joint Review Committee on
Bradley Gehring . . . expires at governor's pleasure
Maury Straub . . . . governor's pleasure

Deaf and Hard of Hearing, Council for the
Thomas O'Connor . . . . .expires 7/1/19
Steven Smart 7/1/19
Lisa D. Woods. 7/1/19
Michelle S. Cordova 7/1/21
Nicole Everson 7/1/21
Karl Nollenberger 7/1/21
Katy M. Schmidt 7/1/21
David H. Seligman. 7/1/21
vacancy

Deferred Compensation Board[1] ($25/day[2])
Gail Hanson . . . . .expires 7/1/18
John M. Scherer 7/1/19
Edward D. Main 7/1/20
Jason A. Rothenberg 7/1/21
Arthur Zimmerman 7/1/21

Dentistry Examining Board[1] ($25/day[2])
Mark T. Braden . . . . expires 7/1/18
Debra Beres. 7/1/20
Dennis Myers. 7/1/20
Matthew R. Bistan[5] 7/1/21
Leonardo Huck. 7/1/21
Wendy M. Pietz[5] 7/1/21
Lisa Bahr[5] 7/1/22
Shaheda Govani[3] 7/1/22
Herbert Michael Kaske[5] 7/1/22
Katherine F. Schrubbe[3]. 7/1/22

Peter Sheild[5] 7/1/22
vacancy

Developmental Disabilities, Board for People with ($50/day[2])
Ramsey A. Lee . . . . .expires 7/1/18
Wendy Ackley. 7/1/19
Lynn Carus .7/1/19
Michael D. Hineberg 7/1/19
Nathaniel Lentz 7/1/19
Leila P. Solati 7/1/19
Carole Stuebe. 7/1/19
Robert Kuhr 7/1/20
David Pinno 7/1/20
L. Lynn Stansberry-Brusnahan 7/1/20
Pam Malin .7/1/21
Amy L. Polsin 7/1/21
Gregory A. Meyer 7/1/22
Elsa Diaz Bautista 7/1/23
Gail M. Bovy 7/1/23
Kedibonye Carpenter. 7/1/23
Patrick Friedrich 7/1/23
Barbara Gadbois 7/1/23
Ashley Mathy 7/1/23
Andy Thain .7/1/23
Tricia Thompson 7/1/23
George Zaske. 7/1/23

Dietitians Affiliated Credentialing Board[1] ($25/day[2])
David Joe . . . . .expires 7/1/18
Scott Krueger[3] 7/1/19
Jill D. Hoyt[3] 7/1/21
Tara LaRowe[5] 7/1/22

Distance Learning Authorization Board
vacancy

Domestic Abuse, Council on[1]
Patricia Ninmann[3] . . . . .expires 7/1/17
Lena C. Taylor 7/1/18
Shirley A. Armstrong[5]. 7/1/19
Susan M. Perry[5]. 7/1/19
Lisa Subeck 7/1/19
Mark M. Thomas[6] 7/1/19
Kevin L. Hamberger[5] 7/1/20
Nela Kalpic[5] 7/1/20
Renee J. Schulz[5] 7/1/20
Susan Sippel[5]. 7/1/20
Alena A. Taylor[5]. 7/1/20
Kathy Flores[3] 7/1/22
vacancy

Dry Cleaner Environmental Response Council
Kevin D. Braden . . . . .expires 7/1/17
Thomas McKay 7/1/17
David Cass. 7/1/18
Jeanne Tarvin 7/1/18
Jim Fitzgerald 7/1/19
Richard W. Klinke. 7/1/19

Economic Development Corp. Authority, Wisconsin[1]
John J. Brogan[3] . . . . expires at governor's pleasure

State officers appointed by the governor, May 15, 2019, continued

Rebecca Cooke[3] . . . . governor's pleasure
Joe Kirgues[3] . . . . governor's pleasure
Eugenia Podestá Losada[3] . . . . governor's pleasure
Henry Newell[3] . . . . governor's pleasure
Thelma Sias[3] . . . . governor's pleasure

Economic Development Corporation Authority, Wisconsin, Chief Executive Officer[1]
Mark Hogan . . . . . . expires at governor's pleasure[4]

Education Commission of the States
Jessica Doyle . . . . . expires at governor's pleasure
Bette Lang . . . . governor's pleasure
Demond Means . . . . governor's pleasure
John Reinemann . . . . governor's pleasure
Amy Traynor . . . . governor's pleasure

Educational Communications Board[1]
Richard Lepping . . . . expires 5/1/17
Karen Schroeder 5/1/19
Rolf Wegenke 5/1/19
David Hutchison[5] 5/1/21
Eileen Littig . . . . . . expires at governor's pleasure

Elections Commission[1] ($115/day[2])
Beverly R. Gill . . . . expires 5/1/19
Julie M. Glancey 5/1/21

Electronic Recording Council
Jodi Helgeson . . . . expires 7/1/18
Michael McDonnell 7/1/18
Staci M. Hoffman 7/1/19
Michael Lenz 7/1/19
Sharon A. Martin 7/1/19
John F. Wilcox 7/1/19
Margo C. Katterhagen 7/1/21

Emergency Management Division, Administrator[1] (group 3 salary[2])
Brian Satula . . . . . . expires at governor's pleasure

Emergency Medical Services Board
Timothy A. Bantes . . . . expires 5/1/19
Carrie L. Meier 5/1/19
Steven W. Zils 5/1/19
Christopher D. Anderson 5/1/20
Jerry R. Biggart 5/1/20
Mark C. Fredrickson 5/1/20
Dustin E. Ridings 5/1/20
Gregory Neal West 5/1/20
Michael Clark 5/1/21
Christopher M. Eberlein 5/1/21
Donald F. Kimlicka 5/1/21

Employee Trust Funds Board[1]
Stephen Arnold[3] . . . . .expires 5/1/23
Katy Lounsbury . . . expires at governor's pleasure

Employment Relations Commission[1] (group 5 salary[2])
James Daley . . . . .expires 3/1/23

Ethics Commission[1] ($115/day[2])
James "Mac" Davis . . . . .expires 5/1/21
Timothy M. Van Akkeren[3] 5/1/24

Federal-State Relations Office, Director (group 3 salary[2])
vacancy

Financial Institutions, Department of, Secretary[1] (group 6 salary[2])
Kathy Blumenfeld[3] . expires at governor's pleasure

Forestry, Council on
Janet Bewley . . . . . expires at governor's pleasure
Dennis G. Brown . . . . governor's pleasure
Troy Brown . . . . governor's pleasure
Matt Dallman . . . . governor's pleasure
Paul J. DeLong . . . . governor's pleasure
James Heerey . . . . governor's pleasure
Thomas Hittle . . . . governor's pleasure
James Hoppe . . . . governor's pleasure
William J. Horvath . . . . governor's pleasure
Mary Hubler . . . . governor's pleasure
James Kerkman . . . . governor's pleasure
Beth Meyers . . . . governor's pleasure
Kenneth Price . . . . governor's pleasure
Mark Rickenbach . . . . governor's pleasure
Robert Rogers . . . . governor's pleasure
Henry Schienebeck . . . . governor's pleasure
Jane Severt . . . . governor's pleasure
Jason Sjostrom . . . . governor's pleasure
Jordan Skiff . . . . governor's pleasure
Jeffrey C. Stier . . . . governor's pleasure
Paul Strong . . . . governor's pleasure
Tom Tiffany . . . . governor's pleasure
Richard Wedepohl . . . . governor's pleasure
Kenneth R. Zabel . . . . governor's pleasure

Fox River Navigational System Authority[1]
Kathryn A. Curren . . . . .expires 7/1/19
John L. Vette 7/1/19
H. Bruce Enke[5] 7/1/20
Jeffery Feldt[5] 7/1/20
S. Timothy Rose[3] 7/1/21
Tim Short[5] 7/1/21

Funeral Directors Examining Board[1] ($25/day[2])
Eric Lengell . . . . expires 7/1/16
Aziz K. Al-Sager 7/1/18
D. Bruce Carlson[3] 7/1/19
Marla Michaelis[5] 7/1/21
Marc A. Eernisse[5] 7/1/22
vacancy

Geologists, Hydrologists and Soil Scientists, Examining Board of Professional[1] ($25/day[2])
Brenda Halminiak . . . . .expires 7/1/12
Randall Hunt 7/1/12
Kenneth Bradbury 7/1/13
William Mode 7/1/13
Richard Beilfuss 7/1/14
Stephanie Williams 7/1/17
6 vacancies

Great Lakes Commission
Dean R. Haen . . . . .expires 7/1/20
Todd Ambs 7/1/23
Noah Roberts . . . . . expires at governor's pleasure

State officers appointed by the governor, May 15, 2019, continued

Great Lakes Protection Fund[1]
Richard Meeusen . . . . .expires 1/9/15
Kevin L. Shafer 1/12/16

Groundwater Coordinating Council
Stephen Diercks . . . . .expires 7/1/17

Group Insurance Board ($25/day[2])
Michael Farrell . . . . .expires 5/1/19
Charles Grapentine 5/1/19
Theodore Neitzke IV 5/1/19
Jennifer L. Stegall 5/1/19
Herschel Day .5/1/21
Nancy L. Thompson 5/1/21
Katy Lounsbury . . . expires at governor's pleasure

Health and Educational Facilities Authority, Wisconsin[1]
James Dietsche . . . . .expires 6/30/19
Robert Van Meeteren 6/30/20
Paul Mathews 6/30/21
Pamela Stanick[5] 6/30/22
James K. Oppermann[3] 7/1/23
Renee E. Anderson[5] 7/1/24
Tim K. Size[3] .7/1/25

Health Care Liability Insurance Plan/Injured Patients and Families Compensation Fund Bd. Of Governors ($50/day[2])
Kim R. Hurtz . . . . .expires 5/1/17
Sridhar V. Vasudevan 5/1/19
Gregory Banaszynski 5/1/20
Carla Borda 5/1/21

Health Services, Department of, Secretary[1] (group 8 salary[2])
Andrea Palm[3] . . . . . expires at governor's pleasure

Hearing and Speech Examining Board[1] ($25/day[2])
Thomas Sather . . . . .expires 7/1/15
Steven Klapperich[5] 7/1/19
Robert R. Broeckert[5] 7/1/20
Barbara Johnson[5] 7/1/21
Thomas J. Krier[5] 7/1/21
5 vacancies

Higher Educational Aids Board
Jeff Cichon . . . . .expires 5/1/18
Stephen D. Willett 5/1/18
Kelsey C. Fenske 5/1/19
Alex M. Hipler 5/1/19
Logan M. Kossel 5/1/19
Steven D. Midthun 5/1/19
Timothy Opgenorth 5/1/19
Jose Delgado .5/1/20
Robert T. Welch 5/1/20
Nathaniel Helm-Quest 5/1/21

Higher Educational Aids Board, Executive Secretary (group 3 salary[2])
Connie L. Hutchison. expires at governor's pleasure

Highway Safety, Council on
J.D. Lind . . . . .expires 7/1/18

Richard G. Van Boxtel 7/1/18
Joseph C. Gonnering 7/1/19
John P. Mesich 7/1/19
Yash Wadhwa .7/1/19
Brian Dean 7/1/20
Robert D. Hinds 7/1/20
Donald Gutkowski 7/1/21
William Neitzel 7/1/21
Kurt Schultz 7/1/21

Historic Preservation Review Board
Bruce Block . . . . .expires 7/1/16
David V. Mollenhoff 7/1/18
Paul Wolter 7/1/18
Kubet Luchterhand 7/1/19
Carlen I. Hatala 7/1/20
Valentine Schute, Jr. 7/1/20
Daniel J. Stephans 7/1/20
Donna Zimmerman 7/1/20
Sissel Schroeder 7/1/21
Sergio M. González 7/1/22
Carol Johnson 7/1/22
Daniel J. Joyce 7/1/22
Neil Prendergast 7/1/22
Melinda J. Young 7/1/22

Housing and Economic Development Authority, Wisconsin[1]
John Horning . . . . .expires 1/1/19
Susan Shore 1/1/20
McArthur Weddle 1/1/20
Raynetta R. Hill[3] 1/1/22
Victoria Parmentier[3] 1/1/22
Ivan Gamboa[3] 1/1/23

Housing and Economic Development Authority, Wisconsin, Executive Director[1] (group 6 salary[2])
Joaquin J. Altoro . . . . .expires 1/3/21

Insurance, Commissioner of[1] (group 6 salary[2])
Mark V. Afable[3] . . . . expires at governor's pleasure

Interoperability Council
Melinda Allen . . . . .expires 5/1/09
Steven Hansen 5/1/13
Lynn Schubert 5/1/13
Jon Freund 5/1/15
Matthew Joski 5/1/15
William Stolte .5/1/15
James D. Formea 5/1/19
Richard G. Van Boxtel 5/1/20
Kirk A. Gunderson 5/1/21
Sean Marschke 5/1/21

Interstate Juvenile Supervision, State Board for
Edward Brooks . . . . .expires 7/1/18
T. Christopher Dee 7/1/19

Invasive Species Council
Hannah Spaul . . . . .expires 7/1/19
Thomas Buechel 7/1/20
Thomas Bressner 7/1/22
Valerie E. Johnson 7/1/22

State officers appointed by the governor, May 15, 2019, continued

Gregory Long. 7/1/22
Mark Renz 7/1/23

Investment and Local Impact Fund Board
Edward Brandis. . . . . .expires 5/1/15
Kelly Klein .5/1/15
David Pajula. 5/1/15
Robert Walesewicz 5/1/16
Leslie Kolesar 5/1/18
Emmer Shields, Jr. 5/1/18
Rick J. Hermus 5/1/20
2 vacancies

Investment Board, State of Wisconsin[1] ($50/day[2])
Mark Doll . . . . .expires 5/1/21
Barbara Nick 5/1/21
Paul Stewart. 5/1/21
Norman Cummings 5/1/23
Timothy R. Sheehy. 5/1/23
David Stein 5/1/23
2 vacancies

Judicial Commission[1] ($25/day[2])
Mark Barrette . . . . .expires 8/1/14
Eileen Burnett 8/1/14
William Cullinan 8/1/14
Steven C. Miller. 8/1/17
vacancy

Judicial Council
Dennis Myers . . . . .expires 7/1/18
Benjamin J. Pliskie. 7/1/19
Christian Gossett. . . expires at governor's pleasure

Kickapoo Reserve Management Board[1] ($25/day[2])
Tracy Littlejohn. . . . . .expires 5/1/12
Adlai Mann 5/1/13
Paul Hayes. 5/1/18
Susan C. Cushing. 5/1/19
Travis M. Downing 7/1/19
David M. Maxwell 5/1/20
Ronald M. Johnson 5/1/20
William L. Quackenbush 5/1/20
Richard T. Wallin 5/1/20
Reggie Nelson 5/1/21
vacancy

Labor and Industry Review Commission[1] (group 5 salary[2])
David B. Falstad . . . . .expires 3/1/21
Georgia E. Maxwell[6]. 3/1/23
Michael Gillick[3, 7]. 3/1/25
vacancy

Labor and Industry Review Commission, General Counsel
Maria Gonzalez Knavel . . . . . expires at governor's pleasure

Laboratory of Hygiene Board
James M. Morrison. . . . . .expires 5/1/18
Robert F. Corliss 5/1/19
Barry E. Irmen. 5/1/19

Jeffery A. Kindrai 5/1/20
3 vacancies

Lake Michigan Commercial Fishing Board
Charles W. Henriksen expires at governor's pleasure
Richard R. Johnson . . . . governor's pleasure
Michael Le Clair . . . . governor's pleasure
Mark Maricque . . . . governor's pleasure
Dan Pawlitzke . . . . governor's pleasure
Brett Schwarz . . . . governor's pleasure
Todd Stuth . . . . governor's pleasure

Lake States Wood Utilization Consortium inactive

Lake Superior Commercial Fishing Board
William Bodin. . . . . expires at governor's pleasure
Maurine Halvorson . . . . governor's pleasure
Craig Hoopman . . . . governor's pleasure
Robert J. Nelson . . . . governor's pleasure
vacancy

Land and Water Conservation Board[1] ($25/day[2])
Mark E. Cupp . . . . .expires 5/1/20
Eric D. Birschbach[3]. 5/1/21
Andrew J. Buttles[3] 5/1/23
Ronald Grasshoff[3] 5/1/23
Bobbie Webster[3] 5/1/23

Law Enforcement Standards Board
James Arts . . . . .expires 5/1/15
Joseph Collins. 5/1/19
Greg G. Giles 5/1/19
Nathan Henriksen 5/1/19
Jean Galasinski 5/1/20
Laura Messner-Washer 5/1/20
Christopher Domagalski. 5/1/21
Jennifer Harper 5/1/21
Kurt Picknell. 5/1/21
Scott R. Parks 5/1/22
Anna Ruzinski. 5/1/22
Edward J. Whealon 5/1/22

Library and Network Development, Council on
Thomas C. Kamenick . . . . .expires 7/1/18
Douglas H. Lay 7/1/18
Kathy Pletcher 7/1/18
Lisa Sterrett 7/1/18
Mary Therese Boyle 7/1/19
Becki George 7/1/19
Svetha S. Hetzler 7/1/19
James F. O'Hagan 7/1/19
Jess M. Ripp 7/1/19
Martha A. Van Pelt 7/1/19
Kristi A. Williams 7/1/19
Terrence Berres 7/1/20
Nick Dimassis 7/1/20
Miriam M. Erickson 7/1/20
Jacqueline Liesch 7/1/20
Bryan McCormick 7/1/21
Dennis Myers 7/1/21
Joan Robb .7/1/21
Jaime Healy-Plotkin 7/1/22

State officers appointed by the governor, May 15, 2019, continued

Lower Fox River Remediation Authority[1] inactive

Lower Wisconsin State Riverway Board[1] ($25/day[2])
Ritchie Brown. . . . . .expires 5/1/17
Gretchen F.G. La Budde. 5/1/17
Gerald Dorscheid[3]. 5/1/19
Ronald J. Leys. 5/1/20
Richard McFarlane. 5/1/21
Frederick Madison[3] 5/1/22
Randall H. Poelma[3] 5/1/22
Steve Wetter 5/1/22
Steve A. Williamson 5/1/22

**Marriage and Family Therapy, Professional
Counseling, and Social Work, Examining Board of[1]**
($25/day[2])
Alice Hanson-Drew . . . . .expires 7/1/13
Peter Fabian. 7/1/18
Allison Gordon 7/1/18
Gregory Winkler[3]. 7/1/19
Bridget Ellingboe 7/1/20
Elizabeth A. Krueger[5] 7/1/20
Tammy H. Scheidegger[5] 7/1/20
Kathleen M. Miller[5] 7/1/21
Kristin Koger[6] 7/1/22
Todd Tedrow[3] 7/1/23
3 vacancies

**Massage Therapy and Bodywork Therapy
Affiliated Credentialing Board[1]** ($25/day[2])
Elizabeth Krizenesky . . . . expires 7/1/2018
Robert Coleman, Jr.[3] 7/1/23
Jaime Ehmer[3] 7/1/23
Carla Hedtke[3] . . . ./1/1/23
3 vacancies

**Medical College of Wisconsin, Incorporated, Board
of Trustees of the[1]**
Ted Kellner. . . . . expires 6/30/21
Jon Hammes 6/30/23

Medical Education Review Committee inactive

Medical Examining Board[1] ($25/day[2])
Mary Jo Capodice . . . . .expires 7/1/18
Kenneth Simons 7/1/18
Rodney Erickson 7/1/19
Robert L. Zoeller 7/1/19
Alaa A. Abd-Elsayed 7/1/20
Michael Carton. 7/1/20
Bradley Kudick 7/1/20
Lee Ann R. Lau[5]. 7/1/20
Timothy Westlake 7/1/20
David Anthony Bryce[6] 7/1/21
Padmaja Doniparthi. 7/1/21
David Roelke 7/1/21
vacancy

Mental Health, Council on
Mishelle O'Shasky . . . . .expires 7/1/13
David Stepien 7/1/15
Ann Catherine Veierstahler 7/1/16
Edward F. Wall 7/1/17

Monique M. Hicks 7/1/18
Richard Immler. 7/1/18
Jacqueline J. Borthwick. 7/1/19
Julie-Anne Braun. 7/1/19
Barbara Buffington 7/1/19
Kathryn Bush 7/1/19
Beth A. Clay 7/1/19
Kimberlee M. Coronado 7/1/19
Inshirah Farhoud. 7/1/19
Mark Lausch. 7/1/19
Charlotte Matteson 7/1/19
Amy L. Polsin 7/1/19
Matthew Strittmater 7/1/19
Donna Wrenn. 7/1/19
Tom Engels .7/1/20
Tracey Hassinger 7/1/20
Daniel C. Kiernan. 7/1/20
Bonnie MacRitchie. 7/1/20
Dori L. Richards. 7/1/20
Lea D. Collins-Worachek 7/1/21
Carol Keen. .7/1/21
Sheli Metzger 7/1/21

**Midwest Interstate Low-Level Radioactive Waste
Commission, Wisconsin Commissioner[1]** ($25/day[2])
vacancy

Midwest Interstate Passenger Rail Commission
Craig Anderson. 1/5/15
Dave Simon . . . . . . expires at governor's pleasure

Midwestern Higher Education Commission
Margaret A. Farrow . . . . .expires 7/1/16
Rolf Wegenke. 7/1/23
Julie Underwood. . . expires at governor's pleasure

Migrant Labor, Council on
Enrique Figueroa. . . . . .expires 7/1/12
Teresa Tellez-Giron. 7/1/13
Steve Ziobro 7/1/13
Richard W. Okray. 7/1/15
Guadalupe Rendon 7/1/16
Lupe G. Martinez. 7/1/18
Jeanine M. McCain. 7/1/19
Melissa K. Cuevas 7/1/20
John I. Bauknecht 7/1/20
Erica A. Kunze. 7/1/20
Kevin Magee 7/1/20

Military and State Relations, Council on
Linda Fournier . . . . expires at governor's pleasure
Daniel Zimmerman . . . . governor's pleasure
vacancy

Milwaukee Child Welfare Partnership Council
Mary Triggiano . . . . .expires 7/1/16
Colleen M. Ellingson. 7/1/17
Sara Purtell Scullen 7/1/17
Delvyn L. Crawford 7/1/18
Willie Johnson, Jr. 7/1/18
Veneshia McKinney-Whitson 7/1/18
Anthony Staskunas 7/1/18
Steve F. Taylor. 7/1/18

State officers appointed by the governor, May 15, 2019, continued

Victor E. Barnett 7/1/19
Christine P. Holmes 7/1/19
James W. Topitzes 7/1/20
Michele M. Bria. 7/1/21
Jameelah A. Love. 7/1/22
Mark Mertens. 7/1/22
Mallory O'Brien. 7/1/22
Anthony E. Shields. 7/1/22

Mississippi River Parkway Commission
Jill Billings . . . . .expires 2/1/20
Dennis Donath 2/1/20
Jean Galasinski 2/1/20
Jaynne L. Lepke. 2/1/20
Alan Lorenz 2/1/20
Howard Marklein 2/1/20
Loren Oldenburg 2/1/20
Sherry Quamme 2/1/20
John Rosenow 2/1/20
David Smith. 2/1/20
Jeff Smith 2/1/20
Thomas Vondrum 2/1/20

National and Community Service Board
Christine Beatty . . . . expires 5/1/17
Lisa Delmore 5/1/17
Kathleen Groat 5/1/17
James M. Langdon. 5/1/17
Amy McDowell 5/1/17
Angela Kringle 5/1/18
Margaret Jane Moore. 5/1/18
Pamela Charles. 5/1/19
Donald P. Dunbar 5/1/19
Anthony F. Hallman 5/1/19
Kate Jaeger 5/1/19
Susan Schwartz. 5/1/19
Robert Griffith 5/1/20
Laura M. Doolin 5/1/20
Daniel Zimmerman 5/1/20
Paula Horning 5/1/21
India McCanse . . . . expires at governor's pleasure

Natural Resources, Department of, Secretary[1]
(group 7 salary[2])
Preston D. Cole[3] . . . expires at governor's pleasure

Natural Resources Board[1]
Gary Zimmer . . . . .expires 5/1/19
Julie Anderson 5/1/21
Frederick Preh 5/1/21
William Bruins 5/1/23
Terry N. Hilgenberg 5/1/23
Gregory J. Kazmierski. 5/1/23
Fred A. Clark[3] 5/1/25

Nonmotorized Recreation and Transportation Trails Council
Rod Bartlow. . . . . . expires at governor's pleasure
William Hauda . . . . governor's pleasure
Anne Murphy . . . . governor's pleasure
Joel Patenaude . . . . governor's pleasure
Debbie Peterson . . . . governor's pleasure
David Phillips . . . . governor's pleasure

Ben Popp . . . . governor's pleasure
Geoffrey Snudden . . . . governor's pleasure
Blake Theisen . . . . governor's pleasure

Nursing, Board of[1] ($25/day[2])
Lillian Nolan. . . . . .expires 7/1/19
Pamela K. White 7/1/19
Beth Smith Houskamp 7/1/20
Jennifer L. Eklof. 7/1/21
Luann Skarlupka 7/1/21
Rosemary P. Dolatowski[5]. 7/1/22
Peter Kallio[3]. 7/1/22
Lisa Pisney[3] 7/1/23
Emily Zentz[3]. 7/1/23

Nursing Home Administrator Examining Board[1] ($25/day[2])
Susan Kinast-Porter . . . . .expires 7/1/09
Kate Bertram 7/1/18
Brittany Cobb. 7/1/18
Sondra L. Norder[3] 7/1/22
5 vacancies

Occupational Therapists Affiliated Credentialing Board[1] ($25/day[2])
Brian Holmquist . . . . .expires 7/1/13
Amy Summers 7/1/18
Laura O'Brien[5] 7/1/19
Terry Erickson[3] 7/1/23
3 vacancies

Off-Highway Motorcycle Council
Kira A. Benkert . . . . .expires 3/1/19
Craig A. Johnson 3/1/19
Robert B. McConnell 3/1/20
Bryan T. Much. 3/1/20
Mitch Winder 3/1/22

Off-Road Vehicle Council
Bryan Much . . . . .expires 3/1/19
David Traczyk. 3/1/20
James Wisneski 3/1/20
Adam Harden. 3/1/21
Rob McConnell. 3/1/21
Michael Biese 3/1/22
Robert A. Donahue 3/1/22

Offender Reentry, Council on
Michael R. Knetzger . . . . expires 7/1/2018
Susan L. Opper 7/1/18
Robert P. Koebele 7/1/19
Angela M. Mancuso 7/1/19
Jonathon W. Nejedlo 7/1/19
Antwayne M. Robertson 7/1/19
Karen J. Cumblad . . expires at governor's pleasure
3 vacancies

Optometry Examining Board[1] ($25/day[2])
Ann Meier Carli . . . . .expires 7/1/14
Mark Jinkins. 7/1/16
Richard L. Foss 7/1/17
Robert C. Schulz[5] 7/1/20
John L. Sterling[5] 7/1/21

State officers appointed by the governor, May 15, 2019, continued

Peter I. Sorce[3]. 7/1/23
vacancy

Parole Commission, Chairperson[1] (group 2 salary[2])
Daniel J. Gabler. . . . . .expires 3/1/19

Perfusionists Examining Council ($25/day[2])
David Cobb . . . . .expires 7/1/10

Pharmacy Examining Board[1] ($25/day[2])
Thaddeus Schumacher. . . . . expires 7/1/19
Franklin J. LaDien[8]. 7/1/20
Philip J. Trapskin[5] 7/1/21
Cathy Winters[5] 7/1/21
John Weitekamp[5] 7/1/22
2 vacancies

Physical Disabilities, Council on
Ron J. Jansen . . . . expires 7/1/18
Gabriel M. Schlieve 7/1/18
Nicole Herda .7/1/19
Robert A. Nissen 7/1/19
Karen E. Secor. 7/1/19
Jason S. Ostrowski 7/1/20
Charles H. Vandenplas 7/1/20
Roberto Escamilla II 7/1/21
Benjamin Barrett. 7/1/22
Jackie Gordon. 7/1/22
Noah Hershkowitz. 7/1/22
Kathleen A. Johnson 7/1/22
Noah Roberts. . . . . expires at governor's pleasure
vacancy

Physical Therapy Examining Board[1] ($25/day[2])
John Greany. . . . . .expires 7/1/19
Shari Berry[5] 7/1/20
Sarah Olson[6] .7/1/21
Kathryn R. Zalewski[5] 7/1/21
vacancy

Physician Assistants, Council on
vacancy

Podiatry Affiliated Credentialing Board[1] ($25/day[2])
Thomas Komp . . . . .expires 7/1/17
3 vacancies

Prison Industries Board[1]
Jose Carrillo . . . . .expires 5/1/14
Bernie Spiegel 5/1/16
Tracey Isensee 5/1/18
James Jackson 5/1/19
James M. Langdon. 5/1/19
Bill Smith. 5/1/19
3 vacancies

Psychology Examining Board[1] ($25/day[2])
Rebecca Anderson . . . . .expires 7/1/18
Daniel Schroeder[3]. 7/1/19
Peter I. Sorce .7/1/20
Marcus P. Desmonde[5]. 7/1/21
David Thompson[5] 7/1/22
vacancy

Public Defender Board[1]
Joseph T. Miotke . . . . .expires 5/1/18
Daniel M. Berkos 5/1/20
Patrick Fiedler. 5/1/20
John J. Hogan. 5/1/20
James Brennan[3] 5/1/22
Regina Dunkin[3] 5/1/22
Ellen Thorn[3]. .5/1/22
Mai N. Xiong[3]. 5/1/22

Public Health Council
Mark Villalpando . . . . .expires 7/1/11
Ann H. Hoffman 7/1/16
William Keeton 7/1/16
Terry Brandenburg. 7/1/17
Mary Dorn 7/1/17
Gary D. Gilmore 7/1/17
Alan Schwartzstein 7/1/17
Michael Wallace 7/1/17
Dale Hippensteel 7/1/18
Eric Krawczyk .7/1/18
Robert Leischow 7/1/18
Joan Theurer .7/1/18
Darlene M. Weis 7/1/19

Public Leadership Board[1]
Bob Cook . . . . .expires 5/1/20
Scott R. Jensen 5/1/20
Gerard Randall 5/1/20
Jason Thompson 5/1/20
Robin J. Vos 5/1/20

Public Records Board
Peter Sorce . . . . . expires at governor's pleasure
2 vacancies

Public Service Commission[1] (group 5 salary[2])
Michael Huebsch . . . . .expires 3/1/21
Ellen Nowak[6] .3/1/23
Rebecca Cameron Valcq[3] 3/1/25

Radiography Examining Board[1] ($25/day[2])
Michele Goodweiler. . . . . .expires 7/1/18
Tracy Marshall[5] 7/1/20
Heidi Nichols .7/1/20
Donald Borst[8]. 7/1/21
3 vacancies

Railroads, Commissioner of[1] (group 5 salary[2])
Yash Wadhwa . . . . .expires 3/1/23

Real Estate Appraisers Board[1] ($25/day[2])
Jennifer M. Espinoza-Coates. . . . . .expires 5/1/19
Steven Miner .5/1/19
Carl Clementi .5/1/20
Dennis Myers .5/1/21
Thomas Kneesel[5]. 5/1/22
Gordon Svendsen[3] 5/1/22
vacancy

Real Estate Curriculum and Examinations, Council on
Kathryne Kuhl . . . . .expires 7/1/15

State officers appointed by the governor, May 15, 2019, continued

Michael M. Grebe 5/1/22
Andrew Petersen. 5/1/22
Scott C. Beightol[6] 5/1/23
Tracey Klein 5/1/23
Robert B. Atwell 5/1/24
Michael T. Jones 5/1/24
Chris Peterson 5/1/25
Gerald Whitburn 5/1/25
Edmund Manydeeds, III[3] 5/1/26
Karen Walsh[3] .5/1/26

Veterans Affairs, Board of[1]
John Gaedke . . . . .expires 5/1/19
Carl Krueger. .5/1/19
Larry Kutschma. 5/1/19
Steven R. Best. 5/1/21
Paul W. Chamberlain 5/1/21
Vern L. Larson. 5/1/21
Leigh Neville-Neil 5/1/21
Alan Richards .5/1/21
John Townsend. 5/1/21

Veterans Affairs, Department of, Secretary[1] (group 6 salary[2])
Mary M. Kolar[3] . . . . expires at governor's pleasure

Veterinary Diagnostic Laboratory Board
Alissa Grenawalt . . . . .expires 5/1/18
James Meronek. 5/1/19
Ray Pawlisch .5/1/19
Sandra C. Madland 5/1/20
Casey Davis 5/1/21
Paul Kunde . . . . . expires at governor's pleasure

Veterinary Examining Board[1] ($25/day[2])
Dana Reimer . . . . .expires 7/1/18
Sheldon Schall 7/1/18
Philip Johnson 7/1/19
Bruce Berth 7/1/20
Kevin S. Kreier 7/1/20
Robert Forbes 7/1/21

Diane Dommer Martin[3] 7/1/23
Lisa Weisensel Nesson[3]. 7/1/23

Waste Facility Siting Board[1] ($35/day[2])
James Schuerman . . . . expires 5/1/2013
Jeanette P. DeKeyser 5/1/18
Dale R. Shaver 5/1/20

Waterways Commission, Wisconsin[1]
Maureen Kinney . . . . .expires 3/1/14
James F. Rooney 3/1/19
Lee Van Zeeland 3/1/20
Ralph C. Brzezinski. 3/1/21
Roger E. Walsh[5]. 3/1/23

Wetland Study Council
Tim Andryk . . . . .expires 7/1/20
Stacy Jepson .7/1/20
Seth Hudson .7/1/21
Thomas Larson 7/1/21
Paul Kent. 7/1/22
Paul Zimmerman 7/1/23
Tracy Hames. .7/1/24
Matthew Howard 7/1/25

Wisconsin Compensation Rating Bureau
Daniel Burazin . . . . expires at governor's pleasure
Chris Reader. . . . . governor's pleasure

Women's Council
Mary Jo Baas . . . . .expires 7/1/18
Brianna N. Buch 7/1/18
Jessie Nicholson 7/1/18
Lisa Armaganian 7/1/19
Patricia M. Cadorin 7/1/19
Karen M. Katz. 7/1/19
Michelle Mettner. 7/1/19
Katherine Mnuk 7/1/19

Workforce Development, Department of, Secretary[1] (group 7 salary[2])
Caleb Frostman[3] . . . expires at governor's pleasure

Note: List includes only appointments made by the governor. Additional members frequently serve ex officio or are appointed by other means. The governor also appoints members of intrastate regional agencies and nonstatutory committees and makes temporary appointments under chapter 17, Wis. Stats., to elected state and county offices when vacancies occur.

Terms are specified by the following statute sections or as otherwise provided by law: s. 15.05 (1), Wis. Stats.—secretaries; s. 15.06 (1), Wis. Stats.—commissioners; s. 15.07 (1), Wis. Stats.—governing boards and attached boards; s. 15.08 (1), Wis. Stats.—examining boards and councils; s. 15.09 (1)—councils.

1. Nominated by the governor and appointed with the advice and consent of the senate. Senate confirmation is required for secretaries of departments, members of commissions and commissioners, governing boards, examining boards, and other boards as designated by statute. 2. Members of boards and councils are reimbursed for actual and necessary expenses incurred in performing their duties. In addition, examining board members receive $25 per day for days worked, and members of certain other boards under s. 15.07 (5), Wis. Stats., receive a per diem as noted in the table. Section 20.923, Wis. Stats., places state officials in one of 10 executive salary groups (ESG) for which salary ranges have been established. Group salary ranges for the period of June 24, 2017 through June 22, 2019, are: Group 1: $60,382–$103,667; Group 2: $65,208–$111,966; Group 3: $70,429–$120,910; Group 4: $76,066–$130,624; Group 5: $82,139–$141,024; Group 6: $88,712–$152,318; Group 7: $95,826–$164,549; Group 8: $103,480–$177,674; Group 9: $111,758–$191,880; Group 10: $120,702–$207,230. 3. Nominated by governor but not yet confirmed by senate. 4. Compensation set by Economic Development Corporation Board. 5. Approved by senate in December 2018; withdrawn by Governor Evers March 22, 2019, after court ruling; reappointed March 28, 2019. Final decision in court case is pending as of the date of this table. 6. Approved by senate in December 2018; withdrawn by Governor Evers March 22, 2019, after court ruling. Final decision in court case is pending as of the date of this table. 7. Succeeds nominee withdrawn by Governor Evers on March 22, 2019. Final decision in court case is pending as of the date of this table. 8. Approved by senate in December 2018; withdrawn by Governor Evers March 22, 2019, after court ruling; reappointed April 2019. Final decision in court case is pending as of the date of this table.

Source: Appointment lists maintained by governor's office and received by the Legislative Reference Bureau on or before May 15, 2019.

Circuit court judges, April 2, 2019

Counties in circuit	Branch	Court location	Judges	Term expires July 31
Adams	—	Friendship	Daniel Glen Wood	2021
Ashland	—	Ashland	Kelly J. McKnight	2024
Barron	1	Barron	James C. Babler	2022
	2	Barron	J. Michael Bitney	2020
	3	Barron	Maureen D. Boyle	2020
Bayfield	—	Washburn	John P. Anderson	2021
Brown	1	Green Bay	Donald R. Zuidmulder	2021
	2	Green Bay	Tom Walsh	2024
	3	Green Bay	Tammy Jo Hock[1]	2019
	4	Green Bay	Kendall M. Kelley	2021
	5	Green Bay	Marc A. Hammer	2021
	6	Green Bay	John P. Zakowski	2024
	7	Green Bay	Timothy A. Hinkfuss[1]	2019
	8	Green Bay	William M. Atkinson	2021
Buffalo, Pepin	—	Alma	Thomas W. Clark	2024
Burnett	—	Siren	Melissia R. Christianson Mogen	2023
Calumet	—	Chilton	Jeffrey S. Froehlich	2024
Chippewa	1	Chippewa Falls	Steven H. Gibbs	2024
	2	Chippewa Falls	James Isaacson	2021
	3	Chippewa Falls	Steven R. Cray	2020
Clark	—	Neillsville	Lyndsey Boon Brunette	2024
Columbia	1	Portage	Todd J. Hepler	2021
	2	Portage	W. Andrew Voigt	2023
	3	Portage	Troy D. Cross	2024
Crawford	—	Prairie du Chien	Lynn Marie Ryder	2022
Dane	1	Madison	Susan M. Crawford	2024
	2	Madison	Josann M. Reynolds	2021
	3	Madison	Valerie L. Bailey-Rihn	2022
	4	Madison	Everett Mitchell	2022
	5	Madison	Nicholas J. McNamara	2022
	6	Madison	Shelley J. Gaylord	2021
	7	Madison	William E. Hanrahan	2020
	8	Madison	Frank D. Remington	2024
	9	Madison	Richard Niess	2023
	10	Madison	Juan B. Colas	2021
	11	Madison	Ellen K. Berz	2024
	12	Madison	Jill J. Karofsky	2023
	13	Madison	Julie Genovese	2021
	14	Madison	John D. Hyland	2022
	15	Madison	Stephen Ehlke	2022
	16	Madison	Rhonda L. Lanford[1]	2019
	17	Madison	Peter C. Anderson	2022
Dodge	1	Juneau	Brian A. Pfitzinger	2020
	2	Juneau	Martin J. De Vries	2023
	3	Juneau	Joseph G. Sciascia[1]	2019
	4	Juneau	Steven Bauer	2020
Door	1	Sturgeon Bay	D. Todd Ehlers	2024
	2	Sturgeon Bay	David L. Weber	2023
Douglas	1	Superior	Kelly J. Thimm	2021
	2	Superior	George L. Glonek	2021
Dunn	1	Menomonie	James M. Peterson	2020
	2	Menomonie	Rod W. Smeltzer	2021
Eau Claire	1	Eau Claire	John F. Manydeeds	2022
	2	Eau Claire	Michael Schumacher	2020
	3	Eau Claire	Emily M. Long	2024
	4	Eau Claire	Jon M. Theisen	2024
	5	Eau Claire	Sarah Harless	2024
Florence, Forest	—	Crandon	Leon D. Stenz	2020

Circuit court judges, April 2, 2019, continued

Counties in circuit	Branch	Court location	Judges	Term expires July 31
Fond du Lac	1	Fond du Lac	Dale L. English	2020
	2	Fond du Lac	Peter L. Grimm	2022
	3	Fond du Lac	Richard J. Nuss	2021
	4	Fond du Lac	Gary R. Sharpe	2022
	5	Fond du Lac	Robert J. Wirtz	2023
Grant	1	Lancaster	Robert P. VanDeHey	2023
	2	Lancaster	Craig R. Day	2021
Green	1	Monroe	Jim Beer	2021
	2	Monroe	Thomas J. Vale	2021
Green Lake	—	Green Lake	Mark Slate	2023
Iowa	—	Dodgeville	Margaret M. Koehler	2022
Iron	—	Hurley	Patrick John Madden	2023
Jackson	—	Black River Falls	Anna L. Becker	2021
Jefferson	1	Jefferson	William V. Gruber[1,2]	2019
	2	Jefferson	William F. Hue[1]	2019
	3	Jefferson	Robert F. Dehring, Jr.	2024
	4	Jefferson	Bennett J. Brantmeier	2023
Juneau	1	Mauston	Stacy A. Smith	2024
	2	Mauston	Paul S. Curran	2020
Kenosha	1	Kenosha	David Mark Bastianelli	2021
	2	Kenosha	Jason A. Rossell	2024
	3	Kenosha	Bruce E. Schroeder	2020
	4	Kenosha	Anthony Milisauskas	2023
	5	Kenosha	David P. Wilk	2021
	6	Kenosha	Mary K. Wagner	2021
	7	Kenosha	Jodi L. Meier	2023
	8	Kenosha	Chad G. Kerkman	2021
Kewaunee	—	Kewaunee	Keith A. Mehn	2022
La Crosse	1	La Crosse	Ramona A. Gonzalez[1]	2019
	2	La Crosse	Elliott Levine[1]	2019
	3	La Crosse	Todd Bjerke[1]	2019
	4	La Crosse	Scott L. Horne[1]	2019
	5	La Crosse	Gloria Doyle	2021
Lafayette	—	Darlington	Duane M. Jorgenson	2021
Langlade	—	Antigo	John Rhode	2021
Lincoln	1	Merrill	Jay R. Tlusty	2022
	2	Merrill	Robert Russell[1]	2019
Manitowoc	1	Manitowoc	Mark R. Rohrer[1]	2019
	2	Manitowoc	Jerilyn M. Dietz	2024
	3	Manitowoc	Bob Dewane	2023
Marathon	1	Wausau	Jill N. Falstad	2021
	2	Wausau	Gregory Huber	2022
	3	Wausau	Lamont K. Jacobson	2020
	4	Wausau	Gregory J. Strasser	2023
	5	Wausau	Mike Moran	2023
Marinette	1	Marinette	David G. Miron	2020
	2	Marinette	James A. Morrison[1]	2019
Marquette	—	Montello	Bernard Ben Bult[3]	2019
Menominee, Shawano	1	Shawano	James R. Habeck	2020
	2	Shawano	William F. Kussel, Jr.	2024
Milwaukee	1	Milwaukee	Maxine Aldridge White	2023
	2	Wauwatosa	Joe Donald	2021
	3	Milwaukee	Clare L. Fiorenza	2021
	4	Milwaukee	Michael J. Hanrahan	2023
	5	Milwaukee	Paul Dedinsky[2]	2020
	6	Milwaukee	Ellen Brostrom	2021
	7	Milwaukee	Thomas J. McAdams	2020
	8	Milwaukee	William Sosnay	2024

Circuit court judges, April 2, 2019, continued

Counties in circuit	Branch	Court location	Judges	Term expires July 31
	9	Milwaukee	Paul R. Van Grunsven	2023
	10	Milwaukee	Michelle Ackerman Havas	2023
	11	Milwaukee	Dave Swanson[1]	2019
	12	Milwaukee	David L. Borowski	2021
	13	Milwaukee	Mary Triggiano	2023
	14	Wauwatosa	Christopher R. Foley	2022
	15	Wauwatosa	J.D. Watts	2021
	16	Milwaukee	Michael J. Dwyer	2021
	17	Milwaukee	Carolina Maria Stark	2024
	18	Milwaukee	Pedro Colón	2023
	19	Milwaukee	Dennis R. Cimpl	2023
	20	Milwaukee	Joseph Wall	2024
	21	Milwaukee	Cynthia M. Davis	2023
	22	Milwaukee	Timothy M. Witkowiak	2021
	23	Milwaukee	Lindsey Grady	2024
	24	Milwaukee	Janet Protasiewicz	2020
	25	Milwaukee	Stephanie Rothstein	2022
	26	Milwaukee	William Pocan[1]	2019
	27	Milwaukee	Kevin E. Martens	2020
	28	Milwaukee	Mark A. Sanders	2024
	29	Milwaukee	Daniel J. Gabler[2]	2020
	30	Milwaukee	Jeffrey A. Conen	2021
	31	Milwaukee	Hannah C. Dugan	2022
	32	Milwaukee	Laura Gramling Perez	2020
	33	Milwaukee	Carl Ashley	2023
	34	Milwaukee	Glenn H. Yamahiro	2022
	35	Milwaukee	Frederick C. Rosa	2023
	36	Milwaukee	Laura Crivello[1,2]	2019
	37	Milwaukee	T. Christopher Dee	2021
	38	Milwaukee	Jeffrey A. Wagner	2024
	39	Milwaukee	Jane Carroll	2024
	40	Milwaukee	Andrew Jones[2,4]	2019
	41	Wauwatosa	Audrey Skwierawski[1,2]	2019
	42	Milwaukee	David A. Hansher	2021
	43	Milwaukee	Marshall B. Murray	2024
	44	Wauwatosa	Gwen Connolly	2022
	45	Milwaukee	Jean Marie Kies	2022
	46	Milwaukee	David Feiss	2021
	47	Milwaukee	Kristy Yang	2023
Monroe	1	Sparta	Todd L. Ziegler[1]	2019
	2	Sparta	Mark L. Goodman	2022
	3	Sparta	Rick Radcliffe	2024
Oconto	1	Oconto	Michael T. Judge	2023
	2	Oconto	Jay N. Conley	2022
Oneida	1	Rhinelander	Patrick F. O'Melia	2020
	2	Rhinelander	Michael H. Bloom	2024
Outagamie	1	Appleton	Mark McGinnis	2023
	2	Appleton	Nancy J. Krueger	2020
	3	Appleton	Mitchell J. Metropulos	2020
	4	Appleton	Gregory B. Gill, Jr.	2024
	5	Appleton	Carrie Schneider	2024
	6	Appleton	Vincent Biskupic	2021
	7	Appleton	John A. Des Jardins	2024
Ozaukee	1	Port Washington	Paul V. Malloy	2021
	2	Port Washington	Joe Voiland[5]	2019
	3	Port Washington	Sandy A. Williams	2021
Pierce	—	Ellsworth	Joe Boles	2022
Polk	1	Balsam Lake	Daniel J. Tolan	2023

Circuit court judges, April 2, 2019, continued

Counties in circuit	Branch	Court location	Judges	Term expires July 31
	2	Balsam Lake	Jeff Anderson	2023
Portage	1	Stevens Point	Thomas B. Eagon	2024
	2	Stevens Point	Robert J. Shannon	2022
	3	Stevens Point	Thomas T. Flugaur	2024
Price	—	Phillips	Kevin G. Klein	2024
Racine	1	Racine	Wynne Laufenberg	2024
	2	Racine	Eugene Gasiorkiewicz	2022
	3	Racine	Maureen Martinez[1,2]	2019
	4	Racine	Mark Nielsen	2022
	5	Racine	Mike Piontek	2024
	6	Racine	David W. Paulson	2021
	7	Racine	Jon E. Fredrickson[1,2]	2019
	8	Racine	Faye M. Flancher	2021
	9	Racine	Robert S. Repischak	2024
	10	Racine	Timothy D. Boyle	2024
Richland	—	Richland Center	Andrew Sharp	2024
Rock	1	Janesville	Karl R. Hanson[1,2]	2019
	2	Janesville	Derrick A. Grubb[1,2]	2019
	3	Janesville	Jeffrey S. Kuglitsch	2024
	4	Janesville	Daniel T. Dillon1	2019
	5	Janesville	Mike Haakenson	2021
	6	Janesville	John M. Wood	2023
	7	Janesville	Barbara W. McCrory	2024
Rusk	—	Ladysmith	Steven P. Anderson	2022
St. Croix	1	Hudson	Scott J. Nordstrand[2]	2020
	2	Hudson	Edward F. Vlack III1	2019
	3	Hudson	Scott R. Needham	2024
	4	Hudson	R. Michael Waterman	2022
Sauk	1	Baraboo	Michael P. Screnock	2022
	2	Baraboo	Wendy J. N. Klicko	2022
	3	Baraboo	Pat Barrett	2024
Sawyer	—	Hayward	John Yackel	2021
Sheboygan	1	Sheboygan	L. Edward Stengel	2021
	2	Sheboygan	Kent Hoffman	2023
	3	Sheboygan	Angela Sutkiewicz	2023
	4	Sheboygan	Rebecca Persick	2021
	5	Sheboygan	Daniel J. Borowski	2023
Taylor	—	Medford	Ann Knox-Bauer	2021
Trempealeau	—	Whitehall	Rian W. Radtke	2023
Vernon	—	Viroqua	Darcy Rood	2023
Vilas	—	Eagle River	Neal A. Nielsen	2022
Walworth	1	Elkhorn	Phillip A. Koss	2024
	2	Elkhorn	Daniel S. Johnson	2022
	3	Elkhorn	Kristine E. Drettwan	2021
	4	Elkhorn	David M. Reddy	2022
Washburn	—	Shell Lake	Eugene D. Harrington	2021
Washington	1	West Bend	James Pouros	2023
	2	West Bend	James K. Muehlbauer	2020
	3	West Bend	Todd Martens	2023
	4	West Bend	Andrew T. Gonring	2024
Waukesha	1	Waukesha	Michael O. Bohren1	2019
	2	Waukesha	Jennifer Dorow	2024
	3	Waukesha	Ralph M. Ramirez	2023
	4	Waukesha	Lloyd V. Carter	2023
	5	Waukesha	Lee Sherman Dreyfus, Jr.	2020
	6	Waukesha	Brad Schimel[1,2]	2019
	7	Waukesha	Maria S. Lazar	2021
	8	Waukesha	Michael P. Maxwell	2021

Circuit court judges, April 2, 2019, continued

Counties in circuit	Branch	Court location	Judges	Term expires July 31
	9	Waukesha	Michael Aprahamian	2021
	10	Waukesha	Paul Bugenhagen, Jr.	2021
	11	Waukesha	William Domina.	2023
	12	Waukesha	Laura Lau.	2024
Waupaca	1	Waupaca	Troy L. Nielsen.	2023
	2	Waupaca	Vicki Taggatz Clussman	2020
	3	Waupaca	Raymond S. Huber	2024
Waushara.	—	Wautoma	Guy Dutcher.	2023
Winnebago	1	Oshkosh	Teresa S. Basiliere.	2024
	2	Oshkosh	Scott C. Woldt	2023
	3	Oshkosh	Barbara Hart Key	2022
	4	Oshkosh	Karen L. Seifert	2024
	5	Oshkosh	John Jorgensen.	2022
	6	Oshkosh	Daniel J. Bissett	2023
Wood	1	Wisconsin Rapids	Gregory J. Potter	2020
	2	Wisconsin Rapids	Nicholas J. Brazeau, Jr.	2024
	3	Wisconsin Rapids	Todd P. Wolf	2021

— Means the circuit has only one branch.

1. Reelected on April 2, 2019, for a six-year term to commence on August 1, 2019. 2. Appointed by the governor. 3. Chad A. Hendee was newly elected on April 2, 2019, for a six-year term to commence on August 1, 2019. 4. Danielle Shelton was newly elected on April 2, 2019, for a six-year term to commence on August 1, 2019. 5. Steve Cain was newly elected on April 2, 2019, for a six-year term to commence on August 1, 2019.

Sources: 2017–2018 Wisconsin Statutes; Wisconsin Elections Commission, department data, April 2019; governor's appointment notices; The Third Branch newsletter, Spring/Summer 2018 and previous issues.

Wisconsin county officers: county clerks, April 2019

	Clerk	Website
Adams	Cheryl Kroening (R)	www.co.adams.wi.us
Ashland.	Heather Schutte (D)	www.co.ashland.wi.us
Barron.	DeeAnn Cook (R)	www.barroncountywi.gov
Bayfield.	Scott S. Fibert (D)	www.bayfieldcounty.org
Brown.	Sandy Juno (R)	www.co.brown.wi.us
Buffalo	Roxann Halverson (D)	www.buffalocounty.com
Burnett	Wanda Hinrichs (D)	www.burnettcounty.com
Calumet	Beth Hauser (R)	www.co.calumet.wi.us
Chippewa	Jaclyn Sadler (D)	www.co.chippewa.wi.us
Clark.	Christina Jensen (R)	www.co.clark.wi.us
Columbia.	Susan Moll (R)	www.co.columbia.wi.us
Crawford	Janet Geisler (R)	www.crawfordcountywi.org
Dane	Scott McDonell (D)	www.countyofdane.com
Dodge	Karen Gibson (R)	www.co.dodge.wi.gov
Door.	Jill Lau (R)	www.co.door.wi.gov
Douglas.	Susan Sandvick (D)	www.douglascountywi.org
Dunn	Julie Wathke (D)	www.co.dunn.wi.us
Eau Claire.	Janet Loomis (D)	www.co.eau-claire.wi.us
Florence	Donna Trudell (R)	www.florencecountywi.com
Fond du Lac	Lisa Freiberg (R)	www.fdlco.wi.gov
Forest	Nora Matuszewski (R)	www.co.forest.wi.gov
Grant	Linda Gebhard (R)	www.co.grant.wi.gov
Green	Michael J. Doyle (I)	www.co.green.wi.gov
Green Lake.	Elizabeth Otto (R)	www.co.green-lake.wi.us

Wisconsin county officers: county clerks, April 2019, continued

	Clerk	Website
Iowa	Gregory T. Klusendorf (D)	www.iowacounty.org
Iron	Michael Saari (D)	www.co.iron.wi.gov
Jackson	Kyle Deno (D)	www.co.jackson.wi.us
Jefferson	Audrey McGraw (A)	www.jeffersoncountywi.gov
Juneau	Terri Treptow (R)	www.co.juneau.wi.gov
Kenosha	Mary Kubicki (D)	www.co.kenosha.wi.us
Kewaunee	Jamie Annoye (D)	www.kewauneeco.org
La Crosse	Ginny Dankmeyer (D)	www.lacrossecounty.org
Lafayette	Carla Jacobson (R)	www.co.lafayette.wi.gov
Langlade	Judy Nagel (D)	www.co.langlade.wi.us
Lincoln	Christopher Marlowe (R)	www.co.lincoln.wi.us
Manitowoc	Jessica Backus (R)	www.co.manitowoc.wi.us
Marathon	Nan Kottke (D)	www.co.marathon.wi.us
Marinette	Kathy Brandt (R)	www.marinettecounty.com
Marquette	Gary L. Sorensen (R)	www.co.marquette.wi.us
Menominee	Sarah Lyons (D)	www.co.menominee.wi.us
Milwaukee	George L. Christenson (D)	https://county.milwaukee.gov
Monroe	Shelley Bohl (R)	www.co.monroe.wi.us
Oconto	Kim Pytleski (R)	www.co.oconto.wi.us
Oneida	Tracy Hartman (R)	www.co.oneida.wi.gov
Outagamie	Lori J. O'Bright (R)	www.outagamie.org
Ozaukee	Julianne Winkelhorst (R)	www.co.ozaukee.wi.us
Pepin	Audrey Bauer (R)	www.co.pepin.wi.us
Pierce	Jamie Feuerhelm (I)	www.co.pierce.wi.us
Polk	Sharon Jorgenson (R)	www.co.polk.wi.us
Portage	Shirley Simonis (D)	www.co.portage.wi.us
Price	Jean Gottwald (D)	www.co.price.wi.us
Racine	Wendy Christensen (R)	https://racinecounty.com
Richland	Victor V. Vlasak (R)	www.co.richland.wi.us
Rock	Lisa Tollefson (D)	www.co.rock.wi.us
Rusk	Loren Beebe (D)	www.ruskcounty.org
St. Croix	Cindy Campbell (D)	www.sccwi.gov
Sauk	Rebecca Evert (R)	www.co.sauk.wi.us
Sawyer	Carol Williamson (R)	www.sawyercountygov.org
Shawano	Pamela Schmidt (R)	www.co.shawano.wi.us
Sheboygan	Jon Dolson (R)	www.sheboygancounty.com
Taylor	Andria Farrand (R)	www.co.taylor.wi.us
Trempealeau	Paul L. Syverson (D)	www.tremplocounty.com
Vernon	Ronald Hoff (R)	www.vernoncounty.org
Vilas	David R. Alleman (R)	www.vilascountywi.gov
Walworth	Kimberly Bushey (R)	www.co.walworth.wi.us
Washburn	Lolita Olson (R)	www.co.washburn.wi.us
Washington	Ashley Reichert (R)	www.co.washington.wi.us
Waukesha	Meg Wartman (R)	www.waukeshacounty.gov
Waupaca	Jill Lodewegen (R)	www.co.waupaca.wi.us
Waushara	Megan Kapp (R)	www.co.waushara.wi.us
Winnebago	Susan Ertmer (R)	www.co.winnebago.wi.us
Wood	Trent Miner (R)	www.co.wood.wi.us

Note: County clerks are elected at the general election for four-year terms.

A–Appointed; D–Democrat; I–Independent; R–Republican.

Source: Data collected from county clerks by Wisconsin Legislative Reference Bureau, April 2019.

Wisconsin county officers: county board chair; executive (or alternative); treasurer, April 2019

	County board chair (# of supervisors)	Executive, administrator, administrative coordinator	Treasurer
Adams	John West (20)	Casey Bradley (AC)	Jani Zander (D)
Ashland	Pete Russo (21)	Jeff Beirl (CA)	Tracey Hoglund (D)
Barron	Louie Okey (29)	Jeff French (CA)	Yvonne Ritchie (R)
Bayfield	Dennis M. Pocernich (13)	Mark Abeles-Allison (CA)	Dan Anderson (D)
Brown	Patrick Moynihan, Jr. (26)	Troy Streckenbach (CE)	Paul Zeller (R)
Buffalo	Mary Anne McMillan Urell (14)	Sonya Hansen (AC)	Tina Anibas (R)
Burnett	Donald Taylor (21)	Nathan Ehalt (CA)	Judith Dykstra (R)
Calumet	Alice Connors (21)	Todd Romenesko (CA)	Mike Schlaak (R)
Chippewa	Leigh Darrow (15)	Randy Scholz (CA)	Patricia Schimmel (D)
Clark	Wayne Hendrickson (29)	Christina M. Jensen (AC)	Mary J. Domanico (R)
Columbia	Vern Gove (28)	Susan Moll (AC)	Deborah A. Raimer (R)
Crawford	Tom Cornford (17)	Dan McWilliams (AC)	Deanne Lutz (D)
Dane	Sharon Corrigan (37)	Joe Parisi (CE)	Adam Gallagher (D)
Dodge	Russell Kottke (33)	Jim Mielke (CA)	Patti Hilker (R)
Door	David Lienau (21)	Ken Pabich (CA)	Jay Zahn (R)
Douglas	Mark Liebaert (21)	Ann Doucette (CA)	Carol Jones (D)
Dunn	David Bartlett (29)	Paul R. Miller (CM)	Doris Meyer (R)
Eau Claire	Nick Smiar (29)	Kathryn Schauf (CA)	Glenda J. Lyons (D)
Florence	Jeanette Bomberg (12)	Donna Trudell (AC)	Donna Liebergen (R)
Fond du Lac	Martin F. Farrell (25)	Allen J. Buechel (CE)	Brenda A. Schneider (R)
Forest	Tom Tallier (21)	Nora Matuszewski (AC)	Christy Conley (D)
Grant	Robert C. Keeney (17)	Linda Gebhard (AC)	Carrie Eastlick (R)
Green	Arthur F. Carter (31)	Michael J. Doyle (AC)	Sherri Hawkins (R)
Green Lake	Harley Reabe (19)	Catherine Schmit (CA)	Amanda R. Toney (R)
Iowa	John M. Meyers (21)	Larry Bierke (CA)	Connie Johnson (D)
Iron	Joe Pinardi (15)	Michael Saari (AC)	Clara Maki (D)
Jackson	Ray Ransom (19)	Kyle Deno (AC)	Jo Anne Forsting (D)
Jefferson	James Schroeder (30)	Ben Wehmeier (CA)	John E. Jensen (R)
Juneau	Alan K. Peterson (21)	None	Denise Giebel (R)
Kenosha	Daniel C. Esposito (23)	Jim Kreuser (CE)	Teri Jacobson (D)
Kewaunee	Robert A. Weidner (20)	Scott Feldt (CA)	Michelle Dax (R)
La Crosse	Tara Johnson (29)	Steve O'Malley (CA)	Amy Twitchell (D)
Lafayette	Jack Sauer (16)	Jack Sauer (AC)	Becky Taylor (R)
Langlade	David Solin (21)	Robin J. Stowe (CC)	Tammy Wilhelm (D)
Lincoln	Robert Lee (22)	Jason Hake (AC)	Diana Petruzates (R)
Manitowoc	Jim Brey (25)	Bob Ziegelbauer (CE)	Amy Kocian (R)
Marathon	Kurt Gibbs (38)	Brad Karger (CA)	Audrey Jensen (R)
Marinette	Mark Anderson (30)	John Lefebvre (CA)	Bev A. Noffke (R)
Marquette	Robert C. Miller (17)	Gary Sorensen (AC)	Diana Campbell (R)
Menominee	Elizabeth Moses (7)	Jeremy Weso (AC)	Louise Madosh (D)
Milwaukee	Theodore Lipscomb, Sr. (18)	Chris Abele (CE)	David Cullen (D)
Monroe	Pete Peterson (16)	Tina Osterberg (CA)	Debra Carney (R)
Oconto	Paul Bednarik (31)	Kevin Hamann (AC)	Tanya Peterson (R)
Oneida	David Hintz (21)	Lisa Charbarneau (AC)	Kristina Ostermann (D)
Outagamie	Jeff Nooyen (36)	Tom Nelson (CE)	Trenten Woelfel (R)
Ozaukee	Lee Schlenvogt (26)	Jason Dzwinel (CA)	Joshua Morrison (R)
Pepin	Steven L. Anderson (12)	Pamela Hansen (AC)	Patricia Scharr (R)
Pierce	Jeff Holst (17)	Jason Matthys (AC)	Kathy Fuchs (R)
Polk	Dean Johansen (15)	Nick Osborne (CA)	Amanda Nissen (D)
Portage	Allen Haga, Jr. (25)	Chris Holman (CE)	Pamela Przybelski (D)
Price	Robert Kopisch (13)	Nicholas Trimner (CA)	Lynn Neeck (D)
Racine	Russell Clark (21)	Jonathan Delagrave (CE)	Jane Nikolai (R)
Richland	Jeanetta Kirkpatrick (21)	Victor V. Vlasak (AC)	Julie Keller (R)
Rock	J. Russell Podzilni (29)	Joshua Smith (CA)	Michelle Roettger (D)
Rusk	David Willingham (19)	Andy Albarado (AC)	Verna Nielsen (R)
St. Croix	Roger Larson (19)	Patrick Thompson (CA)	Denise Anderson (R)

Wisconsin county officers: county board chair; executive (or alternative); treasurer, April 2019, continued

	County board chair (# of supervisors)	Executive, administrator, administrative coordinator	Treasurer
Sauk	Peter Vedro (31)	Alene Kleczek Bolin (AC)	Elizabeth Geoghegan (R)
Sawyer	Tweed Shuman (15)	Thomas Hoff (CA)	Dianne Ince (R)
Shawano	Jerry Erdmann (27)	Brent Miller (AC)	Debra Wallace (R)
Sheboygan	Thomas Wegner (25)	Adam Payne (CA)	Laura Henning-Lorenz (D)
Taylor	Jim Metz (17)	Marie Koerner (AC)	Sarah Holtz (R)
Trempealeau	Timothy Zeglin (17)	Paul L. Syverson (AC)	Laurie Halama (D)
Vernon	Dennis Brault (29)	Ronald Hoff (AC)	Rachel Hanson (R)
Vilas	Ronald De Bruyne (21)	David R. Alleman (AC)	Jerri Radtke (R)
Walworth	Nancy Russell (11)	David Bretl (CA)	Valerie Etzel (R)
Washburn	Thomas Mackie (21)	Lolita Olson (AC)	Nicole Tims (R)
Washington	Donald Kriefall (26)	Joshua Schoemann (CA)	Jane Merten (R)
Waukesha	Paul Decker (25)	Paul Farrow (CE)	Pamela Reeves (R)
Waupaca	Dick Koeppen (27)	Amanda Welch (AC)	Mark Sether (R)
Waushara	Donna Kalata (11)	Robert Sivick (CA)	Elaine Wedell (R)
Winnebago	Shiloh Ramos (36)	Mark Harris (CE)	Mary Krueger (R)
Wood	Douglas Machon (19)	Douglas Machon (AC)	Heather Gehrt (D)

Note: The county board is composed of supervisors who are elected at the nonpartisan spring election for two-year terms (but Milwaukee supervisors elected before 2016 were elected for four-year terms). The county board elects one of its members to be its chair. County executives are elected at the nonpartisan spring election for four-year terms. In lieu of electing a county executive, a county can choose to appoint a county administrator or to designate a county official to serve as the county's administrative coordinator. Treasurers are elected at the general election for four-year terms.

A–appointed to fill a vacancy; AC–administrative coordinator; CA–county administrator; CC–corporation counsel; CE–county executive; CM–county manager; D–Democrat; R–Republican.

Source: Data collected from county clerks by Wisconsin Legislative Reference Bureau, April 2019.

Wisconsin county officers: clerk of circuit court; register of deeds; surveyor, April 2019

	Clerk of circuit court	Register of deeds	Surveyor[1]
Adams	Lori L. Banovec (D)	Jodi Helgeson (R)	Jerol Smart
Ashland	Sandra Paitl (D)	Karen Miller (D)	Patrick McKuen
Barron	Sharon Millermon (R)	Margo Katterhagen (R)	Mark Netterlund
Bayfield	Kay L. Cederberg (D)	Denise Tarasewicz (D)	Patrick McKuen
Brown	John A. Vander Leest (R)	Cheryl Berken (R)	Terry Van Hout
Buffalo	Roselle Schlosser (R)	Carol Burmeister (D)	Joe Nelsen
Burnett	Jacqueline O. Baasch (D)	Jeanine Chell (D)	Jason Towne
Calumet	Connie Daun (R)	Tamara Alten (R)	Bradley Buechel
Chippewa	Karen Hepfler (D)	Marge L. Geissler (R)	Sam Wenz
Clark	Heather Bravener (D)	Peggy L. Walter (R)	Wade Pettit
Columbia	Susan Raimer (R)	Karen A. Manske (R)	Jim Grothman
Crawford	Donna Steiner (D)	Melissa Nagel (D)	Rich Marks
Dane	Carlo Esqueda (D)	Kristi Chlebowski (D)	Dan Frick
Dodge	Lynn Hron (R)	Chris Planasch (R)	Vacant
Door	Connie DeFere (R)	Carey Petersilka (R)	None
Douglas	Michele L. Wick (D)	Tracy Middleton (D)	Matt Johnson
Dunn	Katie Schalley (D)	Heather Kuhn (D)	Thomas Carlson
Eau Claire	Susan Schaffer (D)	Kathryn A. Christenson (D)	Dean Roth
Florence	Tanya Neuens (R)	Laurie J. Boren (R)	None
Fond du Lac	Ramona Geib (R)	James M. Krebs (R)	Peter Kuen
Forest	Penny Carter (D)	Cortney Britten Cleereman (D)	None

Wisconsin county officers: clerk of circuit court; register of deeds; surveyor, April 2019, continued

	Clerk of circuit court	Register of deeds	Surveyor[1]
Grant	Tina McDonald (R)	Marilyn Pierce (R)	Jay P. Adams
Green	Barbara Miller (R)	Cynthia Meudt (R)	None
Green Lake	Amy Thoma (R)	Sarah Guenther (R)	Don Lenz
Iowa	Lia Leahy (R)	Dixie L. Edge (D)	Don Lenz
Iron	Karen Ransanici (D)	Daniel Soine (D)	Todd Maki
Jackson	Jan Moennig (D)	Shari Marg (D)	Ethan Remus
Jefferson	Cindy Hamre Incha (R)	Staci M. Hoffman (R)	Jim Morrow
Juneau	Patty Schluter (R)	Stacy Havill (R)	Gary Dechant
Kenosha	Rebecca Matoska-Mentink (D)	JoEllyn M. Storz (D)	Robert W. Merry
Kewaunee	Rebecca Deterville (D)	Germaine Bertrand (D)	Kip Inman
La Crosse	Pamela Radtke (R)	Cheryl McBride (R)	Bryan Meyer
Lafayette	Trisha Rowe (R)	Joseph G. Boll (R)	Aaron Austin
Langlade	Marilyn Baraniak (D)	Chet Haatvedt (D)	David Tlusty
Lincoln	Marie Peterson (D)	Sarah Koss (R)	Anthony Dallman
Manitowoc	Lynn Zigmunt (D)	Kristi L. Tuesburg (R)	None
Marathon	Shirley Lang (R)	Dean Stratz (R)	Dave Decker
Marinette	Sheila M. Dudka (R)	Renee Miller (R)	None
Marquette	Shari Rudolph (R)	Bette Krueger (R)	Jerry Smart
Menominee	Pamela Frechette (D)	Louise Madosh (D)	None
Milwaukee	John Barrett (D)	Connie Cobb Madsen	Robert W. Merry
Monroe	Shirley Chapiewsky (R)	Deb Brandt (R)	Gary Dechant
Oconto	Michael C. Hodkiewicz (R)	Annette Behringer (R)	Brian Gross
Oneida	Brenda Behrle (R)	Kyle Franson (R)	None
Outagamie	Barb Bocik (R)	Sarah R. Van Camp (R)	David Yurk
Ozaukee	Mary Lou Mueller (R)	Ronald A. Volgt (R)	None
Pepin	Audrey Lieffring (R)	Monica J. Bauer (R)	Cedar Corporation
Pierce	Kerry Feuerhelm (R)	Julie Hines (D)	James Filkins
Polk	Joanne Ritten (R)	Sally Spanel (D)	Steve Geiger
Portage	Lisa M. Roth (D)	Cynthia Wisinski (D)	Thomas Trzinski
Price	Penny Huck (D)	Judith Chizek (D)	Alfred Schneider
Racine	Samuel A. Christensen (R)	Vacant	None
Richland	Stacy Kleist (R)	Susan Triggs (R)	Todd Rummler
Rock	Jackie Gackstatter (D)	Sandy Disrud (D)	Brad Heuer
Rusk	Lori Gorsegner (R)	Carol Johnson (D)	None
St. Croix	Kristi Severson (R)	Beth Pabst (D)	Brian Halling
Sauk	Carrie Wastlick (A)	Brent Bailey (R)	Patrick Dederich
Sawyer	Marge Kelsey (R)	Paula Chisser (R)	Dan Pleoger
Shawano	Susan M. Krueger (R)	Amy Dillenburg (R)	David Yurk
Sheboygan	Melody Lorge (I)	Ellen Schleicher (D)	Jeremy Hildebrand
Taylor	Rose Thums (R)	Sara Nuernberger (D)	Robert Meyer
Trempealeau	Michelle Weisenberger (D)	Rose Ottum (D)	Joe Nelson
Vernon	Sheila Olson (R)	Dawn Nemec (R)	Laurence Johns
Vilas	Beth Soltow (R)	Christine Walker (R)	Thomas Boettcher (R)
Walworth	Kristina Secord (R)	Donna Pruess (R)	Robert W. Merry
Washburn	Shannon Anderson (A)	Renee Bell (R)	Lucas Meier
Washington	Theresa Russell (R)	Sharon Martin (R)	Scott Schmidt
Waukesha	Gina Colletti (R)	James Behrend (R)	Robert W. Merry
Waupaca	Terrie Tews-Liebe (R)	Michael Mazemke (R)	Joseph Glodowski
Waushara	Melissa Zamzow (R)	Heather Schwersenska (R)	Jerry Smart
Winnebago	Melissa Pingel (R)	Natalie Strohmeyer (R)	None
Wood	Cindy Joosten (R)	Tiffany Ringer (R)	Kevin Boyer

Note: Clerks of circuit court, registers of deeds, and surveyors are elected at the general election for four-year terms. In lieu of electing a surveyor, a county can choose to appoint one.

A–Appointed to fill a vacancy; D–Democrat; I–Independent; R–Republican.

1. Surveyors are appointed unless party designation is shown.

Source: Data collected from county clerks by Wisconsin Legislative Reference Bureau, April 2019.

Wisconsin county officers: district attorney; sheriff; coroner (or alternative), April 2019

	District attorney	Sheriff	Coroner/medical examiner
Adams	Tania M. Bonnett (I)	Brent R. York (R)	Marilyn Rogers (ME)
Ashland	David Meany (I)	Mick Brennan (D)	Barbara Beeksma (R)
Barron	Brian Wright (R)	Chris Fitzgerald (D)	Nate Dunston (ME)
Bayfield	Kimberly Lawton (D)	Paul Susienka (D)	Thomas Renz (D)
Brown	David L. Lasee (R)	Todd J. Delain (R)	Vincent Tranchida (ME)
Buffalo	Tom Bilski (R)	Mike Schmidtknecht (R)	Cindy Giese (R)
Burnett	Joseph Schieffer (R)	Tracy Finch (I)	Mike Maloney (ME)
Calumet	Nathan F. Haberman (R)	Mark Wiegert (R)	Michael Klaeser (ME)
Chippewa	Wade C. Newell (R)	James L. Kowalczyk (D)	Ronald Patten (D)
Clark	Kerra Stumbris (D)	Scott Haines (R)	Richard J. Schleifer (R)
Columbia	Brenda Yaskal (D)	Roger Brandner (R)	Angela Hinze (ME)
Crawford	Timothy Baxter (D)	Dale McCullick (D)	Joe Morovits (D)
Dane	Ismael R. Ozanne (D)	David J. Mahoney (D)	Vincent Tranchida (ME)
Dodge	Kurt Klomberg (R)	Dale J. Schmidt (R)	Patrick Schoebel (ME)
Door	Colleen Nordin (R)	Tammy Sternard (D)	Vincent Tranchida (ME)
Douglas	Mark Fruehauf (D)	Thomas Dalbec (D)	Darrell Witt (ME)
Dunn	Andrea Nodolf (R)	Kevin Bygd (R)	Marcie Rosas (ME)
Eau Claire	Gary King (D)	Ron D. Cramer (R)	Marcie Rosas (ME)
Florence	Doug Drexler (D)	Dan Miller (R)	Jeff Rickaby (R)
Fond du Lac	Eric Toney (R)	Ryan F. Waldschmidt (R)	Adam Covach (ME)
Forest	Charles Simono (D)	John Dennee (R)	Crystal Schaub (ME)
Grant	Lisa Riniker (R)	Nate Dreckman (R)	Phyllis Fuerstenberg (R)
Green	Craig Nolen (D)	Jeff Skatrud (D)	Monica Hack (D)
Green Lake	Andrew Christenson (R)	Mark Podoll (R)	John Willett (A)
Iowa	Matthew Allen (D)	Steven R. Michek (R)	Wendell F. Hamlin (R)
Iron	Matthew Tingstad (D)	Paul Samardich (D)	Diane Simonich (D)
Jackson	Daniel Diehn (A)	Duane Waldera (D)	Karla Wood (D)
Jefferson	Susan V. Happ (D)	Paul Milbrath (R)	Nichol Tesch (ME)
Juneau	Kenneth Hamm (R)	Brent Oleson (R)	Myron Oestreich (ME)
Kenosha	Michael Graveley (D)	David Beth (R)	Patrice Hall (ME)
Kewaunee	Andrew Naze (D)	Matthew Joski (R)	Rory Groessl (D)
La Crosse	Tim Gruenke (D)	Jeff Wolf (R)	Tim Candahl (ME)
Lafayette	Jenna Gill (R)	Reginald Gill (R)	Linda Gebhardt (D)
Langlade	Elizabeth R. Gebert (R)	Mark Westen (R)	Larry Shadick (R)
Lincoln	Galen Bayne-Allison (D)	Ken Schneider (R)	Paul Proulx (R)
Manitowoc	Jacalyn LaBre (R)	Daniel Hartwig (R)	Curtis Green (D)
Marathon	Theresa Wetzsteon (D)	Scott Parks (R)	Jessica Blahnik (ME)
Marinette	DeShea D. Morrow (R)	Jerry Sauve (R)	Kalynn Van Ermen (ME)
Marquette	Brian Juech (I)	Joseph Konrath (R)	Thomas Wastart II (R)
Menominee[1]	Gregory Parker (R)	Rebecca Smith (D)	Patrick Roberts (ME)
Milwaukee	John T. Chisholm (D)	Earnell R. Lucas (D)	Brian L. Peterson (ME)
Monroe	Kevin Croninger (R)	Wesley D. Revels (R)	Robert Smith (ME)
Oconto	Ed Burke (R)	Todd Skarban (R)	Vincent Tranchida (ME)
Oneida	Michael Schiek (R)	Grady Hartman (R)	Crystal Schaub (ME)
Outagamie	Melinda Tempelis (R)	Clint C. Kriewaldt (R)	Douglas A. Bartelt (D)
Ozaukee	Adam Y. Gerol (R)	James G. Johnson (R)	Timothy J. Deppisch (R)
Pepin	Jon D. Seifert (R)	Joel D. Wener (R)	Joan Huppert (R)
Pierce	Sean Froelich (D)	Nancy Hove (D)	John Worsing (ME)
Polk	Jeffrey L. Kemp (R)	Brent A. Waak (R)	John Dinnies (ME)
Portage	Louis J. Molepske, Jr. (D)	Michael Lukas (D)	Scott W. Rifleman (ME)
Price	Mark Fuhr (D)	Brian Schmidt (R)	James Dalbesio, III (D)
Racine	Patricia J. Hanson (R)	Christopher Schmaling (R)	Michael Payne (ME)
Richland	Jennifer M. Harper (R)	James Bindl (R)	James C. Rossing (I)
Rock	David J. O'Leary (D)	Troy Knudson (D)	Vincent Tranchida (ME)
Rusk	Annette Barna (D)	Jeffery Wallace (R)	Jim Rassbach (ME)
St. Croix	Michael Nieskes (R)	Scott Knudson (R)	Patty Schachtner (ME)
Sauk	Kevin R. Calkins (I)	Chip Meister (R)	Greg L. Hahn (R)
Sawyer	Bruce R. Poquette (R)	Doug Mrotek (R)	John Froemel (R)

Wisconsin county officers: district attorney; sheriff; coroner (or alternative), April 2019, continued

	District attorney	Sheriff	Coroner/medical examiner
Shawano[1]	Gregory Parker (R)	Adam Bieber (R)	Brian Westfahl (R)
Sheboygan	Joel Urmanski (R)	Cory Roeseler (R)	David Leffin (ME)
Taylor	Kristi Tlusty (D)	Larry Woebbeking (R)	Scott Perrin (ME)
Trempealeau	John Sacia (D)	Brett Semingson (D)	Bonnie Kindschy (D)
Vernon	Timothy Gaskell (R)	John B. Spears (R)	Betty Nigh (R)
Vilas	Martha Milanowski (R)	Joseph A. Fath (R)	Crystal Schaub (ME)
Walworth	Zeke Wiedenfeld (R)	Kurt Picknell (R)	Lynda Biedrzycki (ME)
Washburn	Angeline E. Winton (D)	Dennis Stuart (R)	Angela Pank (A)
Washington	Mark Bensen (R)	Martin Schulteis (R)	Lynda Biedrzycki (ME)
Waukesha	Susan L. Opper (R)	Eric J. Severson (R)	Lynda Biedrzycki (ME)
Waupaca	Veronica Isherwood (R)	Timothy R. Wilz (R)	Barry Tomaras (ME)
Waushara	Steven P. Anderson (R)	Walter Zuehlke (R)	Amanda Thoma (ME)
Winnebago	Christian Gossett (R)	John Matz (R)	Barry Busby (R)
Wood	Craig Lambert (R)	Shawn Becker (R)	Scott Brehm (R)

Note: District attorneys, sheriffs, and coroners are elected at the general election for four-year terms. In lieu of electing a coroner, a county can choose to appoint a medical examiner.

A–Appointed to fill a vacancy; D–Democrat; I–Independent; ME–medical examiner; R–Republican.

1. Menominee and Shawano counties comprise a single prosecutorial unit, served by a single district attorney.

Source: Data collected from county clerks by Wisconsin Legislative Reference Bureau, April 25, 2019.

Tribal chairs and contact information, April 2019

Tribe and chair	Contact information
Bad River Band of Lake Superior Chippewa Mike Wiggins, Jr. (chair)	P.O. Box 39, Odanah 54861-0039 715-682-7111; www.badriver-nsn.gov
Forest County Potawatomi Ned Daniels, Jr. (chair)	P.O. Box 340, Crandon 54520-0346 715-478-7200; www.fcpotawatomi.com
Ho-Chunk Nation Marlon White Eagle (president)	P.O. Box 667, Black River Falls 54615-0667 715-284-9343; www.ho-chunknation.com
Lac Courte Oreilles Band of Lake Superior Chippewa Louis Taylor, Sr. (chair)	13394 W. Trepania Road, Hayward 54843-2186 715-634-8934; www.lcotribe.com
Lac du Flambeau Band of Lake Superior Chippewa Joseph Wildcat, Sr. (president)	P.O. Box 67, Lac du Flambeau 54538-0067 715-588-3303; www.ldftribe.com
Menominee Indian Tribe of Wisconsin Douglas Cox (chair)	P.O. Box 910, Keshena 54135-0910 715-799-5114; www.menominee-nsn.gov
Oneida Nation Tehassi Hill (chair)	P.O. Box 365, Oneida 54155-0365 920-869-4380; www.oneida-nsn.gov
Red Cliff Band of Lake Superior Chippewa Richard Peterson (chair)	88455 Pike Road, Bayfield 54814-0529 715-779-3700; www.redcliff-nsn.gov
St. Croix Chippewa Indians of Wisconsin Lewis Taylor (chair)	24663 Angeline Avenue, Webster 54893-9246 715-349-2195; www.stcciw.com
Sokaogon Chippewa Community Garland McGeshick (chair)	3051 Sand Lake Road, Crandon 54520-8815 715-478-7500; www.sokaogonchippewa.com
Stockbridge-Munsee Band of Mohican Indians Shannon Holsey (president)	P.O. Box 70, Bowler 54416-9801 715-793-4111; www.mohican.com

Sources: Wisconsin State Tribal Relations Initiative, http://witribes.wi.gov [April 2019] and individual tribal websites.

Wisconsin full-time equivalent state government positions

Type of funding	Number of positions[1]
General purpose revenue.	35,349
Program revenue.	19,452
Federal appropriations	10,586
Segregated funds	5,208
Total.	**70,596**

1. Positions authorized by the legislature or under procedures authorized by the legislature as of June 30, 2018. Includes all branches of state government and the UW System.

Source: Wisconsin Department of Administration, Division of Executive Budget and Finance, departmental data.

Wisconsin executive branch employees

Status	Number of employees[1]
Permanent.	29,354
Unclassified	1,145
Limited term.	3,531
Project	128
Seasonal	7
Elected	76
Total.	**34,241**

1. Employees working on a full–time or part–time basis for the executive branch only.

Source: Wisconsin Department of Administration, Division of Executive Budget and Finance, departmental data.

Wisconsin state and local government employment and payrolls, March, 2017

Function	Number of employees		Full-time equivalent[1]	Total payroll ($1,000)
	Full-time	Part-time		
Air and water transport	397	51	418	2,113
Corrections	12,638	1,126	13,345	61,373
Education	131,533	98,187	169,282	761,831
Elementary and secondary	96,343	45,250	119,630	502,716
Higher education institutions.	34,322	52,622	48,566	253,853
Other.	868	315	1,086	5,262
Fire protection	4,310	5,672	4,999	29,175
Government administration (including courts)	14,733	14,010	17,291	85,360
Health and hospitals.	9,456	3,531	11,668	53,167
Highways.	9,520	1,558	9,957	47,903
Housing and community development	943	374	1,050	4,654
Libraries	1,612	3,384	3,090	10,218
Natural resources.	2,897	1,339	3,357	15,021
Parks and recreation.	2,376	2,968	3,182	12,272
Police protection	15,131	2,911	15,989	91,889
Public welfare and social insurance administration	12,634	3,880	15,054	61,748
Sewerage.	1,772	731	1,841	9,516
Solid waste management.	1,338	927	1,444	6,399
Transit.	1,874	148	1,961	7,903

Wisconsin state and local government employment and payrolls, March, 2017, continued

	Number of employees			
Function	Full-time	Part-time	Full-time equivalent[1]	Total payroll ($1,000)
Utilities (electric and water supply).	2,257	325	2,339	11,836
Other	7,528	4,045	8,448	41,313
Total.	232,949	145,167	284,715	1,313,689

1. Full-time equivalent (FTE) is a derived statistic that provides an estimate of a government's total full-time employment by converting part-time employees to a full-time amount.

Source: U.S. Census Bureau, "2017 Government Employment and Payroll Tables," https://www.census.gov/data/tables/2017/econ/apes/annual-apes.html [March 14, 2019].

Wisconsin state and local government employment and payrolls

	Employees (full-time equivalents)			Monthly payroll ($1,000)		
	State	Local	Total	State	Local	Total
2007.	68,714	212,931	281,645	295,616	788,590	1,084,207
2008.	69,019	214,332	283,351	308,878	813,054	1,121,932
2009.	70,457	222,214	292,671	322,316	846,922	1,169,238
2010.	72,428	213,888	286,316	326,643	862,129	1,188,772
2011.	70,891	212,677	283,568	328,658	878,908	1,207,566
2012.	70,851	212,013	282,864	323,080	876,466	1,199,547
2013.	72,347	202,047	274,394	333,207	863,610	1,196,818
2014.	72,551	208,108	280,659	344,334	884,405	1,228,738
2015.	74,383	211,442	285,825	357,334	901,925	1,259,259
2016.	72,676	212,640	285,316	356,014	926,005	1,282,019
2017.	72,899	211,816	284,715	362,633	951,056	1,313,689

Source: U.S. Census Bureau, "2017 Government Employment & Payroll Tables" and previous years, at: https://www.census.gov/data/tables/2017/econ/apes/annual-apes.html [March 14, 2019].

Wisconsin state classified service profile, 2016

Category	Number	Percent
Permanent classified employees	29,410	100.0
Persons with disabilities[1].	1,353	4.6
Women.	14,966	50.9
Racial/ ethnic minorities	3,729	12.7
Black	1,937	6.6
Hispanic.	815	2.8
Asian	803	2.7
American Indian.	174	0.6

Note: Data excludes unclassified, temporary, judicial, and legislative employees and employees in the UW System. Data may not be comparable to prior Blue Book tables.

1. Includes persons with severe disabilities. Disabilities are voluntarily self-reported.

Source: Wisconsin Department of Administration, Division of Personnel Management, *State of Wisconsin Classified Workforce & Affirmative Action Report: Fiscal Years 2015 and 2016.*

PUBLIC FINANCE

Wisconsin state revenues and expenditures

Fiscal year	General fund[1] Revenues ($1,000)	General fund[1] Expenditures ($1,000)	Other funds[2] Revenues ($1,000)	Other funds[2] Expenditures ($1,000)	Total—all funds Revenues ($1,000)	Total—all funds Expenditures ($1,000)	Net surplus or deficit[3] ($1,000)
1971...	1,790,957	1,780,703	929,124	726,545	2,720,081	2,507,247	34,840
1972...	2,096,084	2,031,896	961,970	697,144	3,058,054	2,729,040	116,914
1973...	2,480,748	2,296,679	1,112,600	791,657	3,593,347	3,088,337	217,404
1974...	2,687,517	2,729,854	1,114,326	865,724	3,801,842	3,595,577	241,359
1975...	2,966,532	3,148,968	1,252,422	924,455	4,218,954	4,073,423	78,120
1976...	3,476,690	3,439,062	1,677,155	1,283,467	5,153,846	4,722,529	86,473
1977...	3,807,748	3,712,595	1,887,150	1,376,726	5,694,898	5,089,322	166,587
1978...	4,240,298	3,994,220	1,875,978	1,446,286	6,116,277	5,440,486	407,770
1979...	4,622,611	4,696,263	2,200,365	1,620,899	6,822,976	6,317,162	280,561
1980...	4,900,275	5,027,130	2,481,324	1,809,840	7,381,599	6,836,970	72,627
1981...	5,335,427	5,452,247	2,738,491	1,922,648	8,073,918	7,374,895	14,065
1982...	5,564,585	5,520,811	2,757,388	2,021,266	8,321,974	7,542,078	70,811
1983...	6,036,016	6,302,575	3,905,944	2,288,804	9,941,961	8,591,379	-182,126
1984...	6,966,282	6,360,657	3,614,895	2,528,273	10,581,177	8,888,930	383,085
1985...	7,160,174	7,237,716	4,908,582	2,743,287	12,068,756	9,981,002	314,084
1986...	7,798,367	7,757,063	6,380,605	2,774,683	14,178,972	10,531,747	279,744
1987...	8,133,265	8,205,100	5,061,597	2,693,737	13,194,863	10,898,836	232,733
1988...	8,432,698	8,427,084	3,566,763	2,790,038	11,999,461	11,217,121	216,963
1989...	9,030,466	8,809,189	5,778,125	3,094,116	14,808,591	11,903,305	375,016
1990...	9,418,918	9,464,483	5,483,442	3,287,809	14,902,360	12,752,292	306,452
1991...	10,184,183	10,350,332	5,930,658	3,706,452	16,114,839	14,056,784	113,609
1992...	11,033,948	11,082,220	7,786,483	4,218,565	18,820,431	15,300,785	73,681
1993...	11,828,599	11,708,360	8,192,793	4,596,981	20,021,392	16,305,341	153,540
1994...	12,442,349	12,323,509	5,812,805	4,756,564	18,255,154	17,080,073	234,877
1995...	13,259,772	13,094,450	9,823,810	4,963,553	23,083,582	18,058,003	400,881
1996...	13,804,399	13,648,601	10,038,961	5,057,062	23,843,360	18,705,663	581,690
1997...	14,669,320	14,932,404	12,741,438	5,144,002	27,410,758	20,076,406	386,558
1998...	15,701,212	15,509,615	13,896,719	6,071,649	29,597,931	21,581,264	533,240
1999...	16,252,539	16,098,587	11,847,678	6,864,567	28,100,217	22,963,154	737,748
2000...	18,185,980	18,333,634	14,687,330	8,111,005	32,873,310	26,444,639	574,416
2001...	19,285,734	19,448,417	2,990,770	8,719,341	22,276,504	28,167,758	445,999
2002...	20,850,074	21,248,608	5,920,241	10,395,514	26,770,315	31,644,122	44,469
2003...	20,683,921	20,956,485	10,598,486	11,025,745	31,282,407	31,982,230	-163,608
2004...	22,040,940	21,716,332	19,544,497	12,177,401	41,585,437	33,893,733	127,369
2005...	21,191,600	21,488,178	15,827,541	10,772,231	37,019,141	32,260,409	-131,675
2006...	22,321,870	22,148,049	17,611,450	11,636,031	39,933,320	33,784,080	35,014
2007...	23,123,424	23,205,243	23,140,557	11,329,591	46,263,981	34,534,834	36,467
2008...	23,997,838	24,103,773	4,668,268	12,195,449	28,666,106	36,299,222	110,424
2009...	25,078,246	25,280,016	-4,760,111	13,216,367	20,318,135	38,496,383	-37,167
2010...	26,918,079	26,933,345	19,320,601	13,214,942	46,238,680	40,148,287	99,873
2011...	28,926,518	28,951,824	27,574,543	13,974,915	56,501,061	42,926,739	305,584
2012...	28,557,414	27,379,001	11,959,996	14,158,805	40,517,410	41,537,806	1,115,672
2013...	29,435,181	28,400,745	20,586,682	14,164,382	50,021,863	42,565,127	1,987,605
2014...	29,765,921	30,028,018	26,166,710	15,060,009	55,932,631	45,088,027	1,669,233
2015...	30,622,404	30,861,201	14,096,474	15,437,387	44,718,878	46,298,588	1,359,156
2016...	31,172,186	30,852,156	12,752,252	15,034,976	43,924,438	45,887,132	1,656,065

Wisconsin state revenues and expenditures, continued

Fiscal year	General fund[1] Revenues ($1,000)	Expenditures ($1,000)	Other funds[2] Revenues ($1,000)	Expenditures ($1,000)	Total—all funds Revenues ($1,000)	Expenditures ($1,000)	Net surplus or deficit[3] ($1,000)
2017...	32,390,154	31,891,665	23,285,943	15,099,934	55,676,097	46,991,599	2,254,454
2018...	32,850,441	32,685,469	20,506,458	15,513,335	53,356,899	48,198,804	1,744,973

1. Includes general purpose revenue (GPR), program revenue, and federal funding. 2. Includes special revenue funds (such as conservation and transportation), federal funding, debt service, capital projects, pension and retirement funds, trust and agency funds, and others. 3. Unappropriated (unreserved) balance of the general fund for the fiscal year.

Source: Wisconsin Department of Administration, Division of Executive Budget and Finance, State Controller's Office, *2018 Annual Fiscal Report*, October 15, 2018, and previous editions.

Wisconsin state budget allocations

Revenue type and allocation	Fiscal year 2017–18 ($)	Fiscal year 2018–19 ($)	Fiscal biennium ($)	% of total budget allocations
GENERAL PURPOSE REVENUE	**16,946,921,200**	**17,829,835,700**	**34,776,756,900**	**45.86**
State operations	3,944,240,200	4,156,772,200	8,101,012,400	10.68
Local assistance.	8,695,730,500	9,046,383,200	17,742,113,700	23.39
Aids to individuals and organizations . . .	4,306,950,500	4,626,680,300	8,933,630,800	11.78
PROGRAM REVENUE—TOTAL	**15,632,997,100**	**16,131,690,500**	**31,764,687,600**	**41.88**
State operations	7,076,063,300	7,130,637,000	14,206,700,300	18.73
Local assistance.	1,284,615,000	1,291,503,800	2,576,118,800	3.40
Aids to individuals and organizations . . .	7,272,318,800	7,709,549,700	14,981,868,500	19.75
Program Revenue—federal	**9,688,525,800**	**10,057,467,400**	**19,745,993,200**	**26.04**
State operations.	2,378,779,400	2,387,509,300	4,766,288,700	6.28
Local assistance	1,213,063,700	1,219,987,300	2,433,051,000	3.21
Aids to individuals and organizations . .	6,096,682,700	6,449,970,800	12,546,653,500	16.54
Program Revenue—service	**887,597,100**	**920,821,700**	**1,808,418,800**	**2.38**
State operations.	691,681,500	725,585,700	1,417,267,200	1.87
Local assistance	39,656,100	39,400,800	79,056,900	0.10
Aids to individuals and organizations . .	156,259,500	155,835,200	312,094,700	0.41
Program Revenue—other	**5,056,874,200**	**5,153,401,400**	**10,210,275,600**	**13.46**
State operations.	4,005,602,400	4,017,542,000	8,023,144,400	10.58
Local assistance	31,895,200	32,115,700	64,010,900	0.08
Aids to individuals and organizations . .	1,019,376,600	1,103,743,700	2,123,120,300	2.80
SEGREGATED REVENUE—TOTAL	**4,682,602,700**	**4,614,792,600**	**9,297,395,300**	**12.26**
State operations	2,519,807,800	2,463,390,100	4,983,197,900	6.57
Local assistance	1,414,348,100	1,419,904,800	2,834,252,900	3.74
Aids to individuals and organizations . . .	748,446,800	731,497,700	1,479,944,500	1.95
Segregated Revenue—federal	**1,004,014,000**	**952,682,700**	**1,956,696,700**	**2.58**
State operations.	798,179,600	754,852,100	1,553,031,700	2.05
Local assistance	199,604,500	191,541,900	391,146,400	0.52
Aids to individuals and organizations . .	6,229,900	6,288,700	12,518,600	0.02
Segregated Revenue—local	**115,325,600**	**115,325,600**	**230,651,200**	**0.30**
State operations.	7,452,900	7,452,900	14,905,800	0.02
Local assistance	99,678,500	99,678,500	199,357,000	0.26
Aids to individuals and organizations . .	8,194,200	8,194,200	16,388,400	0.02
Segregated Revenue—service	**99,517,300**	**103,871,900**	**203,389,200**	**0.27**
State operations.	85,517,300	103,871,900	189,389,200	0.25
Aids to individuals and organizations . .	14,000,000	0	14,000,000	0.02
Segregated Revenue—other	**3,463,745,800**	**3,442,912,400**	**6,906,658,200**	**9.11**
State operations.	1,628,658,000	1,597,213,200	3,225,871,200	4.25
Local assistance	1,115,065,100	1,128,684,400	2,243,749,500	2.96
Aids to individuals and organizations . .	720,022,700	717,014,800	1,437,037,500	1.89

Wisconsin state budget allocations, continued

Revenue type and allocation	Fiscal year 2017–18 ($)	Fiscal year 2018–19 ($)	Fiscal biennium ($)	% of total budget allocations
FEDERAL REVENUE—TOTAL	10,692,539,800	11,010,150,100	21,702,689,900	28.62
State operations	3,176,959,000	3,142,361,400	6,319,320,400	8.33
Local assistance.	1,412,668,200	1,411,529,200	2,824,197,400	3.72
Aids to individuals and organizations . . .	6,102,912,600	6,456,259,500	12,559,172,100	16.56
TOTAL—ALL SOURCES	37,262,521,000	38,576,318,800	75,838,839,800	100.00
State operations	13,540,111,300	13,750,799,300	27,290,910,600	35.99
Local assistance.	11,394,693,600	11,757,791,800	23,152,485,400	30.53
Aids to individuals and organizations . . .	12,327,716,100	13,067,727,700	25,395,443,800	33.49

Definitions: **General purpose revenue**—general taxes, miscellaneous receipts, and revenues collected by state agencies that are paid into the general fund, lose their identity, and are available for appropriation by the legislature. **Program revenue**—revenues paid into the general fund and credited by law to an appropriation used to finance a specific program or agency. **Segregated fund revenue**—revenues deposited, by law, into funds other than the general fund and available only for the purposes for which such funds were created. **Federal revenue**—money received from the federal government (may be disbursed either through a segregated fund or through the general fund). **Service revenue**—money transferred between or within state agencies for reimbursement for services rendered or materials purchased. **State operations**—amounts budgeted to operate programs carried out by state government. **Local assistance**—amounts budgeted as state aids to assist programs carried out by local governmental units in Wisconsin.

Source: Wisconsin Department of Administration, State Budget Office, departmental data, March 2019.

Annual appropriation obligations of the state of Wisconsin

Category	Amount of debt issued[1] ($1,000)	Amount outstanding December 15, 2018 ($1,000)
General fund annual appropriation bonds	3,252,620	3,027,935
Master lease obligations	101,214	101,100
Total.	**3,353,834**	**3,129,035**

Note: Appropriation obligations are not general obligations of the state, and they do not constitute "public debt" of the state as that term is used in the Wisconsin Constitution and in the Wisconsin Statutes. The payment of the principal of, and interest on, appropriation obligations is subject to annual appropriation. The state has no legal obligation to make these appropriations and incurs no liability to the owners of the appropriation obligations if it does not do so.

1. Amounts do not include refunding bonds, which do not count against the respective authorizations.

Source: Wisconsin Department of Administration, Division of Executive Budget and Finance, departmental data.

Wisconsin state revenues, all funds

	Fiscal year 2015–16 ($1,000)	Fiscal year 2016–17 ($1,000)	Fiscal year 2017–18 ($1,000)
REVENUES FROM TAXES.	16,394,393	16,831,587	17,393,056
General fund	15,139,330	15,542,153	16,168,750
General purpose revenues	15,097,489	15,517,585	16,144,167
Income taxes.	8,703,852	8,960,453	9,373,042
Individual	7,740,825	8,039,506	8,479,150
Corporation.	963,027	920,947	893,892
Sales and excise taxes	5,774,271	5,929,616	6,128,097
General sales and use.	5,065,762	5,223,935	5,448,118
Cigarette	573,411	564,199	538,898

Wisconsin state revenues, all funds, continued

	Fiscal year 2015–16 ($1,000)	Fiscal year 2016–17 ($1,000)	Fiscal year 2017–18 ($1,000)
Other tobacco products	76,127	80,279	80,202
Liquor and wine	49,991	52,078	51,970
Malt beverage (beer)	8,980	9,125	8,909
Public utility taxes.	360,597	360,473	365,343
Private light, heat, and power.	226,050	229,622	235,390
Municipal light, heat, and power.	3,488	2,895	3,065
Telephone.	76,474	70,783	63,591
Pipeline	37,316	39,727	45,531
Electric cooperative.	11,747	12,046	12,464
Municipal electric	4,947	4,934	4,802
Conservation and regulation	375	349	434
Utility tax (refunds) interest and penalties.	200	117	66
Inheritance and estate taxes	1,745	434	-33
Miscellaneous taxes	257,024	266,609	277,718
Insurance companies (premiums)	177,326	181,584	186,273
Real estate transfer fee.	65,133	70,553	76,600
Lawsuits (courts).	14,491	14,397	14,795
Other.	74	75	50
Program revenues	41,841	24,568	24,583
Fire dues	19,217	20,802	20,570
Pari-mutuel taxes	—	—	—
County expo tax administration	850	854	905
Baseball park administration fee.	454	466	480
Business trust regulation fee	2,059	1,889	2,133
Other.	19,261	557	495
Transportation fund.			
Motor fuel tax	1,037,723	1,044,543	1,065,936
Air-carrier tax	5,103	7,126	6,176
Railroad tax.	38,498	45,323	40,765
Aviation fuel tax.	1,227	1,271	1,338
Other taxes	9,093	10,013	9,005
Conservation fund.			
Forestry mill tax	83,306	85,760	22,335
Forest crop taxes	10,555	10,256	1,318
Motor fuel tax	1	1	1
Dry cleaner fund	—	665	619
Mediation fund.	1	1	1
Petroleum inspection tax	45,798	45,707	51,073
Economic development fund temporary service charges	23,758	38,768	25,739
DEPARTMENT REVENUES.	**26,127,221**	**37,143,936**	**34,461,277**
Intergovernmental revenue.	11,046,123	11,206,587	11,149,472
Licenses and permits	1,816,237	1,846,902	1,779,406
Charges for goods and services	4,188,998	4,236,264	4,457,319
Contributions	3,411,872	3,875,831	3,827,381
Interest and investment income	1,166,878	11,457,291	8,849,596
Gifts and donations	596,606	643,013	667,540
Proceeds from sale of bonds	981,571	834,445	703,623
Other revenues	2,775,527	2,798,022	2,627,829
Other transactions.	143,409	245,581	399,111
TRANSFERS	**1,402,824**	**1,700,574**	**1,502,566**
TOTAL REVENUES	**43,924,438**	**55,676,097**	**53,356,899**

—Represents zero.

Source: Wisconsin Department of Administration, State Controller's Office, *2018 Annual Fiscal Report*, October 15, 2018.

Revenue bonds of the state of Wisconsin

Program funded	Amount of debt authorized ($1,000)	Amount issued[1] ($1,000)	Amount outstanding December 15, 2018 ($1,000)
Transportation facilities and highway projects.	4,055,373	3,845,167	1,768,310
Clean Water/Environmental Improvement Fund.	2,526,700	1,836,245	370,255
Petroleum environmental cleanup	436,000	387,550	27,195
Total.	7,018,073	6,068,962	2,165,760

Note: Revenue bonds are issued for purposes and amounts specifically authorized by the legislature. This debt is not a legal obligation of the state and is not subject to existing debt limitations.

1. Amounts do not include refunding bonds, which do not count against the respective authorizations.

Source: Wisconsin Department of Administration, Division of Executive Budget and Finance, departmental data.

Wisconsin state government expenditures

Function	Fiscal year 2016–17 Amount ($1,000)	Percent	Fiscal year 2017–18 Amount ($1,000)	Percent
Executive total	42,573,246	90.60	43,507,199	90.27
Administration	944,644	2.01	866,765	1.80
Agriculture, Trade and Consumer Protection	92,502	0.20	96,814	0.20
Board on Aging and Long Term Care	3,092	0.01	3,261	0.01
Board for People with Developmental Disabilities	1,373	0.00	3,226	0.01
Child Abuse and Neglect Prevention Board	2,993	0.01	3,842	0.01
Children and Families.	2,139,958	4.55	2,142,058	4.44
Corrections	1,196,582	2.55	1,220,534	2.53
District attorneys.	46,825	0.10	47,192	0.10
Educational Communications Board.	17,543	0.04	19,290	0.04
Elections Commission	6,418	0.01	3,809	0.01
Employee Trust Funds	7,517,149	16.00	7,635,574	15.84
Employment Relations Commission	1,357	0.00	1,069	0.00
Environmental Improvement Program	120,374	0.26	109,845	0.23
Ethics Commission	885	0.00	1,011	0.00
Financial Institutions	18,834	0.04	17,410	0.04
Fox River Navigation System Authority	125	0.00	125	0.00
Governor	3,930	0.01	3,612	0.01
Health Services.	12,062,286	25.67	12,166,717	25.24
Higher Education Aids Board	146,685	0.31	142,019	0.29
Historical Society	25,493	0.05	27,505	0.06
Insurance Commissioner.	40,531	0.09	34,700	0.07
Investment Board	47,904	0.10	46,218	0.10
Justice	151,872	0.32	172,029	0.36
Kickapoo Reserve Management Board	1,061	0.00	1,086	0.00
Labor and Industry Review Commission	2,655	0.01	2,288	0.00
Lieutenant Governor	288	0.00	268	0.00
Lower Wisconsin Riverway.	219	0.00	217	0.00
Medical College of Wisconsin	10,179	0.02	9,823	0.02
Military Affairs	92,295	0.20	114,447	0.24
Natural Resources	589,554	1.25	604,238	1.25
Public Defender	82,498	0.18	88,133	0.18
Public Instruction	6,643,915	14.14	6,700,375	13.90
Public Lands Board	1,342	0.00	1,467	0.00
Public Service Commission	22,863	0.05	31,771	0.07
Revenue	557,419	1.19	604,909	1.26

Wisconsin state government expenditures, continued

Function	Fiscal year 2016–17 Amount ($1,000)	Percent	Fiscal year 2017–18 Amount ($1,000)	Percent
Safety and Professional Services	51,044	0.11	51,537	0.11
Secretary of State	246	0.00	262	0.00
State Fair Park	28,518	0.06	29,904	0.06
Technical College System Board	550,409	1.17	551,112	1.14
Tourism	17,894	0.04	16,333	0.03
Transportation	2,768,887	5.89	3,221,500	6.68
Treasurer	103	0.00	101	0.00
University of Wisconsin	6,055,940	12.89	6,201,687	12.87
Veterans Affairs	143,381	0.31	137,704	0.29
Wisconsin Economic Development Corporation	35,251	0.08	58,682	0.12
Workforce Development	327,931	0.70	314,729	0.65
Total judicial	139,241	0.30	140,284	0.29
Total legislative	68,574	0.15	68,768	0.14
Budget stabilization	0	0.00	33,140	0.07
Shared revenue and tax relief	2,485,851	5.29	2,658,999	5.52
Miscellaneous appropriations	124,192	0.26	126,222	0.26
Program supplements	-178,316	-0.38	-77,346	-0.16
Public debt	837,523	1.78	827,974	1.72
Building Commission	20,641	0.04	26,169	0.05
Building programs	920,646	1.96	887,394	1.84
Total	**46,991,599**		**48,198,804**	

Source: Wisconsin Department of Administration, State Controller's Office, Appendix to Annual Fiscal Report (Budgetary Basis), October 2017 and October 2018.

Debt of the state of Wisconsin, 1980–2017

	Annual debt limit[1] ($1,000)	Amount incurred during calendar year Total ($1,000)	% of debt limit	Amount outstanding, December 31 Total ($1,000)	Per capita ($)	% of state assessed value
1980	813,604	123,500	15.2	1,916,177	407	1.77
1985	922,661	440,955	47.8	2,410,628	508	1.96
1990	1,060,277	484,099	45.7	2,781,071	568	1.97
1995	1,511,536	368,322	24.4	3,305,471	643	1.64
2000	2,147,411	538,795	25.1	4,270,718	796	1.49
2001	2,343,628	485,645	20.7	4,452,626	824	1.42
2002	2,514,949	481,000	19.1	4,682,045	861	1.40
2003	2,705,327	499,030	18.5	4,794,398	876	1.33
2004	2,933,909	664,435	22.6	5,116,439	930	1.31
2005	3,209,502	571,990	17.8	5,445,615	984	1.27
2006	3,517,374	891,285	25.3	5,898,647	1,061	1.26
2007	3,734,403	483,280	12.9	5,893,590	1,052	1.18
2008	3,857,955	493,635	12.8	6,146,978	1,092	1.19
2009	3,839,340	542,765	14.1	6,481,078	1,146	1.27
2010	3,719,281	809,293	21.8	7,407,431	1,303	1.49
2011	3,651,482	896,260	24.5	7,878,628	1,380	1.62
2012	3,533,194	735,585	20.8	8,385,973	1,465	1.78
2013	3,506,269	642,295	18.3	8,344,531	1,453	1.78
2014	3,596,100	598,170	16.6	8,134,099	1,412	1.70
2015	3,679,519	750,475	20.4	8,238,759	1,428	1.68

Debt of the state of Wisconsin, 1980–2017, continued

	Annual debt limit[1] ($1,000)	Amount incurred during calendar year		Amount outstanding, December 31		
		Total ($1,000)	% of debt limit	Total ($1,000)	Per capita ($)	% of state assessed value
2016	3,788,432	713,305	18.8	8,389,198	1,448	1.66
2017	3,944,844	607,975	15.4	8,155,030	1,404	1.55

1. The debt limit for each calendar year is derived through a formula specified in s. 18.05, Wis. Stats.
Source: Wisconsin Department of Administration, Division of Executive Budget and Finance, departmental data.

Debt of the state of Wisconsin, May 31, 2018

Type	Amount outstanding ($1,000)
Tax supported debt	5,844,904
General fund	4,209,945
Segregated funds[1]	1,634,958
Revenue supported debt[2]	1,906,959
Total	7,751,863

1. Includes the Transportation Fund and certain administrative facilities for the Wisconsin Department of Natural Resources.
2. Revenue supported debt includes debt that is issued with initial expectation that revenues and other proceeds from the operation of the programs or facilities financed will amortize the debt without recourse to the general fund.
Source: Wisconsin Department of Administration, Division of Executive Budget and Finance, departmental data.

Debt of Wisconsin state authorities

Authority	Amount outstanding ($1,000)
Wisconsin Health and Educational Facilities Authority	9,372,377[1]
Wisconsin Housing and Economic Development Authority	1,760,263[2]

1. Estimated as of 6/30/19.   2. As of 12/31/18.
Source: Data provided by the respective authorities.

Debt of Wisconsin local governments

Year (Dec. 31)	Counties (mil. dol.)	Cities (mil. dol.)	Villages (mil. dol.)	Towns (mil. dol.)	Total (mil. dol.)
1965	192.5	548.1	22.5	9.2	772.3
1975	261.0	598.7	69.8	26.2	955.7
1985	532.5	1,320.4	227.6	75.2	2,155.7
1995	1,221.6	2,082.8	418.7	193.8	3,916.9
2005	1,753.7	3,718.5	1,098.0	308.5	6,878.8
2010	2,444.8	4,468.2	1,440.1	374.6	8,727.7

Debt of Wisconsin local governments, continued

Year (Dec. 31)	Counties (mil. dol.)	Cities (mil. dol.)	Villages (mil. dol.)	Towns (mil. dol.)	Total (mil. dol.)
2015.	2,378.1	4,713.3	1,560.9	338.6	8,990.9
2016.	2,352.8	5,026.9	1,632.0	341.0	9,352.6
2017.	2,553.3	5,139.0	1,773.7	350.7	9,816.6

Sources: Wisconsin Department of Revenue, *Indebtedness 1981* and previous editions; Wisconsin Department of Revenue, Division of State and Local Finance, Bureau of Local Government Services, *County and Municipal Revenues and Expenditures 2017* and previous editions.

Debt of Wisconsin school districts and technical college districts

Year (June 30)	School districts (mil. dol.)	Technical college districts (mil. dol.)	Total (mil. dol)
1965.	336.6	X	336.6
1975.	798.7	97.2	895.9
1985.	448.7	64.7	513.4
1995.	2,104.9	192.8	2,297.7
2005.	5,335.5	461.4	5,796.9
2010.	4,863.7	510.2	5,373.9
2015.	4,916.4	886.4	5,802.8
2016.	4,989.8	913.4	5,903.2
2017.	5,763.2	916.2	6,679.4
2018.	6,307.8	934.8	7,242.6

X–Not applicable. Technical college districts did not have authority to incur debt prior to 1967.

Sources: Wisconsin Department of Public Instruction, departmental data; Wisconsin Technical College System Board, departmental data.

Federal aids to Wisconsin

Agency administering aid	Aid received by Wisconsin ($1,000)		Disbursed to local governments ($1,000)		Aid to individuals and organizations ($1,000)	
	Fiscal year 2017–18	Fiscal year 2016–17	Fiscal year 2017–18	Fiscal year 2016–17	Fiscal year 2017–18	Fiscal year 2016–17
Administration	178,507	184,469	142,038	182,965	15,279	20,235
Agriculture, Trade and Consumer Protection	12,686	14,413	—	—	—	—
Child Abuse and Neglect Prevention Board	685	786	—	—	516	504
Children and Families	635,416	715,023	113,655	107,533	414,372	426,788
Clean Water Fund Program[1] . . .	134,527	-34,015	58,865	51,802	—	—
Corrections	434	1,648	—	—	—	—
Elections Commission	12,656	365	—	—	—	—
Government Accountability Board	-4,933	376	—	—	—	—
Health Services	6,385,945	6,638,604	158,556	123,441	6,166,663	6,013,710
Higher Educational Aids Board .	—	—	—	—	—	-2

Federal aids to Wisconsin, continued

Agency administering aid	Aid received by Wisconsin ($1,000)		Disbursed to local governments ($1,000)		Aid to individuals and organizations ($1,000)	
	Fiscal year 2017–18	Fiscal year 2016–17	Fiscal year 2017–18	Fiscal year 2016–17	Fiscal year 2017–18	Fiscal year 2016–17
Historical Society.	1,600	1,424	—	—	—	—
Insurance, Commissioner of . . .	-8	525	—	—	—	—
Justice	40,000	34,315	32,194	24,393	1,478	1,008
Military Affairs.	71,004	59,856	15,232	12,040	689	86
Natural Resources	148,490	119,287	7,415	7,809	—	—
People with Developmental Disabilities, Board for	1,493	2,030	—	—	561	203
Public Defender.	104	296	—	—	—	—
Public Instruction.	818,979	808,402	687,055	701,193	60,385	61,869
Public Lands Board.	51	—	51	—	—	—
Public Service Commission. . . .	5,173	6,061	—	—	—	—
Safety and Professional Services	972	549	—	—	—	—
Supreme Court	686	550	—	—	—	—
Technical College System Board	27,095	29,219	23,264	22,934	1,272	1,080
Tourism.	763	1,450	—	—	620	652
Transportation	790,750	627,361	191,562	131,974	6,676	5,053
University of Wisconsin System .	1,621,320	1,624,049	—	—	—	—
Veterans Affairs	2,673	2,522	—	—	—	—
Workforce Development	211,050	219,799	—	—	79,040	73,496
Total.	11,098,121	11,059,363	1,429,888	1,366,085	6,747,552	6,604,682

—represents zero.

Note: Aid is not necessarily disbursed in the same fiscal year in which it is received by the agency. In some cases, aid is received as reimbursement for previous expenditures.

1. Federal aid received by Wisconsin for Clean Water Fund (Environmental Improvement Program, DOA) also includes safe drinking water loan program appropriations.

Source: Wisconsin Department of Administration, State Controller's Office, *Annual Fiscal Report—Appendix*, October 2017 and October 2018.

State payments to local units of government, fiscal year 2018

County[1]	School levy tax credit[2] ($)	Shared revenue payments[3] ($)	Exempt property aid[4] ($)	Total ($)	Per capita[5] Amount ($)	Rank
Adams	4,084,351	1,267,044	45,526	5,396,921	259.64	60
Ashland.	1,963,309	5,997,240	52,936	8,013,486	499.91	1
Barron.	6,887,835	6,754,192	170,970	13,812,997	298.11	37
Bayfield.	3,365,702	1,470,242	10,911	4,846,855	316.23	25
Brown.	33,060,483	27,048,684	5,177,234	65,286,401	250.51	66
Buffalo	1,911,489	2,910,218	59,714	4,881,421	356.33	10
Burnett	3,687,968	1,179,928	22,170	4,890,066	315.33	28
Calumet	6,236,949	3,650,511	562,491	10,449,951	198.45	72
Chippewa	7,962,214	10,876,278	684,607	19,523,099	302.44	35
Clark.	3,093,940	8,092,576	76,953	11,263,468	324.19	19
Columbia.	8,890,936	7,903,995	235,565	17,030,496	298.13	36
Crawford	1,909,279	3,547,234	98,237	5,554,749	331.88	16
Dane	105,361,903	25,407,983	16,192,212	146,962,098	277.02	50
Dodge	10,158,938	12,789,611	453,415	23,401,963	260.17	59
Door.	6,483,991	1,426,078	130,031	8,040,100	282.48	47
Douglas.	5,819,460	11,131,047	129,055	17,079,562	384.30	5

State payments to local units of government, fiscal year 2018, continued

County[1]	School levy tax credit[2] ($)	Shared revenue payments[3] ($)	Exempt property aid[4] ($)	Total ($)	Per capita[5] Amount ($)	Rank
Dunn	4,911,459	8,028,400	184,685	13,124,544	294.16	39
Eau Claire.	12,352,665	13,254,810	1,154,291	26,761,766	260.29	58
Florence	958,618	342,728	5,273	1,306,619	293.36	40
Fond du Lac	12,325,140	14,851,754	1,052,809	28,229,702	271.35	53
Forest	1,953,172	989,272	14,921	2,957,364	320.51	22
Grant	5,399,568	12,493,767	147,751	18,041,086	342.89	11
Green	5,173,031	3,937,930	595,475	9,706,436	262.57	56
Green Lake.	3,283,547	3,132,259	83,521	6,499,327	338.97	15
Iowa	3,658,164	2,402,082	607,712	6,667,958	279.38	49
Iron	1,210,236	1,377,959	4,672	2,592,866	437.91	3
Jackson	2,640,660	3,103,868	92,832	5,837,360	280.64	48
Jefferson	11,584,657	9,317,481	869,657	21,771,796	258.11	61
Juneau	3,794,442	4,930,620	62,052	8,787,115	324.04	20
Kenosha	24,855,268	20,389,282	2,868,294	48,112,844	285.20	44
Kewaunee	2,496,396	3,641,474	56,268	6,194,138	298.00	38
La Crosse	16,751,188	18,125,687	2,480,912	37,357,786	313.42	29
Lafayette	1,940,990	4,477,544	24,627	6,443,160	378.79	7
Langlade	2,429,918	4,130,632	103,178	6,663,728	331.02	17
Lincoln	3,625,435	5,637,812	185,816	9,449,063	327.39	18
Manitowoc.	8,567,052	17,105,404	592,595	26,265,050	322.29	21
Marathon.	17,554,581	19,104,846	2,270,311	38,929,738	286.41	43
Marinette.	5,844,791	9,639,138	211,365	15,695,294	379.28	6
Marquette	2,455,494	1,017,675	54,516	3,527,685	228.95	68
Menominee	544,994	622,988	3,044	1,171,026	275.02	51
Milwaukee	114,952,889	311,703,328	30,074,406	456,730,623	480.58	2
Monroe	4,680,314	8,326,960	146,645	13,153,919	283.72	46
Oconto	5,629,117	4,492,469	80,403	10,201,989	265.15	54
Oneida	9,051,440	1,901,995	129,248	11,082,683	304.61	33
Outagamie.	22,534,600	21,967,679	2,418,855	46,921,135	254.26	62
Ozaukee	17,972,924	6,646,860	780,174	25,399,958	286.46	42
Pepin	1,146,523	1,369,540	15,581	2,531,644	342.53	12
Pierce	5,485,303	5,007,753	94,652	10,587,708	251.96	65
Polk	7,778,659	4,221,632	85,965	12,086,256	272.34	52
Portage.	7,951,219	7,553,580	1,064,768	16,569,567	233.25	67
Price	2,242,490	2,932,680	50,120	5,225,289	372.01	8
Racine.	25,353,314	33,970,727	3,161,418	62,485,458	318.48	23
Richland	1,787,795	3,810,289	57,000	5,655,084	315.59	27
Rock.	17,082,920	32,282,034	1,646,747	51,011,700	318.13	24
Rusk	2,290,937	3,700,383	68,833	6,060,153	410.75	4
St. Croix.	13,413,753	3,909,266	276,927	17,599,946	198.68	71
Sauk.	10,454,679	4,903,063	516,478	15,874,220	252.69	64
Sawyer	4,099,290	1,066,072	21,898	5,187,259	308.25	31
Shawano	5,227,258	5,208,430	111,851	10,547,539	253.21	63
Sheboygan.	15,654,544	17,904,367	1,872,744	35,431,655	305.65	32
Taylor	2,190,218	3,558,652	156,804	5,905,674	284.67	45
Trempealeau.	3,588,166	6,331,389	188,718	10,108,274	339.58	13
Vernon	3,406,405	6,041,918	116,777	9,565,100	316.22	26
Vilas	7,283,918	535,173	29,003	7,848,093	360.48	9
Walworth.	24,364,397	6,556,434	465,515	31,386,346	303.15	34
Washburn	3,603,442	1,283,811	66,933	4,954,187	311.02	30
Washington	20,987,439	5,730,394	1,013,001	27,730,834	203.95	70
Waukesha	87,467,953	11,007,291	6,019,228	104,494,472	260.30	57
Waupaca . . . ., ...	6,822,208	8,226,858	268,705	15,317,771	293.35	41
Waushara.	3,713,605	1,698,072	55,644	5,467,320	223.69	69
Winnebago	19,126,336	21,869,690	4,047,243	45,043,268	264.92	55

State payments to local units of government, fiscal year 2018, continued

County[1]	School levy tax credit[2] ($)	Shared revenue payments[3] ($)	Exempt property aid[4] ($)	Total ($)	Per capita[5] Amount ($)	Rank
Wood	8,465,735	15,563,175	1,335,790	25,364,700	339.02	14
State	**853,000,000**	**884,790,236**	**94,266,672**	**1,832,056,909**	**314.99**	**X**

X–not applicable.

1. Some cities and villages are located in more than one county. In these cases, payments are attributed to the "primary" county, as determined by the Department of Revenue. For example, payments to the city of Appleton are attributed to Outagamie County even though parts of Appleton are located in Calumet and Winnebago Counties. 2. Distributed July 2017. 3. Total of amounts (excluding deductions) distributed July and November 2017. 4. Includes exempt computer aid distributed July 2017. 5. Based on 2018 population estimates.

Sources: Wisconsin Department of Revenue, Division of State and Local Finance, Local Government Services Bureau, departmental data, March 2019; Wisconsin Department of Administration, Demographic Services Center, *Official Final Estimates, January 1, 2018*, October 2018.

Wisconsin general property assessments and tax levies

Year	Full-value assessment of all property (mil. dol.)	% change	Total state and local property taxes levied (mil. dol)	% change	State property tax relief (mil. dol.)	Average full-value tax rate per ($1,000)	% change	Average net tax rate per $1,000 after state tax relief	% change
1900. . . .	630	X	19	X	NA	31	X	NA	X
1910. . . .	2,743	X	31	X	NA	11.18	X	NA	X
1920. . . .	4,571	X	96	X	NA	21.06	X	NA	X
1930. . . .	5,896	X	121	X	NA	20.49	X	NA	X
1940. . . .	4,354	X	110	X	NA	25.26	X	NA	X
1950. . . .	9,201	X	226	X	NA	24.52	X	NA	X
1960. . . .	18,844	X	481	X	NA	25.55	X	NA	X
1970. . . .	34,790	X	1,179	X	140	33.88	X	NA	X
1980. . . .	108,480	X	2,210	X	309	20.37	X	NA	X
1990. . . .	141,370	X	4,388	X	319	31.04	X	28.78	X
2000. . . .	286,321	X	6,605	X	469	23.06	X	21.42	X
2001. . . .	312,484	9.1	7,044	6.7	469	22.54	-2.3	21.03	-1.8
2002. . . .	335,326	7.3	7,364	4.5	469	21.95	-2.6	20.55	-2.3
2003. . . .	360,710	7.6	7,687	4.4	469	21.31	-3.0	20.01	-2.7
2004. . . .	391,188	8.4	8,151	6	469	20.83	-2.2	19.63	-1.9
2005. . . .	427,934	9.4	8,327	2.2	469	19.45	-6.6	18.36	-6.5
2006. . . .	468,983	9.6	8,706	4.6	593	18.56	-4.6	17.29	-5.8
2007. . . .	497,920	6.2	9,251	6.3	672	18.57	0.1	17.22	-0.4
2008. . . .	514,394	3.3	9,667	4.5	747	18.79	1.2	17.34	0.6
2009. . . .	511,912	-0.5	10,106	4.5	747	19.74	5	18.28	5.4
2010. . . .	495,904	-3.1	10,365	2.6	747	20.9	5.9	19.39	6.1
2011. . . .	486,864	-1.8	10,385	0.2	747	21.33	2.1	19.79	2.1
2012. . . .	471,093	-3.2	10,470	0.8	747	22.22	4.2	20.63	4.3
2013. . . .	467,503	-0.8	10,606	1.3	747	22.68	2.1	21.08	2.2
2014. . . .	479,024	2.5	10,384	-2.1	747	21.67	4.4	20.11	4.6
2015. . . .	490,603	2.4	10,620	2.3	853	21.65	0.1	19.91	1.0
2016. . . .	505,124	3.0	10,792	1.6	853	21.37	1.3	19.68	1.2
2017. . . .	525,985	4.1	11,016	2.1	940	20.94	2.0	19.16	2.6

NA–Not available; X–Not applicable.

Source: Wisconsin Department of Revenue, Division of State and Local Finance, Local Government Services, *2017 Town, Village, and City Taxes: Taxes Levied 2017—Collected 2018* and previous issues.

General property assessments, taxes, and rates, 2017

County	Full-value assessment[1] ($)	Total property tax[2] ($)	State property tax credit[3] ($)	Average full-value tax rate per $1,000[4] Gross ($)	Average full-value tax rate per $1,000[4] Net ($)
Adams	2,513,047,500	52,282,590	4,345,262	20.80	19.08
Ashland	1,214,385,900	27,480,175	2,209,774	22.63	20.81
Barron	4,104,693,800	85,541,484	7,782,873	20.84	18.94
Bayfield	2,556,035,700	38,011,074	3,723,831	14.87	13.41
Brown	20,863,710,700	436,451,535	36,608,256	20.92	19.16
Buffalo	1,157,108,700	23,984,249	2,168,035	20.73	18.85
Burnett	2,619,977,600	37,624,546	3,944,953	14.36	12.85
Calumet	4,002,111,800	84,920,945	6,935,138	21.22	19.49
Chippewa	5,328,054,600	91,638,091	8,739,022	17.20	15.56
Clark	2,077,748,400	45,273,078	3,428,532	21.79	20.14
Columbia	5,350,206,600	109,773,396	9,784,504	20.52	18.69
Crawford	1,196,983,000	29,106,814	2,131,678	24.32	22.54
Dane	60,784,157,550	1,379,828,012	119,195,433	22.70	20.74
Dodge	6,375,762,700	140,221,250	11,044,535	21.99	20.26
Door	7,113,624,900	96,465,387	7,233,719	13.56	12.54
Douglas	3,430,449,000	71,552,540	6,512,811	20.86	18.96
Dunn	3,034,074,400	67,904,715	5,406,399	22.38	20.60
Eau Claire	8,295,565,000	172,992,806	14,088,621	20.85	19.16
Florence	627,605,800	11,676,897	1,028,643	18.61	16.97
Fond du Lac	7,404,221,300	164,092,499	13,405,716	22.16	20.35
Forest	1,113,815,000	19,451,785	2,117,285	17.46	15.56
Grant	3,180,242,800	68,267,861	6,029,870	21.47	19.57
Green	2,924,949,800	70,161,415	5,805,794	23.99	22.00
Green Lake	2,277,060,000	41,326,905	3,506,345	18.15	16.61
Iowa	2,013,421,100	47,873,947	3,968,915	23.78	21.81
Iron	944,742,700	15,915,057	1,292,515	16.85	15.48
Jackson	1,649,337,300	34,804,334	3,014,254	21.10	19.27
Jefferson	6,948,833,800	145,975,976	12,751,355	21.01	19.17
Juneau	2,080,178,400	44,703,201	3,988,034	21.49	19.57
Kenosha	14,655,093,000	348,296,201	26,807,826	23.77	21.94
Kewaunee	1,661,920,500	34,329,127	2,891,357	20.66	18.92
La Crosse	9,635,009,700	215,606,268	18,577,012	22.38	20.45
Lafayette	1,149,154,400	27,486,052	2,096,291	23.92	22.09
Langlade	1,688,211,900	31,422,946	2,639,012	18.61	17.05
Lincoln	2,381,987,700	49,169,780	3,930,703	20.64	18.99
Manitowoc	5,287,002,200	112,863,324	9,313,843	21.35	19.59
Marathon	10,590,161,600	236,599,721	19,357,261	22.34	20.51
Marinette	3,843,289,300	68,973,748	6,379,548	17.95	16.29
Marquette	1,588,664,000	31,982,520	2,638,640	20.13	18.47
Menominee	304,250,700	6,160,771	568,269	20.25	18.38
Milwaukee	61,413,297,000	1,700,744,223	124,452,528	27.69	25.67
Monroe	3,301,747,200	69,187,744	5,173,564	20.95	19.39
Oconto	3,792,196,100	67,583,258	6,133,092	17.82	16.20
Oneida	6,867,927,100	93,674,283	9,973,981	13.64	12.19
Outagamie	14,882,910,000	303,957,296	24,813,284	20.42	18.76
Ozaukee	11,735,981,400	203,243,795	19,716,857	17.32	15.64
Pepin	616,444,700	13,778,588	1,266,943	22.35	20.30
Pierce	3,271,381,300	72,595,065	6,214,929	22.19	20.29
Polk	4,530,661,500	87,287,459	8,484,892	19.27	17.39
Portage	5,718,796,400	111,553,819	8,703,190	19.51	17.98
Price	1,376,983,600	27,048,657	2,449,457	19.64	17.86
Racine	14,695,479,800	337,586,807	28,024,591	22.97	21.07
Richland	1,136,481,200	24,886,329	2,001,223	21.90	20.14
Rock	10,907,782,900	265,944,806	18,850,246	24.38	22.65
Rusk	1,217,894,400	25,249,949	2,554,863	20.73	18.63

General property assessments, taxes, and rates, 2017, continued

County	Full-value assessment[1] ($)	Total property tax[2] ($)	State property tax credit[3] ($)	Average full-value tax rate per $1,000[4] Gross ($)	Net ($)
St. Croix.	9,195,173,600	165,583,666	15,525,538	18.01	16.32
Sauk.	7,120,479,000	139,938,793	11,420,415	19.65	18.05
Sawyer	3,496,215,200	40,899,067	4,501,167	11.70	10.41
Shawano	3,096,944,300	60,725,177	5,668,406	19.61	17.78
Sheboygan.	9,228,846,100	195,371,644	16,767,419	21.17	19.35
Taylor.	1,445,462,800	31,843,477	2,450,417	22.03	20.33
Trempealeau.	2,209,706,500	50,307,729	4,041,452	22.77	20.94
Vernon	1,956,310,400	42,971,190	3,674,335	21.97	20.09
Vilas.	6,835,215,600	72,437,903	7,889,250	10.60	9.44
Walworth.	14,156,955,100	261,250,778	26,741,553	18.45	16.56
Washburn	2,488,144,600	40,266,842	3,933,887	16.18	14.60
Washington	14,614,348,100	237,999,396	22,951,984	16.29	14.71
Waukesha	54,158,131,600	911,056,408	96,171,525	16.82	15.05
Waupaca.	4,133,162,800	91,917,447	7,491,961	22.24	20.43
Waushara.	2,513,510,700	45,909,062	4,013,572	18.26	16.67
Winnebago	12,909,954,800	288,974,553	21,269,493	22.38	20.74
Wood.	4,993,169,200	116,125,196	9,282,142	23.26	21.40
Total.	**525,984,545,850**	**11,016,093,428**	**940,000,020**	**20.94**	**19.16**

1. Reflects actual market value of all taxable general property, as determined by the Wisconsin Department of Revenue independent of locally assessed values, which can vary substantially from full value.   2. Includes taxes and special charges levied by schools, counties, cities, villages, towns, special purpose districts, and the State of Wisconsin. It does not include special assessments or other charges.   3. Total amount of school levy tax credit paid by the state to taxing districts and credited to taxpayers on their tax bills. The credit is considered part of the tax payment.   4. A county's average tax rate per $1,000 of assessed valuation (determined by dividing total taxes by equalized value and multiplying by 1,000) is the preferred figure for comparison purposes, rather than the general local property tax rate because the average is based on full market value. Net tax rate per $1,000 reflects the effect of state property tax relief.

Source: Wisconsin Department of Revenue, Division of State and Local Finance, *Town, Village, and City Taxes—2017: Taxes Levied 2017— Collected 2018.*

Municipal property taxes levied in Wisconsin

Year	Total (mil. dol.)	% Residential	% Commercial	% Manufaturing	% Agricultural	% Personal[1]	% Other[2]
1960.	481.4	47.5	13.5	10.7	11.2	16.5	0.6
1965.	664.1	48.4	14.4	10.3	10.6	15.8	0.6
1970.	1,179.0	47.3	15.2	10.4	9.7	16.9	0.5
1975.	1,601.3	50.5	16.8	5.7	10.1	16.2	0.7
1980.	2,210.0	57.7	16.2	4.8	12.5	7.5	1.3
1985.	3,203.5	58.9	17.7	4.7	12.4	4.8	1.6
1990.	4,388.2	60.4	20.2	4.1	8.4	5.5	1.3
1995.	5,738.9	64.8	18.8	3.6	6.7	4.9	1.1
1996.	5,378.0	65.7	18.9	3.6	3.6	4.6	3.7
1997.	5,635.9	66.2	18.7	3.6	3.3	4.5	3.7
1998.	5,975.0	66.5	18.7	3.6	2.9	4.5	3.9
1999.	6,190.9	67.3	18.8	3.7	2.7	3.5	4.0
2000.	6,604.5	67.9	18.9	3.7	1.7	3.4	4.3
2001.	7,043.7	68.1	19.0	3.6	1.6	3.4	4.4
2002.	7,363.6	69.0	18.9	3.5	0.8	3.2	4.6
2003.	7,687.3	69.7	18.8	3.4	0.6	2.9	4.7
2004.	8,150.8	70.3	18.8	3.2	0.5	2.7	4.5
2005.	8,326.7	71.0	18.7	3.0	0.5	2.6	4.2

Municipal property taxes levied in Wisconsin, continued

Year	Total (mil. dol.)	% Residential	% Commercial	% Manufaturing	% Agricultural	% Personal[1]	% Other[2]
2006.	8,706.4	71.4	18.7	2.8	0.5	2.5	4.2
2007.	9,250.3	71.4	18.9	2.7	0.4	2.4	4.2
2008.	9,677.1	70.9	19.2	2.7	0.4	2.6	4.2
2009.	10,105.7	70.4	19.6	2.7	0.4	2.6	4.3
2010.	10,364.6	70.4	19.6	2.8	0.4	2.6	4.3
2011.	10,384.8	70.2	19.7	2.8	0.4	2.5	4.3
2012.	10,469.9	69.6	20.2	2.9	0.4	2.6	4.3
2013.	10,605.5	69.0	20.5	3.0	0.4	2.7	4.3
2014.	10,383.7	68.8	20.8	3.0	0.4	2.8	4.2
2015.	10,620.2	68.6	21.0	3.0	0.4	2.7	4.2
2016.	10,792.1	68.3	21.3	3.0	0.4	2.8	4.2
2017.	11,016.1	68.1	21.7	3.0	0.4	2.7	4.1

1. An exemption for "Line A" business property was phased-in beginning in 1977. "Line A" property was completely exempted by 1981.   2. Beginning in 1996, "Other" includes agricultural property not considered agricultural land for purposes of use value assessment.

Sources: Wisconsin Department of Revenue, Division of State and Local Finance, Local Government Services, *2017 Town, Village and City Taxes: Taxes Levied 2017—Collected 2018*, and previous issues. For 1980 and earlier, *Property Tax*, 1981 and previous issues. 1960 and 1965 data are from Wisconsin Department of Taxation. Percentages may not add up to 100 due to rounding.

Wisconsin general property tax levies, 2017

Type of property	Towns	Villages	Cities	Total
Real estate .	3,216,488,928	1,915,615,995	5,589,676,678	10,721,781,602
Residential .	2,517,616,890	1,425,034,766	3,561,743,780	7,504,395,436
Commercial .	188,320,902	404,505,171	1,801,466,275	2,394,292,349
Manufacturing .	32,979,266	74,439,338	220,934,415	328,353,019
Forest lands .	123,399,848	2,109,097	697,225	126,206,170
Agricultural .	40,483,915	974,605	499,908	41,958,427
Ag forest .	53,918,759	831,567	353,585	55,103,910
Undeveloped .	32,708,652	1,294,070	744,080	34,746,803
Other land and improvements .	227,060,697	6,427,382	3,237,410	236,725,489
Personal property .	41,384,811	49,654,876	203,272,006	294,311,692
Furniture, fixtures, equipment.	8,346,442	20,711,172	91,981,167	121,038,780
Machinery, tools, patterns .	22,064,110	22,304,471	73,573,333	117,941,915
Boats and other watercraft .	147,329	30,901	340,832	519,062
All other personal property .	10,826,930	6,608,331	37,376,674	54,811,935
Total general property taxes.	**3,257,873,771**	**1,965,270,836**	**5,792,948,821**	**11,016,093,428**
Total state tax credit .	336,977,131	167,158,962	435,863,927	940,000,020
Total effective taxes .	**2,920,896,640**	**1,798,111,874**	**5,357,084,894**	**10,076,093,408**

Note: The sums of some columns and rows may differ slightly from the reported totals because the Department of Revenue truncates (rather than rounds) amounts under $1 for individual units of government.

Source: Wisconsin Department of Revenue, Division of State and Local Finance, Bureau of Local Government Services, *Town, Village, and City Taxes—2017: Taxes Levied 2017—Collected 2018*.

Wisconsin Conservation Fund revenues, expenditures, and balances

	2013–14	2014–15	2015–16	2016–17
Opening cash balance	$39,267,307	$37,191,298	$42,685,686	$60,473,125
Revenues	286,915,608	292,932,526	311,640,899	303,038,659
User fees (licenses, registration).	102,118,589	104,820,956	113,182,781	125,634,380
Forestry mill tax.	79,399,769	81,350,401	83,306,027	85,760,413
Federal aids	45,486,239	45,687,437	44,928,485	43,064,052
Motor fuel tax formula	22,842,478	23,574,182	23,681,894	23,086,512
Severance tax	8,985,347	9,263,069	10,555,268	10,150,721
Other revenues (sales, services)	28,083,186	28,236,481	35,986,444	15,342,581
Expenditures	288,991,617	287,438,138	293,853,460	291,600,806
Land and forestry—state	93,368,808	89,769,542	95,214,571	96,581,448
Land and forestry—federal.	15,146,341	17,111,226	16,228,694	16,442,572
Enforcement/science—state.	22,554,512	22,986,382	22,797,824	22,489,837
Enforcement/science—federal	11,257,421	11,246,443	10,166,126	10,324,407
Water management—state	21,704,213	22,638,169	22,601,306	20,970,586
Water management—federal	5,736,280	5,180,222	5,064,936	5,298,995
Conservation aids—state.	29,955,985	32,205,061	31,619,966	34,876,037
Conservation aids—federal	4,250,563	4,867,250	6,309,235	6,613,623
Environmental aids—state	6,722,852	6,287,498	5,892,225	6,316,021
Development/debt service—state	21,065,928	21,958,417	22,218,355	22,854,570
Development/debt service—federal.	6,539,906	3,413,936	6,368,552	1,567,312
Administrative services—state	3,729,519	2,577,149	2,170,431	2,302,533
Administrative services—federal	1,337,961	621,125	437,401	342,926
CAES[1] management—state	24,318,420	24,934,968	26,409,465	26,150,748
CAES[1] management—federal	6,015,817	6,931,415	6,196,326	5,515,622
Other activities—state	15,287,091	14,709,335	14,158,047	12,953,569
Fund Balance	$37,191,298	$42,685,686	$60,473,125	$71,910,978

1. Customer and Employee Services Division.

Source: Wisconsin Department of Administration, Division of Executive Budget and Finance, State Controller's Office, *2017 Annual Fiscal Report (Budgetary Basis) Appendix*, October 15, 2017, and previous editions.

Wisconsin Conservation Fund revenues and expenditures, fiscal year 2017–18

Opening cash balance	$71,910,978
Revenues	338,539,046
User fees (licenses, registrations, recreational fees)	118,204,889
Forestry mill tax.	22,334,529
GPR transfer for forestry mill tax[1]	89,259,577
Federal aids	39,856,736
Motor fuel tax formula	22,362,031
Severance tax	1,318,170
Other revenues (sales, services)	45,203,114
Expenditures	304,450,776
Fish, wildlife, and parks—state	60,188,152
Fish, wildlife, and parks—federal	30,820,435
Forestry—state	50,217,824
Forestry—federal.	3,495,496
Enforcement—state	23,450,604

Wisconsin Conservation Fund revenues and expenditures, fiscal year 2017–18, continued

Enforcement—federal.	6,083,611
Environmental management—state.	1,964,993
Conservation aids—state.	30,854,146
Conservation aids—federal	6,010,268
Environmental aids—state.	7,229,769
Development/debt service—state.	22,677,941
Development/debt service—federal.	1,993,275
Administration—state.	1,991,523
Administration—federal	423,126
Internal and external services—state	35,457,689
Internal and external services—federal.	6,926,777
Other activities—state	14,665,147
Transfers	—
Fund balance	**$105,999,248**

Note: Because of reorganization of the Department of Natural Resources, 2017–18 expenditure categories are not comparable to those of prior years.

1. The forestry mill tax sunset as of January 1, 2017, property tax assessments. 2017 Wisconsin Act 59 provides for a GPR transfer to the conservation fund in an amount comparable to what would have been provided from the tax.

Source: Wisconsin Department of Administration, Division of Executive Budget and Finance, State Controller's Office, *2018 Annual Fiscal Report (Budgetary Basis) Appendix*, October 17, 2018.

Wisconsin Transportation Fund revenues and expenditures

	Fiscal year 2016–17		Fiscal year 2017–18	
Item	State funds ($)	Federal, local, and agency funds ($)	State funds ($)	Federal, local, and agency funds ($)
Opening balance	206,797,181	-798,247,072	219,123,383	-980,770,185
Revenues	1,726,091,565	763,187,961	1,783,904,310	1,007,435,278
Motor fuel taxes.	1,052,187,883	X	1,064,313,224	X
Vehicle registration[1]	465,985,689	X	493,607,554	X
Drivers license fees.	39,379,768	X	39,884,095	X
Motor carrier fees.	3,368,537	X	2,205,668	X
Other motor vehicle fees	25,802,402	X	26,765,446	X
Overweight/ oversize permits	6,185,925	X	6,669,984	X
Investment earnings.	777,943	X	6,387,610	X
Aeronautical taxes and fees	1,945,353	X	1,844,867	X
Public utility tax revenues (aeronautics and railroads)	52,451,223	X	46,940,610	X
Transfers-in[2]	66,840,838	X	73,669,306	X
Miscellaneous	11,166,004	2,449,852	21,615,946	3,763,700
Service center operations.	X	25,488,852	X	26,579,609
State and local highway facilities—federal.	X	560,861,209	X	689,285,451
State and local highway facilities—local	X	25,123,526	X	96,941,867
Major highway development revenue bonds	X	79,438,225	X	73,606,340
Highway administration and planning—federal.	X	827,964	X	3,697,564
Aeronautics—federal	X	23,946,136	X	39,231,608
Aeronautics—local.	X	1,785,083	X	7,513,290

Wisconsin Transportation Fund revenues and expenditures,
continued

Item	Fiscal year 2016–17 State funds ($)	Fiscal year 2016–17 Federal, local, and agency funds ($)	Fiscal year 2017–18 State funds ($)	Fiscal year 2017–18 Federal, local, and agency funds ($)
Railroad assistance—federal	X	1,416,044	X	1,843,034
Railroad assistance—local	X	3,320,206	X	3,726,094
Railroad passenger service—federal . . .	X	179,759	X	66,399
Railroad passenger service—local	X	—	X	1,185
Transit assistance—federal	X	16,034,867	X	13,587,169
Transit assistance—local	X	478,713	X	350,501
Congestion mitigation air quality— federal	X	2,047,477	X	824,563
Congestion mitigation air quality—local	X	101,624	X	210,630
Transportation facilities economic assistance and development—local . . .	X	33,769	X	-374
Transportation alternatives program— federal	X	11,491,400	X	5,771,360
Transportation alternatives program— local	X	1,128,152	X	3,365,153
General administration and planning— federal	X	3,924,169	X	29,009,654
General administration and planning— local	X	38,773	X	166,121
Administrative facilities—revenue bonds	X	1,615,885	X	—
Highway safety—federal	X	927,864	X	7,144,852
Gifts and grants	X	528,412	X	749,508
Expenditures[3]	**1,713,765,362**	**945,711,079**	**1,652,120,001**	**1,256,487,470**
Local assistance	624,578,882	218,290,720	650,411,139	264,355,112
Highway aids	437,552,758	—	458,178,111	—
Local bridge and highway improvement	41,655,194	151,079,685	40,834,407	176,166,880
Mass transit	125,773,447	15,419,375	128,493,765	18,923,334
Railroads	2,658,388	656,583	2,402,412	-853,710
Aeronautics	9,307,411	45,317,556	12,599,465	65,913,852
Highway safety	—	5,814,748	—	4,095,115
Rail passenger service	6,908,980	2,773	4,937,770	109,641
Harbors	722,704	—	2,965,209	—
Transportation alternatives program . .	—	—	—	—
Aids to individuals and organizations . .	9,153,809	15,405,789	9,481,936	11,474,488
Transportation facilities economic assistance and development	4,366,182	46,234	3,814,298	347,688
Railroad crossings	4,265,267	3,323,115	3,933,723	3,694,744
Elderly and disabled	522,360	2,848,982	1,733,915	3,037,687
Freight rail	—	9,187,458	—	4,394,369
State operations	1,059,946,846	712,014,570	972,189,229	980,657,870
Highway improvements	445,906,340	614,892,687	321,927,208	746,958,399
Major highway development—revenue bonds	—	8,749,880	—	176,978,028
Highway maintenance, repair, and traffic operations	261,615,336	17,527,875	285,863,540	6,420,953
Highway administration and planning	14,568,832	2,022,849	14,033,151	1,904,058
Traffic enforcement and inspection . . .	66,115,725	7,376,412	64,285,925	7,141,736
Transportation safety	1,244,325	4,025,335	1,642,969	3,302,066
General administration and planning .	64,208,935	9,535,584	67,172,245	16,876,472
Administrative facilities—revenue bonds	—	5,894,289	—	-2,888,865
Vehicle registration and drivers licensing	72,702,458	478,975	73,417,467	142,012

Wisconsin Transportation Fund revenues and expenditures,
continued

Item	Fiscal year 2016–17		Fiscal year 2017–18	
	State funds ($)	Federal, local, and agency funds ($)	State funds ($)	Federal, local, and agency funds ($)
Vehicle inspection and maintenance . .	2,595,960	—	2,595,960	—
Debt repayment and interest[4]	128,844,739	—	139,647,830	—
Service centers	—	30,002,563	—	20,331,732
Congestion mitigation air quality	—	506,940	—	1,620,251
Miscellaneous	2,144,196	11,001,181	1,602,934	1,871,028
Conservation Fund transfers	20,085,825	—	20,037,697	—
Closing balance	**219,123,384**	**-980,770,190**	**350,907,692**	**-1,229,822,377**

X–not applicable; — represents zero.

1. Section 84.59, Wisconsin Statutes, provides that vehicle registration revenues derived under s. 341.25 are deposited with a trustee in a fund outside the state treasury. Only those revenues not required for the repayment of revenue bond obligations are considered income to the transportation fund. The trustee retained $227.3 million during FY 2017, and $213.4 million during FY 2018. 2. Transfer-in amount for FY 2017 includes $39.1 million general fund, $27.3 million petroleum inspection fund, and $0.4 million conservation fund; and for FY 2018 includes $40.2 million general fund, $30.3 million petroleum inspection fund, and $3.2 million conservation fund. 3. The amounts exclude financial activity relating to general obligation bond funded projects that are reimbursed by the capital improvement fund. 4. 2017 Wisconsin Act 59 (the 2017–2019 biennial budget act) authorized $26.1 million in general obligation bond funding for railroad and harbor improvements. Debt service will be funded by the transportation fund. 2017 Wisconsin Act 58 authorized, contingent upon the receipt of federal moneys for certain purposes, up to $252.4 million in general obligation bond funding for southeast Wisconsin freeway megaprojects.

Source: Wisconsin Department of Administration, Division of Executive Budget and Finance, State Controller's Office, *2018 Annual Fiscal Report (Budgetary Basis) Appendix*, October 17, 2018.

COMMERCE AND INDUSTRY

Value added by manufacturing in Wisconsin

Industry group	2012 ($1,000)	2013 ($1,000)	2014 ($1,000)	2015 ($1,000)	2016 ($1,000)
Food manufacturing.	12,911,973	12,921,206	13,456,814	13,804,143	15,323,526
Machinery manufacturing	11,854,222	10,851,942	11,199,129	10,820,344	10,201,491
Fabricated metal product manufacturing. .	7,920,881	7,926,120	8,178,266	7,907,890	7,693,146
Chemical manufacturing	4,928,734	3,943,563	5,788,557	6,061,961	6,231,740
Paper manufacturing	6,500,354	6,061,120	6,193,379	6,360,489	6,120,441
Computer and electronic product manufacturing	4,789,267	4,928,628	4,792,239	4,488,886	4,709,640
Plastics and rubber products manufacturing	3,713,195	4,103,958	3,946,250	4,061,013	4,422,525
Electrical equipment, appliance, and component manufacturing.	3,903,286	3,906,224	3,913,824	3,920,074	4,100,086
Transportation equipment manufacturing	3,485,497	4,011,747	3,817,121	4,014,721	4,095,890
Printing and related support activities. . . .	3,168,552	3,057,978	2,903,377	2,809,449	2,924,793
Primary metal manufacturing	2,832,415	2,881,892	3,172,064	3,067,135	2,919,110
Nonmetallic mineral product manufacturing	2,067,500	2,127,199	2,286,320	2,335,148	2,446,309
Wood product manufacturing.	1,567,056	1,684,650	1,650,465	1,713,280	2,029,390
Miscellaneous manufacturing	1,612,006	2,807,904	1,771,675	1,752,515	1,732,885
Furniture and related product manufacturing	1,494,873	1,502,942	1,564,026	1,618,473	1,667,070
Beverage and tobacco product manufacturing	1,294,692	1,456,669	1,039,866	990,464	1,101,301
Petroleum and coal products manufacturing	D	D	D	D	863,111
Textile mills	D	D	D	D	162,570
Leather and allied product manufacturing .	D	D	D	D	111,021
Textile product mills	D	D	D	D	81,406
Apparel manufacturing	D	D	D	D	34,234
Total	83,508,979	83,545,379	82,959,072	80,588,078	78,971,684

D–figure withheld to avoid discloser.

1. Total may not add due to the exclusion of manufacturing categories beneath the top twenty highest values.

Source: U.S. Census Bureau, "Annual Survey of Manufacturers, Geographic Area Statistics, 2016" and previous editions, at https://www.census.gov/programs-surveys/asm.html [March 15, 2019].

Value of Wisconsin exports by category

	2016 ($1,000)	2017 ($1,000)	2018 ($1,000)	% change 2017 to 2018
Top 20 categories[1] in 2018	**17,046,709**	**18,252,766**	**17,350,414**	**-4.94**
Industrial machinery, including computers . .	5,205,894	5,400,359	5,736,785	6.23
Electric machinery.	1,977,679	2,220,227	2,572,927	15.89
Optic, photo, medical or surgical instruments	2,335,764	2,201,060	2,153,969	-2.14
Vehicles and parts (not railway).	1,566,089	1,907,643	1,412,195	-25.97
Plastics	1,030,074	1,058,744	1,146,069	8.25
Paper and paperboard	854,617	881,894	888,717	0.77

Value of Wisconsin exports by category, continued

	2016 ($1,000)	2017 ($1,000)	2018 ($1,000)	% change 2017 to 2018
Aircraft, spacecraft, and parts	586,774	749,837	729,701	-2.69
Iron and steel products.	402,579	454,877	456,205	0.29
Miscellaneous chemical products	368,616	400,028	429,654	7.41
Pharmaceutical products	283,603	325,674	393,934	20.96
Miscellaneous food	296,901	331,700	366,214	10.41
Prepared vegetables, fruits, and nuts	314,628	342,027	354,800	3.73
Furniture and bedding	306,247	281,651	307,733	9.26
Salt, sulfur, stone, lime and cement plaster . .	96,075	176,409	289,094	63.88
Dairy, eggs, honey, etc.	251,632	298,612	282,263	-5.48
Books, newspapers, etc.	258,827	281,198	272,384	-3.13
Wood	224,983	255,696	269,773	5.51
Prepared meats and fish	192,628	236,155	245,735	4.06
Beverages, spirits, and vinegar	275,388	227,878	233,221	2.34
Essential oils, perfumes, and cosmetics	217,713	221,096	221,236	0.06
All categories	**21,032,745**	**22,306,123**	**22,709,323**	**1.81**

1. Export categories based on U.S. Census Bureau commodity codes.

Source: Wisconsin Economic Development Corporation, "Wisconsin Export Data," https://wedc.org/export/wisconsin-export-data/ [March 15, 2019].

Value of Wisconsin exports by market

	2016 ($1,000)	2017 ($1,000)	2018 ($1,000)	% change 2017 to 2018
Top 20 markets in 2018	**17,589,811**	**18,483,403**	**19,316,723**	**4.51**
Canada.	6,604,422	6,910,542	7,026,881	1.68
Mexico	3,056,304	3,196,139	3,452,912	8.03
China	1,427,167	1,732,109	1,633,403	-5.70
Germany.	625,131	692,292	814,002	17.58
United Kingdom	814,280	736,600	792,216	7.55
Japan	861,205	788,517	734,269	-6.88
Republic of Korea	478,401	516,504	591,401	14.50
Australia	558,663	558,901	572,808	2.49
France	437,272	454,949	497,963	9.45
Netherlands.	404,444	407,613	448,529	10.04
Belgium	384,274	362,788	397,824	9.66
Brazil	236,099	284,180	392,802	38.22
Italy	242,130	265,025	319,084	20.40
Hong Kong	230,104	318,409	290,796	-8.67
India	248,241	287,358	280,252	-2.47
Thailand	213,251	193,911	267,223	37.81
Singapore	201,160	205,485	221,133	7.62
United Arab Emirates	221,828	190,336	199,496	4.81
Taiwan	185,319	165,830	196,287	18.37
Chile	160,119	215,914	187,439	-13.19
All markets	**21,032,745**	**22,306,123**	**22,709,323**	**1.81**

Source: Wisconsin Economic Development Corporation, "Wisconsin Export Data," https://wedc.org/export/wisconsin-export-data/ [March 15, 2019].

Basic data on Wisconsin corporations

	Transactions[1]			Fees			
	Domestic						
Year[2]	Articles of incorpora- tion filed[3]	Amdts. and restated articles	Foreign corporations licensed	Fees for articles of incorporation	Fees for foreign cor- poration[4]	Other corporation fees[5]	Total fees collected
Calendar							
1905	98	NA	95	NA	NA	NA	$69,312.00
1915	1,043	382	112	$28,287.00	$3,743.00	$89,695.00	121,725
1925	1,438	896	198	57,614	11,139	78,153	146,906
1935	1,272	439	176	30,839	8,956	41,631	81,426
1945	1,120	680	131	31,823	4,826	113,963	150,612
1955	2,537	874	287	89,951	31,146	175,973	297,070
1965	4,063	1,320	401	344,906	120,506	193,844	659,256
Fiscal							
1975	5,976	1,483	663	361,013	386,061	594,498	1,341,572
1980	7,334	1,978	753	373,220	753,461	788,204	1,914,885
1985	7,605	2,359	1,018	485,835	1,142,129	1,371,476	2,999,440
1990	8,387	2,525	1,408	546,550	2,368,900	1,491,104	4,406,554
1995	10,031	2,716	1,507	829,555	4,208,178	2,538,521	7,576,254
2000	21,133	3,088	2,464	2,265,455	6,403,447	3,548,264	12,217,166
2001	20,461	3,064	2,394	2,631,375	6,901,290	3,257,622	12,790,287
2002	22,734	3,145	2,314	2,735,390	6,330,109	3,408,267	12,473,766
2003	26,629	3,057	2,436	3,223,455	7,379,300	5,262,635	15,865,390
2004	31,440	3,644	2,566	3,820,735	6,253,800	6,406,280	16,480,815
2005	33,589	3,595	2,787	4,092,782	6,043,400	5,509,178	15,645,000
2006	33,829	3,711	3,010	4,084,800	8,693,800	4,149,400	16,928,000
2007	32,555	3,596	3,067	1,525,538	5,406,350	6,208,548	17,113,116
2008	31,943	3,401	2,900	1,488,312	5,871,084	7,264,855	18,534,351
2009	27,212	2,273	2,459	5,074,039	7,554,100	5,079,361	17,707,500
2010	27,349	2,231	2,495	5,247,361	8,311,900	5,291,939	18,851,200
2011	28,535	2,210	2,706	10,303,300	7,696,300	723,400	18,723,000
2012	30,014	2,166	2,817	10,599,880	8,345,500	700,200	19,645,500
2013	34,045	2,907	3,100	10,911,200	8,701,600	751,900	20,364,700
2014	35,955	2,917	3,400	11,206,000	9,379,000	784,100	21,369,100
2015	36,576	2,804	3,523	11,746,200	7,820,600	844,400	20,411,200
2016	38,304	3,203	3,701	13,643,500	6,659,700	748,700	21,051,900

Amdts.– Amendments; NA–not available

1. Includes only those corporate entities for which the reporting agency is the office of record. 2. Since 1975, data is computed on a fiscal year basis, ending June 30 of year shown. 3. Beginning in 1997, includes limited liability companies. 4. Since 1975, totals include fees for foreign corporation annual reports. 5. Includes fees for filing annual reports and corporation charter documents other than articles of incorporation.

Sources: Wisconsin Department of Financial Institutions, departmental data for 2000–2016, Feb. 2017; previous data from the Office of the Wisconsin Secretary of State.

Financial institutions operating in Wisconsin

Year[1]	Number	Total deposits ($1,000)	Year[1]	Number	Total deposits ($1,000)
1900.	349	$124,892	1950.	556	2,965,580
1910.	630	268,766	1960.	561	4,385,838
1920.	976	767,534	1970.	602	8,750,823
1930.	936	935,006	1980.	634	24,763,910
1940.	574	993,155	1990.	504	37,588,879

Financial institutions operating in Wisconsin, continued

Year[1]	Number	Total deposits ($1,000)	Year[1]	Number	Total deposits ($1,000)
1995............	449	59,918,000	2009............	302	125,785,000
2000............	365	75,379,000	2010............	299	126,660,000
2001............	337	78,567,000	2011............	296	128,628,000
2002............	328	83,602,000	2012............	295	132,812,000
2003............	319	$95,909,000	2013............	285	129,714,000
2004............	322	$96,111,000	2014............	278	136,508,000
2005............	318	100,643,000	2015............	269	140,261,259
2006............	320	103,511,000	2016............	257	143,503,620
2007............	316	109,734,000	2017............	241	155,033,560
2008............	307	114,838,000	2018............	236	150,113,628

1. Beginning in 1994, data includes federal charter savings associations and state-chartered savings associations, supervised by the U.S. Office of Thrift Supervision, and institutions operating in Wisconsin but headquartered outside the state. Deposits for these years are rounded to nearest thousands of dollars.

Sources: 1950 and earlier: Board of Governors of the Federal Reserve System, All-Bank Statistics, U.S., 1959; 1960: Wisconsin Commissioner of Banks, agency data, December 1965; 1970: Federal Deposit Insurance Corporation, Assets and Liabilities— Commercial and Mutual Savings Banks, June 1971; 1980: Federal Deposit Insurance Corporation, corporate data; 1981–93: Federal Deposit Insurance Corporation, Data Book: Operating Banks and Branches, Book 3, June 30, 1993, and previous issues; 1994 to date: Federal Deposit Insurance Corporation, Summary of Deposits, "State Totals by Charter Class for All Institution Deposits, Deposits of All FDIC-Insured Institutions Operating in Wisconsin," June 30, 2018, and previous issues.

FDIC-insured institutions operating in Wisconsin, June 30, 2018

County	Commercial banks Institutions	Offices	Deposits (mil. dols.)	Savings institutions Institutions	Offices	Deposits (mil. dols.)
Adams	5	6	215	1	1	4
Ashland.	4	9	332	—	—	—
Barron.	9	22	876	1	1	109
Bayfield.	4	11	268	—	—	—
Brown.	17	66	6,944	1	6	143
Buffalo	4	10	291	—	—	—
Burnett	3	7	264	—	—	—
Calumet	7	12	497	1	1	29
Chippewa	12	22	823	1	2	15
Clark.	8	11	369	2	4	148
Columbia.	11	27	1,363	—	—	—
Crawford	5	10	407	—	—	—
Dane	35	161	16,409	4	7	3,144
Dodge	13	30	1,110	2	2	111
Door.	3	12	674	1	2	79
Douglas.	5	9	547	1	1	53
Dunn	8	16	409	—	—	—
Eau Claire.	16	32	2,224	1	1	1
Florence	2	4	111	—	—	—
Fond du Lac	10	32	1,965	1	1	176
Forest	2	6	148	—	—	—
Grant	11	40	1,228	—	—	—
Green	11	20	968	—	—	—
Green Lake.	8	13	681	—	—	—
Iowa.	8	14	462	—	—	—
Iron	2	3	77	—	—	—
Jackson.	3	9	270	—	—	—

FDIC-insured institutions operating in Wisconsin, June 30, 2018, continued

County	Commercial banks			Savings institutions		
	Institutions	Offices	Deposits (mil. dols.)	Institutions	Offices	Deposits (mil. dols.)
Jefferson	13	29	1,193	—	—	—
Juneau	6	14	412	—	—	—
Kenosha	10	35	2,506	1	3	65
Kewaunee	4	12	453	—	—	—
La Crosse	14	38	2,146	—	—	—
Lafayette	8	12	348	—	—	—
Langlade	4	6	90	—	—	—
Lincoln	5	7	282	1	2	118
Manitowoc	10	21	2,059	—	—	—
Marathon	17	50	3,173	3	5	218
Marinette	9	19	836	—	—	—
Marquette	6	9	206	—	—	—
Milwaukee	21	196	42,195	8	44	2,094
Monroe	10	16	750	—	—	—
Oconto	7	14	323	—	—	—
Oneida	8	16	796	—	—	—
Outagamie	21	45	3,293	3	8	229
Ozaukee	12	33	2,544	3	4	118
Pepin	3	3	205	—	—	—
Pierce	8	14	553	—	—	—
Polk	11	14	636	—	—	—
Portage	14	24	1,576	1	1	2
Price	3	5	172	1	1	88
Racine	12	45	3,047	2	6	185
Richland	7	9	263	—	—	—
Rock	17	37	2,705	—	—	—
Rusk	5	8	231	1	1	46
St. Croix	14	25	1,186	—	—	—
Sauk	13	28	1,472	—	—	—
Sawyer	6	9	395	—	—	—
Shawano	9	16	474	—	—	—
Sheboygan	13	37	2,013	—	—	—
Taylor	4	5	245	2	2	174
Trempealeau	9	19	608	—	—	—
Vernon	7	14	446	—	—	—
Vilas	11	14	479	—	—	—
Walworth	15	36	1,599	—	—	—
Washburn	6	8	322	—	—	—
Washington	14	40	2,871	1	1	96
Waukesha	28	151	11,102	7	21	1,347
Waupaca	7	21	849	—	—	—
Waushara	8	11	264	—	—	—
Winnebago	15	34	2,101	2	2	58
Wood	11	23	1,440	4	5	481
Total[1]	**677**	**1,826**	**139,351**	**57**	**135**	**9,331**

Note: Menominee County did not report seperately.

— Represents zero.

1. Total number of institutions is an unduplicated total for institutions operating in more than one county. Deposit figures do not add to state totals due to rounding.

Source: Federal Deposit Insurance Corporation, "Deposits of all FDIC-Insured Institutions: State Totals by County," data as of June 30, 2018, at https://www5.fdic.gov/sod/sodSummary.asp?barItem=3https://www5.fdic.gov/sod/sodInstBranchRpt.asp?sCounty=all&sCityType=USPS&submit1=Continue&barItem=1

Wisconsin financial institutions, June 30, 2018

Type of institution or branch	Insured commercial banks and trust companies				Insured savings institutions		
			State charter				
	Total	National charter	FRS[1] member	FRS non-member	Total	Federal charter	State charter
Headquartered in state	208	22	21	141	24	10	14
Headquartered outside of state	28	10	4	13	1	1	0
Total institutions	236	32	25	154	25	11	14
Total offices	1,971	976	140	720	135	73	62
Total deposits (mil. dol.).	150,114	94,743	10,486	35,556	9,329	6,185	3,144

FRS–Federal Reserve System.

Source: Federal Deposit Insurance Corporation, Summary of Deposits, June 30, 2018, "Individual State Tables—Charter Class," https://www5.fdic.gov/sod/sodSummary.asp?barItem=3 [April 8, 2019].

Wisconsin state-chartered credit unions

Year	Number of credit unions	Total members (% chg. from prior yr.)	Total assets in mil. dols. (% chg. from prior yr.)
1930.	22	4,659 (NA)	0.5 (NA)
1935.	383	57,847 (NA)	2.9 (NA)
1940.	592	153,849 (NA)	11.2 (NA)
1945.	536	144,524 (NA)	19.1 (NA)
1950.	542	193,296 (NA)	42.9 (NA)
1955.	696	292,552 (NA)	120.6 (NA)
1960.	733	363,444 (NA)	206.4 (NA)
1965.	781	493,399 (NA)	346.6 (NA)
1970.	766	628,543 (NA)	480.4 (NA)
1975.	673	805,123 (NA)	875.5 (NA)
1980.	618	1,060,292 (NA)	1,403.8 (NA)
1985.	550	1,261,407 (NA)	2,831.4 (NA)
1990.	440	1,485,109 (4.3)	4,148.8 (8.6)
1995.	384	1,744,696 (1.8)	6,179.2 (7.4)
2000.	340	1,918,729 (1.7)	9,425.9 (7.9)
2001.	326	1,883,387 (-1.8)	10,439.4 (10.8)
2002.	308	1,937,867 (2.9)	11,665.6 (11.7)
2003.	298	1,966,929 (1.5)	12,772.5 (9.5)
2004.	287	1,992,238 (1.3)	13,684.4 (7.1)
2005.	280	2,047,031 (2.8)	14,805.3 (8.2)
2006.	267	2,086,700 (1.9)	15,656.2 (5.7)
2007.	260	2,083,319 (-0.2)	16,543.3 (5.7)
2008.	250	2,118,505 (1.7)	18,182.3 (9.9)
2009.	236	2,164,648 (2.2)	19,719. (8.5)
2010.	223	2,186,471 (1.0)	20,685.4 (4.9)
2011.	203	2,225,892 (1.8)	21,915.6 (5.9)
2012.	187	2,264,788 (1.7)	23,353.8 (6.6)
2013.	171	2,335,239 (3.1)	24,517.9 (5.0)
2014.	160	2,460,025 (5.3)	26,324.6 (7.4)
2015.	150	2,613,667 (6.2)	28,797.1 (9.4)
2016.	143	2,790,644 (6.8)	31,453.3 (9.2)
2017.	129	2,938,267 (5.3)	34,157.2 (8.6)
2018.	125	3,081,193 (4.9)	37,012.0 (8.4)

NA–Not available.

Source: Wisconsin Department of Financial Institutions, Office of Credit Unions, *2018 Year End Credit Union Bulletin*, at: https://www.wdfi.org/_resources/indexed/site/fi/cu/QuarterlyReports/2018/2018YearEndBulletin.pdf [April 2018], and previous editions.

Wisconsin's tribal gaming facilities

Casino	Location	Tribe
Legendary Waters Resort and Casino	Bayfield	Red Cliff Band (Lake Superior Chippewa)
Bad River Casino	Odanah	Bad River Band (Lake Superior Chippewa)
Lake of the Torches Resort Casino . .	Lac du Flambeau	Lac du Flambeau Band (Lake Superior Chippewa)
Sevenwinds Casino	Hayward	Lac Courte Oreilles Band (Lake Superior Chippewa)
Grindstone Creek Casino	Hayward	Lac Courte Oreilles Band (Lake Superior Chippewa)
St. Croix Casino Danbury	Danbury	St. Croix Band (Lake Superior Chippewa)
St. Croix Casino Hertel.	Hertel	St. Croix Band (Lake Superior Chippewa)
St. Croix Casino Turtle Lake.	Turtle Lake	St. Croix Band (Lake Superior Chippewa)
Mole Lake Casino.	Crandon	Sokaogon Chippewa Community
Potawatomi Carter Casino and Hotel.	Carter	Forest County Potawatomi Community
Menominee Casino Resort	Keshena	Menominee Tribe
The Thunderbird	Keshena	Menominee Tribe
North Star Mohican Casino Resort . .	Bowler	Stockbridge-Munsee Band (Mohican Nation)
Ho-Chunk Gaming Wittenberg	Wittenberg	Ho-Chunk Nation
Ho-Chunk Gaming Black River Falls .	Black River Falls	Ho-Chunk Nation
Ho-Chunk Gaming Nekoosa	Nekoosa	Ho-Chunk Nation
Ho-Chunk Gaming Tomah	Tomah	Ho-Chunk Nation
Ho-Chunk Gaming Wisconsin Dells. .	Baraboo	Ho-Chunk Nation
Potawatomi Hotel & Casino	Milwaukee	Forest County Potawatomi Community
Oneida Casino.	Green Bay	Oneida Nation
IMAC Casino/Bingo.	Green Bay	Oneida Nation
Oneida Mason Street Casino.	Green Bay	Oneida Nation
Oneida One-Stop Packerland	Green Bay	Oneida Nation
Oneida Casino Travel Center	Oneida	Oneida Nation

Note: Only Class III gaming facilities regulated by tribal compact are included, pursuant to P.L. 100-497, the Indian Gaming Regulatory Act, which divides gambling into three classes. An additional Ho-Chunk casino in Madison offers Class II gaming. Class I games are social games played solely for prizes of minimal value or traditional forms of Indian gaming played in connection with tribal ceremonies or celebrations. Class II includes bingo or bingo-type games, pull-tabs and punch-boards, and certain nonbanking card games, such as poker. Class III covers all other forms of gaming.

Source: Wisconsin Legislative Fiscal Bureau, Informational Paper 86: *Tribal Gaming in Wisconsin*, January 2019.

EMPLOYMENT AND INCOME

Employment trends in Wisconsin

Year	Labor force (1,000)	Employed (1,000)	Unem-ployed (1,000)	Unem-ployment rate (%)	Total non-farm em-ployment (1,000)	Service providing (1,000)	Goods producing (1,000)	Manu-facturing (1,000)	Trade, trans-portation, and utilities (1,000)
1995	2,859.8	2,750.2	109.6	3.8	2,540.5	1,869.0	671.5	565.4	496.9
1996	2,908.6	2,797.3	111.3	3.8	2,587.7	1,914.2	673.5	564.4	507.2
1997	2,946.1	2,839.0	107.1	3.6	2,623.6	1,940.8	682.8	567.5	511.5
1998	2,983.7	2,887.0	96.7	3.2	2,689.0	1,982.1	706.9	590.2	519.6
1999	2,955.0	2,856.0	99.0	3.4	2,750.6	2,034.2	716.4	592.9	534.2
2000	2,960.2	2,865.5	94.7	3.2	2,814.0	2,090.1	723.9	596.4	548.8
2001	3,004.5	2,887.2	117.2	3.9	2,835.6	2,123.9	711.7	582.9	556.9
2002	3,012.8	2,850.7	162.1	5.4	2,783.2	2,118.0	665.2	537.1	540.3
2003	3,049.8	2,878.7	171.2	5.6	2,773.4	2,130.9	642.5	514.3	535.6
2004	3,047.4	2,885.6	161.7	5.3	2,780.3	2,152.2	628.1	498.4	536.7
2005	3,011.5	2,868.9	142.5	4.7	2,818.6	2,185.9	632.7	501.8	539.0
2006	3,037.4	2,893.8	143.6	4.7	2,849.4	2,210.3	639.1	505.9	542.7
2007	3,084.2	2,934.9	149.3	4.8	2,870.2	2,236.1	634.1	503.0	547.7
2008	3,087.0	2,947.4	139.6	4.5	2,882.6	2,256.6	626.0	499.8	546.4
2009	3,110.4	2,891.3	219.1	7.0	2,808.1	2,228.0	580.1	468.4	527.3
2010	3,083.4	2,797.7	285.8	9.3	2,710.1	2,186.9	523.2	423.8	507.9
2011	3,078.6	2,831.2	247.4	8.0	2,742.2	2,208.2	534.0	438.0	509.1
2012	3,073.3	2,853.5	219.8	7.2	2,756.7	2,208.4	548.3	451.9	512.3
2013	3,078.7	2,864.4	214.3	7.0	2,784.4	2,226.3	558.1	457.7	514.4
2014	3,075.8	2,888.7	187.1	6.1	2,830.5	2,266.0	564.5	460.3	520.5
2015	3,088.4	2,939.4	149.0	4.8	2,873.5	2,293.8	579.7	467.8	526.3
2016	3,116.5	2,983.8	132.7	4.3	2,916.4	2,335.1	581.3	465.9	536.6
2017	3,131.1	3,018.1	113.0	3.6	2,938.4	2,354.5	583.9	465.1	542.5
2018	3,141.4	3,049.2	92.2	2.9	2,967.8	2,370.2	597.6	472.0	544.8
2019	3,127.1	3,033.4	93.7	3.0	2,988.6	2,380.5	608.1	477.5	548.6

Note: Data are estimates that are revised monthly and annually and are seasonally adjusted. Industry classifications in this table are defined by the North American Industry Classification System (NAICS).

Sources: Wisconsin Department of Workforce Development, WisConomy, Wisconsin Labor Market Information Data Access, Local Area Unemployment Statistics at: https://www.jobcenterofwisconsin.com/wisconomy/query and Current Employment Statistics at https://www.jobcenterofwisconsin.com/wisconomy/query#ces_dl [March 19, 2019].

Annual employment in Wisconsin

Industry	2014	2015	2016	2017	2018
Labor force.	3,081,543	3,092,181	3,125,311	3,140,410	3,133,294
Unemployment.	166,551	140,698	125,080	102,957	93,999
Unemployment rate.	5.4%	4.6%	4.0%	3.3%	3.0%
Employment.	2,914,992	2,951,483	3,000,231	3,037,453	3,039,295
Total nonfarm.	2,852,300	2,892,000	2,926,400	2,947,900	2,971,500
Service providing.	2,279,900	2,311,100	2,345,300	2,358,900	2,369,000
Goods producing.	572,400	580,800	581,100	589,100	602,500
Trade, transportation, and utilities	524,200	531,100	539,300	542,300	543,200
Manufacturing	464,700	467,300	464,800	467,300	475,500
Educational and health services.	430,500	436,200	444,800	451,000	456,100
Professional and business services	308,100	315,400	322,600	325,800	326,800
Local government	285,200	283,600	287,200	283,300	285,000
Leisure and hospitality	264,100	270,900	275,900	280,300	282,600
Finance.	150,000	151,200	151,900	152,900	152,900
Other services.	143,300	148,100	149,900	151,400	152,300

Annual employment in Wisconsin, continued

Industry	2014	2015	2016	2017	2018
Construction	103,600	109,400	112,600	117,400	122,200
State government	98,000	96,900	95,600	95,100	93,700
Information	48,000	48,900	49,100	47,900	47,300
Federal government.	28,600	28,800	29,000	29,000	29,100
Natural resources and mining	4,100	4,200	3,800	4,300	4,800

Note: Industry classifications in this table are defined by the North American Industry Classification System (NAICS).

Source: Wisconsin Department of Workforce Development, WisConomy, Wisconsin Labor Market Information Access at: https://www.jobcenterofwisconsin.com/wisconomy/query.

Manufacturing employment in Wisconsin

Industry group	2014	2015	2016	2017	2018
Durable goods	283,500	284,400	280,000	280,300	286,500
Selected detail:					
Fabricated metal product manufacturing.	74,200	74,600	72,900	73,600	76,100
Machinery manufacturing	68,300	67,700	65,500	65,100	67,000
transportation equipment manufacturing	26,700	26,800	26,700	26,800	26,300
Electrical equipment and appliances.	23,700	24,100	23,700	23,800	24,300
Wood product manufacturing.	17,100	17,400	17,500	17,600	17,900
Nondurable goods	181,200	182,900	184,800	187,000	189,000
Selected detail:					
Food manufacturing.	64,300	64,400	65,600	67,700	69,500
Plastics and rubber products manufacturing. . .	31,300	32,000	32,200	32,800	33,700
Paper manufacturing	30,700	30,600	30,400	29,900	29,600
Printing and related support activities.	29,300	29,800	29,700	29,000	28,100
Total.	**464,700**	**467,300**	**464,800**	**467,300**	**475,500**

Source: Department of Workforce Development, WisConomy, Wisconsin Labor Market Information Data Access at: https://www.jobcenterofwisconsin.com/wisconomy/query [March 20, 2019].

Wisconsin personal income

	Personal income (mil. dol.)	Per capita personal income		
		Amount (dol.)	State rank	% of national average
1930.	1,724.7	585	18	95
1935.	1,415.6	461	19	97
1940.	1,723.3	548	21	92
1945.	3,527.0	1,191	22	96
1950.	5,209.0	1,515	24	100
1955.	6,955.7	1,891	21	98
1960.	8,994.3	2,270	20	99
1965.	11,798.4	2,788	22	98
1970.	17,648.8	3,988	21	97
1975.	27,872.0	6,099	25	99
1980.	47,282.0	10,034	20	100
1985.	66,276.7	13,960	28	94
1990.	90,431.2	18,438	24	93
1995.	119,327.1	23,015	24	96
2000.	158,927.6	29,573	20	96
2005.	190,527.6	34,353	21	97

Wisconsin personal income, continued

	Personal income (mil. dol.)	Per capita personal income		
		Amount (dol.)	State rank	% of national average
2010.	221,895.3	38,995	28	95
2015.	268,238.0	46,571	25	95

1. Personal income includes all forms of income received by persons from business establishments; federal, state, and local governments; households and institutions; and foreign countries. Allowance is made for "in-kind" income not received as cash. 2. Per capita personal income is total personal income divided by total midyear population.

Source: U.S. Department of Commerce, Bureau of Economic Analysis, Regional Data, Table SAINC1, Personal Income Summary: Personal Income, Population, Per Capita Personal Income, 2017 and previous editions at https://apps.bea.gov/iTable/iTable.cfm?acrdn=6&isuri=1&reqid=70&step=1#reqid=70&step=1&isuri=1 [March 2019].

Wisconsin personal income, by industry

Industry	2013 (mil.dol.)	2014 (mil.dol.)	2015 (mil.dol.)	2016 (mil.dol.)	2017 (mil.dol.)
Services[1]	59,030	61,235	63,631	66,478	68,663
Manufacturing	33,059	33,829	34,601	34,041	35,294
Government and government enterprises	27,501	28,341	28,453	28,893	29,366
Finance and insurance	11,349	10,989	11,380	12,157	12,676
Retail trade.	10,319	10,751	11,276	11,467	11,780
Construction	9,583	10,452	11,221	11,684	12,572
Wholesale trade	9,107	9,429	9,829	10,076	10,676
Transportation and warehousing	6,227	6,545	6,882	6,924	7,203
Information	3,981	4,300	4,478	4,473	4,591
Farm earnings.	3,091	3,112	2,850	1,999	1,758
Real estate and rental and leasing	2,642	2,667	2,987	3,150	3,094
Utilities	1,534	1,594	1,624	1,563	1,591
Forestry, fishing, and related activities.	485	529	628	653	661
Mining, quarrying, and oil and gas extraction	509	430	311	265	325
Total[2]	247,127	257,572	$268,238	$273,787	$283,636

1. Services includes the following NAICS classification categories: professional, scientific and technical services; management of companies and enterprises; administrative and waste management services; educational services; health care and social assistance; arts, entertainment, and recreation; accommodation and food services; and other services (except government). 2. Total may not add due to rounding.

Source: U.S. Department of Commerce, Bureau of Economic Analysis, Regional Data, "Table SAINC5N: Personal Income by Major Component and Earnings by NAICS Industry," at: https://apps.bea.gov/iTable/iTable.cfm?acrdn=6&isuri=1&reqid=70&step=1#reqid=70&step=1&isuri=1 [March 19, 2019].

Wisconsin adjusted gross income

County	2017 AGI[1] ($)	per return AGI					2017 rank[3]
		2013 ($)	2014 ($)	2015 ($)	2016 ($)	2017 ($)	
Adams	361,771,594	33,770	34,240	35,544	36,292	38,307	68
Ashland.	288,627,337	35,290	35,770	36,628	37,658	38,219	69
Barron.	1,091,761,854	41,420	41,070	43,293	44,329	46,537	41
Bayfield.	353,066,757	42,220	42,490	46,466	44,402	46,050	43
Brown.	8,177,764,317	55,140	56,360	59,421	61,239	62,528	7
Buffalo	285,591,643	39,520	39,590	40,732	40,861	41,796	61
Burnett.	297,891,405	34,980	36,670	38,158	39,356	40,392	66

Wisconsin adjusted gross income, continued

County	2017 AGI[1] ($)	per return AGI					2017 rank[3]
		2013 ($)	2014 ($)	2015 ($)	2016 ($)	2017 ($)	
Calumet	1,467,634,678	57,920	60,060	62,299	62,718	63,548	6
Chippewa	1,559,230,935	44,880	45,960	47,585	49,686	51,372	29
Clark.	673,365,642	39,430	40,200	42,578	40,838	45,156	47
Columbia.	1,654,644,700	48,280	50,080	50,928	52,614	55,170	19
Crawford	338,802,339	35,350	35,500	39,526	41,574	43,320	52
Dane	20,226,279,808	63,890	65,660	68,051	70,303	72,928	3
Dodge	2,203,932,328	47,640	49,120	49,139	49,596	51,596	28
Door.	856,266,497	48,040	49,940	50,845	51,463	54,808	21
Douglas.	938,083,032	41,830	42,890	44,577	45,106	45,675	44
Dunn	1,002,063,992	44,090	45,180	46,468	46,967	50,807	31
Eau Claire.	2,870,598,924	68,660	75,290	57,602	54,543	57,056	12
Florence	91,619,154	38,080	40,590	40,881	44,776	43,900	49
Fond du Lac	2,883,163,205	49,620	51,530	53,402	53,666	56,779	13
Forest	159,151,116	31,280	33,100	35,160	35,742	37,544	70
Grant	993,369,295	39,520	41,030	41,690	41,841	43,177	53
Green	1,039,122,121	49,770	50,180	52,928	52,040	55,858	16
Green Lake.	441,272,989	45,690	44,280	51,836	44,759	46,745	39
Iowa.	621,757,488	47,440	49,470	50,263	50,837	52,209	27
Iron	125,365,215	34,980	36,750	37,477	38,702	39,836	67
Jackson	406,626,651	40,680	42,340	40,717	43,113	43,116	54
Jefferson	2,311,728,712	47,080	48,110	50,124	50,421	56,012	15
Juneau	510,096,603	36,220	36,630	38,654	39,136	41,147	63
Kenosha	4,370,085,181	48,130	49,520	51,439	52,410	53,570	24
Kewaunee	518,021,979	46,160	47,030	48,885	48,394	50,956	30
La Crosse	3,253,790,874	51,070	52,350	53,781	54,610	56,217	14
Lafayette	334,139,912	41,610	40,270	41,924	42,075	42,904	55
Langlade	399,017,121	37,440	37,250	39,353	40,203	41,182	62
Lincoln	664,350,895	42,490	42,330	46,188	44,994	46,158	42
Manitowoc.	2,184,681,195	46,460	47,560	49,208	48,594	54,314	22
Marathon.	3,912,180,775	51,040	52,250	55,310	57,027	57,099	11
Marinette.	866,261,228	38,700	41,710	40,965	41,483	42,162	59
Marquette	326,169,558	38,050	39,250	38,216	40,010	42,631	56
Menominee	14,072,730	15,600	16,470	19,003	17,164	7,415	72
Milwaukee	22,944,629,585	45,620	45,980	48,533	49,692	50,516	32
Monroe	976,661,307	39,850	41,970	42,927	43,661	45,432	45
Oconto	899,678,572	44,030	45,000	47,394	48,296	49,069	34
Oneida	920,907,922	43,460	44,960	46,809	51,505	48,710	35
Outagamie.	5,981,217,914	55,050	56,480	58,774	60,762	62,398	8
Ozaukee	4,624,579,558	93,280	96,420	99,050	99,649	102,425	1
Pepin	188,797,202	46,990	49,930	50,151	48,706	52,444	26
Pierce	1,136,673,863	54,150	55,690	58,918	57,791	58,999	10
Polk	1,020,965,672	43,190	45,200	46,111	46,335	47,955	38
Portage	1,806,865,242	47,550	49,210	51,402	51,056	52,738	25
Price	287,397,807	36,340	38,800	39,992	40,348	40,992	64
Racine.	5,247,654,246	49,890	51,060	52,380	53,002	54,073	23
Richland	337,832,175	36,940	38,710	39,631	40,139	42,415	58
Rock.	4,399,308,982	45,690	45,160	48,142	50,800	54,847	20
Rusk.	245,281,461	33,620	35,870	35,734	36,261	37,534	71
St. Croix.	3,041,080,353	63,260	66,290	68,133	68,823	70,628	4
Sauk.	1,682,024,170	45,000	45,830	47,398	47,658	49,560	33
Sawyer	319,733,611	35,780	37,230	38,373	40,562	40,509	65
Shawano	874,095,715	39,300	40,740	41,421	41,340	44,768	48
Sheboygan.	3,280,543,775	50,220	50,690	53,311	53,418	55,348	18
Taylor.	414,090,956	40,670	42,270	44,184	43,706	45,345	46
Trempealeau.	702,487,091	52,530	47,950	48,587	44,875	46,649	40
Vernon	586,756,313	41,920	40,970	42,168	42,004	43,827	50
Vilas	487,745,329	37,280	39,320	40,998	45,135	43,819	51

Wisconsin adjusted gross income, continued

County	2017 AGI[1] ($)	per return AGI					2017 rank[3]
		2013 ($)	2014 ($)	2015 ($)	2016 ($)	2017 ($)	
Walworth.	2,758,352,093	49,330	55,540	54,723	53,804	55,567	17
Washburn	352,044,491	37,050	38,070	40,835	39,664	41,880	60
Washington	4,691,004,264	61,020	62,340	64,558	65,642	68,180	5
Waukesha	17,831,208,698	78,080	79,410	83,021	85,796	86,671	2
Waupaca	1,256,830,226	44,250	45,140	47,009	46,361	48,262	37
Waushara.	480,653,947	39,230	39,570	40,600	40,765	42,483	57
Winnebago	4,918,215,933	51,090	52,400	54,613	55,890	59,145	9
Wood	1,856,092,646	45,530	45,860	46,653	48,418	48,470	36
Total.	174,549,454,998	50,670	52,050	54,227	55,267	56,698	

1. "Wisconsin adjusted gross income" (AGI) is Wisconsin income as reported to the Wisconsin Department of Revenue for income tax purposes and is based on the federal income tax definition of gross income as modified by certain additions and subtractions required by state law. 2. State totals and state per return figures include amounts not allocated to a particular county. 3. Rankings calculated by Wisconsin Legislative Reference Bureau.

Source: Wisconsin Department of Revenue "Wisconsin Municipal Income Per Return Report, 2017" and earlier reports at https://www.revenue.wi.gov/Pages/Report/i.aspx [March 14, 2019].

Distribution of Wisconsin business establishments, March 2016

Industry	Total employees[1]	Number of establishments by employment size						
		Total	1 to 19	20 to 49	50 to 99	100 to 249	250 to 499	500 or more
Agriculture, forestry, fishing, and hunting	3,314	552	530	17	1	2	1	1
Mining, quarrying, and oil and gas extraction	3,254	175	128	28	12	7	0	0
Utilities	12,704	320	203	58	29	23	3	4
Construction	108,099	13,602	12,587	716	184	77	26	12
Manufacturing	452,798	8,791	5,230	1,565	880	749	232	135
Wholesale trade	120,411	6,954	5,555	891	299	171	31	7
Retail trade.	314,425	19,002	15,596	2,104	745	467	83	7
Transportation and warehousing . .	103,910	5,525	4,536	593	222	133	20	21
Information	55,771	2,486	2,068	247	86	57	14	14
Finance and insurance	138,232	9,126	8,319	487	148	102	35	35
Real estate and rental and leasing .	26,415	4,842	4,603	169	54	15	1	0
Professional, scientific, and technical services	107,316	11,551	10,485	716	202	114	22	12
Management of companies and enterprises	80,072	1,077	677	147	104	72	34	43
Administrative, support, waste management, and remediation services	154,684	7,275	6,130	538	266	235	68	38
Educational services	56,291	1,661	1,258	265	75	36	8	19
Health care and social assistance . .	395,239	15,681	12,498	1,846	690	418	138	91
Arts, entertainment, and recreation	45,105	2,733	2,299	255	102	57	14	6
Accommodation and food services.	238,224	14,599	10,705	2,959	802	109	16	8
Other services (except public administration)	107,710	14,604	13,585	798	157	54	8	2
Industries not classified	355	303	301	2	0	0	0	2
Total.	2,524,329	140,859	117,293	14,401	5,058	2,898	754	455

1. Number of employees for the week including March 12, 2016. Excludes most government and railroad employees and self-employed persons.

Source: U.S. Census Bureau, County Business Patterns, at: https://census.gov/programs-surveys/cbp/data/tables.2016.html [March 14, 2019].

SOCIAL SERVICES

Wisconsin Works (W-2) benefits

County	2017 Avg. mo. paid caseload	2017 Avg. mo. benefit payment ($)	2018 Avg. mo. paid caseload	2018 Avg. mo. benefit payment ($)
Adams	8	469	12	515
Ashland	9	336	8	302
Barron	20	503	15	412
Bayfield	4	334	6	332
Brown	137	410	151	324
Buffalo	2	466	4	436
Burnett	6	445	7	383
Calumet	12	499	9	469
Chippewa	20	396	26	360
Clark	5	460	9	341
Columbia	20	476	21	446
Crawford	7	424	5	419
Dane	217	461	213	424
Dodge	21	468	23	387
Door	14	491	12	421
Douglas	24	433	33	399
Dunn	31	529	27	444
Eau Claire	54	418	53	350
Florence	—	X	1	287
Fond du Lac	78	406	77	315
Forest	7	436	2	571
Grant	32	505	21	393
Green	15	492	10	395
Green Lake	18	490	12	372
Iowa	6	354	7	467
Iron	2	353	0	133
Jackson	6	497	5	400
Jefferson	44	474	35	490
Juneau	17	448	18	528
Kenosha	203	451	192	388
Kewaunee	8	487	8	451
La Crosse	41	385	29	274
Lafayette	5	530	1	463
Langlade	17	378	10	372
Lincoln	8	477	10	314
Manitowoc	25	374	26	300
Marathon	44	380	42	398
Marinette	21	395	21	367
Marquette	7	481	7	531
Menominee	6	344	8	354
Milwaukee	3,586	463	3,309	414
Monroe	10	420	10	410
Oconto	7	401	7	347
Oneida	16	382	22	497
Outagamie	55	482	49	341
Ozaukee	14	572	7	531
Pepin	1	524	2	332
Pierce	9	539	8	314
Polk	14	518	12	409
Portage	13	319	17	393
Price	4	398	4	472

Wisconsin Works (W-2) benefits, continued

County	2017		2018	
	Avg. mo. paid caseload	Avg. mo. benefit payment ($)	Avg. mo. paid caseload	Avg. mo. benefit payment ($)
Racine.	205	407	190	412
Richland	11	401	6	441
Rock.	173	469	123	404
Rusk.	7	359	5	282
St. Croix.	22	471	24	489
Sauk.	6	371	9	335
Sawyer	17	410	21	360
Shawano	73	439	78	414
Sheboygan.	15	491	17	438
Taylor	2	395	1	592
Trempealeau	6	512	5	484
Vernon	5	571	2	449
Vilas	3	474	6	409
Walworth.	59	512	25	535
Washburn	4	361	8	350
Washington	17	375	15	396
Waukesha	76	525	49	477
Waupaca	17	525	16	360
Waushara.	13	452	13	286
Winnebago	98	449	103	378
Wood	44	444	49	395
Total.	**5,820**	**457**	**5,384**	**407**

— represents zero; X–not applicble.

Source: Wisconsin Department of Children and Families, departmental data, March 2019.

Wisconsin Works (W-2) expenditures

W-2 contract agency	Counties served	2017 expenditures ($)	2018 expenditures ($)
Ross IES (www.rossprov.com)	Northern Milwaukee	7,764,470	7,271,649
MAXIMUS (www.maximus.com)	West central Milwaukee	4,917,276	4,207,201
America Works of Wisconsin (www.americaworks.com)	East central Milwaukee	6,766,380	5,559,921
UMOS (www.umos.org)	Southern Milwaukee	6,965,279	5,621,839
Forward Service Corporation (fsc-corp.org)	Adams, Brown, Calumet, Columbia, Dane, Dodge, Door, Florence, Fond du Lac, Forest, Grant, Green, Green Lake, Iowa, Jefferson, Juneau, Kewaunee, Lafayette, Langlade, Lincoln, Manitowoc, Marathon, Marinette, Marquette, Menominee, Oconto, Oneida, Outagamie, Portage, Price, Richland, Rock, Sauk, Shawano, Sheboygan, Taylor, Vilas, Waupaca, Waushara, Winnebago, Wood	11,456,088	10,063,760
ResCare (www.rescare.com)	Kenosha, Ozaukee, Racine, Walworth, Washington, Waukesha	4,194,838	3,512,938

Wisconsin Works (W-2) expenditures, continued

W-2 contract agency	Counties served	2017 expen-ditures ($)	2018 expen-ditures ($)
Workforce Connections (www.workforceconnections.org)	Buffalo, Crawford, Jackson, La Crosse, Monroe, Pepin, Trempealeau, Vernon	595,402	595,896
Workforce Resource, Inc. (workforceresource.org).......	Ashland, Barron, Bayfield, Burnett, Chippewa, Clark, Douglas, Dunn, Eau Claire, Iron, Pierce, Polk, Rusk, Sawyer, St Croix, Washburn	1,949,513	1,751,306
Total..		44,609,246	38,584,509

Source: Wisconsin Department of Children and Families, departmental data, March 2019.

Wisconsin Medicaid and BadgerCare

	Recipients[1]				Expenditures[2]			
			% of 2018 popula-				Per 2018 recipient	
County	Fiscal yr. 2017	Fiscal yr. 2018	tion	Rank	Fiscal yr. 2017	Fiscal yr. 2018	Amount	Rank
Adams	5,468	5,336	25.67	20	$25,565,541	$25,565,673	$4,791	68
Ashland....	6,119	5,985	37.34	3	35,415,842	36,433,905	6,088	19
Barron.....	13,023	12,837	27.70	13	69,242,478	71,421,490	5,564	51
Bayfield....	4,042	3,945	25.74	18	20,999,853	21,587,239	5,472	55
Brown.....	59,839	58,828	22.57	36	303,164,836	317,238,241	5,393	58
Buffalo	2,707	2,738	19.99	49	14,667,928	15,404,416	5,626	47
Burnett	4,573	4,499	29.01	9	18,838,402	19,361,826	4,304	72
Calumet ...	6,197	6,012	11.42	70	31,377,047	30,216,510	5,026	66
Chippewa ..	15,101	14,760	22.87	33	95,227,815	98,965,505	6,705	9
Clark......	7,836	7,773	22.37	39	45,669,847	47,633,882	6,128	15
Columbia...	10,511	10,321	18.07	62	69,788,301	68,492,278	6,636	11
Crawford...	4,074	4,030	24.08	26	21,817,718	22,916,871	5,687	43
Dane	82,927	82,986	15.64	66	525,713,996	495,946,599	5,976	30
Dodge	15,984	15,729	17.49	64	98,656,895	104,728,630	6,658	10
Door......	5,258	5,177	18.19	61	26,890,602	27,925,360	5,394	57
Douglas....	11,610	11,241	25.29	23	63,120,541	64,889,735	5,773	38
Dunn	9,964	10,011	22.44	37	55,165,805	58,870,402	5,881	31
Eau Claire...	23,834	23,704	23.05	32	131,742,502	134,842,573	5,689	42
Florence ...	1,067	1,046	23.48	28	5,009,984	5,390,661	5,154	63
Fond du Lac .	19,781	19,479	18.72	57	114,669,398	117,164,543	6,015	26
Forest.....	2,963	2,868	31.08	5	12,391,642	14,581,917	5,084	65
Grant	10,180	10,020	19.04	55	55,994,415	58,036,860	5,792	37
Green	6,956	6,779	18.34	60	37,951,902	41,129,766	6,067	22
Green Lake..	4,090	4,027	21.00	45	22,657,678	23,353,007	5,799	35
Iowa......	4,507	4,408	18.47	59	25,120,176	24,624,193	5,586	50
Iron	1,686	1,667	28.15	10	10,365,477	9,999,240	5,998	28
Jackson....	5,094	5,089	24.47	25	30,295,266	29,836,075	5,863	32
Jefferson ...	16,008	15,776	18.70	58	107,320,806	112,818,207	7,151	4
Juneau	7,366	7,279	26.84	16	40,094,394	42,176,184	5,794	36
Kenosha ...	44,154	43,161	25.58	21	223,693,883	231,422,884	5,362	59
Kewaunee ..	3,631	3,592	17.28	65	21,722,114	21,930,970	6,106	17

Wisconsin Medicaid and BadgerCare, continued

County	Recipients[1] Fiscal yr. 2017	Fiscal yr. 2018	% of 2018 population	Rank	Expenditures[2] Fiscal yr. 2017	Fiscal yr. 2018	Per 2018 recipient Amount	Rank
La Crosse . . .	25,295	24,562	20.61	46	165,826,527	168,164,913	6,847	7
Lafayette . . .	3,468	3,366	19.79	52	14,251,568	14,859,794	4,415	69
Langlade . . .	6,017	5,961	29.61	8	30,487,283	31,408,599	5,269	60
Lincoln	6,611	6,473	22.43	38	42,880,335	43,648,878	6,743	8
Manitowoc. .	16,298	16,080	19.73	53	93,017,662	96,123,018	5,978	29
Marathon. . .	29,412	29,026	21.35	44	168,099,771	174,468,755	6,011	27
Marinette. . .	11,219	11,042	26.68	17	61,342,792	64,403,569	5,833	33
Marquette . .	3,706	3,794	24.62	24	24,581,507	23,969,946	6,318	13
Menominee .	2,847	2,734	64.21	1	13,455,348	11,842,102	4,331	70
Milwaukee . .	379,452	378,154	39.79	2	2,199,446,739	2,312,601,569	6,116	16
Monroe	10,781	10,714	23.11	30	57,356,977	62,234,608	5,809	34
Oconto	7,580	7,617	19.80	51	41,990,090	42,922,184	5,635	46
Oneida	8,837	8,580	23.58	27	44,036,994	47,548,188	5,542	53
Outagamie. .	32,884	32,342	17.53	63	171,623,470	180,868,057	5,592	49
Ozaukee . . .	8,675	8,616	9.72	72	61,319,744	66,752,834	7,748	2
Pepin	1,486	1,470	19.89	50	9,209,694	8,953,363	6,091	18
Pierce	6,240	6,294	14.98	67	34,435,998	36,035,235	5,725	41
Polk	10,127	10,257	23.11	29	52,883,602	56,992,465	5,556	52
Portage	13,536	13,440	18.92	56	70,385,029	70,368,848	5,236	61
Price	3,875	3,904	27.79	12	23,045,370	23,689,310	6,068	21
Racine.	54,680	54,310	27.68	14	311,816,009	327,071,712	6,022	25
Richland . . .	4,734	4,611	25.73	19	33,918,026	34,609,565	7,506	3
Rock.	45,418	44,985	28.05	11	202,978,452	215,621,334	4,793	67
Rusk	4,504	4,556	30.88	6	24,922,157	25,747,839	5,651	44
St. Croix. . . .	12,204	12,342	13.93	68	66,879,955	69,688,867	5,646	45
Sauk	14,148	14,017	22.31	40	79,721,497	80,696,964	5,757	39
Sawyer	5,778	5,694	33.84	4	27,733,726	29,607,581	5,200	62
Shawano . . .	9,820	9,615	23.08	31	56,033,642	58,142,928	6,047	24
Sheboygan. .	23,789	23,487	20.26	47	130,048,808	135,008,131	5,748	40
Taylor	4,655	4,570	22.03	42	20,282,579	23,447,427	5,131	64
Trempealeau	6,624	6,728	22.60	35	43,030,755	42,060,170	6,252	14
Vernon	6,818	6,744	22.30	41	43,170,622	44,539,812	6,604	12
Vilas	6,048	6,020	27.65	15	23,681,874	26,018,964	4,322	71
Walworth. . .	21,460	20,963	20.25	48	114,467,368	117,792,330	5,619	48
Washburn . .	4,751	4,736	29.73	7	28,199,472	28,811,081	6,083	20
Washington .	16,573	16,258	11.96	69	110,325,574	116,064,036	7,139	6
Waukesha . .	41,758	41,420	10.32	71	285,946,989	295,858,908	7,143	5
Waupaca . . .	11,297	11,326	21.69	43	99,989,316	98,678,678	8,713	1
Waushara. . .	5,735	5,551	22.71	34	29,703,995	30,334,623	5,465	56
Winnebago .	33,518	33,438	19.67	54	179,278,252	184,543,269	5,519	54
Wood	19,448	19,139	25.58	22	112,859,391	116,091,423	6,066	23
Total.	1,358,656	1,346,039	23.14	NA	$7,765,018,041	$8,033,197,520	$5,968	NA

NA–Not applicable.

1. If an individual resided in multiple counties during the year, the individual is counted only in the recipient tally for the last county of residence to avoid double-counting in the statewide total.   2. State totals and state per return figures include amounts not allocated to a particular county.   3. Rankings calculated by Wisconsin Legislative Reference Bureau.   2. The expenditure totals include benefits issued and individuals eligible under BadgerCare+/MA and subprograms CORE, BASIC, Family Planning Only Services, Medicaid Waiver. Costs include: Managed Care Capitation Payments, Fee For Service Payment to providers, and Long Term Care waiver program payments.

Sources: Wisconsin Department of Health Services, departmental data, March 2019; Wisconsin Department of Administration, Division of Intergovernmental Relations, Demographic Services Center, County Population Estimates, January 1, 2018.

BadgerCare and Medical Assistance in Wisconsin

| | Long-term care | | | | Hospitals | | | | Physicians and clinics | | Drugs | | Home care[1] | | Managed care[2] | | Other noninstitutional fee-for-service[3] | | Total provider payments[4,5] | |
| | Nursing homes | | State centers | | Inpatient | | Outpatient | | | | | | | | | | | | | |
Fiscal year	Amt. (mil. $)	% of total	Amt. (mil. $)	% of total	Amt. (mil. $)	% of total	Amt. (mil. $)	% of total	Amt. (mil. $)	% of total	Amt. (mil. $)	% of total	Amt. (mil. $)	% of total	Amt. (mil. $)	% of total	Amt. (mil. $)	% of total	Amt. (mil. $)	Annual % change
1999–2000	906.3	29.8	135.9	4.5	270.6	8.9	55.3	1.8	63.2	2.1	336.5	11.1	498.8	16.4	394.4	13.0	251.8	8.3	3,044.0	NA
2000–01	916.2	27.8	115.3	3.5	297.8	9.0	58.7	1.8	72.4	2.2	373.6	11.4	522.2	15.9	523.6	15.9	280.1	8.5	3,291.8	8.1
2001–02	980.6	26.5	126.9	3.4	333.2	9.0	69.6	1.9	78.7	2.1	432.5	11.7	528.4	14.3	681.8	18.4	319.2	8.6	3,700.9	12.4
2002–03	990.6	25.7	123.9	3.2	332.0	8.6	75.6	2.0	85.2	2.2	494.7	12.9	592.6	15.4	657.9	17.1	334.5	8.7	3,849.2	4.0
2003–04	972.2	21.3	143.0	3.1	338.0	7.4	91.6	2.0	116.9	2.6	700.5	15.4	636.8	14.0	1,013.6	22.2	381.8	8.4	4,558.9	18.4
2004–05	963.8	20.2	117.7	2.5	388.6	8.1	103.7	2.2	133.2	2.8	772.0	16.2	754.9	15.8	873.7	18.3	487.2	10.2	4,777.1	4.8
2005–06	940.1	20.7	111.5	2.5	357.0	7.9	85.8	1.9	104.9	2.3	459.6	10.1	789.2	17.4	1,068.0	23.5	424.2	9.3	4,546.3	-4.8
2006–07	878.2	18.3	111.4	2.3	372.6	7.7	81.6	1.7	111.0	2.3	389.7	8.1	773.6	16.1	1,307.5	27.2	472.3	9.8	4,809.4	5.8
2007–08	837.2	16.3	117.1	2.3	409.7	8.0	85.1	1.7	157.2	3.1	466.3	9.1	812.5	15.8	1,422.3	27.7	599.3	11.7	5,137.5	6.8
2008–09	890.7	14.4	92.0	1.5	602.2	9.7	162.2	2.6	152.6	2.5	621.5	10.0	747.9	12.1	2,089.3	33.8	637.2	10.3	6,188.6	20.5
2009–10	909.5	12.8	148.1	2.1	459.9	6.5	152.8	2.1	188.5	2.6	660.7	9.3	604.5	8.5	2,358.5	33.2	760.2	10.7	7,114.6	15.0
2010–11	842.9	11.2	112.5	1.5	502.5	6.7	188.2	2.5	151.9	2.0	617.6	8.2	599.5	8.0	3,457.1	46.0	1,050.7	14.0	7,522.8	5.7
2011–12	818.8	11.7	127.1	1.8	440.0	6.3	196.3	2.8	166.8	2.4	610.6	8.7	659.0	9.4	2,691.3	38.5	1,288.5	18.4	6,998.4	-7.0
2012–13	819.4	10.8	133.5	1.8	580.6	7.7	208.6	2.8	143.9	1.9	625.8	8.3	784.4	10.4	3,024.3	40.0	1,207.0	16.0	7,553.1	7.9
2013–14	770.0	9.5	128.3	1.6	519.5	6.4	202.5	2.5	187.9	2.3	710.6	8.8	889.1	11.0	3,272.7	40.4	1,355.4	16.7	8,105.8	7.3
2014–15	762.8	9.0	112.5	1.3	564.1	6.6	230.0	2.7	158.3	1.9	876.0	10.3	925.5	10.9	3,531.5	41.5	1,350.5	15.9	8,511.2	5.0
2015–16	713.3	8.2	120.1	1.4	525.9	6.1	201.7	2.3	141.4	1.6	996.0	11.5	920.6	10.6	3,759.2	43.3	1,301.6	15.0	8,680.0	2.0
2016–17	708.0	8.3	108.4	1.3	567.0	6.6	206.8	2.4	170.2	2.0	1,061.9	12.4	903.3	10.6	3,909.4	45.7	917.4	10.7	8,552.5	-1.5
2017–18	685.7	7.7	114.5	1.3	576.4	6.5	194.7	2.2	158.9	1.8	1,139.2	12.8	978.0	11.0	4,043.0	45.4	1,019.6	11.4	8,910.1	4.2

Note: Enrollments in BadgerCare began in July 1999, and expenditures for the program are included in the Medical Assistance figures above. Medical Assistance expenditure data prior to BadgerCare can be found in previous Blue Books.

NA–not available.

1. Home Care includes HCBS waivers. 2. Managed Care includes all capitated programs (BC/BS+, HMOs, CCF/WAM, SSI managed care, PACE/Partnership, Family Care). 3. All noninstitutional fee-for-service acute care not otherwise captured plus local government plus Medicare crossovers. 4. Does not include offsetting recoveries and collections, such as estate recoveries, druge rebates, etc. 5. Total includes expenditures not listed separately.

Source: Wisconsin Department of Health Services, departmental data, March 2019. Data prior to 2006 is from the Wisconsin Legislative Fiscal Bureau.

CORRECTIONAL AND TREATMENT FACILITIES

State corrections populations

Institutions	2018 Avg. pop.	Capacity[1]	Average daily population (fiscal year) 1970	1980	1990	2000	2010	2017
Maximum security (men)	**5,339**	**3,838**	**1,709**	**1,833**	**2,986**	**4,513**	**5,161**	**5,247**
Assessment and evaluation[2]	NA	904	NA	NA	NA	NA	1,214	NA
Columbia Correctional Institution . . .	834	541	NA	NA	477	808	820	827
Dodge Correctional Institution[2]	1,683	1,165	NA	88	551	1,377	341	1640
Green Bay Correctional Institution . . .	1,094	749	755	658	832	1,002	1,089	1,091
Wisconsin Secure Program Facility . . .	470	501	NA	NA	NA	101	461	437
Waupun Correctional Institution	1,258	882	954	1,087	1,126	1,225	1,237	1,252
Medium security	**11,834**	**9,430**	**846**	**938**	**1,771**	**7,281**	**11,242**	**11,823**
Fox Lake Correctional Institution[3] . . .	1,341	979	553	570	785	1,112	1,046	1,339
Jackson Correctional Institution	984	837	NA	NA	NA	971	977	980
Kettle Moraine Correctional Institution	1,179	783	293	368	542	1,233	1,160	1,178
New Lisbon Correctional Institution . .	1,040	950	NA	NA	NA	NA	1,009	1,036
Oshkosh Correctional Institution	2,044	1,494	NA	NA	444	1,859	2,031	2,052
Prairie du Chien Correctional Institution	513	326	NA	NA	NA	297	500	513
Racine Correctional Institution	1,683	1,171	NA	NA	NA	1,414	1,553	1,690
Racine Youthful Offender Correctional Facility.	450	400	NA	NA	NA	395	445	448
Redgranite Correctional Institution . .	1,024	990	NA	NA	NA	NA	1,013	1,017
Stanley Correctional Institution	1,575	1,500	NA	NA	NA	NA	1,509	1,570
Minimum security	**3,303**	**2,230**	**390**	**474**	**1,439**	**2,380**	**3,332**	**3,219**
Chippewa Valley Correctional Treatment Center.	489	450	NA	NA	NA	NA	465	480
Fox Lake Correctional Institution[3] . . .	NA	NA	NA	NA	NA	NA	280	NA
Oakhill Correctional Institution	720	344	NA	198	368	564	677	696
Sturtevant Transitional Facility	147	150	NA	NA	NA	NA	261	145
Wisconsin Correctional Center System (WCCS)[4].	1,947	1,286	390	276	1,071	1,816	1,649	1,898
Detention facility	**1,043**	**460**	**998**	**NA**	**NA**	**NA**	**956**	**1,042**
Milwaukee Secure Detention Facility. .	1,043	460	998	NA	NA	NA	956	1,042
Wisconsin Women's Correctional System[4].	**1,558**	**937**	**141**	**123**	**203**	**644**	**1,262**	**1,461**
Taycheedah Correctional Institution (med./max.)	925	653	141	123	203	644	579	870
Correctional centers (min.)	633	284	NA	NA	NA	NA	683	591
Contract facilities	**436**	**545**	**NA**	**NA**	**78**	**4,665**	**690**	**200**
Intergovernmental contract	28	NA	NA	NA	NA	NA	30	28
In–state.	408	NA	NA	NA	NA	NA	660	172
Other adults.	**66,515**	**NA**	**8,859**	**19,842**	**30,172**	**64,409**	**68,123**	**66,907**
Community residential confinement. .	NA	NA	NA	NA	48	NA	NA	NA
Division of Intensive Sanctions	NA	NA	NA	NA	NA	412	NA	NA
Extended supervision and parole[5] . . .	21,391	NA	4,329	3,045	4,217	8,951	19,783	21,033
Probation.	45,125	NA	4,530	16,797	25,907	55,046	48,340	45,874
Unknown offender type	NA	NA	NA	NA	NA	NA	NA	NA
Juvenile corrections.	**162**	**560**	**446**	**575**	**572**	**904**	**437**	**175**
Copper Lake School[6]	19	29	NA	NA	NA	NA	NA	21
Ethan Allen School[6]	NA	NA	365	306	320	438	207	NA
Lincoln Hills School[6].	138	519	NA	245	252	330	176	150
Southern Oaks Girls School[6]	NA	NA	NA	NA	NA	87	49	NA
Youth Leadership Training Center[7] . . .	NA	NA	NA	NA	NA	40	NA	NA

State corrections populations, continued

Institutions	2018 Avg. pop.	2018 Capac- ity[1]	1970	1980	1990	2000	2010	2017
Sprite program[8].	NA	NA	NA	NA	NA	9	5	NA
Grow Academy[8]	5	12	NA	NA	NA	NA	NA	4
Juvenile correctional camp system. . .	NA	NA	81	24	NA	NA	NA	NA
Other juveniles.	**125**	**NA**	**NA**	**NA**	**NA**	**308**	**265**	**162**
Juvenile aftercare[9]	NA	NA	NA	NA	NA	NA	76	45
Alternate care.	34	NA	NA	NA	NA	174	49	46
Corrective sanctions[9]	NA	NA	NA	NA	NA	134	140	71
Home supervision[9].	56	NA	NA	NA	NA	NA	NA	NA
Alternate care supervision[9]	35	NA	NA	NA	NA	NA	NA	NA
Total.	**90,477**	**NA**	**12,391**	**23,785**	**37,221**	**84,796**	**91,840**	**90,236**

NA–Not available.

1. DOC "rated capacity" is the original design capacity, based on industry standards, plus modifications and expansions. It excludes beds and multiple bunking to accommodate crowding. DHS Care and Treatment Facilities' capacity is "staffed capacity," based on staffing and other budgetary resources rather than number of beds.   2. Dodge CI serves as the assessment and evaluation (A&E) center for sentenced adult felons. A&E for sentenced adult female felons moved from Dodge CI to Taycheedah CI in December 2004.   3. As of December 2011, Fox Lake is exclusively medium security.   4. In July 2005, DOC designated the institutions for female offenders as the Wisconsin Women's Correctional System, which now includes Taycheedah CI and 2 of the minimum security correctional centers. John Burke CC became a male facility in November 2011. A limited number of female inmates are housed at predominantly male St. Croix CC (8). WCCS population statistics prior to 2005 include both male and female inmates. Milwaukee Secure Detention Facility had 36 females.   5. Parole data through 1991 included juveniles; figures from 1992 to date do not include juvenile cases.   6. Ethan Allen and Southern Oaks closed in June 2011; Copper Lake opened in June 2011.   7. Youth Leadership Training Camp program, formerly at Camp Douglas and closed in February 2002, is now part of the program at Lincoln Hills.   8. Sprite program eliminated March 2010. Grow Academy opened June 2014.   9. As a result of 2015 Act 55, Juvenile Aftercare and Corrective Sanctions were consolidated under Community Supervision, which is comprised of two types of supervision: Home Supervision and Alternate Care Supervision.

Sources: Wisconsin Department of Corrections, Fiscal Year Summary Report of Population Movement for 1991 and previous issues, and departmental data, March 2019 and prior years.

State health service institutions populations

Institutions	2018 Avg. pop.	2018 Capac- ity[1]	1970	1980	1990	2000	2010	2017
Mental health institutions (MHI). . . .	**1,184**	**1,286**	**1,354**	**666**	**693**	**1,053**	**1,273**	**1,224**
Mendota MHI	281	288	522	202	266	238	240	281
Winnebago MHI	171	184	574	310	266	279	291	187
Mendota Juvenile Treatment Center . .	28	29	NA	NA	NA	43	29	28
Sand Ridge Secure Treatment Center .	329	400	NA	NA	NA	72	286	352
Central State Hospital	NA	NA	258	154	NA	NA	NA	NA
Wisconsin Resource Center.	375	385	NA	NA	161	421	427	376
Centers for developmentally disabled (CDD)	**351**	**440**	**3,698**	**2,142**	**1,677**	**843**	**448**	**362**
Central Wisconsin CDD	204	255	1,070	731	606	380	258	215
Northern Wisconsin CDD	14	25	1,421	676	495	189	12	13
Southern Wisconsin CDD	133	160	1,207	735	576	274	178	134
Total.	**1,535**	**1,726**	**5,052**	**2,808**	**2,370**	**1,896**	**1,721**	**1,586**

NA–Not available.

Source: Wisconsin Department of Health Services, departmental data, March 2019 and prior years.

MILITARY AND VETERANS AFFAIRS

Wisconsin veterans benefits

		Grants			Loans		
Fiscal year	Total benefits	Economic	Educational	Full-time educational grants	Economic assistance	Personal loans	General obligation bond housing loans
1993....	$22,446,997	$472,302	$512,770	$167,838	$2,673,585	X	$18,620,502
1994....	36,893,647[1]	451,666	716,858	667	2,567,053	X	33,157,403
1995....	114,984,938[1]	552,893	754,052	X	2,544,584	X	111,133,409
1996....	80,581,789	601,030	1,609,350	X	3,189,625	X	75,181,784
1997....	99,984,937	937,294	1,797,649	X	2,401,548	X	94,848,446
1998....	160,760,389	783,664	1,680,881	X	666,575[2]	$10,215,928[2]	147,413,341
1999....	140,457,525	2,263,317	1,447,882	X	X	11,837,974	124,908,352
2000....	143,192,551	3,226,128	1,786,205	X	X	10,802,068	127,378,150
2001....	73,390,596	1,205,846	1,768,452	X	X	9,034,356	61,381,942
2002....	88,227,531	1,925,094	2,822,134	X	X	15,780,270	67,700,033
2003....	83,866,773	1,752,733	2,909,812	X	X	19,792,680	59,411,548
2004....	95,593,212	1,296,310	4,384,642	X	X	11,808,566	78,103,694
2005....	37,428,288	413,564	5,698,107	X	X	2,271,942	29,044,675
2006....	23,935,069	1,052,493	4,751,263	X	X	4,113,262	14,018,050
2007....	48,026,312	678,109	3,715,648	X	X	5,933,810	37,698,745
2008....	59,388,229	1,028,788	2,276,489	X	X	5,081,986	51,000,967
2009....	43,587,113	961,497	1,694,312	X	X	2,764,736	38,166,568
2010....	15,859,166	426,535	1,726,307	X	X	3,133,961	10,572,363
2011....	4,011,393	682,235	1,271,083	X	X	2,058,075	X
2012....	2,531,220	577,061	1,044,751	X	X	909,397	X
2013....	1,242,884	443,312	799,572	X	X	NA	X
2014....	1,181,380	713,279	468,101	X	X	NA	X
2015....	2,450,024	2,005,365	444,659	X	X	NA	X
2016....	2,099,056	1,843,991	255,065	X	X	NA	X
2017....	2,459,211	2,074,031	385,180	X	X	NA	X
2018....	2,674,808	2,562,378	112,430	X	X	NA	X

X–not applicable; NA–not available.

1. Includes $21,444,166 (FY94) and $11,024,956 (FY95) in consumer loans under the Veterans Trust Fund stabilization provision of 1993 Wisconsin Act 16.   2. Personal Loan Program replaced economic assistance loans.

Source: Wisconsin Department of Veterans Affairs, departmental data, April 2019.

Wisconsin Veterans Homes membership, 1888–1974

	Civil and Indian Wars	Spanish-American	World War I		World War II		Korean Conflict		Total
			Men	Women	Men	Women	Men	Women	
1888.........	72	X	X	X	X	X	X	X	72
1890.........	139	X	X	X	X	X	X	v	139
1900.........	680	X	X	X	X	X	X	X	680
1910.........	699	X	X	X	X	X	X	X	699
1920.........	532	X	X	X	X	X	X	X	532
1930.........	254	108	10	14	X	X	X	X	386
1940.........	89	196	101	130	X	X	X	X	516
1950.........	27	156	189	93	5	1	X	X	471
1960.........	4	74	203	94	40	5	X	X	450
1961.........	3	66	221	88	39	8	X	X	427
1962.........	3	66	223	82	52	9	X	X	431

Wisconsin Veterans Homes membership, 1888-1974, continued

	Civil and Indian Wars	Spanish- American	World War I		World War II		Korean Conflict		Total
			Men	Women	Men	Women	Men	Women	
1963.........	3	67	235	87	57	10	X	X	459
1964.........	3	63	237	105	61	16	X	X	485
1965.........	2	62	247	112	77	16	X	X	516
1966.........	1	56	258	112	86	21	X	X	534
1967.........	1	46	272	120	93	20	X	X	555
1968.........	1	48	253	123	93	16	X	X	534
1969.........	1	43	253	145	101	14	X	X	560
1970.........	1	35	279	146	153	20	1	—	635
1971.........	1	39	316	160	184	31	2	—	723
1972.........	—	28	279	155	199	39	2	—	702
1973.........	—	25	285	108	199	37	—	1	715
1974.........	—	21	279	175	185	37	—	2	699

X–not applicable; —represents zero.

Source: Wisconsin Department of Veterans Affairs, departmental data, April 2019.

Wisconsin Veterans Homes membership, 1975-2018

	Spanish- American		World War I		World War II		Korean Conflict		Vietnam		Other eras[1]		Total
	Vets.	Deps.	Vets.	Deps.	Vets.	Deps.	Vets.	Deps.	Vets.	Deps.	Vets.	Deps.	
1975......	1	18	272	171	198	40	3	2	—	—	—	—	705
1976......	1	14	254	167	209	40	2	2	—	—	—	—	689
1977......	1	13	270	164	205	41	4	2	—	—	—	—	700
1978......	1	11	261	158	218	38	3	2	—	—	—	—	692
1979......	1	11	244	146	227	37	4	1	—	—	—	—	672
1980......	1	8	242	144	241	36	5	1	—	—	—	—	678
1981......	—	8	224	139	264	40	8	2	—	—	—	—	685
1982......	—	7	189	124	282	43	11	2	—	—	—	—	658
1983......	—	5	171	111	297	42	14	2	1	—	—	—	643
1984......	—	4	144	97	316	47	21	2	3	—	—	—	634
1985......	—	4	129	102	329	54	28	—	5	—	—	—	651
1986......	—	4	117	92	348	56	35	5	7	—	—	—	664
1987......	—	2	108	84	384	60	36	4	8	—	—	—	686
1988......	—	1	84	76	395	55	45	7	8	—	—	—	671
1989......	—	2	62	75	399	67	50	7	9	1	—	—	672
1990......	—	2	49	65	431	76	62	8	10	1	3	—	707
1991......	—	2	43	57	440	74	69	10	10	2	3	—	710
1992......	—	1	33	44	442	77	82	10	12	1	2	—	704
1993......	—	1	23	41	463	73	94	9	11	1	2	—	718
1994......	—	1	14	33	488	83	99	11	12	2	1	—	744
1995......	—	1	8	31	484	84	99	12	16	2	1	—	738
1996......	—	1	4	24	489	79	103	12	25	1	1	—	739
1997......	—	1	3	20	479	82	107	11	38	1	3	—	744
1998......	—	—	1	17	460	83	123	12	39	1	9	—	745
1999......	—	—	—	12	445	87	128	11	41	3	13	1	741
2000......	—	—	—	10	423	94	132	12	47	4	21	2	745
2001[2].....	—	—	—	9	414	95	133	10	51	3	25	2	742
2002......	—	—	—	8	404	103	130	11	54	2	29	2	744
2003......	—	—	—	7	433	105	140	13	67	3	35	2	805
2004......	—	—	—	3	416	99	148	15	72	3	40	2	798
2005......	—	—	—	2	350	103	144	15	71	3	40	2	730

Wisconsin Veterans Homes membership, 1975–2018, continued

	Spanish-American		World War I		World War II		Korean Conflict		Vietnam		Other eras[1]		Total
	Vets.	Deps.	Vets.	Deps.	Vets.	Deps.	Vets.	Deps.	Vets.	Deps.	Vets.	Deps.	
2006......	—	—	—	1	407	119	164	17	87	5	50	4	854
2007......	—	—	—	1	475	135	173	26	100	8	3	—	921
2008......	—	—	—	1	417	123	177	26	115	7	4	—	870
2009......	—	—	—	1	389	130	193	21	122	8	8	—	947
2010......	—	—	—	1	356	127	176	22	122	8	10	—	892
2011......	—	—	—	1	339	124	170	19	154	12	12	—	904
2012......	—	—	—	1	330	121	180	32	178	11	19	2	953
2013[3].....	—	—	—	1	412	145	286	53	276	16	44	2	1,235
2014......	—	—	—	1	259	128	215	34	262	11	98	4	1,012
2015......	—	—	—	—	308	114	269	49	338	11	43	1	1,133
2016......	—	—	—	—	248	107	255	46	364	14	45	3	1,082
2017......	—	—	—	—	207	93	217	49	376	17	39	9	1,007
2018......	—	—	—	—	157	79	224	46	382	13	44	2	947

Deps.–Dependants; Vets.–Veterans; —represents zero.

1. Other periods of hostilities for which expeditionary medals were awarded.   2. The Wisconsin Veterans Home at King was established in 1887, and the home at Union Grove opened in 2001. Data starting in 2001 includes both homes.   3. Veterans Home at Chippewa Falls opened in 2013. Data starting in 2013 includes veterans homes at King, Union Grove, and Chippewa Falls.

Source: Wisconsin Department of Veterans Affairs, departmental data, April 2019.

Wisconsin National Guard

JOINT UNITS
Joint Force Headquarters Wisconsin
Joint Force Headquarters Detachment–Madison
54th Civil Support Team (WMD)–Madison

ARMY UNITS
Headquarters, Wisconsin Army National Guard–
  Madison
Joint Force Headquarters Separate Units
Recruiting and Retention Battalion–Madison
Det. 1, Recruiting and Retention Battalion–Madison
Det. 2, Recruiting and Retention Battalion–
  Milwaukee
Det. 52, Operational Support Airlift Command–
  Madison
54th Civil Support Team–Madison
505th Trial Defense Team

32nd Infantry Brigade Combat Team
Headquarters and Headquarters Co.–Camp Douglas
1st Battalion, 120th Field Artillery
Headquarters and Headquarters Battery (–)–
  Wisconsin Rapids
Det. 1, Headquarters and Headquarters Company–
  Berlin
Battery A–Marshfield
Battery B–Stevens Point
Battery C–Oconomowoc
3rd Battalion, 126th Infantry–(Michigan Army
  National Guard)

2nd Battalion, 127th Infantry
Headquarters and Headquarters Co. (–)–Appleton
Det. 1, Headquarters Co.–Clintonville
Company A (–)–Waupun
Det. 1, Co. A–Ripon
Company B–Green Bay
Company C–Fond du Lac
Company D–Marinette
1st Battalion, 128th Infantry
Headquarters and Headquarters Co. (–)–Eau Claire
Det. 1, Headquarters Co.–Abbotsford
Company A–Menomonie
Company B (–)–New Richmond
Det. 1, Co. B–Rice Lake
Company C (–)–Arcadia
Det. 1, Co. C–Onalaska
Company D–River Falls
132nd Brigade Support Battalion
Headquarters and Headquarters Co.–Portage
Company A (–) (Distribution)–Janesville
Det. 1, Co. A–Elkhorn
Company B (Maintenance)–Mauston
Company C (Medical)–Racine
Company D (Forward Support)–Madison
Company E (Forward Support)–Antigo
Company F (Forward Support)–Mosinee
Company G (Forward Support)–Waupaca
Company H (Forward Support)–Neillsville
173rd Brigade Engineer Battalion

EDUCATION

University of Wisconsin system fall enrollment

Institution	2012–13	2013–14	2014–15	2015–16	2016–17	2017–18	2017–18 detail Female	Male
Universities	**166,862**	**165,770**	**166,807**	**165,019**	**163,792**	**162,908**	**87,424**	**75,484**
Eau Claire.	11,047	10,907	10,692	10,531	10,705	10,825	6,609	4,216
Undergraduate	10,500	10,388	10,167	9,956	10,043	10,104	6,194	3,910
Graduate	511	464	447	492	584	636	335	301
Professional	36	55	78	83	78	85	80	5
Green Bay	6,790	6,667	6,921	6,779	7,030	7,178	4,689	2,489
Undergraduate	6,611	6,444	6,668	6,528	6,758	6,815	4,466	2,349
Graduate	179	223	253	251	272	363	223	140
La Crosse	10,380	10,502	10,664	10,486	10,624	10,534	5,995	4,539
Undergraduate	9,515	9,684	9,815	9,702	9,737	9,691	5,455	4,236
Graduate	732	686	716	653	757	703	448	255
Professional	133	132	133	131	130	140	92	48
Madison	42,463	42,903	42,865	43,064	42,994	43,450	22,140	21,310
Undergraduate	30,507	30,972	30,990	31,365	31,407	31,872	16,282	15,590
Graduate	9,385	9,405	9,415	9,216	9,134	9,131	4,442	4,689
Professional	2,571	2,526	2,460	2,483	2,453	2,447	1,416	1,031
Milwaukee	29,114	27,784	28,013	27,119	26,011	25,381	13,657	11,724
Undergraduate	24,175	23,004	23,079	22,284	21,375	20,750	10,882	9,868
Graduate	4,819	4,619	4,743	4,639	4,423	4,425	2,613	1,812
Professional	120	161	191	196	213	206	162	44
Oshkosh	13,519	13,902	14,542	14,059	13,955	13,935	8,615	5,320
Undergraduate	12,384	12,623	13,312	12,710	12,479	12,412	7,540	4,872
Graduate	1,102	1,230	1,158	1,269	1,387	1,394	965	429
Professional	33	49	72	80	89	129	110	19
Parkside	4,769	4,617	4,584	4,443	4,399	4,308	2,256	2,052
Undergraduate	4,601	4,489	4,448	4,300	4,276	4,168	2,189	1,979
Graduate	168	128	136	143	123	140	67	73
Platteville.	8,678	8,717	8,901	8,950	8,782	8,558	3,033	5,525
Undergraduate	7,840	7,867	8,047	7,983	7,865	7,621	2,606	5,015
Graduate	838	850	854	967	917	937	427	510
River Falls.	6,447	6,171	6,184	5,958	5,931	6,110	3,757	2,353
Undergraduate	6,046	5,787	5,721	5,507	5,482	5,678	3,463	2,215
Graduate	401	384	463	451	449	432	294	138
Stevens Point	9,677	9,643	9,322	9,255	8,627	8,208	4,429	3,779
Undergraduate	9,296	9,292	8,998	8,857	8,297	7,880	4,187	3,693
Graduate	365	332	304	377	310	307	222	85
Professional	16	19	20	21	20	21	20	1
Stout	9,247	9,286	9,371	9,535	9,619	9,401	4,401	5,000
Undergraduate	8,270	8,180	8,254	8,388	8,398	8,116	3,550	4,566
Graduate	977	1,095	1,091	1,105	1,181	1,246	834	412
Professional	---	11	26	42	40	39	17	22
Superior	2,700	2,656	2,589	2,489	2,487	2,590	1,617	973
Undergraduate	2,550	2,522	2,455	2,362	2,365	2,368	1,462	906
Graduate	150	134	134	127	122	222	155	67
Whitewater	12,031	12,015	12,159	12,351	12,628	12,430	6,226	6,204
Undergraduate	10,752	10,852	10,971	11,142	11,380	11,128	5,490	5,638
Graduate	1,279	1,163	1,188	1,172	1,196	1,251	715	536
Professional	—	—	—	37	52	51	21	30
Colleges	**14,107**	**14,058**	**14,172**	**13,552**	**12,033**	**11,608**	**6,153**	**5,455**
Baraboo/Sauk County	597	580	567	538	523	461	259	202
Barron.	634	603	613	578	497	512	284	228

University of Wisconsin system fall enrollment, continued

Institution	2012–13	2013–14	2014–15	2015–16	2016–17	2017–18	2017–18 detail Female	2017–18 detail Male
Fond du Lac	692	707	627	594	523	563	294	269
Fox Valley.	1,799	1,760	1,702	1,557	1,367	1,286	610	676
Manitowoc.	614	530	461	478	364	334	171	163
Marathon County.	1,275	1,260	1,107	978	841	779	400	379
Marinette.	464	507	495	465	292	289	144	145
Marshfield/Wood County. .	628	650	623	649	535	541	323	218
Richland	523	555	567	528	278	273	141	132
Rock County.	1,305	1,224	1,152	1,155	1,038	908	508	400
Sheboygan.	836	753	770	727	637	560	254	306
Washington County	998	990	937	869	760	730	347	383
Waukesha	2,118	2,175	2,261	2,085	1,868	1,740	847	893
Online Courses	1,624	1,764	2,290	2,351	2,510	2,632	1,571	1,061
System total.	180,969	179,828	180,979	178,571	175,825	174,516	93,577	80,939

— Represents zero.

Sources: University of Wisconsin System, Office of Policy Analysis and Research, Student Statistics reports at https://www.wisconsin.edu/education-reports-statistics/student-statistics/ [March 2019].

University of Wisconsin System budgeted faculty positions,[1] 2017–18

Institution	Professor	Associate professor	Assistant professor	Instructor	Total faculty
Universities	**2,443**	**1,667**	**1,647**	**9**	**5,766**
Eau Claire.	153	119	89	—	362
Green Bay	34	69	62	—	164
La Crosse	99	137	170	—	406
Madison	1,200	384	477	—	2,061
Milwaukee	246	373	125	1	745
Oshkosh	118	102	90	6	317
Parkside.	33	49	40	—	121
Platteville.	103	58	92	—	252
River Falls.	108	40	41	—	189
Stevens Point	142	73	136	2	353
Stout.	79	93	114	—	286
Superior	34	35	36	—	104
Whitewater.	96	136	174	—	406
Colleges	**80**	**123**	**58**	**—**	**261**
Baraboo/Sauk County	1	8	2	—	11
Barron.	1	3	6	—	10
Fond du Lac	3	11	2	—	16
Fox Valley.	12	14	8	—	34
Manitowoc.	5	8	3	—	16
Marathon County.	10	15	3	—	28
Marinette.	3	8	3	—	13
Marshfield/Wood County	4	6	3	—	13
Richland	5	4	-	—	9
Rock County.	6	9	7	—	22
Sheboygan.	4	7	5	—	16
Washington County	10	9	5	—	23
Waukesha	12	20	7	—	39
Other	6	4	4	—	13

University of Wisconsin System budgeted faculty positions,[1]
2017–18, continued

Institution	Professor	Associate professor	Assistant professor	Instructor	Total faculty
Extension	65	100	69	35	269
System total.	2,588	1,890	1,774	44	6,296

Notes: Includes vacant positions. Does not include student assistants. Numbers may not add due to rounding.
—Represents zero.
1. Full-time equivalent (FTE) data used.
Source: University of Wisconsin System, Office of Budget and Planning, *Fact Book 2017–18*, March 2019.

Wisconsin private institutions of higher education fall enrollment

Institution (location)	2013	2014	2015	2016	2017
Universities and colleges	**54,715**	**54,017**	**52,293**	**49,827**	**48,403**
Alverno College (Milwaukee).	2,536	2,389	2,209	2,017	1,942
Beloit College (Beloit)	1,306	1,303	1,358	1,394	1,402
Cardinal Stritch University (Milwaukee)	4,407	3,811	3,176	2,464	2,355
Carroll University (Waukesha)	3,534	3,446	3,508	3,491	3,452
Carthage College (Kenosha)	2,988	2,948	2,978	2,930	2,860
Concordia University Wisconsin (Mequon)	7,943	8,161	8,268	7,721	7,288
Edgewood College (Madison)	2,894	2,980	2,678	2,552	2,221
Lakeland College (Sheboygan)	3,806	4,003	3,677	3,230	2,679
Lawrence University (Appleton).	1,553	1,511	1,557	1,528	1,467
Marian University (Fond du Lac).	2,188	2,130	2,099	1,974	1,971
Marquette University (Milwaukee)	11,782	11,745	11,491	11,294	11,426
Mount Mary University (Milwaukee)	1,481	1,385	1,313	1,404	1,399
Northland College (Ashland).	552	584	541	582	635
Ripon College (Ripon)	904	840	794	793	756
Saint Norbert College (De Pere)	2,222	2,169	2,180	2,211	2,165
Silver Lake College (Manitowoc).	679	629	522	429	475
Viterbo University (La Crosse)	2,762	2,804	2,756	2,699	2,796
Wisconsin Lutheran College (Milwaukee)	1,178	1,179	1,188	1,114	1,114
Technical and professional	**8,569**	**8,678**	**8,873**	**8,466**	**8,208**
Bellin College of Nursing (Green Bay)	325	351	371	430	440
Columbia College of Nursing.	157	151	154	141	122
Herzing University[1] (WI campuses).	3,458	3,444	3,503	3,038	2,700
Medical College of Wisconsin (Milwaukee)	1,212	1,209	1,217	1,297	1,385
Milwaukee Institute of Art & Design (Milwaukee)	667	622	627	630	660
Milwaukee School of Engineering (Milwaukee)	2,658	2,810	2,906	2,846	2,823
Wisconsin School of Professional Psychology (Milwaukee)	92	91	95	84	78
Theological seminaries	**1,272**	**1,262**	**1,247**	**1,291**	**1,321**
Maranatha Baptist University (Watertown)	1,035	1,064	1,059	1,118	1,139
Nashotah House (Nashotah)	124	100	96	88	73
Sacred Heart School of Theology (Hales Corners)	113	98	92	85	109
Tribal colleges	**964**	**912**	**804**	**682**	**496**
College of Menominee Nation (Keshena)	661	560	433	394	285
Lac Courte Oreilles Ojibwa Community College (Hayward)	303	352	371	288	211
Total.	**65,520**	**64,869**	**63,217**	**60,266**	**58,428**

1. For-profit institution.
Sources: National Center for Education Statistics, Integrated Postsecondary Education Data System, https://nces.ed.gov/ipeds/datacenter; U.S. Department of Education, Office of Postsecondary Education, Database of Accredited Postsecondary Institutions and Programs, accredited by the Higher Learning Commission of the North Central Association of Colleges and Schools at: https://www.hlcommission.org/Directory-of-HLC-Institutions.html.

Wisconsin Technical College System enrollment, 2007–2017

School year	Total[1]	Liberal arts transfer	Associate degree	Technical diploma	Vocational adult	Non-post secondary	Community services
2007–08	397,748	22,274	125,044	39,148	203,493	70,585	9,113
2008–09	385,297	24,119	132,128	39,612	182,713	73,198	8,760
2009–10	393,993	27,222	145,547	39,759	178,257	76,325	10,082
2010–11	383,671	28,052	149,249	36,911	167,135	72,176	13,181
2011–12	378,240	27,796	148,017	35,401	166,463	65,506	14,112
2012–13	362,252	26,532	148,548	34,546	149,628	61,552	14,929
2013–14	348,747	25,590	144,915	32,416	143,943	51,902	15,339
2014–15	329,407	23,996	140,380	32,164	134,203	50,782	12,704
2015–16	326,153	22,729	135,593	31,406	134,796	48,794	13,831
2016–17	307,607	21,721	134,543	30,789	119,921	45,885	11,804
2017–18	314,835	21,103	137,562	31,359	124,974	43,325	12,121

1. Unduplicated student headcount.

Sources: Wisconsin Technical College System, *Fact Book 2019* at https://wtcsystem.edu/about-us/resources-publications and previous issues.

Wisconsin Technical College enrollment, 2017

Technical college	Total[1]	Liberal arts transfer	Associate degree	Technical diploma	Vocational adult	Non-post secondary	Community services
Blackhawk	7,872	X	4,144	899	2,773	888	197
Chippewa Valley . . .	18,083	1,197	9,000	2,075	7,201	2,079	X
Fox Valley.	51,524	X	16,952	3,584	30,671	2,139	1,508
Gateway	20,509	X	13,163	2,365	4,508	2,647	9
Lakeshore	10,550	X	3,893	1,154	5,528	915	111
Madison Area	34,145	9,183	15,177	2,841	8,533	6,128	3,474
Mid-State.	7,519	—	4,150	834	2,289	1,106	387
Milwaukee Area. . . .	32,876	9,039	16,315	2,820	5,072	12,671	52
Moraine Park	16,826	X	7,122	1,831	5,529	3,140	1,586
Nicolet Area	5,673	655	1,321	294	2,720	569	1,071
Northcentral.	19,071	X	8,305	1,562	9,115	3,280	X
Northeast Wisconsin	30,503	X	14,886	4,334	13,304	1,366	304
Southwest Wisconsin	7,473	X	3,223	966	3,818	1,254	42
Waukesha County . .	20,111	X	9,242	2,375	7,518	2,058	1,659
Western.	12,383	1,029	6,833	1,612	3,444	2,169	X
Wisconsin Indianhead	19,717	X	3,836	1,813	12,951	916	1,721
Total.	**314,835**	**21,103**	**137,562**	**31,359**	**124,974**	**43,325**	**12,121**

X–Not applicable; —Represents zero.

1. Unduplicated student headcount.

Sources: Wisconsin Technical College System, *Fact Book 2019* at https://wtcsystem.edu/about-us/resources-publications and previous issues.

Wisconsin public high school completion rates, 2017–2018

	Students (rate)			Student detail by race or Hispanic origin[1]					
CESA[2]	Total[3]	Female	Male	American Indian	Asian	Black	Hispanic	White	2 or more
1	17,005 (84.6)	8,638 (87.2)	8,367 (82.2)	NA	692	3,135	2,531	9,890	308
2	10,852 (90.8)	5,396 (92.3)	5,456 (89.3)	NA	278	510	1,084	7,894	167

Wisconsin public high school completion rates, 2017–2018, continued

| | Students (rate) | | | Student detail by race or Hispanic origin[1] | | | | | |
CESA[2]	Total[3]	Female	Male	American Indian	Asian	Black	Hispanic	White	2 or more
3	1,344 (93.6)	614 (94.0)	715 (93.2)	NA	NA	5	NA	577	NA
4	2,489 (94.2)	1,193 (95.4)	1,283 (93.1)	18	86	24	49	1,554	34
5	3,875 (93.1)	1,886 (94.8)	1,989 (91.6)	6	74	22	113	2,701	8
6	7,231 (92.1)	3,617 (94.3)	3,614 (90.1)	6	193	112	404	5,962	35
7	6,092 (91.6)	3,046 (93.1)	3,046 (90.1)	83	238	188	526	4,004	80
8	1,424 (91.3)	727 (92.7)	670 (89.7)	81	NA	NA	22	760	NA
9	2,425 (92.9)	1,159 (95.6)	1,266 (91.1)	31	135	6	34	1,738	25
10	2,435 (90.0)	1,214 (93.2)	1,205 (86.9)	NA	58	22	46	1,360	22
11	3,507 (94.8)	1,747 (95.3)	1,752 (94.2)	NA	21	37	29	2,293	19
12	1,071 (92.0)	521 (92.2)	520 (91.9)	91	NA	7	NA	675	19
Total. . .	59,759 (89.8)	29,817 (91.7)	29,942 (88.0)	585	2,206	4,363	5,598	45,503	1,457
(Rate).				(78.6)	(91.1)	(69.5)	(82.5)	(93.7)	(85.7)

Notes: Percent completion calculated by number of combined completions (diplomas, HSED, certificate) divided by number of students in the 4-year cohort. This table is based on 4-year adjusted cohort completion rates, as required by federal law, and may not be comparable to tables in prior Blue Books. Details may not sum to totals due to privacy rules.

NA–Not available. Includes only students who are identified by race in DPI report. Not all students can be identified by race due to privacy rules relating to small groups.

1. Pacific Islander state total (rate): 47 (94.0). 2. Cooperative Educational Service Agency. 3. Includes students who have completed high school with a diploma, HSED, or other method.

Source: Department of Public Instruction's WISEdash data files, at: http://wise.dpi.wi.gov/wisedash_downloadfiles.

Enrollment in Wisconsin elementary and secondary private schools

Grade level	2009–10	2010–11	2011–12	2012–13	2013–14	2014–15	2015–16	2016–17	2017–18	2018–19
Pre-kinder-garten . . .	13,646	14,737	14,793	14,982	14,204	14,516	14,226	13,572	14,456	14,153
Kindergar-ten	10,161	9,893	9,797	9,994	9,841	9,796	9,529	9,336	9,346	9,381
1	9,975	9,810	9,767	9,492	9,600	9,929	9,658	9,459	9,198	9,384
2	10,006	9,744	9,703	9,487	9,325	9,822	9,855	9,532	9,327	9,201
3	10,026	9,648	9,635	9,462	9,327	9,541	9,769	9,733	9,432	9,347
4	10,179	9,659	9,542	9,320	9,153	9,494	9,425	9,677	9,609	9,444
5	9,957	9,927	9,587	9,450	9,139	9,285	9,403	9,291	9,481	9,598
6	9,672	9,486	9,555	9,233	9,012	9,114	9,105	9,142	9,164	9,400
7	9,377	9,223	9,192	9,157	8,750	8,853	8,827	8,723	8,782	9,030
8	9,486	9,072	9,078	8,909	8,702	8,802	8,747	8,711	8,547	8,731
9	5,980	6,089	5,939	6,159	6,026	6,328	6,389	6,313	6,410	6,406
10	6,043	5,789	5,866	5,917	5,766	5,926	6,072	6,039	6,010	6,177
11	5,770	5,796	5,534	5,677	5,590	5,682	5,795	5,844	5,781	5,889
12	5,496	5,583	5,442	5,217	5,190	5,233	5,250	5,344	5,505	5,536
Ungraded elem. and secondary	1,038	916	1,238	493	176	783	1,087	784	788	863
Total.	126,812	125,372	124,668	122,949	119,801	123,104	123,137	121,500	121,836	122,540

Source: Wisconsin Information System for Education Data Dashboard at http://wisedash.dpi.wi.gov/ [March 2019].

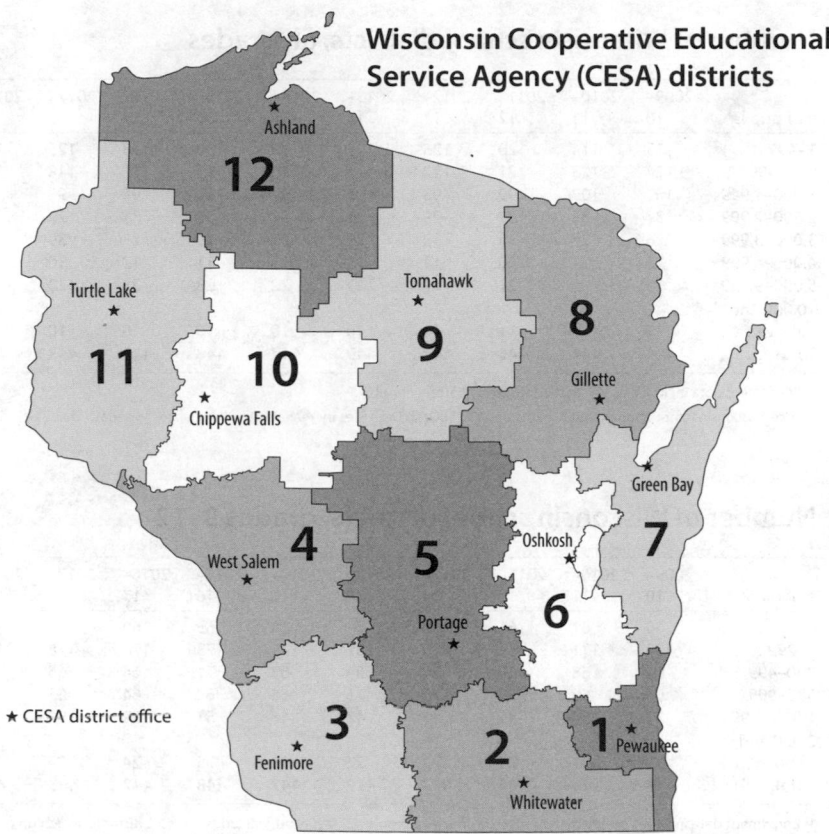

Wisconsin Cooperative Educational Service Agency (CESA) districts

★ CESA district office

Enrollment in Wisconsin elementary and secondary public schools

Grade level	2009–10	2010–11	2011–12	2012–13	2013–14	2014–15	2015–16	2016–17	2017–18	2018–19
Pre-kinder-garten[1] . .	47,054	50,200	54,438	55,008	56,777	55,830	55,907	55,435	55,186	56,096
Kindergar-ten.	61,094	60,721	60,875	62,422	61,522	60,424	58,078	57,331	56,832	56,915
1	60,197	61,262	60,572	61,037	62,479	61,498	60,459	58,224	57,517	57,236
2	59,557	60,226	60,984	60,585	60,999	62,311	61,405	60,523	58,370	57,706
3	60,661	59,981	60,216	61,243	60,697	60,885	62,322	61,749	60,783	58,744
4	61,242	61,015	60,094	60,670	61,393	60,795	60,999	62,407	61,911	61,157
5	60,413	61,420	60,958	60,253	60,768	61,459	60,924	61,207	62,743	62,329
6	60,656	61,053	61,818	61,369	60,505	60,843	61,677	61,264	61,549	63,275
7	60,814	61,264	61,442	62,310	61,814	60,795	61,047	62,170	61,582	62,193
8	61,748	61,337	61,413	61,857	62,721	62,029	61,077	61,428	62,353	61,964
9	69,323	68,383	67,542	67,699	67,985	68,043	67,036	65,847	65,959	66,758
10	68,291	66,490	65,510	64,507	64,958	65,290	65,841	65,137	64,298	64,687
11	70,144	69,076	66,851	66,346	65,450	65,019	64,546	65,269	64,505	63,643
12	71,242	69,858	68,392	67,130	66,346	65,431	65,819	65,832	66,542	66,130
Total[2] . . .	872,436	872,286	871,105	872,436	874,414	870,652	867,137	863,823	860,130	858,833

1. Includes K3 and K4.   2. Totals do not include students with unknown grade levels.

Source: Wisconsin Information System for Education Data Dashboard at http://wisedash.dpi.wi.gov/ [March 2019].

Number of Wisconsin school districts, all grades

# of pupils[1]	2009– 10	2010– 11	2011– 12	2012– 13	2013– 14	2014– 15	2015– 16	2016– 17	2017– 18	2018– 19
1–499	113	114	120	123	125	129	130	123	125	126
500–999 . .	124	123	121	122	123	116	117	117	118	120
1,000–1,999	102	102	99	98	96	97	96	98	98	94
2,000–2,999	37	35	33	29	31	31	32	31	29	32
3,000–3,999	26	27	30	32	29	29	29	28	30	26
4,000–4,999	12	11	10	11	13	13	11	12	10	13
5,000–9,999	19	21	21	21	22	22	23	23	23	23
10,000 and above . . .	11	11	11	11	10	10	10	10	10	10
Total.	444	444	445	447	449	447	448	442	443	444

1. Enrollment data includes nondistrict-sponsored charter schools.
Source: Wisconsin Information System for Education WISEDash Data Files by Year at https://dpi.wi.gov/wisedash/download-files.

Number of Wisconsin school districts, grades 9–12

# of pupils[1]	2009– 10	2010– 11	2011– 12	2012– 13	2013– 14	2014– 15	2015– 16	2016– 17	2017– 18	2018– 19
0[2]	60	61	61	62	64	64	65	60	61	59
1–299	169	171	174	180	181	179	173	178	178	182
300–499 . .	68	68	69	64	64	67	71	64	66	65
500–999 . .	68	69	73	72	71	66	63	64	63	63
1,000–1,999	57	54	45	47	47	48	51	52	51	50
2,000 and above . . .	22	21	23	22	22	23	25	24	24	25
Total.	444	444	445	447	449	447	448	442	443	444

1. Enrollment data includes nondistrict-sponsored charter schools.   2. This group includes the K3-8 districts, which do not have secondary level students.
Source: Wisconsin Information System for Education WISEDash Data Files by Year at https://dpi.wi.gov/wisedash/download-files.

Wisconsin public school salaries

	Instructional staff		Teachers	
Year	Number	Average salary ($)	Number	Average salary ($)
2010–11	63,948	58,159	58,041	54,195
2011–12	61,850	57,649	56,180	53,792
2012–13	62,698	58,999	56,800	55,171
2013–14	62,612	57,777	56,835	53,679
2014–15	61,251	58,518	55,624	54,535
2015–16	60,434	59,111	54,893	54,766
2016.	62,986	58,485	56,937	54,115
2017.	59,866	59,561	54,401	54,998
2018.	61,284	60,657	55,501	55,895

Sources: National Education Association, Rankings of the States 2017 and Estimates of School Statistics 2018, at: http://www.nea.org/rankings-and-estimates, April 2018, and previous issues.

State and local expenditures for Wisconsin public education

Agency/program	2013–14 (mil. dol.)	2014–15 (mil. dol.)	2015–16 (mil. dol.)	2016–17 (mil. dol.)	2017–18 (mil. dol.)
Public elementary and secondary schools[1]	10,749.7	10,971.7	11,057.5	11,274.4	11,557.2
Department of Public Instruction	112.3	132.1	129.5	132.5	137.8
University of Wisconsin System	6,073.9	5,977.9	6,005.4	6,055.9	6,201.7
Wisconsin Technical College System Board	139.4	543.1	543.6	550.4	551.1
Public libraries (local expenditures)[2]	234.9	239.3	248.5	284.0	291.0
Other:					
Educational Communications Board	18.0	17.6	16.6	17.5	19.3
Higher Educational Aids Board	146.9	146.9	140.4	146.7	142.0
Medical College of Wisconsin, Inc. (state funding)	8.4	8.3	8.6	10.2	9.8
State Historical Society	23.4	23.5	23.4	25.5	27.5
Total	**17,506.9**	**18,060.4**	**18,173.5**	**18,497.1**	**18,937.4**
Per capita expenditures[3] (dollars)	3,062	3,150	3,159	3,203	3,275

1. Includes the gross costs of general operations, special projects, debt service, and food service; the net capital projects; and the costs of CESA and County Children with Disabilities Education Board operations. 2. Expenditures are for calendar year ending in the fiscal year shown. 3. Based on total state population. Wisconsin population estimate for 2014: 5,732,981; 2015: 5,753,324; 2016: 5,775,120; 2017: 5,783,278.

Sources: Wisconsin Department of Administration, *Annual Fiscal Report, Appendix (Budgetary Basis)* 2019, and previous issues; Wisconsin Department of Administration, Demographic Services Center, Time Series Population Estimates: County Totals [March 2019]; Wisconsin Department of Public Instruction, Library Service Data, 2019 and previous data; Wisconsin Department of Public Instruction, departmental data.

Wisconsin school district financial data

	State school aid		Gross school levy		Total school costs		Cost per pupil	
Fiscal year	Amount (mil. dol.)	% change	Amount (mil. dol.)	% change	Amount (mil. dol.)	% change	Amount ($)	% change
1999–00	4,226	5.9	2,795	2.2	7,535	3.9	8,679	3.9
2000–01	4,463	5.6	2,928	4.7	7,900	4.8	9,087	4.7
2001–02	4,602	3.1	3,072	4.9	8,349	5.7	9,583	5.5
2002–03	4,775	3.8	3,192	3.9	8,750	4.8	10,035	4.7
2003–04	4,806	0.7	3,368	5.5	8,911	1.8	10,228	1.9
2004–05	4,858	1.1	3,611	7.2	9,216	3.4	10,605	3.7
2005–06	5,159	6.2	3,592	-0.5	9,539	3.5	10,989	3.6
2006–07	5,294	2.6	3,788	5.4	9,903	3.8	11,413	3.9
2007–08	5,340	0.9	4,067	7.4	10,265	3.7	11,894	4.2
2008–09	5,462	2.3	4,279	5.2	10,623	3.5	12,346	3.8
2009–10	5,315	-2.7	4,538	6.0	10,834	2.0	12,624	2.3
2010–11	5,325	0.2	4,693	3.4	11,162	3.0	13,020	3.1
2011–12	4,894	-8.1	4,647	-1.0	10,585	-5.2	12,375	-5.0
2012–13	4,964	1.4	4,656	0.2	10,568	-0.2	12,343	-0.3
2013–14	5,079	2.3	4,694	0.8	10,750	1.7	12,546	1.6
2014–15	5,242	3.2	4,754	1.3	10,972	2.1	12,842	2.4
2015–16	5,244	0.0	4,855	2.1	11,058	0.8	12,942	0.8
2016–17	5,445	3.8	4,858	0.1	11,274	2.0	13,182	1.9
2017–18	5,730	5.2	4,945	1.8	NA	X	NA	X
2018–19	5,900	3.0	4,988	0.9	NA	X	NA	X

NA–Not available; X–Not applicable.

Source: Legislative Fiscal Bureau, Informational Paper 24: *State Aid to School Districts*, January 2019.

Wisconsin home-based private educational enrollments

Grade level	2008–09	2009–10	2010–11	2011–12	2012–13	2013–14	2014–15	2015–16	2016–17	2017–18
1	1,357	1,409	1,127	1,136	1,158	1,197	1,183	1,175	1,214	1,304
2	1,317	1,335	1,164	1,142	1,060	1,144	1,144	1,084	1,133	1,199
3	1,350	1,322	1,179	1,076	1,106	1,077	1,160	1,136	1,147	1,228
4	1,385	1,365	1,098	1,137	1,062	1,095	1,136	1,081	1,191	1,211
5	1,334	1,326	1,155	1,050	1,123	1,087	1,095	1,037	1,118	1,247
6	1,412	1,343	1,189	1,078	1,085	1,089	1,171	1,046	1,131	1,206
7	1,286	1,367	1,160	1,070	1,102	1,035	1,171	1,069	1,119	1,167
8	1,390	1,232	1,149	1,027	1,018	1,053	1,078	983	1,068	1,134
9	1,259	1,316	1,042	1,038	989	996	1,080	933	1,071	1,144
10	1,300	1,183	1,144	917	1,030	996	1,041	936	1,017	1,135
11	1,246	1,184	1,064	1,004	840	993	964	845	1,034	1,104
12	1,076	967	891	703	769	717	820	727	794	886
Ungraded .	3,646	3,700	6,214	5,901	6,122	6,625	6,807	6,698	7,325	7,668
Total.	19,358	19,049	19,576	18,279	18,464	19,104	19,850	18,750	20,362	21,633

Note: A home-based private educational program is a program of educational instruction provided to a child by a child's parent or guardian or by a person designated by the parent or guardian. These programs must provide at least 875 hours of instruction each school year and must offer a sequentially progressive curriculum of fundamental instruction in reading, language arts, mathematics, social studies, science, and health.

Source: Wisconsin Department of Public Instruction, "Home-Based Private Educational Program Enrollment Trends: Enrollment by Grade" at https://dpi.wi.gov/sms/home-based/statistics [March 2019].

Wisconsin charter school enrollments, 2018–2019

CESA[1] district	Total students			American Indian	Asian	Black	Hispanic	Pacific Islander	White	2 or more
	Total	Female	Male							
1	24,061	12,152	11,909	66	2,056	8,710	7,070	10	5,437	712
2	4,324	2,236	2,088	26	94	355	640	3	2,919	287
3	345	174	171	1	3	3	6	0	322	10
4	1,174	583	591	7	17	33	61	0	988	68
5	1,372	634	738	13	26	21	87	2	1,153	70
6	5,158	2,633	2,525	13	294	156	452	3	4,075	165
7	1,674	862	812	11	54	54	282	0	1,147	126
8	187	87	100	23	0	2	3	0	148	11
9	1,701	879	822	13	29	26	62	4	1,529	38
10	1,162	574	588	24	8	40	54	3	971	62
11	1,391	784	607	21	8	71	76	1	1,165	49
12	742	365	377	44	7	6	21	3	626	35
Total.	43,291	21,963	21,328	262	2,596	9,477	8,814	29	20,480	1633

1. Cooperative Educational Service Agency.

Source: Wisconsin Deparment of Public Instructions, Wisconsin Information System for Education at: https://dpi.wi.gov/wisedash/download-files/

AGRICULTURE

Wisconsin's comparative agricultural production, 2017

Commodity	Unit (1,000)	United States Production	United States Leading state	Wisconsin Production	Wisconsin % of U.S.	Wisconsin U.S. rank
All commodities	Dol	371,431,220	California	11,330,883	3.1	9
Livestock and livestock products	Dol	176,034,295	Texas	7,972,042	4.5	6
Crops	Dol	195,396,925	California	3,358,841	1.7	18
Dairy						
Milk production.	Lbs	215,446,000	California	30,320,000	14.1	2
Cheese, total (excluding cottage cheese)	Lbs	12,659,091	Wisconsin	3,365,897	26.6	1
American.	Lbs	5,071,991	Wisconsin	1,016,569	20.0	1
Cheddar	Lbs	3,721,334	Wisconsin	703,960	18.9	1
Italian	Lbs	5,383,864	Wisconsin	1,702,351	31.6	1
Mozzarella	Lbs	4,160,599	California	1,109,289	26.7	2
Dry whey, human food	Lbs	1,017,269	Wisconsin	345,567	34.0	1
Livestock and poultry						
Cattle and calves, all	Head	94,399	Texas	3,500	3.7	9
Milk cows.	Head	9,400	California	1,275	13.6	2
Hogs and pigs, all.	Head	73,695	Iowa	305	0.4	19
Sheep[1]	Head	5,230	Texas	75	1.4	20
Milk goats	Head	380	Wisconsin	47	12.4	1
Chickens	Head	504,536	Iowa	8,514	1.7	17
Broilers	Head	8,913,000	Georgia	53,800	0.6	20
Mink	Pelts	3,305	Wisconsin	1,091	33.0	1
Trout, sold 12" or longer	Lbs	53,286	Idaho	378	0.7	7
Honey	Lbs	147,638	North Dakota	2,968	2.0	15
Eggs	Eggs	105,688,700	Iowa	1,759,400	1.7	17
Crops						
Corn for grain	Bu	14,604,067	Iowa	509,820	3.5	10
Corn for silage	Tons	128,356	Wisconsin	16,720	13.0	1
Oats	Bu	49,391	Minnesota	5,015	10.2	2
Soybeans	Bu	4,391,553	Illinois	100,580	2.3	14
Wheat, winter	Bu	1,269,437	Kansas	11,560	0.9	20
Forage (dry equivalent), all.	Tons	86,692	Texas	7,598	8.8	2
Hay (dry only), all	Tons	131,455	Texas	3,477	2.6	16
Potatoes, all	Cwt	441,307	Idaho	29,145	6.6	3
Cherries, tart	Lbs	259,500	Michigan	11,300	4.4	4
Apples	Lbs	11,406,000	Washington	49,000	0.4	10
Cranberries	Bbl	8,372	Wisconsin	5,372	64.2	1
Maple syrup	Gals	4,271	Vermont	200	4.7	4
Peppermint for oil	Lbs	5,778	Oregon	197	3.4	5
Cabbage, all	Cwt	23,491	California	3,300	14.0	3
Carrots, all	Cwt	30,319	California	2,520	8.3	3
Cucumbers, all	Cwt	19,928	Michigan	688	3.4	8
Pumpkins, all	Cwt	15,660	Illinois	135	0.9	15
Sweet corn, all.	Cwt	79,226	Minnesota	9,592	12.1	3
Green peas, all	Cwt	5,367	Minnesota	968	18.0	3
Snap beans, all	Cwt	18,032	Wisconsin	6,563	36.4	1

Note: Wisconsin is also a leading state in the production of turkeys, ducks, and ginseng; Wisconsin's rank is not available for these commodities.

Bbl–barrels; Bu–bushels; Cwt–hundredweight; Dol–Dollars; Gals–gallons; Lbs–pounds.

1. Tied with Virginia.

Sources: U.S. Department of Agriculture, National Agriculture Statistics Service, "2018 Wisconsin Agricultural Statistics" and U.S. Department of Agriculture, Economic Research Service, "Annual Cash Receipts by Commodity, U.S. and States."

Wisconsin's agricultural cash receipts

Commodity	2014 ($1,000)	2015 ($1,000)	2016 ($1,000)	2017 ($1,000)
All commodities	**12,755,933**	**11,290,089**	**10,748,125**	**11,330,883**
Livestock, dairy, and poultry	**9,401,629**	**8,029,123**	**7,304,501**	**7,972,042**
Meat animals	1,990,709	2,234,309	1,737,302	1,952,288
Cattle and calves	1,854,396	2,128,331	1,639,375	1,829,566
Hogs	136,313	105,978	97,927	122,722
Dairy products, milk	6,745,095	5,121,238	5,014,800	5,443,756
Poultry and eggs	334,719	375,953	255,375	279,597
Broilers	142,879	121,803	108,602	122,944
Farm chickens	504	529	351	162
Eggs	129,992	187,719	79,083	103,278
Miscellaneous livestock	331,105	297,622	297,024	296,401
Honey	6,812	8,466	8,939	8,221
Trout	1,537	1,462	1,558	1,694
Mink pelts	73,207	42,132	39,812	39,610
Wool	263	274	238	215
Crops	**3,354,304**	**3,260,967**	**3,443,624**	**3,358,841**
Food grains	91,825	70,620	72,408	62,943
Wheat	87,428	65,336	66,765	55,806
Feed crops	1,577,730	1,467,082	1,396,351	1,421,306
Barley	1,128	1,033	NA	NA
Corn	1,378,247	1,343,143	1,305,917	1,318,194
Hay	183,098	109,063	84,447	95,958
Oats	15,256	13,842	5,987	7,154
Oil crops	689,426	725,898	983,902	893,484
Soybeans	689,426	725,898	983,902	893,484
Vegetables	456,972	467,525	438,938	447,565
Beans, dry	8,521	9,824	NA	NA
Potatoes, fall	257,078	259,566	281,359	295,050
Beans, snap, processing	57,633	66,472	45,376	35,516
Cabbage	10,295	15,786	13,750	16,467
Carrots	9,569	9,652	10,588	8,820
Corn, sweet	62,212	57,061	48,958	44,537
Cucumbers, processing	10,039	9,538	7,396	4,612
Onions, storage	13,073	10,624	10,624	10,624
Peas, green, processing	26,685	27,110	12,584	10,218
Fruits and nuts	180,650	176,800	203,242	184,547
Apples	31,202	27,825	21,819	26,297
Cherries, tart	4,808	3,049	4,076	2,109
Cranberries	138,370	140,146	177,347	156,141
Strawberries	6,270	5,780	NA	NA
All other crops	357,702	353,042	348,783	348,996
Maple product	6,680	7,117	7,873	6,280
Peppermint oil	3,542	3,507	4,557	3,645
Spearmint oil	1,746	1,586	NA	NA

Note: Bold figures indicate category totals of the commodities immediately following and indicate categories included in next higher level of aggregation. Category totals may include amounts for specific commodities not listed separately or that are not listed to provide confidentiality to large producers in concentrated industries. Prior year's numbers have been revised to reflect updated source data.

NA–Not available.

Source: U.S. Department of Agriculture, Economic Research Service, "Annual Cash Receipts by Commodity, U.S. and States," at http://www.ers.usda.gov/data-products/farm-income-and-wealth-statistics/us-and-state-level-farm-income-and-wealth-statistics-(includes-the-us-farm-income-forecast-for-2015).aspx [November 30, 2016]; and U.S. Department of Agriculture, National Agricultural Statistic Service "2014 Wisconsin Agricultural Statistics," at https://data.ers.usda.gov/reports.aspx?ID=53581#P4ac02090687e44aa93981bc8b2015065_2_16iT0R0x49 [Last updated Nov. 30, 2016].

Wisconsin's agricultural cash receipts, 2017

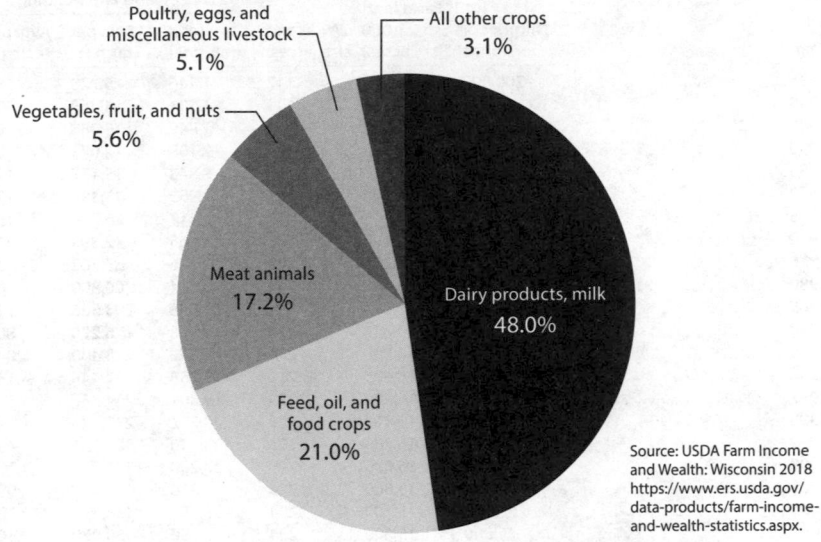

Poultry, eggs, and miscellaneous livestock
5.1%

All other crops
3.1%

Vegetables, fruit, and nuts
5.6%

Meat animals
17.2%

Dairy products, milk
48.0%

Feed, oil, and food crops
21.0%

Source: USDA Farm Income and Wealth: Wisconsin 2018 https://www.ers.usda.gov/data-products/farm-income-and-wealth-statistics.aspx.

Wisconsin's net farm income

Item	2013	2014	2015	2016	2017
Value of agricultural sector production[1] ($1,000)	**13,806,458**	**14,728,661**	**12,970,341**	**12,200,315**	**12,665,225**
Value of crop production.	4,123,863	3,610,826	3,171,503	3,431,471	3,121,434
Value of animals and products production	7,759,108	9,560,469	8,043,040	7,387,687	7,932,138
Farm-related income	1,923,488	1,557,366	1,755,798	1,381,157	1,611,653
Less: Intermediate product expenses[2]	7,332,853	7,898,342	6,890,296	6,904,949	7,158,474
Less: Contract labor expenses	15,282	27,555	26,761	22,903	30,830
Less: Property taxes	400,000	510,000	450,000	380,000	410,000
Less: Motor vehicle registration and licensing fees	15,847	19,783	13,489	17,308	16,234
Plus: Direct government payments.	221,822	92,142	305,627	285,304	134,422
Equals: Gross value added	**6,264,299**	**6,365,123**	**5,895,422**	**5,160,459**	**5,184,110**
Less: Capital consumption (depreciation).	1,202,902	1,584,532	1,383,421	1,431,881	1,287,612
Equals: Net value added[3]	**5,061,397**	**4,780,591**	**4,512,001**	**3,728,579**	**3,896,497**
Less: Payments to stakeholders[4]	1,907,562	2,036,496	1,834,262	2,091,948	2,093,113
Equals: Net farm income[5]	**3,153,835**	**2,744,095**	**2,677,739**	**1,636,630**	**1,803,384**
Number of farms	69,800	69,000	68,900	68,700	68,500
Average net farm income per farm ($).	45,184	39,769	38,864	23,823	26,327

1. Value of agricultural sector output is the gross value of the commodities and services produced within a year. 2. Includes purchases of feed, livestock, poultry, and seed; outlays for fertilizers and lime, pesticides, fuel and electricity; capital repair and maintenance; and marketing, storage, transportation, and other expenses. 3. Net value added is the sector's contribution to the national economy and is the sum of the income from production earned by all factors of production, regardless of ownership. 4. Includes compensation for hired labor, net rent paid to landlords, and interest payments. 5. Net farm income is the farm operators' share of income from the sector's production activities.

Sources: U.S. Department of Agriculture, Economic Research Service, "Value added to the U.S. economy by the agricultural sector via the production of goods and services, Wisconsin, 2010–2019" [Mar. 6, 2019]. U.S. Department of Agriculture, National Agriculture Statistics Service, "2018 Wisconsin Agricultural Statistics" and previous editions at https://www.nass.usda.gov/Statistics_by_State/Wisconsin/Publications/Annual_Statistical_Bulletin/ [September, 2018].

Number, size, and value of farms in Wisconsin

Year	Number of farms	Farm land (1,000 acres)	Avg. farm size (acres)	Value of land and buildings Total (mil. dol.)	Avg. per farm ($)	Avg. per acre ($)
1935.	200,000	23,500	117	1,246	6,228	$53
1940.	187,000	22,900	123	1,191	6,368	52
1945.	178,000	23,600	133	1,440	8,088	61
1950.	174,000	23,600	136	2,100	12,071	89
1955.	155,000	23,200	150	2,343	15,117	101
1960.	138,000	22,200	161	2,953	21,396	133
1965.	124,000	21,400	173	3,317	26,750	155
1970.	110,000	20,100	183	4,663	42,393	232
1975.	100,000	19,300	193	8,376	83,762	434
1980.	93,000	18,600	200	18,674	200,800	1,004
1985.	83,000	17,900	216	16,898	203,586	944
1990.	80,000	17,600	220	14,098	176,220	801
1995.	80,000	16,800	210	17,472	218,400	1,040
1996.	79,000	16,600	210	18,758	237,443	1,130
1997.	79,000	16,500	209	19,305	244,367	1,170
1998.	78,000	16,300	209	20,212	259,128	1,240
1999.	78,000	16,200	208	23,490	301,154	1,450
2000.	77,500	16,000	206	27,200	350,968	1,700
2001.	77,000	15,800	205	30,810	400,130	1,950
2002.	77,000	15,700	204	33,755	438,377	2,150
2003.	76,500	15,600	204	35,880	469,020	2,300
2004.	76,500	15,500	203	38,750	506,536	2,500
2005.	76,500	15,400	201	43,890	573,725	2,850
2006.	76,000	15,300	201	48,960	644,211	3,200
2007.	78,500	15,200	194	57,760	735,796	3,800
2008.	78,000	15,200	195	58,520	750,256	3,850
2009.	78,000	15,200	195	57,000	730,769	3,750
2010.	73,200	14,700	201	53,655	732,992	3,650
2011.	71,200	14,600	205	56,648	795,618	3,880
2012.	69,800	14,600	209	60,006	859,685	4,110
2013.	69,800	14,600	209	59,860	857,593	4,100
2014.	69,000	14,500	210	63,800	924,638	4,400
2015.	68,900	14,400	209	67,680	982,293	4,700
2016.	68,700	14,400	210	68,400	995,633	4,750
2017.	68,500	14,300	209	74,360	1,085,547	5,200

Notes: "Farm" is currently defined as a place that sells, or would normally sell, at least $1,000 of agricultural products during the year. The actual number of farms in Wisconsin peaked at 199,877 in 1935.

Sources: U.S. Department of Agriculture, National Agricultural Statistics Service, "Wisconsin Agricultural Statistics 2018" and prior editions and "Agricultural Land Values and Cash Rents." [September, 2018]

Nonirrigated cropland cash rents

	2013 ($/acre)	2017 ($/acre)	% change		2013 ($/acre)	2017 ($/acre)	% change
Adams	65.50	77.00	17.6	Buffalo	112.00	131.00	17.0
Ashland.	NA	NA	NA	Burnett	39.00	46.00	17.9
Barron.	71.00	83.50	17.6	Calumet	128.00	134.00	4.7
Bayfield.	NA	NA	NA	Chippewa	93.00	117.00	25.8
Brown.	144.00	165.00	14.6	Clark.	87.00	105.00	20.7

Nonirrigated cropland cash rents, continued

	2013 ($/acre)	2017 ($/acre)	% change		2013 ($/acre)	2017 ($/acre)	% change
Columbia.	163.00	189.00	16.0	Oconto	89.00	119.00	33.71
Crawford	131.00	134.00	2.3	Oneida	NA	NA	NA
Dane	163.00	180.00	10.4	Outagamie.	129.00	124.00	-3.88
Dodge	157.00	199.00	26.8	Ozaukee	87.00	NA	NA
Door.	93.50	NA	NA	Pepin	115.00	144.00	25.22
Douglas.	NA	NA	NA	Pierce	121.00	152.00	25.62
Dunn	97.00	102.00	5.2	Polk	68.50	77.00	12.41
Eau Claire.	120.00	88.50	-26.3	Portage.	49.00	66.00	34.69
Florence	NA	NA	NA	Price.	36.00	35.00	-2.78
Fond du Lac	120.00	173.00	44.2	Racine.	122.00	128.00	4.92
Forest	NA	NA	NA	Richland	113.00	107.00	-5.31
Grant	206.00	185.00	-10.2	Rock.	175.00	161.00	-8.00
Green	160.00	164.00	2.5	Rusk	48.00	70.00	45.83
Green Lake.	185.00	133.00	-28.1	St. Croix.	109.00	98.00	-10.09
Iowa	172.00	169.00	-1.7	Sauk.	110.00	127.00	15.45
Iron	NA	NA	NA	Sawyer	40.00	41.50	3.75
Jackson	116.00	108.00	-6.9	Shawano	87.00	99.00	13.79
Jefferson	154.00	148.00	-3.9	Sheboygan.	100.00	108.00	8.00
Juneau	90.00	90.50	0.6	Taylor	70.00	78.00	11.43
Kenosha	128.00	139.00	8.6	Trempealeau	135.00	124.00	-8.15
Kewaunee	120.00	NA	NA	Vernon	117.00	140.00	19.66
La Crosse	127.00	152.00	19.7	Vilas	NA	NA	NA
Lafayette	212.00	230.00	8.5	Walworth.	182.00	184.00	1.10
Langlade	66.00	79.00	19.7	Washburn	49.50	51.00	3.03
Lincoln	44.00	56.00	27.3	Washington	102.00	108.00	5.88
Manitowoc.	127.00	158.00	24.4	Waukesha	NA	128.00	NA
Marathon.	82.00	95.50	16.46	Waupaca	88.00	79.00	-10.23
Marinette.	54.00	66.50	23.15	Waushara.	51.00	53.00	3.92
Marquette	102.00	75.50	-25.98	Winnebago	97.50	91.50	-6.15
Menominee	NA	NA	NA	Wood	61.00	104.00	70.49
Milwaukee	NA	NA	NA	**Total. . . . .**	**82.00**	**133.00**	**62.2**
Monroe	106.00	130.00	22.64				

NA–Not applicable. Data withheld to avoid disclosing details of individual operators.

Source: U.S. Department of Agriculture, National Agriculture Statistics Service, "2018 Wisconsin Agricultural Statistics" and previous editions at https://www.nass.usda.gov/Statistics_by_State/Wisconsin/Publications/Annual_Statistical_Bulletin/ [September, 2018].

Wisconsin agricultural land sales

	Total agricultural land sales[2]				Land continuing in agricultural use, avg. cost per acre ($)		Agricultural land diverted to other uses, avg. cost per acre ($)	
	Number		Avg. cost per acre ($)					
County[1]	2016	2017	2016	2017	2016	2017	2016	2017
Adams	4	5	3,500	3,201	3,500	3,437	NA	2,173
Ashland.	4	12	1,223	1,291	1,223	1,219	NA	1,575
Barron.	34	32	3,218	3,563	3,079	3,563	9,995	NA
Bayfield.	3	8	1,573	975	1,148	975	2,286	NA
Brown.	22	23	10,757	10,219	10,757	10,326	NA	4,800
Buffalo	23	11	4,001	4,120	3,959	4,198	5,137	3,100

Wisconsin agricultural land sales, continued

County[1]	Total agricultural land sales[2]				Land continuing in agricultural use, avg. cost per acre ($)		Agricultural land diverted to other uses, avg. cost per acre ($)	
	Number		Avg. cost per acre ($)					
	2016	2017	2016	2017	2016	2017	2016	2017
Burnett	3	6	1,916	1,755	1,916	1,755	NA	NA
Calumet	12	4	9,734	14,226	9,734	10,918	NA	18,865
Chippewa	16	34	3,967	3,091	3,729	3,053	8,335	4,142
Clark.	28	24	3,960	5,234	3,828	3,653	7,800	10,833
Columbia.	16	19	8,232	6,562	8,013	6,556	10,500	6,676
Crawford	13	8	3,265	3,480	3,268	3,479	3,100	3,500
Dane	24	38	9,693	12,507	9,170	8,458	25,650	16,122
Dodge	23	15	6,467	7,053	6,527	7,053	4,444	NA
Door.	9	6	3,861	3,884	3,845	3,945	4,471	2,200
Douglas.	8	3	908	1,010	908	1,010	NA	NA
Dunn	26	31	3,608	3,150	3,608	3,150	NA	NA
Eau Claire.	12	15	4,171	4,755	3,102	4,445	6,113	6,742
Florence	NA	2	NA	1,145	NA	1,145	NA	NA
Fond du Lac	19	34	7,463	6,487	7,463	6,495	NA	5,942
Forest	NA	1	NA	1,325	NA	NA	NA	1,325
Grant	21	10	5,102	5,662	5,102	5,662	NA	NA
Green	13	21	5,747	6,267	5,866	5,745	4,500	19,950
Green Lake.	10	11	6,748	5,315	6,748	5,369	NA	4,000
Iowa.	21	20	5,049	4,794	5,049	4,794	NA	NA
Iron	1	NA	1,200	NA	NA	NA	1,200	NA
Jackson.	5	12	3,592	5,919	3,566	2,889	4,000	13,018
Jefferson	17	6	7,383	5,826	7,399	5,826	5,800	NA
Juneau	5	9	3,748	3,098	3,748	2,999	NA	3,825
Kenosha	2	4	6,855	7,380	6,855	7,380	NA	NA
Kewaunee	4	10	6,568	6,845	6,568	6,865	NA	5,000
La Crosse.	5	8	3,815	5,973	3,220	4,037	6,575	9,140
Lafayette	17	13	6,805	6,614	6,805	6,614	NA	NA
Langlade	12	7	3,013	3,591	3,013	3,706	NA	2,671
Lincoln	5	4	2,106	2,023	2,339	2,023	1,752	NA
Manitowoc.	7	9	8,348	6,738	8,348	6,738	NA	NA
Marathon.	42	27	3,831	3,892	3,848	3,975	3,320	2,868
Marinette.	9	5	3,610	3,128	3,610	3,082	NA	3,553
Marquette	8	16	3,038	3,602	3,198	3,602	2,641	NA
Monroe	13	15	2,809	4,196	2,809	4,196	NA	NA
Oconto	12	13	4,260	4,079	4,225	4,112	5,126	3,432
Oneida	1	2	1,200	1,456	NA	1,456	1,200	NA
Outagamie.	23	16	7,180	6,675	7,180	6,675	NA	NA
Ozaukee	2	8	6,944	6,985	6,944	6,985	NA	NA
Pepin	4	3	2,049	3,751	2,049	3,850	NA	3,714
Pierce	20	18	3,949	4,189	3,960	4,189	3,731	NA
Polk	21	30	3,132	3,150	3,138	3,126	2,951	4,251
Portage	14	15	3,344	3,349	3,328	3,184	3,557	4,275
Price	2	2	1,230	1,542	1,230	1,542	NA	NA
Racine.	11	10	6,770	7,724	6,770	7,724	NA	NA
Richland	13	10	3,629	3,493	3,586	3,515	3,983	3,000
Rock.	13	23	7,948	7,881	5,383	6,093	34,900	11,566
Rusk.	8	13	1,452	1,540	1,452	1,540	NA	NA
St. Croix.	27	22	4,653	4,341	4,540	4,336	8,095	4,464
Sauk.	31	19	4,069	4,030	4,069	4,073	NA	3,100
Sawyer	1	NA	2,026	NA	2,026	NA	NA	NA
Shawano	18	18	5,626	5,158	5,670	5,158	5,351	NA
Sheboygan.	21	21	6,225	6,450	6,225	6,588	NA	4,851
Taylor	7	11	3,331	3,583	3,331	3,583	NA	NA
Trempealeau.	18	17	4,712	4,373	4,750	4,244	3,354	4,867

Wisconsin agricultural land sales, continued

County[1]	Total agricultural land sales[2]				Land continuing in agricultural use, avg. cost per acre ($)		Agricultural land diverted to other uses, avg. cost per acre ($)	
	Number		Avg. cost per acre ($)					
	2016	2017	2016	2017	2016	2017	2016	2017
Vernon	22	16	3,917	4,021	3,917	4,021	NA	NA
Vilas	NA	1	NA	1,700	NA	1,700	NA	NA
Walworth.	6	13	6,958	7,524	6,958	7,524	NA	NA
Washburn	4	3	2,326	3,004	1,486	3,004	3,434	NA
Washington	11	14	7,353	11,358	7,353	10,088	NA	20,459
Waukesha	1	7	8,051	10,997	NA	11,406	8,051	10,300
Waupaca	17	13	4,186	3,797	4,161	3,784	4,326	3,907
Waushara.	8	9	2,839	3,502	2,839	3,502	NA	NA
Winnebago	21	8	6,671	6,317	6,230	6,317	10,599	NA
Wood	5	8	3,118	3,565	3,118	3,608	NA	3,045
State	878	901	5,306	5,485	5,221	4,960	7,558	10,794

NA–Not available.

1. Menominee and Milwaukee counties had no agricultural sales in years shown.   2. Includes land with and without buildings and other improvements.

Sources: U.S. Department of Agriculture, National Agricultural Statistics Service, "Agricultural Land Sales, Total Agricultural Land, Wisconsin, 2017" and earlier editions, at https://www.nass.usda.gov/Statistics_by_State/Wisconsin/Publications/Land_Sales/index.php/ [Aug 27, 2017].

CONSERVATION

Fish and game harvested, 2017–18

Fish[1]	12,334,465	Gray fox	4,613
Great Lakes trout[2]	96,371	Coyote	47,661
Great Lakes salmon[2]	169,553	Deer (with guns)	227,645
Game and fowl[3]		Deer (with bows)	92,394
Wild turkey	47,276	Bear	4,159
Pheasant	301,490	Duck	404,606
Ruffed grouse	185,336	Canada goose	135,776
Gray partridge	131	**Furbearers[3]**	
Bobwhite quail	524	Muskrat	223,936
Woodcock	69,902	Mink	6,153
Squirrel	204,138	Beaver	18,122
Cottontail rabbit	83,988	River otter	1,515
Snowshoe hare	2,358	Bobcat	574
Doves	56,407	Opossum	15,112
Raccoon	109,433	Skunk	5,325
Red fox	7,813	Fisher	656

1. Data based on 2014–2015 diary survey estimating total fish caught (39,654,149) and total harvested. These are underestimates, because they do not include fish caught or harvested by unlicensed anglers, short-term license holders, or senior citizen discount license holders.   2. Data from Lake Michigan Creel Harvest Tables 2004–18 at https://dnr.wi.gov/topic/fishing/documents/lakemichigan/CreelHarvestTables2004–2018.pdf.   3. Deer, bear, turkey, bobcat, otter, and fisher are all from hunter-registered harvest. Remaining data is from hunter surveys.

Source: Wisconsin Department of Natural Resources, departmental data, April 2019.

Fish and game stocked, 2017–18

Game farm pheasants released	98,164
Warmwater fish produced and distributed (includes fry)	25,799,705
Coldwater fish	2,586,063

Source: Wisconsin Department of Natural Resources, departmental data, April 2019.

Fish and game licenses and recreation permits issued

	2013	2014	2015	2016	2017	2018
Boats actively registered	614,452	628,073	623,796	618,043	630,134	619,319
Snowmobiles actively registered	236,248	222,418	213,325	200,529	223,938	214,661
All-terrain vehicles actively registered	298,857	309,458	320,758	366,987	382,029	400,285
Off-highway motorcycles actively registered	NA	NA	NA	365	2,245	3,608
Gun deer hunting and license tags (including nonresident)[1]	530,256	513,284	515,869	499,312	488,826	472,370
Small game hunting license tags (including nonresident)[1]	135,310	135,635	134,391	129,857	120,103	109,155
Spring turkey licenses (including nonresident)[1]	106,082	97,832	94,056	96,469	93,689	87,429
Fall turkey licenses (including nonresident)[1]	18,455	15,841	14,663	16,006	15,298	21,767
Resident annual fishing licenses[2]	707,285	711,112	721,379	706,688	686,253	652,561
Resident husband and wife fishing licenses	216,920	213,468	211,439	196,332	190,994	187,471
1-day resident fishing licenses	7,591	8,340	8,290	8,784	10,566	9,767
Nonresident annual fishing licenses	107,777	109,525	114,847	120,309	120,563	113,594
Nonresident family annual fishing licenses	64,298	63,652	64,706	57,530	54,324	53,548
15-day nonresident family fishing licenses	31,907	31,622	31,142	25,780	23,282	22,424

Fish and game licenses and recreation permits issued, continued

	2013	2014	2015	2016	2017	2018
15-day nonresident fishing licenses	24,185	23,981	24,087	24,888	24,956	24,973
4-day nonresident fishing licenses	55,562	54,608	56,896	52,670	52,288	51,184
1-day nonresident fishing licenses	59,552	61,965	63,811	61,116	64,394	60,211
Resident sports licenses.	53,982	50,328	48,770	46,144	44,567	48,140
Nonresident sports licenses	3,879	3,639	3,600	3,022	3,147	3,403
2-day Great Lakes fishing licenses	38,936	38,975	37,411	39,751	37,837	36,174
Resident archer's licenses[1]	209,896	171,657	165,025	157,691	143,244	130,524
Nonresident archer's licenses[1].	9,946	8,833	9,077	9,204	8,928	8,782
Guide licenses (residents only)	1,387	1,526	1,552	1,188	1,592	1,789
Conservation patron licenses	45,585	46,633	47,965	50,231	51,889	52,633
Nonresident patron licenses	953	932	973	1,147	1,213	1,039
Resident crossbow[3]	NA	46,224	62,872	58,878	70,855	77,988
Nonresident crossbow[3]	NA	1,250	1,767	1,512	2,093	2,453
Elk license (residents only)	NA	NA	NA	NA	NA	5

Notes: Crossbow data collection started in 2014; data is not available before 2014. The first Wisconsin elk season was held in 2018. DNR began registering off-highway motorcycles in 2016.

NA–Not available.

1. Includes mentored licenses.   2. Includes senior and junior fishing licenses.   3. Includes mentored licenses. Does not include upgrades.

Source: Wisconsin Department of Natural Resources, departmental data, April 2019.

Department of Natural Resources funding sources

	2012–13 ($1,000)	2013–14 ($1,000)	2014–15 ($1,000)	2015–16 ($1,000)	2016–17 ($1,000)	2017–18 ($1,000)
Segregated funds	**356,657**	**369,909**	**361,576**	**412,609**	**432,415**	**427,135**
All-terrain vehicle registration fees	3,849	2,876	3,756	4,635	3,954	5,471
Boat registration fees	5,672	5,002	5,543	5,611	5,165	5,573
Dry cleaner fund	1,533	1,894	757	820	576	572
Endangered resources voluntary payments . .	578	896	549	1,218	1,688	1,422
Environmental improvement fund	891	910	1,358	1,404	1,408	1,729
Environmental management account	47,192	48,451	48,231	52,026	48,057	44,353
Federal aids	54,517	55,352	53,799	93,340	103,659	104,553
Fishing, hunting licenses and permits	69,039	68,564	69,267	64,549	67,524	68,720
Forestry mill tax.	95,023	100,288	97,208	99,721	109,699	98,883
Gifts and donations	557	690	751	620	641	932
Heritage State Parks and Forests Trust Fund . .	61	46	35	42	94	33
Nonpoint source account.	15,752	14,538	15,134	16,135	15,866	15,055
Park stickers and fees	13,077	14,420	13,984	18,676	19,068	21,605
Petroleum storage environmental cleanup fund	5,368	10,570	9,514	11,621	10,964	12,351
Program revenue	28,010	29,061	25,741	26,852	26,937	28,846
Recycling fund	—	1	—	—	—	—
Snowmobile registration fees	2,913	2,840	2,981	2,696	3,737	3,873
Waste management fund.	37	347	198	66	18	438
Water resources account	11,943	12,370	11,981	12,006	12,893	12,306
Wisconsin Natural Resources Magazine	645	799	789	571	467	420
General funds.	**183,714**	**196,163**	**175,297**	**161,753**	**164,092**	**158,356**
General purpose revenue.	119,650	130,130	109,049	102,175	106,900	97,746
Program revenues	19,568	22,470	20,370	18,438	20,227	22,983
Program revenue—services	10,293	11,327	11,051	10,227	9,455	7,860
Federal aids	34,203	32,236	34,827	30,913	27,510	29,767
Total.	**540,370**	**566,072**	**536,873**	**574,362**	**596,507**	**585,491**

—Represents zero.

Source: Wisconsin Department of Natural Resources, departmental data, April 2019.

Department of Natural Resources expenditures

Program	2012–13 ($1,000)	2013–14 ($1,000)	2014–15 ($1,000)	2015–16 ($1,000)	2016–17 ($1,000)	2017–18 ($1,000)
Fish, wildlife, and parks (FWP)*	**84,420**	**85,848**	**89,477**	**85,711**	**87,401**	**85,706**
Wildlife management	20,684	20,759	21,618	20,260	21,248	24,285
Southern forests	5,611	5,597	5,613	5,235	5,540	5,455
Fisheries management	25,377	25,143	27,384	26,060	25,509	26,322
Parks	17,589	18,345	18,010	17,282	17,720	17,842
Endangered resources	4,940	4,650	5,867	6,068	6,648	6,939
Facilities and lands	9,062	10,205	9,911	9,690	9,438	—
Property management	—	—	—	—	—	3,744
FWP program management	1,157	1,149	1,074	1,116	1,298	1,119
Forestry	**50,027**	**56,796**	**52,903**	**53,247**	**61,655**	**53,403**
Public safety*	**45,066**	**42,198**	**41,362**	**39,316**	**40,425**	**36,145**
Law enforcement	32,066	31,809	30,921	30,913	31,230	35,383
Integrated science services	12,112	9,548	9,574	7,617	8,356	—
Enforcement/science program management	888	841	867	786	839	762
Environmental management (EM)*	**76,895**	**74,189**	**74,494**	**70,041**	**69,667**	**72,080**
Drinking and groundwater	12,683	12,553	13,034	12,931	13,464	13,755
Water quality	28,601	24,840	26,444	22,427	22,922	23,299
Air management	13,863	14,622	13,722	14,049	13,366	10,911
Waste and materials management	7,070	8,251	7,434	6,962	7,106	7,159
Remediation and redevelopment	11,761	11,411	11,461	11,140	10,529	15,689
EM program management	2,134	2,512	2,399	2,532	2,280	1,267
Cooperative environmental assistance	783	—	—	—	—	—
Conservation aids*	**43,481**	**42,407**	**42,575**	**45,700**	**43,735**	**44,718**
Fish and wildlife aids	2,147	1,274	1,565	1,578	1,367	848
Forestry aids	10,675	9,440	8,561	9,869	8,571	8,005
Recreational aids	10,674	10,867	12,290	12,730	12,105	13,825
Aids in lieu of taxes	14,723	15,583	15,308	16,916	16,975	17,140
Enforcement aids	2,199	2,277	2,277	2,277	2,277	2,277
Wildlife damage aids	3,063	2,966	2,574	2,330	2,440	2,623
Environmental aids*	**31,214**	**34,113**	**33,630**	**34,643**	**35,803**	**35,669**
Water quality aids	6,561	6,966	6,093	5,807	6,839	6,260
Solid and hazard waste aids	20,844	20,803	21,446	20,163	21,103	20,829
Environmental aids	1,564	7,238	5,067	6,373	5,912	6,509
Environmental planning aids	211	191	232	172	294	365
Nonpoint aids	2,034	−1,085	792	2,128	1,655	1,706
Debt service*	**123,492**	**136,139**	**110,109**	**115,815**	**116,781**	**105,634**
Resource	80,338	89,515	72,382	77,986	87,567	79,399
Environmental	4,827	4,833	4,468	4,725	4,856	4,093
Water quality	32,083	35,330	29,845	29,598	20,766	18,737
Administrative facility	6,244	6,461	3,414	3,506	3,592	3,405
Acquisition and development*	**8,659**	**10,917**	**10,743**	**13,222**	**9,477**	**9,692**
Wildlife	545	1,013	1,384	1,084	995	741
Fish	507	559	1,838	198	751	314
Forestry	2,930	3,650	918	5,323	1,572	285
Southern forests	214	21	317	361	379	327
Parks	1,462	2,475	3,625	1,746	2,310	1,639
Endangered resources	820	1,742	308	847	319	255
Facilities and lands	2,176	1,455	2,153	3,591	3,142	5,531
Property management	—	—	—	—	—	600
Law Enforcement	—	—	163	72	4	—
Customer and employee services	5	—	—	—	—	—
Water resources	—	2	37	—	5	—
Administration*	**23,394**	**24,855**	**22,401**	**23,896**	**21,986**	**24,191**
Administration	1,603	1,727	1,707	1,647	1,906	1,437
Legal services	2,231	2,389	2,369	2,357	2,158	2,210
Management and budget	510	528	547	530	427	640
Facility rental	7,128	7,218	7,336	7,514	7,651	7,498
Nonbudget accounts	11,922	12,993	10,442	11,848	9,844	12,406
Internal services (IS)*	**18,302**	**19,177**	**19,743**	**20,261**	**20,287**	**31,193**

Department of Natural Resources expenditures, continued

Program	2012–13 ($1,000)	2013–14 ($1,000)	2014–15 ($1,000)	2015–16 ($1,000)	2016–17 ($1,000)	2017–18 ($1,000)
Finance	5,989	6,616	7,035	7,633	6,837	6,893
Facilities and lands	—	—	—	—	—	9,164
Technology services	8,237	8,426	8,964	8,917	9,691	8,840
Human resources.	4,076	4,134	3,744	3,711	3,759	2,686
IS Program management	—	—	—	—	—	3,610
External Services (EX)*	**35,288**	**39,129**	**39,969**	**70,221**	**89,170**	**87,062**
Watershed management	13,678	13,834	14,435	13,768	14,455	14,321
Office of communication	1,523	1,823	1,763	979	923	723
Community financial assistance.	5,723	5,915	6,284	41,660	56,611	55,920
Customer & outreach services	11,341	11,128	11,207	7,681	11,143	9,957
Environmental analysis & sustainability :	—	3,393	3,480	3,409	3,084	5,123
EX program management	3,023	3,036	2,800	2,724	2,954	1,018
Total*	**540,238**	**565,768**	**537,406**	**572,073**	**596,387**	**585,493**

*Total of detail immediately following. Totals do not add due to rounding.
—Represents zero.
Source: Wisconsin Department of Natural Resources, departmental data, April 2019.

Department of Natural Resources land acquisition acres

Fiscal year	Northern forests	Southern forests	Natural areas	Parks	Wild rivers	Wildlife mgt.	Fisheries mgt.	Other	Total
1990[1]	975	283	1,278	683	2,490	4,269	2,333	10	12,311
1991.	930	1,567	4,745	1,352	11,832	5,997	1,671	61	28,155
1992.	791	157	3,176	362	15,067	3,940	1,787	226	25,506
1993.	721	298	3,166	624	4,328	5,160	1,475	245	16,018
1994.	396	306	3,288	1,820	3,191	3,137	2,879	563	15,580
1995.	373	370	1,985	271	835	5,052	8,093	633	17,612
1996.	977	398	5,830	1,248	2,012	3,566	2,344	368	16,743
1997.	213	161	2,038	884	2,003	2,929	1,548	332	10,110
1998.	278	81	1,467	107	9,944	4,045	1,133	317	17,372
1999.	815	513	1,904	641	775	2,501	600	209	7,957
2000[2]	496	110	3,301	3,705	16,135	11,800	2,808	136	38,489
2001.	149	194	1,063	4,295	3,558	5,191	2,773	683	17,905
2002.	5,525	208	3,174	1,349	607	4,997	1,595	258	17,713
2003.	35,464	0	5,801	2,029	2,406	3,765	1,880	86	51,432
2004.	4,132	159	1,747	3,060	2,132	7,513	1,177	156	20,076
2005.	6,578	475	7,477	3,842	10,692	5,385	2,308	329	37,086
2006.	18,799	103	2,592	1,823	767	6,022	957	414	31,476
2007.	45,075	171	2,948	713	8,793	3,247	982	192	62,121
2008.	8,722	12	2,288	1,641	2,589	6,515	915	454	23,136
2009.	7,943	1,024	1,844	1,876	1,867	2,150	837	358	17,899
2010.	8,547	37	3,498	1,000	818	3,767	785	73	18,525
2011.	27,070	297	5,845	3,525	2,729	5,560	1,786	5	46,818
2012.	10,866	0	1,804	619	184	892	587	7	14,958
2013.	48,989	247	2,697	891	437	3,046	1,430	157	57,894
2014.	10,283	144	1,346	204	147	4,267	87	283	16,761
2015.	14,446	10	455	1,049	81	1,404	843	218	18,506
2016.	22,340	92	245	358	4	6,671	358	85	30,152
2017.	7,285	44	1,040	359	146	990	355	12	10,231
2018.	20,816	1	4	17	21	844	444	3	22,150
Total.	**309,993**	**7,461**	**78,045**	**40,349**	**106,589**	**124,623**	**46,770**	**6,873**	**720,703**

1. The Warren Knowles-Gaylord Nelson Stewardship Program replaced the Outdoor Recreation Act Program (ORAP) in 1990.
2. The Stewardship 2000 program replaced the Warren Knowles-Gaylord Nelson Stewardship Program in 2000.
Source: Wisconsin Department of Natural Resources, Bureau of Facilities and Lands, departmental data, April 2019.

Department of Natural Resources land acquisition cost

Fiscal year	Northern forests ($1,000)	Southern forests ($1,000)	Natural areas ($1,000)	Parks ($1,000)	Wild rivers ($1,000)	Wildlife mgt. ($1,000)	Fisheries mgt. ($1,000)	Other ($1,000)	Total
1990[1]	395	490	610	727	2,216	1,880	1,951	1	8,269
1991	385	1,675	2,133	384	6,245	3,027	1,498	1,557	16,902
1992	416	398	1,195	461	5,537	2,735	1,530	48	12,320
1993	547	249	1,473	547	1,950	1,636	1,359	31	7,791
1994	178	793	724	902	1,843	2,118	2,315	148	9,021
1995	640	1,315	3,472	762	1,120	3,872	3,688	219	15,087
1996	542	1,036	3,108	2,758	1,413	2,832	2,596	441	14,726
1997	378	617	589	1,168	1,321	2,439	1,757	80	8,349
1998	137	293	2,077	337	11,005	4,331	1,513	1,307	21,001
1999	941	1,170	1,075	1,548	580	3,693	1,534	336	10,878
2000[2]	550	403	3,472	2,734	12,633	9,061	2,861	352	32,066
2001	533	873	2,156	8,605	739	4,251	5,247	420	22,824
2002	13,575	1,105	2,955	3,244	1,095	5,635	4,156	3,822	35,587
2003	7,680	—	3,603	4,105	3,807	3,908	3,976	117	27,196
2004	13,474	579	2,770	5,727	4,629	8,490	3,054	130	38,853
2005	2,418	3,050	4,993	16,693	3,591	8,164	5,034	401	44,345
2006	9,852	1,220	3,642	3,247	1,526	5,574	3,919	81	29,061
2007	20,147	1,081	4,039	6,760	15,864	7,227	3,529	254	58,901
2008	8,734	246	3,004	3,222	5,777	10,016	2,529	135	33,663
2009	6,534	11,325	1,849	8,069	3,729	4,250	2,236	128	38,122
2010	5,867	272	5,448	2,881	2,119	6,693	2,232	122	25,635
2011	12,974	2,023	7,153	4,762	5,416	10,144	4,277	35	46,782
2012	7,426	—	1,836	2,605	369	2,736	1,657	—	16,628
2013	17,412	796	900	3,955	490	5,333	1,660	—	30,547
2014	6,997	742	967	572	410	5,630	249	73	15,640
2015	1,154	30	782	884	899	2,315	1,390	40	7,493
2016	189	660	719	1,273	7	1,328	682	40	4,896
2017	213	250	2,148	74	520	192	369	—	3,767
2018	3	—	—	—	—	60	71	—	134
Total	209,159	101,559	137,761	157,875	165,718	198,438	137,738	79,186	705,354

—Represents zero.

1. The Warren Knowles-Gaylord Nelson Stewardship Program replaced the Outdoor Recreation Act Program (ORAP) in 1990.
2. The Stewardship 2000 program replaced the Warren Knowles-Gaylord Nelson Stewardship Program in 2000.

Source: Wisconsin Department of Natural Resources, Bureau of Facilities and Lands, departmental data, April 2019.

TRANSPORTATION

Highway mileage in Wisconsin, January 1, 2018

County	Total miles	State trunk system	County trunk system	Local roads (city, village, town)	Other roads (parks, forests)
Adams	1,452.25	91.45	226.67	1,134.13	0.00
Ashland.	1,136.56	119.53	91.35	878.23	47.45
Barron.	1,998.00	141.89	290.90	1,565.21	0.00
Bayfield.	2,209.73	155.17	172.81	1,778.96	102.79
Brown.	2,345.40	189.32	360.85	1,789.93	5.30
Buffalo	1,041.74	148.02	317.89	572.44	3.39
Burnett	1,572.58	106.38	220.05	1,205.19	40.96
Calumet	873.92	94.33	133.49	646.10	0.00
Chippewa	2,146.04	210.26	489.25	1,428.41	18.12
Clark.	2,190.01	157.37	300.91	1,684.75	46.98
Columbia.	1,740.05	277.90	357.23	1,103.93	0.99
Crawford	1,089.34	182.78	132.43	768.65	5.48
Dane	4,218.53	401.57	521.44	3,274.19	21.33
Dodge	2,069.76	238.12	538.61	1,281.60	11.43
Door.	1,269.06	101.61	295.55	871.90	0.00
Douglas.	2,095.66	161.27	336.72	1,500.44	97.23
Dunn	1,760.39	205.43	425.12	1,129.84	0.00
Eau Claire.	1,599.33	150.06	420.53	1,010.80	17.94
Florence	553.90	66.84	49.12	378.34	59.60
Fond du Lac	1,792.17	199.53	384.05	1,208.59	0.00
Forest	1,112.42	152.41	109.06	777.84	73.11
Grant	2,127.42	259.08	310.87	1,557.47	0.00
Green	1,262.83	122.45	277.86	862.52	0.00
Green Lake.	703.66	69.97	228.27	405.42	0.00
Iowa.	1,318.77	169.63	364.75	783.13	1.26
Iron	801.27	114.00	67.24	556.86	63.17
Jackson.	1,475.86	185.97	231.24	1,035.11	23.54
Jefferson	1,443.17	179.60	257.27	1,006.30	0.00
Juneau	1,532.84	191.95	234.18	1,095.00	11.71
Kenosha	1,102.21	116.50	252.72	732.99	0.00
Kewaunee	828.44	61.80	219.06	547.58	0.00
La Crosse	1,204.23	156.51	282.09	765.63	0.00
Lafayette	1,158.97	126.79	272.15	760.03	0.00
Langlade	1,159.56	143.36	271.09	736.90	8.21
Lincoln	1,323.05	155.51	270.73	869.56	27.25
Manitowoc.	1,661.89	155.06	283.60	1,223.23	0.00
Marathon.	3,384.64	276.56	614.48	2,487.12	6.48
Marinette.	2,362.53	154.27	334.28	1,641.80	232.18
Marquette	860.30	87.18	237.28	535.77	0.07
Menominee	452.40	40.74	36.51	79.05	296.10
Milwaukee	3,041.72	252.84	141.02	2,629.02	18.84
Monroe	1,732.62	238.30	343.58	1,063.17	87.57
Oconto	2,053.08	149.76	318.51	1,539.16	45.65
Oneida	1,723.59	159.63	171.22	1,352.56	40.18
Outagamie.	2,017.21	186.75	344.02	1,478.94	7.50
Ozaukee	945.43	82.31	155.55	707.57	0.00
Pepin	462.40	48.58	154.72	259.10	0.00
Pierce	1,316.74	164.19	248.65	898.42	5.48
Polk	1,988.11	159.13	331.37	1,487.32	10.29
Portage.	1,902.50	157.72	434.00	1,310.78	0.00
Price	1,446.60	155.24	220.05	1,054.74	16.57
Racine.	1,332.22	152.97	164.77	1,014.48	0.00
Richland	1,130.09	150.14	296.50	683.45	0.00
Rock.	2,088.68	252.61	213.30	1,622.55	0.22

Highway mileage in Wisconsin, January 1, 2018, continued

County	Total miles	State trunk system	County trunk system	Local roads (city, village, town)	Other roads (parks, forests)
Rusk	1,242.42	105.26	255.13	859.68	22.35
St. Croix	1,945.20	205.02	336.07	1,402.43	1.68
Sauk	1,903.92	221.52	308.31	1,294.75	79.34
Sawyer	1,511.32	161.32	228.94	1,092.45	28.61
Shawano	1,766.72	178.84	293.87	1,252.51	41.50
Sheboygan	1,563.24	166.50	449.30	947.44	0.00
Taylor	1,463.52	110.22	248.37	1,081.49	23.44
Trempealeau	1,368.89	176.31	291.90	891.74	8.94
Vernon	1,653.71	214.03	285.22	1,153.36	1.10
Vilas	1,563.10	136.27	204.17	1,135.31	87.35
Walworth	1,534.68	216.15	193.21	1,125.32	0.00
Washburn	1,417.17	137.10	198.75	982.48	98.84
Washington	1,540.42	187.16	182.02	1,171.24	0.00
Waukesha	3,092.12	216.82	407.38	2,467.92	0.00
Waupaca	1,662.38	197.08	333.69	1,131.61	0.00
Waushara	1,331.01	132.32	333.46	865.23	0.00
Winnebago	1,578.05	168.64	220.27	1,189.14	0.00
Wood	1,796.85	185.84	324.41	1,273.99	12.61
Total	**115,546.60**	**11,744.74**	**19,851.43**	**82,090.29**	**1,860.14**

Source: Wisconsin Department of Transportation, Division of Transportation Investment Management, departmental data, March 2019.

Wisconsin road mileage, January 1, 2018

System	Miles	Percent
State trunk highways	11,745	10.2
County trunk highways	19,851	17.2
City streets	13,937	12.1
Village streets	6,532	5.7
Town roads	61,621	53.3
Park, forest, and other roads	1,860	1.6
Total	**115,547**	**100.0**

Surface	Miles	Percent
Bituminous or higher	91,397	79.1
Gravel or soil-surfaced	16,558	14.3
Sealcoat	5,653	4.9
Graded and drained	1,820	1.6
Unimproved	119	0.1
Total	**115,547**	**100.0**

Source: Wisconsin Department of Transportation, Division of Transportation Investment Management, departmental data, March 2019.

Wisconsin harbor commerce tonnage, 2017

Harbors[1]	Crude inedible materials (except fuels)	Coal and lignite	Primary mfd goods	Food and farm products	Petroleum and petroleum products	Chemicals and related products	Mfd equip., machinery, and products	Unknown or other
Lake Superior								
Duluth-Superior	23,276,725	10,328,060	136,442	987,247	—	51,020	3,592	104
Bayfield	46	—	—	—	992	—	12,452	—
La Pointe	46	—	—	—	992	—	12,452	—
Lake Michigan								
Milwaukee	1,423,054	—	850,236	235,944	88,898	—	3,635	68
Green Bay	847,591	434,822	397,747	—	100,918	47,843	—	32

Wisconsin harbor commerce tonnage, 2017, continued

Harbors[1]	Crude inedible materials (except fuels)	Coal and lignite	Primary mfd goods	Food and farm products	Petro-leum and pe-troleum products	Chemi-cals and related products	Mfd equip., machin-ery, and products	Unknown or other
Menominee[2]. .	73,268	—	96,632	—	—	—	1,349	5,663
Manitowoc. . .	26,239	—	106,890	—	—	—	—	—
Detroit Harbor[3]	200	—	—	—	1,621	—	—	4,613
Sturgeon Bay .	—	—	—	—	—	—	20	—
Total.	25,647,169	10,762,882	1,587,947	1,223,191	193,421	98,863	33,500	10,480

Note: Tonnage reported in short tons. One short ton equals 2,000 lbs.
— Represents zero; Mfd–Manufactured.
1. Harbors with reported commerce. 2. Includes tonnage handled at Marinette, Wisconsin. 3. Washington Island.
Source: U.S. Army Corps of Engineers, Navigation Data Center, Ports and Waterways (database), Calendar Year 2017, Region 3, at: http://cwbi-ndc-nav.s3-website-us-east-1.amazonaws.com/files/wcsc/webpub/#/?year=2017&regionId=3 [March 2019].

Motor vehicles in Wisconsin, by type

Fiscal year (ending June 30)	Total	Autos	Trucks[1]	Trailers, semi-trailers	Motor homes	Buses	Motor-cycles	Mopeds
1930.	819,718	700,251	115,883	X	X	554	3,030	X
1935.	722,797	597,197	116,912	5,634	X	498	2,556	X
1940.	874,652	741,583	123,742	5,144	X	675	3,508	X
1945.	828,425	676,978	139,591	6,484	X	1,489	3,883	X
1950.	1,157,221	921,194	209,083	14,124	X	2,465	10,355	X
1955.	1,369,636	1,108,084	227,367	21,643	X	3,337	9,205	X
1960.	1,598,693	1,303,679	246,353	31,502	X	5,184	11,975	X
1965.	1,867,223	1,517,397	269,771	44,017	X	7,218	28,820	X
1970.	2,205,662	1,762,681	317,096	64,065	X	8,178	53,642	X
1975.	2,737,164	2,096,694	425,854	91,609	X	11,897	111,110	X
1980.	3,417,748	2,509,904	558,840	102,256	17,071	13,775	205,786	10,116
1985.	3,372,029	2,310,024	765,852	72,289	17,195	10,325	176,023	20,321
1990.	3,834,608	2,456,175	1,045,583	123,061	21,095	15,081	149,268	24,345
1995.	4,285,753	2,464,358	1,391,374	207,042	22,554	15,593	161,762	23,070
2000.	4,703,294	2,405,408	1,813,385	214,344	24,427	15,587	160,920	17,977
2005.	5,226,584	2,347,042	2,216,863	342,879	22,598	12,478	249,979	34,745
2006.	5,326,157	2,361,853	2,281,988	364,024	22,406	13,174	246,307	36,405
2007.	5,428,629	2,357,616	2,333,538	396,229	21,147	13,516	266,036	40,547
2008.	5,499,872	2,381,911	2,370,655	410,737	20,209	10,736	260,220	45,404
2009.	5,532,953	2,340,991	2,396,470	417,031	20,039	12,685	291,164	54,573
2010.	5,525,794	2,333,029	2,416,295	426,092	19,615	13,376	269,316	48,071
2011.	5,564,794	2,300,243	2,445,056	434,782	18,792	13,745	296,808	55,368
2012.	5,551,411	2,274,596	2,473,072	447,195	18,535	14,169	274,553	49,291
2013.	5,671,185	2,276,007	2,548,029	460,542	18,187	10,598	301,477	56,345
2014.	5,697,808	2,255,966	2,609,402	479,237	18,584	12,615	275,120	46,884
2015.	5,823,555	2,229,199	2,703,329	502,301	18,766	13,324	303,577	53,059
2016.	5,870,311	2,192,295	2,802,029	525,513	18,760	13,739	274,787	43,188
2017.	5,985,094	2,132,984	2,919,745	546,535	18,779	14,138	303,541	49,372
2018.	6,047,860	2,080,739	3,050,820	571,827	19,005	10,164	275,301	40,004

X–Not applicable.
1. "Trucks" includes minivans and sport utility vehicles.
Sources: Wisconsin Secretary of State, *Biennial Report—1928–30*; Wisconsin Highway Commission, *Biennial Reports—1933–35, 1938–40*; Wisconsin Motor Vehicle Department, *Wisconsin Motor Vehicle Registrations—Fiscal Years 1944–45* through *1964–65*; Wisconsin Department of Transportation, *Wisconsin Motor Vehicle Registrations—Fiscal Year 1979–80, 1980*, and previous issues, and *Wisconsin Transportation Facts* (periodical); departmental data, March 2019.

Wisconsin motor vehicle crashes

Year	Total licensed drivers	Crashes[1] Total	Crashes[1] Fatal	Crashes[1] Injury	Persons killed	Persons injured	Miles traveled (millions)	Fatality rate[2]	Fatal crash rate[3]
2001	3,835,549	125,403	684	39,358	764	58,279	57,266	1.33	1.19
2002	3,839,930	129,072	723	39,634	805	57,776	58,745	1.37	1.23
2003	3,933,924	131,191	748	39,413	836	56,882	59,617	1.40	1.25
2004	3,993,348	128,308	714	38,451	784	55,258	60,398	1.31	1.18
2005	4,049,450	125,174	700	37,515	801	53,462	60,018	1.33	1.17
2006	4,066,273	117,877	659	35,296	712	50,236	59,401	1.20	1.11
2007	4,075,764	125,123	655	36,048	737	50,676	59,493	1.24	1.10
2008	4,079,562	125,103	542	33,766	587	46,637	57,462	1.02	0.94
2009	4,085,833	109,991	488	29,907	542	41,589	58,157	0.93	0.84
2010	4,114,622	108,808	517	29,380	562	40,889	59,420	0.95	0.87
2011	4,142,823	112,516	515	28,965	565	40,144	58,554	0.96	0.88
2012	4,171,428	109,385	535	28,453	601	39,370	59,087	1.02	0.91
2013	4,188,194	118,254	491	28,474	527	39,872	59,484	0.89	0.83
2014	4,194,760	119,736	451	28,801	498	39,701	60,044	0.83	0.75
2015	4,206,770	121,613	513	29,845	555	41,653	62,140	0.89	0.83
2016	3,960,597	129,051	524	31,066	588	43,669	63,870	0.92	0.82
2017	4,286,263	139,870	539	30,614	594	42,178	65,324	0.91	0.83
2018	4,288,173	144,082	526	29,934	584	41,092	NA	NA	NA

NA–Not available.

1. A motor vehicle crash is defined as an event caused by a single variable or chain of variables. The property damage threshold for a reportable crash was raised from $500 to $1,000, effective January 1, 1996.   2. Number of fatalities per 100 million vehicle miles traveled.   3. Number of fatal crashes per 100 million vehicle miles traveled.

Source: Wisconsin Department of Transportation, *Wisconsin Traffic Crash Facts*; departmental data, March 2019.

Drivers involved in crashes, 2017

Age of drivers	Total licensed drivers Number	Total licensed drivers % of drivers	Drivers involved in crashes[1] Number	Drivers involved in crashes[1] % of drivers	Drivers by type of crash[1] Fatal	Drivers by type of crash[1] Injury	Drivers by type of crash[1] Property damage
14 and under	—	—	61	0.0	1	22	38
15	—	—	233	0.1	1	81	151
16	40,327	0.9	4,309	2.2	13	1,069	3,227
17	49,430	1.2	5,106	2.6	15	1,330	3,761
18	55,032	1.3	5,454	2.7	24	1,503	3,927
19	57,324	1.3	5,067	2.6	22	1,425	3,620
20	59,265	1.4	4,985	2.5	14	1,410	3,561
21	61,917	1.4	5,045	2.5	21	1,390	3,634
22	63,781	1.5	4,998	2.5	17	1,305	3,676
23	66,391	1.5	4,810	2.4	15	1,248	3,547
24	69,452	1.6	4,600	2.3	16	1,272	3,312
25–34	716,795	16.7	39,269	19.8	166	10,567	28,536
35–44	662,998	15.5	29,705	15.0	106	7,928	21,671
45–54	717,353	16.7	28,083	14.1	127	7,360	20,596
55–64	786,504	18.3	24,929	12.6	114	6,532	18,283
65–74	536,836	12.5	13,430	6.8	63	3,549	9,818
75–84	256,650	6.0	5,952	3.0	48	1,628	4,276
85 and over	86,208	2.0	1,772	0.9	18	489	1,265
Unknown	—	—	10,678	5.4	13	1,466	9,199
Total	4,286,263		198,486		814	51,574	146,098

—Represents zero.

1. Figure indicates the number of times a driver in this age group was involved in a crash. If a driver had more than one crash, the driver would be counted more than once.

Source: Wisconsin Department of Transportation, *Wisconsin Traffic Crash Facts*; departmental data, March 2019.

Fatal crashes on Wisconsin highways and roads

Year	Total	Interstate	State	County	Local
2001	684	35	286	167	196
2002	723	44	310	171	198
2003	748	46	317	174	211
2004	714	47	298	155	214
2005	700	42	284	163	211
2006	659	34	294	128	203
2007	655	43	259	143	210
2008	542	32	225	119	166
2009	488	27	221	93	147
2010	517	32	230	105	150
2011	515	34	236	113	132
2012	535	26	242	103	164
2013	491	26	225	104	136
2014	451	23	198	85	145
2015	513	36	223	93	161
2016	524	31	211	110	172
2017	539	36	230	91	182
2018	526	30	235	108	153

Source: Wisconsin Department of Transportation, *Wisconsin Traffic Crash Facts*; departmental data, March 2019.

Wisconsin motorcycle crashes

Year	Total registered cycles	Cycle crashes Total	Cycle crashes Fatal	Personal injury	Property damage	Cyclist fatalities[1] Total[2]	No helmet	Helmet
2001	201,143	2,285	69	1,928	288	70	53	14
2002	198,495	2,184	73	1,794	317	78	59	15
2003	225,181	2,512	98	2,099	315	100	74	24
2004	221,982	2,423	81	2,015	327	80	60	18
2005	239,938	2,680	91	2,277	312	92	69	22
2006	291,534	2,441	88	2,065	288	93	69	24
2007	322,505	2,788	102	2,331	355	106	70	26
2008	327,938	2,829	86	2,318	425	87	66	19
2009	355,487	2,345	82	1,912	351	82	51	27
2010	343,878	2,426	97	1,959	370	98	72	23
2011	361,893	2,331	79	1,877	375	80	69	5
2012	340,268	2,630	107	2,110	413	112	82	25
2013	367,474	2,150	84	1,705	361	83	60	20
2014	337,637	2,101	63	1,696	342	67	43	21
2015	365,878	2,221	80	1,724	417	81	63	14
2016	334,950	2,250	78	1,733	439	82	62	17
2017	363,094	2,206	73	1,741	392	76	45	27
2018	331,356	2,075	78	1,609	388	81	52	28

1. Number of cyclists killed includes both drivers and passengers. 2. Includes fatalities where there is no data on whether the cyclist was wearing a helmet.
Source: Wisconsin Department of Transportation, *Wisconsin Traffic Crash Facts*; departmental data, March 2019.

Possible contributing circumstances to Wisconsin motor vehicle crashes, 2017

	All crashes				Urban crashes				Rural crashes			
	Total	Fatal	Injury	Property damage	Total	Fatal	Injury	Property damage	Total	Fatal	Injury	Property damage
Driver												
Exceed speed limit	3,259	114	1,437	1,708	1,213	60	549	604	2,046	54	888	1,104
Speed too fast for conditions	10,846	54	2,788	8,004	6,335	41	1,724	4,570	4,511	13	1,064	3,434
Failed to yield right-of-way	19,467	89	6,821	12,557	4,925	57	1,790	3,078	14,542	32	5,031	9,479
Following too close	13,361	11	3,775	9,575	3,927	7	1,141	2,779	9,434	4	2,634	6,796
Improper turn	3,182	5	551	2,626	906	2	181	723	2,276	3	370	1,903
Unsafe backing	7,404	0	346	7,058	2,305	0	95	2,210	5,099	0	251	4,848
Failure to control	20,848	173	6,343	14,332	11,023	131	3,725	7,167	9,825	42	2,618	7,165
Ran off roadway	5,022	77	1,713	3,232	3,375	60	1,250	2,065	1,647	17	463	1,167
Disregarded red light	2,992	18	1,367	1,607	274	2	127	145	2,718	16	1,240	1,462
Disregarded stop sign	2,185	36	959	1,190	902	33	404	465	1,283	3	555	725
Disregarded other traffic control	835	4	291	540	206	3	78	125	629	1	213	415
Disregarded other road markings	414	3	107	304	151	3	45	103	263	0	62	201
Improper overtaking/passing right	772	3	143	626	209	3	44	162	563	0	99	464
Improper overtaking/passing left	945	12	234	699	460	10	130	320	485	2	104	379
Wrong side or wrong way	1,007	48	404	555	508	44	226	238	499	4	178	317
Failure to keep in designated lane	6,937	106	1,863	4,968	3,380	92	1,148	2,140	3,557	14	715	2,828
Operated motor vehicle in aggressive/reckless manner	2,071	55	762	1,254	763	26	297	440	1,308	29	465	814
Operated motor vehicle in inattentive, careless or erratic manner	12,019	49	3,687	8,283	4,771	38	1,594	3,139	7,248	11	2,093	5,144
Swerved or avoided due to wind, slippery surface, motor vehicle, object, non-motorist in roadway, etc.	1,157	9	348	800	731	8	235	488	426	1	113	312
Over-correcting/over-steering	1,615	37	615	963	1,113	30	477	606	502	7	138	357
Racing	82	4	36	42	26	2	10	14	56	2	26	28
Other contributing action	8,325	37	2,282	6,006	2,711	23	838	1,850	5,614	14	1,444	4,156
Highway												
Backup due to prior crash	813	2	219	592	329	2	88	239	484	0	131	353
Backup due to prior nonrecurring incident	454	0	146	308	190	0	68	122	264	0	78	186
Backup due to regular congestion	4,105	2	1,130	2,973	976	0	269	707	3,129	2	861	2,266
Toll booth/plaza related	5	0	2	3	1	0	0	1	4	0	2	2
Road surface condition (wet, icy, snow, slush, etc.)	9,229	34	1,959	7,236	5,434	25	1,165	4,244	3,795	9	794	2,992
Debris prior to crash	175	1	25	149	123	0	18	105	52	1	7	44
Rut, holes, bumps	107	0	40	67	62	0	21	41	45	0	19	26

Work zone (construction/maintenance/utility)	1,176	3	323	850	576	3	156	417	600	0	167	433
Worn, travel-polished surface	10	0	3	7	8	0	2	6	2	0	1	1
Obstruction in roadway	342	0	70	272	180	0	31	149	162	0	39	123
Traffic control device inoperative, missing, or obscured	82	1	24	57	18	1	5	12	64	0	19	45
Narrow shoulder	82	0	25	57	62	0	22	40	20	0	3	17
Low shoulder	53	0	16	37	50	0	15	35	3	0	1	2
Soft shoulder	64	0	27	37	60	0	26	34	4	0	1	3
Nonhighway work	32	0	6	26	15	0	4	11	17	0	2	15
Loose gravel	221	4	122	95	194	4	105	85	27	0	17	10
Rough pavement	14	0	3	10	11	1	3	7	3	0	0	3
Other debris	213	0	29	184	130	0	20	110	83	0	9	74
Sign obscured/miss	8	0	4	4	3	0	2	1	5	0	2	3
Narrow bridge	5	0	1	4	4	0	1	3	1	0	0	1
Visibility obscured	396	1	124	271	164	1	51	112	232	0	73	159
Other	510	2	114	394	207	2	50	155	303	0	64	239
Vehicle												
Brakes	1,495	4	489	1,002	505	3	154	348	990	1	335	654
Exhaust system	27	0	8	19	14	0	2	12	13	0	6	7
Body, doors	325	1	96	228	101	1	29	71	224	0	67	157
Steering	492	2	159	331	213	2	72	139	279	0	87	192
Power train	164	0	38	126	83	1	16	67	81	0	22	59
Suspension	140	3	42	95	59	2	20	37	81	1	22	58
Tires	1,399	10	386	1,003	811	9	224	578	588	1	162	425
Wheels	390	1	83	306	168	1	31	136	222	0	52	170
Head lamps	160	2	75	83	56	2	21	33	104	0	54	50
Turn signals	72	2	25	45	38	1	11	25	34	0	14	20
Tail lamps	67	0	30	37	37	0	18	19	30	0	12	18
Stop lamps	39	0	18	21	21	0	12	9	18	0	6	12
Windows/windshield	190	1	64	125	89	1	25	63	101	0	39	62
Mirrors	60	0	17	43	25	0	8	17	35	0	9	26
Wipers	26	0	12	14	12	0	4	8	14	0	8	6
Coupling device/trailer hitch/safety chains	124	0	17	107	70	0	9	61	54	0	8	46
Disabled due to prior crash	66	0	18	48	29	0	7	22	37	0	11	26
Other disabled	199	2	68	129	67	2	17	48	132	0	51	81
Other	768	5	140	623	362	1	65	296	406	4	75	327

Note: Numbers represent the number of times a possible contributing circumstance was cited and not the total number of accidents.

Source: Wisconsin Department of Transportation, *Wisconsin Traffic Crash Facts*; departmental data, March 2019.

Mass transit systems in Wisconsin, January 2019

Urban bus	Rural/commuter bus	Shared-ride taxi[1]	
Appleton	Bay Area Rural Transit	Baraboo	Portage
Beloit	Dunn County	Beaver Dam	Prairie du Chien
Eau Claire	Kenosha County[3]	Berlin	Prairie du Sac/
Fond du Lac	La Crosse County[3]	Black River Falls	Sauk City
Green Bay	Manitowoc[5]	Chippewa Falls	Reedsburg
Janesville	Marshfield Shuttle[3]	Clark County/Neillsville	Rhinelander
Kenosha	Menominee Regional Transit	Clintonville	Rice Lake
La Crosse	Merrill[5]	Door County	Richland Center
Madison	Oneida-Vilas Counties Transit	Edgerton	Ripon
Milwaukee County[3]	Commission	Fort Atkinson	River Falls
Monona[3]	Ozaukee County Express[3]	Grant County	Shawano
Oshkosh	Platteville[3]	Hartford	Stoughton
Racine[2]	Racine Commuter[3]	Jefferson	Sun Prairie
Sheboygan	Rusk County	La Crosse County	Tomah
Superior[4]	Sauk County	Lake Mills	Viroqua/Westby
Waukesha (city)[3]	Sawyer County	Marinette	Walworth County
Waukesha County[3]	Stevens Point[5]	Marshfield	Washington County
Wausau	Verona	Mauston	Watertown
	Washington County Express[3]	Medford	Waupaca
		Monroe	Waupun
		New Richmond	West Bend
		Onalaska	Whitewater
		Ozaukee County	Wisconsin Rapids
		Plover	

1. Taxi services are privately contracted except for Grant County and the City of Hartford, where they are publicly owned and operated. 2. Privately managed. 3. Privately contracted. (Note: The private service in Waukesha County is an inter-urban service. Waukesha (city) and Waukesha (county) have merged to form Waukesha Metro Transit.) 4. Contracted with Duluth Transit Authority. 5. Moved to "rural" funding tier under WisDOT's criteria for service areas of less than 50,000 in population.

Source: Wisconsin Department of Transportation, Division of Transportation Investment Management, departmental data, March 2019.

Wisconsin urban transit systems

Year	Revenue miles (1,000)	Revenue passengers (1,000)	Operating revenue[1] ($1,000)
1950	53,362	288,996	22,692
1955	42,807	169,129	23,134
1960	34,950	130,299	20,665
1965	32,330	110,979	20,457
1970	28,371	80,172	22,078
1975	26,119	63,587	22,454
1980	33,943	88,756	29,631
1985	31,829	79,540	39,635
1990	33,685	78,215	39,594
1995	30,734	71,875	50,171
2000	42,447	89,821	58,785
2001	46,755	87,729	60,299
2002	48,322	84,874	64,263
2003	47,753	81,650	61,868
2004	46,696	81,812	65,621
2005	52,163	83,545	67,628
2006	51,700	83,913	72,896
2007	51,748	81,229	77,236
2008	52,439	82,953	83,263

Wisconsin urban transit systems, continued

Year	Revenue miles (1,000)	Revenue passengers (1,000)	Operating revenue[1] ($1,000)
2009.	52,488	77,510	82,570
2010.	52,579	74,717	87,288
2011.	52,316	77,533	82,640
2012.	51,214	75,290	83,005
2013.	50,973	74,694	83,522
2014.	52,003	72,281	76,310
2015.	53,268	67,281	71,737
2016.	52,816	63,346	68,149
2017.	54,078	59,955	68,422

1. As recognized by the Wisconsin Department of Transportation.

Sources: Wisconsin Department of Transportation, Division of Transportation Assistance, Bureau of Transit, *Wisconsin Urban Bus System Annual Report 1989* and previous issues; departmental data, March 2019.

Railroad mileage, usage, and revenue in Wisconsin

Year	No. of rail-roads	Mileage operated in Wisconsin[1] Road[2]	Track[3]	Freight traffic Tons (1,000)	Ton-miles[4] (1,000)	Revenue ($1,000)	Passenger traffic Passengers (1,000)	Miles[5] (1,000)	Revenue ($1,000)
1920.	35	7,546	11,615	100,991	9,052,084	92,826.00	20,188	960,569	28,646.00
1930.	27	7,231	11,583	83,672	6,908,656	78,747	4,799	466,154	14,071
1940.	22	6,646	10,484	87,980	6,910,647	69,941	3,952	445,938	8,201
1950.	20	6,337	10,000	121,576	10,850,178	141,762	5,575	646,353	14,933
1960.	18	6,195	9,625	93,475	9,096,855	134,065	3,127	383,457	9,800
1970.	15	5,965	9,127	97,130	13,432,055	191,764	1,463	138,572	4,264
1980[6]	21	5,192	7,990	101,008	14,727,522	453,977	174	1,122	54
1990.	15	4,415	6,125	116,099	14,436,776	455,541	112	783	63
2000.	12	3,548	4,956	151,573	21,321,266	580,678	NA	NA	NA
2001.	13	3,699	5,107	158,881	25,922,949	700,258	NA	NA	NA
2002.	12	3,688	5,095	NA	21,417,016	704,167	NA	NA	NA
2003.	11	3,450	4,643	118,387	26,092,960	667,736	NA	NA	NA
2004.	11	3,417	4,610	106,719	27,408,816	713,951	NA	NA	NA
2005.	11	3,417	4,614	109,214	27,966,142	715,206	NA	NA	NA
2006.	12	3,432	4,634	114,609	28,024,633	717,421	NA	NA	NA
2007.	12	3,430	4,585	109,210	22,942,906	737,119	NA	NA	NA
2008.	12	3,417	4,560	109,207	22,906,152	784,264	NA	NA	NA
2009.	10	3,417	4,571	107,146	20,456,847	762,649	NA	NA	NA
2010.	10	3,408	4,594	108,206	21,394,264	771,203	NA	NA	NA
2011.	10	3,402	4,606	106,527	24,891,634	971,369	NA	NA	NA
2012.	9	3,482	4,669	111,472	25,972,105	1,146,602	NA	NA	NA
2013.	9	3,489	4,676	126,154	28,734,278	1,288,345	NA	NA	NA
2014.	9	3,482	4,668	135,210	30,455,440	1,511,135	NA	NA	NA
2015.	9	3,005	4,176	130,219	29,220,895	1,237,662	NA	NA	NA
2016.	9	3,018	4,189	114,986	27,804,936	994,275	NA	NA	NA
2017.	9	2,995	4,111	138,393	31,589,253	1,155,539	NA	NA	NA

NA–Not available.

1. In order to avoid duplication, mileage shown is exclusive of trackage rights.   2. Road mileage is the measurement of stone roadbed in miles.   3. Track mileage is the measurement of track (2 steel rails) on roadbeds in miles.   4. A ton-mile is the movement of one ton (2,000 pounds) of cargo over the distance of one mile.   5. Passenger miles are the combination of the number of passengers carried on Wisconsin trains and the miles traveled by the passengers while within Wisconsin boundaries.   6. Intercity passenger service operated by Amtrak after May 1, 1971.

Source: Office of the Wisconsin Commissioner of Railroads, departmental data, March 2019.

Wisconsin airport usage by certified air carriers[1]

	2016		2017		2018	
	Passen-gers	Enplaned freight (lb.)	Passen-gers	Enplaned freight (lb.)	Passen-gers	Enplaned freight (lb.)
General Mitchell International (Milwaukee)	3,327,536	80,336,000	3,414,477	79,214,423	3,548,817	79,010,065
Dane County Regional (Madison).	903,155	15,090,373	943,363	13,267,346	1,082,529	14,297,349
Green Bay-Austin Straubel International (Green Bay) . . .	292,868	181,034	283,823	206,259	324,840	155,695
Appleton International (Appleton)	270,633	9,685,052	281,552	10,156,234	360,107	10,978,393
Central Wisconsin (Mosinee) . .	119,222	979,526	116,404	847,160	128,181	771,232
La Crosse Municipal (La Crosse)	94,047	X	92,101	X	98,744	X
Chippewa Valley Regional (Eau Claire)	21,304	X	22,822	X	23,734	X
Rhinelander-Oneida County (Rhinelander)	20,414	1,693,783	23,014	1,501,408	24,931	1,562,840
Total.	5,049,179	107,965,768	5,177,556	105,192,830	5,591,883	106,775,574

X–Not applicable.

1. Wisconsin has eight scheduled air carrier airports. A certified air carrier is an airline that is registered by the Federal Aviation Administration.

Source: Wisconsin Department of Transportation, departmental data, March 2019.

Number of landing facilities in Wisconsin

Type	2016	2018
Airports in the State Airport System (public use)[1]	97	97
Privately owned, public use airports	33	31
Private use airports	421	426
Heliports[2]	154	155
Seaplane bases[2]	27	27

1. Eligible for federal and/or state funding.   2. Public and private.

Source: Wisconsin Department of Transportation, departmental data, March 2019.

NEWS MEDIA

News media correspondents covering the 2019 Legislature

Organization	Correspondents
Print/web	
Associated Press	Scott Bauer, Todd Richmond
Capital Times	Jessie Opoien, Katelyn Ferral
Daily Reporter/Wisconsin Law Journal	Erika Strebel
Isthmus	Judith Davidoff
Milwaukee Journal Sentinel	Molly Beck, Patrick Marley
Wheeler Report	Gwyn Guenther, Trevor Guenther
Wisconsin Catholic Newspapers	Kim Wadas
Wisconsin State Journal	Riley Vetterkind, Mark Sommerhauser
Wispolitics.com	J.R. Ross, Briana Reilly, Alex Moe, Pat Poblete
Spectrum News	Anthony D. DaBruzzi
CBS 58/Telemundo Wisconsin	Victor Jacobo
Radio	
WIBA (Madison)	Robin Colbert
Wisconsin Public Radio	Shawn Johnson, Laurel White
Wisconsin Radio Network	Bob Hague, Raymond Neupert
WOLX	Kitty Dunn
Television	
WisconsinEye	Jon Henkes, Steve Walters, John Schroeder
Wisconsin Public Television	Kathy Bissen, Frederica Freyberg, Andy Moore, Zac Schultz, Christine Sloan-Miller, Andy Soth, Joel Waldinger
WISC-TV (CBS 3) (Madison)	Jessica Arp, Rose Schmidt
WKOW-TV (ABC 27) (Madison)	Tony Galli, Emilee Fannon
WMTV-TV (NBC 15) (Madison)	Ryan Lobenstein, Morgan Wolfe, Caroline Peterson

Source: Data collected by the Wisconsin Legislative Reference Bureau, January 2019.

THE WISCONSIN CONSTITUTION

Last amended at the April 2015 election

Article XIV—Schedule

Section

1. Effect of change from territory to state
2. Territorial laws continued
3. Repealed
4. Repealed
5. Repealed
6. Repealed
7. Repealed
8. Repealed
9. Repealed
10. Repealed
11. Repealed
12. Repealed
13. Common law continued in force
14. Repealed
15. Repealed
16. Implementing revised structure of judicial branch

PREAMBLE

We, the people of Wisconsin, grateful to Almighty God for our freedom, in order to secure its blessings, form a more perfect government, insure domestic tranquility and promote the general welfare, do establish this constitution.

ARTICLE I—Declaration of rights

Equality; inherent rights. Section 1. All people are born equally free and independent, and have certain inherent rights; among these are life, liberty and the pursuit of happiness; to secure these rights, governments are instituted, deriving their just powers from the consent of the governed.

Slavery prohibited. Section 2. There shall be neither slavery, nor involuntary servitude in this state, otherwise than for the punishment of crime, whereof the party shall have been duly convicted.

Free speech; libel. Section 3. Every person may freely speak, write and publish his sentiments on all subjects, being responsible for the abuse of that right, and no laws shall be passed to restrain or abridge the liberty of speech or of the press. In all criminal prosecutions or indictments for libel, the truth may be given in evidence, and if it shall appear to the jury that the matter charged as libelous be true, and was published with good motives and for justifiable ends, the party shall be acquitted; and the jury shall have the right to determine the law and the fact.

Right to assemble and petition. Section 4. The right of the people peaceably to assemble, to consult for the common good, and to petition the government, or any department thereof, shall never be abridged.

Trial by jury; verdict in civil cases. Section 5. The right of trial by jury shall remain inviolate, and shall extend to all cases at law without regard to the amount in controversy; but a jury trial may be waived by the parties in all cases in the manner prescribed by law. Provided, however, that the legislature may, from time to time, by statute provide that a valid verdict, in civil cases, may be based on the votes of a specified number of the jury, not less than five-sixths thereof.

Excessive bail; cruel punishments. Section 6. Excessive bail shall not be required, nor shall excessive fines be imposed, nor cruel and unusual punishments inflicted.

Rights of accused. Section 7. In all criminal prosecutions the accused shall enjoy the right to be heard by himself and counsel; to demand the nature and cause of the accusation against him; to meet the witnesses face to face; to have compulsory process to compel the attendance of witnesses in his behalf; and in prosecutions by indictment, or information, to a speedy public trial by an impartial jury of the county or district wherein the offense shall have been committed; which county or district shall have been previously ascertained by law.

Prosecutions; double jeopardy; self-incrimination; bail; habeas corpus. Section 8. (1) No person may be held to answer for a criminal offense without due process of law, and no person for the same offense may be put twice in jeopardy of punishment, nor may be compelled in any criminal case to be a witness against himself or herself.

(2) All persons, before conviction, shall be eligible for release under reasonable conditions designed to assure their appearance in court, protect members of the community from serious bodily harm or prevent the intimidation of witnesses. Monetary conditions of release may be imposed at or after the initial appearance only upon a finding that there is a reasonable basis to believe that the conditions are necessary to assure appearance in court. The legislature may authorize, by law, courts to revoke a person's release for a violation of a condition of release.

(3) The legislature may by law authorize, but may not require, circuit courts to deny release for a period not to exceed 10 days prior to the hearing required under this subsection to a person who is accused of committing a murder punishable by life imprisonment or a sexual assault punishable by a maximum imprisonment of 20 years, or who is accused of committing or attempting to commit a felony involving serious bodily harm to another or the threat of serious bodily harm to another and who has a previous conviction for committing or attempting to commit a felony involving serious bodily harm to another or the threat of serious bodily harm to another. The legislature may authorize by law, but may not require, circuit courts to continue to deny release to those accused persons for an additional period not to exceed 60 days following the hearing required under this subsection, if there is a requirement that there be a finding by the court based on clear and convincing evidence presented at a hearing that the accused committed the felony and a requirement that there be a finding by the court that available conditions of release will not adequately protect members of the community from serious bodily harm or prevent intimidation of witnesses. Any law enacted under this subsection shall be specific, limited and reasonable. In determining the 10-day and 60-day periods, the court shall omit any period of time found by the court to result from a delay caused by the defendant or a continuance granted which was initiated by the defendant.

(4) The privilege of the writ of habeas corpus shall not be suspended unless, in cases of rebellion or invasion, the public safety requires it.

Remedy for wrongs. Section 9. Every person is entitled to a certain remedy in the laws for all injuries, or wrongs which he may receive in his person, property, or character; he ought to obtain justice freely, and without being obliged to purchase it, completely and without denial, promptly and without delay, conformably to the laws.

Victims of crime. Section 9m. This state shall treat crime victims, as defined by law, with fairness, dignity and respect for their privacy. This state shall ensure that crime victims have all of the following privileges and protections as provided by law: timely disposition of the case; the opportunity to attend court proceedings unless the trial court finds sequestration is necessary to a fair trial for the defendant; reasonable protection from the accused throughout the criminal justice process; notification of court proceedings; the opportunity to confer with the prosecution; the opportunity to make a statement to the court at disposition; restitution; compensation; and information about the outcome of the case and the release of the accused. The legislature shall provide remedies for the violation of this section. Nothing in this section, or in any statute enacted pursuant to this section, shall limit any right of the accused which may be provided by law.

Treason. Section 10. Treason against the state shall consist only in levying war against the same, or in adhering to its enemies, giving them aid and comfort. No person shall be convicted of treason unless on the testimony of two witnesses to the same overt act, or on confession in open court.

Searches and seizures. Section 11. The right of the people to be secure in their persons, houses, papers, and effects against unreasonable searches and seizures shall not be violated; and no warrant shall issue but upon probable cause, supported by oath or affirmation, and particularly describing the place to be searched and the persons or things to be seized.

Attainder; ex post facto; contracts. Section 12. No bill of attainder, ex post facto law, nor any law impairing the obligation of contracts, shall ever be passed, and no conviction shall work corruption of blood or forfeiture of estate.

Private property for public use. Section 13. The property of no person shall be taken for public use without just compensation therefor.

Feudal tenures; leases; alienation. Section 14. All lands within the state are declared to be allodial, and feudal tenures are prohibited. Leases and grants of agricultural land for a longer term than fifteen years in which rent or service of any kind shall be reserved, and all fines and like restraints upon alienation reserved in any grant of land, hereafter made, are declared to be void.

Equal property rights for aliens and citizens. Section 15. No distinction shall ever be made by law between resident aliens and citizens, in reference to the possession, enjoyment or descent of property.

Imprisonment for debt. Section 16. No person shall be imprisoned for debt arising out of or founded on a contract, expressed or implied.

Exemption of property of debtors. Section 17. The privilege of the debtor to enjoy the necessary comforts of life shall be recognized by wholesome laws, exempting a reasonable amount of property from seizure or sale for the payment of any debt or liability hereafter contracted.

Freedom of worship; liberty of conscience; state religion; public funds. Section 18. The right of every person to worship Almighty God according to the dictates of conscience shall never be infringed; nor shall any person be compelled to attend, erect or support any place of worship, or to maintain any ministry, without consent; nor shall any control of, or interference with, the rights of conscience be permitted, or any preference be given by law to any religious establishments or modes of worship; nor shall any money be drawn from the treasury for the benefit of religious societies, or religious or theological seminaries.

Religious tests prohibited. Section 19. No religious tests shall ever be required as a qualification for any office of public trust under the state, and no person shall be rendered incompetent to give evidence in any court of law or equity in consequence of his opinions on the subject of religion.

Military subordinate to civil power. Section 20. The military shall be in strict subordination to the civil power.

Rights of suitors. Section 21. (1) Writs of error shall never be prohibited, and shall be issued by such courts as the legislature designates by law.

(2) In any court of this state, any suitor may prosecute or defend his suit either in his own proper person or by an attorney of the suitor's choice.

Maintenance of free government. Section 22. The blessings of a free government can only be maintained by a firm adherence to justice, moderation, temperance, frugality and virtue, and by frequent recurrence to fundamental principles.

Transportation of school children. Section 23. Nothing in this constitution shall prohibit the legislature from providing for the safety and welfare of children by providing for the transportation of children to and from any parochial or private school or institution of learning.

Use of school buildings. Section 24. Nothing in this constitution shall prohibit the legislature from authorizing, by law, the use of public school buildings by civic, religious or charitable organizations during nonschool hours upon payment by the organization to the school district of reasonable compensation for such use.

Right to keep and bear arms. Section 25. The people have the right to keep and bear arms for security, defense, hunting, recreation or any other lawful purpose.

Right to fish, hunt, trap, and take game. Section 26. The people have the right to fish, hunt, trap, and take game subject only to reasonable restrictions as prescribed by law.

ARTICLE II—Boundaries

State boundary. Section 1. It is hereby ordained and declared that the state of Wisconsin doth consent and accept of the boundaries prescribed in the act of congress entitled "An act to enable the people of Wisconsin territory to form a constitution and state government, and for the admission of such state into the Union," approved August sixth, one thousand eight hundred and forty-six, to wit: Beginning at the northeast corner of the state of Illinois—that is to say, at a point in the center of Lake Michigan where the line of forty-two degrees and thirty minutes of north latitude crosses the same; thence running with the boundary line of the state of Michigan, through Lake Michigan, Green Bay, to the mouth of the Menominee river; thence up the channel of the said river to the Brule river; thence up said last-mentioned river to Lake Brule; thence along the southern shore of Lake Brule in a direct line to the center of the channel between Middle and South Islands, in the Lake of the Desert; thence in a direct line to the head waters of the Montreal river, as marked upon the survey made by Captain Cramm; thence down the main channel of the Montreal river to the middle of Lake Superior; thence through the center of Lake Superior to the mouth of the St. Louis river; thence up the main channel of said river to the first rapids in the same, above the Indian village, according to Nicollet's map; thence due south to the main branch of the river St. Croix; thence down the main channel of said river to the Mississippi; thence down the center of the main channel of that river to the northwest corner of the state of Illinois; thence due east with the northern boundary of the state of Illinois to the place of beginning, as established by "An act to enable the people of the Illinois territory to form a constitution and state government, and for the admission of such state into the Union on an equal footing with the original states," approved April 18th, 1818.

Enabling act accepted. Section 2. The propositions contained in the act of congress are hereby accepted, ratified and confirmed, and shall remain irrevocable without the consent of the United States; and it is hereby ordained that this state shall never interfere with the primary disposal of the soil within the same by the United States, nor with any regulations congress may find necessary for securing the title in such soil to bona fide purchasers thereof; and in no case shall nonresident proprietors be taxed higher than residents. Provided, that nothing in this constitution, or in the act of congress aforesaid, shall in any manner prejudice or affect the right of the state of Wisconsin to 500,000 acres of land granted to said state, and to be hereafter selected and located by and under the act of congress entitled "An act to appropriate the proceeds of the sales of the public lands, and grant pre-emption rights," approved September fourth, one thousand eight hundred and forty-one.

ARTICLE III—Suffrage

Electors. Section 1. Every United States citizen age 18 or older who is a resident of an election district in this state is a qualified elector of that district.

Implementation. Section 2. Laws may be enacted:

(1) Defining residency.

(2) Providing for registration of electors.

(3) Providing for absentee voting.

(4) Excluding from the right of suffrage persons:

(a) Convicted of a felony, unless restored to civil rights.

(b) Adjudged by a court to be incompetent or partially incompetent, unless the judgment specifies that the person is capable of understanding the objective of the elective process or the judgment is set aside.

(5) Subject to ratification by the people at a general election, extending the right of suffrage to additional classes.

Secret ballot. Section 3. All votes shall be by secret ballot.

ARTICLE IV—Legislative

Legislative power. Section 1. The legislative power shall be vested in a senate and assembly.

Legislature, how constituted. Section 2. The number of the members of the assembly shall never be less than fifty-four nor more than one hundred. The senate shall consist of a number not more than one-third nor less than one-fourth of the number of the members of the assembly.

Apportionment. Section 3. At its first session after each enumeration made by the authority of the United States, the legislature shall apportion and district anew the members of the senate and assembly, according to the number of inhabitants.

Representatives to the assembly, how chosen. Section 4. The members of the assembly shall be chosen biennially, by single districts, on the Tuesday succeeding the first Monday of November in even-numbered years, by the qualified electors of the several districts, such districts to be bounded by county, precinct, town or ward lines, to consist of contiguous territory and be in as compact form as practicable.

Senators, how chosen. Section 5. The senators shall be elected by single districts of convenient contiguous territory, at the same time and in the same manner as members of the assembly are required to be chosen; and no assembly district shall be divided in the formation of a senate district. The senate districts shall be numbered in the regular series, and the senators shall be chosen alternately from the odd and even-numbered districts for the term of 4 years.

Qualifications of legislators. Section 6. No person shall be eligible to the legislature who shall not have resided one year within the state, and be a qualified elector in the district which he may be chosen to represent.

Organization of legislature; quorum; compulsory attendance. Section 7. Each house shall be the judge of the elections, returns and qualifications of its own members; and a majority of each shall constitute a quorum to do business, but a smaller number may adjourn from day to day, and may compel the attendance of absent members in such manner and under such penalties as each house may provide.

Rules; contempts; expulsion. Section 8. Each house may determine the rules of its own proceedings, punish for contempt and disorderly behavior, and with the concurrence of two-thirds of all the members elected, expel a member; but no member shall be expelled a second time for the same cause.

Officers. Section 9. **(1)** Each house shall choose its presiding officers from its own members.

(2) The legislature shall provide by law for the establishment of a department of transportation and a transportation fund.

Journals; open doors; adjournments. Section 10. Each house shall keep a journal of its proceedings and publish the same, except such parts as require secrecy. The doors of each house shall be kept open except when the public welfare shall require secrecy. Neither house shall, without consent of the other, adjourn for more than three days.

Meeting of legislature. Section 11. The legislature shall meet at the seat of government at such time as shall be provided by law, unless convened by the governor in special session, and when so convened no business shall be transacted except as shall be necessary to accomplish the special purposes for which it was convened.

Ineligibility of legislators to office. Section 12. No member of the legislature shall, during the term for which he was elected, be appointed or elected to any civil office in the state, which shall have been created, or the emoluments of which shall have been increased, during the term for which he was elected.

Ineligibility of federal officers. Section 13. No person being a member of congress, or holding any military or civil office under the United States, shall be eligible to a seat in the legislature; and if any person shall, after his election as a member of the legislature, be elected to congress, or be appointed to any office, civil or military, under the government of the United States, his acceptance thereof shall vacate his seat. This restriction shall not prohibit a legislator from accepting short periods of active duty as a member of the reserve or from serving in the armed forces during any emergency declared by the executive.

Filling vacancies. Section 14. The governor shall issue writs of election to fill such vacancies as may occur in either house of the legislature.

Exemption from arrest and civil process. Section 15. Members of the legislature shall in all cases, except treason, felony and breach of the peace, be privileged from arrest; nor shall they be subject to any civil process, during the session of the legislature, nor for fifteen days next before the commencement and after the termination of each session.

Privilege in debate. Section 16. No member of the legislature shall be liable in any civil action, or criminal prosecution whatever, for words spoken in debate.

Enactment of laws. Section 17. **(1)** The style of all laws of the state shall be "The people of the state of Wisconsin, represented in senate and assembly, do enact as follows:".

(2) No law shall be enacted except by bill. No law shall be in force until published.

(3) The legislature shall provide by law for the speedy publication of all laws.

Title of private bills. Section 18. No private or local bill which may be passed by the legislature shall embrace more than one subject, and that shall be expressed in the title.

Origin of bills. Section 19. Any bill may originate in either house of the legislature, and a bill passed by one house may be amended by the other.

Yeas and nays. Section 20. The yeas and nays of the members of either house on any question shall, at the request of one-sixth of those present, be entered on the journal.

Powers of county boards. Section 22. The legislature may confer upon the boards of supervisors of the several counties of the state such powers of a local, legislative and administrative character as they shall from time to time prescribe.

Town and county government. Section 23. The legislature shall establish but one system of town government, which shall be as nearly uniform as practicable; but the legislature may provide for the election at large once in every 4 years of a chief executive officer in any county with such powers of an administrative character as they may from time to time prescribe in accordance with this section and shall establish one or more systems of county government.

Chief executive officer to approve or veto resolutions or ordinances; proceedings on veto. Section 23a. Every resolution or ordinance passed by the county board in any county shall, before it becomes effective, be presented to the chief executive officer. If he approves, he shall sign it; if not, he shall return it with his objections, which objections shall be entered at large upon the journal and the board shall proceed to reconsider the matter. Appropriations may be approved in whole or in part by the chief executive officer and the part approved shall become law, and the part objected to shall be returned in the same manner as provided for in other resolutions or ordinances. If, after such reconsideration, two-thirds of the members-elect of the county board agree to pass the resolution or ordinance or the part of the resolution or ordinance objected to, it shall become effective on the date prescribed but not earlier than the date of passage following reconsideration. In all such cases, the votes of the members of the county board shall be determined by ayes and noes and the names of the members voting for or against the resolution or ordinance or the part thereof objected to shall be entered on the journal. If any resolution or ordinance is not returned by the chief executive officer to the county board at its first meeting occurring not less than 6 days, Sundays excepted, after it has been presented to him, it shall become effective unless the county board has recessed or adjourned for a period in excess of 60 days, in which case it shall not be effective without his approval.

Gambling. Section 24. (1) Except as provided in this section, the legislature may not authorize gambling in any form.

(2) Except as otherwise provided by law, the following activities do not constitute consideration as an element of gambling:

(a) To listen to or watch a television or radio program.

(b) To fill out a coupon or entry blank, whether or not proof of purchase is required.

(c) To visit a mercantile establishment or other place without being required to make a purchase or pay an admittance fee.

(3) The legislature may authorize the following bingo games licensed by the state, but all profits shall accrue to the licensed organization and no salaries, fees or profits may be paid to any other organization or person: bingo games operated by religious, charitable, service, fraternal or veterans' organizations or those to which contributions are deductible for federal or state income tax purposes. All moneys received by the state that are attributable to bingo games shall be used for property tax relief for residents of this state as provided by law. The distribution of moneys that are attributable to bingo games may not vary based on the income or age of the person provided the property tax relief. The distribution of moneys that are attributable to bingo games shall not be subject to the uniformity requirement of section 1 of article VIII. In this subsection, the distribution of all moneys attributable to bingo games shall include any earnings on the moneys received by the state that are attributable to bingo games, but shall not include any moneys used for the regulation of, and enforcement of law relating to, bingo games.

(4) The legislature may authorize the following raffle games licensed by the state, but all profits shall accrue to the licensed local organization and no salaries, fees or profits may be paid to any other organization or person: raffle games operated by local religious, charitable, service, fraternal or veterans' organizations or those to which contributions are deductible for federal or state income tax purposes. The legislature shall limit the number of raffles conducted by any such organization.

(5) This section shall not prohibit pari-mutuel on-track betting as provided by law. The state may not own or operate any facility or enterprise for pari-mutuel betting, or lease any state-owned land to any other owner or operator for such purposes. All moneys received by the state that are attributable to pari-mutuel on-track betting shall be used for property tax relief for residents of this state as provided by law. The distribution of moneys that are attributable to pari-mutuel on-track betting may not vary based on the income or age of the person provided the property tax relief. The distribution of moneys that are attributable to pari-mutuel on-track betting shall not be subject to the uniformity requirement of section 1 of article VIII. In this subsection, the distribution of all moneys attributable to pari-mutuel on-track betting shall include any earnings on the moneys received by the state that are attributable to pari-mutuel on-track betting, but shall not include any moneys used for the regulation of, and enforcement of law relating to, pari-mutuel on-track betting.

(6) (a) The legislature may authorize the creation of a lottery to be operated by the state as provided by law. The expenditure of public funds or of revenues derived from lottery operations to engage in promotional advertising of the Wisconsin state lottery is prohibited. Any advertising of the state lottery shall indicate the odds of a specific lottery ticket to be selected as the winning ticket for each prize amount offered. The net proceeds of the state lottery shall be deposited in the treasury of the state, to be used for property tax relief for residents of this state as provided by law. The distribution of the net proceeds of the state lottery may not vary based on the income or age of the person provided the property tax relief. The distribution of the net proceeds of the state lottery shall not be subject to the uniformity requirement of section 1 of article VIII. In this paragraph, the distribution of the net proceeds of the state lottery shall include any earnings on the net proceeds of the state lottery.

(b) The lottery authorized under par. (a) shall be an enterprise that entitles the player, by purchasing a ticket, to participate in a game of chance if: 1) the winning tickets are randomly predetermined and the player reveals preprinted numbers or symbols from which it can be immediately determined whether the ticket is a winning ticket entitling the player to win a prize as prescribed in the features and procedures for the game, including an opportunity to win a prize in a secondary or subsequent chance drawing or game; or 2) the ticket is evidence of the numbers or symbols selected by the player or, at the player's option, selected by a computer, and the player becomes entitled to a prize as prescribed in the features and procedures for the game, including an opportunity to win a prize in a secondary or subsequent chance drawing or game if some or all of the player's symbols or numbers are selected in a chance drawing or game, if the player's ticket is randomly selected by the computer at the time of purchase or if the ticket is selected in a chance drawing.

(c) Notwithstanding the authorization of a state lottery under par. (a), the following games, or games simulating any of the following games, may not be conducted by the state as a lottery: 1) any game in which winners are selected based on the results of a race or sporting event; 2) any banking card game, including blackjack, baccarat or chemin de fer; 3) poker; 4) roulette; 5) craps or any other game that involves rolling dice; 6) keno; 7) bingo 21, bingo jack, bingolet or bingo craps; 8) any game of chance that is placed on a slot machine or any mechanical, electromechanical or electronic device that is generally available to be played at a gambling casino; 9) any game or device that is commonly known as a video game of chance or a video gaming machine or that is commonly considered to be a video gambling machine, unless such machine is a video device operated by the state in a game authorized under par. (a) to permit the sale of tickets through retail outlets under contract with the state and the device does not determine or indicate whether the player has won a prize, other than by verifying that the player's ticket or some or all of the player's symbols or numbers on the player's ticket have been selected in a chance drawing, or by verifying that the player's ticket has been randomly selected by a central system computer at the time of purchase; 10) any game that is similar to a game listed in this paragraph; or 11) any other game that is commonly considered to be a form of gambling and is not, or is not substantially similar to, a game conducted by the state under par. (a). No game conducted by the state under par. (a) may permit a player of the game to purchase a ticket, or to otherwise participate in the game, from a residence by using a computer, telephone or other form of electronic, telecommunication, video or technological aid.

Stationery and printing. Section 25. The legislature shall provide by law that all stationery required for the use of the state, and all printing authorized and required by them to be done for their use, or for the state, shall be let by contract to the lowest bidder, but the legislature may establish a maximum price; no member of the legislature or other state officer shall be interested, either directly or indirectly, in any such contract.

Extra compensation; salary change. Section 26. **(1)** The legislature may not grant any extra compensation to a public officer, agent, servant or contractor after the services have been rendered or the contract has been entered into.

(2) Except as provided in this subsection, the compensation of a public officer may not be increased or diminished during the term of office:

(a) When any increase or decrease in the compensation of justices of the supreme court or judges of any court of record becomes effective as to any such justice or judge, it shall be effective from such date as to every such justice or judge.

(b) Any increase in the compensation of members of the legislature shall take effect, for all senators and representatives to the assembly, after the next general election beginning with the new assembly term.

(3) Subsection (1) shall not apply to increased benefits for persons who have been or shall be granted benefits of any kind under a retirement system when such increased benefits are provided by a legislative act passed on a call of ayes and noes by a three-fourths vote of all the members elected to both houses of the legislature and such act provides for sufficient state funds to cover the costs of the increased benefits.

Suits against state. Section 27. The legislature shall direct by law in what manner and in what courts suits may be brought against the state.

Oath of office. Section 28. Members of the legislature, and all officers, executive and judicial, except such inferior officers as may be by law exempted, shall before they enter upon the duties of their respective offices, take and subscribe an oath or affirmation to support the constitution of the United States and the constitution of the state of Wisconsin, and faithfully to discharge the duties of their respective offices to the best of their ability.

Militia. Section 29. The legislature shall determine what persons shall constitute the militia of the state, and may provide for organizing and disciplining the same in such manner as shall be prescribed by law.

Elections by legislature. Section 30. All elections made by the legislature shall be by roll call vote entered in the journals.

Special and private laws prohibited. Section 31. The legislature is prohibited from enacting any special or private laws in the following cases:

(1) For changing the names of persons, constituting one person the heir at law of another or granting any divorce.

(2) For laying out, opening or altering highways, except in cases of state roads extending into more than one county, and military roads to aid in the construction of which lands may be granted by congress.

(3) For authorizing persons to keep ferries across streams at points wholly within this state.

(4) For authorizing the sale or mortgage of real or personal property of minors or others under disability.

(5) For locating or changing any county seat.

(6) For assessment or collection of taxes or for extending the time for the collection thereof.

(7) For granting corporate powers or privileges, except to cities.

(8) For authorizing the apportionment of any part of the school fund.

(9) For incorporating any city, town or village, or to amend the charter thereof.

General laws on enumerated subjects. Section 32. The legislature may provide by general law for the treatment of any subject for which lawmaking is prohibited by section 31 of this article. Subject to reasonable classifications, such laws shall be uniform in their operation throughout the state.

Auditing of state accounts. Section 33. The legislature shall provide for the auditing of state accounts and may establish such offices and prescribe such duties for the same as it shall deem necessary.

Continuity of civil government. Section 34. The legislature, in order to ensure continuity of state and local governmental operations in periods of emergency resulting from enemy action in the form of an attack, shall (1) forthwith provide for prompt and temporary succession to the powers and duties of public offices, of whatever nature and whether filled by election or appointment, the incumbents of which may become unavailable for carrying on the powers and duties of such offices, and (2) adopt such other measures as may be necessary and proper for attaining the objectives of this section.

ARTICLE V—Executive

Governor; lieutenant governor; term. Section 1. The executive power shall be vested in a governor who shall hold office for 4 years; a lieutenant governor shall be elected at the same time and for the same term.

Eligibility. Section 2. No person except a citizen of the United States and a qualified elector of the state shall be eligible to the office of governor or lieutenant governor.

Election. Section 3. The governor and lieutenant governor shall be elected by the qualified electors of the state at the times and places of choosing members of the legislature. They shall be chosen jointly, by the casting by each voter of a single vote applicable to both offices beginning with the general election in 1970. The persons respectively having the highest number of votes cast jointly for them for governor and lieutenant governor shall be elected; but in case two or more slates shall have an equal and the highest number of votes for governor and lieutenant governor, the two houses of the legislature, at its next annual session shall forthwith, by joint ballot, choose one of the slates so having an equal and the highest number of votes for governor and lieutenant governor. The returns of election for governor and lieutenant governor shall be made in such manner as shall be provided by law.

Powers and duties. Section 4. The governor shall be commander in chief of the military and naval forces of the state. He shall have power to convene the legislature on extraordinary occasions, and in case of invasion, or danger from the prevalence of contagious disease at the seat of government, he may convene them at any other suitable place within the state. He shall communicate to the legislature, at every session, the condition of the state, and recommend such matters to them for their consideration as he may deem expedient. He shall transact all necessary business with the officers of the government, civil and military. He shall expedite all such measures as may be resolved upon by the legislature, and shall take care that the laws be faithfully executed.

Pardoning power. Section 6. The governor shall have power to grant reprieves, commutations and pardons, after conviction, for all offenses, except treason and cases of impeachment, upon such conditions and with such restrictions and limitations as he may think proper, subject to such regulations as may be provided by law relative to the manner of applying for pardons. Upon conviction for treason he shall have the power to suspend the execution of the sentence until the case shall be reported to the legislature at its next meeting, when the legislature shall either pardon, or commute the sentence, direct the execution of the sentence, or grant a further reprieve. He shall annually communicate to the legislature each case of reprieve, commutation or pardon granted, stating the name of the convict, the crime of which he was convicted, the sentence and its date, and the date of the commutation, pardon or reprieve, with his reasons for granting the same.

Lieutenant governor, when governor. Section 7. (1) Upon the governor's death, resignation or removal from office, the lieutenant governor shall become governor for the balance of the unexpired term.

(2) If the governor is absent from this state, impeached, or from mental or physical disease, becomes incapable of performing the duties of the office, the lieutenant governor shall serve as acting governor for the balance of the unexpired term or until the governor returns, the disability ceases or the impeachment is vacated. But when the governor, with the consent of the legislature, shall be out of this state in time of war at the head of the state's military force, the governor shall continue as commander in chief of the military force.

Secretary of state, when governor. Section 8. (1) If there is a vacancy in the office of lieutenant governor and the governor dies, resigns or is removed from office, the secretary of state shall become governor for the balance of the unexpired term.

(2) If there is a vacancy in the office of lieutenant governor and the governor is absent from this state, impeached, or from mental or physical disease becomes incapable of performing the duties of the office, the secretary of state shall serve as acting governor for the balance of the unexpired term or until the governor returns, the disability ceases or the impeachment is vacated.

Governor to approve or veto bills; proceedings on veto. Section 10. (1) (a) Every bill which shall have passed the legislature shall, before it becomes a law, be presented to the governor.

(b) If the governor approves and signs the bill, the bill shall become law. Appropriation bills may be approved in whole or in part by the governor, and the part approved shall become law.

(c) In approving an appropriation bill in part, the governor may not create a new word by rejecting individual letters in the words of the enrolled bill, and may not create a new sentence by combining parts of 2 or more sentences of the enrolled bill.

(2) (a) If the governor rejects the bill, the governor shall return the bill, together with the objections in writing, to the house in which the bill originated. The house of origin shall enter the objections at large upon the journal and proceed to reconsider the bill. If, after such reconsideration, two-thirds of the members present agree to pass the bill notwithstanding the objections of the governor, it shall be sent, together with the objections, to the other house, by which it shall likewise be reconsidered, and if approved by two-thirds of the members present it shall become law.

(b) The rejected part of an appropriation bill, together with the governor's objections in writing, shall be returned to the house in which the bill originated. The house of origin shall enter the objections at large upon the journal and proceed to reconsider the rejected part of the appropriation bill. If, after such reconsideration, two-thirds of the members present agree to approve the rejected part notwithstanding the objections of the governor, it shall be sent, together with the objections, to the other house, by which it shall likewise be reconsidered, and if approved by two-thirds of the members present the rejected part shall become law.

(c) In all such cases the votes of both houses shall be determined by ayes and noes, and the names of the members voting for or against passage of the bill or the rejected part of the bill notwithstanding the objections of the governor shall be entered on the journal of each house respectively.

(3) Any bill not returned by the governor within 6 days (Sundays excepted) after it shall have been presented to the governor shall be law unless the legislature, by final adjournment, prevents the bill's return, in which case it shall not be law.

ARTICLE VI—Administrative

Election of secretary of state, treasurer and attorney general; term. Section 1. The qualified electors of this state, at the times and places of choosing the members of the legislature, shall in 1970 and every 4 years thereafter elect a secretary of state, treasurer and attorney general who shall hold their offices for 4 years.

Secretary of state; duties, compensation. Section 2. The secretary of state shall keep a fair record of the official acts of the legislature and executive department of the state, and shall, when required, lay the same and all matters relative thereto before either branch of the legislature. He shall perform such other duties as shall be assigned him by law. He shall receive as a compensation for his services yearly such sum as shall be provided by law, and shall keep his office at the seat of government.

Treasurer and attorney general; duties, compensation. Section 3. The powers, duties and compensation of the treasurer and attorney general shall be prescribed by law.

County officers; election, terms, removal; vacancies. Section 4. **(1)** (a) Except as provided in pars. (b) and (c) and sub. (2), coroners, registers of deeds, district attorneys, and all other elected county officers, except judicial officers, sheriffs, and chief executive officers, shall be chosen by the electors of the respective counties once in every 2 years.

(b) Beginning with the first general election at which the governor is elected which occurs after the ratification of this paragraph, sheriffs shall be chosen by the electors of the respective counties, or by the electors of all of the respective counties comprising each combination of counties combined by the legislature for that purpose, for the term of 4 years and coroners in counties in which there is a coroner shall be chosen by the electors of the respective counties, or by the electors of all of the respective counties comprising each combination of counties combined by the legislature for that purpose, for the term of 4 years.

(c) Beginning with the first general election at which the president is elected which occurs after the ratification of this paragraph, district attorneys, registers of deeds, county clerks, and treasurers shall be chosen by the electors of the respective counties, or by the electors of all of the respective counties comprising each combination of counties combined by the legislature for that purpose, for the term of 4 years and surveyors in counties in which the office of surveyor is filled by election shall be chosen by the electors of the respective counties, or by the electors of all of the respective counties comprising each combination of counties combined by the legislature for that purpose, for the term of 4 years.

(2) The offices of coroner and surveyor in counties having a population of 500,000 or more are abolished. Counties not having a population of 500,000 shall have the option of retaining the elective office of coroner or instituting a medical examiner system. Two or more counties may institute a joint medical examiner system.

(3) (a) Sheriffs may not hold any other partisan office.

(b) Sheriffs may be required by law to renew their security from time to time, and in default of giving such new security their office shall be deemed vacant.

(4) The governor may remove any elected county officer mentioned in this section except a county clerk, treasurer, or surveyor, giving to the officer a copy of the charges and an opportunity of being heard.

(5) All vacancies in the offices of coroner, register of deeds or district attorney shall be filled by appointment. The person appointed to fill a vacancy shall hold office only for the unexpired portion of the term to which appointed and until a successor shall be elected and qualified.

(6) When a vacancy occurs in the office of sheriff, the vacancy shall be filled by appointment of the governor, and the person appointed shall serve until his or her successor is elected and qualified.

ARTICLE VII—Judiciary

Impeachment; trial. Section 1. The court for the trial of impeachments shall be composed of the senate. The assembly shall have the power of impeaching all civil officers of this state for corrupt conduct in office, or for crimes and misdemeanors; but a majority of all the members elected shall concur in an impeachment. On the trial of an impeachment against the governor, the lieutenant governor shall not act as a member of the court. No judicial officer shall exercise his office, after he shall have been impeached, until his acquittal. Before the trial of an impeachment the members of the court shall take an oath or affirmation truly and impartially to try the impeachment according to evidence; and no person shall be convicted without the concurrence of two-thirds of the members present. Judgment in cases of impeachment shall not extend further than to removal from office, or removal from office and disqualification to hold any office of honor, profit or trust under the state; but the party impeached shall be liable to indictment, trial and punishment according to law.

Court system. Section 2. The judicial power of this state shall be vested in a unified court system consisting of one supreme court, a court of appeals, a circuit court, such trial courts of general uniform statewide jurisdiction as the legislature may create by law, and a municipal court if authorized by the legislature under section 14.

Supreme court: jurisdiction. Section 3. (1) The supreme court shall have superintending and administrative authority over all courts.

(2) The supreme court has appellate jurisdiction over all courts and may hear original actions and proceedings. The supreme court may issue all writs necessary in aid of its jurisdiction.

(3) The supreme court may review judgments and orders of the court of appeals, may remove cases from the court of appeals and may accept cases on certification by the court of appeals.

Supreme court: election, chief justice, court system administration. Section 4. (1) The supreme court shall have 7 members who shall be known as justices of the supreme court. Justices shall be elected for 10-year terms of office commencing with the August 1 next succeeding the election. Only one justice may be elected in any year. Any 4 justices shall constitute a quorum for the conduct of the court's business.

(2) The chief justice of the supreme court shall be elected for a term of 2 years by a majority of the justices then serving on the court. The justice so designated as chief justice may, irrevocably, decline to serve as chief justice or resign as chief justice but continue to serve as a justice of the supreme court.

(3) The chief justice of the supreme court shall be the administrative head of the judicial system and shall exercise this administrative authority pursuant to procedures adopted by the supreme court. The chief justice may assign any judge of a court of record to aid in the proper disposition of judicial business in any court of record except the supreme court.

Court of appeals. Section 5. (1) The legislature shall by law combine the judicial circuits

ARTICLE VIII—Finance

Rule of taxation uniform; income, privilege and occupation taxes. Section 1. The rule of taxation shall be uniform but the legislature may empower cities, villages or towns to collect and return taxes on real estate located therein by optional methods. Taxes shall be levied upon such property with such classifications as to forests and minerals including or separate or severed from the land, as the legislature shall prescribe. Taxation of agricultural land and undeveloped land, both as defined by law, need not be uniform with the taxation of each other nor with the taxation of other real property. Taxation of merchants' stock-in-trade, manufacturers' materials and finished products, and livestock need not be uniform with the taxation of real property and other personal property, but the taxation of all such merchants' stock-in-trade, manufacturers' materials and finished products and livestock shall be uniform, except that the legislature may provide that the value thereof shall be determined on an average basis. Taxes may also be imposed on incomes, privileges and occupations, which taxes may be graduated and progressive, and reasonable exemptions may be provided.

Appropriations; limitation. Section 2. No money shall be paid out of the treasury except in pursuance of an appropriation by law. No appropriation shall be made for the payment of any claim against the state except claims of the United States and judgments, unless filed within six years after the claim accrued

Credit of state. Section 3. Except as provided in s. 7 (2) (a), the credit of the state shall never be given, or loaned, in aid of any individual, association or corporation.

Contracting state debts. Section 4. The state shall never contract any public debt except in the cases and manner herein provided.

Annual tax levy to equal expenses. Section 5. The legislature shall provide for an annual tax sufficient to defray the estimated expenses of the state for each year; and whenever the expenses of any year shall exceed the income, the legislature shall provide for levying a tax for the ensuing year, sufficient, with other sources of income, to pay the deficiency as well as the estimated expenses of such ensuing year.

Public debt for extraordinary expense; taxation. Section 6. For the purpose of defraying extraordinary expenditures the state may contract public debts (but such debts shall never in the aggregate exceed one hundred thousand dollars). Every such debt shall be authorized by law, for some purpose or purposes to be distinctly specified therein; and the vote of a majority of all the members elected to each house, to be taken by yeas and nays, shall be necessary to the passage of such law; and every such law shall provide for levying an annual tax sufficient to pay the annual interest of such debt and the principal within five years from the passage of such law, and shall specially appropriate the proceeds of such taxes to the payment of such principal and interest; and such appropriation shall not be repealed, nor the taxes be postponed or diminished, until the principal and interest of such debt shall have been wholly paid.

Public debt for public defense; bonding for public purposes. Section 7. **(1)** The legislature may also borrow money to repel invasion, suppress insurrection, or defend the state in time of war; but the money thus raised shall be applied exclusively to the object for which the loan was authorized, or to the repayment of the debt thereby created.

(2) Any other provision of this constitution to the contrary notwithstanding:

(a) The state may contract public debt and pledges to the payment thereof its full faith, credit and taxing power:

1. To acquire, construct, develop, extend, enlarge or improve land, waters, property, highways, railways, buildings, equipment or facilities for public purposes.

2. To make funds available for veterans' housing loans.

(b) The aggregate public debt contracted by the state in any calendar year pursuant to paragraph (a) shall not exceed an amount equal to the lesser of:

1. Three-fourths of one per centum of the aggregate value of all taxable property in the state; or

2. Five per centum of the aggregate value of all taxable property in the state less the sum of: a. the aggregate public debt of the state contracted pursuant to this section outstanding as of January 1 of such calendar year after subtracting therefrom the amount of sinking funds on hand on January 1 of such calendar year which are applicable exclusively to repayment of such outstanding public debt and, b. the outstanding indebtedness as of January 1 of such calendar year of any entity of the type described in paragraph (d) to the extent that such indebtedness is supported by or payable from payments out of the treasury of the state.

(c) The state may contract public debt, without limit, to fund or refund the whole or any part of any public debt contracted pursuant to paragraph (a), including any premium payable with respect thereto and any interest to accrue thereon, or to fund or refund the whole or any part of any indebtedness incurred prior to January 1, 1972, by any entity of the type described in paragraph (d), including any premium payable with respect thereto and any interest to accrue thereon.

(d) No money shall be paid out of the treasury, with respect to any lease, sublease or other agreement entered into after January 1, 1971, to the Wisconsin State Agencies Building Corporation, Wisconsin State Colleges Building Corporation, Wisconsin State Public Building Corporation, Wisconsin University Building Corporation or any similar entity existing or operating for similar purposes pursuant to which such nonprofit corporation or such other entity undertakes to finance or provide a facility for use or occupancy by the state or an agency, department or instrumentality thereof.

(e) The legislature shall prescribe all matters relating to the contracting of public debt pursuant to paragraph (a), including: the public purposes for which public debt may be contracted; by vote of a majority of the members elected to each of the 2 houses of the legislature, the amount of public debt which may be contracted for any class of such purposes; the public debt or other indebtedness which may be funded or refunded; the kinds of notes, bonds or other evidence of public debt which may be issued by the state; and the manner in which the aggregate value of all taxable property in the state shall be determined.

(f) The full faith, credit and taxing power of the state are pledged to the payment of all public debt created on behalf of the state pursuant to this section and the legislature shall provide by appropriation for the payment of the interest upon and instalments of principal of all such public debt as the same falls due, but, in any event, suit may be brought against the state to compel such payment.

(g) At any time after January 1, 1972, by vote of a majority of the members elected to each of the 2 houses of the legislature, the legislature may declare that an emergency exists and submit to the people a proposal to authorize the state to contract a specific amount of public debt for a purpose specified in such proposal, without regard to the limit provided in paragraph (b). Any such authorization shall be effective if approved by a majority of the electors voting thereon. Public debt contracted pursuant to such authorization shall thereafter be deemed to have been contracted pursuant to paragraph (a), but neither such public debt nor any public debt contracted to fund or refund such public debt shall be considered in computing the debt limit provided in paragraph (b). Not more than one such authorization shall be thus made in any 2-year period.

Vote on fiscal bills; quorum. Section 8. On the passage in either house of the legislature of any law which imposes, continues or renews a tax, or creates a debt or charge, or makes, continues or renews an appropriation of public or trust money, or releases, discharges or commutes a claim or demand of the state, the question shall be taken by yeas and nays, which shall be duly entered on the journal; and three-fifths of all the members elected to such house shall in all such cases be required to constitute a quorum therein.

Evidences of public debt. Section 9. No scrip, certificate, or other evidence of state debt, whatsoever, shall be issued, except for such debts as are authorized by the sixth and seventh sections of this article.

Internal improvements. Section 10. Except as further provided in this section, the state may never contract any debt for works of internal improvement, or be a party in carrying on such works.

(1) Whenever grants of land or other property shall have been made to the state, especially dedicated by the grant to particular works of internal improvement, the state may carry on such particular works and shall devote thereto the avails of such grants, and may pledge or appropriate the revenues derived from such works in aid of their completion.

(2) The state may appropriate money in the treasury or to be thereafter raised by taxation for:

(a) The construction or improvement of public highways.

(b) The development, improvement and construction of airports or other aeronautical projects.

(c) The acquisition, improvement or construction of veterans' housing.

(d) The improvement of port facilities.

(e) The acquisition, development, improvement or construction of railways and other railroad facilities.

(3) The state may appropriate moneys for the purpose of acquiring, preserving and developing the forests of the state. Of the moneys appropriated under the authority of this subsection in any one year an amount not to exceed two-tenths of one mill of the taxable property of the state as determined by the last preceding state assessment may be raised by a tax on property.

Transportation Fund. Section 11. All funds collected by the state from any taxes or fees levied or imposed for the licensing of motor vehicle operators, for the titling, licensing, or registration of motor vehicles, for motor vehicle fuel, or for the use of roadways, highways, or bridges, and from taxes and fees levied or imposed for aircraft, airline property, or aviation fuel or for railroads or railroad property shall be deposited only into the transportation fund or with a trustee for the benefit of the department of transportation or the holders of transportation-related revenue bonds, except for collections from taxes or fees in existence on December 31, 2010, that were not being deposited in the transportation fund on that date. None of the funds collected or received by the state from any source and deposited into the transportation fund shall be lapsed, further transferred, or appropriated to any program that is not directly administered by the department of transportation in furtherance of the department's responsibility for the planning, promotion, and protection of all transportation systems in the state except for programs for which there was an appropriation from the transportation fund on December 31, 2010. In this section, the term "motor vehicle" does not include any all-terrain vehicles, snowmobiles, or watercraft.

ARTICLE IX—Eminent domain and property of the state

Jurisdiction on rivers and lakes; navigable waters. Section 1. The state shall have concurrent jurisdiction on all rivers and lakes bordering on this state so far as such rivers or lakes shall form a common boundary to the state and any other state or territory now or hereafter to be formed, and bounded by the same; and the river Mississippi and the navigable waters leading into the Mississippi and St. Lawrence, and the carrying places between the same, shall be common highways and forever free, as well to the inhabitants of the state as to the citizens of the United States, without any tax, impost or duty therefor.

Territorial property. Section 2. The title to all lands and other property which have accrued to the territory of Wisconsin by grant, gift, purchase, forfeiture, escheat or otherwise shall vest in the state of Wisconsin.

Ultimate property in lands; escheats. Section 3. The people of the state, in their right of sovereignty, are declared to possess the ultimate property in and to all lands within the jurisdiction of the state; and all lands the title to which shall fail from a defect of heirs shall revert or escheat to the people.

ARTICLE X—Education

Superintendent of public instruction. Section 1. The supervision of public instruction shall be vested in a state superintendent and such other officers as the legislature shall direct; and their qualifications, powers, duties and compensation shall be prescribed by law. The state superintendent shall be chosen by the qualified electors of the state at the same time and in the same manner as members of the supreme court, and shall hold office for 4 years from the succeeding first Monday in July. The term of office, time and manner of electing or appointing all other officers of supervision of public instruction shall be fixed by law.

School fund created; income applied. Section 2. The proceeds of all lands that have been or hereafter may be granted by the United States to this state for educational purposes (except the lands heretofore granted for the purposes of a university) and all moneys and the clear proceeds of all property that may accrue to the state by forfeiture or escheat; and the clear proceeds of all fines collected in the several counties for any breach of the penal laws, and all moneys arising from any grant to the state where the purposes of such grant are not specified, and the 500,000 acres of land to which the state is entitled by the provisions of an act of congress, entitled "An act to appropriate the proceeds of the sales of the public lands and to grant pre-emption rights," approved September 4, 1841; and also the 5 percent of the net proceeds of the public lands to which the state shall become entitled on admission into the union (if congress shall consent to such appropriation of the 2 grants last mentioned) shall be set apart as a separate fund to be called "the school fund," the interest of which and all other revenues derived from the school lands shall be exclusively applied to the following objects, to wit:

(1) To the support and maintenance of common schools, in each school district, and the purchase of suitable libraries and apparatus therefor.

(2) The residue shall be appropriated to the support and maintenance of academies and normal schools, and suitable libraries and apparatus therefor.

District schools; tuition; sectarian instruction; released time. Section 3. The legislature shall provide by law for the establishment of district schools, which shall be as nearly uniform as practicable; and such schools shall be free and without charge for tuition to all children between the ages of 4 and 20 years; and no sectarian instruction shall be allowed therein; but the legislature by law may, for the purpose of religious instruction outside the district schools, authorize the release of students during regular school hours.

Annual school tax. Section 4. Each town and city shall be required to raise by tax, annually, for the support of common schools therein, a sum not less than one-half the amount received by such town or city respectively for school purposes from the income of the school fund.

Income of school fund. Section 5. Provision shall be made by law for the distribution of the income of the school fund among the several towns and cities of the state for the support of common schools therein, in some just proportion to the number of children and youth resident therein between the ages of four and twenty years, and no appropriation shall be made from the school fund to any city or town for the year in which said city or town shall fail to raise such tax; nor to any school district for the year in which a school shall not be maintained at least three months.

State university; support. Section 6. Provision shall be made by law for the establishment of a state university at or near the seat of state government, and for connecting with the same, from time to time, such colleges in different parts of the state as the interests of education may require. The proceeds of all lands that have been or may hereafter be granted by the United States to the state for the support of a university shall be and remain a perpetual fund to be called "the university fund," the interest of which shall be appropriated to the support of the state university, and no sectarian instruction shall be allowed in such university.

Commissioners of public lands. Section 7. The secretary of state, treasurer and attorney general, shall constitute a board of commissioners for the sale of the school and university lands and for the investment of the funds arising therefrom. Any two of said commissioners shall be a quorum for the transaction of all business pertaining to the duties of their office.

Sale of public lands. Section 8. Provision shall be made by law for the sale of all school and university lands after they shall have been appraised; and when any portion of such lands shall be sold and the purchase money shall not be paid at the time of the sale, the commissioners shall take security by mortgage upon the lands sold for the sum remaining unpaid, with seven per cent interest thereon, payable annually at the office of the treasurer. The commissioners shall be authorized to execute a good and sufficient conveyance to all purchasers of such lands, and to discharge any mortgages taken as security, when the sum due thereon shall have been paid. The commissioners shall have power to withhold from sale any portion of such lands when they shall deem it expedient, and shall invest all moneys arising from the sale of such lands, as well as all other university and school funds, in such manner as the legislature shall provide, and shall give such security for the faithful performance of their duties as may be required by law.

ARTICLE XI—Corporations

Corporations; how formed. Section 1. Corporations without banking powers or privileges may be formed under general laws, but shall not be created by special act, except for municipal purposes. All general laws or special acts enacted under the provisions of this section may be altered or repealed by the legislature at any time after their passage.

Property taken by municipality. Section 2. No municipal corporation shall take private property for public use, against the consent of the owner, without the necessity thereof being first established in the manner prescribed by the legislature.

Municipal home rule; debt limit; tax to pay debt. Section 3. (1) Cities and villages organized pursuant to state law may determine their local affairs and government, subject only to this constitution and to such enactments of the legislature of statewide concern as with uniformity shall affect every city or every village. The method of such determination shall be prescribed by the legislature.

(2) No county, city, town, village, school district, sewerage district or other municipal corporation may become indebted in an amount that exceeds an allowable percentage of the taxable property located therein equalized for state purposes as provided by the legislature. In all cases the allowable percentage shall be 5 percent except as specified in pars. (a) and (b):

(a) For any city authorized to issue bonds for school purposes, an additional 10 percent shall be permitted for school purposes only, and in such cases the territory attached to the city for school purposes shall be included in the total taxable property supporting the bonds issued for school purposes.

(b) For any school district which offers no less than grades one to 12 and which at the time of incurring such debt is eligible for the highest level of school aids, 10 percent shall be permitted.

(3) Any county, city, town, village, school district, sewerage district or other municipal corporation incurring any indebtedness under sub. (2) shall, before or at the time of doing so, provide for the collection of a direct annual tax sufficient to pay the interest on such debt as it falls due, and also to pay and discharge the principal thereof within 20 years from the time of contracting the same.

(4) When indebtedness under sub. (2) is incurred in the acquisition of lands by cities, or by counties or sewerage districts having a population of 150,000 or over, for public, municipal purposes, or for the permanent improvement thereof, or to purchase, acquire, construct, extend, add to or improve a sewage collection or treatment system which services all or a part of such city or county, the city, county or sewerage district incurring the indebtedness shall, before or at the time of so doing, provide for the collection of a direct annual tax sufficient to pay the interest on such debt as it falls due, and also to pay and discharge the principal thereof within a period not exceeding 50 years from the time of contracting the same.

(5) An indebtedness created for the purpose of purchasing, acquiring, leasing, constructing, extending, adding to, improving, conducting, controlling, operating or managing a public utility of a town, village, city or special district, and secured solely by the property or income of such public utility, and whereby no municipal liability is created, shall not be considered an indebtedness of such town, village, city or special district, and shall not be included in arriving at the debt limitation under sub. (2).

Acquisition of lands by state and subdivisions; sale of excess. Section 3a. The state or any of its counties, cities, towns or villages may acquire by gift, dedication, purchase, or condemnation lands for establishing, laying out, widening, enlarging, extending, and maintaining memorial grounds, streets, highways, squares, parkways, boulevards, parks, playgrounds, sites for public buildings, and reservations in and about and along and leading to any or all of the same; and after the establishment, layout, and completion of such improvements, may convey any such real estate thus acquired and not necessary for such improvements, with reservations concerning the future use and occupation of such real estate, so as to protect such public works and improvements, and their environs, and to preserve the view, appearance, light, air, and usefulness of such public works. If the governing body of a county, city, town or village elects to accept a gift or dedication of land made on condition that the land be devoted to a special purpose and the condition subsequently becomes impossible or impracticable, such governing body may by resolution or ordinance enacted by a two-thirds vote of its members elect either to grant the land back to the donor or dedicator or his heirs or accept from the donor or dedicator or his heirs a grant relieving the county, city, town or village of the condition; however, if the donor or dedicator or his heirs are unknown or cannot be found, such resolution or ordinance may provide for the commencement of proceedings in the manner and in the courts as the legislature shall designate for the purpose of relieving the county, city, town or village from the condition of the gift or dedication.

General banking law. Section 4. The legislature may enact a general banking law for the creation of banks, and for the regulation and supervision of the banking business.

ARTICLE XII—Amendments

Constitutional amendments. Section 1. Any amendment or amendments to this constitution may be proposed in either house of the legislature, and if the same shall be agreed to by a majority of the members elected to each of the two houses, such proposed amendment or amendments shall be entered on their journals, with the yeas and nays taken thereon, and referred to the legislature to be chosen at the next general election, and shall be published for three months previous to the time of holding such election; and if, in the legislature so next chosen, such proposed amendment or amendments shall be agreed to by a majority of all the members elected to each house, then it shall be the duty of the legislature to submit such proposed amendment or amendments to the people in such manner and at such time as the legislature shall prescribe; and if the people shall approve and ratify such amendment or amendments by a majority of the electors voting thereon, such amendment or amendments shall become part of the constitution; provided, that if more than one amendment be submitted, they shall be submitted in such manner that the people may vote for or against such amendments separately.

Constitutional conventions. Section 2. If at any time a majority of the senate and assembly shall deem it necessary to call a convention to revise or change this constitution, they shall recommend to the electors to vote for or against a convention at the next election for members of the legislature. And if it shall appear that a majority of the electors voting thereon have voted for a convention, the legislature shall, at its next session, provide for calling such convention.

ARTICLE XIII—Miscellaneous provisions

Political year; elections. Section 1. The political year for this state shall commence on the first Monday of January in each year, and the general election shall be held on the Tuesday next succeeding the first Monday of November in even-numbered years.

Eligibility to office. Section 3. (1) No member of congress and no person holding any office of profit or trust under the United States except postmaster, or under any foreign power, shall be eligible to any office of trust, profit or honor in this state.

(2) No person convicted of a felony, in any court within the United States, no person convicted in federal court of a crime designated, at the time of commission, under federal law as a misdemeanor involving a violation of public trust and no person convicted, in a court of a state, of a crime designated, at the time of commission, under the law of the state as a misdemeanor involving a violation of public trust shall be eligible to any office of trust, profit or honor in this state unless pardoned of the conviction.

(3) No person may seek to have placed on any ballot for a state or local elective office in this state the name of a person convicted of a felony, in any court within the United States, the name of a person convicted in federal court of a crime designated, at the time of commission, under federal law as a misdemeanor involving a violation of public trust or the name of a person convicted, in a court of a state, of a crime designated, at the time of commission, under the law of the state as a misdemeanor involving a violation of public trust, unless the person named for the ballot has been pardoned of the conviction.

Great seal. Section 4. It shall be the duty of the legislature to provide a great seal for the state, which shall be kept by the secretary of state, and all official acts of the governor, his approbation of the laws excepted, shall be thereby authenticated.

Legislative officers. Section 6. The elective officers of the legislature, other than the presiding officers, shall be a chief clerk and a sergeant at arms, to be elected by each house.

Division of counties. Section 7. No county with an area of nine hundred square miles or less shall be divided or have any part stricken therefrom, without submitting the question to a vote of the people of the county, nor unless a majority of all the legal voters of the county voting on the question shall vote for the same.

Removal of county seats. Section 8. No county seat shall be removed until the point to which it is proposed to be removed shall be fixed by law, and a majority of the voters of the county voting on the question shall have voted in favor of its removal to such point.

Election or appointment of statutory officers. Section 9. All county officers whose election or appointment is not provided for by this constitution shall be elected by the electors of the respective counties, or appointed by the boards of supervisors, or other county authorities, as the legislature shall direct. All city, town and village officers whose election or appointment is not provided for by this constitution shall be elected by the electors of such cities, towns and villages, or of some division thereof, or appointed by such authorities thereof as the legislature shall designate for that purpose. All other officers whose election or appointment is not provided for by this constitution, and all officers whose offices may hereafter be created by law, shall be elected by the people or appointed, as the legislature may direct.

Vacancies in office. Section 10. **(1)** The legislature may declare the cases in which any office shall be deemed vacant, and also the manner of filling the vacancy, where no provision is made for that purpose in this constitution.

(2) Whenever there is a vacancy in the office of lieutenant governor, the governor shall nominate a successor to serve for the balance of the unexpired term, who shall take office after confirmation by the senate and by the assembly.

Passes, franks and privileges. Section 11. No person, association, copartnership, or corporation, shall promise, offer or give, for any purpose, to any political committee, or any member or employe thereof, to any candidate for, or incumbent of any office or position under the constitution or laws, or under any ordinance of any town or municipality, of this state, or to any person at the request or for the advantage of all or any of them, any free pass or frank, or any privilege withheld from any person, for the traveling accommodation or transportation of any person or property, or the transmission of any message or communication.

No political committee, and no member or employee thereof, no candidate for and no incumbent of any office or position under the constitution or laws, or under any ordinance of any town or municipality of this state, shall ask for, or accept, from any person, association, copartnership, or corporation, or use, in any manner, or for any purpose, any free pass or frank, or any privilege withheld from any person, for the traveling accommodation or transportation of any person or property, or the transmission of any message or communication.

Any violation of any of the above provisions shall be bribery and punished as provided by law, and if any officer or any member of the legislature be guilty thereof, his office shall become vacant.

No person within the purview of this act shall be privileged from testifying in relation to anything therein prohibited; and no person having so testified shall be liable to any prosecution or punishment for any offense concerning which he was required to give his testimony or produce any documentary evidence.

Notaries public and regular employees of a railroad or other public utilities who are candidates for or hold public offices for which the annual compensation is not more than three hundred dollars to whom no passes or privileges are extended beyond those which are extended to other regular employees of such corporations are excepted from the provisions of this section.

Recall of elective officers. Section 12. The qualified electors of the state, of any congressional, judicial or legislative district or of any county may petition for the recall of any incumbent elective officer after the first year of the term for which the incumbent was elected, by filing a petition with the filing officer with whom the nomination petition to the office in the primary is filed, demanding the recall of the incumbent.

(1) The recall petition shall be signed by electors equalling at least twenty-five percent of the vote cast for the office of governor at the last preceding election, in the state, county or district which the incumbent represents.

(2) The filing officer with whom the recall petition is filed shall call a recall election for the Tuesday of the 6th week after the date of filing the petition or, if that Tuesday is a legal holiday, on the first day after that Tuesday which is not a legal holiday.

(3) The incumbent shall continue to perform the duties of the office until the recall election results are officially declared.

(4) Unless the incumbent declines within 10 days after the filing of the petition, the incumbent shall without filing be deemed to have filed for the recall election. Other candidates may file for the office in the manner provided by law for special elections. For the purpose of conducting elections under this section:

(a) When more than 2 persons compete for a nonpartisan office, a recall primary shall be held. The 2 persons receiving the highest number of votes in the recall primary shall be the 2 candidates in the recall election, except that if any candidate receives a majority of the total number of votes cast in the recall primary, that candidate shall assume the office for the remainder of the term and a recall election shall not be held.

(b) For any partisan office, a recall primary shall be held for each political party which is by law entitled to a separate ballot and from which more than one candidate competes for the party's nomination in the recall election. The person receiving the highest number of votes in the recall primary for each political party shall be that party's candidate in the recall election. Independent candidates and candidates representing political parties not entitled by law to a separate ballot shall be shown on the ballot for the recall election only.

(c) When a recall primary is required, the date specified under sub. (2) shall be the date of the recall primary and the recall election shall be held on the Tuesday of the 4th week after the recall primary or, if that Tuesday is a legal holiday, on the first day after that Tuesday which is not a legal holiday.

(5) The person who receives the highest number of votes in the recall election shall be elected for the remainder of the term.

(6) After one such petition and recall election, no further recall petition shall be filed against the same officer during the term for which he was elected.

(7) This section shall be self-executing and mandatory. Laws may be enacted to facilitate its operation but no law shall be enacted to hamper, restrict or impair the right of recall.

Marriage. Section 13. Only a marriage between one man and one woman shall be valid or recognized as a marriage in this state. A legal status identical or substantially similar to that of marriage for unmarried individuals shall not be valid or recognized in this state.

ARTICLE XIV—Schedule

Effect of change from territory to state. Section 1. That no inconvenience may arise by reason of a change from a territorial to a permanent state government, it is declared that all rights, actions, prosecutions, judgments, claims and contracts, as well of individuals as of bodies corporate, shall continue as if no such change had taken place; and all process which may be issued under the authority of the territory of Wisconsin previous to its admission into the union of the United States shall be as valid as if issued in the name of the state.

Territorial laws continued. Section 2. All laws now in force in the territory of Wisconsin which are not repugnant to this constitution shall remain in force until they expire by their own limitation or be altered or repealed by the legislature.

Common law continued in force. Section 13. Such parts of the common law as are now in force in the territory of Wisconsin, not inconsistent with this constitution, shall be and continue part of the law of this state until altered or suspended by the legislature.

Implementing revised structure of judicial branch. Section 16. **(4)** The terms of office of justices of the supreme court serving on August 1, 1978, shall expire on the July 31 next preceding the first Monday in January on which such terms would otherwise have expired, but such advancement of the date of term expiration shall not impair any retirement rights vested in any such justice if the term had expired on the first Monday in January.

Criminal Justice Coordinating Council,
177
Criminal Penalties, Joint Review
Committee on, 151–52, 627
Crowley, David, representative, **38**, 609,
612

Dallet, Rebecca Frank, supreme court
justice, **10**, 485, 615–18
Darling, Alberta, senator, **43**, 626
Deaf and Hard of Hearing, Council for
the, 204, 627
Deaf and Hard-of-Hearing Education
Council, 222
Deferred Compensation Board, 199–200,
627
Democratic Party of Wisconsin, 560
Dentistry Examining Board, 230, 627
Detainers, Interstate Agreement on, 263
Dietitians Affiliated Credentialing Board,
230, 627
Direct Primary Care, Legislative Council
Study Committee on, 160–61
Disabilities
Blind and Visual Impairment
Education Council, 221
Blindness, Council on, 204
Deaf and Hard of Hearing, Council for
the, 204
Deaf and Hard-of-Hearing Education
Council, 222, 627
Developmental Disabilities, Board for
People with, 187, 627
Disabilities, Governor's Committee for
People with, 177
Physical Disabilities, Council on, 206,
633
Special Education, Council on, 222
vocational rehabilitation, 179, 180
Disability Board, 174–75
Distance Learning Authorization Board,
206–7, 627
District attorneys, 646–47
Dittrich, Barbara, representative, **60**, 610,
613
Domestic Abuse, Governor's Council on,
194, 627

Domestic relations, significant legislation,
2017 session, 409
Doyle, Steve, representative, **121**, 130,
611, 615
Dry Cleaner Environmental Response
Council, 215–16, 627
Duchow, Cindi, representative, **125**, 611,
615
Duffy, Sean, U.S. representative, **18**, 510,
513, 568, 571
Dwelling Code Council, Uniform, 229,
635
Dyslexia, Legislative Council Study
Committee on the Identification and
Management of, 162–63

Early Childhood Advisory Council, 177
Early Intervention Interagency
Coordinating Council (Birth to
Three), 178
Eau Claire campus, UW System, 240
Economic development, significant
legislation, 2017 session, 409
Edming, James, representative, **113**, 610,
615
Education, 389–97
Commission of the States, 257, 628
significant legislation, 2017 session,
409–12
statistics, 692–700
See also Public Education; Public
Instruction, Department of; Schools
Educational Communications Board,
197–98, 628
Elections
absentee voting, 373, 413
attorney general, 600–603
campaign finance, 373–78
circuit court judges, 622–24
Congress, U.S., 116th, 563–72
constitutional amendments, historical
table, 498–503
county clerk duties, 367–69
court of appeals judges, 620–22
Elections Commission, 367–68, 628
Employment and income, statistics,
675–79